Strategic Management

We work with leading authors to develop the
strongest educational materials in business,
bringing cutting-edge thinking and best learning
practice to a global market.

Under a range of well-known imprints, including
Financial Times Prentice Hall, we craft high-quality
print and electronic publications which help
readers to understand and apply their content,
whether studying or at work.

To find out more about the complete range of our
publishing please visit us on the World Wide Web at:
www.pearsoneduc.com

Strategic Management

An Introduction to Business and Corporate Strategy

Paul Finlay

FINANCIAL TIMES
Prentice Hall

An imprint of **Pearson Education**

Harlow, England · London · New York · Reading, Massachusetts · San Francisco · Toronto · Don Mills, Ontario · Sydney
Tokyo · Singapore · Hong Kong · Seoul · Taipei · Cape Town · Madrid · Mexico City · Amsterdam · Munich · Paris · Milan

Pearson Education Limited
Edinburgh Gate
Harlow
Essex CM20 2JE
England

and Associated Companies around the World

Visit us on the World Wide Web at:
www.pearsoneduc.com

First published 2000

ISBN 0 201 39827 3

British Library Cataloguing in Publication Data
A CIP catalogue record for this book can be obtained from the British Library.

Library of Congress Cataloging-in-Publication Data
Finlay, Paul N.
    Strategic management : an introduction to business and corporate strategy / Paul Finlay.
        p.   cm.
    Includes bibliographical references and index.
    ISBN 0–201–39827–3 (pbk. : alk. paper)
    1. Industrial management.   2. Strategic planning.   3. Industrial management – Case
studies.   4. Strategic planning – Case studies.   I. Title.

HD31.F5229 1999
658.4'012 – dc21   99–049462

10 9 8 7 6 5 4 3 2 1
04 03 02 01 00

Printed and bound by Grafos S.A.,
Arte sobre papel, Barcelona, Spain

To Ann, Mike, Sam, Steve and Susie

Contents

Acknowledgements

A book of this length, incorporating as it does ideas picked up over several years, has benefited enormously from the help of a great number of people: it's impossible to name them all.

I would first like to thank members of my family: my wife Ann and daughter Susie for their proofreading of chapters and for making many valuable suggestions regarding the readability of the text; and to my brother John for his help with historical features and other facts, and with editing two of the chapters.

My thanks are due to my colleagues at the Business School, Loughborough University, in particular Grahame Boocock, Mark Davies, Cathy Hart, Malcolm Hill, Peter Jennings, Ruth King, Malcolm Kirkup, Peter Lawrence and Mohammed Rafiq. Also to Phil Herbert of Loughborough Computer Services and Gareth Griffiths of Manchester Metropolitan University for their help with the IT aspects of Chapter 7. Also thanks to David Nichols of Rhône-Poulenc Rorer for help with understanding the workings of the pharmaceutical industry, and Kevin Waring of ADtranz, with whom I many times debated the finer points of strategic management.

In 1998, Eve Poole, at that time studying at the Management School, University of Edinburgh, and now working for Deloitte Consulting, won the 1998 AMBA Student of the Year Award with her dissertation entitled 'Machiavelli for management: Lessons from *The Prince* for business leadership'. I am deeply indebted to Eve for allowing me to use her work in Section 4.6. I have also made fairly extensive use of the PhD thesis of Douglas McConchie, for which access I'm most grateful.

This book contains 18 major cases, without which the book would be much the poorer: they are of major significance in providing the scope for developing the art of strategic management. Without the contributions from people within the firms the cases would have lacked much of their richness. Thus I am very much indebted to the following for the time they made available to me to facilitate the writing of the cases:

GSM Graphic Arts	Barry Dodd, Andrew Hall and Rudy Pearce
Shane McGill and One-shot	Shane McGill
Dutton Engineering	Ken Lewis of Dutton Engineering (Woodside) Limited and Mike Nash and Tina Mason of Business Excellence Training
BDHTBWA	Roger Ward
Eversheds	John Sarginson and Simon Slater
Pearson Education	Richard Beaumont, Peter Brimacombe, Claire Tavernier and Andy Ware

ARM Ltd	Robin Saxby
ITNET	Claire Forrest
Pearson plc	Peter Brimacombe and Claire Tavernier

I am also indebted to the authors and co-authors of the cases:

The Life and Times of an Entrepreneur	Peter Jennings of the Business School, Loughborough University
BDHTBWA	Mark Davies of the Business School, Loughborough University
The Gallup Organisation	Jonathan Hill of the Gallup Organisation
Rose Bearings	David Shore, MBA student, studying at the Lincoln Campus of the University of Lincolnshire and Humberside
Wynnstay & Clwyd Farmers plc	Nimal Wijayaratna of the Business School, Loughborough University
Superdrug	Helene Hill of the Department of Retailing and Marketing, Manchester Metropolitan University
ITNET	Grahame Boocock of the Business School, Loughborough University
Powergen and Thorntons	David Jennings of Nottingham Trent University
ADtranz (UK & Ireland)	Kevin Waring of ADtranz (UK & Ireland)
European Telecommunications Champions	Willem Hulsink of the Erasmus University Rotterdam and Andrew Davies of University of Sussex

Finally, for all the help she has given me with the preparation of the text and also in tracking down information sources, I would particularly like to thank my secretary Julie Collett for all her time and trouble.

We are grateful to the following for permission to reproduce copyright material:

Auburn House Publishing for an extract from *Rumor in the Marketplace: The Social Psychology of Commercial Hearsay* by F. Koenig (1985); the author Bill Bryson for an adapted extract from the article 'Of Mice and Millions', first published in *The Observer Magazine* 28.3.93, reproduced as 'Case Study: The Euro Disney encounter' in *Understanding Marketing* by Mark Davies (Prentice Hall, 1997); the author Simon Caulkin for the article 'It's bigger than Turkey, Thailand or Denmark – but it's not a country . . .', first published in *The Observer* 8.3.98; the Controller of Her Majesty's Stationery Office for statistics from Table 1 from *Small and Medium Enterprise (SME) Statistics for the United Kingdom, 1996* (Department of Trade and Industry, 1997), Crown copyright; Deutsche Bank, Frankfurt, for 'Deutsche Bank Strategic Planning Framework 1997 GD Investment Banking (IB)'; the author John Dunn for adapted extracts from the article 'Bringing up flat-top baby', first published in *The Guardian* 26.1.99; EMI Small Business Research and Consultancy for data from *The European Observatory for SMEs, Fifth Annual Report* (EIM/ENSR, Zoetermeer,

1997); Elsevier Science Ltd for a Figure from the article 'Acquisitions – Techniques for Measuring Strategic Fit' by C.J. Clarke from *Long Range Planning*, Vol. 20, No. 3 (1987), and a Figure from the article 'Benchmarking: The Japanese Experience' by Yoshinobu Ohinata from *Long Range Planning*, Vol. 27, No. 4 (1994); Financial Times for the article 'Victims of "groupthink" by R. Chote from *Financial Times* 7.9.98, a Figure from the article 'Retailers warned over web delays' by Jean Eaglesham from *Financial Times* 7.1.99, the articles 'BP overcomes fear of the "too difficult box" ' by Vanessa Houlder from *Financial Times* 15.4.98, 'Two blueprints for the Engine of Progress' by Peter Marsh from *Financial Times* 2.7.98, 'Open up in a company crisis' by Virginia Matthews from *Financial Times* 26.11.97, and 'A strategist who has everything to play for' by S. Wagstyl and G. Bowley from *Financial Times* 20.4.98, and adapted extracts from the article 'At the cutting edge' by John Willman from *Financial Times* 20.4.98; Gee Publishing for an extract from *The Financial Aspects of Corporate Governance*, Stock Exchange Council (1992); the author, Jules Goddard for an extract and an adapted extract from the article 'The Essential Nature of Strategy' from *London Business School Journal* (Autumn, 1986); The Guardian for the articles 'Ecstasy test kit immoral says drugs tsar' by Amelia Gentleman from *The Guardian* 28.5.98 and 'A dirty business bogged down in a moral and political mire' by John Vidal from *The Guardian* 15.8.98, and an illustrated extract from the article 'Channel Tunnel Fire' from *The Guardian* 20.11.96; Harvard Business Review for two exhibits and an adapted exhibit from the article 'Profit Pools. A Fresh Look At Strategy' by Orit Gadiesh and James L. Gilbert from *Harvard Business Review* (May–June, 1998), Copyright © 1998 by the President and Fellows of Harvard College, all rights reserved, an adapted exhibit from 'Understanding Your Organization's Character' by Roger Harrison from *Harvard Business Review* (May–June, 1972), Copyright © 1972 by the President and Fellows of Harvard College, all rights reserved, an adapted exhibit from the article 'The Core Competence of the Corporation' by C.K. Prahalad and Gary Hamel from *Harvard Business Review* (May–June, 1990), Copyright © 1990 by the President and Fellows of Harvard College, all rights reserved, and an adapted exhibit from the article 'Successful Change Programs Begin With Results' by Robert H. Schaffer and Harvey A. Thomson from *Harvard Business Review* (Jan–Feb, 1992), Copyright © 1992 by the President and Fellows of Harvard College, all rights reserved; Houghton Mifflin Company for a Figure from *Industrial Market Structure and Economic Performance* by F.M. Scherer and David Ross, 3rd Edition (1990), Copyright © 1990 by Houghton Mifflin Company; The Independent for an extract from the article 'Cadbury aims for exactly the right mix' by Richard Phillips from *The Independent on Sunday* 12.4.98, and the articles 'Globalisation: the facts behind the myth' by David Miles from *The Independent* 22.12.97 and 'The battle of the beakers' by Roger Trapp from *The Independent* 23.12.97; Jossey-Bass Inc., Publishers, for an extract and an adapted exhibit from *Organizational Culture and Leadership* by Edgar H. Schein, 2nd Edition (1992), Copyright © 1992 Jossey-Bass Inc.; KPMG for a Figure from *KPMG Consulting Pricing Policy White Paper*, EMU Unit – KPMG Consulting Reference: /a7724 (KPMG Consulting Survey, 1999) and Figures from *Knowledge Management Research Report 1998*; the author John Kay for the article 'The future is not what it used to be' from *Financial Times* 8.7.98; the author Alice Lam for two slightly adapted Figures from *Tacit Knowledge, Organisational Learning and Innovation: A Societal Perspective*, Danish Research Unit for Industrial Dynamics,

DRUID Working Paper No. 98–22 (1998); Macmillan Press Ltd and The Free Press, New York, for Figures from *The Competitive Advantage of Nations* by M.E. Porter (1998); Macmillan Press, New York, for an extract from *Ethical Managing: Rules and Results* by Neil F. Brady (1990); the author George Monbiot for the article 'Law and the profits of PR', first published in *The Guardian* 21.8.97; The Observer for adapted extracts from the article 'How the biscuits strategy crumbled' by Heather Connon from *The Observer* 14.3.99, the article 'Manager's maxim' by Sir John Egan from *The Observer* 12.4.98, and an extract from the article 'Suits in a league of their own' by Stefan Szymanski from *The Observer* 1.11.98; Oxford University Press for a Figure and an extract from *Foundations of Corporate Success* by John Kay (1993); Pearson Education Ltd for extracts from *Intellectual Property* by D. Bainbridge, 2nd Edition (1994), a Figure from *Managing Organizational Change* by C.A. Carnall (1990), adapted extracts from *Understanding Marketing* by Mark Davies (1998), an extract from *The Strategy Process: Concepts, Contexts, Cases* by Henry Mintzberg and James Brian Quinn (1991), an extract and Figures from *Management and Organisational Behaviour* by L.J. Mullins, 5th Edition (1999), and an extract from *Mastering Management* (1997); PIMS Associates Ltd for exhibits from 'Calibrating the Cost (?) of Gaining Market Share' by R.D. Buzzell and B.T. Gale, *The PIMS Letter on Business Strategy*, No. 37, and an exhibit from 'The Unprofitability of "Modern" Technology and What to Do About It' by Sidney Schoeffler, *The PIMS Letter on Business Strategy*, No. 2; Plenum Publishing Corporation for a Figure from the article 'The strategic management of change' by D. Dunphy and D. Stace from *Human Relations*, Vol. 46, No. 8 (1993); Prentice-Hall, Inc. for an extract from *International Business: Environments and Operations* by John D. Daniels and Lee H. Radeburgh, 8th Edition (1998); the author, Rachelle Thackray for the article 'Reinventing the wheel' from *The Independent on Sunday* 22.3.98; United Nations for a Figure from *World Population Projections to 2150*, Population Division of the Department of Economic and Social Affairs at the United Nations Secretariat (1998); John Wiley & Sons Ltd for a Figure from the article 'The creation of momentum for change through the process of strategic issue diagnosis' by Jane E. Dutton and Robert B. Duncan from *Strategic Management Journal* Vol. IX (1987); Rolls-Royce plc for an extract by W. Budjinski from a Rolls-Royce plc/EDS publications (May 1998). We have been unable to trace the copyright holder in *Strategic Management* by G.G. Dess and A. Miller (McGraw-Hill, 1993) and would appreciate any information that would enable us to do so.

Whilst every effort has been made to trace the owners of copyright material, in a few cases this has proved impossible and we take this opportunity to offer our apologies to any copyright holders whose rights we may have unwittingly infringed.

Rationale and road map
for the book

When studying a new subject it's important to know what the author is emphasising and what they expect of you. It's also important to understand the rationale for the chapter sequence and why the chapters are grouped in the way they are. This chapter covers these two important points.

LEARNING
OUTCOMES

When you have worked through this preliminary chapter, you should be able to:

- describe the characteristics of strategic management models and know their general strengths and weaknesses;

- distinguish between the two sides of strategic management – the art and the science;

- describe the collage view of strategic management;

- describe how differing views will be treated and understand why a good knowledge of strategic management terminology is an important part of the book's learning objectives;

- explain why the bulk of the book concentrates on business-level strategic management;

- list the main elements of strategic management, explain the positioning of the chapters and describe the linkages between the chapters and these main elements.

1 Introduction

This preliminary chapter explains the rationale for the form and content of this book and describes how the book is structured and laid out. An overarching theme is that strategic management is both an art and a science and that successful strategic management requires a judicious blend of the two. The chapter begins by reviewing the characteristics of models in the physical sciences, engineering and social sciences as a prelude to considering the form of the models that constitute the science of strategic management. The art of strategic management, and how it melds with the science, is explained through use of the analogy of creating collages. With this background, the treatment of content is discussed – how differing views are to be treated, terminology, learning objectives and the prior knowledge that is assumed.

This rationale for the book's contents is followed by a 'road map' for the rest of the book and a rationale for the sequencing of chapters. The split of the book into three portions is described, as well as the contents of each group of chapters and of the chapters themselves within these groups.

2 The science of strategic management

2.1 Models as simplifications

Anyone involved in strategic management, and thus taking *responsibility for the overall direction of an organisation*, must simplify their world or they will be swamped by all the stimuli they receive. In other words, they must develop models of their world. Models are simplifications of reality, with unnecessary detail discarded so that the fundamentals can be seen more clearly. The map of the London Underground placed at the back of almost all UK diaries is a very good example of a model. It's a wonderful simplification to help travellers. The rail lines don't run in the straight lines shown on the map, but that's just the point – to put in the twists and turns of the track would be more realistic but would obscure the core message that the map gives. And the map probably doesn't tell you all you need to know when travelling. It doesn't give train times, tell you where the toilets are, or the provision made at particular stations for disabled people.

A useful model shows only the fundamentals and doesn't cloud the issue with detail. Models can be considered as 'cognitive coathangers' – frameworks upon which we can hang our own particular thoughts. The 'science' of this book is about the form and content of the models of strategic management; the 'art' of this book is about their appropriate use.

2.2 Types of model

The map of the London Underground is a descriptive model – it describes the linkages between stations in the network but says nothing about how the system might change with differing inputs. There are other types of model – prescriptive models – that tell you what to do in defined circumstances. As well as this split, models may also be categorised according to their level of abstraction. There are physical models that are almost identical to the real thing, such as those that car assemblers create before a car is put into production. However, our concern is with conceptual models rather than physical ones, often in the form of pictures or diagrams. When understood, these models become mental models – representations of reality within a person's head.

2.3 Models in science and engineering

Scientists have sets of models covering portions of the physical world. For example, physicists have models of the way electrons move through materials and how the sun radiates heat and light. Biologists have models of plant growth. One of the quests of scientists is to fit these models together into bigger units like a well-fitting jigsaw. These models differ from the descriptive models such as the Underground map since they do more than describe – they are used to predict. Ohm's law, which relates the electric current flowing in a conductor to the applied voltage, is a good example of a predictive model. Predictive models allow you to move from the present situation to see what a new one would look like.

Engineers also have many models: for example, civil engineers use models about the strength of materials and the stresses in structures. However, the fitting together of the models isn't as good as in the sciences, because uncontrollable features of the real world intrude – civil engineers have to take account of ill-defined specifications and particular site conditions. So although engineers are working with a jigsaw of models, it's not a perfect jigsaw: it's a jigsaw with well-recognised pieces that don't fit together exactly, and the art is in the fitting. As with most scientific models, engineering models are predictive, used to predict the form of many of the features of a bridge, for instance.

Social scientists also have models: of how children learn, for example, and of what conditions predispose people to criminal activities. However, because of the centrality of people, the models of social scientists tend to be much weaker both descriptively and predictively than scientific and engineering models; they have many fewer well-defined pieces in their jigsaw. The social science models deal with people in general, and they need to be tailored to an individual's circumstances if they are to be applied usefully to them.

<table>
<tr><td>DISCUSSION POINT 1</td><td>The map of the London Underground shows that if you get on a Circle Line train at South Kensington, the next station going anti-clockwise will be Sloane Square. Why is this map not a predictive model?</td></tr>
</table>

2.4 Strategic management models

Strategic management also has its models. The ubiquitous budget is sometimes not recognised for what it is – a financial model of the firm. In the main, the models of strategic management are much more like the models in the social sciences than those in the physical and biological sciences and engineering. And as with social science models, they need to be fleshed out with the particulars of a situation to be useful.

In general, the models of strategic management aren't powerful enough to allow prediction directly, and thus the main purposes of the models are to aid understanding and to help structure debate about strategic matters. Put another way, the models in strategic management provide the *means of thinking* strategically about matters; they don't provide the *ends* in the sense of providing *the* answer. They focus attention on the important items.

<table>
<tr><td>KEY CONCEPT</td><td>Scientists have very powerful predictive models, in part because the situations in which they are working can be controlled. In less well-controlled situations, where the environment and/or individuals are a major consideration, the models become less precise in their power to predict other than general features. Strategic management models are similar to models used in the social sciences – they provide the cognitive coathanger around which the flesh of the particular situation needs to be placed.</td></tr>
</table>

3   The art of strategic management

3.1   Collages

Collages are works of art created through merging together pieces of different materials. There are four requirements in creating an appealing collage. First, the overall artistic design must be conceived, although not necessarily in detail. Second, the materials to be used must be selected from the very large number of possible materials. Third, the materials need to be shaped to fit the artistic need. Finally, the pieces must be placed in an artful arrangement.

In the past, strategic management and particularly strategy formulation have been considered to be like doing a jigsaw with every piece in place and in only one place.[1] However, it has now been realised that strategic management is more like a collage than a jigsaw, as shown in Exhibit 1 – and the approach to crafting strategy is analogous to creating a collage. The comparison is illustrated in Exhibit 2. Just as there are some rules for the creation of a collage, the juxtaposition of colours for example, there are some rules for combining the models of strategic management. For example, the markets in which a firm is operating will almost always be linked to the economy and not divorced from it.

EXHIBIT 1

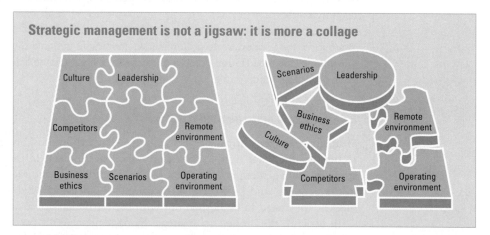

Strategic management is not a jigsaw: it is more a collage

Culture · Leadership · Competitors · Remote environment · Business ethics · Scenarios · Operating environment

Scenarios · Leadership · Business ethics · Culture · Remote environment · Competitors · Operating environment

EXHIBIT 2

The collage view of strategic management

Work of art	Strategic management
• Conceive the overall artistic design	• Strategic thinking to conceive the vision and main organisational goals
• Select the range of materials that might be used and understand their characteristics	• Identify the models that might be useful and understand their strengths and weaknesses
• Shape the materials into pieces to fit the artistic need	• Tailor and flesh out the models to suit the particular requirements and context
• Place the pieces in an artful arrangement	• Link the 'fleshed-out' models to form a coherent whole and thus a coherent strategy

In fact, the strategic management process is akin to a dynamic collage, a creation where the pieces are like Post-it notes that can be readjusted in a creative manner as new issues emerge that call for strategy to be reviewed and possibly changed.

3.2   The stance taken in this book

The stance taken in this book is that strategic management is both a science and an art. The science is contained in the models that have been constructed to help understanding; the models for environmental and competitor analysis, for example, are pieces of the collage. The models allow deductive reasoning, thinking from the general situations that have given rise to the models in the first place to the particular situation that is faced at the moment. However, every organisation is different, and so the models used are likely to be different, or applied differently. The art is in selecting the appropriate models and in adding the necessary detail. This perspective stresses the point that there aren't any general prescriptions in strategic management that can be applied without concern for the context.

A strand in this stance is that the scientific part (the models) can be taught, but the art (trimming and putting the models together) cannot. Fortunately, although the art can't be taught it can be learned. The main portions of the book are concerned mainly with the taught part, with the learning coming from using the case studies, from discussion with fellow students and from your own reflection in the light of your own experiences.

KEY CONCEPT   The overarching view is that there are helpful 'universals' that can be taught, but that each particular situation requires the universals to be tailored in a particular way. The art of good strategic management is to know the bits of the strategic management collage – the models – to select those models that are useful, tailor them to suit the situation and fit them together with other, similarly tailored models in the most appropriate way.

DISCUSSION   There is a saying, *'There's nothing so practical as a good theory.'* How does this apply to
POINT 2   the discussion above about strategic management models?

4   The treatment of content

4.1   The treatment of opposing views

There are many approaches to strategic management teaching and learning, and many inputs to the subject from other disciples. Much is common to all (or almost all) approaches, but there are several differences of emphasis. The discussion of stakeholders' rights in Section 1.7 of Chapter 1 illustrates this. So there is a problem of deciding which approach to adopt. One extreme is to champion a single approach to the exclusion of all others. This, however, would not fit with the collage view of strategic management.

Why would championing of only one approach offend the collage view of strategic management?

The other extreme is to try deliberately to introduce all (or most) alternative views, but this would tend to be tedious. The approach used in the book takes a middle ground: a prescriptive approach to some extent (no doubt reflecting my prejudices), yet still indicating the weaknesses of the selected approach, that contrary views exist and indicating where these can be found in the further readings. Hopefully, this provides enough of a firm framework in an introductory book for you to feel confident that you are learning something of value, yet for you to be aware of views different from the favoured one.

4.2 The importance of language: precision and definitions

There is an important maxim, 'freedom lies just beyond discipline'. The great artists have freedom because they are disciplined enough to have mastered the basic brush strokes. Similarly, you can't express yourself in any language until you have mastered the basic vocabulary and basic syntax.

It's the same with strategic management: it's vital for you to master the basic terminology before you can form useful constructs and, perhaps more importantly, develop your learning through discussion with others. Thus the important concepts and terms are defined when they first occur and reinforced through the self-check sections at the end of each chapter. Terms are brought together in the glossary at the back of the book. Terminology is also stressed in many of the computer-aided exercises that your lecturer can make available to you.

4.3 Learning objectives

It isn't possible for someone to become a complete strategist solely through reading one book on strategic management. The learning objectives associated with this book are thus more modest and are for you:

- to become aware of the importance and characteristics of strategic management in all forms of organisation;
- to appreciate the contribution you can make to strategic management in your business career at many levels in organisation;
- to know a range of strategic management models and to understand their strengths and weaknesses;
- to have the confidence to be able to tailor the models as appropriate;
- to be sensitive to the 'softer' issues of strategic management, for example organisational culture and business ethics.

References to further reading are provided at the end of each chapter if you wish to explore a subject in more depth.

4.4 Prior knowledge

It is assumed that you have at least a basic knowledge of business in general, and of marketing and finance in particular. Given the characteristics of the organisational environment, this analysis will overwhelmingly be qualitative, so there is no requirement for you to be an expert in mathematics or quantitative methods.

5   A road map to the rest of this book

5.1   Business vs corporation

The main units of analysis in strategic management are the business and the corporation, which consists of several businesses. Exhibit 3 sets out some information on the distribution of firm size in the EU and the UK.

DISCUSSION
POINT 4

What are the main messages contained in Exhibit 3?

Approaching 50% of employed people – excluding the self-employed – work in very small and small enterprises. It is almost certain that these will be businesses and also unlikely that medium-sized enterprises are corporations. Thus it is quite likely that you will work in a business. Even if you join a corporation, almost certainly you will be working at the business level. For these reasons alone, the emphasis in an introductory strategic management text should be on the business. To use a military analogy, not to focus on the business level would be like the Army concentrating all its initial officer training on the needs of generals and field marshals, rather than giving them the skills to be good lieutenants, captains, majors and colonels.

A second reason for the emphasis on the business level is that business-level strategic management is more complex than at the corporate level – and thus more needs to be learned about it. A third reason for the focus is that it's at the business level where almost all the value in a corporation is created.[2] Thus the main emphasis in this book will lie with business-level strategic management. Exhibit 4 illustrates this.

The first four chapters are concerned with the internal context, and this is applicable at both the business and corporate levels. The next ten chapters are concerned with the business level, and only the last three are concerned with the different

EXHIBIT 3

The distribution of firms by size (1996)						
No. of enterprises (1,000) No. of employees in group	Single	Very small 2–9	Small 10–49	Medium 50–249	Large 250+	Total
EU	*8,500	*8,785	1,105	165	35	18,590
UK	2,517	1,010	165	26	7	3,724
Employment (1,000)						
EU	*8,500	*28,500	21,110	15,070	38,220	111,410
UK	2,856	3,553	3,199	2,601	8,746	20,954

ˣestimated

Source: SME Statistics Unit (1997),[3] The European Observatory for SMEs (1997)[4]

emphases associated with strategic management at the corporate level – often called *parenting*.

5.2 The main elements of strategic management

Exhibit 4 illustrates the five main elements of strategic management – although at first glance there might appear to be only four main elements. There is **picturing the future** – the analysis of the organisation's environment into handleable 'chunks' and the subsequent synthesis of these 'chunks' to provide coherent views of the future, involving the organisation's markets, the political climate, the legal framework, etc. The second element is **organisation position determination,** in which the organisation seeks to understand how it is positioned *vis-à-vis* its competitors to face the issues that it thinks might arise in the future. With this understanding of the future and of the

EXHIBIT 4

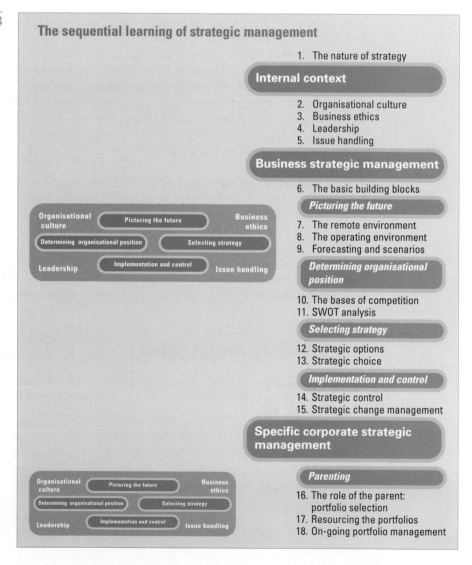

The sequential learning of strategic management

1. The nature of strategy

Internal context

2. Organisational culture
3. Business ethics
4. Leadership
5. Issue handling

Business strategic management

6. The basic building blocks

Picturing the future

7. The remote environment
8. The operating environment
9. Forecasting and scenarios

Determining organisational position

10. The bases of competition
11. SWOT analysis

Selecting strategy

12. Strategic options
13. Strategic choice

Implementation and control

14. Strategic control
15. Strategic change management

Specific corporate strategic management

Parenting

16. The role of the parent: portfolio selection
17. Resourcing the portfolios
18. On-going portfolio management

Organisational culture | Picturing the future | Business ethics
Determining organisational position | Selecting strategy
Leadership | Implementation and control | Issue handling

organisation's place within it, the organisation can move on to **selecting strategy**. Following selection will come **implementation and control** – first carrying out the activities necessary to achieve the chosen goals, and then seeking to keep the strategy as intended and/or reacting to emergent issues.

These four elements are unlikely in practice to be thought about and developed in a fixed sequential fashion, with each element completed and set in stone before the next stage is started – although strong sequential features are likely to exist. It is difficult to control something before it has been implemented, for example.

These four elements don't take place in a vacuum: all of them are affected by the organisational culture, including the ethical stance adopted. They are also strongly affected by the characteristics of the personnel in the organisation, especially those of the leaders. The style of leadership, particularly the strategic vision and the way issues are handled, is of great importance in strategic management. These factors constitute what will be termed the **internal context**, which infuses the other four elements of strategic management. The management of the internal context is the fifth main element of strategic management.

KEY CONCEPT   The five main elements of strategic management are picturing the future, organisational position determination, selecting strategy, implementation and control, and the managing of the internal context.

While the five elements of strategic management are unlikely *in practice* to be considered in a fixed sequence, *for learning* about the subject it is both convenient and necessary to present the material in a sequential manner. This unravelling is shown in Exhibit 4.

5.3 *The internal context (Chapters 2–5)*

Organisational culture is concerned with organisational behaviour, values and assumptions. One particularly important feature of culture, and for this reason given its own chapter, is **business ethics**, concerned as it is with both how employees are treated within an organisation and how the organisation deals with outside interests, with customers, government, the general public, etc. Recognising the cultural 'capabilities' of the organisation and making and keeping efficient and effective in a very competitive world with good ethical practices is one of the real challenges of strategic management.

Leaders are people who seek out opportunities in their quest for increased effectiveness. Fairly obviously then, **leadership** is required in organisations as well as management, not only at board level but also at lower levels in the organisation. While decisions need to be taken that affect the long-term well-being of the organisation, decision taking is often the outcome of a rather fuzzy and indistinct process involving much deliberation, hesitation and controversy, and is best embedded in organisational learning. Thus, rather than seeing leaders as taking decisions, it is more appropriate to see organisations as handling issues. Consequently, the cognitive, psychological and organisational aspects of **issue handling** need to be considered and understood.

5.4 The Building blocks of business strategy (Chapter 6)

Before getting into detail about business strategy formulation and implementation, it is useful to discuss the basic ideas underpinning much of it, so that the subsequent exploration can proceed more easily. This is what is done in Chapter 6.

5.5 Picturing the future (Chapters 7–9)

Before making a considered strategic choice, every organisation needs to have a view of its environment. In strategic management however, it is inappropriate to focus solely on today's environment: the future must be considered, since whether a course of action turns out to be 'good' or 'bad' depends not on *current* conditions but on *future* conditions. There are a great many factors in the environment of a business and it is necessary to have a structure to make sense of them.

Any business can be considered to be operating in two environments. First there is what is termed the **remote environment**, consisting of such things as government pressure and actions, information technology developments and demographic trends. It wouldn't be expected that a business would have any significant influence over the remote environment.

There is also the **operating environment**, consisting of such factors as the markets that the business is operating in, its competitors, its suppliers and other stakeholders over which a business would have some influence. **Forecasts** and **scenarios** take the rather static and fragmented view of the future that comes out of the analyses of the operating and remote environments and melds them together in a dynamic fashion to produce a set of views of the future – scenarios.

5.6 Determining organisational position (Chapters 10 and 11)

Scenarios encapsulate the environmental issues facing a business. The analysis of the **bases of competition** in Chapter 10 identifies where the critical factors lie. The next stage is to determine the relative standings of competing businesses in the future environment in terms of these critical factors. These findings are then assessed to produce a table listing the Strengths and Weaknesses of the business's position and the Opportunities and Threats that it faces through a **SWOT analysis**.

The way in which Chapters 7 to 11 fit together to lead up to the SWOT analysis is shown in Exhibit 5.

5.7 Strategy selection (Chapters 12 and 13)

The results of the SWOT analysis provide the springboard for **strategy selection**. There are many 'generic' strategic options open to a business. These include the method of competition (e.g. low price, high differentiation), the proposed direction (e.g. to expand overseas, to consolidate) and the method of doing it (e.g. through closer links with suppliers, using internal resources). The pros and cons of these various methods need to be considered in a **strategic options** analysis as a prelude to making an appropriate specific strategic choice. The **strategic choice** process will examine the strategic fit, feasibility and acceptability of the various generic options that make up the strategic pathway for a particular organisation.

EXHIBIT 5

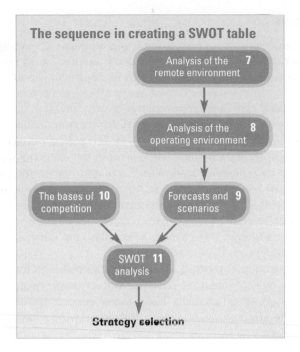

The sequence in creating a SWOT table

Analysis of the remote environment **7**

Analysis of the operating environment **8**

The bases of **10** competition

Forecasts and **9** scenarios

SWOT **11** analysis

Strategy selection

5.8 Strategic implementation and control (Chapters 14 and 15)

However good a strategy may be in the abstract, it is unlikely to be implemented unless considerable thought is given to the human resource implications. The penultimate chapter in treating business-level strategic management concerns **strategic change management**, particularly important as the demands on leader-managers are for constant change. What also needs to be considered is how the objectives should be monitored, how frequently they should be monitored and how the findings should most appropriately be reported. This is the area of **strategic control**.

5.9 Corporate strategic management – parenting (Chapters 16–18)

Many businesses are grouped within corporations, and the corporate head office – or parent – has a significant role to play. These three chapters deal with those aspects of parenting that are unique to the parent. Thus, although parents will be involved with change management they are not uniquely so, for example, and their concerns are equally those of business-level strategic managers and will have been explored in Chapter 14.

The **role of the parent** and **portfolio selection** are considered first. Chapter 17 is concerned with **resourcing the portfolios**, where the demands arising from the business and competences portfolios are explored. The final chapter is concerned with **ongoing portfolio management**, where the continuing parental roles in all their forms are considered.

5.10 Summary

SUMMARY
- Strategic management isn't like completing a jigsaw; it's more like creating a collage, with the same four stages – goal determination, model identification, model tailoring and model integration. Strategic management is both an art and a science. The scientific aspects may be viewed as assembling the pieces of a collage: the art is to arrange the pieces in an appropriately creative manner. EXHIBIT 1, EXHIBIT 2
- The number of people employed in small businesses, the number of businesses in corporations, the greater complexity of business-level strategic management and the value-creating capacity of businesses mean that the great majority of this book is given over to exploring business-level strategic management. EXHIBIT 3
- The book is laid out in three main sections. Chapters 2–5 cover what is termed the internal context – the features of the organisation that colour all it does. Chapters 7–15 explore business strategic management. Chapters 16–18 cover those aspects of corporate strategic management where the emphasis is significantly different from the business level. EXHIBIT 4
- There are five main elements in strategic management: picturing the future, organisation position determination, selecting strategy, implementation and control, and managing the internal context. The internal context provides both some of the pieces of the strategic management collage and the glue that holds the pieces together. EXHIBIT 4
- The SWOT table is a summary of the position of a business within its environment. It's a pivotal point within strategy development. EXHIBIT 5
- There are many learning aids within each chapter, which are listed in Exhibits 6 and 7. EXHIBIT 6, EXHIBIT 7

5.11 Self-check

SELF-CHECK
1 Reconsider the learning outcomes for this chapter. Check that you feel confident that you can carry out the activities listed there.
2 Having read this chapter you should be able to define the following terms:

model	cognitive coathanger	collage

5.12 Mini-case

MINI-CASE

Phoney strategists (after Goddard)[5]

The phoney strategist defines himself; he is the man who calls himself a professional, an expert, an insider. But thinking and investing strategically do not require expertise. There is no body of arcane knowledge that stands to the strategist as biology stands to the physician or physics to the engineer. The strategist, like the artist and the scientist but unlike the cook, does not have a recipe. There is no method as such; certainly no method for having an idea, telling a story, or inventing a good enough myth by which the firm can define its competitive stance over the next year or two; only a method for testing, much later, its efficacy. The need for a formula, or even proof, is the surest sign of a man unsuited to the strategic task.

Who then are the impostors? Who are the culprits?

- All those formulae. All those who see strategy as a kind of cooking rather than a kind of science; or as painting by numbers rather than painting by imagination.
- Peters and Waterman with their principles of excellence (these are now, of course, the rules that need to be broken for profit to be made).
- Michael Porter with his generic strategies, each appropriate to different stages of the industry life cycle.
- Boston Consulting Group, with its assorted animals and investment rules.
- But by far the worst of all, the most damaging idea ever put into the tender and innocent minds of businessmen, the dreaded MBO: management by objectives, invented as a kind of meccano for the child manager unable to structure his thoughts, let alone his strategy.

Strategic thinking does not, and cannot, work to a system. On the contrary, it is the tool the manager has at his disposal to overturn systems, to question deeply held assumptions, and to think and perform 'the impossible'.

Discussion point 5

What is the link between the 'rules' discussed above and the models of strategic management?

- The argument about impostors appears to be one against learning 'the rules' of strategic management. Do you agree with what is said about the impostors? And do you agree that you are wasting your time learning these rules?

5.13   *Notes and References*

NOTES AND
REFERENCES

1 Although strategic management – especially strategic thinking – isn't a jigsaw, one of the aims of strategic managment is to make present-day operations something akin to a jigsaw, as a move to efficiency.

2 Rumelt, R.P., 'How much does industry matter?' *Strategic Management Journal*, Vol.12, 1991, pp 167–85.

3 Statistical Bulletin, *Small and Medium Enterprise (SME) Statistics for the United Kingdom, 1996*. SME Statistics Unit, Department of Trade and Industry, July 1997, URN 97/92.

4 European Network for SME Research, EIM/ENSR, *The European Observatory for SMEs*, Fifth Annual Report, Zoetermeer 1997.

5 Goddard, J. This is a transcript of an after-dinner talk given by Jules Goddard to the participants on the Strategic Investment Decision Programme, London Business School, May 1986.

6   The consequences of the clear split between the treatment of business and corporate strategic management

There are two main reasons for making a distinct split between business- and corporate-level strategy. First, it makes it easier to understand each area. Second, it prevents an inappropriate focus on the sensational, the big mergers and corporate upheavals, and concentrates instead on those areas where most leader-managers are active most of the time.

However, this clear split made for pedagogic reasons does have a few slightly disturbing consequences for the treatment of topics. The main ones concern those features that may exceptionally be the concern of business and are treated as though they are solely corporate matters, and thus not treated in Chapters 7–15 but in the final three chapters. These features are:

- mergers and acquisitions and alliances;
- long-term sources of funds;
- large changes in business capability, treated as tantamount to the creation of another business and thus the province of the parent.

7 How to use this book

Chapter 1 provides an overview of strategic management. It is therefore a chapter that you are strongly urged to read before tackling any others.

Each chapter has a very similar format. Each begins with a **fronting page**, which places the chapter in the context of the whole book and in the group of which it's a part. A **contents list** of the main sections of the chapter is provided together with a short description of the chapter sequence. The chapter proper then begins with a **short statement** explaining why the material is important and a set of learning objectives.

Discussion points appear throughout each chapter. Their inclusion is motivated by the belief that for anyone to understand something they have to have internalised it. While you can use these discussion points on your own, the best way for most people to internalise an idea is to articulate it. With present-day class sizes it's well-nigh impossible for most students to do this in formal lecture and tutorial sessions. Perhaps the most appropriate way is for you to get together in small groups with your fellow students to discuss the chapters, and these discussion points are a way of focusing that discussion.

The discussion points only deal with matters introduced and explored in that chapter. This is because your course may not follow quite the same sequence as the book and to link chapters may be inappropriate. As students often experience difficulty in integrating the various topics in strategic management courses, some integrating discussion points are presented at the end of each chapter in a **further discussion points** section.

Exhibits, the diagrams set throughout the text, play a very significant role. They really are worth a thousand words in the sense that they show the main features, with detail removed. It's suggested that after a quick read through of the chapter, you begin your more detailed understanding by ensuring that you understand these diagrams. To help with this, the summary of the main points given at the end of each chapter is linked to the associated exhibit. These diagrams are the 'cognitive coathangers' on which you can hang the details in the text.

Material is thus summarised in the diagrams and in the summary itself. Further mini-summaries are set as **key concepts** throughout the text.

There is a self-check section immediately after the summary in which you are encouraged to check on your understanding of the main learning objectives and the key terms introduced in the chapter.

In most chapters, one or two **mini-cases** are provided that get you to think further about important issues in the chapter. Assignments using material outside of the book are also offered. In particular, the GSM case, which is the first main case in the section towards the back of the book, is treated as a 'backbone' case, and questions are asked about it in most chapters.

Further readings are provided for those of you who wish to follow up a particular point, and **chapter notes and references** follow. It's in these two sections where views that may differ from those expressed in the book are referenced.

All these points are illustrated in Exhibits 6 and 7. Exhibit 6 identifies the important features of the fronting page that introduces each chapter and places the chapter within the context of the book and strategic management. Exhibit 7 indicates the main features of the text in each chapter and the learning aids incorporated.

EXHIBIT 6

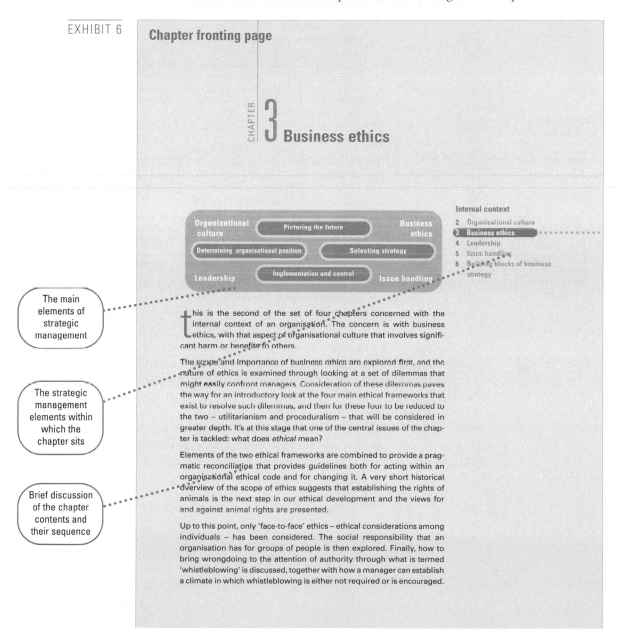

Chapter fronting page

CHAPTER **3** Business ethics

Organisational culture — Picturing the future — Business ethics

Determining organisational position — Selecting strategy

Leadership — Implementation and control — Issue handling

Internal context
2 Organisational culture
3 **Business ethics**
4 Leadership
5 Issue handling
6 Building blocks of business strategy

The main elements of strategic management

The strategic management elements within which the chapter sits

Brief discussion of the chapter contents and their sequence

This is the second of the set of four chapters concerned with the internal context of an organisation. The concern is with business ethics, with that aspect of organisational culture that involves significant harm or benefits to others.

The scope and importance of business ethics are explored first, and the nature of ethics is examined through looking at a set of dilemmas that might easily confront managers. Consideration of these dilemmas paves the way for an introductory look at the four main ethical frameworks that exist to resolve such dilemmas, and then for these four to be reduced to the two – utilitarianism and proceduralism – that will be considered in greater depth. It's at this stage that one of the central issues of the chapter is tackled: what does *ethical* mean?

Elements of the two ethical frameworks are combined to provide a pragmatic reconciliation that provides guidelines both for acting within an organisational ethical code and for changing it. A very short historical overview of the scope of ethics suggests that establishing the rights of animals is the next step in our ethical development and the views for and against animal rights are presented.

Up to this point, only 'face-to-face' ethics – ethical considerations among individuals – has been considered. The social responsibility that an organisation has for groups of people is then explored. Finally, how to bring wrongdoing to the attention of authority through what is termed 'whistleblowing' is discussed, together with how a manager can establish a climate in which whistleblowing is either not required or is encouraged.

EXHIBIT 7

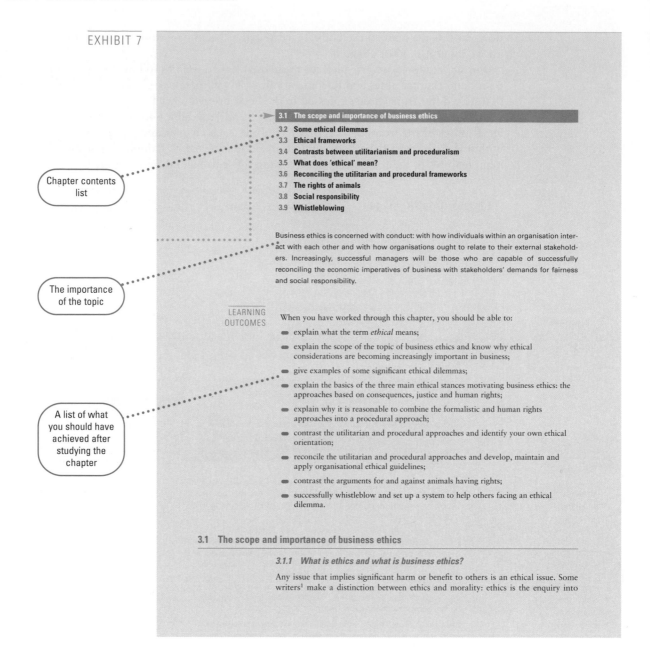

3.1 **The scope and importance of business ethics**
3.2 **Some ethical dilemmas**
3.3 **Ethical frameworks**
3.4 **Contrasts between utilitarianism and proceduralism**
3.5 **What does 'ethical' mean?**
3.6 **Reconciling the utilitarian and procedural frameworks**
3.7 **The rights of animals**
3.8 **Social responsibility**
3.9 **Whistleblowing**

Business ethics is concerned with conduct: with how individuals within an organisation inter-act with each other and with how organisations ought to relate to their external stakehold-ers. Increasingly, successful managers will be those who are capable of successfully reconciling the economic imperatives of business with stakeholders' demands for fairness and social responsibility.

Chapter contents list

The importance of the topic

A list of what you should have achieved after studying the chapter

LEARNING
OUTCOMES

When you have worked through this chapter, you should be able to:

- explain what the term *ethical* means;
- explain the scope of the topic of business ethics and know why ethical considerations are becoming increasingly important in business;
- give examples of some significant ethical dilemmas;
- explain the basics of the three main ethical stances motivating business ethics: the approaches based on consequences, justice and human rights;
- explain why it is reasonable to combine the formalistic and human rights approaches into a procedural approach;
- contrast the utilitarian and procedural approaches and identify your own ethical orientation;
- reconcile the utilitarian and procedural approaches and develop, maintain and apply organisational ethical guidelines;
- contrast the arguments for and against animals having rights;
- successfully whistleblow and set up a system to help others facing an ethical dilemma.

3.1 The scope and importance of business ethics

3.1.1 What is ethics and what is business ethics?

Any issue that implies significant harm or benefit to others is an ethical issue. Some writers[1] make a distinction between ethics and morality: ethics is the enquiry into morality and morality is what is being enquired about. Another distinction is that ethics is about 'public' rules and regulations and that morals are personal. These distinctions won't be made here, and the terms *ethics* and *morality* and *ethical* and *moral* will be used interchangeably.

While fundamental ethical principles will remain unchanged wherever they are applied, the specifics of their application and the specific dilemmas that are being confronted will vary with the context. Just as medical ethics is concerned with the application of ethics in medical contexts, business ethics is concerned with the application of ethics in business contexts. While business ethics will be grounded in general ethical principles, no company that defines 'right' and 'wrong' in terms that would satisfy the most demanding of contemporary individual consciences would survive for very long. The economic imperatives of business are what make business ethics different from ethics in other areas.

There are two intertwined considerations in business ethics that are of concern to senior management.

DISCUSSION POINT 3.1

Reflect on the issues you have confronted over the past few months, in both your business and personal life. How many of them involved harm or benefit to other individuals? How many involved *significant* harm or benefit?

• Should we be considering *business* ethics or should we be considering *corporate* or indeed *organisational* ethics?

First, just as the firm is a legal entity, one view of business ethics is that a firm is also exhibit a moral entity. In this view the organisation, perhaps through its senior managers, should determine how the company deals with the outside world. A firm should act morally because the very enterprise of business presupposes that the participants in business transactions subscribe to a set of agreed moral norms. If they didn't and, for example, fraud and deception were commonplace in commercial transactions, it would be very difficult to conduct business. Every transaction would need some form of tight contract and lawyers would grow exceedingly rich. A second view is that the sole purpose of a profit-seeking firm is to seek profit for the shareholders and that managers should work towards this end. The firm is an inanimate construction and can't and shouldn't take on a moral stance. In this view the firm would be legally obliged only to act according to the law in its dealings with outsiders. However it is regarded, legally or morally, there is a requirement on senior managers to define the relationships between the firm and its environment.

KEY CONCEPT

An ethical issue is any issue that implies significant harm or benefit to another individual. Business ethics is concerned with the way moral issues are handled within a business environment, and thus within economic imperatives. Business ethics gives rise to two concerns for managers; they have to determine both the ethical stance that the firm takes to its external stakeholders and the moral climate within the organisation to guide the actions of employees.

Points for personal consideration and group discussion

Interim summary of the key point of the preceding sections

SUMMARY   The resolution of ethical dilemmas is likely to become a more important part of a manager's working life and thus it is very important for them to reflect on what is involved. In summary:

- To say that something is *ethical* hasn't much objective significance; what is ethical is in the eye of the beholder. However, the one firm statement that can be made is that the notion of ethics carries with it the idea of something bigger than the individual: the concept of universality.
- Business ethics is concerned with the moral climate within the organisation and with how the organisation deals with outside stakeholders. While the laws of the land and the dominant ethics are usually broadly in line, there is never likely to be perfect overlap.   EXHIBIT 3.1
- There are four generic ethical frameworks that might be used in business situations: the theological, the utilitarian, the formalistic and an approach based on human rights. In practice the formalistic and human rights approaches can be treated together, and termed the procedural approach. Together, the utilitarian and procedural approaches provide the framework within which a business can frame its ethical position. No ethical position can be objectively considered better than any other.   EXHIBIT 3.2, EXHIBIT 3.5, EXHIBIT 3.6, EXHIBIT 3.7
- The scope of business ethics is increasing to include a concern for animals and for future generations.
- Social responsibility is concerned with how the organisation treats its secondary stakeholders. Four areas of concern can be identified: environmental, exploitation, sustainability and influence.   EXHIBIT 3.8
- Successful whistleblowing is difficult to achieve. It is the responsibility of senior management to establish a climate in which the primary stakeholders can bring unethical behaviour to the attention of senior management.   EXHIBIT 3.9

SELF-CHECK   1 Reconsider the learning outcomes for this chapter. Check that you feel confident that you can carry out the activities listed there.
2 Having read this chapter, you should be able to define the following terms:

ethical	human rights	utilitarianism
ethics	proceduralism	whistleblowing
formalism		

MINI-CASE 3.2

Animal rights

Ape rights not wrong[21]

Great apes may soon have some of the rights previously reserved only for humans, if a group of New Zealand scientists and activists succeed.

They have asked their parliament to grant the right to life to man's closest relatives, which include chimpanzees, gorillas and orang-utans.

The Great Ape Project argues that the apes are genetically very close to humans and part of the same animal family. 'There's now a mountain of evidence that the great apes are as intelligent as young human children,' said theoretical biologist David Penny.

Discussion point 3.11

Is genetic closeness a guide to ethical behaviour? Is closeness in intelligence to children a criterion?

Are animal rights the logical next step in social evolution?

Recap and review of the main points in the chapter

Itemising the linking diagrams

Self-check on learning outcomes, terminology and the effect of environmental unpredictability

Mini-case to help consolidate learning

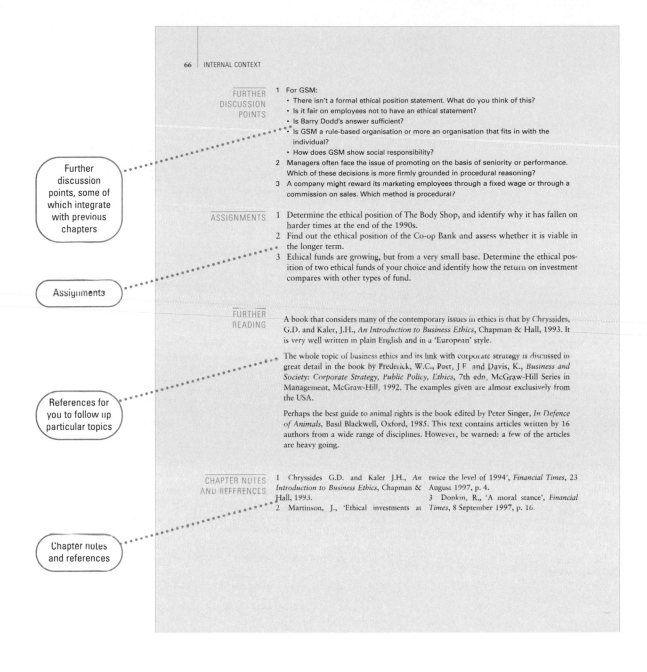

66 | INTERNAL CONTEXT

FURTHER DISCUSSION POINTS

1 For GSM:
   • There isn't a formal ethical position statement. What do you think of this?
   • Is it fair on employees not to have an ethical statement?
   • Is Barry Dodd's answer sufficient?
   • Is GSM a rule-based organisation or more an organisation that fits in with the individual?
   • How does GSM show social responsibility?
2 Managers often face the issue of promoting on the basis of seniority or performance. Which of these decisions is more firmly grounded in procedural reasoning?
3 A company might reward its marketing employees through a fixed wage or through a commission on sales. Which method is procedural?

ASSIGNMENTS

1 Determine the ethical position of The Body Shop, and identify why it has fallen on harder times at the end of the 1990s.
2 Find out the ethical position of the Co-op Bank and assess whether it is viable in the longer term.
3 Ethical funds are growing, but from a very small base. Determine the ethical position of two ethical funds of your choice and identify how the return on investment compares with other types of fund.

FURTHER READING

A book that considers many of the contemporary issues in ethics is that by Chryssides, G.D. and Kaler, J.H., *An Introduction to Business Ethics*, Chapman & Hall, 1993. It is very well written in plain English and in a 'European' style.

The whole topic of business ethics and its link with corporate strategy is discussed in great detail in the book by Frederick, W.C., Post, J.F. and Davis, K., *Business and Society: Corporate Strategy, Public Policy, Ethics*, 7th edn, McGraw-Hill Series in Management, McGraw-Hill, 1992. The examples given are almost exclusively from the USA.

Perhaps the best guide to animal rights is the book edited by Peter Singer, *In Defence of Animals*, Basil Blackwell, Oxford, 1985. This text contains articles written by 16 authors from a wide range of disciplines. However, be warned: a few of the articles are heavy going.

CHAPTER NOTES AND REFERENCES

1 Chryssides G.D. and Kaler J.H., *An Introduction to Business Ethics*, Chapman & Hall, 1993.
2 Martinson, J., 'Ethical investments at twice the level of 1994', *Financial Times*, 23 August 1997, p. 4.
3 Donkin, R., 'A moral stance', *Financial Times*, 8 September 1997, p. 16.

Further discussion points, some of which integrate with previous chapters

Assignments

References for you to follow up particular topics

Chapter notes and references

Introduction

1 The nature of strategic management

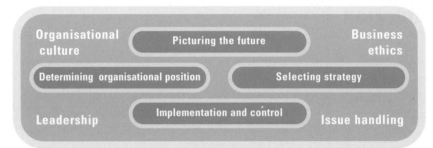

this opening chapter begins with a consideration of the importance of strategic management and of who should be involved in its formulation and implementation. The strategic concerns of the two main levels of strategic management, the business and the corporation, are explored, and the differences in emphasis between strategy for profit-seeking and not-for-profit organisations are discussed.

The features of the environment that affect strategy are then considered and the scope and characteristics of strategic management itself are explored. Different views concerning the rights of stakeholders are discussed.

The discussion to this point has not included formal definitions of terms; these are now introduced. Two important distinctions are considered: the different ways in which strategy can be developed and the difference between strategy and tactics. This discussion brings home the point that little is totally cut and dried in strategic management, and that there are many grey areas.

Strategic management is concerned with the overall direction of an organisation and as such it is a vital management activity. The present trends in business mean that many more managers than previously have the opportunity and responsibility to contribute to the strategic management of their organisations: strategic management is far too important and complex to be left solely in the hands of the board of directors. To make a useful contribution, however, managers must understand their role in the strategic management process and how strategic management differs from other forms of management.

LEARNING
OUTCOMES

When you have worked through this chapter, you should be able to:

- explain the importance of strategic management and the trends leading to greater involvement of a larger number of people in strategy development;

- describe the main strategic concerns at the two main levels of strategic management both for profit-seeking and not-for-profit organisations;

- characterise the environment within which strategic management has to operate;

- describe the scope and characteristics of strategic management;

- explain the two sides of the stakeholder debate and have a view of your own on this issue;

- explain the difference between strategic planning and strategic thinking and between strategy and tactics.

1.1 The importance of strategic management

Organisations are groupings of people and resources created for a purpose and, in general, running any organisation – your local garage, a multinational company or a university – is a complex activity. It is complex because a lot of information from many sources needs to be considered in order to understand the organisation and the situation it finds itself in and take reasoned action. There are outside interests; for a university these include the interests of government, local education authorities, prospective students and their potential employers. There are the aspirations and skills of the students and staff, the suitability and state of repair of the buildings and so forth. There will also be concerns about what the organisation is aiming to do and the balance between carrying out present activities and preparing for different, future ones. As this list illustrates, many views on many different sorts of thing have somehow to be combined: there is a need to juggle apples and pears. Someone, or much more likely a group of people, must handle this complexity and the ambiguity that is often associated with information from multiple sources, and be responsible for the overall direction of the organisation.

Responsibility for the overall direction of the organisation sums up what strategic management is about. In small businesses this is a responsibility for the livelihood of the owners, the employees and their families. In large organisations it means responsibility not only for large financial investments but also for the jobs and well-being of perhaps thousands of people, possibly around the world, who might be affected directly by the firm's operations. Thus strategic management truly is important, concerned as it is with the sustained well-being of the organisation and with the groups and individuals affected by its activities.

1.2 Who should be concerned with strategic management?

Having said that strategic management is concerned with the overall direction of the whole organisation, it should be stressed that a board of directors isn't the only group of people who are involved in or should know about strategic management, and neither are those who are working in a strategic planning department as specialist planners. But these are exceptional positions; most people will be operating in the functions, such as marketing and operations. It might be felt that managers in the functions will only be contributing in a peripheral manner to strategic management, if at all. However, this isn't the case. The number of people who might contribute to strategic management has increased considerably over the past decade. The trend towards a larger number of more autonomous units with the people in them responsible for unit strategy has played a part. There has also been delayering, where the number of people between the top and bottom of an organisation has been reduced. Everyone is now nearer the top of their organisations and thus closer to those with ultimate strategic responsibility, and the emphasis on empowerment gives employees the freedom to get on with contributing to the running of their organisation without detailed interference from above. A further impetus towards wider involvement has been the realisation that the implementation of change is far easier to carry out successfully if those responsible for the implementation, and those affected by it, have contributed to the thinking that has led to the change.

A further motivation for non-board managers to develop strategic management skills and strategic understanding is the realisation that much of strategy is a 'bottom-up' process, whereby each subunit within an organisation initiates much of its own strategy and this contribution is consolidated with other subunit strategies to form the organisational strategy. It is clear why this should be so: lower-level managers are much more in touch with many of the main stakeholders, with customers and suppliers for example. Lower-level managers have the vital role of being the organisation's antennae, picking up trends in the environment, especially the marketplace, interpreting this information and ensuring that it is passed to the senior managers who can authorise action.

Although specialist strategic planners can be very useful in providing information and offering models to senior managers as well as helping to control the sequence of the strategic management process, it's important to realise that they should be *on tap and not on top*. Managers must not abdicate their responsibility for strategic management to such staffers: they have to implement the strategy, and they have the knowledge of the organisation and its environment that planning staff rarely have.

1.3   Levels of strategic management

1.3.1   Corporate, business and functional levels

Saying that strategic management is about taking responsibility for the overall direction of the organisation may seem simple enough, but it isn't completely obvious what should be considered to be 'the organisation'.

Profit-seeking organisations are in existence to generate returns to shareholders by satisfying customer needs. They do this by engaging in at least one conversion process, converting inputs to something of a higher value. At its simplest, a car assembler such as Ford or Peugeot can be considered to be converting a set of car components into a whole car; an advertising agency converts a proposal into an advertising campaign; a street trader converts articles from one location to a more convenient one.

A starting point in establishing the types of organisation that can reasonably call for strategic management is to focus on the conversion processes. Except for the smallest, organisations have within them functions – such as marketing, operations and personnel. Large high-street retailers often have logistics and buying functions. Below the functional level there are the subfunctions; for example, merchandising and quality assurance are subfunctions within the buying function, as shown in Exhibit 1.1. The functions and subfunctions are all units that are concerned with conversions of some sort: the question is, should they be considered organisations in strategic management terms?

There are many books about the functions that include the words *strategy* or *strategic* in their title: examples are *human resource strategy* and *strategic marketing*. However, it should be realised that these phrases are simply shorthand for *the human resource/marketing dimension of business strategy*. Strategic management is needed at the functional levels, but it must be part of, and not independent of, business strategic management. It would be madness for a marketing function to establish a strategy that demanded more financial support than the business could provide, or more production facilities than were available. Such considerations have led to the realisation that an organisation in strategic management terms must be one that can sensibly operate independently of other organisations. This isn't the case for a function, but it is true for a business. Thus we *can* talk of business strategy but not of functional strategy, only of the contributions that the functions can make to business strategy.

Organisations engaged in more than one business are corporations. Prior to 1988, BAT Industries was active in both tobacco and insurance and thus it consists of at least two businesses. Abbey National includes three businesses – retail banking,

EXHIBIT 1.1

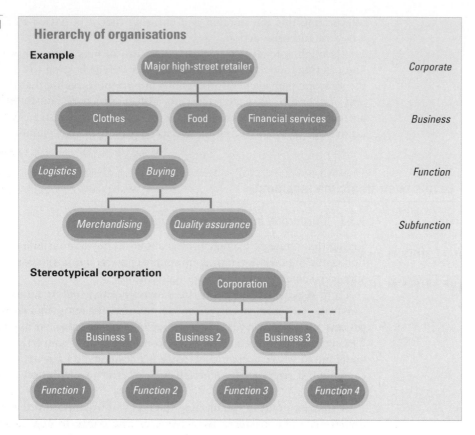

Hierarchy of organisations

insurance and treasury operations. The European engineering giant ABB Asea Brown Boveri is a collection of 1300 businesses.[1] Thus there is a level of strategic management above that of the business: the corporate level. A corporation is also an organisation in strategic management terms. A stereotypical organisational hierarchy is shown in Exhibit 1.1. The relationships between the functions and the business will tend to be much more intimate than that between a business and its parent corporation.

1.3.2 Corporate and business concerns

Although people working in the functions and indeed the subfunctions may be concerned with strategy, it can be seen that there are two distinct levels of strategic management, with the business level separate from, yet working within, the corporate strategy. While both the corporate and business levels will have some concern for and some input into most strategic aspects of the organisation, the primary strategic responsibilities of the corporate and business levels are different. They are summarised in Exhibit 1.2.

The main question a corporation must ask itself is what businesses it should be in, i.e. what should be its portfolio of businesses. A further very important consideration is the building up of competences that can be used in several of its businesses and provide the bases for future businesses. The Japanese see microchips as the *rice of*

EXHIBIT 1.2

Major concerns in strategic management

Level	Main concerns
Corporate	What businesses should we be in? Which competencies do we need to develop?
Business	How do we compete? Which capabilities do we need to develop?
Not-for-profit organisation	How do we develop and maintain good relationships with stakeholders?

industry, feeding competitive advantage into every product:[2] to many Japanese companies expertise in microchips would be seen as a competence that needs corporate support.

The corporate level is only peripherally concerned with competing, since it hasn't got the usual set of competitors or customers: it's the businesses that have these. Managers at the business level are seldom asking whether they should be in the business they are in; they *are* in that business and generally have to accept this state of affairs. At the business level, the main strategic concern is with how the business should compete and with the development of the capabilities it requires.

Note that the questions 'What businesses should we be in?' and 'How do we compete?' are both part of the bigger question, 'How do we add value?' Except perhaps for some very special cases, organisations all seek to add value: that is to say, the value of the output is greater than the value (costs) of the inputs and the processes.

DISCUSSION
POINT 1.1

Consider your university and your department. Which, if any, is a business and which a corporation?

● Can you think of an organisation that isn't in existence to add value?

1.4 Not-for-profit organisations

Even not-for-profit organisations (e.g. government departments, universities and charities) are 'in the business' of carrying out a conversion – for example, among other things a university converts academic staff time, lecture room facilities, library facilities, etc. into a learning environment – and the term 'business' will be applied equally to their activities. Not-for-profit organisations should be in the business of adding value, even if not creating profits.

However, there is a difference in emphasis between not-for-profit organisations and profit-seeking ones, and this difference is contained in Exhibit 1.2. There is no difference at the corporate level, where the concerns lie with the business and competency portfolios. But at the business level the main question that a profit seeking business will be asking – 'How do we compete?' – will be replaced by 'How do we develop and maintain good relationships with our stakeholders?' This isn't to say that not-for-profit organisations never compete: charities compete for government grants and for the contributions of individuals, and universities compete for students and for research funding. It's also not to say that profit-seeking organisations aren't concerned with relationships; indeed, the question of how well a business competes is closely linked to the quality of its relationships with stakeholders. The important point is not that one type of business does something that the other doesn't; it's that the emphases are different.

KEY CONCEPT | Recent trends mean that many managers have considerable opportunity to contribute to the formulation of strategy. There are two main levels of strategic management, the corporate and the business. Both are seeking to add value. The main questions that the corporation is seeking to answer are 'What businesses should we be in?' and 'Which competencies do we need to develop?' The main questions that the profit-seeking business is seeking to answer are 'How do we compete?' and 'Which capabilities do we need to develop?' Not-for-profit organisations will downplay the competitive aspect and put a greater emphasis on the question 'How do we develop and maintain good relationships with stakeholders?'

1.5 The environment of strategic management

Each functional area within an organisation has to take account of factors external to it. However, it's at the strategic level where environmental concerns are the greatest, since the functions are cushioned from the full force of the environment by the rest of the organisation. If the environment was unchanging or was changing in well-recognised ways, then much of strategic management would be straightforward – and boring. It's the unpredictability of the future that makes strategy so absorbing, and it's the characteristics of this unpredictability that affect the form of the strategic management process.

The predictability of an environment may be characterised by the influence of five components, as shown in Exhibit 1.3. Complexity and dynamism differ from the other three components as the situations in which they arise are intrinsically understandable. The complexity in the environment can be understood by carrying out more detailed analyses, while the dynamism can be understood through faster analy-

EXHIBIT 1.3

The components of predictability in the environment

Chaos	the situation in which broad patterns are predictable but within these broad patterns detailed features are completely unknowable
Complexity	reflects the need to mesh together many different forms of information to achieve understanding as a prerequisite for taking reasoned action
Dynamism	the rate of change of features in the environment
Turbulence	the situation whereby the environment changes in unpredictable ways
Uncertainty	reflected in the number of feasible futures facing an organisation

sis. In practice, however, the level of complexity and the degree of change may make it impossible for an organisation to cope fully.

Complexity and turbulence are similar in that they describe situations where the links between cause and effect are difficult to discern. They differ in that complex situations are those for which there are many cause-and-effect relationships that can be understood, at least in theory, from an analysis of past events, whereas in a turbulent environment the interactions between many different causes and effects make it such that no one is in a position to make predictions. The Asian economic crisis that began in 1997 is an example of turbulence.

Turbulence and chaos characterise situations where the future is unknowable, however detailed the analysis may be. The defining difference between turbulence and chaos is that in chaos the general patterns are repeated (although the detail isn't), whereas with turbulence there are no discernible patterns to help predict the future. For example, the weather patterns we experience are chaotic, in that although firm predictions of what the weather will be like on any particular day in any particular year aren't possible, it is possible to predict reasonably accurately the average daily temperature for a day in any specific period and the likely range of temperature values that might reasonably occur. The predictions of the averages come from an analysis of past data. Turbulence, however, doesn't follow any past patterns; it consists of one-off events coming 'out of the blue'. Turbulent weather arises from some incident like a massive volcanic eruption, as happened when Mount Pinatubo erupted in 1991 and lowered the average temperature in the northern hemisphere by a measurable amount, or with the tsunami that struck Papua New Guinea in 1998.

KEY CONCEPT   Uncertainty can be considered as the organisation's 'residual' lack of knowledge. It comprises the intrinsically unknowable, turbulence and the detail in chaos, together with that which is intrinsically knowable but that the organisation doesn't know, i.e. with complexity and dynamism. Greater *organisational agility* will allow competitors to obtain competitive advantage in the face of the intrinsically unknowable. Greater *understanding* will allow a competitive advantage in the face of the intrinsically knowable.

1.6 The scope and characteristics of strategic management

The degree of importance of strategic management and the environmental uncertainty are not the only facets that distinguish strategic management from other forms of management. Six further distinguishing characteristics can be identified, and they are summarised in Exhibit 1.4. This isn't to say that these features are absent at other levels within an organisation, but only that they aren't present with the same intensity.

- Long-term orientation   Decisions taken in the present will be played out in the future; in the case of strategic decisions, in the longer term. What *long term* means isn't obvious, as it depends on the type of business: a fast-moving consumer goods manufacturer (of fashion items, for example) will have a time horizon of perhaps only a few months, while a firm operating in shipbuilding or aircraft manufacture will typically have a time horizon of years; the aero engine

EXHIBIT 1.4

The characteristics of strategic management

Importance	Qualitative emphasis
Environmental uncertainty	Matching the organisation and its environment
Long-term orientation	Transformational as well as incremental change
External orientation	Relationships

manufacturer Rolls-Royce takes a 30-year view. So there's no fixed period that can be considered long term. Furthermore, the organisation's situation may dictate what long term means: a week may be long term for an organisation in dire trouble. Whatever the organisational circumstances, however, the time horizon for a corporation will almost certainly be longer than that of its constituent businesses and that of a business longer than that of its functions.

It's important for managers involved in strategy formulation to adopt an appropriate time horizon: too narrow and they will be accused of short-termism; too long and they will be considered blue-sky dreamers.

- What underlying characteristics of a business and its environment do you think will determine an appropriate time horizon?

- External orientation   The emphasis on matching the organisation with its environment indicates that strategic managers must be externally aware, and this is indeed the case. Senior managers typically spend 50% or more of their time interacting with people and interests outside of their organisation and with considering external issues.[3]

- Qualitative emphasis   Strategic management is about the future – and often about a very uncertain future. Detailed calculations are seldom called for: what's the use of landscape gardening when there's an earthquake about to occur? This emphasis on 'the big picture' rather than on detail means that most of strategic management, especially the determination of strategy, is qualitative in nature, with relatively little emphasis on the quantitative. Numbers are used in two ways. First, in a very broad way to establish the 'ballpark' in which the organisation should be thinking – financial considerations should inhibit the local corner shop from thinking about taking on the giant supermarket chains; a local garage proprietor shouldn't consider for too long whether to acquire the Ford Motor Company. Second, numbers are used in a more detailed way to establish the feasibility of proposed courses of action; they are used as a 'sanity check' on qualitative proposals. This isn't to say that numbers aren't vital for day-to-day decision making, only that they aren't the mainspring for strategic thinking and that their downplaying distinguishes the strategic from the operational.

- Matching the organisation and its environment   Strategic management involves matching the organisation to its environment. Matching takes two forms:

  - The organisation alters itself and the products and services it offers in order to match the needs of customers in its chosen marketplace. This is the

market-based approach, so called because the organisation looks to the marketplace to see how it should act and how it should evolve. Most businesses have to operate a market-based approach if they are to stay viable in the market in which they currently operate.

- The organisation identifies where its strengths lie and chooses those activities that play to these strengths. This is the **resource-based approach,** whereby the organisation considers its resources and capabilities to determine what it should do, rather than looking to the characteristics of a particular market to determine what to do. Of course, an organisation following a resource-based approach mustn't fall into the trap of providing a product or a service for which there is no demand.

Most organisations have to be content with working within an environment over which they have little influence, and thus with matching their activities to their chosen environment. However, some organisations are so innovative that they determine what the future will turn out to be. Examples of this are 3M with its range of products that 'seek markets', and Microsoft with what are effectively world standards for PCs, first with MS-DOS (disk operating system) and then Windows. There is a belief that the dominance of office-based personal computers will give way early in the 2000s to digital appliances that have radio connectivity built in. The formation of the joint venture Symbian in 1998 between the mobile phone giants Nokia, Ericsson and Motorola, which make 75% of the world's mobile phones, and Psion, which will provide the necessary software, is an attempt by these organisations to set the standards for personal communications in the next decade.[4]

KEY CONCEPT In general, the matching of an organisation with its environment takes two forms. In the market-based approach the organisation adjusts to fit the market it is in. In the resource-based approach the organisation finds the market that best suits its capabilities.

DISCUSSION
POINT 1.3 Can you think of organisations other than those cited above that have 'made the future'?
Why is the third approach termed a *hybrid approach*?
Can you think of any big decisions in your life that depended on numbers? Which degree course to take? Who your partner should be?

- Incremental and transformational change   Strategic change isn't simply the 'big-bang' changes that make the newspaper headlines, the mega-takeover or the ousting of a managing director after an organisation has incurred enormous losses. It's often about slow, apparently unexciting, incremental change, the sort practised over many years by Marks & Spencer, the family-owned small firms of the German Mittelstand[5] and many Japanese companies.[6] However, what distinguishes strategic concerns from others is that strategic change *can* be revolutionary, often termed *transformational*, whereas non-strategic change is almost always evolutionary.

It is important to realise that the resources for future developments often depend on doing well today, on establishing a good reputation and generating profits to fuel future growth. Thus strategic management can't solely look at the far future; it must also be concerned with the present and near future. And this represents a significant tension in most organisations – perhaps *the* main tension. Continuing to do well what you're currently doing generally requires evolution, since no organisation can stand completely still, while gearing up for new things requires transformation. So evolution and the potential for transformation must co-exist. The following quote from Pascale nicely sums up this tension.[7]

> Nothing fails like success. Winning organizations – whether the Israeli Army, the US Olympic Committee in its heyday, expanding young enterprises or established global corporations – are locked in the embrace of a potentially deadly paradox. This is because great strengths are inevitably the root of weakness. Organizations have a tendency to do what they best know how to do; they are, if you will, the ultimate conservatives. Couple this with the tendency of dedicated and energetic leadership to drive the organization to be still better at what it already does well, and we propel ourselves on a trajectory toward excess. Results may be positive and profitable in the short run, but excesses are fatal over time. The golden adage 'Stick to your knitting' becomes an epitaph. This is because our fixation on 'what is' obscures that other aggravating necessity of worrying about 'what isn't' and 'what might be'.

However, the consequences of the reverse situation, where attention is diverted from the present activities – 'the knitting' – into new ventures, is vividly shown in Exhibit 1.5.

- Relationships   An important part of a strategic manager's job is to understand the contribution that relationships with stakeholders can make to the well-being of the organisation and to establish and maintain good relationships with them. The success of Japanese companies has alerted people to the vital contribution that both internal and external relationships can make to organisational competiveness and success.

KEY CONCEPT   Strategic management is concerned with matters that are important in that they affect the long-term welfare of the whole organisation. While many features of strategic management are present at other levels within an organisation, they aren't present with the same intensity. The environment with which strategists are wrestling is characterised by chaos, complexity, dynamism, turbulence and uncertainty. The strategic management process can be characterised as being complex with a long-term and external orientation and with a qualitative emphasis. Major strategic management concerns are with matching the organisation and its environment, initiating and handling both evolutionary and transformational change, managing the organisation's relationships with stakeholders, and balancing short- and long-term considerations.

EXHIBIT 1.5

How a biscuits strategy crumbled [8]

When Eric Nicoli, chief executive of United Biscuit, took over at UB in 1991, it had sales of £3 billion and pre-tax profits of £211.3 million, and its UK McVitie's biscuits business had margins of 15.7%. In 1998 it reported sales of £1.7 billion, pre-tax profits of £110.1 million and margins of 11.5% at McVitie's. To be fair to Nicoli, the reduction in sales and profits was partly because UB had sold off large chunks of its activities, but this was forced on the group by its abysmal performance and for that Nicoli must bear the blame.

UB is still struggling to recover from the effects of three key strategic mistakes made by Nicoli and his team in the early 1990s. First, it was so confident of its pre-eminent position in British biscuits – where it still has over half the market – that it thought it could keep pushing up its margins for ever, at the expense of boring things like marketing and product development. Second, it developed grandiose ambitions to be a global player and rushed out on a spending spree, snapping up biscuit and snack businesses from Poland to China. And third, it failed to appreciate the strength of Frito Lay, the crisps and snacks business owned by PepsiCo, which dominates most of the markets into which UB was expanding.

The results of the strategic errors soon became all too clear. Customers got tired of paying ever higher prices, particularly when they could buy supermarket own brands (some of them actually made by McVitie's) far cheaper. And they were easily tempted away by the more interesting products on offer from the likes of Cadbury and Fox, both more successful than UB in new product development. McVitie's profits collapsed from £92.9 million in 1992 to £57.1 million in 1995 and even in 1996 they had crept up only to £60.5 million.

Internationally, UB was spreading itself too thinly across too many fronts instead of focusing on areas where it could have a real advantage. No sooner had it sorted out one set of problems than another set appeared. One analyst cites frozen foods – its ranges include Ross Foods and the Linda McCartney vegetarian products – as an example of businesses where Nicoli should have bitten the bullet and sold.

1.7 Stakeholders

The previous section ended with the view that a significant strategic concern is the organisation's relationships with its stakeholders. While there's really no controversy in suggesting that any organisation would be so foolhardy as to ignore the groups and individuals who could help it to thrive – or alternatively damage its prospects – there is controversy about the *rights* of stakeholders in profit-seeking organisations. This controversy has been nicely summed up in the pages of the journal *Long Range Planning*.[9,10]

Argenti sets out the case against non-shareholders having special rights. He stresses that 'the sole purpose of all human organizations is to deliver a satisfactory benefit to a specific set of human beings. Thus the purpose of a school is, solely and exclusively, to educate children (and is categorically not there for the teachers, publishers of text-books or the local builder).' Correspondingly, the sole purpose of a profit-seeking organisation is to make returns for its owners, the shareholders. Argenti points out that there may be very many stakeholder groups – there may be a great number of different types of supplier, for example, differentiated by size, support given, previous conduct, etc., and all with different demands on the organisation. In this confusion, Argenti plumps for two sorts of stakeholder: the shareholders, who are the intended beneficiaries, the people for whom the organisation was set up, and collateral stakeholders, the stakeholders who will also benefit from the operations of the organisation but have no rights to control it. Argenti is reiterating the classic view of capitalism; it is the shareholders of profit-seeking organisations who own the company and it is they who are in a different position to all other interested parties. And this difference is enshrined in law: the legal position of shareholders is different to that of other stakeholders.

Campbell concentrates on the purpose of an organisation to support his contention that stakeholders other than shareholders should have a say in how an organisation is run. He challenges Argenti by asking, 'Does a school's purpose change when it is privately owned?' He then counters the view that there is a myriad of stakeholders by differentiating between *active* and *passive* stakeholders. Active stakeholders are the providers of capital (shareholders and lenders of finance), customers, employees and suppliers. They are active because they all operate in markets – markets for the firms' products/services, finance, information, labour and supplies/services. According to Campbell, active stakeholders are, or can be, involved in the daily activities of the company and thus can directly affect its performance. On the other hand, passive stakeholders, for example government and pressure groups, have a less direct involvement. One nice distinction between the two types of stakeholder is that active stakeholders always want more (greater dividends, more pay, lower prices), the passive stakeholders simply want the company to perform to some acceptable level – for example, to pay its taxes, not to pollute the environment, not to exploit child labour.

To Campbell, the active stakeholders are the ones who should be allowed and encouraged to participate in the running of the firm; the purpose of an organisation can't really be to give the maximum returns to shareholders. A firm in the steel industry has the purpose of making steel, and to keep a clear view of such a purpose helps identify the relationships that the firm should have with its active stakeholders.

The two types of stakeholder are shown in Exhibit 1.6. They have been termed *primary* (rather than intended beneficiaries or active stakeholders) and *secondary* (rather than collateral or passive stakeholders). The term *secondary* has been chosen not because these stakeholders are necessarily less important than the primary ones, but because they are affected by the by-products of the organisation's activities. The terms *primary* and *secondary* are considered to be the most appropriate and will be used in this book.

DISCUSSION
POINT 1.4

Reflect on the above debate. Which view do you support, or do you have another view?
* Do you consider that the terms *primary* and *secondary* are more appropriate terms than *intended beneficiaries* and *collateral stakeholders*, or *active* and *passive stakeholders*?

An interesting form of stakeholder is the *common-interest organisation*.[11] These groups exist to distort the market in favour of their members and include the professions, trade associations and trade unions.

EXHIBIT 1.6

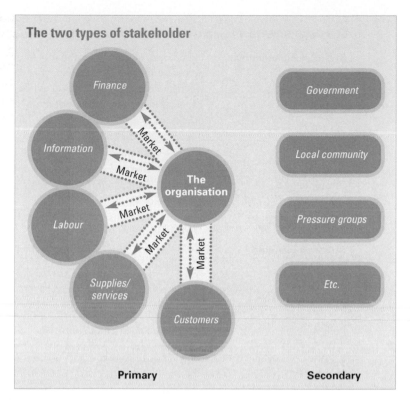

The two types of stakeholder

Finance

Government

Information

Local community

Market

Market

The organisation

Labour

Market

Pressure groups

Market

Market

Supplies/ services

Etc.

Customers

Primary   **Secondary**

1.8 Some formal definitions

All the previous sections give some sense of a definition of strategic management and its components. However, given that this book has *strategic management* in its title, it really is necessary to define the term formally. Formally, strategic management is the process of managing the mix of ends and means that serve to define *what* the organisation is (or wishes to be), *where* it's going, *when* it wants to get there, and *how* in general it's going to get there. The *what*, *where* and *when* in this definition concern the goals of the organisation: the *how* concerns the means of attaining the goals. Additionally, strategic management is concerned with *monitoring* and *controlling* both the goals and the means.

Formal definitions for the key terms in strategic management are set out in Exhibit 1.7. Strategy is taken to include both the organisational goals and the means by which they are to be achieved: strategic goals and strategic pathways[12] together comprise the strategy of an organisation. However, you should be aware that some writers expressly exclude goal formulation from strategy, i.e. they are using the term *strategy* where *strategic pathway* is used here, and they don't have a single term to cover the formulation of both the goals and the means of attaining them. The reason that it's considered better to encompass both means and ends in the one term *strategy* is because means and ends are intimately bound together: if you don't have the means to realise your preferred goals, then the goals will have to be changed. A firm wanting to expand overseas and thinking of targeting South-east Asia would have to change its target – and perhaps even its overall goal – if it couldn't find the funding to support the venture.

EXHIBIT 1.7

Key definitions in strategic management

Strategic management	the process of managing the mix of goals and strategic pathways that serve to define what the organisation is (or wishes to be), where it's going, when it wants to get there and how in general it is to get there. It also includes the processes of monitoring and controlling the strategy of the organisation
Strategy	the long-term direction and scope of an organisation. It is the combination of strategic goals and strategic pathways
Strategic goal	where the organisation wishes to go and when it wishes to get there
Strategic pathway	a pattern of actions (the means) used to attain a strategic goal (an end)
Strategic planning	the systematic process through which strategic thinking is formalised and plans devised to support strategy implementation
Strategic thinking	the creative thinking and learning process that allows the organisation to be positioned for maximum effect
Policy	a rule or guideline that expresses the limits within which action may occur
Plan	a set of proposed actions

There is a huge distinction between strategic thinking and strategic planning. Strategic thinking is a creative process involving learning and can't be systematised. In contrast, strategic planning is a *systematic process through which strategic thinking is formalised and plans devised to support strategy*. It can be seen from this that strategic planning is concerned with strategy implementation, not with its formulation, and that it will follow from strategic thinking. Strategic planning should provide an integrative framework for other forms of planning and is a necessary preliminary to project planning, operational planning and budgeting.

Policies are rules or guidelines that express the limits within which action should occur. For example, a corporation may specify that a firm will not operate outside the EU, or the senior management of a university may specify that an engineering department must use the accountancy expertise of staff in its business school instead of employing its own accountancy lecturers. A plan is a set of detailed actions by which an aim is to be achieved: for example, setting out how a firm will acquire new premises will require many detailed processes, such as searching out possible properties, calculating any refurbishment needed, and how people will transfer to the new site.

1.9 Intended and emergent strategy

One way in which strategy may be determined is through strategic planning. The so-called **planning approach** produces an intended strategy, whereby a set of actions is planned to achieve well-defined organisational goals, and it's intended to follow the plan through to realisation. In practice, reassessment of the strategy is undertaken from time to time, often annually according to an established planning timescale. In this approach, the strategic pathway is the set of policies and plans for attaining the strategic goals. The way in which this may be done in practice is sketched in Exhibit 1.8. This also illustrates the point that short-term, tactical considerations may mean that it's sometimes necessary to make short-term deviations from an intended strategy. It may be necessary to abandon an intended strategy in the light of insurmountable obstacles; the intended strategy then becomes unrealised.

A second approach to formulating strategy is to recognise that you will never know how the environment will change and that the strategy should develop to take changing environmental conditions into account, i.e. strategy emerges as conditions change. In this **emergent approach**, the strategic pathway is the pattern of events in the life of the organisation, seen after the event. An emergent strategy is sketched in Exhibit 1.8.

An example of an emergent strategy concerns a business school that had one person within it who had a professional interest in the car industry. Teaching contact with an MBA student who worked in the industry led first to support for research, then to some support for an undergraduate degree and later to sponsorship from one of the major car manufacturers. From tiny acorns a largish operation developed that became part of the school's mainstream activities. The Tory Party manifesto in 1979 had no mention of privatisation although, after the initial sell-off of state assets, it then gradually emerged to become a central plank of policy. A considerable number of organisations have spawned businesses from their IT activities: Experian, Europe's largest credit-scoring agency, evolved out of Great Universal Stores, and ITNET was formed by a management buyout from Cadbury Schweppes. Both are examples of emergent strategies.

Perhaps the most famous example is that of Honda when it first entered the US motorcycle market.[13] It had intended to enter with the large motorbikes that dominated the market. In this it was unsuccessful. However, what did catch the eye of Californians was the 50cc motorbikes that the Honda personnel themselves drove to get to work. Honda started to sell these small machines and a new and highly successful strategy emerged.

EXHIBIT 1.8

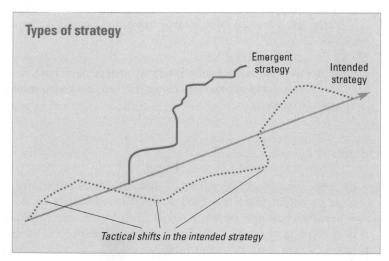

Types of strategy

Emergent strategy

Intended strategy

Tactical shifts in the intended strategy

DISCUSSION
POINT 1.5
Which usage do you prefer: strategy to include both means and ends or simply to refer to means?
- Can there be such a thing as an unrealised emergent strategy?

A strategy emerges because a person or informal grouping pushes for this to occur. Thus often an emergent strategy is developed from below the top level in an organisation; in contrast, it's often the leaders who develop intended strategy. In practice, both intended and emergent strategies tend to be followed simultaneously and they combine to form the actual strategy, as illustrated in Exhibit 1.9.

EXHIBIT 1.9

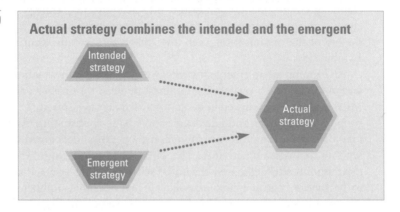

Actual strategy combines the intended and the emergent

Except for very special organisations, there will always be some features of an organisation's future well-being that need to be planned in advance, sometimes well in advance; Rolls-Royce had to nurture its core engineering skills over many years in order to develop state-of-the-art aero engines, for example. However, organisations would be remiss if they didn't take advantage of opportunities as they emerge. When the communist regimes rather unexpectedly fell in Eastern Europe in the late 1980s and early 1990s, and in the wake of the Asian economic crisis that began in 1997, it was sensible for firms to assess the situation and to grasp the opportunities that these events offered, whatever their intended strategies might have been at the time. The example given in Exhibit 1.10 shows how intended and emergent processes are allied.

DISCUSSION
POINT 1.6
What do you think happens to an emergent strategy over time?
- Can you think of any organisations where there is no need to have any form of intended strategy?

1.10 Strategy vs tactics

It's important to get a feel for the difference between strategy and tactics. A good, short definition of strategy used by the British Army is *not in the face of the enemy*, with tactics being the opposite: *in the face of the enemy*. Military commanders would be thinking and acting strategically if they were involved in determining the composition of their country's armed forces, defining overall equipment requirements, etc.

EXHIBIT 1.10

The development of strategy at Deutsche Bank[14]

At Deutsche Bank the yearly operational and financial reviews take place during September through December and involve a considerable number of managers. The strategic planning process follows on immediately after. It's a two-month process involving only the board and planning staff which sets out to identify resources for the next five years. It looks at competitors, from Sainsbury's to Microsoft to other banking competitors; it covers tangibles and intangibles; and it studies capabilities, weaknesses and possibilities. It's a qualitative process, with more words and with few quantative guidelines. Only a few key ratios are used: RoE, RoA, cost–income ratio and capital adequacy ratio.

However, a certain pragmatism to the limits of the strategic review and the strategic planning process are born in mind, as this quote from a Deutsche Bank director illustrates:

It's not that you run around and say, well, let's wait for the strategy department to come and define our strategic aims and targets and then OK, we'll try to fulfil them. I guess that you have something like an ongoing process: you take a look at retail banking especially in Germany and you will find something that is evolving incredibly fast, so if you wait for certain points in time to start to do strategic planning you would be totally lost. So what we are doing is telling people why we are doing this and not doing that. So I guess strategic planning today is more or less something like the point in time where you state where you stand, because. . . . you are already walking while you are planning where to go.

Prepared by Douglas McConchie from interviews, 1998

They would be acting tactically when they have a group of soldiers under their command and are holding a position in battle with no further reinforcements or support forthcoming. Business managers would be acting strategically when deciding on the range of services to market and acting tactically when they had to meet specified objectives within the budget set for them, for example by dropping prices in order to counter competitive moves. An analogy that might help further to make the distinction between strategic and tactical is the difference between climate and weather. Climate is a long-term consideration and changes in it, such as global warming, have long-term implications; by contrast, weather is about the next week or the next few days.

The rules of cause and effect tend to apply very directly in tactical situations: if you want more output you know that you can achieve this by adding a further shift or by working overtime. In strategic situations, cause-and-effect relationships are weaker and/or are more difficult to discern. Effects may be separated by a considerable period of time from causes, and thus there is considerable scope for the environment to shift in unexpected ways between the impetus and the result. In considering strategy, intuition, pattern recognition and being sensitive to small stimuli are important.

Many distinctions made in strategic management are not clear-cut and the distinction between strategy and tactics is no exception: one person's strategy can be another person's tactics. If a corporation sets down policies for a business (for example only to operate in France, or only to make and sell garden furniture), prescribes its resources and states the expected financial returns, then from the corporate point of view the actions of the business would appear to be purely tactical. From a business point of view, however, these policies are constraints within which the business can act strategically. The current move to more autonomous units implies that corporations are setting policies loose enough for their businesses to act strategically.

KEY CONCEPT   Strategic management includes determining the strategy of the organisation, both its strategic goals and the associated strategic pathways. Strategy can develop in two distinct ways. First there is the planned approach, whereby an intended strategy is devised and implemented. The second approach is the evolution of emergent strategy through a reaction to events and the taking of opportunities. An actual strategy generally contains elements of both intended and emergent approaches.

While it can be said that one person's strategy is another person's tactics, the military distinction is useful: strategy is *not in the face of the enemy*, while tactics is the opposite, *in the face of the enemy*.

DISCUSSION   Consider the position of a football manager/coach. When would they be thinking
POINT 1.7   strategically and when tactically?
              ● Consider your actions over the past few years. When were you acting strategically and
                when tactically?

SUMMARY   ● Strategic management is concerned with the overall direction of an organisation. Recent trends mean that managers will have considerable opportunity to contribute to this level of management. There are two main levels of strategic management – the corporate and the business. Both are seeking to add value. The main questions that the corporation is seeking to answer are 'What businesses should we be in?' and 'Which competencies do we need to develop?' The main questions that the profit-seeking business is seeking to answer are 'How do we compete?' and 'Which capabilities do we need to develop?' Not-for-profit organisations put a greater emphasis on the question 'How do we develop and maintain good relationships with stakeholders?'   EXHIBIT 1.1, EXHIBIT 1.2
● The environment within which strategic management takes place is characterised by chaos, complexity, dynamism, turbulence and uncertainty to a far greater extent than any functional environment.   EXHIBIT 1.3
● The strategic management process can be characterised as being complex, with a long-term and external orientation and with a qualitative emphasis. Significant strategic management concerns are with matching the organisation and its environment, initiating and handling revolutionary change, managing the organisation's relationships with stakeholders and balancing short- and longer-term considerations.   EXHIBIT 1.4
● Two types of stakeholder can be recognised. The primary stakeholders are those who operate in markets and are always wanting more from the organisation. The secondary stakeholders are those who don't operate in markets and whose concern is that the organisation performs to acceptable standards.   EXHIBIT 1.6
● Some key defintions concerned with strategy and strategy formulation are set out in Exhibit 1.7.   EXHIBIT 1.7

- Strategy can be developed in two main ways: through a planned approach and through an emergent approach. In practice, both intended and emergent strategies tend to be followed simultaneously and they combine to form the actual strategy. EXHIBIT 1.8, EXHIBIT 1.9
- Many tensions exist in most organisations. A very important one – perhaps the main one – is that between doing what is currently being done while at the same time gearing up to do new things. Senior managers have to balance an efficient present with an effective future; evolution with transformation and efficiency with effectiveness.

SELF-CHECK

1 Reconsider the learning outcomes for this chapter. Check that you feel confident that you can carry out the activities listed there.

2 Be sure that you know the meaning of the following terms:

business	market-based approach	strategic pathway
chaos	plan	strategic planning
common-interest organisation	policy	strategic thinking
complexity	primary stakeholder	strategy
corporation	resource-based approach	tactics
dynamism	secondary stakeholder	turbulence
emergent strategy	strategic goal	uncertainty
intended strategy	strategic management	

MINI-CASE 1.1

Allegro Computer Peripherals plc

Background

Allegro Computer Peripherals was formed in 1975 by the three current directors, Beresford Shute, the managing and marketing director, Bill Smith the production and research director, and Nigel Spackman, the finance director. They had been schoolboy friends, with Beresford and Bill going to the same university to study electrical engineering. The impetus to set up the company had come from the research work in which they had been engaged as postgraduate students. Nigel Spackman's career had followed a different course: he became a qualified financial accountant through evening study while working for several light engineering companies. In 1985 Allegro went public, with five million shares sold. Between them, the directors own 55% of these shares, with Beresford being the largest single holder with 25%.

Allegro is involved in manufacturing and selling accessories for computers. There has been a gradual build-up of activity, into such items as VDUs and communication devices, and these still form the main part of Allegro's activities. However, a big change started two years ago when it was decided to manufacture and sell a 'vocal input adaptor', a device for accepting speech directly as computer input. This device had come out of a joint research and development programme with the local university. Sales of the adaptor had been modest until now, but market research has shown that there is considerable potential for such an adaptor, with sales in the European Union perhaps rising to around a million a year within five years, possibly even more in due course. The possibilities in the USA appear equally exciting.

The present situation

The close relationships that had existed between the three men since boyhood had been maintained. They always met first thing every Monday morning to discuss how things looked for Allegro over the next month and to plan the activities of the factory and sales-force over the next week.

Production and research

Bill Smith's responsibilities cover the production function's areas of materials purchasing, manufacturing and distribution. Additionally, he is responsible for the 15 engineering graduates engaged in research and development and for maintaining and developing the close relationships established with the local university.

The factory is co-located with the head office in a small market town in Leicestershire, 10–15 miles from the cities of Derby, Nottingham and Leicester. The factory has been developed from the brewery buildings that were on the site. The town has good road and rail links.

The factory is currently working at 80% capacity on a normal day shift. Overtime working is possible, to produce a further 20%, and double-shift working is a further possibility. Allegro owns some land adjacent to the factory that is currently not used and, with planning permission, the factory could be extended if demand warranted it.

The company employs a total of 200 workers. There is a shortage of skilled labour, and competition among the town's manufacturers is keen. Bill has first-class factory and materials procurement managers reporting to him; however, the rapid development of the company has led to there being no formal training or promotional schemes in place for the factory staff. The personnel function is carried out by one rather junior employee.

Marketing and sales

Currently, Allegro is selling 12,600 vocal input adaptors per quarter and holds a 15% market share of the UK market. There are at least two other sellers in the market besides Allegro, with Betatron the current market leader at around 50% of the UK market. Betatron has been involved in many segments of the electronics industry for many years and is effectively the price setter for vocal input adaptors. It's expected that it will charge a price of around £500 for its adaptor, gradually increasing the price over the next two years to around £550. Betatron has a significant presence in the rest of Europe.

Promotion of Allegro's products is handled by an experienced multimedia agency. Currently, promotional spend is around £100 per unit.

Specially trained sales representatives do all the selling and provide after-sales service and support. On average, each salesperson is considered to be able to make 100 sales per quarter under normal operating conditions.

The main current issues

Towards the end of one of the regular Monday morning meetings, Beresford raised the question of the lack of a strategy for Allegro. He was concerned that little attention was being paid to the possibilities offered by the vocal input adaptor.

'I think we're all agreed that we've got a very exciting product with our vocal input adaptor. From all the reports and the comments in the technical press, our model's streets ahead of Betatron's, so we should really make headway in the market during the next few months.' He paused to see the reaction of the others.

'Totally agreed,' said Bill. 'Our R&D boys have done a really great job.'

'Yes, a great product, but we must be careful not to over-extend ourselves financially,' cautioned Nigel. 'Many a growing company like ours has put profits before cash flow – and come a cropper as a result.'

Beresford had expected this. He knew both Bill and Nigel very well: technocratic Bill and prudent Nigel. 'What we've got here is not only a terrific product protected very ably through patents, but the possibility of using it to make Allegro a major player in the computer peripherals industry. If we want to do that then we've got to start to think on a much wider scale than we have done previously. We've got to think globally.'

'By globally you mean the EC and the USA don't you?' queried Bill.

'Yes, I do,' replied Beresford. 'We must move quickly to capitalise on our position.'

'If we think and act globally, then we're going to need much greater financial backing than we currently have,' interjected Nigel. 'This must mean either taking out loans from the bank, and thus exposing ourselves should profits fall, or selling equity. Selling equity will dilute our holdings, possibly leading to the loss of our controlling interest. Remember that we agreed when we went public that we would always retain more than 50% of the shares between us.'

'Large changes in our financial position may not be needed,' replied Beresford. 'If we're agreed to go all out for a dominant position there are several possibilities for production and distribution that require little extra finance from ourselves. For example, couldn't we move to double- or even triple-shift working in the factory, or subcontract work – or move into a licensing agreement with one of the bigger boys. And a fashionable avenue of sales and distribution is to franchise activities.' He felt confident in this, as he had recently been on two marketing courses.

'You are theorising about manufacturing,' interjected Bill vehemently. 'Let's look at the volumes involved. Currently we're expecting to manufacture around 50,000 adaptors this year. This would take our UK market share to about 20%. The EU market alone is around five times as big and the US market would appear to be similar. So to get a 20% share of all three markets would require a manufacturing capacity of about ten times our current operation. We are also in a growing market, so the further demands will be even greater. With a lot of effort we could increase production by possibly three times. This leads to an awful lot of production to be obtained elsewhere. And remember,' he added darkly, 'for agreeing to double-shift working the union will demand a 20% pay rise for all shift workers; going to triple shift would cost us even more.'

Nigel raised another objection. 'Although we believe that we've got excellent patent protection, the protection may not be quite as good as we think in protecting us from competition; other designs for the adaptor coming along may do the same thing in a better or cheaper way.'

Beresford saw his chance. 'So if we want to move we have to move very, very quickly,' he interposed. 'If we're to go strongly with the vocal input adaptor it'll have enormous impact on the whole company, and if we get it wrong it could lead to the end of the company. What I suggest is that we call in some outside consultant to help us decide what to do.'

'Yes,' said Nigel. 'I'm very happy to spend a day or two with a consultant to look at all the issues. But there's an awful lot of things to discuss. If we attack the US market there's the £–$ exchange rate to consider; if we link up with an American operator we may be excluded from the European Commission's initiatives just as Fujitsu has been; and we know little of the US market. And let's not forget the small matter of our stock-market rating: we'll need to manage any expansion plans very carefully to keep our share price up in case we wish to obtain funds from the City.'

'And what about you, Bill?' asked Beresford. 'Would you be happy to call in a consultant?'

'Certainly I would,' replied Bill. 'The suggestions you are making could spell the end of the company unless we get them right. An outsider could be a great help – give us a wider and more dispassionate view. Do you have any ideas on who we should call in to help?'

'Good,' Beresford summed up. 'How about my setting up a meeting for us and the consultant. I do know someone whom I'd like us to try: her name's Helen Bailey, and she's had quite a lot of experience in helping companies to expand quickly. Is that OK?'

The meeting was about to break up when Beresford's secretary entered and handed him a fax. 'Looks interesting Beri,' she said, 'and very relevant to your meeting, I guess.'

Beresford glanced at the fax and then read it more carefully. 'You're right,' he replied, and then turned to the other two directors. 'IBM has just announced that it has obtained a controlling interest in Betatron.'

This created a thoughtful hush around the table. 'Perhaps we should start negotiations with Bill Gates – or David Potter of Psion,' quipped Bill, 'then we could all retire to the Bahamas.'

Many a true word spoken in jest!

Discussion point 1.8

The three board members of Allegro Computer Peripherals have a set of difficult decisions to make. Acting as a consultant to the board, you are asked to

a   identify the main factors that the board will have to take into account in order to arrive at a decision;

b   identify the concepts and techniques that you have already met in your course that might help you if you were Helen Bailey.

MINI-CASE 1.2

The difference between a common-or-garden plan and a strategic plan[15]

The strategic plan adopts a contrary style of thinking – it works against the grain. Huysman, the Victorian novelist, called his most famous novel *Au Rebours* – rubbing against the hairs of the skin. Good strategic plans rub against the hairs: they are counter-intuitive, and counter-rational. They consciously and purposefully apply the principle of contrarianism.

The kernel of a strategic plan is the rule that it breaks – the orthodoxy that the firm is choosing to challenge. Without a clear definition of the myth that drives the competitors and the truth that is the future touchstone of the firm's own future operating principle, the plan cannot be called strategic. It's just another one of those boring documents that we have all seen (and probably written) full of pious platitudes signifying nothing. As Philip Larkin said of the modern novel: 'A beginning, a muddle, and an end.'

The other defining property of a strategic plan is that the analytical section is devoted to dispelling the myth by which the competitors live; it cannot, by definition, lead to the truth by which the firm itself is choosing to live. This has to be a jump of the imagination. A plan that doesn't make such a jump is a fraud. In other words, a strategy cannot be fully rationalised. It has to be an act of faith. This is the central message of the modern philosophy of science. No general statement, not even the simplest generalisation, can be derived from raw data without some imaginative effort on the part of the mind. Einstein suggested, 'A theory can be proved by experiment; but no path leads from experiment to the birth of a theory.'

The phoney strategy is the one that's written according to a method. The conclusions follow from the facts. It is all utterly rational and sensible. So sensible that it's what everyone else is thinking and doing. Strategic plans start at the point where rationality and 'being sensible' leave off. This is the country of the entrepreneur, the man who, like Medawar's famous description of the scientist, has to depart from the truth (by telling stories and the like) if only to arrive at a new truth.

Discussion point 1.9

Do you agree that 'the kernel of a strategic plan is the rule that it breaks?'

- Must a strategic plan have an analytical section that dispels the myths believed by competitors?
- Must a strategy contain original thinking?

1 Having read the GSM case:
   - Summarise GSM's strategy in 50 words or less.
   - Is GSM following an intended or an emergent strategy?
   - What do you think of the criteria for start-up?
   - A company must look after both its present activities and the future. What has GSM been doing to do both?
   - Strategic management is about prioritising. What evidence is there that GSM has prioritised?

2 The strategic management environment was characterised as chaotic, complex, dynamic and turbulent – all generally increasing the level of uncertainty facing strategic managers. However, not all business environments are the same. Reflect on how changes in the environmental characteristics might affect how a strategy would be developed.

3 What sort of strategy would you associate with the dynamic collage view of strategy as described in Section 3.1 of the Rationale and Road Map?

4 In picturing the future, the environment is usually split into two – into the remote and operating environments. Where would you expect to position the primary and secondary stakeholders in these two environments?

5 What do you think of the view that strategists have to be concerned with both an efficient present and an effective future for their organisation?

6 In what ways is strategic management different from capital budgeting?

1 Obtain the annual report and accounts over several years for a company of your choice (these may be available on the Internet). For this company, determine to what extent it has been following an emergent or an intended strategy.

2 Determine from a large company's report and accounts whether it is a corporation or a business. If it is a corporation, how is it structured?

3 Compare and contrast the strategic concerns of one profit-seeking business of your choice with those of a not-for-profit organisation.

The predictability of the environment in which strategic management is practised, particularly chaos, is dealt with in considerable detail by Ralph Stacey in Stacey, R.D., *Strategic Management and Organisational Dynamics*, 2nd edn, Financial Times Pitman Publishing, London, 1996.

The debate between John Argenti and Andrew Campbell in the pages of *Long Range Planning*, Vol. 30, No. 3, June 1997, pp. 442–5 and 446–9) sums up very nicely the main points for both views on the role and rights of stakeholders.

Different forms of strategy and definitions of strategy are considered by Charles Hofer and Dan Schendel in Hofer, C.W. and Schendel, D., *Strategy Formulation and Analytical Concepts*, West Publishing, 1978.

CHAPTER NOTES
AND REFERENCES

1 Peters, T., *Liberation Management: Necessary Disorganization for the Nanosecond Nineties*, Macmillan, 1992, p. 45.

2 Hampden-Turner, C. and Trompenaars, F., *The Seven Cultures of Capitalism: Value Systems for Creating Wealth in the United States, Britain, Japan, Germany, France, Sweden, and the Netherlands*, Doubleday, 1993.

3 Hickson, D.J., Butler, R.J., Cray, D., Mallory, G.R. and Wilson, D.C., *Top Decisions: Strategic Decision Making in Organizations*, Basil Blackwell, 1986.

4 Barnett, A.A., 'Hand-held wizard pulls mat from under Gates', *The Observer*, Business, 28 June 1998, p. 3.

5. Simon, H., *Hidden Champions: Lessons from 500 of the World's Best Unknown Companies*, Harvard Business School Press, 1996.

6 Nonaka, I. and Takeuchi, T., *The Knowledge-Creating Company: How Japanese Companies Create the Dynamics of Innovation*, Oxford University Press, 1995.

7 Pascale, R.T., *Managing on the Edge: How Successful Companies Use Conflict to Stay Ahead*, Viking, Penguin Group, 1990, p. 11.

8 Connon, H., 'How a biscuits strategy crumbled', abridged from *The Observer*, Business, 14 March 1999, p. 4.

9 Argenti, J., 'Stakeholders: the case against', *Long Range Planning*, Vol. 30, No. 3, June 1997, pp. 442–5.

10 Campbell, A., 'Stakeholders: the case in favour', *Long Range Planning*, Vol. 30, No. 3, June 1997, pp. 446–9.

11 Olson, M., *The Rise and Decline of Nations*, Yale University Press, 1982.

12 The term *strategic pathway* seems to have been first used in Bowman, C. and Faulkner, D., *Competitive and Corporate Strategy*, Irwin, 1997.

13 Pascale, R.T., 'Perspectives on strategy: the real story behind Honda's success', *Californian Management Review*, Vol. 26, No. 3, 1984, pp. 47–72.

14 McConchie, D.R., 'Patterns of strategic control: an investigation of British, French and German retail banking practice', PhD thesis, Loughborough University, October 1998.

15 This is a transcript of an after-dinner talk given by Jules Goddard to the participants on the Strategic Investment Decision Programme, London Business School, May 1986.

PART 1

Internal context

CHAPTER **2** **Organisational culture**

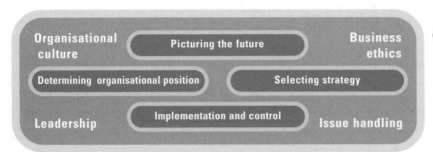

This is the first of a set of four chapters concerned with the internal context of an organisation. The concern is with organisational culture – with the assumptions, values and norms of behaviour existing within an organisation. Culture is given this pre-eminent position as the first chapter after the scene setting of Chapter 1 since it colours everything that the organisation does: the sort of leaders it selects, how issues are handled, its attitude to risk, the control systems it uses, etc. It is an important determinant of the form of the organisation's chosen strategy and of how this strategy is implemented.

The concept of culture is first explored and its components examined. This paves the way for national and ethnic cultural differences to be considered. These differences in turn provide the backdrop for a consideration of other influences that help determine organisational culture. Three classifications of organisational culture are described, and from these a six-dimensional composite of important organisational values is constructed. The manifestations of organisational culture are captured through the use of the web of behaviours. These norms are then mapped on to the underlying organisational values to form the cultural web.

Organisations are groupings of people and resources created for a purpose. This purpose is very often an economic one, but organisations are also social systems in which people have non-economic, personal needs. Current trends in developed economies, particularly the shift towards knowledge-based enterprises, mean that employees are now generally recognised as being an organisation's most important asset. 'Culture' is the glue that unconsciously binds members of a group and guides their actions, and the recognition of the differences in national and ethnic cultures is becoming increasingly important as workforce heterogeneity increases, particularly in those organisations that are operating internationally. The culture of an organisation has the potential for providing a competitive advantage, and managers who fail to understand the culture of their organisation will find that successful strategic management is difficult to achieve.

LEARNING
OUTCOMES

When you have worked through this chapter, you should be able to:

- describe what *culture* is and recognise why it's important that managers understand the important cultural features in their organisations;

- explain the three levels of culture – the three rings of the 'cultural onion';

- list national and ethnic cultural differences and appreciate how these might affect the appropriate way for managers to act;

- explain the determinants of the cultural differences in organisations;

- describe the three categories of organisational culture as put forward by Miles and Snow, Deal and Kennedy, and Harrison/Handy;

- understand that the cultural web is made up of the intertwining of the components of the web of behaviours and the web of beliefs and be able to list the components of both webs;

- be able to use the cultural web to characterise an organisation and to identify the current norms and values so that change activity can be targeted.

2.1 The concept of culture

2.1.1 The meaning of 'culture'

All groups of people face the same basic 'relationship dilemmas': how to relate to other human beings, how to relate to time and how to relate to nature.[1] How groups have resolved these dilemmas in the past determines their culture, and they will seek to resolve current dilemmas within this cultural framework. Consider the dilemma of rewarding good performance. Performance-related pay schemes can work well in the USA, the UK and the Netherlands where an individualistic approach is accepted; they're considerably less successful in more communitarian countries such as France, Germany and large parts of Asia. A further dilemma is how to organise to carry out projects. The introduction of matrix organisations, whereby an employee reports to two bosses (one responsible for the task, such as the launch of a new product, and one responsible for the function, such as accounts or marketing), has been a failure in Italy: there bosses are like fathers, and you can't have two fathers.[2]

These two examples illustrate the national/ethnic differences between the way people see things and make meanings of what they see, and how they act. Organisations within a nation, even within the same industry, also show cultural differences, as Exhibit 2.1 illustrates. There are even cultural differences in the same business; an example would be an entrepreneurial marketing department and a technically oriented research centre. This is to be expected, since culture is unique to an organisation owing to the path-dependent history of the organisation.[3]

EXHIBIT 2.1

The Lloyds–TSB Group

In 1995 Lloyds Bank and the Trustee Savings Bank (TSB) agreed to merge. This made it the biggest bank in the UK and the sixth biggest in Europe. The retail banking businesses showed several cultural differences.

In Lloyds there was an authoritarian chief executive who issued diktats on what should be done. This led to decisions being questioned before implementation: what had been agreed and what had to be done weren't clear. In contrast, at the TSB there was a small community of top managers who would discuss and debate issues until agreement was reached: all would have agreed the implementation steps required and implementation would proceed smoothly.

Lloyds' people characterised TSB people as being a bit slap-happy: they just get on and do something and then think about it afterwards – the *ready, fire, aim* approach. The TSB's people saw Lloyds' people as doing a lot of planning, a lot of thinking and reflection and then maybe doing something – the *plan, plan, plan and maybe do* approach.

The staff at Lloyds were what might be called institutionalised – in many cases their qualifications and experiences were specific to Lloyds. In contrast, the TSB had realised that it wouldn't be possible for the bank to offer jobs for life and that people would have to learn to exist with increasing levels of uncertainty. So there was official encouragement for the staff to get external qualifications. Although this made them more marketable – and thus more footloose – it provided the bank with a better-qualified workforce and made staff more willing to accept change.

The TSB was a very results-oriented organisation. Specific objectives and associated milestones were set and monitored against. There was a stigma associated with missing these targets. In Lloyds, targets were the basis for debate.

Prepared by Douglas McConchie from interviews, 1998

2.1.2 The cultural 'onion'

There are many definitions of *culture*.[4,5] Some address the bases of culture and some its manifestations. A good, brief definition is that culture is the shared norms of behaviour, values and assumptions that knit a community together. It has been described as *collective mental programming*.[6] Culture is a property of a group, not of an individual, although it will be individuals who will 'carry it around'. Culture will determine how a person sees the world.

It's very useful and illuminating to explore the different facets of culture. Culture can be likened to an onion with three layers, as illustrated in Exhibit 2.2. In the outer ring of the cultural onion are those aspects of culture that are readily apparent – the norms of behaviour. Norms are the behaviours acceptable to members of a group. The different ways in which people use the formal and informal version of you (*du* or *Sie* in German, *tu* or *vous* in French, *tú* or *usted* in Spanish) and the habit in France of shaking hands every time you meet someone are indications of national norms. Examples of norms in business are how lateness and absenteeism are treated, how tolerant the organisation is of individuals' use of company stationery and telephones for private purposes, the attitude to alcohol consumption in the workplace, the rules governing who gets a company car and how large a desk a manager is entitled to. Of course, norms aren't always adhered to by everyone and they can change over time, and there is a distinction between espoused norms and 'norms-in-use'. Norms-in-use are the behaviours actually practised; espoused norms are the behaviours that are officially stated as required.[7]

The second ring of the cultural onion involves values. These are of two sorts. There is the ethical stance that is taken about what is good and just: for example, 'last in first out' when considering redundancies. They are also the organisation's general goals and ideals, such as 'it's best to promote from within' and 'it's vital to be number 1 in every market'. Values are about how the group aspires to behave, with its processes, and what the group aspires to achieve, with its results. Values are more general than norms and generally provide the basis for several norms.

Two examples should make the distinction between values and norms clear. Japanese will generally bow when meeting superiors. If they do this because it's

EXHIBIT 2.2

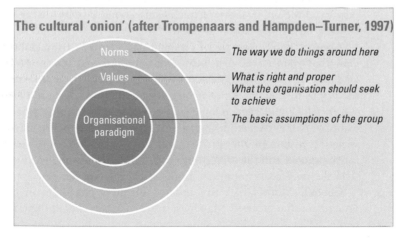

The cultural 'onion' (after Trompenaars and Hampden–Turner, 1997)

conventional behaviour, then bowing is simply a norm. An underlying associated value of respect for the superior would also show itself in other norms, such as genuinely agreeing with their views and seeking their advice. Managers working long hours because it's expected of them are meeting a norm; if they did it because they believed that they wanted to do a good job and that required long hours to be worked, then long-hour working would be an expression of values.

2.1.3 Paradigms

At the core of the onion are the basic or implicit assumptions that members of an organisation unconsciously carry around with them. The fashionable term for this shared mindset is *paradigm*. Following Kuhn,[8] a paradigm may be defined as a constellation of concepts and perceptions shared by a group that determines how the group views the world. Thus a paradigm acts as the lens through which the group looks at the world and it therefore determines what the members of the group perceive. There has to have been enough shared experience to have led to a shared view, and this shared view has to have worked for long enough to have come to be taken for granted and to have dropped out of awareness. The shared view then becomes a set of assumptions about how the world works. Culture in this sense is a learned product of group experience.[9] So what may have started off as a tentative view of the working of a part of the world becomes an assumption and invisible, and it drops out of consciousness.

The set of assumptions is normally beneath the group's level of awareness and therefore is rarely questioned. The significance of a paradigm is that only the outsider or a very reflective person can detect it. What sets the assumptions in the paradigm apart from values is that values can be debated and discussed, whereas challenging the assumptions in the paradigm will generally be treated as stupid and too absurd to respond to. The assumptions in the paradigm are generally non-negotiable but may have to be examined when the organisation is in crisis.

Kuhn gives an example of the change of paradigm in physics at the turn of the twentieth century. Traditional physics considered matter sometimes as waves and sometimes as particles, whereas in the 'new' physics matter was viewed as patterns of energy – the fundamental building blocks of the universe – with the dimensions of space, time and mass as secondary derivatives. Relativity theory in the 'new' physics disproved the universality of Euclidean geometry, with distance shortening and time slowing near to the speed of light.

Another good example of clashing paradigms is from politics. Fascism takes the view that people are born weak and bad, and that it's the responsibility of the few leaders that there are to decide what is required for the 'masses'. Communism takes the opposite view, that people are essentially good but are corrupted by society; get society right and then people will automatically exhibit good behaviour. Another example is the marked difference in 'separations' between European and East Asian societies. In Europe the spiritual and the secular don't mix very much – Sundays are for the sacred and the sacred isn't to be brought into the workplace – whereas in East Asia the two facets are much more closely interwoven.

General Motors had an outdated business paradigm in the 1980s: it couldn't understand the success of Japanese and European cars in the USA because of the erroneous belief shared by its senior management about what the US public wanted.[10]

IBM effectively 'gave away' the operating system for PCs because its culture valued hardware much more highly than software. In 1998, the UK *Sun* newspaper continued to 'out' gay members of parliament when the nation had accepted that sexual orientation was a personal matter and didn't affect the ability of the politicians to do their job.[11]

Five examples of basic assumptions that might contribute to a paradigm and be associated with business values and norms are set out in Exhibit 2.3. Values and the organisational paradigm are both beliefs, and one group's paradigm can be another group's values; the distinction would lie in the openness to challenge what the organisation recognises and permits.

During the 1990s a great deal was written about *paradigm shift*, and the term was applied quite often to rather small changes in organisational activity, such as becoming more customer-focused. It would seem more reasonable to restrict this term to the very large changes – such as those from Newtonian to quantum physics and from fascism to communism – and to use the term *paradigm adjustment* for the smaller changes, which are much more common and involve the change of just one or two assumptions in the paradigm.

EXHIBIT 2.3

Examples of paradigms, values and norms

Element of culture	Example 1	Example 2	Example 3	Example 4	Example 5
Assumption within a paradigm	A focus on outcomes yields greater impact on an organisation than attention to processes	Ours is not a global industry	Humans are basically bad	Businesses should be run for the benefit of the shareholders	Bosses should manage: they know best
Value	Control the 'bottom' line	Only look at national competitors	Strong and extensive control systems are needed	Maximising shareholder value is the overriding goal	Hierarchy is valuable. To obey orders is right
Norm	Payment by results. Focus on meeting targets	Directors' pay should be based on national market share	Pencil butts must be shown before new pencils can be obtained	Large pay differentials and profit-related pay are appropriate	Don't socialise with the bosses. Suggestions are not welcome

KEY CONCEPT Culture is a way of thinking and doing that is shared to a greater or lesser degree by all group members. At its deepest level – the organisational paradigm – culture is the largely invisible, guiding set of assumptions that determines what a group of people think and do when they don't reflect about what they're thinking or doing. Values are about what is good and just, and are what the group aspires to socially and economically. Norms are about what is acceptable and unacceptable behaviour. In moving outwards from the core of the cultural 'onion', the move is from the implicit and intangible to the explicit and tangible facets of culture.

2.1.4 The merit in understanding an organisation's culture

The merit of understanding the culture of others isn't simply to avoid the embarrassing gaffes that can occur between different peoples. At the national and ethnic levels, an understanding can allow managers to work with the grain rather than against it when they are in a culture that isn't their own.

Within an organisation a manager can do more than simply understand the culture and work within it. They have the power to alter it. The merit of the cultural onion should now be apparent. The norms are the manifestations of the deeper aspects of culture. It's easy to see and describe the norms and relatively easy to alter them through managerial action. For example, managers can change reward systems to promote certain behaviours and can impose sanctions to prevent others. But this is only altering behaviour and specific behaviour at that; it isn't altering more fundamental attitudes. Stopping expense account fiddling through the implementation of strict control measures is unlikely to alter the underlying belief that stealing from your employee is OK. More subtle beliefs are even more difficult to alter. There could easily be overt compliance, but covert non-acceptance.

An appreciation of the norms is likely to provide insights into the underlying values, and it may be appropriate to use these insights in order to alter the values. Instead of asking 'What is happening?' to find out the norms, the question is now 'Why is it happening?' or 'What drives this behaviour?' If this sort of questioning unearths the underlying values, then more fundamental change might be possible. All the sorts of fiddling might be stopped or reduced rather than simply the inflation of expense accounts: long-distance private telephone calls, office stationery for home use, fiddling time sheets, reporting sick when perfectly healthy and so on might all be reduced or even eliminated if there were a change in the underlying value.

More ambitiously, managers might attempt to change the organisational paradigm. But they should be careful. It's not obvious that culture can be 'actively' changed at the level of the organisational paradigm. Perhaps all that can be done is to understand and to work with the grain.

The value of understanding organisational culture has been well expressed by Schein:[12] 'If we give culture its due, if we take an inquiring attitude toward the deciphering of culture, if we respect what culture is and what functions it serves, we will find that it is a potentially friendly animal that can be tamed and made to work for us.'

2.2 National and ethnic cultures

Differences in the culture of businesses derive to some extent from the cultures of the wider community in which they operate – of the nation/ethnic group. That there are cultural differences between nations and ethnic groups is fairly obvious: take the importance placed on family values in Italy, on logic in French education, on engineering in Germany, epitomised by the slogan *Vorsprung durch Technik*, and the reverence afforded to business cards in Japan. National and ethnic cultural differences derive from the interaction of a whole host of factors, for example the richness of the region's agriculture, the climate, the size and density of the population, experiences of war, famine and other calamities. National and ethnic differences will now be explored.

2.2.1 The Hofstede and Bond findings

Hofstede[13] reviewed his original research (first reported in 1980) into the views of 116,000 IBM staff operating in 50 countries and augmented it with later findings.[14] Most of the differences in national culture could be explained using five dimensions.

- Power distance – the extent to which the less powerful members of organisations and institutions (like the family or a business) accept and expect that power would be distributed unequally in the group. In countries where there is a small power distance, there is a close interdependence between boss and subordinate, with subordinates quite ready to discuss and argue with approachable bosses. Where there is high power distance, there is in practice an acceptance of strong leaders and centralised power.

- Individualism – the extent to which the ties between individuals are loose or strong. Where the ties are loose, everyone is expected to look after only themselves and their immediate families. Strong ties are associated with strongly cohesive groups that have broader and more diffuse commitments, and the organisations and institutions protect the individual in return for unquestioning loyalty.

- Gender roles – the extent to which gender roles are clearly distinct, demonstrated by the extent to which men are supposed to have 'masculine' traits such as toughness, assertiveness and focus on material success, while women are associated with 'feminine' traits such as co-operation, modesty and concern for the quality of life.

- Uncertainty avoidance – the extent to which the members of a culture feel threatened by uncertain or unknown situations. People of some nationalities seek to have a well-ordered existence and feel worried in unstructured situations, those that are novel, unknown, uncertain and different from the usual. They would adhere closely to rules and accepted practices and tend to have a belief in absolute truth.

- Confucian dynamism – the extent to which East and South-East Asian societies stress perseverance, thrift, having a sense of shame and, in particular, a long-term orientation.

The research findings are summarised in Exhibit 2.4 for a selection of the countries investigated. All the scores are relative, with around 100 points separating the highest and lowest possible scores on each dimension. The higher the score, the more of that trait that was shown: for example, Belgium scores more highly than Austria on 'acceptability of power distance', meaning that the respondents from Belgium accepted an unequal distribution of power more readily than did the Austrians. Reading across for Great Britain, we find that the British would be characterised as wishing to work on an equal footing with their bosses, being rather individual, recognising gender differences far more than the Scandinavians for example, able to tolerate high levels of uncertainty and tending to take a short-term view.

DISCUSSION
POINT 2.1

How might a manager use the information in Exhibit 2.4?
- Some commentators have used the Hofstede and Bond scores in Exhibit 2.4 to suggest a link between individualism and national wealth. In which direction do you think causality operates?

EXHIBIT 2.4

Cultural differences across nationalities (adapted from Hofstede, 1991)

Country	Acceptability of power distance	Individualism	Gender roles	Uncertainty avoidance	Confucian dynamism
Austria	11	55	79	70	
Belgium	65	75	54	94	
Denmark	18	74	16	23	
Finland	33	63	26	59	
France	68	71	43	86	
Germany (West)	35	67	66	65	31
Great Britain	35	89	66	35	25
Hong Kong	68	25	57	29	96
India	77	48	56	40	61
Ireland	28	70	68	35	
Italy	50	76	70	75	
Japan	54	46	95	92	80
Netherlands	38	80	14	53	44
Norway	31	69	8	50	
Spain	57	51	42	86	
Sweden	31	71	5	29	33
United States	40	91	62	46	29

Note: the higher the scores the more of the trait. Data not available for many countries on the Confucian dynamism dimension.

2.2.2 Trompenaars and Hampden-Turner's findings

Trompenaars and Hampden-Turner[15] have reported the results of their study of national differences from a database of 30,000 business people of many nationalities covering many industries. They grouped the differences between cultures under three main headings: relationships with other people, attitudes to time and attitudes to nature.

Relationships with other people

Trompenaars and Hampden-Turner subdivided these relationships into five 'tensions':

- Rules versus relationships   some cultures take the view that universal laws should apply. This view tends to the use of tight contracts rather than to relying on relationships between people when engaged in business. Others take the view that, instead of believing that there is only one right way, the person should act in a way that fits the particular, often exceptional, circumstances. A person's obligations of friendship, for example, may easily override a concern for universality. One consequence for international business is that reward systems imposed on affiliates from head office may well be counter-productive.

- The group versus the individual   this was one of the explanatory dimensions found by Hofstede and Bond – the extent to which the ties between individuals were loose or strong. The relative emphasis on individuality and on the community is a tension that exists in the EU between the UK, the Netherlands and Scandinavian countries, which tend to stress individuality, and most of the rest of the EU, which puts more emphasis on a communitarian approach. In cultures that put an emphasis on the group, it would be expected that several people would attend meetings and they would see themselves as delegates, bound by the wishes of their group. In more individually inclined cultures, single decision makers are common and decisions are made quickly. The group decision making in group-oriented cultures tends to take longer, but implementation of the decision tends to be quicker.

- Lack of emotion versus show of emotion   in some cultures it is expected that emotion be expressed, in others the showing of emotions is considered 'uncultured'. Where the expression of emotion is frowned on, the use of humour, understatement and irony should be severely restricted.

- Specific relationships versus diffuse relationships   in some cultures the relationships between people are narrowly defined to fit a specific context: no business talk at the golf course, no religiousness in business. This can be contrasted with other, more inclusive cultures, where all aspects of a relationship intertwine. In these it takes much longer to forge a relationship as much more information has to be shared – and longer to enact business as all aspects of the relationship have to be enquired about before 'getting down to business'. Where specific relationships dominate, the expectation is for specific target setting, a striving for efficiency and for meetings structured in terms of agendas and time management.

- Status through achievement versus status through ascription   in some societies, status is accorded to a person's *track record* – to what have they achieved – with little or no concern with qualifications or family background. In other cultures, what a person is, rather than what they can do, is important: have they been to the right university, the Haute Ecole Polytechnique or INSEAD, or are they part of a well-known family? In achievement-oriented businesses it would be expected that managers would be of differing ages and gender and for decisions to be challenged on technical and functional grounds.

Attitudes to time

In some cultures, what has been achieved in the past isn't of much importance: the focus is on the future and making future plans. Other cultures place more importance on history and the past. To quote Trompenaars and Hampden-Turner:[16]

> With respect to time, the American Dream is the French Nightmare. Americans gener- ally start from zero and what matters is their present performance and their plan to 'make it' in the future. This is *nouveau riche* for the French, who prefer the *ancien pauvre*; they have an enormous sense of the past and relatively less focus on the pres- ent and future than Americans.

Some cultures view time as linear, as a sequence of events. Other cultures view time more as circular, linking the past, present and future. The sequential-time thinker will tend to separate means clearly from ends and plan each link in the chain. The circu- lar thinker won't work with intertwined means and ends. One view of time is that the immediate future is achievable through personal effort yet the longer-term isn't, since too many things can happen. In this view, short-term planning is in order, with the future taken care of through a succession of short-term activities.

Attitudes to the environment

Two broad attitudes to the environment can be discerned. One is to see it as some- thing to be controlled and exploited; in business this leads to the entrepreneur who overcomes environmental forces to succeed with the product or service that they are offering. The other view of the environment is to see it as something that must be adapted to; in business this leads to taking notice of customers continually and appraising the business environment.

DISCUSSION
POINT 2.2

How might the two different views of time lead to different attitudes towards recruitment of outside staff as opposed to home-grown talent?

2.2.3 The Laurent[17] findings

Several further dimensions of national culture have been researched by Laurent. Some of these are shown in Exhibit 2.5. Columns A to G are the results for the selected statements:

A It is important for a manager to have at hand precise answers to most of the questions that his subordinates may raise about their work.

B Most managers seem more motivated by obtaining power than by achieving objectives.

C Through their professional activity, managers play an important political role in society.

D The main reason for having a hierarchical structure is that everyone knows who has authority over whom.

EXHIBIT 2.5

Some national differences (after Laurent, 1986)

Country	Positive responses %						
	A	B	C	D	E	F	G
Belgium	44			36	64	84	27
Denmark	23	25	32		40		19
France	53	56	76	45	64	83	24
Germany	46	29	47	24	26	79	16
Netherlands	17	26	45	38	38	60	17
Italy	66	63	74	50	69	81	41
Sweden	10	42	54	26	46	54	4
Switzerland	38	51	65	24	29	75	18
UK	27	32	40	38	44	74	13
USA	18	36	52	18	22	54	6

E Today there seems to be an authority crisis in organisations.

F An organisational structure in which subordinates have two direct bosses should be avoided at all costs.

G Most organisations would be better off if conflict could be eliminated for ever.

As an example of reading this table, consider column G. This indicates that while 41% of Italians believed that 'most organisations would be better off if conflict could be eliminated for ever', only 4% of Swedes believed this.

Major differences between US, French, German, Japanese and UK management have been described by Lawrence[18] and may be summarised as follows:

- In the USA, the drivers of business are personal success and company profit. Ambition is universally recognised as 'a good thing'. Organisations tend to be short-termist, relying on equity finance rather than debt finance. Profit is the rationale overriding almost all other considerations; hence the reporting of profits at very short intervals, often quarterly. The marketing and finance functions are pre-eminent.

- In France, management is about the application of educated cleverness with managers needing to be qualified educationally, capable of carrying out sophisticated analysis and synthesis and good at logical argument. Intellectual virtuosity is a key feature: managers must demonstrate their ability. Organisations tend to be formal and bureaucratic. There is close co-operation between government and industry.

- In Germany, management is about engineering knowledge or specialist skills, known as *Technik*, and their application. Experts are recruited as managers, with acquired specialist knowledge and relevant job experience being prized.

Promotion depends on specific knowledge, experience and demonstrable achievement. Organisations tend to be organised functionally and have few layers of general management.

- In the UK, management is about individuals and their leadership ability, rather than the system. People with the right human qualities are presumed to be capable of management. Managers are recruited and promoted on the basis of general credentials, e.g. social and political skills, judgement, charisma and the ubiquitous British humour, rather than on their engineering or other specialist abilities. Organisations tend to be short-termist, relying on equity finance rather than debt finance. Profit is the rationale; hence the use of profit centres.

- In Japan, management is seen as a process not as a series of discrete decisions; the thinking is long-term. Recruitment is from the top universities, in a similar fashion to the recruitment in France from the *grandes écoles*. Loyalty to the company is high, with commitment to the team, and in the large companies managers have a job for life. There is very close contact between business and government.

DISCUSSION POINT 2.3 Summarise the differences in the cultures of France, Germany and the UK as found by Hofstede and Bond, and Laurent and Lawrence.

- Give examples of how these differences might find expression in the way in which the different nationalities approach business.

2.2.4 Education and training and labour markets

Of particular significance to knowledge-based organisations is the role of the formal education and qualification system and the form of the labour market organisation in the host country.[19] A two-by-two matrix classifying the four types of host is shown in Exhibit 2.6.

The type of education and training can be characterised as either elitist or egalitarian. In an elitist system little attention is given to the general education and vocational training of the majority of the workforce – the emphasis is on academic rather than on practical skills. A two-tier system of education is established, with a widespread lack of formal intermediate skills and qualifications amongst the general

EXHIBIT 2.6

Influence of education and training and labour markets in the host societies (from Lam, 1998)

		Labour markets	
		Occupation based	*Organisation based*
Education and training	*Elitist*	Professional model	Bureaucratic model
	Egalitarian	Occupational community model	Organisational community model

Source: Adapted from Lam A., Tacit knowledge, Organisational Learning and Innovation, pp 23–7[19]

workforce. This in turn generates social distance within organisations between the academically and less academically educated. Examples of elitist systems would be France, the UK and the USA.

In contrast, egalitarian systems are characterised by a deep and widespread vocational education, epitomised by the esteemed apprenticeship system in Germany. An important feature of such systems is that they provide a large number of well-qualified middle-level workers who are able to operate in a fairly autonomous manner. Japan is also an egalitarian society in this respect.

Labour markets can be considered as either occupation-based or organisation-based. The occupation-based labour market offers high job mobility, with knowledge, learning and careers sought in a series of organisations rather than in a single organisation. Formal education and training play a large part in making an individual marketable, and knowledge and skills are owned by the individual.

In organisation-based labour markets, long-term employment is in the same organisation, and career progression is through a series of interconnected jobs. Knowledge and skills are generated though on-the-job training.

Labour markets may change, and there is some indication that there is a move away from the organisation-based towards the occupation-based, as illustrated in Exhibit 2.7.

EXHIBIT 2.7

Changes in labour market focus

Banking used to be a generalist trade, so that you could do many different jobs in the bank. I think there is a big trend today, probably influenced by Anglo-Saxon companies, American especially, in that the trend is to specialisation. So there you have more individuality, you have less faithfulness to the company. An international fiscal specialist might work for BA, BNP and then ICI – what is interesting for this person is that they want to be at the edge of international tax and the fact that this is done through BNP or ICI is secondary. It's a culture of specialists who work together for a time but never merge.

A BNP bank strategist[20]

2.2.5 Similarities of cultures

Throughout childhood, future employees will be learning – often unconsciously – the culture of their communities, and will naturally take their culture with them into the workplace. Thus national and ethnic cultures are likely to be powerful determinants of organisational culture. However, the differences between nationalities shouldn't be overemphasised – there are a great many similarities in the cultures of nations, as Exhibit 2.8 illustrates. And there are many subcultures within any national or ethnic culture – professional people have a different view of life from landowners; women from men.

KEY CONCEPT   The several investigations of national and ethnic cultures have uncovered the many differences of emphasis placed on values: for example, on how cultures view time and the environment, and how they cope with uncertainty and power distance. These findings all suggest that managers need to understand cultural values in order to manage and lead a group successfully. Although the differences in culture can be marked, there is also a great deal of commonality: much of human nature is the same worldwide.

EXHIBIT 2.8

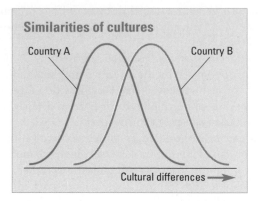

Similarities of cultures

Country A

Country B

Cultural differences ⟶

EXHIBIT 2.9

Culture in the Crédit Agricole

The Crédit Agricole, founded in 1894, was originally conceived for farmers who were excluded from the current banking system: people to whom the capitalist banks of the period wouldn't lend money. It was conceived on the collective capital of the excluded individuals. In our case the bankers' maxim *debts make the assets of a bank* is reversed – here it's the assets that make the debts. These two aspects of our history make for two strong cultural features: we don't choose our customers nor do we select our market. And we are a structurally balanced bank – assets equal liabilities. The third important cultural feature is that all the directors and managers in the Crédit Agricole have been employees of the Crédit Agricole for long periods of time. They have attended many in-house training programmes, so there is great homogeneity within the management team.

Interview with one of the directors of Crédit Agricole, prepared by Douglas McConchie, 1998

2.3 The determinants of organisational culture

Just as countries and ethnic groups can have distinct cultures, so can organisations,[21] as Exhibit 2.9 testifies. Managers who wish to get the best out of the people in their organisations need to be attuned to the organisational culture. This is particularly important when carrying out strategic change: the change sought may clash with the prevailing culture and so resistance must be expected. It shouldn't be assumed that culture is uniform within an organisation. Just as nationally we wouldn't expect those who support right-wing political parties to be culturally identical to those who support left-wing parties, organisations can easily have several significantly different cultures: perhaps the control culture of the accountancy department, the entrepreneurial culture of the sales department and the engineering orientation of the production department.

2.3.1 The merit of a strong culture

Culture is the glue that unconsciously binds members of a group and guides their actions. If the culture is aligned to the direction that the organisation wishes to go in, then this is a powerful means for achieving the strategy. However, a powerful culture may be inappropriate. A culture that strongly believes in the maxim 'if it ain't broke don't fix it' is not going to be well attuned to an environment that calls for rapid innovation.

2.3.2 The determinants of organisational culture

Every organisation is unique since the combination of personalities and events – both past and present – will have produced a unique balance of factors that is the organisational culture. Thus it wouldn't be expected that national and ethnic factors, although very powerful, would be the only influences on organisational culture. Indeed, two commentators go so far as to write:

> The particular industry is more important in structuring executive perceptions, defining issues and developments, and in the shaping of strategy than is the national culture of the country.[22]

This is perhaps a little strong. Major determinants of organisational culture are the following:

- Technology   The technology used in a firm can have a profound effect on work patterns and thus on culture. A jobbing shop, in which each job is an individual piece of work and where the design and production skills of several people are involved, can bring people together in a way that production-line activity never can. Technology can concentrate people and this leads quite naturally to concerted action, as seen most vividly in union activity. A feature of retailing is the low power of the unions, in part because their members aren't concentrated as they are in factories. The more complex the technical system, the more elaborate and professional the support staff. The way in which co-ordination between individuals and groups is exercised determines the appropriate form of organisation and thus significantly affects the culture. The more formalised the work the more bureaucratic the operations and thus the more similar they would be. For example, it would be expected that an oil refinery would be operated in a very similar way all over the world.[23]

- Leadership and the power structure   Leadership and power in an organisation have a considerable impact on the organisational culture, and a particularly powerful force is the make-up of the senior management team. In Germany, engineers and lawyers are well represented on the boards of companies; in the UK, while engineers do make it to the top, economists and historians are well to the fore.[24] The greater the external control exerted on an organisation (e.g. by a corporate parent or government), the more centralised and formalised its structure.

- Market factors   The factors most significant to success will tend to be reflected in the make-up of the board of directors of an organisation. A tobacco company is likely to stress marketing and finance, and the composition of the board will reflect this. A company with an IT director on its board is likely to see information as more important than one that doesn't.

- Ownership and history of the organisation   Businesses in which the owner takes a 'hands-on' role are likely to have a different culture from those where ownership is divorced from management. Where ownership and management are separate, management will tend to seek to maximise its own rewards at the expense of the shareholder. An organisation that has seen nothing but success will have a view of life completely different from a company that has suffered job losses and loss of market share.

- Organisational age and size   The older and larger an organisation, the more formalised its behaviour and the more likely it is to be bureaucratic. The larger an organisation, the larger the size of its average unit and the more specialised the jobs and units within it.[25] Each specialisation is likely to be accompanied by an appropriate culture, and thus various cultures will flourish in the organisation.

- Environment   The more dynamic an organisation's environment, the more its culture needs to be one that supports flexibility. The more complex an organisation's environment, the more decentralised its structure is likely to be, with a consequent development of cultural diversity.

KEY CONCEPT   The culture of a community is bound to influence the culture in the workplace. However, the particular features of the business – technology, leadership and the power structure, market forces, ownership, history, age and size, and the form of the environment – all help to define the organisational culture and moderate the influence of national and ethnic factors.

2.4   Classifications of organisational culture

Three classifications of organisational culture are reviewed in this section. In all cases, the authors have selected the dimensions, usually only two, that most completely characterise organisations.

2.4.1   Miles and Snow's classification

Miles and Snow[26] put forward four organisational types, categorised by their approach to innovation and to risk:

- Defenders   are organisations in which the managers are experts in their organisation's limited area of operation but tend not to search outside their current areas for new opportunities. These companies deliberately maintain an environment in which a stable form of organisation is appropriate – and they do this by 'sealing off' narrowly defined market segments. Such organisations seldom make major adjustments to their operations: their focus is on increasing efficiency.

- Prospectors   are organisations that continually search for market opportunities, regularly experimenting with potential responses to emerging environmental trends. The emphasis isn't on efficiency but on innovation.

- Analysers   are organisations that exhibit both defender and prospector characteristics. In stable situations, these organisations operate through the use of formalised structures and processes. In more dynamic settings, they tend to be followers, watching their competitors closely and copying their most promising innovations.

- Reactors   are organisations in which managers are impotent in the face of the change and uncertainty that they perceive. The managers lack a coherent strategy and only react when they are forced to do so. Reactors are not viable organisations in the longer term.

2.4.2 Deal and Kennedy's classification

According to Deal and Kennedy,[27] organisational cultures can be characterised according to two factors: the degree of risk associated with the organisation's activities, and the speed with which the organisation and its employees get feedback on whether their actions were successful or not. From these two dimensions, these authors recognise four types of culture:

- **The tough-guy, macho culture**   In this culture individuals regularly take high risks and get quick feedback on whether their actions are right or wrong. Fortunes can be made overnight. The whole of the entertainment industry would seem to have this culture, with extravagantly financed films, expensively assembled football teams and high-profile TV scheduling as examples. Within a short time the appropriateness of these endeavours will be apparent – the film is a box-office flop, the football team languishes in the lower reaches of its league and the TV schedule makes the viewers turn off. Venture capitalists, currency dealers and many young Internet entrepreneurs would seem to fit into this category as well. Inside the organisation the pressures will be intense, with every meeting becoming a trial of wills between the tough guys, resulting in early 'burn-out' for the survivors and high staff turnover as the losers leave.

- **The work hard, play hard culture**   Employees in this culture live in an environment of small risks, quick feedback and a high level of activity. Sales reps and retailers would seem to live completely in this world. Factory workers are often in this culture as they are making a series of small decisions throughout the day; the risks are small since they work within well-defined procedures and controls. Such organisations are centred on customers and they will satisfy their needs through team activities. Team working will be encouraged through team playing – through games, meetings, promotions, beer busts and away-days. This culture is appropriate for action-driven people who thrive on quick, tangible feedback.

- **The bet-your-company culture**   Organisations with this culture experience high risk but with slow feedback. Examples would be those organisations that invest large sums in research and development projects with a long timescale, such as pharmaceutical companies and aero engine manufacturers. A particularly high-profile case is that of Apple Computers, with the whole company bet (twice, as it happens) on the success of a single machine. With such long timescales and the inherent risks, the handling of significant issues will be a very deliberate process by the most senior members of the organisation. This culture leads to high-quality inventions and major scientific breakthroughs.

- **The process culture**   Organisations such as retail banks, insurance companies, the utilities and much of government are examples of the process culture, characterised by low risk and slow feedback. Employees find it difficult to measure their output and so they concentrate on how they do their work – on the process. Procedures become an end in themselves and people tend to develop a 'cover your back' mentality, where memos are sent about everything. Process cultures are appropriate where there is a need for consistency of treatment.

DISCUSSION
POINT 2.4

Which form of culture as described by Deal and Kennedy would best characterise a) the Army, b) a university and c) a police service?

2.4.3 The Harrison/Handy classification

Harrison[28] and later Handy[29] describe four types of culture, characterised by the concentration of power and hierarchy, the relationship of the individual to the organisation and the centrality of tasks or of the individual:

- Personal culture   The personal culture revolves around individuals who come together in an organisation only because it furthers their own ambitions; the organisation provides the medium in which they can thrive. The individuals have little loyalty to the organisation. Although not many organisations can exist with the full manifestation of this sort of culture, examples of organisations where the personal culture is strong are currency dealers, universities and barristers' chambers. Controls are well-nigh impossible to impose, and any that are used can only work through consent. Influence is shared by individuals and power is expert power. Change for individuals can be very rapid, but as the organisation can't generally sack anyone, organisational change can be slow.

- Power culture   In this form of culture power is all that matters and instructions emanate from the top of the organisation. An entrepreneurial organisation would typically be of this type. The junk bond operation headed by Michael Milken during the 1980s was a typical example. The essence is that good people are hired and allowed to get on with their jobs with only minimal – usually financial – control held at the centre. The advantage is rapid response to changing circumstances; the weakness is the idiosyncratic nature of the changes.

- Role culture   As the name suggests, in a role culture the role of every person is well defined. The organisation is a bureaucracy. The organisation is formally structured – probably with several levels of hierarchy – and relies on committees for decision making. The organisation puts an emphasis on procedures and fairness. Although bureaucracy is now often considered something to be avoided at all costs, it still has a very important role to play. It's impossible to build tens of thousands of cars to a uniform specification without it – although it's probably impossible to design a successful car with it. The role culture provides for efficiency if not effectiveness. Change is likely to be slow.

- Task culture   A task culture is most frequently found in small organisations whose members have come together because of some shared values or goal. Examples are research teams and high-risk businesses. In a task culture the organisation focuses on successfully completing well-defined projects or tasks. The formal organisational structure is but a very weak guide to the structures that are put in place in an *ad hoc* way to tackle the issues as they arise. The structure is one of project teams and one that allows considerable flexibility within the organisation. Influence is based on expert power and is widely dispersed. Change can be fast. NASA, the US space agency, made great use of tasks to put a man on the moon. Advertising agencies and consultancies are other good examples of task cultures.

DISCUSSION
POINT 2.5
Which form of culture as described by Harrison/Handy would best characterise a) the Army, b) a university and c) a police service?

Harrison has identified the basic tension in all organisations between the values and structural qualities that advance the interests of the individual and those that advance the interests of the organisation. He identified three interests that are primarily individual and three that are primarily organisational. These six interests are shown as the white headings of Exhibit 2.10. As an example of reading this table, the role culture provides high security against deprivation for the individual, low opportunities for their voluntary commitment and poor opportunities for them to pursue their own growth. For the organisation the role culture offers a moderate to low response to environmental issues, a low ability to react to environmental complexity and change, yet a high level of internal integration.

2.4.4 Approaches to learning

The developed world has entered a phase where knowledge and the knowledge worker are the dominant creators of wealth.[30] In this situation it has become recognised that ensuring that the organisation increases its knowledge base over time is a necessity. Just as being able to read is a metacompetence, so is the learning that underpins the continual change to business activities and processes that the organisation requires to survive.

One view of culture is that it is the totality of the shared learning of an organisation[31] and thus cultural change comes about through organisational learning. Organisational learning isn't simply the approach the personnel department takes to employees obtaining qualifications – although this is no doubt important – but how the organisation organises to continually renew itself. A major strategic advantage – perhaps the *only* sustainable long-term advantage – that an organisation can have is to learn faster than its competitors.[32] Organisations need to be learning organisations, and knowledge needs to be fostered by individual and organisational learning. It all starts with the individual and then is extended to the unit and perhaps to the whole organisation.

KEY CONCEPT | Miles and Snow's classification of organisational culture is primarily based on innovation, with a dichotomy between innovation and efficiency – the new and the current. Deal and Kennedy's is based on the risk that is associated with an organisation's activities and the speed with which feedback is obtained. Harrison and Handy's is based on how organisations differ primarily in terms of power and control and the individual versus the organisation. To more completely characterise an organisation, its approach to learning should also be considered.

DISCUSSION
POINT 2.6
What are the links between the Miles and Snow, Deal and Kennedy and Harrison/Handy classifications of organisation culture?

2.4.5 The web of beliefs

All of the three classifications of organisational cultural style are simplistic. No organisation will fit exactly into one or other of the categories in the classifications, and in any one organisation it is likely that portions of it will have different cultures – for

EXHIBIT 2.10

Interests of individuals and the organisation (Harrison, 1972)

A Interests of individuals	Security against economic, political and psychological deprivation	Opportunities for voluntary commitment to worthwhile goals	Opportunities to pursue one's own growth and development independent of organisation goals
Power culture	Low: At the pleasure of the autocrat	Low: Unless one is in a sufficiently high position to determine organisation goals	Low: Unless one is in a sufficiently high position to determine organisation goals
Role culture	High: Secured by law, custom and procedure	Low: Even if, at times, one is in a high position	Low: Organisation goals are relatively rigid and activities are closely prescribed
Task culture	Moderate: Psychological deprivation can occur when an individual's contributions are redundant	High: A major basis of the individual's relationship to the organisation	Low: The individual should not be in the organisation if he does not subscribe to some of its goals
Person culture	High: The individual's welfare is the major concern	High: But only if the individual is capable of generating his own goals	High: Organisation goals are determined by individual needs

B Interests of the organisation	Effective response to dangerous, threatening environments	Dealing rapidly and effectively with environmental complexity and change	Internal integration and co-ordination of effort – if necessary, at the expense of individual needs
Power culture	High: The organisation tends to be perpetually ready for a fight	Moderate to low: Depends on size, pyramidal communication channels are easily overloaded	High: Effective control emanates from the top
Role culture	Moderate to low: The organisation is slow to mobilise to meet increases in threat	Low: Slow to change programmed procedures; communication channels are easily overloaded	High: Features a carefully planned rational system of work

Exhibit 2.10 (continued)			
Task culture	Moderate to high: The organisation may be slow to make decisions but produces highly competent responses	High: Flexible assignment of resources and short communication channels facilitate adaptation	Moderate: Integrated by common goal; but flexible, shifting structure may make co-ordination difficult
Person culture	Low: The organisation is slow to become aware of threat and slow to mobilise effort against it	High: But response is erratic; assignment of resources to problems depends greatly on individual needs and interests	Low: A common goal is difficult to achieve and activities may shift with individual interests

example, using the Deal and Kennedy framework, an R&D department is likely to have a bet-your-company culture, while the sales department will tend towards a work hard, play hard culture. These cultural types can exist side by side – often in tension – within a unit. For example, project teams often overlie a role culture, as would be expected where the new (represented by the project team) is working to change the current organisation, which is likely to be operating with well-defined roles.

There is a great deal in common in the Miles and Snow, Deal and Kennedy and Harrison/Handy classifications, and in the findings of Trompenaars and Hampden-Turner – but some features are different. Combining their characteristics determines the six segments of Exhibit 2.11, which sum up the main organisational beliefs.

EXHIBIT 2.11

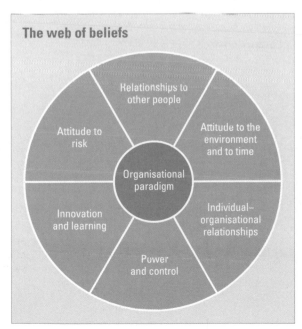

The approaches of Trompenaars, Hampden-Turner and Handy identified relationships between people, of people to their environment and to time as important cultural values. Both identified the link of the individual to the organisation (the task orientation–person orientation dichotomy) and power and control. Miles and Snow contribute two further significant values concerned with an organisation's approach to learning and innovation and its approach to risk.

2.5 Identifying an organisational culture

Of key importance to the manager is to recognise the culture of their own organisation and of organisations with which they are going to have a close relationship, perhaps through a business alliance, as a supplier, or as an organisation that they might join in a career move. The norms are what will be fairly readily identified, although it's the beliefs that really need to be understood. As norms are the windows to the values, norm recognition is required and this needs to be linked to the organisational value and to the paradigm.

2.5.1 The web of behaviours

The norms of an organisation are expressed – and indeed transmitted – in many ways, often unwritten and informally. Common modes of transmission have been identified by Kilmann[33] and Johnson[34] and have been succinctly expressed in the web of behaviours, as shown in Exhibit 2.12. The web of behaviours is concerned with the manifestations of culture – the behaviours in the organisation – and has six components:

- Symbols   A symbol is someone or something that represents a particular quality or idea. Symbols abound in all organisations: the size and shape of offices, the size and make of company car, the titles in use. Never a day seems to go by without it being announced that an organisation has (usually at exorbitant expense) changed its corporate logo. In Germany the use of old script signifies old-fashioned and conservative values – perhaps OK for a brand of beer or for a

EXHIBIT 2.12

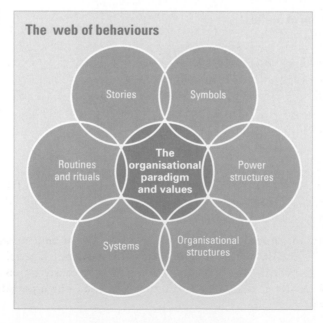

staid bank, but hardly likely to be appropriate for an IT company. BA dropped, then partially reinstated, the Union flag from the livery on its aircraft, since it wanted to be considered a global rather than a British airline. The language that is used to describe people both inside and outside the organisation can be very revealing. Advertising agencies divide their staff into *suits* (the account managers), *creatives* (the artistic personnel) and *intellectuals* (the programme chasers).

- Power structures   The dominant coalition is the obvious source of power in an organisation and this is generally, but not always, formed by the board or by a section of it. In some cultures seniority and age are the most significant source of power. It may be that a group has power through its expertise. In fast-moving consumer goods the dominant coalition will tend to be the marketers; at the corporate level financial personnel are likely to be dominant. The power of individuals and groups is likely to become more significant in knowledge-based organisations, where individual or group expert knowledge is the source of most of the value in the business.

- Organisational structure   Organisational structures may not truly represent the way people work in an organisation, but they can reflect hierarchical thinking. The number of organisational levels signifies an extensive hierarchy. People in an organisation may have more than one reporting line; for example, a computer specialist may report both to their functional boss and to the boss of the department in which they are working. In large teaching hospitals the control of information systems has been bedevilled by organisational structures: doctors were provided with money, hardware and software for information systems by the university, by the National Health Service, and by firms selling to the hospital and firms for whom doctors were carrying out consultancy.

- Systems   Systems play very important roles in most organisations. Significant systems are:

  - *Control systems*   These are the sets of procedures established to constrain activities and to ensure conformance. They indicate the freedom that people have. Manifestations to look for are who and what are controlled and what size of activity is measured. Furthermore, a useful guide is to assess whether the measures are predominantly financial or whether other, perhaps softer, factors are controlled. It's useful to explore whether the control systems are accepted by the controlled or whether they are simply tolerated and something to be circumvented.

  - *Reward systems*   These are the carrots and sticks so that those in power can foster their view of how the organisation should develop. A reward system geared very closely to results and to individuals will produce a different outcome from one that is more relaxed about meeting short-term objectives and that links reward to group success.

  - *Information systems*   The old adage 'information is power' is very apposite. The way in which information is made available to people is of considerable significance. An organisation that puts little constraint on information indicates an open structure and one that has a high potential to be a learning organisation.

- *Issue-handling systems*   These consist of the set of procedures that an organisation uses to handle issues. What should be considered is who is involved and the process by which issues are handled. With the move to knowledge-based organisations, there is a need to move to *fair process*,[35] to use issue-handling processes that individuals feel are fair even if they haven't achieved the decision that they were seeking.

- *Organisational learning systems*   These are the processes that are in place both to support individual learning and, perhaps more importantly, to help the organisation learn and retain its learning: for example, organised rotation of staff in project teams or through the functions are indications of a learning organisation. The formal appreciation of the role of business intelligence systems whereby the general business environment, particularly that of customers and competitors, is monitored is another indicator.

- **Routines and rituals**   All organisations must have some routine behaviours or working together would be very difficult as you would never be sure of what anyone would do. In the right place routines lead to efficiency. They can say a lot about an organisation. For example, if design engineers always go to the offices of the production engineers, this probably indicates the lower status of the designers. Organisations tend to have rituals to emphasise events. Several forms of ritual are listed in Exhibit 2.13. Those that are promoted in the organisation can say a great deal about the organisation. For example, does the organisation have procedures for handling complaints from staff?

EXHIBIT 2.13

Types of ritual[36] (adapted from Trice and Beyer, 1984)

	Role	Examples
Rites of passage	Consolidate and promote social roles and interaction	• Induction courses • Certificates awarded on completion of training
Rites of enhancement	Recognise efforts benefiting the organisation	• Award ceremonies for best-performing salesperson
Rites of renewal	Reassure that something is being done	• Unveil a new strategy; move to a new building
Rites of integration	Encourage shared commitment	• Beer busts • Christmas parties • Corporate newsletter
Rites of conflict reduction	Reduce conflict and aggression	• Collective bargaining • Staff associations
Rites of degradation	Publicly acknowledge problems	• Sacking the chief executive • Dissolving a project team
Rites of challenge	'Throwing down the gauntlet'	• The John Lewis Partnership and its complaints procedure

- Stories   The stories that members of an organisation tell about the past can provide a good view on what people feel is important. The stories are about heroes and villains and revolve around successes, failures and crises. The company 3M places a very great emphasis on innovation; Art Fry, the inventor of the Post-it note, is one of the heroes and his success is frequently referred to.

2.5.2   Combining the webs of behaviours and beliefs – the cultural web

The cultural web is concerned with the manifestations of culture – the behaviours in the organisation. As remarked, what is important is to use these indications to understand the deeper aspects of culture that have given rise to them – the beliefs, the values and the paradigm. Each value could find expression in all or any of the elements of the cultural web. This is illustrated in Exhibit 2.14 through the six circles that overlap each of the main values.

The manifestations allow us a window to the organisational values. As values are more general than norms, the insights provided by the norms allow us to estimate what the norms will be in new situations.

As an example, a set of norms that tell you about the underlying values concerning innovation and learning is listed in Exhibit 2.15.

KEY CONCEPT   The web of behaviours provides a checklist by which the tangible aspects of organisational culture can be recognised. This web provides a window on the web of beliefs – the organisational values and the organisational paradigm. Together, the web of behaviours and the web of beliefs constitute the cultural web.

2.5.3   Organisational climate

It is important to realise that there is a difference between organisational culture and climate. Climate is to do with the quality of the general feelings that people have about the culture and about what they are asked to do.

The climate is the sum of two main features of the organisation:

- Staff morale   Morale can be viewed in terms of the mental attitudes that people have towards their tasks and responsibilities. Morale will suffer if people think that their job is unimportant, there is little sense of group pride, management seems indifferent to staff welfare and rewards aren't fair and individualised.[37]

- The commitment of the workforce   Organisational commitment can be viewed as an individual's psychological bond to the organisation, including a sense of job involvement, loyalty and a belief in the values of the organisation.[38]

SUMMARY
- Organisational culture is the customary way of thinking and doing things that is shared to a greater or lesser degree by all of the organisation's members. Culture shows itself in layers – like an onion. The outer layer is the explicit culture, the norms, enclosing the more implicit and intangible inner layers of values and the organisational paradigm. Cultural beliefs are group responses to relationships between people and people's relationships with the environment and with time.

EXHIBIT 2.14

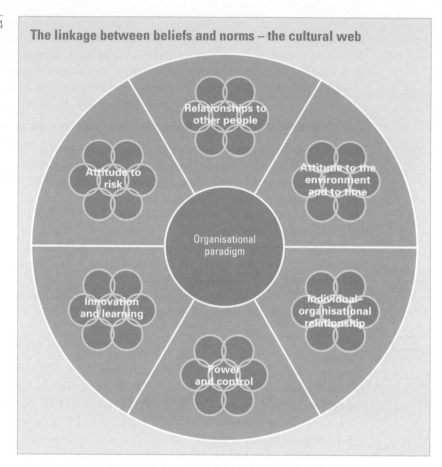

The linkage between beliefs and norms – the cultural web

Relationships to other people

Attitude to risk

Attitude to the environment and to time

Organisational paradigm

Innovation and learning

Individual–organisational relationship

Power and control

Strong cultures may become dangerous because they tend to be a force for maintaining the status quo. EXHIBIT 2.2

- There is considerable overlap between the cultural characteristics of different nationalities and ethnic groups. While national and ethnic culture are important determinants of organisational culture, in the developed world they appear to be less powerful influences than the prevailing culture of the industry in which the organisation is operating. EXHIBIT 2.8

- Organisations can be categorised in terms of culture. Miles and Snow categorise organisations as defenders, prospectors, analysers and reactors, according to their approaches to innovation and risk. Deal and Kennedy characterise organisations according to the degree of risk associated with their activities, and the speed with which the organisation and its employees get feedback on whether their actions were successful or not. Harrison/Handy characterised organisations according to the concentration of power and hierarchy, the relationship of the individual to the organisation and the centrality of tasks or of the person. The interests of individuals and of the organisation are catered for in different ways depending on the type of organisation. EXHIBIT 2.10

- The norms of an organisation will be manifest in six main areas, the components of the web of behaviours: symbols, power structures, organisational structures,

EXHIBIT 2.15

Manifestations in the cultural web indicating an organisation that emphasised innovation and learning

Elements of the cultural web	Examples
Symbols	Qualifications on office door nameplates
Power structures	Generally egalitarian but with professionals/specialists having great influence, IT board director
Organisational structures	Project teams much in evidence, mixing of functional people, matrix organisation, status of IT department
Systems	Light touch on project budgets, flexible use of resources, financial increments when qualifications achieved, use of technology in issue handling, formal competitive intelligence system
Routines and rituals	Celebration of project completions, celebration of outstanding intellectual achievement
Stories	Concern innovators

DISCUSSION POINT 2.7

Repeat Exhibit 2.15 to illustrate an organisation that places an emphasis on traditional values.

systems, routines and rituals, and stories. The web of behaviours provides the windows on the web of beliefs that underpin them. Six main beliefs have been identified: relationships to people, attitudes to the environment and to time, the relationship of the individual to the organisation, power and control, innovation and learning, and attitude to risk. Together, the webs of behaviours and beliefs constitute the cultural web.   EXHIBIT 2.11, EXHIBIT 2.12, EXHIBIT 2.14

SELF-CHECK

1 Reconsider the learning outcomes for this chapter. Check that you feel confident that you can carry out the activities listed there.

2 Having read this chapter, you should be able to define the following terms:

belief	norm	power structure
behaviour	occupation-based	symbol
climate	labour market	value
cultural web	organisation-based	web of behaviours
cultural onion	labour market	web of beliefs
culture	organisational structure	
mindset	paradigm	

Parris-Rogers International (PRI)[39]

In June 1996, a car bomb in Saudi Arabia killed 19 US servicemen. The victims were among approximately 9000 US troops remaining in Saudi Arabia, Kuwait, Bahrain and the United Arab Emirates since the end of the 1991 Gulf War to liberate Kuwait from Iraq. Although no group claimed responsibility for the blast, most analysts reasoned that cultural conflict was an underlying cause. Traditionalists wanted to rid the area of Western influences, such as music, entertainment and dress, which they considered immoral. At the same time, a Western-educated middle class was questioning many of the traditional rules. The cultural conflict and accommodation are illustrated by the rules imposed by the US Army on female troops during the war. They were not permitted to jog, drive or show their legs outside the military base. In deference to US sensitivities, Saudi Arabia suspended beheadings in central squares during the Gulf crisis.

A few years earlier, Parris-Rogers International (PRI), a British publishing house, sold its floundering Bahraini operations. This branch had been set up to edit the first telephone and business directories for five Arab states on or near the Arabian peninsula, plus the seven autonomous divisions making up the United Arab Emirates. Although the US Army had protocol officers to advise it on accepted behaviour, PRI had no such guidance. Further, although the Saudis were willing to make some accommodations to assure the defence of their country, PRI's directories were less important to the 12 Arab states. The ensuing lack of understanding between the Arab states and PRI and PRI's failure to adapt to a different culture contributed directly to the company's failure.

Most Middle Eastern oil-producing countries have an acute shortage of local personnel, so many foreign workers have been hired. They now make up a large portion of the population in those countries. In the United Arab Emirates in 1995, for example, 70% of the population was foreign, mainly from India and Pakistan. In Saudi Arabia, about 40% was foreign. Thus when PRI could not find sufficient qualified people locally, it filled four key positions through advertisements in London newspapers. Angela Clarke, an Englishwoman, was hired as editor and researcher, and three young Englishmen were hired as salesmen. The four new hires left immediately for Bahrain. None had visited the Middle East before; all expected to carry out business as usual.

The salesmen, hired on a commission basis, expected that by moving aggressively they could make the same number of calls as they normally could in the UK. They were used to working about eight hours a day, to having the undivided attention of potential clients, and to restricting most conversation to the specifics of the business transaction.

The salesmen found instead an entirely different situation. There was less time to sell, first, because the Muslims were required to pray five times a day and, second, because the workday was reduced even further during the sacred ninth month of the Muslim year, Ramadan, when there is fasting from sunrise to sunset. The Muslim year is based on a lunar rather than a solar calendar; thus Ramadan may begin in different solar months, such as in January for 1997, or December 1997 for 1998. Moreover, the start of Ramadan is based on the sighting of a new moon; thus longitudinal, latitudinal and weather conditions usually cause the start to vary by a day or two among countries and cannot be determined in advance. The salesmen also felt that Arabs placed little importance on appointments. Appointments seldom began at the scheduled time. When the salesmen finally got in to see Arab businessmen, they were often expected to go to a café where the Arabs would engage in what seemed to them to be idle chitchat. Whether in a café or in the office, drinking coffee or tea seemed to take precedence over business matters. The Arabs also frequently diverted their attention to friends who joined them at the café or in the office.

Angela Clarke also encountered considerable resistance as she sought to do her job.

Since she was paid a salary instead of commission, PRI had to bear all of the expenses resulting from her work being thwarted in unexpected ways. It had based its budgets for preparing the directories on its English experience. In Bahrain, however, preparing such books turned out to be more time-consuming and costly. For example, in a traditional Middle Eastern city there are no street names or building numbers. Thus, before getting to the expected directory work, Clarke had to take a census of Bahraini establishments, identifying the location of each with such prepositions as 'below', 'above', or 'in front of' some meaningful landmark.

Clarke encountered other problems because she was a single woman. She was in charge of the research in all 12 states and had planned to hire freelance assistants in most of them. But her advertisements to hire such assistants were answered by personal harassment and obscene telephone calls. In addition, Saudi authorities denied her entry to Saudi Arabia, while her visa for Oman took six weeks to process each time she went there. These experiences were particularly frustrating for her because both Saudi Arabia and Oman sometimes eased the entry of a single woman when her business was of high local priority and/or when she would be serving as a housemaid or nanny, where her only contact would be with women and children. In the states she could enter, Clarke was sometimes required to stay only in hotels that government officials had approved for foreign women, and even there, she was prohibited from eating in the dining room unless accompanied by the hotel manager.

PRI's salesmen never adjusted to working in the new environment. Instead of pushing PRI to review its commission scheme, they tried to change the way the Arab businessmen dealt with them. For example, after a few months they refused to join their potential clients for refreshments and began showing their irritation at 'irrelevant' conversations, delays and interruptions from outsiders. The Arab businessmen responded negatively. In fact, PRI received so many complaints from them that the salesmen had to be replaced. By then, however, irrevocable damage had been done to PRI's sales.

Clarke fared better, thanks to her compromises with Arab customs. She began wearing a wedding ring and registering at hotels as a married woman. When travelling, she ate meals in her room, conducted meetings in conference rooms, and had all incoming calls screened by the hotel operators. To avoid arrest by decency patrols, she wore long-sleeved blouses and below-the-knee skirts in plain blue or beige. Still, in spite of her compromises, her inability to enter Saudi Arabia caused PRI to send in her place a salesman, who was not trained to do the research.

The rapidly growing number of foreigners in the Middle East has created adjustment problems for both the foreigners and the local societies. In many cases, foreigners are expected to conform; in others, they are allowed to pursue their own customs in isolation from the local populace. For example, according to traditional Islamic standards, most Western television programming is immoral. However, in some places foreigners are permitted to acquire unscramblers to view Western programmes; local people are not. At the same time, although satellite dishes are technically illegal in Saudi Arabia, these 'devils' dishes' – a term used by hard-line Islamic fundamentalists – are seen on rooftops everywhere. Nevertheless, the BBC axed its Arabic Television Service in 1996 because of disagreements over programme content. This led a BBC executive to remark, 'Looking at the partners involved, the Saudis and the BBC, who would have thought two such different cultures could comfortably co-exist?'

The Saudi government has also had second thoughts about some of its culture's double standards. For example, at one time male and female hotel guests were allowed to swim in the same pools in Saudi Arabia. This permission was rescinded, however, because Saudis frequent the hotels. It was feared they might be corrupted by viewing 'decadent' behaviour. In addition, when Angela Clarke and the salesmen first arrived in Bahrain, there were prohibitions on the sale of pork products, including imported canned foods. This prohibition was later modified, but grocers had to stock pork products in separate rooms in which only non-Muslims could work or shop.

These dual and changing standards for foreigners and citizens hamper foreign efforts to adapt. The situation has been further complicated because the Middle East is going through a period of substantial, but uneven, economic and social transformation. As contact increases between Arabs and Westerners, cultural borrowing and meshing of certain aspects of traditional and modern behaviour will increase. These changes are liable to come slowly, perhaps more so than many think.

Discussion point 2.8

List the different business practices in the Middle East and Western Europe.

- List the adjustments to Middle Eastern cultural norms made by Angela Clarke. Was she 'selling out' in any way?
- Is there an obvious line where further adjustments wouldn't be appropriate? What about what Westerners might call bribery?

FURTHER
DISCUSSION
POINTS

1 From the GSM case:
   - Is culture transferable?
   - In Section 2.3.2 the main determinants of organisational culture were listed. Having read the GSM case, would you add to the list?
   - How does GSM motivate its employees?
   - How does GSM empower its employees?
   - What is the dominant sort of culture in Harrison and Handy and Miles and Snow's terminologies?
   - Is GSM operating an occupation-based or an organisation-based labour market?
2 The categories of organisational culture of Harrison and Handy, Deal and Kennedy, and Miles and Snow have been described in this chapter. Which categories of organisation would you expect to follow an intended approach to strategy and which an emergent approach introduced in Section 1.9?
3 Trompenaars and Hampden-Turner identify two attitudes to time. How do these link to the two approaches to strategy formulation outlined in Section 1.9?
4 Trompenaars and Hampden-Turner identify two attitudes to the environment. How do these link to the organisation–environment matching and types of change discussed in Section 1.6?
5 Do differing management styles have implications for operational efficiency when comparing, say, a factory in Japan with one in France?
6 Do you believe that achievements or qualifications should be the main consideration when recruiting managers?

ASSIGNMENTS

1 Map how the culture of Dutton Engineering (one of the cases in this book) changed over the decade to 1999.
2 Using Exhibit 2.14 as a guide, map out the cultural web for an organisation of your choice. (It is unlikely that you will be able to find an 'entry' for all categories.)

FURTHER READING

The first part of this chapter owes a considerable amount to a book by Fons Trompenaars and Charles Hampden-Turner, *Riding the Waves of Culture: Understanding Cultural Diversity in Business*, Nicholas Brealey Publishing, 1997. This book includes many fascinating charts showing the scores on many traits of different nationalities. If you are involved internationally, it could be very beneficial to look at the broad differences between people of your own nationality and those of the people with whom you are about to interact.

Management in several countries in Europe have been considered by Peter Lawrence in a series of books. Anyone intending to work in one of these countries would be well advised to read the appropriate book: he has written books on East Germany, France, Germany, the Netherlands, Israel, Sweden and the USA. Additionally, there is a book covering Western Europe (P. Lawrence and V. Edwards, *Management in Western Europe*, Macmillan Business, 1999).

CHAPTER NOTES AND REFERENCES

1 Hampden-Turner, C. and Trompenaars, F., *The Seven Cultures of Capitalism: Value Systems for Creating Wealth in the United States, Britain, Japan, Germany, France, Sweden, and the Netherlands*, Doubleday, 1993.

2 Trompenaars, F. and Hampden-Turner, C., *Riding the Waves of Culture: Understanding Cultural Diversity in Business*, Nicholas Brealey Publishing, 1997.

3 Fiol, M., 'Managing culture as a competitive weapon with interorganizational information systems resource: an identity-based view of competitive advantage', *Journal of Management*, 17, 1991, pp. 191–211.

4 Schein, E., *Organizational Culture and Leadership: A Dynamic View*, Jossey-Bass, 1985, p. 6.

5 Schall, M.S., 'A communication-rules approach to organizational culture', *Administrative Science Quarterly*, Vol. 28, 1983, pp. 557–81.

6 Hofstede, G., *Culture's Consequences*, Sage, 1980.

7 Argyris, C. and Schon, D.A., *Organizational Learning*, Addison-Wesley, 1978. They use the rather confusing terms 'espoused theory' and 'espoused theories-in-use'.

8 Kuhn, T.S., *The Structure of Scientific Revolutions*, University of Chicago Press, 1970.

9 Schall, *op. cit.*

10 Loomis, C.J., 'Dinosaurs', *Fortune*, 3 May 1993, pp. 32–8.

11 Gapper, J., 'Sun is accused of missing new dawn in attitudes to homosexuals', *Financial Times*, 11 November 1998, p. 9.

12 Schein, E., 'How culture forms, develops, and changes', in Kilmann *et al.*, *op. cit.*, p. 46.

13 Hofstede, G., *Cultures and Organizations: Software of the Mind*, McGraw-Hill, 1991.

14 Hofstede, G. and Bond, M.I1., 'The Confucius connection: from cultural roots to economic growth', *Organisational Dynamics*, 16, 4, 1998, pp. 4–21.

15 Of the employees in their sample, 75% were managers, with a preponderance of large organisations.

16 Trompenaars, F. and Hampden-Turner, C., *op. cit.* 1997, p. 10.

17 Laurent, A., 'Cultural diversity of Western conceptions of management', *International Studies of Management and Organisations*, Vol. XIII, No. 1–2, pp. 75–96, 1983.

18 Lawrence, P., 'Management across borders', in Woods, M. (ed.), *International Business*, Chapman & Hall, 1995.

19 Lam, A., 'Tacit knowledge, organisational learning and innovation: a societal perspective', Danish Research Unit for Industrial Dynamics, Druid working paper No. 98–22,

1998 paper presented at the *British Academy of Management Conference*, Nottingham, 14–16 September 1998.

20 McConchie, D.R., 'Patterns of strategic control: an investigation of British, French and German retail banking practice', PhD thesis, Loughborough University, October 1998, p. 19.

21 The word *organisation* comes from the Greek *orgon*, meaning instrument, thus an organisation is an instrument to accomplish a task. This is a Western view. (Hampden-Turner, C. and Trompenaars, F., *op. cit.*, 1993, p. 34.) Other nationalities, particularly the East Asians, see organisations as meetings of people with a social goal.

22 Edwards, V. and Lawrence, P.A., 'Country versus industry: the dynamics of strategic differentiation', *Proceedings of the 25th Annual Meeting of the Western Decision Sciences Institute*, Seattle, USA, April 1996, pp. 136–43.

23 This finding is supported by McConchie, D. 'European retail banks', PhD thesis, Loughborough University, 1998.

24 Barry, R., 'History shakers', *Guardian Higher Education*, 16 February 1999, page iv.

25 Mintzberg, H., Quinn, J.B. and Ghoshal, S., *The Strategy Process*, European edn, Prentice Hall International, 1995, pp. 350–71.

26 Miles, R.E. and Snow, C.C., *Organizational Strategy, Structure, and Process*, McGraw-Hill Series in Management, McGraw-Hill, 1978.

27 Deal, T.E. and Kennedy, A.A., *Corporate Cultures: The Rites and Rituals of Corporate Life*, Addison-Wesley, 1982.

28 Harrison, R., 'Understanding your organization's character', *Harvard Business Review*, May–June 1972, pp. 119–28.

29 Handy, C., *Understanding Organisations*, 4th edn, Penguin Books, 1993.

30 Drucker, P.F., *Post-capitalist Society*, Butterworth Heinemann, 1993.

31 Schein, E., *op. cit.*, 1986, p. 19.

32 Stata, R., 'Organisational learning – the key to management innovation', *Sloan Management Review*, Vol. 30, Spring 1989, pp. 63–74.

33 Kilmann, R.H., Saxton, M.J., Serpa, R. and Associates, *Gaining Control of the Corporate Culture*, Jossey-Bass, 1986.

34 Johnson, G., 'Managing strategic change – strategy, culture and action', *Long Range Planning*, Vol. 25, No. 1, 1992, pp. 28–36. Johnson termed this the 'cultural web'.

35 Kim, W.C. and Mauborgne, R., 'Fair process: managing in the knowledge economy', *Harvard Business Review*, July–August 1997, pp. 65–75.

36 Trice, H.M. and Beyer, J.M., 'Using six organisational rites to change culture', in Kilmann *et al.*, *op. cit.*

37 Petrick, J.E. and Manning, G.E., 'How to manage morale', *Personnel Journal*, Vol. 69, No. 10, October 1990, pp. 83–8.

38 O'Reilly, C., 'Corporations, culture and commitment: motivation and social control in organizations', in Steers, R.M. and Porter, L.W. (eds), *Motivation and Work Behavior*, 5th edn, McGraw-Hill, 1991, pp. 242–55.

39 Daniels, J.D. and Radebaugh, L.H., *International Business Environments and Operations*, 8th edn, Addison-Wesley, 1998, pp. 58–61.

3 Business ethics

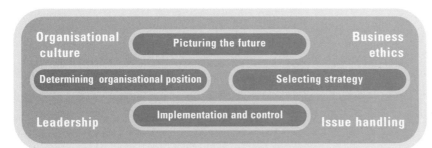

his is the second of the set of four chapters concerned with the internal context of an organisation. The concern is with business ethics, with that aspect of organisational culture that involves significant harm or benefit to others.

The scope and importance of business ethics are explored first, and the nature of ethics is examined through looking at a set of dilemmas that might easily confront managers. Consideration of these dilemmas paves the way for an introductory look at the four main ethical frameworks that exist to resolve such dilemmas, and then for these four to be reduced to the two – utilitarianism and proceduralism – that will be considered in greater depth. It's at this stage that one of the central issues of the chapter is tackled: what does *ethical* mean?

Elements of the two ethical frameworks are combined to provide a pragmatic reconciliation that provides guidelines both for acting within an organisational ethical code and for changing it. A very short historical overview of the scope of ethics suggests that establishing the rights of animals is the next step in our ethical development and the views for and against animal rights are presented.

Up to this point, only 'face-to-face' ethics – ethical considerations among individuals – has been considered. The social responsibility that an organisation has for groups of people is then explored. Finally, how to bring wrongdoing to the attention of authority through what is termed 'whistleblowing' is discussed, together with how a manager can establish a climate in which whistleblowing is either not required or is encouraged.

Business ethics is concerned with conduct: with how individuals within an organisation interact with each other and with how organisations ought to relate to their external stakeholders. Increasingly, successful managers will be those who are capable of successfully reconciling the economic imperatives of business with stakeholders' demands for fairness and social responsibility.

LEARNING
OUTCOMES

When you have worked through this chapter, you should be able to:

- explain what the term *ethical* means;

- explain the scope of the topic of business ethics and know why ethical considerations are becoming increasingly important in business;

- give examples of some significant ethical dilemmas;

- explain the basics of the three main ethical stances motivating business ethics: the approaches based on consequences, justice and human rights;

- explain why it is reasonable to combine the formalistic and human rights approaches into a procedural approach;

- contrast the utilitarian and procedural approaches and identify your own ethical orientation;

- reconcile the utilitarian and procedural approaches and develop, maintain and apply organisational ethical guidelines;

- contrast the arguments for and against animals having rights;

- successfully whistleblow and set up a system to help others facing an ethical dilemma.

3.1 The scope and importance of business ethics

3.1.1 What is ethics and what is business ethics?

Any issue that implies significant harm or benefit to others is an ethical issue. Some writers[1] make a distinction between ethics and morality: ethics is the enquiry into morality and morality is what is being enquired about. Another distinction is that ethics is about 'public' rules and regulations and that morals are personal. These distinctions won't be made here, and the terms *ethics* and *morality* and *ethical* and *moral* will be used interchangeably.

While fundamental ethical principles will remain unchanged wherever they are applied, the specifics of their application and the specific dilemmas that are being confronted will vary with the context. Just as medical ethics is concerned with the application of ethics in medical contexts, business ethics is concerned with the application of ethics in business contexts. While business ethics will be grounded in general ethical principles, no company that defines 'right' and 'wrong' in terms that would satisfy the most demanding of contemporary individual consciences would survive for very long. The economic imperatives of business are what make business ethics different from ethics in other areas.

There are two intertwined considerations in business ethics that are of concern to senior management. First, just as the firm is a legal entity, one view of business ethics is that a firm also exhibit a moral entity. In this view the organisation, perhaps through its senior managers, should determine how the company deals with the outside world. A firm should act morally because the very enterprise of business presupposes that the participants in business transactions subscribe to a set of agreed moral norms. If they didn't and, for example, fraud and deception were commonplace in commercial transactions, it would be very difficult to conduct business. Every transaction would need some form of tight contract and lawyers would grow exceedingly rich. A second view is that the sole purpose of a profit-seeking firm is to seek profit for the shareholders and that managers should work towards this end. The firm is an inanimate construction and can't and shouldn't take on a moral stance. In this view the firm would be legally obliged only to act according to the law in its dealings with outsiders. However it is regarded, legally or morally, there is a requirement on senior managers to define the relationships between the firm and its environment.

The second consideration for senior management is to establish the moral climate within the organisation. Individual employees can't be expected to resolve moral issues within or on behalf of the organisation on their own. Thus, managers have to consider their ethics both as individuals and as the setters of the business ethics framework within which employees should act.

DISCUSSION
POINT 3.1

Reflect on the issues you have confronted over the past few months, in both your business and personal life. How many of them involved harm or benefit to other individuals? How many involved *significant* harm or benefit?

- Should we be considering *business* ethics or should we be considering *corporate* or indeed *organisational* ethics?

3.1.2   The growing importance of ethics

In the past, the morality of a workforce – and indeed of whole nations – was fairly homogeneous. In northern Europe the traditional ethic was a Christian Protestant one; in southern Europe a Catholic one predominated. With globalisation, the migration of large numbers of people from one part of the globe to another, and with people turning towards less established forms of belief, many people are more and more likely to be working with colleagues who have ethical views different from their own. This in itself means that ethical considerations are becoming more important; but they are also becoming more important – or at least their consequences are – because there is far more scrutiny than previously of the behaviour of individuals and of businesses from both inside and outside the organisation.

A further reason for managers to take ethical considerations seriously is that in general *good ethics is good business*. Consider The Body Shop: its whole marketing strategy has been built around a set of moral stances, for example no pollution and no testing of its products on animals. Ethical funds allow investors to buy into a portfolio of shares that typically exclude investments in tobacco, alcohol, military manufacturers and sometimes oil companies. Although still only a tiny fraction of the total unit and investment trust funds, the amount of money invested in ethical funds almost doubled in the UK in the period 1994–1997.[2] Here the fund managers are presenting an ethical stance, and indeed that is the main selling point of their products.

The growing concern for companies to review their ethical stances makes it even more important that managers consider the ethical dimension to their actions. Many ethical programmes in the USA have been developed in response to the Federal sentencing guidelines laid down in 1991. These guidelines cover establishing codes of ethics, carrying out ethical audits and the duty of senior executives to take responsibility for ethics. If companies follow the guidelines they may find themselves in a better position legally if charged with malpractice.[3] Around 10% of large UK firms are experimenting with ethical audits to ensure that their business practices are aligned with the ethical principles they espouse.

Within this developing situation, managers will be called on more and more often to resolve moral conflicts and to establish an appropriate moral climate in and for the organisation.

DISCUSSION POINT 3.2
Why should ethical issues concern the individual manager? Why should ethics not be considered a specialism like the law and thus a manager would consult a specialist when an ethical issue arises?

KEY CONCEPT
An ethical issue is any issue that implies significant harm or benefit to another individual. Business ethics is concerned with the way moral issues are handled within a business environment, and thus within economic imperatives. Business ethics gives rise to two concerns for managers: they have to determine both the ethical stance that the firm takes to its external stakeholders and the moral climate within the organisation to guide the actions of employees.

3.2 Some ethical dilemmas

Ethical considerations pose many dilemmas, and it's not obvious how to resolve them. To get a feel for the most common business dilemmas, it's useful to introduce them through a set of questions.

● Is the only requirement on your firm to act within the law?   In the mid-1990s Burger King came under severe criticism in the UK when it was revealed that at one of its branches its already poorly paid workers weren't paid when business was slack, although they had to remain on the firm's premises during the periods when they weren't being paid. (The firm replied to accusations of unethical practice by saying that not to pay people in this way yet demand that they be available to work at a moment's notice wasn't company policy – an overzealous manager had imposed this practice locally.) As it wasn't illegal to act in this way, was the local management right to do as it did?

This dilemma raises the question of a possible clash between legality and ethics. If something is legal, is it necessarily ethical? If it's ethical, is it necessarily legal? Exhibit 3.1 illustrates the point that in most countries the 'laws of the land' are generally in line with the ethical stance of the dominant culture: not surprisingly, as the pervading morality has usually been the main force in shaping the law. But should you break the law if you think it's morally right to do so? Some people do take the view that all laws should be obeyed, and that effort should be made to change a law rather than to disobey it. But what obligation did anyone have to obey the apartheid laws that used to be in place in South Africa? The dilemma is between obeying a 'legal' law or a 'moral' law.

EXHIBIT 3.1

The overlap between ethics and the law

Ethics   The law

● How should an organisation operate in order to protect the environment? Should an organisation simply comply with the law or should it do more than the law requires to take due regard of the well-being of future generations? Some commentators are of the view that profit-seeking organisations are in the business of maximising returns to shareholders, and that it's unethical for a business to do anything other than what is in the best interests of the shareholders as long as it is within the law; in other words, 'the business of business is business.[4] According to this position the law 'sums up' society's view on environmental matters (and indeed any other matters external to the organisation), and all the organisation needs to do is comply with the law. The dilemma here is between the economic imperatives of a business and the concerns of stakeholders other than shareholders.

Don't businesses have to obey the 'law of the land' first and restrict the application of ethical considerations to areas of operation that the law doesn't cover?

● Is it ethical for a manager to risk the security of their company by breaking the law they believe to be unethical?

- Do you agree with the view that 'the business of business is business'? What are the likely consequences in terms of legislation if this view became the prevailing view in society?
- Do you agree that 'good ethics is good business'?

- Would you ever offer or accept a bribe when working in Western Europe?   Very often the initial public stance of people when asked this question is to say *no* very firmly. However, their private stance might be different. The more reflective begin to wonder what is a bribe and what isn't. A bribe is something valuable (usually an amount of money) given to someone to persuade them to do something that they wouldn't do otherwise and whose acceptance is not to be disclosed. So what about accepting a bottle of whisky from a supplier at Christmas, especially if this is the 'done thing'? This may be OK as it might not affect how you do business with the supplier: you may continue to act in the best interests of your organisation. But if bigger gifts are involved there might well be a conflict between personal and organisational interests. Dennis Skinner, a long-serving and well-respected member of the UK parliament, won't even accept a cup of tea from a journalist, believing that any sort of gift, even a small and public one, is a form of bribe, in that it tends to buy or corrupt. The phrase 'there's no such thing as a free lunch' springs to mind. However, most people aren't as pure as Dennis Skinner and see the issue as simply a question of magnitude: of relative rather than absolute behaviour. A small gift merely oils relationships. Here the dilemma revolves around the size of a gift and the influence that's being sought.

- Would you ever offer or accept a bribe in a country where bribery is commonplace?   In some countries bribery is so common it's a way of life. In parts of East Asia bribes are known as easy money or hush money, in Western Asia as baksheesh. European and American business people say that unless you pay these bribes you can't do business there: 'when in Rome, do as the Romans do'. If a foreign subsidiary of your company is operating in a country in which it is legally permissible to employ slave labour, should your company take advantage of this facility? This question raises the issue of relativities: are all ethical stances as 'good' as others? Should you necessarily judge others by your own standards? Is one set of ethics 'better' than another?

- Are you honest, even when this may hurt someone's feelings?   This question faces squarely one of the main issues in ethics. Ethics isn't normally about right and wrong: it's about choosing between two 'right' things. The answers to the *individual* questions 'should I be honest?' and 'should I seek not to hurt people's feelings?' are likely to be an unequivocal *yes* in both cases. On the other hand, a combination of these questions poses a dilemma for which no clear-cut resolution is possible. How to act will depend on the circumstances and on the relative strengths with which you hold each of the two views: how strongly you believe in honesty at (almost) any costs and how strongly you don't want to hurt someone's feelings. The dilemma here is the choice between two 'rights'. This example illustrates the point that we need to use ethical frameworks flexibly.

- How would you select people to be made redundant?   Suppose that there is a need to 'downsize' in your organisation and some people are to be made redundant. Would you retain the mix of employees that will be most cost-effective? Or would you operate on the common rule of 'last in, first out'? Here there is a (potential) conflict of efficiency and fairness. If you opt to retain the most cost-effective mix of employees, you are putting efficiency above fairness to employees who have worked longer with the firm and who are likely to be older – and possibly have more family and other commitments. Or do you take the fair view and give little or no consideration to the profitability – and possibly long-term survival – of the organisation and 'look after' these long-serving employees? The dilemma here is between fairness and economic efficiency – perhaps the central dilemma distinguishing business ethics from other types of ethics.

- Would you falsify some data relating to the safety of a product if your boss asked you to?   Would you go along with the boss, although you know it is both illegal and misleading to falsify the data, because it would seem to help the organisation? Or would you refuse, although this may adversely affect your promotion prospects? Here is a case of a clash between the organisation (in the shape of the boss) and the individual. Of course, as with much in ethics it isn't clear-cut. If the 'adjustment' that the boss wants is a complete and very misleading falsehood, then the individual may, and indeed should, not do as requested. But what if it's an omission that is called for or a massaging of the data or being economical with the truth or engaging in creative accounting? Then there is a real dilemma – one between the organisation and the individual (and another between the business and external stakeholders).

KEY CONCEPT   Ethics generally has a close but by no means complete correspondence with 'the law'. Ethics is concerned with context or situational aspects, with relativism and the application of conflicting 'good' rules/laws. Business ethics is concerned with the potential clash between efficiency and fairness and with the dilemmas posed to individuals when their organisation calls for what they see as unacceptable ethical behaviour.

3.3   Ethical frameworks

Ethics can be defined as the rules or principles that define right and wrong. The obvious difficulty with this definition is in knowing what is right, especially when there is a clash of 'rights', as has been amply shown by the dilemmas in the previous section. There are various versions of what is right. One person's moral behaviour may appear immoral to others.

An overarching rationale of all ethical frameworks is redressing the balance in society between the strong and the weak: historically, ethical rules were framed to curb the excesses of rulers. There are many ethical frameworks to help guide people through the moral dilemmas that they will meet in business. The four main ones are set out in Exhibit 3.2. Before you read the discussion about them, you might like to complete the questionnaire in Exhibit 3.3 (on page 70), which, as will become apparent later, will help you to identify your own ethical standpoint.

EXHIBIT 3.2

Ethical frameworks

Ethical framework	Overall rationale
Theology	driven by divine command
Utilitarianism	driven by consequences
Formalism	driven by what is just and by duty
Human rights	driven by what is a 'right'

3.3.1 Theology

Although many people's actions are motivated by religious beliefs, theology won't be given much consideration here. This doesn't mean that it's not important to an individual, simply that in the European and North American contexts it's not helpful in business. A religious framework obviously has the potential for structuring the behaviour of a group if all parties agree with its underlying rationale, but where this doesn't apply, theology can't provide a means of resolving conflict, because it relies on faith. There is thus generally a need to look to the other three frameworks to find a way forward.

DISCUSSION
POINT 3.4

It was said previously that business ethics would be based on individual ethics. If this is so, how is it possible to ignore religious ethics, which many people may take with them into the workplace?

3.3.2 Utilitarianism[5]

Jeremy Bentham (1748–1832) was responsible for the systematic development of utilitarianism.[6] Utilitarianism is about *utility*, which is simply another word for usefulness, so utilitarianism is concerned with the usefulness of actions.

Utilitarianism asserts that what is right is that which brings the best overall results; what is wrong is that which doesn't. This is the greatest happiness principle, often summed up in the phrase 'the greatest good for the greatest number'. Utilitarianism is concerned with results, outcomes and consequences and as such is very context-dependent. Actions are judged solely on their outcomes or forecast outcomes. For example, murdering someone is moral if it produces good results: it's immoral if it gets bad results.

(Almost) all actions result in a balance between benefits and disbenefits. Benefits are such things as pleasure, advantage, happiness, profit and wealth; disbenefits are such things as cost, disadvantage, harm and pain. The management tool of cost–benefit analysis is an example of utilitarianism in action, whereby all benefits and disbenefits are brought together in a common 'currency' – usually, but not always, money – so that the feasible option offering the greatest utility (the greatest net benefit) can be identified.

EXHIBIT 3.3

Survey of ethical orientation[7] (Brady, 1990)

Instructions: Each of the following statements can be completed in two ways. Think about each alternative, and circle the one that better represents your feelings.

1 Persons' actions should be described in terms of being
   a) good or bad
   b) right or wrong
2 When making an ethical decision, one should pay attention to
   a) one's conscience
   b) others' needs, wants and desires
3 Solutions to ethical problems are usually
   a) some shade of grey
   b) black and white
4 It is of more value to societies to
   a) follow stable traditions and maintain a distinctive identity
   b) be responsive and adapt to new conditions as the world changes
5 When thinking through ethical problems, I prefer to
   a) develop practical, workable alternatives
   b) make reasonable distinctions and clarifications
6 When people disagree over ethical matters, I strive for
   a) some point(s) of agreement
   b) workable compromises
7 Uttering a falsehood is wrong because
   a) depending on the results, it can lead to further problems
   b) it wouldn't be right for anyone to lie
8 Thinking of occupations, I would rather be a
   a) wise judge, applying the law with fairness and impartiality
   b) benevolent legislator, seeking an improved life for all
9 I would rather be known as a person who
   a) has accomplished a lot and achieved much
   b) has integrity and is a person of principle
10 The aim of science should be
   a) to discover the truth
   b) to solve existing problems
11 Whether a person is a liar is
   a) a matter of degree
   b) a question of kind (either yes or no)
12 A nation should pay more attention to its
   a) heritage, its roots
   b) its future, its potential
13 It is more important to be
   a) happy
   b) worthy
14 Unethical behaviour is best described as
   a) violation of a principle of law
   b) causing some degree of harm
15 The purpose of government should be
   a) to promote the best possible life for its citizens
   b) to secure justice and fair treatment

3.3.3 Formalism[8]

Formalism was most fully developed by the philosopher Immanuel Kant (1724–1804).[9] Kant objected to utilitarianism on the grounds that true moral judgements are independent of what any particular individual or group thinks or wants. Formalism is thus very different from utilitarianism, in that formalism is based on universal moral principles. A person following a formalistic approach would select the course of action that most closely conforms to a set of ethical rules, i.e. they would act according to a moral code. Behaviour is judged by considering personal motives, not by the results stemming from a person's behaviour. Thus someone who is lax about implementing health and safety legislation would be deemed to be acting unethically according to formalism, whether or not anyone was killed or injured in a consequent accident.

The idea of duty – i.e. following a set of universally applicable rules – is central to formalism and it is duty that determines whether a motive is ethical or not. Under formalism, the praiseworthiness of personal motives isn't sufficient for them to be considered moral. Kindness is generally admirable, but unless it's shown for reasons of principle and out of a sense of duty, it isn't necessarily ethical. If a person held to the principle that people should stand on their own feet and earn their own living, then to give money to a beggar might be kind – but it wouldn't be ethical according to formalism.

A major principle of formalism is that the set of laws (moral code) applies to everyone equally, i.e. the laws are universal. The universality of laws is what Kant called the 'categorical imperative', which may be stated as:

> No one should act unless they are willing to have the rule under which they act apply to everyone, including themselves.

For instance, nepotism would not be allowed since, although it's something that you might like to be applied to yourself and your relations, you can see that it wouldn't be a good law to apply to the whole of society. You are duty-bound to respect the confidences of others because you would like them to be bound by the same considerations. You are duty-bound not to spread rumours about other people if you don't want rumours to be spread about yourself.

DISCUSSION
POINT 3.5

In utilitarianism actions are judged solely on their outcomes. Under utilitarianism, do you feel that *telling* the truth can in some, perhaps many, circumstances be considered *im*moral?
- How would a utilitarian judge the morality of driving after drinking alcohol?
- The laws within formalism are considered *just* because everyone is treated the same. Is a law *just* simply because it's applied to everyone? What about individual circumstances?

3.3.4 Human rights

A *right* is an entitlement for a person or group of people to be treated in a certain way. The basic concept behind the idea of human rights is that *natural laws* exist that take priority over any laws devised by humans. Natural laws give rights to humans because humans are valuable in themselves and not simply because they can be used by others. Although many thinkers contributed to the human rights approach to ethics, the key figure was John Locke (1632–1714), whose writings were influential in getting human rights embodied in the American Declaration of Independence in 1776, in the framing of the French Declaration of the Rights of Man in 1789 and, by extension, the Universal Declaration of Human Rights in 1948.

What should be considered a human right is not a simple question. The most basic of human rights are the right to life – and thus, by extension, to food, clothing and shelter – and to liberty. There is perhaps little disagreement that these are indeed human rights, although what levels of food, clothing and shelter are adequate are frequently disputed. However, there is intense controversy over what other rights might be. Do people have the right to a minimum wage, or should the market be allowed to dictate wage rates? Do people have the right to welfare payments when they are disabled or unemployed, or should everyone be individually responsible for insuring against these twists of fate? Do employees have the right to be consulted on changes to their work environment? As can be imagined, the list is almost endless.

One of the problems with arguing from the position of rights is the same as with formalism: rights can often clash. Many people would consider it to be a right to be able to walk the streets without being molested. Some states believe that to support this right they must retain capital punishment. Thus the right to life is taken away from some individuals in order to advance the right for street safety for others. In business, an employee's right to privacy might be in conflict with the organisation's wish to safeguard its assets from theft by implementing rules to dismiss any employee convicted of criminal activity, even when that activity hasn't involved the organisation. Here there is a clash between the right to privacy and the right to safeguard (shareholders') property.

3.3.5 Formalism and human rights: proceduralism

The ethical frameworks based on formalism and human rights have much in common. First, both are concerned with establishing a set of universal rules based on what is just or right in governing human interactions. Indeed, an alternative view of the categorical imperative emphasises respect for the individual as a human being rather than an object. As Kant put it: 'Act in such a way that you treat humanity . . . never simply as a means, but always at the same time as an end.'[10] Thus everyone has a duty to act fairly to people because they are humans.

Second, formalism and the approach based on human rights are 'mirror images' of each other. Where there is a human right then there is a duty to respect it and this duty finds expression in a formalistic rule. A right is morality seen from the point of view of the recipient of an action; a duty is morality from the point of view of the person performing the action. The right of someone to welfare payments has its complement in the duty on others to pay taxes. Third, neither formalism nor the human rights approach is concerned with consequences, and both emphasise the individual rather than the group. Because of their close similarities these two approaches will be combined into what will be termed the **procedural approach**.

KEY CONCEPT There are three ethical frameworks that can be used to help with ethical issues in business. These are the utilitarian, formalistic and human rights approaches. The formalistic and human rights approaches are very similar and in practice they may usefully be combined into what is termed the procedural approach. While utilitarianism is concerned with ends, the procedural approach is concerned with means and motives. Much of personnel policy in organisations is based on the notion of consistent treatment of employees and thus much of it is procedural.

3.4 Contrasts between utilitarianism and proceduralism

Before discussing the differences between utilitarianism and proceduralism, it's a good time to use your responses to the questions in Exhibit 3.3 to identify your own ethical orientation. The scoring procedure is set out in Exhibit 3.4.

There isn't a score, and thus an orientation, that is good or bad, right or wrong, better or worse than any other. The score simply reflects where your ethical orientation lies between extreme utilitarianism and extreme proceduralism. The value of knowing your own ethical orientation and how you arrived at it is that it should help when you have to work with other people who have an orientation that may be different to your own – and that you will be able to estimate. If you do have a significantly different orientation to colleagues at work, you are forewarned that you can't assume that they will necessarily think as you do.

EXHIBIT 3.4

Calculating your ethical orientation (after Brady, 1990)

Score = Odd As + Even Bs − 8

Odd As For all the odd-numbered questions, add up the number of cases where you have selected the first (the a) answer.

Even Bs For all the even numbered questions, add up the number of cases where you have selected the second (the b) answer.

With this score you can now determine your ethical orientation using the following 'grid':

$+7 \geq$ Score $\geq +5$ strongly utilitarian
$+4 \geq$ Score $\geq +2$ moderately utilitarian
$+1 \geq$ Score ≥ -2 middling
$-2 \geq$ Score ≥ -4 moderately proceduralist
$-5 \geq$ Score ≥ -8 strongly proceduralist

DISCUSSION
POINT 3.6

What do you consider are the rights of students at a university?

- How can it be said that the human rights approach isn't concerned with consequences? One human right is the right to life and to remain alive is a consequence, for example.
- Estimate the ethical orientation of another person (perhaps by answering the questionnaire in Exhibit 3.3 as if you were they). Then, if they are willing, ask them to fill in the questionnaire and let you see the results. Was your estimate accurate?

3.4.1 Psychological contrasts

The significant contrasts between utilitarianism and proceduralism are summarised in Exhibit 3.5. The first point here is that utilitarians are concerned with relativities and frame ethical issues as questions of where along a continuum of outcomes a choice should be made. For example, they would judge a misdemeanour by an employee on the range from *not very serious* to *grounds for dismissal*. The proceduralists will have none of this. To them everything is clear-cut and the question is how to categorise: is it a misdemeanour or not? The utilitarian is constantly looking forward, not ham-

EXHIBIT 3.5

Contrasts between utilitarianism and proceduralism

Utilitarianism	Proceduralism
Resolves questions of degree	Resolves questions of kind
Forward looking	Backward looking
Case by case	Consistency, pattern
Democratic	Authoritarian
Fluid	Rigid
Compromise	Consensus
Rules of thumb	Principles

pered by past decisions and thus they're open to change. Proceduralists are always looking at the past, because they consider past patterns and take the rules that have been developed in the past and apply them in the present. The proceduralists, in their quest for universal fairness, look for consistency, whereas the utilitarian is pragmatic, viewing every issue on its merits – a case-by-case approach. The procedural approach is naturally rigid and authoritarian as it involves the application of fixed rules to everyone, and the rules are likely to have been made by the powerful to their own advantage. By contrast, utilitarianism takes everyone's view into account (at least to obtain those of the *greatest number*) and in this way is democratic. While utilitarians seek compromise and are happy to use rules of thumb when handling issues, the proceduralist can't do so. You can't compromise on principles: what you must do is seek consensus between all affected parties to form the rules.

You could be an extreme utilitarian and a colleague could be strongly proceduralist. Neither position is better than the other, just different. And it doesn't necessarily mean that you disagree about everything; for example, you could agree that low pay is wrong but for different reasons.

3.4.2 Relative strengths and weaknesses

Both the utilitarian and procedural approaches have their strengths and weaknesses. By and large, utilitarianism is strong where proceduralism is weak and vice versa. Utilitarianism is liberal (not prejudiced), in that equal importance is given to every person's view and it is forward-looking. Utilitarianism is based on what people want (or what most people want – remember that the aim is the greatest good for the greatest number) and it is 'rational'.

On the other hand, proceduralism is fair and just in that everyone is treated equally according to universally applicable laws. Proceduralism calls for an explicit codification of a set of principles, which utilitarianism doesn't, since it is context-dependent and deals with ethical issues on a case-by-case basis. The advantage of a set of precise and self-consistent principles is that it encourages a coherent shared understanding by all those who abide by them. It also has the advantage of setting down what individuals should do.

The main weakness of utilitarianism is that of fairness. Utilitarianism can lead to a total disregard for the good of minorities, a situation that most of us today would consider unacceptable. In extreme cases the application of utilitarianism has been used to justify genocide, such as the Nazis instigation of the Holocaust. Utilitarianism cannot deal with the question of fairness, the underpinning of proceduralism.

Proceduralism has the opposite weaknesses. It's all very well to define an unconditional law, such as 'Thou shalt not kill', but the world is really too complex for such simple rules. The simple rule has to be augmented with conditions such as 'it's acceptable to kill in self-defence', and 'it's acceptable to kill to defend your country'. However, every condition needs to be defined. For example, what constitutes self-defence enough to kill – when someone is in your house and won't leave? When you're in a fight in a pub? And what does defence of your country mean? In order to cope with complexity, the rules have to be equally complex. In most civil services of old, the 'rule book' was very thick; if any error occurred a future occurrence was prevented – in theory – by writing an additional rule specifically to stop its recurrence. This tendency to complexity is one of the main weaknesses of proceduralism. Further difficulties are that proceduralism ignores individual differences, and there is a tendency to dogmatism over what is right and wrong because a law or a rule says so.

KEY CONCEPT There are several very powerful psychological contrasts between utilitarianism and proceduralism. Utilitarianism is concerned with the ends achieved for a group, proceduralism with the procedures (motives and means) adopted by people in their relations with individuals. The strengths and weaknesses of utilitarianism and proceduralism are complementary.

DISCUSSION POINT 3.7 What reasons could the utilitarian and the proceduralist put forward to support the view that low pay is wrong?
- What do you understand by the term 'rational'?

3.5 What does 'ethical' mean?

At this point we need to address the main question that has been running through this chapter: 'What does it mean to say some action is ethical/unethical?' In fact, it means very little. In general discussion it's now come to mean 'to act according to the dominant, and thus expected, rules of society', with society being widely interpreted: an organisation is a society, the nation is a society and so on. However, this can hardly be a good approach for an organisation or an individual to take.

The one concrete thing that can be said is that an ethical action is something that the perpetrator **can defend in terms of more than self-interest**. The notion of ethics carries with it the idea of something bigger than the individual, seeking some sort of universality. The phrases 'Do unto others as you would be done by' and 'Love thy neighbour as thyself' sum up this aspect of ethics. If you were to make some employees redundant *because* this will ensure the survival of the firm, this is probably an ethical action, defensible on the grounds of the greatest good for all stakeholders taken together. However, if you had done it simply to enhance your performance-related pay, then you would have been acting unethically. Thus ethics is often about curbing your own selfish wants, it's about not being egotistical.

This view of ethics can have some rather disturbing aspects. If a group of Nazis were to murder someone so that they could take over their property, they would be acting unethically. However, if they did it because they believed that the German nation or indeed the world as a whole would benefit, then it could be argued that they were acting ethically.

DISCUSSION
POINT 3.8

What argument would you put forward to counter the view that to act ethically is to act according to the (dominant) rules of society?

- What do you think of the line of reasoning that holds that someone who acts as a Nazi may be acting ethically?

3.6   Reconciling the utilitarian and procedural frameworks

3.6.1   The need for both approaches

The existence of organisational rules implies that a procedural approach is being taken to the running of the organisation, at least in part. However, the rules are less likely to cover new ventures or new conditions. If an organisation decides to establish an operation overseas for example, or if environmental conditions change rapidly, the flexibility of the utilitarian approach is needed. A business run solely on procedural ethics is likely to be economically inefficient and thus run the risk of going out of business. So the procedural and utilitarian approaches must go hand in hand: the skill is striking the appropriate balance.

To strike that balance requires a manager to take into account the different abilities and needs of the stakeholders to bring about as much good as possible for them (i.e. the utilitarian approach) in ways that at the same time recognise the common features of individuals, respect their rights and cater for their need for fairness (the procedural approach). The dilemma for the business manager is adequately to take into account both the differences between people and their similarities, while recognising the economic goals of the organisation.

It should be acknowledged that the balance between the procedural and the utilitarian can change over time. For instance, from its inception in 1948 up to the early 1990s, a principle of the UK National Health Service was that all people were treated the same. With the introduction of fund-holding GPs, some patients were given priority over others in the interests of efficiency.

3.6.2   The principles of benefaction and membership: maximin

The principle of benefaction

Organisations maintain a 'background' of established procedures within which employees operate. However, there is a need to cope with matters that don't neatly fit these procedures. One thing that doesn't neatly fit some procedures is the fact that humans aren't all the same. The *principle of benefaction* focuses on people's differences and on their different situations. It simply says: 'Make an exception to a rule when greater overall good or satisfaction will occur by doing so'. For example, the rule might be that all employees must start work at 9am every workday. It may be that public transport is such that for one person it's much easier to start at either 8:45 or 9:15 and adjust their lunch break to accommodate this different quarter of an hour. If the employee were allowed to start at other than 9am and this had no significant effect on the working of their unit, then this should be allowed under the principle of benefaction. Although the principle of benefaction would appear to be pure utilitarianism, it is applied in association with a rule: the rule is the 'anchor' around which small shifts are allowed. As the implementor of the rules, the manager is the benefactor.

The principle of membership

In contrast to the principle of benefaction, the *principle of membership* focuses on people's similarities. This principle says that people should be treated the same because the unit in which they work assumes some sort of similarity among the workforce, in outlook and common aspiration. So although one employee may not have worked as hard as others, they get the same group bonus as everyone else. The application of the principle of membership takes the harsh edge off a fully utilitarian approach.

The use of the principles of membership and benefaction to bring about a (partial) reconciliation of the utilitarian and procedural approaches is depicted in Exhibit 3.6. US and North-western Europeans tend to start with a universal law and bend it to particular situations, especially where friends are involved. The Japanese and other East Asian cultures value harmony over the rule of an 'iron' law. What might appear devious to the outsider is seeking to put relationships first and universality second.[11]

EXHIBIT 3.6

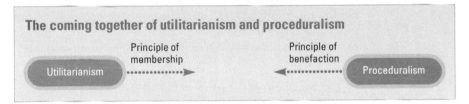

The coming together of utilitarianism and proceduralism

Utilitarianism ····· Principle of membership ·····→ ←····· Principle of benefaction ····· Proceduralism

The maximin approach

Rawls[12] has put forward an interesting procedure for reconciling the utilitarian (efficiency-driven) and procedural (rights/fairness-driven) approaches. He accepts that efficiency demands incentives, that incentives almost certainly mean differential rewards and that these result in inequalities. To prevent the inequalities becoming too great yet supporting them as a necessary requirement for improved efficiency, he proposed that inequalities are permitted only if they result in a greater good for the *poorest*. For example, consider a situation in which the profits of a firm are to be divided between ten people. If the profit is £400 and this is split equally among all ten people, each gets £40. This isn't as good for the poorest (or for the richest for that matter) as the situation where profits are £900 and the poorest get a fifteenth of it, i.e. £60, and the richest get a fifth of it, i.e. £180. (Of course, getting a fifteenth of £900 is worse for the poorest than getting a tenth of £900, but a tenth division of the profits is unlikely to provide the incentives to achieve the £900 profit in the first place.) The change from the one-tenth equal distributions to the spread of distribution between one-fifth and one-fifteenth results in the poorest being better off. Thus, if the unequal rewards produce the £900 profit, the associated inequality is justified. What Rawls is proposing is the maximin principle: distribute the profits so as to *maxi*mise the *min*imum amount that anyone receives.

DISCUSSION
POINT 3.9

How does Rawls' approach complement the principles of benefaction and membership?

3.6.3 Guidelines for action within an existing ethical framework

Generally, managers are called on to operate within an ethical framework that has already been established in their organisation. The framework will involve both procedural and utilitarian components. Guidelines for the manager when faced with an issue are set out in Exhibit 3.7.

The first step in any issue is as far as possible to establish the 'facts', particularly who is involved and how they might be affected. The term 'facts' is put in inverted commas because many so-called facts will turn out to be opinions and/or interpretations. Remember, there are always (at least) two sides to every story. The next step is to identify the rules that are in operation. If care isn't taken, a proposed action might cut across current company ethical policy or breach the law. Then consider the ethical aspects of the issues and any proposed actions from both the procedural and utilitarian points of view. From the procedural viewpoint the personal motives of the people involved need to be examined. Whether the proposed action could be applied as a universal rule needs to be assessed and the related questions 'are people's rights being respected?' and 'is the proposed action just and fair?' answered. From the utilitarian viewpoint the calculation of the likely benefits and disbenefits of all stakeholders takes into account the economic well-being of the organisation, both in the short and longer terms. Armed with this information, apply one or all of the principles of benefaction, membership and maximin as appropriate.

EXHIBIT 3.7

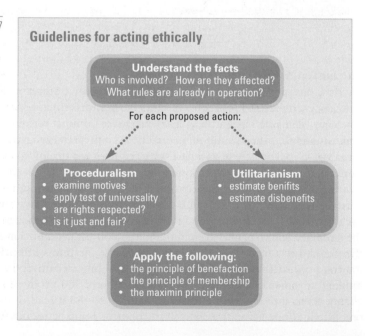

3.6.4   Maintaining an existing ethical framework

Senior management has the responsibility for the moral climate within the organisation and this includes maintaining the organisation's ethical framework, which will often be written down as a code of ethical practice. From time to time this will mean reassessing the code. For example, a company intending to expand overseas may need to incorporate guidelines on how employees should deal with bribery; a new production process may call for a reassessment of the way employees are moved between jobs. In general, the longer the time horizon for the proposal, the more procedural and less economic a proposal can be and still be acceptable.

KEY CONCEPT   In practical business situations there is a need to combine the procedural and utilitarian approaches when addressing ethical issues. Often a procedural framework has already been established and issues are approached flexibly within this framework, using the principles of benefaction, membership and maximin where appropriate but always aware of the (economic) needs of the organisation. Managers also have the responsibility to maintain the relevance of the organisation's code of ethical practice.

3.7   The rights of animals

All of this chapter so far has been concerned with relations between humans. Before moving on to discuss the rights (if any) of animals, we should pause to reflect on how the scope of ethics, certainly Western ethics, has undergone dramatic change over the years. In early times, members of a tribe, class or caste were protected by ethical rules but outsiders could be treated in any way whatsoever. Only 150 years ago, the indigenous population of Australia was hunted and killed by European settlers, so much so that the Aborigines of Tasmania were completely wiped out. Gradually the scope of who was included in the protection offered by ethical considerations was widened to include everyone in a nation and recently the whole human race. The actions in Tasmania would now generally be recognised as being morally wrong. Perhaps we are ready to embrace animals within our ethical considerations.

It is estimated that millions of animal experiments are performed each year in universities and other research establishments to support research and development in the cosmetic, pharmaceutical, medical and defence industries.[13] Thus the ethical aspects of using animals can be a concern to managers in many businesses. That animal rights is now hotly debated may in part be a result of the loosening of the grip of Christianity on Western thought. Historically, the Judaeo-Christian tradition hasn't been strong in recognising animal rights; indeed, it holds to the view that humans have dominion over other animals.[14] However, the Buddhist idea of compassion extends to animals as well as to humans, and the increasing general interest in Buddhism may be influencing the animal rights movement. Many movements go through the three stages of ridicule, discussion and adoption; perhaps the animal rights movement is at the same position as was anti-racism 150 years ago, moving from ridicule to discussion or even towards acceptance.

In Section 3.3 the question of the rights of humans was raised. People had rights because they were human and humans were valuable in themselves. When considering human rights, the question that had to be answered was whether one group (marked by gender, race, etc.) was fundamentally different in kind from another. The equivalent question when considering the issue of animal rights is 'are animals and humans fundamentally different in kind?' To answer this question there is a need to identify one or more characteristics that differentiate animals from humans. Apparently obvious characteristics are the ability to reason, to write and to speak. The reason that these are *apparently* obvious characteristics is that on examination they aren't strong differentiators, because whatever characteristics are chosen some humans will fail the test. For example, a person born with severe brain damage can't reason as well as a chimpanzee or a dog and they can't live unsupported lives. They are accorded (human) rights solely because they are genetically/biologically human, *not* because of how they can or do act. The question is whether this line of reasoning is the same as that used when confronting racism and sexism.[15]

Taking the line that animals have rights doesn't mean that animals have *the same* rights as humans. For example, no one suggests that animals should have the right to vote or freedom of worship. But there is a demand from animal rights campaigners that *equal consideration* should be given to animals as to humans. For example, it might be considered important to test a new shampoo by squirting it into eyes under controlled conditions. Should animals or humans be used in the testing? Some animal rights campaigners would judge who to use on the basis of whose suffering would be the greater. Those who either don't believe in animal rights or who believe human considerations always take precedence over those of animals would test on animals without considering the relative degrees of suffering.

3.8 Social responsibility

3.8.1 'Face-to-face' ethics and social responsibility

Business ethics is concerned with how an organisation interacts with all its stakeholders. In Chapter 1 two types of stakeholder were identified. The primary stakeholders are the owners, customers, employees and suppliers who can directly affect the organisation's performance through their involvement in its daily activities. The primary stakeholders are usually dealt with as individuals, and ethical considerations with respect to them are considered 'face-to-face' ethics. It is this form of ethics that has dominated the discussions in this chapter so far.

Social responsibility is the branch of business ethics that is concerned with the interaction of the organisation with its secondary stakeholders. The secondary stakeholders are rarely dealt with as individuals; much more often, as the term *social responsibility* suggests, they are dealt with as groups or organisations: governments, the inhabitants of a particular geographical region, pressure groups, etc. Social responsibility is concerned with what economists term 'externalities', costs not absorbed in the product or service and not paid for directly by the customer but borne by the wider community. A simple example of an externality is the smoke emissions generated by a power station: the cost of not cleaning up the emissions falls on the wider public through increased air pollution which, among other things, gives rise to illnesses and acid rain damage to forests and buildings.

3.8.2 Areas of social responsibility

Four main areas of social responsibility can be identified, depending on the sorts of groups affected. These are set out in Exhibit 3.8.

By and large, environmental issues (which include what are often termed green issues) are of concern because they affect the lives of people currently alive.[16] The list of such issues is almost endless. It includes all forms of pollution, such as air pollution from motor cars, which have been strongly implicated in the growth in the number of people suffering from asthma, water pollution killing fish and pesticide overuse destroying wildlife. Paper makers and chemical manufacturers are examples of firms that are frequently accused of damaging the local environment through emissions. Perhaps the most widely publicised issue of this sort is the thinning of the Earth's ozone layer, which protects us from the sun's harmful ultra-violet rays, brought about by the use of chlorofluorocarbons (CFCs). This example illustrates the point that the effect of apparently localised environmental issues may in fact sometimes be very extensive.

Exploitation is often concerned with the treatment of people in poorer countries, who typically have little power and who are not protected by health and safety legislation. However, as was shown by the ethical dilemma concerning the UK fast-food outlet described in Section 3.2, exploitation is also a concern in developed countries and has been one of the drivers for a minimum wage. The issue of exploitation is most often confronted where the final consumer is closely involved. Finch[17] describes how millions of pairs of shoes sold in Europe are produced under slave labour conditions in China, Vietnam and Brazil. The charges against the practices are that workers only had two or three rest days per month and three days holiday a year, and that children were exposed to industrial glues without protection. The report Finch cites is putting pressure on UK distributors to force their suppliers to alter their working practices. It is in the area of exploitation that issues of human rights appear to be at their strongest.

Issues of the environment and exploitation tend to be those that affect the here and now. The issue of sustainability is generally of longer-term concern. Sustainability issues affect future generations and are potentially extremely important. One highly publicised issue here is the enhanced greenhouse effect, the warming of the Earth due to the industrial production of carbon dioxide and other gases. Where companies are directly exploiting the world's natural resources – through mining or oil extraction, for example – the concern of pressure groups is that irreplaceable resources are being

EXHIBIT 3.8

Areas of social responsibilty

Type of issue	Groups most affected
Environmental	the general public in a locality
Exploitation	workers – usually in foreign countries
Sustainability	future generations
Influence	any group

squandered. This is particularly an accusation levelled at the oil companies, which, through their poor operating techniques, leave a lot of oil in the ground that can't subsequently be extracted. The main issue here is with the rights of future generations.

A further consideration for companies is that they are being criticised not for what they are doing but for what they fail to do: sins of omission rather than commission. Given the power of multinational companies, often more powerful than sovereign states, this sort of pressure is likely to increase.

The nature of the pressure for social responsibility seems to depend on how close the firm's activities are to the consumer. Those dealing with raw materials are open to charges of non-sustainability, those dealing with more refined products are open to charges of not considering the environment, while those near to the consumer are open to charges of human rights abuses.

KEY CONCEPT Concerns for animals and future generations are growing. Thus the definition of an ethical issue as any issue that implies significant harm or benefit to others is only complete if 'others' is taken to include a concern for animals and for future generations. Social responsibility concerns are also growing. Three 'sins of commission' have been identified involving the disbenefits felt by the general public in a given locality, the exploitation of employees and the sustainability of the world resources for future generations. Of increasing importance as commercial organisations become more powerful is the 'sin of omission', an organisation not using its power to prevent wrongdoing.

3.9   Whistleblowing

During their working lives, many employees will become aware of what they consider unethical practices in or by their own organisations. This issue has already been highlighted as a dilemma in Section 3.2. If the issue is potentially of little significance, then perhaps it isn't worth making a fuss. But suppose it's potentially of major significance? Managers have two clear responsibilities here. Their first responsibility is to be prepared to 'blow the whistle' on other staff. The second responsibility falling to senior management is to set up a system in their organisation to help people report on others who might be acting unethically.[18]

3.9.1   Whistleblowing on others

Senior staff have available sanctions to discipline junior staff and thus whistleblowing is only an issue involving staff over whom the potential whistleblower has no effective control. Given that it is an issue you think you should do something about, what is the best way of proceeding to 'blow the whistle'? The first thing to remember is that it's far better to act as soon as the issue arises so that a small issue can be nipped in the bud. Early on, fewer people are committed and fewer will close ranks. Guidelines of the form shown in Exhibit 3.9 provide an appropriate approach to whistleblowing.

EXHIBIT 3.9

> **Guidelines for whistleblowing**
>
> * Make a rough estimate of the harm that could be done if the issue were ignored.
> * Reflect on your own motives for whistleblowing, ensuring that they aren't dominated by self-interest – for example, out of spite for someone.
> * Find out the organisation's procedures for handling employees' ethical concerns.
> * Try to establish whether the issue is illegal as well as unethical. If it's both, then this alters the power situation between yourself and the organisation.
> * Estimate the consequences to you personally – in terms of your career both within your current organisation and when looking for jobs in the future.
> * See if there is a way of stopping the abuse by acting anonymously.
> * Make sure that the facts you will be citing are indeed facts, and that where possible there is more than one piece of corroborative evidence.
> * Seek out other people who could corroborate your story.
> * Use the hierarchy within your own organisation to channel your concerns.
> * If this fails use other established channels, – e.g. a trade union or staff association.
> * As a last resort use external channels.

It's important to remember that whistleblowers often suffer in terms of their jobs if they stay with the organisation within which they are blowing the whistle, and afterwards if they choose to leave their organisation and seek a job elsewhere. So whistleblowing isn't for the faint-hearted. Recently, the law in the UK has been changed so that whistleblowers will be eligible for unlimited compensation. The ceiling had been £50,000 and this limit was seen as deterring senior executives, who are often best placed to blow the whistle, from sounding the alarm.

3.9.2 Setting up a structure to support whistleblowing

If senior management wishes to prevent ethical misconduct, it's incumbent on it to set up a system that allows people who believe that there is wrongdoing to express this as soon as possible, before much damage has occurred. One approach is to follow the path chosen by the John Lewis Partnership. As well as the normal hierarchical routes for communication, 'committees of communication' are held between four and six times a year to provide a link between the chairman and all the partners (employees) of the firm who aren't managers. At these committee meetings any issue can be raised and the chairman's answers are published in the partnership's in-house magazine. Any partner can write, either signed or anonymously, to the correspondence columns of the weekly magazines that are produced at branch and partnership (company) levels. For letters that require it, a comment must be made by the principal director most closely concerned with the issue and then published. An example of an issue that was raised in this way was a partner querying the close personal relationship between a general manager and a registrar, saying that this compromised the registrar's independence and their ability to safeguard the privacy of partners.[19]

While such a 'bureaucratic' arrangement may suit a large organisation, it would seem less appropriate in a small firm. Perhaps the most appropriate approach is to have an 'ethical suggestion box', which must be opened only when at least two directors are present.

SUMMARY The resolution of ethical dilemmas is likely to become a more important part of a manager's working life and thus it is very important for them to reflect on what is involved. In summary:

- To say that something is *ethical* hasn't much objective significance; what is ethical is in the eye of the beholder. However, the one firm statement that can be made is that the notion of ethics carries with it the idea of something bigger than the individual: the concept of universality.
- Business ethics is concerned with the moral climate within the organisation and with how the organisation deals with outside stakeholders. While the laws of the land and the dominant ethics are usually broadly in line, there is never likely to be perfect overlap.   EXHIBIT 3.1
- There are four generic ethical frameworks that might be used in business situations: the theological, the utilitarian, the formalistic and an approach based on human rights. In practice the formalistic and human rights approaches can be treated together, and termed the procedural approach. Together, the utilitarian and procedural approaches provide the framework within which a business can frame its ethical position. No ethical position can be objectively considered better than any other.   EXHIBIT 3.2, EXHIBIT 3.5, EXHIBIT 3.6, EXHIBIT 3.7
- The scope of business ethics is increasing to include a concern for animals and for future generations.
- Social responsibility is concerned with how the organisation treats its secondary stakeholders. Four areas of concern can be identified: environmental, exploitation, sustainability and influence.   EXHIBIT 3.8
- Successful whistleblowing is difficult to achieve. It is the responsibility of senior management to establish a climate in which the primary stakeholders can bring unethical behaviour to the attention of senior management.   EXHIBIT 3.9

SELF-CHECK
1 Reconsider the learning outcomes for this chapter. Check that you feel confident that you can carry out the activities listed there.
2 Having read this chapter, you should be able to define the following terms:

bribe	formalism	principle of membership
ethical	human rights	proceduralism
ethics	maximin	utilitarianism
externality	principle of benefaction	whistleblowing

MINI-CASE 3.1

The ecstasy test kit

Ecstasy test kit immoral says drugs tsar[20]

A new kit which allows drug users to test whether they have been sold pure ecstasy pills was condemned yesterday as an 'immoral money-making venture' by the 'drugs tsar' Keith Hellawell. He said he would investigate why the company selling the kits had been granted a licence. But Dylan Trump, the co-founder of EZ Test, a Brighton-based company which markets the pocket-sized kit, insisted that he was providing a useful service to established drug users, rather than encouraging anyone to start taking ecstasy. The product was a practical way of helping users to ensure their ecstasy was not contaminated, he said, and would lead to safer drug use.

A tiny scraping from the tablet is mixed with chemicals provided in the £5 kit. If there is no reaction, the pill is likely to contain a large quantity of contaminants. A change in the sample's colour indicates the main drug it contains, which can then be identified according to a chart provided.

'We are not condoning drug use, necessarily,' Mr Trump said. 'But about 500,000 people already take ecstasy every weekend. This is just a method of harm reduction – like providing clean needles for heroin users, or free condoms.' Ecstasy is a loose term; it used to refer to a drug called MDMA, but because the demand for it has been so high and because the manufacture of it is wholly unregulated, makers are passing off as ecstasy a number of other drugs. This means you are crossing your fingers every time you take a pill, because you have no idea what is in it. 'It is the unexpected experience that can lead to panic attacks and can be dangerous.' The kit explained the physical and mental effects that might be caused by different kinds of drug, he said. 'A lot of health problems associated with drug taking are due to a lack of information. If people know in advance that they are likely to overheat or drink too much water, then they'll know how to counteract that.'

Mr Hellawell, who is in charge of Britain's anti-drug strategy, was not impressed by these arguments. The test itself was extremely crude, he said, and would pick up only a limited number of substances. Even a pure ecstasy tablet could be life-threatening. 'I think it is immoral – just a money-making venture on the back of the trend in young people taking drugs,' he said. His views were echoed by Paul Betts, founder of Action for Drugs Awareness and father of Leah, who died after taking ecstasy at her 18th birthday party in 1995. 'As far as I know, nobody has ever died from taking a bad tablet,' said Mr Betts. 'It is the drug itself which is dangerous, so all this test is really telling you is that you're taking a dangerous substance. This is a money-making con which is lining someone's pocket.'

Discussion point 3.10

Do you think that selling the ecstasy test kit is immoral or not? Apply the guidelines for acting ethically (Exhibit 3.7) to this newspaper report.

MINI-CASE 3.2

Animal rights

Ape rights not wrong[21]

Great apes may soon have some of the rights previously reserved only for humans, if a group of New Zealand scientists and activists succeed.

They have asked their parliament to grant the right to life to man's closest relatives, which include chimpanzees, gorillas and orang-utans.

The Great Ape Project argues that the apes are genetically very close to humans and part of the same animal family. 'There's now a mountain of evidence that the great apes are as intelligent as young human children,' said theoretical biologist David Penny.

Discussion point 3.11

Is genetic closeness a guide to ethical behaviour? Is closeness in intelligence to children a criterion?

Are animal rights the logical next step in social evolution?

A dirty business

A dirty business bogged down in a moral and political mire[22]

Oil is a dirty business, with a habit of polluting both the physical and the political environment, and the global oil map is littered with international and local conflicts, human rights abuses, environmental disasters and power politics. The oil companies insist they are not responsible for the governments with which they must work, and argue that they cannot interfere in internal politics. But the only way they can extract oil in what are known as 'frontier regions' is to operate as political, moral and economic allies of the weakest or most barbarous and illegitimate regimes on Earth.

It has led to growing opposition from human rights and environmental groups, and accusations that they destabilise regions and help to foster corrupt regimes. The International Federation of Human Rights Leagues in 1996 accused Total of condoning widescale human rights violations by the Burmese military junta, which evicted 30,000 people, opened labour camps and used summary executions, rape and torture to build a pipeline. Total, 5% owned by the French government, denied the charges. Shell and other oil companies working in Nigeria have been accused of complicity with an illegitimate government and turning a blind eye to civil outrages which culminated in the deaths of several thousand people, the judicial murders of the writer Ken Saro Wiwa and other Ogonis, and the expulsion of Nigeria from the Commonwealth in 1996. Shell denied the charges. Since then, it has launched enquiries and tried to clean up its act. Other companies, including Chevron and BP, long worked with the apartheid regime in South Africa and war-torn governments in Angola and Algeria.

The industry considers Columbia the most dangerous country in which to operate – Shell is pulling out of new explorations to protect its image and its investments – but the next international flashpoint is predicted to be in the Caspian region. Here BP/Amoco is the main corporate player in an increasingly turbulent political arena which involves Azerbaijan, Kazakhstan, Turkmenistan, Afghanistan and Pakistan. Oil companies will have to work with the Islamic fundamentalist Taliban in Afghanistan.

Oil is one of the most potent local destabilising forces. Because it is such a large, visible investment in often desperately poor countries, the companies attract dissident and revolutionary groups, who attack them to destabilise their governments. Human rights and social issues will dominate future oil extraction, says Edward Morse, who heads the New York-based Energy Intelligence Group. One area where the companies are compromised, he says, is land rights. Much new oil has been found on territory claimed by indigenous groups. Oil finds disturb their cultures, and exacerbate ethnic and land-use tensions. Building a supply road into a remote area can wreak social havoc. It is not just BP which has problems in the Amazon basin. Texaco, Conoco and Occidental have had pipelines and installations attacked.

The industry has historically liked to operate in a *laissez-faire* style, trying to avoid regulation or control, and its record on the environment is 'shameful', Mr Morse says. It is now much more aware of environmental obligations. 'The industry fought the clean-up of toxic wastes, the campaigns for lower emission levels and alternative fuels, and the disposal of obsolete platforms.' It also continues to lobby against social goals set by governments, seeks to overturn laws protecting wilderness areas, and tries to scupper global agreements to avoid global warming from the burning of fossil fuels. 'The industry has a serious image problem,' Mr Morse wrote in *Index on Censorship* last year. 'It has a good story to tell, but it needs to overcome decades of bad habits.'

Discussion point 3.12

What social responsibility does Shell have in Nigeria?

FURTHER
DISCUSSION
POINTS

1 For GSM:
  • There isn't a formal ethical position statement. What do you think of this?
  • Is it fair on employees not to have an ethical statement?
  • Is Barry Dodd's answer sufficient?
  • Is GSM a rule-based organisation or more an organisation that fits in with the individual?
  • How does GSM show social responsibility?

2 Managers often face the issue of promoting on the basis of seniority or performance. Which of these decisions is more firmly grounded in procedural reasoning?

3 A company might reward its marketing employees through a fixed wage or through a commission on sales. Which method is procedural?

4 'We are quite used to managing processes to ensure quality is maintained, financial controls are maintained and we run safe operations, and we do this in integrated ways. I think that we should consider ethics in that light – it has to be something that grows out of ordinary management processes and emphases.'[23] What do you think of this view? How would you go about ensuring that 'ethics grows out of ordinary management processes and emphases'?

5 'It makes no sense to respond to an ethical question with an economic answer: for example, to respond to a query whether an action was fair with the answer that targets on margins had to be met.'[24] What do you think of this view?

6 Tight legislation of financial services through the various financial services acts and the need for financial services staff to be qualified and in many cases individually registered with regulatory bodies takes care of moral and ethical issues. Discuss.

7 'Levi Strauss is not in the human rights business.'[25] Discuss.

ASSIGNMENTS

1 Determine the ethical position of The Body Shop, and identify why it has fallen on harder times at the end of the 1990s.

2 Find out the ethical position of the Co-op Bank and assess whether it is viable in the longer term.

3 Ethical funds are growing, but from a very small base. Determine the ethical position of two ethical funds of your choice and identify how the return on investment compares with other types of fund.

FURTHER
READING

A book that considers many of the contemporary issues in ethics is that by Chryssides, G.D. and Kaler, J.H., *An Introduction to Business Ethics*, Chapman & Hall, 1993. It is very well written in plain English and in a 'European' style.

The whole topic of business ethics and its link with corporate strategy is discussed in great detail in the book by Frederick, W.C., Post, J.E. and Davis, K., *Business and Society: Corporate Strategy, Public Policy, Ethics*, 7th edn, McGraw-Hill Series in Management, McGraw-Hill, 1992. The examples given are almost exclusively from the USA.

Perhaps the best guide to animal rights is the book edited by Peter Singer, *In Defence of Animals*, Basil Blackwell, Oxford, 1985. This text contains articles written by 16 authors from a wide range of disciplines. However, be warned: a few of the articles are heavy going.

CHAPTER NOTES
AND REFERENCES

1 Chryssides G.D. and Kaler J.H., *An Introduction to Business Ethics*, Chapman & Hall, 1993.

2 Martinson, J., 'Ethical investments at twice the level of 1994', *Financial Times*, 23 August 1997, p. 4.

3 Donkin, R., 'A moral stance', *Financial Times*, 8 September 1997, p. 16.

4 Often attributed to Professor Milton Friedman.

5 Utilitarianism is by far the best-known form of the more general ethical approach known as consequentialism. Other forms of consequentialism moderate the full utilitarian approach, through such measures as incorporating some elements of formalism and by giving more weight to disbenefits than to benefits (for example, giving more emphasis to the elimination of pain than to the gratification of pleasure).

6 See, for example, Acton, H.B. (ed.), *Mill, J.S.: Utilitarianism, on Liberty, Considerations on Representative Government*, Dent, 1991.

7 Brady, F.N., *Ethical Managing: Rules and Results*, Macmillan, 1990, pp. 211–13.

8 Formalism is by far the best-known form of the more general ethical framework known as deontology (from the Greek meaning *duty*).

9 See, for example, Paton, H.J. (trans.) *The Moral Law: Kant's Groundwork of the Metaphysic of Morals*, Hutchinson, 1948, and Harper & Row, 1964.

10 *Ibid.*, p. 96.

11 Hampden-Turner, C. and Trompenaars, F., *The Seven Cultures of Capitalism: Value Systems for Creating Wealth in the United States, Britain, Japan, Germany, France, Sweden, and the Netherlands*, Doubleday, 1993, p. 106.

12 Rawls, J., *A Theory of Justice*, Oxford University Press, 1972.

13 Coleman, V., *Why Animal Experiments Must Stop and How You Can Help Stop Them*, Green Print, 1991.

14 Genesis, I, 26.

15 Discrimination between animals and humans because of biological differences is termed specieism.

16 This isn't always the case, and some environmental issues are issues because they might affect future generations.

17 Finch, J, 'Just how clean are your shoes?' *The Guardian*, 12 September 1997, p. 21.

18 Although it might be thought that internal auditors fulfil this role, the code of conduct for the UK Institute of Internal Auditors expressly advises its members not to blow the whistle externally, since the person involved is likely to find great difficulty in finding a new job.

19 *The Gazette*, John Lewis Partnership, Vol. 79, No. 41, 8 November 1997, p. 1079.

20 Gentleman, A., 'Ecstacy kit test immoral says drugs tsar', *The Guardian*, 28 May 1998, p. 6.

21 Reuters, 'Ape rights not wrong', as quoted in *The Guardian*, 31 October 1998, p. 16.

22. Vidal, J., 'A dirty business bogged down in a moral and political mire', *The Guardian*, 15 August 1998, p. 5.

23 Wright, C., director of public affairs, ARCO Chemical Europe, in *1. Why Ethics in Business*, in the Executive Video Channel Ltd series 'Ethical Management', Cheshire, 1994.

24 Drummond, J., managing director, Integrity Works, in *1. Why Ethics in Business*, in the Executive Video Channel Ltd series, 'Ethical Management', Cheshire, 1994.

25 Peter Jacobi, President of Levi Strauss, on the company's decision to manufacture again in China. As quoted in 'Sayings of the week', *The Observer*, 12 April 1998, p. 25.

CHAPTER 4 Leadership

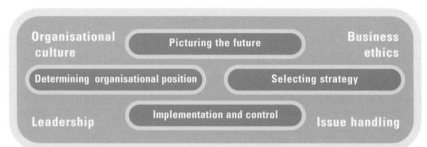

Organisational culture
Picturing the future
Business ethics
Determining organisational position
Selecting strategy
Leadership
Implementation and control
Issue handling

Internal context

2   Organisational culture
3   Business ethics
4   **Leadership**
5   Issue handling
6   Building blocks of business
    strategy

t his is the third of the four chapters concerned with the internal context of an organisation. The concern is with leadership, which is necessary in all organisations.

The changing nature of the workforce and the needs of the knowledge workers who are the main resources of knowledge-based businesses are considered first. The differences between managers and leaders are explored and the myths of leadership are examined. The conclusion is that many managers can and should act as leaders and that the need is for leader-managers rather than simply leaders or managers. Leader-manager styles are then considered and this is followed by an examination of the sources of power open to them. This leads on to a consideration of Machiavellianism, where non-ethical behaviour is deemed desirable. Leader-managers very seldom operate alone: they tend to operate within and through a team of senior managers, who constitute the top team. The effects of the composition of this team and the political aspects of leadership are explored. Finally, the role of leader-managers as entrepreneurs and intrapreneurs is reviewed.

The new forms of organisation appropriate to knowledge-based economies call for new ways of managing and leading – ways that seek buy-in from employees rather than relying on forms of coercion. Leadership and management are very different: leaders operate on the emotional and spiritual resources of the organisation, whereas managers deal with the physical resources. Senior managers need both leadership and management skills: they need to be leader-managers. Leader-managers also need to be entrepreneurs in order to achieve the continual renewal necessary for the long-term well-being of their organisations. Leadership and entrepreneurship can both be learned, and those who aspire to be leader-managers will need to recognise the requirements of leadership and hone the relevant skills.

LEARNING
OUTCOMES

When you have worked through this chapter, you should be able to:

- explain the difference between leadership and management;
- summarise the findings of Bennis and Nanus, which suggest that many people can make effective leaders;
- describe the characteristics of good leader-managers;
- explain the importance of a clear vision in leadership, know the characteristics of a good vision, and explain how a leader-manager can share it;
- define and describe leadership styles;
- summarise the forms of power that are open to a leader-manager;
- explain the importance of the top team in an organisation;
- understand the main features of Machiavellianism;
- describe the characteristics of entrepreneurs and intrapreneurs.

4.1 New ways of running organisations

4.1.1 The new organisation

Until the end of the 1960s, developed economies were still predominantly industrial. In the stable conditions that then prevailed, the future could be predicted with relative certainty and it thus made sense for organisations, particularly large ones, to opt for efficiency. Often this search for increased efficiency led to the establishment of detailed procedures whereby every action was prescribed. In such an environment, machines and machine-like activities ruled the lives of many people, and the important consideration was to ensure that employees understood how to perform the machine-like tasks that were asked of them. Bosses were often autocratic: to ask the question 'What is the organisation's purpose?' or 'Is the organisation acting responsibly?' would be considered at best irrelevant, at worst dangerous.

Since the 1960s the majority of people in developed economies have been employed in the service rather than the industrial sectors. Not only has there been this switch in the relative importance of the sectors, there has also been an increase within each to employing more knowledge workers.[1] These workers are highly educated and often possess skills that their managers don't possess or possibly don't even know much about. For example, hospital managers know little about the medicines and clinical procedures used by the specialist medical staff whom they manage. These shifts brought with them the realisation that considering employees as simply a cost was no longer appropriate; now, people really were the most important resource of the organisation. Knowledge workers demand a meaning in their work beyond pay and a career ladder, and need to be sensitively led to produce their best.

The Internet and intranets are democratising the workforce and there is the potential for everyone to have access to all the company data and to receive all the company messages. Hierarchies now have less meaning: for example, people who wouldn't dream of knocking on the boss's door will cheerfully e-mail them. Hierarchies will have difficulty surviving in companies driven by innovation, immediacy and Internet working.[2] The Net generation (Ngeneration) is used to sharing information and will resist working in organisations, where one result of a hierarchy is the restriction of information. The capacity to manage 'knowledge-based intellect' is becoming a critical skill for managers.

Advances in information technology and globalisation have meant that there has been an increase in the pace of change. This enhanced dynamism, coupled with the demands and aspirations of more knowledge workers, has meant that the way in which organisations were led and managed in the industrial past – through 'command and control' methods – has become inappropriate. The need to change is well documented by Peters and Waterman[3] in their classic *In Search of Excellence* and by many others. A common sense of direction together with a knowledgeable and committed workforce are more appropriate than a set of prescribed procedures.

4.1.2 Management and leadership

Graduates in or about to enter business or industry will almost certainly be seeking eventually to become managers, responsible for the activities of others. The more ambitious may already see themselves in the near or middle futures as being responsible for changing an organisation – and thus leading it. Thus there is a need to consider both the demands of management and the demands of leadership.

To manage means 'to bring about, to accomplish, to deal with problems, to have responsibility for, to control, to conduct'. Managers are dealing with the physical resources of an organisation, its capital, raw materials, technology and the demonstrable skills of the workforce. They are concerned with efficiency and mastering routines. They are the people who resolve issues as they arise: they do things right, working within defined policies.

On the other hand, *to lead* is 'to go in front, to show the way, to influence, guide in direction, course, action and opinions'. Leaders are people who are concerned with effectiveness: they do the right things and make policy.

DISCUSSION
POINT 4.1

What is the difference between efficiency and effectiveness?

Leaders operate on the emotional and spiritual resources of the organisation – they deal with its values, commitment and aspirations.[4] Zaleznik[5] distinguishes between managers and leaders when he writes:

> Managers aim to shift balances of power toward solutions acceptable as compromises amongst conflicting values ... [while] leaders develop fresh ideas to long-standing problems and open issues to new options.

He could have extended this since leaders are also issue *finders*: they seek issues in their search for opportunities. Thus the characteristics of managers and leaders are very different.

KEY CONCEPT
Strategic management is more than simply managing – it also involves leadership. This is one aspect that distinguishes strategic management from other forms of management and is why strategic managers are *leader-managers*.[6] Leadership is the process of moving a group in some direction through mostly non-coercive means, with effective leadership producing change that is in the long-term best interests of the group.

4.2 The myths of leadership

We can probably all cite great leaders. The politicians Bismarck, Churchill and Kennedy spring readily to mind, as do the great military commanders Eisenhower, Montgomery, Napoleon and Rommel. In the business world, we have such figures as Ray Kroc, the inspiration behind McDonald's, John Welch of General Electric, Richard Branson of Virgin, Gerhard Schmid of MobilCom and Lord Weinstock, the former chairman of GEC.

Seeing this roll call of the greats may make mere mortals feel somewhat fazed – these people appear to have something that ordinary people simply can never aspire to. If this were the case, then to discuss leadership would be of little practical value since you either have it or you don't, and there is little that can be done about the situation. Because this is a common feeling, it's very important to be aware of the findings of Bennis and Nanus.[7] They researched 90 successful US leaders and established the following:

- Leadership is not a rare activity   By definition, there are few people who are *great* in their chosen profession – there are few great painters, few great musicians and few *great* leaders. But just as there are many people who can paint or play musical instruments more than adequately, there are a great many people demonstrating good leadership, as you can see by those who are active in the unions at work and those who run churches, gardening clubs and other local organisations. Many people are practising leadership in all walks of life; there are a great many leaders.

- **Leaders are not generally born – they make themselves** While some people have more natural abilities than others and *great* people *may* possess more of an aptitude for their chosen activity, almost all people have some ability in most human activities. And these abilities can be improved – sometimes markedly – through practice and enhanced motivation. Leadership is no different: *great* leaders may be as rare as great violinists, but almost everyone has leadership potential, and leadership skills can be learned.

- **There isn't a leader 'type'** Bennis and Nanus were struck by just how different the 90 successful leaders were. In their words:

> Our leaders were all 'too human'; they were short and tall, articulate and inarticulate, dressed for success and dressed for failure, there was virtually nothing in terms of physical appearance, personality or style that set them apart from their followers.

In particular, there were only a very few leaders whom Bennis and Nanus described as charismatic. So the picture of all or even many business leaders being like Richard Branson, or even Robert Maxwell, is a false one. This picture is reinforced by some military commanders: the very low-key nature of Eisenhower, the showmanship of Montgomery, the craftiness of Rommel.

- **Leaders don't exist only at the top of an organisation** Leadership is obviously one of the responsibilities of the chairman of a board and of the chief executive. However, strategic management is required at the functional as well as at the business and corporate levels, and teams are the preferred groupings to implement strategic change. So the scope for exercising leadership is quite extensive.

KEY CONCEPT The myths of leadership are that leadership is a rare activity, that leaders are born not made, that there is a leadership 'type' and that leadership is required only at the top of an organisation. None is true: leadership can be learned and mere mortals can be leaders.

4.3 The characteristics of leaders

Given that leadership can be learned, it's important if you are aspiring to take a prominent role in an organisation to understand what leadership entails and how you can improve your own leadership skills. One important research finding is that informal groups tend to select a leader who most represents the group's needs and values. Thus the captain of a sports team is very often the best player; the head of a university department generally has a good track record of research and is someone who knows how their university hierarchy operates.

Think of a leader you know who has been elected by the group to which they belong. What are the group's needs and what are the values that the leader represents?

The fact that these leaders are chosen to reflect the group's aspirations and values means that they have many advantages as the leader. However, the problem for heads of bigger organisations is that they cannot hope to represent the values and needs of all the groups contained in them in the same intimate way. Their task of representing the people in the group is a much greater one, and leaders must have characteristics other than simply representing group members' aspirations.

Research findings[8,9,10] suggest that successful leaders in complex organisations must have the following three attributes:

- they must have a strongly held vision;
- they must be able to communicate that vision;
- they must be able to convert the vision into reality.

4.3.1   The role and characteristics of a vision

One thing seems to come out of all the research: the leader must have a vision:[11] 'If there is a spark of genius in the leadership function it lies in the ability to assemble – from all the images, signals etc. – a clearly articulated vision of the future.' To a leader, a vision is a reality that has not yet come to be.[12] As Pascale[13] puts it, 'a vision is such that it allows you to act as if you are standing in the future, managing the present from the future.' These phrases sum up the graphic nature of a vision.

A leader may have a vision, but for it to be useful in energising an organisation it must have certain characteristics:

- A vision needs to be *credible*. If a leader presents what is perceived to be an impossible view of the future for the organisation, people will naturally reject it. In the late 1990s Oxford University was given multimillion-pound donations to set up a business school. Given the moneys available and the association with a prestigious university, the vision the incoming director had of making Oxford a world-class business school was perfectly plausible. If the director of a business school in a former polytechnic had the same vision, it would be unlikely to be afforded the same credibility. Kay[14] warns against relying on vision. All too easily a vision-based strategy can become a wish-driven one: a strategy based on what you would like the organisation to be rather than what it is and what it can be. The vision must be based on the organisation's strengths.

- The *timescale* associated with the vision must fit the timescale of the organisation. If the average employment duration in an organisation is only a few months, then a vision that extends to many years is unlikely to be heeded. At the opposite end of this spectrum, leaders in organisations offering lifetime employment, as IBM and the major Japanese companies have traditionally done, can have a vision that extends over a great many years and one to which the ordinary employee can relate. What is important is for the vision to be broken down into appealing shorter-term milestones, with employees asked to concentrate on a single area: one year the concentration might be on quality, the next on customer service.[15]

Suggest a vision for the UK, and for your business school.

- Think of a leader, perhaps yourself. What are the timescales associated with their/your vision? Is the vision broken down into shorter-term milestones?

- The vision needs to offer *an attractive and challenging future*, a condition that is better in some important ways than what currently exists. This attraction could appeal in a very simple and direct way: higher market share and/or increased profitability, both linked to increased remuneration. However, how much better if the vision is challenging to stretch the organisation to do better and to feel better about this achievement. For example, university departments in the UK are now judged and scored on their research performance. A leader who simply had a vision to achieve a high score is not providing much of a vision; a leader who focused research on an uplifting theme, for example research to help a disadvantaged group in society, would have a vision to which many researchers could relate.

Vision would seem to be a necessary requirement for a successful leader, but vision alone isn't sufficient. Although Napoleon is generally considered a great general, he did undertake the disastrous march on Moscow and a subsequent even more disastrous retreat. Clive Sinclair was a very inventive and innovative creator, responsible for the digital watch and the first home computer in the UK. Then he had the vision of a very cheap 'car', the C5, which was a complete disaster. It had a canvas cape as a car body, it couldn't accommodate any passengers and the driver sat about 15cm from the road – rather worrying when you met large lorries. What these two stories illustrate is that vision must be allied with an analysis of the real world and tested against it. 'An accurate picture of current reality is just as important as a compelling picture of a desired future.'[16]

While a vision may be energising it may be energising in a negative way. Hitler's Aryan vision is likely to appeal to some people, but obviously not to all, and will be considered evil by most. Thus there is an ethical dimension to a vision.

KEY CONCEPT   A vision is an overarching goal that provides a challenging yet credible picture of the future and the place of the organisation within it. Vision is a necessary requirement for a successful leader, but vision alone isn't sufficient.

4.3.2 Communicating the vision

Many commentators[17,18,19] have highlighted the importance of the leader communicating their vision – and thus being able to get people to 'buy in' to it. The vision is successfully shared if the leader's vision also becomes the organisational vision, in the sense that most of the people in the organisation share it. It's important to articulate the vision in a way that resonates with the values of employees, indicates how each individual can contribute to its achievement and encourages public recognition and reward for success.[20]

In a famous article, Mintzberg[21] examined the activities of American chief executives and also quoted from similar British studies. He concluded that the classical view of a manager as almost totally occupied in organising, planning and controlling the operations of an enterprise just did not stand up to investigation: a large part of a manager's time was spent performing many other roles, of which Mintzberg identified a total of 10. One such role is the figurehead, in which the manager carries out ceremonial duties, such as presiding at Christmas dinner and attending employees' retirement parties. Another role is in liaison, with the manager making contacts outside their own unit.

Not only does Mintzberg's work show that a leader-manager has many roles to play, it also highlights the fragmentary nature of management work. In his words, management activities are characterised by 'brevity, variety and discontinuity'. In support of this contention, he cites his research findings in which half of the activities engaged in by the chief executives lasted less than nine minutes, and only 10% exceeded one hour. The chief executives met a steady stream of callers from the moment they arrived in the morning until they left in the evening.

DISCUSSION
POINT 4.1

Reflect on how many people you could have communicated a vision to over the course of an average working day, either in your personal life or when working in an organisation.

Management work is thus characterised by many brief segments of action, almost always involving interactions with people and often with people in the organisation. These segments may be *ad hoc*, one-off activities, but more often than not they will form part of a continuous thread of issue-handling actions. Mintzberg found that the chief executives he studied supervised as many as 50 projects at the same time and, to quote him again, the chief executive 'is like a juggler, he keeps a number of projects in the air: periodically, one comes down, is given a new burst of energy, and is sent back into orbit.' So leader-managers have a great many opportunities for reinforcing employees' understanding and commitment to the vision during their working day. Ways that this can be done include the following:

- Communicate the vision through use of the cultural web. When BA removed the Union flag from the tail fins of its aircraft, it was demonstrating that it wished to be seen as a world, not merely a British, airline. The move to open-plan offices can indicate a vision that includes closer teamworking and a more democratic organisation.

- Encapsulate the vision in a short phrase, perhaps a slogan that can be remembered easily. Sometimes the slogan is attached to the organisation's logo. Examples are 'MARU-C', the Japanese for 'Surround Caterpillar' (Komatsu, a strong competitor of the Caterpillar earth-moving company); 'Solutions for Business' (Coopers and Lybrand management consultancy); 'Improvement through inspection' (UK Office for Standards in Education); 'To be one of the world's leading independent gas and electricity companies' (PowerGen, 1997); 'To be the outstanding financial services company in the UK' (Abbey National). When he took over at British Airways in the early 1980s, Sir Colin Marshall coined the slogan 'The world's favourite airline'. In April 1990, Matsushita officially announced to the outside world its corporate vision of becoming 'a possibility-searching company'.[22] A declaration can be as powerful as a slogan. A very powerful declaration of a vision was that made by President Kennedy in 1961 when he famously declared 'this nation should commit itself to landing a man on the moon and returning him safely to Earth before the decade is out.'

- Use the vision to create meaning for people. Over the long term people are not motivated by being pushed: they are motivated by the desire for achievement. The vision statements given above are examples of this. John Major, British prime minister in the early 1990s, and his 'Back to Basics' campaign illustrate the use of a slogan to encapsulate what was considered a vision but was a flop. It was a flop because the message that it contained wasn't understood: what were the basics that people were meant to get back to?

DISCUSSION
POINT 4.5

Can you think of an organisation's vision 'slogan' – perhaps of the organisation in which you have worked? If you can't, what does this say about the vision?

- Consider a vision of an organisation that you know. Does it create meaning?

- 'Walk the talk'. However good the vision, simply having a slogan or making a declaration isn't sufficient. The leader needs to use all reasonable steps to emphasise aspects of the vision as it affects employees and to communicate their own commitment to the vision. They also need to communicate their commitment to the process of realising the vision – to the actions needed. As Mintzberg has shown, they have many opportunities for doing this. One organisation has taken the opportunity to state its vision on the calendars it issues to all staff; another has had the vision printed on office coffee mugs.

- The leader should be engaged in *enrolling* people to become part of something by choice[23] rather than trying to sell the vision. Selling is trying to get someone to do something that they might not do if they were in full possession of the facts. A leader can't exhort people to change. What they can do is to use the organisational culture to support the vision.

- Using e-mail, voicemail and videos and perhaps video-conferencing allows a leader-manager to get the message across in the personalised way that is needed. In one large company the senior manager carried around a brown leather binder with tabs for relevant project groupings. He used the information in the binder to manage the agendas of regular meetings that he held to discuss changing market conditions and review proposed action plans with his subordinates. The binder represented those things that were important to him – and thus to subordinates. He used a photograph of himself for the firm's annual report to push this message: the binder rested prominently under his hands.[24]

4.3.3 Specific characteristics

Although there doesn't seem to be one leadership 'type', to convert a vision success-fully into reality requires the characteristics of the leader listed in Exhibit 4.1. These are described below.

- Integrity and strong personal ethics   Integrity is concerned with 'wholeness' and it concerns the leader's ability to see the whole picture and act consistently with that picture. To do this, they will need to have worked out a coherent ethical

EXHIBIT 4.1

> **Characteristics of a leader**
>
> - Integrity and strong personal ethics
> - Respect for others
> - Energy, perseverance and courage
> - Team-building skills
> - The ability to learn from their mistakes
> - The ability to see beyond simple cause-and-effect relationships
> - The ability to empower people

position. Thus a leader acting with integrity will use the same logic when seeking to persuade people of a course of action (although the style of presentation may differ depending on the audience). They are reliable and their actions show a consistent interpretation of the vision. A set of interviews of more than 40 business leaders published in 1998 indicated that nearly 80% identified the ability to inspire trust as the most important quality of leadership.[25]

- **Respect for others** Trust in a leader is dependent on the leader showing respect for others. This is revealed by the leader having the ability to recognise people for what they are, treating them with courtesy and having a positive belief in them.

- **Energy, perseverance and courage** An inescapable requirement of effective leaders is that they possess more than an average amount of energy. This was seen famously in Margaret Thatcher, British prime minister during the 1980s, who needed only a few hours sleep per night. A leader needs to be resilient, and able to bounce back after failure – there will be failures on the way to realising the vision. This resilience requires that the leader shouldn't need constant approval or recognition, because they are unlikely to get it.

- **Team-building skills** The difference between managers and leaders is nicely summed up by Snyder, Dowd and Houghton:[26] 'It's managers who meet a new situation by forming a committee: leaders build up teams of people. A team has a vision: a committee has an agenda.'

- **The ability to learn from their mistakes** Leaders themselves shouldn't think in terms of failure. All successes and lack of success are seen as learning experiences from which they develop and improve their skills.

- **The ability to see beyond simple cause-and-effect relationships** The leader's vision is their view of the future. The trouble with trying to envisage the future is that cause-and-effect relationships are difficult to determine. One reason for this difficulty is that sometimes the effects are not directly linked to the causes; sometimes the effects occur at different times and possibly in different places from the causes. Leaders need to be able to discern patterns in their environment, so pattern recognition is an important attribute of the leader.

- **The ability to empower people** The leader needs to be able to make others feel stronger and more capable than previously. This enhanced capability empowers subordinates and encourages them to take on more responsibility and to strive for greater performance. A leader needs to establish a culture in which people aren't disciplined for mistakes – as long as the mistakes occur when the person is acting in the best interests of the organisation. There is considerable evidence that men and women exercise leadership in different ways. John Sculley, ex-CEO of Apple Computers and chairman of Spectrum Information Technologies,[27] takes the view that men lead largely by pulling power inwards in a hierarchical fashion: women lead more from the vantage point of being in the centre and disseminating power outwards. Leaders should make their pronouncements about means ambiguous and about ends general in order to allow others to be creative.

Leadership is about aligning organisational strategy and human behaviour. There will be blocks to human activity that the leader-manager should seek to remove or at least ameliorate. Four such blocks and the appropriate approach that the leader-manager might employ are set out in Exhibit 4.2.

EXHIBIT 4.2

Human behaviour, organisational blocks and suitable responses for leader-managers[28]

Employee desires to	Organisational blocks	Leader-managerial responses
Contribute	Unsure of purpose	Communicate core values and mission
Do right	Pressure or temptation	Specify and enforce ethical and other company rules
Achieve	Lack of focus or resources	Build and support clear objectives
Create	Lack of opportunity or afraid of risk	Open organisational dialogue to trigger learning

4.3.4   Keeping the faith

The previous sections may have suggested that the successful leader is always involved in either starting up an organisation or transforming one that isn't performing very well. The view that a useful vision promises a future better than the present certainly seems to imply this. But what of leaders that follow on from others who were great leaders; for example, what of the chairmen of Marks & Spencer who followed on from Simon Marks, the founder? They don't appear to have been particularly innovative (which isn't to say that Marks & Spencer hasn't developed over the years), but they do appear to have adhered to the principles established by the founder – they have kept the faith and kept it alive throughout the organisation.

DISCUSSION POINT 4.6

Can you think of any other examples of leaders 'keeping the faith'?

One chief executive's view of leadership is set out in Exhibit 4.3.

EXHIBIT 4.3

Manager's maxim (John Egan, chief executive, British Airports Authority)[29]

Much of senior management is about leadership – starting, of course, with a vision. The leader must share his or her conviction about where the company is going, why and how, across the whole of the business, and also with business partners and other stakeholders, so that their creative energies are harnessed towards one end – the mission of the company.

Leadership calls for a positive attitude towards the future; an overriding belief in people, balance in one's own life (leadership is not about obsession), personal health and fitness, and willingness to engage in lifelong learning.

Even in the latter part of my career I have never stopped trying to learn, listening to new ideas.

The leader should also act as coach, helping people to succeed by encouragement, not through fear. Only then will people be persuaded to bring their brains to work as well as their hands and feet.

The leader should always be looking out for the 'reflective layer'. This happens when ideas from both the top and the 'shop floor' are blocked by middle management, who either don't want to understand or don't want to change. The result is that the ideas bounce back from whence they came. Middle management, above all, has to be motivated to welcome and encourage change.

Finally, leadership must be related to specific objectives. There has to be a clear understanding of the required outputs and achievements, recognised through key performance indicators and yearly business plans and a clear determination to achieve them.

KEY CONCEPT   To be successful a leader must be able to communicate their vision. Their daily activities offer many opportunities for them to do this. A leader also needs to be able to convert the vision into reality. This requires integrity, energy, team-building skills and the abilities to learn from mistakes, to build teams, to empower people and to see beyond simple cause-and-effect relations. It also requires the leader to act ethically and with integrity.

4.4 Leadership styles

Leadership styles can be categorised by the relative emphasis that the leader puts on the task and on the welfare and abilities of the people undertaking the task. A leader with a task-related orientation would be concerned with the organisation and with procedures. The leader who is people-related would be concerned with the feelings, attitudes and emotions of the people in the organisation.[30] These two dimensions allow leaders to be categorised as using one of four broad styles, shown in Exhibit 4.4.

Leaders who are highly task-oriented with little consideration for the feelings of the group would fit the upper right box and be termed *autocratic*. Their 'opposites' would be those whose main concern was with the group's feelings and relatively little concern for the task – these would be following a *human relations* style. Leaders scor-

EXHIBIT 4.4

Styles of leadership (adapted from Cook *et al.*, 1977)

Task-related orientation

		Low	High
People-related orientation	Low	*Laissez-faire*	Autocratic
	High	Human relations	Enrolling

ing high on both dimensions would be showing an *enrolling* style, while those scoring low on both dimensions would be following a *laissez-faire* style.

Toffler[31] believes that the 'strong' leader is now an anachronism. He bases this on the view that the complexity of issues that leaders currently face involve too many interest groups with too many dependencies. This calls for negotiation and the handling of issues by groups of people, not for autocratic behaviour. According to Blake and Moulton,[32] the enrolling style is most effective. However, it would seem that the situation in which the leader finds him/herself would be a strong contributory factor to which style they might adopt, particularly the ability and motivation of the leader's immediate subordinates. If the subordinates lacked motivation, then a more strongly people-related style would seem most appropriate; if they lacked ability, then a stronger task orientation by the leader would be applicable.

DISCUSSION POINT 4.7

Which styles in Exhibit 4.4 are closest to a managerial outlook and which to a more leadership outlook?

• If the leader's subordinates lacked both motivation and ability, what might be the appropriate leadership style?

The discussion so far suggests that the effective leader is a wonderful human being, a cross between a saint and a genius. The assumption is that everyone will recognise this goodness and respond to it in a positive way, rather than taking advantage of it; no one will be opposed to the 'good' leader. However, to quote Crainer,[33] 'In the world of leadership, the gulf between theory and practice is cavernous.' Leaders must expect resistance to their leadership. Thus they need to have sources of power – the subject of the next section – and use it in ways that might at first sight appear immoral – the subject of Section 4.6.

4.5   Sources of power

Power is the capacity to make someone else act according to your own preferences when the other person doesn't want to. Power is the potential to influence; influence is the application of power. Every leader needs power and at the same time needs to be aware of the power structures in the organisation. Wrapp[34] suggests that when considering a change in strategy the successful leader plots the position of various individuals and units on a scale from outspoken support to determined, sometimes bitter and often well-hidden opposition. In the middle are what Wrapp calls *corridors of comparative indifference*, pathways peopled by units with little concern for what might happen. The skilled leader moves along these pathways; if blocked, they pause until the pathway clears.

EXHIBIT 4.5

Sources of power

- Coercive power
- Expert power
- Legitimate power
- Referent power
- Reward power
- Personal power
- Connection power

French and Raven[35] identify five sources of power, listed in Exhibit 4.5:

- Coercive power is based on the ability to 'wield the big stick'. Examples would be passing a well-qualified candidate over for promotion, transferring someone to an undesirable job and publicly ridiculing an employee.

- Expert power comes from the superior expertise that the leader has (or is believed to have) and that is needed in the organisation. The technologists who start up small companies will typically have such expertise.

- Legitimate power is the power that comes from the socially accepted duty for people to do as the leader says. Whatever other powers they may have, it is accepted that the chief executive has certain powers, not because of who they are but because of the position the shareholders and others have given them. Sometimes these powers are legally determined, such as the power to demand an audit of the organisation. The owner of a business will naturally have legitimate power.

- Referent power is the power that comes to someone who is a role model for others, someone whom others seek to emulate.

- Reward power is based on the ability to award 'carrots' and is thus the opposite of coercive power. Examples would be giving a larger than normal office to someone, a financial bonus or accelerated promotion.

To these can be added the following:[36,37]

- Personal power, supported and trusted by their colleagues and subordinates.

- Connection power, which results from personal and professional access to key people and information.

DISCUSSION
POINT 4.8

Which of these types of power are strongly linked to the position of the leader in the organisation? Which are linked to the individual?

KEY CONCEPT Power can be defined as the capacity to make someone else act according to your own preferences when that isn't in accordance with what they want to do. Power is the potential to influence; influence is the application of power.

4.6 Business politics: Machiavellianism[38]

To call someone *Machiavellian* is normally considered an insult, indicating immorality and cunning. Machiavelli is best remembered for his book *The Prince*,[39] in which he sets out his views on political statecraft, advising political leaders how to acquire power, resist aggression and control subordinates. The part of his book that jars with present-day views is that Machiavelli saw that when power is at stake, questions of morality are irrelevant and lying, deceit and manipulation are legitimate tactics. There have been several books written on this theme stressing that what Machiavelli wrote is still relevant today, both in general and for business. Machiavelli was writing about what people did, not about what they perhaps should do from a moral perspective.

The Prince contains three specific leadership themes. The first can be given the short-hand term *immoral deeds*, as it derives chiefly from the chapters in which Machiavelli explains why a leader must be prepared to act immorally in the interests of the state. The second theme is *being prepared*, which reflects Machiavelli's concern that leaders should at all times be poised for battle. The third theme is *reputation*: even if a leader is prepared to act immorally in the interests of the state and is well prepared to act, they can only take full advantage of opportunities if they have a good reputation. Without this a leader runs the risk of being seen as self-seeking and opportunistic, and therefore, in Machiavelli's experience, is likely to fail.

4.6.1 Immoral deeds

Machiavelli claims that 'how men live is so different from how they should live that a leader who does not do what is generally done, but persists in doing what ought to be done, will undermine his power rather than maintain it.' Because of this difference between theory and practice, Machiavelli's leaders must be prepared to vary their conduct as the winds of fortune and changing circumstances constrain them. They should stick with ethical conduct if possible, but be prepared to act unethically when this becomes necessary.

Examples of immoral deeds coming good are by their nature difficult to find, as only failed unethical behaviour comes to light. One celebrated example of a firm acting unethically and being found out was British Airways. Worried by the appearance of Virgin Airlines on the money-spinning transatlantic routes, British Airways tried to undermine Virgin by blackening the name of its boss, Richard Branson, and trying to steal its business by lying about cancelled flights.

There are four sorts of immoral deed that Machiavelli excuses:

- **Meanness** Machiavelli maintains that meanness is a vice that enables a leader to rule. Stanley Kalms, chairman of electrical goods retailer Dixons, echoes this in his assertion that 'fair is a word I have never heard voiced in a pricing meeting.'[40]

- Cruelty   Machiavelli regards mercifulness as detrimental to effective rule, noting that good ends justify the use of cruel means – being cruel to be kind. He argues for making an example of one dissenter to avoid the bloodshed of a full-blown civil war. In the British Airways–Virgin case, Brian Basham, British Airways' public relations consultant at the time of the scandal, was scapegoated, being the only culprit to be named in British Airways' apology to Virgin.[41]

- Not keeping promises   Machiavelli rejects the absolute requirement to keep a promise, partly on the grounds that leaders need flexibility to facilitate responsiveness to change and partly because other people won't keep their promises so there is no need for you to keep yours. In the business world there is little evidence that keeping promises is the best policy. Bhide and Stevenson[42] found that treachery could pay and that there was no compelling economic reason to tell the truth or to keep one's word – and that punishment for the treacherous in the business world is neither swift nor sure. Prior to the sale of Rover in 1994, Rover had a strategic alliance and several joint ventures with Honda. These, and a 20% stake, gave Honda the right to be informed of any intent on the part of British Aerospace to sell Rover and be offered first refusal of the balance of the equity. Honda was only notified of the impending sale to BMW in January 1994, once British Aerospace had accepted BMW's offer in principle, effectively forestalling any opposition. This breach of trust led to Honda disposing of its stake in Rover a month later.[43]

- Love, fear and hatred   Machiavelli's first point on the subject of subordinates' attitudes is that it's safer for the leader to be feared than to be loved. He takes this view because he sets great store on the leader having control, and while the generation of fear is under the control of the leader, generating affection can only be controlled weakly. Machiavelli exhorts the leader to tread the narrow path between engendering fear and hatred in their people; fear leads to respect while hatred leads to rebellion. Machiavelli sees hate as personal and direct, whereas fear is at one remove: you hate someone who has wronged you, but fear them for wronging others. Thus, if you do wrong someone then there is a need to prevent effective revenge, and this means either caressing or crushing them. This has been a view taken by many dictators: crushing enemies to prevent revenge also instils fear in any other potential dissenters. If fear should degenerate into hatred, Machiavelli proffers the advice to strive assiduously to avoid the hatred of the most powerful.

On the subject of fear, Machiavelli would have approved of Henry Ford of the Ford Motor Company. He established a sociological department to monitor employee behaviour, whose spies investigated the private lives of his workers. Gangsters and bully boys enforced plant discipline and staff were sacked for driving any car other than a Ford. No smiling or talking was allowed on the factory floor and according to one commentator, 'so close was the supervision in the factory that workers devised the "Ford whisper", a means of talking without moving the lips.' Ford even issued two edicts, banning the consumption of alcohol in employees' homes and requiring all employees to grow potatoes in their garden or yard. The incentive of $5 a day pay ensured that there was a ready supply of informants to ensure that any rebels were weeded out. Not surprisingly, staff turnover was high (423% in 1913).[44,45] This sort of divide-and-rule approach to management is certainly not advocated today, where top-down directives are considered to inculcate fear, distrust and internal competitiveness, which reduces collaboration and co-operation.[46]

Machiavelli would also approve of MBWA – management by walking about – management walkabouts that are invariably unplanned and thus create a climate of expectancy and fear.

DISCUSSION
POINT 4.9

Should leader-managers consider fairness in their pricing decisions?

4.6.2 Preparedness

The second of the leadership themes in *The Prince* is the need for a leader always to be prepared for battle. In business, this means that they need to be closely focused on their important stakeholders, particularly on customers and competitors, and to have the capabilities and competencies to react to events. Little more need be said about this here, as much of this book is about preparedness.

4.6.3 Reputation

Machiavelli saw a good reputation as making ruling easier and thus was concerned with how a leader should act in order to enhance their reputation. In this sense, he was one of the first public relations gurus. Reputation is important in management, as the exercise of power depends on the perceptions of the followers. Underpinning all of Machiavelli's advice about reputation was his belief that reputation can be wholly separated from actuality; a leader may be rotten to the core but, given their position, they can enjoy an excellent reputation as long as they control the people's perceptions. They can control this in the following ways:

- Wisdom   Machiavelli saw it as vital for a leader to be perceived as having great intelligence. Because this is best illustrated through the company they keep, they should surround themselves with people of the highest calibre, and of course loyalty. They should also maintain a close inner circle to obtain access to advice without losing respect. In business this advice endorses the use of senior management advisory groups and the use of consultants.

- Constancy   Machiavelli stressed the value of sticking with decisions and courses of action, thoughts echoed by Marks & Spencer's Clinton Silver: 'Having made a decision you must stand by it. You can't lead with uncertainty and equivocation.'[47]

- Awe and loyalty   Machiavelli stresses the importance of impressing those around you with feasts and spectacles, a point not lost on Richard Branson with his balloon and power boat escapades. Machiavelli also recommends that leaders should reward and punish in ways that will be much talked about. A 100-person IBM sales branch rented out a stadium for the evening so that each salesperson could run through the tunnel, have their name put up on the scoreboard, and be applauded by colleagues, friends and family.[48]

  Leaders should distance themselves from their subjects/subordinates, which is a problem for royalty even today. Thus it could be seen as a grave mistake for the younger UK royals to take part in a version of the TV game show *It's a*

Knockout. This is why very few people should be allowed to enter the 'holy of holies' that is the chairperson's office in the great corporations. It's also the reason that managing by walking about can't be undertaken frequently or the mystique of senior managers will be broken.

- Internal competition   Machiavelli was a great believer in internal competition, seeing it as a means of ensuring that no concerted challenges develop and as a means of getting people to provide the leader with information on others. Peters and Waterman[49] point out that internal competition has long been a feature of many successful businesses. Henry Ford made great use of internal competition, going as far as encouraging disharmony and bickering among his most important henchmen.

- Buffer mechanism   Leaders need to put in place mechanisms and institutions to keep themselves apart from necessities perceived as being in some way unpleasant by the public. This was illustrated by Gordon Brown, the UK Chancellor of the Exchequer, passing control of interest rates to the Bank of England. And when royalty is seen to do something appealing, that reflects their good taste and character; when they do something unappealing, they are portrayed as having been misinformed or badly advised.

- Superordinate goals   The leaders of countries often use an external threat to solidify support at home. Slobodan Milosovic, the Serb president, found his support greatly increased and internal dissension greatly reduced once the NATO aircraft began bombing targets in Serbia in 1999. An external threat or a superordinate goal can help to marshal employees' efforts and keep them too busy to plot against the chief.

4.6.4   How Machiavellian are you?

Exhibit 4.6 is a questionnaire that lets you determine your own 'level of Machiavellianism'.[50] Average scores for managers are reported[51] to lie in the range of 85 to 98, with the majority of US adults scoring around 85.

4.7   Top teams

Although it has been stressed that leadership is practised at many levels in organisations, strategic leadership at the very top of an enterprise poses some particular problems. The head of the enterprise – the managing director in the UK, the chief executive officer (CEO) in the USA, the general manager elsewhere – has to lead a multifunctional activity involving marketing, operations, finance and all the other functions. While the chief executive should try to reach out to all employees, what they must do is work closely with direct subordinates, and lead and manage through them. Kay[52] makes an interesting contrast between the US and UK views on leadership and those of the rest of Europe. In the USA and UK (and to some extent in France), the chief executive is seen as the master of the organisation and business success is effectively realising the chief executive's vision. In Japan and most of the rest of Europe, senior executives are seen as the servants of the organisation and success is seen as maximising the value of an organisation's distinctive capabilities.

EXHIBIT 4.6

How Machiavellian are you? (Christie and Geis, 1970)

1   The best way to handle people is to tell them what they want to hear

2   When you ask someone to do something for you, it is best to give the real reasons for wanting it rather than giving reasons which might carry more weight

3   Anyone who completely trusts anyone else is asking for trouble

4   It is hard to get ahead without cutting corners here and there

5   Honesty is the best policy in all cases

6   It is safest to assume that all people have a vicious streak and it will come out when they are given a chance

7   Never tell anyone the real reason you did something unless it is useful to do so

8   One should take action only when sure it is morally right

9   It is wise to flatter important people

10 All in all, it is better to be humble and honest than be important and dishonest

11 Barnum was very wrong when he said there's a sucker born every minute

12 People suffering from incurable diseases should have the choice of being put painlessly to death

13 It is possible to be good in all respects

14 Most people are basically good and kind

15 There is no excuse for lying to someone else

16 Most people forget more easily the death of their father than the loss of their inheritance

17 Most people who get ahead in the world lead clean, moral lives

18 Generally speaking, people won't work hard unless they are forced to do so

19 The biggest difference between most criminals and other people is that criminals are stupid enough to get caught

20 Most people are brave

The chief executive has to lead a complex integrative process and has to do it with people who in general possess much greater expertise about the functions than they do. These people are likely to constitute the board of directors, but another group could constitute the top team – the dominant coalition.[53] So while the characteristics of the chief executive are important, so too are those of the dominant coalition – perhaps even more so. Hambrick[54] gives several examples of research findings that demonstrate the effect that the characteristics of the top team have on organisational performance: for example, the values of the members of the top team affect the organisation's level of innovation; the length of time for which people are members of the top team affects the way strategic issues are handled.

Strongly agree	Agree	Mildly agree	Neutral	Mildly disagree	Disagree	Strongly disagree
7 ☐	6 ☐	5 ☐	4 ☐	3 ☐	2 ☐	1 ☐
1 ☐	2 ☐	3 ☐	4 ☐	5 ☐	6 ☐	7 ☐
7 ☐	6 ☐	5 ☐	4 ☐	3 ☐	2 ☐	1 ☐
7 ☐	6 ☐	5 ☐	4 ☐	3 ☐	2 ☐	1 ☐
1 ☐	2 ☐	3 ☐	4 ☐	5 ☐	6 ☐	7 ☐
7 ☐	6 ☐	5 ☐	4 ☐	3 ☐	2 ☐	1 ☐
7 ☐	6 ☐	5 ☐	4 ☐	3 ☐	2 ☐	1 ☐
1 ☐	2 ☐	3 ☐	4 ☐	5 ☐	6 ☐	7 ☐
7 ☐	6 ☐	5 ☐	4 ☐	3 ☐	2 ☐	1 ☐
1 ☐	2 ☐	3 ☐	4 ☐	5 ☐	6 ☐	7 ☐
1 ☐	2 ☐	3 ☐	4 ☐	5 ☐	6 ☐	7 ☐
7 ☐	6 ☐	5 ☐	4 ☐	3 ☐	2 ☐	1 ☐
1 ☐	2 ☐	3 ☐	4 ☐	5 ☐	6 ☐	7 ☐
1 ☐	2 ☐	3 ☐	4 ☐	5 ☐	6 ☐	7 ☐
1 ☐	2 ☐	3 ☐	4 ☐	5 ☐	6 ☐	7 ☐
7 ☐	6 ☐	5 ☐	4 ☐	3 ☐	2 ☐	1 ☐
1 ☐	2 ☐	3 ☐	4 ☐	5 ☐	6 ☐	7 ☐
7 ☐	6 ☐	5 ☐	4 ☐	3 ☐	2 ☐	1 ☐
7 ☐	6 ☐	5 ☐	4 ☐	3 ☐	2 ☐	1 ☐
1 ☐	2 ☐	3 ☐	4 ☐	5 ☐	6 ☐	7 ☐

Peterson *et al.*[55] examined nine leading US companies over the period from the late 1970s to the early 1990s. They found that the chief executive's characteristics play an important and effective role when they are able to foster similar strong values among other members of the dominant coalition. They found that successful companies had 'healthy group dynamics', meaning that the group had openness to new information, cohesiveness, willingness to take risks, strong ethics and decentralised decision making. These findings back up earlier work that the team characteristics have a larger effect on organisational performance than do those of the chief executive.[56]

Top teams have repertoires: a set of routines governing the behaviour of top managers.[57] Breakdown of the repertoires appears to set in when intended actions produce significant unintended consequences that can't be ignored by top management. The ability of a top team to transform its repertoire is positively associated with a moderate homogeneity of the top team. Too much homogeneity supports the inertia of established repertoires; too little prevents the team forming shared repertoires.

Repertoires may change gradually,[58,59] while in other cases the change may be imposed by people who enter the top management team (or try to do so). This typically happens in hostile takeovers or when a sudden change is enforced by government.

One very important role for the dominant coalition is to ensure that the organisation adapts to changing circumstances. Adaptation calls for the organisation to renew itself – and for the dominant coalition to change its repertoire. Whether the dominant coalition is able to do this depends to some degree on its composition, which is affected by the characteristics of the organisation and the industry it is in: for example, the firm's diversification posture affects the mix of functional areas represented in the top management team; and the age of an industry affects the ages of the top team.[60]

There is some evidence that homogeneity in the top team aids performance when the environment is stable but competitively intense, and that heterogeneity aids performance when the environment is turbulent. This fits the notion that in a drive for efficiency the top team should all be 'singing from the same hymn sheet' to support current operations, but providing a multitude of viewpoints when facing a less certain future. A positive relationship between innovation and the average amount of education and the diversity of functional backgrounds of people in the top team has been found,[61] although others are much less certain about such a relationship.[62]

The reason for the success in innovation of heterogeneous teams doesn't simply reside in the diversity of functional backgrounds. The different aspects of the strategic management process call for different cognitive styles – for different ways of thinking. People gather and evaluate information in different ways. For example, the identification of opportunities needs people who can think 'outside of the box', people who aren't restricted by the mindset of the rest of the group. Since an individual's way of thinking is very difficult to change,[63] the only sure way to get different ways of thinking into a team is through the selection of the team members.

Wrapp[34] has some interesting views on the interaction between the chief executive and the rest of the top team. He makes the point that a skilful manager doesn't make specific objectives for the rest of the top team – these are left somewhat open to allow subordinates to determine what they should be in line with strategy, and the chief executive has given the sense of strategic direction through his vision. Wrapp also has the view that 'the chief executive is a spotter of opportunities and relationships in the stream of operating problems and decisions.' This doesn't mean that chief executives aren't planners, but what they do is encourage their subordinates to plan.

4.8 Entrepreneurship and intrapreneurship

4.8.1 Entrepreneurship

Entrepreneurship is what an entrepreneur does, and it's easiest when trying to understand what entrepreneurship is to concentrate on the characteristics of entrepreneurs. The six characteristics listed in Exhibit 4.7 stand out as being closely associated with

EXHIBIT 4.7

> ### The characteristics of entrepreneurs
>
> - Risk taking
> - Innovative
> - Opportunity seeking
> - Happy with change
> - Power and independence seeking
> - Possessing a strong need to achieve

entrepreneurs and, when combined in sufficient strength, can be considered to characterise the entrepreneur:

- **Risk taking**   Taking risks is an attribute that most people would intuitively associate with an entrepreneur. However, investors and gamblers, who wouldn't usually consider themselves to be entrepreneurs, also take financial risks. The difference is that entrepreneurs are directly linked to the creation of one or more business processes, rather than having an arm's-length relationship to them, as the investor would have.

- **Innovative**   It would be expected that entrepreneurs would be innovative. Drucker[64] links entrepreneurship with the management of innovation. He writes:

  > Innovation is the specific tool of entrepreneurs, the means by which they exploit change as an opportunity for a different business or a different service.... Entrepreneurs need to search purposefully for the sources of innovation, the changes and their symptoms that indicate opportunities for successful innovation.

- **Opportunity seeking**   The entrepreneur's strategy is dominated by a search for opportunities.[65] Thus they need to be closely associated with many people who can provide them with the chance to identify the market openings. They also need to be well aware of what they can offer and where their capabilities can best be used. Drucker[66] writes:

  > To succeed, innovators must build on their strengths ... Which of these opportunities fits me, fits this company, puts to work what we (or I) are good at and have shown capacity for in performance?

- **Happy with change**   Entrepreneurs see change as the norm and as healthy and thus they are ready to adapt to new conditions.

- **Power and independence seeking**   Entrepreneurs are often driven by their need to be 'their own boss'. They need to be confident in their own abilities. They also often seek the power that goes with independence and success.

- **Possessing a strong need to achieve**   Entrepreneurs need to feel that they are creating something new and valuable – a new product or service or a new organisation – or simply creating a large amount of money.

Thus we are now in a position to create a definition of an entrepreneur: *an entrepreneur is a person with a strong need for achievement, who continually seeks opportunities where they can innovate and drive change, and who seeks the power and independence necessary for success.*

It might be thought that all small firms are necessarily entrepreneurial. However, the distinguishing feature of an entrepreneurial enterprise is that it's based on innovation and has potential for growth. So the leader-managers of small businesses need not be entrepreneurs, as the average local corner shop demonstrates.

4.8.2 Types and personalities of entrepreneurs

When discussing the personal characteristics of leaders, it was stressed that there were few if any personal characteristics that would indicate whether someone would be a successful leader or not. While to be a successful entrepreneur takes many factors such as hard work, drive and ambition, the same lack of a definite personality type appears to be true of entrepreneurs.[67,68] The careful and reserved introvert is just as likely to be successful as the more extrovert, although the extrovert's success will be more noticeable. As with leadership, entrepreneurial ability can be learned.

The *need to achieve* and *seeking power* and *independence* have been used to compare entrepreneurs with other managers and to indicate that there are two types of entrepreneur. This is shown in Exhibit 4.8.[69] One type is the independent entrepreneur, who is more interested in independence than power. Firms with such an interest will tend to remain small or to grow only slowly, since their wish for independence means that they will restrict financial borrowings and retain all or most of the equity. Sometimes they don't wish to grow; many (family-owned) firms in the German *Mittelstand* seem to be happy to stay the size they now are.

The second type of entrepreneur is more concerned with power than with independence. This means that they are happy to give up independence – perhaps through borrowing to finance growth – in order to achieve growth.

There is a tendency to see entrepreneurship as restricted to individuals setting up their own firms from scratch. But entrepreneurs can also be found at the top of large organisations, Lee Iacocca's rejuvenation of Chrysler and Jan Carlzon's turnaround of Scandinavian Airlines System being examples.

Wickham[70] has identified those factors that encourage someone to become an entrepreneur, both the 'pull' factors that attract people to be entrepreneurs and the 'push' factors that encourage people to leave what they are currently doing and become entrepreneurs. These are shown in Exhibit 4.9.

EXHIBIT 4.8

Types of entrepreneur (adapted from Ettiger, 1983)

		Independence/power	
		Dominant need for independence	*Dominant need for power*
	Weak	Professionals	Managers
Need to achieve			
	Strong	Independent Entrepreneurs	Entrepreneurs who make organisations

EXHIBIT 4.9

> ## 'Pull' and 'Push' factors for entrepreneurs (adapted from Wickham, 1998)
>
> ### 'Pull' factors
>
> Financial rewards from entrepreneurship
> The freedom to work for yourself
> The sense of achievement from running your own venture
> The freedom to pursue a personal invention
> A desire for social standing
>
> ### 'Push' factors
>
> The limited financial rewards in conventional jobs
> Being unemployed in the established economy
> Job insecurity
> Career limitations and setbacks in a conventional job
> The inability to pursue a personal invention
> Being a misfit in an established organisation

4.8.3 Intrapreneurship

The realisation that leadership can be practised at many levels in organisations can be extended to include entrepreneurship. When entrepreneurship is carried out below the highest level in large organisations it is called intrapreneurship.[71] The conditions for intrapreneuring have been well described by Pinchot and are laid out as a set of questions in Exhibit 4.10.

EXHIBIT 4.10

> ## Tests to decide if an organisation would support intrapreneuring (adapted from Pinchot, 1985)
>
> - Does the organisation encourage the self-appointed intrapreneur?
> - Does the organisation provide ways for intrapreneurs to stay with their intraprises?
> - Are the people in the organisation permitted to do the job in their own way, or do they have to constantly stop to explain their actions and ask for permission?
> - Has the organisation evolved quick and informal ways to access the resources to try new ideas?
> - Has the organisation developed ways to manage many small and experimental products and businesses?
> - Are the systems set up to encourage risk taking and to tolerate mistakes?
> - Can your organisation decide to try something and stick with the experiment long enough to see if it will work, even when that may take years and several false starts?
> - Are people in the organisation more concerned with new ideas or with defending their turf?
> - How easy is it to form functionally complete, autonomous teams in the organisation?
> - Do intrapreneurs in the organisation face internal monopolies or are they free to use resources of other parts of the organisation and outside suppliers if they choose?

One role for leader-managers is to ensure that their organisation is able to adapt and renew itself. Renewal is concerned with change and in many cases with intra- and entrepreneurship. It can be seen from Exhibit 4.10 that intrapreneurial activity requires policies and practices to support it. In particular, the organisation must be made receptive to innovation, and perceive change as an opportunity and not a threat. It also needs an organisational structure and an incentives and rewards policy that support intrapreneurial activity. Systematic measurement, or at least appraisal, of a company's performance as innovator is also necessary if innovation is to flourish.[72]

SUMMARY

- Managers are dealing with the physical resources of an organisation, with its capital, raw materials, technology and the demonstrable skills of the workforce. They are concerned with efficiency and mastering routines. Leaders operate on the emotional and spiritual resources of the organisation and are concerned with effectiveness. Thus the characteristics of managers and leaders are very different. Strategic management requires leader-managers.
- Research has exploded four myths of leadership: that leadership is a rare ability, that leaders are born not made, that there is a leadership type and that leaders only exist at the top of organisations. Very importantly, leadership skills can be learned.
- Although there doesn't seem to be one leadership 'type', leaders do need to possess certain characteristics. Leaders must also have four vital attributes to be successful: they must have a strongly held vision, they must be able to communicate that vision – particularly to the top team – and they must be able to convert the vision into reality. Additionally, an accurate picture of reality is a prerequisite for success. EXHIBIT 4.1, EXHIBIT 4.2
- Four leadership styles have been identified, categorised by the relative emphasis that the leader puts on completing the task and on the treatment of people. In order to bring about change, leader-managers need power. Seven sources of power have been identified. EXHIBIT 4.4, EXHIBIT 4.5
- The gulf between the theory and practice of leadership is very wide. Machiavelli wrote about what leaders did, not about what was ethically sound. He identified the willingness to undertake immoral deeds, preparedness, and the maintenance of reputation as vital for successful leaders.
- Six characteritics stand out as being closely asociated with entrepreneurs. An entrepreneur is a person who seeks opportunity and drives change to create new value. There is not a clear entrepreneurial 'type' and entrepreneurship can be learned. The *need to achieve* and *seeking power and independence* have been used to compare entrepreneurs with other managers and to indicate that there are two types of entrepreneur. Leader-managers need to be intrapreneurs in order to lead the continual renewal required for the long-term survival of their organisations. There are many 'pull' and 'push' factors associated with entrepreneurship. EXHIBIT 4.7, EXHIBIT 4.8, EXHIBIT 4.9, EXHIBIT 4.10

SELF-CHECK

1 Reconsider the learning outcomes for this chapter. Check that you feel confident that you can carry out the activities listed there.
2 Having read this chapter, you should be able to define the following terms:

coercive power	leader-manager	power
connection power	leadership	referent power
entrepreneurship	legitimate power	repertoire
expert power	Machiavellian	reward power
intrapreneurship	manager	vision
leader	personal power	

MINI-CASE

Managers[73]

Managers are the heroes of the corporate economy. They are lionised by politicians and endlessly studied in management schools, but do they make a difference?

For several years I have been studying the relationship between the economic performance and on-the-pitch success of football clubs. One use to which this analysis can be put is to evaluate the contribution of managers to the success of organisations and to understand why some managers succeed and others fail.

In theory a successful manager is simply someone who can take the same set of inputs and turn them into something of greater value than anyone else. Measuring the impact of managers in practice is difficult because in most industries both the inputs and outputs come in non-standard forms and because the evaluation of performance so often depends on the context.

These problems cannot be avoided even if we base comparisons only on profitability. Our evaluation of a manager whose business reports a £1 million profit this year will vary according to the size of the company and its profits in previous years. In most industries the circumstances surrounding individual corporations are so diverse as to render realistic comparisons impractical.

The football industry is different. In England and Wales the leading corporations (still nostalgically called clubs) compete in a league system. This provides a controlled set of contests, which renders the outcome of competition comparable for each team, an unassailable indicator of relative performance.

Of course, the equality of opportunity of each club is limited by its resources, which are devoted primarily to buying players. Human inputs are notoriously unpredictable in their performance and the market for labour is often a lottery. When a manager hires a worker it is difficult to know what he or she is getting. References are almost always favourable and qualifications are often irrelevant. Again, the football industry is different. The characteristics of players are generally well known, and the most important work the player does (playing in cup or league matches) can be fully monitored. Because of this there is a more or less perfect market for players. Players are paid what they are worth, which can be measured by their contribution to enhancing league performance. I have used regression analysis to study the performance of 41 clubs over the past 16 years. This shows that the wage spending of clubs can account for 80–90% of the variation in league performance over time. Disgruntled fans notwithstanding, in football you generally get what you pay for.

The first question to ask about a football manager is this: is he or she capable of raising the performance of the club above the level implied by the wage spend alone?

The answer in general is no. If wages account for 80–90% of performance, the extra explanatory power added by including the manager in the regression is about 2%. However, not all managers are the same and we can rank managers according to their relative impact on performance.

Using my database I have compiled a list of the top 10 managers. As can be seen, the names are not necessarily fashionable, but then the data gives no special weight to recent events. For example, since the database only runs to the end of the 1996–97 season, Kenny Dalglish's interlude at Newcastle is not included.

These are statistical estimates of performance, not personal judgements. Most importantly, regression analysis irons out the effect of a big purse. Thus Dalglish is top of the pile not merely because he ran clubs with big budgets: he achieved more at those clubs he managed than would have been expected given his spending on wages.

However, several managers appear largely because of their ability to extract above-average performance from limited resources (Kinnear, McMenemy and Bassett).

George Graham does not quite make it into the top 10, because Arsenal was actually among the biggest spenders during his tenure.

The analysis even allows us to place a value on a good manager, by measuring the difference in league position that would be expected with an average manager compared with that under a top manager. The gap in expected league position could always be made up by buying more players, and from this we can estimate the worth of the manager.

For example, at present a club with an average manager and £15 million to spend on salaries could expect to achieve a mid-table position in the Premier League. In the hands of Alex Ferguson, £15 million would be expected to yield a league position of third. Coming third with an average manager would require a wage bill of £32 million, so the added value of Alex Ferguson in today's money is about £17 million.

One interesting fact that emerged in this research is that experience does not appear to count for much. Most managers have short careers (an average 2.7 years and falling) and the survivors are those who did better than average in their first few years.

However, the lifetime career performance of long-lived managers was not markedly better than those with short careers, implying that performance actually deteriorates over time.

The managerial merry-go-round is an expensive and painful way of finding out who is good at the job. If it were possible to predict who would make it as a top manager a good deal of anguish could be saved all round.

Since almost all managers are former professional players it is possible to examine their past careers to look for factors that indicate likely success. Contrary to received opinion, Scottish managers are on average no more successful than their southern counterparts.

The strongest predictor of success as a manager is to have won international honours as a player. Forwards are also more likely to have successful careers. But overall, successful managers are extremely difficult to predict.

Aces of clubs: Top 10 football managers to 1997

Rank	Name	Clubs managed in database period
1	Kenny Dalglish	Blackburn, Liverpool
2	Joe Kinnear	Wimbledon
3	Lawrie McMenemy	Southampton
4	Howard Kendall	Everton, Sheffield United
5	Alex Ferguson	Manchester United
6	Keith Burkenshaw	Tottenham, West Bromwich
7	Dave Bassett	Sheffield United, Wimbledon
8	Trevor Francis	Birmingham, Sheffield Wednesday
9	Bruce Rioch	Arsenal, Bolton
10	Kevin Keegan	Newcastle

Discussion point 4.10

What are the lessons concerning football managers and their clubs from this article?
- What does this article tell us about leader-managers in business? Should more emphasis be placed on team building? What does it say about how a leader-manager should act with a team of knowledge workers?

FURTHER
DISCUSSION
POINTS

1   For GSM:
- Has Barry Dodd got a vision?
- How have Barry Dodd and the works managers empowered people?
- How does Barry Dodd fit the characteristics of leaders?
- What is the leadership style?
- Are the composition of the top team and its method of working appropriate?
- What sort of entrepreneur is Barry Dodd and what forces drove him there?

2   In Chapter 1, the strategic management environment was characterised as chaotic, complex, dynamic and turbulent – all generally increasing the level of uncertainty facing leader-managers. However, not all business environments are the same. Reflect on how changes in the environmental characteristics might affect the way leadership is exercised in the organisation.

3   What is the relationship between the repertoires of top teams and a paradigm as discussed in Chapter 2?

4   Two types of entrepreneur are described in Section 4.8.2. Which form of culture as described in Chapter 2 would fit most appropriately?

ASSIGNMENTS

1   Compare and contrast the characteristics and leadership styles of Shane McGill in the Shane McGill and One-Shot case, Ken Lewis of Dutton Engineering and Robin Saxby of ARM.

2   For an organisation of your choice, determine the background of its board of directors and judge whether the board has the appropriate breadth of experience for the environment in which the organisation is operating.

FURTHER
READING

A personal account from Sir John Harvey-Jones, the former managing director and chairman of ICI, provides interesting insights into leadership in a large multinational: John Harvey-Jones, *Making it Happen: Reflections on Leadership*, Fontana/Collins, 1988. Examples of the leadership of Ray Kroc of McDonald's, Sam Walton of Wal-Mart and Walt Disney and Michael Eisner of Disney Corporation are described in the book by Neil H. Snyder, James J. Dowd Jr and Dianne Morse Houghton, *Vision, Values and Courage: Leadership for Quality Management*, Free Press, 1994.

A book that is written for managers and is practical rather than academic in emphasis is the book by John P. Kotter, *Leading Change*, Harvard Business School Press, 1996. More academic treatments of the topic of leadership are given in the special edition on leadership of the *Strategic Management Journal*, Vol. 10, 1989.

A very readable text on entrepreneurship is that by Philip Wickham, *Strategic Entrepreneurship: A Decision-making Approach to New Venture Creation and Management*, Financial Times Pitman Publishing, 1998. An international perspective is given in the book edited by Alison Morrison, *Entrepreneurship: An International Perspective*, Butterworth Heinemann, 1998.

CHAPTER NOTES
AND REFERENCES

1 Drucker, P.F., *Post-capitalist Society*, Butterworth Heinemann, 1993.

2 Shillingford, J., 'FT telecoms', *Financial Times*, 10 June 1998, p. 11.

3 Peters, T.J. and Waterman, R.H., *In Search of Excellence*, Harper & Row, 1982.

4 Bennis, W. and Nanus, B., *Leaders: The Strategies for Taking Charge*, Harper & Row, 1985, p. 21.

5 Zaleznik, A. 'Managers and leaders: are they different?' *Harvard Business Review*, March–April 1992, pp. 129, 131.

6 Williamson, J.N. (ed.), *The Leader-Manager*, Wilson Learning Corporation, John Wiley & Sons, 1986.

7 Bennis, W. and Nanus, B., *op. cit.*, p. 44

8 *Ibid.*

9 Snyder, N.H., Dowd, J.J., Jr and Houghton, D.M., *Vision, Values and Courage: Leadership for Quality Management*, Free Press, 1994, p. 18.

10 Senge, P., 'The leader's new work: building learning organisations', *Sloan Management Review*, Fall 1990, p. 13.

11 Bennis, W., 'Managing the dream: leadership in the 21st century', *Training*, May 1990, p. 44.

12 Snyder, N.H., *et al.*, *op. cit.*

13 Pascale, R.T., *Transformation*, BBC Enterprises video, 1994.

14 Kay, J., *Foundations of Corporate Success: How Business Strategies Add Value*, Oxford University Press, 1993.

15 Hamel, G. and Prahalad, C.K., 'Strategic intent', *Harvard Business Review*, May–June 1989, pp. 63–76.

16 Pascale, R.T., *op. cit.*

17 Pedler, M., Burgoyne, J. and Boydell, T., *The Learning Company*, McGraw-Hill, 1991.

18 Brown, J.S., 'Research that re-invents the corporation', *Harvard Business Review*, Jan–Feb 1991, pp. 115–25.

19 Nonaka, I., 'The knowledge-creating company', *Harvard Business Review*, Nov–Dec 1991, pp. 97–104.

20 Kotter, J.P., *A Force for Change*, Free Press, 1992.

21 Mintzberg, H. 'The manager's job: folklore and fact', *Harvard Business Review*, July–August 1975, pp. 49–61.

22 Nonaka, I. and Takeuchi, T., *The Knowledge-Creating Company: How Japanese Companies Create the Dynamics of Innovation*, Oxford University Press, 1995, p. 115.

23 Senge, P., *op. cit.*, p. 218.

24 Simons, R., *Levers of Control: How Managers Use Innovative Control Systems to Drive Strategic Renewal*, Harvard Business School Press, 1995, p. 98.

25 O'Reilly, S., 'Leaders are developed, not born', *The Sunday Times*, Business, 8 February 1998, p. 7.

26 Snyder, N.H., *et al.*, *op. cit.* p. 16.

27 Sculley, J., 'Manager's maxim', *The Observer*, 17 May 1998, Page I of 'Work' in the Business section.

28 Simons, R, *op. cit.*, p. 173.

29 Egan, J., 'Manager's maxim', *The Observer*, 12 April 1998, Page I of 'Work' in the Business section.

30 Cook, C.W., Hunsaker, P.L. and Coffey, R.E., *Management and Organizational Behavior*, 2nd edn, Irwin, 1997.

31 Toffler, A., *The Third Wave*, Collins, 1980, p. 413.

32 Blake and Mouton, 1964.

33 Crainer, S. (ed.) *Leaders on Leadership*, Institute of Management, 1996, p. 12.

34 Wrapp, H.E., 'Good managers don't make policy decisions', in Mintzberg, H. and Quinn, J.B. (eds), *Concepts, Contexts, Cases*, 2nd edn, Prentice-Hall International Series, 1991, pp. 32–8.

35 French, J.R.P. and Raven, B., 'The bases of social power', in Cartwright, D. (ed.), *Studies in Social Power*, Michigan Institute for Social Research, 1959, pp. 150–67.

36 Kakabadse, A., *Culture of the Social Services*, Gower, 1982.

37 Thompson, J.L. *Strategic Management Awareness and Change*, 2nd edn, Chapman & Hall, 1993, p. 89.

38 A great deal of this section is based on Eve Poole's MBA dissertation, 'Machiavelli for management: lessons from *The Prince* for business leadership'. This was written by Eve while she was studying at the University of Edinburgh Management School, where she won the AMBA Student of the Year Award. I am deeply indebted to Eve for allowing me to

use her ideas, examples, sources and terminology in this way.

39 Machiavelli, N., *The Prince*, by G. Bull (trans.), Penguin Books, 1961.

40 Quoted by Kay in *Prospect*, March 1998, p. 25.

41 *Financial Times*, 19 December 1996. Basham subsequently had his name cleared in the libel courts.

42 Bhide, A. and Stevenson, H.H., 'Why be honest if honesty doesn't pay?', *Harvard Business Review*, Vol. 68, No. 5, 1990, pp. 121–9.

43 Potter, N.S., 'The BMW acquisition of the Rover Group', University of Birmingham, 1995.

44 Corbett, J.M., *Critical Cases in Organisational Behaviour*, Macmillan, 1994, p. 123.

45 Garraty, J.A. and McCaughey, R.A., *The American Nation*, Harper & Row, 1987.

46 Drucker, P.F., Dyson, E., Handy, C., Sells, P. and Sage, P.M., 'Looking ahead, implications for the present', *Harvard Business Review*, Vol. 75, No. 5, Sept–Oct 1997, pp. 18–28.

47 Crainer, S., *op. cit.*, p. 175.

48 Peters, T.J. and Waterman, R.H., *op. cit.*, pp. xxiv and 71.

49 *Ibid.*, p. 114.

50 Christie, R. and Geis, F.L., *Studies in Machiavellianism*, Academic Press, 1970, p. 17 (slightly modified so as not to be gender-specific).

51 Graham, J.H., 'Machiavellian project managers: do they perform better?' *International Journal of Project Management*, Vol. 14, No. 2, 1996, pp. 67–74.

52 Kay, J., *op. cit.*, p. 15.

53 Cyert, R.M. and March, J.G., *A Behavioral Theory of the Firm*, Prentice-Hall, 1963.

54 Hambrick, D.C., 'Guest editor's introduction: putting top managers back in the strategic picture', *Strategic Management Journal*, Vol. 10, 1989, pp. 5–15.

55 Peterson, R.S., Owens, P.D., Tetlock, P.E., Fan, E.T. and Mortorance, P., 'Group dynamics in top management teams: groupthink, vigilance and alternative models of organizational failure and success', *Organizational Behaviour and Human Decision Processes*, Vol. 13, No. 2–3, 1998, pp. 272–305.

56 Bantel, K.A. and Jackson, S.E., 'Top management and innovations in banking: does the composition of the top team make a difference?', *Strategic Management Journal*, Vol. 10, 1989, pp. 107–24.

57 Romme, A.G.L., 'Vertical integration as organizational strategy formation', *Organisation Studies*, Vol. 11, No. 2, 1990, pp. 239–60.

58 Johnson, G., *Strategic Change and the Management Process*, Basil Blackwell, 1987.

59 Lewis, G., *Corporate Strategy in Action*, Routledge, 1988.

60 Hambrick, D.C., *op. cit.*

61 Bantel, K.A. and Jackson, S.E., *op. cit.*

62 Pettigrew, A.M., 'On studying managerial elites', *Strategic Management Journal*, Vol. 13, 1992, pp. 163–82.

63 Myers, I.B. and McCaulley, M.H., *Manual: A Guide to the Development and Use of the Myers-Briggs Type Indicator*, Consulting Psychologists Press, 1985.

64 Drucker, P.F., *Innovation and Entrepreneurship: Practice and Principles*, Heinemann, 1985, p. 17.

65 Mintzberg, H., 'Strategy making in three modes', *Californian Management Review*, Winter 1973.

66 Drucker, P.F., *op. cit.*, p 127.

67 *Ibid.*, p. 23.

68 Wickham, P.A., *Strategic Entrepreneurship: A Decision-making Approach to New Venture Creation and Management*, Financial Times Pitman Publishing, 1998, p. 23.

69 Ettinger, J.C. 'Some Belgian evidence on entrepreneurial personality', *European Small Business Journal*, Vol. 1, 1983, pp. 48–56.

70 Wickham, P.A., *op. cit.*, p. 49.

71 Pinchot III, G., *Intrapreneuring: Why You Don't Have to Leave the Corporation to Become an Entrepreneur*, Harper & Row, 1985. The tests are taken from pp. 198 and 199.

72 Drucker, P.F., *op. cit.*, p. 138.

73 From Szymanski, S. 'Suits in a league of their own', *The Observer*, 1 November 1998, 'Work', p. 1.

5 Issue handling

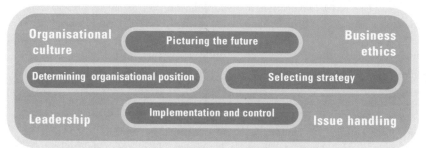

this is the last of the four chapters concerned with the internal context of an organisation. The concern is with the way in which issues and decisions are handled.

A definition of an *issue* is first addressed and a model of the process of issue handling is presented and discussed. This discussion explores how awareness of the existence of potential issues comes about and how people react to this information. The two ways of responding positively – through programmed response and through seeking understanding – are then described.

The interrelated concepts of information, knowledge and learning are next explored. Individual mental models and individual learning are considered and, since individual knowledge is the source of all organisational learning, this leads on naturally to considerations of the *learning organisation*. The particular decision-making concerns of senior leader-managers in top teams is considered, and the support that is available for group processes is then discussed.

A very significant role for leader-managers is to establish ways within their organisation for handling appropriately all the sorts of issues that confront it – those that are incremental and those that are transformational, the singular and the recurring. Appropriate issue handling calls for knowledge and this in turn calls for learning. A prevalent view is that the ability to learn faster than competitors may be the only truly sustainable competitive advantage. If this view is accepted, then a prime task for leader-managers is to foster learning within their organisations: to develop a knowledge-creating and thus a learning organisation.

LEARNING
OUTCOMES

When you have worked through this chapter, you should be able to:

- explain what an issue is and give examples;

- list the ways of responding to an issue;

- explain the five-phase model of issue handling and explain what takes place in each phase;

- describe the forms of programmed response;

- describe how people seek understanding of issues;

- explain the rational and incremental forms of issue handling and relate them to the intended and emergent forms of strategy formulation;

- understand the three levels of understanding and changes to mental models;

- describe the role of the organisation in creating knowledge;

- describe the forms of group support systems that might help organisations to *disagree without being disagreeable*.

5.1 Issues

5.1.1 Problems, decisions and issues

'Issue handling' isn't a well-known term in strategic management; much more common are such terms as *problem solving* and *decision making*. So there's a need to explain why the term is used here. Consider first *problem solving*. Very generally, problem solving can be considered as the process of finding a way of moving from a less to a more satisfactory state. This is fine, except that the opportunity for a leader-manager to increase market share, to increase profits or to reduce costs would not normally be considered a problem, and few leader-managers would term it so. Consider now the term *decision making*. Sometimes decision making is considered rather narrowly as simply making a selection between various courses of action; at other times it is taken to include aspects such as the need to obtain further information. However, even in this wider use, the term 'decision making' is too narrow for what leader-managers are involved in. Decisions do need to be taken that affect the long-term well-being of the organisation, but decision taking is often the outcome of a rather fuzzy and indistinct process involving much deliberation, hesitation and controversy. Also, leader-managers face few decisions where well-defined choices are presented at well-defined times.[1]

In order to get over these difficulties, it is easier and more appropriate to consider opportunities, problems, decision situations and threats – in fact any aspect of organisational life that potentially must be dealt with – under the generic term 'issue'. The term *decision taking* will be retained to imply the irrevocable commitment of resources, which is one aspect of issue handling. What leader-managers are often facing are long-term issues interspersed with decision points, as illustrated in Exhibit 5.1. For example, 'external' issues that might affect many organisations are globalisation and the demographic changes affecting their markets, while organisations are often concerned with 'internal' issues such as enhancing quality, reducing waste and shortening lead times. These aren't 'one-off' events but long-lasting – perhaps never-ending – concerns. Even 'one-off' events such as the result of a general election are likely to have long-term consequences and demand many organisational decisions.

Formally, an issue is a trend or an event that:

- potentially could have a high impact on the organisation's overall performance;
- is controversial, in that it's likely that reasonable people may have different views about its probability of occurrence and on the most appropriate way to handle it.

EXHIBIT 5.1

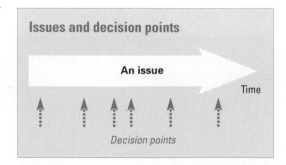

Issues and decision points

An issue

Time

Decision points

An issue is something that indicates that the status quo has or is likely to change, and that this change might make the current strategy (either the strategic goals, the strategic pathways or both) ineffective and consequently inappropriate.

DISCUSSION
POINT 5.1 Reflect on matters that have affected you personally over the last few years. Were any of them issues as defined above? Take 'the organisation' to be yourself here when using the definition of 'strategic issue'.

5.1.2 Types of decision

Two types of decision can be identified on the basis of the size of the change that is sought. The first are the largish and often step changes, which are usually the result of top-team deliberations since they are likely to have significant resource implications. These changes are shown as the top line in Exhibit 5.2. In a small company the large decisions might involve the introduction of a new machine tool or a new computer system, to support the issues of achieving greater flexibility and reducing lead times. A larger company may make the decision to acquire another company in support of its quest to become global.

However, such high-profile events and actions are not the only concern for leader-managers. The Japanese, with their *kaizen* or continuous improvement philosophy, have shown the importance of detail and how what might seem like simple, purely tactical, changes can build up to provide a strategic competitive advantage (the lower line in Exhibit 5.2). Two examples of *kaizen* are the rearrangement of a work area to reduce walking between jobs and a reduction in the amount of paperwork associated with a job. Establishing and maintaining the conditions within which continuous improvement can take place is a very important aspect of the leader-manager's job. This is about establishing a learning organisation, learning for everyone in the organisation.

We see again the thread that flows through the view of strategic management taken in this book: that the short term must be balanced with the long term. Leader-managers must be concerned with the on-going, the present and the short-term future, as this is the wellspring of their longer-term future. They need to be concerned with ensuring that the organisation's present activities are performed well: with incremental change, with keeping close to their customers, with enhancing and extending the skills and processes of their units. However, they also must be concerned with changes concerning the broad shape of the organisation: with enlargements (or contractions) of the organisation's activities, and not simply with honing existing operations.

EXHIBIT 5.2

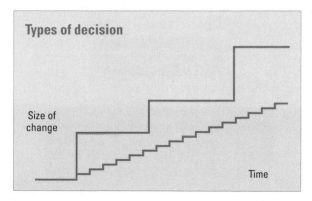

Types of decision

Size of change

Time

Issues often have long-term consequences. Leader-managers need to put the emphasis on issues being handled rather than on decisions being made. They need to put in place the organisational context to support the organisation in continually upgrading its performance: its operating performance to support the present and short-term future, but also upgrading its strategic thinking to help ensure its longer-term future.

5.2 The process of issue handling

It is generally recognised that the process of issue handling involves the five phases of awareness, programmed response, seeking understanding, decision taking and action. These phases are shown in Exhibit 5.3, together with the stages within each phase.[2]

In the awareness phase, environmental signals are first recognised as suggesting that there may be an issue to be considered. Then follows a diagnostic stage, when some sort of sense is made of the signals and a preliminary decision is made as to how to handle the issue, if at all; it may be that the issue is not considered worthy of any further concern. Should the decision be taken that the issue must be dealt with, there are two main ways of handling it: to make an immediate response or to be more reflective. It may appear that leader-managers should always be reflective, but the hurly-burly of organisational life prevents this except in a limited number of cases.

EXHIBIT 5.3

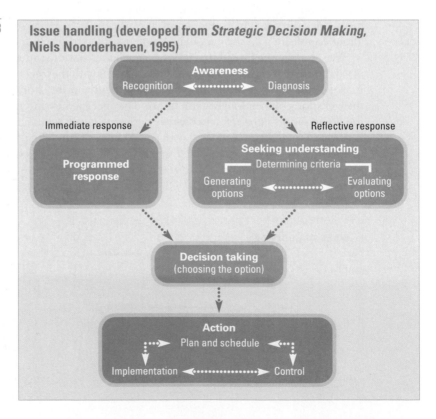

Issue handling (developed from *Strategic Decision Making*, Niels Noorderhaven, 1995)

Time and attention are always in short supply and for some issues leader-managers take short cuts and operate 'on autopilot', relying on routinised/programmed responses. In other cases, leader-managers need to reflect on those issues where reflection is likely to be most useful.

In organisations, this reflection and subsequent enhanced understanding will hopefully result in an enhanced and shared understanding between its members. With options evaluated in the light of the strategic goals, there is then the selection of one option – the act of decision taking, where resources are irrevocably committed. This is followed by the action phase, where the chosen option is implemented. Following implementation, the efficacy of the choice is reviewed (through the control process).

In this chapter, the first three phases of the process are considered, i.e. awareness, programmed response and seeking understanding. The characteristics of specific strategic options and the action phase will be considered in detail in later chapters. When discussing the phases and stages, it must be realised that issue handling is complex and the process is an iterative one, especially within a phase, and this is why the arrows between stages in a phase in Exhibit 5.3 are double-headed.

5.3 Awareness

There are two stages in the awareness phase – recognition and diagnosis.

5.3.1 Recognition

Recognition is the detection of one or more signals from the environment and their interpretation as harbingers of an issue. The signals could arise from both formal and informal sources, with the organisation's stakeholders as one particularly important source. Formal sources might be the profit and loss account indicating unacceptable performance or a business intelligence system indicating that competitors are about to launch a new product. Environmental analysis – especially scenario writing – can play an important role in identifying emerging issues. Informal sources might be gossip on the golf course, rumours at a business convention or a piece of information on rivals picked up by a salesperson during a visit to a client. The signals might simply manifest themselves as feelings in one or more individuals of unease, imbalance, inconsistency, or may come from a formal gap analysis, such as a strengths, weaknesses, opportunities and threats analysis. Put generally, issues are tied to a feeling that there is some form of performance gap, and the triggering serves to focus attention on it. These triggering stimuli are shown on the left-hand side of Exhibit 5.4.[3]

Note that it is only possible for people to interpret a signal as indicating the presence of a potential issue if they have an appropriate overall view of the issue situation. For example, a person without any medical knowledge would be quite unable to detect whether someone with a temperature of 38°C was likely to be ill or not; probably they would not even be aware that temperature is often an important symptom! They would be unable to detect the issue because they have no model of the workings of the human body to guide their thoughts. Similarly, it would be well-nigh impossible for someone with no knowledge of car manufacture to know why or even

EXHIBIT 5.4

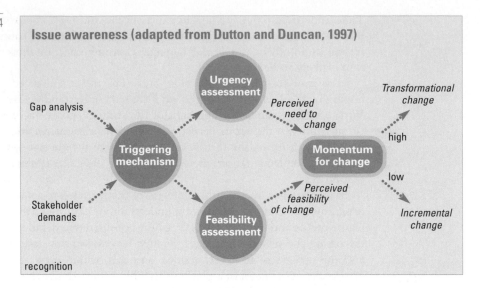

Issue awareness (adapted from Dutton and Duncan, 1997)

whether a car plant was working efficiently or not, and if it wasn't, what to do about it. This is why leader-managers are employed and paid for their experience; they have a broad view that allows them to pick out the wheat from the chaff.

5.3.2 Diagnosis

Once a potential strategic issue has been recognised, the question is what makes leader-managers take one potential issue seriously while not bothering with others. Organisations do not have the time to attend to all potential issues, thus there has to be some selection.

While individuals are likely to recognise potential issues, it is generally a group which diagnoses the next stage. According to Dutton and Duncan,[4] issue diagnosis involves two main interpretations. There is an interpretation of *issue urgency*, the urgency to take action, and there is an interpretation of the *feasibility of action*, the feasibility of being able to take the appropriate action. On the basis of these assessments a momentum for change is created. Momentum for change refers to the level of effort and commitment that leader-managers are willing to devote to action designed to handle an issue. Note that at this stage all that the leader-manager is doing is making a gross judgement about the possibility of successfully handling the issue; they aren't into the detail of implementation. These judgements will be formed by their experiences, which will affect how they interpret the issue. For example, a similar issue successfully handled previously might be seen as an opportunity; if nothing like it has been encountered before, then the issue may be seen as a threat.

Issue urgency

Issue urgency is related to the perceived cost of not taking action. There are four aspects to issue urgency:

● Importance   Importance will be reflected in the damage that the organisation in general and the dominant coalition in particular will experience if the issue is wrongly handled. Ultimately, importance is about how threatening the issue is to the survival of the dominant coalition.

- Time pressures   Deadlines may be embedded in an issue. Deadlines would arise, for example, if a competitor was known to be launching a revolutionary product in a month's time, or if compliance to new regulations will become mandatory by the end of the year.

- Persistence   This is the time over which the issue is likely to be significant.

- Visibility   How easy is it for stakeholders, both inside and outside the organisation, to recognise that the organisation is confronted by the issue? This is the issue of visibility. Visibility has two facets. First, it is related to the publicity surrounding an issue and how exposed the organisation is to it. For example, when Greenpeace highlighted Shell's position over the redundant *Brent Spar* oil rig, the issue became very significant. The same was true of Mercedes after it was found that the small car it had just introduced was unstable when carrying out high-speed turns; this was front-page news in 1997 and led to the withdrawal of the car from the market. Second, the responsibility that management feels for the situation will also be important and add to the issue urgency. This will be particularly marked if specific senior leader-managers are held responsible for the issue arising, perhaps by not taking action earlier.

Feasibility of action

If it is considered feasible to handle the issue, then management is willing to confront it and to invest the necessary effort to handle it. If management considers that the appropriate action is infeasible, then it is likely that the issue will be ignored. There are two aspects of feasibility:

- Perceived understanding will be reflected in the confidence that leader-managers have that they understand the cause-and-effect relationships that are operating. For example, many organisations are now grappling with the consequences of Internet developments. If leader-managers understand or feel they could understand the effect that these might have on their organisation, their feeling of being able to harness the Internet will tend to be high. Note that the important point for generating a momentum for change is the *perception* that leader-managers have of their understanding, not their *real* understanding. Of course, if they think that they have a good understanding of an issue but do not, then although they will be energised to take action, they are likely to take inappropriate action.

- Perceived capability is the view that resources will be available to carry out the change needed. If a business has no resources to hire an Internet specialist, then management will feel powerless to act and will perceive Internet developments as a threat: something that their competitors may use to put them at a disadvantage.

5.4   Ways of responding to an issue

The above discussion implies that there are many ways of dealing with issues.[5] One response to an issue is to *absolve* it by ignoring it and hoping that it will go away. A small example may make this clear. Consider a firm faced with a sudden decline in demand for its products. The issue is what to do. This issue could be absolved simply by ignoring it, hoping that the decrease is a 'blip' and that demand will soon return to its former level. (Actually, absolving isn't such a bad idea – issues have life cycles and do disappear.)

Second, where action follows, a programmed response is **pre-resolving** the issue in that an apparently appropriate response is effectively made prior to the issue arising. If the firm had successfully met such sudden declines in demand before, it might use the rules it had developed previously, for example to increase the level of advertising.

Another 'response' is to **dissolve** the issue by changing the context in which it has arisen. If the firm decided to move out of the business in which it is currently involved, the need to respond to declining sales would no longer be an issue, although obviously other issues would now arise.

To **solve** this issue would require finding the best solution. This in turn would require management to review fully both customer requirements and what competitors are doing so as to be able to specify the potential demand completely and precisely. The firm would also need to assess all feasible ways of altering its market offering. This could be an extremely time-consuming task, and even if an optimum match between the new offering and demand could be found, it's very unlikely that the choice would remain optimum for long; customer requirements are likely to change, and certainly competitors would do new things.

This little example should suggest that the search for the best answer is often a search that is not worth the effort. Most leader-managers have realised that optimising part of a issue is not necessarily very useful. An answer that is sensible and understandable and not grossly wrong – resolving or being 'good enough' – is the stuff of a great deal of management activity. In the example of falling demand, to **resolve** the issue the firm would need only to have identified broadly the key features of the situation. This process would not be nearly so time-consuming as optimising and would suggest reasonable action within an appropriate timescale.

KEY CONCEPT   Awareness is the first phase of strategic issue handling. It consists of two stages, recognition and diagnosis. Recognition results from the realisation that there is some sort of performance gap. Diagnosis leads to a momentum for change when the dominant coalition judges the issue to be urgent and believes that the organisation has the capability to handle it successfully. There are five ways of handling issues following awareness: absolving, dissolving, resolving, pre-resolving and solving. Absolving is where the issue is ignored. Dissolving occurs when the context in which the issue arises is changed so as to eliminate the issue. Resolving is where an answer that is good enough is all that is sought. Pre-resolving is a form of resolving where the response to the issue has already been internalised by the decision taker. Solving is where an optimum or best solution is obtained.

5.5 Programmed response

Once diagnosis has taken place and the issue is 'on the agenda', there are two options available: a reflective approach or a more immediate programmed response. These immediate responses are 'cognitive short-cuts' or *heuristics*, whereby a set of decision

EXHIBIT 5.5

Programmed responses (adapted from *Strategic Decision Making*, Niels Noorderhaven, 1995)

	Individual programmed responses	*Organisational progammed responses*
Based on previous rational decisions	Individual routine behaviour	Organisational rules and procedures
Arational	Mindless habits	Paradigm and shared values

rules has been internalised and is used when the individual or organisation thinks appropriate. Heuristics are rules of thumb. There is a search for responses that have been used in what appear to the leader-manager to be similar previous situations. This requires managers to scan their individual and organisational memory and the environment for fit.

The types of programmed response are shown in Exhibit 5.5.[6]

5.5.1 Individual programmed responses

One form of individual programmed response is where the response to an issue is based on previous rational behaviour. *Rational* is taken as meaning that someone is open to evidence and uses logical analysis in coming to conclusions. An example of a response based on previous rational behaviour would be if you are reading, the natural light deteriorates and you switch on a lamp; you have found previously that to switch on the lamp does actually help and you do that without thinking. A sales leader-manager faced with falling sales will look for answers that have worked before – if in similar past situations they have responded by cutting prices, then they will tend to do the same this time. This is what leader-managers are paid to do, to use their judgement based on experience.

A second form of individual programmed response is arational programmed response. In contrast to rational programmed response, this is a response that no one could logically argue the case for. Habits are routinised behaviours: dressing in a certain way for work, following the same route to work every day, someone always starting the working day with a cigarette, a leader-manager asking for detailed computer printouts each week but never using them. The problem with a habit is that it's often difficult for the person themselves to recognise it in themselves – although other people will do!

DISCUSSION POINT 5.2

Is *arational* the same as *irrational*?
* Describe a habit or someone you know, either in your private or business lives.

5.5.2 Group programmed responses – organisational rules and paradigms

Groups may also tackle issues through programmed responses. One form of organisational programmed response is the rational one, whereby issues are handled within the framework of organisational rules and procedures. One great advantage of rules and procedures is that they allow large sections of organisational activity to be 'automated' and thus free leader-managers for non-routinised activities. The case of employee time-keeping provides an example. If flexitime is worked there are usually rules governing it – every employee must be in the office between 9:30 and 12 noon and 2 and 4:30pm and work 37 hours per week, for example. Another example lies in the routines involved in running meetings. In both cases, the 'rules' forestall repeatedly 'reinventing the wheel' about such things as negotiating work times or how to conduct a meeting.

The second form of organisational programmed response is the type of activity stemming from the organisational paradigm and shared beliefs – responses embedded in the organisational culture.

KEY CONCEPT   Programmed responses are internalised ways of reacting to issues. The arational forms are generally unrecognised and transparent. Paradigms tend to cement the status quo – very valuable in some circumstances but worryingly dangerous in others.

5.6   Seeking understanding – generating and evaluating options – and decision taking

In the more reflective or at least more considered approach, when options are to be generated, there is a need to create a new response. There are several approaches to reflective strategic issue handling and these will now be discussed. The main distinction is between the so-called *rational* and *incremental* approaches.

5.6.1   Rational issue handling

Technical rationality

In process terms, *technical rationality* assumes that a decision taker confronts an issue with known objectives. They then gather appropriate information, develop a set of options and select the optimum one. Suppose a firm requires more production capacity. There may be several options open – buy or lease more machines, subcontract, build or lease a new factory unit, and so on. If the decision taker's preference was simply to spend as little money as possible (a preference for cheapness), then the technically rational approach would be to choose the option that cost the least. Such an approach is considered 'technically rational', as the option chosen is objectively best given the preferences of the people involved. The main characteristics of the technical rational approach are set out in Exhibit 5.6. The technical rational approach tends to be deterministic but need not necessarily be so.

Bounded rationality

A modification of the rational approach is the *bounded rational* approach. Here, although the objective is known and fixed over time, cognitive and informational limitations 'bound' (i.e. limit) the level of rationality employed in handling the issue. After all, we are all 'cognitive cripples' working to some form of timescale. Within bounded rationality the number of options that are considered tends to be limited, and the search for options tends to stop when a satisfactory option is found. A satisfactory option is one that meets the aspirations of the decision takers. This is in con-

EXHIBIT 5.6

The technical rational approach

- Issues are clearly diagnosed and so this aspect is not a problem
- Objectives remain fixed over time
- There are no limitations on information
- Cognitive ability is not a limitation
- There are no political or behavioural considerations
- The move to a solution is through a sequential, step-by-step logical process
- There are no time or cost considerations governing the issue-handling process
- All feasible options are considered

trast to the technical rational approach, where there is no limit on the search for options, with a striving to find the optimum; in the bounded rational approach the search is for an option that is 'good enough' rather than the best one. The bounded rational approach has the characteristics set out in Exhibit 5.7.

EXHIBIT 5.7

The bounded rational approach

- Although the issue is relatively well defined, there remains some need to structure it
- The approach is rational within known constraints of time, cognitive ability, information availability and cost
- 'Rules of thumb' are used as well as technical rationality
- Limited search for options stops when a 'good enough' option has been found

5.6.2 Incremental issue handling

In the strategic management context, both of the rational approaches discussed above suggest a top-down approach, with strategy formulation and issue handling taken by the top one or few people in the organisation. A very different view is taken in the incrementalist approaches.

Logical incrementalism

Logical incrementalism takes the view that leader-managers simply don't have the capability to understand many of the activities of the organisation and for them to attempt to decide what all subsystems should be doing is inappropriate. Also, leader-managers can't know enough to be able to adapt to unexpected environmental changes. Rather, strategy emerges from the strategies desired by the organisational subsystems: it's 'bottom-up', with initiatives coming from lower-level management. Note that a subsystem may be equivalent to a function or subfunction, but it's really any source of influence in the organisation and thus need not necessarily be linked to the formal organisational structure. The major characteristics of logical incrementalism are listed in Exhibit 5.8.

The following quote from Quinn[7] nicely sums up logical incrementalism:

'Logical incrementalism' is not 'muddling' as most people use that word. It is conscious, purposeful, proactive, good management. Properly managed, it allows the

EXHIBIT 5.8

The logical incrementalist approach

- Managers have a clear view of the long-term strategic goals but cannot foresee many of the consequences of their actions
- Managers have only a limited capability to control strategy making and/or implementation
- Issue handling is fragmented, with no fundamental reassessment of strategy
- Change is incremental, proceeding by trial and error, with the means gradually worked out
- What is desirable is based on a comparison with the present situation
- Strategies for the organisation emerge out of subsystem strategies
- Overall co-ordination is achieved through formal planning procedures and managers' associations with the subsystems

executive to bind together the contributions of rational systematic analysis, political and power theories, and organisational behaviour concepts. It helps executives achieve cohesion and identify with new directions. It allows them to deal with power relationships and individual behaviour needs, and permits them to use the best possible informational and analytical inputs in choosing their major courses of action.

Obviously, there is a problem with allowing strategy to be developed from within subsystems; unless efforts are made, the organisational strategy is likely to be a mishmash of unco-ordinated initiatives. However, there are two main mechanisms whereby overall co-ordination is achieved. First, leader-managers are personally involved with many subsystems and thus can informally pass on knowledge about initiatives around the organisation. Second, alongside emerging strategies there will almost always be some form of formal planning procedure that forces leader-managers to look ahead and give at least a little consideration to the strategies of other subsystems.

With such an approach, it isn't surprising that different 'logics' apply to the determination of 'substrategies' within the organisation, since there is no reason why one subsystem should work the same way as another; indeed, for all subsystems to work in the same way is likely to be inappropriate.

How might the marketing and operations functions develop strategy in different ways and develop different strategies?
- In what way is logical incrementalism *logical*?

Disjointed incrementalism[8]

A more extreme version of incrementalism is disjointed incrementalism. Here issue handling and formulation of strategy are incoherent, in that those responsible for organisational direction don't bother to look far ahead (lip service is all that's paid to any formal planning process), nor do they make much effort to co-ordinate what they are doing with other leader-managers. Instead, the concentration of senior leader-managers is on their own goals within a short time horizon – months rather than years – the long term being heavily discounted.

As with logical incrementalism, there are problems of ensuring that the strategies of the subsystems have some sort of reasonable fit to the organisational strategy. With disjointed incrementalism this co-ordination comes about through negative co-ordination,[9] meaning that precautions are taken to ensure that the decisions of the subsystems aren't in flat contradiction with each other. This should be contrasted with the planning approach to strategy formulation, where there is positive co-ordination, with all subsystems 'singing from the same hymn sheet'.

The main characteristics of the disjointed incrementalist approach are listed in Exhibit 5.9. This approach sees organisations as 'organised anarchies' characterised by extreme ambiguity. First, the issue handlers have inconsistent and ill-defined preferences, tending to discover their goals through action rather than through thought. Second, leader-managers have only a loose understanding of means and ends, and thus trial-and-error learning is the dominant method of gaining knowledge. Third, there is fluid participation in the handling of the issue: participants come and go from the decision process and thus anticipating who will be involved in the process is difficult. A strategy that emerges under disjointed incrementalism is considered a 'success' when it has widespread support. Decisions are made when an issue happens to meet with a set of people and a set of feasible alternatives.

EXHIBIT 5.9

The disjointed incrementalist approach

- Organisations are organised anarchies with a variety of inconsistent and ill-defined preferences
- Issues and those who might handle them interact more or less at random
- Power is dispersed and not well defined, with the consequence that the individuals who are involved in handling an issue vary over time
- Cause-and-effect relations are not understood, with the organisational learning coming from trial and error
- Overall co-ordination of subsystem strategic direction is through negative 'co-ordination'

DISCUSSION POINT 5.4

Give concrete examples of the situations under which each of the four ways of seeking understanding might be applicable.

- How can disjointed incrementalism be part of strategic management when strategic management is supposed to be considering the well-being of the organisation as a whole in the long term?
- In Section 5.6.1, *rational* issue handling was considered. This suggests that incremental issue handling isn't rational. Reflect on the definition of *rational* given earlier: is incremental issue handling rational or not?
- How do the views of means and ends change in the four ways of seeking understanding?

KEY CONCEPT

There are two main ways in which leader-managers seek understanding of issues: using the rational and incremental approaches. In the rational approach both ends and means are fairly well known and, very broadly, analysis starts from a blank sheet of paper. In the incremental approach ends and means are less well recognised or, in the extreme, aren't known at all. Change is heavily influenced by the present situation and is incremental.

5.7 Information, knowledge and learning

A prerequisite for any rational response to an issue is knowledge. Knowledge has become recognised as the prerequisite for wealth creation for the developed world, where it has been realised that knowledge and the knowledge worker are the dominant creators of wealth. This requires both individuals and organisations to update their knowledge continuously.

5.7.1 Information and knowledge

In a business context, information may be defined as data that are perceived by an employee to be of use or potential use in their job. Knowledge is the result of internalising information; it is the outcome of meshing together and reconciling pieces of information. Accounting principles are available to all and as such are information; it is their internalisation in a person's brain that changes information into knowledge.

Thus information can be considered as the raw material from which knowledge is produced. Unlike information, knowledge is anchored in the beliefs and commitment of its holder. It is essentially related to human action and is a function of a particular stance, perspective and intention;[10] knowledge is to 'some end'.

The distinction between information and knowledge can be paralleled in the distinction between information and knowledge workers.[11] Information workers process information without significant modification: for example, people working in a call centre are information workers. On the other hand, knowledge workers add value to the original information: for example, by interpreting the outputs from a linear programming application or by explaining the causes of an adverse variance.

5.7.2 Tacit and explicit knowledge

Knowledge can be considered to be of two kinds. Some knowledge can be formalised so that it can be passed on in codified form.[12] Engineering formulae and accounting conventions are examples. This is **explicit knowledge**: it tends to be public, defined, documented and objective. However, in almost all activities explicit knowledge isn't the only form of knowledge required, particularly to carry out the activity well. What's also required is **tacit knowledge**, knowledge that is personal, ill- or undefined and subjective. This is seen most readily in skills that come from doing, and nowhere is this better seen than in sports. The science of striking a golf ball or of sailing has been fully explored and is available to any golfer or sailor. But what separates the excellent from the merely competent is the application of tacit knowledge; the ability of a golfer to recognise the lie of the ball, to select the appropriate club and to adjust for the slope and speed of the green; the recognition by the yachtsman of an imminent change in wind direction and how and when to adjust the sails to meet it.

There are three main differences between tacit and explicit knowledge. First, they differ in their ease of communication. Explicit knowledge can be easily communicated and made available widely because it is 'objective' knowledge. Tacit knowledge is 'subjective' knowledge that resides in an individual and so can't be communicated through objective means; the main means of transmission is close interaction between people, the master–apprentice relationship, to build up understanding. Second, the two forms of knowledge differ in how they are created. Explicit knowledge can be generated through formal study, whereas tacit knowledge can only be created through practical experience, through 'learning by doing'. Third, tacit and explicit knowledge differ in their potential for aggregation and appropriation; for example, explicit knowledge can be stored in computers and used by many people. This isn't the case with tacit knowledge.

Organisations often wish to take tacit knowledge and turn it into explicit knowledge – in this way they can centralise and more easily control business processes. The problem with doing this is that knowledge becomes standardised and the organisation may have difficulty responding to new threats and opportunities. Explicit knowledge is inevitably a selection of the tacit knowledge available, and it is bound to be less rich than the original.[13]

DISCUSSION
POINT 5.5 Strategic management is both an art and a science. Which part do you think represents tacit knowledge and which explicit?

The greater importance traditionally placed on explicit knowledge in Anglo-Saxon cultures means that the most easily codifiable aspects of management will tend to dominate management thinking: accounting, finance, economics and law will be far more influential than will human resources, employee relations and creativity.[14] The Germans, Dutch and Swedes make a distinction between *Wissenschaft*, literally knowledgemanship, and *Technik*, the making and running of things. Both are of equal status, with *Wissenschaft* used to improve *Technik*. *Technik* includes everything necessary to make techniques work, and good leader-management. The Japanese put a great deal of emphasis on tacit knowledge.

5.7.3 Individual and organisational knowledge

As well as splitting knowledge into the two types – tacit and explicit – it's also useful to split it into knowledge that resides in the individual and that which resides within the group. The types of knowledge contained within these two dimensions are shown in Exhibit 5.10.[15]

At the level of the individual, explicit knowledge is the formal theoretical knowledge that is contained within an individual's brain, such things as accounting principles and how to do certain operations in a spreadsheet. This is termed *embrained knowledge* and is concerned with 'knowing'. Tacit individual knowledge is termed

EXHIBIT 5.10

Types and ownership of knowledge (from Lam, 1998)

		Ownership of knowledge	
		Individual	*Group*
Type of knowledge	*Explicit*	Embrained knowledge	Encoded knowledge
	Tacit	Embodied knowledge	Embedded knowledge

Source: Adapted from Lam A., Tacit Knowledge, Organisational Learning and Innovation . . . pp 9–11[14]

embodied knowledge; it is action-oriented knowhow created from hands-on experience. It is about 'doing', and the creation of tacit knowledge is inseparable from its application.

At the level of the group, explicit knowledge is termed *encoded knowledge* and would include such things as manuals, written-down procedures and company-specific spreadsheet templates. *Embedded knowledge* is tacit knowledge that is held within the group. It resides within the group's routines, the relationships within the group and the group culture.

5.7.4 Learning

Knowledge is a prerequisite for initiating and coping with rational change and is created through learning. Learning is the detection and correction of those deficiencies in knowledge that make an individual or organisation less efficient and effective than it might be.[16] Learning can take place at both the individual and organisational levels; however, as the origin of organisational learning is individual learning, it is important first to consider the learning process of the individual.

5.8 Individual mental models and individual learning

5.8.1 Individual mental models

People use mental models of the situations they find themselves in both when deciding whether an issue should come 'on the agenda' and when handling it. A person's mindset is the complete set of their mental models. The mapping of the 'real' world and a person's mindset are depicted in Exhibit 5.11. Some of the mental models in the mindset consist of fairly well-understood sets of cause-and-effect relationships, and these are illustrated in the mindset as well-defined shapes, representing such things as spreadsheet financial planning models, budgetary systems, forecasting methods and the organisational pay structure. The less well-defined shapes represent less well-defined models, such as what success means in the organisation, or what the values are.

The defined portions of the mindset exist within a 'jelly' of broader concepts and feelings, which are often expressed as metaphors. Thinking in terms of a metaphor

EXHIBIT 5.11

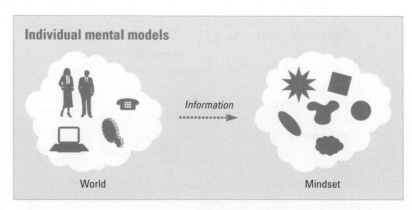

helps many business people understand their organisation by providing the 'big picture' of how it works. For example, business competition is often thought of in military terms, such as offensive, encirclement, attack and campaign (and the original meaning of the word *strategy* was 'the art of the general'), with the organisation seen as an army at war. It's important to bear in mind that metaphors offer a partial comparison: commercial organisations are not exactly like armies, and business competition isn't exactly like warfare. Metaphors concentrate on the similarities and ignore the differences.

The classical metaphor used in business is of the organisation as a machine: the expressions 'the market mechanism' and 'the value chain' are machine metaphors. In certain circumstances, considering an organisation as a machine is likely to be appropriate – for example, where the business processes are simple and straightforward and every product or service is meant to be identical and where the environment is not changing rapidly or in a turbulent fashion. As firms in developed economies move towards knowledge-based enterprises, however, the machine metaphor is likely to be a less valuable way of viewing the world. Morgan[17] has identified eight metaphors for the workings of organisations, viewing them as brains, cultures, machines, organisms, political systems, psychic prisons, instruments of domination and of flux and transformation. Perhaps viewing an organisation as a brain or as in flux and transformation would be more valuable than viewing it as a machine. However, as Morgan points out, the value of using more than one metaphor is that it allows a person or an organisation to view issues from more than one 'angle', making issue handling open to more than one interpretation.

DISCUSSION
POINT 5.6

Give examples of where thinking of an organisation as being like a machine might be appropriate.
- Are metaphors paradigms?
- Where do metaphors fit into Exhibit 5.11?

5.8.2 Modes of learning

In Exhibit 5.11 information comes to the mindset from the 'real' world. This information, the raw material for knowledge creation, is likely to call for focus on one part of the mindset – on one or two mental models within it. An issue may be dealt with in a pre-programmed manner, using recipes to deal with it, or it may be tackled in a more reflective way, perhaps using the tools of strategic management. It would be expected that the mindset would be changed as a result of the new information. These changes in the mindset are learning.

Single- and double-loop learning

How much learning accompanies a change in mindset depends on the circumstances. People are constantly engaged in the cycle of implementation, monitoring to obtain feedback information on the consequences, understanding this information and then implementing once more, as shown in the upper diagram in Exhibit 5.12. Any learning in this mode of operating has been termed *single-loop learning*.[18] The learning that takes place is rather superficial, in the sense that it leaves untouched the 'mindset jelly' – the deeper mental models that we all carry around with us.

Single-loop learning provides model enhancement: any learning that takes place is

EXHIBIT 5.12

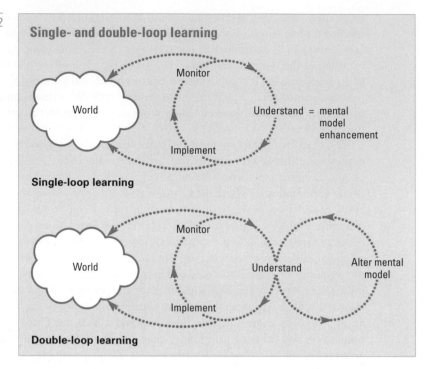

Single- and double-loop learning

Single-loop learning

Double-loop learning

through monitoring the effects of a decision and adjusting the mental model accordingly. This produces only *shallow learning*, – enhancements to the person's mental model sufficient to keep the business processes for which they are responsible matched to a situation that is changing slowly and in ways that can be closely predicted. Suppose that organisational performance is seen to be unsatisfactory and that costs are becoming unsustainable: the mental model might immediately suggest that labour costs must be reduced and a no-hiring policy might be implemented. The consequence on costs would be monitored, and learning would occur if cost savings differed from the expected. The learning would be a fuller understanding of the known cause-and-effect relationships; the mental model would be enhanced but not radically changed.

Single-loop learning is incremental and evolutionary in that changes are within the existing mindset. Sometimes, particularly when the recipe that is adopted in single-loop learning doesn't seem to be working any more, more profound learning is invoked, termed *double-loop learning*. This is also shown in Exhibit 5.12. In double-loop learning the change is revolutionary – the mental model is transformed. Here the fundamental pattern of thinking is changed. When the issue of cost is considered, for example, transformational learning would take place if it was realised that the market has moved from being a price-conscious one to one that demands innovative products. The whole basis of competition would be reassessed.

The characteristics of single- and double-loop learning are summarised in Exhibit 5.13.

Recall recent cases in which you have learned through single- and double-loop learning.

EXHIBIT 5.13

Modes of learning

Type of learning	Type of change to the mental model	Form	Example from	to
Single-loop	Enhancement	Altering a cause-and-effect relationship	A 2% change in advertising spend will cause a 10% change in sales	A 5% change in advertising spend will cause a 10% change in sales
Double-loop	Transformation	Altering an assumption in the mindset	Belief in the command-and-control form of management	Belief in the value of participation by the workforce

KEY CONCEPT Learning is the same as a change in a mental model. There are two broad types of learning: single-loop learning within the existing mindset and double-loop learning, where one or more assumptions in the mindset is changed. In double-loop learning there is model transformation, whereby there is a move to a new pattern of thinking. Model transformation is revolutionary change.

5.8.3 Systems thinking

A prerequisite for profound learning is systems thinking. Senge[19] has most recently been associated with this view, but considerable understanding of systems has emerged over the last few decades. Much thinking in Europe and the Americas has traditionally been reductionist, whereby an issue is broken down into smaller, handleable 'chunks' and understanding of the characteristics of these smaller chunks is sought. The assumption is that the whole can be understood by combining the understanding of the parts. A more holistic approach has traditionally been taken in Asian societies.[20]

The problem with reductionist thinking is that the whole is often more than the sum of the parts; for example, a hand is more than the sum of the nerves, muscles, molecules, etc. of which it's composed. Surrounding and embedded within the parts are ephemeral factors such as organisation and control that make a hand a hand rather than a leg. A similar situation exists within organisations, with the ephemeral factors residing largely within the internal context.

As well as the sum being greater than the parts, two other aspects of systems thinking are important. The first is interconnectivity: few processes are completely isolated from others around them, and so the leader-managers in charge must take into consideration the impact of their actions on others. The other is feedback, whereby the outputs of processes at any one time will be affected by the residual influence of past outputs. This is particularly obvious in relationships; building up good relationships in one period will result in a better reception for actions in a subsequent period.

5.9 Learning organisations

5.9.1 Knowledge-intensive firms and learning organisations

In the last several years there has been a growing interest in knowledge-intensive firms[21] such as advertising agencies and management consultancies, where the firm's resources overwhelmingly lie in knowledge rather than more tangible assets. These firms have to be learning organisations, as they must keep their knowledge up to date. However, while knowledge-intensive firms may exhibit the most extreme forms of knowledge usage, all firms need to upgrade their knowledge base, and thus Stata's[22] view of the sustainability of competitive advantage would appear to be universally applicable: 'The ability to learn faster than competitors may be the only truly sustainable competitive advantage.'

If this view is accepted, even if only in part, then a prime task for leader-managers is to foster learning within their organisation; indeed, to turn their organisation into a learning organisation. A learning organisation may be defined as 'an organisation skilled in continually seeking out knowledge deficiencies, acquiring, creating, spreading and managing knowledge, and expert at modifying its behaviour to reflect its new knowledge.'

DISCUSSION POINT 5.8

The definition of a learning organisation doesn't include *destroying* knowledge. Should this be a part of learning?

Thus a learning organisation is dealing with knowledge. Some of this knowledge will remain simply individual knowledge, some will become organisational knowledge. In setting up a learning organisation, leader-managers have to sustain individual learning and establish procedures and the appropriate climate to encourage organisational learning.

Each element of the first part of the definition of a learning organisation will be discussed in the next three subsections: seeking out knowledge deficiencies; acquiring knowledge; and creating, spreading and managing knowledge.

5.9.2 Seeking out knowledge deficiencies

For an organisation to sustain itself, it must recognise that it faces gaps or challenges, mismatches between what it currently is or does and what it wishes to do or be. The challenge will often come from outside the organisation, shown through falling sales or threats from aggressive competitors, for example. However, it could also be generated by leader-managers to stimulate the organisation through setting 'impossible' tasks, an approach apparently favoured by Japanese firms.[23] In short, the organisation is given a challenge, whereby variation and creative chaos are fed into it. The challenge will provide the purpose that is vital for learning and spark creativity.

5.9.3 Acquiring information and knowledge from outside the organisation

Knowledge can be acquired by taking information into the organisation for its subsequent interpretation. It can also be acquired by introducing people with the required knowledge into the organisation. The main methods of knowledge acquisition are described below.

Accessing public domain information

Very large amounts of information are now available to organisations, some free from government and some through payment to the many organisations that exist to provide information. The Internet is rapidly becoming an enormous repository of information, although the quality is variable and often unvalidated.

Carrying out market research and business intelligence activity

Traditional market research methods are used to obtain codified information about the firm from a customer and potential customer perspective. Focus groups are becoming more significant in unearthing tacit knowledge. Business intelligence systems use formalised methods and activities to obtain information on business trends, especially the actions of competitors.

Engaging in benchmarking

A formalised way of obtaining knowledge about business processes is **benchmarking**, whereby a business compares its operations with those of similar organisations elsewhere.[24] The Department of Trade and Industry in the UK has a scheme, 'Inside UK Enterprise',[25] whereby companies invite people from other organisations to visit them and learn from their experiences. Although access to direct competitors may not be possible, where a business is part of a corporation benchmarking can be undertaken between the associated businesses; for example, BAT Industries has carried out benchmarking among its many cigarette-making factories around the world. Benchmarking can also be carried out between noncompetitors in the same business; for example, a local brewery in the south-west of England could compare its operations with those of a local brewery in the west of Scotland. Benchmarking can also be across industries; for example, both car parts operations and electronic component factoring demand great attention to fulfilling customer orders, inventory and quality control. Thus a firm engaged in supplying car parts could benchmark itself against an electronics component supplier.

DISCUSSION
POINT 5.9

How does seeking knowledge deficiencies link to Exhibit 5.4?

- If you wished to benchmark the operations of a business school, what other organisations could you chose for comparison?

Gathering information through relationships

Stakeholders, particularly customers, are excellent sources of information on knowledge deficiencies. Thus it's important to develop the organisational capability to pick up weak signals from them. The key individuals in this capability are not only salespersons but also many of the employees engaged in the firm's operations. Some firms have such close relationships with their business customers that their employees sometimes work inside their customers' premises.

It's also very important that leader-managers are involved in their business environment through membership of local and national associations: the local chamber of commerce, their particular trade association and perhaps learned societies.

Introducing diversity into an organisation

Leader-managers must have at least as many potential responses as the number of potential disturbances in the environment. One aspect of this is that there must be a range of diverse thinking among the dominant coalition for the organisation at least to think of ways of dealing with environmental changes. Blinkered thinking isn't going to be able to keep the organisation viable.

There are two main methods of introducing diversity into an organisation:

- **Recruit new people**   This is often the response of a failing organisation – to sack the managing director and other senior staff and recruit others who seem more in tune with the environment. But such recruitment can also be done when things are going well to deliberately introduce new ways of thinking into the organisation. One common approach is to appoint non-executive directors to the board. This should introduce new ways of thinking, and it often brings with it relationships that are very important to the firm. This is one of the reasons that serving politicians and ex-ministers find a ready home on the boards of many companies in the UK and many other countries.

- **Employ consultants**   Consultants will generally have been actively engaged in an area for several years and will be able to introduce best practice to the organisation. If they are part of a large consultancy practice, the individual consultants will be able to call on many forms of expertise. Apart from their cost, the weakness of consultants is that they have a tendency to apply a standardised approach to the organisation they are seeking to advise, rather than a more individualised one tailored to the particular circumstances in which the company finds itself.

5.9.4   *The organisation's role in creating and spreading knowledge*

An organisation can establish the appropriate conditions for creating and spreading knowledge in two broad ways. First, it can support individual learning. Second, it can establish the conditions whereby individual knowledge becomes converted into group knowledge. This involves knowledge management.

Individual learning

Individual learning is the source of organisational learning. Five conditions seem to be important to encourage individual learning:

- **Provide a purpose for learning**   Knowledge is the reconciliation and meshing together of pieces of information, and how they are reconciled and meshed together will depend on why it is being done. Thus the person creating knowledge must have a purpose, and from the organisation's view it's obviously useful if the individual's purpose coincides closely with that of the organisation. Purpose focuses debate and guides the information that needs to be obtained and the knowledge that is to be created, acquired and managed.

DISCUSSION
POINT 5.10

How can an organisation provide a purpose for its employees?

- Provide education and training   Since personal mastery is one element of the learning organisation,[26] the organisation should provide facilities for people to receive the appropriate education and training.

- Give time to search out information and digest it into knowledge   People need an environment in which they can fail yet be able to use the learning gained from the experience. The story is told of a promising junior IBM executive who lost $10 million in a new venture. When he was called into the chief executive's office he blurted out, 'I guess you want my resignation.' To which the boss replied, 'You can't be serious. We've just spent $10 million educating you!'[27]

- Provide an appropriate level of autonomy   Individuals will unearth more tacit knowledge the greater the level of autonomy they are allowed.[28] They will also tend to take a wider view of their activities and thus understand where their activities fit into those of the whole organisation.

- Encourage redundant information   Redundancy of information means that information not of immediate use is made available. This could be done by establishing a knowledge base with effectively universal access. The greater the redundancy of information provided to people, the greater the learning.

Knowledge management

An organisation will have two concerns should learning remain solely with the individual. First, there is the worry that the organisation won't be able to continue appropriating this knowledge if the employee leaves the company; the individual will take the value with them. Exhibit 5.14a shows what organisations thought the effect of a key employee leaving had been.[29] These findings were for the large organisations; the consequences for small firms would be expected to be much greater.

The second concern is that the organisation is failing to exploit individual knowledge, because it isn't being shared with others. Exhibit 5.14b indicates the reasons for problems associated with sharing knowledge in companies with some experience of knowledge management. Contrary to previous findings,[30] where the main barriers to knowledge sharing were perceived to be cultural and personal, in only a relatively small number of cases is the culture considered to be a barrier to knowledge sharing; in general, the main concern is with the time individuals have to share knowledge.

 EXHIBIT 5.14A

The effect of a key employee leaving the organisation

base: all respondents (100)

- Lost knowledge of best practice in specific area — 49%
- Damaged relationship with key client/supplier — 43%
- Lost information vital to the running of the business — 14%
- Lost significant income — 13%

Source: KPMG Management Consulting, 'Knowledge management', research report, 1998.

EXHIBIT 5.14B

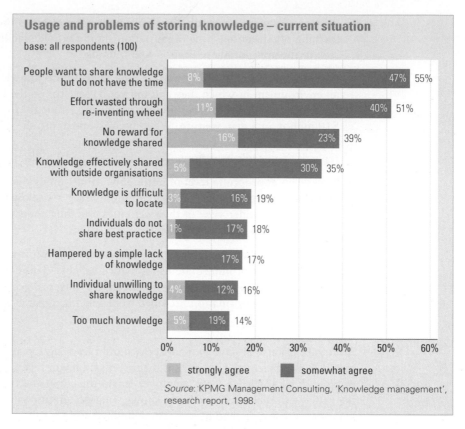

Usage and problems of storing knowledge – current situation

base: all respondents (100)

	strongly agree	somewhat agree	total
People want to share knowledge but do not have the time	8%	47%	55%
Effort wasted through re-inventing wheel	11%	40%	51%
No reward for knowledge shared	16%	23%	39%
Knowledge effectively shared with outside organisations	5%	30%	35%
Knowledge is difficult to locate	3%	16%	19%
Individuals do not share best practice	1%	17%	18%
Hampered by a simple lack of knowledge		17%	17%
Individual unwilling to share knowledge	4%	12%	16%
Too much knowledge	5%	19%	14%

strongly agree   somewhat agree

Source: KPMG Management Consulting, 'Knowledge management', research report, 1998.

This could be a consequence of the delayering and lean staffing that have occurred over the past decade.

Knowledge management is the systematic capture and structuring of knowledge within an organisation in order to improve business performance. There appear to be two dominant modes of knowledge management, depending on the role played by explicit and tacit knowledge.[31] These modes are dominant, but each is not used to the exclusion of the other. The first is what has been termed a codified knowledge management strategy, whereby the firm lays great importance on 'downloading' tacit and personal knowledge and making it explicit for reuse by others. Hansen *et al.* describe the situation at the Center for Business Knowledge at management consultants Ernst & Young.[32] Here 250 people manage an electronic repository and help consultants find and use information. The sort of information stored there consists of such things as interview guides, work schedules, market segmentation data and presentations made to clients. So, for example, a consultant wishing to put together a proposal to a client could access the relevant market segment data and view the past presentations made on similar subjects. Thus the reusability of past efforts could be high.

The second dominant mode of knowledge sharing puts the emphasis on tacit knowledge. This is termed a *personalised* knowledge-sharing strategy, since the sharing takes place through personal contact, not through codified documentation. Bain, the Boston Consulting Group and McKinsey use the personalised approach. When given an assignment, a consultant in such a firm would first access a database providing information on the skills and experience of all the company employees.

From this list they would decide whom they would like to include in their network of contacts to help tackle the assignment. The consultant would then meet them personally, and through videoconferencing, e-mail and telephone. This culture of networking is supported and reinforced by moving people between offices, supporting a culture in which consultants are expected to return phone calls from colleagues promptly, and by keeping the register of expertise current.

What is known as data mining, but is far better termed 'knowledge discovery in databases', is now becoming an important feature in many organisations. Data mining allows firms with large amounts of data to use such esoteric statistical techniques as neural nets to unearth patterns in the data. For example, an insurance company has used its database on customers to unearth a linkage between fraudulent claims made and a combination of other variables, such as the age of the policy holder and where they live.

5.10 Particulars for top teams

5.10.1 Political concerns

So far the broad way in which issues are handled and the general features of learning organisations have been considered. Now we look at the particular concerns of the top team, the dominant coalition in an organisation.

An important aspect of the process of strategic issue handling is that decisions are only rarely taken by the lone leader-manager. Overwhelmingly, decisions are taken only after consultation involving many people in many interest units, and senior leader-managers spend a considerable amount of time dealing with conflicting views and with different areas of expertise. In the case of strategic issues, these are handled by the dominant coalition. A coalition is an informal group of people pursuing shared objectives. Most often the dominant coalition is composed of some members of the board of directors or is a group of leader-managers at the head of an important unit. The members of the dominant coalition will inevitably bring to the activity their own cognitive and psychological capabilities and styles, and their own prejudices, and they will be doing so within group and organisational contexts.

Politics plays a large role in strategic issue handling. The political view[33] holds that organisations are comprised of people with partly conflicting preferences, and that decisions are the result of a process in which the preferences of the most powerful people triumph. The leader-managers often attempt to change the power structure by engaging in political tactics such as coalition formation, the strategic use of information and the employment of outside experts.

KEY CONCEPT Strategic issue handling involves both the cognitive and psychological characteristics of the individual members of the dominant coalition. These individual characteristics are employed within an organisational context in which politics plays a significant role.

5.10.2 Top team issues

The most comprehensive study of strategic issue handling was undertaken in the 1980s by a team from Bradford University.[34] Their study looked at 150 decisions in both profit-seeking and not-for-profit UK organisations. Of the outcomes 138 were positive, to do something; seven were to maintain the status quo (e.g. not to make a takeover bid, not to relocate); and five were negative, such as to close retail outlets, to close a hospital. The average organisation in the study employed 2600 people, with the smallest employing 100.

The issues that were considered by the leader-managers have been placed into ten categories, which are listed and described in Exhibit 5.15. It can be seen that leader-managers were involved in a wide range of issues – from 'big-bang' issues such as buying new-generation aircraft to the rather more 'incremental' ones such as changing the source of component supplies.

The ten categories label the issues but don't say much about their characteristics. The issues could be classified along two main dimensions. First, there is the rarity of likely meetings between the group of senior leader-managers on similar issues, indicated by the number of times per year that such an issue occurs.

Rarity is an important feature of an issue, since it's very likely that leader-managers have 'set responses' to the commonly occurring issues but not to those that occur rarely. The rarity with which issues arise is set out in Exhibit 5.15.

The second dimension that was used to categorise an issue was its consequentiality. Consequentiality has four components:

- Radicality   how much things would be changed in the organisation as a consequence of the associated decision.
- Seriousness   how bad it would be for the organisation if things went wrong.
- Diffusion   the number of criteria by which the correctness of the decision was judged (e.g. costs, morale, market share).
- Persistence[35]   how far ahead the people handling the issue looked when considering the consequences of the options they were considering.

The rankings of the consequentiality of issues are shown in the final column of Exhibit 5.15. In the study the persistence averaged 8.1 years, with a maximum of 20 years. Note that persistence is not the same as the elapsed time over which issues were considered. This averaged 12.4 days, with a maximum of four years.

The Bradford team identified three types of issue: **vortex issues,** so called because they tended to suck many people into the activity, which were complex and controversial; **tractable issues,** which were unusual but not very controversial; and **familiar issues,** which were the least complex and only mildly controversial. The characteristics of these three forms of issue are listed in Exhibit 5.16. Note that the strongly controversial nature of some issues means that they are likely to be politically charged.

DISCUSSION POINT 5.11

Summarise the important findings in Exhibits 5.15 and 5.16.
- Which of the Hickson *et al.* types of issue listed in Exhibit 5.15 would you think were most likely to be vortex issues?

KEY CONCEPT

In its study the Bradford team identified three types of strategic issue handled by top teams: the vortex, the tractable and the familiar. These types were categorised mainly according to their complexity and the level of controversy that surrounds them, although other factors played a part.

EXHIBIT 5.15

Issues for top teams (adapted from Hickson *et al.*, 1991)

Issue category	Examples	Rarity*	Consequentiality†
Boundaries	Purchases of, and mergings with, other organisations, e.g. whether to buy a subsidiary company, to merge colleges.	6	7
Controls	Planning, budgeting and requisite data processing, e.g. what the five-year 'strategic plan' or annual 'business plan' are to be, whether to purchase a computer.	7	5
Domains	Marketing and distribution, e.g. whether to bypass wholesalers and distribute direct, introduce 'no-charge' banking, standardise a name for all branches of the company.	8	6
Inputs	Finance and other supplies, e.g. whether to raise funds by a share issue, or (local government) by a lottery, or to change the sources of supply of components.	10	10
Locations	Site and sites dispersal, e.g. whether to build a new plant abroad, to move the company's principal offices, to reduce dispersal (by closing branches).	3	1
Personnel	Job assessment, training, unions, e.g. whether to make a first productivity agreement, to use consultants to regrade all staff, to resist unionisation.	4	8
Products	New products, e.g. whether to launch a new beer, a new glass-impregnated cement, or to generate electricity.	9	2
Reorganisations	Internal restructurings, e.g. whether to insert regional level between branches and headquarters, merge departments, change overseas branches into subsidiaries ('domestication' in host nations).	1	3
Services	New, expanded or reduced services, e.g. whether to launch a novel form of interdisciplinary university degree, to increase municipal housing, to decrease European air services.	2	9
Technologies	Equipment and/or premises, e.g. whether to invest in new machinery and buildings, buy 'new-generation' aircraft, close geriatric wards.	5	4

* 1 = rarest: 10 = most common. † 1 = most consequential, 10 = least consequential

EXHIBIT 5.16

The characteristics of the three types of strategic issue (adapted from Hickson et al., 1991)

Vortex issues	*Most complex* Serious consequences Involves many internal interest groups and external stakeholders *Most controversial* Contentious Heavily influenced by external stakeholders
Tractable issues	*Mildly complex* Less serious consequences There are consequences to many internal interest groups Fewer interested parties Are met rarely *Least controversial* Little contention Interested parties have roughly equal influence
Familiar issues	*Least complex* Commonly met Limited consequences *Mildly controversial* Mainly influenced by internal interest groups Uneven influence across the interest groups

5.11 Support for group processes

5.11.1 The requirement for support

It's at the highest levels in an organisation where issue handlers meet a more diverse set of stakeholders and where the vortex issues are generally handled. Although when it comes to *action* the ideal is for all of the dominant coalition *to* sing from the same hymn sheet – for consensus – this is not what is required in the *thinking* that goes on before a decision is taken. What is needed is contention[36] and a way of keeping this alive. Thus the concern isn't so much with the output from the decision making but with the process.

The question of how an organisation nurtures the required dialectic breaks down into two further questions. First, how do you get the divergent views and different mindsets into an organisation? This has been discussed in Section 4.7 and again in Section 5.9.3. The second is how you get the different mindsets to share their views with each other in a constructive way.

The second consideration is how you get the diversity to blossom, as in many organisations the natural focus is on suppressing controversy, and in the process encouraging a bunker mentality.[37] A major quest is to establish the appropriate group processes, bearing in mind that the team has to work together in the future. In Pascale's words, 'How do you get people to disagree without being disagreeable?'[38]

5.11.2 The strengths and weaknesses of group processes

Issue handling in large organisations is very much an interactive process. The issues faced are complex, requiring many informational inputs, and have widespread repercussions; and implementation is difficult. So very often issue handling is performed by a group. The advantages of using a group of people are that the group has more information and knowledge than any individual, and implementation becomes easier if the implementors have been involved in the issue discussions. The disadvantages are that it takes more time and effort than individual issue handling, and compromise is often sought rather than a clear-cut decision. Furthermore, group processes suffer from the weaknesses listed in Exhibit 5.17.

Conventional meetings are associated with disorganised and unfocused activity, domination by one or two members of the group and the consequent inhibition of others, and the social pressures to conform. The aim of group support systems (GSS) is to reduce these 'process losses', and especially to help a more democratic issue-handling process to emerge, and reduce the muddling through apparent in many group meetings.

As well as rewarding the individuals and the team, a GSS also needs to be able to facilitate negotiation between members of the team while the group session is underway, rather than simply as a result of informal discussions after the session. Although a GSS could be used to seek compromise, the ideal is to develop consensus about what should be done. If consensus or an amicable compromise is achieved, then this should provide the context to facilitate the conversion of agreement into a commitment to action. The emphasis is on sufficing rather than achieving a 'best' decision.

It is now becoming more common to use a trained facilitator to improve the

EXHIBIT 5.17

Dynamics observed in group processes[39]		
Behaviour	**Description**	**Explanation**
Groupthink	Small groups behave and make decisions as if they were infallible	Group closes itself off from outside information
Risky shift	Groups make decisions that pose higher risk than individuals do on their own	Assumption of protection by size of group, diffusion of blame
Commitment errors	Individuals take on tasks that are difficult and fail to adjust goals or expectations as work progresses	Individuals fear embarrassment or group sanctions
Goal-setting errors	Groups frequently set more difficult goals after a failure	Compensation for past performance
The Abilene paradox	The group as a whole adopts a course of action contrary to the desires of most or all individual members	Members remain silent because they perceive agreement of other members or fear separation from the group if they disagree

quality of meetings, and there has also been considerable progress towards using information technology. For either to be successful they should offer one or more of:

- communication facilities between participants;
- enhanced modelling and interface facilities to permit voting and ranking for developing consensus;
- both qualitative and quantitative decision aids, as appropriate;
- decision aids with which the participants are comfortable;
- decision aids that are transparent in operation, so that the participants will understand and use the results;
- decision aids that are flexible, so that they do not constrain problem formulation.

They should also help to reduce the dysfunctional group processes listed in Exhibit 5.17.

5.11.3   Group support tools[40]

Four types of group support system (GSS) will be considered: keypad systems, the approaches that may be described as workstation systems, soft systems modelling and cognitive mapping.

Keypad systems

In keypad systems each member of the group is provided with a personal handset that generally provides a two-line display and a numeric keypad. Typically, the numeric keypad is configured like a telephone layout and in appearance can be likened to a mobile phone. The keypads are linked to a central micoprocessor either by cable or by radio. One example is TeamWorker.

Typically, a facilitator will have agreed with the person calling the meeting on the questions that will be asked of the group. This is particularly likely to occur in situations where the activities are well structured, as in the case of beer- and lager-tasting panels for which keypad systems have been used. In other cases, the questions to be considered will emerge during the initial portion of the meeting and be input to the computer either by the facilitator or by an assistant.

Following the posing of a question the participants will be asked to respond using the keypad. The computer takes all the responses and then displays them on a public screen. At the simplest level, histograms can be displayed indicating the spread of responses. More sophisticated and informative displays may result from splitting up the whole set of responses; for example, it is common for the responses to be grouped according to the number of the handset, such as handsets numbered 1–9 given to salespeople and handsets numbered 10–15 to accountants. Then a distinction can be made between the responses of the two groups, which may stimulate a useful discussion.

Workstation systems

GSS offering high levels of technical support have been developed, notably by IBM. This groupware operates with a set of PCs linked by a local area network providing for direct individual input and for individual and aggregated information to be displayed to the group on a public screen. A typical set of modules is shown in Exhibit

EXHIBIT 5.18

Some of the modules in workstation systems	
LIST	This module combines ideas from each participant into one, publicly displayed list. Each participant enters their ideas at their PC independently of each other and thus in parallel.
BRAINSTORM	Similar to LIST, but with the ideas displayed publicly as they are typed in by the participant. Individuals can use this public list to further ideas.
DISCUSS	A publicly displayed list of all the ideas that the participants wish to discuss. The facilities include a timer to ensure that discussion time is allocated appropriately.
EDIT	A means of editing inputs.
ORGANISE	An outliner allowing ideas to be organised prior to further discussion.
RATE	This module enables each participant to rate an item, and for these individual ratings to be combined, and for histograms and an average rating to be displayed.
RANK	The same as RATE, but with participants ranking items in order.
VOTE	Used to register a yes or no vote for a particular item.

5.18. The sequencing of the modules is called 'script writing', with the module chosen to support the particular issue situation.

Participants can draft ideas privately at their workstations, passing promising suggestions to the public screen for discussion by the group, while quietly discarding, without embarrassment, suggestions that they think are weak. The display of many ideas on a public screen leads to productive discussions. When voting takes place, individual preferences can be expressed confidentially – a valuable feature if it is difficult to express views contrary to the dominant person or group. An action plan is formulated at the close of the meeting including concisely documented recommendations for future activity and assigning actions to be carried out by each of the participants. Because much of the communication is electronic, a permanent record of the session is automatically created.

Soft systems modelling (SSM)

SSM has been refined over many years by Checkland and his collaborators.[41] The facilitator's first consideration is to identify the issue owners and then to work with them to unearth those patterns, themes or features that encapsulate the symptoms of the situation, i.e. what makes people angry or depressed or produces other strong emotions. Working from these responses, the next step is to develop theoretical systems that, if implemented, would help resolve the issue.

These theoretical systems are only in a notional form at this stage. The next stage in SSM is to produce several 'root definitions' that specify concisely what the relevant system should be. There could be many root definitions, because there may be many perceptions about the issue. Consider a country's educational system: the stakeholders, with very differing objectives, include the government, children and adult users, teachers, law enforcement agencies, and religious bodies. It's very likely that each group could write a significantly different root definition of the same situation.

For example, a business systems planning system might have as one of its root definitions: 'a company-accepted method for determining the information systems needed to support the organisation's business needs and for the prioritising of information systems developments.' Working from this root definition, a conceptual model is created of what the real-world system will look like to match the root definition. This model is compared with the situation being analysed (and this may be an existing real-world system), with this comparison defining and focusing debate.

SODA and cognitive maps

Eden and his collaborators[42] have spent many years developing the ideas of cognitive mapping. Cognitive mapping is a technique set within an overriding SODA methodology that has been used extensively to help top teams handle messy strategic issues. Typically, the facilitator in a cognitive mapping process will discuss with each member of the issue-handling team their thoughts about the issue. A map will be drawn up reflecting (mapping) each participant's thought processes, particularly their cause-and-effect thinking. The cognitive map is a network of ideas that can be developed from written and spoken statements.

The individual cognitive map for each member of the issue-handling team would be input to a computer, and from the 'overlap' of these maps the areas of agreement and those of contention can be identified. It is the areas of contention that are then focused on in subsequent group sessions.

SUMMARY
- Leader-managers are making decisions within the context of long-running issues. Two types of decision can be recognised: the incremental and the transformational. Leader-managers need to put in place the context to support the organisation in continually upgrading its performance, both its operating performance to support the present and short-term future and its strategic thinking to help ensure its longer-term future. EXHIBIT 5.1, EXHIBIT 5.2
- Empirical research into issue handling clearly indicates that:
  - many issues follow the basic phases of awareness, understanding and action but they cycle through these stages, frequently repeating and often going deeper into analysis and following different paths in fits and starts;
  - perceived understanding about an issue and management's perception that it can do something sensible about it are the drivers for management to put effort into handling the issue; EXHIBITS 5.3 TO EXHIBIT 5.9
  - leader-managers, both individually and in groups, make widespread use of pre-programmed responses when reacting to issues;
  - there are four different approaches to gaining understanding of an issue. These are the technical rational, bounded rational, incremental and disjointed incremental approaches. There is widespread use of the bounded rational rather than the technical rational approach. Leader-managers generally seek a satisfactory option rather than the best.
- Knowledge can be placed in four categories: embrained and embodied for individual knowledge; encoded and embedded for organisational knowledge. Individual learning is the result of change to a person's mental model, with information enriching the embrained knowledge that is their mental model. There are two forms of learning, single-loop learning, where the mental model is enhanced, and double-loop learning, where the fundamentals of the mental model are changed

and the model is transformed. Enhanced forms of learning are associated with doing things better and with ordinary management. Revolutionary learning is associated with doing things differently and with extraordinary management. EXHIBITS 5.10 TO EXHIBIT 5.13

- A learning organisation is an organisation skilled in continually seeking out knowledge deficiencies as well as acquiring, creating, spreading and managing knowledge, and expert at modifying its behaviour to reflect its new knowledge. The organisation should support both individual and organisational learning. One of the leader-manager's tasks is to ensure that knowledge is retained within the organisation and the damage caused to the organisation's knowledge base through staff leaving is minimised. EXHIBIT 5.14

- The most senior management teams in an organisation deal with a wide range of issues. These have been classified into three types: vortex, tractable and familiar. Top teams need support in what can be complex decision issues, and several types of group support systems are available. One aim of such systems is to prevent groupthink; another is to allow people to disagree without being disagreeable. EXHIBITS 5.15 TO EXHIBIT 5.18

SELF-CHECK

1 Reconsider the learning outcomes for this chapter. Check that you feel confident that you can carry out the activities listed there.

2 Having read this chapter, you should be able to define the following terms:

absolve	information	resolve
decision making	issue	single-loop learning
decision taking	issue handling	soft information
dissolve	knowledge	solve
dominant coalition	paradigm	tacit knowledge
double-loop learning	pre-resolve	tractable issue
explicit knowledge	problem solving	vortex issue
familiar issue	programmed response	
heuristic	rational	

MINI-CASE

Victims of 'groupthink'[43]

With financial markets around the world in turmoil, it would be reassuring to know there was a safe hand on the economic tiller at home. But when the Bank of England's monetary policy committee navigates its course for interest rates this week, there will be nine hands on the tiller – and not all of them necessarily pulling in the same direction.

Is this cause for concern? Social psychologists have long debated which take better decisions: groups or individuals. Are two heads better than one or do too many cooks spoil the broth? As these conflicting adages imply, they have failed to reach a clear-cut answer.

Nonetheless, given that in many countries interest rates are set by committee, economists should pay more attention to the implications of group decision making in trying to understand how monetary policy operates. Committees behave differently from individuals. And one committee will behave differently from another, depending on the rules, informal norms and personalities involved.

Evaluating the 'quality' of decision making is fraught with difficulty because laboratory experiments in social psychology are necessarily somewhat artificial. But the consensus that emerges from several studies is that groups make better decisions than their average member would have done in isolation. However, they perform less effectively than the attributes of all their members imply: they are less than the sum of their parts.

In the early 1970s, the academic Irving Janis carried out a pioneering analysis of group decision making by looking at a series of US foreign policy decisions from 1940 onwards. He concluded that when the outcome was poor – the attempted invasion of Cuba at the Bay of Pigs in 1961 and the bombing of North Vietnam in 1965, for example – the decision-making process had been marked by undesirable features, which he labelled 'groupthink'.

- The decision makers formed a highly cohesive group that put pressure on internal dissenters to conform to the consensus view.
- The group developed an illusion of unanimity and correctness that in turn fostered a reluctance to evaluate alternative policies.
- The group negatively stereotyped outsiders who disagreed with its views.
- The group was almost always dominated by a highly directive leader.

These characteristics are not unheard-of in the marble committee rooms of the world's central banks. The consensus-seeking behaviour they promote is aggravated by other characteristics that differentiate central bank committees from other groups, such as juries or public inquiries.

First, the membership of central bank committees changes relatively slowly. This allows time for informal norms of behaviour to develop and for a cohesive 'insider' culture to develop.

Second, a committee setting interest rates is essentially taking the same decision repeatedly. The body of information on which decisions are based may change relatively little between meetings. This means that an individual committee member may be reluctant to alter his or her opinion in the face of changing circumstances – it might give the impression that they have simply conceded the superiority of someone else's argument.

Combined with the innate caution of all career central bankers, these characteristics mean that monetary policy committees may respond sluggishly to changing economic events. As Alan Blinder, former vice-chairman of the US Federal Reserve, has argued: 'Decision-making by committee may contribute to systematic policy errors by inducing the central bank to maintain its policy stance too long.'

This may help explain why independent central banks – many of which make policy by committee – have been found to preside over deeper recessions and reduce inflation at greater cost to jobs and incomes than those subservient to politicians.

The Bank of England fell victim to sluggishness and inertia in the early months of its independence last year. It raised interest rates too slowly in the face of strong domestic demand, although its job was made more difficult by the government's failure to impose a bigger increase in consumer taxes.

Does this imply that the monetary policy committee will be equally tardy in reducing interest rates to a neutral position as economic activity weakens, thereby exacerbating the looming downturn? Not necessarily.

Since the spring of this year the behaviour of the committee has changed remarkably. After months of unanimity, almost every decision has been disputed, and on two occasions Eddie George, the governor, has been forced to use his casting vote to break a deadlock.

The committee's critics have been appalled. They accuse it of incoherence, unpredictability and a lack of leadership. They lament that the policy is in the hands of unworldly academics with no sense of collective responsibility. Maybe so, but this is a price well worth paying to avoid the damaging inertia that results from a consensus-seeking culture.

But why has the monetary policy committee developed a culture so much more tolerant of dissent than that of other central banks? One reason is that the committee members – career central bankers and outside academics alike – have a clearly quantified inflation target and are held *individually* to account for the policies they recommend to hit it.

The monetary policy process in the UK is also highly transparent, with votes published in detailed minutes of the monthly meetings. Committee members cannot hide behind a consensus view. The same should be true of the Fed, where votes are also recorded publicly. But as Professor Blinder has observed: 'There is a tradition that dissent is a huge deal.' This reflects the fact that Fed chairmen hold enormous informal sway over committee members, one of the elements of 'groupthink'. Few of Mr George's colleagues, by contrast, are burdened by any sense of inferiority.

This analysis of group decision making contains good and bad news for Gordon Brown, the chancellor. It suggests that the Bank of England may avoid some of the mistakes of other independent central banks, but it also highlights a danger in his desire to join Europe's single currency.

The European Central Bank is more independent than the UK's but less transparent and more insistent on collective responsibility. Its interest rate setting will suffer as a result.

Discussion point 5.12

What suggestions do you have for improving decision making in the central banks?

* Apparently, there is a tradition that dissent is a huge deal in central bank decision making. Is dissent a good or a bad thing in this context?

FURTHER DISCUSSION POINTS

1 For GSM:
   • What were the issues that GSM had been confronting over the last decade?
   • What form of issue handling was taking place?
   • Who was taking the decisions?
   • What evidence is there that the firm was a learning organisation?
   • What sort of knowledge is there in GSM?
   • What does GSM's recruitment practice say about qualifications?
   • How were teams affecting strategy?
2 In what ways is strategic issue handling different from tactical issue handling?
3 In Chapter 1 the two ways of formulating strategy were discussed – the intended and the emergent. Which of the methods of seeking understanding do you think would be used in each of these two ways of forming strategy?
4 In Chapter 2 the 'cultural onion' was considered. How do single- and double-loop learning link to changes in the layers of the onion?

ASSIGNMENTS

1 Consider someone working in Birmingham and living in Nottingham, a distance of 50 miles. They wish to keep doing this, yet public transport between the two places is difficult and their partner wants use of the car to ferry their children to school. Another car seemed to be called for. The issue then became what car to buy. How could this issue be absolved, dissolved, pre-resolved, resolved and solved?
2 Reflect on how you yourselves, working as a group, have gone about handling the issues that you've been confronted with. What sort of issue-handling process did you use? How did it compare with those explored in this chapter?

FURTHER
READING

An excellent and very readable book on all forms of strategic decision making is that by Niels Noorderhaven, *Strategic Decision Making*, Addison-Wesley, 1995. Unfortunately, at the time this book is going to press, Niels' book is out of print.

The book by Gareth Morgan, *Images of Organization*, 2nd edn, Sage, 1997, is essential reading to provide many competing views of organisations – competing and yet complementary.

Richard Tanner Pascale, *Managing on the Edge: How Successful Companies Use Conflict to Stay Ahead*, Viking, Penguin Group, 1990, is an excellent book that discusses operating at the edge between the evolutionary and the revolutionary. Ralph Stacey puts the case in more systematic terms and in terms of chaos theory (Ralph D. Stacey, *Strategic Management and Organisational Dynamics*, 2nd edn, Financial Times Pitman Publishing, 1996). Both books are easy reading for such a potentially difficult subject.

CHAPTER NOTES
AND REFERENCES

1 Beach L.R., 'Four revolutions in behavioral decision theory', in Chemers, M.M. and Ayman, R. (eds), *Leadership Theory and Research, Perspectives and Directions*, Academic Press, 1993, pp. 271–92.
2 Noorderhaven, N., *Strategic Decision Making*, Addison-Wesley, 1995, p. 20.
3 Dutton, J.E. and Duncan, R.B., 'The creation of momentum for change through the process for strategic issue diagnosis', *Strategic Management Journal*, Vol. 8, 1987, pp. 279–95.
4 *Ibid.*
5 Ackoff, R.L., 'The art and science of mess management', *Interfaces*, Vol. 11, No. 1, 1981, pp. 20–6. Ackoff describes dissolving, resolving and solving.
6 Noorderhaven, N., *op. cit.*, p. 55.
7 Quinn, J.B., 'Logical incrementalism', *Sloan Management Review*, No. 20, Fall 1978, pp. 7–21. This quote has been slightly changed to make it less gender-specific.
8 An extreme 'political' view of organisations and of disjointed incrementalism is the garbage-can approach (described in Eisenhardt, K.H. and Zbaracki, M.J., 'Strategic decision making', *Strategic Management Journal*, Vol. 13, 1992, pp. 17–32.
9 Noorderhaven, N., *op. cit.*, p. 20.
10 Nonaka, I. and Takeuchi, H., *The Knowledge-Creating Company: How Japanese Companies Create the Dynamics of Innovation*, Oxford University Press, 1995, pp. 89–99.

11 Scott Morton, M.S., (ed.), *The Corporation of the 1990s: Information Technology and Organizational Transformation*, Oxford University Press, 1991.
12 Once the knowledge becomes codified, it then becomes information.
13 Adapted from Lam, A., 'Tacit knowledge, organisational learning and innovation: a societal perspective', Danish Research Unit for Industrial Dynamics, DRUID Working Paper No. 98–22, pp. 6–7.
14 Hampden-Turner, C. and Trompenaars, F., *The Seven Cultures of Capitalism: Value Systems for Creating Wealth in the United States, Britain, Japan, Germany, France, Sweden, and the Netherlands*, Doubleday, 1993, pp. 25, 233.
15 Considerable use has been made here of the paper by Lam, A., 'Tacit knowledge, organisational learning and innovation: a societal perspective', Danish Research Unit for Industrial Dynamics, DRUID Working Paper No. 98–22 (ISBN 87–7873–060–0), Aalborg University, Denmark. The paper was read at the British Academy of Management conference, Nottingham, 14–16 September 1998.
16 Argyris, C., 'Single-loop and double-loop models in research on decision making', *Administrative Science Quarterly*, Vol. 21, September 1976, pp. 363–76.
17 Morgan, G., *Images of Organization*, 2nd edn, Sage, 1997.
18 Argyris, C., *op. cit.*

19 Senge, P., 'The leader's new work: building learning organisations', *Sloan Management Review*, Fall 1990, p. 13.

20 Hampden-Turner, C. and Trompenaars, F., *op. cit.*, p. 174.

21 Other terms are knowledge-based organisation (Winch, G. and Schneider, E., 'Managing the knowledge based organisation', *Journal of Management Studies*, Vol. 20, No. 6, 1993, pp. 923–37); the knowhow company (Sveiby, K.E. and Lloyd, T., *Managing Know-How*, Bloomsbury, 1987) and the knowledge-creating company (Nonaka, I. and Takeuchi, H., *op. cit.*).

22 Stata, R., 'Organizational learning – the key to management innovation', *Sloan Management Review*, Vol. 30, Spring 1989, pp. 63–74.

23 Nonaka, I. and Takeuchi, H., *op. cit.*, p. 74.

24 Clayton, T. and Luchs, B., 'Strategic benchmarking at ICI Fibres', *Long Range Planning*, Vol. 27, No. 3, 1994, pp. 54–63.

25 Department of Trade and Industry, *Inside UK Enterprise*, 1999.

26 Senge, P., *op. cit.*

27 Bennis, W. and Nanus, B., *Leaders: The Strategies for Taking Charge*, Harper & Row, 1985, p. 76.

28 Nonaka, I. and Takeuchi, H., *op. cit.*

29 KPMG Management Consultancy, 'Knowledge management', research report, 1998, p. 7.

30 *The Knowledge Barrier*, Information Systems Research Center, Cranfield School of Management, September 1997.

31 Hansen, M.T., Nohria, N. and Tierney, T., 'What's your strategy for managing knowledge?', *Harvard Business Review*, March–April 1999, pp. 106–16.

32 *Ibid.*

33 Eisenhardt, K.M. and Zbaracki, M.J., *op. cit.*

34 Hickson, D.J., Butler, R.J., Cray, D., Mallory, G.R. and Wilson, D.C., *Top Decisions: Strategic Decision Making in Organizations*, Basil Blackwell, 1986; and in Cray, D., Mallory, G.R., Butler, R.J., Hickson, D.J. and Wilson, D.C., 'Explaining decision processes', *Journal of Management Studies*, Vol. 28, 1991, pp. 227–51.

35 Note that in the original the term *endurance* was used. The term *persistence* is used here because it has the same meaning as that used by Dutton and Duncan later in the chapter.

36 Pascale, R.T., *Managing on the Edge: How Successful Companies Use Conflict to Stay Ahead*, Viking, Penguin Group, 1990.

37 The term 'bunker mentality' arises, I believe, from the end of the Second World War, when Hitler and his trusted confidants were holed up in a bunker in Berlin. They had completely lost a grip on reality, issuing orders to army units that no longer existed. The expression was also used about Margaret Thatcher in her last days as the British prime minister, depending on a few confidants who were trusted because they held similar views to her own.

38 Pascale, R.T., *Transformation*, BBC Enterprises video, 1994.

39 Kettelhut, M.C., 'JAD methodology and group dynamics', Information Systems Management, winter 1993, pp. 46–53.

40 Jessup, L.M. and Valacich, J.S., *Group Support Systems: New Perspectives*, Macmillan, 1992, and special issue of the *European Journal of Operational Research*, Vol. 46, No. 2, on group decision and negotiation support systems.

41 Checkland, P., *Systems Thinking, Systems Practice*, Wiley, 1981.

42 Eden, C. and Radford, J., *Tackling Strategic Problems: The Role of Group Decision Support*, Sage, 1990.

43 Chote, R., 'Victims of "groupthink"', Economics Notebook, *Financial Times*, 7 September 1998, p. 20.

6 Building blocks of business strategy

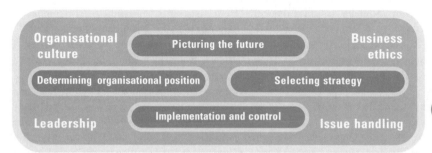

The previous four chapters described the internal context of strategic management – the context within which all organisational activity takes place. We are now moving on to look at strategy formulation and implementation at the level of the business.

In this chapter many of the basic ideas necessary to thinking strategically are introduced and discussed. The *organisational* distinction between business and corporation is considered first. This distinction is barely adequate for purposes of strategic analysis, however, and a deeper distinction between business and corporate is needed. This is achieved through considering businesses as made up of processes and capabilities. The rationale for not making a distinction between products and services is then explored. Finally, the role and components of mission statements are discussed and the characteristics of strategic goals are considered.

Before considering any subject, it's important to understand its basic elements. Although some of the basic elements of strategic management were discussed in Chapter 1, it is valuable to consider some further aspects in detail before looking closely at strategy formulation and implementation. In particular, the distinction between the business and corporate levels and the role and composition of business missions and goals can usefully be explored.

LEARNING
OUTCOMES

When you have worked through this chapter, you should be able to:

- name the two forms of environment and explain the rationale for the split between them;

- justify the rejection of *industry* and *segment* as major units of analysis;

- explain the linkage between resources, processes and capabilities and the difference between a business and a corporation in terms of processes;

- explain the rationale for considering *offers* rather than *products/services in markets* and describe the three forms of offer development;

- debate the inadequacy of profit as the purpose of an organisation;

- explain what a mission and a mission statement are, state why organisations have mission statements, and outline what makes a good mission statement;

- explain what makes a good strategic goal;

- develop a mission statement together with appropriate goals.

6.1 The characteristics of businesses

In Chapter 1 the distinction between a corporation and a business was introduced. Because we are moving on to consider the formulation of business strategy, we need to revisit the topic to get a better understanding of what a business is.

A business may be a 'stand-alone' operation such as the corner newsagent or the local garage, or it may be part of a larger organisation. Two such larger groupings are shown in Exhibit 6.1. The first shows the very simple organisational structure of a high-street retailer, with the businesses reporting directly to the corporate centre.

EXHIBIT 6.1

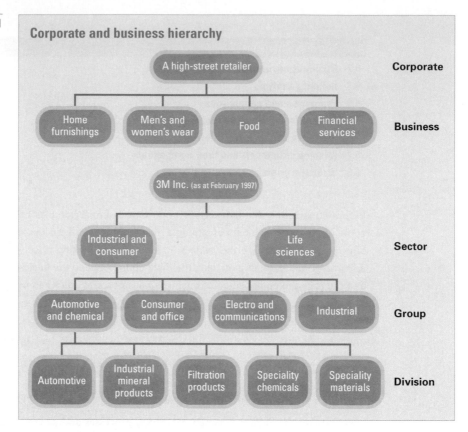

Corporate and business hierarchy

A high-street retailer — Corporate

Home furnishings | Men's and women's wear | Food | Financial services — Business

3M Inc. (as at February 1997)

Industrial and consumer | Life sciences — Sector

Automotive and chemical | Consumer and office | Electro and communications | Industrial — Group

Automotive | Industrial mineral products | Filtration products | Speciality chemicals | Speciality materials — Division

More complex is the company 3M, part of whose organisational structure is shown in Exhibit 6.1. Here there are four levels of strategic management. The corporation is divided into two sectors. The industrial and consumer sector is shown further split into four groups. The automotive and chemical group contains five divisions. Although this is unusual terminology, the divisions are businesses. The reason for a hierarchy such as this is partly for control purposes and partly because of the association there is between parts of the organisation: the five businesses within the automotive and chemical group have, in general, stronger associations – and thus the potential for synergies and the development of new products – than they do with businesses in other groups. As management of the units above the business level corresponds more closely to corporate than to business-level strategic management, it's appropriate for discussion of these levels to be deferred until the corporate level is considered in Part 3.

6.1.2 Strategic business units

A corporation is the total legal entity, in general consisting of several businesses. A business within a corporation is generally termed a strategic business unit (SBU). An SBU may be defined[1] as a unit that:

- has a distinctive business mission, sensibly independent of that of any other business in the corporation;

- offers a well-defined product or service in a well-defined market (and is not predominantly a supplier to other units in the corporation);
- is able to manage its strategy in a manner that is independent of other businesses within the corporation (although not of the strategy of the corporation itself);
- contains all the important components essential to the conduct of its business mission, for example technology, operations and marketing.

Thus in accounting terms an SBU corresponds to a profit centre – a unit that is responsible for the generation of profit. (The corporation is an investment centre – the unit that, among other things, decides what to do with the profits that the businesses have generated.) It can be seen that this definition of an SBU, although it includes reference to the corporation of which it is a part, is a definition that can easily be applied to 'stand-alone' businesses. Throughout Part 2 of this book the term *business* will be used to mean any business unit, whether 'stand-alone' or a strategic business unit that is part of a corporation.

DISCUSSION
POINT 6 1

Do you think it is appropriate to say that all strategic management above business level is closer to corporate strategic management than to business strategic management?

- Does this definition of an SBU encompass not-for-profit organisations (such as charities and government departments)?
- An SBU corresponds broadly to a profit centre and doesn't have control over major investments of the profits it generates. How can it be appropriate to consider a 'stand-alone' business in the same light as an SBU when a 'stand-alone' business does have control over its investment decisions?

The above distinction between business and corporation stresses the organisational distinction. The operational distinction is shown by the main questions a corporation and a business ask themselves: 'What businesses should we be in?' for the corporation and 'How do we compete?' for the business.

6.1.3 Sub-business-level strategy

Functions such as the marketing and IT departments wouldn't be a sensible unit for strategic analysis, since these functions only *contribute* to strategy, they can't sensibly have a strategy of their own.

6.2 Business environments

Every business is engaged in at least one conversion process, converting inputs to outputs. While doing this it is operating in an environment consisting of a great many influences, some of which are sketched in Exhibit 6.2.

This environment includes all the stakeholders that the business has or potentially will have in the future. One particularly important feature for strategy formulation is how to analyse the external environment in order to make sense of it. The first consideration concerns the level of influence that the business can have on the elements

EXHIBIT 6.2

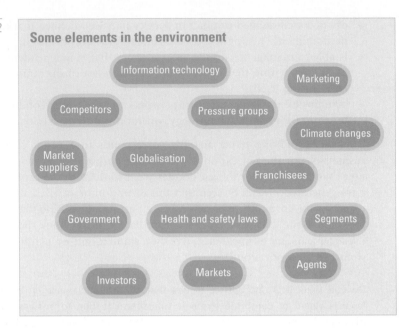

Some elements in the environment

Information technology

Marketing

Competitors

Pressure groups

Climate changes

Market suppliers

Globalisation

Franchisees

Government

Health and safety laws

Segments

Agents

Investors

Markets

in its environment and vice versa. The areas where the business can influence and where it's being influenced point the way to where tools of analysis are most needed.

6.2.1 The two environments for a business

The elements in the external environment can be classified by the level of influence that they have on the business and the business has on them. For some elements the influence is two-way, since the business can influence some of the elements in the environment and they influence the business. There are other elements in the environment where the influence is one-way, as the business can't influence them but they have a significant impact on the business. It needs to be borne in mind that what is being sought is a model of the environment – a simplification of it. Thus we would only include those elements where the impact is significant.

Based on this view of significant influence, any organisation can be considered to be operating in two environments. First there is the **operating environment,** consisting of such factors as the markets that the business is operating in, its competitors, its suppliers and other stakeholders: elements over which the organisation would have some influence.

There is also the **remote environment,** consisting of such items as government pressure and actions, information technology developments and demographic trends. It wouldn't be expected that a business would have any significant influence over the remote environment, although changes there may affect the business and its operating environment. In this respect, the individual businesses in the operating environment are like small boats floating in a remote environmental 'sea', having to adapt to whatever the elements throw at them.

The two environments and the place of the business within them are shown in Exhibit 6.3.

EXHIBIT 6.3

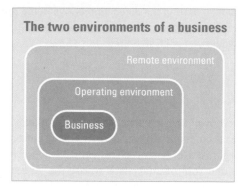

The two environments of a business

Remote environment

Operating environment

Business

KEY CONCEPT   A business can be considered to have two environments, depending on the direction of the influences between the business and the elements within them. First there is the *operating environment*, composed of elements that the organisation can influence and that also influence the business. Second there is the *remote environment*, composed of elements on which the individual business has no significant influence but which may have a major effect on the operating environment and on the business.

6.2.2 Which to consider first – the operating or the remote environment?

In an environmental analysis it's not obvious which of the two environments should be considered first: the operating environment and then the remote environment, or vice versa. The rationale for considering the operating environment *before* the remote environment is that many features of the remote environment are specific to the operating environment – and consequently to the business that's the focus of the analysis. For example, changes in the laws relating to drug patent life are vitally important to pharmaceutical companies but are of no concern to garage proprietors; a trend for people to keep a car for longer before replacement is of concern to garages but not to the drug companies. Thus the logical progression is from the organisation to its operating environment to the remote environment. If you don't know the organisation and the operating environment you're in, you can't sensibly talk about the remote environment. This line of reasoning emphasises current activities and supports a market-led approach to strategy.

The rationale for considering the remote environment first is that the analysis shouldn't start by concentrating solely on current activities. There are some factors in the remote environment – IT is an obvious example – that will affect all (or almost all) businesses, and it is only by considering these first that the analysis can be open-minded enough to capture fully the consequences of these forces for the business and lead to new thinking.

DISCUSSION
POINT 6.2
Do you see any problems with making the distinction between the operating and remote environments?

- Which environment would you analyse first?

6.3   Industry analysis

Splitting the environment into two on the grounds of influence is a step forward in structuring the 'mess' that confronts the strategist, because it has separated those features over which the organisation has no significant influence from those over which it has. One possible further tool of analysis is to use the characteristics of the industry within which the business is operating to help in the competitive analysis. This possibility should be investigated, since there is a great deal of industry data collected by governments that might be a great help.

Both the EU and US Standard Industrial Classifications[2] (SIC) group businesses mainly on the basis of technology rather than on the basis of similar competitive dynamics. Thus businesses with common markets would be broken apart under the SIC classification. A portion of the EU and US categories associated with the lowest level of classification for aircraft is reproduced in Exhibit 6.4. Note the that range of items under the (most detailed) four-digit categories 35.30 and 3721 includes fixed-wing aircraft, helicopters, balloons and hang-gliders.

While the SIC classifications are precise and no doubt suitable for the purposes for which they were devised, they have little to offer to aid strategic analyses. Feigenbaum et al.[3] make the point:

> An industry as conventionally understood produces a range of different products, all of which are not close substitutes, and uses a variety of technical production processes. It therefore becomes unclear where the boundaries of an industry should be drawn. However, two criteria are commonly used to define these boundaries: markets and technologies. The technological criterion focuses upon the classification of industries according to their similarity of processes.

With IT changing the basis of competition,[4] it is very relevant to quote Keen[5] in his discussion of the role of information technology in changing competition:

> There is hardly a single industry that can ignore the threat from or the need to co-operate with firms from outside its own. Regardless of the level of sustainability of the competitive edge, business innovation via telecommunications makes the word 'industry' meaningless.

It will be apparent from the examples in Exhibit 6.4 that even a four-digit subclassification of an industry doesn't include any of the market features: would one seriously expect that hang-gliders are in the same market as helicopters? In this chapter, the term 'industry' will be used in a very general way when vagueness is a virtue. It won't be used in formal analysis.

The businesses in an industry can sometimes act together to establish and maintain the legitimacy of a whole industry or simply as a lobbying group to protect common interests. Examples here are the tobacco industry and the nuclear power industry over many decades, and the more recent example of the cable companies getting together to trumpet the advantages of their technology.

DISCUSSION
POINT 6.3
What is the car industry? What is the financial services industry?

EXHIBIT 6.4

Example of the EU and US industrial classifications

EU Classification of Economic Activities

35.30 MANUFACTURE OF AIRCRAFT AND SPACECRAFT
This class includes:
- manufacture of aeroplanes for the transport of goods or passengers, for use by the defence forces, for sport or for other purposes
- manufacture of helicopters
- manufacture of gliders, hang-gliders
- manufacture of dirigibles and balloons
- manufacture of parts and accessories of the aircraft of this class:

  - major assemblies such as fuselages, wings, doors, control surfaces, landing gear, fuel tanks, nacelles, etc.
  - aircrews, helicopter rotors and propelled rotor blades
  - motors and engines of a kind typically found on aircraft
  - parts of turbo-jets and turbo-propellers

- manufacture of aircraft launching gear, deck arresters, etc.
- manufacture of ground flying trainers

US Standard Industrial Classification

3721 AIRCRAFT
Establishments primarily engaged in manufacturing or assembling complete aircraft. This industry also includes establishments owned by aircraft manufacturers and primarily engaged in research and development on aircraft, whether from enterprise funds or on a contract or fee basis. Also included are establishments engaged in repairing and rebuilding aircraft on a factory basis. Establishments primarily engaged in manufacturing engines and other aircraft parts and auxiliary equipment are classified in industries 3724 and 3728; and those manufacturing guided missiles and space vehicles and parts are classified in industry group 376. Establishments primarily engaged in the repair of aircraft, except on a factory basis, are classified in Transportation, industry 4581; and research and development on aircraft by establishments not owned by aircraft manufacturers are classified in Services, industry 8731.

Aircraft	Dirigibles
Airplanes, fixed or rotary wing	Gliders (aircraft)
Airships	Hang-gliders
Autogiros	Helicopters
Balloons (aircraft)	Research and development on aircraft
Blimps	by the manufacturers

6.4 Processes and capabilities

6.4.1 The components of a process

A **process** is a series of actions taken in order to convert inputs to something of greater value, so the term *process* is shorthand for *conversion process*. Every process combines four resources to a greater or lesser extent: basic assets, explicit knowledge, tacit knowledge and procedures.

- Basic assets are the building blocks of the organisation, which can be recognised and evaluated by outsiders. They consist of tangible assets, assets that the organisation owns that generally have been bought. Examples are plant and machinery and cash; they have a book value. Basic assets also include intangible assets such as reputation and brand strength. Looking at the example of a small garage, basic assets would be the equipment used in the repair of cars, e.g. ramps, test equipment, its buildings and its reputation.

- Explicit knowledge is knowledge that can and has been codified and is in the public domain. Examples would be the laws of physics, the legal obligations of companies and the knowledge of how to undertake stock control. For a garage, explicit knowledge would include car-servicing schedules and instructions describing the workings of car engines.

- Tacit knowledge is knowledge that can't be codified or that is very difficult to codify. Skill, the ability to do something well, especially because it has been learned and practised, is one form of tacit knowledge. Skill may reside in individuals or it may reside in the organisation as a whole. One example of skill residing in an individual is the knowhow that experienced mechanics have of the cause of unusual faults in specific makes of car. Individual skills are also very evident in advertising agencies, in financial trading and in the bosses of small companies. In contrast, much of the skill in a firm such as Marks & Spencer is organisational skill, for example how to establish profitable relationships with suppliers.

- Procedure provides the ability to co-ordinate the basic assets, explicit and tacit knowledge to perform a process. A garage procedure would be that involved in dealing with a client bringing their car in for repair, with logging the car in and estimating the cost of the repair. Where procedures are written down – and thus codified – they may be copied by competitors.

With these definitions, we have the picture shown in Exhibit 6.5. A **process** is performed by using a **procedure** to combine **basic assets** with **explicit** and **tacit knowledge**. The process is designed and undertaken within the internal context of the business – in particular the organisational culture.

DISCUSSION POINT 6.4
Should intangibles such as reputation and brand strength be considered elements of a process?
- What is the strategic management rationale for splitting knowledge into explicit and tacit knowledge?
- Is a procedure knowledge?

EXHIBIT 6.5

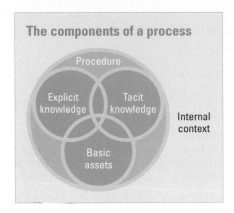

The components of a process

6.4.2 *Sets of business processes*

In a business, processes are generally linked together. One obvious set of processes is that combining the inputs of components, their assembly and the distribution of the finished products. Processes link together to form a set that delivers a product or service to the customer. Such a set of linked processes is termed a **capability**. A capability is more than the sum of the individual processes, since the individual processes need to be combined and co-ordinated. A firm could have efficient individual processes but poor capabilities if the individual processes weren't appropriately linked. As Stalk[6] puts it:

> To succeed, a company must weave its key business processes into hard-to-imitate strategic capabilities that distinguish it from its competitors. Competitive success depends on transforming a company's key processes into strategic capabilities that consistently provide superior value to the customer.

Two processes out of many associated with the production of Post-it notes by the 3M Company are shown in Exhibit 6.6 to illustrate how processes are combined to form a capability. A capability in a small garage would involve the processes of recruitment, training and retention of skilled mechanics.

In the 3M example, process B, in which adhesive is applied to paper, could be used to add adhesive to other products – for example, labels for packaging. Thus processes aren't restricted to one capability. The linkage between the resources in a process and the linkages between processes and capabilities and that between the capabilities and the whole business are shown in Exhibit 6.7. Together, the resources, processes and capabilities are the assets of the business, both the individual resources and the relationships between them. Some of these will be important to strategy: these are **strategic resources**. It's often the linkages between the parts that provide competitive advantage.

An example from aero engine manufacture shows this very well. Apparently, the availability of spares plays little part in the (sales) decision by airlines which buy the engines; what is very important is whether the new engines are delivered on time. This means that there is a tremendous pressure to take parts that were meant for spares stock and use these in the manufacture of new engines. However, the consequent inability to supply spares quickly when an engine needs overhaul is damaging to long-

EXHIBIT 6.6

Processes in the making of Post-it notes

	Processes	
	Process A	Process B
Resources	Producing and dispatching adhesives	Applying adhesives to paper
Basic assets	Factory Machines Raw materials Vehicles	Factory Machines Operatives Paper
Tacit knowledge	Knowledge of peculiarities of the machines used in the production process	
Explicit knowledge	Adhesives Production process Transportation	Adhesives Paper Production process
Procedures	Ability to integrate resources and technologies	Ability to integrate resources and technologies
	Process A	Process B
Capability	to produce Post-It notes	

EXHIBIT 6.7

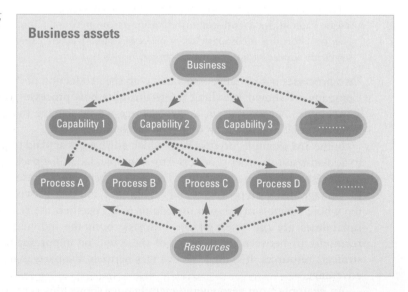

Business assets

term relationships. The way in which the aero engine manufacturers organise operations, sales, marketing and spares service may be vital to maintaining the good relations that will provide tomorrow's orders. Getting the balance right between these activities provides a competitive advantage.

KEY CONCEPT   Every business must engage in at least one conversion process, utilising some or all of four types of resource: basic assets, explicit knowledge, tacit knowledge and a procedure knitting the three together. Except in the simplest of businesses, processes are linked together to form capabilities – a set of processes that delivers a product or service to the customer.

As a postscript to the discussion on capabilities, it's perhaps useful to mention competences, because the two are often confused. As with a capability, a competence is a conversion process combining elements of the four basic resources. The difference lies in the focus. A capability is geared to satisfying a specific stakeholder target, most usually the customers. A competence is geared to meeting ill-specified opportunities in the future. An analogy is the difference between training and education: training is to gain expertise in a specific skill to be used in the short term, while education is to gain general abilities that might be used in many spheres of activity in the longer-term future. This analogy suggests that competences are a concern for a corporation, since they are abilities that will be used to initiate new businesses. Competences will be considered in much more detail when corporate issues are discussed.

Thus the distinction is clear. A business is managing a portfolio of products and services and a portfolio of processes; a corporation is managing a portfolio of businesses and a portfolio of competences.

6.5 Product/service and market developments

6.5.1 A capability view of the difference between the corporation and the business

It would be expected that a business would be continually improving its product or service – either to keep up with or get ahead of the competition. This is *product* or *service enhancement*. For example, a maker of microwave ovens might make the oven a little more powerful, or may add a more sophisticated timing mechanism to it. A small garage might provide a customer waiting room.

A business may decide to extend its product/service range by offering different versions of its one basic product or service: a maker of microwaves for the French market might make ovens of various capacities to be targeted at the same market segment as the original product or service, for example. The garage might add a special form of engine tuning to its repertoire. This sort of product or service change is *product* or *service extension*. Alternatively, the business may decide to enter a different market to the one it's currently in. This would be the case, for example, if the microwave oven maker decided to move from the French domestic market into a similar domestic market, say into Germany or the UK. This sort of move is *market extension*.

With product, service and market enhancements and extensions the changes are rather limited and all can be accommodated within the current capabilities of the business. Enhancements entail the upgrading of current processes; extensions may mean a radical overhaul of one or more of the processes and/or the addition of a new process *within* the existing capability.

More significant change occurs when the business decides to *enlarge* its activities, either by fundamentally changing its portfolio of products or services or by enlarging the portfolio of markets it serves or perhaps by doing both.[7] With all forms of enlargement the risks are likely to be greater than with extensions, mainly because the organisation has to develop or otherwise gain access to new capabilities. The need to access additional processes to develop new capabilities is likely to call for the establishment of a further business. The link between enhancements, extensions and enlargements is illustrated in Exhibit 6.8. The microwave oven manufacturer would be engaged in product enlargement if it moved into manufacturing and selling industrial gas-fired ovens, the garage if it moved into car hire.

EXHIBIT 6.8

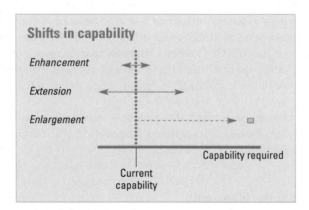

DISCUSSION
POINT 6.5

What additional resources would the microwave oven manufacturer need to acquire in order to successfully carry out the move from domestic microwave manufacture to manufacturing and selling industrial gas-fired ovens?

Examples of product/service enhancements, extensions and enlargements are provided in Exhibit 6.9.

6.5.2 Corporate thinking in business strategic management

In an organisation that is structured as a corporation, the corporate 'parent' is the primary source of corporate thinking about such matters as the businesses to be engaged in. Considerations of the role of the parent are considered in Part 3, which is concerned with *established* corporations. However, every business needs on occasion to be thinking beyond its present business, if only to consider how it can build on its current strategic resources by entering new business areas.

Unless intending to exit a competitive arena, an existing business needs to be continually following a market-led approach to sustain that business; it must enhance its products/services, and it is under pressure to extend its processes. Some of the time it should also be asking where else it can use its strategic assets (possibly with augmentations), i.e. some of the time it should be considering a competence-based approach.

EXHIBIT 6.9

Reinventing the wheel[8]

In an industry which has been chugging along for more than 100 years, it might seem like uphill work to reinvent the wheel and find new markets. 'It's a mature product, and there's not going to be a sudden leap forward in technology,' admits Mr Smith, who joined the Continental Tyre Group as UK managing director four years ago, after a stint as commercial director at Leyland Daf.

Nevertheless, he has made significant inroads into company philosophy, pumping in new life through a series of initiatives which he hopes will increase Continental's market share. Part of Hanover-based Continental AG, it is fourth behind Goodyear, Pirelli and Michelin.

Two key elements in his approach are the manipulation of a growing trend for out-sourcing and a strategic building-up of his brand by cashing in on association with companies such as Volkswagen. He believes he has been something of a catalyst in a traditionally staid industry, a claim endorsed by colleagues, who say he is a live wire and unafraid to demolish established practices. He says: 'I was surprised by how old-fashioned the industry was. There was a lack of challenge, and some employees were unwilling to come forward with ideas. I have challenged them to give of their best. There's a real buzz being in a company that's doing well.'

The sticking point is determining the way forward in a mature market. 'Anyone can get a level of proficiency in making a tyre, and the consumer takes the product for granted. You have to look at your core competencies and say "What more can we do with related products?" We don't want to give up on tyres, but the real growth is in associated products. You work with your suppliers and customers to see what extra you can do for them.

'When I came on board, I set about looking for what I could offer that wasn't the tyre. When people came along excited about a new tread pattern, of course I valued the technological improvement and was pleased to offer it to the customer, but the main thrust was "I have got to be different and better for other reasons"'.

One thing he noticed was that individual tyre dealers needed a helping hand when it came to replacing a tyre on a vehicle. 'It's quite a complex business to choose the right size and fit it to the right wheel. But it is a simple step for us to provide sub-assembly and create machinery that could deliver the complete wheel and tyre.'

And Continental has done so, teaming up with a software company to provide dealers with the wherewithal to access original tyre specifications through their computers. The company is also working with car manufacturers Volkswagen and Mercedes-Benz to develop engineering systems including ISAD, a German acronym for a unit which eliminates the need for a heavy starter motor and dampens noise from the engine.

Meanwhile, Brian Smith's eagle eye was sharp to spot the opportunity to assist fleet operators who, he deduced, would be more than happy to have wheel worries taken off their hands. 'Fitting tyres is not a pleasure, and what they would like is for someone to say "I will take on management of your tyres and guarantee you quality at a cost".' Thus, the Tyre Management System (TMS) was born, and is now used with thousands of UK fleet vehicles, monitoring everything from tyre pressure to tread. 'I don't sell the tyre to the customer; I manage the customer's vehicles. He knows I know how to get better mileage and safety,' says Mr Smith.

Another initiative has been a waste-management system for tyre dealers and garages. 'They had old filters, catalytic converters, brake shields and dirty rags. We had to understand what was needed and what we could offer. But now I can go to a truck operator and say "I can help you, sir".'

Such packages seem attractive to those wishing to out-source. But while the concept, one of the most fashionable business buzzwords around, has droves of followers, there are doubters. Bob Aylott, principal consultant at KPMG Management Consulting, warned that while many organisations out-source in the belief that they will gain control over operational costs and service levels, this could prove misleading. 'Out-sourcing appears to be the most commercially viable choice as cost benefits can be achieved through avoiding recruitment costs, eliminating capital requirements and sharing risks,' he says.

'[But] the organisation must be able to absorb the changes that the supplier will inevitably bring to the client. The client must work to ensure that changes are made with the organisation, not to the organisation. In order for an out-sourcing agreement to be successful, the organisation must be prepared to spend management time – a commitment which is not always foreseen. It can be a success, but only if it is systematically managed through all its stages.'

Brian Smith acknowledges the need for a partnership between supplier and client; to that end, many of his clients were invited to a forum in Hanover in February, at which the 1800 guests included Germany's potential chancellor, Gerhard Schröeder.

Meanwhile, the process is working two-way, with Continental's UK arm out-sourcing parts of its business, such as distribution. 'My job is tyres and related services,' says Mr Smith. 'I haven't got the core competency to distribute.'

Discussion point 6.6

Map out which changes you think are offer enhancements, offer extensions and offer enlargements.

KEY CONCEPT Three kinds of product/service and market development can be identified. Product/service *enhancements* are small-scale changes to a product/service. They are often the changes that are required to keep the product/service viable in the current marketplace and require little in the way of changes to current processes. Product/service or market *extensions* are changes larger than enhancements and are achieved through extensions to the **processes** that the business already possesses. Product/service or market *enlargements* require access to new **capabilities** and thus generally lead to the creation of a new business.

An important consequence of the process- and capability-based view is that it's very important when considering potential competitors for leader-managers to look at organisations that have processes similar to their own businesses; these have operations close to those of their own firms.

6.6 Products, services and offers

6.6.1 The similarity between products and services

In general, products can be considered to be tangible things whose ownership changes when they are bought. Services are less tangible and generally don't result in the customer owning anything that has a resale value, for example a meal in a restaurant or a haircut. However, even for a product there are many cases where you aren't simply buying something tangible: what you are buying is a bundle of features, many of which are intangible. One view of this is shown in Exhibit 6.10. There is the core product or service that provides the core benefit. If you were buying a personal computer the core product would be the computer itself, made up of VDU, keyboard, disk storage, etc., and two of the benefits would be that it would allow you to write letters and do calculations in your home. While some people can simply buy a computer and use it independently right away, many require additional services. The core product, the computer, would be augmented by the sorts of things listed in Exhibit 6.10: equipment set-up, whereby the parts of the computer are connected together, the disks formatted, etc.; after-sales service, including perhaps freephone numbers at the dealers in case of difficulty; an on-going relationship to let buyers know of software and hardware upgrades; information on new software games packages as they become available; and equipment repairs. Note that many of the augmentations are the addition of services, but this need not be so: the different letters in different languages mean that different keyboards would be needed in different markets.

Some augmentations are extremely intangible, for example 'lifestyle' augmentations. Cars and cigarettes are heavily into promoting 'lifestyle': BMW sees its cars as epitomising male sexuality, while the Marlboro man appeals to the cowboy in many of us.

It is generally augmented products – products directly bundled with services – that are bought today, and in affluent societies the service portion is increasing. This increase in the service content isn't limited to consumer goods, as Exhibit 6.11 testifies. The aero engines offered by the big three manufacturers (General Electric, Pratt and Witney and Rolls-Royce) are technically almost the same and sell at roughly the same price. Differentiation and order-winning features are based on non-technical issues such as reputation, after-sales service and the financial package that can be put together. Because of the significant service content of many products, it makes little sense to make a distinction between products and services, and the term *offer* will be used for both. Only where the distinction needs to be made explicitly will the terms *product* or *service* be used.

The particular augmentations to basic offers will reflect those things that are valued by the potential buyers in the particular market that the provider is targeting.

EXHIBIT 6.10

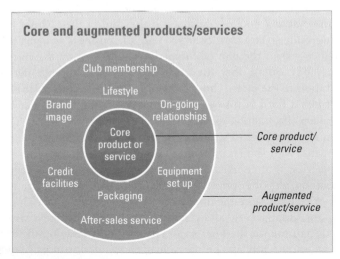

EXHIBIT 6.11

The service content in engineering[9]

Sir Christopher Lewington, chairman of TI, the UK engineering company with interests in mechanical seals and fluid-handling systems for cars and refrigerator, says TI is a 'service company which happens to be in engineering.'

A large part of the sales of Dürr, the German company which is the world leader in automated painting systems for car plants, comes from service-related activities such as helping to supervise the system after it has been installed.

Stephen Howard, chief executive of Cookson, the UK engineering and materials company specialising in systems for improving the efficiencies of electronics and steel production, says: 'The environment in engineering has moved to helping customers improve their business through enabling technologies. You won't get very far in engineering just selling standard products.'

Given that it's almost always the augmented offer that is purchased, it generally makes little sense to talk of offers separately from the associated market. For this reason, and to prevent the constant use of bulky terminology, the simple term *offer* will be used to mean an augmented offer in a market.

KEY CONCEPT Customers generally buy augmented products and services. The characteristics of the potential buyers in the target market determine the augmentations that will accompany a core product or service. As many augmentation of products are services, the distinction between products and services becomes blurred. Unless the distinction between products and services needs to be made, augmented products and augmented services will both be termed *offers*.

6.6.2 The basis of competitive strategy: business or offer?

The main unit of analysis in this book is the business. From the discussion of processes and capabilities, it can be seen that a business would generally have capabilities that share a pool of processes; if they didn't they would be separate businesses. It's not quite so straightforward to take the business as being the main unit of analysis, since it isn't the unit of competition – as seen by the customer. In general, customers buy offers; they don't buy businesses, although the business may impart reputation to the offer. Thus competition in the marketplace is at the offer level: you don't buy a Ford Focus because Ford has a range of other cars but because you like the Focus. The market for the Focus isn't the market for all Ford cars; indeed, Ford will make an effort to segment the market so that its cars don't compete with each other, just with similar offers from other car manufacturers.

The view that competitive strategy equates to offer strategy emphasises the offer value above the offer price. While the offer characteristics are specific to the offer, the offer price isn't, since the offer price depends on the underlying cost base of the business, not simply on the direct costs that can be associated with the particular offer. To concentrate on the offer to the relative downplaying of the business as a whole puts an undue emphasis on one side of the value-for-money equation – on the external, where revenues are generated, and downplay the internal, where costs are incurred. Competitive strategy requires both sides to be considered together. Thus the business level remains the appropriate major unit of analysis. To choose the offer as the unit of analysis would be to suggest that there is such a thing as a marketing strategy decoupled from the rest of the business, a contention already rejected.

6.7 Mission statements and their components

6.7.1 Missions and visions

A vision is a reality that has not yet come to be.[10] An organisational vision is sometimes termed its *strategic intent*. Rolls-Royce plc states its strategic intent to be 'to make Rolls-Royce the world's leading high integrity power systems company for the next century.' Virgin has the vision 'to be the number 1 entertainment and service provider.' On the announcement of the Ford takeover of Volvo car interests in 1999, William Clay Ford Jr is quoted as saying, 'Our 21st century vision is to become the world's leading consumer company for automotive products in 1999.'[11]

While a vision is meant to inspire, it isn't very helpful in the shorter term. Many organisations now understand that their stakeholders need to know what the organisation stands for and why they should give the organisation their loyalty. What is required is a 'road map', and this is very often articulated in a **mission statement**. The difference between a mission and a vision is that the mission is about behaviour and actions for the present and immediate future; a vision sketches out a much longer-term future, perhaps even an ideal that can never be achieved. The two are intertwined, since they should be self-supporting. The vision is likely to enter the mission as one of the strategic goals of the organisation or as one of its main values.

KEY CONCEPT | A vision or strategic intent is a view of a future reality that the organisation seeks. A mission statement is an enduring declaration of the broad directions that the organisation wishes to follow. A mission statement is a 'road map' for stakeholders.

DISCUSSION POINT 6.7 | Can you think of reasons why it might be inappropriate for an organisation to have a mission statement?

A mission should say what the strategic boundaries are. Simons[12] quotes the following examples:

- We will not undertake any activities that do not fit our four families of products.
- Jack Welch, CEO of General Electric, states very firmly: 'We won't be in any business in which it can't achieve a number one or number two market position.'
- Profit – not volume – will be our creed.

6.7.2 The components of a mission statement

Five components can be recognised for a mission statement,[13] as illustrated in Exhibit 6.12.

EXHIBIT 6.12

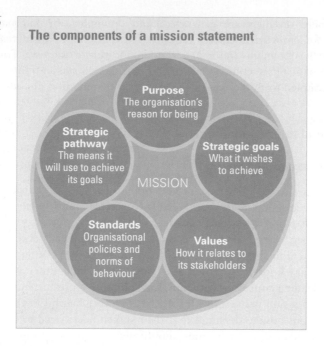

The components of a mission statement

Purpose
The organisation's reason for being

Strategic pathway
The means it will use to achieve its goals

Strategic goals
What it wishes to achieve

MISSION

Standards
Organisational policies and norms of behaviour

Values
How it relates to its stakeholders

Purpose

In their famous book *In Search of Excellence*, Peters and Waterman[14] write:

> Whatever the case, we find it compelling that so many thinkers from so many fields agree on the dominant need of human beings to find meaning and transcend mundane things.

Peters and Waterman see people as needing a significant purpose for what they do, and this applies to their business activities as well as in their personal lives. People can't live by bread alone. In commercial organisations profit or some closely related financial measure is often seen as the purpose of the organisation. Boots plc is an example of a company that has maximising shareholder value (share value and dividends) as the focus of its mission. However, the following quote from Sir Adrian Cadbury[15] quite beautifully sums up the inadequacy of this view:

> An answer that is sometimes given to the question of what is the purpose of an enterprise is that it is to make a profit. Clearly, profitability is essential to survive, but as a definition of purpose it is illogical, unhelpful and uninspiring. Illogical, because profit is the outcome of succeeding in your purpose and not therefore the purpose itself. Unhelpful, because it gives no guidance as to what activities to pursue or not pursue – does it mean literally anything, provided it is profitable and within the law? Uninspiring, because 'we are here to make a profit' is not much of a rallying cry to those working on the shop or office floor.

For some people in business, especially some entrepreneurs and owner-managers, profit may well be the driving force for their business activity. However, in larger organisations financial measures are unlikely in themselves to provide a useful purpose even for profit-seeking organisations – and of course, they are of little value at all to not-for-profit ones. So there is a need to look for 'bigger' aims than simply financial returns – aims that inspire and that every employee can understand and relate to their jobs, which means non-financial as well as financial aims.

A second reason that Cadbury was so scathing of profit as the overarching purpose is that this really only appeals to one stakeholder – the shareholders. It's much better if all stakeholders can find inspiration in the purpose. However, a mission statement must encapsulate the commercial realities that are often the primary concern of shareholders.

The purpose of an organisation is its 'reason for being', what might be considered its overarching strategic aim. Examples of organisational purposes are set out in Exhibit 6.13. The value of setting down the organisational purpose is that it indicates the business areas that the organisation is in (or seeks to enter) and this indicates to stakeholders the boundaries and limitations it is placing on its intended actions. This is particularly useful for subordinate units, as it sets the bounds within which they are allowed to operate.

It is also useful for individuals. Knowledge can only have meaning if it is 'for a purpose'. Thus the person creating knowledge must have a purpose – and from the organisation's view it's obviously useful if the personal purpose coincides closely with that of the organisation. Thus the organisation must have a purpose recognised by the individual, and one reason for articulating visions and missions is to provide a common purpose. Purpose focuses debate and guides the information that needs to be obtained and the knowledge that is to be created, acquired and managed.

DISCUSSION
POINT 6.8

How might the view that organisations are in existence to undertake a conversion process to satisfy customer needs fit with the statement of purpose in a mission statement?

EXHIBIT 6.13

Statements of purpose

Statement of corporate purpose for the Office for Standards in Education (OFSTED)

The purpose of OFSTED is to improve standards of achievement and quality of education through regular independent inspection, public reporting and informed advice.

Purpose of Abbey National

To achieve above-average growth in shareholder value over the long term. This can only be accomplished if we meet the needs of our customers, our staff and all of the other stakeholders in our business. (Note that this purpose only makes sense when coupled with its vision: 'To be the outstanding financial services company in the UK'.)

Purpose of Matsushita Electric

The purpose of an enterprise is to contribute to society by supplying goods of high quality at low prices in ample quantity. The happiness of man is built on mental stability and material affluence. To serve the foundation of happiness, through making man's life affluent with an inexpensive and inexhaustible supply of life's necessities like water, is the duty of a manufacturer. The purpose of the enterprise is to materialise the duty and consequently contribute to society.

Strategic goals

Formally writing down the purpose of an organisation is helpful in that it sets out the scope of the organisation's operations. The strategic goals are likely to have far-reaching consequences for many stakeholders, and thus it's useful to indicate in the mission statement broadly what they are: a broad indication of the organisation's offers and customers. An important point is that goals are about priorities; a list of goals would probably be the same for most organisations in the same industry, but the emphasis given to each would be expected to differ.

Strategic pathways

Outlining the strategic pathways will provide guidance as to how the organisation means to attain its strategic goals. An organisation might specify that it will proceed through internal development rather than out-sourcing – an important consideration to employees thinking of spending a significant part of their working lives with the company.

Values

The purpose and the strategic goals and pathways set out the broad scope of activities and the way in which the organisation wishes to operate within this scope. A further feature of many mission statements is an affirmation of the organisation's values. Values are what the organisation considers important in its dealings with its stake-holders: its customers, employees, etc. The values express the organisation's ethical stance. As with goals, values are about priorities; a list of values would probably be the same for most organisations in the same industry, but the priorities would be different.

Values represent boundaries on behaviour, similar to the boundaries on strategic activity. They are most needed when there is a lack of trust in the organisation, per-haps because of a lack of shared experience or low homogeneity among employees, or in loosely coupled organisations where shared values can't be assumed.[16]

Standards

Many mission statements include a statement of the standards of the organisation: what the outside world can expect of the organisation as a whole and what is expected of employees in their dealings both with external stakeholders and within the organisation: in short, organisational policies and the norms of individual behaviour.

A further purpose of a mission statement is to encourage the search for value cre-ation. This is likely to permit an almost unlimited area of search. Thus there is a need to channel this search through establishing policies. The domain of activity for the organisation also needs to be specified so time is not wasted exploring avenues that don't fit with the current activities or the strategy. Whereas the mission encourages search, policies generally tend to be negative or a set of prohibitions, like nine of the ten commandments. Paradoxically, these prohibitions are liberating; are the brakes on a car to slow it down or to allow it to go fast? The policies also specify how employees should behave.

The purpose, strategic goals and pathways, values, and standards of an organisation should be in harmony with each other. For example, if a university had as one element of its purpose 'to establish an excellent learning environment for students' but had a policy that 'the only way staff will be promoted is through excellent research', there would appear to be a lack of coherence.

6.7.3 An example of a mission statement

A simple, hypothetical mission statement may help to consolidate these ideas. Consider a large hospital. Its purpose may be 'to provide world-class healthcare to the people in our region'. Its strategy may include the strategic goal 'to have a nationally ranked renal unit in operation within the next three years', with its chosen strategic pathway being 'to recruit and retain three top-quality surgeons'. Its values may include 'respect for patients' and 'consideration for staff'. And the standards might find expression in such policies as 'waiting times for surgery will never be more than three months' (for patients) and 'disagreements on staff duties will be handled through arbitration' (staff matters) and in behaviour such as 'all nursing staff will wear full uniform while on duty'.

The mission statement for the Ford Motor Company is shown in Exhibit 6.14.

6.7.4 The style and format of a good mission statement

While a good mission statement will include each of the five components detailed above, it also has to have some measure of permanence to it. A mission statement would be of limited value if it changed with every move that the organisation made or with every environmental change. This need for permanence means that although the mission has to be specific enough to provide real guidance to people, it also has to be vague enough to encourage initiative and to remain relevant under a wide range of conditions. The consensus view would seem to be that a mission statement should:

- be limited enough to exclude some ventures;
- be broad enough to allow for creative growth;
- generate enthusiasm from all stakeholders;
- encapsulate commercial realities;
- have personality, to distinguish the specific organisation from others;
- be memorable (only details specific to individual stakeholders can realistically be memorised);
- be achievable, within a reasonable timescale (although firm dates need not be specified).

That a mission statement needs a measure of permanence doesn't mean that it should never be changed. An interesting change of mission was made by the Royal Automobile Club (RAC) in 1997. For years it had been the car drivers' champion, opposing speed limits, seat belts and driving tests.[17] In 1997, it signalled that the car must be tamed and it began promoting the idea of the civilised city. The RAC realised that its members are not just motorists: they also cycle, walk and use public transport. As it now puts it,[18] 'We favour travel over traffic and mobility over motoring.' The organisation is now putting its weight behind measures to limit the use of cars, especially in towns; as a small example, it's selling a bicycle that folds up and can be carried in the boot of a car.

A questionnaire and checklist that can be used to critique any proposed mission statement is given as Exhibit 6.15.

EXHIBIT 6.14

The Ford Motor Company

Company mission, values, and guiding principles

MISSION

Ford Motor Company is a worldwide leader in automotive and financial products and services. Our mission is to improve continually our products and services to meet our customers' needs, allowing us to prosper as a business and to provide a reasonable return for our stockholders, the owners of our business.

VALUES

How we accomplish our mission is as important as the mission itself. Fundamental to success for the Company are these basic values:

- **People** Our people are the source of our strength. They provide our corporate intelligence and determine our reputation and vitality. Involvement and teamwork are our core human values.
- **Products** Our products are the end result of our efforts, and they should be the best in serving customers worldwide. As our products are viewed, so are we viewed.
- **Profits** Profits are the ultimate measure of how efficiently we provide customers with the best products for their needs. Profits are required to survive and grow.

GUIDING PRINCIPLES

- **Quality comes first** To achieve customer satisfaction, the quality of our products and services must be our number one priority.
- **Customers are the focus of everything we do** Our work must be done with our customers in mind, providing better products and services than our competition.
- **Continuous improvement is essential to our success** We must strive for excellence in everything we do: in our products, in their safety and value – and in our services, our human relations, our competitiveness, and our profitability.
- **Employee involvement is our way of life** We are a team. We must treat each other with trust and respect.
- **Dealers and suppliers are our partners** The Company must maintain mutually beneficial relationships with dealers, suppliers and other business associates.
- **Integrity is never compromised** The conduct of our Company worldwide must be pursued in a manner that is socially responsible and commands respect for its integrity and for its positive contributions to society. Our doors are open to men and women alike without discrimination and without regard to ethnic origin or personal beliefs.

6.8 Strategic goals

6.8.1 The scope of strategic goals

A vision is a reality that has yet to be achieved. A purpose is the overarching aim of the organisation, its reason for existence. A goal is a general statement of direction.

One fairly obvious criterion for a suitable goal is that it should be relevant to the mission: if a goal doesn't link with the mission then there is something wrong – with the mission, with the goal or perhaps with both. Given the concern with *strategic*

EXHIBIT 6.15

The quality of a mission statement[19]

1 Purpose
Does the statement:

- describe a purpose that is greater than the interests of individual stakeholder groups?
- describe the organisation's responsibilities to its stakeholders?
- specify the business in such a way as to channel management effort appropriately?
- specify business areas vaguely enough to allow for creative growth?

2 Strategy – goals and pathways
Does the statement:

- include realistic strategic goals of the organisation?
- prioritise the strategic goals?
- describe the means that the organisation proposes to use to attain its goals?
- identify any new capabilities that the organisation will have to develop or obtain?

3 Values
Does the statement:

- state the things that the organisation believes in (its ethical position)?
- prioritise these organisational values?

4 Standards
Does the statement:

- provide information on organisational policies that is of use to stakeholders?
- provide information to guide individual employee behaviour?

5 Integrity

- Overall, do the purpose, strategy, values and standards align with one another?

6 Character and personality

- Does the statement indicate an organisation that is different from other organisations in the same competitive arena?
- Are the main parts of the statement memorable?
- Is the statement easy to read?

goals, another required attribute is that they capture what is important to the organisation, and thus that they are related to the factors that have a significant impact on the organisation's survival and well-being. Another criterion for the set of goals is that some of the goals must be concerned with the financial health of the organisation. Historically, the goals of profit-seeking firms reflected this concern and were strongly financially oriented. More recently, there has been a move to consider other criteria. In this respect commercial organisations have moved closer to not-for-profit organisations, which traditionally tended to play down the financial side of their operations. However, as not-for-profit organisations have been forced by pressures from government and elsewhere to consider financial aspects more clearly and closely, there has been a general convergence of the goals used in the two types of organisation.

The concern for non-financial goals to complement the financial ones has found its most popular reflection in the concept of the balanced scorecard.[20] This considers four main areas of concern to organisations, two external and two internal. The two external perspectives focus on how well the organisation is doing when looked at from the financial – mainly shareholder – perspective and the customer point of view. The internal perspectives are concerned with current business processes and with how the organisation is developing itself for the future. However, a wider view would suggest that it is important to consider all the stakeholders, including the general populace. Doing this produces the extended scorecard which is shown in Exhibit 6.16.

On the left-hand side is the internal perspective. First, there are concerns for employees, both as individuals and as groups – such as clerical staff, engineers and the unions. Second, there is consideration of the organisation's current business processes, what it must get right to thrive. Finally, there is the forward-looking perspective concerned with innovation and learning, both in terms of new offers that the organisation might provide and new processes that it is developing and might adopt. This perspective is how the organisation is progressing as a learning organisation.

On the right-hand side of Exhibit 6.15 are the external perspectives. Very importantly, there is the customer perspective: not only that of current customers but also

EXHIBIT 6.16

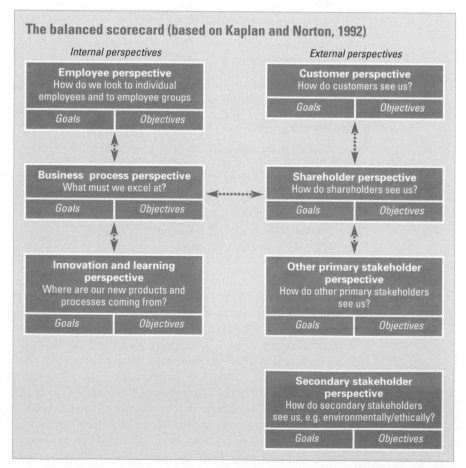

The balanced scorecard (based on Kaplan and Norton, 1992)

Internal perspectives

Employee perspective
How do we look to individual employees and to employee groups

Goals | *Objectives*

Business process perspective
What must we excel at?

Goals | *Objectives*

Innovation and learning perspective
Where are our new products and processes coming from?

Goals | *Objectives*

External perspectives

Customer perspective
How do customers see us?

Goals | *Objectives*

Shareholder perspective
How do shareholders see us?

Goals | *Objectives*

Other primary stakeholder perspective
How do other primary stakeholders see us?

Goals | *Objectives*

Secondary stakeholder perspective
How do secondary stakeholders see us, e.g. environmentally/ethically?

Goals | *Objectives*

of potential customers. Second, there is the perspective of the shareholders to consider – the owners of the enterprise. Third, there is what has been labelled 'other primary stakeholder perspective', which takes into account primary external stakeholders other than the shareholders and customers. Finally, there needs to be a consideration of how the organisation looks to secondary stakeholders, in particular in an environmental and ethical audit – the perspective of the general citizen, or perhaps reflected through governmental concerns. Note that all of the perspectives are the views of the parties cited; they are not the organisation's own perspectives.

The perspectives identified in Exhibit 6.16 are listed and explained in Exhibit 6.17, together with examples of goals for each perspective. The objectives associated with strategic goals are considered in Chapter 15.

DISCUSSION POINT 6.9

Why is the scorecard in Exhibit 6.16 described as *balanced*?
- Which of the perspectives in Exhibit 6.16 would not be from the point of view of the parties cited?
- Give examples of goals for *other primary stakeholders* and for *social* responsibility for an oil company.

EXHIBIT 6.17

Perspectives and goals

Perspective	Explanation	Examples of goals
Employees	The view that individual employees and groups of them have of the organisation	To maintain good employee relations
Business processes	The performance of key internal business processes in terms of quality, speed and productivity	The speedy implementation of new and enhanced information systems
Innovation	The ability of the organisation to improve continuously and innovate in its products, services and processes	Increase the % of revenues from new services
Customer	The view that current and potential customers have of our products, services and aftersales service	Enhance customer satisfaction
Shareholder	The view that shareholders, particularly the institutional shareholders, take of the organisation	Increase shareholder value in line with other businesses in the same sector
Other primary stakeholders	The view that primary stakeholders other than employees, customers and shareholders take of the organisation	
Social responsibility	The view that governments and environmental pressure groups take of the organisation's environmental impact, its operations overseas, etc.	

6.8.2 Economic measures of success

Not-for-profit organisations would not measure their success in economic terms: a church might measure its success by the number of its regular attenders, an overseas charity by the number of villages for which it secured clean water. However, commercial businesses would and indeed must do so, otherwise they will cease to grow and, in the extreme, cease to exist.

Underpinning all the measures of economic success is the ability of the business to add value. Added value is the difference between the value of the firm's outputs and the combined costs of the inputs it uses and the processes it undertakes, as shown in Exhibit 6.18. The value of the firm's inputs includes the costs of all inputs – of materials, information, labour and capital. The value of the firm's outputs to the firm is the total revenue that is obtained. This measure has three valuable features: it emphasises the processes and capabilities approach; it underscores one, and in some people's eyes *the* central, purpose of business activity; and it can be linked closely with competitive advantage. The competitive advantage of one firm can be judged by comparing the added value it produces against the added value of the marginal firm against which it is competing. The marginal firm is the one that is just finding it worthwhile to remain in the market. In a contestable market the marginal firm won't be making any added value – its outputs will be sold at cost – and thus competitive advantage is measured by the other firm's added value. In a protected market the marginal firm may be absorbing value, as will be the case where it operates when its operating costs equal its revenues; i.e. when it isn't covering its cost of capital out of its operations. In an extreme case, none of the firms could be producing added value yet they could still be profitable, due to government subsidy for example.

The links between the main measures of financial success for an organisation are set out in Exhibit 6.19.[21] While the question of which financial measures to use is very important over the short term – and they need to be tailored to the audience – over the longer term many of the measures amount to almost the same thing, or at the very least serve to pull the firm in the same direction.

6.8.3 Intellectual capital

In 1999, Microsoft became the largest company in the world as evaluated on its share price, although its tangible assets are little more than a few office buildings. The very high valuations put on Internet shares are also not backed by tangible assets but

EXHIBIT 6.18

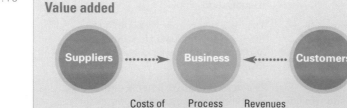

Value added

Suppliers ·······▶ Business ◀······· Customers

Costs of inputs   Process costs   Revenues

added value = revenues – (cost of all inputs + process costs)

EXHIBIT 6.19

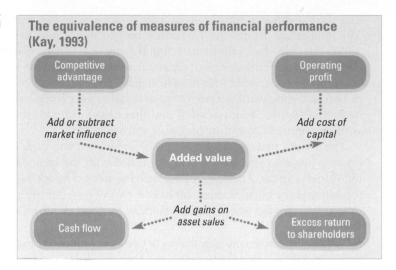

The equivalence of measures of financial performance (Kay, 1993)

reflect a belief in their future earning power. These ratings rely on the hidden assets – the intellectual capital in the organisations. While such examples are extreme, it is now becoming recognised that the intellectual capital in almost any organisation is the seed corn for future prosperity. Thus there is a quest to include it in financial statements and in the balanced scorecard.

Exhibit 6.20 sets out an evaluation scheme for intellectual capital. The market value of a firm is composed of its financial capital – as measured by its book value or some variant of it – and its intellectual capital. The intellectual capital includes such

EXHIBIT 6.20

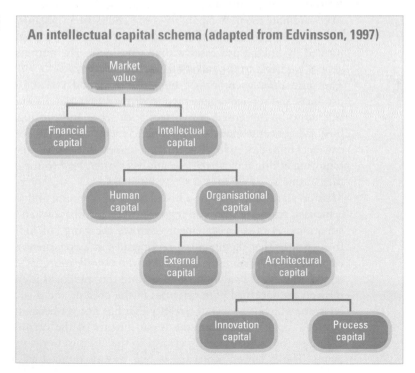

An intellectual capital schema (adapted from Edvinsson, 1997)

items as patents, trademarks, computer systems, customer databases and alliances. The intellectual capital can be further broken down into that capital that resides within the individual – the human capital – and that which resides in the organisation itself. Edvinsson[22] has described organisational capital as what is left behind when the staff go home, i.e. what isn't in their heads. The organisational capital is composed of two elements: that associated with external relationships – such as customer databases and supplier relationships – and that associated with the firm's architecture – with the internal context, its processes and structures.

The architectual capital can in turn be subdivided into capital associated with processes – process capital – and that associated with the future and with innovation – innovation capital. Although the balanced scorecard hasn't been subdivided further, the importance of intellectual capital to an organisation means that the scorecard should be extended when there are sufficiently good measures to make it workable.

SUMMARY

- A business can be considered to have two environments. First, there is the *operating environment*, composed of elements that the organisation can influence and that also influence the business. Second, there is the *remote environment*, composed of elements on which the individual business has no significant influence but that may have a major effect on the operating environment and on the business. EXHIBIT 6.3

- The business and corporation are the two appropriate levels of business analysis. Functions and subfunctions can't sensibly have a strategy on their own, and strategy at the level of the offer ignores the links between offers in a portfolio and the common cost base. Industry is either too nebulous a concept or linked too rigidly to operations and too little to the dynamics of the market to be useful for purposes of statistical analysis. EXHIBIT 6.4

- A process is made up of basic assets, tacit and explicit knowledge and a procedure to co-ordinate them. A capability is the ability of an organisation to combine business processes to deliver something that is valued by a customer. Capabilities are formed by linking processes within a business. The outputs from capabilities are generally visible to the stakeholders. EXHIBITS 6.5 TO 6.7

- The term *offer* encompasses both products and services and invariably means products and services augmented to fit market requirements. An offer can be considered to be composed of two facets: the core and the augmented offer. Current business concerns include offer enhancements and extensions, which the business can accommodate within its present capabilities. Offer enlargements are those requiring additional capabilities and very often lead to the establishment of a further business. EXHIBITS 6.8 TO EXHIBIT 6.10

- Mission statements provide a broad sense of direction and should be able to evoke a focused response from the organisation's members when they confront unusual situations. A mission statement narrows the range of individual discretion and thus ensures that the organisation operates in a consistent manner. There are five elements to a mission: the purpose of the organisation, its strategic goals, its strategic pathway, the values it espouses and the standards it expects of employees. A mission is concerned with activities in the present and near future. It differs from a vision, which is a view of a reality that has not yet been attained. EXHIBIT 6.12

- Strategic goals encapsulate the broad intents of the organisation and should be linked to the factors that are critical to the organisation's present and future well-being. The balanced scorecard is one way of doing this. Various measures are available to evaluate the financial success of a commercial business, each suitable for a particular purpose and for particular audiences. Added value is the most appropriate financial measure to use; adding value is a core rationale for the business, and added value can be related to competitive advantage.   EXHIBITS 6.16 TO EXHIBIT 6.19

- With intellectual capital now far outweighing tangible assets in very many organisations, there is a pressing need to ensure that intellectual capital is identified and safeguarded.   EXHIBIT 6.20

SELF-CHECK   1 Reconsider the learning outcomes for this chapter. Check that you feel confident that you can carry out the activities listed there.

2 Having read this chapter, you should be able to define the following terms:

balanced scorecard	offer	purpose in a mission
basic asset	offer enhancement	remote environment
business	offer enlargement	resource
capability	offer extension	service
core product	operating environment	strategic asset
corporation	procedure	strategic business unit
industry	process	strategic goal
intellectual capital	produce	value

MINI-CASE

GUS develops a winner

Great Universal Stores (GUS) has for many years been the UK's major mail-order shopping organisation with, for example, its Kays and GUSCO brands. By the late 1970s it had grown to such an extent that it received around five million applications a year for its various brand catalogues. It also operated the General Guarantee Company, offering motor finance. This meant that it had information on many millions of UK residents, not only postal information but also, because it had to safeguard its operations, on their creditworthiness.

During the 1970s, GUS developed an internal Credit Account Information Sharing (CAIS; pronounced 'keys') network to allow any of its constituent businesses to access the customer information held by any of the others. For example, when a customer applied for a motor finance loan, the General Guarantee Company could reference any mail-order accounts of GUS associates and use this information in its lending decisions. In 1980, realising the potential of the data it possessed and after an approach it received from a high-street bank to carry out creditworthiness checks, GUS set up its customer database as a free-standing business called CCN, and CAIS was extended to include the bank's data.

CCN offered a consistent and valid set of public-domain data relating to millions of UK citizens: addresses, county court judgments, electoral roll information, etc., together with past credit histories. It was continually augmenting the scope of its database. In the main, CCN's clients were the banks and hire-purchase companies. CCN also provided consultancy in the analysis and use of this data, for example the building of credit-scoring models tailored to the particular needs of clients. CCN also used its database for market segmentation, for example to provide targeted mailing lists.

Early in the 1980s, CCN began to involve itself in management systems to carry out real-time authorisations of card transactions, for example for credit-card companies. In

1983, having been a purely UK operation like its parent, CCN began to set up offices in Europe and the Pacific Rim to offer consultancy in credit scoring. However, it didn't initially possess the databases for these areas required to offer a full credit-rating and scoring service.

From the mid-1980s, CCN further developed its software to manage the interface that clients had with its databases. This was quickly followed by risk-management software, which clients could use themselves to analyse, model and implement policies towards credit-seeking clients.

Throughout the 1980s and 1990s, CCN continued to expand the CAIS network. This had become a grouping of clients of CCN – mostly external to GUS – who realised that if they shared information on their clients with each other, they were each likely to safeguard themselves better against fraud and bad debt. The members of the group operated 'rules of reciprocity' under which they agreed to post data to the CCN-controlled database in exchange for access to the data posted by others. Restrictions were placed on the use to which the data could be put; for example, companies weren't allowed to use the data to directly target rivals' customers.

In the late 1980s, CCN developed MOSAIC, a database and associated software that classified each postal code in the UK according to 50 lifestyle groupings: large new houses occupied by 'corporate careerists', inner-city rented accommodation occupied by young people – the 'rootless renters' – 'pebbledash suburbia' for middle-class families, and so on. MOSAIC allows an area, such as Greater Manchester, to be depicted according to types of people, and thus buying patterns.

At this time, CCN also developed its suite of Strategy Manager software. The suite includes a module to allow company risk managers to use their own PCs to create and change the rules they wished to apply in their risk-management policies and then hand the file to the IT department to be processed against the database of applicants. A second module provides portfolio management determining clients' balances, the minimum payment due, etc., and initiates any procedures that are needed, such as collection procedures.

In 1992, CCN entered the US market by taking a stake in MDS, a 200-person agency located in Atlanta, Georgia. MDS, with its analytical and consulting base, gave CCN entry into the US financial sector. Later, CCN obtained full control of MDS.

In June 1997, GUS bought the firm Experian, the second-largest data bureau in the USA, and amalgamated CCN with Experian under the latter's name but the former's control. This combined Experian's established capability to provide US data similar to that possessed by CCN with CCN's advanced software and analytical services. GUS continued to acquire firms to support Experian's core activities. Towards the end of 1997, Metromail, a US direct mailing and marketing company, was acquired. In 1997, Experian acquired GOAD, a group specialising in recording the location of every retail outlet in each of the top 120 UK shopping centres. It also bought COREF in France, a consultancy group providing consultancy services to the banking industry. In 1999, Experian acquired the Argentinian business information suppliers ADDO Sistemas de Decisión SA and Fidelitas SA to establish it as one of the region's major suppliers of commercial and consumer credit information.

Experian now has a turnover in excess of £1 billion and accounts for around a third of GUS's profits.

Discussion point 6.10

Which of the moves that CCN/Experian has made have been offer enhancements, which offer extensions and which offer enlargements?

What capabilities does Experian currently possess?

What competencies does Experian currently possess?

1 For GSM:
   • Make two lists of GSM's capabilities and competencies.
   • What capabilities/competencies did the purchase of Wetherby give GSM?
2 In which environment would you place the primary stakeholders? The secondary stakeholders? (Section 1.7 might help here).
3 Would it be appropriate for an organisation to have a mission statement if it were following an emergent strategy (Section 1.9)?
4 How do the elements of the cultural onion enter the mission statement?
5 What additional resources would the local garage need to acquire in order to successfully carry out a move into servicing commercial vehicles?
6 It's not always easy to pick out the components of a mission from a mission statement. What are the purpose, strategic goals, strategic pathway, values and standards demonstrated in the Ford mission statement (page 180)?

Obtain your university's mission statement and use the checklist in Exhibit 6.15 to assess its worth.

The view of the pre-eminence of the offer in developing business strategy is most forcibly put by Shiv Mathur and Alfred Kenyon in their recent book, *Creating Value: Shaping Tomorrow's Business*, Butterworth Heinemann, 1997.

An interesting read on the subject of missions is the book by Andrew Campbell and Kiran Tawadey, *Mission and Business Philosophy: Winning Employee Commitment*, Heinemann Professional, 1990.

That added value is the most appropriate measure of business success is well argued by John Kay in his book *Foundations of Corporate Success: How Business Strategies Add Value*, Oxford University Press, 1993.

1 Following Salveson, M.E., 'The management of strategy', *Long Range Planning*, Vol. 7, No. 1, February 1974, pp. 19–26.

2 *International Standard Industrial Classification of all Economic Activities*, 3rd revision, Statistical Office of the United Nations, Statistical Papers, series M, No. 4 Rev. 3, United Nations 1990, Department of International Economic and Social Affairs, Publishing Division, New York; and *Standard Industrial Classification Manual 1987*, Executive Office of the President, Office of Management and Budget, National Technical Information Service, PB87–100012, Springfield, Va., USA.

3 Feigenbaum, A., McGee, J. and Thomas, H., 'Exploring the link between strategic groups and competitive strategy', Faculty working paper No. 1238, College of Commerce and Business Administration, University of Illinois, 1986.

4 Porter, M.E. and Millar, V.E., 'How information gives you competitive advantage', *Harvard Business Review*, July–Aug 1985, pp. 149–60.

5 Keen, P.G.W., *Competing in Time: Using Telecommunications for Competitive Advantage*, Ballinger, 1988.

6 Stalk, G., Evans, P. and Shulman, L., 'Competing on capabilities', *Harvard Business Review*, March–April 1992.

7 When an organisation decides to enlarge both its product/service and market portfolios at the same time, it is termed diversification.

8 Thackray, R., 'Reinventing the wheel', *Independent on Sunday*, 'Smart Moves', 22 March 1998, p. 4.

9 Marsh, P., 'Moving into a higher gear', *Financial Times*, 'Survey: World Engineering' 24 June 1998, p. 1.

10 Snyder, N.H., Dowd, J.J. Jr and

Houghton, D.M., *Vision, Values and Courage: Leadership for Quality Management*, Free Press, 1994, p. 18.

11 Quoted in *The Guardian*, 29 January 1999, p. 19.

12 Simons, R., *Levers of Control: How Managers Use Innovative Control Systems to Drive Strategic Renewal*, Harvard Business School Press, 1995, p. 135.

13 Based on Campbell, A. and Tawadey, K., *Mission and Business Philosophy: Winning Employee Commitment*, Heinemann Professional, 1990. In their view, a mission statement has four elements: purpose, company values, standards and behaviours.

14 Peters, T.J. and Waterman, R.H. Jr, *In Search of Excellence: Lessons from America's Best-run Companies*, Harper & Row, 1982.

15 Cadbury, Sir Adrian, *Lancaster University Esmee Fairbairn Distinguished Lecture Series*, 7 November 1991.

16 Kanter, R.M., *Men and Women of the Corporation*, Basic Books, 1977, pp. 49–55.

17 *The Guardian*, 19 February 1997.

18 RAC, news release, 17 April 1997.

19 This questionnaire is based on the Ashridge Strategic Management Centre's 'Do you have a good mission statement?'

20 Kaplan, R.S. and Norton, D.P., 'The balanced scorecard – measures that drive performance', *Harvard Business Review*, Jan–Feb 1992, pp. 71–9. In 1996, several US business leaders wrote that they found it particularly useful (*Harvard Business Review*, 'Letters to the Editor', March–April, 1996, pp. 168–71).

21 Kay, J., *Foundations of Corporate Success: How Business Strategies Add Value*, Oxford University Press, 1993.

22 Edvinsson, L., 'Developing intellectual capital at skandia', *Long Range Planning*, Vol. 30, No. 3, 1997, pp. 366–73. He used different names for some of the items in his hierarchy; they have been changed to retain the same terminology across chapters.

PART 2

Picturing the future

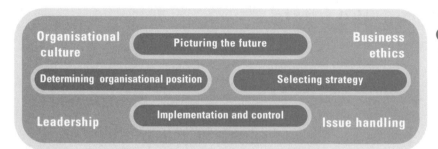

t his chapter is the first of three chapters concerned with the process of 'picturing the future', with deriving views of the environment within which the organisation is and will be operating. The concern in this chapter is with the remote environment, with that part of the environment that the organisation can't influence, but which can have a powerful influence on its operating environment.

The chapter begins with an exploration of what is meant by the remote environment for a business, followed by a consideration of the waves of change, the megatrends, that underpin the current changes in the remote environment. Information technology and internationalisation are the two main drivers for change, and each of these is explored. Attention is then focused on the individual elements of the remote environment. These elements constitute the DEEPLIST checklist: **D**emographic, **E**conomic, **E**nvironmental, **P**olitical, **L**egal, **I**nformational, **S**ocial and **T**echnological.

The environment of a business can be split into two parts: the remote environment and the operating environment. While it is generally changes in the operating environment that most concern businesses, the origins of most of these changes lie in the remote environment. Thus the ways in which the remote environment might develop must be understood.

LEARNING
OUTCOMES

When you have worked through this chapter, you should be able to:

- describe what the remote environment for a business is and explain its relationship to a business's operating environment;

- state the differences in the characteristics of the second and third waves of change and understand their significance;

- describe the convergence of computer, telephony and television technologies and explain their significance;

- explain internationalisation and understand the sceptics' view on the level of globalisation;

- list the eight DEEPLIST elements and appreciate the sorts of factors that would be included in each;

- identify the set of DEEPLIST elements appropriate for a specific business.

7.1 The remote environment

As we saw in Chapter 6, a business can be considered to have two environments. First there is the operating environment, involving components that the business can influence and that also influence the business. Second there is the remote environment, involving components on which the individual business has no significant influence, but which can have a major effect on the operating environment and on the business. In this respect the individual businesses in the operating environment are like small boats floating in a remote environmental 'sea', having to adapt to whatever the elements throw at them. Changes in the remote environment affect businesses indirectly through changes in the operating environment: for example, political or social changes induce changes in market conditions and technological change provokes the emergence of substitute offers.

While it's generally changes in the operating environment that most concern businesses, strategists must concern themselves with the remote environment because strategic issues – significant trends and events – generally originate there. An example of a trend would be the increase in the ageing populations in most countries in the developed world. An example of a strategic event would be an approaching general election.

In one sense the remote environment is the same for all organisations, since all organisations, wherever they are located in the world, are affected in some way by the ageing population in the developed world and the results of elections in major countries. However, some will be affected in a strong and direct way, others in a weak and much less direct way. In order not to be swamped by all the detail in the remote environment, every organisation will have to pick out of it those elements that are of particular concern and that warrant further attention; in short, the remote environment needs to be modelled.

Consider the following examples of environmental modelling. Recent changes in drug patent laws have considerably affected the operating environment of pharmaceutical companies but aren't likely to have concerned motor manufacturers. Conversely, the recent alteration in the vehicle registration system in the UK whereby car registration prefix letters are changed twice yearly will clearly affect the car industry but is unlikely to be of any significant concern to pharmaceutical companies. A firm producing gardening equipment wouldn't be too concerned with changes in teenage demographics, while it should be concerned with the number of people taking early retirement. A new government may have plans to restrict the activities of factory farming, which is not likely to be of great significance to a newspaper wholesaler but is obviously quite a concern for many farmers.

Before moving on, it should be recognised that every issue is likely to have a differential impact on individual businesses that are carrying out the same sort of activity. For example, the former UK vehicle-licensing regime with its annually changing licence plate letter was originally called for by the car industry itself as a means of boosting sales. The surge in demand when the plates changed each year meant that car manufacturers needed to build up stocks of cars. Since sales in the UK constitute a large proportion of the sales of UK producers but a relatively small proportion of sales for continental European and East Asian producers, these strains were felt differentially. Differential effects such as these are considered in Chapter 10; in this chapter the concern isn't with the remote environment of a specific business but with the remote environment for all competing businesses.

DISCUSSION
POINT 7.1
The ageing population and an imminent general election are strategic issues that can potentially affect all businesses active in the UK. Can you think of other such wide-ranging developments?
- Can you think of 'specific' issues in the remote environment affecting a) universities, b) food retailers?

KEY CONCEPT
The term *remote environment* is shorthand for *remote environment for a business*. The remote environment is a model of those elements in the environment that may affect the business's operating environment but that the business can't significantly influence. The remote environment is likely to be substantially the same for all competing businesses operating within the same national economy.

7.2 Waves of change – the megatrends

The remote environment for all competing businesses is the focus of this chapter. For most, but by no means all, this means a timeframe of perhaps five to ten years. However, before looking at appropriate 'models' of such remote environments, it's very useful to get a feel for the megatrends that underpin them, trends that may take decades to work themselves through. Historians, particularly economic historians, can shed light on trends of historic proportions.

7.2.1 The third wave

Toffler examined long-term trends in his trilogy of books. Some of his specific predictions of what the future would hold have not turned out as he suggested, but the overall scope of his work has a great deal of merit.

Toffler's 1980 book is called *The Third Wave*.[1] He applies the wave metaphor because he wishes to see beneath the raging surface of change to distinguish those changes that are merely transitional and cosmetic from those that are truly revolutionary. The first wave was the change from a hunter gatherer existence to a more settled agricultural way of life. The second wave was the industrialisation that occurred in (mainly) Europe and North America between the eighteenth and mid-twentieth centuries.

Second-wave society was heavily dependent on concentrated fossil fuels for its energy sources, factory production for its goods, the nuclear family for social stability, the corporation as the main means of wealth creation and mass education to supply the labour for the factories. Mass education and the mass media contributed to social cohesion (and to social engineering). There was a wide gulf between production and consumption: almost no one produced the items they consumed. The whole organisation was managed by a set of elites, governments, civil servants and corporations whose task was to integrate the elements into a whole. In particular, the nation-state was a second-wave creation, particularly matched to the size and scope of second-wave economies.

In developed countries, we haven't left behind all traces of the first two waves; indeed, we are in the middle of a struggle between the industrial and the post-industrial modes of thought and lifestyles, mingled together with a nostalgic view among some for an agricultural way of life.

According to Toffler, the characteristics of the third wave are almost diametrically opposed to those of the second wave, as shown in Exhibit 7.1. Although standardisation of measurement in production has been retained, there has been a move away from the production of millions of identical products to providing much greater choice. For example, UK supermarkets stock around half a dozen types of table salt; there are around 250 models of car on sale in most European countries. There has been a demassification of the media, as shown by the upsurge in the number of specialist periodicals and the number of TV channels now available. And whereas in the second wave the recipients of goods and services were passive, having a negligible *individual* impact on the offers they bought, the move now is towards incorporating individual tastes into their production. The purchase of a new kitchen is a good example of this, whereby the technology exists for the customer to input to its design. As Amis[2] says, 'We live in a karaoke age. You don't listen to your favourite singer. You become your favourite singer.'

EXHIBIT 7.1

The forces of the second wave (Toffler, 1980)

Force	Consequences
Standardisation	Standardisation of measurements; millions of identical products
Specialisation	Specialists within manufacturing and in the professions
Synchronisation	Groups of workers working together at the same time
Concentration	Concentrated energy sources, cities, factories, schools, hospitals, mental asylums and of capital
Maximisation	Quest for efficiency and bigness
Centralisation	New management methods in business and politics

Standardised norms of behaviour haven't been retained; there is considerable individualism and pluralism of outlook and behaviour. This is perhaps most obviously reflected in the many forms of sexual relationship that are now openly accepted.

Specialisation is a very significant feature of the second wave. Instead of an individual or their family taking responsibility for their own food, clothing, education, health, etc., large numbers of specialisms became established by people who would do this for them: specialist farmers, teachers, doctors, lawyers, etc. In the third wave, individuals are taking back some of these responsibilities. This is shown, for example, in the increasing concern people have to take responsibility for their own health, reflected in their preoccupation with diet and exercise, and the pressure exerted by governments for individuals to take responsibility for funding their old age.

There has been a move away from synchronisation and concentration. Toffler sees office workers as the last surge of the second wave; they are the factory workers of the present. The rise in the number of people employed in call centres is a recent example of this surge. With the facilities offered by information technology, the need to maintain synchronisation of same-place/same-time working is no longer so pressing. The reduction in concentration is seen in the more modern energy sources that provide both electricity and heat to a local community.

DISCUSSION
POINT 7.2

Can you think of further examples of the move towards individualised products?
- What other examples can you give of individuals taking back responsibilities?
- What other forms of desynchronisation can you think of?
- Can you think of other examples of a reduction in concentration in our lives?

The second wave was characterised by a concern for efficiency. This led to massive manufacturing operations, built without consideration of the needs of the people who had to work there. This partly reflected the fact that second-wave manufacture was based on the production of very large numbers of identical products from a mass of individual pieces, whereas third-wave processes (in which the overwhelming majority of people are employed in the manufacturing industries of developed economies) are much more holistic in concept, concentrating on one-off or short-run products; examples are aero engines, mainframe computers, pharmaceuticals, high-tech polymers and plastics.

As the move from second-wave to knowledge jobs continues, management methods need to change. Centralisation made sense when the environment was changing slowly and there was a need to concentrate and maximise. The move nowadays is towards much smaller units that are more autonomous and more in control of their own destiny. The failure of communism reflects this at the international level.

7.2.2   The knowledge age

We are entering the third wave of human endeavour, which is variously termed post-modern and post-capitalist; sometimes it is referred to as 'the information age', but a better term is 'the knowledge age'.

The knowledge age is one where the rare resource is knowledge and no longer capital[3]: this is why it's alternatively termed *post-capital*. Many observers[4,5,6] consider 1956 as a watershed: it was the year in which, for the first time in US history, white-collar workers in technical, managerial and clerical jobs outnumbered blue-collar workers. The next year was also fateful; it was the year in which the first satellite was launched (the Russian *sputnik*), leading to the development of communications satellites, which form a major element in the global communications infrastructure.

According to Drucker, from 1750 to 1900 knowledge was applied to making more efficient machines. From 1900 to 1975 knowledge was applied to the organisation of work, i.e. making groups of resources more efficent through, for example, production line working and the use of time-and-motion study. This application of knowledge to work led to the productivity revolution, which is responsible for the high standards of living in the developed world. Applying knowledge to finding out how existing resources can best be used to produce results is, in effect, what we mean by management. But knowledge is now also being applied systematically to define what new knowledge is needed. It is being applied, in other words, to systematic innovation.

Drucker views the future as both non-socialist and non-capitalist. In his view, the market will remain the effective integrator of *economic* activity, but *society* has already moved into the post-capitalist age. In the new economy the vast majority of workers would be either knowledge or service workers. The *economic* challenge of third-wave society is how to make the knowledge worker productive; the *social* challenge will be the dignity of service workers.

DISCUSSION POINT 7.3 Do you think that 'knowledge age' is a better term than 'information age'?

7.2.3   Megatrends and the remote environment

In Exhibit 7.2 the megatrends are shown influencing and being part of the remote environment that 'surrounds' the operating environment in which a business operates. Note that there will be trends and events that don't necessarily have their origins in the shift from second to third waves, or if they do the influence is very weak. One example of this is the ageing of the populations in the developed world; a second is the imposition of changes in a national tax regime. So the remote environment is a mix of both third-wave characteristics and other trends.

EXHIBIT 7.2

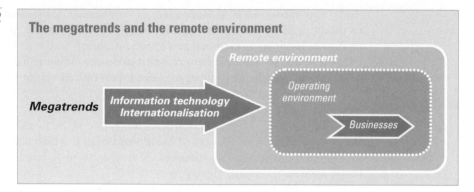

The megatrends and the remote environment

KEY CONCEPT   The remote environment for a business is both informed and formed by megatrends. These megatrends are very long-term trends of interest to virtually all businesses, while the remote environment is shorter-term and will also contain issues
that are of concern only to sets of competitive businesses. We are at the beginning
of the knowledge age, where knowledge is being applied to knowledge. Capital isn't
a limit on production; the limit is our imagination.

In Exhibit 7.2 two main forces are shown driving the megatrends to change the
remote environment. These two forces will now be considered.

7.3   Information technology

Microsoft is one of the largest organisations in the world and Bill Gates, one of its
founders and the main shareholder, is now the richest individual in the world, estimated to be worth $100 billion in mid-1999. The company that produced the Internet
search engine Yahoo! was valued in mid-1999 at $30 billion – remarkable for a
company that has had great difficulty making any profits at all since it was founded
in 1996. These two examples illustrate how much IT has been and will continue to
be a very powerful business driver.

IT has been an enormous factor for change over the last 20 years and will almost
certainly be the biggest single influence on business over the next few decades, fundamentally changing how businesses operate, indeed possibly the nature of business
altogether.

7.3.1   The convergence of communications technologies

The real excitement in IT over recent years has been the convergence of three communications technologies: telephony, television (and radio) and the Internet. This
convergence may bring about the merging of the three means of communication so
that eventually you won't need to have a separate phone, TV and computer; you will
be able to choose to have only one piece of equipment, with one network doing all.
But perhaps not. Murdoch's[7] view about the convergence of TV and the PC is that

'TV will continue to be the medium for "lean-back" leisure rather than "lean-forward" interaction. Both pieces of technology will happily sit together in the home of the future, fulfilling different needs for their owners.'

The convergence of the three communications technologies has come about because telephony and television (and radio) have followed computing technology and 'gone digital'. This means that the codification of data into zeros and ones (bits), which has been the basis of computers from their inception, has been extended to telephony and television, so that voice messages and images are transmitted using the same coding as that used in computers. The main developments in IT are described in Exhibit 7.3.

7.3.2 Television and radio

Digital TV won't only provide mobility and better-quality reception: the real revolution will be in the content that can be provided. Viewers can have the choice of

EXHIBIT 7.3

IT developments

The transistor, the basis for modern computers, was discovered in 1947. Computing and communications have developed enormously over the subsequent 50 years. The increase in computing power – measured by the number of instructions per second that a processor can carry out – has over three decades followed Moore's law, named after Gordon Moore, co-founder of Intel, the world's leading maker of computer chips. In 1965 Moore forecast that computing power would double every 18 months to two years. This has meant, for example, that between 1960 and 1990 the cost of a unit of computing fell by 99%.[8] Computer power is now 8000 times less expensive that it was 30 years ago. 'If we had similar progress in automotive technology, today you could buy a Lexus for about $2, it would travel at the speed of sound and go about 600 miles on a thimble-full of gas.'[9] (But see the riposte.[10])

Computing technology has been one of the main drivers of the convergence; the other is the rapid development of fibre-optic[11] and wireless technologies, both satellite and land-based. While computer technology provides processing power and the means of routing signals along the appropriate communication 'roads', these roads are increasingly fibre-optic and wireless. Fibre-optic cables are made from filaments of glass fibres, each only the thickness of a human hair and from glass that is so pure that a sheet 70 miles thick would be as clear as a windowpane.[12] The filaments carry the bits as very small pulses of light. Fibre-optic and satellite channels support the revolution in communications because they provide what is termed broad bandwidth. Bandwidth is the number of bits per second that can pass through a channel. There is a comparable law to Moore's for fibre optics – currently, bandwidth is tripling every year.[13]

At the beginning of 1999, Internet traffic exceeded voice traffic in both the USA and the UK. The cost of transferring a terabyte (a million million bytes, equivalent to 300 million pages of text) is estimated to fall from $80,000 in 1998 to $300 by 2003.[14]

For those of you who are interested in collecting 'laws', there is Metcalfe's law, promulagated by Robert Metcalfe, who founded 3Com, the US networking equipment manufacturer: 'The value of a network is proportional to the square of the number of nodes in the network.'

Discussion point 7.4

Where does this exhibit suggest we are in the development of the knowledge age?

perhaps 500 channels, some dedicated to narrow interest, along the lines of Cable News Network, which provides news around the clock, and Sky Sports, dedicated to sports and nothing else. The markets for news and sport – and for many such transmissions – is almost endless. CNN now has seven channels, one devoted to sports news and one specially designed to show in airports (presumably without news of plane crashes!). Such channels are able to be strongly branded. The development of TV would appear to be following the development of department stores and boutiques, with the traditional networks as the department stores, poorly branded and losing market share to the narrowly focused boutique channels.[15]

TV is making strong inroads into developing economies. China already has more cable television subscribers than any other country bar the USA, and India has more homes with cable TV than with a telephone.[16]

7.3.3 The Internet

The Internet grew out of the communication needs of the research and university communities between the 1960s and 1980s. The term *Internet* is a shortened version of *international network of computers*.

The Internet is the infrastructure linking the computers of the world together in a network of networks consisting of links and nodes. A national road system is an analogous network of networks. In any city there are roads (the links) and roundabouts and crossroads (the nodes) forming a network. Each city network is linked to other city networks via highways. The networks of the Internet operate under the Transmission Control Protocol/International Protocol (TCP/IP), a standard protocol that is recognised by virtually all computers.

Often the term *World Wide Web* (WWW), or simply the Web, is used synonymously with the Internet. However, Web applications are only one category of application where data are transmitted across the Internet; others are e-mail, voicemail and electronic data interchange (EDI). Although e-mail, voicemail and EDI can and are run on the Internet *outside* of the Web – and indeed outside of the Internet – rather confusingly, perhaps, they are also available *within* the Web.

Since it has become available to the general public, penetration of the Internet has been exceedingly fast. As Koenig writes:[17]

> It took 38 years for the radio to reach 50 million US listeners, and 13 years for the television to reach 50 million viewers. It has taken only 5 years since the internet got going for real in the US in 1993 for the internet to acquire 50 million users.

It's worth noting the increase in the activity possible to the recipients in this quote; first they were listeners, then listeners and viewers and now users.

7.3.4 Intranets and extranets

Overloading of the capacity of the Internet by 'leisure surfers' is a problem. It may mean that a two-tier system develops, with business class for those willing to pay for high-quality service. The congestion is also being tackled through the use of private internets. For reasons of cost, security and speed, some companies operate their own local area networks (LANs), which link people over small distances, say up to 5 km, and thus cover a large factory site or a university campus. Wide area networks

(WANs) link sites over a greater distance. Companies are using Internet and Web technologies on these dedicated networks as they are cheaper to use than the older technologies and aren't proprietary (owned by a software house). Networks conforming to the TCP/IP that are used exclusively within a single organisation are termed *intranets*. Intranets are themselves often networks of networks: an office network may reside within a functional network, which itself may be part of a company network, which may be linked within a corporate network.

Increasingly, companies are linking electronically through private networks with external stakeholders, e.g. suppliers, agents and customers. For example, many of the main motor manufacturers have demanded that their major suppliers be linked electronically. Where these private networks use the TCP/IP, they are termed *extranets*.

7.3.5 The end of the PC-centric era?

To most people, Internet access is via a PC and thus the importance of the PC has increased as the use of the Internet has increased. However, the centrality of the PC is being threatened by other modes of communication, by other forms of what are termed *information appliances*. An information appliance is any device that can be connected via a network to a source of information. Digital TV allows easy access to the Internet, and the situation is rapidly developing where most people will carry several Internet enabled devices capable of doing some of the things traditionally done by PCs.[18] Mobile phones can now access the Internet. In 1998, NCR and Knowledge Laboratory developed a 'concept microwave' that plugs into the Internet, with a touch-sensitive screen and built-in Internet browser, arguing that a microwave is located in the kitchen where people are often doing such things as household administration, sorting out bills and writing shopping lists.[19] In 1999, Electrolux was preparing to launch its ScreenFridge with a 'home management centre'. The argument put forward is that the fridge is the most visited place in the home. Games machines and of course televisions are other information appliances that could be used to access the Internet.

7.3.6 How widespread will Internet usage be?

It's very difficult to estimate the scope of Internet usage. Many commentators have provided estimates that vary widely and these need to be updated often. One estimate is for 300 million households worldwide on-line by 2005, with roughly a third of these in Europe, a third in the USA and a third elsewhere.[20] The overall consensus is that business-to-business e-commerce will grow rapidly; estimating consumer usage is more problematical.

At the beginning of 1999, the projected size of the UK on-line retail market excluding financial services was forecast as shown in Exhibit 7.4.[21] The important feature to note is that a decade after the beginning of the Internet proper, only a very small percentage of overall sales is forecast to be transacted via the Internet. The overall value of the UK retail sector is around €230 billion[22] (£150 billion in round figures), which puts the volume of Internet shopping into perspective. Apparently, shoppers like shopping, but there are often reasons linked to the characteristics of the offer. Offers that can be specified precisely and in a manner that can be easily understood will be sold readily on the Internet. These are products such as computer software and

EXHIBIT 7.4

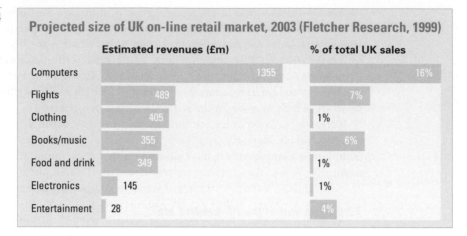

Projected size of UK on-line retail market, 2003 (Fletcher Research, 1999)

	Estimated revenues (£m)	% of total UK sales
Computers	1355	16%
Flights	489	7%
Clothing	405	1%
Books/music	355	6%
Food and drink	349	1%
Electronics	145	1%
Entertainment	28	4%

hardware, books, discs, videos and sheet music, music recordings and films; and services such as financial services – insurance, banking and investments, travel and betting. A second consideration is that the value of transactions is often too low to justify the cost of maintaining a transaction-based website.

There are three main inhibitors to the rapid development of consumer e-commerce in Europe: the far-from-full penetration of PCs in the home (although TV has a much greater penetration); relatively high local telecommunication tariffs; and doubts about Internet security concerning payments.

The potential of the Internet is immense, but what can easily be overlooked is that this potential may take some years to be achieved. Customer inertia can be high. A cautionary tale come from the introduction of credit cards. The first cards were introduced into the UK in 1963, with the publicity that this was the beginning of the end of the cheque. But it wasn't until 1990 that a fall in the number of cheque transactions occurred.

7.3.7 US domination of the Internet

The USA is likely to dominate the new communications technologies in the medium term. Houlder[23] writes that in 1997, American businesses and consumers made nearly 90% of all Internet purchases. US businesses account for 70% of all websites and 93% of Web revenues. The Americans have low telephone tariffs, with local call charges not usually based on the length of the call, and wide ownership of personal computers. They have an average 30% higher standard of living than Europeans. They use/speak the world's most widely spoken second language and the language of business – English – and are comfortable with mail-order shopping and credit-card ordering. With technological convergence, the intellectual property industries such as the film industry and popular music, in which the USA excels, will become more valuable. Microsoft, Intel, Oracle and Yahoo! are all American companies. Finally, there are 100 million TV households in the USA, most currently watching poor-quality analogue transmissions. The Americans will see a much greater benefit than Europeans in the move to digital TV, with its higher picture quality, and are thus likely to switch to it faster and in larger numbers.

We are approaching a situation where virtually free telecommunications have collapsed distance. The convergence of computer, telephone and TV technologies and the almost universal acceptance of Internet and Web technologies means that information is more readily available than ever before. Satellite communications mean that geography ceases to be a significant inhibitor of information access.

7.4 Internationalisation and globalisation

The second main driver of the third wave is internationalisation. The popular term for this is 'globalisation', but globalisation is only one form of internationalistion, one that encompasses the whole globe. While there are activities that can be considered global – and IT is a clear example of this – there are many others that are continental or regional in scope, and others that remain national or subnational.

7.4.1 The rise of internationalisation

Between 1930 and 1990, the average revenue per mile in air transport fell from US¢68 to ¢11 (in 1990 dollars). Between the early 1980s and 1996, the unit cost of sea freight fell by 70% in real terms.[24] The cost of communications has fallen dramatically over the last few decades, and communication is expected to become virtually free in the medium term. The Internet is also rapidly becoming a force in business.

It is the decline in the costs of transport and telecommunications that has made the growing integration of national economies feasible. The progress has been greatly helped by the liberalisation of trade between countries and blocs. During the 1990s the EU has become a tariff-free zone within its borders, many of its members have joined together to use a common currency, and the Union may soon be expanded to possibly 21 member states. The North American Free Trade Area and the Association of South-East Asian Nations have been established. The Uruguay round of multinational trade negotiations and many bilateral arrangements have substantially reduced inter-country tariffs and quotas. These technological and political changes have helped the cause of the international economy.

As long ago as 1983, Levitt[25] wrote:

> the same single standardized products – autos, steel, chemicals, petroleum, cement, agricultural commodities and equipment, industrial and commercial construction, banking, insurance, computers, semiconductors, transport, electronic instruments, pharmaceuticals and telecommunications – [are sold] largely in the same single ways everywhere.

Levitt may be overstating the case somewhat, concentrating on industrial products rather than consumer products and services. For example, although wholesale banking services are sold in a similar way in all advanced countries, this is certainly not the case with retail (high-street) banking. But Levitt certainly has a case: young urban professionals in London probably have more in common with their opposite numbers in Hong Kong than they do with farm workers in Scotland.

While the obvious starting point for any strategic analysis is to consider competition to be global, this global stance couldn't sensibly be held for long in many cases, for example when considering the operations of a corner shop. The point of starting global is so that analysis won't be inappropriately limited to current national or regional boundaries – it would include the possibility of competition from as yet unrecognised firms abroad, and the possibility of a firm developing internationally itself.

Some products/services do have global markets, others have regional ones and some are very local. Aerospace, pharmaceuticals and cars are probably global products; airlines and telecoms benefit from a large network. English has now become established as the international business language, and Western values have been spread around the globe through television, videos and films. For example, in 1999 it was estimated that one billion people in 144 countries regularly watch the TV programme *Baywatch*.[26] Many films and musical recordings tend to be global in appeal.

However, the construction industry, which relies on local labour and local materials, operates locally, except for some specialism such as tunnelling and the design and building of skyscrapers. Newspapers are a product that shows the whole gamut of geographic spread: there are newspapers for small localities (e.g. the *Wuppertal Nachrichten*, the *Nottingham Evening Post*), regions (e.g. *Ouest-France*, *Le Provençal*, *Frankfurter Allgemeine Zeitung*, *Süd Deutsche Zeitung*, *Yorkshire Post*), national newspapers (e.g. *Le Monde*, *Die Zeit*, *El Païs*, *Corriera della Serra*, *The Times*) and continental newspapers (e.g. *USA Today*). There is possibly one general-interest global newspaper in the *International Herald Tribune*, printed in Paris, and there are three for the global financial community (*The Financial Times*, *The Wall Street Journal* and *The Economist*).

DISCUSSION
POINT 7.5

Can you give other examples of offers that are local, national, continental and global?

There has perhaps been an overemphasis on the extent of internationalisation and in particular of globalisation. For example, in 1950 the ratio of exports to global output was 7%, in 1973 it was 11% and in the early 1990s around 14%.[27] The volume of international activity is increasing, but the proportion of international trade is only doing so rather slowly. In 1999, after almost a decade of a tariff-free EU, the prices of cars vary among its members by close to 50%,[28] illustrating that internationalisation in production and products isn't the same as the internationalisation of markets. Exhibit 7.5 sets out very clearly the concerns of those who are sceptical about what they see as the popular overemphasis on globalisation.

7.5 The remote environment for a business

7.5.1 The DEEPLIST checklist

The remote environment can perhaps most easily be modelled through using the DEEPLIST checklist[30] shown in Exhibit 7.6. Although it's useful to consider the remote environment under the eight categories in this list, as with many cases in strategic management the categorisation isn't water-tight and some features could sensibly be included in more than one category, or indeed *should* be included in more than one category. The issues are highly interrelated and thus an issue in one category may influence another. For example, increased wealth (economic dimension) may

EXHIBIT 7.5

Globalisation: the facts behind the myth[29]

There is a scene in one of the films by the great American comedian WC Fields which goes something like this: Fields, as usual playing a wealthy sourpuss, is sitting by the fire in his comfortable home. It is a winter during the American depression. An unshaven, bedraggled figure knocks on the door. Barely able to speak with cold, he says: 'I haven't eaten in a week.' Fields, scowling, replies 'force yourself!' and shuts the door.

As an economist I like this scene; it is an excellent example of a common phenomenon: wilful misinterpretation of evidence in one's favour. The dramatically overused, and much abused, notion of 'globalisation' is largely based on misinterpretation of evidence; and the concept is most frequently used by those with a vested interest of one sort or another.

For example, governments, when in power (though rarely when in opposition), frequently claim they are constrained by global forces. 'We cannot ban tobacco advertising in Formula One racing since. . .' or 'There is no point in our banning exports of arms to that country because of the global market. . .' And what better way for corporate spokesmen and women to justify an attempt at changing work practices or gaining acceptance for a small pay settlement than by saying that in a global market failure to compete will result in death.

How can the claims of the globalists be assessed? Is it true that in the last 10 to 20 years there have been such changes in technology, in the nature of traded goods and the way materials, information and people move around the globe that the world is now a dramatically different place than it was 50 or even 20 years ago?

Hermann Goering once, famously, said: 'When I hear the word culture I reach for my gun.' When I hear the word 'globalisation' I reach for the *Annual Abstract of Statistics*. And what statistics reveal is that the claim that there is a global world marketplace in most commodities is hard to square with the facts.

Consider, first, the allocation of accumulated wealth across different asset classes. Portfolio theory says that diversification is a good thing. Suppose we live in a world with no barriers to international portfolio diversification. It would seem to follow that the portfolio of wealth held by the private sector in various countries should be fairly widely internationally diversified.

A chart reveals a picture of portfolio allocation dramatically at odds with this. It shows the proportion of the total wealth held by the personal sectors in the major economies that is in the form of claims on governments or companies in foreign countries. I use here a very wide definition of financial assets – it includes direct ownership by households of equities, bank deposits and bonds; but it also includes all the assets held by pension funds, life insurance companies, mutual funds and so on on behalf of the personal sector. The chart reveals that in Europe, typically only about 5 per cent of the overall financial assets of the private sector are international. The UK and the Netherlands stand out as countries with an unusually high degree of international diversification; but even there only around 15 per cent of assets are claims on foreign governments or companies.

Labour is dramatically less mobile than financial wealth. Indeed labour mobility now is probably lower than for much of the past 150 years. For those who are relatively well-off (almost anyone in a developed country) a combination of inertia and familiarity with one's own culture and language make the option of moving to another country to work fairly unattractive for most people. For those who are far from comfortable (in developing countries the vast majority), immigration restrictions rule out the option of moving to countries where standards of living are dramatically higher.

It is plausible, of course, that physical capital (the location of factories and offices) is more mobile than human capital. Is there a global market here? In fact the degree of mobility of capital may well be no greater than 100 years ago. Consider the recent evidence from the UK. The UK has been one of the most successful countries in Europe in attracting foreign direct investment. Over the last 10 years the level of foreign direct investment in the UK has averaged about £12 billion a year. But that still only represents a little over 10 per cent of domestic fixed investment over that period. So one of the most successful developed countries in attracting inward investment still finds that about 90 per cent of its capital formation is done by nationals.

This observation fits in with the empirical evidence first uncovered over 15 years ago by Martin Feldstein and Charles Horioka. They found an extremely high correlation between changes in physical investment in countries and changes in domestic saving. The implication of their finding was that most investment in developed countries gets financed from domestic saving. Most studies continue to find a very significant correlation between national saving and investment.

Of course it would be absurd to argue that all this means economies are insulated from world economic developments. But the claim of the globalists seems to be that there has, fairly recently, been some dramatic change in the degree of integration of world markets. Two forces – one worldwide and the other specific to Europe – are often argued to be behind this. First, technology has so increased the ease with which information can be transferred that the physical location of many operations is often now irrelevant. Second, and specific to Europe, the creation of the single market, the abolition of many tariffs and the imminent creation of a single currency area have (it is argued) had a massive impact.

I doubt whether either of these factors is really that new or has caused a huge jump in market integration. In the second half of the nineteenth century there were few capital or trade restrictions between the capitalist countries. For much of that period there also, effectively, existed a single currency (the gold standard). And for much of the nineteenth century there were huge movements of workers between countries (largely from Europe to America).

At the same time there were enormous flows of capital between countries. And in the 40 years from 1861 to 1901 the pace of technological change was stunning. In those four decades the following were invented: the telephone, the internal combustion engine, the microphone, the electric locomotive, the motor car, the aeroplane, the radio transmitter. It is far from obvious that in the period since 1960 there has been such a change in technology.

In fact, claims about globalisation are themselves not particularly new. I am old enough to remember Labour politicians in the mid-1960s blaming many of the country's economic ills on the 'gnomes of Zurich' – the faceless operators of the global levers of economic power. And there is a much longer tradition of politicians being prey to the dark forces of foreign financiers.

So the next time you hear someone pontificating about globalisation ask yourself just what they are trying to make you believe, and why.

Discussion point 7.6

This exhibit discusses the internationalisation of accumulated wealth, labour mobility and the movement of physical capital, and suggests that globalisation may not be as important as many commentators suggest. Do you believe that globalisation will be a major force in business over the next one or two decades? For all businesses?

EXHIBIT 7.6

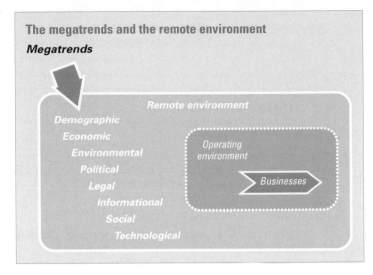

The megatrends and the remote environment

Megatrends

Remote environment

Demographic
Economic
Environmental
Political
Legal
Informational
Social
Technological

Operating environment

Businesses

cause an increase in car ownership (social dimension), leading to a demand for more out-of-town shopping centres (social and economic dimensions), putting pressure on governments to ease planning permission (political dimension). 'Miscategorisation' doesn't really matter as long as all significant issues are identified.

The following consideration of the elements of the DEEPLIST environment can't possibly be anything like exhaustive; the best that can be done is to indicate examples in each area to illustrate the sort of factors that might be included in each category.

7.5.2 Demographic

Demographics is concerned with mapping the characteristics of human populations, with such factors as the distribution of ages, gender and the ethnic mix, and with income distributions. These factors are the determinants of many of the long-term changes in society. One major statistic is the estimate that there are more people alive today than have ever lived, which is a very sobering thought; if this is true, one euphemism for dying, *joining the majority*, no longer applies. In developed countries a significant concern is the size of the ageing population. The data in Exhibit 7.7 show projections of the world population under five 'fertility' scenarios.

Demographics would also include, for example, the composition of the labour force – the distribution between sectors and standards of education and training.

7.5.3 Economic

The issues in the economic environment include such matters as the tax and monetary regimes that national and international governments employ, and the state of economic activity, as reflected in such measures as industrial output, consumption levels, price movements, inflation and exchange rates. Economics is also concerned with structural shifts in the economy, for example the move from 'smokestack' to knowledge-based industries and from manufacturing into services. The shift from manufacturing to services links into another trend – away from transaction-oriented links between producer and customer towards the relationship-oriented links associated with the provision of services.

EXHIBIT 7.7

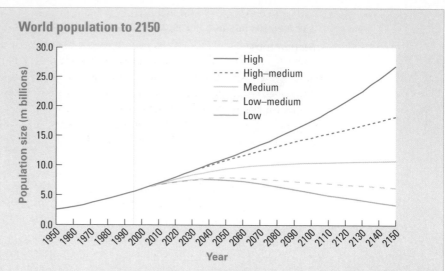

World population to 2150

Population size (m billions)

- High
- High–medium
- Medium
- Low–medium
- Low

Year

Source: Population Division of the Department of Economic and Social Affairs at the United Nations Secretariat, *World Population Projections to 2150* (United Nations, New York, 1998).

The fertility gap separating the high- and low-fertility scenarios is about one child. The high-fertility scenario assumes that total fertility rates will converge by 2050 to between 2.50 and 2.60 children per woman, and the low-fertility scenario assumes that the total fertility rates will eventually stabilise at levels between 1.35 and 1.60 children per woman. According to the high-fertility scenario, world population will grow to 11.2 billion by 2050, 17.5 billion by 2100 and 27.0 billion by 2150. The low-fertility scenario is in sharp contrast and shows a world population increasing to 7.7 billion persons by 2050 but then declining to 5.6 billion in 2100 and eventually falling to 3.6 billion by 2150.

There are two intermediate scenarios, the high/medium- and low/medium-fertility scenarios, which assume that fertility rates will follow the high and the low patterns, respectively, until about 2025, after which they converge to 10% above replacement level (in the high/medium-fertility extension) and 10% below replacement level (in the low/medium-fertility extension). According to these two scenarios, world population in 2150 would reach 18.3 billion and 6.4 billion, respectively.

The constant-fertility scenario presents the results of future world population growth if fertility rates were to remain at 1990–1995 levels until 2150. The results highlighted the unsustainability of the current situation: world population under the constant-fertility scenario would reach 296 billion by 2150.

Economics is also about the comparative advantage of nations, the costs of operating in different countries. With enhanced world trade it might be expected that inequalities between different parts of the world would be falling, but this doesn't seem to be the case. The share of the poorest fifth of the world's population in global income dropped from 2.3% to 1.4% during the 1990s.[31]

IT has made the financial markets into global markets, with money capable of being transferred very rapidly from one financial centre to another. Every working day, well over a trillion dollars is traded on the global currency markets.[32] This has made it far harder to isolate national and regional economies.

The curbs on greenhouse gases agreed at Kyoto in 1997 will have an impact on the world's energy producers that will take years or even decades to emerge fully. Some expect a general rise in energy prices as governments resort to higher taxes to cut fossil fuel demand. Oil will probably bear the maximum inpact as the ordinary motorist is an easier target than industry. The Kyoto agreement is likely to help natural gas sales and accelerate the trend to replace coal-fired power plants with gas-fired ones.

The 'third way' popularised by Tony Blair and seemingly taken up with alacrity by many other European countries has several core ideas, which seem likely to form the economic landscape over the next decade or so. These include deregulation and privatisation, free trade, flexible labour markets, smaller safety nets and fiscal austerity.[33] A distinct theme is that the economic losers must be carried into the mainstream of economic life and not left behind. Thus income distribution isn't seen as the way forward; rather, the idea is to make it easier for those who would normally be considered losers – the unemployed and the uneducated – to find work and thus become winners. Work is the core responsibility – with governments called upon to provide access to the necessary job skills, and individuals to work hard.

7.5.4 Environmental

The consequences of global warming found perhaps their most evocative embodiment for British people in the massive fall of rock at Beachy Head – the white cliffs of Sussex – during the night of Sunday morning, 10 January 1999. This fall was caused by bigger waves than normal in the English Channel and unusually heavy rains, both of which were blamed on global warming.[34] Worldwide, hurricanes with a ferocity that was predicted to occur once in 100 years are now occurring once a decade. Sea levels are expected to rise over the whole world, submerging entire sets of islands such as the Maldives and inundating low-level land in such places as Bangladesh and East Anglia in the UK due to thermal expansion of the oceans and to melting glaciers and, in the case of East Anglia, the tipping of the whole of the UK towards the east. The link between global warming and the burning of fossil fuels gave rise to the political developments at Kyoto.

Another worrying trend is the thinning of the ozone layer that protects the Earth's surface from harmful radiation. Acid rain is a further example of action at a distance, as is the pollution of common seas and oceans. Half the world's rivers and lakes are seriously polluted, and that includes the freshwater lakes in Europe. As Hampden-Turner and Trompenaars[35] quite nicely point out, 'unless we control pollution, instead of wealth we will have illth'.

7.5.5 Political

The political environment may be broadly defined as the arena within which different interest groups compete for attention and resources to advance their own values, interests and goals.[36] It is also concerned with the scope of territorial governance, with freedoms and with the reach of the state.

One of the most significant developments over the last two decades has been the pluralism of political groupings that have found expression – supranational, national, district and tribal. Many of these are tending to outflank the nation-state, with some observers[37,38] taking the view that the nation-state is becoming simply an administrative rather than a political unit. The major powers of a state have traditionally lain in control of its currency and its armed forces. Few if any of the countries of Western Europe, for example, still retain these powers in any effective form. Regionalism results from the economies of scale associated with third-wave industries (reflected in the spate of merger activity in the EU). There is an increase in tribalism epitomised by the setting up of national assemblies in Scotland and Wales, Basque and Catalan separatism in Spain, and the break-up of the Soviet Union.

At the other end of the scale there are the lowering of trade barriers and the rise of large groupings such as the EU and NAFTA. The collapse of communism has left the USA as the only superpower. The USA is also the global policeman, as the leadership it showed in the European dispute in former Yugoslavia testifies. It is also the most powerful economy, although Japan or the EU might supplant it in the distant future. The country or bloc in this powerful position tends to write the rules of world trade to its own advantage.[39]

The changes being wrought in the EU are good and pertinent examples of the effect of politics on the business environment. For example, the push by some countries of the EU for very close integration of tax regimes and for common health and safety laws will have widespread consequences for business. The development of the EU and the common currency in many of the member states have changed the regulatory climate with regards to transborder merger and acquisition activity. There are an increasing number of pan-European institutions, for example the European Medicines Evaluation Agency and the European Central Bank.

Deregulation is also a significant factor in all EU countries and in the former communist countries in Eastern Europe. This brings powerful competitors into certain sectors such as the utilities and airlines.

Whereas in the past the state took care of old age and illness, this has become politically unacceptable and people will be required to make their own provision. The political dimension also takes into account the infrastructure of the nation or region. For example, the form of the transport system, the number of new roads and subventions to encourage rail travel, and decisions concerning the number, siting and size of out-of-town shopping centres are all political decisions.

7.5.6 Legal

The legal environment consists of the body of laws and regulations that affect business together with the institutions that administer and enforce them. Thus all the regulatory requirements – for example health and safety, information disclosure, maternity and paternity legislation and the laws governing the dismissal of employees – are considered part of the legal environment.

Regulations governing business are widespread; they include those on vehicle emissions, the use of pesticides, where smoking is permitted and many, many more. Privatisation programmes have included regulation, in the UK through such regulators as Oftel (the Office of Telecommunications) and Offer (the Office of Electricity Regulation).

Of major concern to business is the issue of governance, how enterprises should organise both to control themselves internally and to account responsibly to those agencies that can make a legitimate demand for accountability. Over the last decade there have been the Cadbury,[40] Greenbury[41] and Hampel[42] reports in the UK dealing with various aspects of governance.

There is a growing 'compensation culture' in which people readily take to the law courts to claim compensation for what has traditionally been considered an act of God or an accident. This is the culture that someone else is always to blame and that life should be risk-free. Thus we see police officers successfully suing for trauma associated with the Hillsborough football disaster of 1989; in 1999 there were around 4000 police compensation claims worth £40 million making their way through the UK courts. A doctor sued for pricking her finger on a needle, which led to her incapacitation through 'needle phobia'. A man who killed his mother was awarded £45,000 against a health authority deemed to have negligently discharged him from hospital. A senior social worker was awarded £175,000 for psychological stress due to the nature of his job.[43] The growing litigation fever in the UK has been encouraged by the introduction of no-win/no-fee arrangements for lawyers.

7.5.7 Informational

While the technological side of the informational business environment is treated as falling within the technological environment (see Section 7.5.9), the impact of information as the raw material in a knowledge-based economy is so great that it needs to be considered in its own right. There are many sources of information external to organisations that businesses can now access and make use of: on the Internet and through access to (commercial) databases and to firms making use of databases. For example, Experian offers a database of around 100 million records in the UK alone associated with the creditworthiness of individuals. It is becoming ever easier to use IT to pinpoint bad risks – the people who will cost the insurers money. For example, bad medical risks will be identified by genetic testing, and houses liable to subsidence will be identified from geological survey. So the old principle of a large cross-section of people pooling their risk is being replaced by individual risk identification. This will have consequences for many members of the community.

The ready transmission of business data has been greatly helped by English now being established as the world's commercial language, and the second language of a great many people.

7.5.8 Social

In contradistinction to the demographic environment, which is concerned with the structure of populations, the social dimension of the business environment is concerned with people's needs, wants and aspirations – with lifestyles and with the 'shapers' of markets. One strong trend in developed societies is the increased refinement of consumer requirements.

Women have probably never had equality with men at any period, but now a measure of equality has been attained in Western countries and women are pushing for change all over the world. Other traditions are being eroded, as the viewing figures for *Baywatch*, a series about lifeguards in California featuring scantily clad actors, might suggest. However, this has led to a counter-blast from fundamentalists, both religious and lay. Fundamentalism calls for a return to basic scripture, to be read in a literal manner, and the doctrines derived from this reading to be applied to social, political and economic life.

A widespread change has been the shift away from the historic 9–5 hours of employment to a much more flexible form. One manifestation is the so-called *24-hour society*, where many people are working at any hour during the day and night. Supermarkets are now open to midnight on a regular basis, leisure venues are open to the early hours, the Internet and other forms of IT allow people to order books or to bank in the middle of the night. Apparently more than 25% of UK shoppers are likely to shop after 6 pm and more than one million people in the UK work between 9 pm and 11 pm.[44] The driving forces for these changes include the young, affluent and time-pressured, especially single people living in cities.

In the UK, more people are living alone than ever before: in 1996 the number of one-person households was just under 30%, by 2016 it is estimated to reach 36%.

Within this statistic is the surprising one that 40% of adult women were living without a partner.[45] There are several causes for this: people are living longer after their partner has died, there are more divorces and people are marrying later. The number of young adults is due to rise, and they will have the income to support themselves in their own accommodation. This rise in one-person households has driven the government to plan for millions more dwellings over the next two decades, with the consequent pressure on land use and infrastructure. In business terms, people living alone is likely to increase demand for houses, for the infrastructure that supports new houses and for such things as fast food, home security and nursing agencies.

7.5.9 Technological

Technological change is the most visible and pervasive form of change in society, as it brings in its wake new products, processes and materials. It directly affects every aspect of society and alters the rules of international trade and competition.[46] The technological dimension of the environment can broadly be considered to encompass science and the translation of this scientific knowledge into innovation – new products, processes and materials.

While there is a generally held belief that technological change is accelerating and that we're living through the most dramatically changing times, perhaps this isn't in fact the case, as Exhibit 7.8 suggests.

Although IT is perhaps the main technological driver for change in business practice, other major changes appear to be widespread. Advances in biotechnology are likely to have the most profound affect on human existence of all the advances now occurring; genetic engineering is likely to revolutionise the drug and medical industries, insurance and indeed our whole thinking about what it is that is intrinsically human.

Developments in IT

The developments in IT, particularly the Internet, are megatrends that impinge directly on the operating environment, and as such the discussion in Section 7.3 applies equally well here. Features in the IT remote environment of particular significance are the following:

- Gates' contention[48] is that for a company to beat the competition it needs to develop a world-class digital nervous system, the technological version of the human nervous system. With such a system every piece of information is in digital form, and the information systems are so arranged that information flows effortlessly and seamlessly through the organisation. His view is that a number in digital form is the start of meaningful thought and the making of relationships; a number on a piece of paper isn't.

- Digitisation is also producing a convergence between consumer electronics and information technology. The significance of this is that some of the characteristics of the consumer electronics industry are likely to be absorbed into the IT sector, for example more user-friendly offers, greater price sensitivity and more offer styling.

- Electronic data interchange (EDI) is the electronic transmission of data without manual intervention. Until the late 1990s, EDI was established using proprietary software, with the substantial set-up cost that that entailed; this deterred all but the large organisations. This software was also rather inflexible. However, Web technologies make EDI much easier to carry out and much less costly, opening up EDI to the smaller company.

EXHIBIT 7.8

The future is not what it used to be[47]

Everyone knows that technology is advancing at an unprecedented rate. In the USA it is even argued that there is a 'new economy' or a 'new economic paradigm', in which innovation has freed us from the laws of economics which hitherto restricted growth.

And yet there is a problem with this argument. The best measure we have of the rate of technological change is the rate at which productivity is increasing – particularly in those countries, like the USA, which are at the frontiers of efficiency and application of technology. And productivity growth has not gone up. In the USA, and in most other developed countries, productivity has risen by less in the 25 years or so since 1970 than it did in the 25 years before that.

Now many of the proponents of the 'new economic paradigm' are aware of this difficulty. They argue that the statistics are simply wrong: they fail to reflect properly the impact of technology on growth and output. There is probably something in this argument. But to make it stick, you would have to demonstrate not only that we are underestimating the value of improvement in the quality of goods we buy – which is plausible – but that we are underestimating by more, much more, than we did in the past.

There is another possible explanation. It is that we are victims of our own hype, and that technology is not moving forward today any faster than it did in earlier decades.

After all, someone who lived from 1860 to 1960 would have seen horse transport replaced by cars and aeroplanes, would have watched electricity and everything powered by it introduced into their home, and might have lived in 1960 because they had not died from contaminated water, smallpox or infectious diseases – which is what would very probably have happened if they had been born a century earlier. They could never have expected to see or hear Abraham Lincoln, but the voice and moving image of John Kennedy was in their living room. Besides all this, Internet shopping seems a rather minor novelty. That thought was stimulated when I stumbled across a dusty copy of a 1967 report from the futurologists of the Hudson Institute, *The Next 33 Years – A Framework for Speculation* by H Kahn and A J Wiener (Daedalus, 1967). They had drawn on historical trends in innovation to suggest changes that would 'almost certainly' occur before the end of the century. They got a lot right.

They forecast general use of automation and cybernation in management and production, and development of high-speed data processing. They anticipated universal real-time credit, audit and banking systems. They thought we would have facsimile machines, and high-quality reproduction in black and white and colour. Communication would be transformed by personal pagers (perhaps even two-way pocket phones).

It is amusing that the too ubiquitous mobile phone was regarded as a way-out invention. Like many people in the 1960s, these futurologists correctly sensed that information technology would be important, and their expectations about what it would achieve were surprisingly prescient.

What they did not anticipate was miniaturisation, or that processing would become so cheap that we would have our own personal computers rather than a terminal to a central mega-computer. But once you move outside the field of electronics, very few of the innovations they anticipated have occurred.

Take transport. They expected us to have personal flying platforms and inexpensive road-free (and facility-free) transportation. We would traverse longer distances in super-helicopters and giant supersonic jets, and enjoy interplanetary travel. In reality, developments in transport have been modest. In 1939, you crossed the Atlantic in an ocean liner; in 1969, you could do so in six hours in a jumbo jet. In 1999, the seats are more comfortable and the flight attendants friendlier, but the service is essentially the same.

Or take fuel and power. The Hudson Institute anticipated new sources of power for fixed installations – magneto-hydrodynamic, thermionic and thermoelectric, and radio-active; for ground transportation – storage battery, fuel-cell propulsion, or support by electromagnetic fields; and a large expansion of controlled nuclear power. In practice, most power is still generated by burning fossil fuels to make electricity; cars still have petrol engines; and trains are propelled by diesel engines or overhead electricity supplies.

They expected our lifestyle to be transformed. We would have relatively effective appetite and weight control. We would benefit from human hibernation, controlled mechanisms for relaxation and sleep, and chemical methods for improved memory and learning, and enjoy programmed dreams. And there would be non-harmful methods of overindulging. I wish they had been right.

The list of things that have not happened goes on. We do not light cities by artificial moons, or have any significant influence on the weather. The fabrics we wear have not changed much. We still do not mine the oceans, and we certainly do not have undersea colonies. Automated grocery and department stores are technically feasible, but we do not want them.

If you had been writing in 1966, and had projected the pace of historical development in the creation of new materials, in transport, in pharmacology and in lifestyle changes, you would have anticipated far more than occurred, which is what the Hudson Institute did. In only one – admittedly large – area would you have underestimated the pace of change. Perhaps we have been misled by one extraordinary sector – electronics – into exaggerating the rate at which the world is changing. Perhaps the story the statistics tell us is true.

Discussion point 7.7

In its day, the Hudson Institute was considered the foremost futurology establishment in the world. What does this exhibit suggest we should do about considering the remote environment?

- Video conferencing, which allows people in different locations to hold 'virtual' meetings, thus reducing the need for people to travel to the same location, is becoming far more widespread in business.

- There are four billion microchips in the world and relatively few of these are in PCs;[49] the rest are in products. Microwave ovens now have microprocessors to provide automatic cooking programmes through which the user simply selects the type of food and keys in the weight; the oven will select the appropriate power level and cooking time. Sharp's Viewcook microwave comes with 200 pre-programmed recipes, each telling you the ingredients required and what to do with them.[50] There are talking microwaves for the elderly and visually impaired. Cars provide a further example where the use of microprocessors is widespread: controls that respond to voice can dial a number on the mobile phone, turn on the radio and adjust the internal temperature. Satellite navigation systems advise on less congested routes and automatically send out a call for help in an emergency together with the car's exact location; and there is also radar-guided cruise control, as well as electronic cards carried by the driver that replace the ignition and door keys and act at a distance.

- IT hasn't only made a huge impact on products: services have been influenced as well. Customer profiling is now becoming commonplace, made possible by new storage devices and access software. Credit scoring for potential consumers has been standard for some time, and this is developing into risk managment. In the insurance field sophisticated software is being used to cut down risk. Retailers are using loyalty cards and other means to develop relationship marketing.

DISCUSSION
POINT 7.8

Bill Gates apparently sees digitised numbers as the focus for learning. Do you think he is right to say this about strategic matters?

7.5.10   An example of a DEEPLIST checklist

Note that what is included in the DEEPLIST environment needs to be tailored to the timeframe of the target business; for a business involved in heavy industry this could be many years, while for a fashion boutique it could be a few months. An example of a DEEPLIST analysis that might apply to the aero engine maker Rolls-Royce plc is shown in Exhibit 7.9. Note that if a firm is operating in different countries, it could face several different DEEPLIST environments.

EXHIBIT 7.9

A DEEPLIST table for Rolls-Royce plc

Demographic

Disposable incomes
Increased numbers of mature people

Economic

Business cycles
Globalisation of markets
Economic climate
Disposable income of leisure flyers
Interest rates
Fuel tax rates

Environmental

Upper atmospheric pollution and the
   ozone layer
Noise restrictions near airports

Political

Government policy on subsidies
Restrictions on airport usage
Political stability in customer countries
Government and EU policies on airline
   alliances and mergers

Legal

Airworthiness certification requirements
Environmental legislation

Informational

Databases on airworthiness

Social

Amount of leisure time
Concern with night-time aircraft takeoffs
Desire for air travel

Technological

IT developments – decision conferencing
Advanced computer-aided design
New materials for blades and other
   components

Note that in Exhibit 7.9 the values of the issues aren't given: *disposable incomes* are listed and not *increase in disposable incomes*. All that has been done here is to identify strategic issues. The attachment of values to these issues at this stage would suggest that they could be forecast, which in most cases they can't. Attributing values to the issues will be undertaken when scenarios are considered in Chapter 9.

SUMMARY

- The term *remote environment* is shorthand for *remote environment for a business*. The remote environment is a model of those elements in the environment that may affect the business's operating environment but which the business can't significantly influence. Changes in the remote environment affect businesses through changes in the operating environment; for example, political or social changes induce changes in market conditions and technological change provokes the emergence of substitutes.

- The main changes from second-wave society to the third wave result mainly from advances in technology, particularly the advent of information technology in its many guises and internationalisation. Major shifts are away from standardisation, specialisation, synchronisation, concentration, maximisation and centralisation. EXHIBIT 7.1

- The remote environment includes and reflects the influence of megatrends. However, there will be trends and events that don't necessarily have their origins in the shift from second to third waves – or if they do, the influence is very weak. Thus the remote environment is a mix of both third-wave characteristics displacing those of the second wave and other trends. EXHIBIT 7.2

- The main source of wealth in the third wave is knowledge. Markets rather than political groupings dominate economic activity, although culturally there is a rise in small groupings and in individualism.

- Internet technology will make the cost of transmitting data and information anywhere in the world practically cost-free. Together with improved software, this will have the effect of destroying distance. The convergence of the three technologies – computers, telephony and television – will open up vast opportunities to change the way business is conducted. However, the speed of uptake of the Internet could easily have been overestimated. EXHIBIT 7.3, EXHIBIT 7.4

- Internationalisation is increasing and extending to global activities in some cases such as IT, car manufacturing and consultancy services. However, it's easy to ignore the vast amount of activity that isn't yet international and perhaps never will be. EXHIBIT 7.5

- The acronym DEEPLIST stands for Demographic, Economic, Environmental, Political, Legal, Informational, Social and Technological. This checklist is useful in identifying the factors in the environment that might change the environment within which an organisation is operating. EXHIBIT 7.6, EXHIBIT 7.9

SELF-CHECK

1 Reconsider the learning outcomes for this chapter. Check that you feel confident that you can carry out the activities listed there.

2 Having read this chapter, you should be able to define the following terms:

DEEPLIST	internationalisation	megatrend
extranet	Internet	post-capitalist
globalisation	intranet	World Wide Web
information appliance	knowledge age	

FURTHER
DISCUSSION
POINTS

1 What are the trends in GSM's remote environment?
2 Andy Law, chairman of St Luke's advertising agency, goes further than Toffler. 'Mr Law's view of history takes humans from agrarian and industrial eras to the Communications Age, which he says ends in 2000. Now the world has entered a "Creative Age", which benefits from free-thinking, flexibility, imagination and enjoyment.'[51] Do you believe that this is the case?
3 Is globalisation a reality for most companies or are those with global pretensions making almost all their money in a single market?
4 There is a call to 'think global, act local'. How difficult is this to achieve?

ASSIGNMENTS

1 For a business of your choice, construct a DEEPLIST environmental list.
2 Outline the economic indicators that may be used to assess the characteristics of the economic dimension for the car industry. Explain how such indicators affect motor manufacturers and dealerships.
3 Explain how a) car dealerships have been affected by changes in the remote environment over the last ten years, b) they might be affected over the next ten years.

FURTHER
READING

Alvin Toffler has produced books at the start of each of the last three decades. *Future Shock* (Random House) appeared in 1970, followed by *The Third Wave* in 1980 (Collins) and *Power Shift* in 1990 (Bantam Books). All are very readable and thought-provoking. Will there be a fourth book in 2000?

Frances Cairncross writes very interestingly on the history and the convergence of telephony, television and the Internet in her book *The Death of Distance*, published by Orion Business, 1997.

Michel Feneyrol, *Telecommunication in the 21st Century*, Springer, 1996 gives a very clear account of the information technology that is around now and can be expected to be developed in the next few decades. It has a French flavour.

For those interested in a history of the Internet, a very readable though detailed account is given by Daniel Dern, *The Internet Guide for New Users*, McGraw-Hill, 1994.

CHAPTER NOTES
AND REFERENCES

1 Toffler, A., *The Third Wave*, Collins, 1980.
2 Martin Amis, quoted in 'For the record', *The Independent on Sunday*, 5 October 1997, p. 23.
3 Drucker P.F., *Post-capitalist Society*, Butterworth Heinemann, 1993.
4 Toffler, A., *op. cit.*
5 Drucker, P.F., *op. cit.*
6 Naisbitt, J., *Megatrends: Ten New Directions Transforming our Lives*, Macdonald, 1984; and Naisbitt, J. and Aburdene, P., *Megatrends 2000: Ten New Directions for the 1990s*, William Morrow, 1990.

7 Murdoch, E., quoted in *The Guardian*, 'Media', 31 August 1998, p. 2.
8 Wolf, M., 'The heart of the new world economy', *Financial Times*, 1 October 1997, p. 16.
9 Pritchett, J., *The Employee Handbook of New Work Habits for a Radically Changing World*, Pritchett and Associates, 1997.
10 At a recent computer expo, Bill Gates reportedly compared the computer industry with the auto industry and stated: 'If GM had kept up with technology like the computer industry has, we would all be driving twenty-five dollar cars that got 1000 miles to the gallon.' In response to his comments, General Motors issued a press release stating:

'If GM had developed technology like Microsoft, we would all be driving cars with the following characteristics:

a) For no reason whatsoever your car would crash twice a day.

b) Every time they repainted the lines on the road you would have to buy a new car.

c) Occasionally your car would die on the freeway for no reason, and you would just accept this, restart and drive on.

d) Occasionally, executing a maneuver such as a left turn would cause your car to shut down and refuse to restart, in which case you would have to reinstall the engine.

e) Only one person at a time could use the car, unless you bought Car95 or CarNT. But then you would have to buy more seats.

f) Macintosh would make a car that was powered by the sun, reliable, five times as fast, and twice as easy to drive, but would only run on five percent of the roads.

g) The oil, water temperature and alternator warning lights would be replaced by a single *general car default* warning light.

h) New seats would force everyone to have the same size derriere.

i) The airbag system would say 'Are you sure?' before going off.

j) Occasionally, for no reason whatsoever, your car would lock you out and refuse to let you in until you simultaneously lifted the door handle, turned the key, and grabbed hold of the radio antenna.

k) GM would require all car buyers to also purchase a deluxe set of Rand McNally road maps (now a GM subsidiary), even though they neither need them nor want them. Attempting to delete this option would immediately cause the car's performance to diminish by 50% or more. Moreover, GM would become a target for investigation by the Justice Department.

l) Everytime GM introduced a new model car buyers would have to learn how to drive all over again because none of the controls would operate in the same manner as the old car.

m) You'd press the 'start' button to shut off the engine.

11 The term *fibre-optic* seems to be used interchangeably with *optical fibre*.

12 Cairncross, F., *The Death of Distance*, Orion Business, 1997, p. 5.

13 Shillingford, J., 'FT telecoms', *Financial Times*, 10 June 1998, p. 15.

14 Taylor, P., 'How the Internet will reshape worldwide business activity', *Financial Times*, 'Survey Information Technology', 7 April 1999, pp. I–II.

15 Cairncross, F., *op. cit.*, p. 68.

16 *Ibid.*, p. 63.

17 Koenig, P., 'The irresistible force', *The Independent on Sunday*, Bloomberg Business, 5 July 1998, p. 3.

18 Caulkin, S, 'In e-commerce, the 'e' is not for ecstacy', *The Observer*, 'Work', 20 September 1998, pp. I and VIII.

19 Murphy, D., 'Surfing with the oven', *Financial Times*, 18 September 1998, p. 12.

20 Datamonitor/IDC, quoted in *Financial Times*, Survey Information Technology', 7 April 1999, p. 1.

21 Fletcher Research, *Window Shopping*, quoted in Eaglesham, J., 'Retailers warned over web delays', *Financial Times*, 7 January 1999.

22 'Corporate intelligence on retailing', as reported in *The European Retail Handbook 1998*.

23 Houlder, V., 'Surfing in the wake of the Americans', *Financial Times*, 17 June 1998, p. 14.

24 Naisbitt, J., *op. cit.*

25 Levitt, T., 'The globalization of markets', *Harvard Business Review*, Vol. 61, No. 3, May–June, 1983, pp. 92–102.

26 Hobson, W., 'Hobson's choice', *The Independent on Sunday*, 'Culture', 11 April 1999, p. 2.

27 Naisbitt, J., *op. cit.*

28 Bowley, G., 'On the road to price con-

vergence', *Financial Times*, 12 November 1998, p. 45; and Bannister, N., 'UK cars most expensive in Europe', *The Guardian*, 2 February 1999, p. 2.

29   Miles, D, 'Globalisation: the facts behind the myth', *The Independent*, 22 December 1997, p. 19.

30   It is conventional to consider the remote environment as consisting of four main elements – political, economic, social and technological – and to look for issues in each element. This is why an analysis of the remote environment is sometimes loosely called a *PEST analysis*. A deficiency in using the PEST framework is that it doesn't easily accommodate natural events and trends such as global warming and earthquakes, legal issues, and the importance of information in the knowledge age. Note that some writers like specifically to include an environmental and others a legal dimension (a PESTEL analysis?). However, both acronyms are meaningless, whereas the acronym DEEPLIST resonates with the remoteness of the remote environment.

31   Reich, R. 'We must still tax and spend', *New Statesman*, 1 May 1999, pp. 13–14.

32   Gittens, A.. First Reith Lecture, *Runaway World*, 11 April 1999.

32   *Ibid.*

33   *Ibid.*

34   McCarthy, M., 'Beachy Head cliff collapses into the sea', *The Independent*, 12 January 1999, p. 5.

35   Hampden-Turner, C. and Trompenaars, F., *The Seven Cultures of Capitalism: Value Systems for Creating Wealth in the United States, Britain, Japan, Germany, France, Sweden, and the Netherlands*, Doubleday, 1993, p. 199.

36   Fahey, L. and Narayanan, V.K., *Macroenvironmental Analysis for Strategic Management*, West Publishing, 1986.

37   Toffler, A., *op. cit.*

38   Drucker, P.F., *op. cit.*

39   Thurow, L.C., *Head-to-head: The Coming Economic Battle among Japan, Europe and America*, Morrow, 1992.

40   The Cadbury Committee, *The Financial Aspects of Corporate Governance*, Stock Exchange Council, London, 1992.

41   Study Group on Directors' Remuneration, *Directors' Remuneration: Report of a Study Group Chaired by Sir Richard Greenbury*, Gee Publishing, July 1995.

42   Committee on Corporate Governance, final report (the Hampel Report), chairman: Sir Ronald Hampel, Gee, 1998.

43   Toynbee, P., 'A culture of compensation makes victims of us all', *The Guardian*, 21 April 1999, p. 18, quoting from Furedi, F., *In Courting Mistrust: The Hidden Growth of a Culture of Litigation in Britain*, Centre for Policy Studies, 1999.

44   The Future Foundation *The 24-Hour Society*, NTC Publications, 1998.

45   Clements, M., *The Improvised Woman: Single Women Reinventing Single Life*, Norton, 1999.

46   Fahey, L. and Narayaran, V.K., *op. cit.*

47   Kay, J., 'The future is not what it used to be', *Financial Times*, 8 July 1998, p. 13.

48   Gates, B. (with Collins Hemingway), *Business @ the Speed of Thought: Using a Digital Nervous System*, Warner Books, 1999.

49   Murphy, D., *op. cit.*

50   *Ibid.*

51   Abrams, H., 'A Creative Age manifesto', *Financial Post*, Canada, 11 January 1999, p. C4.

8 The operating environment

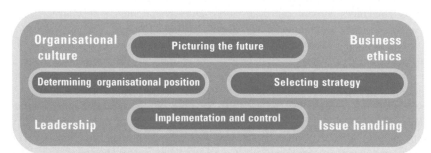

his chapter is the second of the three concerned with 'picturing the future'. The concern is with the operating environment, with that part of the environment that the organisation can influence.

The exploration of the operating environment begins with a consideration of the arena within which the organisation is competing and of the value chains of which the competitive arena is a part. These value chains, together with the secondary stakeholders, form the operating environment for the organisation.

The part of the operating environment that most intimately affects the competitive arena, the immediate operating environment, is explored in detail, followed by a consideration of the rest of the operating environment. Finally, operating environmental analyses for not-for-profit organisations are discussed.

The formulation of strategy can only be sensibly undertaken after an assessment of the organisation's operating environment, and the identification of the forces that directly affect its chances of success. The influences on a business are extensive and there is a need for a framework to help with their analysis. This chapter provides such a framework, which is vital for any leader-manager if they are to identify the significant factors in their operating environment.

LEARNING OUTCOMES

When you have worked through this chapter, you should be able to:

- identify the competitive arena and value chains for a specific business;

- describe the Porterian five forces model and list the factors that should be taken into account when assessing the strength of each of the five forces;

- explain the meaning of a substitute in strategic management and the difference between the use of the term in strategic management and in marketing;

- apply the five forces model of the immediate operating environment to a real situation;

- explain the deficiencies and limitations of the five forces model as the sole means of analysing a business's environment;

- extend the analysis to include the whole of the operating environment;

- identify when it would be advantageous to include potential competitors in the competitive arena;

- understand the significance of the changes that information technology can make to the forces in the value chain.

8.1 The competitive arena

In this chapter we are going to explore how to undertake a structural analysis of the operating environment. By a structural analysis is meant that we are going to look at the main elements of the operating environment in order to identify those that are strategically significant – the significant operating factors. We are addressing the question 'How attractive is the operating environment as a place to do business?' This is the second step towards deriving views of the future in which the business will be operating.

Except perhaps for very special organisations, all perform a conversion process and seek to add value – the value of the output is greater than the value (costs) of the inputs and of the process. A car assembler such as Ford or Peugeot converts a set of car components into a whole car to satisfy customers' need for personal, powered transport.

Any specific business won't generally be the only one carrying out the same conversion process: there will be others doing effectively the same thing – certainly others satisfying the same customer need – and thus providing competition. For example, Arbed/CSI of Luxembourg, CORUS (British Steel and Hoogovens), Thyssen/Krupp of Germany and Usinor of France are all competing in carrying out the conversion of iron ore into sheet steel; Ford, Peugeot, Toyota and VW are all competing in the assembly of parts to satisfy the need for cars. Even not-for-profit organisations will generally have competitors (the 100+ UK higher education establishments are all competitors to some degree, and charity shops such as Oxfam and Help the Aged are also fighting among themselves for income.[1] These competing businesses can be considered to be operating in the same **competitive arena**: all are satisfying the same broad customer need.

8.2 Value chain basics

Generally, the conversion process undertaken by the set of businesses in a competitive arena doesn't exist on its own: it is rare for something 'raw' to be finally consumed after only one conversion process. There is normally a set of conversion processes linked together in a chain. This is called the **value chain**. In Exhibit 8.1 each circle represents a **competitive arena**, where all directly competing businesses (shown by the ⏝ symbol) are located and where they are undertaking conversion processes to satisfy very similar customer needs. Note that the value chain shown in Exhibit 8.1 has four competitive arenas: it starts with the really raw 'things' (for which naturally there are no suppliers), followed by three other competitive arenas. The value chain is completed by the consumers, those who 'use up' the final offer. The arrows represent the logistics of the situation, with ever more refined offers passing **downstream**. **Upstream** is the opposite direction – towards the source of the value-creating process.

DISCUSSION POINT 8.1

What conversion process is an insurance company involved in? Or a retail bank? Or an airline? And what customer need are they satisfying?

- How many businesses are shown as active in the first competitive arena in Exhibit 8.1?
- Should the 'consumers' box' in Exhibit 8.1 be shown containing businesses (the ⏝ symbol)?

EXHIBIT 8.1

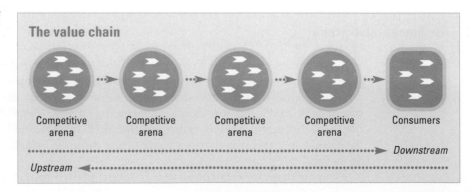

The value chain

Competitive arena   Competitive arena   Competitive arena   Competitive arena   Consumers

Downstream

Upstream

EXHIBIT 8.2

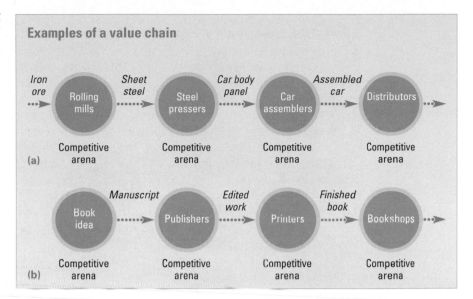

Examples of a value chain

Before moving on, it is important to recognise that the value chains shown in Exhibits 8.1 and 8.2 are very simple ones: they are very simple because each of the competitive arenas is shown feeding into only one other competitive arena. However, consider car assemblers. They take in a great many components, from a host of suppliers operating in different competitive arenas (tyres, electric motors, body panels, batteries, upholstery, glass, etc.), as shown in Exhibit 8.3. In 1997 Ford Europe had around 800 suppliers supplying items that were used in its cars. Equally, the businesses in a competitive arena can have customers in many different competitive arenas; a customer chain for electric motor manufacturers is shown in Exhibit 8.4. From Exhibits 8.3 and 8.4 we can see that there can be many different value chains merging into/coming out of the competitive arena in which a business is operating. All relevant value chains are part of the operating environment of a business.

Two examples of value chains are shown in Exhibit 8.2. In the first case iron ore is converted in a rolling mill into sheet steel, the sheet steel is pressed into a car body panel, which is assembled into a car by the car manufacturer. The car is then taken by distributors. In the second case a book idea is transformed through various stages into a finished book in a bookshop.

KEY CONCEPT A *value chain* is the chain of conversion processes from the initial 'raw' thing or concept through to the final consumption of the associated product or service. A *competitive arena* is formed by the totality of businesses that are involved in satisfying broadly the same customer needs. A value chain will generally include several competitive arenas.

DISCUSSION POINT 8.2

What might be the inputs to *Tyres* and *Batteries* in Exhibit 8.3?
- What might be further inputs to the aircraft builders in Exhibit 8.4?

EXHIBIT 8.3

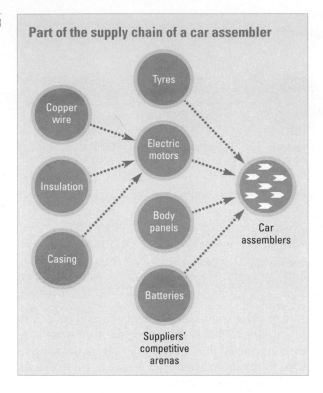

Part of the supply chain of a car assembler

EXHIBIT 8.4

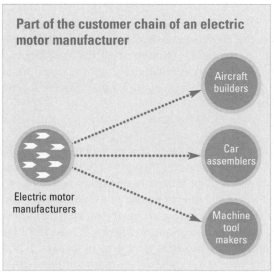

Part of the customer chain of an electric motor manufacturer

8.3 Operating environment basics

8.3.1 A note on terminology

Much of the structural analysis of the operating environment owes its origins to Porter.[2] Before moving on we should consider four terms introduced by Porter that

EXHIBIT 8.5

Terminology

Porter (1980)	This book
Value system	Value chain
Value chain	Value link
Buyer	Buyer/customer
Industry	Competitive arena

are either used differently or replaced by other terms in this and other chapters. His four terms and their replacements are listed in Exhibit 8.5. First, what he termed the *value system* is called the *value chain* here. This change is made for two reasons. The linkage of competitive arenas together forms what looks like a chain much more than a system. Second, the word 'chain' fits with the use of the term as it is used in supply chain management, defined by Potts[3] (1994) as 'the physical management of materials from suppliers to the customers' warehouses'.[4] The second change, the use of the term *value link* that will be met in Chapter 12, is better to describe activities *within* individual businesses as it reinforces the position of a business as an element in the value chain. 'System' and 'chain' don't provide an integrating picture: 'chain' and 'link' do.

Third, Porter uses the term *buyer* rather than *customer*. 'Customer' might be preferred as it is a more common term and the term *buyer* suggests a specific role within a business, whereas a customer may also be a private individual. Buyer and customer will be used interchangeably.

Fourth, Porter and many other writers use the term *industry* where *competitive arena* is used here. The reason for this is very clear, as described in Chapter 6: the term 'industry' is either too hazy a concept or is inappropriately defined to be useful in strategic analysis.

8.3.2 Defining the competitive arena

A competitive arena consists of all the directly competing businesses that seek to satisfy very similar customer needs. This may seem very clear-cut, but some clarification is needed. The Ford Motor Company is producing cars and lorries; are these conversion processes taking place in the same or in different competitive arenas? Ford makes its own starter motors, although these are made by other manufacturers for other car assemblers. What are the competitive arenas here?

There is no hard-and-fast rule as to how to define a competitive arena: what is important is to define it in a way that provides an illuminating analysis. A good starting point is to ask what is the broad customer requirement that is being satisfied.

In the case of cars it might be personal, weather-proof transportation; for some electric motor manufacturers it might be to provide the means of generating electricity on moving vehicles; for an insurance company it might be to carry individual risk. With this starting point, the competitive arena would naturally contain all the businesses that are competing directly to satisfy the identified customer need. *Directly competing* means that if one business gained market share, one or more other businesses would automatically lose market share.

There is the problem of a firm that is vertically integrated, i.e. it carries out several of the conversion processes in a value chain. For example, ICI Paints makes its own resins,[5] one of the basic ingredients of paint; is ICI Paints in the resin or in the paint-making competitive arena? It could be in both. If it makes resins only for itself, then its resin operations couldn't be considered a business and thus it wouldn't be in the resin competitive arena at all. On the other hand, if all paint makers made their own resins (and no one else did), then it wouldn't be sensible to attempt to separate resin manufacture from the whole operation. If there are resin manufacturers who do not manufacture paint and who supply paint makers, then there is a resin competitive arena and ICI's resin operation should be placed within it; after all, ICI could supply resins to other paint manufacturers and presumably buy (some of) its own from these other manufacturers.

A further complication comes about with segmentation, where a business treats different customers differently. Gold-card status for borrowers with low risk and Mondeos for salespeople are examples of segmentation. The touchstone of whether segmentation should act to differentiate competitive arenas is whether the operations to satisfy each segment can be considered a business – obviously each segment has a well-defined set of customers, but do they have sensibly separable production facilities and overhead apportionment? If not, it's unlikely that it would be appropriate to treat them as separate businesses and thus they should be treated as operating in the same competitive arena. A consultant suggested to a tobacco firm that it organise itself into businesses according to segment; this was rejected by the board as it would have meant that the factories would have to be segmented and this would prove very inefficient, given the fluctuations in demand that occurred over the year.

DISCUSSION
POINT 8.3

Where might you expect to see the broad customer requirement written down?
- Would you think that the car and truck operations of Ford should be treated as operating in different competitive arenas?

There is also the consideration of whether obviously *potential* competitors should be included in the competitive arena. The rationale would be that although not competitors at the moment, they would only need to change their operations in a relatively minor way to become so. For example, a firm making starter motors for cars might choose to diversify into other forms of electric motor – windscreen wiper motors or heaters for cars, or motors for aircraft or for domestic use. A consideration of potential competitors is particularly necessary when the current barrier to direct competition is geographical. This is linked to whether the competitive arena should be considered as including businesses all over the world or restricted to businesses in the same region – or are national, subnational or local areas appropriate? As a starting point, it's probably best to consider that all competitive arenas are global. However, this is just a starting point: it would be poor analysis to continue with this starting point if the analysis were being carried out for a local garage. But when you realise that at the height of the strawberry season in the UK, Californian strawberries can be marketed 10p a punnet cheaper than the home-grown variety, or that India is the home of many computer programming firms offering their services worldwide, then many competitive arenas that a few years ago were national or subnational have now become international.

KEY CONCEPT

There is no hard-and-fast way of defining a competitive arena: it should be defined in a way that provides an illuminating analysis. Difficulties in definition arise from firms being vertically integrated (i.e. operating in more than one competitive arena in the value chain), with segmentation and with the inclusion of potential competitors. The competitors and potential competitors are businesses; it doesn't make sense to talk of a competitive arena of corporations or of functions.

DISCUSSION
POINT 8.4

Why does it not make sense to talk of competitive arena of corporations or of functions?

8.3.3 Markets and the immediate operating environment

Let us return now to the simple case of the operating environment consisting of a single value chain, as shown in Exhibit 8.6. Again, each circle represents a competitive arena and the individual businesses are shown by the ⊃ symbol. The competitive arena of interest will be termed the *focus* competitive arena, and this is located centrally in Exhibit 8.6.

Note that in Exhibits 8.1 to 8.4 the arrows represented the flow of offers: logistically, logically and chronologically they move from left to right in the exhibits, i.e. downstream. In Exhibit 8.6, however, these arrows represent the **forces** operating in the value chain. They represent the relative **bargaining power** between the competitive areas, and they point both ways to illustrate the two-way nature of the forces. For example, while the businesses in the focus competitive arena influence customers in the customers' competitive arena, the customers in their turn also influence the focus competitive arena. The businesses in each competitive arena are operating in two markets: that with their customers and that with their suppliers. The market is the linkage between the competitive arena and its customers.

It is likely that the adjoining competitive arenas will have the strongest impact on each other: quite naturally, as they contain the market forces. As shown in Exhibit 8.6, these markets lie within what has been termed the **immediate operating environment**.[6] Note that it's in the market where the offers are treated as separate offers – it's in the competitive arena where the businesses are competing.

EXHIBIT 8.6

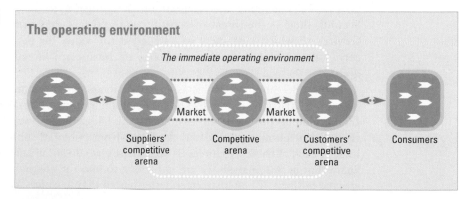

The operating environment

The immediate operating environment

Market   Market

Suppliers'   Competitive   Customers'   Consumers
competitive   arena   competitive
arena   arena

8.3.4 Perfect competition

There is a certain amount of profit in the value chain associated with the value that is being created. However, it isn't necessarily the case that the profit goes to those who create the value; it's the power of the various competitive arenas that determines which arena keeps the lion's share of the profits. Economists have identified perfect competition – the situation in the market that ensures that the customer gets the goods they want at the lowest price – and correspondingly the producers obtain just those profits that allow them to continue to exist but to do no better than that. The conditions of perfect competition[7] are that:

- all products are the same, there is no differentiation;
- customers have full information about the price of the offers from all producers;
- there is nothing to prevent firms entering the market;
- there is nothing to prevent firms leaving the market;
- each producer produces only a very small part of the total offer in the market, and thus no producer can significantly affect the price of offers. All the producers are what are termed *price takers*.

One reason for strategic managers to consider the forces in the operating environment is because they are trying to *prevent* perfect competition or anything approaching it. The purpose of the analysis is to identify the strength of the forces and to see how those that are harming profitability can be reduced or bypassed, and how those that might aid profitability can be protected and augmented.

8.4 The immediate operating environment

The immediate operating environment includes the customers of and suppliers to the businesses in the focus competitive arena. There are also considerations of the in-fighting between the businesses inside the competitive arena, with their rivalry.[8] However, there are two other forces. First, there is the threat of entry into the competitive arena: if the competitive arena is a profitable one to be in, then other firms might wish to enter. They will pose a significant threat of entry if the barriers to entry are low. It is one of the main considerations for all the businesses in the arena to ensure where possible that high barriers can be erected and maintained. Of course, the firms that wish to enter will try to reduce any barriers – and so will governments if there are suggestions of collusion to inhibit free competition. Second, there is the threat of substitutes: the threat that firms will offer goods or services to which customers will switch if the value for money they offer is perceived to be higher than that offered by businesses already in the competitive arena.

Exhibit 8.7 summarises this as Porter's famous five forces model of the immediate operating environment, the five forces being the rivalry within the competitive arena, the bargaining power of the customers, the bargaining power of the suppliers, the threat of potential entrants, and the threat from potential substitutes.[9] We will now look at each of these five forces in turn. Before we do so, it's important to stress once again that in this analysis we are *not* trying to find the answer to the question 'Is the specific business X better/stronger/better placed than business Y?' We are undertaking

EXHIBIT 8.7

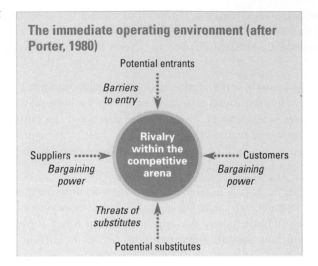

The immediate operating environment (after Porter, 1980)

Potential entrants

Barriers to entry

Rivalry within the competitive arena

Suppliers ......

Bargaining power

...... Customers

Bargaining power

Threats of substitutes

Potential substitutes

a *structural* analysis of the arena to assess what the forces are that are acting on it and within it in order to see whether it's hard or easy for the **generality** of businesses in it to make satisfactory profits.

KEY CONCEPT

The immediate operating environment is that part of the operating environment that includes the customers and suppliers and the other businesses operating in the competitive arena. Analysis of the forces of the operating environment includes the barriers to entry into the competitive arena and the threat of substitutes.

8.4.1 Intensity of rivalry

Here we are looking inside the competitive arena and considering those aspects of it that will suggest how much competition there is between the businesses there. It's important to do this, as the greater the in-fighting there is between the businesses for market share and profits, the more margins will be eroded. This erosion will come about through the greater costs incurred for such things as enhanced advertising and the acceptance of lower prices. The profitability of the whole of the competitive arena will correspondingly be reduced.

The factors that intensify the rivalry are as follows:

- If the businesses are equally balanced in terms of the market power they have
  It's easiest to see the consequences of equally balanced competitors by first
  considering the reverse: the situation where the competitive arena is dominated
  by one business. Often this domination will be associated with market share, but
  it may not be; for instance, a business with a small market share may have the
  power to lower prices below the norm through the results of innovation or
  through having a rich parent which is willing to support short-term losses, as
  News International has been willing to do with *The Times* newspaper during the
  1990s. In general, when domination occurs, all other businesses will have to fall
  in line with what the dominant player wants. Where there is no dominant player

– as with UK food retailing, where all of the big five supermarkets are of comparable size – there is fierce fighting for market share and profits. In such oligopolistic cases, a major concern is with the action–reaction between the players.

- **When the growth of the market is slow**   When a market is growing rapidly, it's fairly easy to increase sales without necessarily taking sales from anyone else. Of course, a business may be losing market share, but the impact is masked somewhat by the increasing absolute sales. Fast market growth can also be associated with a lack of supply, and this would tend to mean that prices and margins can be increased.

- **If there are high exit barriers**   From an economic perspective, a firm should exit the competitive arena when it could use its resources more profitably elsewhere. Whether there are opportunities in other competitive arenas will depend on how specific the capabilities are to its current activities. If the capabilities of the business are not very specific – and thus they can be used in many other activities – then the firm will exit the competitive arena as soon as it becomes difficult to make profits there and engage in more profitable ventures. This then removes a business from the competitive arena and reduces the overall production capacity, something likely to improve the profitability of the remaining businesses. On the other hand, if there were no better use for the capabilities (i.e. in any other competitive arena the firm's capabilities, either whole or broken up, would be worth less than they are currently), then the firm should continue to operate as long as its revenues are greater than its operating costs. For a firm to operate in this way is unhelpful for the competitive arena as a whole, since businesses want to obtain revenues that are significantly above operating costs to cover overheads and provide profits. Perhaps the best contemporary example of high exit barriers is that of the Channel Tunnel: billions of pounds in sunk costs have ensured that the operating costs of the tunnel are very low compared with those of the ferry operators. The tunnel also has 'infinite' asset specificity; what other use is there for it? So unless there is such an increase in cross-Channel traffic that the tunnel is operating at capacity and the ferries are needed to cope with the excess, sell your shares in the Dover, Folkestone and Calais harbour boards.

  Economic factors are not the only reasons that firms find it difficult to exit a competitive arena. The European steel industry in the 1980s and 1990s was a case of too many suppliers with too much capacity. Over the last decades, the problems with unemployment have meant that the political will has often been lacking to reform the industry.

  A stand-alone business will tend not to exit as this is the only business that it is in. There may be emotional ties as well, and this can be especially inhibiting with family firms. The links that a business has to its corporation may inhibit exit. This may occur where there is some form of synergy between the operations of the business and those of other businesses; the corporation may need a portfolio of interests. For example, many UK civil engineering firms are engaged in both house building and construction: house building provides good profits but is demanding of cash, while the construction business is the opposite.

- **When it's difficult to differentiate the product or service**   If a product or service is truly undifferentiated – what is often termed a commodity – then we have one of the conditions for perfect competition. This is something that no business wants, since then the only way to 'differentiate' a commodity is on price – by cutting margins and thus profits. Examples of undifferentiated products are fertilisers and cement. One way that an item becomes a commodity is through legislation: for example, if legislation were imposed to make all cars have airbags fitted as standard. Another way is when a well-defined standard is put in place: for example, when an item is specified as a national or European standard. In the building industry, many items such as bricks, concrete blocks, electrical fittings and drainage materials have a national standard designator attached and civil engineering projects specify to the standard. It is then very difficult for any supplier to supply an item with different characteristics that would differentiate its offer, since any higher performance would tend to be beyond specification and a higher price couldn't be obtained.

- **When the fixed costs are high**   When fixed costs are high the business will need to sell a large quantity to cover them, i.e. the break-even point will be high. The upshot of this is lower returns, as amply demonstrated by the findings of the PIMS programme[10] and shown in Exhibit 8.8. This shows a plot of return on investment against the ratio of investment to sales (termed the investment intensity). The figures on the x-axis represent the values of investment intensity that partition the sample into five equal portions; for example, 20% of the businesses in the sample have an investment intensity lower than 36%. With high fixed costs (reflected in a high investment intensity) the mode of competition changes: it may be very beneficial for society as a whole that investments are made to add more value, but the value doesn't accrue to the firms themselves. PIMS suggests that price wars develop in a search for the volume sales needed to cover fixed costs, and that the employees remaining after the introduction of the extra investment demand more pay. One example of this situation is the introduction of information technology in banks; in general the banks haven't gained from this, although customers have.

EXHIBIT 8.8

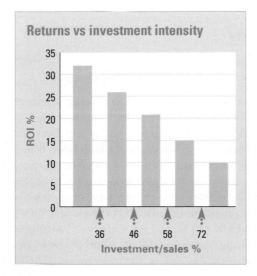

- Where large increments in capacity are required to obtain more output   In some competitive arenas, it is not possible to obtain small increments of output, for example by working overtime or buying another machine. This is particularly so in what are termed process industries such as paper making and oil, where the product is made in large, continuously operated plant. Unless there is some form of signalling between the businesses, in boom times many players build more capacity and overcapacity results, especially in any subsequent lean times. This was happening in UK electricity generation during the mid-1990s: power stations are run continuously and the new power stations being built to provide incremental extra electricity cost around £250 million. There is expected to be considerable overcapacity in electricity generation in the UK from the early 2000s.

- When rivals are different in origins and 'personalities'   The communications industry provides a good example of different personalities, often people with different ethnic and social backgrounds. In the UK media, for example, there were the part-Iraqi Eddie Shah and his local and national attempts to initiate the production of newspapers using cutting-edge information technology, the émigré Robert Maxwell and his 'unorthodox' business practices, Rupert Murdoch, an Australian and latterly US citizen, and Conrad Black, Canadian owner of the *Daily Telegraph*. With such different backgrounds there will not be an agreed way of operating in the competitive arena; there is a higher level of anarchy, with competition in many different ways.

DISCUSSION
POINT 8.5

Would you advise your friends to sell any shares they might have in the cross-channel ferry companies? Why?

- What sort of differentiation might be possible for a maker of commodity items such as bricks and concrete blocks?
- What distinguishes a process industry from other industries?
- What other process 'industries' can you think of where large increments in capacity are required?

8.4.2 Power of buyers

In general, buyers are in a strong position to bargain with the businesses in the target competitive arena if one or more of the following applies:

- They are concentrated   In this context, concentration means that a few firms are responsible for the majority of market transactions. The extreme case of concentration of buyers is monopsony – many suppliers and only one customer. This situation operated for many years in the defence field in many countries, with only the government as a customer for defence contractors. It applies now with the UK government and lawyers who work within Legal Aid. A less extreme form of concentration lies in the grocery supermarkets in the UK, where just a few retailers dominate the market. In the mid-1990s the six top multiple food retailers in the UK (Asda, Iceland, Safeway, Sainsburys, Somerfield and Tesco) were responsible for around 65% of all grocery sales:[11] they and the other multiples[12] together sold over 80% of groceries.[13] Concentration can be enhanced by smaller businesses 'clubbing together' to increase their buying power. Examples of such groupings are the UK local authority combined purchasing schemes and those of farmers for buying fertiliser, seeds, etc. There is an increasing concentration of airlines; for example, BA has acquired equity stakes in USAir, Qantas and TAT and seeks to merge with American Airlines, and SAS is allied to several European airlines. This is bad news for aero engine manufacturers.

- **They purchase large quantities**   If a customer buys in large quantities then they can demand discounts on their purchases – and it's obviously in its interests to spend effort to achieve this, as large amounts are at stake. The purchases will tend to be large if the buyers are concentrated. An added twist to this is that large buyers are likely to have sophisticated purchasing departments. A small manufacturer of compressed-air equipment has one of the large car assemblers as a customer. This assembler, because of the expertise of its purchasing department, is able to drive a hard bargain with the manufacturer.

- **They buy standard products**   If products are standard, then one of the conditions for perfect competition is satisfied, and thus profits are likely to be depressed. With a standard product any business in the competitive arena will be much the same as another, and so if one business tries to increase its prices the customers will simply buy the same item elsewhere. Raw materials are a particular problem, as these tend to be undifferentiable.

- **They can integrate backwards**   All customers have to make the decision whether to make or buy their inputs. **Backward integration** occurs when buyers extend the scope of their operations to carry out the conversion process being undertaken by the businesses in the competitive arena immediately upstream of themselves. Examples of backward integration are car manufacturers making more car components, paint manufacturers manufacturing their own resins and food retailers owning their own canneries. The balance in the make-or-buy decision will shift to 'make' if buyers see businesses in upstream competitive arenas making large profits. During the 1990s the trend has been in the opposite direction with the move to out-sourcing.

- **They have full information**   Information is power, it is said. It is this realisation that lies behind the apocryphal story that Nathan Rothschild, the British banker, made a great deal of money by knowing the result of the Battle of Waterloo before anyone else in London by uniquely using carrier pigeons released from the battlefield as soon as the result of the battle was known. If buyers have full information, another of the conditions for perfect competition is fulfilled and thus profits are likely to be low. Note that full information doesn't only mean information about the characteristics of the offer itself: it means information about the suppliers, about their margins, costs and state of their order books.

A good example of where the buyer has full information is where bidding (especially sealed bidding) is involved. This is the case with construction firms. If a health authority requires a new hospital, an architect will be used to specify precisely what is required of the building. The construction companies will bid against this specification in sealed bids. The health authority will know all of the bids, and unless there is collusion between the construction firms, no firm will know any other bid. The power is firmly in the hands of the health authority. Indeed, during the recession of the early 1990s, the bids had to be itemised and each bid was scrutinised to determine the lowest price for each *component* of the tender. The construction firm tendering the lowest overall bid would have its bid accepted as long as it reduced the price of individual items to be the same as the lowest of all the other bids. Power indeed! It will be interesting to see whether the advent of telephone shopping swings the balance towards consumers as information becomes more readily available to them.

DISCUSSION
POINT 8.6

How might construction companies break the grip of their clients?

- **They are hard pressed for cash**   This aspect of buyer power is often stated as buyers earning low profits or low margins, but this force is equally applicable to not-for-profit organisations which are operating within tight budget constraints. If the buyers haven't got much money then they must be very careful in how they use what they have, and this includes the costs of their inputs. Thus they are forced to be hard bargainers with their suppliers.

- **Purchases form a significant fraction of product/service cost**   This is a variant of the previous factor. Consider car manufacturers. If they are purchasing small bolts of which they use only one per car, then they are unlikely to be bothered about the bolt's cost – perhaps a ten-thousandth part of the car's sale price. The engine, however, costs around 10–15% of the sales price, so car manufacturers need to watch this cost very carefully indeed. An interesting case is Lycra. In most offers Lycra constitutes only a small percentage of the total fabric, yet it can give the required flexible features. Thus fabric makers aren't really bothered by how much Lycra costs them, and this is reflected in Lycra being the world's most profitable fibre.

- **Quality is unimportant**   It's easiest to see the consequences of quality being unimportant by first considering the reverse: the situation where quality *is* important. If you are seriously ill or if you are in deep trouble with the law, quality is likely to be important to you and you will pay a lot for the best surgeon or lawyer. A good business example is in oil exploration: the costs of drilling are very high and the oil companies wish to use the best expertise possible to map and interpret the geological information that is obtained from their drilling programmes. Schlumberger is a firm that can demand very high fees for doing this sort of work as it is the world's best, and poor interpretation is likely to be very, very costly for the oil companies. You pay for quality, but if quality is unimportant then buyers are able to shop around among suppliers as many suppliers can supply 'average' products and services.

- **There are low switching costs**   Switching costs are the costs incurred when a buyer replaces one supplier with another. In the mid-1990s one of the factors inhibiting the switch from British Telecom (BT) to the cable telephone companies was that if you changed you couldn't retain your BT telephone number. As the price differential for many customers was small, this need to inform everyone that your number had changed proved quite an effective disincentive to switching. Naturally, the alternative providers sought to get the UK Office of Telecommunications to allow the retention of numbers. Similar switching costs are associated with changing your bank – having to change the standing orders and direct debits, for example. Indeed, some banks now offer to make these changes for you if you switch to them, so reducing or eliminating switching costs. In certain circumstances the pharmaceuticals acceptability regimes (the Federal Drugs Administration in the USA and the European Medicines Evaluation Agency) will specify that the raw materials for drugs must come from certain suppliers.

8.4.3   Power of suppliers

In many ways the power of suppliers is the mirror image of the power of buyers, since suppliers supply to buyers and buyers buy from suppliers. Thus suppliers will be powerful if they are concentrated, they supply in small quantities to many buyers and their products are differentiated. They are also powerful if they can feasibly integrate forwards, if quality is important to their customers and switching costs are high. They will be forced to act powerfully if they are hard pressed for cash.

While suppliers are the mirror images of buyers, it is worth saying a little more about four of the forces:

- Concentration of suppliers   The extreme case of supplier concentration is monopoly – one supplier and many buyers. This is the situation that many businesses seek, for as any basic economics textbook illustrates, a monopolist can obtain monopolistic, i.e. very good, profits. Most governments actively oppose such restrictions on competition (for example, through the Competition Commission in the UK). However, due partly to customer inertia, British Telecom and British Gas were able to hang on to their quasi-monopolies long after privatisation.

- Forward integration   Forward integration is the process whereby suppliers extend their operations to carry out the conversion process being undertaken by their customers. All suppliers have to make the decision whether to extend their operations to include those of their current customers. The balance in the decision will shift to move forwards (downstream) into adjacent competitive arenas if they see their customers making large profits.

- Non-standard products   If the suppliers supply differentiated products, then there is pressure on the buyer to take them. If a supermarket wants to sell Kellogg's cornflakes, then it will have to get these from Kellogg. If it simply wants to sell cornflakes, then it can get these from many suppliers.

- Suppression of information   The buyer would like full information, but it is often in the interests of the supplier not to give this. A good example of this was the mis-selling of pensions in the UK during the early 1990s. The insurance companies, or perhaps just some of their employees, were able to obtain large commissions through selling inappropriate pensions to people, mainly by not disclosing information about administration costs.

Types of supplier

Suppliers to a competitive arena are not simply the obvious ones supplying materials (including components) used in their offers: they include suppliers of finance, people and information, and there is a market associated with each. This is shown in Exhibit 8.9. Equifax, for example, provides personal information, Reuters and Bloomberg provide business information.

8.4.4 Barriers to entry[14]

Barriers to entry provide a 'force' different from the three we have already considered, where the players were already identified. Here we are talking about the threat of new businesses coming into the competitive arena, which they will be tempted to do if the businesses already there are earning high returns. If they enter they are likely to depress the earnings of existing businesses. They will be inhibited from entering if the barriers to entry are high, and this will be the case if one of the following applies:

- There are large economies of scale   Economies of scale refer to the reduced costs per offer associated with higher volumes of output per given period, i.e. operating costs are lower for the 'big players' because they can spread their overheads over many sales. If there are large economies of scale, then new entrants will either have to come in on a big scale or accept a cost disadvantage, which they will have to overcome through differentiation. The reverse can also apply. New entrants into electrical generation in the mid-1990s had access to new technologies and could generate electricity more cheaply than the incumbents.

EXHIBIT 8.9

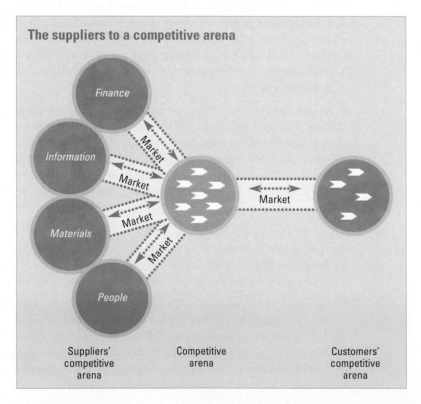

The suppliers to a competitive arena

Finance

Information

Materials

People

Market

Market

Market

Market

Market

Suppliers' competitive arena

Competitive arena

Customers' competitive arena

EXHIBIT 8.10

Economies of scale

Economies of scale can occur in many elements of business activities, for example:

Operations	the economies of scale in volume car manufacture are such that it has only become possible for *countries* such as South Korea and Malaysia to enter this competitive arena; the costs for a commercial firm are too great.
Purchasing	large firms are able to press for substantial discounts.
Marketing	all the cigarette, soft drinks, beauty preparation and detergent manufacturers make very similar core offers. Thus they *all* make a considerable effort to differentiate themselves, generally through advertising. Within the competitive arena this is somewhat self-defeating, as it puts up the cost of offers. However, outside of the arena it pays dividends since it acts as a barrier to entry: potential entrants will have to match – and indeed more than match – the efforts put into differentiation by the established players, especially if reputation needs to be established, and this is difficult to do. The need to carry high inventories is also a consideration. TV advertising is often necessary to establish an offer, and to be efficient the business must be operating in most of the region covered by the TV station.
Research and development	large firms are able to undertake R&D on a scale that is not open to smaller firms. Even 'big' firms may be at a grave disadvantage. In 1996, General Motors spent over $8 billion and Ford almost $6 billion on R&D. In 1999, GEC, which had recently moved strongly into Internet technology, was reported as spending around £1 billion a year on R&D, while Lucent, one of its largest rivals, was spending more than £10 billion.[15]

Economies of scale are greatly enhanced if there is a **natural monopoly**. Some competitive arenas are natural monopolies in that it doesn't make sense for there to be more than one business. One obvious source of monopoly is where the geographical area of activity is restricted, either locally or over a wider area. Although car ownership is eroding the power of location somewhat, the corner or village shop, the fast-food outlet and public house are often located where it wouldn't make sense for there to be competition – and this is especially so where the goods are perishable. Geography is another powerful force for the creation of a natural monopoly, and this has been particularly true with the utilities; it hardly makes sense to have competition in the water industry, for example.

An associated concept, and one that is in practice linked to economies of scale, is **economies of scope**. A firm with a portfolio of offers is at an advantage over a firm that has only a single offer, as it is able to spread some of its costs over more offers, thus lowering the cost per offer.

- There are high risks associated with the capabilities that need to be acquired
  Lippman and Rumelt[16] postulate the theory of 'uncertain imitability': the greater the uncertainty potential entrants feel about how successful businesses 'do it', the more inhibited they will be in entering the competitive arena.

- **Experience is important**   The established players may have advantages that come with being in the competitive arena at or for a particular time. One aspect is what is termed the learning or experience curve: a business can have an advantage because it has learned how to make a product better or more cheaply by doing it many times. Unit costs in manufacturing have been found to decline on average by around 15% with each doubling of cumulative output. The experience curve is likely to apply where many people are involved in intricate tasks, for example aircraft manufacture, and computer design and manufacture. While the reduction of costs with production experience is well documented, that with services is less so. However, this doesn't seem to have stopped people applying the concept of an experience curve to services.

- **Relationships with suppliers are important**   Incumbents will have established good relationships with their suppliers, perhaps a synergistic relationship. Marks & Spencer has a very close relationship with many clothing manufacturers, and an entrant would need to match this or compensate for it in some way.

- **Access to advertising and distribution channels is restricted**   There is something of a chicken-and-egg situation for food manufacturers trying to get into supermarkets. They need 5% market share before the retailers will stock their products, but they need to get on the supermarket shelves before they can establish a 5% market share. When they were first introduced, digital watches couldn't use the conventional jewellers and thus they had to use supermarkets and garages. When Fujitsu wished to enter the UK market with mainframe computers it experienced considerable difficulty. In the early 1980s, ICL hadn't got a suitable computer to upgrade its customers and 'badge-engineered' the Fujitsu machine, i.e. put the ICL logo on Fujitsu machines. Later, this allowed Fujitsu to supply the next generation of computers to what were effectively its own customers. Pubs and tied houses are another example of a restriction on channel access.

- **Government and EU policy protects incumbents**   Legal restraints on competition are widespread, with patents being possibly the most obvious example. But there are many more, particularly in the regulated European markets. One example is the availability of landing and take-off slots at major airports. The allocation of such slots was determined many years ago, and established airlines such as British Airways hang on jealously to their very large quota. For many years the relative newcomer Virgin Atlantic had been petitioning the British government for access rights at Heathrow and had been forced to use what it considers the inferior Gatwick Airport. Dairy quotas to limit production of dairy products and fishing quotas to conserve fish stocks are both examples of EU legislation that supports the incumbents. In the mid-1990s the UK government announced that planning permission wouldn't be given for further out-of-town shopping centres and supermarkets. This would obviously help the incumbents, which had such outlets or planning permissions for them already agreed. A new entrant into the aero engines business requires certification of its engines and needs to demonstrate proven levels of reliability in service. Existing engine manufacturers can obtain certification on the basis of actual experience or using experience from similar designs that have already been certified, something not available to new entrants.

● Retaliation is expected to be fierce   If the established firms are very committed to the competitive arena, then entrants should expect retaliation. This is what appeared to have happened to both Laker Airlines and Virgin Atlantic when they took on British Airways.

DISCUSSION
POINT 8.7

Which part of the electricity industry would you think is a natural monopoly?
● Is the Post Office a natural monopoly?
● Can you think of businesses where there is a powerful 'pull' of a large number of customers – and thus towards monopoly?
● What other factors are there about the capabilities that might make them risky?
● What is the difference between reduced costs because of economies of scale and reduced costs because of experience?
● Why are low margins and/or low profits for incumbent businesses not considered a barrier to entry?

The forces operating in the operating environment are summarised in Exhibit 8.11, including the threat of substitutes, which will now be considered.

8.4.5   Threat of substitutes

Substitutes are important because customers will always be prepared to consider offers that provide better value for money than those made available by the present incumbents of the competitive arena. They will switch as long as switching costs and the associated risks aren't excessive.

In one sense, everything is a substitute for everything else, since all offers are competing for the same customer cash. A new computer with a new car, a Chinese takeaway with dry cleaning. For purposes of analysis, however, there is a need to restrict the focus. The restriction is made by looking fairly narrowly at customer needs: in the case of the computer/car the need may be status; in the case of a Chinese takeaway/pizza the need can be considered to be a quick meal. Care must be taken with the focus; it's very important not to under- or overfocus.

It's important to spend a little time discussing what a substitute is. If one considers almost any *specific* product or service – a Ford Focus, or an insurance policy from General Accident, for example – then a substitute for these would be a VW Golf and similar cover from Allianz. But it's important to realise that these are **marketing** substitutes – substitutes in the marketplace in which a customer replaces one car or insurance policy with one from *another business already in the competitive arena*. Such substitutes have been considered when discussing the power of buyers. This is purely substituting one offer for another that is very similar.

The competitive arena consists of all businesses satisfying the same general customer need. If this general need should diminish the reduction isn't a substitute. For example, if a less stressful life reduced the number of people suffering from stomach ulcers, this is not a substitute for an anti-ulcer drug such as Tagamet or indeed for anti-ulcer drugs in general; it is simply a reduction in the need for anti-ulcer medication, a reduction in demand.

What we are concerned with in this analysis is to understand the forces operating on the competitive arena *as a whole*. Thus we are concerned with offers that threaten to take demand away from the *totality of the businesses* currently in the competitive

EXHIBIT 8.11

The sources of power in the immediate operating environment

The barriers to entry will be high if:

- there are large economies of scale
- the assets are risky
- experience is important
- relationships with suppliers are important
- access to advertising and distribution channels is restricted
- there is protective governmental policy
- the retaliation is expected to be fierce

The threat of substitutes will be low if:

- they do not offer significantly better value for money than the current encumbents
- switching costs are high

Rivalry will be intense if:

- the businesses are equally balanced
- the growth of the market is slow
- there are high exit barriers
- it is difficult to differentiate the product/service
- fixed costs are high
- large increments in capacity are needed
- rivals are different in origins and personality

Suppliers can act powerfully if:

- they are concentrated
- they sell small quantities
- they sell non-standard products
- they can integrate forwards
- they can suppress information
- they are hard pressed for cash
- quality is important
- there are high switching costs
- purchasing departments are unsophisticated

Buyers can act powerfully if:

- they are concentrated
- they purchase large quantities
- they buy standard products
- they can integrate backwards
- they have full information
- they are hard pressed for cash
- purchases form a significant fraction of product/service cost
- quality is unimportant
- there are low switching costs

arena. But this is not simply taking demand away from the incumbent businesses, because potential entrants will be threatening to do the same. The difference between the substitute and the entrant is that the entrant will satisfy the customer need in a *similar* manner to the incumbents; the substitutes will do it in a *different* manner. For example, before it became operational Eurotunnel was a threatening substitute to ferry operations as it operated in a different manner. At one time margarine was a threatening substitute for butter, because the suppliers and manufacturing process were completely different to those of the incumbents (the dairy industry).

Digital watches satisfied one of the needs of customers, to tell the time, in a very different way to that of the conventional analogue watch. The Swiss watchmakers' skills lay in mechanical design, metal working and the organisation of a multitude of small suppliers throughout Switzerland. These capabilities were almost completely devalued by the digital watches coming from the electronics companies. This example highlights the nub of what a strategic management substitute is: the firm offering the substitute operates in a different way to the incumbents. The threat that a substitute poses is that it devalues the skills that the incumbents possess: a substitute destroys capability. This isn't the case with entrants, who tend to be broadly capability-neutral.

DISCUSSION POINT 8.8

Who are the suppliers and what are the methods of production in butter and margarine?
- Most car manufacturers make their own engines and buy in their (steel) body panels. If a new ceramic material was developed and engines could be made out of it, would this development appear to be a substitute to the car manufacturers?
- If a new plastic material was developed for body panels, would this be a substitute?

Note that once customers start buying from substitute businesses, the substitute businesses then enter the competitive arena: they are no longer threats as they are inside the competitive arena. When Eurotunnel opened it ceased being a threat of substitute and joined the ferries in the 'channel crossing' competitive arena.

KEY CONCEPT   A strategic management substitute is different from a marketing substitute. A marketing substitute only concerns the offer. A strategic management substitute poses the threat of devaluing the capabilities that all the incumbents possess. Capability devaluation isn't the case with entrants, who tend to be broadly capability-neutral.

8.4.6 Competitive and strategic groups

Sometimes it's reasonable to consider the competitive arena as homogeneous, i.e. all the businesses in it can be considered the same and it would be expected that they would all react in a similar way to environmental changes. This may be the approximate position in the manufacture of large aero engines, where there are only three companies worldwide which are competing with each other. However, in general the competitive arena is heterogeneous. First, there are businesses in it that are servicing different segments of the market. For example, Mercedes and BMW are servicing a different segment of the car market to Ford and Vauxhall with their family cars and are not direct competitors. Mercedes and BMW are in one **competitive group**, with family cars in another. (The businesses in a competitive group are such that if one business improves its market share one or more of the others in the group loses it.) Note that many firms compete in several competitive groups with different offers.

Strategic thinking is about the future, and the strategist should be looking at future competitors – and in particular at businesses that aren't competing now but might in the future, i.e. at potential groups of competitors. We have already looked at the threat of future competitors to the incumbent businesses when we considered the threat of entrants and that of substitutes.

However, the most likely source of new competition will be from businesses that are not yet competing but have most of the capabilities that are needed. In section 8.3.2 it was suggested that potential competitors should be included in the competitive arena. For example, Rolls-Royce would be remiss if it didn't consider the manufacturers of small aero engines in its competitive arena (especially if they are Japanese), since they are likely future competitors. The competitors to the national brewers of canned and bottled beers are not the pharmaceutical companies or the car assemblers; they are brewers already operating in other countries. Groups of businesses that have similar capabilities, whether or not they are competing at the present, are termed **strategic groups**.

Note that if the competitive arena is international, then one feature determining strategic groups might be the national regime under which the firms are operating, since they are likely to have different remote environments. A good example of this is the pressure on manufacturing firms when interest rates rise and/or the national currency strengthens *vis-à-vis* competitors in other countries.

KEY DEFINITIONS A competitive group is composed of those businesses that are competing to serve a defined market segment.[17] A strategic group is a group of businesses where the businesses within the group resemble each other in their capabilities more closely than any other business outside the group, and they are likely to respond similarly to environmental changes and be similarly advantaged/disadvantaged by such changes.

Both competitive and strategic groups are separated by **mobility barriers**. These are similar, although smaller than the barriers to entry discussed in Section 8.4.4. Exhibit 8.12 shows four strategic groups within the competitive arena, with mobility barriers between two of them. In practice, there would be mobility barriers between all of the strategic groups. The businesses H, A and B are in the same group, with C making up a group on its own.

EXHIBIT 8.12

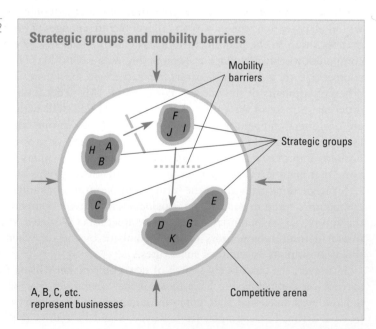

8.5 The value chain outside the immediate operating environment

8.5.1 Influence in the value chain

So far we have discussed the immediate operating environment. This is where the main interest of many businesses will lie. However, businesses should be concerned with influencing groups and individuals further afield, both downstream and upstream of their own competitive arena.

The main influence is downstream through advertising. For example, raw material suppliers may seek to influence the final consumer, as ICI did with the kitchen surface laminate Formica many years ago and manufacturers are now trying to do with a new material for kitchen work surfaces, Corian. This was also done by the manufacturers of artificial sweetener Nutrasweet when the consumer couldn't buy the product directly, only when buying cakes, biscuits and other products. Food manufacturers such as Heinz and Cadbury attempt to reduce the power of the supermarkets through branding, essentially appealing to consumers to put pressure on the supermarkets to stock their products. So in terms of the forces in Exhibit 8.6 the businesses in one competitive arena 'leapfrog' the competitive arena 'next in line' to attempt to reduce the power of the businesses in the adjoining competitive arena. Daewoo cut out the normal car distributors and sells directly to the public, as does Dell with computers. Thus the strategist does need to keep the whole of the operating environment in mind, as it is often through new relationships that competitive advantage can be obtained.

8.5.2 Secondary stakeholders

In Chapter 1 the distinction was made between primary and secondary stakeholders. The main distinction was that the primary stakeholders operated in markets, whereas the secondary stakeholders didn't. However, the secondary stakeholders are still important – potentially very important – to the well-being of a business, and they must be considered as part of the operating environment. Thus Exhibit 8.6 needs to be augmented to include the secondary stakeholders. The full operating environment is shown in Exhibit 8.13, where all the types of supplier stakeholder are encompassed within the one competitive arena.

EXHIBIT 8.13

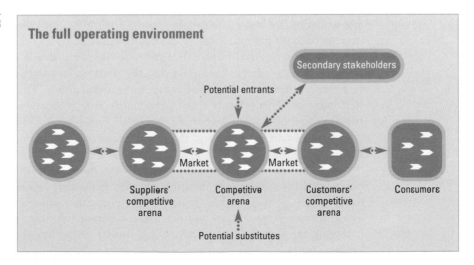

In 1997 the aid agency Cafod produced a report[18] in which it described how millions of pairs of shoes sold in the UK are produced under slave labour conditions in China, Vietnam and Brazil. This was a case of a secondary stakeholder – a pressure group – exerting pressure on the UK distributors. It was also an example of reverse pressure, whereby the distributors are being asked to exert pressure upstream in the value chain to force their suppliers to alter their working practices.

8.5.3 The effects of IT

As early as 1985, Porter and Millar[19] described how information technology (IT) was and would alter the balance of power in and around the competitive arena, although at that time they weren't able to consider the influence of the Internet. The effect of IT, and particularly the Internet and e-commerce, on the elements of the operating environment (Exhibit 8.13) will now be considered. It could well be that the Internet will become a 'naturally concentrating medium' in which a few companies meet the needs of large segments of the global market.

Effect on buyer and supplier power

Electronic data interchange (EDI) has been used by large organisations for many years – by the large supermarkets, car assemblers and pharmaceuticals distributors for example – but its complexity, high up-front cost and inflexibility have inhibited its general use. It was estimated in 1998[20] that only 2% of UK companies use EDI, yet all have a telephone line and most have a PC. The cheapness of Internet technology allows many more suppliers to establish electronic business-to-business links, which the costs of proprietary EDI software inhibited. Carrefour, the French retailing group, has more than 100,000 lines of stock to consider, negotiate about and order. It is using an extranet linked to some of its suppliers and is hoping to link them all. The claim is that the system has produced time savings of 20% for the buyers by eliminating the time spent preparing and faxing requests for proposals. It has also ended disputes with suppliers over mislaid faxes.

Cisco, a networking products company, provides an intranet to support its sales staff and distribution processes. Customers can order and configure products electronically. Between January and October 1997, the company increased the percentage of orders treated electronically from 13 to 30% and estimated that it achieved savings of $200 million. Sales support calls were cut by 25,000.[21]

The Internet allows buyers to determine the price, availability and some of the features of rival offers. This will bring the markets to something closer to the perfect market that the firms in any competitive arena abhor. Thus the power of buyers will increase. This is likely to be particularly true of business-to-business transactions, where offers can be closely specified. Exhibit 8.14 indicates the size of the savings that can be made and the effort required to implement a fully fledged IT system.

Selling to consumers on the Internet provides more difficulties than selling to businesses, but the same broad principle applies. Items that can be highly specified will most readily be sold, such as books, where you either know exactly what you want or the author you want, or you determine whether you want to buy the book after browsing through the details. Music has similar properties. Travel – especially over known routes – is also appropriate for Internet selling.

EXHIBIT 8.14

BP overcomes fear of the 'too difficult' box[22]

It was called the 'billion dollar challenge'. In 1996 BP, the international oil group, decided that it could save $1 billion from the $15 billion a year that it spent on goods and services. The key was information. BP could only make these savings by getting an overview of all its spending decisions. Once it had the full picture, it could negotiate better deals with its main suppliers. But two years ago, identifying those opportunities was difficult as there was no single place in which all the purchasing data were gathered. 'The whole thing tended to be put into the "too difficult" box,' says Chris Browning, the former procurement manager for BP Oil (Europe) in charge of the project.

There was a need to build a computer system to collate information about who was buying what from whom. BP tackled this problem by building a data warehouse – information from many sources in analysable form. PA Consulting was brought in to manage Project Oyster. It built a data warehouse to reside in an Oracle database running on a Unix server. Any registered user within BP could access the information using a Web browser across BP's intranet. Users as far afield as Australia, Alaska and Azerbaijan can interrogate the system to find if a potential supplier is doing business elsewhere in the group or if another supplier offers better terms. BP procurement managers can use this information to aggregate purchases and to negotiate better terms.

An important consequence is that BP can rationalise its supplier base. 'It could easily be seen as a big stick to beat suppliers,' says Steve Davenport of PA. But he argues that it allows suppliers to develop a more collaborative mode of working with BP. 'The real value of Oyster is in the second-tier suppliers,' says Mr Davenport. 'For heads of procurement, it is pretty obvious who are the top 20 suppliers. But look one level down, they don't actually know who are the next 20.'

The project – awarded the 1997 UK Management Consultancies Association's business improvement award, IT category – is judged a success by BP. But it has had to overcome many political and organisational obstacles. One advantage was that it did not require much effort to input purchasing data as these could be transferred from accounting systems. The system also overcame a potential problem in the way suppliers' names were described in different parts of the organisation. PA Consulting had to set up a sophisticated 'fuzzy logic' data-matching system that could, for example, recognise that IBM was the same company as International Business Machines.

The convenience and relatively low cost of the system has made it popular within BP. Data from 20 countries are in the system, now used by 700 people all around the group. Within a year of the system's introduction, savings of at least $15 million were made, equivalent to five times the project's cost.

A further source of advantage to buyers will be offered through the development of *agents* or *bots*, software that can intelligently search the Internet for sites and combine the resultant information in a way easily understandable to the user. Retailers can try to stifle the problem of agents and bots – or individuals themselves from determining the best offers – by bundling many features into the augmented offer.

The most important issue for a seller is how to get Internet users to visit its site. Just as with on-line airline reservation systems of old, where the trick for the airlines was to get their flights on to the first screen at the travel agents, consumer marketing on the Internet has to be concerned with getting well positioned within a well-used search engine.

E-commerce allows suppliers to obtain a great deal of information about their customers' likes, dislikes and habits, enhancing the role of relationship marketing. Relationships can be strengthened and loyalty increased through using IT to offer increased value. One of the appeals of Internet bookseller Amazon, for example, is that it provides space for book reviews posted by other readers. However, coupling retailers' data with the vast amounts of personal data held by such agencies as credit-scoring firms could lead to a considerable loss of personal freedom.

Effect on entry barriers

The low costs associated with Internet operations will reduce the barriers to entry for small players. This has occurred in periodical publishing, as shown by the mass of specialist periodicals now on offer. The Internet permits what had been local operators to supply almost anywhere in the world. This both increases the scale of the suppliers' operations and is likely to reduce costs.

Effect on the threat of substitutes

The value of the assets of established businesses can be seriously undermined by the use of IT. The phone as well as Internet operations have discounted the value of bank branches, for example, and allowed non-traditional players into banking and insurance. Share transactions by Internet have substantially affected transaction costs and the role of brokers.

Disintermediation

'Disintermediation' is the term used by economists to describe the situation whereby intermediaries cease to have a role, i.e. a link in the value chain is removed or bypassed. For example, insurance brokers are intermediaries who act between the client wanting insurance and the insurance companies covering the risk: the broker matches the client's profile with the most suitable offer from the insurance companies. With the Internet, it could well be that such intermediaries disappear – or transform themselves into something different.

In the USA, independent travel agents handled 80% of US airline reservations in 1996; by 1998 their share was 52%.[23] Airlines have cut their commissions to travel agents as more customers book on-line. The US booksellers Amazon and Barnes & Noble have bypassed much of the value chain through their Internet sites, ironically becoming a new form of intermediary. Dell Computer, which is a direct sales outfit, rejected selling through retailers and now sells $5 million worth of personal computers a day via its website.[24] Note that it was Amazon rather than WH Smith or its US equivalent that set up the first Internet bookshop; it was Direct Line that transformed the insurance market, not one of the established players. In the case of WH Smith, it feared devaluing its own stores; the insurance companies were worried about upsetting the brokers. In 1997, 11% of all new cars in the USA were bought via the Internet: to many American car buyers, dealers are becoming simply pick-up points.[25]

Secondary stakeholders

Since secondary stakeholders aren't asking for more of anything, simply that the business performs to some acceptable level, the effect of IT on the relationship between the firm and the secondary stakeholders is likely to be small. However, firms are now routinely supplying their annual reports over the Internet, and government regulations are also available there.

Pressure groups have successfully mobilised their resources through the use of the Internet. In 1998, groups against the Multilateral Agreement on Investment being negotiated at the Organisation for Economic Co-operation and Development formed a loose coalition. The coalition included trade unionists, environmental and human rights lobbyists and groups opposed to globalisation. They condemned the proposed agreement as a secret conspiracy to ensure global domination by multinational companies. Their campaign was a strong element in getting the agreement taken off the immediate agenda.[26] Also in 1998, it was reported that the Zapatista guerrillas in Mexico were using the Internet to spread their concerns and programmes for economic and social reform, which were being suppressed in the mainstream media.[27]

8.5.4 Feedback in the value chain

The strategist needs to keep the whole of the value chain in mind for another reason – the feedback loops that might operate in it. Senge[28] describes what he terms the beer game: he asks people to play roles in the value chain of beer from brewery, through the wholesaler and retailer to the final consumer. Buying patterns to cope with perceived swings in demand and in the face of perceived bottlenecks in supply mean that small swings in one part of the value chain can lead to very large swings elsewhere. Thus the strategist should also look at the dynamics of the system of which they are a part, not simply at the relatively static picture provided by the five forces model and its extensions.

DISCUSSION
POINT 8.11

Can you think of examples – other than branding – where pressure is exerted on a competitive arena that isn't from the direct customer of the businesses in the competitive arena?
- Can you think of other examples where pressure is exerted on a competitive arena that isn't from the direct supplier of the businesses in the competitive arena?

8.6 Operating environmental analysis for not-for-profit organisations

The analysis of the operating environment described above relies heavily, but not exclusively, on the five forces model of Porter, which was derived for profit-seeking organisations competing with rivals in markets. The customers were rather easy to identify (at least they paid money) and suppliers were mainly the suppliers of goods and services consumed in the conversion process within the target competitive arena. With not-for-profit organisations, the analysis needs to be rather more subtle.

Consider a charity such as the Royal Society for the Protection of Birds (RSPB), which is paid for by the annual subscriptions of members. The customers may seem to be the members, but on the other hand they are the main suppliers (of money) and they ask the professionals at the RSPB to act on their behalf. The members are customers, but so are the government and the general public. The Royal National Institute for the Blind is financially supported very strongly by the UK government, which is thus one of its major suppliers, but the government is also one of its major buyers in the sense of the five forces model: the visually impaired consume the services but the government pays. The government is also a powerful force in the remote environment, and this further complicates the picture.

Perhaps a better alternative for not-for-profit organisations is to identify the demands of each stakeholder, without giving the emphasis to competitors, suppliers and threats of entry that is appropriate when analysing commercial enterprises.

SUMMARY

- The focus of attention in analysing the operating environment of a business is the competitive arena in which the business operates, together with the value chains within which it lies. The questions being addressed are 'How attractive is the operating environment as a place to do business?' and 'What significant operating factors can be identified?' The operating environment can be further subdivided into an immediate operating environment and the remainder of the value chains. EXHIBIT 8.1, EXHIBIT 8.6, EXHIBIT 8.7

- The competitive arena consists of businesses satisfying broadly the same customer need. There is no hard-and-fast way of defining a competitive arena: it should be defined in a way that provides an illuminating analysis. Difficulties in definition arise from organisations being vertically integrated, with segmentation and with the inclusion of potential competitors.

- The immediate operating environment can be analysed using Porter's five forces model. This considers the power of customers and of suppliers, the rivalry in the competitive arena, the barriers to entry and the threat of substitution. The five forces model provides a series of checklists to help the strategist determine how strong the forces are that are operating on and within the competitive arena. These checklists are in the form of 'the greater is X the smaller is Y'. There is no quantification in the original Porter analysis; the PIMS programme provides this to some extent. EXHIBIT 8.7, EXHIBIT 8.8, EXHIBIT 8.9, EXHIBIT 8.13

- It is often useful to consider the competitive arena as divided into groups of businesses. Competitive groups are groups of businesses targeting the same segment of the market. Strategic groups are groups of businesses that are likely to respond similarly to environmental changes and be similarly advantaged/disadvantaged by such changes. EXHIBIT 8.12

- The full operating environment consists of the full set of value chains and the secondary stakeholders. EXHIBIT 8.13

SELF-CHECK

1 Reconsider the learning outcomes for this chapter. Check that you feel confident that you can carry out the activities listed there.

2 Having read this chapter, you should be able to define the following terms:

competitive arena	immediate operating environment	strategic group
competitive group	industry	strategic management
disintermediation	marketing substitute	substitute
economies of scale	perfect competition	value chain
economies of scope	significant operating factor	value link

Fisons Pharmaceuticals

General background

Very broadly, the pharmaceutical industry manufactures and sells four types of product. First, there are the so-called ethicals, which are drugs that can only be obtained via a prescription from a doctor (for example, Intal). They are also known as 'prescription' drugs. Then there are the 'over-the-counter' (OTC) drugs, which can be obtained without a prescription. OTC drugs are of two types: one type can only be obtained from a pharmacist (for example Nurofen), while the other can be obtained through any outlet (for example paracetamol). The fourth type is healthcare products such as diet supplements, suntan creams and toothpastes. Drugs are further subdivided into 'generics' and 'proprietary' (also termed 'non-generics'). Generics are a general class of chemical (such as aspirin), while a proprietary drug is one that has the same active ingredient but has been given a brand name by the manufacturer (e.g. Aspro).

Prescription drugs typically provide 30% margins, OTC only 15%. The marketing process in the OTC and healthcare markets is very different to that for ethicals, with branding and promotion the key. General practitioners (GPs) are responsible for prescribing 80% of all ethical drugs in the UK and therefore the drug companies place a great deal of emphasis on influencing them.

Prior to 1985, doctors in the UK had complete discretion as to the drugs they prescribed for their patients, notwithstanding the government's advisory list of pharmaceuticals that could be prescribed. In 1985, the government separated drugs into those on a 'white list' and those on a 'black list', with the aim of reducing its overall drugs bill. Those on the white list consisted of the cheaper versions of drugs, generally the generic varieties, those on the black list were proprietary drugs and could only be prescribed in special circumstances. The differences in price between chemically equivalent drugs on the two lists were often marked: for example, the generic drug paracetamol would be around one-third the price of the chemically equivalent proprietary drugs Panadol and Hedex.

Although the Clinton administration's attempts to reform US healthcare may have floundered, the insurance and health management organisations that play a role akin to government agencies and departments in Europe have become more vigilant about costs. Consequently, drug prices have fallen in the USA over the last two years.

A significant part of the drugs companies' success lies in their ability to chemically synthesise compounds from simpler, cheap and widely available compounds. However, some observers believe that the key growth business in the future is likely to be in biotechnology. UK industry, which has led the market in pharmaceuticals and currently develops and manufactures around 30% of world sales, is not in the vanguard in this area.

The development and validation of new drugs

The processes by which new drugs are developed and marketed are broadly the same in most developed countries. Once a firm has an idea for a product it will attempt to protect its interests through patents, which provide protection for 20 years after the patent has been granted.

Once a drug has been synthesised, it must first be tested. Before this testing is carried out, the test regime must be notified to governmental authorities (the Medicines Control Agency in the UK, the FDA in the USA and the fledgling European Medicines Evaluation Agency for Europe[a]). Testing will usually take place on animals and then later on human volunteers. Finally, testing on patients will be carried out through doctors. These final tests

---

a   As yet the national drug agencies work independently and thus the drug firms must deal with many of them in order to obtain wide coverage.

will be spread over many years, with results constantly being fed back to the government authority. The whole development time is a minimum of seven years, with ten to twelve years being common. Thus patent protection on drugs is typically eight to ten years after market launch.

Failure in drug development is common. Out of 10,000 compounds that are considered, only one makes it to the prescribing list. The average cost for research and development of a single drug is of the order of £100–150 million. However, the rewards for success are correspondingly great.

Fisons' history

The discovery of the anti-allergy compound disodium cromoglycate (DSCG) in the late 1960s led to Fisons developing Intal for the treatment of asthma. The first follow-on DSCG product was Rynacrom, first marketed in the early 1970s for the treatment of nasal inflammation caused by allergy. Fisons' strategy in the 1980s was initially to focus on developing products directly based on DSCG, and in 1984 Opticrom for the treatment of eye allergies was launched, followed by the alimentary tract product Nalcrom. Fisons then extended its offers with the launch of Tilade in 1986 for the improved treatment of asthma and other diseases of the air passages. Tilade was considered a new compound, although its base chemical, nedocromil sodium, is a close relative of DSCG. In 1993, the steroid Tipredane was licensed from Bristol-Myers-Squibb and evaluated as a treatment of asthma. Throughout the latter part of the 1980s and during the 1990s, considerable R&D effort was expended on the design of improved delivery devices.

Fisons' present position

As Fisons moved into the mid-1990s its focus was overwhelmingly on the treatment of allergies, particular those connected with asthma, and on ethical and proprietary drugs based on DSCG. This can be seen from its pharmaceutical portfolio set out in Exhibit 8.15. The 'other category' includes approximately £100 million from its healthcare activities, with such products as the Sanatogen vitamin supplement range and Desenex, a leading athlete's foot cure in the USA.

Exhibit 8.15 Fisons' pharmaceutical portfolio

Brand	Active ingredient	Sales (£ million)
Intal	Disodium cromoglycate (DSCG)	195
Rynacrom	Disodium cromoglycate (DSCG)	44
Opticrom	Disodium cromoglycate (DSCG)	41
Tilade	nedocromil sodium	31
Others		135
Total		446

Allergies are a hypersensitivity to substances that most people hardly notice: the reaction to pollen that results in hayfever is perhaps the most well-known allergy in the UK. Asthma is characterised by difficulty in breathing caused by restrictions in the size of the bronchial passages. It is thought that both Intal and Tilade help allergic asthmatics by inhibiting the release of histamine activated by an allergic reaction that causes swelling of the bronchial tubes. This mode of action distinguishes Intal and Tilade from all other anti-asthmatic drugs. They are also prophylactic and should be taken regularly to prevent asthma attacks; they are of no use once an attack is underway.

The pharmaceuticals market is essentially global. In 1994 worldwide drug sales were estimated to be worth £130 billion. Total drug sales are growing at 10% per year. Part of this growth is caused by the increase in the number of elderly people; part is due to the greater affluence of developing countries. The world market for ethical drugs for the respiratory system was estimated to be $8.5 billion in 1994. In the developed world over the last decade there has been a marked increase in the incidence of allergic diseases, including asthma and hayfever. The cause of these increases is disputed: air pollution (especially that from vehicles), air conditioning and diet have all been suggested. In the UK, it is estimated that as many as one in seven schoolchildren has asthma attacks, with about half this number continuing into adulthood. Hayfever, virtually unknown in the UK until the mid-nineteenth century, is even more common; again, age brings reduced symptoms. In Japan, allergic rhinitis, an allergic inflammation of the nose, was virtually unknown in the 1950s but now affects 10% of the population. The position is similar in continental Europe and the USA.

The anti-asthma market is in the process of change. It is now being seen as more important to treat the underlying cause of the disease rather than the symptoms. This is leading to a growth in the use of steroids, of which Becotide is an example.

Fisons' standing in relation to other companies and products in anti-asthmatics is shown in Exhibit 8.16. The patents on its new range of Intal aerosol formulations will expire by the year 2000. Ventolin came off patent in the UK in 1987 and in the USA in 1989, but is still the market leader in 1993. Glaxo has two new drugs, Serevent and Flixonase, which are expected to achieve significant sales.

Exhibit 8.16 Worldwide sales of anti-asthmatics, 1993

Brand	Treatment	Company	Revenue ($ million)	Market share (%)
Ventolin	Salbutamol	Glaxo	702	15
Becotide	Beclomethasone	Glaxo	454	10
Proventil	Salbutamol	Schering-Plough	370	8
Zaditen	Ketotifen	Sandoz	295	6
Intal	DSCG	Fisons	234	5
Theo-Dur	Theophylline	Schering-Plough	211	4
Atrovent	Ipratropium bromide	B-Ingelheim	187	4
Pulmicort	Budesonide	Astra	178	4
Others			2050	44
Total			4681	100

In 1994 Fisons spent around £70 million on research and development at its laboratories in Loughborough, UK, and in Rochester, USA. During the same period, Glaxo spent £858 million on research on a turnover of £5.6 billion; Zeneca spent £300 million on a turnover of almost £2 billion.

Discussion point 8.10

Carry out an operating environmental analysis for Fisons Pharmaceuticals.

1 For GSM:
   • It says in the case that competitors are ill-defined. Why does it say this?
   • Barry Dodd talks about industries – is this appropriate?
   • Which arena(s) is GSM competing in?
   • Sketch out the operating environment for GSM.
   • What evidence is there to suggest that the competitive arenas in which GSM operates might be profitable arenas?
   • How have the car assemblers' processes changed over the years?
   • How do you think a recession will change the operating environment as far as GSM is concerned?
2 How does Exhibit 8.9 relate to Exhibit 1.6?
3 The attractions of electronic commerce aren't equally strong for all forms of offer. What are the characteristics of offers that suggest that they might be made available via the Internet?
4 List the weaknesses of the five forces model if it were put forward as the only tool for analysing the operating environment.

1 Draw up value chains for each of the following:
   a)   an airline such as British Airways;
   b)   a building society;
   c)   electrical power generation and distribution in the UK.
2 Select a business of your choice. Identify how developments in IT are currently changing the forces in and around its competitive arena. Sketch out how the competitive arena is likely to be affected by IT over the next decade.

The obvious starting point in further reading about a structural analysis of the operating environment is with the guru Michael Porter and his *Competitive Strategy* book (Porter, M.E., *Competitive Strategy: Techniques for Analyzing Industries and Competitors*, Free Press, 1980). Although Porter provides the framework for the analysis, he doesn't provide any quantitative measures of the effects.

The PIMS programme does this through the data it has collected over many years. The book by Buzzell and Gale (Buzzell, R.D. and Gale, B.T., *The PIMS Principles: Linking Strategy to Performance*, Free Press, 1987) describes the methodology adopted in the programme and the results from it. Fully up-to-date results are available on subscription from the Strategic Planning Institute.

CHAPTER NOTES AND REFERENCES

1   It is difficult, however, to find direct competitors for the Royal Society for the Protection of Birds and the Royal National Institute for the Blind.

2   Porter, M.E., *Competitive Strategy: Techniques for Analyzing Industries and Competitors*, Free Press, 1980.

3   Potts, J., *Reengineering the Business*, BBC for Business video, BBC Enterprises, 1994.

4   Unfortunately, this use of chain clashes with the commonly used term *chain of supermarkets*, which isn't a chain at all.

5   IMD 'The world paint industry 1992', International Management Development Institute, Lausanne, Switzerland; distributed by the European Case Clearing House, Cranfield University (No. 393–138–5), 1993.

6   It could be that the business in any competitive arena could have an impact on the target competitive arena and, conversely, the businesses there could use their influence on the competitive arenas that don't abut their own. The forces acting on the target competitive arena from outside the immediate operating environment will be considered later.

7   Lipsey, R.G. and Chrystal, K.A., *An Introduction to Positive Economics*, 8th edn, Oxford University Press, 1995, Chapter 12.

8   Porter, M.E., *op. cit.*

9   *Ibid.*

10   Buzzell R.D. and Gale, B.T., *The PIMS Principles: Linking Strategy to Performance*, Free Press, 1987, p. 143; and Schoeffler, S., 'The unprofitability of "modern" technology and what to do about it', *The PIMSLetter*, No.2, The Strategic Planning Institute, 1980. The PIMS (Profit Impact of Market Strategy) programme is a non-profit organisation aimed at advancing strategic management practice. The programme is run by the Strategic Planning Institute, with offices in Boston (USA), London and several other cities. Its database consists of data on around 3000 businesses, overwhelmingly within corporations. The institute applies three validation tests to its findings: are they statistically significant, do they conform to best available theory and do they make sense to knowledgeable business people?

11   Nielsen, *The Retail Pocket Book 1996*, NTC Publications, 1995.

12   'Other multiples' are defined as having ten or more outlets under common ownership.

13   The concentration in Germany was comparable, while in Italy it was far less (Nielsen, *op. cit.*).

14   Note that Porter (*op. cit.*) used the expression 'threat of entry'. However, although it is the profitability or future profitability that might get firms to think of entering a competitive arena; it is the barriers to entry that inhibit entry and put the prospective profitability into perspective.

15   Koenig, P., 'GEC mounts net offensive', *The Independent on Sunday*, 'Business', 2 May 1999, p. 3; and Cookson, C., 'Financial community develops a taste for industrial research', *Financial Times*, 20 January 1998, p. 1 (quoting Company Reports, Edinburgh).

16   Lippman, S.R. and Rumelt, R.P., 'Uncertain imitability: an analysis of interfirm differences in efficiency under competition', *Bell Journal of Economics*, Vol. 13, No. 2, 1982, pp. 418–38.

17   Cunningham, M.T. and Culligan, K.R., 'Strategies for declining industries', *The Journal of Business Strategy*, Vol. 1, No. 2, 1980, pp. 20–34.

18   Finch, J., 'Just how clean are your shoes? *The Guardian*, 12 September 1997, p. 21.

19   Porter, M.E. and Millar, V.E., 'How information gives you competitive advantage', *Harvard Business Review*, July–Aug 1985, pp. 149–60.

20   Moran, J., *Financial Times*, Review of Enterprise Computing, 25 February 1998, p. 4.

21   *Ibid.*

22   Houlder, V. 'BP overcomes fear of the "too difficult" box', *Financial Times*, 25 April 1998, p. 16.

23   Taylor, J., *Financial Times*, 3 June 1998.

24   *Ibid.*

25   Doyle, P., *The Guardian*, 7 March 1998, p. 31.

26   Jonquières, G. de, 'Network guerrillas', *Financial Times*, 30 April 1998, p. 20.

27   Vidal, J., 'Modem warefare', *The Guardian*, 'Society', 13 January 1998, p. 4.

28   Senge, P.M., *The Fifth Discipline: The Art and Practice of the Learning Organization*, Doubleday, 1990, pp. 27–54.

9 Forecasting and scenarios

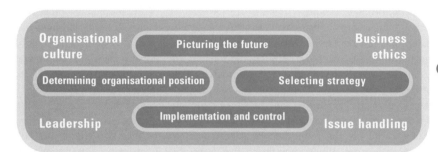

this chapter is the last of the three concerned with the process of 'picturing the future'. Whereas Chapters 7 and 8 are concerned with **analysis**, this chapter is concerned with **synthesis**. Picturing the future isn't simply environmental analysis, it's also about bringing the elements of the analysis together to develop coherent views of how the future may turn out.

The chapter opens with a look at forecasting, which is the traditional way in which views of the future are derived. Three forecasting methods are introduced and the combination of methods is discussed. For the longer term, however, forecasting isn't appropriate and another way of 'picturing the future' is needed. This is through the development of scenarios.

The form of a scenario is first examined and the composition of the scenario-building team discussed. The appropriate number of scenarios and their timeframe are considered. This is then followed by considering the steps in scenario building, stressing the learning aspect of the process. Scenario thinking and what should be included in a set of scenarios are then explored. Finally, the role of scenarios in formulating and selecting strategy is considered.

Every leader-manager needs to 'picture the future' – to take a view of the state(s) in which the organisation may be operating when the decisions they are taking today will come into effect. Forecasting has a role in strategic management, but for anything but the near future scenarios are needed to provide appropriate views. The process of developing scenarios is very useful for encouraging contributions from many different sources, for developing strategic thinking and for advancing organisational learning. The scenarios themselves allow the robustness of proposed strategies to be tested.

LEARNING
OUTCOMES

When you have worked through this chapter, you should be able to:

- explain what time series forecasting is, the assumptions underlying it and the limitations of its application in strategic management;

- explain what causal forecasting is, the assumptions underlying it and the limitations of its application in strategic management;

- describe the Delphi technique and explain where it can usefully be applied;

- explain why organisations are turning to scenarios to 'picture their future';

- decide on the number of scenarios to choose as a preliminary to carrying out strategy formulation;

- determine the appropriate timescale for a set of scenarios;

- write scenarios;

- know how scenarios can be used in strategy formulation.

9.1 Forms of future environmental pictures

In Chapter 7 the process of analysing the remote environment for trends and events was explored. In Chapter 8 a structural analysis provided a rather static view of the forces in the operating environment. Because change in the operating environment is usually generated from changes in the remote environment, a more dynamic view of the operating environment can be obtained by linking the two environments. This linking is through forecasts and scenarios, the third and final step in the development of 'views of the future'.

Everyone needs to consider the future, since whether a decision turns out to be 'good' or 'bad' depends not on *current* but on *future* conditions. Although managers and their organisations do survive without taking heed of the future, many pay severe penalties: sales may be prejudiced through inadequate raw material availability; extra costs may be incurred because a lack of production capacity forces expensive overtime to be worked; an acquisition may be a great mistake if the market subsequently experiences a sharp decline. In the early 1990s British Gas wished to secure its supplies of natural gas. However, it incorrectly forecast higher prices than those that actually occurred and signed long-term contracts on what turned out to be very disadvantageous terms compared with those secured by its competitors.

When you are looking a short distance into the future, it is likely that the future will be quite similar to the past and thus it will be relatively straightforward and appropriate to extend the past fairly directly into the future. In such circumstances it's quite reasonable to ask questions such as 'What will our sales be next month?' and 'What will the €–$ exchange rate be this time next year?' and to expect a fairly definite answer. This is the realm of forecasting. As you look further and further into the future, however, the uncertainty about what the future may look like generally increases. It then becomes unreasonable to expect any sort of definite answer; forecasting becomes inappropriate and we must turn to a completely different way of 'picturing the future': we are in the realm of scenarios. Scenarios will be considered in the second part of this chapter, after we have had a look at those forecasting methods that are useful in strategic management.

9.2   Forecasting

9.2.1   Forecasting methods

Forecasting isn't a magic art, it's a systematic way of combining managerial judgement with past data to say something rational about the future. It's rarely possible to forecast with unerring accuracy and precision, since there will almost always be some factors that affect the future that we don't know about, and these show up as forecasting errors. The effects of these errors will generally be absorbed by the 'slacks' in the organisation – holding stocks, the use of exceptional overtime working, etc. However, the bigger the errors in forecasting, the greater these 'slacks' must be and the greater the associated costs. The challenge in forecasting is to reduce the errors.

There are three types of forecasting methods that are useful in strategic management. All forecasting is based on the past, but the three methods utilise the data and understanding that exist about the past in very different ways. These types are explained in Exhibit 9.1.

Which of these three approaches to adopt will depend on the circumstances, on the level of understanding surrounding the variable whose value is being forecast and on the time ahead that is being considered.

9.2.2   Time series forecasting

A time series is a set of data values for a single variable collected at equally spaced intervals of time. Examples are the monthly sales of soft drinks and the daily move-

EXHIBIT 9.1

The major types of forecasting

- **Time series forecasting**, where future data values are obtained simply by extending past data.
- **Causal forecasting**, where future data values are obtained from extending past, explicitly formulated cause-and-effect relationships.
- **Judgemental forecasting**, where future data values are obtained in situations where little directly relevant experience exists and where it is hard to articulate this experience.

ment of share prices. The fundamental assumption underpinning time series forecasting methods is that future data values will be extensions of a past time series. The methods don't depend on any deep understanding of the underlying causes giving rise to the data values; almost all there is to know about the future is contained in the set of data values that *happen* to have occurred in the past.

Although there are many different specific time series forecasting techniques, most of them are only of value for forecasting a very short period ahead and thus are of little or no value in strategic management. One technique that is of value in business strategic thinking, however, is the technique of *time series decomposition*. This technique assumes that the *past* data can be decomposed (broken down) into components. Thus we can write:

past data = a combination of components + (unexplained) random fluctuations

The technique further assumes that these components can be recombined to provide *future* data values, and so:

future data = a recombination of the components

One example of a time series is shown in Exhibit 9.2a. The particular choice of components into which to decompose the series will depend on the specifics of the situation. However, there is a 'standard set' of components to be considered and these are sketched in Exhibit 9.2b–e (Exhibit 9.2f will be considered later).

One component, often the most important, is the trend – a *continuous* increase or decrease in the data. In Exhibit 9.2b the trend is shown as increasing with time. What distinguishes a trend from cycles and seasonal variations is that these variations are wave-like movements that repeat themselves. Seasonal variations are a special case of cyclical variations where the periodicity of the cycle is one year. Even in our rather artificial lives, the seasons of the year still play a major role, reflected in the availability of fresh foods, the sale of consumer goods and the choice of leisure activities.

For this reason the seasonal component is picked out and given greater emphasis than the other cyclical components, which have periodicities other than a year. Examples of non-annual cyclical variations are the full business cycle for developed economies, which is sometimes termed the Kitchin cycle and has a periodicity of three–five years. Some economists believe that the most important cycle is one of about 50 years due to major technological innovations. According to this view, the cycle of information technology that we are currently experiencing will only have run its course around the year 2030. On a smaller scale than this are the cycles of stocks of raw materials and finished goods, with many cycles lasting about two years.

It's very unlikely that the trend, the seasonal and cyclical variations will completely

EXHIBIT 9.2

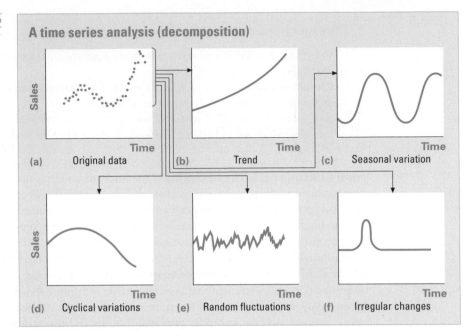

A time series analysis (decomposition)

(a) Original data (b) Trend (c) Seasonal variation

(d) Cyclical variations (e) Random fluctuations (f) Irregular changes

describe the past data: some unexplained contribution, the random fluctuations, will remain. These fluctuations are sketched in Exhibit 9.2e. As long as the random fluctuations are small compared with the trend and the explained variations, however, then time series decomposition may be a reasonable technique for forecasting. (But beware, here we are talking about randomness in the past data; you would expect the errors in forecast values to grow the further into the future you look until a point is reached when it's no longer valid to use time series analysis as a method of forecasting, because the past is no longer a good guide to the future.)

The data for Exhibit 9.2 were decomposed by subtracting components from the full data. Thus the future value of the variable can be determined by adding together the contribution from each component, although any past irregular changes (9.2f) should not be included unless they are likely to recur in the future. Thus if sales are being forecast:

sales = trend + seasonal variation+ cyclical variations

One aspect of this additive combination of components is that the sizes of the seasonal and cyclical variations are assumed to be independent of the size of the trend, so the size of a seasonal peak wouldn't be linked to average annual sales. If it was believed that the size of the seasonal peak was linked to the size of the trend, then a non-additive combination of components would be more appropriate. Consideration of such combinations is beyond the scope of our present discussion, however.

KEY CONCEPT   The fundamental assumption underpinning time series forecasting is that future data values will be extensions of past data values: almost all there is to know about the future is contained in the set of data values that *happen* to have arisen in the past.

DISCUSSION
POINT 9.1

List three products or services that aren't seasonal.

- Can you think of any product or service that has a cycle different from one or two years?

9.2.3 Causal forecasting

As with time series methods, causal forecasting is concerned with quantitative data, with how many pairs of shoes to make over the next few years rather than with what the fashionable styles might be. Causal methods provide a more sophisticated type of forecast than time series methods, since the cause-and-effect links between variables are used to make the forecasts. For a clear-cut example, consider the time series shown in Exhibit 9.3a, where for simplicity no seasonal or cyclical components are present; there is simply a trend. In Exhibit 9.3a this trend has been extrapolated as the lower curve using a time series forecasting technique. Suppose our understanding was that sales are dependent on disposable income,[a] shown in Exhibit 9.3b. Suppose also that a general election is likely to take place in the near future and that it's our experience that chancellors of the exchequer are very prone to increasing disposable income in the hope of staying in power. The forecast view of disposable income is shown in Exhibit 9.3c. Now the situation looks very different: whereas the time series method forecasts a continuing decline in sales (as shown by the lower line in Exhibit 9.3a), the causal method forecasts a sharp rise (as shown by the upper line in Exhibit 9.3a).

Causal methods are particularly useful when one of the variables in the cause-and-effect relationship is what is termed 'a leading indicator'. A leading indicator is a variable where a change in its value precedes (or leads) a change in the variable that you want to know about. The number of new housing starts is a leading indicator for sales of domestic appliances such as refrigerators and washing machines, because people tend to buy these when they move into a new home; an upturn in car sales is a leading indicator for sheet steel demand. Possibly the most colourful leading indicator was that suggested by the nineteenth-century economist Jevons, who believed that sunspot activity could be used to predict a nation's economic performance. (Actually, since sunspots influence the weather and the weather in turn influences agricultural

EXHIBIT 9.3

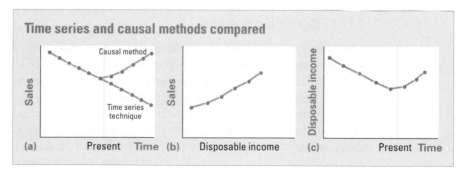

a   Crudely, the amount of money we have left 'in our pocket' after 'fixed' items such as rent, rates, electricity, heating, etc. have been paid for.

yields, this was not too stupid a theory at a time when agriculture played a very large part in the national life.) Leading indicators are fine as long as there is enough lead-time between cause and effect for appropriate action to be taken and the value of the leading indicator can be predicted reasonably accurately and fairly easily. There is an undoubted link between UK beer sales and the maximum daily temperature, but are weather forecasts good enough and long-term enough to allow the brewers to act on them?

DISCUSSION POINT 9.2

What other leading indicators can you think of? Is the timescale such that these indicators can be acted on?

There is no requirement for casual relationships to be linked only to time series (although of course there will always be a time element; we are *fore*casting, after all). For example, a firm's expected sales might be causally linked to the ratio of its advertising spend to that of its competitors.

The value of causal methods is that they encapsulate more fundamental patterns from the past than do time series forecasting methods; they use our understanding of past cause-and-effect relationships as well as the data values that happen to have occurred. Time series methods are applicable only if the (rather unknown) variables that have given rise to the data in the past are repeated exactly as before in the same strength and with the same consequences. In contrast, causal methods only require that the cause-and-effect patterns exhibited in the past are repeated: the *value* of any particular variable can be far different from that previously experienced. For example, if it was known that advertising spend by competitors was to be doubled in the future, time series forecasting would pick up the consequences of this only **after** the event; causal methods could **predict** them.

KEY CONCEPT

Causal forecasting uses understanding of the cause-and-effect relationships between variables to make a forecast. These relationships allow a wide range of values of variables to be considered. A particularly powerful use of causal methods is with leading indicators.

9.2.4 Combining forecasts

It might seem that combining the results from more than one type of forecasting method would be a good idea, in that the combined forecast is likely to be more accurate that any of the methods used singly. Judgement would be used to apply weightings to each component in the combination.

It's important to reflect on how much judgement has already been used with time series and causal forecasting methods *prior to getting the forecast results* – that is to say, before ever predicting future values. Consider time series forecasting. First a judgement will have to be made to decide which data to use: should daily, weekly or monthly values be used? Then a decision will need to be made as to which particular time series technique would be most appropriate: additive or non-additive time series decomposition, for example. The decomposition in Exhibit 9.2 featured an *irregular* component (Exhibit 9.2f): this blip might have been due to a strike at a competitor's factory limiting its supply, or the result of a special promotion by your own firm. It would be appropriate to exercise judgement and remove such a special blip *before* determining the other components, and thus prior to extrapolating into the future.

Considerable judgement must also be used with causal methods: for example, which variables are significant, which sets of data should be used to determine the values of any coefficients in the cause-and-effect relationships, and what to do with any irregularities in the data.

For judgement to be usefully included in quantitative methods and their forecasts, the person exercising that judgement should be incorporating information not captured in the data points or in the causal relationships. Since the data and causal relationships already contain past information, it's very often information about the future that judgement is providing. You might know that a new tax is to be levied in the near future, or that competitors will be aggressively marketing revamped products during the next few years. Judgement would be used to take account of this new information.

DISCUSSION
POINT 9.3

If you have ever done any quantitative forecasting, how did you incorporate judgement into your forecasts?

KEY CONCEPT

There are three ways of combining judgement with quantitative forecasting methods (time series and causal). The first is combining the *results* from different techniques. The second is to use judgement to decide, *prior to getting the results*, what is the most appropriate forecasting technique to use and then accept unmodified the results that are generated. The third is to modify the results of quantitative forecasts *after* they have been produced, in the light of new future conditions. In practice, combinations of these three methods are used as appropriate.

9.2.5 Judgemental forecasting

When suitable past data do not exist for time series forecasting to be used and cause-and-effect relationships are insufficiently understood to employ causal forecasting techniques successfully, then reliance must be placed on judgement alone. Surveys of corporate forecasting practice show that most important forecasts involve judgement.[1] When a very new product or service is launched, for example the launch of Internet services in the 1990s, demand could hardly be estimated at all; even Bill Gates got it wrong. Here, experience of the launch of electronic consumer goods or of telephone banking might be a guide, but it's very likely that this experience could not be articulated and would be translated simply into a 'gut feeling'.[2]

Although there is evidence that group decision making can make effective use of the combined knowledge of a group of people, there is also a lot of evidence that groupthink and the dominance of one or two individuals can be so strong that group knowledge is often wasted. One sophisticated method of judgemental forecasting that gets around this problem is the Delphi technique, developed in the 1950s by Olaf Helmer of the Rand Corporation in California and named after the famous Oracle of Delphi in ancient Greece. The method is used to determine answers to one or more specific questions about the future. For example, suppose a firm wanted to know the answer to the following question: 'By what date will 50% of the world's population have access to a video recorder?' The method would operate as follows.

First a co-ordinator would be appointed. They would then select a panel of appropriate experts; for the video recorder example these might include electronics experts, salespeople with experience in selling in undeveloped countries, politicians and experts in demographics. To prevent the dominance by one or more individuals that often occurs in committees, the experts never meet and indeed do not even know who the other participants in the exercise are. Each expert would be asked to state their view (a date) and to give reasons for their answer. The responses would be collected and collated by the co-ordinator and the numerical data would perhaps be graphed. The graph and the reasons for any extreme views would be transmitted to all the experts without attributing their source. The experts could then be asked to review their forecasts in the light of the new information: some may revise their initial forecast, others may give further reasons why they are sticking with their original view. The process would be continued until no significant shift in responses occurred. This is usually after two or three iterations of the question–answer routine. The end result is a consensus of views grouped around a middle point.

> KEY CONCEPT Judgemental forecasts are appropriate when no suitable past data exist for time series forecasting and when quantifiable cause-and-effect relationships are insufficiently understood. The rather pompous term 'jury of expert opinion' is sometimes used to describe groups of people engaged in group thinking – when, for example, they are seeking a forecast. The Delphi technique is a suitable means of obtaining expert opinion, although it can be a costly approach.

9.2.6 Predetermined, self-defeating and self-fulfilling forecasts

Three types of forecast can be identified.[3] First there is the 'predetermined' forecast, based on variables already known; this is hardly a forecast at all, more a mechanical extension of present data. For example, the number of secondary schoolchildren in the UK in 2010 is already known very accurately since, except for some small uncertainty regarding immigration and emigration, almost all are currently in UK primary schools. Thomas Cook, the travel agent, is facing a form of predetermined forecast. It relies heavily for its revenues and profits on supplying foreign currencies and the issuing of travellers' cheques. With the advent of a common European currency and the further spread of cash dispensers and the use of credit cards, these markets are 'predetermined' to fall very markedly.

Second, there is the 'self-defeating' forecast, whereby if everyone believes that something will happen, their behaviour changes and this then 'defeats' the forecast. For example, suppose an oil shortage is forecast and this leads to the imposition of strict oil conservation measures. If these measures are successful, the potential shortage is prevented and the forecast has been 'defeated' – through publicising itself. The other side of this behaviour-changing coin is the third type of forecast, the 'self-fulfilling' forecast. If many people believe that the price of a particular share is going to fall, there will be a lot of selling of this share and this selling will indeed cause the price to drop. If it is rumoured that there is going to be a shortage of some type of goods, people buy far more than they need and this results in shops selling out, exactly as forecast.

DISCUSSION
POINT 9.4

From your experience, what timescales would typically be associated with each of the three types of forecasting? Can you think of other predetermined forecasts?

- Can you think of other self-defeating and self-fulfilling forecasts?

9.3 The weakness of forecasting

Forecasting methods are attempting to predict the 'most likely'. Sometimes the forecasts will include an estimate of the confidence that the forecaster has of the forecast (e.g. plus or minus 10%). However, as the planning horizon increases, predictions such as these that rely so strongly on the past (particularly on past data) become less and less convincing and we come to the situation shown in Exhibit 9.4. As the time-frame that is being considered gets longer, the range of possible futures widens.

Forecasting is a dangerous activity. In his video series, Pascale[4] gives four examples of forecasts made by experts in their field that turned out to be hopelessly wrong:

1880   Thomas Edison, inventor and entrepreneur: 'The phonograph is not of any commercial value'.
1920   Robert Millikan, Nobel prize-winning physicist: 'There is no likelihood that man can tap into the power of the atom'.
1927   Harry Warner, movie producer: 'Who the hell wants to hear an actor talk?' (about putting a soundtrack on to silent movies).
1943   Thomas Watson, chairman of IBM: 'I think there is a world market for about five computers'.

EXHIBIT 9.4

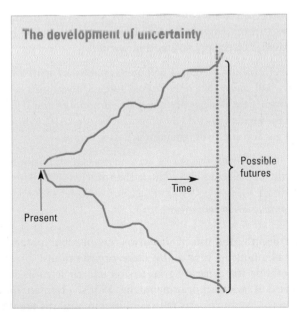

The development of uncertainty

Possible futures

Time

Present

to which can be added:

1936   Sir Harold Gillies, leading British plastic surgeon: 'There are four plastic surgeons in the country and I can't think that there can be room for more.'[5]

1985   Massachusetts Institute of Technology study *Global Energy Futures*: 'The supply of oil will fail to meet increasing demand before the year 2000, most probably between 1985 and 1995, even if energy prices rise 50% above current levels in real terms.'[6]

With even the experts getting things so hopelessly wrong, there's a need to turn to something else 'to get a handle on the future': we need to consider scenarios. Scenarios and forecasts differ fundamentally, because forecasts are based on the belief that the future can be predicted; scenarios are based on the belief that it can't. Indeed, it's no coincidence that the big push for the use of scenarios came from the turmoil of the 1970s and the realisation of how useless single-point forecasts were in many situations. And the world hasn't become any less uncertain since.

DISCUSSION POINT 9.5   Do you believe that the world has become more or less uncertain or stayed the same? Give reasons for your view.

KEY CONCEPT   Scenarios and forecasts differ fundamentally. Forecasts are made assuming that the future can be predicted; scenarios are generated on the assumption that it can't.

9.4 Scenarios

9.4.1 What are scenarios?

During the early 1990s, after the collapse of the Soviet Union, a British producer of land-based gas turbine engines (not aero or marine engines) considered the market situation in Russia. Company strategists[7] wrote:

> It's likely that dictatorial control will be re-established with a very nationalistic orientation. This will mean that only limited foreign investment will be allowed. Limited foreign investment will mean that the state monopoly natural gas producer (Gazprom) will undertake no new gas field development before 2010. Consequently the market for land-based gas turbines will remain much as it is now.

Surprising as it may seem, this set of statements is a scenario; it's a narrative providing an internally consistent view of how the future might plausibly turn out.

DISCUSSION POINT 9.6   What does *internally consistent* mean?

Over the last decade, the use of scenarios has become a standard aid for strategic thinking and planning in very many large organisations. As with the Delphi technique, the methods for generating scenarios had their roots in the activities of the California-based Rand Corporation in the 1950s. Herman Kahn, their originator, says that the term 'scenario' was first used by him and his team to de-glamourise the concept of writing narratives. They kept saying 'It's only a scenario', the kind of thing that is produced by Hollywood film writers – only a framework, not a blueprint. The main thrust for the use of scenarios in business came from the Shell Oil Company's use of them in the 1970s, when it developed a process whereby the scenarios were intimately liked to strategy formulation.

The view of the future that is required is a view of the operating environment within which the organisation developing the scenario thinks it might be operating. Changes in the operating environment are most often driven by changes in the remote environment, by changes in the DEEPLIST factors. Thus very often the relationships in a scenario link remote with operating environmental variables, and these are expressed as causal relationships. The gas turbine scenario provides an example:

> Limited foreign investment will mean that Gazprom will undertake no new gas field development before 2010. *Here the value* (limited) *of a remote environmental variable* (foreign investment) *affects the value* (no) *of an operating environmental variable* (new gas field development).

The purpose of writing scenarios isn't to provide or improve the precision of planning; rather, it's to improve the appreciation that managers have of possible future environments – and to get them to face up to the uncertainty inherent in the future. Scenarios are not data-rich: most of the information needed to develop them is qualitative and generally known to leader-managers already.

KEY CONCEPT | A scenario is an internally consistent narrative of how the future might plausibly turn out. The variables to consider in a scenario are those where the strategic uncertainties are the greatest. These variables are generally easy to identify, but it's often difficult to predict their values. The benefit of scenarios is mainly in their development, which is aimed at individual and organisational learning.

9.4.2 The elements of scenarios

The scenario presented in the previous section is a very simple one and doesn't include much of the logic underlying its creation. In fact, it's little more than a statement of the end-state – the situation at the end of the timeframe being considered.

As shown in Exhibit 9.5,[8] a scenario would normally include the story by which the present develops into the future end-state, together with the logic underpinning it. The story and the logic give credibility to the end-states and, very importantly, support the main reason for scenario development – organisational learning. In order to learn it is necessary for the logic associated with each end-state to be discussed, debated and understood (although not necessarily agreed with).

9.4.3 The scenario-building team

As with so much of strategic management, much of the value of scenarios is in the process by which they are built. Thus the composition of the team of people building the scenarios and the way they interact are very important. On the one hand the more people involved the better, but too many can inhibit debate. Certainly all the key

EXHIBIT 9.5

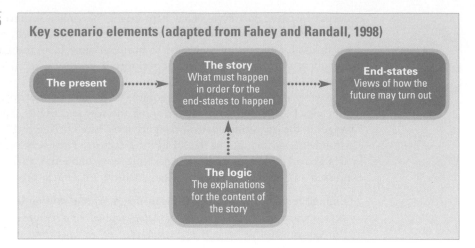

Key scenario elements (adapted from Fahey and Randall, 1998)

leader-managers should be involved in the scenario-building process in order for them to 'own' the set of scenarios, to understand the rationale behind them, to know how any chosen strategy fits with the future, and for their thinking and learning to be expanded in the process.

The interactions between the participants needs careful planning and channelling. The use of a trained facilitator could be very valuable, and group support systems can provide useful help.

KEY CONCEPT | A scenario consists of a statement of an end-state and a story explaining how this end-state has developed, together with the underlying logic. The team building the scenarios should include all key leader-managers.

9.5 The number of scenarios and scenario timeframes

9.5.1 The number of scenarios

Given the volatility of the situation in the former Soviet Union, the gas turbine company would be ill-advised to rely on the one scenario; if it did so, it would in fact be forecasting. So there is a need for a set of scenarios. A balance needs to be struck between the enormous number of scenarios that could theoretically be written and the limited number that can be managed by a group of strategists. Given that the purpose of scenarios is to improve the appreciation that managers have of possible future environments, there is a need to span the possible futures, as depicted in Exhibit 9.4.

Scenarios link remote and operating variables and the situation is as depicted in Exhibit 9.6, where the operating environment is shown 'embedded' in the DEEPLIST remote environment. This whole picture is shown replicated three times at the bottom of the exhibit to represent three scenarios that might be generated to provide a range of futures spanning the possibilities.

The consensus seems to be to develop between two and four scenarios. The

EXHIBIT 9.6

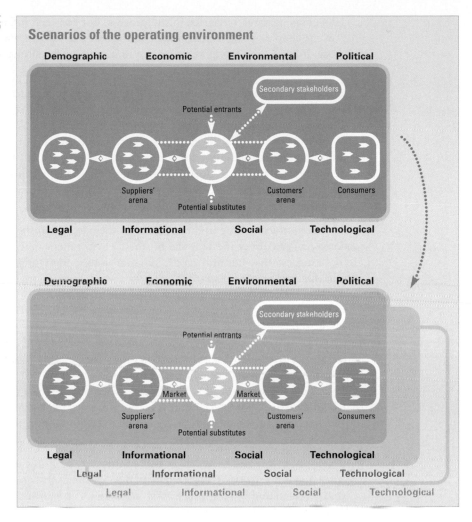

Scenarios of the operating environment

problem with using only two scenarios is that one will almost certainly be very optimistic and the other very pessimistic. The middle of three scenarios is likely to be the 'most likely' or a 'surprise-free' scenario ('surprise-free' generally meaning an extrapolation of current trends). The problem with three scenarios is that the strategic focus will very likely be on the middle one unless great care is taken. However, in most organisations there is likely to be a strong need to include the 'most probable' or at least a 'likely' scenario to maintain the credibility of the strategic management process; a group of leader-managers has to be very sophisticated to realise that a concentration on the 'most probable' future is very limiting. A choice of four scenarios helps prevent any such inappropriate focus.

The number and scope of the scenarios should be chosen to:

• keep (almost) every member of the strategy development team 'on board', allowing each to 'live' with at least one of the scenarios. Suppose that the inflation rate is crucially significant and that some members of the team think inflation will average 2% over the next five years, some think 5% and others

10%. Having three scenarios in the process, one for each inflation value, will prevent people opting out, considering the exercise to be a waste of time – with those dropping out using as an excuse that none of the situations being considered is plausible.

- encourage wide-ranging thinking, calling attention to a large range of possibilities
The difficulty here is how 'extreme' the 'wide-ranging' thinking should be. Choosing either situations that have only a very remote possibility of occurring (a nuclear war, say, in the case of gas turbines in Russia) or those that are little more than extrapolations of the present should be avoided. It's impossible to define precisely what to do: a rule of thumb would be to choose extremes that are 'unlikely but possible', which probably translates into situations with something like a 1 in 20 chance of occurring.

A not unimportant feature of the scenarios is the names that they are given. Evocative scenario names convey the way the business environment may change. Schwarz and Ogilvy[9] suggest that cultural icons, popular songs, films and TV shows are often memorable and cite one set of scenarios named after Beatles recordings, *A Hard Day's Night*, *Help*, *Magical Mystery Tour* and *Imagine*.

9.5.2 The timeframe for scenarios

There are no hard-and-fast rules to determine the suitable timeframe for scenarios, but the following guidelines will probably help.

The *minimum time* ahead is likely to be when any forecast is becoming so diffuse that strategists lack confidence that it is useful for strategic thinking.

The *maximum time* ahead is governed by the following factors:

- The timescale over which resources are to be committed   Scenarios are developed to provide views of possible futures; the futures in which the consequences of proposed decisions will work themselves out. If it takes ten years to plan and build a power station, then the scenario should cover at least this period of time. In the fashion and many service industries, the resource commitments are for much shorter periods.

- The time over which benefits from the decision would be expected to accrue
Using the example of the power station again, the revenues from the investment would only come through after the station had begun to generate electricity and then over the working life of the station, say 30 years. Perhaps the scenario should cover this whole period. Aero engine manufacturers have to think 20–30 years ahead, especially as their main source of profits is not from the sale of engines but from aftersales service.

- The inertia in the organisation   If an organisation has great flexibility, then it can get by with considering only a very short time horizon; in the ultimate it could take no heed of the future and simply react to events. However, if a venture requires skilled team working, for example, then it's necessary to consider exactly what capabilities will be required and build them up ready for action. This is certainly the case in many engineering companies.

9.6   Steps in scenario building

9.6.1   The broad approaches

Although there are many ways of building scenarios,[10] two broad approaches are recognised. First there is the bottom-up approach, whereby the important issues are identified, a range of future feasible values is attached to each and then scenarios are developed by combining the values of the issues. For example, suppose that the result of an approaching general election and the €–$ exchange rate were the only two important issues. Then the values associated with the election might be *Party A wins, Party B wins* and *a coalition between Parties A and C*, and the exchange rate values might be taken as *1:1* and *1:1.3*. Scenarios would be built by combining one value from each variable, e.g. *Party A wins* and the exchange rate is *1:1*.

The second broad approach starts with 'themes' for the end-states (for example, in a particular situation it might be appropriate to consider the three themes 'high tech', 'low tech' and 'constant trends'). Important issues are then identified and values for these variables are chosen that would correspond to these different themes.

In both approaches the strategic issues or drivers of change need to be identified, and for this to occur the purpose of creating the scenarios must first be established. The purpose may be wide-ranging, such as 'What will the EU look like in the future?', or more focused to support a key decision facing the organisation: 'Should we enter the Russian power market?' or 'Should we put new shops in central city shopping malls?'

9.6.2   Selecting the drivers

The main reason for building scenarios is because of the uncertainty that the organisation faces. Scenarios need to take these uncertainties into account when they are concerned with factors with a potentially high strategic impact. In short, what must be included in the scenarios are the strategic uncertainties.

In terms of uncertainty, there are two types of factor in scenarios. First there are **predetermined factors**, which are constants or variables that vary in a known way. These factors don't distinguish scenarios from each other but are the assumptions underlying all the scenarios. Second there are **scenario variables**, whose values do differentiate scenarios from each other. Thus scenario variables would feature in all scenarios, but often with different values in each.

EXHIBIT 9.7

The drivers of change

| | | Degree of uncertainty in the value of variables | |
		Low	High
	High	Predetermined factor	Scenario variable
Level of strategic impact	Low	Don't include in scenarios	Don't include in scenarios but monitor

Exhibit 9.7 indicates that those variables that are thought to have a high level of strategic impact should be in the scenarios, as either predetermined factors or scenario variables. Those thought likely to have a low strategic impact should not be included. However, when the uncertainty in the value of a variable is high, then the variable should be monitored to ensure that it doesn't attain values that will make a chosen strategy ineffective.

9.6.3 Determining suitable end-states

Of the two broad approaches to building scenarios, generally the more useful and usually the easier approach is the 'thematic' or top-down approach. Returning to the gas turbine example, four themes were considered. The first was *the Western investors' dream*, which is a highly optimistic scenario for Western investors, one where almost everything that can go right does so. The second is the opposite, the *Western investors' nightmare*, when almost everything that can go wrong does so. Then there were two less extreme views: *the middle ground* and *a modest tale*. With these four themes identified, the characteristics that would correspond to them are considered and written down.

The important factors in the environment are the position and role of Gazprom; political and economic stability in Russia; the Russian attitude to foreign investment; and Gazprom's new gas field development strategy. The year 2010 is considered the appropriate time horizon. For all scenarios, it's assumed that Gazprom is kept intact and remains monopolistic.

The four end-states corresponding to these themes can be written as follows:

- The Western investors' dream   a relatively stable, capitalist economy with foreign investment welcomed. Gazprom plans to develop new gas fields from 2000.

- The Western investors' nightmare   the political and economic situation is chaotic and foreign investment isn't welcome. Gazprom isn't intending to develop any new gas fields prior to 2010.

- The middle ground   the political and economic situation is relative stable. The Russians are taking a cautious attitude to foreign investment. Gazprom plans to develop new gas fields from 2000.

- A modest tale   the political and economic situation is stable. The Russians are taking a cautious attitude to foreign investment. Gazprom isn't planning to develop any new gas fields prior to 2010.

DISCUSSION
POINT 9.7

Is gas field development without foreign investment a possible scenario?
    Do all the scenarios in a set have to involve the same timeframe?
    Is there a predetermined factor underlying the end-states?

Let's consider what has been done to develop the four gas turbine end-states. The eight-step process has been as follows:

1 Define the purpose   The purpose of writing the scenarios is to determine whether a new market should be entered (*what is the situation associated with entering the Russian market for land-based gas turbines?*).

2 Set the 'tone' of the scenario themes   (*the Western investors' dream; the Western investors' nightmare; the middle ground; a modest tale*).

3 Identify the important factors in the environment   (*the role of Gazprom; political and economic stability; attitude to foreign investment; Gazprom's gas field development strategy*). Guidelines to help select the variables to include and those to discard are:
   - discard variables having a low probability of occurrence and low potential impact (as shown in Exhibit 9.7);
   - include an event that is likely to happen or have an impact in the next few years rather than one that might not happen or will only be significant towards the end of the time horizon;
   - don't include disaster events;
   - aggregate variables where possible: for example, factors associated with economic activity – exchange rates, GDP, inflation rate – can be combined into an aggregated variable of, say, 'economic health'.

4 Determine an appropriate time horizon   (*the year 2010*).

5 Identify and give values to the predetermined factors   (e.g. *the role of Gazprom*).

6 Review the number of end-states in the light of the number and range of values of the environmental variables (here, remain with *four*).

7 Determine plausible ranges of values for the scenario variables that correspond to the tone of each scenario (e.g. *stable, relatively stable, chaotic* for political and economic stability). Guidelines here are:
   - reject values so extreme that they appear absurd;
   - if a value lies between the marginal and the absurd, then use it.

8 Write down the cause-and-effect relationships for each set of remote and operating environmental variables and collect them into a narrative. Check the narrative for self-consistency.

9.6.4 Fleshing out the narrative[11]

End-states can be written that are simple 'one-liners', for example: 'The Internet will allow our products to be sold at half of today's prices', or 'Genetically modified foods will be outlawed in the next three years'. This is the case where one very powerful issue can be identified. The gas turbine end-states are slightly more extensive but, although adequate for their purpose, they are still very simple ones: they are almost uni-dimensional in that the only variables concern the very broad economic and political situation. In general, it would be expected that many of the issues identified in each of the eight DEEPLIST components of the remote environment would feature in the scenarios and be linked to the important elements of the operating environment. It would also be expected that the story and the logics would be included in the written scenario. An example of a complete scenario is shown in Exhibit 9.8.

DISCUSSION
POINT 9.8

Why would you not expect all of the issues identified in the analysis of the remote environment to feature in the scenarios?

EXHIBIT 9.8

Northeast Consulting 10th Anniversary Future Mapping, 17–18 June 1998, Boston, Massachusetts[12]

On 17 and 18 June 1998, twenty-two senior executives, managers and entrepreneurs gathered to map the future of computing and communications in 2005. This group represented a broad cross-section of the industry, including venture capital companies, hardware and software product creators, service providers, enterprise IT organisations, and consultants. This report summarises the essential points of the debate.

End-state summaries

The four end-states used in this workshop reflected input from approximately twenty interviews as well as past Northeast Consulting work with large enterprises, vendors and service providers. Input from previous Future Mapping workshops on this same subject was also used. The end-states look at the evolution of computing and communications industries, technologies and markets, as well as their impact on society, government and individuals. We should note that they represent a decidedly US-centric point of view. This was a conscious choice, as we did not feel we could do justice in one workshop to all the issues of a multinational setting for such a broad set of topics. Short summaries of each end-state follow:

2005 A: CONSUMER AND EMBEDDED MARKETS LEAD
Inexpensive CPUs and wireless nets, combined with the digitisation of just about everything, have resulted in a proliferation of network appliances and smart products as well as new services that support them. Personal, home and embedded markets are the drivers of volume and innovation.

2005 B: FUNDAMENTAL TECHNOLOGY ADVANCES
The massive computing and communication advances of the '80s and '90s were almost all built on fundamental technology advances from the late '60s and '70s. A new round of similarly profound technology innovations (e.g. wireless nets, optoelectronics and semiconductors) during the '90s laid the groundwork for extraordinary capacity, robustness and performance leaps in the '00s. The distributed control, adaptive behaviour and federated solutions pioneered by the Internet are the underlying architectural paradigm.

2005 C: UTILITIES AND VIRTUAL COMPANIES
Web-based delivery of a variety of business and consumer services enables the proliferation of virtual enterprises; many product businesses turn into service businesses. The rise of massive global IT service providers creates computing utilities.

2005 D: E-BUSINESS REVOLUTION
E-business profoundly affects enterprises of all types, with the computer and communications industries leading the transformation. E-business applications are the major source of investment and innovation.

Each of five teams of delegates was asked to devise a story and associated logics for one of the end-states. The story and logics for the first end-state are given below.

2005 A: CONSUMER AND EMBEDDED MARKETS LEAD:
Main themes: Inexpensive CPUs and wireless nets combined with the digitisation of just about everything have resulted in a proliferation of network appliances and smart products as well as new services supporting them. Personal and embedded markets are the drivers of volume and innovation.

Customer environment: Increasingly, business and consumer markets overlap. Home-based computing is a major market, with a growing number of residences having some form of LAN. WebTV, Internet radio, digital photography and other digital forms of previously analogue media have broadened personal computing far beyond the PC. Advanced virtual-reality arcades and home game systems lead the adoption of immersion systems. Everything from toys to toasters to traffic lights is smart and communicates. Many gizmos feature seamless integration with remote databases, including exact location awareness (via GPS or wireless microcell). The Web is now a major, global entertainment medium, even broadcasting live events. Just as Enterprise IT departments finish standardising PC computing on Wintel, they are faced with a proliferation of diverse, communicating, embedded (e.g. lab equipment) and personal devices, which increasingly require integration with corporate systems. Knowledge workers have many different means of accessing information services, all highly customisable to individual preferences. Internal efficiencies are increased by smart-asset tags to track equipment, smart badges to locate employees and smart buildings to lower energy usage. Backing all this intelligence are large, centrally managed servers that support the storage and transaction needs of gizmo users and smart products. Diverse network appliances and widespread embedded, networked intelligence in all consumer and business environments create an entirely new kind of networking challenge beyond traditional LANs.

Systems: The PC is just one of many ways to access the Net. Web standards apply broadly, but digital TV (DTV) is a Web alternative that reaches major consumer market segments; likewise, embedded industrial markets have their own standards. Network services proliferate as consumers are offered a number of ways to get broadband multimedia services. New user-interface technologies support keyboardless access to information and services. DSPs are widely used, providing powerful, inexpensive, 3-D multimedia. Mobility is expected by most new clients: wearable body networks and computers are popular with sick people, young people, and workers who need hands-free operation. Large-scale server clusters running NT, UNIX or OS/390 are the basis of centralised services, but client systems are highly diverse. A new tier of ubiquitous, mostly narrowband networks (e.g. powerline-based networks, infrared) connect smart products and network applications, making them surprisingly knowledgeable and responsive to their environments.

Industry structure: The largest volume markets are for consumers as well as for enabling technologies, such as wireless network links, that support both embedded and commercial markets. Wintel architecture is just one of many popular and successful product families. Asian consumer electronics and toy companies play a major role. Prices have fallen due to component volumes and the scale economies of centralised services for storage and processing. Previously analogue media such as TV, film, radio, printing and photography expand to overlap each other as well as traditional computing and communications markets. Brand matters in this world of many media and many choices. Most Internet services are enriched with content and are advertising-supported.

Socio-culture: The proliferation of networked intelligence has meant an ongoing balancing act between convenience and personal privacy; the trade-offs are made on a country-by-country and person-by-person basis. Physical location is far less critical in work, school and social life; lifestyles adjust accordingly. Nearly everyone is working (or schooling) from home at least some of the time. New user interfaces reinforce a shift from written to visual/oral communication. Education (in the USA as well as in developing countries) is a major beneficiary, as intelligent, adaptive appliances make learning both fun and challenging.

Discussion point 9.9

Identify the scenario variables and place them into each of the DEEPLIST categories.

9.6.5 The treatment of competitors

In very general terms the driving forces can be considered to be of two types: those that are not affected by the actions of the organisation considering the future, and those that emanate from agencies that will react to what the organisation attempts to do (such as competitors). In the eight-step approach described above, only the non-reactive driving forces have been considered. It might seem odd that at this stage the behaviour of competitors hasn't been considered, since in deciding on a particular strategy the plausible moves of competitors *must* be taken into account. However, the appropriate stage to do this is after the sources of comparative advantage have been considered and when the scenarios are melded together with the comparative strengths and weaknesses of competitors to form a strengths, weaknesses opportunities and threats (SWOT) table. These considerations are explored in the next two chapters.

9.7 Scenario thinking and the content of scenarios

So far we have considered the form and purpose of scenarios and their appropriate number and timeframe. We now consider the content of scenarios – not the specific content, because this will depend on the particular situation – but the form of the content. Again, we can only provide some guidelines, and these are:

- Challenge assumptions   Hidden in every person and organisation are assumptions about the world that may not really apply; these are inappropriate mindsets and paradigms. For example, it was once thought that only a very small proportion of people could ever be taught to read. For many years during the 1970s and 1980s the British Labour Party, or at least influential portions of it, hung on to the view that the voters wanted nationalisation and, as we know, this view was fatally flawed. So it's most important to try to unearth the assumptions and to build at least one scenario that 'offends conventional wisdom'.

- Ask fundamental questions about markets and consumers   Consumers buy offers for very basic reasons: you can't buck economics or the market for long. Ask if the offers provide value for money for however much the customer is willing to pay.

- Discount extrapolations and downplay historical precedent   Putting a strong emphasis on historical precedent is likely to lead to scenarios that are alike and similar to extrapolatory forecasts.

- Beware of technological wonder   The case of the introduction of credit cards in the UK is worth repeating. When they were introduced in 1968, the view was that within a few years writing cheques would be a thing of the past. In fact, it wasn't until 1990 that the level of cheques written fell; until then the number had risen every year. It had taken more than 20 years for a simple change to make a major impact.

- Don't include the proposed plans of the organisation in the scenario   Inclusion of such plans will obscure one of the main reason for writing scenarios: to provide possible future 'backcloths' against which to test proposed strategic plans.

- **Don't assign probabilities to events or trends**   Intuitively it might seem a good idea to assign probabilities to parts of scenarios, leading to placing a probability of occurrence on the scenarios themselves. This isn't advised. Assigning probabilities is very difficult to do, and working with conditional probabilities is highly problematic; both will cause the planning team to spend a lot of energy for no real advantage. The main rationale for building scenarios should be kept in mind: to stretch thinking, enhance individual and organisational learning, and provide 'backcloths' to test out strategic options.

DISCUSSION POINT 9.10   How does the scenario in Exhibit 9.8 stand up to this list of dos and don'ts?

9.8   The use of scenarios in strategy formulation

Scenarios provide the backcloths against which proposed strategies can be viewed and tested, allowing any proposed strategy to be tested against more than one view of the future. They provide an estimate of the 'space' within which a strategy will remain suitable/robust. A proposed strategy may be wonderful in one future but very poor in another. A second strategy may be reasonable in all futures. If the decision makers are risk takers, they may opt for the first strategy; if they are somewhat risk-averse, they may opt for the second.

This space within which a strategy remains viable suggests where organisational monitoring effort might be applied, which is a very important aspect of strategic control.

SUMMARY
- When there are a lot of quantitative past data about a fairly stable business process, then the use of time series techniques will generally provide useful forecasts. Causal methods have the added advantage of allowing for the forecasting of more extreme situations than had been experienced in the past. Both forms of forecasting have the advantage of making efficient use of past data, being reliable in the sense of always producing the same forecast with the same data, and less prone to bias than purely judgemental forecasting methods. In cases where hard data do not exist or where the basic causal patterns from the past are unlikely to apply in the future, formal quantitative methods have little to offer and pure judgemental methods are then needed.   EXHIBITS 9.1 TO 9.3
- Forecasts are generally useful when you're 'near to home', near to both the present in time and in what you are intending to do. As you move further away from the present and what the firm is currently engaged in, it doesn't become possible to forecast the future and another way of viewing the future is needed: this is done through the use of scenarios.   EXHIBIT 9.4
- Scenarios and forecasts differ fundamentally. Forecasts are made assuming that the future can be predicted; scenarios are generated on the assumption that it can't. Forecasting is fundamentally a consensus-seeking activity, whereas scenario development aims to encourage differing views.
- Scenarios are narratives of how the future may turn out. They consist of end-

states, the story of how the end-states have been reached from the present situation, together with the logics underpinning the story. Their primary purpose is to develop strategic thinking and individual and organisational learning and to act as 'backcloths' against which strategic options can be tested. Their use can help leader-managers to remain committed to the strategic planning process, since scenarios encourage several views of the future to be 'carried forward' through to option generation and choice.   EXHIBIT 9.5, EXHIBIT 9.6

- A good set of scenarios should span possible, but not outlandish, futures. There are two types of factor in scenarios: the predetermined factors, which are constants or variables that vary in a known way, and the scenario variables, whose differing values differentiate scenarios from each other. If the set of scenarios is well enough selected, the future should hold few surprises.   EXHIBIT 9.4, EXHIBIT 9.7

SELF-CHECK

1   Reconsider the learning outcomes for this chapter. Check that you feel confident that you can carry out the activities listed there.

2   Having read this chapter, you should be able to define the following terms:

causal forecasting	predetermined factor	scenario variable
Delphi technique	predetermined forecast	self-defeating forecast
forecast	scenario	self-fulfilling forecast
judgemental forecasting	scenario end-state	statistical forecasting
leading indicator	scenario logic	time series analysis

MINI-CASE

UK higher education funding

Research and teaching audits

The main governmental funding for universities is channeled through higher education funding councils (HEFCs), with one each for England, Northern Ireland, Scotland and Wales. Two measures are being used by each HEFC to assess universities: a measure of research quality and a measure of teaching quality. The standing of a business school depends heavily on its research rating. Research assessment exercises (RAEs) were conducted in 1986, 1989, 1992 and 1996, with the next scheduled for 2001. The first teaching quality assessment for business schools was made during 1993 and 1994, with the next scheduled for the year 2001.

RESEARCH ASSESSMENT EXERCISE
In the last RAE, a seven-point scale was used (1, 2, 3b, 3a, 4, 5 and 5*), with the worst research departments scoring 1 and the best 5*. Around 25% of business departments scored in the highest three categories. The funding for research from the HEFCs after 1992 was dependent on the RAE scores, and in England the relationship was a linear one, e.g. departments achieving a 4 rating received twice the funding per staff member than those departments recording a 2 score (roughly £3000 per staff member per year as against £1500). In Scotland, the funding council did not opt for the linear scale but favoured more strongly the highest-scoring departments. After the 1996 RAE the English formula for funding was no funding for departments rated 1 and 2, some funding for 3b departments and thereafter broadly a 50% increase in funding for each point on the scale. An overall reduction of 10% in research funding is widely forecast.

Traditionally, the former polytechnics were not given substantial funding to carry out 'academic' research, although, like all universities, they could obtain funds from industry and commerce to support 'applied' research. The former polytechnics did not take part in the RAEs of 1986 and 1989. They did not score well in the 1992 RAE, although some matched the 'old' universities in 1996.

TEACHING QUALITY AUDIT (TQA)

Effectively, the TQA only made two categories of award: satisfactory and excellent. Roughly 20% of business schools were considered 'excellent'. It is unlikely that any funding will be associated with these ratings, although an excellent rating may attract more and/or better-qualified undergraduate applications. However, it is government and university policy that will dictate whether a university will be allowed to take more undergraduates. The method of appraisal has been severely criticised, and a radically changed method will be used in future to assess business departments.

The remote environment

From 1979, UK governments have consistently held the view that any sector in receipt of government funds must be held accountable for these funds. This demand for greater accountability has been seen in the National Health Service and schools and is now being seen in the university sector. It has spawned the research and teaching audits referred to above. UK governments have also been fairly consistent with regard to education First, they have declared an aim of having 40% of 18-year-olds in further and higher education and are now seeking to increase this still further. Second, they wish to support only a relatively few centres of excellence in research. While the older universities traditionally had around 30% of staff costs given for research, this level of funding is considered inappropriate as the number of university staff increases markedly. Some observers consider that the government has the goal that no more than 10% of departments in any one discipline would receive government funding for research.

There has been continuous reduction in the funding associated with undergraduates – both the funding from local education authorities to students as maintenance grants and the funding given via the HEFCs to universities as fees. Over the last few years, the funding to universities for each undergraduate has fallen by an average of 3% a year and is expected to fall by at least that amount over the next five years; it could be by much more. Student loans are now the norm, and it is expected that many universities will charge students 'top-up' fees in the near future. The universities are very expensive compared with the further education institutions, many of which now offer all or parts of degree courses. Some universities are offering two-year degrees with teaching in the summer months. The cost of one year's undergraduate study in business studies (full fees and accommodation) per year is around £7000. There is no limit to what can be charged for postgraduate taught courses and for research degrees apart from the dictates of market forces.

The vast majority of undergraduates have traditionally come from the 18–21 age group. An increase in the size of this group will occur at the end of the next five years. There is an increase in mature students as undergraduates and a large increase in the number of students wanting to study business subjects. With fees paid by students rising and maintenance grants falling, some observers predict that English students will tend to follow the international norm and study at their home university. This will not be possible for 'specialist courses' such as sports science, library studies and some engineering subjects, but is very likely for business studies.

Because of the move to mass higher and further education, there have been exhortations to use IT much more. The opportunities opened up through the information superhighway are potentially very great, with students holding part-time jobs, living in their 'home' area and selecting their modules from 'a greatly extended Open University'.

The XX Business School

The University of XX's Business School (XXBS) is currently the largest department in XX with around 50 academic staff members. It has an annual intake of around 300 full-time equivalent (FTE) undergraduates into the five courses that it itself offers, and its staff teach a further 150 undergraduate students in other departments. Two postgraduate degrees are offered with an all-up annual intake of around 50. In 1999, there were approximately 40 full-time equivalent research students working towards an MPhil or a PhD.

For the academic year 1997/8, XXBS's budget is around £3 million, with £2 million received from government, 80% of which is associated with undergraduate teaching and 20% with research. Some £300,000 was generated by running non-certificated courses for external organisations. This latter income has been severely reduced by recession. The remainder came from special grants and postgraduate teaching.

In the 1992 RAE, XXBS achieved a 4; in the 1996 RAE it received a 3a grading, one of only two business schools out of the 100 in the UK to drop a grade. In November 1994, XXBS was considered 'excellent' in the TQA.

Discussion point 9.11

Identify one predetermined factor and two scenario variables in this narrative.

- Write scenarios for the appropriate timeframe to help the XX Business School in its strategic planning.

FURTHER
DISCUSSION
POINTS

1 For the GSM case:
   - What form of forecasting does GSM do? Is it appropriate?
   - What type of scenario building is undertaken? Is it appropriate?
2 In Chapter 1 the strategic management environment was characterised as chaotic, complex, dynamic and turbulent – all generally increasing the level of uncertainty facing leader-managers. However, not all business environments are the same. Reflect on how changes in the environmental characteristics might affect the approach taken to developing forecasts and scenarios.
3 If someone said to you 'a scenario got the future wrong', would you reply?
4 Which methods for picturing the future would you associate with functional, business and corporate-level strategic planning?
5 Why is the use of only one scenario in strategic planning simply a forecast?
6 How might the Delphi technique be used in scenario building?
7 In the gas turbine example, why is *new gas field development* an operating environmental variable?

ASSIGNMENTS

1 Develop a set of scenarios for GSM or for any of the companies described in the cases provided towards the end of the book.
2 Go to the Northeast Consulting website (hppt://www.ncri.com/pubwork.html) and look at other scenarios that it has been working on. Select one set of scenarios and critique it.

FURTHER READING

Liam Fahey and Robert M. Randall, *Learning from the Future: Competitive Foresight Scenarios*, John Wiley, 1998, provides many examples of where scenarios have been used and especially how they are linked with strategy development and choice.

The book by Gill Ringland, *Scenario Planning: Managing for the Future*, John Wiley, 1998, provides a fine overview of scenario development and use, and case histories of scenario development in several organisations including British Airways, the UK's National Health Service, Shell and Electrolux. There is also coverage of how the Internet might develop written in 1997, which makes interesting reading in the light of subsequent developments.

There are a great many books that describe and explain forecasting methods. Jeffrey Jarrett's *Business Forecasting Methods*, 2nd edn, Basil Blackwell, Oxford, 1991, is a good and very readable book. For combining forecasts one source is Scott Armstrong, J. and Collopy, F., 'Integration of statistical methods and judgement for time series forecasting: principles from empirical research' in Wright, G. and Goodwin, P. (eds) *Forecasting and Judgement*, John Wiley, 1997.

With scenarios there is less choice. Perhaps the best option is to look at the book by Robert Dyson, *Strategic Planning: Models and Analytical Techniques*, John Wiley, 1990.

Bennis, W and Nanus, B., *Leaders: the Strategies for Taking Charge*, Harper & Row, 1985, pp. 167–83 provides a good blow-by-blow account of the development and use of scenarios.

CHAPTER NOTES AND REFERENCES

1 Bunn, D. and Wright, G., 'Interaction of judgmental and statistical forecasting methods – issues and analysis', *Management Science*, Vol. 37, No. 5, 1991 pp. 501–18.

2 This is the technical term for managerial hunch or intuition.

3 Beck P.W., 'Corporate planning for an uncertain future', *Long Range Planning*, Vol. 15, No. 8, August 1982, pp. 12–21.

4 Pascale, R.T., *Transformation*, BBC Enterprises video, 1994.

5 Connolly, C. 'Review of *Venus Envy: A History of Cosmetic Surgery* by Elizabeth Haiken', *The Observer Review*, 11 January 1998, p. 17.

6 Marsh, B., 'Using scenarios to identify, analyze, and manage uncertainty?' Chapter 3 of Fahey, L. and Randall, R.M. (eds), *Learning from the Future: Competitive Foresight Scenarios*, John Wiley, 1998.

7 I am indebted to members of an MBA cohort for this example.

8 Fahey, L. and Randall, R.M., 'What is scenario learning?' Chapter 1 in Fahey, L. and Randall, R.M. (eds), *Learning from the Future: Competitive Foresight Scenarios*, John Wiley, 1998.

9 Schwarz, P. and Ogilvy, J.A., 'Plotting your scenarios', Chapter 4 of Fahey, L. and Randall, R.M., (eds), *Learning from the Future: Competitive Foresight Scenarios*, John Wiley, 1998.

10 Marsh, B., *op. cit.*

11 Fahey, L. and Randall, R.M., *op. cit.*

12 I am indebted to Northeast Consulting of Boston, Mass., for directing me to this set of scenarios, which it has made public on the Internet. The Northeast Consulting website is at hppt://www.ncri.com, with the public scenarios available at hppt://www.ncri.com/pubwork.html.

PART 3

Determining organisation position

CHAPTER

10 The bases of competition

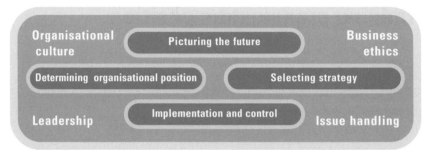

t his is the first of two chapters determining the position of a business *vis-à-vis* the competition. The concern in this chapter is with the dimensions on which a firm's competitive positioning should be judged.

The main focus for a competitive analysis is introduced. The links between the critical features of an offer, the significant operating factors of the operating environment and a firm's strategic resources are explored. The characteristics of critical offer features and of strategic resources are then considered in detail, particularly of the two strategic resources within which a business is operating at any moment of time, its structural assets and reputation.

The focus then shifts to considering both offer and process innovation, which are supported by two further strategic resources, the firm's (internal) architecture and its (external) relationships. A model of business, the value link, is introduced, and its place within the value chain is explained. This model is used to introduce a detailed discussion of the architecture and relationships.

Posing the question of how a business compares with its direct competitors leads on to two further major questions: 'What are the critical features in an offer that lead to sales?' and 'What are the attributes of the business that permits it to be able to provide these features?' These are vital questions that need answering, because leader-managers can't hope to operate effectively if they don't realise where competitive advantage lies and are thus unable to apply their limited business resources in the most appropriate way.

LEARNING
OUTCOMES

When you have worked through this chapter, you should be able to:

- explain the main focus for a competitive analysis;
- describe the linkages between critical offer features, significant operating factors and strategic resources;
- describe what critical offer features are and explain their two forms;
- describe the four types of strategic resources;
- list and explain the sources of structural assets;
- explain the types of offer for which reputation is important;
- draw and describe the elements of the value link;
- explain the importance of internal architecture to competitive positioning;
- explain the importance of external relationships to competitive positioning.

10.1 The main focus for competitive analysis

In Chapter 7, the main trends in the remote environment were discussed. In Chapter 8, the concern was whether a competitive arena is a good place for the *generality* of businesses to do business in. Coupling these two analyses produces scenarios (Chapter 9) giving broad views of the future operating environment. There was no concern with any specific business, simply with all the businesses in the competitive arena treated in aggregate. In this approach, the structure of the operating environment is the determinator of profitability.

EXHIBIT 10.1

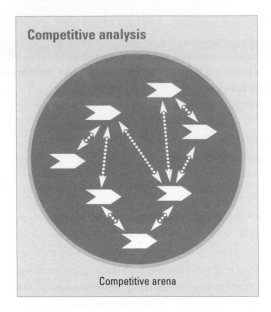

Competitive analysis

Competitive arena

We turn now to the second question associated with the standing of a business: 'How does the target business compare with direct competitors?' This calls for a more detailed analysis of the competitive arena than was carried out in Section 8.4.1, where rivalry was considered. Now questions are of the form 'How does Peugeot compare with Ford, Toyota and Renault?' and 'In what ways is McDonald's better than Burger King, better than Pizza Hut, better than ...?' This form of comparison is illustrated in Exhibit 10.1. This line of questioning is an expression of the *resource-based* view, which asserts that competitive advantage rests more on the firm's possession of resources – its basic assets, knowledge and capabilities – than in the structural features of its operating environment. Note that this is still an external analysis, since the main focus is the relative standing of all the businesses in the competitive arena, with actual and potential direct competitors.

DISCUSSION
POINT 10.1

In the statement above, *direct* competitors are mentioned. This suggests that there are indirect competitors. Who might these be?

In a competitive analysis the aim is to identify the relative strengths and weaknesses of all the competing businesses, both the present competitors and those that might be competitors in the future. The capabilities of competitors can be obtained by asking the opinions of important stakeholders and specific employees – for example, sales personnel who are engaged with competitors on a daily basis. Tapping these sources of information is very valuable, particularly in the short term. However, there are great advantages in allying such an informal approach to a more formal competitive analysis in order to seek out the fundamental sources of success. If the analysis doesn't focus on what is important to success, there is little potential for appropriately prioritising managerial effort.

10.2 Critical offer features, significant operating factors and strategic resources

10.2.1 Critical offer features

Customers don't buy a business, they buy an offer. They buy an offer because they see the features it possessses as providing more value for money than alternative offers. Those features that must be present for an offer to appear credible and win sales are termed the **critical offer features**.

10.2.2 Significant operating factors

It is important to consider critical offer features, since competing well today provides the wherewithal to establish a strong future position. However, it's also vital to look beyond the critical offer features to the fundamentals of the business's operations – the sources of the critical offer features required in the future. All competitive arenas will have associated with them some factors that are very significant for doing business there. These **significant operating factors** will be different in different competitive arenas. For example, during the 1960s and 1970s economies of scale were critical in steel and shipbuilding, and raw material sourcing was a critical feature for fertiliser manufacture; in the 1980s seating/fare management using computer reservation systems was vital for the airlines. In the 1990s distribution has been of overriding importance to brewers, and to film makers, especially in Europe.[1] Any business that wasn't strong in these critically important factors was competitively disadvantaged. The significant operating factors are the concern of all the businesses in the competitive arena. However, some businesses are better placed with regard to them than others.

10.2.3 Strategic resources

A business's ability to achieve a strong competitive position hinges on how well its **strategic resources** support the offer features that are critical to success within the chosen competitive arena. The strategic resources are the source of the critical offer features.

There are four types of strategic resource.[2] These are:

- Structural assets   the advantage a business enjoys because of the structure of the competitive arena. The advantage is not associated with current superior performance, it is about the legacy of largely fortuitous positioning. For example, a business may be able to hold on to an advantage it obtained if government placed restrictions on firms entering the competitive arena. Businesses located in one country may be beneficiaries of a benign governmental regime, while ones in other countries may be handicapped.

- Reputation   the way in which the market deals with offer features that customers cannot easily determine for themselves.

- Internal architecture   the linkages between resources within a business. These are not restricted to the relationships between people but include all the linkages within and between the organisation's processes and capabilities.

- External relationships   the relationships that the firm enjoys with its external stakeholders. These are most often relationships between people but can be wider than that – for example, e-commerce between suppliers and buyers.

EXHIBIT 10.2

The strategic resources of Marks & Spencer[3] (based on Collis and Montgomery, 1995)

The critical offer features for Marks & Spencer are reputation, high-quality merchandise, no-quibble take-backs and knowledgeable staff. These are achieved through the following strategic resources:

Type	Strategic resource	Marks & Spencer's position
Structural asset	Occupancy costs	Freehold locations, 1% occupancy costs versus a 3–9% industry average
Reputation	Reputation	Customer recognition with minimal advertising, no promotional sales
Internal architecture	Labour costs	Employee loyalty, lower labour turnover: 8.7% labour costs versus 10–20% industry average
	Quality of employees	Fewer layers of hierarchy than competition
External relationships	Input costs	Suppliers have lower costs and provide high quality of goods sold

The strategic resources of Marks & Spencer as they appeared in 1996 are presented in Exhibit 10.2. Note that reputation is both a critical offer feature and a strategic resource.[a]

10.2.4 The static links between critical offer features, significant operating factors and strategic resources

The link between critical offer features, significant operating factors and strategic resources is shown in Exhibit 10.3. In general, the significant operating factors won't be seen by the customers; for example, low distribution costs are not seen directly by customers, although they are likely to make an indirect contribution to the offer's value for money. Strategic resources such as many of the firm's external relationships will also generally not be seen by the customer, although again, the consequences of these relationships are likely to be ultimately appreciated by them. On the other hand, a characteristic may be a strategic resource, a significant operating factor and a critical offer feature: for example, the location of a restaurant or a university.

What significant resource other than reputation was also a critical offer feature for Marks & Spencer?

---

a At the end of 1999, things are quite different. What had been strategic resources, such as relationships with UK suppliers, turned out to be a millstone, as these suppliers couldn't compete on price with overseas manufacturers.

EXHIBIT 10.3

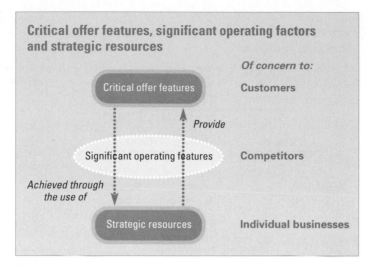

Critical offer features, significant operating factors and strategic resources

KEY CONCEPT   Critical offer features are associated with an offer and allow it to compete effectively. The critical offer features arise from the firm being strongly positioned with
respect to the significant operating factors. Underpinning this strong positioning are
the strategic resources that a business possesses. One important skill in strategic
management is to align the firm's strategic resources with the significant operating
factors, and thus be able to provide the necessary critical offer features.

10.2.5 The dynamic between the critical offer features, significant operating factors and strategic resources

Strategic resources are the fundamental bases of competition in the competitive arena.
No two businesses will be exactly alike in the strategic resources they command, since
these depend on the history of the business and the personalities within it. Exhibit
10.4 extends Exhibit 10.3 to illustrate the further connections between the critical
offer features, the significant operating factors and the strategic resources.

Specific critical offer features will obviously depend on the characteristics of the
particular customers being targeted. At the general level, however, critical offer features must provide value for money to customers and be based on an appropriate
combination of value and price.

The significant operating factors reflect the characteristics of the competitive
arena – perhaps low distribution costs are important, perhaps it's control of the
quality of inputs. But what is the same in all competitive arenas is that the significant operating factors will determine the balance between the offer features and
business costs.

The achievement of the appropriate balance between features and costs is based on
the strategic resources that the business has. Although structural assets can provide
some of the offer features, Exhibit 10.4 illustrates the broad point that there are only
two main ways of providing greater than average offer features: through reputation
and through innovation used to improve the offer. It also shows that there are only

EXHIBIT 10.4

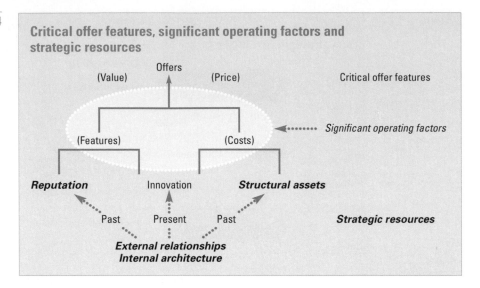

Critical offer features, significant operating factors and strategic resources

two main routes to achieving lower than average costs: by using structural assets and through innovation when this is used to improve efficiency.

There is a significant difference between the four types of strategic resources. The most fundamental features of the business, its internal architecture and external relationships, support reputation, the power to innovate and the structural assets. Past activities and events will have established the business's reputation and the structural assets and thus reputation and structural assets are the givens at any particular time. The present internal architecture and external relationships are available to provide the innovation needed for changes to the way the business operates.

KEY CONCEPT

At any point in time, a business *works within* its reputation and structural assets. So in the short term the business has to take the reputation and structural assets as fixed. At the same point in time, it *uses* its internal architecture and external relationships to provide and support its offers. Reputation and offer innovation are the two main routes to improving offer features. Structural assets and process innovation are the two main routes to reducing costs.

Exhibit 10.4 introduced the linkages between the critical offer features, significant operating factors and strategic resources. What it didn't show is any of the time dependency that exists between the three elements. This dynamic is shown in Exhibit 10.5.

In the short term the main concern isn't with the significant operating factors. These are taken as given and the concern is with providing appropriate critical offer features. In the longer term, however, the concerns are very different: here the firm has to consider the *future* significant operating factors and determine the strategic resources it needs to be successful in this future. An important point is that the firm shouldn't attempt to develop its strategic resources closely in line with future critical

EXHIBIT 10.5

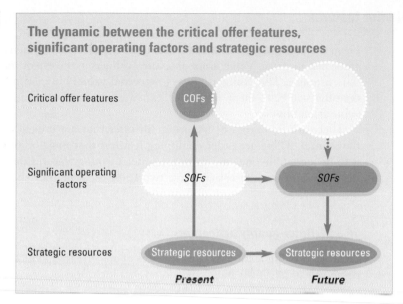

The dynamic between the critical offer features, significant operating factors and strategic resources

Critical offer features — COFs

Significant operating factors — SOFs → SOFs

Strategic resources — Strategic resources → Strategic resources

Present   Future

offer features, because it's unlikely that it can realistically have any detailed idea of what these might be.

In the late 1980s, the Japanese government decided that the industries that would be of most significance in the early decades of the 2000s would be electronics, aerospace and biotechnology. It didn't know precisely the form of the critical offer features, but it knew it had to have a significant presence in these areas. It was looking at the significant operating factors and not bothering with the critical offer features, as these would take care of themselves as the future unfolded. The same holds for companies. A car assembler may be fighting for current sales through sophisticated customer financing arrangements, but if it sees that the future significant operating factors will be low costs and sophisticated electronics, then it must work on its strategic resources to attain the necessary low costs and to acquire an appropriate capability in electronics.

DISCUSSION POINT 10.3

Reflect on Exhibit 10.5. Why are the circles indicating the critical offer features put in *faint* and drawn as getting larger?

- Why are the arrows pointing the way they are, particularly the arrows related to the future?

KEY CONCEPT

Offer features are what are seen by the customer. The firm uses its strategic resources to provide these features. The strategic resources will be able to provide the features if they match the characteristics of the operating environment.

While the leader-manager has to be mindful of developing the strategic resources required for the future, it's also very necessary for them to consider the (present) critical offer features. It is success in the marketplace today that provides the wherewithal to build future assets. The tension between present and future performance is ever present within organisations.

10.3   Critical offer features

From the point of view of a customer, there are two main dimensions to any offer: its value and its price. Value is not absolute– value is in the eye of the customer or potential customer. Thus value is always perceived value: how useful the customer thinks the offer will be to them. Because it's *always* perceived value, it will simply be termed **value** from now on.

There are two types of feature in an offer that are critical to its acceptability in the market. There are order-qualifying features that must be present in the offer for it to be a credible one, and there are order-winning features that then achieve a sale. It's important to differentiate these two features, since they should be managed very differently.

10.3.1   Order-qualifying features

Order-qualifying features are the features of an offer that must be present or there will be no sale at all. A car must have doors that lock, windscreen wipers and lights or no one will buy it. A theatre must have seats and offer a warm environment or it would soon have no patrons. The psychologist Hertzberg[4] dubbed these the hygiene factors: things that are only of concern if they are absent. The relationship between the 'amount' of an order-qualifying feature and the value/satisfaction it brings is shown in Exhibit 10.6. The important thing to notice is that when the 'amount' of a feature doesn't meet the threshold then there is strong dissatisfaction. Once the threshold is reached, however, the dissatisfaction disappears: it isn't replaced by satisfaction but simply by indifference. Order-qualifying features are switches that, when set, prevent a potential customer from 'switching off'.

A very important consideration with order-qualifying features is that it's against the interests of the business to supply more than the threshold amount. If the business provided the quantity Q in Exhibit 10.6, rather than the minimum required by the customer, it would cost the business more but with no corresponding extra value perceived by the customer. Providing an extra amount of an order-qualifying feature reduces a business's profits.

EXHIBIT 10.6

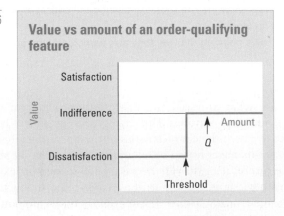

10.3.2 Order-winning features

In contrast to order-qualifying features – where to be over the threshold is all that is required – order-winning features are such that customer value increases the greater the amount of a positive feature there is or the lower the amount of a negative one. For example, the greater the fuel economy, the more that many customers will value a car; the lower the road noise the greater the satisfaction. Sample relationships between value and the amount of three order-winning features are shown in Exhibit 10.7.

EXHIBIT 10.7

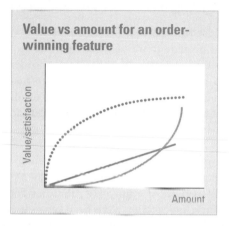

Value vs amount for an order-winning feature

Value/satisfaction

Amount

10.3.3 The migration of order-winning features to order-qualifying features

One problem that all businesses have is that over time what were order-winning features become order-qualifying ones. For example, when you go to a supermarket you are provided with free plastic bags at the checkout. At one time this was an order-winning feature, but now you would only remark on the bags if they weren't provided. In car manufacture the quality of cars has improved greatly over the last two decades, so much so that the Japanese advantage in quality is of much less significance now than previously; quality differences are no longer critical and other factors such as price have become more significant. This demonstrates the tendency as a market matures for quality to become an order-qualifying feature and for price to become an order-winning feature.

An important way in which an order-winning feature is converted into an order-qualifying feature is when new legislation is enacted or a new, widely acknowledged standard is established. If legislation forced all car manufacturers to put airbags in their cars, then simply having an airbag wouldn't confer any competitive advantage. If a new European standard for the composition of fertiliser were to be agreed, then it's likely that any advantage that fertiliser composition might have had would be lost.

KEY CONCEPT   There are two types of critical offer feature. Order-qualifying features must be present at a threshold level for a sale to be possible. Order-winning features arise where the likelihood of making the sale depends on the magnitude of the feature. Over time, order-winning features tend to become order-qualifying ones.

DISCUSSION
POINT 10.4

What is the minimum amount required of the order-qualifying feature in Exhibit 10.6?

- What might be the order-winning features for some commodity items like oil, gas and electricity?
- Can you think of features that have turned from order-winning to order-qualifying in cars? In air travel?
- What might be critical offer features for your business school? Which are order-qualifying and which order-winning?

10.3.4 Managing order-winning and order-qualifying features

Order-qualifying features are features that must be present for an offer to be credible in the marketplace. Yet to provide more of them than are required by the customer represents an unnecessary cost. Thus the management of order-qualifying features is aimed at providing them at the lowest cost and in this the business should seek efficiency. Ford has recognised that it has been providing 'needlessly unique' elements in its cars: for example, it has reduced the number of alternative car horns from 33 to three, steering wheels from 50 to three, batteries from 44 to 14 and cigarette lighters from 15 to one.[5]

The teaching quality audit performance measure currently being used in UK universities grades university departments on a 24-point scale. Departments that score highly will almost certainly be part of a university that has good IT, library and student support provision. Thus, unless they have been woefully inept, all departments of the 'older' (i.e. not the former polytechnic) universities, which have traditionally received better funding from government, will score 20+ points. Unless you believe that students will distinguish between departments on whether they have 22 or 23 points, teaching quality has certainly moved to order-qualifying status, with 20 points perhaps being the order-qualifying level. If this is so, then once a department thinks that the threshold has been comfortably achieved, it should put its efforts into something else.

Order-winning features are very different. The business requirement is to identify the form of the relationship between value and amount that applies to each element of the bundle of features that the organisation is thinking of putting into its offer, and to seek an appropriate combination of the features that balance overall value against the costs of providing it.

10.4 Strategic resources

DISCUSSION
POINT 10.5

Logically, there should be a discussion of the significant operating factors at this point. Why do you think one isn't given?

The concern of a business in the longer term lies with the development of the strategic resources that allow the firm to be successful in its future chosen competitive arena, where the most important characteristics of that arena are summed up by its significant operating factors.

The exploration of the operating environment in Chapter 8 identified the forces in the operating environment affecting *all* of the businesses in the competitive arena, which are reflected in the average profitability. We now seek to discover the ways in which a particular business can improve its competitive position over and above the average of the businesses with which it is competing, through the possession of appropriate strategic resources: its structural assets, reputation, internal architecture and external relationships.

10.4.1 Structural assets

Structural assets are assets that arise from the structure of the competitive arena. They arise from past events and activities and are associated with the position in which the firm finds itself: they are not a reflection of its current competitive success. The structural assets reflect the fact that firms rarely compete on a 'level playing field': at any point, some businesses have built-in advantages, and they will be able to use these better endowments either to lower costs or, less frequently, to provide extra features in their offers.

Six sources of structural assets are economies of scale and scope, proprietary standards, sunk costs, subsidy, regulation, and first-mover advantages.

Economies of scale and scope

Economies of scale and scope featured as barriers to entry into the competitive arena (Section 8.4.4). If scale economies are significant to potential entrants then they are also likely to be significant to the incumbents, both in the efficiency of their operations and in the power they wield over suppliers and customers.

There are some situations in which the greater the number of customers the better it is for all of them. Telecommunications is an obvious example. There is a great advantage in all systems using the same set of telephone numbers; if this didn't happen then once one telecommunications company (in Europe, almost always the previous state monopoly) had more customers than the other companies, no one would wish to use the other companies because of the small number of people with whom they could communicate. There is a powerful 'pull' in a large number of customers. Dating agencies are another example: an agency with only a few people on its books is at a great disadvantage compared with an agency with a large number of clients.

Proprietary standards

Every firm needs to match its activities with the business environment within which it's operating, and one form of matching is where a firm 'made the future' by establishing what the future would look like. Proprietary standards can do this, leading naturally to monopoly and to a form of economy of scale. This happened when Matsushita supported JVC's VHS format, which became the standard for video recorders.

It is interesting to reflect on the position of knowledge-based businesses. Such businesses tend to have what economists call *returns to scale*: the bigger the scale of operations the greater the proportionate returns. Microsoft effectively has a monopoly in PC operating systems. Unlike Apple, it allowed and indeed encouraged applications software developers to use its proprietary operating system software and in so doing vastly increased the demand for its own products. In the same way, Sun Microsystems may soon have a standard with its Java Internet software. Many firms produce compatible software and thus reinforce the position of the standard.

Sunk costs

Sunk costs are simply costs that have been incurred and can't be retrieved. Firms with the greatest sunk costs are likely to be better positioned than those that haven't made the past investments. Outlays will often have been incurred to reduce the costs of day-to-day operations; a good example of this is the operating costs of the Channel Tunnel shuttle compared with those of the ferry companies. The experience curve and the establishment of strong brands are also associated with sunk costs. For the same current outlays, the firm without the investment that the sunk costs imply will be disadvantaged.

Subsidy

Government subsidies are widespread. General Electric and Pratt & Witney reportedly get a subsidy of 80% of their R&D spending from US government agencies – worth around $700 million a year. In 1999, rival car companies complained to the EU that the British government was illegally subsidising Rover when it offered BMW around £150 million to help keep open the Rover plant in Longbridge.

Regulation

There are many competitive arenas that are subject to governmental or EU regulation. Almost universally, the governments in the EU states have had a monopoly in telecommunications and large parts of the energy industry. In some countries state monopolies have been set up for tax-gathering reasons (the tobacco manufacturing industries of France and Italy are examples). The alcohol industry is regulated in many countries: in some Scandinavian countries the state has a monopoly on its manufacture and distribution. With privatisation and the directives from the EU, the state monopolies are slowly being eroded, but often this comes with increased regulation: witness the many OFs (Office of Gas Supply, Office of Electricity Regulation, etc.) in the UK.

The advantages from regulation often go to the long-established firms. In 1998, when the EU gave its verdict on the then-proposed merger between British Airways and American Airlines, the authorities were happy with the merger as long as the two airlines released some of their landing rights at London's Heathrow Airport, which were very valuable structural assets and something neither airline wished to lose. The lack of slots has been a bone of contention with the newer airlines such as Virgin Atlantic, which have little access to Heathrow and have to use the less acceptable alternative London airport at Gatwick.

The position of the recently privatised utilities throughout Europe shows how the structure of the competitive arena is still influenced by the monopoly positions inherited on privatisation.

First-mover advantages

Some firms have an advantage because they were the first to do something and often regulation prevents imitation. UK supermarkets that now own out-of-town sites are better positioned than those that don't, since there has been a ban on any more sites being made available. In 1999, when Wal-Mart, the US food retailer, had ambitions to enter the UK food retail market, it had to buy a UK supermarket chain, as it wouldn't be allowed to start operating from greenfield sites. It achieved this when it acquired Asda.

Some first-mover advantages spring from natural monopoly, where it makes sense to have only one operator. The utilities tend to fall into this category.

Many offers, especially those with a high intellectual content, need effort to learn how to use them. Thus once learned there is a natural tendency to stick with what you know unless the new offer is considerably better. Thus there is 'stickiness' in the market and an established player can use this to extend its offers (as Microsoft has done with its various Windows variants and with its Internet Explorer).

<table>
<tr><td>KEY CONCEPT</td><td>Structural assets are those assets that arise from the structure of the competitive arena and are enjoyed differentially by the businesses in it; firms rarely compete on a 'level playing field'. There are six main sources of structural assets: economies of scale and scope, proprietary standards, sunk costs, subsidy, regulation, and first-mover advantages.</td></tr>
</table>

<table>
<tr><td>DISCUSSION POINT 10.6</td><td>What is the difference between sunk costs and economies of scale?</td></tr>
</table>

10.4.2 Reputation

Reputation is the way in which the market deals with attributes of offer quality that customers cannot easily determine for themselves.[6] A good reputation is something that all businesses would like to have, but in some cases a good reputation is much more valuable than in others. Consider buying fresh vegetables. It's useful for the greengrocer to build up a reputation for quality as it keeps their shop on the list of retailers that potential consumers will buy from. But this reputation for quality has to be closely and consistently linked to value, because the customer can easily see if quality starts to decline: most purchasers have the necessary knowledge to know whether a cabbage is limp or not. On the other hand, reputation is particularly important to banks, which operate on the basis of only being able to pay out a fraction of the total deposits at any one time. If a bank's reputation suddenly becomes suspect, depositors seek to withdraw their money, and if enough do so the bank will have to cease trading.

Items like fresh vegetables are termed **search offers** as the customer can determine value for money by simply searching through the items on offer. A second class of purchases are **immediate experience offers**. Unlike search offers their value cannot be determined by the customer by inspection. Whereas the value of fresh vegetables can be readily seen, that of canned vegetables cannot. Although the reputation of the brand name on the can usually plays a part in getting the first purchase, the value of reputation isn't very significant as the value can be recognised immediately after purchase, and if the value for money is low then there will be no repeat purchases.

A third class of offers are **long-term experience offers**, whose value can be determined only after extensive personal experience. For example, it's difficult to know whether a doctor is good or not until you have had several years experience with them. Since it's estimated that roughly 70% of ailments that people go to the doctor about clear up spontaneously, this is quite difficult. Only in the long term do you know whether a medicine to lower cholesterol levels is working or whether medication to ward off stomach pains won't cause long-term damage.

The fourth class of offers are the **no-experience offers**, where no personal experience can be obtained at all, because the purchases tend to be one-off with no repetition. For many years a successful sales slogan for a double-glazing company was 'Fit the best. Fit Everest. You only fit double glazing once.' Perhaps this is not strictly true, since people more readily change homes nowadays, but it is probably still close to the mark.

Definitions and examples of these four types of offer are given in Exhibit 10.8.

Kay[7] cites car-hire firms in foreign cities as a good example of long-term experience offers that are supported by reputation. The well-known firms such as Hertz and Avis are able to charge a premium price for car hire not necessarily because their service is any better than the local firms but because a stranger in a foreign city can't readily know the quality of the service they might get from them. What the names Hertz and Avis do is to reassure the hirer that the service they will get will be of a high minimum standard.

Thus we see that some types of offer need to be supported more strongly by reputation than others. For those that aren't, the business would be wasting resources trying to establish a reputation.

Reputation is not only of significance with regard to customers. When ICI was in the limelight as Europe's biggest manufacturer of ozone-damaging CFCs, its reputation as a reputable company helped it to obtain support from governments for the position it was taking and allowed it to continue with the manufacture of these gases while it searched for a solution through the development of ozone-friendly substitutes.

EXHIBIT 10.8

Types of offer and the importance of reputation

Type of offer	Use of knowledge	Examples
Search	Where knowledge of the *specific* offer about to be bought can be obtained from inspection of the offer itself before or during purchase	Clothes Fresh vegetables
Immediate experience	Where knowledge of the offer quality becomes evident immediately after consumption, but not before purchase	Beer Canned vegetables Painkillers
Long-term experience	Where it takes a long time to ascertain the value of the offer from individual experience	Some medicines Professional advice Car hire in a foreign city
No experience	Where it is impossible to ascertain the value of the offer from individual experience	Double glazing

KEY CONCEPT   Reputation is a way of signalling an offer's value. It is especially powerful when supporting long-term and no-experience offers. Reputation can be associated with the name of an individual, a brand, a business or a corporation.

DISCUSSION
POINT 10.7
Should clothes be considered a search offer?

- Where would you place the following in the classification given in Exhibit 10.8: a university degree course, a cafe, security services, a deodorant, car hire in your local city, funeral services?
- Which types of offer might be those where it would be a waste of time creating a good reputation?
- Can you think of a reputation that is associated with an individual? With a brand? With a business? With a corporation?

10.5 Innovation

10.5.1   Invention, innovation and change

Invention is the act of creating or producing through use of the imagination,[8] while innovation is the commercial exploitation of an invention. Thus an innovation does not necessarily mean that a firm has to be the inventor. Whereas stock markets may respond to inventions – this seems to have occured in biotechnology to some extent – customer markets don't: they respond to developments and innovations.

An innovation may be a new product (such as the Dyson vacuum cleaner) or a new way of producing the product (Pilkington's float glass process for producing plate glass). It may be a new service (distance learning in higher education) or a new way of organising the delivery of a service (using the Internet). It may be a change in the way the organisation is structured or a change in the way employees are recruited.

While all innovation is change, not all change is innovation. Although not a clear-cut distinction, the difference between innovation and change is that innovation must have some element of being the first, of being unique. Thus the first introduction of a computerised order entry system would be innovative; subsequent installations would necessitate change but wouldn't be innovative. The first to introduce something new into one competitive arena that already exists in another would be considered innovative for two reasons – it is intended to gain an advantage over competitors and it is adapting the innovation to new circumstances. However, success doesn't always go to the fleet of foot: it's often better to be a fast second rather then an innovator. Remember, pioneers tend to get arrows in their backs.

Two forms of innovation are recognised: offer innovation where an offer is extended or enlarged, and process innovation, associated not with the offer itself but with the way in which the business processes are undertaken. Gillette has successfully done both, as Exhibit 10.9 shows.

10.5.2   Offer innovation

It has been estimated that out of 3000 ideas for products, 300 will be worth experimenting with, 125 become projects, 17 become actual products and just one will be profitable.[9] Failure in drug development is common: out of every 10,000 compounds that are considered, only one makes it to the prescribing list. Most are quickly discarded, but some fail at the final hurdle. This happened in 1993 to Boots with the heart drug Manoplax when it was found that, although it was effective in some patients, it worsened the life expectancy of others. Boots wrote off £100 million, and

EXHIBIT 10.9

Innovation – Gillette and its Mach3 razor[10]

In the world of fast-moving consumer goods, innovation has long been recognised as one way of staying ahead of competitors. Another is marketing. Gillette, the US company that dominates the global shaving products market, attempts to combine both.

In April 1998 it announced Mach3, its latest wet-shave razor, which it expects will capture more than a quarter of the market with claims of a closer shave with less skin irritation. The Boston-based company has invested more than $1 billion (£600 million) in the new product, including a $300 million advertising budget for the first year alone. Devised by advertising agency BBDO, it offers a package of television, radio, print and poster advertisements that all play on the supersonic theme in the Mach3 name. Loud, brash and unmissable, it hammers home the message that the new product breaks through the performance barrier with three sonic booms in the soundtrack.

Gillette has launched a razor about every nine years since it introduced the first twin-blade razor, Trac II, in 1971. In 1977 the Atra added a pivoting head and in 1990 the Sensor's spring-mounted blades promised an even closer shave. The Sensor later added rubber microfins to stretch the skin taut. Sensor produced sales of $6 billion worldwide, selling almost 400 million razors and more than eight billion blades. It has helped Gillette establish dominance over the wet-shave market in North America and Western Europe, with 70% of sales.

Mach3 adds a third blade to the cartridge, and 35 other features and elements. These include a diamond-like carbon coating on the blades, which make them thinner, and a lubricating strip, which deposits vitamin E on the skin and changes colour when empty to remind the shaver to replace the cartridge. 'Each of these is protected by patents, making it next to impossible for competitors to copy,' says Bob King, head of the company's North Atlantic group, which covers the USA and Western Europe.

Gillette has installed a production line to reduce unit costs on its more complex new product. Using advanced robotics, it makes the cartridges in a continuous process similar to that used in bottling soft drinks. With no stopping and starting, ten cartridges are made every second, each checked by computer. Output will be 600 million a year from the Boston plant, which will double to 1.2 billion when production begins at Gillette's Berlin factory. This will allow Mach3 to be launched in more than 100 markets by the end of next year – a roll-out that took more than four years with Sensor.

The company expects Mach3 to attract millions of new users from competitors. But three-quarters of those who buy this latest product will already be Gillette customers – including people using the company's disposable razors. Pre-launch market research, says the company, shows consumers are willing to pay the $6.50–$7 price (about £4) for a razor and two cartridges. Unlike most other makers of consumer products, Gillette does not withdraw older products when it introduces the latest generation. 'We're still selling brands that are 25 and 18 years old,' says Mr Darman. 'Mach3 will soon be number one in every market, with a 20-30 per cent share. But Sensor will be the second biggest brand by a large margin.'

This approach recognises that many consumers are unwilling to trade up every time Gillette improves the technology. An increasing number of men are described by the company as 'high-interest users', spending an average of £75 a year on shaving tackle, gels and aftershave lotions. But the typical 'low-interest user', with a pack of disposables and a can of own-label shaving foam, has to be persuaded to raise his annual spending of £16.71.

Work is already underway on the next-generation razor. The company aims to maintain its dominance by continuing an innovation strategy that has largely excluded the own-label producers and cut-price copycats that have been so successful in most similar product markets.

Discussion point 10.8

In what way is marketing different from innovation, as the first paragraph suggests? List the ways in which Gillette has made offer and process innovations.

this setback caused it to dispose of its pharmaceutical interests. It is estimated that only 40% of drugs are sufficiently successful to cover their R&D costs.

Innovation can be expensive. The average cost for research and development of a single drug is of the order of £100–150 million. A new car production line costs in the order of £500 million to establish. A new microchip plant will cost in the order of £1 billion.

Offer changes can be initiated to reduce the costs of the offer. This may simply be a degradation in offer features that the producer thinks won't be noticed by the customer. This approach can be dangerous. In the 1980s, some chocolate manufacturers decided to hold the price of their chocolate bars steady and to maintain margins in the face of increasing input costs by reducing the size of the bars. This shaving of the bars went unnoticed for a time and then customers realised what was happening. This gave an opportunity for Nestlé to introduce a new, larger bar – Yorkie – which has been an enduring success.

So innovation can be risky, and it can be expensive. It can also be hard for the business to appropriate the gains. Philips has been the technological leader in audio cassettes, video recorders, compact discs and DAT, but has failed to keep the rewards that 'should' have gone to it. The Swiss watch industry developed the first digital watch yet failed to exploit it, with devastating consequences. The problem is that it's relatively easy to copy offer innovations: new offers are public and thus competitors can scrutinise them. This is especially true of products, since competitors are adept at what is termed *reverse engineering*, that is, they get hold of the product and analyse it in detail to see how it was made and then manufacture it themselves. The time it takes for a competitor to bring copied products to market are shown for Japanese manufacturers in Exhibit 10.10.

With these very short lead times, one way for a business to succeed through product innovation is to be committed to bringing out new variants *continuously*. Casio changes its products about every six months. In 1996, the company 3M obtained nearly 30% of its revenues from products introduced within the past four years.[12] *Cycle time* – the time to convert a customer need into a product that satisfies that need or the time it takes to convert an idea into a product that is ready for market – is an important competitive weapon.

EXHIBIT 10.10

Development of 'me too' products[11]

Products			Delay in the followers' marketing (months)
Photographic film	Fuji	14	
Concentrated detergent	Kao	11	
Dry beer	Asahi	11	
Headphone stereo set	Sony	7	
Electronic notebook	Casio	7	
Compact convertible	Honda	6	
Personal fax machine	Matsushita	4	

10.5.3 Process innovation

The process by which a product is made or a service is delivered is much less public than are offers, often being hidden within the organisation. Thus process innovation coupled with a suitable internal architecture can be a potent weapon. The 3M factory where Post-it notes are made is prohibited to all but a few key personnel, as one of the advantages to 3M is the process technology that it uses to make the notes.

Process innovations to reduce costs may affect any part of the business. These process innovations often go under the title of *business process re-engineering*. The widespread introduction of computers has caused extensive re-engineering in the financial services industry. The move from mechanical to electronic watches was a move that reduced the number of parts in inbound logistics and assembly. Use of data-entry terminals by salespeople has revolutionised the process of order entry and reduced its costs.

Process innovation can come from carrying out the process many times, characterised by the learning curve. The classic case is aircraft manufacture, and that for one aircraft is shown in Exhibit 10.11a:[13] the cost per aircraft drops with each aircraft built, with a drop of around 30% for each doubling of output.[b] Note that the costs in Exhibit 10.11 are on a logarithmic scale.

Kay[14] makes an interesting juxtaposition of the B-29 graph with that for broiler chickens. This graph is shown as Exhibit 10.11b. As he points out:

> The only similarity between chickens and aircraft is that both have wings. The industry-wide adoption of battery rearing, supported by the use of antibiotics, turned chicken from a luxury product into a commodity staple. The market for chicken grew rapidly. While the causality in one case runs from output to costs, in the other it runs from costs to output. That difference is critical to the strategic implications. The world aircraft market is, and is likely to remain, dominated by Boeing. The market for broiler chickens is, and is likely to remain, both local and fragmented. Anyone induced by the experience curve to aspire to be the Boeing of the broilers would be sadly misled. We need to look behind the experience curve at what drives costs in particular industries.

DISCUSSION POINT 10.9

What is the direction of the cause-and-effect relationship between cost and output for broiler chickens?

KEY CONCEPT

A firm is innovative when it does something that is new in its competitive arena. An offer innovation is where a new product or service is introduced or where an offer is augmented. Product innovations are easily copied if they are not protected. Process innovation is concerned with augmenting the way in which the organisation operates. In general, the gains from process innovation are more easily appropriated by the organisation implementing them than are product innovations.

---

b   Note also that such a curve incorporates the learning associated with the particular aeroplane and with learning in the aircraft industry generally.

EXHIBIT 10.11

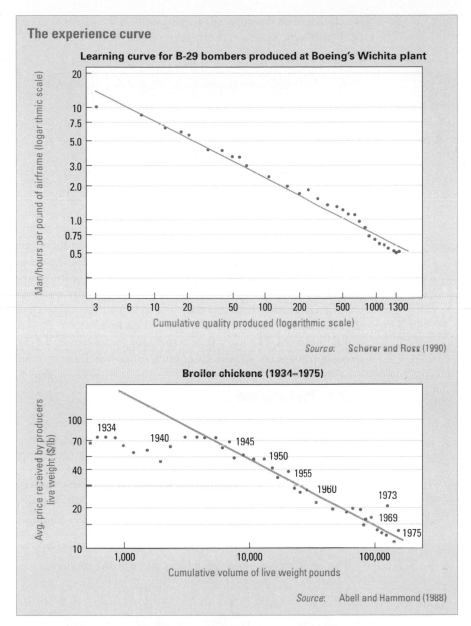

The experience curve

Learning curve for B-29 bombers produced at Boeing's Wichita plant

Man/hours per pound of airframe (logarithmic scale)

Cumulative quality produced (logarithmic scale)

Source: Scherer and Ross (1990)

Broiler chickens (1934–1975)

Avg. price received by producers live weight ($/lb)

Cumulative volume of live weight pounds

Source: Abell and Hammond (1988)

10.5.4 The forces for innovation

Porter[15] suggests that any firm seeking to compete through innovation should seek to operate where the pressures for innovation are the most intense. He suggests that the firm should:

- sell to the most sophisticated and demanding buyers;
- seek out buyers with the most difficult needs;
- establish norms of exceeding the toughest regulatory standards;

- source from the most advanced suppliers;
- benchmark against outstanding competitors;
- treat employees as permanent.

DISCUSSION
POINT 10.10

Why should treating employees as permanent help innovation?

10.6 A model of a business – the value link

10.6.1 The place of the value link

Innovation relies on internal architecture and external relationships. Before considering these two strategic resources, it is valuable to consider a model of a business that emphasises the architecture and the relationships, and look at the way a business combines its processes. This model is the value link. Its importance is that it allows us to look at a business in a way that readily links to business processes. This allows the strengths and weaknesses of a business *vis-à-vis* its competitors to be identified and allows the resources required for strategic change to be recognised.

The connection between the value link and the value chain is shown in Exhibit 10.12. The ⊃ symbol represents the value link, which is a representation of an individual business. The individual businesses are shown in the circles that represent the competitive arena, and the set of circles together illustrate a value chain.

10.6.2 The value link

Porter[16] introduced a version of what is here termed the value link to describe manufacturing firms in the late 1970s. Twenty years later, business is conducted rather differently, with less emphasis on manufacturing, a greater emphasis on marketing in general, and relationship marketing in particular, and, very importantly for strategic management, more concern for nurturing relationships with stakeholders.

The importance of stakeholder relationships is reflected in the model of the business (the value link) that is shown in Exhibit 10.13. The link is composed of three

EXHIBIT 10.12

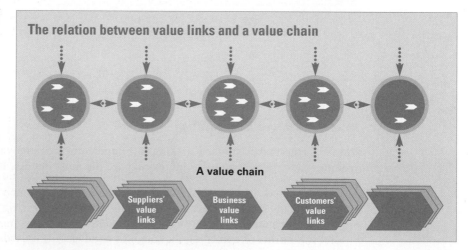

The relation between value links and a value chain

A value chain

Suppliers' value links

Business value links

Customers' value links

EXHIBIT 10.13

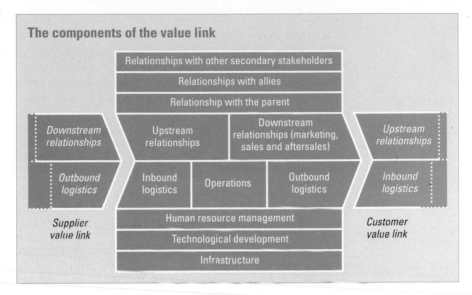

The components of the value link

Relationships with other secondary stakeholders

Relationships with allies

Relationship with the parent

| *Downstream relationships* | Upstream relationships | Downstream relationships (marketing, sales and aftersales) | | *Upstream relationships* |
| *Outbound logistics* | Inbound logistics | Operations | Outbound logistics | *Inbound logistics* |

Human resource management

Technological development

Infrastructure

Supplier value link

Customer value link

types of relationship; the internal architecture encompassing relationships within the business itself; the relationships with external stakeholders within the value chain; and relationships with those stakeholders outside the value chain (parent, allies and secondary stakeholders).

DISCUSSION POINT 10.11

Identify the three sets of relationships in Exhibit 10.13.

- The value link strongly reflects the view that relationships are very significant to a business. Reputation has been treated separately, outside of the value link. Is this appropriate?

10.6.3 Primary activities

There are three primary activities in the value link that are concerned with a firm's on-going business. These are inbound logistics, operations and outbound logistics. These three activities are different from the others in the value link because all the others could cease and the business could keep operating (albeit only in the short term).

- Inbound logistics is concerned with receiving and storing the inputs needed for operations. The subactivities within this process for a manufacturer are such things as quality control, materials reception and handling, stock control, and the movement of the received goods forward to operations. For financial services, it would involve such things as access to finance and to information.

- Operations is concerned with the conversion of the inputs into the core offers that the business makes to customers. The subactivities within operations for manufacturers are such things as machining, packaging, assembly, quality control and the movement of finished products to storage. In retailing, they would be such things as shelf filling and checkout operations. For financial services, operations would include such things as the processing of insurance claims.

● Outbound logistics are concerned with distributing the offer to the customer next in line in the value chain. Outbound logistics would also involve non-core offer features, for example the installation of a fitted kitchen. For services, the concern with outbound logistics can often include bringing the customer to the service point. This would be the case for organisers of concerts and sporting events. For supermarket services, they would be such things as providing trolleys, and dedicated buses to get the shoppers to and from home. For financial services, this would include dispatching documentation and sales information.

10.6.4 Support activities

In any business there are not only the primary activities described above but there are also three further activities to support them. These support activities are:

● Technological development   A technology is information about scientific, business or industrial methods, or information about the use and/or application of these methods. Porter[17] stresses that every process uses some technology: for example information technology in the office, management science in scheduling the movement of goods, using forklift trucks in warehouse operations and lorries for distribution. There is also the technology in the offers themselves. Technologies often combine a number of more fundamental technologies involving different scientific principles, for example machining involves mechanics, metallurgy and the electronics associated with computer-controlled equipment. Technology is generally an organisational attribute, one residing in the organisation rather than with an individual.

   While technological development would naturally be associated with the well-defined activities labelled 'research and development', any development in the offers or business processes would be considered a technological development; for example, a consultancy may develop a system for making better use of office space, through the use of IT and hot desking; a manufacturer may find a way of rearranging workflows to reduce the time taken in operations. The installation of a new management information system or a new assembly line would be further examples.

DISCUSSION
POINT 10.12 How are technological development and innovation related?

● Human resource management   Human resource management isn't concerned just with the individual but also with organisational development. Human resource management includes recruitment, developing salary and wage structures, and training. Marks & Spencer, IBM and many Japanese firms offer lifetime employment, placing importance on seniority, giving on-the-job training specific to the firm and enterprise-focused unionism. All are aspects of human resource management.

● Infrastructure   is concerned with those features that are business-wide. The infrastructure includes the overall direction of the business and overall financial control. Among other things it is involved with the formal way in which the business is organised – with the structure of the functions and subfunctions and the organisation of the processes within them. Organisational structure is the sum total of ways in which the organisation divides its labour into distinct tasks and then achieves co-ordination between them.[18]

10.7 Architecture and its components

10.7.1 The scope of architecture

Architecture includes much more than the organisational structure of an organisation: it encompasses all the relationships within a business, between all forms of resources and within and between processes. Architecture is a fundamental factor in a business, representing a strategic resource just as much as the more basic resources, as Exhibit 10.14 illustrates.

10.7.2 Types of architecture

How the relationships between processes are managed is of vital importance, and thus one of the main decisions that organisations have to make is how they structure and organise themselves. One well-known classification of organisations is that of Mintzberg,[19] who developed a classification based on how the tension between the division of labour and the necessary associated co-ordination is handled. He has developed a standard organisational template, which is reproduced as Exhibit 10.15 He sees the people in the organisation as being of five types:

EXHIBIT 10.14

Examples of the non-structural aspects of internal architecture

Rover–BMW

In 1998, under intense pressure from its parent company, BMW, the unions at Rover Group agreed to change their working practices to those operating in the BMW plants. Rover was working the traditional fixed hours with overtime worked when demand was high. On the other hand, BMW worked flexible hours whereby employees contract to work a set number of hours per year, but work shorter hours when demand is low and longer hours when demand is high. No overtime is worked. It was estimated that this flexible method of working at Rover would result in a 15% increase in productivity (output per person hour).

The *Mittelstand*

The *Mittelstand* is the term used to describe the three million, mainly manufacturing, small to medium-sized businesses in Germany. These companies account for half of the country's industrial turnover. According to Professor Brun-Hagen Hennerkes of the University of Stuttgart, the most important reason for the success of the *Mittelstand* has been their family-owned managerial structure, which leads to strong relationships between workers and owners and a flat hierarchical structure. This encourages greater worker motivation and leads to a high degree of flexibility and innovation with lower unionisation and less bureaucracy.[20, 21]

EXHIBIT 10.15

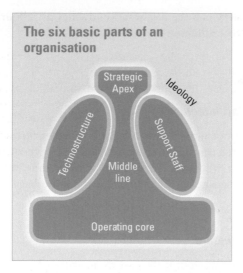

The six basic parts of an organisation

- The operational core   the people in an organisation who carry out the basic, day-to-day processes that are needed to enable the business to make the offers that it does. They are the people who work on the factory floor, as bank tellers and as shop assistants.

- The strategic apex   the senior leader-managers who have a higher responsibility than functional or project management and oversee the whole of the business operations. They will tend to constitute the board of directors of a firm.

- The middle line   consisting of the leader-managers other than those in the strategic apex who supervise the operating core and other managers.

- The support staff   who provide various internal services such as secretarial support and catering facilities.

- The technostructure   consisting of analysts and other professional people who are not in the line of management but who are involved in what are often termed 'staff' jobs, such as IT specialists, accountants and personnel officers. They differ from support staff because they are concerned with supporting change, which isn't usually a significant role for support staff.

These five types of employee would come together in different mixtures and strengths to create different organisational forms, differing as to how the parts of the organisation are co-ordinated and reflecting the relative power of the five types of employee. Although Mintzberg identified seven different forms, only four of these are of particular significance here. These are:

- The entrepreneurial organisation   characterised by usually one, but occasionally a few, dominant individuals and an operating core that is supervised directly from the top. This is typical of the small firm. Communications and control are informal and the systems are simple. This form of organisation can be very effective in simple environments, where the vision and drive of the entrepreneur are of paramount importance. As the environment becomes more complex, however, it is unlikely that the dominant individual(s) will have sufficient knowledge to operate effectively.

- **The machine organisation** characterised by a large technostructure and a large middle-management core needed to control the organisation through standardisation of processes. Typical examples would be where mass production is involved, for example large-scale factory-based work such as car assemblers, or delivery services. It can be the appropriate structure when the environment is not changing rapidly and where its complexity requires sophisticated analysis. It is appropriate where efficiency and cost leadership are important.

- **The professional organisation** characterised by very few middle managers and a large core of professionals. Co-ordination comes from standardisation of the knowledge and skills of the workers – usually first developed outside of the organisation and then through institutionalised training. In this sense it is bureaucratic, but without the centralisation found in the machine organisation and imposed by the central management line. The interesting point about this form of organisation is that a lot of control is retained by the professionals and by the institutions of which they are members. Typical examples are law practices and universities. This sort of organisation is appropriate when environments are stable and complex. The type of co-ordination is inimical to innovation.

- **The adhocracy** which Mintzberg also terms the innovative organisation. This form of organisation relies on mutual adjustment among its highly trained and highly specialised experts, through task forces, project teams and matrix structures. Typical examples of innovative organisations would be film makers and consultancies. Power is distributed unevenly in the organisation according to expertise and need. It's an appropriate organisation where the environment is both dynamic and complex, and where the issues to be tackled are novel.

To Mintzberg's categorisation can be added the type that has been called the J-firm or the **J-form organisation** by Aoki[22] and by Lam.[23] This form is prevalent in Japan and differs markedly in the way in which knowledge is created and embedded in the organisation, rather than residing with individuals. Much of the co-ordination comes from horizontal co-ordination facilitated through the extensive use of semi-autonomous project groups whose members are drawn from many functions. It would appear to be an organisational form well equipped to respond well in either stable or dynamic conditions, but it may have difficulty responding in turbulent times.

The dominant form of knowledge in the J-form organisation is that embedded in its operating routines and shared culture. Firms that have the J-form of organisation have been termed *knowledge-creating companies* by Nonaka and Takeuchi.[24] A primary feature of J-form organisations is that non-hierarchical project teams, consisting of people from various functions, operate in parallel with the formal hierarchical structure. This allows the members of the project teams who will be engaged in the new activities to feed back and embed their new knowledge into the 'normal' organisational structure, and thus combine the new with the old. The stability and efficiency of the organisation are married to the flexibility of the project teams.

Nonaka and Takeuchi use the term *hypertext organisation*, borrowed from computer science, to describe the easy and dynamic way in which people can interact with the different layers in their organisation.

It's not just Japanese or East Asian firms that actively follow a knowledge-creating way. Simon[25] reports this also for the German *Mittelstand*, the set of medium-sized companies that don't achieve much publicity but contribute so much to the German economy.

Within the broad typology of Mintzberg, Aoki and Lam there are smaller-scale but nevertheless important considerations regarding how the elements interact with each other. For example, a requirement of enterprise computing is to treat an organisation's IT systems as indivisible, and to provide end-to-end solutions to problems such as maintainability and interoperability. Should IT personnel be located and controlled centrally, or should they be located within the departments and sections that need their support?

EXHIBIT 10.16

Five business organisational forms (based on Mintzberg, 1991; Aoki, 1988; and Lam, 1998)

Internal features				Suitable environmental conditions	
Organisational form	Dominant type of knowledge	Main co-ordinating mechanism	Key part of the organisation	Simple/ complex	Stable/ dynamic/ turbulent
Entrepreneurial	Embrained/ embodied in the strategic apex	Direct from the strategic apex	Strategic apex	Simple	Dynamic
Machine organisation	Encoded	Standardisation of work processes	Technostructure	Complex	Stable
Professional organisation	Embrained	Standardisation of knowledge and skills	Operating core	Complex	Stable
Adhocracy	Embodied	Little formal standardisation. Direct interaction and mutual adjustment	Operating core	Complex	Dynamic
J-form	Embedded	Horizontal co-ordination and mutual adjustment	Semi-autonomous project groups	Complex	Non-turbulent

KEY CONCEPT

Five organisational forms have been described that support the tension that exists between the division of labour and the need to co-ordinate activities. One organisational form may be relevant to the whole organisation, but it could be that differing forms are applicable to different functions and processes.

DISCUSSION
POINT 10.13

How do the five types of people that Mintzberg identified in organisations fit into the 11 elements of the value link?

- Within a manufacturing organisation, which organisational form might be most appropriate for operations and which for offer development?

10.8 External relationships

10.8.1 Clusters

Porter[26] looked into the question of why some nations – or rather the firms within some nations – are better placed competitively than others. One of his most significant findings was that successful firms belong to clusters. Examples of very localised clusters are the financial expertise in the City of London and diamond dealers located in Antwerp. The clusters in southern Germany and in northern Italy, as shown in Exhibit 10.17, are examples of slightly more widely dispersed clusters.

Porter identified two main reasons for and advantages of clustering:

- Clusters facilitate information flows   There are personal relationships due to schooling and military service; there are ties through the scientific community or professional associations; there are community ties due to close geographical proximity; there are trade associations encompassing many of the firms in the clusters.

- Clusters are sources of goal congruence   There are family or quasi-family ties between firms; there is common ownership within an industrial group; ownerships of partial equity stakes are common; there are interlocking directorships; and the norms of behaviour help cohesion through such things as a belief in the value of long-term relationships.

Clusters generate a great deal of synergy. The rivalry between firms has a greater intensity than would be the case if they were more physically dispersed. Suppliers can help with a firm's research and development and can provide the skills and information that more isolated businesses have difficulty in gaining access to. For example, there are many contributors to the production of facsimile machines: copier technology, photographic equipment, telecommunications equipment and office machines. If the expertise in these areas is close at hand, this can greatly help product development.

DISCUSSION
POINT 10.14

Can you give two further examples of clusters?

- Do you think that geographical clustering is important in the age of the Internet and teleconferencing?

EXHIBIT 10.17A

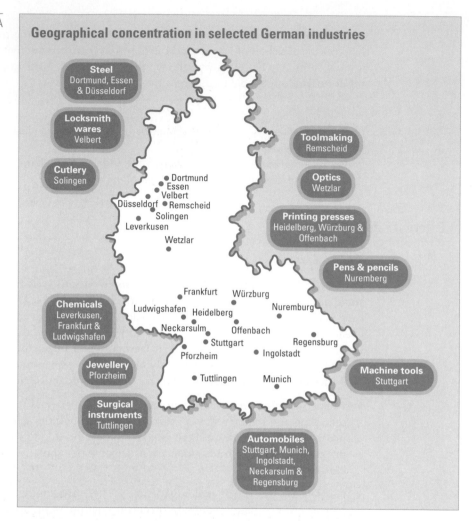

Geographical concentration in selected German industries

- **Steel** — Dortmund, Essen & Düsseldorf
- **Locksmith wares** — Velbert
- **Cutlery** — Solingen
- **Toolmaking** — Remscheid
- **Optics** — Wetzlar
- **Printing presses** — Heidelberg, Würzburg & Offenbach
- **Pens & pencils** — Nuremberg
- **Chemicals** — Leverkusen, Frankfurt & Ludwigshafen
- **Jewellery** — Pforzheim
- **Machine tools** — Stuttgart
- **Surgical instruments** — Tuttlingen
- **Automobiles** — Stuttgart, Munich, Ingolstadt, Neckarsulm & Regensburg

10.8.2 Relationships within the value chain

The analysis of the operating environment in Chapter 8 involved markets and contractual arrangements between suppliers and buyers. In contractual transactions, the detailed conditions under which a purchase is made are determined beforehand. This is actually the case when you go into a shop to buy an item: there are conditions laid down covering the legal rights of both buyer and seller, and if there is a disagreement between them then the final remedy is to go to law. Contracts provide little in the way of flexibility in the interaction between the parties involved. Over the last decade there has been a recognisable shift from contract-based transactions to relational ones. In relationships, any agreement is a much looser arrangement than with a contract; it's like a marriage where general agreements are understood rather than laid down, and the partners are expected to resolve difficulties without going to law or other outside agencies. Relationships can involve very close liaison with suppliers – for example, joint design – or be limited to activities involving one area of business (for example an agreement on joint distribution) or simply informal help when required.

EXHIBIT 10.17B

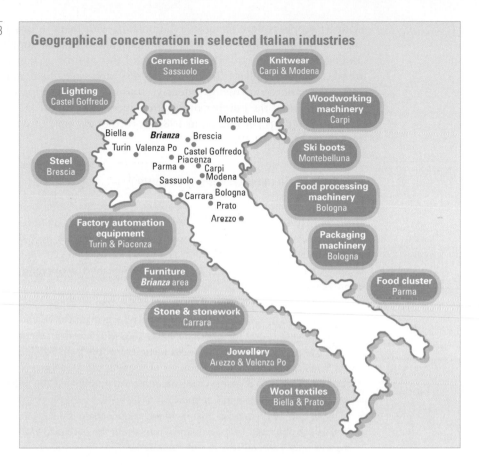

The importance of considering relationships is that while until fairly recently competition was between firms, now the complexity of offers is such that wealth is better created through co-operation, through clusters and through value-adding chains.[27] Japanese firms have long realised the value of external contacts. Japanese companies have continually turned to their suppliers, customers, distributors, government agencies and even competitors for any new insights or clues they may have to offer. The Japanese collaborate and compete, but at different levels: they collaborate in basic research and in trade negotiations, but compete with offers.

Relationships in banking differ markedly between countries. In the UK and the USA, banks tend to rely on classic contracts making lending decisions based on assets and project feasibility. In contrast, German and Japanese banks share directorships and cross-holdings of shares, giving rise to strong relationships between banks and non-financial firms; in such situations lending decisions are based more on intangibles.[28]

10.8.3 Upstream relationships

Upstream relationships are associated primarily with the suppliers who directly supply the businesses in the competitive arena, but they might be more extensive. They're primarily concerned with supply chain management, with procurement and with developing supplier relationships. Marks & Spencer has worked for many years with its suppliers developing its relationships with them in order to get the goods it wants.[29] Japanese firms have long done the same with their suppliers, allowing them, among other things, to bring in successful just-in-time systems. Xerox reduced the number of its suppliers from 5000 to 480 and demanded that every supplier be 'process-qualified', involving extensive training in quality management.[30] This programme reduced the number of defective incoming parts from 10,000 per million in 1980 to 200 parts per million in 1989. A further example of what is involved is illustrated in Exhibit 10.18.

EXHIBIT 10.18

Supply chain management at Cadbury[31]

For Cadbury, the chocolate arm of Cadbury Schweppes, Easter is one of the busiest times of the year alongside Christmas. By the close of business on Easter Thursday 1998, it had shipped 350 million Easter eggs in all shapes and sizes, from the familiar Creme Egg retailing at 29p each to the Milk Tray egg, which sells for £20. Most were delivered to 29,000 delivery points across the country, while a third were exported. In total, we gorged ourselves on £250 million worth of eggs.

To squeeze every ounce of profit out of this one-off binge requires timing and co-ordination. So it is not just marketing the products that needs careful planning. Each year, Cadbury has to purchase about 60,000 tonnes of cocoa from West Africa. Another 180 million litres of milk is bought into its factories, mostly from Herefordshire, while to satisfy the British sweet tooth, 80,000 tonnes of sugar is added to the mix. In total, Cadbury will spend £300 million a year on raw materials. An additional £200 million a year goes on gas, electricity, water and transport.

How Cadbury manages this extended supply chain is a key element in the money it makes out of Easter. This discipline – managing the purchase and supply functions – is increasingly a central concern of management in big companies across the board, from manufacturers, to insurance companies and banks.

To ensure the least wastage, Cadbury's logistics department has conducted a review of its supply chain over the last five years. Andy Phythian, logistics manager at the Bournville factory in Birmingham, is responsible for running the whole operation with military-style precision. He says the goal of the review was to 'improve the level of service, at greater speed with less cost.'

Sir Dominic Cadbury, the company's chairman, sums up a view that is catching on across a wide range of businesses: 'The market has changed, customer requirements have changed, and the only way we can keep up with the customer and end consumer is by seeing that all the supply chain is moving at the same speed and to the same standard on all fronts.' Purchasing and supply, he says, used to be a separate function, 'but I do not see it that way now. It has entered the mainstream.'

Cadbury reduced its packaging suppliers from 45 to 22 after the five-year review. To incentivise the remaining suppliers, it gave them three-year contracts to improve relationships and the quality of service. As a result, its packaging costs fell by 16%. It also halved the number of non-edible materials suppliers it relies on from 3000 to 1500.

Peter Thompson, the director-general of the Chartered Institute of Purchasing and Supply, the body responsible for developing and raising managerial skills in this area, sees Cadbury's efforts reflecting a broad trend. 'A company with thousands of suppliers has no chance of managing them pro-actively,' he says.

10.8.4 Downstream relationships

Whereas outbound logistics is concerned with specific sales, downstream relationships are concerned with activities not directly associated with a *specific* sale. They are longer-term relationships, and often extend further down the value chain than with businesses in adjacent competitive arenas. Aftersales are all those activities that enhance or maintain the offer after sale – such as providing spare parts, repairs to products and training. Although aftersales service is associated with current offers, it has additional value to the firm by building future customer relationships.

Recent developments have been those in relationship marketing, whereby the supplier builds up information and knowledge about its customers. Well-known examples of this are the loyalty cards introduced by supermarkets and the airlines' frequent-flier programmes.

Relationships with competitors

Although the car industry would appear to be rather cut-throat, the huge number of relationships within it illustrates the way in which companies collaborate, very often on a shared risk and reward basis. In manufacturing, this is often to defray R&D expenditure. Rolls-Royce plc works with its nominal arch-enemy Pratt & Whitney in the design of portions of its engines. Nokia, Motorola, Ericsson and NEC jointly operate the Yokosuka Research Park, 50 km south of Tokyo, to enhance their advanced technology.[32] In Europe, the 'big five' multinationals which dominate the European music business (Bertlesmann, EMI, PolyGram, Sony and Warner) have looked to pool distribution. SAS reports obtaining the benefits of synergy from its membership of the STAR alliance with Air Canada, Lufthansa, Thai Airways, United Airlines and Varig (of Brazil) in the areas of aircraft maintenance, catering and ticketing.

A common form of co-operative relationship between competitors is that within trade associations or similar groupings. The National Farmers' Union and the Tobacco Manufacturers' Association are just two UK examples. An interesting case is the consortium of 35 steelmakers that has spent $22 million on producing an ultra-light steel auto body.[33] The results of the project were first unveiled at the Geneva motor show in March 1998: a car body that was 25% lighter than conventional steel bodies with no production cost penalties. This collaboration was fuelled by the need for car makers to react to pressure to produce lighter cars that are more fuel-efficient and less polluting, and by the efforts of the aluminium producers seeking to produce car bodies much lighter than conventional steel bodies. As another example, in 1998 the Saudi government was reported to be setting up an informal cartel to try to control oil production in order to safeguard its income.[34]

10.8.5 Relationships outside of the value chain

Relationships within a corporation

A business that is part of a corporation has potentially many sources of support that stand-alone businesses don't have. The corporation, because of the scope of its activities, may be able to obtain funds and buy supplies at lower cost than stand-alone businesses. Services, such as IT, might be provided centrally. The corporation may be able to coach the business to superior performance. There may be synergy between the business and the other businesses within the corporation. The rationale for BSkyB bidding £625 million for Manchester United in 1998 was built on synergy. News International owns 40% of BSkyB and fully owns the rights to schedule the screening of rugby league and cricket in the UK. News International owns a baseball team and a basketball team in the USA. The intention was to follow the same path with football to drive BSkyB sales.

To realise the potential of corporate membership, the business needs to ensure that its relationships with the corporate centre, known as the parent, are appropriate. There are many examples of bad parents – parents which depress the profits of businesses through their influence – so striking the right balance between support and suffocation is important.

Relationships with potential allies

Much of the emphasis within strategy has been on competition, with little thought given to achieving success through collaboration with organisations outside the value chain. For example, Saga, a leisure group providing services for older people, has an affinity arrangement with the telecommunications firm Worldcom.

Relationships with secondary stakeholders

It is obviously important to establish and maintain good relationships between a business and all its stakeholders, if you define stakeholders as any person or organisation that can harm or help the business. One significant stakeholder is government, with relationships helped along by lobbying. One example is the success of Air France in obtaining a £2 billion subvention from the French government.

Porter[35] has stressed the role that government can play in setting standards, particularly health and safely standards. Firms operating in the country with the toughest standards will be in a good position to capitalise on the upgrading of other countries that will follow:

> The demanding home market is partly manifested in tough product standards, known as DIN (*Deutsche Industrie Norm*). DIN are consistently amongst the most stringent of any nation (within Germany their difficulty and level of detail is the subject of many amusing stories) ... German environmental regulations are today the most stringent in some fields and spending on environmental protection is by far the highest in Europe. Germany is very early in setting demanding standards and environmental regulations, and other nations follow.

SUMMARY

- Competitive analysis is concerned with how one firm compares with another along strategically significant dimensions. The leader-manager has to balance two things. It is very necessary for them to consider the (present) critical offer features, since it is success in the marketplace today that provides the wherewithal to build future assets. They also must be mindful of developing the strategic resources required for the future.   EXHIBIT 10.1
- It is fundamentally important to distinguish between offer features, operating factors and strategic resources. Offer features are the results of business activity that are of concern to the customer. Significant operating factors are associated with a competitive arena and are of concern to competitors. The strategic resources are peculiar to each particular business. The skill of strategic management is to align

the firm's strategic resources with the significant operating factors and with the critical offer features. Offer features represent the *results* of strategic positioning. EXHIBIT 10.3, EXHIBIT 10.4, EXHIBIT 10.5

- There are two types of critical offer feature. Order-qualifying features must be present at a threshold level for a sale to be possible; these features should be managed for low cost. Order-winning features are the source of differentiation and should be managed for the value they provide. EXHIBIT 10.6, EXHIBIT 10.7

- There are four fundamental sources of strategic positioning: structural assets, reputation, internal architecture and external relationships. Structural assets and reputation are strategic resources developed in the past and used in the present. Internal architecture and external relationships are assets to be used in the present. The importance of these sources varies, depending on the type of business.

- Offers can be distinguished by the importance of reputation to their value. These are search, immediate experience, long-term experience and no-experience offers. EXHIBIT 10.8

- Invention is the act of creating or producing through use of the imagination, while innovation is the commercial exploitation of an invention. Whereas stock markets may respond to inventions, customer markets don't: they respond to developments and innovations. EXHIBIT 10.9, EXHIBIT 10.10

- A useful model for viewing business relationships is the value link, which models the linkages that exist between various parts of the business and between the business and external stakeholders. There are eleven main elements in the value link, split into those concerned with the internal architecture, those concerned with external relationships within the value chain and those concerned with relationships with stakeholders outside the value chain. All eleven activities are undertaken through the use of resources in processes that are combined into capabilities. EXHIBIT 10.12, EXHIBIT 10.13

- The value link considers the organisation from a process perspective. A second view of architecture considers organisations as consisting of five types of people, with the appropriate organisational form based on how the tension between the division of labour and co-ordination is handled. EXHIBIT 10.15, EXHIBIT 10.16

- The relations that exist between a business and its external stakeholders are vital for the well-being of the firm. Clusters of firms in the same industry seem to provide advantages to all the participants. EXHIBIT 10.17

SELF-CHECK

1 Reconsider the learning outcomes for this chapter. Check that you feel confident that you can carry out the activities listed there.

2 Having read this chapter, you should be able to define the following terms:

cluster	order-qualifying feature	reverse engineering
critical offer feature	order-winning feature	significant operating factor
cycle time	organisational structure	strategic resource
(external) relationship	reputation	structural asset
(internal) architecture	resource-based view of the firm	value link

The Eurodisney encounter[36]

Eurodisney opened in the summer of 1992. Since Florida's Disney World and Epcot attracted many visitors from Europe, it appeared that locating a theme park in Europe would be a sensible choice. However, its specific location within France, 20 miles east of Paris, has proved to be rather less than spectacular.

Many continental Europeans have an aversion to queues (unlike their American counterparts) and tend to be rather less well disciplined in standing in line. Somehow consumers are more receptive to a theme park concept providing entertainment in the form of fun, mystique and fantasy in the outdoors if it is accompanied by warm sunshine. The French weather, particularly north of the Loire, is decidedly more fickle than Florida.

Perhaps Disney did not clarify its marketing concept for the European culture. When Eurodisney first arrived, Parisians were hostile to the Americanism of Mickey Mouse and all it stood for, with some French intellectuals branding it as 'a cultural Chernobyl'.

Whilst prior experiences had shown that Americans and Japanese adopt new products quickly, the French were far more reserved. Significantly, 95% of continental Europeans and French had never been to a Disney park and so awareness was low. Boosting attendance amongst the French is problematical. Whilst most nationalities treat the park with the enthusiasm of an assault course, staying until the close, the French are perplexingly casual sometimes, turning up towards closing time or leaving early if the weather deteriorates. They are also unpredictable, making planning for unexpected increases in demand a difficult burden to cater for.

Disney has been disciplined in attempting to transfer core Disney values and themes into Europe. Nowhere in the Disney park can you see the outside world, with not a glimpse of litter, delivery vans or stacks of deliveries. The world of Disney appears to be timeless and self-sustaining.

A more sinister discipline appears to be the recruitment and training policies of how its contact staff deal with the public. Their list of don'ts is long. They're not allowed to smoke, chew gum, wear flashy jewellery, tint their hair an unnatural shade, possess a visible tattoo or be fat. Their code of conduct is stricter than the Mormons, with no long or facial hair. Even the executives appear to be cloned to the rule book.

The world of Disney is further individualised with its own language. Thus shops are referred to as 'retail entertainment centres', waitresses are 'quality hosts', employees are 'cast members' and queues are endowed with the title of 'pre-entertainment areas'.

Since the opening of the theme park, Disney has been refining its product. Early visitors complained of few Disney characters, so these were increased. The shortage of rides and other shows is also being extended. Visitors can now not only meet Mickey Mouse but see where he lives.

Discussion point 10.14

What sort of internal architecture does Disney have?

- What problems does Eurodisney face beyond those expected of a company selling a product?
- How does Eurodisney use search, immediate experience and long-term experience qualities to develop consumer confidence in the Eurodisney offer?

1 For GSM:
 • What are GSM's critical offer features? Which are order-qualifying and which order-winning features?
 • It is said that strategic resources are the basis for competitive success. These are structural assets, reputation, internal architecture and external relationships. What evidence is there that GSM has developed these strategic resources?
 • It is said that overtime isn't determined by customer demand, it is determined by the standard of living that people think they should have. If overtime isn't forthcoming in the normal way, people are clever enough to manage matters to get it. Employees at GSM work overtime. What do you think of this? Is GMS missing a trick here?
 • How does the company meet fluctuations in demand?
 • What evidence is there that GSM is innovative?
 • What sort of organisational form is GSM?

2 In Chapter 1 the strategic management environment was characterised as chaotic, complex, dynamic and turbulent – all generally increasing the level of uncertainty facing leader-managers. However, not all business environments are the same. Reflect on how changes in the environmental characteristics might affect the relative importance of the bases of competition.

3 In Chapter 2, three different classifications of organisation were presented: Harrison/Handy, Deal and Kennedy, and Miles and Snow. Why do you think Mintzberg's and Lam's classifications weren't presented there and are presented here?

4 Power was discussed in Section 4.5. How are the forms of power related to the forms of organisation?

5 Two men are in the wilderness and they see a bear coming towards them. One of the men takes off his rucksack, gets his trainers out of it and starts putting them on. The other says, 'You don't think that you'll outrun a bear, do you?' And the first man says 'I don't need to outrun the bear, all I need to do is outrun you.' Does this sum up strategic positioning?

6 In Chapter 7 the view was expressed that developments in IT are destroying distance. How does this match with Porter's view on the value of clusters?

7 Do you think that a core offer will always equate to an order-qualifying feature, while all the augmentations in the augmented offer will be order-winning features?

8 Why is the adhocracy poor at accumulating tacit knowledge and the J-firm so good?

9 How innovative do you think each of the five different kinds of organisation is likely to be?

1 Four models of a firm and its environment have been described. These are:
 • the model of business processes and capabilities, which was discussed in Chapter 6;
 • the model of the two environments of a business, described in Chapter 6;
 • the model of the operating environment, described in Chapter 8;
 • the model of the value link provided in this chapter.
 Link these models together to create a complete pictorial model of a business.

2 For two businesses in the same competitive arena of your choice, compare the configurations of their value links.

FURTHER
READING

The discussion on sources of competitive advantage owes much to the books by John Kay, which are easy reading. In 1993 he wrote *Foundations of Corporate Success: How Business Strategies Add Value*, Oxford University Press, with a European perspective and with mainly European examples. In 1995, the book was effectively re-released as a second edition but with American examples, under the title *Why Firms Succeed*, Oxford University Press.

The sources of advantage to firms within nations, in particular the power of clusters, are examined in detail by Michael Porter in his book *The Competitive Advantage of Nations*, Macmillan, 1990.

CHAPTER NOTES
AND REFERENCES

1   Glaister, D., 'A narrow field of view', *The Guardian*, 10 February 1998, p. 15.

2   I'm indebted to the book by John Kay (Kay, J., *Foundations of Corporate Success: How Business Strategies Add Value*, Oxford University Press, 1993) for the identification of strategic resources, which he terms 'strategic assets'. This slight change in terminology was made to fit in with usage in previous chapters.

3   Collis, D.J. and Montgomery, C.A., 'Competing on resources: strategy in the 1990s', *Harvard Business Review*, July–August 1995, pp. 119–28.

4   Hertzberg, F., Mausner, B. and Snyderman, B.B., *The Motivation to Work*, 2nd edn, Chapman & Hall, 1959.

5   Potter, N.S., *The Global Car Industry: Preparing for the 21st Century*, ECCH Collection, 396–074–1, 1996.

6   Kay, J., *op. cit.*, pp. 87–8.

7   *Ibid.*

8   Davis, S.M., 'Transforming organizations: the key to strategy is context', in Williamson, J.N. (ed.), *The Leader-Manager*, Wilson Learning Corporation, John Wiley, 1986, pp. 105–24.

9   Unattributed, *The Observer*, 'Work' in the business section, 12 April 1998, pp. I and VIII.

10   Extract from Willman, J., 'At the cutting edge', *Financial Times*, 20 April 1998, p. 15.

11   Ohinata, Y., 'Benchmarking: the Japanese experience', *Long Range Planning*, Vol. 27, No. 4, August 1994, pp. 48–53.

12   3M Annual Report and Accounts, 1997.

13   Scherer, F.M. and Ross, D., *Industrial Market Structure and Economic Performance*, 3rd edn, Houghton Mifflin.

14   Kay, J., *op. cit.*, p. 117.

15   Porter, M.E., *The Competitive Advantage of Nations*, Macmillan, 1990.

16   Porter, M.E., *Competitive Strategy: Techniques for Analyzing Industries and Competitors*, Free Press, 1980.

17   Porter, M.E., in De Wit, B. and Meyer, R. (eds), *Strategy: Process, Content, Context: An International Perspective*, West Publishing Company, 1994.

18   Mintzberg, H., *The Structuring of Organizations*, Prentice Hall, 1979, p. 2.

19   Mintzberg, H., 'The structuring of organizations', in Mintzberg, H. and Quinn, J.B. (eds), *The Strategy Process: Concepts, Contexts, Cases*, 2nd edn, Prentice Hall International, 1991, pp. 330–50.

20   Simon, H., *Hidden Champions: Lessons from 500 of the World's Best Unknown Companies*, Harvard Business School Press, 1996.

21   Bowley, G., 'Industry's hidden winners', *Financial Times*, 'World Economy and Finance', 19 September 1997, p. 12.

22   Aoki, M., *Information, Incentives and Bargaining in the Japanese Economy*, Cambridge University Press, 1988.

23   Lam, A., 'Tacit knowledge, organisational learning and innovation: a societal perspective', Danish Research Unit for Industrial Dynamics, DRUID Working Paper No. 98–22 (ISBN 87–7873–060–0), Aalborg University, Denmark, 1998.

24   Nonaka, I. and Takeuchi, T., *The Knowledge-Creating Company: How*

Japanese Companies Create the Dynamics of Innovation, Oxford University Press, 1995, p. 5.

25 Simon, H., *op. cit.*

26 Porter, M.E., *op. cit.*, 1990.

27 Hampden-Turner, C. and Trompenaars, F., *The Seven Cultures of Capitalism: Value Systems for Creating Wealth in the United States, Britain, Japan, Germany, France, Sweden, and the Netherlands*, Doubleday, 1993, p. 200.

28 Heffernan, S., *Modern Banking in Theory and Practice*, John Wiley, 1996.

29 Collis, D.J. and Montgomery, C.A., *op. cit.*

30 Snyder, N.H., Dowd, L.J. Jr, Houghton, D.H., *Vision, Values and Courage: Leadership for Quality Management*, Free Press, 1994, p. 157.

31 Phillips, R., 'Cadbury aims for exactly the right mix', *The Independent on Sunday*, Business Bloomberg, 12 April 1998, p. 2.

32 Barnett, A., 'Wired in a world without frontiers', *The Observer*, 'Business', 12 October 1997, p. 7.

33 Griffiths, G., 'Steel gets tough on aluminium', *Financial Times*, 5 March 1998, p. 21; and unattributed, 'Steelmakers offer car with less metal', *The Guardian*, 5 March 1988, p. 20.

34 Corzine, R., 'Saudis signal new informal alliance of oil exporters', *Financial Times*, 26 July 1998, p. 1.

35 Porter, M.E., *op. cit.*, 1990, p. 372.

36 Davies, M., *Understanding Marketing*, Prentice Hall, 1998; case adapted from 'Of Mice and Millions', *Observer Magazine*, 28 March 1993, pp. 16–23.

11 SWOT analysis

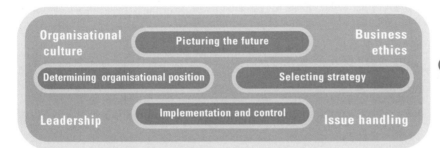

his chapter is the second of two concerned with determining the position of a business *vis-à-vis* its competitors. It links the knowledge of the bases of competition considered in the last chapter with the scenarios discussed in Chapter 9. The result of a SWOT analysis is a SWOT table, which is a concise statement of the situation in which the firm finds itself.

The characteristics of a **S**trengths, **W**eaknesses, **O**pportunities and **T**hreats table and the associated analysis are first described and the difficulties in carrying out a formal analysis are explored. The relatively easy task of building a SWOT table for the short term is described. Then a five-step approach to the much more difficult task of building a SWOT table for the longer term is outlined. This outline is followed by an extended example in which each step in the approach is discussed in depth. Finally, the relative emphases to be placed on internal and external factors is considered briefly, and sensitivity analysis is broached.

Many leader-managers find it useful to encapsulate the position of their organisation in a concise statement of its strengths and weaknesses *vis-à-vis* the competition and the opportunities and threats that it faces in its environment. They do this by constructing a SWOT table. A SWOT table provides a useful springboard for the identification of strategy, since it identifies the weaknesses that need to be strengthened, the strengths that can be used for competitive advantage, the opportunities that can be used to the organisation's advantage, and the threats that it needs to guard against.

LEARNING
OUTCOMES

When you have worked through this chapter, you should be able to:

- explain what strategists are seeking to achieve through a SWOT analysis;

- determine who are the present key competitors and who the future competitors are likely to be;

- explain the focus on critical offer features when developing a SWOT table for the near future, and the focus on significant operating factors and strategic resources when considering a SWOT table for the longer term;

- construct SWOT tables for both the short and longer terms.

11.1 SWOT analysis and its difficulties

11.1.1 What is a SWOT analysis?

In Chapters 7 and 8 the remote and operating environments of a business were considered. Together these analyses were used to produce pictures of the future – scenarios – as described in Chapter 9. In Chapter 10 the bases of competition were examined to identify where sources of competitive advantage would lie. Together they provide the information necessary to assess organisational position. Prior to thinking about formulating strategy, it can be useful to bring this information together to provide a summarised view of where a business stands. A useful form of this concise view is a SWOT table, a table setting out the business's Strengths and Weaknesses and the Opportunities and Threats that it faces.[1] An example of a SWOT table for a no-frills airline is given in Exhibit 11.1.

It is very common in practice to begin the process of formulating strategy by asking the participants in a rather informal way to draw up a SWOT table for their organisation through what is termed a SWOT analysis. Such a process can be valuable in

EXHIBIT 11.1

An example of a SWOT table for a no-frills airline

Strengths

- Airports used are better than those used by the other no-frills airlines
- Management skills
- Lower costs than established airlines
- Ease of booking flights
- Recognised logo
- IT facilities
- Better than average employee relations

Weaknesses

- Airports used are worse than those used by the big carriers
- Reputation for punctuality
- Cash flows
- No safety record yet established
- Poorer than average customer service

Opportunities

- Strong business demand for cheap air fares
- Strong leisure demand for cheap air fares
- The Internet
- Many secondary airports underused

Threats

- The further entry of subsidiaries of the big carriers
- Higher airport charges

getting the participants quickly and fully engaged in strategy formulation. However, this informality produces a strong tendency to consider only the present and short-term future by focusing on the present critical offer features and the present significant operating factors. This is what has occurred in Exhibit 11.1, which is a SWOT table applicable to the short term and derived from thinking about the short term. A short-term SWOT has its uses, but what is obligatory for longer-term strategy formulation is a SWOT table that focuses on the longer term – on the future significant operating factors and the strategic resources that the firm will need.

11.1.2 The problem in identifying strengths and weaknesses

A competitive analysis provides the basis for a comparison of the businesses in the competitive arena. It isn't a straightforward matter to determine what is a strength and what is a weakness in such a comparison, however, since any assessment must be made bearing in mind the organisational environment. Suppose a business takes the view that incorporating additional IT functionality into its products is needed, and it has £200,000 that it can allocate to building up its expertise in this area. Is this £200,000 a strength? It is, if competitors have a lesser amount and if the extra that the business has can make a significant difference. On the other hand, it's a weakness if competitors are willing to spend more and this larger spend can bring much greater functionality. This example illustrates that any strength must be judged *vis-à-vis* the competitors in the context of the environment. To quote Collis and Montgomery:[2] 'The greatest mistake managers make when evaluating their resources is failing to assess them relative to competitors.'

11.1.3 The problem in identifying opportunities and threats

The external environment is the source of the opportunities and threats facing the business, with scenarios encapsulating the environmental issues. In all the chapters so far, events and trends in the environment have been termed *issues* rather than opportunities or threats. This has been deliberate, since it's not possible to determine whether an issue is an opportunity or a threat until a full picture of the business's situation has emerged. Consider the following issue: the UK government decides to give less financial support to undergraduates. Is this a threat or an opportunity to a particular university? It's likely to be a threat to a university that isn't located close to a conurbation (attractive to students who wish to save money by living at home or who hope to find part-time work) or one that isn't seriously engaged in distance learning. On the other hand, it's an opportunity (or perhaps only a lesser threat) for those that are. This small example illustrates that whether an issue is a threat or an opportunity depends on the relative strengths of the competing businesses.

11.1.4 Critical offer features, significant operating factors and strategic resources

It is relatively easy to construct a SWOT table for the near future driven by the present critical offer features and the present significant operating factors; it's much harder to construct one that focuses on the truly strategic and the longer term.

Exhibit 10.5 is reproduced as Exhibit 11.2. This illustrates the important point that it's the future significant operating factors that need to be focused on, mainly because these are the part of the future that can sensibly be considered. The future critical offer features can't be known with any certainty and to use them could be very misleading. Thus, although knowledge of the present and future critical offer features

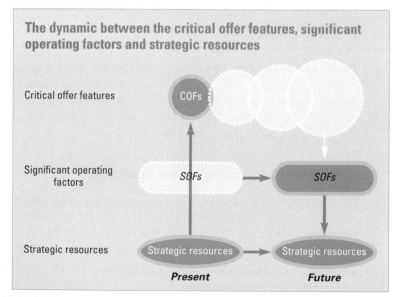

The dynamic between the critical offer features, significant operating factors and strategic resources

does play a part in determining strategic position, it's the significant operating factors and the strategic resources needed to operate effectively in the future that are of paramount concern.

DISCUSSION
POINT 11.1

If you have previously carried out a SWOT analysis, reflect on whether you could state unambiguously what was a strength and what was a weakness, what was a threat and what was an opportunity.

KEY CONCEPT

In the main, a Strengths, Weaknesses, Opportunities and Threats analysis derives from more detailed analyses. A comparison with competitors unearths the strengths and weaknesses. The (external) environment is the source of opportunities and threats. The concern in developing a SWOT table for the short-term future is likely to be the present critical offer features and significant operating factors. The concern in developing a SWOT table for the longer term is the future significant operating factors and the strategic resources needed to operate successfully in this future.

The interdependence of the SWOT elements – for example, what is a strength depends on the environmental context as well as on the relative standing of competitors – means that it's not really possible to provide a set of mechanical procedures to cover all aspects of producing a SWOT table. However, it is possible to mechanise several of the individual steps. Whether a mechanised path is followed or not, a pattern of thinking can be identified that will enable the important elements of the SWOT table to be identified. Like so many techniques in strategic management, the importance is not the SWOT table itself but the understanding that should be obtained by the process of building it. Throughout the building of the SWOT table, management judgement is of overwhelming importance.

11.2 An approach to building a short-term SWOT table

The process of building a short-term SWOT table involves the identification of present competitors, critical offer features and significant operating factors. Identifying the present competitors stimulates the identification of the present critical offer features and significant operating factors, and the present strategic resources, since they can be found through answering the question 'Why are the successful competitors successful?'[3]

11.2.1 Step 1 – identifying present competitors

It is relatively easy to determine present competitors: they are the businesses that are in the same competitive group as the target business for which the SWOT analysis is being carried out. However, it is especially important to identify *key* competitors. One way of determining the key competitors for a business is to generate the following lists:[4]

- List the businesses with closely similar offers.
- List the businesses that serve closely similar customer needs.

- List the businesses with a similar geographical scope.
- List, in order of market share, those businesses with higher market share than the target business.

It has been suggested[5] that key competitors will be those that appear in the top three of any one list and those that appear on more than one list.

11.2.2   Step 2 – identifying present critical offer features

Managers knowledgeable about the markets will be those whose experience would be used to identify the critical offer features. It may be that a large number of offer features are identified initially, but to focus debate there is a need to restrict the list only to those that are critical, i.e. those that have a significant effect on sales success. They are likely to include order-winning features.

DISCUSSION
POINT 11.2

Why have the order-winning features been picked out as present critical offer features rather than the order-qualifying features? Is there any point in including order-qualifying features in a SWOT table?

11.2.3   Step 3 – identifying present significant operating factors

The significant operating factors are those characteristics of the operating environment where all successful businesses must have strong positions. Significant operating factors will have been detected in an operating environmental analysis of the sort discussed in Chapter 8, as the significant forces in the competitive arena will have been identified. However, it should be realised that it's the relative endowments of businesses in the competitive arena, rather than the average position, that are significant in determining the significant operating factors. If all competitors are equally endowed, a significant force isn't a significant operating factor, since it doesn't differentiate between competitors.

11.2.4   Step 4 – identifying the present strategic resources

The present strategic resources will be assessed in relation to competitors and in the light of the significant operating factors. For example, if a significant operating factor for a watch maker was the constant addition of many additional features, then styling and/or skills in electronics might be called for.

11.2.5   Step 5 – identifying the present issues

The present issues are those that have to be reacted to fairly immediately to support the firm's operations in the short term. They will be identified through forecasting and a knowledge of likely future events. Management judgement would be used to decide which features of the firm are strengths and weaknesses and which issues are opportunities and which are threats, and thus to create a SWOT table in the form shown in Exhibit 11.1.

11.3 An approach to building a longer-term SWOT table

The rest of this chapter will focus on building a SWOT table suitable for the longer term. It will thus focus on future significant operating factors and the firm's strategic resources rather than the critical offer features. To support the building of a longer-term SWOT table, the five-step process indicated in Exhibit 11.3 is suggested. Step 1 is similar to that in the development of a short-term SWOT table. In step 2, the future significant operating factors are identified by taking into account the changes that the strategic issues will cause to the significant operating factors. In step 3, the strategic resources that will be needed in the future are identified through the interplay of present strategic resources and future significant operating factors. In step 4, the strategic resources are split into strengths and weaknesses by comparing the firm's strategic resources with those of future competitors. In the light of these strengths and weaknesses, the issues can be separated into opportunities and threats (step 5). There is likely to be some iteration in steps 4 and 5.

EXHIBIT 11.3

Steps to building a longer-term SWOT table

Step

1 Determining the present situation
2 Present significant operating factors ············▶ Future significant operating factors
3 Present strategic resources ·····················▶ Future strategic resources required
4 Future strategic resources required ···········▶ Strengths and weaknesses
5 Issues ··▶ Opportunities and threats

11.3.1 Step 1 – determining the present situation

As with developing a short-term SWOT table, the present significant operating factors and the present competitors will have been identified. This will be used in steps 2 and 4, respectively.

11.3.2 Step 2 – determining the future significant operating factors

The future significant operating factors will be determined through the interplay between the present significant operating factors and the strategic issues. For example, until towards the end of the 1980s, very large power stations had been favoured by the one large UK electricity generator – the Central Electricity Generating Board (CEGB). A firm such as International Combustion of Derby was one of the few companies that could manufacture the massive boilers necessary for these stations. Then the situation changed drastically. The CEGB was broken up and privatised, and technological and social changes favoured the much smaller, locally sited combined heat and power stations. The significant operating factors had changed and the strategic resources of International Combustion were strategic no more, as very large boilers were no longer required.

11.3.3   Step 3 – determining the future strategic resource needs

Determination of the future strategic resources needed to compete effectively in the competitive arena of the future is the nub of a SWOT analysis for the longer term. Three further examples will illustrate how identification of the strategic resources comes out of identification of the significant operating factors to augment the example given above of electricity generation.

Car manufacture

One scenario for a car manufacturer when viewing the early 2000s might include increased globalisation, increased importance of relationship marketing and increased customer environmental awareness. These issues would be reflected in necessary changes in strategic resources, with, for example, more emphasis placed on global branding (reputation), on aftersales service (external relationships) and on the development of electronic engine management systems (architecture).

Retail banking

Until recently, one of the biggest advantages that the retail banks had – and a feature that protected them from new entrants – was their high-street branch networks. With automatic teller machines in many convenient locations and with telebanking, these branches are no longer the asset they were; indeed, they are becoming an expensive liability. This would imply that the banks need to augment their strategic resources in the area of non-branch distribution, using other 'physical' outlets such as supermarkets, and telephone, Internet and PC banking (architecture).

Supermarkets and branding

The rise in the power of the supermarkets has meant that the balance of power has shifted from producers to retailers, and only the producers with very strong brands are able to resist supermarket pressure. Thus the value of powerful brands has increased over the last decade or so, and that of weak brands has fallen. The strategic resources needed by manufacturers are an excellent reputation (reputation) or a very low cost base (architecture).

11.3.4   Step 4 – establishing strengths and weaknesses

The strengths and weaknesses in a longer-term SWOT table are the *present* strategic resources looked at in the light of the *future* significant operating factors. As strengths and weaknesses are relative to *future* competitors, future competitors need to be identified to enable the strengths and weaknesses to be unearthed.

Identifying future competitors

The most likely future competitors are the present competitors: after all, there is considerable inertia in most organisations and sometimes in customers – it is said that there's more chance of your being divorced than of changing your bank account.[6] The next most likely future competitors are the businesses that are not in the same competitive group as the target business but are already operating within the same competitive arena.

DISCUSSION
POINT 11.3 Where would you look for the next most likely group of future competitors after the present ones and those within the same competitive arena?

The important feature when seeking to identify future competitors is not only to consider the changing significant operating factors and how these might swing the balance of advantage to new players but also what the businesses in the competitive arena are really providing to the customer. Such an analysis was used to identify the substitutes to the businesses in the competitive arena. The development of some relatively simple technology to allow the mains electricity grid to be used to access the Internet introduced a potential competitor to the established cable, satellite and deregulated telephone companies from an unexpected source.[7] It was competition because it satisfied the same customer requirements as the present incumbents of the competitive arena. So the touchstone is to look at what the offer *does* rather than what it *is*. The electricity distribution companies weren't simply suppliers of electricity, they were electrical wave and impulse carriers into virtually all homes in the developed world.

Separating strategic resources into strengths and weaknesses

In the light of the future competitors, present strategic resources will be assessed to determine whether they are strengths or weaknesses in the future situation. This might require the collection of further data on competitors, perhaps through benchmarking. The assessment of strengths and weaknesses may be done formally through the creation of a table, as illustrated later.

11.3.5 Step 5 – establishing opportunities and threats

Once the strengths and weaknesses have been identified, it is useful to separate the issues into opportunities and threats. The opportunities are there to be taken advantage of, while threats need to be guarded against; thus they are both important inputs to strategy formulation. It may be that it's appropriate for the organisation to manage its relationships with its stakeholders to reduce the threats and augment the opportunities. One threat to tobacco companies is a more stringent advertising code: the companies try to mitigate this threat through legal challenge by their trade organisation[8] and through political lobbying and other public relations methods. The convergence of entertainment, communications and computers offers many opportunities, especially if the opportunities can be widened through successful political lobbying, as Rupert Murdoch seems able to do.

KEY CONCEPT   In a longer-term SWOT table, an organisation's strengths and weaknesses describe its *present* relative standing in terms of strategic resources to likely *future* competitors within an operating environment characterised by the *future* significant operating factors. These future significant operating factors are identified by looking at the present significant operating factors and considering how environmental issues will change and augment them.

11.4 An example of creating a longer-term SWOT table

Many organisations would use the pattern of thinking described above in a rather informal way to produce a SWOT table. Some organisations employ a more formal approach, and the formality of the five-step approach is now illustrated through the use of an extended example. The example is of an airline – which we'll call Speedijet – offering no-frills fares in Europe.

11.4.1 Step 1 – determining the present position

Identifying the present competitors

It is easy to identify the present competitors: they are all those airlines operating in Europe. One strategic group would be composed of all the no-frills airlines that are offering fares much lower than the established airlines such as BA and the national carriers in continental Europe, which consitute another strategic group. Thus the present competitors to Speedijet would include EasyJet, Go and Ryanair, together with all the national carriers. The number of competitors is likely to be large, and the form of culling suggested in Section 11.2 might be appropriate.

Identifying the present critical offer features

From considering the success of these airlines and from market research data, it is judged that the present critical offer features from the point of view of Speedijet are the airports used, ticket price, availability of flights, availability of seats on the flights, reputation for punctuality, ease of booking a flight, and reputation for safety.

Identifying the present significant operating factors

The present significant operating factors have been assessed, and are listed in the first column in Exhibit 11.4.

11.4.2 Step 2 – determining the future significant operating factors

The issues

An environmental analysis might have thrown up the eight strategic issues set out in the second column of Exhibit 11.4. It is considered that the no-frills airline Go, which is a subsidiary of BA, was set up in order to put the independent no-frills airlines out of business, with BA subsidising Go's activities.[9] Thus the EU stance on cross-subsidy is very important.

The effective embargo on the no-frills airlines using the central airports such as Heathrow, and the poorer airport facilities and access by road and rail at the smaller airports that the no-frills airlines have to use, are both major issues. The monitoring of aircraft safety is to be tightened. The Channel Tunnel and pollution and congestion fears are bringing about a renaissance in rail travel. The EU and national government stances on noise could be significantly altered in the medium term. The EU, national government and union stances on aircrew costs could be significant; currently, the social cost of using aircrew registered in continental Europe is an inhibiting factor, and if aircrew could be registered in the UK or Ireland the costs to the

EXHIBIT 11.4

The link between present and future significant operating factors

Present significant operating factors	Strategic issues	Future significant operating factors
1 Much lower costs than the established airlines	• EU stance on cross-subsidy by parents • Availability of central airports	1 Airports used
2 Punctuality	• Airport facilities and ease of land access • Safety monitoring of aircraft to a common European standard	2 Much lower costs than the major carriers 3 Cross-subsidy by parent airlines 4 Number of flights offered by the major carriers
3 Airports used	• Renaissance in rail travel	5 Punctuality
4 Perceived safety	• EU/national government stance on noise pollution • EU/national government/union stance on aircrew registration • Demand for both business and leisure travel	

airlines would be much lower. The demand for low-cost business and leisure travel is strong.

The future significant operating factors

The issues will change the significant operating factors, perhaps to those shown in column 3 of Exhibit 11.4. This shows the addition of two new factors: the cross-subsidy by parent airlines and the number of flights offered by the established airlines. This latter significant operating factor comes about because, in the face of the threat from no-frills airlines in the USA, the established carriers flew many more flights than usual on the routes where they were being challenged, a tactic that was successful in limiting the number of passengers that the no-frills airlines could persuade to change allegiance and travel with them. The importance of the significant operating factors has also changed; the airports that the no-frills airlines can use form the most important factor, driven by the expected tightening of noise pollution regulations and the renaissance in rail travel using central city termini. The enhanced monitoring of aircraft standards has meant that no airline, including the no-frills airlines, needs to concern itself with public perceptions of safety, since this is guaranteed by the European standards authority. Thus safety ceases to be a significant operating factor in the future.

11.4.3 Step 3 – determining the future strategic resource needs

The five future significant operating factors are listed in the first column of Exhibit 11.5. For each, the strategic resources needed to establish a strong competitive position have been listed in column 2, with the type of strategic resource indicated in column 3.

DISCUSSION
POINT 11.4

Why do you think there are no entries for *structural assets* in column 3 of Exhibit 11.5?
- Can you think of a strategic resource that could be used to combat the large number of flights that the big carriers might put on as a spoiling tactic?

The assumption in creating the third column is that Speedijet has all of the resources in house. Where this wasn't the case, as perhaps it wouldn't be for the legal activity, then the strategic resource would be in external relationships.

11.4.4 Step 4 – establishing strengths and weaknesses

Identifying future competitors

Future competitors are likely to include the present competitors. However, apart from

EXHIBIT 11.5

The strategic resources needed in the future

Future significant operating factors	Strategic resource needed to establish a strong competitive position	Type of strategic resource
Airports used	Lobbying of national governments and EU commissioners	External relationships
Much lower costs than the major carriers	Lean manning	Architecture
	Crew costs	Architecture, external relationships
	IT skills	Architecture
	Aircraft scheduling	Architecture
	Marketing to fill capacity	Architecture
	Efficient ticketing	Architecture
	Fast maintenance	Architecture
Cross-subsidy by parent airlines	Legal skill	Architecture
	Close monitoring of main carriers' operations	Architecture, external relations
	Lobbying of EU commissioners	External relationships
Number of flights offered by the major carriers Punctuality	Efficient maintenance	Architecture
	Crew rostering	Architecture
	Extra aircrew	Architecture
	Publicising of punctuality	External relationships

SouthWest airlines, the no-frills airlines that were born out of the US deregulation in the early 1990s have all failed, so it is unlikely that the major US airlines will create no-frills airlines in Europe.

Future competitors are likely to include subsidiaries of the national carriers in continental Europe as they become denationalised over the coming years. Coupling the future strategic resources needed with the likely future competitors will allow the strengths and weaknesses of Speedijet to be established. Exhibit 11.6 is the resulting strengths and weaknesses table. SJ is Speedijet, B is Go, and C and D are two other no-frills airlines. Managerial judgement is used to establish the ratings of Speedijet and each competing airline for each future strategic resource on a scale of +2 to −2. This rating suggests, for example, that Speedijet is strong on lean staffing and crew costs, but weak on aircraft maintenence and legal skills. It is neither strong nor weak compared with competitors on publicity or punctuality.

11.4.5 Step 5 – establishing opportunities and threats

An example of a SWOT table for Speedijet is given in Exhibit 11.7. What are opportunities and what are threats will be determined by inspection of the relative standing

EXHIBIT 11.6

Strengths and weaknesses

Future strategic resource requirements	Future competitors				
	SJ	B	C	D	S/W
1 Lobbying of national governments and EU commissioners on airports used	+2	+1	+1	0	S
2 Lean manning	+2	−1	+1	+1	S
3 Crew costs	+2	−2	+1	0	S
4 IT skills	−1	0	+2	+1	W
5 Marketing to fill capacity	+1	+2	−1	−1	W
6 Efficient ticketing	+2	+2	−2	0	S
7 Fast maintenance	−1	+1	−2	0	W
8 Legal skill	+1	+2	0	0	W
9 Close monitoring of the major carriers' operations	−1	+2	1	−1	W
10 Lobbying of EU commission on cross-subsidy	0	+1	1	0	S
11 Efficient maintenance	+1	+2	−1	0	W
12 Crew rostering	−1	+1	−2	0	S
13 Extra aircrew	+1	+2	−2	0	W
14 Publicity on punctuality	+2	+2	0	0	−

EXHIBIT 11.7

An example of a SWOT table for a no-frills airline

Strengths

- Lobbying of national governments and EU on airports used
- Lean manning
- Crew costs
- Efficient ticketing
- Lobbying of national governments and EU on cross-subsidy
- Crew rostering

Weaknesses

- IT skills
- Marketing to fill capacity
- Speed of maintenance
- Legal skills
- Monitoring of major carriers
- Efficiency of maintenance
- Extra aircrew

Opportunities

- Tightening of safety monitoring of aircraft to a common European standard
- EU stance on aircrew registration softens
- Increasing demand for both business and leisure travel

Threats

- EU stance on cross-subsidy remains weak
- Airport facilities and ease of land access do not improve
- Renaissance of rail travel
- EU/national government stance on noise pollution stiffens

of Speedijet on the issues set out in Exhibit 11.4. The availability of central airports is not included in the SWOT table, because it is not considered either an opportunity or a threat. Note that the issues listed in the SWOT table include a firm statement on each issue; the issue is *safety monitoring of aircraft to a common European standard*, whereas the entry in the SWOT table is that applicable to one scenario, e.g. *tightening of safety monitoring of aircraft to a common European standard*.

11.4.6 The new SWOT table

Note that the strengths and weaknesses are internal factors and must be relative to competitors, rather than an absolute view. This shift to a comparator frame of reference may suggest to an organisation that it would be fruitful to spend some time comparing itself against competitors to see whether it really is as good as it thinks it is.

Also note that the opportunities and threats are in the environment – they *aren't* actions that the business might carry out. For example, it would be inappropriate to have as an opportunity a statement such as *move to register aircrew in the UK or in Ireland*: the appropriate entry is *EU stance on aircrew registrations softens*. The SWOT table suggests strategic direction but doesn't contain it.

11.5 Further considerations

11.5.1 Relative emphasis in a SWOT table

The strengths and weaknesses are identified from considering assets, processes and

capabilities: opportunities and threats from a structural analysis. The relative emphasis to put into these two aspects of position determination will depend on the environmental dynamism. Stalk *et al.*[10] take a very strong line:

> When the economy was relatively static, strategy could afford to be static. In a world
> characterised by durable products, stable customer needs, well-defined national and
> regional markets, and clearly defined competitors, competition was a 'war of position'
> in which companies occupied competitive space like squares on a chessboard.
>
> Competition is now a 'war of movement' in which success depends on anticipation
> of market trends and quick response to changing customer needs. Successful competi-
> tors move quickly in and out of products, markets, and sometimes even entire busi-
> nesses – a process more akin to an interactive video game than to chess. In such an
> environment, the essence of strategy is *not* the structure of a company's products and
> markets but the dynamics of its behavior.

DISCUSSION
POINT 11.5

This view would seem to play down the role of environmental analysis. What do you feel
about this?

11.5.2 Sensitivity analysis

The whole of the discussion in this chapter so far has assumed one view of the
future – one scenario. The whole point about scenarios is that the future can't be predicted and that a set of scenarios is needed to force consideration of alternative
futures. Thus it would be inappropriate to carry out the SWOT analysis for one scenario only. One approach is to repeat the analysis for each scenario. However, this
can be very time-consuming, and a short-cut is to consider the effect that different
values of the scenario variables might have on the entries in the SWOT table. The
effect of the significant variables can then be debated to revise the SWOT table
entries.

SUMMARY
- A **S**trengths, **W**eaknesses, **O**pportunities and **T**hreats (SWOT) table provides a
  framework for organising either intuitive information or the results of more
  formal analyses to establish an organisation's strategic position in its environment
  and vis-à-vis its competitors. The production of a SWOT table isn't easy: a great
  deal of mental discipline is needed. What is a strength and what is a weakness is
  relative to competitors in the context of the environment. And what is an opportunity and what is a threat is relative to the environment in the context of the
  position vis-à-vis competitors.
- The tension between the near and more distant futures is evident in the building
  of a SWOT table. The concern in developing a SWOT table for the near future is
  likely to be the critical offer features and the present significant operating factors.
  The concern in developing a SWOT table for the longer term is with future significant operating factors and with strategic resources.   EXHIBIT 11.2
- There are five main steps in arriving at a SWOT table appropriate for the short
  term:

- identify the present competitors;
- identify the present critical offer features;
- identify the present significant operating factors;
- identify the present strategic resources;
- identify the present issues and divide them into opportunities and threats.
- There are also five main steps in arriving at a longer-term SWOT table:
  - identify the present situation;
  - identify the future significant operating factors;
  - identify the future strategic resource requirements;
  - determine where the organisation's strengths and weaknesses lie in respect to the future strategic resource requirements;
  - divide the issues into opportunities and threats.   EXHIBIT 11.2
- The determination of present competitors is fairly easy; determining future competitors is more difficult. Future competitors will include those whose strategic resources make them well placed with regard to the future significant operating factors.
- In arriving at a SWOT table, considerable judgement will have been exercised by leader-managers. The table will have been developed within the mindset and paradigm of the participants. This could lead to a blinkered vision of the organis-

EXHIBIT 11.8

SWOT table for a retail bank

Strengths

- Traditional family-based relationships
- Customer inertia
- Branch network
- Product range
- Management skills/resources
- Processing technology
- Communication network
- Brand image
- Trustworthy reputation

Weaknesses

- High level of fixed costs
- Poor level of customer services
- Lack of customer information
- Product, not market, focus
- Lacks brand strength
- Lack of flexibility to respond
- Traditional management practices
- Complexity of operations

Opportunities

- Develop enhanced customer service
- Develop effective marketing systems
- Reduced cost structures
- New distribution opportunities
- Market/product/customer segmentation
- Product innovation
- Social changes
- Brand positioning/strengthening

Threats

- New market entry competition
- New technologies
- Product innovations
- Changing customer attitudes/needs
- Innovative delivery systems
- Legislation

ational position. There may be several SWOT tables depending on the number of views of the future (scenarios) that are considered.

1 Reconsider the learning outcomes for this chapter. Check that you feel confident that you can carry out the activities listed there.

2 Having read this chapter, you should be able to define the terms *SWOT analysis* and *SWOT table*.

1 In Chapter 1 the strategic management environment was characterised as chaotic, complex, dynamic and turbulent – all generally increasing the level of uncertainty facing leader-managers. However, not all business environments are the same. Reflect on how changes in the environmental characteristics might affect the approach taken to the carrying out of a SWOT analysis.

2 Critique the SWOT table set out in Exhibit 11.8 for a typical retail bank.[11]

3 How would you label the group of businesses that are not present competitors yet are in the same competitive arena?

4 The identification of the critical success factors and significant operating features are activities in developing a SWOT table. In your reading in previous chapters, where do you think these will have been identified and used?

1 For GSM carry out a SWOT analysis – both for current operations and for five years hence.

2 Carry out a SWOT analysis for your university department. It is suggested that you restrict yourselves to one major activity, such as the undergraduate or post-graduate programmes.

1 In the USA, the acronym TOWS is more popular than SWOT. TOWS stands for the same elements, Threats, Opportunities, Weaknesses and Strengths. The TOWS acronym suggests that the analysis starts with the environment, whereas SWOT suggests that the analysis starts with the comparison of competitors.

2 Collis, D.J. and Montgomery, C.A., 'Competing on resources: strategy in the 1990s', *Harvard Business Review*, July–August 1994, pp. 118–28.

3 The identification of present competitors is also the starting point for identifying future competitors.

4 Rue, L.W. and Holland, P.G., *Strategic Management: Concepts and Experiences*, 2nd edn, Management Series, McGraw-Hill, 1989, p. 116.

5 *Ibid.*

6 Research carried out by the Abbey National bank in the summer of 1998, quoted in S. Pritchard, 'Go on, divorce the bank', *The Independent on Sunday*, section 2, 24 January 1999, p. 18.

7 Bannister, N., 'British team discovers the Internet's holy grail', *The Guardian*, 1997 p. 1.

8 Willman, J., 'Tobacco groups to challenge EU ban', *Financial Times*, 22 September 1998, p. 1.

9 EasyJet has already appealed to the EU authorities claiming that British Airways is doing just that.

10 Stalk, G., Evans, P. and Shulman, L.E., 'Competing on capabilities – the new rules of corporate strategy', *Harvard Business Review*, March–April 1992, pp. 57–69.

11 Goldrick, P.J. and Greenland, S.J.,

Pragma Consulting, 1994, quoted in D. McConchie, 'Patterns of strategic control: an investigation of British, French and German retail banking practice', PhD thesis, Loughborough University, 1998.

PART 4

Selecting strategy

CHAPTER **12** **Strategic options**

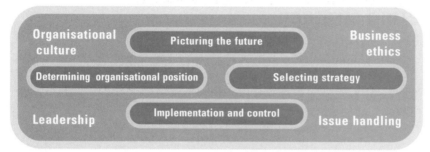

█ n Chapters 7 to 11 the position of a business *vis-à-vis* its environment
| and its competitors was considered, and encapsulated in one or more
█ SWOT tables. These tables provide a basis for selecting strategy.

This chapter is the first of two chapters concerned with strategy selection, with choosing the strategic pathway by which a business moves
towards its goals. In this chapter the characteristics of the possibilities
open to all businesses will be explored, i.e. the generic options. In the
next chapter the way in which a business might choose its particular
combination of options to form a strategic pathway will be considered.

The chapter begins with an overview of possible options and how they
can be built into a pathway. Five areas of choice are identified and these
are discussed in turn. First, the portfolio of offers that the business
makes is considered. Then the offer positioning possibilities are
explored, both in terms of market share and in terms of price–value combinations. While this considers market position there is also the need to
review the business position, and thus capability and cost considerations are discussed. This is followed by a review of the broad forms of
access to the non-financial resources required to implement the strategy. These broad forms are considered in three areas: upstream with
supplies and suppliers, downstream with logistics and customers, and
with the in-sourcing and out-sourcing that alters the scope of a firm's
support activities within the value link. Finally, the sources of funds to
support any augmentation of capabilities and activities are considered.

Strategy consists of strategic goals and the means of achieving these goals – a strategic pathway. A strategic pathway is a coherent set of options in offer positioning and resource selection. The choice of strategic pathway is an extremely important aspect of a leader-manager's job, and thus it's vital that the appropriateness of the options open to them are fully understood before the choice is made.

LEARNING
OUTCOMES

When you have worked through this chapter, you should be able to:

- describe the five fundamental areas where options exist when selecting a strategic pathway;

- explain the importance of market share and describe the market share options for a business's present offers;

- understand offer positioning and explain the relationship between price, value and consumer surplus;

- explain what is involved in the management of a portfolio of offers;

- argue whether to buy, do it yourself or collaborate to obtain access to the non-financial assets that a firm needs;

- appreciate the characteristics of the sources of funds available.

12.1   Strategic options and pathways

The vision and other business goals and the organisational position encapsulated in a SWOT table will provide the focus within which search for an appropriate strategic pathway should take place. A strategic pathway is the set of choices made in each of five interrelated areas:

- The portfolio of offers   The business must decide on the number and range of its offers and thus on the possibilities of augmenting its present offers or reducing them.[a]

---

a   In this chapter it is assumed that the leader-manager is working in an established business making at least one offer.

- **The offer positioning**   The business must consider its overall position in its market. A conventional way of doing this is to view position in terms of market share. The business must also decide how each offer should be positioned in terms of value and price.

- **The resources required**   The business needs to identify the resources, processes and capabilities it requires to support the offer positioning.

- **The form of access to resources**   How the business will obtain the use of the non-financial resources necessary to achieve its strategic goals.

- **The source of funds**   Where the business will obtain the finance to gain access to the non-financial resources it needs.

These considerations form a broad sequence, as shown in Exhibit 12.1.[1] A specific pathway is built up from choices for each element. For example, Boots the Chemist has chosen to extend its offers by entering the Dutch market. It chooses to do this by positioning itself slightly upmarket, matching the average price for healthcare products in the Netherlands.[2] It needs to develop a knowledge of the Dutch market and it's doing this through developing its own in-house resources (developing its store layout team in the subtleties of the Dutch shopper). The required funding will come from retained profits. This example is a simple pathway, with only one choice for each element. There can be mixed strategic pathways: for example, Boots is not only developing its own in-house resources but also buying in consultancy expertise.

It should be stressed that the sequence shown in Exhibit 12.1 wouldn't necessarily be followed rigidly from left to right when choosing a pathway, i.e. first decide on the portfolio of offers and freeze this decision, then decide on the appropriate offer positioning for each offer and freeze these, and so on. There will be considerable iteration;

EXHIBIT 12.1

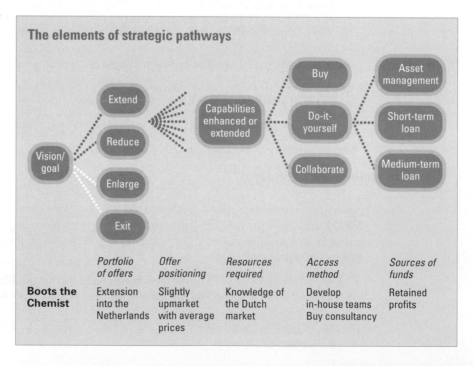

The elements of strategic pathways

	Portfolio of offers	Offer positioning	Resources required	Access method	Sources of funds
Boots the Chemist	Extension into the Netherlands	Slightly upmarket with average prices	Knowledge of the Dutch market	Develop in-house teams Buy consultancy	Retained profits

for example, the funding available may not support a pathway that involves extending the range of offers.

12.2 The portfolio of offers the business makes

12.2.1 The options

The possible changes to the portfolio of offers that a business can make are indicated in Exhibit 12.2. The central position is around the present, which is to continue to make the same offers as the business is doing currently. Extending the offers will be accompanied by an extension to the firm's existing capabilities. Reducing the offers is likely to be accompanied by a reduction in its capabilities.

EXHIBIT 12.2

Changes in the portfolio of offers

Exit | Reduce offers | Stay with present offers | Extend offers | Enlarge offers

← Reduction in offers | Increase in offers →

12.2.2 Offer extensions and reductions

Offer extensions are becoming increasingly important. Offers are increasingly forming 'food chains', as the Japanese call them,[3] or 'offer generations'. The number of starts and finishes is decreasing, with a tendency for them to be replaced by continuous incremental developments.

Offer extensions may be differentiated by whether they are predominantly extensions to the core product or service, generally simply called product extensions, or whether the emphasis is on market extensions. Product extension would particularly suit a firm that had a strong brand and is prepared to undertake what is known as *brand stretching* – using a well-respected brand name with the new offers. However, brand stretching can be dangerous. Mercedes is in danger of destroying the value of its brand name by using its name on the smaller cars that it has introduced. In contrast, BMW resisted using its name on Rover cars after it bought the Rover company in 1994, and Volkswagen has retained the brand names on its Audi, Seat, Skoda and VW ranges.

Market extension occurs when an offer is introduced into a market segment other than the one where it's currently positioned. The UK supermarkets are engaging in market extensions because they're seeing their 'traditional' areas becoming saturated. For example, Sainsbury is encouraging village shops to stock its brands, and Esso and Tesco are combining to provide local stores on garage forecourts. In both cases, new types of customer are being sought. Through recent expansions, Boots is apparently making a similar offer to its UK offers in the Netherlands and South-east Asia.

DISCUSSION
POINT 12.1
Which form of offer extension is likely to be the riskier?

12.2.3 Exit and offer enlargements

A business can enlarge its offers or alternatively exit the competitive arena. But consistent with the definition of business and corporation, enlarging or exiting the competitive arena is a corporate decision. If the business only has one offer and it decides to exit, to cease trading, this is still a corporate decision, although in this case the business and the corporation are the same entity.

12.3 Offer positioning in terms of market share

12.3.1 Profit and market share approaches

Profits and market share are the two main goals for many businesses. Traditionally the Japanese have seen market share as the precursor of profits, whereas the Anglo-Saxon view is to concentrate more on profits *per se*.[4] The differences in a market share-led approach and one focused on profits and profitability are:

- Market share measures what has been put into a relationship, profits what has been taken out.
- Market share faces outwards to the community, profitability faces inwards towards owners.
- In the market share approach, customers are ends in themselves. In profit calculations, customers are a means to the end.
- A focus on market share provides a quicker signalling system to the business – any changes show up sooner in shifting customer needs than is the case with a profit-oriented approach.
- The greater the market share, the more customers and possibly suppliers there are to learn from.

It is commonplace to use market share as a proxy for success, so the relationship between market share and financial returns needs to be explored.

12.3.2 Market share and business performance

There's strong evidence that market share and financial return are associated, as the findings from the PIMS programme[5] shown in Exhibit 12.3 illustrate. Exhibit 12.3a indicates that market share is strongly associated with profitability as measured by return on investment. This is why strategists place such a large emphasis on market share and why market share is often used to characterise the choices that a business is making. However, Exhibit 12.3b shows that within the overall figures there is still success available to small market share businesses. In Exhibit 12.3b relative market share means relative to the combined market share of the competitors with the three largest market shares. This is why relative market shares of over 100% are possible.[6]

DISCUSSION
POINT 12.2
What do Exhibits 12.3a and b tell you?
- It is said that customers buy offers, they don't buy businesses. If this is so, what is the value of results such as the PIMS findings in Exhibit 12.3, which is showing returns on

EXHIBIT 12.3

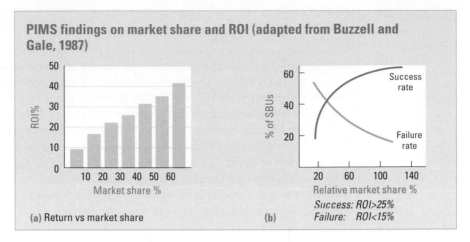

PIMS findings on market share and ROI (adapted from Buzzell and Gale, 1987)

(a) Return vs market share

(b)

Success: ROI>25%
Failure: ROI<15%

investment to a *business*? What do market share and relative market share refer to in these graphs – share of what?

The assumption that large market share leads to enhanced profits has been roundly attacked by Kay:[7] his view is that a large market share is the *result* of success rather than a cause of it. Over the very long term this is probably true, but in the shorter term it would seem that there is a certain amount of circularity in the arguments. Large market share will provide economies of scale and market power, and this will allow the business to enjoy lower than average costs. This cost position can be used to increase value for money in the company's offers, and if this is done its market share is likely to increase still further. However, this progression, shown in Exhibit 12.4, isn't necessarily sustainable in the long term, especially in turbulent times, when fleetness of foot and innovation are so important.

EXHIBIT 12.4

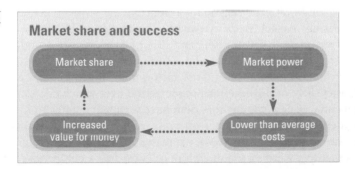

Market share and success

Market share ······> Market power

Increased value for money <······ Lower than average costs

12.3.3 The market share options

There are three basic options when offer positioning is considered in terms of market share: to maintain market share, to increase it or to let it fall. Which is appropriate revolves around how the firm sees its future and how it sees the importance of market share, i.e. where it lies on Exhibit 12.3b.

EXHIBIT 12.5

The curry implosion[8]

After 20 years of spectacular growth which has seen 8000 Indian restaurants in the UK in 1997, restaurant openings have plateaued. The British love affair with Indian cuisine has not faltered, but there is increasing competition from supermarkets for cheap, high-standard, ready-made Indian meals and an increasing sophistication from customers, who are no longer willing to pay for similar anglicised food in restaurants. Additionally, the service offered by the restaurants has slipped; indeed Iqbal Wahheb, when editor of the trade journal *Tandoori*, lambasted Indian waiters for being 'miserable gits' who made eating out akin to attending a funeral. Many Indian restaurants are still in the deprived areas where the low rents made it possible for poor immigrants to start up, and potential customers do not now wish to travel there. Also, there is a problem of getting staff as second-generation Anglo-Asians are reluctant to run the family restaurant.

Maintain market share

A firm may simply seek to maintain market share – to **consolidate**. But a firm is unlikely to maintain market share if it does nothing; to stay exactly the same is not a viable option in the longer term, as competitors will enhance their own offers and thus the firm's offer will degrade relative to theirs. Order-winning features become order-qualifying features and new order-winning features are introduced as customer demands change and new technologies emerge. Thus firms have to run fast simply to stand still; they have to enhance their capabilities or they will lose market share and/or they will lose margin. Cosmetics company Yardley went into receivership in 1998 because it failed to modernise its appeal – and its ageing customer base was also going into liquidation! Exhibit 12.5 illustrates the consequences that not upgrading capabilities can have on a whole set of businesses.

Increase market share

A firm can increase market share either by reducing prices or by increasing perceived value, or by doing both of these together or sequentially. A term often used for increasing market share is **market penetration.** The PIMS findings[9] on the link between market penetration (and loss of market share) and changes in return on investment are shown in Exhibit 12.6a.

Exhibit 12.6b indicates those factors that affect changes in market share. Large market share at the beginning of the period over which change is being measured and the entry of new competitors both have a negative impact on market share, i.e. they reduce it. All the other factors increase market share. Surprisingly perhaps, among all of the businesses in the PIMS database, changes in relative prices among the major competitors were rare; although price is used as a competitive weapon in some markets, in most markets price changes by one competitor are apparently matched by rivals, so that relative prices tend to remain unchanged.

While the costs of gaining share are often high, PIMS found that it was also the case that most businesses that gain market share improve their profitability at the same time. PIMS found that businesses that made the biggest year-on-year gains in share improved their return on investment by an average of 4%. The joint movement of profitability and market share is attributed to two factors. The first is that a business's competitive position improves because of competitor inertia or mistakes: for

EXHIBIT 12.6

Changes in market share and changes in ROI

Change in ROI (points)

Change in market share (%)

Note: Changes are from year to year. The figures shown for ROI are differences between the ROI increases or decreases for each business and the overall average change in ROI among PIMS businesses for a given year.

Factors related to market share changes

Variables	Observed impact on market share*
Beginning competitive position:	
Market share, beginning of period	–
Relative new products	+
Relative product quality	+
Relative customer service	+
Changes during period:	
Relative new products	+
Relative product quality	+
Relative customer service	+
Sales force expenditures**	–
Advertising expenditures**	+
Promotion expenditures**	+
Other marketing expenditures**	+
Uncontrollable events:	
Entry of new competitors	–
Exit of competitors	+

*   Market share changes are from year to year. The measure used is the percentage change from the preceding year. For example, an increase of 2 share points is a 10% change for a business with a beginning market share of 20.

** Changes in sales force, advertising and promotion expenditures are relative to the growth rate of the business unit's served market.

example, the relative quality of one business can rise because the quality of a competitor has fallen. The second is that rising and falling trends in market share usually persist for several years, and many year-on-year gains or losses reflect moves made in the past, which may involve little or no current costs.

A Lloyds TSB director[10] tells what his bank did to increase its market share:

> In the mid 1990s we moved customers who had historically had accounts paying only 1–2% into high interest accounts. This of course had an adverse impact on profitability and the City hated it initially, and then two years later praised us for our great sense: we retained customers and were then selling them more things and so the strategy worked.

Allow market share to fall

The third way forward is not to enhance the offer features and to accept that the value for money in the offer will decline as competitors upgrade, and that the offer will lose market share. The attraction of this is that money will be saved through not upgrading the associated capabilities. This so-called **harvesting** strategy isn't necessarily a bad idea in certain circumstances: why throw good money after bad? If senior management thinks that an offer faces insurmountable long-term competitive disadvantages, it shouldn't persist in what it's doing: it should make the most of the difficult situation and move to get the best it can before exiting. This would appear to be the situation facing many small EU farmers as they await disadvantageous changes in the Common Agricultural Policy and the entry of low-cost East European producers into the EU.

KEY CONCEPT | There are three 'market share' options. These are to **increase market share**: to **consolidate** – maintain market share; and to **harvest** – allowing market share to fall and reap the short-term benefits that will come from not needing to upgrade capabilities.

DISCUSSION POINT 12.3

Why is market share considered an important feature of offer positioning?
- Why are efforts to increase market share not likely to dent profits?
- Why is a business that doesn't enhance its offers likely to lose margin?
- One apparent possibility not considered above is the sale of the firm. Is this the same thing as withdrawal from the market?

12.4   Offer positioning in terms of price and value

Having decided on its portfolio of offers and the market share position it seeks, a further choice in determining a strategic pathway is how the company wishes to compete in its chosen segments – how it wishes to position each of its offers *vis-à-vis* its competitors. Before considering these choices, however, it is useful to consider what is meant by an offer.

12.4.1 What is a single offer?

Although the business remains the main unit of analysis, the pricing and characteristics of the offers it makes are obviously very important, as is how they should be managed. But what constitutes an offer; for example, should a 75cl bottle of wine be considered a different offer from a litre bottle of the same wine? Are a vacuum cleaner and the replacement bags two separate offers? If the answer is *yes*, then each of the pair of items would be treated separately and thus managers would have a portfolio of offers to manage (in this case consisting of just two offers); if the answer is *no*, then the pair of items would be treated as one offer. There are two tests to apply to determine whether two offers should be considered a single offer or not:[11]

- one offer serves as a close substitute for the other;
- the two offers complement each other.

The two bottles of wine would be considered as one offer on the basis of close substitutability. The vacuum cleaner and its replacement bags would be seen as a single offer on the grounds of complementing each other: you buy one and subsequently you are 'forced' to buy the other. The tests boil down to whether the prices that the pair of items can command are determined together: if yes then the items are one; if not then they are separate.

DISCUSSION POINT 12.4 What offer(s) are customers buying when they go to a supermarket? What about fleet car buyers?

12.4.2 Value and price

Price is related to value but not in a completely straightforward way. There is the price that a customer is *prepared to pay* and there is the price that they *do* pay. The price that a customer is prepared to pay is the same as the value, while the price that they do pay is simply the price. Economists call the difference between the value and the price the *consumer surplus*. Thus:

Price that a customer is prepared to pay = price that a customer does pay + consumer surplus

or

Value = price + consumer surplus

The higher the value/price ratio, the larger the value for money that customers perceive they are receiving.

DISCUSSION POINT 12.5 Would *consumer surplus* be better termed *customer surplus*?
- Is the value/price ratio the same as a value-added/price ratio?

Airlines provide a good example of how consumer surpluses can be kept low. You can get cheap flights if you stay at your destination over the weekend – just the sort of offer to appeal to people wanting a weekend break but not to the business traveller. The weekend restriction allows the airlines to keep the price of weekday flights at the high levels that the business market will support, and thus prevent business people from enjoying large consumer surpluses. The weekend reductions allow the use of capacity that would otherwise be idle. Conversely, the organisers of many sporting events (such as Wimbledon and the World Cup) lose a great deal in consumer surplus since they sell many seats at the same price irrespective of the value of the tickets to different customers. Many customers are prepared to pay a great deal more than the face value of the ticket and this of course allows the ticket touts to flourish. They get the consumer surplus 'lost' by the organisers.

It is important to realise that a price doesn't just mean the purchase price; it also includes the costs incurred thereafter: the price of a car includes the purchase price and the maintenance costs, petrol, tax, repairs, membership of a motoring association, etc.

KEY CONCEPT | From a customer's point of view, value and price are the two dimensions to any offer. Value is always perceived value, it is how useful the customer thinks the offer will be to them. Value is the price that a customer is *prepared to pay*. Consumer surplus is the difference between value and the price actually paid. The value/price ratio is a measure of value for money.

12.4.3 Value–price combinations

What is vital in any strategy is for managers to establish the appropriate price–value combination for their offers. A start in exploring appropriate combinations can usefully be made by considering the possible combinations of price and value for a simple offer, one that has only one significant distinguishing feature (other than price). An approximation to this situation might be domestic refrigerators, where the only distinguishing feature between offers is the storage capacity.

Several positions in the value–price space are drawn in Exhibit 12.7. Consider position A. This combination of value and price is one where the offer has a higher than average value with a lower than average price. This will be seen by customers as representing greater value for money than an offer at position D. Similarly, a product at position B will be seen as better value for money than one at C.

EXHIBIT 12.7

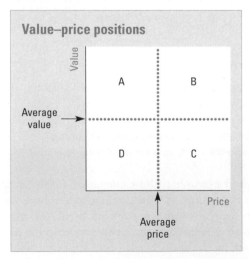

Value–price positions

Position C is where an above-average price is asked for an offer providing below-average value. An offer positioned at C where value is based on only one feature isn't sustainable over time, because for the same price the customer could have the higher-value offer located at B, or could pay the price associated with position D and obtain the same value.

What are the consequences in revenue and market terms for the business offering offer A in a rational market, with B, C and D as the only competitors?

- What if there isn't any feature, other than price, to distinguish offers? How would Exhibit 12.7 look?

12.4.4 Value–price positioning of real offers

In the previous section, the relationship between value and price was explored for a very simple offer, an offer with only one distinguishing feature. With only one distinguishing feature it is possible to say unequivocally that some positions in the value–price space aren't viable, except possibly in the very short term.

In most offers, however, what is being offered is not one distinguishing feature but a bundle of features, and *value* expresses how an individual customer appraises the bundle. That is to say, differentiation is occurring along many dimensions. For example, a mortgage might be differentiated by the size of the deposit required, the payment period, the interest charged, and the conditions surrounding defaulting on payments. Exhibit 12.8 illustrates this explicitly by showing the cluster of value–price positions: this is indicated by the 'cloud'. In general, several positions within the cloud would be taken by offers from competitors. The cloud represents all the positions within the value space that appeal to at least one target customer. Thus an offer that provides less than average value to the *average* customer can still sell at an above-average price (presumably to a small number of customers) if the offer has more of at least one order-winning feature than all other competing offers.

Consider an offer selling at the average price and providing average quality. There are several changes that a business might make to this value–price position. First there

EXHIBIT 12.8

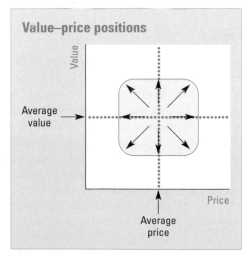

Value–price positions

are the four simple strategies, altering only one of price and value and keeping the other constant, i.e. movement along the horizontal and vertical axes of Exhibit 12.8. *Increasing price* without increasing value will result in increased unit revenue and loss of market share.[12] Conversely, *reducing price* without increasing value will result in reduced unit revenue and increased market share.

Increasing value without changing the price is likely to result in an increase in market share. However, the business will generally incur greater costs in providing this enhanced quality.

DISCUSSION
POINT 12.7

What are the consequences of decreasing value without changing the price?
- Where do the large carriers and the no-frills airlines position themselves in Exhibit 12.8?

There are of course hybrid strategies whereby both the value and price are altered, and this twin approach is very common.

Differentiation of an offer from those of competitors has been achieved when the offer can command a premium price. Another way of looking at differentiation is that it makes an offer less price-sensitive. Differentiation can also be considered as removing competition – the greater the differentation, the fewer competitors there will be. How many competitors are there for Rolls-Royce cars?

12.5 Capability and cost considerations

12.5.1 Capability considerations

Offer enhancement will generally call for a change in the capabilities in the business, typically the upgrading of one or two resources to upgrade a current capability. Offer extensions will entail larger changes, perhaps a fundamental change to a process or even a new process. For example, Boots will need to gain knowledge of the Dutch market when extending into the Netherlands, and Mercedes required additional production processes to support the smaller class A cars it introduced. The renewal and augmentation of resources, processes and capabilities need to match the firm's new offer positioning.

12.5.2 Cost considerations

Many value–price positions are feasible in *market terms* in the sense that customers can be found for the offers. This would certainly occur if above-average value were offered at a below-average price. However, such a position may be unsustainable in *business terms* because it may be that the below-average price puts too great a strain on the business's margins. So the sustainability of a market position is not simply dictated by the market: it's also determined by the cost base of the firm. Of course, the business may have large reserves that can enable it to sustain a loss-making position for a considerable period of time. These reserves may be associated with the corporation to which the business belongs: an example is the pricing of *The Times* newspaper at a loss during the mid-1990s by Rupert Murdoch in an attempt to drive *The Independent* out of business. Exhibit 12.9 lists the possible ways of achieving a low cost position.

EXHIBIT 12.9

Ways of achieving a low cost position

Economies of scale	The reduction in unit costs that occurs as the total number of units produced *per period* increases
Economies of scope	The spreading of costs across many offers
Gains from experience	The reduction in unit costs that occurs as the *cumulative* number of units produced during the lifetime of the business increases
Relatively lower input costs	The use of lower-cost inputs (raw materials and components, finance, information and people) than competitors
Offer innovations	Changes to the offer itself that reduce costs
Process innovations	Changes in the business processes that reduce costs
Collaboration	Spreading the cost with other organisations, including the corporation of which the business is a part

12.6 Access to non-financial resources

How a business obtains access to the non-financial assets it needs, the resources, processes and capabilities to support its intended portfolio of offers, is a further option in the strategic pathway. The phrase 'obtains access to' is used rather than 'acquires' because the business need not own the assets it uses. The finance required to support access will be considered in Section 12.10.

There are three broad ways for a business to gain access to the resources it needs: to buy them, produce them itself (DIY) or collaborate with others in their development. Definitions of these three ways are set out in Exhibit 12.10. The choices between buy, DIY and collaborate lie in:

- dealings upstream in the value chain – with suppliers (region A in Exhibit 12.11, which is a reproduction of Exhibit 10.13);
- dealings downstream in the value chain – with distributors and customers (region B); and
- the scope of the support activities within the value link (region C).

These three areas are considered in the next three sections.

EXHIBIT 12.10

The three modes of access to resources

Buy	Gaining access to the results of another firm's capabilities through market transactions
DIY	Maintain/develop own capabilities through redeployment of current resources or by bringing new resources in house and integrating them into current processes
Collaborate	Augment own capabilities with the resources of another organisation through relationships

EXHIBIT 12.11

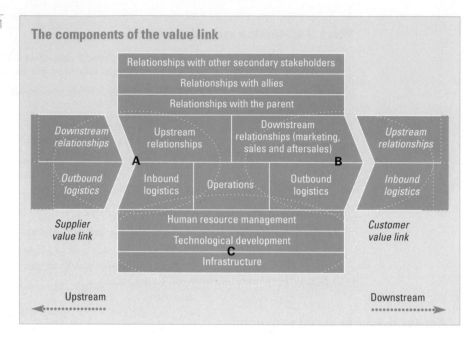

The components of the value link

12.7 Upstream considerations – supplies and suppliers

One choice that has traditionally faced every business is whether to carry out a process itself (DIY), or whether to buy in the results of that process. The view taken by Williamson[13] and others is that the choice between carrying out a process in house and buying lies in the balance of the costs of production/development and those associated with transactions, including the associated risks and uncertainty.

12.7.1 The production/development costs of buy and DIY

Considerations in the buy/DIY decision are as follows:

- Potential suppliers are likely to be producing at a much greater rate than the buying firm, since in general they are supplying many customers and thus enjoy economies of scale that aren't open to the firm itself. These economies of scale should lower costs. This reasoning would suggest that Ford should make its own car engines and that Rolls-Royce, with its very small sales of cars, should opt to buy the engines it needs (as it has done for many years, from BMW).

- The supplier is likely to have specialist expertise that the firm itself can't hope to have. Given its focus, the supplier is likely to have engaged in more extensive benchmarking than would have occurred in house and thus ensure that its operations are state of the art. It would also be expected that the processes would get full management attention from the supplier, which is unlikely when an activity isn't a core activity.

- The supplier can generally support cyclical demand more easily than can an in-house facility, since they are likely to be facing the combined cyclical demands from businesses in several industries.

- A major production consideration concerns the specificity of the assets involved. If the assets needed to carry out the processes are very specific – they have little applicability elsewhere – then it's very unlikely that any firm will wish to supply, and the associated process must be conducted in house. An example is the carbon-fibre blades used in Rolls-Royce aero engines.

12.7.2 Transaction costs

The costs of transactions arise from the effort that must be put into specifying what is required and subsequently co-ordinating delivery, monitoring quality and carrying out a host of other activities. If the product or service required is of a standard or near-standard design, then specification will be straightforward and the transaction costs will be low. However, with sophisticated and idiosyncratic products and services a specification isn't straightforward; for example, there needs to be a great deal of negotiation between the firm and its suppliers in the design and development of many car components. Thus transaction costs can be high.

The cost of supplies isn't the same as the price that that the supplier is paid; there can be many additional costs associated with acquiring a good or a service. Price is only the tip of the iceberg, as Exhibit 12.12 illustrates.[14]

EXHIBIT 12.12

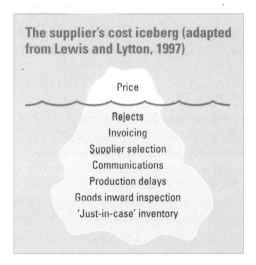

The supplier's cost iceberg (adapted from Lewis and Lytton, 1997)

Price

Rejects
Invoicing
Supplier selection
Communications
Production delays
Goods inward inspection
'Just-in-case' inventory

12.7.3 Supplier relationships

A firm runs several risks when using an outside supplier. First there is the risk of opportunism whereby the supplier pushes up prices or otherwise forces a change in its favour once the client is 'captured'. There is the risk of late or non-delivery, with perhaps considerable knock-on effects, and the risk of the leakage of commercially sensitive information to competitors. As the risks increase the decision will swing towards DIY, or to developing exceptional relationships with the suppliers.

In the wake of the Japanese success with *kanban* and just-in-time approaches, there has been increased interest in moving away from market contracts towards the development of supplier relationships. Although the building of relationships takes time, it may well be worth it when the total costs and the hidden benefits are taken into account, as listed in Exhibit 12.13.

Given that building up supplier relationships takes time and effort, it is important to select the appropriate ones. Exhibit 12.14 illustrates the effort that Dutton Engineering, a firm with a turnover of £2.2 million, takes with its suppliers.

EXHIBIT 12.13

Contrast between traditional and partnership sourcing[15] (developed from Lewis and Lytton, 1997)

Traditional market-based sourcing	Partnership sourcing
• Win/lose confrontation • Price is dominant • Need to check quality • If poor performance, need to find another supplier • Need to renegotiate at regular intervals	• Win/win relationship and mutual profitability • Total cost is dominant • Quality is assured • Work together to improve performance, especially that involving product/service design • Supplier knows present and future requirements • Able to use partners' expertise • Lower stocks and so smaller overdraft • Simpler delivery systems

EXHIBIT 12.14

Supplier assessment at Dutton engineering

Because supplier relationships are so important to Dutton, and because it expects to put a considerable effort into developing a relationship, it is very careful who it selects as suppliers. Dutton's procedure to find top-class suppliers is very thorough. First, some trial business is conducted with suppliers who have ISO 9000 or similar accreditation. If this trial is successful, Dutton gets a team together from the parts of the business that will be directly affected, and it reviews all aspects of the potential supplier's performance. Very many features are considered and placed within the formula:

supplier rating = $(0.3 \times \text{culture}) + (0.25 \times \text{product quality}) + (0.25 \times \text{delivery}) + (0.2 \times \text{price})$

The highest weighting is given to 'culture', with Dutton arguing that it would find it difficult to have a long-term relationship with another organisation that worked in a different way. The cultural assessment includes judging the quality of the paperwork it sends out, how the firm responds to problems and how pro-active it is. Equal weightings are given to product quality, the technical aspects of the supplier's products, and delivery performance. Price is only weighted at 20%; Dutton has found that if the other three factors are not good then any price advantages tend not to be translated into cost advantages. The consequences of deficiencies in cultural fit, quality and delivery performance are likely to outweigh any price advantages.

12.8   Downstream relationships

Just as with suppliers, the firm has the choice to buy, DIY or collaborate downstream in the value chain. These connections are often contractual in nature but overlaid with an on-going developmental relationship. Examples of such relationships include:

- The use of agents   Agents don't normally own the goods they sell. They generally carry stock and take responsibility for credit risks. Although they tend not to be involved in promotional marketing, they would normally distribute catalogues and price lists.

- The use of distributors   Distributors have exclusive or preferential rights to purchase the goods and services they sell. Their remuneration comes from the differences between the purchase and resale price of the offer. They provide all or some of aftersales service, market feedback, forecasting and sales reports, and sales and distribution management. The use of dealers is commonplace in car retailing.

- Licensing   A licence usually gives the rights to manufacture an offer. The licenser should ensure that it produces at least as much volume as the licensee, or the licensee will gain knowledge and improve its operations much more than the licenser. It's also important that the licenser keeps back its technology, as pharmaceutical companies do by not disclosing their R&D.

- Franchising   The franchise holder undertakes specific activities such as manufacturing, distribution and selling. The franchiser is responsible for the brand name, marketing, etc. Examples are Coca-Cola, Tie Rack, Burger King, KFC and Thornton's chocolates. Some UK universities have franchised some of their degree courses to further education colleges.

- Customer relationships   General Electric, the US engineering group, offers long-term maintenance contracts to utilities, basing its revenues on a share of the money that the customer saves through improvements in servicing.[16] The Body Shop was operating a similar sort of arrangement with its distributor in the UK.

12.9   The scope of support activities – in-sourcing and out-sourcing

In-sourcing and *out-sourcing* are both *processes* to change the scope of the business. With in-sourcing, activities are brought into the business's value link, while with out-sourcing they are removed from it. While the terms *in-sourced* and *out-sourced* can be applied to any process, they are usually, but not invariably, applied to support activities. In-sourcing and out-sourcing are in contrast to other buy/DIY/collaborate decisions which tend to involve the primary activities in the value link.

Out-sourcing is the practice of handing over the management and operation of certain processes to a third party, and it has been much in vogue during the last decade. (Facilities management is another term that is sometimes used for out-sourcing.) Examples are the out-sourcing of catering facilities, office cleaning and information technology. Even a company as large as IBM is heavily out-sourced; it effectively out-sourced the MS-DOS PC operating system to what is now Microsoft, part of its hard-disk manufacturing operation to Quantum and its PC microprocessor design to Intel.

Exhibit 12.15 illustrates the reasons for outsourcing the IT function at Rolls-Royce plc.

EXHIBIT 12.15

Rolls-Royce plc IT Out-sourcing to Electronic Data Systems[17]

Rolls-Royce wanted to focus efforts on its area of expertise – making and selling engines – not designing software and buying IT hardware. The search began for a partner who would have access to all the new information technologies and the world's best practice in process improvement and IT deployment.

We looked for a partner who could help us increase added value by deploying IT more effectively (a change management issue) as well as taking over the existing IT infrastructure. EDS was selected because it is world leader in this type of engagement and has substantial aerospace industry experience.

As part of the agreement EDS shares the costs of funding a business improvement programme, which plays a key role in the aerospace businesses' 'better performance faster' activity. In return, it will also share in the tangible benefits resulting from improved performance.

In essence, it is a long-term risk-sharing partnership. Rolls-Royce, EDS and its consultancy arm AT Kearney will share both the risks and rewards involved.

Discussion point 12.8

What are the dangers for Rolls-Royce plc in out-sourcing its IT?
● Should Rolls-Royce keep any of its IT developments in house?

KEY CONCEPT Using the market has the advantages that it allows the business to avoid dis-economies of scale and retain flexibility. The downside of using markets is that the transaction costs tend to be higher than if done in house, the flexibility over speci-fication is lower, and organisational learning may be hampered. When opportunism and high uncertainty are absent, it is only for idiosyncratic transactions and where a supplier doesn't have any significant economies of scale that the goods or services should be provided in house. In all other situations, use of markets with some form of contract yet with strong supplier relationships would appear to be preferable.

12.10 Sources of funds

12.10.1 Types of funds

Whatever method is used to gain access to additional non-financial resources, fund-ing will be required. Conventionally, funding is considered to be short, medium or long term, although the definitions aren't totally clear-cut. Short-term funds are those to cover normal operations and can be taken to mean finance available for up to one year. Medium-term funds are those available for between one and five years, with long-term greater than five years. Short- and medium-term funds will tend to be used for organisational enhancement and extension and thus they are the sources most likely to be used by businesses. Long-term funds are more associated with enlargements and thus are much more likely to be a corporate concern; as such, their discussion will be deferred until Chapter 17.

12.10.2 Asset management

Perhaps at first sight it may seem rather odd to consider asset management as a source of funds. Good asset management is concerned with ensuring efficient operations and as such reduces the need to seek funding elsewhere. There are several areas where good asset management can reduce this need:

- Stock control   Stock levels, both for raw materials and finished goods, can be kept low through efficient operations. Just-in-time systems whereby stock is made available a very short time before it is needed, the sort of operation pioneered by Toyota and now used by all the large car assemblers, are perhaps the ultimate in keeping low stock levels. Efficient scheduling can enable little, or no, finished goods stock to be held, especially with the relationships that develop with customers.

- Trade credit   Trade credit is the credit obtained from suppliers or given to customers. It is a widespread practice in the UK and a necessary term of trade; most suppliers would lose considerable custom if they reduced their credit terms below the norm. However, both the supplier credit taken and the customer credit extended need to be managed in order to reduce the working capital required by the business. There are dangers to keeping creditors waiting, and it isn't ethical, nor is it advisable, if the firm is trying to build good relations with its suppliers.

- Deferred tax   While tax is all but inevitable, deferred payment is one way in which cash can be retained in the business.

- Retained profits   The most common way of funding developments is to use the profits that the business generates rather than take it out of the business, either the owner-manager taking the money or it being given to shareholders as dividends. The pressure on senior management to provide large dividend payments is against retention, since there's always the temptation to show regular advances in dividend per share. High retention policies will be favoured by firms that can't offset their advance corporation tax.

12.10.3 Short-term external sources of funds

In most businesses, even the best asset management isn't sufficient to provide all the finance required. There are several external sources of short-term finance open to a business:

- Overdrafts   These are sources of short-term funds made available by the banks. They are by far the most popular source of short-term funds for UK business.[18] Overdrafts are very flexible, as portions of the outstanding sum can be paid back at any time, and interest is only payable on the negative balance outstanding rather than on the agreed maximum facility. However, overdrafts are unreliable, as the interest rate is variable and in theory the bank can demand repayment at any time and at very short notice. (In practice, the bank may wish to avoid the stigma of driving a firm into liquidation, which the demand for repayment at short notice is bound to stimulate.) Banks will normally require an overdraft to be secured against company or personal assets.

- Factoring   Although there are several variants in factoring, the same principle applies – the debts owing to the company, usually customers yet to pay for offers received, are used to obtain funds earlier than would be the case if the business waited for payment in the normal way. A third party, a factor, often takes responsibility for all the invoicing and debt collection. For this they receive a percentage of the invoice value. Factors can also provide protection against bad debts. The merit of factoring is that the firm is sure of its cash flow and it isn't involved in chasing up bad debts, which factors have more skill in doing. Certain companies, the high-street banks for instance, use factors to distance themselves from the damage to their reputation that might be incurred through being associated with some of the less publicity-worthy aspects of debt collection.

- Bills of exchange   Bills of exchange are IOUs and are a commitment to pay a specified sum at a later date. They can be referred to as bills, drafts or acceptances and often come with a label, for example bank drafts, bank bills, time drafts and bankers' acceptances. The simplest form of bill is the post-dated cheque. If an offer is received on 1 January and a cheque dated 1 March is sent to the supplier, the supplier is giving the buyer two months credit, since the bank will only honour the cheque on or after 1 March. The supplier can retain the cheque when it is received in January or it can be sold at a lower or discounted rate to a bank or discount house, and the money obtained used in the business. A *commercial* bill of exchange is prepared by the supplier and is now used mainly for overseas trade, where there might be a long delay between the sending and reception of an offer. Bills are traded on the money market by the commercial banks.

12.10.2   Medium-term finance

- Bank term loans   These are loans offered by banks for periods longer than one year. The loan is made for a fixed period of time, with repayment either as a lump sum at the end of the period or through periodic instalments. They can be arranged at variable or fixed rates of interest. For variable rate loans, the rate is usually 2–5% above the bank's base rate, depending on the credit rating of the client.

- Hire purchase   Hire purchase would be used for such things as the purchase of equipment. A hire purchase company, typically a finance company, buys the equipment, which the firm can then use in return for a series of rental payments. After all the payments have been made the firm will become the owner of the equipment. The benefit to the firm is that the cash flow is smoother, with a set of payments over time rather than the full purchase price at the beginning. Security on the loan resides in the equipment itself.

- Leasing   Leasing is a very popular source of finance[19] and is similar to hire purchase. The difference is that at the end of the lease period, the firm using the equipment (the lessee) doesn't become the owner of it. It's quite common for the lessee to be given the option of extending the original lease at the end of the initial period. The rental payments during this extension are often extremely low and are referred to as 'peppercorn rents'. As well as the advantage of smoother cash flows and the immediate use of the equipment, leasing can have tax advantages. If a firm isn't producing taxable profits it won't be immediately able to obtain investment allowances; on the other hand, the firm leasing out the equipment will be making profits and will be able to obtain these allowances. Thus the cost of the equipment to the lessor is less than to the lessee. With equipment such as computers and company cars, where to be up to date is important, the lessor frees the lessee from the burden of constant change.

- Sale and leaseback   With sale and leaseback, a business can convert some of its assets into funds and continue to be able to have use of them. A company might sell a building, to an insurance company for example, and at the same time lease the building back from it. This provides an immediate, and probably large, cash inflow to the firm, but with a subsequent set of rental payments. There is also the loss of any capital appreciation associated with the asset.

- Mortgaging property   Rather than sale and leaseback, a firm might choose to mortgage its property. This is identical in principle to the individual buying their house, but with an insurance or investment company or pension fund supplying the finance rather than a building society. Repayments can be spread over a long period of time. The advantage of a mortgage over a sale and leaseback scheme is that the benefits of ownership are retained, which can be quite valuable if property values are rising.

DISCUSSION
POINT 12.9

What are the disadvantages of a mortgage over sale and leaseback?

- Loan guarantee scheme   This scheme was introduced into the UK to help smaller firms with little or no record of obtaining medium-term finance, mainly because of lack of security. It resembles schemes operating successfully in other European countries.[20] Banks provide loans of from two to ten years to firms and the government guarantees to refund between 70 and 85% of the loan if the firm fails. The borrower pays a premium to the government (typically around 3% more than the bank's commercial rate).

- Corporate venturing   This is a form of capital injection that a large company can make into a small company. The large company might take an equity stake, usually a minority equity stake, to gain access to the small company's innovative R&D or to an innovative product. The advantage of corporate venturing is that if the corporation restricts itself to ventures near to its competencies, it will be in a far better position to understand the situation than will a bank, which is unlikely to have the expertise to be able to evaluate the business prospects. 3M receives a great many unsolicited bids for corporate venture finance from inventors, as apparently does Shell.[21]

- Venture capitalists   There are two forms of venture capitalist. First there are

EXHIBIT 12.16

Bringing up flat-top baby[22]

Dick Cooper has been approached with takeover offers. He has been paid not to talk, his premises have been broken into, and he has nearly lost his house. He has also collected more air miles than he cares to remember co-ordinating a private research programme over three continents. But now, after five years of struggle, the 52-year-old's dream of producing the world's first affordable wall-mounted TV screen is becoming a reality.

At the beginning of 1999, he is set to sign a technology partnership with a large American ceramics company to complete development of his 'vision tiles'. These are solid-state, colour-display circuits, about the size of a bathroom tile and a few millimetres thick, that can be assembled side by side to make a flat-panel TV and computer display screens of virtually any size.

In April 1999, Mr Cooper was planning to unveil a £1 million pilot assembly laboratory that will produce a flat panel display every 20 minutes, with robot arms snapping tiles together like an Airfix kit. By the summer, P1, a prototype palm-top computer screen, should be ready. It will be followed at the end of the year by P2, a prototype flat-panel display for a desk-top computer. This could mean the end of liquid crystal displays and a massive $40 to $50 billion market, says Mr Cooper.

'In one month a UK venture capital company offered to take control of us for £2 million and a Japanese flat-panel display manufacturer wanted to buy us out.' Although the Japanese offered him a lot more money than the venture capital company, it wanted him to go and work in Japan. 'I don't like Japan, the weather's terrible,' Mr Cooper says.

He did not take up the offer of venture capital because he was not prepared to take on a secondary role with his baby. 'The price was so expensive – they wanted control. And they didn't have the expertise to support us through our development programme.' British venture capital companies are naïve about high technology, he says. 'We were showing them the holy grail and they didn't have a clue what we were offering them. It was a waste of time talking to them.'

As a result, he says, Ceravision has turned down over £5 million of venture capital funding. Then three months ago, a US company paid Ceravision $300,000 for rights to the desk-top monitor application. 'Not to develop it, but to stop us talking to anyone else about it. They wanted us to do it for them eventually, but wanted a "put" option for three months so that we didn't talk to anyone else.' Negotiations are now underway with that company to take the P2 desk-top display prototype into production within two years.

It was while Cooper was working for Alcoa in the USA, developing a production line to encapsulate Intel's first Pentium computer chip, that he came up with the idea of the 'vision tile' and his dream of a flat TV screen hung on the wall like a picture.

Funding for Ceravision has all come from private investors. Two initial rounds of a few hundred thousand, both oversubscribed, he says, came from friends and small investors. But last year Ceravision raised a third tranche of funding worth around £2 million. There are now 20 shareholders in the company, including a group of Americans living in London and a group of British expatriates in the Middle East.

'We have some very wealthy, skilled and experienced backers who have supported us unflinchingly,' says Mr Reynolds, Cooper's partner. 'We're in the lucky position of being able to turn down venture capital. But we worked hard around the world to get the right funding in place.'

Mr Cooper and Mr Reynolds hold most of the shares. The board has been strengthened by the appointment of a chairman, Daniel Taylor, who set up Hewlett-Packard's European operations.

Ceravision, which now employs four people in the USA and five in the UK, is based at the government-run Rutherford Appleton Laboratory research facilities in Didcot. In a ground-breaking deal for Ceravision 18 months ago, RAL took an equity stake in the company in return for use of office space and RAL's chip fabrication equipment. 'It's the only place in Europe that can do the microstructure we need until we can afford to produce our own equipment,' says Mr Cooper. 'To buy the equipment would cost us £20 million.' He says its stake in Ceravision has been 'character-forming' for RAL.

Although Ceravision has patented everything it can about its flat-screen process, Messrs Reynolds and Cooper recognise that their patents are only worth what they are prepared to spend defending them. 'We have had some issues of security recently. We've got a lot of people upset and one or two companies have tried to find out what we're doing. We have had break-ins.' But, unfazed by the prospect of giving Britain a major lead in display technology, he says there is only one thing bothering him: 'Nostradamus. He predicts the end of the world in May.'

Discussion point 12.10

List the sources of funds that Dick Cooper has used to support his 'baby's' development.

- If British venture capitalists are naïve about high technology, what alternatives are open to people like Dick Cooper?

individuals who obtain funds from a variety of sources and pool these to support projects for a specified period of time and then liquidate them. These are sometimes termed 'angels' and are frequently used to support West End theatrical shows. Second are the subsidiaries of major financial institutions, banks and insurance companies, that channel money into risky enterprises. Examples are Apax, Cinven, Candover and CVC. Apax Partners backed Chris Evans when he bought Virgin Radio and Kelvin MacKenzie when he bought out Talk Radio. It owns PPL Therapeutics, the biotechnology firm that famously cloned Dolly the sheep. CVC acquired businesses worth around £5 billion in the two years 1997 and 1998, operates in 22 countries and employs more than 45,000 people in such firms as William Hill (bookmakers), Britton Group (plastics) and Smurfit Condat (paper).[23] Venture capitalists are usually interested in providing funds of £250,000 or over, generally to existing companies with high growth potential. This capital is cheaper than bank finance and also the capitalist will provide a partner with business expertise. However, accepting this sort of finance will tend to mean loss of control.

Experiences with venture capitalists and with using other forms of finance are illustrated in Exhibit 12.16.

SUMMARY

- Strategic options are the broad choices open to a business. The set of options that the business selects constitutes its strategic pathway. There are five main considerations for leader-managers when they are thinking about possible strategic pathways. These are:
  - the portfolio of offers that the business makes;

- • the positioning of its offers in the market;
- • the resources required to support these offers;
- • the form of access to non-financial resources;
- • the source of funds. EXHIBIT 12.1, EXHIBIT 12.2
- • Offer positioning is both in terms of market share and in terms of value and price. There are three market share options: market penetration, consolidation and harvesting. EXHIBIT 12.3, EXHIBIT 12.4, EXHIBIT 12.6
- • Value and price determine the offer positioning. *Business positioning* integrates the offer positioning with the cost base that will support the value–price combination chosen. EXHIBITS 12.7 TO 12.9
- • There are three broad options for gaining access to non-financial resources: to buy the results of another firm's capabilities, to acquire the resource yourself, or to collaborate with others to provide the resources needed through the development of relationships. These modes are used to obtain access to supplies, distribute offers and to reduce the cost of/enhance the quality of the firm's processes. EXHIBIT 12.10, EXHIBIT 12.11
- • Supplies can cost much more than their price as the supplies iceberg demonstrates. Good relationships with suppliers have many advantages, in terms of overall costs and organisational learning. EXHIBITS 12.12 TO 12.14
- • Insourcing and outsourcing are both processes to change the scope of the business. The terms are generally applied to support functions. With insourcing activities are brought into the business's value link, while in outsourcing they are removed from it.
- • There are three main sources of funds for businesses: asset managment, short-term funds for up to a year, and medium-term funds for up to five years.

SELF-CHECK

1 Reconsider the learning outcomes for this chapter. Check that you feel confident that you can carry out the activities listed there.

2 Having read this chapter, you should be able to define the following terms:

agent	distributor	mortgage
bank term loan	DIY (access to resources)	out-sourcing
bill of exchange	factoring	overdraft
brand stretching	franchising	price
buy (access to resources)	harvesting	sale and leaseback
collaborate (access to resources)	hire purchase	trade credit
consolidation	in-sourcing	value
consumer surplus	leasing	value link
corporate venturing	licensing	venture capitalist
deferred tax	market penetration	

MINI-CASE 12.1

Virtuality[24]

By wearing a special headset it's possible to experience a computer-generated three-dimensional world. Instead of visualising a 2-D image from a computer screen, the image appears everywhere. This experience is known as virtual reality (VR). It is an industry that is evolving rapidly.

Virtuality Group plc, with subsidiaries in the UK, the USA and Japan, is the leading supplier of VR systems and software in the location-based entertainment market, with an estimated 75% global market share. Location-based entertainment is an out-of-home centre in which people may be attracted to the leisure services offered, such as theme parks and family entertainment centres. Virtuality's systems have been installed not only in amusement arcades but also in retail outlets, cafés, bars and theatres.

In May 1993, Virtuality signed a licensing agreement with Sega of Japan for use in its interactive game centres and arcades, 50 of which are planned to open by the year 2000. The first model was demonstrated at an amusement machine exhibition in Japan in October. In the home VR market, Virtuality has a licensing agreement with Takara, in which it has customised a head-mounted display suitable for use as a personal viewing device. Licensing offers an opportunity for strategic partners to share in the technological know-how of Virtuality, but under the terms and conditions agreed between both partners. Licensing offers Virtuality not only development fees but future royalties on sales.

Despite a recent cyclical downturn in the out-of-home entertainment business, the future of Virtuality appears bright. Innovation and product development are improving the quality of VR technology and making it more affordable as new consumer markets are sought. For example, new head-mounted displays are 20% the weight of previous models. Also, the improving price/performance ratio of VR computing is increasing the demand in the home market. Demand is set to grow with rising consumer expectations of their graphics requirements, as the Internet becomes progressively more integrated with 3-D images and VR environments.

Virtuality is now focusing on exploiting its higher-margin industrial applications. Many industrial applications generate higher margins because of customised specifications required to match client needs. It is building relationships leading to further licensing agreements. A wide variety of applications are possible, as town planners, architects, interior designers and property developers are finding uses for it. Car, ship and airline manufacturers have used VR to test ergonomic factors in the early design stages.

Virtuality also provides a range of software, which it sells for entertainment and industrial applications. Applications include sports simulation and medical training. Today, the company is a leading developer of VR software and has systems in more than 40 countries, and an estimated 50 million people have played its games.

Discussion point 12.11

List Virtuality's portfolio of offers.

- Where might it make offer extensions?
- What new resources would be needed to support these extensions?
- What is the value of licensing to Virtuality?

MINI-CASE 12.2

That'll be the Daewoo[25]

Daewoo is an $8.4 billion Seoul-based shipbuilding and electronics conglomerate which is also one of Asia's biggest firms. Despite its size, its roots are surprisingly recent. It was founded in 1967 by Kim Woo Chong with three associates and $18,000 of capital. Daewoo cars arrived in Europe in April 1995 with some fresh sales techniques (no dealerships, no salesmen). They launched the most successful launch in the history of British mass motoring, with the aim of obtaining 1% market share. By March 1996 it had reached that goal. In a European market which was sluggish during 1995, Korean manufacturers doubled their share, in which established Korean makers, Hyundai and Kia, had also improved sales. Whilst the Europeans have improved the quality of their cars and cut costs, the Koreans can afford to drop prices with less restrictive import controls than their Japanese competitors, which are currently set at 10% of the market. Consequently, during 1995, the Japanese manufacturers, such as Toyota, Mazda and Nissan, have lost sales.

Despite the Japanese believing they have the edge in advanced technology over their Korean competitors, the Japanese are lobbying behind the scenes for a relaxation of European controls or tighter controls on Korean exports to Europe. British car firms have great difficulty in selling cars in Korea (due to problems in setting up distribution networks and the abnormally high tariffs and taxes), whereas in Japan, land and labour are scarce and expensive for manufacturing, and loyalty is entrenched for home-made motors.

Daewoo's ambitions are to enter the USA by 1997 with bargain-based cars selling in mass merchandisers such as Sears and K mart, with estimated sales at 100,000 units per year. It is currently investing in plants in Eastern Europe, where labour is cheap, for export to Britain. Plants and distribution deals are also planned for Russia, India, China, Iran and the Philippines. However, feedback on the Korean-based Kia and Hyundai has been disappointing in the States, suggesting improvements required in customer satisfaction and perceived quality. One commentator suggested Korean cars have an image problem there, although there are benefits to be claimed in becoming established in the American market.

The demand for cars in the States attracts volume producers. The intensified competition attracted by the huge demand for cars in the States presents a challenge to any volume producer. This competition also encourages constant refinement. Whilst there is always room for a better mouse-trap, the demand based on affordability will come mostly from the emerging economies of the former Soviet Union and other Eastern bloc areas, India and South America. The costs of production and marketing are generally lower in these countries. A recent success has been the agreement to sell its cars to the government in Moscow, designed for a state-run taxi service.

Discussion point 12.12

Why is Daewoo successful in European markets and will this necessarily follow in the USA?

- How is Daewoo positioning its offers?
- Which capabilities did Daewoo need to enter the UK market, and which of the capabilities that the encumbents had did it bypass?

FURTHER
DISCUSSION
POINTS

1 For GSM:
- Use Exhibit 12.1 to sketch out the strategic pathway associated with the Primographic purchase.
- What is GSM's portfolio of offers?
- How is GSM giving value to its customers?
- What might be GSM's next offer enhancements and extensions?
- What new capabilities might it need to make this extension?

2 Charles Baillie, CEO of Toronto-Dominion Bank, responding (in January 1999) to the engagement of his competitors, the Royal Bank of Canada and the Bank of Montreal, said: 'You succeed by being smarter. Size is not a strategy, it's a statistic.'[25] What is your view on this?

3 In Section 12.4.3, would the single distinguishing feature be an order-qualifying or an order-winning feature?

ASSIGNMENTS

1 For an organisation of your choice, identify the offers made and the offer positioning.
2 For an organisation of your choice, determine the components of the supplier's cost iceberg.
3 Follow up an out-sourcing agreement in an organisation of your choice. Identify the advantages and disadvantages compared with carrying out the activity in house.

FURTHER READING

The arguments against economies of scale are well presented by John Kay in his book *Foundations of Corporate Success: How Business Strategies Add Value*, Oxford University Press, 1993.

Two books are suggested to those wishing to consider sources of funding in more detail and to see worked examples. These are Richard Pike and Bill Neale, *Corporate Finance and Investment: Decisions and Strategies*, 2nd edn, Prentice Hall, 1996) and J.M. Samuels, F.M. Wilkes and R.E. Brayshaw, *Financial Management & Decision Making*, International Thomson Business Press, 1999.

CHAPTER NOTES AND REFERENCES

1 It's useful to reiterate the position taken in this book, that the emphasis in Chapters 6–15 inclusive is on the business level. Consequently, offer enlargements, access methods involving full-blown alliances and longer-term financial funding arrangements are all considered to be corporate rather than business activities and thus left until Chapters 16–18.

2 As Boots is entering a new market it would be increasing its market share.

3 Hampden-Turner, C. and Trompenaars, F., *The Seven Cultures of Capitalism: Value Systems for Creating Wealth in the United States, Britain, Japan, Germany, France, Sweden, and the Netherlands*, Doubleday, 1993, p. 67.

4 *Ibid.*, p. 186.

5 Buzzell, R.D. and Gale, B.T., *The PIMS Principles: Linking Strategy to Performance*, Free Press, 1987, p. 94.

6 For example, if a firm had 40% market share and its three main rivals held 16%, 12% and 7% of the market, then the firm's relative market share would be 114% (40/(16+12+7) × 100 = 114).

7 Kay, J., *Foundations of Corporate Success: How Business Strategies Add Value*, Oxford University Press, 1993. Kay considers the diseconomies of scale and the sizes of firms that survive, and the optimum size derived from engineering estimates.

8 Buzzell, R.D. and Gale, B.T., *op. cit.*, pp. 190–91; and *PIMS Letter*, No. 37, 'Calibrating the Cost(?) of Gaining Market Share', The Strategic Planning Institute, 1986.

9 Rowe, M., 'Has the great British curry house finally had its chips?' *The Independent on Sunday*, 14 February 1999, p. 3.

10 McConchie, D.R., 'Patterns of strategic control: an investigation of British, French and German retail banking practice', PhD thesis, Loughborough University, 1998.

11 Mathur, S.S. and Kenyon, A., *Creating Value: Shaping Tomorrow's Business*, Butterworth-Heinemann, 1997, pp. 55–60.

12 Unless the offer is what economists term a superior good, one where a high price signals high quality and results in increased sales.

13 Williamson, O.E., *Markets and Hierarchies*, The Free Press, 1975; and *The Economic Institutions of Capitalism*, The Free Press, 1985.

14 Lewis, K. and Lytton, S., *How to Transform Your Company and Enjoy It!*, 2nd edn, Management Books 2000, 1997, p. 93.

15 *Ibid.*, p. 96.

16 Wagstyl, S., 'When even a rival can be a best friend', *Financial Times*, 'The Global Company', 22 October 1997, p. 17.

17 Budjinski, W. Director of Information Technology Rolls-Royce plc, Rolls-Royce/EDS publication issued May 1998.

18 Samuels, J.M., Wilkes, F.M. and Brayshaw, R.E., *Financial Management and*

Decision Making, International Thomson Business Press, 1999, p. 411 reports that: 'A survey in 1994 indicated that 70% of UK business relies heavily on overdrafts, compared with 37% in Germany relying on short-term funds.'

19   *Ibid.*, p. 429 states when considering the UK that 'leasing accounts for between 20% and 25% of all new assets acquired.'

20   Pike, R. and Neale, B., *Corporate Finance and Investment: Decisions and Strategies*, 2nd edn, Prentice Hall, 1996, p. 400.

21   *Ibid.*, p. 468.

22   Extract from Dunn, J., 'Bringing up flat-top baby', *The Guardian*, 26 January 1999, p. 22.

23   Finch, J. and Buckingham, L., 'New breed dares to differ', *Finance Guardian*, 27 February 1999, p. 28.

24   Davies, M., *Understanding Marketing*, Prentice Hall, 1998, pp. 182–3.

25   *Ibid.*, pp. 57–8.

26   Quoted in the 'Financial Post' section of *National Post* (Canada), 2 January 1999, p. D4.

CHAPTER **13** **Strategic choice**

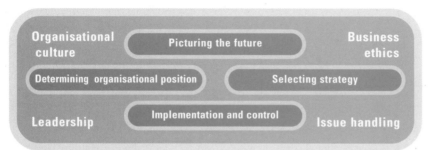

t his is the second chapter concerned with the selection of strategy. In the previous chapter the characteristics of the possible choices facing all businesses were discussed; i.e. the generic options in each area of choice. In this chapter we explore how a business might choose the particular set of options that will constitute its chosen strategic pathway.

The chapter opens with a consideration of the types of screening that are required to ensure that a theoretically possible strategy is a suitable one. The first form of screening is an audit of strategic fit, for which examples are first given and then the underlying principles are discussed. Major considerations are that any competitive advantage that the business obtains is sustained and that the value associated with the advantage accrues to the firm rather than to others. One area of particular concern is the protection of intellectual property rights. Following these considerations of strategic fit, two other tests of the suitability of a strategic pathway are considered. Feasibility is concerned with whether the resources necessary to implement the proposed strategy can be accessed. Acceptability is concerned with whether stakeholders will be supportive of the proposals.

The particular set of choices that determine a firm's strategic pathway often involve significant investments, generally include major resource allocations and frequently alter the basis of competitive advantage. Choosing the most appropriate options for a business's strategic pathway is thus among the most important activities that leader-managers engage in. Thus it is crucial that all aspects of the suitability of a proposed strategy are fully explored.

LEARNING
OUTCOMES

When you have worked through this chapter, you should be able to:

- list and describe the three tests of suitability that should be applied to any proposed strategy;

- explain how the four types of strategic resource contribute to strategic fit;

- describe the factors that affect the sustainability and appropriability of competitive advantage;

- describe the main forms of intellectual property rights;

- check that a proposed strategic pathway is feasible;

- check that a proposed strategic pathway is acceptable.

13.1 The main considerations in determining strategic suitability

SWOT analyses sum up the strengths and weaknesses of a firm and the opportunities and threats that it faces. They encapsulate both the firm's short-term and its longer-term future situation. Thus the important features of the firm's position *vis-à-vis* both its competitors and the environment have been assessed. The strategic options discussed in the previous chapter suggest a range of possible choices. Together, the SWOT analyses and a knowledge of the possible options provide a great many plausible strategic pathways. To judge whether any particular initially plausible pathway is practical and appropriate, it needs to pass three different screening processes, or audits:

- Audit of strategic fit   This is concerned with the fit between what is proposed and the organisation's aspirations and capabilities, and whether the proposed strategy is a suitable response to environmental events and trends.

- **Feasibility audit** This is concerned with whether the intended strategy can be implemented: with whether the resources can be obtained and with whether processes can be devised to support the proposed new pathway within suitable timescales.

- **Acceptability audit** This is concerned with how acceptable the strategy would be to all the organisational stakeholders. The concern would primarily be with the outcomes of the strategy, but not exclusively so: process considerations would also play a part. A particular concern is the risk that each group of shareholders will be running.

Although the search for a strategic pathway will be triggered by the vision the business has and the business goals it has set itself, Exhibit 13.1 indicates that the vision and goals don't necessarily remain inviolate as the search for a strategic pathway proceeds. The search will first be within the chosen vision and goals, but if no appropriate pathway can be found, then the vision and goals will need to be changed and the search for an appropriate pathway resumed.

13.2 Examples of strategic fit

To appreciate the concept of strategic fit, several examples will be given, mainly revolving around the choices of market share and offer extensions and reductions.

EXHIBIT 13.1

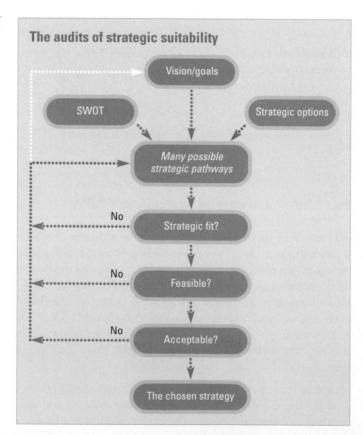

The audits of strategic suitability

Vision/goals

SWOT

Strategic options

Many possible strategic pathways

Strategic fit? — No

Feasible? — No

Acceptable? — No

The chosen strategy

The examples present simple clear-cut reasons for a choice; in practice, many factors will influence the choice of pathway.

13.2.1 Market share considerations[1]

Consolidation occurs when a business decides to maintain its market share. This option would appear to fit strategically when:

- an owner-manager wishes their firm to remain the same size as it is now, for example because they are near retirement, or because they don't wish to relinquish control to others;
- market share isn't an important driver of profit;
- no funding is available to support market penetration or offer extensions.

Market penetration occurs when market share is increased in one of the segments the firm is currently addressing. This option would appear to fit strategically when:

- current markets are not saturated for the types of offer the firm is making;
- present customers can be induced to buy more;
- increased economies of scale provide significant competitive advantages;
- the firm has spare production or distribution capacity.

Harvesting occurs when the market share is allowed to decline. This option would appear to fit strategically when:

- there is no money available for the enhancements needed to retain market share;
- the firm's markets are being hit by cheap imports;
- the firm's reputation has suffered and can't be reclaimed.

13.2.2 Offer extension and reduction

Offer extension can take two forms, depending on where the emphasis in development is placed.[2]

Market development is where the emphasis is on new markets, with the same or similar product/services as are currently offered. This option would appear to fit strategically when:

- good new channels of distribution are available;
- the business is strong in marketing;
- it has superior products to its competitors;
- unsaturated markets exist;
- the business has excess production capacity;
- the competitive arena is becoming global;
- economies of scale are significant.

Product/service development is where the emphasis is on developing the product/service itself, with the offer placed in the firm's current markets. This option would appear to fit strategically when:

- the firm's or its brand's reputation is high, and this reputation can feasibly be attached to new offers, i.e. brand stretching;

- the competitive arena is characterised by rapid technological developments;
- major competitors offer better-quality products at comparable prices;
- the business has especially strong research and development capabilities;
- economies of scope are significant.

Offer reduction is where the business decides to reduce its portfolio of offers. This option would appear to fit strategically when:

- there are few economies of scope or scale and the offer isn't profitable;
- the support budget would be better used elsewhere;
- the offer is cannibalising other offers that provide better margins.

13.3 Tests of strategic fit

The above examples give a flavour of the areas where strategic fit could exist. We now move on to consider more formally a wide range of criteria that should be used to test the strategic fit of a proposed strategic pathway.

13.3.1 Types of fit

Exhibit 13.2 summarises the questions that need to be answered in determining strategic fit. A significant consideration is the match between the business and its environment, both in the short and longer terms. In the short term, the concern is primarily with offer and process enhancements; in the longer term with offer and process extensions. Both approaches need to be considered when determining the appropriate strategic pathway.

A second main considerations is with 'internal' matters; how the proposed strategy fits with the vision and goals, with the other offers in the business portfolio, and with how the strategic resources will be changed if the proposed strategy is implemented. Finally, the sustainability of the proposed strategy and whether the firm can appropriate the rewards of it need to be addressed.

EXHIBIT 13.2

Assessing strategic fit

Sustainability and appropriability?

How does it leave the strategic resources?

Synergy of portfolio?

Fit to vision/ goals?

Proposed strategy

Fit to strategic resources?

Fit to the short-term environment?

Fit to the longer-term environment

From SWOT analyses

13.3.2   Fit with strategic resources and with the environment

A significant consideration with any new strategy is whether it fits with the firm's current strategic resources. If a proposed strategy requires strategic resources that are dissimilar to the current strategic resources, requiring a large number of augmentations to the firm's capabilities, then the proposed strategy is unlikely to be suitable.

The three items on the right-hand side of Exhibit 13.2 would be expected to be derived from SWOT analyses, where the strengths and weaknesses would be based on the strategic resources, and the opportunities and threats would surface from an environmental analysis. Thus little will be said about this except to discuss the special role played by reputation and competitor reactions.

Reputation

Value is composed of two portions: the value that is intrinsic to the offer, and that would be recognised as such by customers if they had sufficient trials to determine it, and the value that is associated with the reputation of the offer. Thus:

$$\text{Value} = \text{Intrinsic value} + \text{reputation value}$$

Redrawing Exhibit 12.7 as Exhibit 13.3 illustrates the power of reputation.

EXHIBIT 13.3

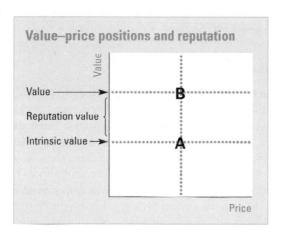

Suppose that an offer was positioned at position A, offering only intrinsic value, i.e. with no reputation. By contrast, another offer (B) has the same intrinsic value but also the reputation value as shown. The value of reputation enhances the value over and above the intrinsic value, allowing the offer to be positioned at B and anywhere else along the value line, allowing a higher price to be charged without losing sales. Alternatively, the intrinsic value could be lowered while maintaining price.

The power of reputation doesn't just have an impact on the firm's offers and its customers. Reputation can also be associated with the business or with its owner. This reputation can be very valuable in dealing with other stakeholders, particularly with banks and other sources of funds, which see a good reputation as enhancing the firm's creditworthiness and thus adjust their interest rates accordingly.

Competitor reaction

The analysis so far hasn't emphasised the interactive nature of market behaviour. Neither customers nor competitors are going to stand idly by as a competitor changes its portfolio of offers and its offer positioning.

In a monopoly or in a perfect market, competitor reactions are of little concern or are easy to discern. They are also of little concern where the market is led by one firm, which is so strongly positioned that it sets prices and generally provides an 'orderly market'. Where competitor reactions are significant is when an oligopoly exists in which no one player is dominant. In such a market there's no stable relationship between price and sales level since no definite assumptions can be made about the future behaviour of competitors: behaviour is psychologically based in the minds of the dominant coalitions in the competitors. Some competitors will be risk takers, others risk-averse. Some will want a quiet life, while others revel in publicity. Flair in predicting and anticipating moves of opponents is thus an important attribute of leader-managers; an army commander in the field always wants to know the identity of the commander who opposes them.

Game theory can be used to understand the theoretical possibilities of moves and countermoves in oligopolistic situations, but it provides little help in practice.[3]

DISCUSSION
POINT 13.1

What can be said about the elasticity of demand if increased sales compensate for the reduced unit revenues?

- Why are competitor reactions of little concern or are easy to discern in a monopoly or where there is perfect competition?

13.3.3 Fit with the vision and goals

A vision is a view of where the organisation wishes to go and to be. Although both vision and goals may change, and indeed should change if necessary, they should have a degree of permanence. As such, it would be expected that a strategic pathway would fit with them. If a small retailer had the goal to be the number one retailer of health and beauty products in the UK within five years, then a strategic pathway that wouldn't tolerate a dilution of the owners' equity probably exhibits poor strategic fit. If there was a sudden influx of cheap imports, a response that simply involved cost cutting is unlikely to provide a good fit; a good fit might be to harvest the main offer, and undertake product and market development to move into a niche, concentrating on very high-quality products.

13.3.4 Synergy: the portfolio of offers

In one sense, the managing of a single-offer business operating in a single market is easy: all the efforts of the business are channelled into the single activity, and the focus is very obvious. When the firm has a portfolio of offers there is the problem of apportioning resources between them.

Overlap and cannibalism

If the business decides to extend its offers it will be addressing one or more different market segments. Such an offer extension is illustrated in Exhibit 13.4. The dotted line expresses the average value–price line over the whole of the market. For example,

EXHIBIT 13.4

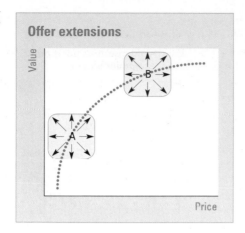

Offer extensions

Exhibit 13.4 could be covering the whole of the German car market, with Bentley, Maybach and Rolls-Royce at the top right and the Ka and Swatch at the bottom left. The cloud around position A could represent the small family car market, that around position B the company car market for middle managers. For both, the considerations of value for money discussed in Section 12.4 will of course apply, although the actual value-for-money positioning of the offers will not be the same – the Ford Ka doesn't have the same value-for-money positioning as the Ford Cougar. It's very important that any overlap between these two clouds is minimal, since as the overlap increases, there is then an increasing probability of cannibalism, whereby one offer eats away the customers for the other.

DISCUSSION POINT 13.2

Does the broad shape of the curve in Exhibit 13.4 look sensible? Or should it be roughly linear or perhaps 'curve' the other way?

● Risk is one of the main concerns of management. How do you see the riskiness of the moves away from a present offer, from a present product/service in a present market?

The BCG growth–share matrix

With a portfolio of offers, there is a need to assess the position of all the offers in order to decide on how much and what types of support they need. A very well-known portfolio model is the Boston Consultancy Group's (BCG) growth–share matrix,[4] reproduced as Exhibit 13.5.

This matrix is derived from the simple proposition that there are only two factors that determine the 'goodness' of an offer's market position: the growth rate of the segment it serves (the *growth* part of growth–share) and the relative market share that the offer enjoys (the *share* part of growth–share). Splitting each of these two factors into *high* and *low* produces the matrix. Thus four types of offer are recognised. The *stars* are offers enjoying a high segment share in a segment that is growing rapidly, while the *cash cows* have high segment share but the segment growth rate is small or even in decline. The offers with low segment share are the *question marks*, which are in a high-growth segment, and the *dogs*, which are offers that exist in low-growth segments.

The whole idea of portfolio management is that offers in one quadrant of the matrix support the others. For example, when the segment growth rate is low (a

EXHIBIT 13.5

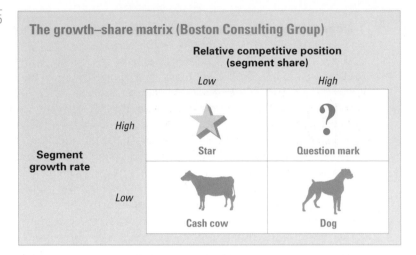

The growth–share matrix (Boston Consulting Group)

mature market) and an offer enjoys a large market share, then it will be a cash cow, generating lots of cash. This cash may then be used to support the question mark offers, which need cash to gain market share, i.e. they need to be strongly supported to change them into stars. In this way today's successes provide for tomorrow's successes. Note that a dog, which may be needing lots of the cash that the other offers are generating, is a prime candidate for disposal. However, it may be that a dog should be retained in the portfolio if it helps support the other offers, for example by complementing the other offers in some way. Exhibit 13.6 illustrates this.

As time passes, offers will change their position in the BCG matrix, under the pressure of competition and changing market conditions as the offer moves through its life cycle. Many offers will start as question marks, and the business needs to decide if it's going to support them sufficiently for them to become stars or whether it will cut its losses and discontinue them. As markets mature, stars will (hopefully) become cash cows.

EXHIBIT 13.6

The portfolio effect[5]

If a product is admired it can have a halo effect on all other products in the firm's portfolio. A very good example is the Volvo 850T5, which is a super-fast estate – faster than a Ferrari in fourth gear. It is not going to sell in any great number, perhaps a couple of hundred cars a year, but the halo effect on other parts of the Volvo range, and in shifting customer perceptions of what Volvo now means, have been quite significant.

Do you agree that the two factors used in the BCG matrix determine the 'goodness' of an offer's market position?

● In the rationale to this book, strategic management models were described as being generally too vague for prediction: their use was as 'cognitive coathangers'. Do you think this description should be applied to the BCG matrix?

Excellence

Over the last decade it has become a commonplace to read in mission statements and to hear company chairpersons and chief executives saying that they believe in *excellence*. 'Excellence in all we do' does have an appealing ring to it, but it is vacuous because it can mean a great many things: does it mean the best, near to the best, within the top 10%, or simply better than average?

If the concept does mean anything at all, it *could* be a driver for a single-offer firm. Linford Christie was the sporting equivalent of a single-offer business: he ran the 100 metres and that was that. So he *had* to seek to be the best, to be excellent by any definition of the term. Consider Daly Thompson or any other Olympic decathlon champion, however. He wasn't and didn't attempt to be the best or anything like it in any of the ten activities that make up the decathlon. He chose the combination of achievement that maximised his total score. And he would adjust his training to achieve that score. Suppose that his overall score could be increased by the same amount in either of two ways: reducing his time for the 100-metre sprint by 0.02 of a second or by throwing the javelin a further 5 metres. If he felt that a small amount of specialist training could feasibly reduce his sprinting time, yet he was on his limits in the javelin, it wouldn't make sense for him to spend much time trying to improve his javelin throws: any extra available time should be spent on specialist sprint training. On no account should a decathlete or a business with a portfolio of offers attempt to be 'excellent in all they do', because they can't do it. They should manage the portfolio for maximum overall performance.

KEY CONCEPT Segmentation subdivides the total market into parts in which customer characteristics are similar. When operating in more than one segment, care needs to be taken that one offer doesn't cannibalise another. When managing a portfolio of offers, the focus shouldn't be on the excellence with any individual offer, but on the overall performance of the business.

13.3.5 How might a strategic pathway leave the strategic resources?

We now wish to consider how the proposed strategic pathway might leave the strategic resources for use in the future: we are looking at the bold arrow in Exhibit 13.7 (a reproduction of Exhibit 10.5).

Structural assets

Structural assets arise from economies of scale and scope, proprietary standards, sunk costs, subsidy, regulation, and first-mover advantages. No firm would voluntarily follow a strategy that would reduce the advantages that they provide. British Airways' alliance with American Airlines stumbled when BA realised that it would have to give up many of the coveted landing slots at Heathrow Airport that it had historically held. For many years IBM was able to impose its standards on the rest of the computer industry, but this has now been very much reduced, particularly in the PC market, where it 'gave away' the rights to its operating system to what is now Microsoft. A strategy that didn't maintain market share might cause a firm to lose the economies of scale it possessed; failure to extend its offer portfolio when competitors were doing so might pass the advantages of scope to them.

EXHIBIT 13.7

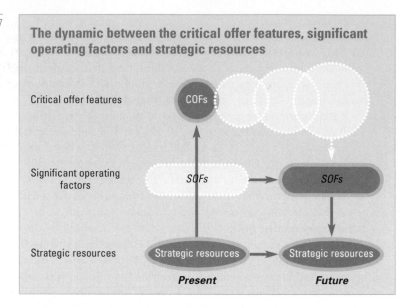

The dynamic between the critical offer features, significant operating factors and strategic resources

Reputation

What is sought by some businesses is to have a reputation for giving value for money without incurring the associated costs. They reduce the intrinsic value through cost-cutting measures and rely on their reputation to keep their prices high. Kay[6] cites the case of Hilton Hotels milking its reputation for high-quality accommodation for many years and gradually diminishing its reputation until it was no longer considered an upmarket hotel chain, and thus could no longer command a premium price. In the 1990s some UK universities, under pressure to earn more revenue, started to franchise courses overseas with inappropriate supervision of standards. This threatened to tarnish the high reputation of all UK universities – and of course damage their future earnings. But no doubt it was good for the errant institutions over the short term.

The experience of Gucci as illustrated in Exhibit 13.8 should act as a warning about spreading a brand reputation too far, and a caution against believing that an increased market share will automatically increase profits.

Architecture

One concern with a strategic pathway that reduces the activities of the firm, through out-sourcing for example, is with the capabilities that are being lost or not developed. If a firm uses another firm to undertake all its manufacturing for example, it loses much of the knowledge about the product itself – vital in organisational learning, particularly for offer development. Rolls-Royce plc has recognised three categories of goods and services. There are the goods/services whose design and manufacture can both be out-sourced; there are goods/services whose manufacture can be out-sourced but whose design must be kept in house; and there are goods/services where both the design and manufacture must remain in house. In this way, insensitive, non-core goods/services can be obtained at the lowest cost in the market, while the core capabilities associated with the sensitive core goods/services are retained and augmented in house.

EXHIBIT 13.8

Gucci's gulch: the problem with growth[7]

For most managers today, growth is the holy grail. When charting strategy, they focus on ways to expand revenues, believing (or at least hoping) that higher sales will bring higher profits. The assumption is that a company able to capture a large proportion of revenues in an industry – a large market share – will reap scale efficiencies, brand awareness, or other advantages that will translate directly into greater profits. If you can grow faster than your competitors, the thinking goes, profits will surely follow.

There is one problem with this logic: it is wrong. Profits do not necessarily follow revenues. Consider the recent experience of Gucci, one of the world's top names in luxury leather goods. In the 1980s, Gucci sought to capitalise on its prestigious brand by launching an aggressive strategy of revenue growth. It added a set of lower-priced canvas goods to its product line. It pushed its goods heavily into department stores and duty-free channels. And it allowed its name to appear on a host of licensed items such as watches, eyeglasses and perfumes. The strategy worked – sales soared – but it carried a high price: Gucci's indiscriminate approach to expanding its products and channels tarnished its sterling brand. Sales of its high-end goods fell, leading to an erosion of profitability. Although the company was eventually able to retrench and recover, it lost a whole generation of image-conscious shoppers in some countries.

Gucci's misstep highlights the problem with growth: the strategies businesses use to expand their top line often have the unintended consequence of eroding their bottom line. Gucci attempted to extend its brand to gain sales – a common growth strategy – but ended up alienating its most profitable customer segments and attracting new segments that were less profitable. It was left with a larger set of customers but a much less attractive customer mix.

One of the criticisms of many business reengineering programmes is that they failed to understand the role that tacit knowledge plays in processes, and the changes undertaken failed to retain the tacit knowledge in the firm. Given that tacit knowledge is often difficult to discern, this is a worrying feature for anyone seeking to change an organisation.

External relationships

The concern with allowing others to carry out distribution of offers was considered in Chapter 12. If a business relies on strong relationships with its customers and suppliers, rather than simply operating on a market-based contract, it must nurture these relationships and make sure that the strategic pathway it chooses doesn't damage them. In 1999, Abbey National became the first bank in the UK to charge customers for paying bills at its branches. The publicised reason for this was to prevent the branches from becoming overloaded. It was a rational approach by the bank since over-the-counter transactions are costly, but customers were antagonised. The need to nurture strong relationships is also very evident with secondary stakeholders. A strategy that embarrassed a government, for example, is unlikely to help the firm when it comes to political lobbying.

13.4 Sustainability and appropriability

A significant question about any changes that a business makes is whether the business can profit from its activities. Where a change leads to a competitive advantage, the advantage is of little value if it's only held for a short time. Thus a main concern with any proposed strategic pathway is its sustainability. Competitive advantage is also of little use to the firm if the associated rewards aren't kept by the business itself. Thus a second main concern is with appropriability.

13.4.1 Sustainability

A sustainable competitive advantage will have been achieved when a firm receives a return on investment that is greater than the norm for its competitors, and when this enhanced return persists for a period long enough to alter the relative standing of the firm among its rivals. Sustainability depends on three factors:

- Durability   No advantage is sustainable in perpetuity, as competitors will eventually succeed in imitating it. Even without competitors striving to imitate an innovation, the increasing pace of technological change shortens the useful life of technological resources and knowhow. Social change can rapidly make an offer unsaleable. However, reputation has the potential of providing a long-lasting advantage, as the standing of such household names and market leaders as Rolls-Royce, Kellogg, Heinz, Nestlé and Cadbury testifies. Indeed, Rolls-Royce cars maintain their reputation of being the best cars in the world even though this hasn't been true since the end of the First World War.[8] So high is their reputation that the word 'Rolls-Royce' has even become part of the language, a byword for exceptional quality.[9]

- Transparency   A competitor attempting to imitate what the innovative firm is doing has to understand what is being done and how it can be done. The harder it is for outsiders to understand how the firm does what it does, the lower the confidence the potential imitators have that they understand what is needed,[10] and the less likely are they to attempt to copy the innovation. The contrast between the ease of identifying and understanding offer and process innovations was discussed in Chapter 12. The imitators may be able to identify the results of the business processes, but the potential imitators have to understand the capabilities underlying these results. If the competitive advantage relies on only a single process or a single capability then it will be fairly easy for a rival to understand what is going on; if it relies on a complex set of interacting capabilities then this is much more difficult.

- Replicability   Once a rival has understood the capabilities needed, they will need to get the resources together to replicate it. If these can be obtained openly in markets, then replicability is relatively easy. This is one reason that bread-and-butter IT applications don't give competitive advantage.[11] As with transparency, it's much more difficult to replicate a complex set of capabilities than to copy a simple set. The problem for the replicator is that a complex capability arises from the co-operative efforts of teams, and teams are much less mobile than are individuals. However, teams sometimes move from one firm to another, a feature that seems to be particularly prevalent in the financial services industry.

DISCUSSION
POINT 13.4 Why should the movement of teams be more prevalent in the financial services industry than in manufacturing?

13.4.2 Appropriability

A sustainable competitive advantage is of little value if the firm can't appropriate the rewards that 'should' come to it as the generators of this advantage. This problem wasn't acute when the capabilities that gave rise to the advantage relied mostly on resources and systems: these were 'owned' by the firm and remained with the firm. However, as we move to a knowledge-based society, it is knowledge that is significant, particularly the tacit knowledge and skills 'owned' by individuals. This makes for a very dangerous situation for knowledge-based firms. Financial whizz kids can readily move firms if they aren't given the appropriate remuneration, stars in the world of academe can easily move from one university to another, star footballers can easily change clubs. When advertising executives leave one agency, perhaps to set up on their own, there is little to stop them taking their client list with them.

It might be expected that if all the firms in a competitive arena were to change together – investing large sums to become more efficient, say – then all the firms in the arena should benefit. In fact, the evidence suggests that they all lose.

The most powerful evidence is shown in Exhibit 13.9[12] (a repeat of Exhibit 8.8). This shows a plot of return on investment against the ratio of investment to sales (termed the investment intensity). The figures on the x-axis represent the values of investment intensity that partition the sample into five equal portions; for example, 20% of the businesses in the sample have an investment intensity lower than 36%. What this graph indicates is that there is a very strong and negative link between high investment intensity and returns. From this evidence, it doesn't pay to be in a busi-

EXHIBIT 13.9

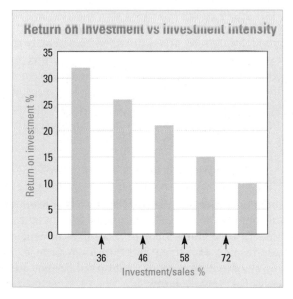

ness where high investment is needed. This applies to the airline industry, for example, where high investments are needed by the established airlines with their aircraft, reservation systems and ticketing services.

DISCUSSION POINT 13.5 How can the graph in Exhibit 13.9 be reconciled with the use of discounting methods of investment appraisal, where investments are only made when they make positive returns?

13.5 Intellectual property

The term *intellectual property* relates to assets that can be traded (bought and sold, hired or rented) and that are intangible, as opposed to the physical assets such as buildings, machinery or stock.[13] It is concerned with creative activities and with commercial reputation and goodwill.[14] Intellectual property rights put the owner of the right in a privileged position whereby they can exploit the right and at the same time prevent others doing things that might undermine it, i.e. they can sustain and appropriate the value associated with their intellectual property.

There are several forms of intellectual property, and Bainbridge[15] has provided the classification of these that is reproduced in Exhibit 13.10.

EXHIBIT 13.10

A classification of intellectual property (from Bainbridge, 1994)

Formalities required?	Creative		Commercial reputation
	Artistic	Commercial	
Yes	Registered designs	Patents	Trade marks
No	Copyright	Design right	Passing off
		Breach of confidence	

A major element of the classification is whether formal application and registration procedures are required to obtain the intellectual property right. Where such formalities aren't required, legal protection is provided immediately the intellectual property is created. The second main distinction is between the protection of creative activities and the protection of commercial reputation. The creative activities can usefully be further subdivided into those that are artistic, such as a piece of music or a book, and commercial, such as a new offer or a new way of producing an offer.

The seven main types of intellectual property for which protection is legally available are shown in Exhibit 13.10[16] and described below.

Registered designs

A design is a monopoly right for the outward visual appearance of a product or set of products. This right would typically be sought when a new article isn't sufficiently novel or inventive to be granted a patent. Examples of articles that might be registered designs are display packaging and bathroom fittings. A registered design is additional to any copyright protection. A registered design can last for up to 25 years through a process of five-yearly renewals.

Copyright

Copyright provides automatic rights to the creators of the following kinds of original materials:

- literary works (e.g. books, computer manuals, articles in newspapers and instruction manuals), but not names or titles;
- artistic, dramatic and musical works;
- sound recordings, which may be recordings of other copyright works;
- films;
- broadcasts and cable programmes.

A copyright doesn't protect an idea; it protects (tangible) expressions of an idea and so other people are free to create similar works if they do so by their own efforts. In the UK the copyright lasts for 50 years after its creation or 50 years after the author's death depending on the type of work. International protection of copyright is maintained mainly through the Berne Copyright Convention and the Universal Copyright Convention. Under these conventions, foreigners can sue in the courts of the countries that are signatories to the conventions.

Patents

A patent for an invention is granted by governments – national or supranational such as the EU – and operates only within the government's jurisdiction. A patent is concerned with the technical and functional aspects of a product such as a new car engine or a process such as one for making float plate glass. It gives the inventor the right for a period of time (up to 20 years) to stop other people from making, using or selling the invention without the permission of the patent holder. Patents are only granted where there is significant novelty and inventiveness in the proposal. The European Patent Convention, operated by the European Patent Office in Munich, accepts applications for patents covering all EU member states, although national patents can still be obtained through national patent offices.

It isn't an easy matter to make patents secure. The drug companies aim to achieve this through four patent routes. A whole group of chemicals may be protected; the specific process of chemical synthesis that is to be used and also all other known methods of synthesis may be protected; the product may be patented; and there is the possibility of patenting the design of the delivery device (for example Fisons' Spinhaler). Patents provide protection for 20 years after the patent has been granted. However, while patents have given considerable protection in pharmaceuticals, they tend to be weak forms of protection in many other areas, although Gillette seem to have achieved a great deal of protection for its Mach3 razor (see Exhibit 10.9).

Establishing and maintaining patents is not necessarily simple, as Exhibit 13.11 indicates.

Design rights

While registered designs apply to visually appealing characteristics, design rights apply to facets that are functional. Examples of articles to which design rights might be applicable would be a new design for a kitchen roll dispenser or for a new type of lawnmower grass-catching box. There is considerable overlap between design rights and registered designs; it's not obvious, for example, whether the housing for a new type of computer (such as the iMac) would attract a registered design for its visually

EXHIBIT 13.11

Battle of the beakers[17]

For somebody who has apparently solved a problem that has bedevilled generations of parents, Mandy Haberman is remarkably underwhelmed.

Mrs Haberman invented a valve for a spill-proof child's trainer cup. That was the easy part. Taking out a patent on the design and bringing it to market was harder: she had to spend a small fortune and then she became embroiled in a legal case when one of the world's leading makers of baby accessories introduced a similar product.

For now, Mrs Haberman and V&A Marketing, the company with which she teamed up to make and market the Spill-Proof Anywayup Cup, are victorious. Earlier this month, the High Court upheld their claim against Jackel International, maker of Tommee Tippee, for alleged copying of her patented invention. But she is not basking in the success – and not just because Jackel has been granted leave to appeal, so that she has to wait an anxious three weeks to see if it decides to go to the Court of Appeal.

She says the legal process of challenging a company the size of Jackel has been daunting. 'I believed that the grant of a patent fully protected my product, it was horrendous to discover that Tommee Tippee had infringed my patent and that it was able to question the validity of my patent in court. Fortunately, the action has been successful and should give confidence to other small inventors.'

The saga began in 1990, when she was at a friend's house with her youngest child. Another visitor was there with her toddler, who was in constant danger of staining the carpets by shaking her beaker around. 'I thought, there must be a better way,' says Mrs Haberman.

She was familiar with other products that dealt with the problem by having lids that could be turned to close, or required an inner lid to be inserted when the child was not using it. With all of them, 'you had to intervene to make them seal.'

Having previously been involved in inventing a feeder for babies with sucking problems, she applied the same thinking and came up with the idea of a valve fitted to the cup lid. Made of a very thin soft membrane, this would open when the baby sucked and close when it stopped – preventing spills. The invention was recognised by the Design Council last July, when it made the cup a 'millennium product' for being among the most innovative products designed and produced in Britain.

Once she had developed the idea she joined up with V&A, and in 1995 they made a number of prototypes to show at exhibitions. The two events they attended produced £10,000 worth of advance orders. As Mrs Haberman says: 'We felt we had to make it.'

They found a company to which they subcontracted the manufacturing and went into production – putting the first orders out in March 1996. The initial interest at the exhibitions was reflected in rapidly rising sales. After a short while the product was being sold in Tesco.

With demand growing, the cup was redesigned by Sebastian Conran and V&A decided to invest in its own factory. While Mrs Haberman continued to work from her home in Hertfordshire, V&A Plastics, as the new unit was called, was opened in Cardiff, employing 70 people making and packaging about 60,000 cups a week.

Then, on 11 August 1998, Mrs Haberman saw a Tommee Tippee cup that looked a lot like hers – or at least like the early prototype. By 14 August a writ had been served on Jackel, but the damage had already been done. 'Our market fell from underneath us,' says Mrs Haberman. Sales nearly halved. 'It was an ordeal and I never want to go through anything like that again.'

For the moment, the heat is off. Thanks to an injunction preventing further infringement of the patent, the threat of lay-offs for the workers in Cardiff has been lifted. And, while the High Court assesses the level of damages and costs Jackel will have to pay if it decides not to pursue the case, Mrs Haberman and V&A are looking ahead. A new cup is due in June and there are also plans for a range of tableware called Anyware.

Jackel is thought likely to go for the appeal, which would be heard in about 18 months. Meanwhile, it says it has substituted the valve system with two alternative 'tried and tested' leakproof systems. David Jones, UK marketing director, said in a statement that the company was 'naturally extremely disappointed by the ruling' and added that it had a long history of new product development. 'We have always welcomed competition and will continue to provide the best range of cups and accessories on the market.'

Mrs Haberman's solicitor, the City firm of Paisner & Co., said the case showed how 'small companies can successfully protect their creativity, however powerful their competitor.'

But it is clear that for all the entreaties for inventors to take out patents, this onerous process is not enough to ensure protection. Because judges tend to favour challenges to patents unless the product is genuinely innovative, individuals need to get advice on the best way to take out a patent and be ready to square up to powerful rivals.

This is a situation familiar to the likes of James Dyson, who endured many setbacks before being hailed an 'instant success' for his bagless vacuum cleaner. But it is not highlighted by ministers stressing the importance of innovation.

Discussion point 13.6

What are your views on the strategic fit of the new products?

attractive appearance or a design right for its new functionality, or perhaps both. Design rights can last for 15 years.

Trade marks

A trade mark is any sign that distinguishes the offers of one particular organisation or sole trader from those of other organisations and sole traders. A sign generally consists of words and graphics but can include pictures, sounds and smells. Registration of trade marks began in 1876 in the UK, the first trade mark being the Bass Red Triangle label.

There have been interesting developments with the Internet. In Britain and Switzerland, for example, it's rather arbitrary who gets to assign domain names. This means that in some countries company and brand names can be assigned to people who don't have any rights to use these names outside of the Internet. Thus the huge intellectual property that lies in brands is at risk.[18]

Passing off

As with trade mark law, passing off is concerned with preventing the offers of one business being confused with those of another: with protecting reputation and goodwill. In general elections it has been known for candidates to register new political parties with names that are almost identical to those of established parties, thereby confusing the voters. The unauthorised application of cartoon characters such as Disney characters to T-shirts and other merchandise is an area of increasing significance. Passing off can only be challenged when a reputation has been established.

Breach of confidence

The term *intellectual property* is also used to cover information and knowledge such as customer lists, knowhow and trade secrets. The protection of such information is covered to some extent by the law of breach of confidence. This is significant, as it is often the only form of protection when something is still in its infancy.

Bainbridge[19] has described the life of an invention as shown in Exhibit 13.12. Note that the solid lines indicate the duration of the right, while the broken lines signify that the right still exists but in a weaker form.

Consider the steps to granting a patent for a product. Even at the stage when an inventor first gets an idea for a new offer or process, they will have some rights through the laws on breach of confidence. Once the idea is expressed in a tangible form, they can ask for copyright. After preliminary negotiations with potential manufacturers and as the ideas become more concrete, a patent can be applied for. Once a patent has been granted, the copyright weakens but is still in force. Once articles have been produced, the manufacturer or the inventor can apply for trade-mark protection. Once a reputation has been established for the product, then challenges to passing off can be instigated if necessary.

13.6 Feasibility

Following the audit of strategic fit, the second screening on the suitability of a proposed strategic pathway is whether the necessary resources can be obtained and the necessary changes implemented. This is one of the few areas in strategic management where there needs to be a concern with detail and with numbers. It might seem odd to say this, because it might be felt that this concern would have been included within the comparative analysis that is part of a SWOT analysis. However, the analysis of one's own business that is done as part of the comparative analysis is at the detail that is known of the competitors; it doesn't make sense in a *comparative* analysis to treat your own business at a finer level of detail than that possible for the competing businesses. In contrast, the analysis involved in assessing feasibility is detailed, and focused on the feasibility of carrying out one or more specific choices in the strategic pathway.

13.6.1 Obtaining resources

Developing the resources needed

Any new business strategy will be accompanied by augmentations to capabilities. This will require either new resources or the redeployment of currently available resources. In either case, the feasibility of a new strategy will depend on how large the changes need to be; fairly obviously, if only small changes are required, the feasibility of successfully implementing the changes is likely to be high.

EXHIBIT 13.12

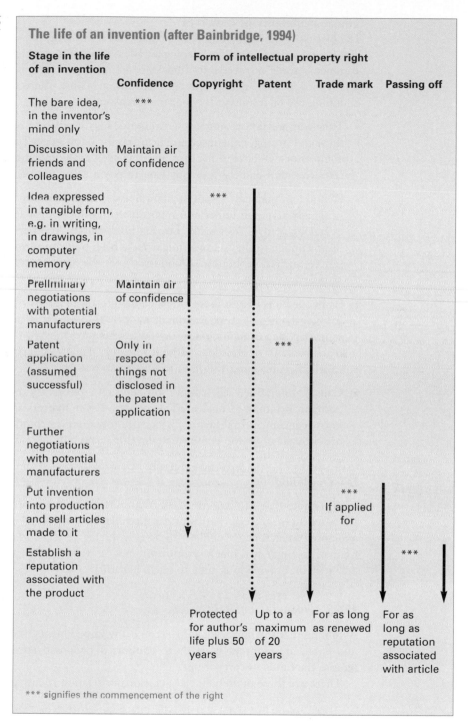

The life of an invention (after Bainbridge, 1994)

Stage in the life of an invention	Form of intellectual property right				
	Confidence	Copyright	Patent	Trade mark	Passing off
The bare idea, in the inventor's mind only	***				
Discussion with friends and colleagues	Maintain air of confidence				
Idea expressed in tangible form, e.g. in writing, in drawings, in computer memory		***			
Preliminary negotiations with potential manufacturers	Maintain air of confidence				
Patent application (assumed successful)	Only in respect of things not disclosed in the patent application		***		
Further negotiations with potential manufacturers					
Put invention into production and sell articles made to it				*** If applied for	
Establish a reputation associated with the product					***
		Protected for author's life plus 50 years	Up to a maximum of 20 years	For as long as renewed	For as long as reputation associated with article

*** signifies the commencement of the right

The unavailability of resources

The discussion of sustainability of a competitive advantage was directed at the factors that would aid a business in keeping an advantage for a useful period of time. Similar arguments apply in reverse to a business attempting to obtain resources to nullify a disadvantage. Even if the funding is readily available, there may be a difficulty in obtaining use of resources for four main reasons:[20]

- Time compression economics   A resource may need to be built up over time through learning, experience and firm-specific knowledge. This implies that a competitor will have difficulty replicating such a resource through use of its current resources, and that the firm may have to pay a premium if it wishes to buy it.

- Historic uniqueness   Some structural assets are inherently unique or were originally acquired under non-replicable conditions, such as distinctive location or having control over a sole raw material source. Another source of disadvantage to the follower might have been built up through being a first mover, such as reputation, brand loyalty or the power to establish industrial standards.

- Embeddedness of resources   The value of a resource may be inextricably linked to the presence of another, complementary resource. It is claimed that in university departments, research and teaching are inextricably linked: that teaching can't be excellent without research. Thus a department that seeks to be excellent at teaching will have to undertake research.

- Causal ambiguity   The connection between a business's resources and its performance may be unclear. This occurs in such matters as culture, tacit knowledge and social factors, which are too complex to understand, or which are thought to be too complex to develop, especially in combination.

13.6.2   Cultural fit

It is possible that the culture of an organisation makes it problematical whether a proposed new strategic pathway can feasibly be implemented. For example, Miles and Snow's reactors are unlikely to be able to change to a prospecting role; Deal and Kennedy's tough guy, macho culture will not be well suited to a strategy that involves activities that take a long time to reach maturity.

13.6.3   Financial feasibility

Assuming that the business can overcome any impediments to obtaining access to the non-financial resources it needs to support a proposed strategic pathway, it will require the funds to carry it out.

There are three main financial questions in relation to any proposed strategy:

Does it make financial sense?

This is the requirement to assess whether the specific funds directly associated with the proposed strategic pathway are being used wisely; i.e. whether at a minimum the return on investment won't be negative, and that there is no better use for the funds. There are a range of methods to support such decisions,[21] in particular calculation of the net present value of the investment and the payback period. One area of considerable concern to many businesses is their investment in IT, particularly as those IT investments that would purportedly save money have now been made (the back-office systems), and the major investments are now with front-office applications and with aiding decision making. Both these areas are where the benefits are difficult to determine, particularly before the event.

What funds are needed?

The second element of determining the financial feasibility of a strategic pathway is to determine the external funding needed. A funds-flow analysis is required to determine this. All businesses, but particularly small businesses, need to be watchful of their cash position. Thus a significant concern is the timing of the costs and the associated revenues: typically with new activities, there is a large up-front cost followed by a relatively slow, and hopefully steady, revenue stream. However profitable a future activity might be, the timings of cash flows may preclude its being undertaken.

Consideration of a firm's funds flow should also consider where cash outflows might be reduced and inflows maximised through improved asset management.

Can the funds be obtained?

A funds-flow analysis will indicate the timing of cash inflows and outflows, and thus indicate the timing of any necessary cash injections. However, the firm still has to obtain the required funding. This is generally not too difficult where it has tangible assets that can be used as security for a loan. Where tangible assets aren't available, however, and the loan needs to be based on future cash flows, getting a loan can be much more difficult. This is often the case with high-technology startups. Exhibit 12.16 (Bringing up flat-top baby) illustrated how difficult it can be, especially if the owners don't want to part with any of the equity in the company.

13.7 Acceptability

Following the audits of strategic fit and feasibility, an acceptability audit should be undertaken. Acceptability is concerned with the views of all stakeholders, particularly with those who are powerful and are willing to use their power.

13.7.1 Relationships with internal stakeholders

It is hard to see any changes in the offers that a business makes in today's dynamic environment that don't require a change in working practices, since processes will have to be altered to match the new requirements. Thus it's very likely that one of the most significant stakeholder groups that must accept a new strategic pathway are the employees. A good example of change is that undertaken at Dutton Engineering (a case in this book). Employees had to become team members. The teams were given responsibility for on-going customer relations and had to take responsibility for the quality of their own work. Payments were changed from weekly wages to monthly salary, and earnings differentials were narrowed. The factory moved to flexible working and annualised hours. They needed to embrace the *kaizen* approach and to operate just-in-time supplier systems.

13.7.2 Relationships with external stakeholders

It should be recognised that as a firm moves into offer extensions, it should be expected that each increment in added value will tend to be smaller than the previous one. For example, as supermarkets expand they move into the best locations available, but each best location tends to be poorer than the last.[22] The external stakeholders need to be aware that this tailing-off of margins is likely to occur.

DISCUSSION
POINT 13.7

If there is a tailing-off of margins, why should stakeholders wish to support the strategy?

Financial relationships

There are four types of external stakeholder who have an interest in the financial performance of the firm. There are the people who own it, the owner-managers and shareholders. There is the stock market, with its analysts and prospective owners. There are those who have lent money to it, the banks and other sources of funds, and there are those authorities who have a duty to see that it operates in an appropriate manner, the tax authorities and, in the UK, the Department of Trade and Industry. These four groups of stakeholders judge the performance of the firm in different ways and thus have differing views on whether a proposed strategy is acceptable.

The owner-manager will often be concerned with the short term and wish to generate cash, both for their own salary and for immediate investment; to them, cash flow is the important consideration. Shareholders, both actual and prospective, are concerned with the medium term. A measure that has become particularly popular in the last decade is shareholder value. Shareholder value is the sum of the value of the shares and any after-tax profits that are not already included in the share price. The share price will be a reflection of the future cash flows that the market expects from the company, discounted at the cost of capital. At a minimum, the discounted net cash flows should be such that the net present value of the firm is greater than zero.

The stock market is interested in financial value, the net present value of the expected future cash flows over the lifetime of the organisation. Maintaining good relationships with market analysts and the managers of the large pension funds can be very significant for chairmen and chief executives, especially of the larger firms, which are closely scrutinised.

The lenders of money to the firm, primarily the banks, will often be concerned with the collateral that the firm can offer when the loan is being made. Once made, a significant consideration is whether the cash flows to be generated by the firm will be adequate to service the loan.

The financial authorities are primarily concerned with the stewardship of the firm and with securing the tax that governments have levied. In this case the concern is with the past and with such accounting measures as profit and returns on assets.

Supplier and customer relationships

While some proposed strategies may call only for changes to the firm's internal architecture, some will affect the relationships with suppliers and many will affect those with customers. The imposition of charges by Abbey National upset some customers, although the resultant smaller queues would be appreciated by the remainder. What is perceived to be unethical behaviour can also alienate customers, as shown by boycotts in supermarkets against food from unacceptable regimes and what could be seen as a lack of social responsibility in the supermarkets' acceptance of genetically modified foods.

The Internet represents a dilemma for many companies. If they don't use the Internet they will lose business to competitors which do. If they do use it, they risk damaging long-standing business relationships with suppliers and buyers who yield the bulk of their current revenue. This is why the upstart has a great chance. It was Direct Line that pioneered telephone selling of insurance, not the established players, who didn't want to upset the brokers providing the bulk of their income. Dell had already ceased using retailers by the time it went on the Internet and so didn't have the same problem. Banks with their high-street outlets face a similar dilemma, as do airlines with travel agents.

13.7.3 Risk management

While the returns connected with a proposed strategy are obviously important, so too are the associated risks. The risk can be particularly high when a firm is undertaking long-term innovation, such as occurs in the aerospace and pharmaceuticals industries. It is also high if there are large strategic uncertainties. However, a firm must take risks; if it doesn't, it can end up with no profit from its activities. This situation is akin to someone who insures for everything and then finds that they have no money on which to live. However, the risks taken should be identified and assessed.

The power of scenario development is that it highlights the strategic uncertainties, and a proposed strategy will have been selected in the knowledge of the 'strategic space' within which the strategy is thought to remain viable. It is likely that presenting this information will make a proposed strategy more acceptable to some of the more sophisticated stakeholders.

Useful insights into the risk being run by the firm if the proposed strategy was adopted would be obtained by calculating the future values of the key financial ratios. Two particularly important ratios are the gearing and liquidity ratios. A strategy that required increased medium-term funding would increase the firm's gearing and increase the risk the firm was running, because it would have consistently to generate the cash to cover the interest payment on the loan.

Liquidity considerations are an important feature when evaluating expansion strategies, particularly for small businesses. When a firm is doing well and securing a large number of orders, there is the danger of overtrading. Since suppliers need to be paid before payment is received from customers, the bank overdraft is likely to need to be increased, with the consequent extra interest payments, which may be difficult to make.

Although scenarios and SWOT tables will have identified the general risks associated with major changes in strategic direction, more specific risks will remain, associated with both incremental change and on-going management. For example, a change in a supplier brings new and different risks, as does using a new marketing services agency. It is the responsibility of leader-managers to identify such risks and to see how they can be reduced or their effects ameliorated through risk management. Risk management includes risk assessment, contingency planning and crisis control. (Together, the planning associated with the building of scenarios and SWOT tables, and risk management form what has recently been termed *business continuity management*. Contingency planning and crisis control are discussed in Chapter 15).

Interestingly, law firms are in the forefront of risk assessment, seeing the legal position as underpinning the rights and relationships in virtually every area of business. Eversheds, one of the world's largest law firms, has produced a checklist of questions that firms should ask themselves when they are considering the risks they are running, in terms of the damage both to asset value and to relationships. Its list is shown in Exhibit 13.13. Of particular concern to the many companies that are engaging in e-commerce is the risks they run from unauthorised access and fraud. Authorisation, firewalls, encryption and other forms of protection need to be considered, and computer viruses need to be protected against.

EXHIBIT 13.13

The risks being run

Assets

* *Product liability*   A mishandled product recall can severely damage brand and market share. What contingency plans do you have to respond to product failure?
* *Facilities*   How would a fire or flood at a major manufacturing plant affect your operations? Do you have the appropriate collateral warranties in place in the event of defects in the design or construction of premises?
* *Plant*   If critical new equipment does not perform to specification on delivery can you reject it and order a replacement elsewhere, or must you accept the supplier's offers to repair despite the delay and potential loss of scheduled production?
* *Environmental*   What is your exposure to civil claims and criminal liability arising from environmental damage or occupation of contaminated land?
* *Information technology*   Businesses are increasingly dependent on systems. What would happen to your operation in the event of systems failure?
* *Confidential information*   What steps do you take to secure confidential information such as customer lists, pricing details or expansion plans?
* *Intellectual property*   Trade marks and patents may be among your most valuable assets. Are they protected? How do you deal with infringement?

Relationships

* *Contractual relationships*   Do you operate a just-in-time stock system? If so, could delays in the supply of even minor items cause disproportionate damage?
* *Out-sourcing*   Out-sourcing critical areas and securing long-term partnering relationships to maintain business growth is well recognised as a means of managing risk. It also has dangers. Have you weighed them up?
* *Disputes*   The risk and potential magnitude of claims is escalating, particularly for businesses operating in the United States. Do you have a policy that enables you to assess and address disputes before they develop?
* *Insolvency*   Many successful businesses are brought down by the insolvency of trading partners. How do you minimise your exposure when a key customer or supplier runs into financial difficulties?
* *Competition*   Is your business at risk of investigation or a dawn raid for anti-competitive conduct? Are you prepared?
* *Regulatory*   The number and scope of regulatory and government bodies ranging

from the Financial Services Authority to Trading Standards, the Stock Exchange and the Data Protection Office, continue to expand. Does your company manage its contacts with these authorities in a careful and informed manner?

SUMMARY

- There are three tests that leader-managers should apply to assess the suitability of any proposed strategic pathway. These are the strategic fit – how the organisation matches its vision/goals and strategic resources to its short- and medium-term environments; its feasibility – can the strategic pathway be delivered in practice; and its acceptability to (powerful) stakeholders. Very generally, strategic fit is concerned with the market position of offers and identifying resource need. Feasibility is concerned with the likelihood of obtaining access to the resources needed to support them. EXHIBIT 13.1, EXHIBIT 13.2

- The derivation of SWOT tables will automatically provide some testing of strategic fit. Further tests to apply are those for synergy, fit with the business vision and goals, sustainability and appropriability, and how the strategic pathway leaves the strategic resources. Of particular concern is the role of reputation in adding value. EXHIBIT 13.3, EXHIBIT 13.4

- To turn an advantage into a worthwhile competitive advantage requires that the advantage be both sustainable and appropriable. Sustainability depends on the durability, transparency and replicability of the underlying capability.

- Intellectual property is becoming more significant as we move into the knowledge age. There are many forms of intellectual property right and various durations of protection. EXHIBIT 13.10, EXHIBIT 13.12

- The feasibility audit is concerned with establishing that the wherewithal is available to carry out the strategy and that the resources needed can be made available. The feasibility is likely to be enhanced if the required resources are already available in house. A proposed strategy will have a lower feasibility if the necessary resources aren't currently in house and not readily available in the marketplace. This lack of a market in resources arises because they are characterised by time compression economics, historical uniqueness, embeddedness and causal ambiguity.

- Acceptability is concerned with how the stakeholders will judge the proposed strategy. Internal stakeholders are likely to judge the strategy in terms of how it affects their job security and job satisfaction. External stakeholders will judge the proposals primarily in terms of the financial returns that the strategy is expected to generate. All stakeholders will be concerned with the risks that are being run, associated with the major changes in strategy and with incremental change and on-going management.

SELF-CHECK

1 Reconsider the learning outcomes for this chapter. Check that you feel confident that you can carry out the activities listed there.

2 Having read this chapter, you should be able to define the following terms:

acceptability	feasibility	registered design
appropriability	intellectual property	strategic fit
breach of confidence	passing off	sustainability
copyright	patent	trade mark
design right		

The Story of Dean LeBaron[24] (revisited)

In this we can learn from the story of a very successful American investment manager Dean LeBaron, founder in 1969 of Batterymarch Financial Management of Boston.

It's the story of a fortune being made in a market – the capital market – in which consistently high returns are meant to be impossible, or at least highly improbable. And the way in which LeBaron made his fortune is interesting. If we understand the kind of strategy by which someone like LeBaron makes money in a highly efficient market like the New York Stock Exchange, then we're in a better position to define the properties of strategies that earn supernormal profits in relatively inefficient markets such as product and service markets.

From this story I want to take four ideas:

1. the virtues that turn an ordinary plan into a strategic plan;
2. the minimal conditions for making money in a product market;
3. a set of rules for detecting charlatans and impostors, whether they take the form of strategies or strategists; and
4. some of the prime culprits.

Before 1969, LeBaron was a highly successful fund manager running Keystone Custodian Growth, one of biggest mutual funds in America. Gradually, however, he became convinced that share prices are all taking a random walk and that therefore they are unpredictable; his 'expertise' was therefore founded on a myth. He set up Batterymarch on a completely new basis: not one of trying to beat the market through forecasting the unforecastable but simply one of matching the performance of the stock market as a whole. His was the first index fund. It was made up of 250 stocks which closely approximated the behaviour of the 500 tracked by Standard and Poor's. By dispensing with the need to employ expensive analysts and by minimising the buying and selling of stocks, he was able to beat the average return on professionally managed money.

LeBaron outperformed the experts by doing nothing. His computer picked the stocks, assembled the portfolio and then, more or less, sat on it. This meant far fewer commissions as well as lower commissions. By embracing the efficient market hypothesis he was able to claim that he did not spend time on things over which essentially he had no control.

But how do you follow an act like that? LeBaron found that many of his clients were unhappy that, whilst beating the experts, they didn't beat the average. So LeBaron developed a second-line strategy designed to beat the average and satisfy the greedy. What he did was to look for the common factor that united the analysts, so that he could play a different tune. The big players in the market were overinvesting in big companies and underinvesting in smaller ones, if only because such huge sums of money could only be used by buying into huge companies. Small companies would have to be taken over completely in such circumstances, and this would break one of their basic rules about diversification and minimisation of risk. LeBaron deduced that therefore a lot of the smaller companies, especially those listed on the American, not the New York, Stock Exchange, would be selling at a significant discount from their 'true' price. LeBaron based a portfolio on just such stocks. He called it his 'two-tier market theory'. Unfortunately for him, unlike his index fund, it was quickly imitated. LeBaron lost his competitive edge almost as soon as he had invented it.

So now he is still trying to find a system, a strategy, for beating the index fund. And he thinks he has found it. This is how he recently described it:

> We've been valuing companies by replacement costs. Valuing companies that way runs counter to everything the institutional investors are doing at the moment. It has caused us to buy things like steel stocks and rubber stocks – companies with lots of

physical assets and no earnings – which are not considered terribly attractive by the institutions. It has given us a portfolio which satisfies our desire to be different. We tested that assumption by showing the portfolio to our friends at the institutions and they said Ugh! That really appealed to us.

When our clients started criticising us for buying these stocks, it reinforced our notion. We felt we were being sufficiently contrary. Contrarianism therefore is the name I wish to use to describe this against the grain investment strategy.

LeBaron's strategy of contrarianism finds its ultimate expression in his concept of the bankrupt portfolio – the hottest thing since mutual funds. Based on the theory that institutions undervalue the potentially bankrupt company by classing it as an imprudent holding, LeBaron sees immense potential in his new fund. 'It's very hard these days for a large company to go bankrupt. Chrysler has tried very hard but it still has to succeed.' So has Continental Illinois. Nor is bankruptcy itself necessarily a bad thing. Penn Central is now a very powerful real-estate company. Unfortunately, there are very few takers for his new imprudent fund. It's an idea ahead of its time.

Discussion point 13.8

For each of the activities undertaken by LeBaron, decide what provided sustainable advantage.

FURTHER DISCUSSION POINTS

1 In Chapter 1 the strategic management environment was characterised as chaotic, complex, dynamic and turbulent – all generally increasing the level of uncertainty facing leader-managers. However, not all business environments are the same. Reflect on how changes in the environmental characteristics might affect the choice of strategic pathway made by the organisation and the approach taken to making the choice.

2 For GSM:
   Use Exhibit 13.2 to assess the strategic fit of GSM's close linkage with Ford.
   - What examples are there of synergy between the offers that GSM makes?
   - How does GSM sustain its advantage?
   - There is no protection of the intellectual property rights. Is this a mistake? What could GSM do to protect itself?
   - What is your view of GSM's open pricing policy?
   - How risky are the GSM operations?

3 What is the place of scenario building in the testing of strategies for fit, acceptability and feasibility?

ASSIGNMENTS

1 Choose a business that is currently in the news and, using Exhibit 13.2 as a framework, determine whether the strategic pathways that have or are being chosen are strategically suitable.

2 Analyse how each of the following organisations is sustaining and appropriating the value associated with their advantages:
   - Shane McGill;
   - The entrepreneur;
   - Eversheds;
   - ITNet.

FURTHER READING

John Kay has looked at games theory to describe competitor behaviour in his book *Foundations of Corporate Success: How Business Strategies Add Value*, Oxford University Press, 1993.

The book by David Bainbridge, *Intellectual Property*, 2nd edn, Financial Times Pitman Publishing, 1994, discusses intellectual property in great detail. Considerable information is also available on the Patent Office website at www.patent.gov.uk.

CHAPTER NOTES AND REFERENCES

1 This section has been derived with some input from David, F.R., 'How do we choose among alternative growth strategies?' *Managerial Planning*, Vol. 33, No. 4, January–February 1985, pp. 14–17, 22.

2 Chapter 6 said that it's not generally useful to distinguish between products/services and markets, since the augmented products/services would be augmented to suit the market. However, this is a case where a distinction is apposite.

3 Kay, J., *Foundations of Corporate Success: How Business Strategies Add Value*, Oxford University Press, 1993, discusses the use of two-person game theory in business situations.

4 Henderson, B.D., *The Experience Curve – Reviewed. IV. The Growth Share Matrix of the Product Portfolio*, Boston Consulting Group, 1973. The growth–share matrix is given a very full treatment in Hax, A.C. and Majluf, N.S., *Strategic Management: An Integrative Perspective*, Prentice Hall, 1984.

5 McConchie, D.R., 'Patterns of strategic control: an investigation of British, French and German retail banking practice', PhD thesis, Loughborough University, 1998, p. 276.

6 Kay, J., *op. cit.*, p. 98.

7 Gadiesh, O. and Gilbert, J.L., 'Gucci's gulch: the problem with growth' in 'profit pools: A fresh look at strategy', *Harvard Business Review*, May–June 1998, pp. 139–47.

8 Green, G., 'Rolls-Royce once built the best car in the world', *The Independent*, 12 September 1998, p. 9.

9 *Ibid.*

10 Reed, R. and DeFillippi, R., 'Causal ambiguity, barriers to imitation and sustainable competitive advantage', *Academy of Management Review*, 15, 1990, pp. 88–102.

11 Rumelt, R.P., 'Towards a strategic theory of the firm', in Lamb, R. (ed.) *Competitive Strategic Management*, Prentice Hall, 1984, pp. 556–70. Rumelt sees a business surviving imitation if it can erect what he terms *isolating mechanisms*. These are similar to barriers to entry and mobility barriers between strategic groups.

12 Buzzell, R.D. and Gale, B.T., *The PIMS Principles: Linking Strategy to Performance*, Free Press, 1987, p. 143; and Schoeffler, S., 'The unprofitability of "modern" technology and what to do about it', *The PIMS Letter*, No. 2, The Strategic Planning Institute, 1980.

13 The Patent Office website (www.patent.gov.uk), accessed 9 April 1998.

14 Bainbridge, D., *Intellectual Property*, 2nd edn, Financial Times Pitman Publishing, 1994, pp. 3–4.

15 *Ibid.*, p. 4.

16 There are other types of intellectual property that are of less general interest, such as the rights in performance for live performances and plant variety protection.

17 Trapp, R., 'Battle of the beakers', *The Independent on Sunday*, Section 2, 24 January 1999, p. 24.

18 McGookin, *Financial Times*, 3 June 1998.

19 Bainbridge, D., *op. cit.*, p. 19.

20 Rumelt, R.P., *op. cit.*

21 For example, Wood, F. and Sangster, A., *Business Accounting* 2, Financial Times Pitman Publishing, 1999, Chapter 46.

22 This is not always the case, since there can be remote environmental shifts, for example when out-of-town sites were first made available.

23 Eversheds Business Risk Services, Eversheds, Leeds. (eversheds.com)

24 This is a transcript of an after-dinner talk given by Jules Goddard to the participants on the Strategic Investment Decision Programme, London Business School, May 1986.

PART 5

Implementation and control

14 Strategic change management

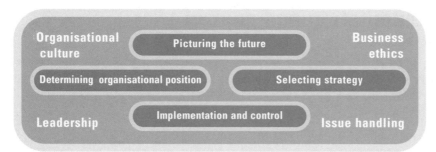

this is the first of two chapters concerned with strategic implementation and control. The focus is on the process of implementing changes in strategy.

The chapter begins with a consideration of the two main types of strategic change, followed by a discussion of the fundamentals of change processes, including how learning to support change can be engendered in the organisation. Practical considerations of how to begin implementing strategic change are then considered: how people react to change situations and where the leader-manager might best strike the balance between changing behaviours directly or changing them through changes in beliefs. The styles of change management that are appropriate to different types of change and contexts are then explored. The mechanisms that can be used in the different stages of an organisation's life are discussed. Finally, the roles of the change agent and middle managers in the change programme are described.

Since the only constant in the business lives of leader-managers will be change, the ability to handle strategic change is a fundamental skill. There are two main considerations. The first is to set up the conditions so that organisational learning, the precursor to much effective change, is enhanced. This will allow incremental learning, and thus purposeful incremental change, to take place on a continuous basis. The second concern is with the changes that are initiated by leader-managers and that may need to be imposed. Knowing where and how to direct their efforts to best overcome resistance to change is an important attribute for the modern leader-manager, and the widespread use of project teams means that skills in project management have become a key requirement.

LEARNING
OUTCOMES

When you have worked through this chapter, you should be able to:

- describe the two types of strategic change and explain the phases of the change process;

- describe the methods and structures by which organisational learning can be encouraged;

- explain the assumptions underlying belief-driven and behaviour-driven approaches to change management, and describe the designed-involvement and results-driven programmes for change;

- manage the change process that people go through when their work processes are changed;

- select the change-management style that fits the context under which change is taking place;

- list and explain the characteristics required of a change agent.

14.1 The types of strategic change

All organisations need continually to undertake operational change in order to renew those parts of the organisation that grow old and die. They also need to undertake strategic renewal in order to adjust to changing environmental factors. Where environmental change is slow and/or small, organisational change is likely to be in small incremental steps. The changes that the organisation needs to undertake are likely to be larger, however, where the environmental changes are larger or because there has been strategic drift. It is no longer appropriate to call these large changes *incremental*: the changes are transformational. Thus organisations have to be prepared to undertake both incremental change and transformational change. Although the changes will find expression in changed behaviours, processes and outputs, it should be recognised that for change to be lasting it must come about in people's minds; their mental models must change.

The saying 'The only certainty is uncertainty; the only constant is change' applies very much to management today. It indicates that change is a journey, not an event. It's something that is always with us.

14.1.1 Incremental change

By far the most frequent sort of change in organisations is incremental change. Incremental change alters the outer ring of the cultural onion, the behaviours, and doesn't disturb the more deeply held beliefs in an organisation. Examples of incremental change are producing more of something, doing something slightly differently and doing things better.

Although incremental change may be initiated by leader-managers, much incremental change is originated by the people most intimately connected with the organisation's processes, offers and customers. If they are suitably empowered, they can bring about the required change themselves. Incremental change will tend to be reactive, or pro-active with a short time horizon.

Incremental change is associated with management rather than leadership, since management operates close to equilibrium and stability. Incremental change doesn't lead to a change in the implicit underlying assumptions of the organisational paradigm. Management is concerned with linear systems in which cause-and-effect relationships are easily recognisable by the experienced manager. In terms of control, the task of management is to deal with negative feedback, keeping an on-going situation *in control*. Management is also concerned with efficiency. The characteristics of situations where incremental change will occur and will need to be handled are summarised in the first column of Exhibit 14.1.

EXHIBIT 14.1

Differences between incremental and transformational change[1] (adapted from Stacey, 1996)

Incremental change	Transformational change
Doing things better or doing more of them	Doing things very differently or doing different things
Stability	Close to instability
Paradigm unaffected	Paradigm changed
Linearity	Non-linearity, circularity
Cause–effect is easily recognisable	Cause–effect is obscure
Keep in control – negative feedback	Push out of control – positive feedback
Efficiency	Effectiveness
	Enlightenment

14.1.2 Transformational change

Transformational change involves changing one or more assumptions in the organisational paradigm, and with it the values of the organisation. Examples are the changes in the processes associated with doing things very differently, and with undertaking very different activities. A company coming under severe competition may be forced to adjust its paradigm.

The main differences between the situations appropriate for incremental management and transformational leadership can be seen by comparing the two lists in Exhibit 14.1. In general, transformational change will be a top-down process, initiated and possibly imposed by the top team, although it's certainly possible that a series of incremental changes may be seen with hindsight to have constituted a transformation. Transformation is associated with leadership. Here the leader is dealing with positive feedback, driving the organisation out of control in the sense that it is being driven out of its familiar ways to a position where it is operating close to the edge of instability, and close to a new equilibrium where the organisation is likely to be doing something very differently.

KEY CONCEPT   Two types of change can be recognised: incremental change, which takes place without disturbing the underlying organisational paradigm, and transformational change, which upsets elements of this paradigm. In general, leading incremental change requires management, while leading transformational change requires leadership. All change requires an alteration to mental models – and thus to knowledge – involving unfreezing of existing concepts, changing to the new, and subsequently freezing the new in place.

DISCUSSION   Which of incremental and transformational change would you associate more strongly with
POINT 14.1   an intended strategy and which with an emergent stategy?

14.2 The change process

14.2.1 A model of the change process

The basic process of change involved in both incremental and transformational change is one of unfreezing, change and refreezing.[2]

Unfreezing

The change process begins with the loosening of the hold of the established behaviour, value or paradigm because there is a feeling that change is needed and feasible. Three ingredients must be present to some degree for unfreezing to take place:[3]

- serious discomfort because there is evidence that doesn't support the current ways of thinking and/or doing;
- the connection of this discomforting information to important goals and ideals;
- enough 'psychological safety' to support action. It is important that a group is able to see the possibility of resolving the issue without the group having to be disbanded or dismembered.

If certain levels of profits and customer satisfaction are important organisational goals, two examples of discomforting information would be decreased profits and increased customer complaints. It's a common trick of politicians to invoke an external threat – real or not – to change values and behaviour, and this device is open to leader-managers. Nonaka and Takeuchi[4] recount how senior Japanese managers put their middle managers under severe pressure by presenting them with very stiff challenges in order to force change. A new leader with a new vision may be a catalyst for change because they see the main issues in a way that allows for their resolution: the new leader is providing the psychological safety that the group will survive, keeping its integrity intact. However, without a period of prior discomfort it may well be that the visionary leader won't be listened to; people are only ready to listen when they feel something is wrong and/or they could do better.

Change

Following unfreezing, change can then take place. The deeper the ring of the cultural onion that is being changed, however, the more difficult it is to bring about change. However, the deeper the ring of the onion that is changed, the more lasting and fundamental the change is likely to be – and the more general are the consequences. If behavioural change is coerced, the change is unlikely to last when the coercion is removed, as shown by the inability of communism to survive the totalitarian regimes that coerced whole nations for 50 years.

Unless it is done in an unthinking manner, to do something new requires that the mental models of an individual and/or of a group be altered, i.e. that knowledge is created. Knowledge is the reconciliation and meshing together of pieces of information. How they are reconciled and meshed together will depend on why it is being done and so the person creating knowledge must have a purpose. Thus it's important that the leader-manager makes very clear the purpose of change.

Refreezing

Following change, the new ways of thought and behaviour need to be locked in place, in the process termed *refreezing*. For refreezing to take place, confirmatory information needs to be provided to show that the new behaviours and/or beliefs more closely mirror the perceived reality. If such information isn't forthcoming, then coping, together with a search for a new approach, will continue. The importance of confirmatory evidence means that leader-managers should ensure that it is provided. One way of doing this is to ensure that the change programme includes some *quick hits* so that some success comes early in the programme, rather than there being an extended period of uncertainty when success in unclear. Once sufficient confirmatory information has been gained, then the situation will stabilise until further uncomfortable information triggers off the whole unfreezing–change–refreezing process once more.

14.2.2 Learning that supports incremental change

Simons[5] has put forward an interesting view of how to encourage organisational learning through the use of a control system. The idea is that an organisational control system should be used interactively, with its outputs the focus of discussion and learning. Most organisations will have several control systems already set up that could be used: for example budgetary systems, sales systems, cost-accounting systems, personnel systems, brand-revenue systems and project-monitoring systems.

Using an available control system has the obvious advantages that it's already in existence and people are familiar with it. Simons believes that there are four necessary features of a good interactive control system.[6] These are that the information generated by the system needs to:

- be of recurring importance to the highest levels of management;
- demand frequent and regular attention from operating managers at all levels;
- be interpreted and discussed in face-to-face meetings of superiors, subordinates and peers;
- be a catalyst for the continual challenge and debate of underlying assumptions and action plans.

The most appropriate control system to use interactively would be one that focuses on those variables whose values are uncertain and where these uncertainties could have serious consequences; in other words, the appropriate system is one that will highlight the strategic uncertainties. If a significant strategic uncertainty was the costs of inputs, then an appropriate interactive control system would be one containing current cost information and predicted prices. If the main strategic uncertainty was the future actions of competitors, then a system that reported on their activities, on such things as gains in market share, prices and other developments, would be the most appropriate.

Simons provides three reasons why only one of the organisation's control systems should be used rather than two or more. The first is that interactive control systems are time-consuming to use and leader-managers have limited time. The second reason is that individuals can process only a limited amount of information and using more than one system might cause information overload. Third, using several control systems might cause the dreaded *paralysis by analysis* and is likely to place people under great stress.[7]

14.2.3 Learning that supports transformational change

Putting middle managers under pressure in order to force learning as Nonaka and Takeuchi describe and the use of control systems for learning as suggested by Simons appear very suitable for incremental change and thus for keeping the organisation in line with the environment defined by the business and markets in which it is already engaged. They are appropriate vehicles for producing emergent strategies. However, these approaches appear less able to help with anticipating changes in the longer term, and thus with devising intended strategy.

The quest is to set up an 'engine for enquiry and renewal'[8] to encourage identification of elements of the organisational paradigm prior to their challenge and subsequent possible amendment. Pascale's view is that the engine for renewal is to be found in cultivating the 'tensions' that exist in all organisations and to move from a black-and-white, either/or frame of mind to one that can see different poles of a situation at the same time. For example, in most organisations there is a tension between the emphasis to be placed on the near and distant futures. To handle these tensions, Pascale sees the need for logical disputation, and he considers that one of the roles of the leader-manager is to organise 'constructive debate around the tensions' both to maintain the viability of current operations and to move the organisation to an appropriate future position. The building of scenarios would appear to offer one appropriate springboard for strategy. Group support systems offer one way to provide the process support that the group needs.

DISCUSSION
POINT 14.2

Are scenarios a form of interactive control system?

14.2.4   Difficulties in discussing change issues

Whichever sort of change takes place, incremental or transformational, the same basic process of change is involved. It is generally important for the people who are affected by the change to discuss what the change means for them. However, the difficulty in discussing and debating change issues depends on the circumstances.

People are much more ready to debate and discuss some things than others. This hinges on which ring of the cultural onion is being worked on. Bowman[9] has described these as zones of debate, as shown in Exhibit 14.2. This diagram is valid for both individuals[10] and for groups. People are reasonably happy discussing norms of behaviour but less so with discussing values. Values may be discussed, but generally this would be outside of formal meetings, as values often concern vested interests and personal reputations. But to make significant progress there is a need to 'surface' prevailing mental models and challenge them in order to build a shared vision.[11] In general, however, the core assumptions in the organisational paradigm aren't discussed, often because they are never surfaced. However, the greater the feeling of crisis, the more people may feel that they must challenge elements of the paradigm, since the paradigm is failing them.

EXHIBIT 14.2

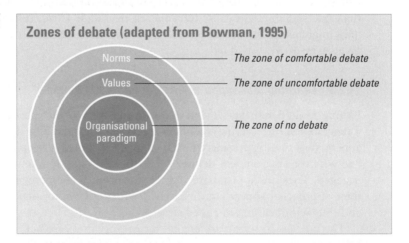

Zones of debate (adapted from Bowman, 1995)

Norms ——————— *The zone of comfortable debate*

Values ——————— *The zone of uncomfortable debate*

Organisational paradigm ——————— *The zone of no debate*

14.3   Implementing strategic change

14.3.1   Unfreezing

A learning organisation is an organisation skilled in continually seeking out knowledge deficiencies, acquiring, creating, spreading and managing knowledge, and *expert at modifying its behaviour to reflect its new knowledge*. We now turn our attention to the italicised part of this definition, to the process of change. Note that in the definition of a learning organisation the term 'behaviour' is used rather than other aspects of culture. This doesn't mean that change shouldn't work on beliefs, simply that behaviour *must* be changed if the organisation is to adapt. Behavioural change may result from changes in values or from changes in the organisational paradigm.

The starting point for any change is to unfreeze the current behaviour and/or belief (values and elements of the organisational paradigm). While this requires that the group realise that change is necessary, there are two further requirements for change to be brought about: there needs to be the will to undertake the change process and also the resources to carry out the change. In a learning organisation any associated incremental changes will occur almost automatically as long as the resources are available, since the need for change and the desire for change will evolve together. In this case, the main concern for the people driving change, termed *change agents,* is to tap into the organisational will and obtain the necessary resources. The reverse is the case with top-down change, since the senior managers can make the resources available: here, the main concern is with the change management process itself.

14.3.2 Enablers of and impediments to change

When any change is being considered, it's important to consider the forces involved, those that are driving change and those that are impeding it. Very often the drivers for change are economic: to increase market share, to increase profits, to expand into new markets. And very often they can be argued for logically even if the main drivers in practice are likely to be personal ambition. In contrast, the impediments are more often emotional and based on personal gains and losses.[12] A leader-manager must expect resistance to some if not many of the changes that they are seeking to bring about, and a forcefield analysis is a good start to see where resistance to change might lie and where to seek allies.

A force-field diagram such as that shown in Exhibit 14.3 shows the balance between the forces driving change and those inhibiting it. The particular example is from a medium-sized engineering firm that wished to move towards a learning organisation driven by enhanced competition and the demands of its parent company. The changes included moving people into different roles and reducing the sharp demarcation between departments, especially with the setting up of project teams. The

EXHIBIT 14.3

An example of force-field analysis

Forces driving change

- Enhanced competition
- Profit demands from the parent company
- Need for cost reductions
- Need to move to become a learning organisation
- Frustrations felt by junior managers

Forces inhibiting change

- Status of departmental managers dependent on the number of staff reporting to them
- Inability or unwillingness of some staff to learn new skills
- Lack of IT knowledge

analysis indicated that major resistance could be expected from the departmental managers, with lesser but still significant inhibitors being the resistance of some staff to learning new skills and a lack of knowledge of IT. To reduce the forces inhibiting change, the departmental managers were given an assurance of no salary cuts whatever their subsequent position and number of people they had reporting to them. The roles of the junior managers were enhanced, and they were empowered to take on more problem-solving roles. Training, particularly in IT, was strengthened. Approximately 25 people who couldn't fit into the new multitasking structure were either made redundant or given early retirement.

One aspect that is particularly important in change management is the role of a strong culture, especially when the changes sought are transformational. Whereas a strong culture is valuable when the culture is in line with strategy, it isn't valuable when there is misalignment – as IBM found in the 1980s when strategic drift had set in.

14.3.3 People's reaction to change

Almost everyone will feel some sort of stress when facing and enacting change. An important requirement for the change agent is to be able to empathise with people who are undergoing change and to manage their self-esteem, what individuals feel about themselves. Esteem will suffer in many cases because skills will be devalued before other skills are fully learned. Part of the empathy is to understand the phases that affect people who are undergoing the unfreezing–change–refreezing process. A model of the change process, termed *the coping cycle*, as it affects the people involved in change is shown in Exhibit 14.4.

The first stage of the coping cycle is **denial**. The tendency to deny the validity of new ideas, at least initially, does seem to be a general reaction to the announcement of change.[13] The responses are along the lines of 'Why fix it if it isn't broken?' and 'We have always done it that way'. Managing change in past-oriented cultures, typical of Asian societies, poses considerable challenges.[14]

Paradoxically perhaps, self-esteem could rise during the period of denial as the advantages of the present job and the value of the group are emphasised. Performance levels relative to some 'normal' fiduciary level could go up or down due to the

EXHIBIT 14.4

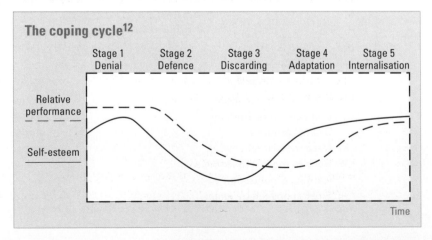

The coping cycle[12]

combination of this increased self-esteem and the energy expended through discussing the impending changes. If change occurs without warning, then the performance loss could be large.

The second stage of the coping cycle is **defence**, where the individuals have to come to terms with the fact that change is going to take place. This phase is often accompanied by a feeling of frustration and depression as the individual doesn't know what to do. This can lead to defensive reactions. Both self-esteem and performance are likely to suffer significantly.

Defence and denial have focused on the past. In stage three of the coping process the focus is on the change to the future, on **discarding** the past and looking forward. If possible, it's valuable to allow people to experiment or experience the future: through visits to organisations operating in the 'future' way, 'playing through' the possibilities by using a computer simulation or, where a new or enhanced computer information system is to be installed, allowing staff to play around with it. In this way a positive attitude to change may develop, and the change may begin to be seen as inevitable and/or may begin to be seen as for the better. Self-esteem begins to recover as people begin to resolve problems and take the initiative, but performance may continue to drop, not least because this is often the time when the old processes must be carried out while the new ones are being phased in.

The fourth stage of the coping process is **adaptation**. Here a process of testing and adaptation takes place: adaptation of the individual to the new working practices and adaptation of the practices as people learn about them. It's often a trial-and-error process, and the build-up of skill can be slow and frustrating. If a group is involved – as is likely with strategic change – then the strength of the group will support the individuals within it. It's important to allow people to have control over how the activities are carried out as long as the required outputs are achieved.

The final stage, **internalising**, corresponds to the refreezing stage when individuals internalise the changes as they become part of 'normal' behaviour. Relative performance will return to 'normal', although this could mean that the absolute output is much better than before the new method of working was introduced. The group has re-established itself as a well-functioning team and built team strength as a result of the problems it has faced and overcome.

It should be noted that the 'buy-in' to change often follows the marketing model, with first the innovators, then the early adopters, followed by the majority and then finally the laggards. The innovators are the leaders of change and thus in the early days of change the leader-manager should seek out such people and make sure that their acceptance of change is noticed by others, particularly by the early adopters who will be looking to the innovators to see what's happening. As time progresses, the next group that the leader-manager should focus on are the early adopters, and later the majority and the laggards.

KEY CONCEPT People facing change often go through five phases as they discard the old and internalise the new: denial, defence, discarding, adaptation and internalising. It's important for the change agent to recognise the stages that individuals have reached and to empathise with the difficulties they may be having.

14.3.4 Where to place the emphasis for change

Leader-managers wishing to initiate change must decide where to start the change process: with change to the paradigm, to values or to behaviour. While incremental change is almost solely concerned with changes in behaviour, this isn't the case with transformational change, where a change in beliefs is needed. The contrasting assumptions concerning effecting change at the belief and behavioural levels are set out in Exhibit 14.5.[15]

Many commentators agree that for leader-managers to consider change to the deeper levels of culture, they need to think in terms of years rather than months.[16] With the rate of change in many organisations today, it probably isn't reasonable to work on the deeper levels of cultural change alone.

Schaffer and Thomson[17] contrast two approaches to change management, the designed-involvement and result-driven approaches, as shown in Exhibit 14.6. While designed-involvement programmes and results-driven programmes share common methods for initiating change, they differ very significantly in philosophy. The designed-involvement approach is much longer-term than is the results-driven approach.

Schaffer and Thomson's obvious preference for the results-driven approach may indicate a US or Anglo-Saxon bias. They describe approaches such as total quality management and continuous improvement as 'rain dance' approaches to change, because like the rain dance they allow participants to feel good about what they are doing, while making little or no measurable contribution to organisational performance.

EXHIBIT 14.5

Contrasting assumptions about change (adapted from Beer *et al.*, 1990)

	Belief change	Behaviour change
Causes of beliefs and behaviours	Problems in behaviour arise from individual knowledge, attitudes and beliefs	Individual knowledge, attitudes and beliefs are shaped by recurring patterns of behaviour
Target for change: beliefs or behaviours	The primary target of renewal should be attitudes and ideas; actual behaviour should be secondary	The primary target of renewal should be behaviour; attitudes and ideas should be secondary
Target for change: individual or organisation	The target for renewal should be at the individual level	The target for renewal should be at the organisational level, with roles, responsibilities and relationships
How change can be effected	Behaviour can be isolated and changed individually	The effects of the organisation on the individual are greater than those of the individual on the organisation, thus emphasis should be on organisational change

EXHIBIT 14.6

Comparing improvement efforts (after Schaffer and Thomson, 1992)

Designed-involvement programmes	Results-driven programmes
1 The improvement effort is defined mainly in long-term, global terms. ('We are going to be viewed as number one in quality in our industry.')	1 There are measurable short-term performance improvement goals, even though the effort is a long-term, sustaining one. ('Within 60 days, we will be paying 95% of claims within 10 days.')
2 Management takes action steps because they are 'correct' and fit the programme's philosophy. ('I want every manager in the division involved in an action.')	2 Management takes action steps because they appear to lead directly toward some improved results. ('Let's put together a small group to work with you to solve this machine downtime problem.')
3 The programme's champion(s) counsels patience and fortitude. ('Don't be looking for results this year or next year. This is a long-term process, not a quick fix.')	3 The mood is one of impatience. Management wants to see results now, even though the change process is a long-term commitment. ('If we can't eliminate at least half of the cost disadvantage within the next three months, we should consider closing the plant.')
4 Staff experts and consultants indoctrinate everyone into the mystique and vocabulary of the programme. ('It will be a Tower of Babel if we try to work on these problems before everyone, managers and employees alike, has been through the quality training and has a common vocabulary and a common tool kit.')	4 Staff experts and consultants help managers achieve results. ('We could probably work up a way to measure customer attitudes on delivery service within a week or two so that you can start improving it.')
5 Staff experts and consultants urge managers and employees to have faith in the approach and to support it. ('True employee involvement will take a lot of time and a lot of effort, and though it may be a real struggle for managers, they need to understand that it is essential to become a total quality company.')	5 Managers and employees are encouraged to make certain for themselves that the approach actually yields results. ('Why don't you send a few of your people to the quality course to test out whether it really helps them to achieve their improvement goals in the next month or two?')
6 The procedure requires management to make big investments up front – before results have been demonstrated. ('During the first year, we expect to concentrate on awareness building and skill training. Then, while managers begin to diagnose problems and opportunities in their areas, a consultant will be surveying all of our customers to get their views on the 14 critical dimensions of service. And then . . .')	6 Relatively little investment is needed to get the process started; conviction builds as results materialise. ("Let's see if this approach can help us increase sales of high-end products in a couple of branches. If it does, we can take the method to the other branches.')

Business process re-engineering (BPR) is one results-driven approach, with the emphasis on processes and the results of processes rather than on attitudes.[18] The starting point for BPR is the blank piece of paper, what ought to be if you totally ignored the current situation. Thus the history and the internal context of the organisation are ignored. Re-engineering also dismisses the barriers to change that will arise as functional boundaries are displaced and career ladders and personal empires are removed.

In practice, a balance between the designed-involvement and results-driven approaches is probably wise. One approach where time permits would be to begin by working on the norms of behaviour, but if possible allowing groups to fine-tune their own ways of working. When some success has been achieved, the leader-manager could try working on the values that underpin the norms and other behaviours. For example, suppose that petty fiddling of expenses, stationery, etc. was going on. A start could be made by rigorously vetting all expense claims. The underlying value that employees might have is that taking from the firm is not robbery. If a bonus scheme was introduced whereby all employees gained from increased profits, and thus from fewer losses, this might reduce the fiddling as well as other sorts of loss. In the John Lewis Partnership, notices are apparently sometimes put near light switches saying 'Turn this light off – you're spending my bonus.'[19] The final stage might be to work on the paradigm, although this is a long-term effort. At all stages, however, it's important for leader-managers to be sensitive about culture, at the very least working with the grain wherever possible.

DISCUSSION POINT 14.3   Schaffer and Thomson consider two approaches to change: the designed-involvement and the results-driven. Which of these is more closely linked to the view that beliefs are the more appropriate focus of change?

14.4 Appropriate change-management styles

The leader-manager must decide where to place the emphasis between altering behaviours and altering beliefs. In general, organisations will act differently when facing the same environmental change, because they will have different resources and different cultures and are likely to be positioned in strategically different ways. The specific manner in which they react to change will be contingent on the position in which they find themselves.

Four styles of change management have been be identified by Dunphy and Stace.[20] The **collaborative style** is one in which there is full input from all members of the group to the change required. A smaller level of participation occurs with the **consultative style**, where the people involved and affected by the proposed changes are asked for their views. The third style is the **directive style**, whereby people are told what they are to do and they are reasonably happy with the changes. The final style is the **coercive style**, where people aren't happy with the proposed changes and resist them.

The approaches of Nonaka and Takeuchi[21] and Simons[22] and that described in the last section might have suggested that a considerable level of participation is appropriate in all change situations, but this isn't the case. The appropriate style of change management is contingent on four factors: the *magnitude of the change*, whether it's incremental or transformational; the *fit of the organisation to its environment*; the *time available for discussion*; and the *support for change within the organisation*. The

EXHIBIT 14.7

Change management styles (after Dunphy and Stace, 1993)

		Type of change	
		Incremental change	Transformational change
Style of change management	Collaborative/ consultative	Participative evolution	Charismatic transformation
	Directive/ coercive	Forced evolution	Dictatorial transformation

appropriate and/or actual process of enacting the two types of change is shown in Exhibit 14.7.

- Participative evolution is most appropriate for incremental change when an organisation broadly matches its environment and only minor adjustments are required. It's also the appropriate response when there is a poorish fit between the organisation and its environment but time is available for people to participate and key individuals and groups favour change. The appropriate style of change management would be collaborative or consultative.

- Forced evolution is most appropriate for incremental change under similar conditions of organisational–environmental fit and time availability as for participative evolution. However, this is the appropriate approach when key interests oppose change. The appropriate style of change management would be directive or coercive.

- Charismatic transformation is most appropriate when there is a substantial mismatch between an organisation and its environment, when there is little time for extensive participation but there is support for radical change within the organisation. The appropriate style of change management would be collaborative or consultative.

- Dictatorial transformation is most appropriate when an organisation doesn't match its environment, there is no time for extensive participation and there is little or no support for radical change, but radical change is vital for organisational well-being. When an organisation is performing so badly that the chief executive is sacked, the new chief executive is often appointed to carry out a dictatorial transformation. The autocrat needs a clear vision of the organisational goals but should let the people in the organisation who know the operational details decide on the means of achieving it. The situation is like a ship in a storm; the captain knows the port he wants to shelter in but he uses the expertise of the first mate to take the most appropriate course. The appropriate style of change management would be directive or coercive.

Different styles of change management are likely to be appropriate at different times in an organisation's existence, and the appropriate approach wouldn't necessarily be the same for all parts of an organisation.

14.5 Change mechanisms

Whichever *style* of change leadership is adopted, the appropriate *mechanisms* to use depend on the stage of organisational development. Exhibit 14.8 sets out the view of Schein.[23]

EXHIBIT 14.8

Cultural change mechanisms (after Schein, 1992)

Organisational stage	Change mechanism
Founding and early growth	1 Incremental change through evolution 2 Change through insight 3 Change through promotion from within the culture
Midlife	4 Change through systematic promotion from selected subcultures 5 Planned change through organisation development projects and the creation of learning structures 6 Change through technological development
Maturity and decline	7 Change through infusion of outsiders 8 Unfreezing through scandal and myth explosion 9 Destruction and rebirth

14.5.1 Founding and early growth

During founding and early growth, incremental change will occur through the normal growth pattern, with the founder delegating authority for example. Change through insight will occur when senior managers reflect on their own experiences and on external stimuli, for example from consultants and from attending courses and trade shows. These tend to preserve and enhance the existing culture, in the sense that the leader-managers don't change and their perceptions are developed rather than transformed. In contrast, the third change mechanism involves promoting managers already within the organisation who have views that match better what are seen as the new situation that the organisation is facing. Because of their knowledge of the organisation they are acceptable, whereas an outside appointment might not be. Senior managers need to have recognised the behaviours and beliefs that they wish the new appointments to foster in order to do this effectively.

14.5.2 Midlife

When an organisation reaches midlife, it has become larger and more complex. Much more of the culture will be taken for granted and included in well-established routines. While the three change mechanisms open to it when it was younger are still available, the complexity provides further opportunities. For example, promotion of insiders with appropriate differing views is now easier, since the organisation is likely to have developed distinct subcultures.

Organisation development is a process whereby an organisation deliberately sets out on a road to organisational learning. The internal context is deliberately designed to enhance learning and to build on success.

Schein[24] gives the following example of a deliberately designed internal context:

> When Procter & Gamble decided to change the way it manufactured various products, it started with a staff group that was empowered to design a whole new plant. The staff was even allowed to hire the plant manager so that they could ensure that he or she would be a person with genuinely different assumptions from those that had traditionally prevailed in the company. Such a manager was hired, and the new plant was successful. Now the problem was how to spread the innovation. The staff group decided to apprentice young, high-potential plant managers to the new plant manager. After a few years these managers understood the new system well enough to be moved out into other new plants to introduce the system. Only when a number of such new plants were working successfully were these managers, who were now experienced, moved into old unionised plants that would require a longer period of conversion. It took almost twenty years before the last of these plants was converted to the new system.

Technological change has been observed to be a method of bringing about organisational change and this is particularly true of developments in IT. Electronic mail provides an example, often making organisations more open; people have access to much more information than before, and they are willing to e-mail superiors who they would never have dared to meet or send a written memo to.

14.5.3 Maturity and decline

Particularly when there is a feeling of decline or strategic drift, change can often best be brought about by introducing outsiders into positions of authority in the organisation. The changes will be particularly dramatic if the organisation is facing a turnaround situation. People who cling to the old ways of working are forced out of the organisation. This process will be hastened if scandal has surrounded the previous incumbents or if myths, part of the paradigm, have been exposed.

An extreme form of change is destruction and rebirth. An example of this was during the 1980s when Rupert Murdoch moved his newspaper offices across London from Fleet Street to Wapping. In so doing he completely changed the culture: for example, information technology was widely introduced in production and the electricians' union replaced the printers'. The old habits of strikes and double manning by printers ceased.

KEY CONCEPT   The appropriate style of change management is contingent on four factors: the magnitude of the change, whether incremental or transformational; the fit of the organisation to its environment; the time available for discussion; and the support for change within the organisation. The change mechanisms open to a leader-manager differ depending on the stage of growth of the organisation; however, those particular to one stage can also be used in subsequent stages.

14.6 Roles in the change process

14.6.1 The agents of change and the change agent

An *agent of change* can be defined as the person who seeks to initiate and manage a planned change process.[25] There are likely to be several agents of change involved with any one change process, people who move in and out of importance as the change progresses. Davenport[26] has identified several 'players' in the change process:

- the advocate, who proposes change;
- the sponsor, who legitimises change;
- the targets, who are the people who undergo change;
- the change agents, who implement change;
- the process owner, who is typically the most senior target.

Thus the *change agent* has the specific role of implementing change. The change agent is the individual or group who carries through change in an organisation. In many cases the change agent(s) is an employee of the organisation and is given special responsibilities. Often, however, external consultants may be recruited to effect change, and this might involve a team of people. Thus when the term 'change agent' is used it shouldn't necessarily be inferred that there is only one person involved or that they are company employees. While one person is often the source of an idea or invention, a team is generally required to innovate. When change is being considered, it should be realised that five roles are being played out: one individual may play all roles (as a chief executive might, even being the target); alternatively each role might be played by a different person or group, and thus many people are likely to be involved.

If the change agent is the chief executive, some of the problems with strategic change management will disappear or be significantly reduced; for example, in many situations there should be little difficulty in getting the resources required to bring about change. However, many chief executives haven't the time to be closely involved with any one specific change programme and some haven't the inclination, thus they delegate the task to others. Change agents need not be a member of the top team, but they are almost always leader-managers. They have a particularly difficult task. It's as well to recall the oft-quoted extract from Machiavelli:[27]

> there is nothing more difficult to take in hand, more perilous to conduct, or more uncertain in its success, than to take the lead in the introduction of a new order of things. Because the innovator has for enemies all those who have done well under the old conditions, and only lukewarm defenders in those who may do well under the new.

The requirements of a successful change agent are listed in Exhibit 14.9, grouped into five areas. The initial objectives could change as conditions, or rather perceptions of conditions, alter, and the change agent needs to be sensitive to this. Coupled with this is the need for a strong political awareness to understand the ebbs and flows of interest and power around the change programme, and to be sensitive to people's feelings. Communication and negotiation skills will be paramount in reconciling the many demands that change makes on an organisation. While invention is from within the individual, the team members must tune in to a force outside of themselves[28] and

EXHIBIT 14.9

The requirements of a change agent[29]

Relating to objectives

1 Sensitivity to the way changes in senior personnel, management perceptions and business conditions impact the goals of the change programme.
2 Clarity in defining objectives.
3 Flexibility in responding to changing conditions.

Political awareness

4 Being aware of potential coalitions and understanding their significance.
5 Continually ensuring that more senior management are backing the team.
6 Balancing conflicting goals and perceptions.
7 Being aware of the extent of their own power.

Sensitivity

8 Being able to empathise with people undergoing a change process.
9 Sensitivity to the organisational context in terms of where the forces for change and inhibiting forces might come from, and in the style of change process that will be acceptable.

Communication and negotiation

10 Networking skills to establish and maintain the appropriate contacts within and outside the organisation.
11 Communication skills to inform team members, superiors and networkers of progress and needs.
12 Ability to enrol others in plans and ideas.
13 Negotiating with key individuals within the organisation for resources.

Team building and leadership

14 Team-building abilities to identify key potential team members, enrol them and motivate them to ensure they work as a team.
15 Team management to define team members' responsibilities and delegate authority accordingly.
16 Team leadership to provide a vision for the future.

Individual characteristics

17 Enthusiasm for the change.
18 Tolerance of ambiguity, being able to work effectively and efficiently in an uncertain environment.

thus team-building skills will also be a significant attribute. Finally, it is vital that the change agent is enthusiastic and able to tolerate ambiguity.

14.6.2 Tactics for and against change

The mechanisms described in Section 14.5 were 'overt' and often planned moves to introduce change into an organisation. But the change agent will need to employ tactics to counter the often covert resistance to change which they must expect. Exhibit 14.10 lists many of the moves that might be made to counter change and also the moves to counter these countermoves.

EXHIBIT 14.10

Countermoves and counter-countermoves to change[30]

Countermoves

- **Divert resources** Give other priorities to staff who will be key to the project's success.
- **Exploit inertia** Request that something else needs to happen before progress can be made on the project – for example, wait until a report is ready, wait for a committee to deliberate.
- **Keep goals vague and complex** This widens the number of people who might think they will be adversely affected by the proposals and thus the number of potential 'resisters'.
- **Great idea – let's do it properly** Involve so many representatives and consultants that there will be a great many differing views and conflicting interests.
- **Dissipate energies** Get people to conduct surveys, collect data, write reports, make overseas trips.
- **Reduce the credibility of the change agent** Spread damaging rumours about past activities and lack of success, particularly among the lukewarm supporters of the change programme.
- **Do not declare resistance** Openly declaring resistance to the proposed change gives the change agent knowledge of the opposition and of the rationale they are putting forward.

Countering countermoves to change

- **Establish clear objectives and a clear programme of activities** The use of computer project management software can be a great help in establishing the programme.
- **Create a prior 'felt need'** If people want change because they have had the reasons explained to them, then resistance is likely to be minimal.
- **Rely on face-to-face communication** A personal approach is usually more effective in winning agreement and understanding than the impersonal e-mail or memo.
- **Exploit a crisis** A crisis, especially if it is seen to arise from outside the organisation and can be seen to be connected to the change being pursued, can be used to rally support.
- **Seek support early on** Obtain top management support and cultivate key players in the organisation prior to getting deeply involved in the detail of the project. Co-opting opponents may be tactically useful.
- **Get a steering committee set up** This committee will act to support the project team when it's formed. It must include senior management and key players in the organisation.

14.6.3 Middle managers

Hampden-Turner and Trompenaars[31] make the point that in the USA, the top team specifies the strategy in a very precise way: top management knows or thinks it knows what is required. In such a situation middle managers are the implementors of highly defined change; their role is to assemble the resources required, make plans to implement the change, and control costs and resource usage. They are likely to be seen as inhibitors of change, especially as the precise specification of the change developed by the top team has probably been made without full knowledge of the capabilities required.

In contrast, Japanese senior management takes a less precise approach to strategy. Hampden-Turner and Trompenaars illustrate this by contrasting the Japanese approach, where the senior managers would say to middle managers 'We are going to make a microprocessor – what kind of microprocessors would you like the firm to make?' with the US approach, in which senior managers would tell middle managers 'This is the new microprocessor we want'.

Nonaka and Takeuchi[32] describe the role of the middle manager in the more flexible Japanese situation. They take the broad vision of top managers and combine it with the detailed, often tacit, knowledge from front-line employees, such as salespersons and factory operatives, to make the vision a reality. Many modern businesses are now taking this view, as Exhibit 14.11 illustrates. Thus middle managers have a very creative and pivotal role in modern business, much more than the downsizers and lean-management gurus would have us believe.

EXHIBIT 14.11

The role of middle managers[33]

Recent consulting engagements have suggested that the middle manager today is increasingly the linchpin of strategic and competitive competence. Those men and women are the key to balancing tensions within the organisation through becoming the stabilisers who make enduring change possible and the source of real-time strategies. They have become the link between strategy and action – in short, the very opposite of the notion of middle managers as bureaucratic time servers and the narrow and repetitive conductors of information

One problem that middle managers have as the initiators of change is in obtaining the ear of top management to acquire the resources they need to support the change. Another problem is that technical people have difficulty in finding ways to translate their technical ideas into a form that allows senior management to evaluate them.[34]

14.6.4 Project teams[35]

A project can be considered to be a set of processes aimed at achieving a well-defined objective within a specified timescale. Thus the building of a new car production line would be a project; running the line would not.

Project management has long been recognised as a specialist field; indeed, there are project management qualifications and professional project management organisations. Traditionally, the term has been associated with large and long-timescale civil engineering projects such as the construction of the Channel Tunnel and the Millennium Dome. However, the concern for rapid response has led to the demand for organisations to be flexible, able to cope with complexity and at ease with innovating and initiating change. As long ago as 1969, Bennis[36] argued that one of the key descriptive terms for a flexible, organic organisational structure is that it's temporary. He claims that 'these structures will be adaptive, rapidly-changing temporary systems. They will be project teams organised around problems to be solved by groups of relative strangers with diverse professional skills.' Thus very often the project team will only exist for the time of the project, being disbanded once the project is completed.

The use of project teams to tackle complex issues is widespread throughout business,[37,38] so much so that there is the view that management has become very much project-based management – at least for all leader-managers when they are involved in change. This widespread use of project teams means that skill in project management has become one of the key requirements for leader-managers.

One complication for project leader-managers is the requirement to work with colleagues over whom they have no direct authority. This is particularly apparent in the public sector when a project team is set up with members from several public agencies. For example, a project team to consider how to reduce youth crime might involve schools, youth employment agencies, the police, the local chamber of trade and a host of other organisations. Another complication lies in the inclusion of individuals in the project team from units that haven't empowered them to act on behalf of their unit and require them to report back before anything can be agreed. There are individuals who expect to be consulted fully before others take action and introduce changes that will affect them. The need for the project leader-manager to be aware of the power they themselves have and to use it appropriately is very evident in these situations.

DISCUSSION
POINT 14.4

In what ways do the roles of project leader-managers and change agents differ?

Spreading knowledge

Moving people through the organisation in a structured way is common in firm-based labour markets such as Germany and Japan, where an individual's career is framed by the firm rather than by professional qualifications. In this way, when a person becomes a leader-manager they have a very wide knowledge of many aspects of the company and share a common mindset with other leader-managers. Similarly, the composition of project teams can be designed so that the tacit knowledge generated and spread through team discussions will automatically be spread throughout the organisation when the team members go back to their 'home' units and discuss what they have been doing. During teamwork, prevailing mental models will have been surfaced and challenged and new and shared knowledge will have been developed.

SUMMARY

- Change is a journey not an event, and on this journey organisations face two types of strategic change, incremental and transformational. In general, incremental change is a managerial issue, transformational change is a leadership issue. The general change process of unfreezing–change–refreezing is the same for both types of change, but the part of the culture that is changed is likely to differ. Three 'zones of debate' are recognised, which differ in the ease with which they are open to discussion. EXHIBIT 14.1, EXHIBIT 14.2
- A force-field analysis can illustrate which are the drivers and which are the inhibitors of change. EXHIBIT 14.3
- People facing change often go through five phases as they discard the old and internalise the new: denial, defence, discarding, adaption and internalising. It is important for the change agent to recognise the stages that individuals have reached and to empathise with the difficulties they may be having. EXHIBIT 14.4

- There are two opposing views on how to effect change in organisations. One approach is to focus on behaviours in the belief that individual knowledge, attitudes and beliefs are shaped by recurring patterns of behaviour, and the primary target of renewal should be behaviours. The other sees problems in behaviour arising from individual beliefs, so the primary target of renewal should be beliefs. EXHIBIT 14.5, EXHIBIT 14.6
- The appropriate style of change management is contingent on four factors: the magnitude of the change, incremental or transformational; the fit of the organisation to its environment; the time available for discussion; and the support for change within the organisation. EXHIBIT 14.7
- There are many cultural change mechanisms that leader-managers can use to bring about change. The role of the change agent is a demanding one, with special emphasis on interpersonal and political skills. In particular, they must be adept at recognising blocking tactics used by people who are resistant to change. EXHIBITS 14.8 TO 14.10
- Organisational learning is developed by using project teams and a control system. If an organisation can establish either of these mechanisms, then incremental change almost becomes a way of life. Transformational learning is not helped so much by project or operational control systems, and here there needs to be learning about the longer term through such activities as scenario building.

SELF-CHECK

1 Reconsider the learning outcomes for this chapter. Check that you feel confident that you can carry out the activities listed there.

2 Having read this chapter, you should be able to define the following terms:

agent of change	internalisation	transformational change
change agent	learning organisation	unfreezing
charismatic transformation	participative evolution	zone of comfortable debate
dictatorial transformation	project	zone of disturbing debate
forced evolution	refreezing	zone of uncomfortable debate
incremental change		

MINI-CASE

Organisational culture change – the BCM story (Mullins[39])

For many organisations the 'old' ways of doing business simply cannot continue if the company is to survive in today's global market. For many years organisations thrived and prospered by focusing their efforts on their 'core' competencies – basically doing one thing and doing it very well. The organisation needed to support this business focus tended to emphasise issues such as structure, procedures and loyalty to the organisation. A hierarchical structure, with layers of management each responsible for a specific area of the business, was very effective in this environment.

For example, in a traditional manufacturing environment each producing unit had a supervisor – responsible for organising and controlling both the flow of work and the people doing the work. The training programmes developed to support these supervisors tended to focus on issues such as effective employee discipline, evaluating employees, and other skills designed to improve the supervisor's skill at doing the job. Little or no attention was paid to developing the supervisors' skills in areas such as interpersonal communications and working with other people.

The speed of communication and transportation, coupled with the emergence of many former 'colonial' states as major competitors in the world economy, has caused a dramatic shift in the environment of manufacturing throughout the world. The scale of this change may very well be viewed by historians as being of at least the magnitude of the Industrial Revolution, and possibly even greater in its scope and impact on the workplace.

Change at BCM

Boots the Chemist (BTC) is a long-established company, well known in the UK high street for its retailing activity serviced by in-house production facilities – a typical vertically integrated company. This integrated relationship allowed the production people to concentrate on technical excellence, rather than seeking outlets for their production in the open market.

In the late 1980s and early 1990s Boots underwent a major reorganisation, splitting the business into strategic business units (SBUs). This split the retail, healthcare and manufacturing functions of Boots into separate divisions and required each SBU, including Boots Contract Manufacturing (BCM), to function as a stand-alone profit centre.

Top management at BCM began the process of becoming a profit centre by conducting an exhaustive analysis of the organisation and of the needs of their new customers. Customers were seeking flexibility and reliability in their producers to make the competitive difference when seeking a supplier of products. Benchmarking surveys of other organisations throughout the UK and other countries suggested five major new strategies for BCM, all of which have required initiative, drive and patience. The first was to turn the organisation into one that was totally customer-focused. Second, as good customer service has become of paramount importance in retaining and developing BCM's customer base, there was a need to develop cross-functional processes to improve product development and reduce customer lead times. The third strategy was to establish key performance indicators[a] in order to challenge the organisation's effectiveness. This is being driven through all levels of the organisation, across all functions, and represents the commitment to continuously improve business performance. Fourth, there was room to improve production efficiency through investment in new plant. This was done. But supporting this investment in new plant and equipment also required tapping the talents and enthusiasm of the people. In order to achieve this fifth goal, it was decided to move the organisation in the direction of team-working. This approach offered new answers to old problems, involved employees in every level of the production process, and released management from merely controlling the minute-by-minute activities of the workforce.

Three decisions made early in the process were critical to the team building that was to follow:

1 It was decided that the 'supervisors' – brought up on a diet of 'direct and control' – were unlikely to be the team leaders of the future. It was not that their skills for the job were wrong, just that the environment had changed and those skills were obsolete. A completely new set of competencies was developed for the team leaders, and an assessment centre was designed to select people for these key positions.

2 The second decision was to align the production and engineering management functions within each department by assigning technicians to each team. Before team-working, engineering and production had two entirely independent management structures at the department level, which only came together at the factory level. Thus the impact of losing all the 'craft/apprenticeship' heritage was the most devastating element of team-working for the technicians to come to grips with. In addition, the majority of the technicians had to undergo more technical training so

---

[a] Equivalent to the objectives in a balanced scorecard.

that they could truly become multi-skilled. For some of the fitters this has required a substantial amount of additional training.

3   The third decision had major ramifications for the packaging floor. Previously there had been six separate pay grades, with assignment to the grades being based on the skill level required for each position. So many grades tended to create confusion and competition within each department. The decision was made to simplify the grading structure by concentrating on three grades, and to provide training opportunities to upgrade over time.

Team building at BCM

Paralleling the revolution in the structure of the organisation has been a major revolution in the field of training and development. BCM has been very supportive of employee development programmes, including programmes such as basic reading skills and a formalised NVQ framework available to all employees. While traditional training methods are fine for teaching these 'skills', they do not fully address the specific issues that BCM needed, including taking responsibility for one's own actions, empowerment, and learning to value each other's contributions. One increasingly popular method of training has been the use of 'experiential' methods. Experiential (or experience-based) training focuses on 'learning by doing'. For example, to train a group in problem-solving methods, traditional training would probably include a video on problem solving, followed by a lecture on the steps to solving a problem. A creative trainer might finish with a case study or 'hands-on' problem for the group to solve. Some participants would learn a lot, but some would learn very little because they were not engaged in the process.

An experiential training programme would emphasise the involvement of *all* participants right from the start. The group would be given an activity which required them to actually solve a problem. In this way the group would 'learn' as they actually did the activity. Failure would cause them to replan, while success would allow them to begin to develop a process for team problem solving that works and is transferable to the work setting.

BCM management chose an experiential programme to provide core teamwork training for both team leaders and the teams themselves. The specifics of the programmes are described in Exhibits 14.12 and 14.13. The overall programme is large – over 60 programmes will be run in a period of approximately one year.

Some issues crucial to the overall success of the team-building programme take place immediately after the training sessions are over. The teams generally meet their manager the day after the programme to discuss those work issues identified during training and to help 'verify' to the team the belief that things can move forward by connecting issues and learning from the course to the workplace. This is a critical 'first step' in bringing the skills taught during training back to the work setting. Follow-up training is also a critical part of the team-building process. Two full-time facilitators have been appointed. Their main focus has been working with management helping them to take ownership of the whole process, both before and after the team-building event.

Discussion point 14.5

List the new strategies for BCM.

- Identify the new form of (internal) architecture.
- If you had to evaluate the BCM change programme, what would you look for?

Laurie Mullins is grateful to John Campbell, Executive and Staff Training Ltd; Julian Page, Boots the Chemist; and Richard J Wagner, University of Wisconsin, Whitewater, USA, for providing this information.

EXHIBIT 14.12

Team leader programmes

Outcomes

- Develop management skills.
- Understand the difference between supervision and team leadership.
- Become a team themselves.
- Practise the skills of team leadership, including:
  - the value of people's contribution to the group;
  - improving communication skills;
  - developing group planning and problem-solving skills;
  - learning to take responsibility for one's own actions.

Description

- Length – four days.
- Participants – department team leaders (6), immediate managers (2) and department engineer.
- Team leaders all come from one department.
- Location – hotel (they spend three nights at the hotel).
- Methodology – experiential – following Kolb's learning cycle.

Day 1

- Set the scene for the four days.
- Agree on ground rules for risk taking and feedback.
- Become familiar with experiential process and theory through the use of several experiential activities.

Day 2

- Three experiential activities ranging in length from $1\frac{1}{2}$ to 3 hours each.
- In-depth review of each activity by the team.
- Feedback for the team leader responsible for each activity.
- Theory building by the team to uncover what works well for them.
- Linking of activities to actual situations encountered at BCM.
- Managers do not 'control' the activities but are encouraged to act as a 'coach' to the team leader in charge of each activity. Managers also facilitate discussion during the feedback sessions.
- Participants maintain a 'learning log' to record key learning points and relate these to actual work situations where possible.
- Final activity – completion of Belbin self-perception questionnaires.

Day 3

- Results of self-perception questionnaires to teams and individuals.
- Discussion of how best to use the range of roles and to cover deficiencies noted from questionnaires.
- Completion of three experiential activities and follow-up as per day 2.
- Final activity – complete observer forms for each other to build on the self-perception information.

Day 4

- Feedback and discussion of updated team profile.
- Final three-hour experiential activity, focusing on team process and outcomes, is conducted.
- Teams are encouraged to identify how they will maintain their 'leader team' back at work. The maintenance of the 'leader team' has been shown to be an important criterion for success of the two-day 'team programme'.
- Development of a 'take-away' product which can be used to link the two-day team programme to the leader programme. This can be a five-minute video, a mission statement, or something of the team's choosing.
- Final activity – development of an individual action plan by each team leader.
- Department manager reviews the 'take-away' product and the individual action plans, and closes the overall programme.

EXHIBIT 14.13

Team programmes

Outcomes

- Learn the advantages and process of teamwork.
- Become a team themselves.
- Practise the skills of teamwork, including:
    - the value of people's contribution to the group;
    - improving communication skills;
    - developing group planning and problem-solving skills;
    - learning to take responsibility for one's own actions.

Description

- Length – two days.
- Participants – all members of the team and the team leader. Overall size varies from eight to 20 or more, depending on the production environment.
- Location – the hotel where the team leader attended the programme (they spend one night at the hotel, which becomes a sort of team training home).
- Methodology – experiential – following Kolb's learning cycle.

Note: Most departments consist of six production teams, but some contain as few as two, and some as many as eight teams. The team programmes immediately follow the team leaders' programme, so that all teams are trained within a four-week period.

Day 1

- Set the scene for the two days.
- Divide the large team into sub-teams of five or six to assure maximum involvement in each phase of training (team leader moves from team to team).
- Complete three short (30–40 minutes) experiential tasks.
- In-depth review of each exercise by the team focusing on how the team is functioning, the need for clarity of purpose, the value of planning and the value of each individual's contribution to the exercise.

- Final task – group plans a project and commits the plan to paper. Groups then swap plans and each group 'tries' to complete the plans given them by one of the other groups.
- Debriefing of the final event – looking at complexities of communication and the need to take responsibility for the quality of our own, rather than judge the actions of others.

Day 2

- Large-scale, full group exercise led by the team leader fills the morning. The team leader participated in a similar exercise during the team leader course, but the 'packaging' of this one is different. The focus of this exercise is on managing complex jobs in a dynamic environment with a large team. This exercise is the critical phase of the entire programme and forces the team to focus on clearly understanding the requirements of the task, planning, communication, quality and personal responsibility.

- Review of exercise. This focuses on what each individual could have done differently to take responsibility for moving the team forward, rather than leaving it up to the team leader.

- The parallel of this exercise to the new work setting is clearly discussed during the debriefing process.

- Brainstorming exercise. The afternoon begins with small group sessions to identify work issues which need to be dealt with. These range from maintaining the level of training to day-to-day operational issues to organisational questions. The team is encouraged to take responsibility for those issues it can deal with, and to refer issues to the team leader when needed. The managers close the session, and discuss those issues which need management's attention.

FURTHER DISCUSSION POINTS

1 In Chapter 1 the strategic management environment was characterised as chaotic, complex, dynamic and turbulent – all generally increasing the level of uncertainty facing leader-managers. However, not all business environments are the same. Reflect on how changes in the environmental characteristics might affect the approach taken to strategic change management.

2 For GSM:
   - How is change carried out?
   - How do the teams get agreement for the resources to carry out change?
   - Is the way in which change is carried out more inclined to the designed-involvement or the results-driven approaches?
   - Who are the change agents?
   - What change mechanisms are used?

3 For leader-managers to consider change to the deeper levels of culture they need to think in terms of years rather than months. How would this affect a leader-manager seeking change depending on the labour-market conditions operating in the country that they are operating in (see Section 2.2.4)?

4 How does Exhibit 14.2 link with the 'cultural onion' of Exhibit 2.2?

5 In Section 2.2.3 the differences in business culture in France, Germany, the UK and the USA were summarised. How do you think the attributes of a change agent would differ across these countries?

6 How does the change process of unfreezing, change and refreezing link to the view of issue awareness described in Section 5.3?

7 What is the role of *vision* in change management?

8 How do incremental and transformational change link to offer developments: to enhancements, extensions and enlargements as described in Sections 6.5 and 6.6?

ASSIGNMENT   From the Dutton Engineering case:
- highlight the main barriers to change and how they were overcome;
- identify the responsibilities of the teams and the team leaders at the end of 1999;
- what evidence is there that *The Dutton Way* has been met?

FURTHER
READING

The books by John Kotter (*Leading Change*, Harvard Business School, 1996) and by Dave Buchanan and Dave Boddy (*The Expertise of the Change Agent: Public Performance and Backstage Activity*, Prentice Hall, 1992) cover most of the ground concerning the roles of leader-managers in change programmes. Kotter's book is written for managers and is practical rather than academic in emphasis.

Barbara Senior's book *Organisational Change* (Pitman Publishing, 1997) also covers the topic of strategic change very fully and describes much of the 'how' of change.

Chapters 4 and 5 of Ikujiro Nonaka and Hirotaka Takeuchi's book *The Knowledge-Creating Company: How Japanese Companies Create the Dynamics of Innovation*, Oxford University Press, 1995) describe knowledge creation through project teams in Japanese companies.

Colin Carnall covers fully the way in which people react to the stresses and opportunities of change in *Managing Organizational Change*, Prentice Hall, 1990.

CHAPTER NOTES
AND REFERENCES

1 This exhibit is an adaptation from Stacey R.D., *Strategic Management and Organisational Dynamics*, 2nd edn, Financial Times Pitman Publishing, 1996.

2 Schein, E.H., *Organizational Culture and Leadership*, 2nd edn, Jossey-Bass, Chapters 15 and 16, developing the original theory of Lewin, K., 'Group decision and social change', in Newcombe, T.N. and Hartley, E.L. (eds), *Readings in Social Psychology*, Holt, Rinehart & Winston, 1947.

3 *Ibid.*

4 Nonaka, I. and Takeuchi, H., *The Knowledge-Creating Company: How Japanese Companies Create the Dynamics of Innovation*, Oxford University Press, 1995.

5 Simons, R., 'How top managers use control systems as levers of strategic renewal', *Strategic Management Journal*, Vol. 15, No. 3, 1994, pp. 169–89.

6 *Ibid.*, p. 97.

7 *Ibid.*, p. 117.

8 Pascale, R.T., *Managing on the Edge: How Successful Companies Use Conflict to Stay Ahead*, Viking, 1990.

9 Bowman, C., 'Strategy workshops and top team commitment to strategic change', *Journal of Managerial Psychology*, Vol. 10, No. 8, 1995, pp. 4–12.

10 For an individual, *organisational paradigm* should be changed to *mindset* in Exhibit 14.2.

11 Senge, P.M, 'The leader's new work: building learning organisations', *Sloan Management Review*, Vol. 32, No 1, Fall 1990, pp. 7–23.

12 Lewin, K., 'Group decision and social change', in Newcombe, T.N. and Hartley, E.L. (eds), *Readings in Social Psychology*, Holt, Rinehart & Winston, 1947.

13 Carnall, C.A., *Managing Organizational Change*, Prentice Hall, 1990, p. 142.

14 Trompenaars, F. and Hampden-Turner, C., *Riding the Waves of Culture: Understanding Cultural Diversity in Business*, Nicholas Brealey Publishing, 1997, p. 133.

15 This exhibit has been adapted from Beer, M., Eisenstat, R.A. and Spector, B., 'Why change programs don't produce change', *Harvard Business Review*, November–December 1990, pp. 158–66.

16 Schein, E.H., *op. cit.*

17 Schaffer, R.H. and Thomson, H.A., 'Successful change programs begin with results', *Harvard Business Review*, January–February 1992, pp. 80–9. In their original paper they used the term *activity-centred* rather than *designed-involvement* used in this book. This change has been made so as not to confuse the designed-involvement programmes with business processes and activities that were introduced in Chapter 6.

18 Hammer, M. and Champy, J., *Re-engineering the Corporation: A Manifesto for Business Revolution*, Nicholas Brealey Publishing, 1993.

19 Whitty, E., Principal Registrar, Waitrose (John Lewis Partnership), *Ethical Management 1 – Why Ethics in Business*, Executive Business Channel, 1994.

20 Dunphy, D. and Stace, D., 'The strategic management of corporate change', *Human Relations*, Vol. 46, No. 8, 1993, pp. 905–20.

21 Nonaka, I. and Takeuchi, H., *op. cit.*

22 Simons, R., *op. cit.*

23 Schein, E.H., *op. cit.*, p. 304.

24 *Ibid.*

25 Hunsaker, P.L. and Cook, C.W., *Managing Organizational Behaviour*, Addison-Wesley, 1986, p. 669.

26 Davenport, T.H., *Process Innovation: Re-engineering Work Through IT*, Harvard Business School Press, 1993.

27 Machiavelli, N., *The Prince*, Wordsworth Editions, 1993.

28 Hampden-Turner, C. and Trompenaars, F., *The Seven Cultures of Capitalism: Value Systems for Creating Wealth in the United States, Britain, Japan, Germany, France, Sweden, and the Netherlands*, Doubleday, 1993, p. 67.

29 Adapted from Buchanan, D. and Boddy, D., *The Expertise of the Change Agent: Public Performance and Backstage Activity*, Prentice Hall, 1992, pp. 92–3.

30 *Ibid.*, pp. 78–9.

31 Hampden-Turner, C. and Trompenaars, F., *op. cit.*, p. 98.

32 Nonaka, I. and Takeuchi, H., *op. cit.*

33 Robertson, B. and Holec, J., 'The middle manager is alive and well and doing more to add value: a survey in France, Germany, Spain, the UK and the US of the new roles of today's middle managers', Price Waterhouse Coopers, 1998, p. 4.

34 Cash, J.I. and McFarlan, F.W., *Competing through Information Technology*, Harvard Business School Video Series, 1989.

35 This section relies heavily on Buchanan, D., 'Theories of change', Loughborough University Business School Research Series, paper 1994: 5, 1994.

36 Bennis, W.G., *Organizational Development: Its Nature, Origins, and Prospects*, Addison-Wesley, 1969, p. 34. The original term *task forces* has been replaced by the term *project teams*.

37 Obeng, E., 'Avoiding the fast-track pitfalls', *Sunday Times*, 'Finance' 11 March 1994, p. 1.

38 Kanter, R.M., *When Giants Learn to Dance: Mastering the Challenges of Strategy, Management and Careers in the 1990s*, Simon & Schuster, 1989.

39 Mullins, L.J., *Management and Organisational Behaviour*, 5th edn, Financial Times Pitman Publishing, 1999, pp. 831–5.

CHAPTER

15 **Strategic control**

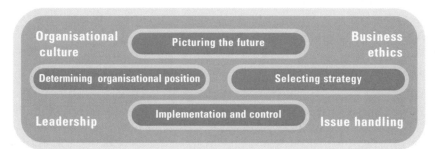

Organisational culture
Picturing the future
Business ethics
Determining organisational position
Selecting strategy
Leadership
Implementation and control
Issue handling

Implementation and control

14 Strategic change management

15 Strategic control

this is the second chapter devoted to implementation and control. The concern is with the processes of controlling all aspects of organisational activity. Although strategic control needs to be exercised throughout the life of an organisation, it is particularly important to reconsider the appropriate forms of control to adopt when change is about to take place and immediately after it has occurred.

The chapter opens with a consideration of the fundamentals of reactive control and with how it is applied in organisations. The success of many control systems hinges on the quality of the objectives that they use and the characteristics of good objectives need to be considered. The discussion then moves on to consider pro-active control, which is control to prevent the development of an imbalance between what is wanted and what transpires. The fusing of reactive and pro-active controls leads to the identification of six types of strategic control available to a business: assumption, surveillance, climate, implementation, operational and crisis control. These six types are considered in detail. Finally, the characteristics of business control systems are reviewed.

The purpose of all forms of strategic control is to identify whether the organisation should continue with its current strategy or modify it in the light of changed circumstances. Controls can take many forms: those that apply after the event and those that aim to anticipate events; those that are internal and those imposed from outside; those that rely on formal quantitative objectives and those that rely on looser mechanisms; those that are planned and those that are reactions to crises.

Controls bring out the tensions in organisations: between the on-going and the future, coercion and motivation, efficiency and freedom, rewards and punishments, and the mandatory and the suggested. Unless appropriately applied, controls can easily lead to counter-productive behaviour, so it is vital that leader-managers understand the pros and cons of different forms of control and strike the appropriate balance between them.

LEARNING
OUTCOMES

When you have worked through this chapter, you should be able to:

- describe reactive cybernetic control, list the assumptions underlying it and explain why it might not be appropriate to apply such control to all aspects of business;

- critically assess the characteristics of objectives, understand their link with goals, and list the main differences between financial and non-financial objectives;

- describe pro-active control and understand why it is so important in strategic management;

- list the six forms of strategic control systems and characterise each of them;

- explain the place of both reactive and proactive public relations in strategic control.

15.1 The fundamentals of control

15.1.1 *A working definition of* control

A starting point in a consideration of control in business is to consider the control of designed physical systems,[1] i.e. systems not involving humans and that have been designed by engineers.[a] Engineers have long understood the need to control their creations, and the science of cybernetics is concerned with the control of machinery. The term *cybernetics* comes from the Greek word meaning 'steersman', and this derivation gives a flavour of the nature of control.[2] The origin of the word 'control' is the French term meaning 'inspection', and control has this connotation in several European languages.[3] However, control is a word with many different interpretations and nuances, including 'checking' and 'testing', and is linked to the idea of 'domination', 'power' and 'regulation' and 'monitoring'. Indeed, '57 varieties' of meaning for the word 'control' have been identified.[4] While a fuller definition of control will be developed as the discussion in the chapter unfolds, a working definition of control for designed physical systems will be taken as 'to keep within prescribed limits'.

15.1.2 A domestic central heating system

Many of the basic principles of control in designed physical systems can be illustrated by considering the operation of a domestic central heating system, and this system will be used as an extended example. One type of system uses a gas-fired boiler to heat water that circulates through radiators and eventually heats the air in the house. A sensor measures the air temperature at a suitable point in the house, and a comparison is made in a thermostat between this measurement and a desired value – the objective. If the measured temperature is below the objective temperature, then a signal is sent for the gas to be turned on. This causes the water to be heated, the radiators to get hot and the air temperature to rise. The heating continues until the sensor records a temperature equal or just above the preset value, when the gas is turned off.

A model of such a central heating system is shown in Exhibit 15.1. The process (to heat the air) has two inputs: an environmental input, which cannot be controlled (heat leaving the house is modelled as incoming cold) and a controllable input (gas, whose rate of input to the boiler can be controlled). The output from the process (ultimately the air temperature in the house) is measured and compared in the comparator (the thermostat) with an objective (the preset temperature). If the measured output differs from the objective in what is considered to be an undesirable way (the air temperature falls below the objective), then a signal is sent to the actuator (the gas valve) to alter the input (the gas) to the process.

EXHIBIT 15.1

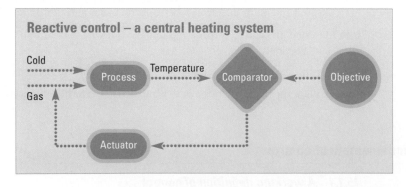

a   Physical systems such as the solar system and biological systems aren't considered as designed physical systems as they haven't been designed by humans.

15.1.3 Reactive control

The domestic central heating example illustrates many of the important features of control. What is happening is that information specifying the difference (or variance) between an objective value and that actually achieved is being used to signal a change to an input; information is being fed back from the output to influence the input.

This type of control provides **reactive control**: control is exercised *after* a variance between objective and actual has occurred; the house must cool below the required temperature before action is taken. In practical systems the signal to switch on the boiler will not be sent unless the difference between the objective and actual temperatures is a degree or so, and there will be a lag between the boiler coming on and the house temperature attaining the required value. Overshoot or overcompensation will also occur. These deficiencies are illustrated in Exhibit 15.2 and are a general feature of all systems controlled retroactively.

The feedback shown in Exhibit 15.1 is termed **negative feedback** as the signal fed back *negates* the variance that has been detected. In the central heating system just described, a signal to open the gas valve, and thus to start heating the house, would be sent when the house temperature was below the preset temperature; the resultant rise in temperature would reduce this difference until, when no difference between the objective and the actual temperature is detected, a signal would be sent to switch the gas off.

Feedback can also be positive. **Positive feedback** acts in a reverse way to negative feedback: rather than negate the variance between objective and actual, it increases the size of the variance. This is generally considered undesirable, as continuing positive feedback tends to send the process out of equilibrium. The central heating would go 'out of equilibrium' if a signal were sent to increase the gas input when the temperature was above the objective, producing ever higher temperatures. The consequences of positive feedback can sometimes be heard at concerts when the loudspeakers 'howl'; the microphone is sending a signal to the loudspeakers, where it is amplified, and this amplified sound is picked up by the microphone and amplified once more, and so a vicious cycle of amplification is established. Although these two examples suggest that positive feedback is always to be avoided, this isn't the case; situations where positive feedback can be advantageous are discussed in Section 15.11.3.

 EXHIBIT 15.2

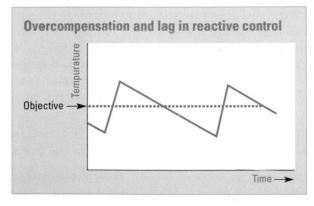

Overcompensation and lag in reactive control

15.1.4 Insulation

Double glazing and cavity wall insulation are important elements in any domestic heating system, but they are only capable of slowing down the effect of changes in the environment. Insulation alone is well suited to counter short-term random and cyclical environmental change, but it isn't appropriate for longer-term changes.

KEY CONCEPT   Reactive control is invoked only after an undesirable state of affairs has been detected. The most common form of feedback is negative feedback, which is used to remove (negate) any difference between the objective and the actual. Insulation is a means of moderating the link between (environmental) cause and (system) effect.

DISCUSSION POINT 15.1   Consider one type of business control system that you are familiar with. How are its main elements related to those of a domestic central heating system?
- What is the equivalent of insulation in a business?

15.2   Control in organisations

15.2.1   Difficulties with cybernetic control systems

While management is concerned with the effective use of all types of resource, the most difficult management issues often concern human resources and thus the control of human activity systems.[5] As can be imagined, organisations show facets not present in designed physical systems; in particular, the processes are different.

Processes can be split into two types.[6] There are structured processes, defined as stable, repetitive activities or procedures that can be systematised, such as clerical or assembly-line tasks. The second type are unstructured processes, which are novel activities requiring judgement. Examples of unstructured activities are those associated with the leadership roles of leader-managers, one-off projects, and many of the activities of knowledge workers, for example in research and development and in legal and public relations practice.

The domestic central heating system as described above is a cybernetic control system because the objectives and the rules of operation have been defined outside the system. It is the kind of control system appropriate to designed physical systems and for structured activities in human activity systems, although the human element in these means that they are unlikely to be effective on their own. For organisations engaging in many unstructured activities, however, sometimes called managed or discretionary organisations, the applicability of cybernetic control systems is questionable. This is because cybernetic control relies on the four basic assumptions itemised in Exhibit 15.3.

15.2.2   Assumption 1 – objectives can be devised and can be stated precisely

Most organisations do not start off with ready-made objectives for their processes; they begin with broad, rather imprecisely stated goals. For example, a business organ-

EXHIBIT 15.3

The assumptions underlying reactive cybernetic control

* Objectives can be devised and can be stated precisely.
* Achievement can be measured and an acceptable measure of variance can be calculated.
* Variance information can be fed back.
* The feedback is sufficient to maintain control.

isation may see its primary goal as survival, with other goals likely to include an adequate profit, a certain market share and providing useful and interesting work for the employees. Such goals must be hardened into precisely defined objectives to act as cybernetic control objectives.

Sometimes this is straightforward; for example, a car assembler would have little difficulty in setting objectives in terms of cars produced per shift or cars produced per person hour, but in other cases it can be very difficult. Although some of the outputs of a personnel department can be precisely defined, such as the number of employees recruited or the number of wrongful dismissal cases brought against the company, the outputs of its many other roles, such as responsibility for employee development and training, are much more difficult to specify. Such difficulties appear with most unstructured activities. Substitute or surrogate measures may be used as output measures for unstructured activities, for example absentee rates used as surrogate measures for morale, or number of employees sent on training courses for employee development.

Multiple objectives

It is rarely possible to devise a single objective for an organisation, although shareholder value is sometimes touted as such. Most organisations have multiple objectives encompassing the concerns of all major stakeholders and associated with the main business processses. Multiple objectives aren't necessarily a problem in themselves but become so when they are conflicting. Profit may seem to be the one and only objective of a commercial enterprise but, generally, higher profits in one year have to be tempered by the need to pay for such things as restructuring and the development of enhanced capabilities that put the organisation in a better position for the future. To cope with clashing objectives, organisations tend to fix on minimum acceptable values for each objective. This is shown in Exhibit 15.4 for two semi-conflicting objectives. The acceptable region is one where both minimum market share and profit are attainable and it is in this region where the actual objectives will lie.

Personal and group objectives

While organisations don't have objectives, only individuals do, what pass for organisational objectives are those of the dominant individual or coalition.[7] Not surprisingly, it isn't to be expected that all individuals in an organisation will have the same objectives. There is likely to be objective alignment on central issues, or else an individual would either not join or not remain in the organisation. However, there might be opposition to other organisational objectives, for example where redundancy is concerned or with sales to a country governed by what is considered to be a reprehensible regime.

EXHIBIT 15.4

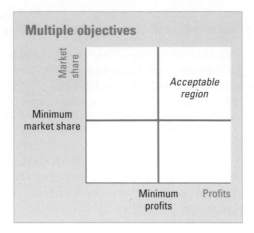

Not only may individual objectives not align with those of the organisation, the norms of a group may also not align. A group may have strong feelings about what constitutes a fair day's work, for example. Many employees belong to professional and other organisations, for example the trade unions, the Law Society and the accounting bodies. These organisations have rules and regulations covering their members' conduct. Such rules may differ from organisational objectives, and thus can have a significant effect on control as well as on strategy.

Management by objectives

The misalignment of individual, group and professional norms and objectives with those of the organisation are likely to induce unhealthy tensions within an organis-ation. Management by objectives (MBO) is a technique that, through personal com-mitment, attempts to defuse these tensions.

In MBO, each subordinate develops their own set of objectives. Concurrently, their boss will have developed a set of objectives for their unit that is consistent with the organisational objectives. In the light of the unit's objectives, the boss and subordi-nate then reassess and develop the subordinate's objectives until agreement is reached. The subordinate will later be evaluated against each agreed objective.

Proceeding in this way, a subordinate has much greater control over their own objectives than in conventional control systems, and thus they are more likely to be motivated to meet them. Also, an agreed set of quantifiable objectives allows evalu-ation to be made against achievement, rather than by subjective assessments coloured by the way the subordinate goes about their job. However, the time taken to obtain agreement on a set of objectives with many subordinates can be too demanding for many managers, and too demanding for the organisation, which needs perhaps three to five years to implement MBO successfully. More fundamental, however, is the assumption made in MBO that the decomposition of goals into separate objectives can actually be achieved. Where this isn't the case, MBO can be stultifying.

15.2.3 Assumption 2 – achievement can be measured and an acceptable measure of variance can be calculated

If an objective cannot be set, then there is little point in measuring achievement as part of the control process. However, even with an agreed objective, the interpretation of achievement may be problematical. The level of sales is likely to be one of the objectives set for a sales manager. If actual sales are less than the objective, is this because of failings by the manager or because conditions under which the sales were forecast have changed? The difficulty in interpreting variances and ascribing causation becomes exacerbated with the use of surrogate measures as objectives. For example, if a firm was interested in measuring morale and used absentee rates as a surrogate measure for morale, then the measure may be invalidated if a flu epidemic occurred; crude use of the raw figures on absenteeism would lead to the view that morale had slumped. A further concern is that an organisation will tend to measure those things that can be measured precisely and those that can be measured easily: these may not be the important things. Using the appropriate measures is vital. A very important 'rule' to remember is 'What gets measured gets managed'.

15.2.4 Assumption 3 – variance information can be fed back

Unstructured activities

Unstructured activities are those that have a considerable element of judgement and uniqueness. In such cases direct feedback of information isn't possible, as exactly the same activities are never repeated; rather, indirect feedback takes place through the accumulation of knowledge of how similar activities might be performed in the future. Such a link between past and on going activities is a far cry from the direct feedback implicit in cybernetic control. Because the form of the variance is likely to be complex in unstructured situations, there is the distinct possibility that communication of it could be flawed.

Service organisations

Organisations providing services and perishable products rather than products with a long shelf life face a complex situation when feeding back variance information. When a customer is buying a service, they are buying a complex bundle of features, and high customer impact results from their appropriate combination. Identifying which feature of the bundle to associate with a particular variance poses problems.

If a service is consumed simultaneously or almost immediately it is produced, there will be little or no chance to check the quality of the products before sale. In this case we have something close to what is termed **open-loop control** as illustrated in Exhibit 15.5, with no (direct) feedback. Where the product is perishable, forecasting, scheduling and process quality control are all very important, and 'right first time' is a necessary requirement. When there is a high labour content in the service, it is difficult to maintain consistency of objectives between employees.

EXHIBIT 15.5

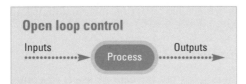

Open loop control

Inputs ··········▶ Process ··········▶ Outputs

15.2.5 Assumption 4 – the feedback is sufficient to maintain control

The simple domestic central heating system described earlier would be powerless to effect control if the environmental temperature went above the objective; control would then only be possible with an air-conditioning system. This illustrates a very important concept: a system can only be expected to perform control if the control variables are at least as effective in altering the system outputs as are the environmental variables whose effects are to be countered. This, in slightly simplified form, is the law of requisite variety.[8] Without sufficient control variables, the controller has been given responsibility without power: the two need to be balanced. It isn't sensible to hold a manager responsible for the total labour costs incurred in their department, for example if a company-wide wage agreement over which they have had no influence comes into force. All they can be held responsible for are some of the factors making up these costs, for example the number of people employed in their department, perhaps, or the amount of overtime worked.

DISCUSSION POINT 15.2

What are the dangers of using surrogate measures?

- Open-loop control was introduced in assumption 3. This implies that there is such a thing as closed-loop control. Where have you met this before?
- How might international management make the four assumptions of cybernetic control more difficult to meet?

15.2.6 Adaptive control

A simple central heating system relies on cybernetic control in that the controls are set from outside. A central heating system that includes the tenant with the power to change things if there is unexpected environmental change is an example of an adaptive process, a process in which some or all the control is exercised by the process itself. Hofstede[9] likens this to the actions of a biological cell, whereby, within wide limits, the cell controls itself and adapts to its environment. If the government decided to operate a policy to conserve fossil fuels and used high VAT rates to drive up the price of gas, an adaptive process could adapt to this (perhaps by lowering the thermostat setting), while a cybernetic system couldn't. Adaptive systems tend to be more flexible and adaptable than are cybernetic ones; however, they tend to be slow to implement since the rules of self-control have to be learned.[10] The tenant has to learn the pattern of causes and effects in the central heating system before they can make reasoned judgements about controlling their process. This is a simple learning situation; it's often much more difficult in a complex business situation, and thus training and organisational learning are necessary for the empowerment that accompanies being part of an adaptive system.

The emphasis here is on formal controls that are acting on formal/explicit knowledge. Informal controls are needed to act on informal/tacit knowledge.

15.2.7 Hierarchies of controls

The discussion above highlights the concept of levels of control: the tenant controls the central heating system through setting the objective, and the government influences the way the tenant runs the system through its price-setting policy. This concept of levels of control is an extremely important one in business, and it can be summed up by the aphorism 'Even the boss has a boss'.

So far two methods of controlling the temperature of the house have been mentioned: to alter the input (in this case the quantity and/or price of the gas used), or to alter the objective itself (change the required temperature). A third method of exercising control is to change the process itself, to alter the process by which inputs are converted to outputs. In the central heating case, a violent rise in gas prices might call for a more efficient gas boiler to be installed, a boiler that doesn't use gas, or simply to install better insulation.

KEY CONCEPT A system controlled cybernetically relies on the control mechanism set by others. In contrast, an adaptive system is able to control itself. It's only able to do this if it understands how its system works and the relationships between its system and its environment. Both cybernetic and adaptive control systems generally use reactive control.

15.3 Strategic objectives

15.3.1 The characteristics of a good strategic objective

A vital component of a control system, particularly a cybernetic one, is appropriate objectives. An objective is a goal that can be measured, and it is expected that there would be at least one objective associate with each goal. Exhibit 15.6 takes part of Exhibit 6.16 and extends it to illustrate objectives. The evidence is that three to four objectives per goal are appropriate.[11]

DISCUSSION POINT 15.3 How might an organisation derive the appropriate objectives?
- Provide objectives for shareholders' goals and goals and objectives appropriate for social responsibility in order to complete Exhibit 15.6.

Objectives have two main elements; a dimension, such as the *number of disputes*; and one or more values, such as *5% for the next three years*. Objectives need to be relevant to the organisational mission and to be measurable. However, an objective needs to be more than relevant and measurable to be a good objective; it needs to provide a suitable REMIT for leader-managers to support what they are trying to achieve for their organisations. The characteristics of a good objective are set out in Exhibit 15.7.

While one of the main uses of reactive control systems is for diagnosis – identifying non-planned behaviour – another is that they should energise people because they provide a challenge that is achievable. Exhibit 15.8 shows the well-established link between the difficulty of an objective and its energising properties.[12,13] Neither very easy nor very difficult objectives motivate people; the trick is to set objectives somewhere in the middle.

Left to their own devices, managers will choose highly achievable 'official' goals for themselves to improve the predictability of their forecasts, ensure that there are only a few negative variances for their superiors to focus on and allow for organis-

EXHIBIT 15.6

Goals and objectives

Perspective	Examples of goals	Examples of objectives
Employees	• To maintain good employee relations	• Reduce disputes by 5% each year for the next three years • Reduce absenteeism to below 3% by next year
Business processes	• The speedy implementation of new and enhanced information systems	• All agreed enhancements to be completed within agreed timescale starting at year end
Innovation	• Increase the % of revenues from new services	• 30% of revenues to be obtained from services introduced in the preceding three years, to be achieved three years hence
Customer	• Enhance customer satisfaction	• Reduce customer complaints by 10% per year starting this year • Complaints to be answered within three working days of receipt, starting immediately • 95% of customers to be retained from one year to the next, with the current year as the base year
Shareholder	• Increase shareholder value in line with other businesses in the same sector	
Social responsibility		

ational slack to allow for experimentation. It's vital for motivation, of course, that the people being motivated can influence the value of the measure that is achieved. If this isn't so, or isn't perceived to be so, then the objective won't motivate.

Care needs to be taken to ensure that a measure captures the relevant features; it needs to have the appropriate level of completeness. If a sales manager trying to increase market share chose only to measure the number of sales visits made by their salesforce, then this could lead to dysfunctional behaviour on the part of the salesforce, with easy-to-visit outlets visited rather than the more difficult but perhaps more rewarding outlets in terms of sales. If the measure was too inclusive, measuring total sales or overall profitability for example, then it would be unlikely to be motivational.

An objective should be chosen so that any deviation between the value achieved

EXHIBIT 15.7

The characteristics of a good objective

- Relevant   directly related to the overall task/mission of the organisation
  - Energising   presents an achievable and stretching target and thus is motivating
    - Measurable   allows achievement to be recognised
      - Insightful   improves learning
        - Timed   defines when performance should have been achieved

EXHIBIT 15.8

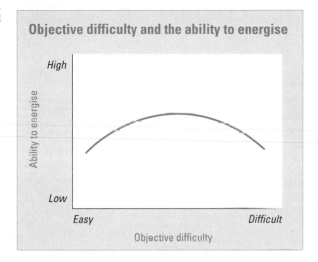

Objective difficulty and the ability to energise

and the objective will initiate thinking that leads to insights into how the unit operates and its relationships with its environment. The objective should also have a duration attached: it's no good setting an objective of doubling turnover, for example, if there is no limit to the time that can be taken in its achievement. Obviously, the timescale should be both relevant and realistic.

KEY CONCEPT   A goal is a general statement of intent, while an objective is a well-defined commitment to achieve. A good objective provides a manager with a REMIT: it has the characteristics of being Relevant, Energising, Measurable, Insightful and Timed.

DISCUSSION POINT 15.4

Can a goal have more than one quantifiable measure associated with it?
- Can you think of a goal for which there's no feasible objective?

15.3.2   Differences between financial and non-financial objectives

The main differences between financial and non-financial objectives are listed in Exhibit 15.9.[14] Financial measures have the attraction that they are relatively few in number, standardised through accounting convention, (almost) universally understood and together provide a coherent set of measures: profits are directly linked to total revenues and total costs; total revenues are linked to sales price and sales

EXHIBIT 15.9

Differences between financial and non-financial objectives (adapted from Meyer, 1996)

Financial measures	Non-financial measures
• Few	• Many – and multiply rapidly
• Standardised	• Anarchic – non-standardised
• Closely related to each other (e.g. financial ratios)	• Unrelated, frequently unconnected
• Few innovations	• Endlessly inventable
• Limited pressure to increase the number of measures	• Driven by internal, non-financial, functional interests (e.g. manufacturing, marketing) and external initiatives (e.g. ISO 9000)
• Not closely linked to the processes that people carry out	• Closely linked to the processes that people carry out
• Direct linkage to (usually past) financial performance	• Linkage to financial performance may require statistical evidence acquired over years
• Generally discriminate between good and bad performance	• Tend to 'run down' with use over time

volume; total costs are linked to variable and fixed costs; and so on. Non-financial measures are deficient in all these areas. On the other hand, financial measures aren't often closely related to the processes that people are engaged in, so they lack motivational power. Non-financial measures tend to 'run down' over time, in that they eventually become obsolete as the processes with which they are associated change.

15.4 Pro-active control

15.4.1 The fundamental of pro-active control

So far the discussion has been about reactive control, which is what people often mean when they use the term control. Reactive controls have the inherent weakness that an objective will have been missed before action is taken to remedy the situation. A more subtle form of control is **pro-active control**, whereby the environment is monitored and the organisation changes its processes *before* the environment significantly affects it. Some sophisticated central heating systems have such a facility: a thermometer placed outside the house measures the rate of change of the outside temperature, and if the temperature is falling a signal is *fed forward* to activate the boiler before the extra cold seeps into the house and before the (internal) thermostat has registered any fall in temperature. This is shown in the top portion of Exhibit 15.10. The monitoring of the environment (the change in the outside temperature) allows compensation to be made for the otherwise inevitable lag between an internal temperature fall and the resultant injection of heat to restore the required temperature. The modulations shown in Exhibit 15.2 will be reduced and smoothed out.

EXHIBIT 15.10

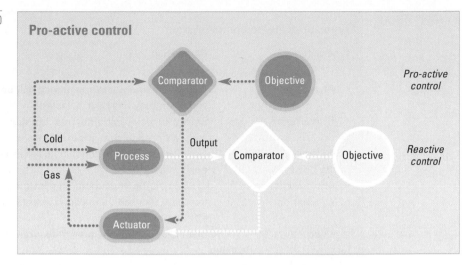

Pro-active control provides the possibility of protecting processes from a severe buffeting caused by environmental change: to use a nautical analogy, the hatches are battened down and the sails trimmed before the main force of the storm reaches the ship.

KEY CONCEPT   Reactive control is invoked only after an undesirable state of affairs has been reached. It involves feeding information back from the output of the process to alter the inputs. Pro-active control is a way of preparing the organisation for environmental change, involving feeding forward information from the environment to the process and its inputs. For most organisations a combination of both types of method of control will be used. Both cybernetic and adaptive systems can utilise reactive and/or pro-active control.

15.4.2 Combining reactive and pro-active control

The preceding discussion indicates that effective strategic control has to combine controls that apply after the event and those that try to anticipate events. These considerations lead to a fuller definition of control than the working definition: strategic control is now defined as 'the continuous critical evaluation of plans, inputs, processes and outputs to provide information for future action'.[15] Thus control isn't seen as episodic, although for practical reasons there is likely to be some strong periodicity in the reporting period; rather, it's performed simultaneously with strategic thinking.

15.4.3 Forms of strategic control

Effective strategic control is concerned both with controlling the present processes and with preparing for the future. It combines the reactive with the pro-active. To do this appropriately, leader-managers need to employ the six types of strategic control listed

EXHIBIT 15.11

Types of strategic control system

Type of control	Description
Pro-active	
• Assumption	focused environmental monitoring of the assumptions under which strategy has been selected
• Surveillance	unfocused environmental monitoring in order to provide early warning of changes in the business environment
• Climate	aimed at establishing and maintaining a favourable business environment
• Implementation	focused on the implementation of strategic change
• Operational	internally focused on making the present processes more effective and efficient
• Crisis	managing potentially damaging, rapidly arising issues
Reactive	

in Exhibit 15.11. The types are ordered broadly according to their degree of pro-activity, with assumption control considered the most pro-active and crisis control the least.

15.5 Assumption control

Assumption control focuses on the values of the variables used in building scenarios. Scenarios are composed of two types of variable: predetermined variables, whose values are deemed to be the same for all scenarios; and scenario variables, whose values differ between scenarios. Scenarios are used to test the robustness of possible strategies, and in this testing the organisation is taking a (single) view of the value of the predetermined variables and a view of the range of values taken by the scenario variables, i.e. within which the strategy remains suitable. The monitoring of the continuing suitability of a strategy requires the monitoring of the value of sensitive variables. Assumption control is thus concentrating on strategic uncertainties.[16]

For example, suppose that a European firm is experiencing increasing demand for its products in the USA, and that two possibilities are proposed to cater for this: either to open a new factory in the USA or to continue to export from its home base in Europe. Two important factors in the scenarios are the level of protectionism that the US government might impose against foreign manufactures and the €–$ exchange rate. When developing scenarios, three levels of protectionism were considered and two values for the exchange rate, as illustrated in Exhibit 15.12.

Suppose that the strategy to open the factory in the USA would appear to be the better option as long as the €–$ exchange rate stayed above 1:0.8 and if the threatened level of protectionism stayed high. Then the company would monitor to see if the predictions of the level of protectionism and the €–$ rate continued to remain within the bounds shown in Exhibit 15.12. If it looked as though these bounds would be broken, then the decision to open the factory in the USA might be rescinded.

EXHIBIT 15.12

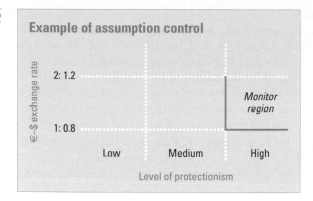

Example of assumption control

15.6 Surveillance control

Assumption control will be fairly blinkered even though the scenario planning will have helped to consider events of low probability but of potentially high impact. Surveillance control is 'early warning control', akin to picking up a blob on a radar screen. Surveillance control is a broad search and its diffuseness means that it's not a job that can be left to a single individual or group. Many people in the organisation should be involved in scanning both the remote and operating environments. This will often occur quite naturally: for example, salespersons meeting their customers and finding out about competitors, specialists reading their specialist journals, and many of the workforce watching news and current affairs programmes on TV. The problem is with channelling this knowledge to the places where it can be acted on. Establishing a business intelligence unit is one way of doing this, although this formal approach is only really open to large organisations.

15.7 Climate control

In Chapter 6, a sharp distinction was made between the operating and remote environments, with the remote environment that part of the environment where *individual* businesses have no influence. In fact, the distinction isn't quite as watertight as that, and firms use public relations to influence elements in the remote environment.

15.7.1 A definition of public relations

The Institute of Public Relations[17] states: 'Public relations practice is the discipline which looks after reputation with the aim of earning understanding and support, and influencing opinion and behaviour.'

Note that the term *public relations* is used in at least two senses. First, it's about the *quality* of the relationships with those who constitute an organisation's publics. Second, it's about the *ways and means* used to achieve favourable relationships.

DISCUSSION
POINT 15.5

The term *publics* hasn't occurred yet in this book. What term has been used instead?

Two types of public relations activity can be identified. First, there is reactive public relations, concerned with rapidly rising issues, such as crisis management and rumour control. These will be considered in Section 15.10. Second, there is pro-active public relations, which aims to generate an appropriate climate within which on-going business strategies can be developed and enacted.

Before moving on, it is worth contrasting public relations with the two associated areas of advertising and publicity. Advertising is specifically directed at businesses and individuals downstream in the value chain, whereas public relations encompasses much wider interests. However, since both are concerned with reputation, advertising and public relations have a common interest. It is important that the functions responsible for advertising and for public relations co-ordinate their actions and responses.

Publicity is an act or public device designed to attract public attention or support.[18] So there is no clear distinction between public relations and publicity, but publicity tends to be short term and is not necessarily positive for the organisation. The most important distinction, however, is that publicity isn't controlled by the organisation; rather, it originates from other sources.

15.7.2 Pro-active public relations

Much of public relations associated with politics is carried out by trade associations and trade unions, generally focused on a topical issue; for example, the Tobacco Alliance, which represents independent retailers in the UK, is attempting to get the UK government to act more diligently to prevent tobacco being smuggled into the UK; the National Farmers' Union is trying to get an easier time for beef farmers in the wake of the BSE problems, and the Union of Communication Workers has been working towards preventing privatisation of the Post Office.

Much of public relations is about establishing a good climate to achieve understanding and support, and to influence opinion and behaviour. Sometimes public relations is a long-term effort and not targeted on any particular issue, as suggested by Exhibit 15.13, and conducted over many years by trade associations such as the Tobacco Manufacturers' Association. Sometimes it is in connection with a specific issue, as in the case of ICI and CFCs in Exhibit 15.15.

To enhance public relations, it is necessary to understand the stakeholders, determine the messages that you wish to give them, and then select the appropriate

EXHIBIT 15.13

The need for an improved corporate image[19]

A survey by an international consultancy revealed that responses to different publics or audiences (such as a complaining customer, a potential employee, a fund raiser for charities, a personal investor) varied in promptness, tone, accuracy and completeness both across companies and significantly across departments within the same organisation. This would suggest that, while firms are attending to the direct effects of advertising and promotions, their total effectiveness is undermined by the indirect effects of word of mouth, resulting in an unsatisfactory corporate image that could harm their reputation. Most organisations need to respond more positively to these people.

channels of communication to pass these messages to them. It is often important to use public relations consultants when framing the public relations campaign. They are helpful in marshalling arguments and determining the best channels of communication to use. They often have personal contacts with people in high places. It is also helpful to use experts, who have the authority that comes from being an expert and allow the organisation, through them, to communicate with lesser experts and so on, cascading information through to the stakeholders.

15.7.3 Understanding stakeholder concerns

It is important to determine who the important stakeholders are and understand their demands and aspirations. A four-step approach to the initial management of stakeholders is sketched in Exhibit 15.14.

The first step is to determine who the directly affected stakeholders are, because the stakeholders with the most to lose from the organisation's actions are most likely to be within this group. Having identified these stakeholders, the second step is to assess their power to influence events. The third step is to determine the attitudes of the stakeholders, particularly those that are powerful. The most important thing is to determine whether the powerful stakeholders will use their power and, if so, in what way. In particular, it is important to identify those stakeholders whose views can be changed; it is not too useful to preach to the converted or to those who are implacably opposed to what the organisation seeks to do. Finally, it can be very useful to enlist influential allies who may not be initially concerned with the issue but who can be shown that there can be consequences for them. In the early 1990s, the then Tory government was keen to privatise the Post Office. The Union of Communication Workers sought successfully to widen its attack on these proposals by enlisting the Women's Institute, whose members were concerned with the effect that privatisation might have on rural postal services. Another interesting ally was the Royal National Institute for the Blind (RNIB). During the eight months of its Post Office campaign, the RNIB set up a team of eight people to campaign against privatisation. They did this because Michael Heseltine, the minister responsible for the privatisation, wouldn't commit the firms who might run the post-privatisation postal services to continue free postage for materials for the blind (worth £30–40 million a year to the RNIB).

EXHIBIT 15.14

Stakeholder management

- **Identify the directly affected stakeholders** – the groups and individuals that the organisation seeks to influence.
- **Determine the strengths of the stakeholders** – and thus what should be the main focus for relationship building.
- **Find out the attitudes and behaviours of the stakeholders** – who is indifferent, who is sympathetic and who is unsympathetic.
- **Decide which parties can be included in an enlarged platform of support** – are there any parties who can be drawn into the issue and who would support your cause?

15.7.4 Determining the messages and selecting channels of communication

Having identified and characterised the stakeholders, the next stage is to determine the messages that should be put across to each of them. Anyone responsible for determining the content and style of these messages should bear in mind the following points:

- Have a positive and credible message.

- Ensure that the stance is and appears to be socially responsible. In particular, it is very useful if the organisation can shift itself from being seen as the source of a problem to be seen as providing the solution to it.

- Ensure understanding of the issues. This can be difficult if the issue is an esoteric one, for example one requiring a fairly deep understanding of physics or medicine.

- Tailor the message to the recipient. Although it is not proposed that contradictory messages should be given to different stakeholders, it's important to emphasise those aspects of issues that each public sees as important.

- Tailor the channels of communication needed to match the messages that are to be transmitted and the stakeholders being targeted. It is important to select suitable mouthpieces and brief them well. A cascaded approach to influence should be considered; for example, use the scientific journals to place information about scientific matters that will be 'picked up' by the more general press and by television.

Many of these points are illustrated by Exhibit 15.15.

15.8 Implementation control

Implementation control is concerned with the implemention of strategic change and thus with whether the strategy remains 'on track'. When implementing new ventures, there is a need to establish objectives on the way to implementation. These objectives are often called *milestones*. Given that new ventures are invariably developed using a project team, control will be exercised through the project planning and control systems.

15.9 Operational control

Although on-going operational control is unlikely to be strategic in itself, what is strategic is that it is the responsibility of leader-managers to devise and implement appropriate operational control systems. All the features of Sections 15.1 throught 15.4 would apply to operational controls.

15.9.1 The characteristics of a good operational control system

A good operational control system needs to assist the organisation to be both efficient and effective. To do this it needs to be both attention-conserving and attention-enhancing. A good control system needs to be an attention-conserving device to allow businesses to operate without constant monitoring. It allows leader-managers to be freed from the mundane and 'in-control' areas by the staff professionals (e.g. account-

EXHIBIT 15.15

CFCs, the ozone layer and ICI[20]

A series of high-profile incidents such as the death of North Sea seals as a result of a mysterious virus and the Alaskan oil spillage saw a heightening of public interest in 'green issues' during the 1980s. At the end of the decade environmental issues had moved to the top of the political agenda, so much so that in 1988 Mrs Thatcher, the then prime minister, was reported as having 'turned green'. One particular concern related to the damage being caused to the ozone layer shielding the Earth from the sun's harmful radiations, which among other things cause skin cancer. A group of man-made chemicals called chlorofluorocarbons (CFCs), used in aerosols, refrigerators, air conditioners and plastic foams, were implicated as the main culprits causing the damage.

Some scientists had been aware of the thinning of the ozone layer since the early 1970s. However, little conclusive evidence as to the cause of the depletion had been established. The hypothesis that chlorine released by CFCs in the upper atmosphere could cause a thinning of the layer had first been put forward in 1974. Individual research teams had worked to clarify the situation and had been helped by the CFC producers who, by the late 1980s, had donated US$23 million to help with this scientific activity. The evidence was somewhat contradictory, as might be expected with such a technically complex area, with satellite measurements showing considerable ozone depletion, whereas ground-based measurements showed no such weakening. In 1987, the US National Aeronautics and Space Administration (NASA) brought together key scientific groups as the Ozone Trends Panel to examine the available evidence on ozone depletion. The conclusion was far from conclusive; however, the panel reported that there appeared to be a small but significant downward trend in the thickness and extent of the ozone layer and that CFCs were likely to be the main culprit.

The panel report had two main consequences. First, in September 1987 the Montreal Protocol was signed. This represented the first international agreement to protect the global environment and was intended to control the future world use and production of CFCs. Its initial stipulation was for a 50% reduction in CFC consumption from 1986 levels, although there were some short-term exemptions for developing countries. It was accepted that the protocol would very likely have to be modified as new scientific evidence was accumulated.

The second main consequence of the panel report was a massive concern throughout the developed world orchestrated by powerful pressure groups such as Friends of the Earth. These groups often had high media skills and very close relations with the media. Public concern was fuelled by further scientific evidence supporting the view that CFCs were having a deleterious effect on the ozone layer and by alarmist reporting of the issue, particularly by the tabloid press.

Imperial Chemical Industries (ICI) was one of the largest chemical producers in the world and the largest producer of CFCs in Europe. ICI fully supported the Montreal Protocol and called for a review of control measures that would take account of the latest scientific research. It recognised the desirability of stopping all production of CFCs, but only when the industry had successfully developed environmentally friendly substitutes for CFCs in their many important uses. This position may have been rational and based on the best available scientific evidence but it was not one that found favour with the environmental pressure groups or the media – and through them with the public.

ICI was in the forefront of research and development into safer alternatives to CFCs and had invested £30 million in two chemical plants that would produce such alternatives. This fact was almost totally overlooked in the popular movement against all producers of environmentally damaging products and indeed was little known to customers who were worried that ICI would cease to supply them with CFCs.

ICI realised that it had to respond to the issue of CFCs, which was receiving massive media coverage. This was an issue that was damaging its reputation as a responsible, socially concerned organisation.

Discussion point 15.6

Suppose that you were asked to help ICI to handle the public relations aspects surrounding the issue of CFC production. You are asked to:
- decide the stance that ICI should take;
- identify the publics that need to be addressed and rank them in order of importance; and
- determine the messages that would be appropriate for each public.

ants and sales administrators) who keep the system working smoothly. Staff professionals are the gatekeepers for diagnostic control systems, providing integrity for data input and preventing reports being distorted.

However, a good control system needs to be more than a diagnostic system. It needs to be an insightful one that supports learning. For this to occur, the control system needs to be an attention enhancer, in contrast to the diagnostic system, which is attention-conserving. Attention is greatly enhanced if the information system is interactive, whereby causes and effects can be explored. One example of such a system would be a spreadsheet, another would be an executive information system (EIS).

EIS, sometimes known as boardroom systems, provide selected and summarised information in a form suitable for senior executives. They are geared to doing three principal tasks: exception reporting, 'drilling down' and trend determination. Exception reporting is facilitated by allowing users to set tolerance limits for the values of key variables; should these limits be exceeded, then the area on screen will be highlighted. Drill-down permits managers to examine information in more and more detail in a logical progression. To investigate an identified problem the user would move progressively through the screens, going into more and more detail until the source of the problem is found. Trend analysis allows current and historical data to be analysed and forecasts to be made.

15.9.2 Responsibility centres

So far, the discussion and diagrams have indicated that a single process is controlled. In practice it could be a single process, but much more usually control is exercised over a set of processes. Accountants term these 'responsibility centres'. Formally, a hierarchy of three control centres is conventionally used by accountants, and these are listed in Exhibit 15.16.

A cost centre is a responsibility centre in which the managers can influence the costs incurred, but they would have little if any influence on the revenues associated with their activities, mainly because the link is indirect. Typical cost centres would be a section in a factory and a offer-development department. The main problem with establishing a cost centre is in allocating the indirect costs to it, for example the costs of the services that support the cost centre such as accounting and personnel services.

EXHIBIT 15.16

Types of responsibility centre

- **Cost centre** responsible for costs incurred
- **Profit centre** responsible for costs incurred and revenues generated
- **Investment centre** responsible for costs incurred, revenues generated and investments made

DISCUSSION
POINT 15.7

What sort of support services might need to be allocated to a primary process?

The managers of profit centres are responsible not only for their unit's costs but also for the associated revenues, and thus for most aspects of the profits generated. Typically, strategic business units within a corporation would be profit centres and so might individual products or product lines within a business. The problems of cost allocation remain broadly the same as with cost centres. The managers of investment centres are reponsible not only for the profit their unit is making but also for investments made, and thus for the return on investment.

The problem remains as to what processes should constitute a responsibility centre. At one extreme, the lowest possible identifiable 'subprocess' might be controlled for costs, e.g. control of the issuing of stationery and the use of photocopiers. At the other extreme, business profits may be all that are controlled.

There is also a need to incentivise the attainment of objectives through rewards and the withholding of rewards. Here a significant concern is that between rewarding the individual or rewarding the group. If it's the group that is rewarded, then there is the problem of defining the group.

15.10   Crisis control

In strategic management a crisis may be defined as an event that occurs without specific warning and to which the organisation has to react. A survey in 1997[21] found that 75% of UK companies had already experienced what they considered to be a company crisis, and 84% now considered crisis management to be a senior management responsibility.

Crisis control relies on both pro-active and reactive control. It is pro-active in that, although the precise form of the crisis will be unknown, broad elements of many crisis situations will be, and these can be planned for through risk management and particularly *contingency planning*. Crisis control is also reactive in that the specifics of the situations must be dealt with as they unfold.

15.10.1   Contingency planning and product recalls

Contingency planning

Contingency planning is 'just-in-case' planning, planning for events that it is hoped won't happen but might. These events take many forms, as Exhibits 13.13 and 15.17 indicate, but for any one business the types most likely to occur can be assessed. The Channel Tunnel fire of 1996 is an example of a crisis that was envisaged and planned for. Crises involve two forms of threat. There are also those directly involving the internal processes of the organisation, with health and safety for example. There are those that concern an organisation's outputs, contamination in its offers or damage from their use.

Product recalls

It is probable that product recall is the most common form of crisis, and it appears to be on the increase.[22] Obviously, one way of reducing the chance of having to recall a product is through excellent quality management and extensive consumer testing prior to product launch. However, as BMW illustrated in the middle of 1999 when it had to recall 280,000 of its 3-Series saloons because of problems with the brakes and airbags, even the best-run companies can get it wrong. Exhibit 15.17 illustrates many types of product recall.

EXHIBIT 15.17

Open up in a company crisis[23]

In recent days [written in November 1997] Mercedes-Benz has halted production on its A class cars, J. Sainsbury has become a target for incendiary attacks and Amstel beer has again been forced to recall its product, as some was found to contain glass fragments.

With a nearly 300% increase in product recalls in the UK since 1995, no organisation, it seems, can discount the possibility of such headaches.

According to a report* by crisis management specialists Infoplan International, food products, cars and electrical appliances have become especially vulnerable to recalls in the past 18 months – usually the direct result of damaged, dangerous or contaminated products.

While the term 'crisis management' is usually associated with dramatic problems such as Perrier's benzene contamination seven years ago or, more recently, the Channel Tunnel fire, Infoplan makes the point that for most UK companies, product recalls will be a bigger problem.

Such recalls are running at more than 16 a month, says Infoplan, with 298 in Britain in the past 18 months alone. They relate to everything from hidden peanuts in confectionery to wiring faults in objective lamps.

Daphne Barrett, Infoplan chairman and author of the report, says 'It was only five or so years ago that product recalls would be hidden at the bottom of a newspaper column – almost as if the company involved didn't want people to know that something had gone wrong.

'Today, such recalls are shouted from the rooftops and are given half a page or more in both the tabloid and the quality press. The message appears to be getting through that the consequence of not coming clean about a problem that affects your consumers is far more dire than simple honesty.'

More than 90% of the 500 leading UK companies surveyed for the report said they were prepared for a possible crisis such as product failure, criminal activity including blackmail or terrorism, a health or safety alert, or a major accident.

The survey, conducted over the past 18 months, found that 75% of UK companies have already experienced what they consider to be a company crisis, with most saying they have successfully put their own crisis plan to test.

Eighty-four per cent now consider crisis management a senior management responsibility, compared with the 58% who said the same in Infoplan's last survey two years ago. Just under half the respondents said that seven was the maximum number for an efficient crisis management team, while 5% of companies believed that up to 100 people would be needed.

Infoplan notes that 1996 was a particularly difficult year for car companies, while 1997 has so far seen the spotlight fall, once again, on food.

The car incidents in 1996 included: Volkswagen's recall of 105,000 cars in Britain after the discovery of a cooling system fault; Dunlop being criticised by a High Court judge after concealing problems with a faulty tyre; 200,000 Ford Fiestas recalled because of possible seat-belt faults; and Vauxhall's recall of more than 30,000 Fronteras after exhaust problems were detected.

The food industry was, says Infoplan, 'under almost constant attack in 1996 and throughout much of 1997 as well.'

Aside from BSE and *E. coli* outbreaks, 1996 saw: a big product recall from Walker's Snack Foods because of glass fragments in crisps; a food poisoning alert in central London hotels and restaurants over infected mussels; brands of honey linked to infant botulism; attacks on peanut butter manufacturers because of escalating allergy fears; lamb mince with up to 10% beef found in supermarket chains and butchers' shops.

Recalls have become almost as common in other areas in the past months: Hotpoint was accused of shredding clothes in its washing machines; Ikea withdrew a range of over-boiling kettles; Remington recalled its Professional 1600 hairdryer model 'for safety reasons'; and Matsui recalled a 14-inch colour TV after the discovery of a fire hazard.

Not all company crises are so grave, says Infoplan. One of the problems that gained most media attention was the withdrawal, by C&A, the clothing chain, of thousands of pairs of men's underpants when it was found that a manufacturing error had put the opening in the wrong place.

Discussion point 15.8

List the types of crisis that Matthews cites above.

● What are the reasons for the increase in product recalls?

* *The 1997 Review of Crisis and Risk Management*

Contact: Infoplan International, Ludgate House, 107 Fleet Street, London EC4A 2AB.

There are many features that are applicable to all recalls. First, one senior person should be made responsible for contingency planning. An obvious candidate would be the main person responsible for downstream relationships. This person will need to put in place measures to ease a recall should this become necessary. They could seek to alter designs so that components can be easily replaced. Less ambitiously, the firm should build traceability into the product through ensuring that products and parts of products contain individual serial numbers that enable time and place of manufacture to be established unequivocally. Traceability also means that the organisation's information systems must be capable of allowing identification of wholesalers, retailers and customers who may have bought the product. The aero engine companies have had to have near perfect traceability for many years to comply with air safety requirements. Another task for the recall manager would be to identify and brief all personnel who might be needed should a recall be necessary.

Once the company has become aware of the issue, it needs to identify the real source of the problem. The issue may appear to be a product fault but it could be something else; for example, the issue may be a false perception where the most appropriate response would be to refute the charges, as an unnecessary recall will tend to be costly and give credibility to the issue. If it proves to be a product fault, then there is the question of what action to take. The consequences of the fault are obviously highly significant; a fault that is merely irritating wouldn't cause the same level of concern as one that is life-threatening. If a recall appears warranted, consideration must be given to its extent; should all products over an extended period be recalled or perhaps only those produced over a very limited time period or only those sold in one country? A repair or retrofit offer may be appropriate. An optional recall might be appropriate, with the chance for customers to have a replacement or money back.

15.10.2   The public relations aspects of crisis management

As well as contingency planning to obviate a crisis and to be in a better position to react to it should it arise, there is a need to handle the public relations aspects once the crisis has occurred. This is reactive public relations, concerned with protecting the reputation of an organisation in the face of a suddenly emerging and potentially damaging issue. There are six main elements to the public relations side of crisis management and these can be combined and summarised in the CRUNCH mnemonic of Exhibit 15.18.

EXHIBIT 15.18

The CRUNCH mnemonic

- **C**ontingency plan
  - **R**eact fast
    - **U**se experts
      - **N**urture the media
        - **C**entralise control
          - **H**uman interest and concern emphasised

It is important to **contingency plan** – to have a plan in place that covers the other five public relations aspects of a crisis. Obviously, not all crises can be foreseen, but some can and can be planned for. This form of contingency planning will have considered a range of types of crisis and will have identified the publics who will need to be addressed: shareholders, customers, buyers, victims, etc. It should also have considered the messages that should be given and the types of media that will be seeking information.

It is vital to **react fast** or, to be more precise, to be seen to be doing something quickly. Setting up telephone hotlines and publicising the numbers widely can be valuable. However, it is important that in reacting quickly the real problem, and people's perceptions of it, are fully understood.

It is advisable to **use experts**, particularly if they aren't directly involved with the organisation facing the crisis. Experts can often present a more convincing message than can the organisation itself.

It is important to **nurture the media**. They are likely to provide the most persuasive channels of communication and it's important to keep them 'on-side'. Silence breeds suspicion and lets rumour breed. To prevent this, the media should be given access to the crisis site or production facility, if there is one, to photos where appropriate, and to other sorts of information. In this way the messages given by the media are to some extent under the control of the organisation.

An organisation that doesn't **centralise control** in a crisis is asking for problems. It's very important not only to have just one centre controlling the handling of the (real) crisis but also to have no more than one voice responsible for all media briefings and all other information dissemination, so that consistency of the messages is maintained.

Many stakeholders – particularly the general public – will be much more interested in the human side of a crisis than with more abstract features. Thus **human interest and concern** should be emphasised if possible. The concern of the organisation for any individual suffering, hardship or loss should also be emphasised. The genuine concern of interested parties shouldn't be underestimated.

The effect of the good or bad previous standing of the organisation is considerable. A good reputation can be very helpful in that it sets the context within which any current campaign is viewed. Being recognised as a socially responsible organisation, for example, allows the organisation to carry conviction when setting out its case. This was the position of ICI when it got caught up in concerns over CFCs and the ozone layer.

15.10.3   Rumour control

Rumour is a proposition that is unverified and in general circulation.[24] Being unverified doesn't mean that a rumour is untrue, only that it isn't known whether it is or not.

Koenig[25] has analysed a great many rumours in the USA, ranging from worms in McDonald's beefburgers and the poprock sweets that 'made kids' stomachs explode' through to Ray Kroc, the president of McDonald's allegedly supporting the Church of Satan, and Procter & Gamble's 'Man on the Moon' charge. He identified three categories of information in commercial rumours:

- The target – the offers, policies and personalities associated with businesses.
- The allegation – there are two forms: *conspiracy rumours*, which allege policies or practices that are deemed threatening or unethical; and *contamination rumours*, which claim that an offer is harmful or undesirable.
- The cited source – rumours associated with an authoritative source to provide credibility: a TV show, a celebrity or a relation 'who knows about these things', for example.

Allport and Postman[26] developed a formula linking the amount of rumour in circulation with the importance/interest attached to it by the people transmitting the rumour, and the ambiguity of the evidence about the topic:

$$\text{amount of rumour} = \text{importance/interest to the transmitters} \times \text{ambiguity of the topic}$$

Thus if the rumour isn't interesting, it will not be transmitted. Similarly, ambiguity indicates that a situation is unclear, and if a situation is unambiguous, then any rumour will die away.

An ambiguous situation can arise because there is more than one source providing information that differs, thus creating confusion. Censorship and conspiracy are other conditions giving rise to ambiguous situations. Thus a way to avoid rumour is for there to be one and only one source for official information and for this source to be as open as possible.

Koenig has experience of many rumours and of the problems of leaving them to 'burn out on their own' and tackling them head on. He has distilled his experiences into the checklist that is reproduced as Exhibit 15.19.

KEY CONCEPT   Effective strategic control require the use of six types of control. Assumption control is narrowly focused on the values of the key variables on which the strategy is based. Surveillance control is weakly focused, concerned with identifying emergent issues. Climate control is concerned with establishing and maintaining a climate that is benevolent to the organisation's interest. All three are forms of pro-active control.

Implementation control is concerned with controlling strategic change; operational control with control of the on-going, present processes. Both rely primarily on reactive control. Crisis control is concerned with managing suddenly emerging issues, and relies on both pro-active and reactive elements.

EXHIBIT 15.19

Synopsis of recommended steps in rumour control (Koenig, 1985)

Alert procedure

1   On first hearing a rumour, note the location and wording of the allegation and target.

2   Keep alert for any other rumours to see if the original report was spurious.

3   If rumours increase to ten or more, send requests to distributors, franchise managers, and whoever else meets the public to find out who told the rumour to the person reporting it. It is important to specify the regional boundaries of the problem and the characteristics of the participating population. Distribute forms that can be filled out for the above information, as well as fact sheets rebutting the rumour.

4   Check with competitors to see if they share the problem. Try to find out if the target has moved from your company to them or from them to yours, or if it has spread throughout the industry.

Evaluation

1   Check for a drop in sales or a slowdown in sales increase.

2   Monitor person-hours required to answer phone calls and mail.

3   Keep tabs on the morale of company personnel by meeting people in the corporation. Do they feel harassed? Do they feel that management is doing enough to help them?

4   Design a marketing survey to find out what percentage of the public believes any part of the rumour.

5   Make an assessment of the threat or potential threat the rumour poses to profits. Is the corporation in danger of appearing to be an inept, impotent and passive victim of the rumour problem? How much is management's image affected by the way things are going? The next move is a judgement call. If it seems that something more should be done, then it is time to move to the next square.

Launch a media campaign

1   Assemble all facts about the extent of the problem to present to co-workers and superiors. Be prepared for resistance from people who support the myth that 'pussyfooting is the best policy'.

2   Based on information gathered in the previous phases, decide on the geographical regions for implementing the campaign. If it is a local rumour, treat it locally; if it is a national rumour, treat it nationally.

3   Based on information gathered in the previous phases, decide on the demographic features of the carrying population.

4   Select appropriate media outlets and construct appropriate messages.

5   Decide on what points to refute. (Don't deny *more* than is in the allegation.) If the allegation is of the contamination variety, be careful not to bring any offensive association or to trigger potential 'residuals' in the refutation.

6   Two important points to make in any campaign are that the allegations are *untrue* and *unjust*. It should be implied that the company's business is not suffering, but that 'what's right is right!' and that people who pass on the rumour are 'going against the American sense of fair play!'

7   Line up spokespeople such as scientists, civic and/or religious leaders, rumour experts – whoever you think appropriate – to make statements on the company's behalf.

DISCUSSION
POINT 15.8 Koenig considers that there are two forms of allegation. Which of the conspiracy and contamination rumours involves a firm's outputs and which its processes?

15.11 Modelling and positive feedback

15.11.1 The six types of control

Six types of strategic control have been identified and their characteristics are summarised in Exhibit 15.20.

15.11.2 Modelling and the design of a control system

The design of a control system calls for the link between the related parts to be known: in the case of the central heating system, it is necessary to know that an increase of the amount of gas to the boiler will ultimately enable the house temperature to reach the objective temperature. The relations specifying links such as these form a model of how the process will perform for various combinations of the control and environmental variables. Without a knowledge of these relations, the designer would not be able to design: also the controller would be controlling in the dark, unsure of the effect that their setting of control levels would have on system performance.

Adding this requirement for a model of the control system to the 'picture' of a reactive control system itself produces Exhibit 15.21. A similar picture would apply to pro-active control; however, to include this in Exhibit 15.21 would cloud the picture.

The designer would use a model of the control system to investigate the types of control that might be installed, testing each possibility against a range of values of the environmental variables. For example, environmental temperatures higher than the required temperature could be tried on the central heating control system. If this were done with a conventional heating system, the controls would not be adequate to cope; the system's only response to such conditions would be not to make matters worse (i.e. not to switch the boiler on). An air-conditioning system able to extract heat from the house would be needed to get the house temperature back under control. Thus the model has allowed this possibility to be examined before the process is installed; if it were deemed important to prevent a rise of temperature above the objective temperature, then a conventional central heating system would not be a sound choice.

15.11.3 Positive feedback

Positive feedback is the situation whereby information regarding the output is fed back in such a way as to *increase* the difference between the objective and the output, ultimately driving the process out of equilibrium. In Section 15.1.3 positive feedback was introduced with the contention that it wasn't always disadvantageous. The reason why positive feedback may be advantageous is that it may be important that the present organisation be forced into another state,[27,28] into a state that better fits with its environment. Positive feedback can produce this sort of change, but negative feedback can't. The argument is to put an organisation under pressure to change. This is the rationale for Japanese companies setting 'impossible' goals for their project teams, which forces them to change their way of thinking and the way they do things. This is also the logic behind Porter's[29] assertion that firms should compete where the competition is fiercest. Pascale[30] and Stacey[31] point out that a firm has both to be in

EXHIBIT 15.20

Strategic control

	Assumption	Surveillance	Climate	Implementation	Operational	Crisis
Purpose	To ensure that planned strategy remains appropriate Reactive	To quickly pick up weak signals Pro-active	To generate and maintain a receptive climate for the business Pro-active	To keep strategy on track Diagnosis Reactive	To ensure efficient on-going operations Almost always reactive	To limit the damage to the business – its reputation and the claims against it Reactive and pro-active
People involved	Top management	Top management People in contact with all stakeholders	Public relations	Project managers Middle managers	Operating core	Designated central control
Focus	Narrow	Diffuse	Narrow	Narrow	Narrow	Narrow
Information source	Predetermined groups or individuals – internal and external	Varied and not prescribed except for business information systems	People in the know and influential external stakeholders	Project managers	Internal	The pro-active element could be contingency planning The reactive portion comes from outside stakeholders, particularly the media
Form of information acquisition	Monitoring	External to the organisation	Monitoring	Internal to the organisation	Monitoring internal operations	Wide-ranging, but mainly customers
Process periodicity	Periodically and triggered	Triggered	On-going with bursts of special activity	Milestones Project management	On-going with some periodicity	Episodic

EXHIBIT 15.21

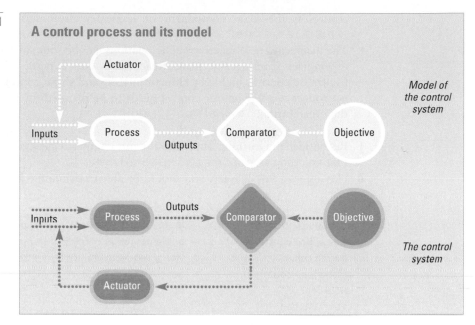

A control process and its model

Actuator

Model of
the control
system

Inputs

Process

Outputs

Comparator

Objective

Outputs

Inputs

Process

Comparator

Objective

The control
system

Actuator

control and on the verge of instability: being in control safeguards the on-going processes and the present revenues of the firm; being on the verge of instability provides
the prospect of engaging in new processes and future prosperity.

SUMMARY
- Reactive control is invoked only after an undesirable state of affairs has been
reached. It involves feeding information back from the output to the process
and/or its inputs. Pro-active control is the way of preparing the organisation for
environmental change. It involves feeding forward information from the environment to the process and/or its inputs. For most organisations both methods of control will be used. Both cybernetic and adaptive systems may utilise reactive and
pro-active control.

- Many business control systems are reactive and cybernetic and, although broadly
appropriate for structured activities, are often inapplicable to unstructured ones.
Multiple objectives are a particular concern, particularly the tensions between individual objectives and those of the organisation.   EXHIBIT 15.1, EXHIBITS 15.3 TO 15.5

- Objectives are commitments to achieve and these commitments should have the
characteristics of being **R**elevant, **E**nergising, **M**easurable, **I**nsightful and **T**imed.
Objectives need to be chosen carefully so as to strike the appropriate balance
between ease of attainment and the ability to energise.   EXHIBITS 15.6 TO 15.8

- Financial objectives have the attraction of providing a coherent, objective frame-
work for assessing the achievement of the economic goals of the organisation.
However, they often lack the motivational power of non-financial objectives.
Three types of financial control centre are generally recognised.   EXHIBIT 15.9,
EXHIBIT 15.10

- Pro-active control is control such that environmental influences are observed
before they affect the organisation, thus giving the organisation time to respond.
This form of control includes assumption, surveillance and climate. Reactive

control is the main component of implementation and operational control.
EXHIBIT 15.9, EXHIBITS 15.11 TO 15.13, EXHIBIT 15.20, EXHIBIT 15.21

- The main aspects of reactive public relations can be summarised in the CRUNCH mnemonic: Contingency plan, React fast, Use experts, Nurture the media, Centralise control, highlight Human interest and show concern. A growing issue is product recall. Rumour control needs to be planned for to prevent damage to the organisation. EXHIBIT 15.18, EXHIBIT 15.19

SELF-CHECK

1 Reconsider the learning outcomes for this chapter. Check that you feel confident that you can carry out the activities listed there.

2 Having read this chapter, you should be able to define the following terms:

adaptive control	human activity system	pro-active control
assumption control	implementation control	publicity
climate control	law of requisite variety	public relations
closed loop control	negative feedback	reactive control
crisis control	objective	rumour
cybernetic control	open loop control	structured process
designed physical system	operational control	surveillance control
feedback	positive feedback	unstructured process
feed forward		

MINI-CASE

The Channel Tunnel fire

When the Channel Tunnel began operation in 1994 the operators, Eurotunnel, were naturally keen to stress the wealth of built-in safety features capable of dealing with every eventuality, from collision to terrorist bomb – and fire. The late evening news programmes on Monday 18 November 1996 carried the news of the first major incident: there had been a serious fire in the Channel Tunnel. The chronology of the incident and relevant details are set out below and in the exhibit.

The fire started aboard a lorry carrying flammable goods on a nearly half-mile-long HGV (heavy goods vehicle) train travelling from Calais to Folkestone. The HGVs are carried in semi-open wagons whose design had been criticised by the Channel Tunnel Safety Authority in 1991: the authority had insisted that wagons of this design should be phased out by March 1994 but, after pressure from Eurotunnel, the decision was reversed. With a speed and intensity that shocked firefighters and health and safety agencies, the fire quickly spread to five other vehicles before the train was brought to a halt in the tunnel and the emergency services were alerted. No one was in the lorries, as the drivers are required to leave their vehicles and to move into a restaurant car at the front of the train. However, the halting of the train allowed the smoke from the fire to settle around the restaurant car. The smoke seeped into the car and was inhaled by the people in there.

Three companies that were most affected by the fire – Eurostar, the company carrying passengers through the tunnel; Le Shuttle carrying cars and HGVs; and Eurotunnel, which operates the tunnel – agreed to centralise control to handle the information sought by the media, with Eurotunnel in control in both France and the UK. The media were informed very soon after 10pm that the fire had occurred and a helpline for relatives and others seeking information was immediately set up. Pictures of the charred wagons were released to the media on Thursday, and pictures of the scene of the disaster were made available on the Friday.

Emile Grard, the *chef de train*, gave a press conference on the Tuesday. He was sitting in the restaurant car with other passengers when the fire alarm first went off. When he opened the carriage door he was confronted by clouds of black smoke. He shut the door and told everyone not to panic. One or two drivers tried to smash windows, which M. Grard was able to prevent, pointing out that opening windows would make matters worse by letting in more smoke. 'The smoke was toxic and I told everyone to get paper serviettes, soak them in water and hold them over their faces,' he recounted. M. Grard got out of the restaurant car and was able to make out the luminous arrows that are marked along the whole length of the tunnel and use them to lead the passengers and train crew to safety in the service tunnel. He said that the evacuation procedure had worked like clockwork. 'We have carried out exercises plenty of times for just this sort of thing and it worked very well. In fact, when it all started some of the passengers thought it was just a drill. We made it, and nobody was really injured.'

Two questions were immediately raised about safety in the tunnel. First, why the train didn't carry on to Folkestone, where it would have been much easier to fight the fire; it had been surmised that the fire disabled the engine and thus the train had to stop in the tunnel. Second, whether the HGV wagons are safe; Eurotunnel expressed confidence in the safety of the wagons and said that it would continue with that wagon design in the future.

Eurotunnel, which was losing £1 million a day in revenue while the tunnel was closed, wanted to start Eurostar services as soon as possible. However, this move was condemned by the leader of Britain's firefighters as premature – there needed to be a comprehensive tightening of safety systems before any restarting of Eurotunnel services. Colin Brown, deputy research director of the Consumers' Association, said that Eurotunnel's operating licence should be withdrawn following what he described as a fiasco.

Discussion point 15.9

Eurotunnel faced a crisis. Suppose you are a consultant in the public relations side of crisis management:

* What do you think of the crisis management skills of Eurotunnel: what did Eurotunnel do right, what did it do wrong, and what extra things should it have done?
* It is Saturday 23 November 1996. What would you suggest that Eurotunnel, Le Shuttle and Eurostar do now in terms of strategic control?

FURTHER DISCUSSION POINTS

1 For the GSM case:
   * What forms of strategic control are in evidence?
   * What type of control centres are the factories?
   * What evidence is there of controls being linked to tasks that people perform?
   * How are rumours internal to GSM dealt with?
2 In Chapter 1 the strategic management environment was characterised as chaotic, complex, dynamic and turbulent – all generally increasing the level of uncertainty facing leader-managers. However, not all business environments are the same. Reflect on how changes in environmental characteristics might affect the approach taken to strategic control.
3 It has been said that the quality of the dialogue around performance is much more important than the mechanics of control. Do you agree?

EXHIBIT 15.22

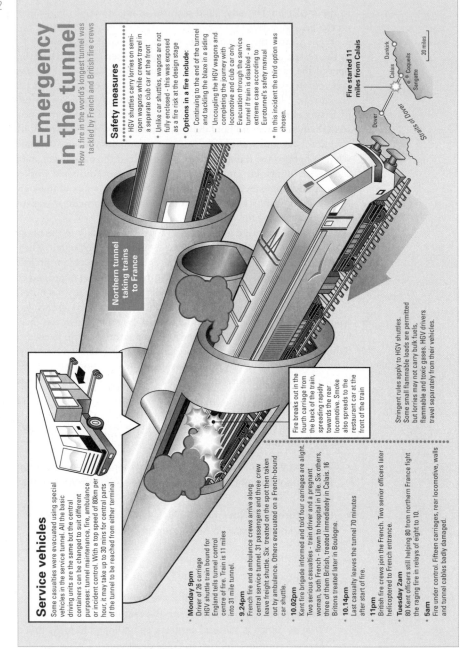

Emergency in the tunnel

How a fire in the world's longest tunnel was tackled by French and British fire crews

Safety measures

- HGV shuttles carry lorries on semi-open wagons while crews travel in a separate club car at the front
- Unlike car shuttles, wagons are not fully enclosed - this was exposed as a fire risk at the design stage
- **Options in a fire include:**
  - Continuing to the end of the tunnel and tackling the blaze in a siding
  - Uncoupling the HGV wagons and completing the journey with locomotive and club car only
  - Evacuation through the service tunnel if train is disabled - an extreme case according to Eurotunnel's safety manual
- In this incident the third option was chosen.

Northern tunnel taking trains to France

Fire started 11 miles from Calais

Calais · Dunkirk · Coquelles · Sangatte · Dover · Straits of Dover

20 miles

Service vehicles

Some casualties were evacuated using special vehicles in the service tunnel. All the basic driving units are the same but the central containers can be changed to suit different purposes: tunnel maintenance, fire, ambulance or incident control. With a top speed of 80km per hour, it may take up to 30 mins for central parts of the tunnel to be reached from either terminal

- **Monday 9pm**
  Driver of 26 carriage HGV shuttle train bound for England tells tunnel control centre of fire. Train is 11 miles into 31 mile tunnel.

- **9.24pm**
  French fire and ambulance crews arrive along central service tunnel. 31 passengers and three crew leave freight shuttle. Six treated on the spot then taken out by ambulance. Others evacuated on a French-bound car shuttle.

- **10.02pm**
  Kent fire brigade informed and told four carriages are alight. Two serious casualties - train driver and a pregnant woman, both French - flown to hospital in Lille. Six others, three of them British, treated immediately in Calais. 16 Britons treated later in Boulogne.

- **10.14pm**
  Last casualty leaves the tunnel 70 minutes after start of fire.

- **11pm**
  British fire crews join the French. Two senior officers later helicoptered to French entrance.

- **Tuesday 2am**
  80 Kent officers still helping 80 from northern France fight the raging fire in relays of eight to 10.

- **5am**
  Fire under control. Fifteen carriages, rear locomotive, walls and tunnel cables badly damaged.

Fire breaks out in the fourth carriage from the back of the train, spreading rapidly towards the rear locomotive. Smoke also spreads to the restaurant car at the front of the train

Stringent rules apply to HGV shuttles. Some small flammable loads are permitted but lorries may not carry bulk fuels, flammable and toxic gases. HGV drivers travel separately from their vehicles.

4 There is an aphorism that hard measures are soft (i.e. easy to deal with); soft measures are hard (i.e. difficult to deal with). Does this fit with your experiences?

5 The relationship between objectives, the purpose of the organisation and the environment has been written as *Objectives = Purpose + Environment*. What is your view on this?

ASSIGNMENTS

1 You hear a rumour that your company has donated roadside hoarding sites to a certain political party so that it can display prominently its pre-election propaganda. Your company has not done this, and you don't want a large proportion of the electorate who won't vote for this party to believe this. What would you do?

2 Identify the objectives for the Ford Motor Company as given in the mission statement in Chapter 6. Are they suitably framed?

FURTHER READING

A very readable account of financial control systems in everyday use is that given by Frank Wood and Alan Sangster in Frank Wood's *Business Accounting* 2, 8th edn, Financial Times Management, 1999.

A short, very interesting and amusing account of rumours and how they are generated and their consequences is the book by Fredrick Koenig, *Rumor in the Marketplace: the Social Psychology of Commercial Hearsay*, Auburn House Publishing, 1985.

CHAPTER NOTES AND REFERENCES

1 Checkland, P., *Systems Thinking, Systems Practice*, John Wiley, 1981.

2 Norbert Wiener appears to have been the first person to apply the term 'cybernetics' to the control of systems in his book *Cybernetics*, John Wiley, 1948.

3 Hofstede, G., *The Game of Budget Control*, Tavistock, 1968, p. 9.

4 Rathe, W.A., 'Management controls in business', in Malcolm, G.G. and Rowe, A.J. (eds), *Management Control Systems*, John Wiley, 1959, pp. 28–62.

5 Checkland, P., *op. cit.*

6 Dermer, J., *Management Planning and Control Systems: Advanced Concepts and Cases*, Irwin, 1977.

7 Perrow, C., *Organisational Analysis: A Sociological View*, Tavistock, 1970, p. 134.

8 Ross Ashby enunciated the law of requisite variety, that for a system to be able to maintain itself it must have at least as much variety as the environment in which it's operating (1970, *An Introduction to Cybernetics*, University Paperbacks). *Requisite variety* is Ross Ashby's way of describing *the required power to change things*: the power that the controller requires so that they can counter the variation in the environment and thus effect the required level of control.

9 Hofstede, G., 'The poverty of management control philosophy', *Academy of Management Review*, Vol. 3. No. 3. July 1978, pp. 450–61.

10 *Ibid.*

11 Edvinsson, L., 'Developing intellectual capital at Skandia', *Long Range Planning*, Vol. 30, No. 3, 1997, pp. 366–73.

12 Hofstede, G., *op. cit.* 1968, pp. 154–5.

13 Hopwood, A.G., *Accounting and Human Behaviour*, Prentice Hall, 1974, pp. 61–2.

14 Meyer, M., 'Pitfalls in choosing non-financial measures', *Antidote*, No. 1, 1996, p. 1.

15 Schreyögg, G. and Steinmann, H., 'Strategic control: a new perspective', *Academy of Management Review*, Vol. 12, No. 1, 1987, pp. 91–103.

16 Simons, R., 'How top managers use control systems as levers of strategic renewal', *Strategic Management Journal*, Vol. 15, No. 3, 1994, pp. 169–89.

17 Institute of Public Relations, *Professionalism in Practice*, IPR, 1995.

18   *Webster's Collegiate Dictionary*, 1989, p. 690.

19   Aldersey-Williams, H., 'Letters that say a lot', *Financial Times*, 19 October 1995, p. 15.

20   Based on Dewhurst, P., 'Environmental crisis: CFCs and the ozone layer – how ICI handled a major public issue', Case 5 in Moss, D. (ed.), *Public Relations in Practice: A Casebook*, Routledge, 1990.

21   Matthews, V., 'Open up in a company crisis', *Financial Times*, 26 November 1997, p. 19.

22   *Ibid.*

23   *Ibid.*

24   Rosnow, R. and Fine, G., *Rumor and Gossip*, Elsevier, 1976.

25   Koenig, F., *Rumor in the Marketplace: The Social Psychology of Commercial Hearsay*, Auburn House Publishing, 1985.

26   Allport, G. and Postman, L.J., *The Psychology of Rumor*, Henry Holt, 1947. The formula that they devised was based on wartime rumours. Koenig casts doubt on whether this formula is applicable to all sort of rumour.

27   Pascale, R.T., *Managing on the Edge: How Successful Companies Use Conflict to Stay Ahead*, Viking, 1990.

28   Stacey, R.D., *Strategic Management and Organisational Dynamics*, 2nd edn, Financial Times Pitman Publishing, 1996.

29   Porter, M.E., *The Competitive Advantage of Nations*, The Free Press/Macmillan, 1990.

30   Pascale, R.T., *op. cit.*

31   Stacey, R.D., *op. cit.*

PART 6

Parenting

16 The roles of the parent: portfolio identification

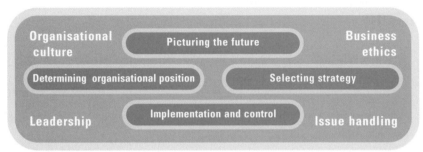

This chapter is the first of a set of three that consider the distinct characteristics of corporate strategic management, i.e. those aspects that aren't present at the business level. This unique contribution is termed 'parenting'.

The chapter begins by revisiting the differences between business and corporation, explains what a parent is and illustrates the power of corporations. The question of whether parents add value is then explored. Parental strategic activities are contrasted with business strategic activities, and four main parental roles are identified. Two are explored in this chapter: the role of the parent in determining the general direction of the corporation, and the identification of the appropriate business and competence portfolios.

The role of the parent in setting corporate direction is first considered. Then the rationale for portfolio selection is explored, with both false and rational grounds discussed. Forms of diversification are examined. The impetus and impediments to entering new markets, particularly international markets, are explored and this is followed by considering the basis for developing new offers based on competences.

The previous sections emphasise the growth of a corporation. In the last section radical changes to the structure of corporations that reduce the role of the parent are considered – demerger, divestiture and liquidation.

The third and fourth parenting roles – the establishment of portfolios and on-going portfolio management – are explored in Chapters 17 and 18.

Since over half of all business activity in developed countries is carried out by corporations, which are often economically more powerful than nations, it's vital for the world's economic well-being that corporate strategy be well founded. Furthermore, there is a high probability that anyone entering employment today will work for a corporation at some time in their working lives. To understand how corporations function is thus very important from both economic and career perspectives.

LEARNING
OUTCOMES

When you have worked through this chapter, you should be able to:

- explain the relationship of a parent to the corporation;

- compare and contrast the strategic management activities of parents and businesses;

- list the 13 parental roles and know what each involves;

- explain the tests for appropriateness in a corporation's SBU portfolio;

- explain the situations in which the various forms of diversification are appropriate;

- explain demerger, divestment and liquidation and the situations in which they might be contemplated.

16.1   The importance and rationale of corporate strategic management

16.1.1   Corporation and business

Before considering corporate strategic management, it's useful to reaffirm the difference between a corporation and a business. Businesses within a corporation are termed strategic business units (SBUs); they are units that provide significantly different offers and can operate independently of the rest of the enterprise (or could do so with only minor additions to their activities). Exhibit 16.1, which is a reproduction of Exhibit 6.8, re-emphasises that a business should be considered a corporation when it includes at least two significantly different capabilities in its portfolio.

EXHIBIT 16.1

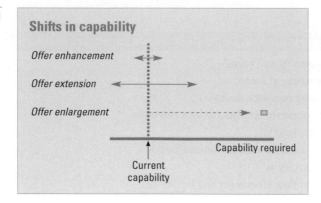

16.1.2 Parents

The people outside the individual SBUs are corporate personnel, who together can be likened to acting as a parent[1] 'looking after' and nurturing its offspring, which are the businesses. When the term *corporation* is used it includes the whole enterprise; the term *parent* will be used to mean the people in the corporation who aren't affiliated to any of the constituent businesses. The parent is what is 'left over' after the businesses have been extracted from the total organisation. Corporate strategy is about what the parent can and should do to add value.

16.1.3 The power of corporations

Corporations wield tremendous financial and political power. Exhibit 16.2 illustrates this point, showing the world's top economic entities.[2] This exhibit should make crystal clear why good corporate strategic management is so important, on a par with the need for good government.

16.2 Do parents add value?

The role of the parent is to add value over and above the value that the SBUs within the corporate portfolio would generate on their own. Thus at the very minimum the parent shouldn't cost more than the increased profits that arise from the parental influence on the SBUs. However, the obvious costs of even the most bloated corporate hierarchy will seldom be a large consideration. What are important are the hidden costs and constraints: an SBU must explain its decisions to top management, spend time complying with planning and other corporate systems, live with the constraints imposed by the parent, and forgo the opportunity to motivate employees with direct equity ownership.[3]

What is also vital is the corporate strategy the parent pursues, for example which businesses it has in its portfolio and how it controls them. An ill-chosen acquisition or merger, such as that between Mindscape and Pearson or those made in the USA by several British companies, can be very damaging to profitability, as also, but in a less obvious way, is the retention of a business that isn't performing as well as it should.

EXHIBIT 16.2

It's bigger than Turkey, Thailand or Denmark – but it's not a country (Caulkin, 1998)

In the late seventies, a French civil servant declared that IBM had all the attributes it needed to become a world power. You might think the troubles that beset Big Blue during the eighties had knocked that scare story on the head.

But the truth is that, even diminished, IBM is *still* a world power. Its 1995 sales of $71.9 billion were greater than the GDP of all but 40 nation-states – about the same as the Philippines and half as much again as Iran and Ireland.

IBM is just 18th among the world's biggest corporations. The real corporate leviathans – Japan's Mitsubishi and Mitsui, with sales of more than $180 billion each – just miss the world's economic top 20, not far behind Indonesia and Sweden. Economically speaking, Mitsubishi is more than half the size of Russia or Australia.

The world's giant firms represent scarcely conceivable concentrations of market power. Two weeks ago, Microsoft passed the $200 billion mark in terms of market capitalisation, and its PC partner, Intel, is not far behind.

This is not just abstract power. One commentator has written: 'By making ordinary business decisions, managers now have more power than most sovereign governments to determine where people will live; what work they will do – if any; what they will eat, drink and wear; what sorts of knowledge they will accumulate; and what kinds of society their children will inherit.'

Should size matter to anyone except those trying to manage these monsters? Is the current wave of mergers, making big even bigger, different from previous ones? And can markets and the managers of the colossi be trusted to produce outcomes that benefit the world as well as themselves?

Optimists might argue that the growth in size and sophistication of the joint stock corporation has, over the past 200 years, coincided with a massive upsurge in well-being which (with setbacks) now embraces much of the globe. Large companies have many positive qualities, including better pay, more stability and the ability to do a lot of R&D.

Moreover, market capitalism appears not only to go rather well with democracy but actually to require it. In 1790, as the Industrial Revolution was gathering pace, there were just three liberal democracies in the world. Two centuries later, that number has risen to around 80, including 45 of the top 50 economies.

Why change a winning formula? Merger mania, optimists might add, is nothing new. Companies are always trying out new combinations of businesses. In any case, what markets put together they often pull apart again. For every Diageo, Commercial Union/General Accident or Coopers & Lybrand/Price Waterhouse there is an ICI/Zeneca (and now ICI again), a Thorn/EMI, a Hanson, a BTR or an Inchcape.

It is important to separate short-term from long-term considerations here. All the merger waves of the past have died away – and this one will be no exception. The more big companies merge, the greater the pressures on competitors to join in. The inevitable result is that too many companies are chasing too few targets, which creates prices unrelated to reality and sustained only by the expectation of yet more deals.

But the longer-term trends are not so reassuring. Companies *are* becoming more powerful, not only at the level of what we eat and drink, but in every dimension of our lives.

The world's top economic entities – country/company by GDP/sales

		$bn			$bn
1	United States	7100	31	Thailand	160
2	Japan	4964	32	Denmark	156
3	Germany	2252	33	Hong Kong	142
4	France	1451	34	Ford Motor (USA)	137
5	United Kingdom	1095	35	Norway	136
6	Italy	1088	36	Saudi Arabia	134
7	China	745	37	South Africa	131
8	Brazil	580	38	Toyota Motor (Japan)	111
9	Canada	574	39	Exxon (USA)	110
10	Spain	532	40	Royal Dutch/Shell	110
11	South Korea	435	41	Burma	108
12	Netherlands	371	42	Poland	108
13	Australia	338	43	Finland	105
14	Russia	332	44	Nissho Iwai (Japan)	98
15	India	320	45	Portugal	97
16	Mexico	305	46	Wal-Mart Stores (USA)	94
17	Switzerland	286	47	Israel	88
18	Argentina	278	48	Greece	86
19	Taiwan	260	49	Hitachi (Japan)	84
20	Belgium	251	50	Ukraine	84
21	Austria	217	51	Nippon Life Insurance	83
22	Sweden	210	52	Nippon Telegraph and Telephone	82
23	Indonesia	190	53	Singapore	80
24	Mitsubishi (Japan)	184	54	AT&T (USA)	79
25	Mitsui (Japan)	181	55	Malaysia	78
26	Otochu (Japan)	169	56	Daimler-Benz (Germany)	72
27	Turkey	169	57	Philippines	72
28	General Motors (USA)	169	58	IBM (USA)	72
29	Sumitomo (Japan)	168	59	Matsushita Electric Industrial (Japan)	71
30	Marubeni (Japan)	161	60	General Electric (USA)	70

Source: *The Economist*

In a new book on the future of the corporation (*The Emperor's Nightingale: Restoring the Integrity of the Corporation*, Capstone, £18.99) American shareholder activist and governance specialist Robert Monks warns against a warmly anthropomorphic view of companies and their aims.

By virtue of their charter and their constitution, he argues, companies are a kind of artificial life form, not constrained by the laws of nature. Unlike mortals, companies are characterised by a drive for unlimited life, size and power.

Monks gives many examples of the way the drives manifest themselves: the extraordinary growth of executive reward; the remarkable incidence of wrongdoing in even the most admired companies; and particularly, in the growth of corporate political power. Think of Rupert Murdoch's News Corporation (452 in the global big company league).

Less obviously, think of EDS, the American computer services company (67 in the world), without which many of Whitehall's computers would grind to a halt. It is inconceivable now that Whitehall could ever reconstitute the knowledge to run its own computers again, or even frame the possibility of doing so. In effect, EDS (one of ten companies 'named and shamed' for corporate governance failings by the California Public Employees Retirement System) has been incorporated into the machinery of government.

Most of all, companies attempt at every stage to frame in their favour the rules by which they operate. A case in point is the new Multinational Agreement on Investment, which will severely limit the ability of governments to set conditions for inward investment by foreign companies.

Relentlessly externalising the political, social and environmental costs of its activities, the corporation has outstripped the limitations of accounting and accountability to become what Monks calls a 'machine for transferring risks to others'. It is, he goes on 'An externalising machine, in the same way that a shark is a killing machine – no malevolence, no intentional harm, just something designed with sublime efficiency for self-preservation, which it accomplishes without any capacity to factor in the consequences for others.'

In the conventional economic model, size does not matter so long as the company is accountable to the market, which judges impartially between competing offerings.

But this does not work any more. In the first place, beyond a certain size companies are too big to be allowed to go bust – take Chrysler, for example. Second, in some areas the recently identified phenomenon of increasing returns or 'lock-in' means the market is not an impartial arbiter. Once a certain mass is reached, it rewards bigness, not goodness.

The paradigm for 'lock-in' is the qwerty keyboard: its original rationale is long gone, but it is now impossible to change. The best-known commercial example is the VHS video format.

Size *does* matter. None of these great corporate entities is accountable to those whose lives they affect, as the vast majority of national entities are. What is more, the very qualities that make the corporation so productive – its creativity, energy and flexibility – make it particularly adept at co-opting those economic and social accountabilities which do exist to its own advantage.

The revisions of company law planned by President of the Board of Trade Margaret Beckett should take into account the fact that as companies continue to grow, the economic and political frameworks within which they operate must change too. Otherwise Frankenstein will end up controlling its creator.

Discussion point 16.1

Why might the rankings overestimate the power of countries and underestimate the power of corporations?
* Which sort of activities lead to increasing returns to scale?

There are two strong indications that parents don't always add value to their SBUs. The hostile takeovers in the 1980s, whereby the predator could pay a hefty premium for its prize and still make a great deal of money out of the subsequent splitting of the business portfolio, indicated that the parent was subtracting value: the parts were worth more than the whole. More recently, the spate of successful management buyouts, whereby the incumbent managers buy an SBU from the corporation and make significant profits from the business's subsequent rise in value, again attests to the fact that some businesses are underperforming when part of a corporation.

Quantitative evidence concerning the value created by parents is hard to come by. Perhaps the best source is the line-of-business data collected for US manufacturing during the early 1970s. Analysis shows conclusively that parents added nothing significant to the profitability of the corporation: value was being added by the SBUs, not by the parent.[4]

The reasons why parents might subtract value aren't hard to imagine. Parents can spend only a fraction of the time thinking about an SBU that the managers of the SBU itself can spend. So unless the SBU managers are abysmal, it is likely that they will know more about their business and how it works than the parents. It's also likely that a parent works within a framework that's the same for all SBUs. Goold and his colleagues write that they have found no successful parents that apply basically different value-creation insights and parenting characteristics in different parts of their portfolios.[5] However, this common approach could be fatal. Applying the same policies where there is a portfolio of businesses in different parts of their life cycles or where the portfolio spans many different countries are examples where SBUs require different treatments.

There is another significant reason for surmising that SBUs might perform less well in a corporation than outside it. An SBU in a highly profitable corporation is unlikely to be subject to the same discipline as a business that has to face the full might of the marketplace. It's in the interests of managers of an SBU to 'massage the truth' in presenting a case for corporate investment, for example.

While these are some of the reasons for supposing that parents can very easily subtract value, a parent certainly has the potential to add considerably to the performance of its SBUs. In contrast to the line-of-business findings noted above, the 1970s was a time when Japanese corporations were beginning to show the strength that was to make their SBUs such formidable competitors in the subsequent decades. They appeared to pursue parenting policies that were successful in augmenting SBU competitiveness.

EXHIBIT 16.3

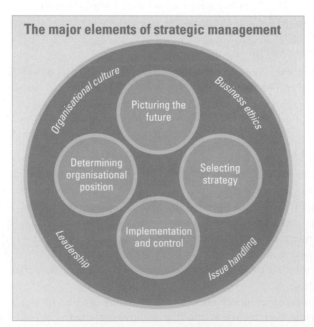

The major elements of strategic management

16.3 The scope of parenting

16.3.1 Contrast with the business level

The main elements of corporate strategic management are the same as those for business strategic management (as shown in Exhibit 16.3). However, there are some different emphases, which will now be explored.

Internal context

The parent is responsible for the overall corporate strategic direction. This includes setting the corporate vision, mission, culture and ethics, and providing leadership and handling issues; exactly the same elements as at the business level. Thus little will be added to what has already been written in Chapters 2 to 5, except to discuss setting the corporate direction.

Picturing the future

The concern for a business when picturing the future is with its operating environment and the relevant remote environment: demographics, the economic features, the environmental framework, etc. A corporation doesn't make anything and doesn't have the customers and suppliers that a business has,[a] and thus it doesn't have an operating environment that in any meaningful way corresponds to the operating environment of a business. It is the relationships of the corporation with its secondary stakeholders that are of major significance. However, the parent may seek to influence its environment in a way not available to the constituent businesses; for example, if a corporation has several operations in one particular country, the parent may try to influence features in that country to the corporation's advantage.

DISCUSSION POINT 16.2

How true is it to say that a corporation doesn't have an operating environment that in any meaningful way corresponds to the operating environment of a business?

- Does a corporation have only *secondary* stakeholders? Identify any primary stakeholders.

A corporation's remote environment is largely the sum of the remote environments of its constituent SBUs, although the parent will almost certainly consider a longer time horizon than the SBUs. Thus, although some cash and profit forecasting will be undertaken, the long-range perspective will suggest an emphasis on scenario building, bringing together the scenarios of its SBUs in a somewhat broader form. The concern is for what Fahey and Randall[6] describe as 'paramount issues', issues that are above those affecting any individual SBU and that span many businesses.

Determining organisational position

A business is concerned with establishing its position *vis-à-vis* its competitors and with two portfolios: its portfolio of offers and its portfolio of capabilities. The parent is also concerned with two portfolios: with its portfolio of SBUs, concerned with which businesses the corporation has and should have, and its portfolio of compe-

---

a   Parents are sometimes in competition, for instance when a business is put up for sale. But this is a very different form of competition to that faced by businesses.

tences. A competence is akin to a capability in that it is a set of business processes; it is unlike a capability in that it's not 'owned' by the business but is 'owned' by the corporation. For example, a corporation may make an electronic device that is used in offers made by many SBUs, and the corporation would have the responsibility of identifying this as a competence and nurturing it. (A competence is the seed corn for SBUs and will be used to develop future offers.) Japanese firms call microchips the rice of industry, as they are feeding competitive advantage into every product;[7] the design and manufacture of microchips is a competence. Thus alongside a consideration of the portfolio of SBUs is a consideration of the portfolio of (corporate) competencies. Any SWOT table that the parent produces would consider the strengths and weaknesses of both the SBUs and the competencies of the corporation as a whole.

Selecting strategy

There are two elements to selecting corporate strategy. First, there is the **basis** on which the portfolios will be founded. It's likely that the portfolio of SBUs and that of competences will complement each other and thus have the same basis. For example, Sharp produces a host of consumer electronics that are supported through expertise in liquid crystal displays, microminiaturisation and basic electronics. Daimler–Chrysler produces a great many offers that are associated with transportation, and supports them with competences in mechanical and electrical engineering.

Second, there is the **strategic pathway** by which the corporate goals are to be attained. Businesses are concerned with offer enhancements and offer extensions and with getting the resources to back these: with make-or-buy decisions, co-operation within their value chains, and short- and medium-term funding. The parent faces similar resource allocation problems, but the access paths to resources are different: mergers and acquisitions, formal alliances and long-term funding.

Implementation and control

Whichever strategic pathway is chosen, there will be a need for a parent to monitor and control, as with any business. Special parenting concerns will be with establishing and nurturing alliances and with post-acquisition activity. One additional requirement concerns corporate governance, how the parent should organise itself both to control its SBUs and to account responsibly to those agencies that can make a legitimate demand for accountability.

KEY CONCEPT   The main elements of strategic management are fundamentally the same at the corporate and business levels. The emphases are different, however, with a parent concerned with a portfolio of businesses rather than a portfolio of offers, and with its competences rather than with capabilities.

16.3.2 The parenting roles

Exhibit 16.4 summarises the areas where a parent has a role over and above that of the SBUs. Four main parenting roles can be identified, 13 roles in all. First there are the considerations that the parent must have for the general direction of the corporation. Second there is the concern for identifying the SBU and competence portfolios,

EXHIBIT 16.4

The roles of a parent

Setting corporate direction

Identifying the appropriate SBU and competence portfolios

Determining the portfolio of SBUs
Determining the portfolio of competences

Establishing the SBUs and competences

Internal development
Carrying through mergers and acquisitions
Initiating alliances

On-going portfolio management

Determining the organisational structure
Supporting strategic alliances
Providing corporation-wide services
Improving individual SBU performance
Developing the relationships between SBUs
Nurturing competences
Maintaining appropriate corporate governance arrangements

which generally would support one another and therefore should be considered together. Third there is the responsibility for establishing the SBU and competence portfolios. Finally there is the need to consider on-going parental concerns for both the SBUs and the competences: determining the organisational structure, supporting strategic alliances, and so on.

16.3.3 The spectrum of parents

Not all parents act in the same way. At one extreme there is the corporation where there is a seamless fusing of parental and other activities. Many Japanese corporations would seem to come close to this situation with their J-form organisations and cross-holdings between many companies. Thus some parents may be carrying out many or all the parenting roles listed in Exhibit 16.4.

At the other extreme is the 'hands-off' parent, which is involved in determining the portfolio of businesses in which the corporation engages and then letting the leader-managers in each SBU run it in almost any way they think fit as long as well-specified control targets are met. This approach to parenting is one that doesn't consider competences at all and isn't interested in synergies between businesses. Here the corporation is based on the leadership/managerial skills residing in the parent. For example, during the 1980s, Hanson Trust was very successful in buying and subsequently rejuvenating underperforming companies through keen deal making and robust management of the subsequently acquired companies. BTR was another case in point.[8] Such parents have been termed *corporate catalysts*.[9] There are also the passive investors, who may intervene to put pressure on management but who play no role in the day-to-day running of the corporation. These are institutions such as the pension funds and individual investors, of whom Warren Buffett with Berkshire Hathaway is possibly the prime example.

16.4 Setting corporate direction

A vision sets out the long-term goal or ideal for an organisation; a mission provides a 'road map' of what to do on the way to achieving it. A corporate mission statement is particularly useful at setting down the corporate 'theme' or basis for the corporate portfolios and thus the statement acts as a linking force. While a business mission statement should consider products, markets and customers, a corporation doesn't have any of these, and so there are likely to be significant differences between the forms of business and corporate mission statements.

Difficulties with forming a corporate mission statement can arise because:

- the corporate mission of a diversified corporation will tend to be rather bland, with the mission statement either long-winded to cover all business areas or a short 'slogan' to avoid becoming overly specific in any particular area. Lord Hanson of Hanson Trust had a corporate mission that was simply to create maximum profits for his shareholders;
- it may not be feasible to cover all stakeholders in all the businesses;
- ethical and cultural considerations are likely to differ markedly between businesses if the corporation is a multinational.

It is quite appropriate for an organisation to have a mission statement for each and every strategic level, as the two mission statements from 3M in Exhibit 16.5 illustrate.

EXHIBIT 16.5

3M hierarchy of missions

Corporate vision and values

VISION
To be the most innovative enterprise and the preferred supplier.

VALUES
Satisfy customers with superior quality, value and service.
Provide investors with an attractive return through sustained, quality growth.
Respect our social and physical environment.
Be a company employees are proud to be part of.

CUSTOMER SERVICES
Our mission is to know our customers and clients, create service value, and deliver satisfaction to achieve competitive advantage.

DISCUSSION POINT 16.3

Is it appropriate to have a vision at the corporate level but only a mission at lower levels?

EXHIBIT 16.6

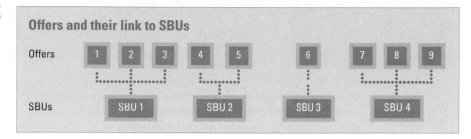

Offers and their link to SBUs

16.5 The rationale for SBU portfolio selection

Offers and SBUs are linked, as shown in Exhibit 16.6. A significant concern for a parent is whether to add another SBU or remove one. In doing so the parent is considering whether to enlarge or reduce a set of offers made by the enterprise.

Offer enhancements and extensions are associated with rather limited change; both cases would be a business concern, as new capabilities wouldn't be needed. However, more significant change occurs when the organisation decides on offer enlargement, for example to develop a distinctly new product or service or to move into and develop a new market. In both cases the risks and rewards are likely to be greater than with extensions, mainly because the organisation has to obtain access to one or more new capabilities.

16.5.1 Conglomerates and conglomerate diversification

An enterprise is termed *diversified* when it has more than one SBU in its portfolio. Two types of diversification can be recognised: related and unrelated. Related diversification is where the SBUs have something in common and thus the opportunity exists to transfer skills or share activities between them; unrelated diversifications don't offer such oppportunities.

Some corporations do consist of SBUs that have little in common: at one time Hanson Trust included battery making in Europe, coal mines between the USA and tobacco manufacture in the UK. A corporation with little or no relatedness between the SBUs in its portfolio is termed a *conglomerate*. The difference between a conglomerate and other forms of diversification is that it is financial or managerial considerations that are paramount, rather than any commonality of markets, products or technology. Examples of conglomerate diversifications are an SBU paying a lot of tax paired with one that has unused tax credits: and a parent good at turning round ailing companies buying an underperforming firm.

Conglomerate diversification would appear to fit strategically when:

- an organisation's basic industry is experiencing declining sales and profits;
- an organisation has the capital and managerial talent needed to compete successfully in a new business area;
- the organisation has the opportunity to purchase an unrelated business that is an attractive investment opportunity;
- there exists financial synergy between the businesses;
- government action may be against concentration in a single market.

16.5.2 Poor reasons for portfolio selection

There are two rationales that are often put forward to support the case for conglomerate diversification: the spreading of risk and the importance of size.

Spreading of risk

With a portfolio of businesses, risk can be spread: one area of business suffering a downturn might well be counterbalanced by another doing well. This is especially true where the businesses are prone to cycles of activity. While this line of reasoning may well appeal to senior managers, it has little merit for shareholders. In English-speaking countries the vast majority of investments are made by people or organisations who hold a portfolio of shares in many enterprises. For example, pension funds and other institutions in the UK hold around 70% of all shares traded on the stock market; in the USA it is around 60%. Thus shareholders are fully and easily able to spread their risk by holding the portfolio that suits them, and this is especially true with accessible Internet trading significantly lowering transaction costs. There is no need for the managers of enterprises to do this for investors. In countries such as Germany and Japan, where banks hold much of the business equity, the banks have spread their risk through their own portfolios.

The value of size

Size, usually taken to mean market capitalisation, has also been put forward as a rationale for unrelated diversification. The argument is that the larger the market capitalisation, the more power the corporation will have in supplier and buyer markets. While there are break points that can be obtained as an enterprise gets larger, these advantages tend to be relatively small. Kay[10] has made out a reasonably compelling case for why the gains from size tend to be small and overemphasised.

Of perhaps greater significance is using reputation to move into new areas of business. The UK supermarkets, Marks & Spencer and Virgin are examples of companies that have such good reputations that they have moved into an area where reputation is just about all – financial services. This is corporate branding, providing considerable benefits, but it can be dangerous: Branson is running a grave risk by attaching the Virgin name to an unpopular train service. Disney saw its Disney brand as standing for family values and family entertainment. When it wanted to move into more adult films, such as *Good Morning Vietnam* and *Dead Poet's Society*, it used the brand Touchstone rather than stretch the Disney brand.

16.5.3 Valid reasons for SBU portfolio selection[11]

Adding or subtracting an SBU from the corporate portfolio is the same as adding or subtracting one or more capabilities. The economic decision to change the portfolio hinges on the value of the corporation with and without the SBU. Whether to add or subtract an SBU depends on whether the decision passes two tests.

The **better-off test** poses the question: 'Is the corporation better off with the SBU?' Better off means that the corporation will be adding more value with the SBU in its portfolio that without it. The problem in practice is calculating the likely future value. What should be considered are the future profitability of the competitive arena, the cost of entering or exiting the arena, and whether there is sufficient relatedness in the corporation for the SBU to thrive there.

However, the ultimate test of a parent is the **best-owner test**. This test poses the question to leader-managers: 'Are we the best possible parent?' or 'Does the SBU create more value either as a stand-alone business or as part of another corporation than it does within the corporation?[b] This best-owner test assumes that the SBU can be sold for a value greater than its value to the corporation. The merit of applying this test is that it will push leader-managers to have SBUs in their portfolio for positive reasons – help prevent them hanging on to an SBU through inertia when it would better be divested. The better-owner test could certainly be passed in the case of the acquisition of Rolls-Royce motor cars by Volkswagen in 1998: Rolls-Royce motor cars within the car maker Volkswagen would certainly be adding greater value than the same firm when located within Vickers, which didn't have the resources to develop the new cars that were required. Both Vickers and Volkswagen would appear to have gained from the transfer of ownership.

16.6 Diversification

Although size can offer some advantages to the corporation, the costs of diversification can be significant. Thus it is unlikely that unrelated diversified corporations will add value unless there are managerial or financial synergies. The 'better-off' and 'best-owner' tests are effectively tests of relatedness: the closeness of the set of offers – markets or product/services – that the SBUs make or will make in the future, which in turn means a closeness of the processes underpinning them.

16.6.1 Diversification and integration

A corporation diversifies when it changes the scope of its capabilities to such an extent that it is adding a new SBU to its portfolio. If there is no relatedness in the offers made by the new SBU and the rest of the portfolio, then this would be a conglomerate diversification. Where there is some form of relatedness, two broad types of diversification are recognised, as illustrated in Exhibit 16.7:

- Vertical diversification – enlarging capabilities in order to undertake operations in a different competitive arena in the same value chain in which an SBU is currently operating. An example of vertical diversification would be an airline underaking the operations of a travel agent.

- horizontal diversification – enlarging capabilities in order to undertake operations in a different competitive arena in a value chain related, but not directly, to that in which an SBU is currently operating. Horizontal diversification is related diversification, where the relatedness is complementary. An example would be a car manufacturer moving to offer car insurance.

Once having diversified, the corporation has the option of how closely it fuses its operations together. One extreme is to integrate the operations of the new business fully with the original. In this case the diversification is integration.

---

b   Because of the not inconsiderable costs of transferring an SBU from one corporation to another, this ultimate test is likely to be rather too severe.

EXHIBIT 16.7

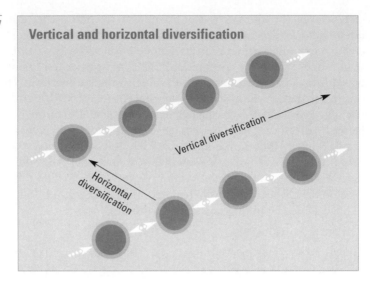

Vertical and horizontal diversification

Vertical diversification

Horizontal diversification

Thus 'vertical integration' is the term used where a company's operations in one competitive arena are used mainly by the same company's operations in another arena and the two operations are intimately linked. Vertically integrated companies are enterprises that carry out all, or a significant proportion, of the activities in a value chain and fuse them together in the sense that the outputs from one activity are exclusively the inputs to the next activity in the value chain. The oil companies have historically been vertically integrated, carrying out exploration, oilfield development, oil refining, retailing and marketing.

Horizontal integration is where two businesses are run as one: if the car manufacturer allowed its car insurance service to operate independently and offer insurance to owners of cars other than their own, this would be horizontal diversification, but not integration. When one company acquires another in exactly the same line of business and then combines the two, this is integration and is sometimes termed horizontal integration. However, while there is integration there is no diversification.

Although integration, particularly vertical integration, is common, what has become more popular over the last two decades is to treat the different businesses as profit centres and to allow each business to trade as if it were a stand-alone business, or something akin to that. Thus there is no need for businesses to buy from each other and the businesses are allowed and indeed encouraged to sell their offers to outsiders.

16.6.2 Vertical diversification

Vertical diversification is most often used to describe the move into activities that are extensions of its primary activities. It has two forms. There is forward diversification, whereby the business takes on the activities of the competitive arena further down the value chain (downstream). An example of forward diversification for a car assembler would be if it distributed cars. There is backward diversification, whereby the business takes on the activities of the competitive arena upstream of its competitive arena. An example of backward diversification is a motor manufacturer deciding to make the electric motors it has hitherto bought from a supplier.

Forward diversification[12]

This option would appear to fit strategically when:

- an organisation's present distributors are especially expensive, unreliable or incapable of meeting the firm's distribution needs;
- the availability of quality distributors is so limited as to offer a competitive advantage to those firms that diversify forwards;
- an organisation has both the capital and human resources needed to manage the new business of distributing its own offers;
- the advantages of stable production are particularly high: this is a consideration because an organisation can increase the predictability of the demand for its output through forward diversification;
- present distributors or retailers have high profit margins: this situation suggests that a company could profitably distribute its own products and price them more competitively by diversifying forwards;
- the organisation wishes to get closer to its customers, to learn of their requirements at first hand.

Backward diversification

This option would appear to fit strategically when:

- an organisation's present suppliers are especially expensive, unreliable or incapable of meeting the firm's needs for parts, components, assemblies or raw materials;
- the number of suppliers is few and the number of competitors is many;
- an organisation has both the capital and human resources needed to manage the new business of supplying its own raw materials and components;
- the advantages of stable prices, quality and quantity are particularly important;
- present suppliers have high profit margins, which suggests that the business of supplying products or services in the given industry is a worthwhile venture.

DISCUSSION POINT 16.4

List two highly vertically integrated organisations other than the oil companies.

Is vertical integration simply the exact opposite of out-sourcing?

In what ways does forward integration differ from offer enlargement?

Is vertical integration a related or an unrelated diversification?

16.6.3 Horizontal diversification

Horizontal diversification is when a firm moves into providing offers that complement its current offers. So, for example, a brewer might move into manufacturing snack foods, a car manufacturer might offer car finance. Porter[13] takes the view that horizontal diversification should be 'a co-ordinated set of goals and policies across distinct but interrelated business units' and 'without a horizontal strategy there is no convincing rationale for the existence of a diversified firm because it is little better than a mutual fund.'[c]

Horizontal diversification would appear to fit strategically when:

---

c   Equivalent to a unit trust in the UK.

- revenues derived from an organisation's current products or services would be significantly increased by adding the new set of offers;
- an organisation's present channels of distribution can be used to market the new products to current customers;
- new, but related, offers could be offered at highly competitive prices;
- new, but related, offers have seasonal sales levels that counterbalance an organisation's existing peaks and troughs;
- related competitive arenas are more profitable than that currently occupied.

KEY CONCEPT | Vertical diversification includes both backward diversification, when a business moves to undertake the activities of its suppliers, and forward diversification, when a business moves to undertake the activities of its distributors and/or buyers. Vertically integrated companies are enterprises that carry out all, or a significant proportion, of the activities in a value chain and where the outputs of one activity are used (almost) exclusively as the inputs to the next activity in the value chain.

Horizontal diversification occurs when a firm moves into activities that complement one of its current activities.

16.6.4 Identifying suitable competitive arenas for diversification

Profit pools

A value chain may be viewed as a progressive addition of value as items move from one competitive arena to another. Value is added as the items move downstream, and those adding the value get rewarded in the form of profits. However, life isn't necessarily fair: those adding the greatest value don't necessarily reap the greatest rewards. Lying in the set of value chains associated with a competitive area are what Gadiesh and Gilbert term *profit pools*:[14] pools of profit in the value-adding revenue stream. The pools are associated with competitive arenas.

Gadiesh and Gilbert analysed the car and personal computer industries, and their breakdown of these industries into profit pools is reproduced in Exhibits 16.8 and 16.9. In these diagrams, operating margins (closely associated with profits) are shown for each of the main areas of activity in the two industries. The area in each element of the histogram reflects the total operating margin within that portion of the industry; for example, the largest total operating margin in the car industry lies in car insurance (and this is why Kwikfit moved into car insurance in the mid-1990s, made possible by its database of satisfied customers from its replacement tyre and exhaust service). The profit pools in the car industry indicate that car manufacturing is a low-margin business and new car dealerships are especially so. The saving grace for car manufacturers is that there are a relatively small number of firms sharing a large revenue stream; this isn't the case with dealerships. On the other hand, car leasing, loans and insurance offer much better margins. Thus car manufacturers should consider entering these areas (which they have done: Ford, for instance, has generated almost half its profits over the last ten years from financing[15]).

Many of the players in the car industry can alter the businesses they are in and move, in part, into more lucrative competitive arenas elsewhere. The personal computer area shows a different use of profit pool analysis. The most profitable areas are

EXHIBIT 16.8

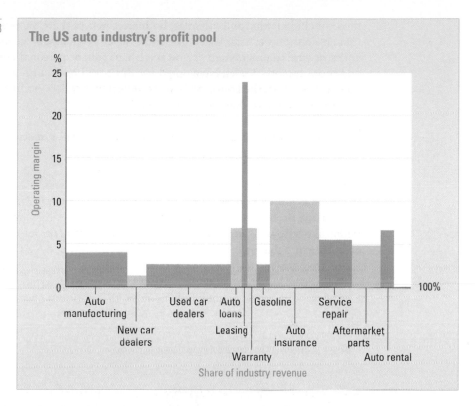

The US auto industry's profit pool

EXHIBIT 16.9

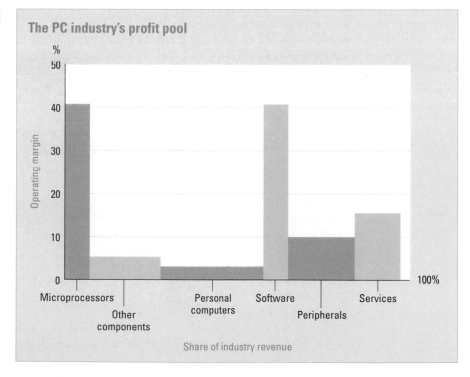

The PC industry's profit pool

those of chip making and software, both areas where there are monopolies. Given the vast strength of the established players, it would be suicidal to take on the processor and software manufacturers if you were a maker of personal computers. Both Dell and more recently Viglen have opted for direct selling – cutting out the retailers and selling directly to the consumer – reasoning that retailers both cut into margins and acted as a barrier to their customers.

DISCUSSION POINT 16.5 Do the arguments for profit pool analysis refer to relatedness directly in the value chain or to relatedness outside of the value chain?

SWOT analyses

A business will explore the ways in which it can best deploy its resources within the competitive arena within which it's currently operating. As part of this process it will undertake a SWOT analysis. Competitors within the current competitive arena and customers are the main focus. The process of producing a SWOT table for a business is illustrated in the top portion of Exhibit 16.10.

When considering whether to diversify, an approach identical to that described in Chapters 7–11 would be undertaken, but with a corporate perspective. The resources

EXHIBIT 16.10

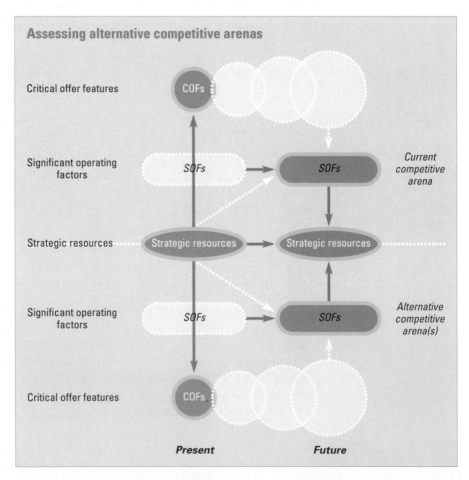

of the organisation – especially its set of unique capabilities and competences – are identified and used to determine the environment in which it might profitably operate. Put another way, the strengths of the organisation are not matched to the competitive area of current SBUs; rather, markets are sought in which the strengths will find a productive outlet. The process of producing a SWOT table in this approach is illustrated in the lower portion of Exhibit 16.10.

16.7 New markets and internationalisation

Market enlargements can be within the present geographical area but to a different clientele. In the 1980s Lex, the distributor of car parts for Volvo, decided to move into the distribution of electronic components. It did this because it saw that most of the processes it used to deliver car parts – the relationship with suppliers, the stock control of many small parts, the invoicing systems – could all be used with little change for electronic parts. The diamond smugglers operating between Antwerp and London have been finding this activity less lucrative and have turned to smuggling hard drugs. Their knowledge of the shadier sides of both cities and of how to evade customs with small packages are cited as reasons for the shift.

The second form of market enlargement is when a new geographical area is selected, very often for the same or very similar products/services. This form of market enlargement is of particular interest with the thrust to internationalisation – and particularly globalisation.

16.7.1 Reasons for internationalisation

There are four reasons for a firm to move away from a purely domestic operation:[16]

- To gain access to new customers for current products or services   With the reduction in product and technological life cycles, it is important that firms are able to market their products/services to as many customers as possible so as to recoup their investment. Other companies will capitalise in other markets on the innovation of companies that remain wedded to their domestic market.

- To retain present customers   National customers require national suppliers and, by extension, global customers require global suppliers. The largest companies in the UK and the USA (the FT 100 and Fortune 500 companies respectively) are overwhelmingly operating internationally, and any company that wishes to deal with them will have to offer an international approach. The perceived need for telecommunications companies to provide a global service to their global customers has been the main driving force for the expansion strategies of the telecommunications companies, such as British Telecom and Worldcom. One of the reasons put forward for the mergers between the large consultancy/accounting firms such as Price Waterhouse and Coopers & Lybrand, and Deloitte & Touche and Tohmatsu in the 1990s, was the need to have global reach to service their global clients. Thus global operations beget more global operations.

- To augment current competences   Being active in another country can be used to augment competences. Porter[17] argues that firms ought to seek out the most demanding markets so that they are forced to keep their competences up with the best in the world. Being global also allows firms to tap into a great deal of intellectual capital – a significant driver of future success.

- **To gain access to low-cost factors of production**   The main factors sought are low-cost labour and low-cost raw materials. However, with freight costs falling, being physically close to sources of raw materials has ceased to be as important as previously. For some firms there is also a need to have access to the cheapest sources of capital, and this has driven a firm such as Hoechst, the Frankfurt-based chemicals and drugs group, to seek a listing on the New York Stock Exchange.

There are three questions that an organisation needs to answer when considering moving into geographically new markets:

- Do we need to create new variants of the products for the new markets?
- Are the distribution channels adequate and are there trade barriers?
- What are the demands of the host country's government?

16.7.2   Barriers to international operations

There are still barriers to international operations. These are as follows:

- **Tariffs and quotas**   Some governments place barriers on the range or quantity of imports. The EU has set quotas on Japanese car imports and on textiles.

- **Foreign ownership rules**   Companies wishing to set up in another country, often a developing country, are forced to accept major shareholdings being held by locals. It was for this reason that Coca-Cola pulled out of India.

- **Foreign languages**   English may be the language of business, but it's not generally the language of the marketplace. At the very least, packaging will need to be altered. Occasionally a brand name can't be used in all countries (for example Irish Mist in Germany, Pschitt anywhere except in France).

- **Local regulations**   These may mean that different forms of packaging need to be used, that sales quantities need to be changed and perhaps the characteristics of the product need to be altered (for example, electrical appliances and different forms of electricity supply).

- **Local tastes**   While it's probably true that in many respects the financial traders in London have more in common with their opposite numbers in New York and Tokyo than their neighbours in East London, there are differences in national and regional tastes. One of the failures of UK firms operating in the USA is to believe that the USA is a homogeneous culture. US marketers of consumer products see New England as very different from California, and both as very different from the Deep South.

- **Transport costs**   These may affect low-value, high-volume/high-mass products such as cement and paper.

- **Different currencies**   Currency instability can be a problem, especially when dealing with less developed countries.

- **Tax and other financial regimes**   Some countries forbid companies taking revenues out of the country and impose special taxation rules on foreign-owned companies.

16.8 Competences

There will be a common thread between the capabilities of the SBUs in related diversified corporations, and experience in one area of the corporation can help create an advantage in another. It would also be expected that the portfolio of businesses would rest on the competences that the corporation has or intends to obtain access to. In this way, the rather ephemeral capabilities of the businesses are linked to the more enduring competences from which future offers will come.

16.8.1 Sets of corporate processes

Prahalad and Hamel[18] define a **competence** as collective learning in the organisation, especially how to co-ordinate diverse production skills and integrate multiple streams of technologies. A competence is the linking of processes that themselves are a meld of procedures, explicit and tacit knowledge, and basic assets. A competence can be used to support the activities of several SBUs, and it is for this reason that a competence is considered a corporate rather than a business concern.

Prahalad and Hamel use the metaphor of a tree to describe the relationship between SBUs and competences. Their view is reproduced in Exhibit 16.11. The SBUs are the branches of a tree and the offers are the leaves. The competences are the roots of the tree. This view emphasises that the competences are not very obvious to outsiders and also that they need to be nurtured in order to sustain a healthy show of leaves and branches and to produce new growth in the future – the future offers. By nurturing the roots, the tree grows larger every year. Hampden-Turner and Trompenaars[19] provide another metaphor: the competences are like a gene pool, with offers fashioned from the myriad of genes in the pool.

The company 3M has many competences: in one annual report it mentions 'over

EXHIBIT 16.11

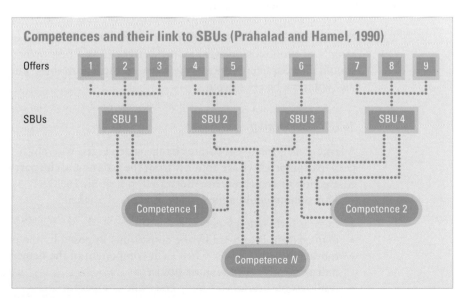

Competences and their link to SBUs (Prahalad and Hamel, 1990)

EXHIBIT 16.12

A selection of 3M's competences

Adhesives	Melt-blown non-woven materials	Speciality chemicals
Microreplication	Wire connectors	Abrasives
Fluorochemicals	Micro-interconnections	Laser imaging
Tapes	Resins	Substrates
Medical delivery, aerosols	Medical delivery, subdermal	Filtration technology
Molecular discovery	Micro-encapsulation	

two dozen core competences', in another 'over 30', and in another 'many'.[20] Some of 3M's competences are listed in Exhibit 16.12.

Micro-replication is one of the competences that 3M believes has a very bright future. It is the process whereby microscopic 3-D patterns are replicated on plastic films and other surfaces. Micro-replication is being used to make structured abrasives with four times the abrasion wear of ordinary sandpapers, more effective reflective sheeting for road traffic signs, brighter laptop computer screens using less power, fasteners for disposable nappies, films that prevent alteration of ID cards and security badges, and paints that reduce the drag on ships and aircraft. These offers cover a very wide range of markets – and the SBUs that service them.

KEY CONCEPT   A capability resides in an SBU and its outputs are generally visible to stakeholders. A competence is 'owned' by the parent; in contrast to a capability, it's rarely visible to external stakeholders. Competences can be looked on as the roots of a tree or alternatively as a gene pool.

16.9   Demerging, divestment and liquidation

Most of the discussion so far in this chapter has dealt with expansion of a corporation's portfolios. However, as the better-off and best-owner tests indicated, firms should also consider reducing the scope of their portfolios. Three forms of 'downsizing' will now be considered.

16.9.1   Demerging

A large-scale form of corporate change is demerger, whereby a set of related SBUs and perhaps competences are split off from the parent and the parts then exist separately. A selection of demergers are illustrated in Exhibit 16.13.

This option would appear to fit strategically when:

● there is little synergy between the SBUs;
● management is fettered by the constraints imposed by the parent;
● funding becomes easier when each component of the demerger can act independently when seeking funds;
● it allows businesses to supply erstwhile competitors.

EXHIBIT 16.13

Examples of demergers

In 1993 ICI, Britain's biggest manufacturing company, split its activities into two separately quoted companies. The ICI name was retained for the heavy chemicals, paints and explosives interests, while the new name Zeneca was coined for the biosciences interests – pharmaceuticals, agrochemicals and seeds. The rationale was to enable each company to respond better to economic circumstances and to the great shifts and rationalisations likely to come in the international chemical industry. It was also thought that the biosciences would find it easier to raise cash on its own than as part of a corporation with a more mature range of businesses.[21]

At the end of August 1998, shares in BAT Industries were trading at 500p when it demerged its tobacco and insurance interests. Its insurance interests (including Allied Dunbar, Eagle Star and Threadneedle in the UK and Farmers Insurance in the US) were simultaneously merged with Zurich Insurance to become Allied Zurich. The tobacco arm reverted to using the name British American Tobacco. On 11 January 1999 when British American Tobacco announced its merger with Rothmans, shares in the tobacco interests were worth 626p and Allied Zurich were worth 987p. This was an effective rise in value of 300%.

In 1999 General Motors, the world's leading car maker, demerged its Delphi Automotive Systems division. Delphi supplies a full range of components to GM factories worldwide and itself ranks among the top 30 US companies in the Fortune 500, with sales of $28.4 billion in 1998. Delphi's chief executive, J.T. Battonberg III, said that the main purpose of floating the company as an independent business was to pick up more sales from other car manufacturers which have been reluctant to buy from a company that was owned 100% by GM. He also said that the demerger would give Delphi greater freedom and mean that it was no longer competing with other parts of GM for resources. For the same reasons, Ford is planning to demerge its inhouse automotive components business, Visteon.[22]

16.9.2 Divestment[d]

When an SBU or a competence fails the 'retain' tests (the better-off and best-owner tests described in Section 16.5.3), it should be divested. This can occur when the resources don't exist for the corporation to continue in that business or with that competence. This occurred in the late 1980s when Boots realised that it hadn't the resources to stand the risks entailed in pharmaceutical research and development and sold off this competence.

Two particular forms of divestment are noteworthy. A management buyout (MBO) occurs when the current management of a business purchases the business assets from the corporation of which it is a part. Most MBOs are of underperforming SBUs or where the parent no longer feels that the SBU is a valuable part of the corporate portfolio. A management buyin (MBI) occurs when a management team from one organ-

---

d   The terms *vertical* and *horizontal disintegration*, whereby a firm ceases to carry out an activity, never seem to be used.

isation buys an equity stake in an existing company and takes over managerial control. In both cases, funding is most likely to come from venture capitalists and the banks.

Divestment would appear to fit strategically when:

- an SBU needs more resources to be competitive than the company can provide;
- an SBU is responsible for an organisation's overall poor performance;
- an SBU is a misfit with the rest of the organisation: this can result from radically different markets, customers, managers, employees, values or needs;
- a large amount of cash is needed quickly and cannot be reasonably obtained from other sources;
- an acquisition can't be carried through unless the divestment takes place. An example is BAT's forced divestment of cigarette and roll-your-own tobacco and paper brands in Australia to win regulatory approval from the Australian Competition and Consumer Commission for its merger with Rothmans.[23]

16.9.3 Liquidation

A more severe form of divestment is liquidation, whereby the assets associated with an SBU are dispersed. This option would appear to fit strategically when:

- opportunities exist within the corporation to utilise the SBU's/competence's resources more profitably;
- the organisation's only alternative is bankruptcy. Liquidation represents an orderly and planned means of obtaining the greatest possible cash for an organisation's assets. A company can legally declare bankruptcy first and then liquidate various resources to raise needed capital.

SUMMARY

- A corporation consists of two or more businesses, thus it involves two or more distinct capabilities. The parent is that part of the corporation not directly associated with any individual business. Parents have the potential to add value, but there are powerful reasons why this may not occur. EXHIBIT 16.1
- The main elements of corporate strategic management are broadly the same as those for business strategic management. However, there are very significant differences in emphasis. In particular, whereas a business is concerned with its portfolios of offers and capabilities, the parent is concerned with its portfolio of SBUs and its portfolio of (corporate) competences. EXHIBIT 16.3
- Thirteen parental roles have been identified, grouped into four main areas. These main areas are setting corporate direction, identifying the SBU and competence portfolios, establishing these portfolios, and on-going portfolio management. EXHIBIT 16.4
- A corporate mission statement is likely to differ considerably from those of its constituent businesses. This mainly arises from the corporation not having well-recognised suppliers and buyers and needing to take a wider and longer-term view. EXHIBIT 16.5
- The rationale that diversification reduces risk is invalid. The rationale that company size will provide a large advantage is often overstated. Valid reasons for adding an SBU to a corporate portfolio or retaining one in it are whether the corporation and SBU combination passes the better-off and best-owner tests. EXHIBIT 16.6

- Conglomerate diversifications will be appropriate when financial synergies or managerial abilities can produce value. Two types of diversification that are related in terms of markets and/or products/services are recognised – vertical and horizontal diversification. The analysis of profit pools will help identify appropriate diversification directions. While there are powerful reasons for a company to expand internationally, impediments still remain.   EXHIBITS 16.7 TO 16.9
- Competences are linked processes that are developed and nurtured by the parent. Competences are generally not obvious to external stakeholders. They can be likened to the roots of a tree or to a gene pool.   EXHIBIT 16.11, EXHIBIT 16.12
- As the better-off and best-owner tests indicate, parents should also consider reducing the scope of their portfolios. There are three forms of corporate 'downsizing': demerging, whereby a company splits its activities into two or more self-standing groups; divestment, whereby an SBU or competence is sold off; and liquidation, whereby the assets of an SBU or competence are broken up and either sold or used elsewhere in the organisation.

SELF-CHECK

1 Reconsider the learning outcomes for this chapter. Check that you feel confident that you can carry out the activities listed there.

2 Having read this chapter, you should be able to define the following terms:

best-owner test	divestment	parenting
better-off test	horizontal diversification	portfolio
competence	horizontal integration	related diversified
conglomerate	liquidation	relatedness
corporate branding	management buyin (MBI)	unrelated diversified
demerger	management buyout (MBO)	vertical diversification
diversified	parent	vertical integration

MINI-CASE 16.1

Pearson plc and Mrs Scardino: 1997–mid 1999

At the beginning of 1997, Pearson plc was an international media group with interests in publishing, TV production, broadcasting, and electronic and multimedia businesses. The group focused on three key markets worldwide: information, education and entertainment.

Information   The information division encompassed a worldwide portfolio of information services. Its printed products included national and international business newspapers, professional books, magazines and periodicals. It also provided information services. The major holdings were:

- Financial Times Newspapers printed in ten centres covering Europe, North America and Asia
- Financial Times Information providing electronic business and specialist financial information worldwide.
- *Les Echos* France's leading business daily newspaper and the flagship of a group that includes many other business and professional titles, including a twice-weekly medical newspaper.
- Recoletos one of Spain's leading newspaper and magazine publishers. Its titles include the country's premier business daily and sports daily and a daily newspaper for doctors.

- Pearson Professional   publishes books, periodicals and screen-based services for professional communities worldwide under FT, Pitman Publishing and Churchill Livingstone brand names.

Education   The education division is one of the world's top three educational publishers, selling books, multimedia and learning programmes in the school, higher education, professional and English-language teaching markets throughout the world. The major holdings were:

- Addison Wesley Longman   publishes teaching products in many major markets in the USA and throughout the world for elementary and secondary schools, colleges and computer science and engineering professionals. AWL is also the largest publisher of American and British English language teaching materials.

Entertainment   The entertainment division produced, distributed and broadcast television programmes, was a leading international trade book publisher, ran visitor attractions and produced consumer magazines, videos and software. The major holdings were:

- Penguin   publishes English-language consumer books, fiction and non-fiction, in hardcover and paperback. Joined by Putnam Berkley, the US trade publisher.
- The Tussauds Group   is the largest European operator of visitor attractions specialising in exhibitions and theme parks, including Madam Tussauds, Alton Towers, Warwick Castle, Chessington World of Adventure and a 40% holding in Port Aventura, a theme park near Barcelona.
- Pearson New Entertainment   publishes special-interest consumer magazines, videos and related new media especially for 'boys of all ages'.
- Mindscape   develops and publishes consumer software for personal computers and video game systems.
- Pearson Television   was the UK's largest international television producer. It sold its formats worldwide and also had interest in distribution and broadcasting. It produced and sold programmes under the Thames, Grundy, Alomo, Witzend and ACI brands. It had a 24% stake in the UK's Channel 5.

Investment banking   Pearson had a shareholding in Lazard Partners, a 50% interest in Lazard Brothers and a 9% stake in the partnership profits of Lazard Frères, Paris and Lazard Frères, New York.

Marjorie Scardino took over as Pearson plc's chief executive in January 1997. Since then to mid-1999, the changes wrought by Mrs Scardino are chronicled in Exhibit 1, p. 704.

Discussion point 16.6

Identify the augmentations that Mrs Scardino has made in terms of the four levels of relatedness.

MINI-CASE 16.2

A strategist who has everything to play for[24]

Heinrich von Pierer, chief executive of Siemens, the electrical engineering group, still believes in one of the oldest principles of German management: that there is no contradiction between the interests of workers and shareholders.

'Only a profitable company can secure jobs,' says Mr von Pierer. 'Only well-motivated people can earn good profits. These are two sides of the same coin.'

But, as he is the first to admit, he is finding it difficult to put this philosophy into practice in the competitive business environment of the 1990s. He often finds himself appearing on the political pages of German newspapers defending the company from workers' criticism while at the same time being quoted on the financial pages explaining the same decisions in terms shareholders will understand. Not for nothing has he earned a reputation as a conciliator and Chancellor Helmut Kohl's favourite manager.

Mr von Pierer, a tall, athletic man who plays tennis 'to win', dismisses suggestions that Siemens is reacting too slowly to the fast-moving shifts in the global business environment of the 1990s. 'This company has changed more in the last three years than it did in the previous 50 years,' he retorts, rattling off figures to back his claims.

He describes the changes he has pushed through Siemens' sprawling empire since taking office in 1992; he has sold businesses with a combined turnover of DM7.5 billion (£2.5 billion) and acquired others with total sales of DM13 billion. And, he says, 'this is not the end of the story.' He has closed more than 30 smaller operations and reduced the Siemens workforce by 60,000 to 386,000, strikes and demonstrations notwithstanding. Moreover, many of the cuts have come in Germany, where business leaders are under political pressure not to upset the economic and social order.

Mr von Pierer knows he has some way to go before he can claim victory. Satisfying workers and shareholders is hard enough, but even more urgent is the need to respond to global competition. Without more profit the company will be unable to finance its international expansion fast enough to keep up with rivals. Mr von Pierer insists that, in spite of recent setbacks such as the economic crisis in East Asia, he aims to meet his self-imposed target of return on capital of 15% by 2000. This compares with less than 10% in the year to September 1997.

Investors are impatient. Although Siemens' share price has doubled in the past five years, it has fallen by nearly 40% against the German market. Swantje Conrad, analyst at US bank JP Morgan in London, wants to see more action. 'There is currently no evidence that Siemens is actively considering a radical refocusing of the company. There is a significant risk that the degree of restructuring may not go as far as many investors want.'

Another analyst says: 'We just doubt Siemens' management can really prioritise time and allocation of capital among the different groups. If it were split up then management could focus better.'

The core of Mr von Pierer's strategy remains the belief that the Siemens group, with its 16 divisions, is more than the sum of its parts. He does not believe that the company should, as some analysts have proposed, spin off parts, such as the medical equipment operations, that have required extensive restructuring in recent years. 'I believe in the synergies of the group,' he says.

Siemens executives argue that, although the group is often seen as a conglomerate, almost all businesses are in electrics or electronics. Moreover, in infrastructure-related equipment, which accounts for a big part of turnover, sales in one division often lead to sales in another, particularly in developing countries. 'This is a real strength for us,' says Mr von Pierer.

Mr von Pierer concedes that in the past Siemens has dissipated its strength by spreading itself too thinly. That is the reason for his recent disposals. The company's divisions must be 'market leaders', he says, occupying first, second or third place in global markets. Already companies accounting for two-thirds of the group's DM107 billion turnover are in such positions. The aim is to raise the proportion to 80% within three years.

Successful divisions are being bolstered by investment and acquisition. In semiconductors, Siemens has spent DM2.8 billion on two new chip plants in the UK and the USA (the second a joint venture with Motorola). In medical equipment, it has backed the development of new forms of ultrasound equipment. In building automation, it has turned a business struggling for market share into a world leader by the DM3 billion acquisition of the industrial activities of Switzerland's Elektrowatt. In power generation, it beat powerful rivals in the race to buy, for $1.5 billion, the generation unit of Westinghouse of the USA.

At the same time, Mr von Pierer is trying to reduce Siemens' dependence on Germany, which the company's critics have long seen as a weakness. In the next few years, he wants to reduce Germany's share in group turnover from 35% to 25%. Western Europe as a whole should fall from 65% to 50%, with expansion coming mainly in North and South America, as well as Asia.

Mr von Pierer believes Siemens is more adventurous geographically than its critics recognise. He is irritated by negative comparisons with ABB, the Swiss–Swedish engineering group, which is often seen as a model of a globalised multinational. 'We have more people in Asia than ABB,' he says. In Russia the group operates from more locations than any other Western company except Coca-Cola.

A crucial challenge is retaining the confidence of the group's German workers after heavy job losses. No further big reductions are planned, but over the next five years 'the tendency will be for further decline,' Mr von Pierer says.

The company is also reducing the costs of those it retains, introducing flexible working patterns. With nationwide concern about unemployment, Mr von Pierer finds trade unions more willing to accept plant-by-plant deals. Siemens has recently won from IG Metall, the metalworkers' union, an agreement for flexible working that will reduce costs by up to one-fifth.

He insists the expansion of overseas production should not be seen as a threat to German jobs. Factory posts in China, India, Russia and elsewhere create software engineering posts in Germany, he says. Thus, in Mr von Pierer's view, globalisation is as good for workers as it is for shareholders. The demands of the two sides of industry can be balanced.

Discussion point 16.7

Which parenting roles is Mr von Pierer undertaking?
- What is Siemens' corporate strategy?
- What sorts of diversification has Siemens made?
- What sorts of reduction in the scope of Siemens have been made and are called for?

FURTHER DISCUSSION POINTS

1 For GSM:
  - Are there strategic business units in GSM? If so, what are they?
  - If there are SBUs, do they have their own strategies?
  - What form of relatedness were the acquisitions?
2 In Chapter 1 the strategic management environment was characterised as chaotic, complex, dynamic and turbulent – all generally increasing the level of uncertainty facing leader-managers. However, not all business environments are the same. Reflect on how changes in the environmental characteristics might affect how the parent operates with its constituent businesses.
3 Reassess Exhibit 6.15 to see how it needs modification as a test of the appropriateness of a corporate mission statement.

ASSIGNMENT

Obtain a set of annual reports and accounts for an FT 100 corporation covering three or more years. Analyse these to identify:
  a)   the roles undertaken by the parent;
  b)   its portfolio of businesses;
  c)   its portfolio of competences;
and then unearth:
  d)   the basis for its portfolio of businesses.

FURTHER
READING

The book by Michael Goold, Andrew Campbell and Marcus Alexander, *Corporate-level Strategy: Creating Value in the Multibusiness Company*, John Wiley, 1994, considers many aspects of corporate-level strategic management.

Bob de Wit and Ron Meyer, *Strategy, Process, Content, Context: An International Perspective*, West Publishing, 1994, contains articles by many eminent strategists concerning the role of the parent.

A review of the features of mission statements for companies with various levels of diversification is presented by Rebecca Morris, 'Developing a mission for a diversified company', *Long Range Planning*, Vol. 29, No. 1, 1996, pp. 103–15.

CHAPTER NOTES
AND REFERENCES

1 Goold, M., Campbell, A. and Alexander, M., *Corporate-level Strategy: Creating Value in the Multibusiness Company*, John Wiley, 1994, p. 399.

2 Caulkin, S., 'It's bigger than Turkey, Thailand or Denmark – but it's not a country . . .', *The Observer*, 8 March 1998, p. 9.

3 Porter, M.E., 'From competitive advantage to corporate strategy', *Harvard Business Review*, May–June, 1987, pp. 43–59.

4 Rumelt, R.P., 'How much does industry matter?' *Strategic Management Journal*, Vol. 12, No. 3, pp. 167–86.

5 Goold, M., Campbell, A. and Alexander, M., *op. cit.*, p. 283.

6 Fahey, L. and Randall, R.M., 'What is scenario learning?', chapter 1 in Fahey, L. and Randall, R.M. (eds), *Learning from the Future: Competitive Foresight Scenarios*, John Wiley, 1998, p. 32.

7 Hampden-Turner, C. and Trompenaars, F., *The Seven Cultures of Capitalism: Value Systems for Creating Wealth in the United States, Britain, Japan, Germany, France, Sweden, and the Netherlands*, Doubleday, 1993, p. 198.

8 Goold, M., Campbell, A. and Alexander, M., *op. cit.*, p. 67.

9 Mathur, S.S. and Kenyon, A., *Creating Value: Shaping Tomorrow's Business*, Butterworth-Heinemann, 1997, pp. 289–90.

10 Kay, J., *Foundations of Corporate Success: How Business Strategies Add Value*, Oxford University Press, 1993.

11 Goold, M., Campbell, A. and Alexander, M., *op. cit.*, pp. 7–8; Mathur, S.S. and Kenyon, A., *op. cit.*, pp. 289–90; Porter, M.E., *op. cit.*, 1987, pp. 43–59.

12 Adapted from David, F.R., 'How do we choose among alternative growth strategies?' *Managerial Planning*, Vol. 33, No. 4, January–February 1985, pp. 14–17, 22.

13 Porter, M.E., *Competitive Advantage*, Free Press, 1985, pp. 318–19.

14 Gadiesh, O. and Gilbert, J.L., 'Profit pools: a fresh look at strategy', *Harvard Business Review*, May–June 1998, pp. 139–47.

15 *Ibid.*

16 Barney, J.B., *Gaining and Sustaining Competitive Advantage*, Addison-Wesley, 1997.

17 Porter, M.E., *The Competitive Advantage of Nations*, Macmillan, 1990, chapter 11.

18 Prahalad, C.K. and Hamel, G., 'The core competence of the corporation', *Harvard Business Review*, May–June 1990, pp. 79–91.

19 Hampden-Turner, C. and Trompenaars, F., *op. cit.*, p. 140.

20 3M Company, Annual Report and Accounts, 1996–8.

21 Kennedy, C., 'The ICI demerger: unlocking shareholder value', *Long Range Planning*, Vol. 26, No. 2, 1993, pp. 10–16.

22 Harrison, M., 'Float values GM's Delphi at \$9.6bn', *The Independent*, 6 February 1999, p. 19.

23 Blackwell, D., 'BAT deals to clear way for Rothmans takeover', *Financial Times*, 20 May 1999, p. 28.

24 Wagstyl, S. and Bowley, G., 'A strategist who has everything to play for', *Financial Times*, 20 April 1998, p. 6.

17 Establishing the portfolios

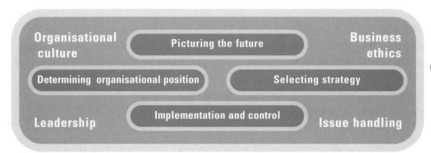

This chapter is the second of the set of three that considers the distinct characteristics of parenting. The setting of the general direction of the corporation and the identification of the SBU and competence portfolios were considered in the preceding chapter. This chapter deals with establishing the chosen portfolios.

The chapter begins by exploring the two main concerns with how to gain access to the resources needed to enlarge the portfolios. The first concern is with the three broad forms of access available: internal development, acquisition/merger and alliance. Each of these is considered in detail – their advantages and disadvantages and the processes involved.

The second concern – the sources of funds to support the access to non-financial resources needed to support the establishment of the portfolios – are then explored.

If corporate strategy calls for enlargement of the corporate portfolios, there is a need to gain access to additional resources. This in turn requires access to the funds that can allow this access to be achieved. Given that many of the moves necessary to enlarge its portfolios are often of major significance to the corporation, it is vital that leader-managers choose the most appropriate strategic pathway – and thus understand the advantages and disadvantages of the possibilities open to them.

LEARNING
OUTCOMES

When you have worked through this chapter, you should be able to:

- explain the strengths and weaknesses of internal development as a means of achieving corporate goals, and describe the process of internal development;

- explain the strengths and weaknesses of acquisition as a means of achieving corporate goals, and describe the process of acquisition;

- describe the three main forms of alliance;

- explain the strengths and weaknesses of forming an alliance as a means of achieving corporate goals, and describe the process of alliance formation;

- provide evidence for the success of each sourcing option;

- describe the characteristics of the sources of long-term funds.

17.1 The main questions regarding portfolio enlargement

17.1.1 The two questions

Once the parent has identified the appropriate scope of the corporation's SBU and competence portfolios, it will need to choose a strategic pathway to establish them. If the decision is to enlarge the portfolios, the parent will need to gain access to the required capabilities and competences. There are two main considerations:

- The form of access   This area of choice is about how the parent will obtain control/ use of the capabilities and/or competences necessary to enlarge its portfolios.
- The source of funds   This concerns where to obtain the funds to allow access to the required non-financial resources.

EXHIBIT 17.1

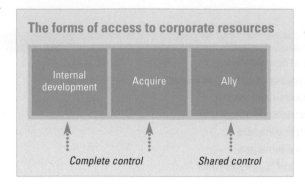

The forms of access to corporate resources

Internal development | Acquire | Ally

Complete control | *Shared control*

17.1.2 Forms of access

There are three broad forms of access to non-financial resources. The first is **internal development**, whereby the capabilities and competences are developed in house. This can be achieved either by redeploying resources that are already available in the corporation or by buying in individual resources or processes. In both cases, the parent will meld the resources into the required sets of new processes.

A second form of access to resources is through the **acquisition** of a complete SBU or competence – often both at the same time. Finally there is the **alliance**, whereby the parent doesn't achieve full control over a new set of resources and must work in co-operation with one or more other organisations. Examples of acquisitions and alliances are given in Exhibit 17.2. This also shows that two companies competing very directly can take very different pathways towards the future.

17.2 Internal development

When an organisation itself develops the required new capabilities to enlarge its business portfolio, resources and/or processes will either be transferred from one part of the corporation to another or bought in. It's very likely that a (corporate) competence will be applied in a new area.

An extreme example of internal development is the virtual organisation, in which all the necessary resources and processes are brought together from scratch. Once the need for the output from the capability has been exhausted, the virtual organisation dissolves itself. An example of a (virtually) virtual organisation occurs in the making of a film – the producer gets together the financial backing, assembles the cast and the camera crews, etc. and makes the film. The group then splits up after the filming has been completed.

When using internal development as the chosen route to enlarging the portfolio of competences, the consideration is with internal research and development. This may be a centralised function or may be dispersed throught the organisation.

17.2.1 The advantages and disadvantages of internal development

The advantages and disadvantages to an organisation of using internal development as a route to portfolio enlargement are the following:

EXHIBIT 17.2

Two blueprints for the engine of progress[1]

There are few better examples of the different approaches to gaining a foothold in unfamiliar markets or technologies than the battle for dominance in the large diesel engines sector, in which Caterpillar and Cummins Engines, two big engineering companies in the USA, compete head-on.

Caterpillar is best known for its earthmoving equipment, of which it is the world's leading maker, but last year it gained a quarter of its near $19 billion sales through diesel engines. These are sold to customers in power generation, shipbuilding, trucks and industrial machinery, and are directly related to the engines Caterpillar builds for its own use.

Cummins focuses far more on engines and derives most of its nearly $6 billion annual revenues from these products, which are sold to customers similar to Caterpillar's. With both companies about the same size in terms of revenues from diesels, Cummins is slightly ahead in units – Caterpillar generally sells its engines with additional equipment to fit them to specific applications, which pushes up prices.

According to industry statistics, Cummins is the world's biggest maker of large diesels (more than 200hp) in units. Caterpillar is in third position with Navistar, the US truckmaker, between them.

Caterpillar and Cummins differ in their stance on moving into new markets through joining up with other businesses. In the past decade, Cummins has formulated a strategy based on joint ventures with outside groups – including customers and competitors.

For instance, Cummins is building a new family of engines for power generation with Wartsila of Finland and runs an engine factory in the USA jointly with Case, the big US tractor and construction machine supplier. In 1996, Cummins formed a $300 million joint venture with Fiat, the Italian automotive group, to develop and make engines for tractors, buses and trucks, to be fitted early next decade. It also has several partnerships with Komatsu, the big Japanese company, which is second to Caterpillar in excavators and a big engine builder in its own right.

Caterpillar, meanwhile, has taken a determinedly go it alone approach, preferring to stay in complete control of its new engine ventures. In the past two years, it has spent more than $2 billion buying engine companies worldwide – including MaK of Germany and Perkins of the UK, makers of very large engines for electricity generation and ships, and of smaller engines suited for fitting to new families of compact construction machines, respectively.

The high cost of adapting diesel technologies for use in new types of product is driving the decisions of Caterpillar and Cummins. Both companies have spent billions of dollars since the 1930s developing their diesel knowhow. Building a new series of engines with different applications can cost an extra $300–400 million. Much of this cost is linked to modern techniques to satisfy fuel consumption demands and pollution controls.

Buying existing companies can often be less expensive than trying to develop the new applications independently, according to Gerald Shaheen, head of Caterpillar's engine products division. 'This technology does not come cheap,' he says.

He adds that Caterpillar has generally aimed for complete control of its new engine ventures, partly to safeguard what it regards as proprietary knowhow, which feeds directly into the engines it uses internally for its construction equipment.

Managers in both parts of Caterpillar's engines business – concerned with customers inside and outside the company – are encouraged to share development and manufacturing ideas, which the company sees as vital to sustaining a competitive advantage in its machinery business.

Cummins has taken a more flexible stance, with its smaller financial base precluding the kinds of acquisition Caterpillar has opted for in recent years. Its managerial bias is also more oriented towards collaboration – virtually all its sales are built around some kind of partnership with customers, who buy engines for fitting into their own products.

Even so, Jim Henderson, Cummins chairman and chief executive, says the company has had to learn a new, more open way of sharing information with its worldwide collaborators. 'I would not have imagined 10 years ago that I would spend so much time as I do now travelling the world and talking to partners on new engine ventures,' he says.

The new approach has not always been easy. In the past decade, Cummins had to take the tough step of shutting down its own US-based development programme on large generator engines in favour of the new project with Wartsila. This involved teaming up on a new production operation for the engines in France. But the company has probably benefited from lessons learned in its long, and sometimes turbulent, partnership with Komatsu. It formed its first joint venture, purely on manufacturing, with this company as far back as 1961.

Strains appeared in the 1980s as the Japanese group sought to loosen the ties with Cummins on engines by radical price cutting in the latter's home market in North America. In one episode in 1987, the then Komatsu president described Cummins as 'the enemy' at a ceremony to open a US factory. But relations have clearly become a lot more cordial. In the past few weeks, the two companies have announced a joint venture to collaborate on small engines in a move which Mr Henderson regards as an important element in his company's efforts to branch out into new businesses.

Discussion point 17.1

What are the strategic pathways chosen by Caterpillar and Cummins?
- Why are Caterpillar and Cummins taking these different approaches to growth?
- Which approach is the more appropriate?

- There is likely to be minimal change to on-going activities. Very importantly, there are unlikely to be the cultural problems associated with either an acquisition or an alliance.

- The cash flow will probably be more uniform than would occur with an acquisition. With an acquisition, and to a lesser extent with an alliance, the cash flows tend to be lumpy.

- Internal development is likely to be slower than if acquisition had been used, and probably slower than developing an alliance. The PIMS programme[2] investigated the time it took start-up ventures to achieve profitability and found that on average it took eight years and that half the start-ups didn't have a positive cash flow during this time. These data were for business start-ups within the large, mainly manufacturing, corporations that contributed to the PIMS database; such long periods wouldn't be expected in non-manufacturing

EXHIBIT 17.3

Adolescent businesses (Buzzell and Gale, 1987)			
	Years 1 and 2	Years 3 and 4	Mature SBUs
Performance measures %			
ROI	−40	−14	
Cash flow/investment	−80	−29	
Pre-tax profit/sales	−39	−10	
Gross margin/sales	+15	+28	
Expense ratios %			
R&D/sales	19	8	3
Marketing/sales	38	22	10
Purchases/sales	46	44	39
Manufacturing/sales	26	25	29

businesses.[a] Further information on adolescent businesses is shown in Exhibit 17.3.

DISCUSSION
POINT 17.2

When using internal development as part of a strategic pathway, some further resources are very likely to be bought in. At what level of buying in does internal development become acquisition?

* Is the creation of the virtual organisation internal development, acquisition followed by divestment, or simply out-sourcing?

17.3 The process of internal development

The sort of internal development considered here isn't that which accompanies offer enhancements and extensions: it is the sort that accompanies offer enlargements and so is concerned with the development of new capabilities and/or competences.

17.3.1 Internal sources of ideas

Within certain cultures, many suggestions for offer enlargements will come from employees, as 3M has encouraged for many years.[3] 3M employs a loose–tight approach whereby employees are encouraged to work on research projects with their own or 'stolen' resources. This is the 'loose' part. The 'tight' part is the very strict corporate controls that are imposed when it comes to developing the initiative, since generally research isn't costly: the real costs are incurred in the development phase. The excerpts given in Exhibit 17.4 from ARM Ltd, a designer of microchips, and ITNET, a supplier of IT out-sourcing services, testify to a similar 'bottom-up' approach. In both cases there is an automatic *product champion*[5] who is likely to be willing to develop the idea.

Another form of internal development is where an idea is generated by the board and a person is recruited to carry the idea forward. This occurs in Pearson, as shown in Exhibit 17.4.

Another way of using internal development is to allow customers to lead in the way the market is developing. This requires the company to build and then develop

---

a   Or to stand-alone businesses that have to withstand the force of the financial markets.

EXHIBIT 17.4

The sources of new businesses[4]

ARM Ltd All developments are apparently coming from below the top team. As CEO Robin Saxby explains: 'All the board says is "The industry is going this way, have you thought of this?" We set direction, we hire people and we set up the mechanism for them to get approval for resources. Anyone in the company can put a proposal to the board. Someone puts up a proposal saying the competition is doing this or that, I think this is very important etc., here's my project proposal, and they will argue for it. Then I ask the finance director what the financial risk is and the company secretary about the legal aspects. If we're convinced, we sanction the resources.'

ITNET New product areas are popping up in the company. Claire Forrest, director of corporate marketing and strategy, explains: 'ITNET has a monthly development executive meeting where the management team looks at projects, new organisation structures, problems, etc. Anyone can present their ideas at this meeting. Generally, they would have discussed this with me and/or the business development manager and between them worked with the individual to build a case for the initiative and positioned it within ITNET's strategy. One such presentation was from someone who had an idea about a product for the Internet, which the board agreed to give space and time to nurture.'

Pearson plc In January 1999 it was decided to establish Financial Times Management. This was a business that brought together the distance-learning management education operations of the Financial Times group with the extensive intellectual properties of Pearson Education. It's aimed at providing both individual and company training. The newly appointed head reports directly to the CEO, Mrs Scardino, which illustrates the Pearson approach to fledgling businesses of great potential. New businesses are left alone to get on with things – and can thus react very speedily – but at the same time they have direct access to resources should they be needed. This approach can only be used in a few key strategic areas, but it can be, and has been, employed at levels other than the very top of Pearson; for example, the head of the new animation business reports directly to the chief executive of Pearson Television.

good client relationships. The strength of this is that there is a strong focus for learning.

Whatever the source of the initial idea, it is very common for a task or project team to be set up to report back on the feasibility of the ongoing project, to determine the further resources required and to set up the procedures for getting and melding the resources into an internal team.

17.3.2   Internationalising

Ohmae[6] believes that there are five steps for any firm seeking to become a truly global company, which are:

- export to where the company can expect the best returns. The home base stays in the mother country. Agents or distributors would be used;
- set up marketing, sales and aftersales service facilities in the countries where goods/services are being sold to provide local responsiveness;

- relocate some production facilities to key markets and/or to low-cost/high-efficiency locations to take advantage of economies of scope;
- transfer some head office functions (such as R&D, engineering and customer financing) to the key markets to allow for both local responsiveness and economies of scope;
- remove any distinction between the home country and others and emphasise the identity of the company.

KEY CONCEPT   Internal development occurs when individual resources are brought together within the organisation to construct the required capabilities and/or competences. The main advantages of internal development over the other possibilities are the lack of problems of cultural fit, and smooth cash flows; the disadvantage is the time it takes to develop the required capabilities and/or competences.

17.4 Acquisition and merger

17.4.1 The terminology of acquisitions and mergers

The process by which a corporation obtains control over a complete SBU or competence may be described as being by acquisition, merger or takeover. A merger is the coming together of two organisations, often of a broadly similar size. Negotiations are generally friendly, as the coming together is mutually desired and instigated. In contrast, an acquisition is the purchase of one company by another, with the acquirer usually considerably larger than the company acquired. A takeover is a hostile acquisition – an acquisition where the directors of the target company don't wish their firm to be acquired.

Although there are some differences in the formal accounting for mergers and acquisitions, their close similarity means that they can generally be treated as the same. Thus for strategic management purposes the terms *acquire* and *acquisition* may be used interchangeably with the terms *merge* and *merger*.[b] A major difference between a merger and an acquisition, however, is the phenomenon of two bosses in a merger between equals. This happened in the mergers of Travelers and Citicorp, Monsanto and American Home Products and Daimler-Benz and Chrysler. In general, such joint bosses are the exception, and the arrangement is seldom durable. However, both Shell and Unilever have had joint bosses for many years.

17.4.2 Waves of acquisition

Acquisition activity seems to go in waves. In the mid-1980s high-street takeovers were common in the UK; the mid-1990s saw mergers among solicitors, financial services and the banks. In the late 1990s Internet and communications, fine chemicals and cars were the sectors with large merger activity.

At the turn of the twentieth century acquisitions were to create enterprises to dominate national economies (or in the case of the USA, a continental economy); today

b It is recognised that an acquisition may not be fused with other SBUs. In this case there is no merger. With no linkages, the acquisition would effectively be a conglomerate diversification.

the acquisitions are often to fit a global scale. During the 1960s and 1970s acquisitions tended to be conglomerate acquisitions carried out for financial reasons; an acquirer such as BTR or Hanson purchased undervalued assets and managed them more successfully. During the late 1990s the reasons for acquisition were much more marketing- or competence-led, giving companies the reach and scale that they think will be needed in the years ahead. The need to have global reach to service global corporations has been the main rationale for the growth of the large accounting firms. The need to keep abreast of genetic engineering developments has driven the big pharmaceutical companies to acquire small bioscience firms.

17.4.3   The advantages and disadvantages of acquisitions

The advantages
Acquisition has some significant advantages over both internal development and alliances as a route towards gaining access to resources. They are:

- **High-speed access to resources**   The speed with which a new SBU or competence can be added to the corporate portfolio is high. This is particularly true of brands: an acquisition can provide a powerful brand name that could take years to establish through internal development.

- **Less likelihood of retaliation from competitors**   An acquisition only changes the ownership of an SBU and thus doesn't alter the capacity of the competitive arena as successful internal development would. Thus less reaction from competitors might be expected.

- **They can block a competitor**   An acquisition can block off a capability or competence from a competitor. There was general agreement among commentators that one reason for the (abortive) Kingfisher bid for Asda in 1999 was that it would remove a possible acquisition target from Wal-Mart, the giant US retailer apparently aiming to continue to enter Europe (which it did by acquiring Asda from under the noses of Kingfisher in mid-1999).

- **They can help to restructure the operating environment**   Acquisition can be used as a means of restructuring the operating environment. At the end of the 1990s, car manufacturers had an overcapacity for 15 million cars per year. Overcapacity and the need to reduce it was one of the driving forces for the worldwide wave of car mergers, and for the mergers among European steel companies.

These advantages are summarised in Exhibit 17.5.

DISCUSSION
POINT 17.3

Why are economies of scale not included under the advantages in Exhibit 17.5?
- If you were a senior leader-manager, what other advantages could you think of?

The disadvantages
Also summarised in Exhibit 17.5 are the several significant disadvantages associated with acquisition:

- **Cultural mismatch**   There is bound to be some cultural mismatch between any two organisations, and this is exemplified in the merger between Lloyds and TSB

EXHIBIT 17.5

The advantages and disadvantages of mergers and acquisitions

Advantages	Disadvantages
High-speed access to resources	Cultural mismatch
Less likelihood of retaliation from competitors	Mismatch in managerial salaries
Can block competition	Heightened risk
Can help restructure the operating environment	Disposal of assets

as described in Section 2.1. A lack of fit can be significant in knowledge-based businesses, where the value of the business resides in individuals. When a large, well-established British bank bought a trading company, the cultural mismatch was palpable, as shown in Exhibit 17.6,[7] and this mismatch led to failure: the value of the trading company lay in its people and, dissatisfied with the merger, they simply left the organisation, thus stripping the bank of its value. Some commentators expect Asda and Wal-Mart to have a good cultural fit, since Asda's chairman and previously its CEO, Archie Norman, greatly admired Wal-Mart's style and way of operating, visited Wal-Mart's executives and copied several of its innovations. Other commentators aren't so sure,[8] viewing Wal-Mart's growth as stemming from its operating in the most parochial manner, until fairly recently restricted to mid-town America and with 'old-fashioned'

EXHIBIT 17.6

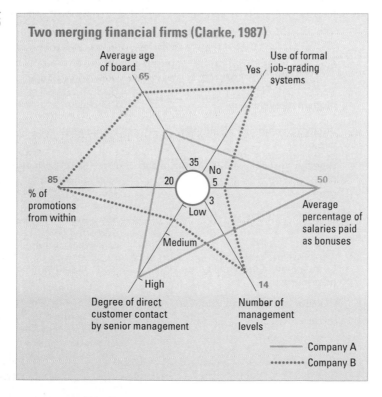

Two merging financial firms (Clarke, 1987)

American virtues. In Germany, Wal-Mart's working practices have not been acceptable to all its German employees.[9]

- **Mismatch in managerial salaries**   One significant area of cultural mismatch involves managerial salaries. For example, the very high salaries of US senior managers compared with those of the Germans were a serious concern in the Daimler–Chrysler merger of 1998.

- **Heightened risk**   Unless very great care is taken, the acquirer won't know all there is to know about the organisation it seeks to buy. Thus there is a risk associated with the purchase. This risk will be much reduced if the organisations have been working with each other prior to the acquisition, or where the features of the competitive arena are known, such as is the case where two airlines or car companies agree to merge. Sometimes an acquisition brings with it assets that the buyer doesn't want but is forced to purchase at the same time. The acquirer would generally have difficulty valuing these assets, since they would be outside its area of expertise.

- **Disposal of assets**   Government and/or EU restrictions may force the buyer to dispose of assets it had prior to the acquisition. This has happened several times in brewery acquisitions in the UK, where the buyer is not allowed a monopoly of pubs in specified areas.

17.4.4   The empirical evidence for acquisition success

The economic success of acquisitions has been principally assessed by four methods. A selection of results is shown in Exhibit 17.7. As a broad generalisation, 50% of

EXHIBIT 17.7

The success of acquisitions and mergers	
Method of evaluation	**Conclusion and comments**
Subjective opinions of company personnel	Around half were successful[10]
Whether the acquired SBU is retained in the long term	More then 50% divested when in entirely new industries More than 60% divested when in new fields More than 70% divested when in unrelated fields[11] More divested than retained[12]
Comparison of profitability pre- and post-merger	Nil to negative effect[13]
Effect on stock market valuation	Positive initial impact[14] Success rate 50%; neither the price paid nor the strategy adopted had any impact on success[15] (return to shareholders in deals worth $500m or more)

acquisitions are failures and, overall, there is little or no gain in the medium term when all parties are considered. This might appear to be unacceptable, but it should be recognised that of all the investments made by a firm, a failure rate of 50% might be good. For example, the failure rate of drugs is very high indeed,[16] and research shows that two-thirds of offers launched in the main European markets fail within their first 12 months.[17] There is some evidence that the overall success of acquisitions is improving, partly because there has been a move away from acquisitions that support conglomerate diversification to those that support related diversification.[18]

While the overall economic consequences are important, so are those to the different groups of stakeholders. Broadly, the picture is that the shareholders of the acquiring firm seem to neither gain nor lose. Although there tends to be a rise in the share price of the acquiring firm when an acquisition is announced, when the deal has been done the shareholders in the acquiring firms in the UK only approximately break even.[19] The shareholders of the victim, however, generally do well; acquisitions provide large gains for the target's shareholders:[20] premiums as large as 30% in the USA, and around 20% in the UK.

The employees in the buyer tend to do well, with senior managers particularly well rewarded through greater responsibilities, status and remuneration. In a merger the senior managers in the acquired firm are likely to be retained, while in a takeover they are likely to be ousted or leave of their own accord. Research suggests that the departure of executives lowers the performance of the acquired firm, through the loss of in-depth understanding of the values, strengths of key employees and implicit contracts.[21] With cost reductions often the stated rationale for acquisitions, employees of the victim and to some extent the buyer are in danger of losing their jobs.

DISCUSSION
POINT 17.4

Why might you expect the share price of the acquired firm to rise by 20–30%?
- What does the success or otherwise of acquisitions say about the transferability of managerial expertise?

17.5 Undertaking an acquisition

A framework by which the likelihood of success for a proposed acquisition might be gauged is set out in Exhibit 17.8. The success of an acquisition depends on both the context in which it takes place and the process by which the acquisition is carried out.

17.5.1 The context of an acquisition

Studies show that six features of the context play a part in determining the success of an acquisition:

- Strategy doesn't refer to the strategy itself; rather, it refers to the buyer having a clear idea of its strategic direction, and thus of where the acquisition will fit its current SBU and competence portfolios. Opportunistic buying correlates with failure.

- Relatedness measures the closeness of the acquired firm's activities to those of the buyer. While theory would unambiguously suggest that the closer the relatedness the more the chance of success – or rather, perhaps, the lower the

EXHIBIT 17.8

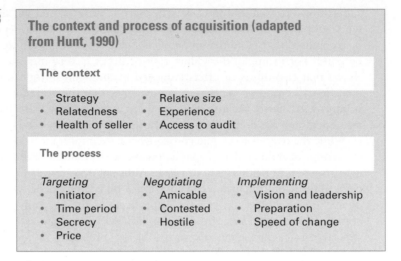

The context and process of acquisition (adapted from Hunt, 1990)

The context

- Strategy
- Relatedness
- Health of seller
- Relative size
- Experience
- Access to audit

The process

Targeting	Negotiating	Implementing
• Initiator	• Amicable	• Vision and leadership
• Time period	• Contested	• Preparation
• Secrecy	• Hostile	• Speed of change
• Price		

chance of failure – the empirical evidence isn't overwhelming, with some studies showing that success is strongly linked to relatedness[22] and others showing a more tentative linkage.[23] Overall, studies indicate that:

- relatedness doesn't harm success;
- horizontal integration generally leads to success;
- conglomerate diversification is unlikely to lead to success;
- cross-border acquisitions work well for core businesses and within geographical areas where the buyer is already operating.[24]

- Health of seller   In Hunt's study the health of the seller was based on its pre-bid profitability and on its general and marketing management strengths, and its technical capabilities. Hunt's and other studies indicate fairly conclusively that purchasing unhealthy companies is a recipe for failure.

- Relative size   If the buyer is very much larger than the seller in terms of turnover, the failure rate is high.[25,26] However, 'very much larger' means that the seller has a turnover of less than 2% of the buyer.

- Experience   It might be expected that a firm that has experience of acquisitions would learn and become more successful. In general this doesn't appear to be the case. However, in certain conditions, for example where there is a hostile bid, experience appears to help.[27]

- Access to audit   The ability of the buyer to audit the strengths and weaknesses of the seller, both financially and in terms of non-financial resources, appears to be a very significant feature of successful acquisitions.[28]

What reasons can you give why:

a)   purchasing unhealthy companies is a recipe for failure;

b)   a mismatch in the relative size of the buyer and seller might lead to failure;

c)   a mismatch in the relative size of the buyer and seller might lead to success;

d)   experience of acquisitions doesn't generally correlate with success?

17.5.2 The acquisition process

Three phases of the acquisition process can be identified:

- Targeting   Some research has found that the *initiator* of the deal – the buyer or seller – played a role in determining success,[29] while other research found no such linkage:[30] the thought that a seller-initiated acquisition indicates a wish to dispose of a basically unsound business doesn't seem to be borne out. Rushed acquisitions have a higher failure rate than those assessed over a longer time period. On average, targeting/observing the seller lasted around two years.[31] Two further considerations are of course the two *prices* that the buyer and seller think acceptable and the level of *secrecy* that needs to surround this phase – and the negotiation phase.

- Negotiating   The second phase is when a bid has been lodged and serious negotiations begin. It is in this phase that the expectations of both the buyer and particularly the seller are formed and embedded, and these can have a significant influence as the negotiations unfold and implementation begins. In particular, an amicable bid allows for a more open and unhurried discussion and less secrecy. The high bid premiums associated with hostile bids are unlikely to occur, and the high commissions to financial advisers may not need to be paid.

- Implementing   This third phase is perhaps the most sensitive. There are three vital features of implementation. First, **vision** and **leadership**. Leadership[32] and the need to communicate widely the vision of what the new enterprise will be both inside and outside the organisation have been highlighted as vital ingredients to acquisition success.[33] The need to communicate is illustrated by Cable and Wireless, which installed an intranet linking 14,000 staff to enable the rapid integration of the four businesss – Bell Cablemedia, Mercury Communications, Nyrex CableComms and Videotron – which had been brought together to form the company.[34]

  The second important factor for success is *meticulous preparation*. The changes that need to be made to the merging organisational structures, their processes and culture must be planned in detail. Shortly after Daimler and Chrysler merged in 1998, the merged company set up more than 100 'integration teams' to implement the detail of the merger and extract the savings that it was thought could be made.[35]

  Culture is a particularly significant area in which meticulous preparation is vital.[36] When a bid has been amicable, the seller's staff are likely to have had some prior warning of the acquisition, and the emphasis here is for the buyer to welcome the seller's staff as members of the team. In a hostile bid, the staff may be alienated from the buyer. When the seller is unhealthy, staff may be enrolled to a more effective firm and feel liberated as a consequence. Cross-border acquisitions are likely to pose particularly difficult cultural issues. How to deal with managers and differential pay is another important consideration. There also needs to be meticulous planning of information systems if the two businesses are to merge their activities.

  The third vital ingredient of successful acquisition concerns the *speed of change*. Staff in both organisations will be expecting change to occur and, if there are shareholders, they will have been promised change. Rapid changes are likely if the seller has been underperforming; less rapid changes will be called for if the seller is healthy with a good management team.

17.5.3 Defences against hostile acquisitions

Given what tends to happen to managers of acquired companies, they will tend to resist acquisitions and particularly takeovers. There are many defences against a (hostile) takeover, and the main ones are set out in Exhibit 17.9.

> KEY CONCEPT   Acquisitions are a rapid means of enlarging a corporation's portfolio. However, there are risks attached to them. The success of a merger is positively correlated to several contextual factors, of which the most important are a clear buyer strategy, relatedness, the health of the seller and access to audit. The success of an acquisition is also positively correlated to several process factors, of which the most important are the time for decision, an amicable bid, vision, leadership and meticulous preparation.

17.6   Strategic alliances

17.6.1   What is a strategic alliance?

Businesses build relationships with varying degrees of formality, but these aren't the same type of collaboration that parents engage in when they develop a strategic alliance. The significant difference is in the form of ownership, with a (corporate) alliance involving equity. Without an equity exchange, the collaboration is a relationship. For an alliance to be considered strategic, there are four main 'tests':

- The extent of resource commitment   If this is not a significant proportion of the overall resources of the partners, it would be difficult to argue that the investment is strategic.
- The level of interdependence   Simple supply or subcontracting arrangements, for example, almost never exhibit a sufficiently high degree of interdependence to be considered strategic alliances.
- The time frame   Short-term, *ad hoc* relationships would normally not be strategic.
- The centrality of the alliance to the strategic objectives and purposes of the partners   An alliance must be sufficiently central to the business of at least one of the partners for it to be considered strategically important. Speculative, opportunistic and peripheral activities would generally not be considered to be strategic. The provisioning of transport or cleaning services via a joint venture would not be strategic for a bank, for example.

With these considerations, a strategic alliance may be defined[38] as 'a durable relationship involving equity shareholders established between two or more independent firms involving the sharing or pooling of resources for undertaking activities of strategic importance to one or more of the partners.'

EXHIBIT 17.9

The language of takeovers[37]

Slang is popular in mergers and acquisitions. For example, a *pigeon* (highly vulnerable target) or *sleeping beauty* (more desirable than a pigeon) might take a *cyanide pill* (take on a huge long-term debt on the condition that the debt falls due immediately upon the firm's acquisition) so that it can avoid being *raped* (being subjected to a forcible hostile takeover, sometimes accompanied by looting the target's profitability) by a *shark* (extremely predatory takeover artist) using *hired guns* (lawyers, merger and acquisition specialists, and certain investment bankers).

The following are some of the moves made by leader-managers to prevent a hostile takeover:

Scorched earth Selling off key assets in an effort to purposely make the business unattractive to sharks. The assets sold are referred to as the *crown jewels* because they are often those which make the company most attractive in the first place. When sharks threaten, crown jewels may be offered at greatly reduced prices to ensure a quick sale. Obviously, this defence could result in mortally wounding the corporation.

White knight In order to avoid being acquired in a hostile (unwanted) takeover, managers approach a third firm about acquisition. In order to induce this 'white knight' to rescue the corporation, it is often offered the targeted firm's stock on very favourable terms – sometimes much less than the price the shark was offering or the price other stockholders must pay. When the friendly acquiring firm buys only a portion of the corporation, it is known as a *white squire*.

Greenmail Financial inducements offered by the threatened firm to stop a shark from acquiring it. The inducement is commonly an offer to buy back (usually at an attractive premium) any of the corporation's stock the shark has already purchased in exchange for the shark's guarantee that it will not threaten the defending firm. Again, this is special treatment offered only to selected stockholders.

Golden parachute High pay packages, often running three times normal annual compensation, promised to executives fired as a result of a takeover. Sharks are repelled by the idea of having the management team of the acquired corporation leave *en masse* – especially if they leave with so much cash.

Poison pills Any of a number of devices aimed at reducing the worth of a company once it has been taken over. For instance, a clause requiring that huge dividend payments be made upon takeover would raise the effective cost of the acquisition, because the shark would have to allow for the cost of meeting the payments. Because there are so many ways to sabotage the future operations of a business, poison pills remain the most popular form of shark repellent.

Pac-man A defence based on trying to consume the hunting shark before it attacks. In this situation, offence becomes defence and the hunter becomes the hunted. The risk in using this tactic is that it sometimes sets up a cycle of bid and counterbid in which the price of both firms escalates. When this happens, the 'winner' of the bidding war may be saddled with more debt than it can hope to service.

17.6.2 Types of alliance

There are three main forms of alliance.

Joint venture

A joint venture is an arrangement whereby two or more independent firms establish a legally separate company. The parent organisations will provide the finance and other needs initially, but it is expected that the joint venture will become totally free-standing in time. This is the most popular form of alliance. Joint ventures aren't all identical, however; they differ according to the dependence of the joint venture on the parent companies for centrally provided services, management expertise and other operational support.

Strategic investment in a partner

The key characteristic of this type of alliance is a firm taking a minority equity stake in another, rather than making an investment in plant and equipment, technology development, etc. This form of alliance is popular with large companies taking a position in small high-tech firms, for example pharmaceutical companies taking a position in (small) genetic engineering firms. In some circumstances this type of investment will lead to a full acquisition in the longer term, which may not be currently possible due to government/legal restrictions, market conditions, lack of funds, etc. An example of a strategic investment in a partner is Stagecoach's purchase of a 35% shareholding in Sogin, an Italian bus operator, in mid-1999. In Stagecoach's case, it has the option of increasing its stake to 45% but may not be able to move further because 55% of the shares are held by the Italian state railway.

In other situations strategic investment in a partner may be a reciprocal arrangement where both companies take a stake in the other with a view to long-term and very close collaboration. This is particularly characteristic of the *keiretsu* system in Japan, whereby companies maintain long-standing business ties with each other that are often cemented by mutual ownership of some of each other's shares.

An equity investment could result in the investing firm taking one or more seats on the board of the firm in which it is investing if its stake is sufficiently large, and could even lead to organisational changes such as rationalising sales and engineering departments to realise scale economies.

Consortium

A special sort of strategic alliance is the consortium, which is a collaboration between a number of partners for a very specific purpose. This purpose is usually a project, where the collaboration runs for the duration of the project. Examples of joint ventures are the building of the Channel Tunnel and the European Airbus project. Consortia tend to be joint ventures.

17.6.3 Alliance activity

Impetus

There was a considerable build-up of cross-border alliances in the 1990s. There are four main drivers:

- The blurring of national boundaries, giving rise to greater competition. The development of the EU and the North American Free Trade Area are examples of political and economic factors that have reduced the economic separateness of nation-states – and the protection that this affords nationally operating companies. However, it hasn't as yet had much effect on the cultural separateness that divides nations and suggests that collaboration with indigenous partners is likely to be appropriate, especially with consumer offers.

- Political requirements   Some countries, such as India, demand some local ownership in foreign companies entering the country. One option in satisfying this demand is for the foreign company to forge an alliance with a local company.

- Information technology is compressing time and distance, allowing collaboration between physically separated organisations (as the collaboration between Roll-Royce plc operating in the UK and General Electric operating in the USA illustrates).

- Globalisation   Many companies see the need to operate globally but do not have the resources to achieve the necessary presence.

17.6.4   The advantages and disadvantages of alliances[39]

The advantages
The advantages of alliances over internal development and acquisition are as follows:

- Access to complementary resources   Offers have become increasingly complex and companies need access to a wide range of competences and capabilities that they themselves don't possess and have little likelihood of possessing. For example, supermarkets have teamed up with banks to offer financial services. The need for extra expertise is especially required with IT, now included in many offers from firms that have no deep expertise in IT.

- Sharing of resource requirements and risk   Some opportunities look potentially very profitable but require very large resources to carry them out and/or are accompanied by large risks. In such cases, an alliance is an appropriate means of obtaining the resources and reducing the risks to any one member of the alliance. The Alaskan pipeline and the Channel Tunnel are examples of reward/risk sharing. In many fields, research and development costs have risen greatly and this is also a driver for spreading costs between partners.

- Speeds market access   Firms need access to all the important markets of the world to prevent competitors maintaining a comfortable home base from which to attack them. They also need simultaneous access to these markets, since competitive advantage is often fleeting and without fast access, their offers will be imitated and thus they will not appropriate the full gains.

- Reduces political difficulties   An alliance can provide a foreign company with the opportunity for obtaining local management, thereby reducing risks such as expropriation and harassment by host-country officials.

- Enhances competences   To remain competitive in the long run, a firm must ensure that its competences are continuously upgraded rather than allowed to remain stagnant or even erode over time. An alliance can help with this upgrading process, especially if a company considering an alliance identifies the competences it wishes to enhance. Learning is a major feature of successful alliances.[40]

- Provides defence   When two or more smaller firms have trouble competing with a large firm, an alliance may provide the market power to compete successfully.

These advantages are listed in Exhibit 17.10.

The disadvantages
The disadvantages of alliances are also listed in Exhibit 17.10. These are as follows:

- The costs of establishing and maintaining the alliance   The costs associated with an alliance may be large, as senior management will be involved together with a highly qualified team. One view is that these costs tend to outweigh the gains from an alliance:[41]

  Alliances are a tempting solution to the dilemma of a firm seeking home-based advantages of another nation without giving up its own. This is rarely a solution. They can achieve selective benefits but they always involve significant costs in terms of co-ordination, reconciling goals with an independent entity, creating a competitor and giving up profits. These costs make many alliances temporary and destined to fail. Alliances tend to ensure mediocrity since they deter the firms' own efforts to upgrade.

- Damage to capabilities and competences   The possibility of damaging the capabilities and competences is alluded to in the above quote. If a partner takes over the marketing of another firm's products, then the producer has lost its feel for the marketplace and thus for what is needed in the way of offer development.

EXHIBIT 17.10

The advantages and disadvantages of alliances

Advantages	Disadvantages
Access to complementary resources	The cost of establishing and maintaining the alliance
Sharing of resource requirements and risk	Damage to capabilities and competences
Speeds market access	Long development time
Reduces political difficulties	May be forced to sell assets
Enhances competences	
Provides defence	

- **Long development time** The time to establish an alliance can be long, especially for it to be established well enough to achieve significant profitability. This is especially true of alliances with East Asian partners.

- **May be forced to sell assets** Government restrictions may force the buyer to sell some of its own assets.

KEY CONCEPT Strategic alliances are fundamentally different from acquisitions and require a different level of understanding. While achieving full control, acquisitions bring to the acquirer all parts of the acquired entity – both strengths and weaknesses – whereas alliances match strength to strength and balance control with collaboration.

17.7 Alliance formation

The main steps necessary in initiating an alliance are listed in Exhibit 17.11.

17.7.1 Internal strategic analysis

It is vital that any company seeking an alliance has clear and strategically sound reasons for doing so. It ought to have clear financial, product and market objectives and goals, and a firm understanding of the business risks. Similarly, it is equally important that a company considers whether it wants to protect one or more of its competences, possibly by taking a 'black box' approach where a set of processes is performed within the company rather than within the alliance, which only sees the result of the processes.[42] The 'black box' approach is likely to raise issues of lack of trust and openness, particularly in alliances involving sophisticated technology.

Alliances will take a number of years to be successful. A long-term view creates the necessary environment for those involved to take the time to resolve the many issues that are almost bound to arise.

EXHIBIT 17.11

Major steps in initiating an alliance

Phase	Goal
Internal strategic analysis	Classifying what is sought and what can be shared
Partner assessment	Unearthing strengths and weaknesses
Preparation of the joint business case	Establishing the operational details
Preparation of the alliance contract	Determining the state restrictions on actions

17.7.2 Partner assessment

Partner selection is one of the most important criteria distinguishing successful and unsuccessful joint ventures.[43] Exhibit 17.12 illustrates the five most important features of a successful alliance.[44] These are:

- **Compatible goals**   It is commonsensical that if the partners to an alliance have incompatible goals it's unlikely that the alliance will flourish. The failure of cross-border alliances where the parties were competing in the same markets has been recorded.[45]

- **Commensurate risk**   It is important that both parties hold roughly the same measure of risk, for this will be a powerful factor keeping the motivation of the parties at a similar level. If one party would be relatively unscathed by the failure of the alliance while the other party would be severely affected by it, it's unlikely that the same amount of managerial time and effort would be devoted by both parties.

- **Co-operative culture**   Doz[46] discusses the substantial problems that mismatched partners can create for an alliance. He analyses one collaboration in particular, between Ciba-Geigy of Switzerland and Alza of the USA, and the problems they experienced in developing an advanced drug delivery system because of the significant differences between the two companies' management styles. At the time of the alliance (mid-1970s to early 1980s) Ciba-Geigy was a large bureaucratic organisation that insisted on a high degree of centralised control external to the alliance's management team, while Alza was a much smaller, entrepreneurial and innovative company that expected the management team to run the venture unhindered. The differences were so entrenched that they eventually led to the alliance failing after considerable efforts to improve the manner in which it was managed.

- **Complemetary skills**   It is important that the assessment is focused primarily on the partner's strengths and weaknesses as they pertain to the alliance, rather than on areas that will have little influence on its success. The choice of selection

EXHIBIT 17.12

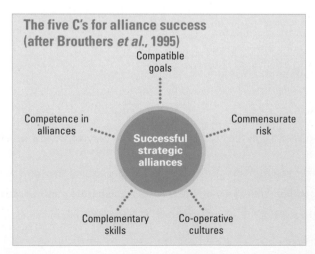

The five C's for alliance success (after Brouthers *et al.*, 1995)

Compatible goals

Competence in alliances

Commensurate risk

Successful strategic alliances

Complementary skills

Co-operative cultures

criteria should be driven by the reason for collaborating identified in the strategic analysis. For example, 'can the firm in question provide the required market access or key technological input?' 'Do its current products and perceived strategy match the objectives and goals that have been identified for the alliance?' It can be argued that a partner's strengths in complementary skills and markets are fundamentally more important than their weaknesses in particular areas, if these areas can be adequately covered by the other collaborating party.[47]

- Competences in alliances   Analysis of a large number of US alliances[48] suggests that alliance experience increases the return on investment that is likely to be achieved from an alliance, with average ROI figures increasing from 10% for inexperienced firms to close to 20% for those with considerable knowledge. By extension, it would be reasonable to infer that experience increases the absolute likelihood of the alliance succeeding rather than failing. In cross-border alliances, those between strong and weak companies rarely work:[49] it would be expected that this would be the case in most forms of alliance.

DISCUSSION
POINT 17.6

What reasons can you give for experience increasing the success of alliances but apparently not generally increasing the success of acquisitions?

17.7.3   Preparation of the joint business case

There is a great deal of consensus on the preparation of a detailed, agreed business plan being one of, if not the, most important factors influencing whether an alliance is successful.[50,51] Five factors appear to be particularly important:

- Governance arrangements should be addressed early on   Control and dominance of an alliance are issues that need to be discussed and understood at the outset. Dominant parent alliances and 'independent' alliances (which receive almost no interference from any parent) are more successful than shared management ventures, where all the parents participate actively.

- Set and agree realistic targets   Targets should be set for all the major objectives of the alliance, including financial performance, funds to be repatriated to the parent companies, target market shares, the products that the alliance will produce, and quality standards.

- Detailed quantification of partner contributions   This would include such things as capital, land and buildings, fixed assets and working capital, technical expertise, including manufacturing and engineering processes, patents and intellectual property, business and market expertise, and access to distribution channels.

- Task definitions   These should be explicit and clear, preferably modular and with clearly defined boundaries, and appropriately supported within each partner organisation, ideally with a named 'champion'. Typical areas of responsibility would be engineering, procurement, manufacturing, quality control, research and development, and marketing.

- Management team   The management structure must be clear, and cross-fertilisation of various functional activities will improve trust and communication. An advantage is to retain continuity of key interface managers. Failures in alliances between Western and Japanese companies, where they have occurred, have been attributed primarily to Western partners choosing insufficiently experienced staff for the project, involving them at short notice and not being as committed to the venture as the Japanese partner.[52]

17.7.4   Preparation of the alliance contract

Once the partners have prepared a business plan and agreed it as a basis for forming an alliance, a legal contract will be drawn up between the parties. There is disagreement as to the amount of attention the contract should receive. It has been argued that excessive focus on the contract can breed a 'who owns what' mentality that distracts efforts away from value creation and growing the alliance for the greater good. Conversely, it can also be argued that considerable effort should be focused on producing a well-defined contract to ensure that important issues are not left undefined. This is particularly important in cross-cultural alliances, where issues that it would normally be possible to solve on the basis of 'commonly held beliefs' may be more troublesome to clarify as the applicable 'beliefs' may not be commonly held. The operational reality is that, in large, publicly quoted companies that have defined commercial and legal functions, there will be a significant focus on producing a well-defined contract – more so than there may be in smaller companies with less skill in these areas.

Each contract is likely to include many clauses that are specific to the particular alliance. However, a number of points would generally be included to ensure that each party's position is suitably protected:

- Restrictions   The contract should limit the transfer of competences to other parties, particularly if the alliance should fail, to prevent the other partner competing directly with the alliance, and to prevent the other partner establishing further alliances to compete in the same or connected markets.

- Intellectual property rights   The contract should provide guidance on how the intellectual property rights of each party would be released to the alliance. It would also specify how the intellectual property rights developed in the alliance would be owned and used by the partners.

- Dispute settlement and exit strategy   The contract should address the question of how disputes are to be settled, which may include external arbitration or the involvement of executives from the parent companies. It also should consider the situation where one partner wants to liquidate its shareholding in the alliance. Thus the contract may include pre-emption rights for the other party to buy out its partner, or a commitment to continue contributing resources for a period of time to act as a disincentive for withdrawal.

- Accounting and financial standards   Specification of agreed standards in the contract will help ensure that both partners can accurately monitor the performance of the alliance. The standards would cover such matters as the accounting standards employed, the currencies to be used in reports, the frequency of financial statement preparation and the form of audit and review.

KEY CONCEPT   There are four main phases in initiating an alliance: establishing what is sought and what is to be shared; the partner's strengths and weaknesses; the operational details; and the restrictions on actions. Partner assessment and preparation of the joint business case are perhaps the two most important phases.

17.8 Sources of long-term funds

Whatever method is used to gain access to additional non-financial resources, funding will be required. The concerns of the parent will almost certainly be long-term and thus the appropriate funding focus will also be long-term (although this isn't to say that there won't be short-term considerations arising from the activities of the corporation's businesses).

A major form of long-term funding is internal – from retained profits.[c] The other main forms are external: equity (the sale of shares in the company) and debt (the sale of bonds by a company or a term loan). 'Hybrid' forms of funding that combine characteristics of both equity and debt funding are also available.

17.8.1 Equity finance

Equity is ownership of all or part of a commercial enterprise through holding shares in it. Although rights can be prescribed in many ways, in general the owner of a share is entitled to vote at general meetings, to obtain payment of dividends out of profits, and to the ultimate repayment of capital if the company should go into liquidation. When a company is formed it may issue ordinary shares, with the money raised used to fund the company's activities.

Stock exchange

If the company requires a large amount of new capital then it will need to *go public* and become a public limited company – a plc in the UK. The most obvious sources of equity funding are the stock exchange that exists in most countries, usually in the commercial capital – London, New York, Milan and Paris for example. In becoming *quoted* a company will get a full listing on the stock exchange. The costs involved in going public aren't trivial, starting at around £300,000,[53] and a listed company has to abide by the rules of the exchange.

Although the most high-profile sources of capital, stock exchanges tend to cater only for large enterprises. For example, the number of companies quoted on the London Stock Exchange in 1999 was around 2500, 500 of which don't have their head office in the UK. The vast majority of companies must obtain equity finance elsewhere:

---

c   More precisely, internal finance comes from retained profits and depreciation provision, as depreciation doesn't involve a cash outflow.

- Private placing   Well-established companies can obtain equity-based funding by using a stockbroker or issuing house to buy their shares and sell them to their clients (termed *placing*).

- Alternative Investment Market   The Alternative Investment Market (AIM) was set up by the London Stock Exchange to provide a market in the shares of small and/or youthful companies for which full listing would be inappropriate or unobtainable. In mid-1999 there were just over 300 companies listed. One disadvantage of being involved in the AIM is that a company must appoint a nominated adviser to help ensure compliance with the AIM's rules and a nominated broker to carry out share transactions – all additional and on-going costs. The cost for a company of obtaining a quote on the AIM can be as low as £100,000 but would approach £350,000 for a company with a complex structure.[54]

17.8.2   Long-term debt finance

Debentures[d]

Companies can raise finance based on their assets by issuing debentures. Here, the company agrees to meet a series of interest payments and pay back the sum borrowed at the end of a fixed period – usually more than ten years. The lender has security based on the borrower's assets. If the security is through what is termed *a floating charge*, then the borrower can dispose of assets as they please; if it is through *a fixed charge*, the security lies with specified assets and the borrower isn't at liberty to dispose of these. Debenture holders have priority over ordinary shareholders in the event of company liquidation.

At the end of 1996, IBM issued an $850 million 'century bond', where payment of the sum borrowed could be in 100 years time. These bonds were attractive because they offered high interest; the IBM bonds offered 7.22%, while a 30-year US Treasury bond was offering 6.42%. The Walt Disney Corporation, Coca-Cola and Yale University have also issued long-maturing bonds.[56]

Unsecured loan stock

These are similar to debentures. However, the loan isn't secured on the firm's assets and so quite naturally with the enhanced risk the interest payments are considerably higher than with a secured loan – typically 3–6% higher. This high rate of interest imposes the requirement that the borrower performs well over many years.

Two types of bond are of special interest. *Eurobonds* are bonds issued by companies outside of the currency in which they are denominated. For example, a US company may issue bonds denominated in US$ in Frankfurt. Funding via eurobonds is only available to big, creditworthy companies. *Junk bonds* are high-risk bonds that tend to be issued by smaller, perhaps not very creditworthy companies; but with high risks come high returns, on average.

---

d   The terminology of debt finance isn't straightforward. The term *debenture* includes debenture stock and bonds in the Companies Acts. It is quite common for the terms *debenture* and *bond* to be used interchangeably. Company debentures can also be referred to as *loan stock*. Usually, *debentures* refer to secured loans, *loan stock* to less secure loans.[55]

Bank term loans

These loans are made for a fixed period of time, with repayment either as a lump sum at the end of the period or through periodic instalments. They can be arranged at variable or fixed rates of interest. For variable rate loans, the rate is usually 2–5% above the bank's base rate, depending on the credit rating of the client.

17.8.3 Hybrid long-term funding arrangements

There are several funding arrangements that combine some equity and some loan components. Convertible loan stock and warrants give a flavour of what is on offer. Convertible loan stock offers an agreement whereby the lender obtains interest payments together with the opportunity to buy shares in the borrower at a specified price within a stated time period. Warrants are similar, but with the difference that the interest receipts cease if the right to buy the shares is exercised.

KEY CONCEPT   The combination of forms of financing that a company employs will depend on its situation. Its tax position and the amount of operating and capital gearing will all play a part in its funding decisions.

SUMMARY
- There are three broad avenues for a parent to acquire new capabilities (new businesses) and competences: internal development, acquisition/merger and alliance. Both internal development and acquisitions involve the corporation obtaining complete control of the resources that it is using.   EXHIBIT 17.1
- With internal development, individual resources are either bought in and melded with other resources to produce the necessary capabilities and competences or redeployed from other parts of the corporation. The main advantage of internal development is the relative lack of cultural problems; the main problem is the time it takes.   EXHIBIT 17.3
- With acquisitions, whole new businesses or competences are brought into the corporation. The main advantage of acquisition is the speed with which a business or competence can be obtained; the main disadvantages are the potential for a cultural clash between the established and the new and the lack of knowledge that the acquirer might have of the acquiree.   EXHIBIT 17.4
- Very broadly, 50% of acquisitions are successful. The success of acquisitions is positively correlated to several contextual factors, of which the most important are a clear buyer strategy, relatedness, the health of the seller and access to audit. Success of an acquisition is also positively correlated to several process factors, of which the most important are the time for decision, an amicable bid, vision, leadership and meticulous preparation.   EXHIBITS 17.5 TO 17.8
- There are many ways in which the leader-managers in a firm can hinder a takeover.   EXHIBIT 17.9
- Assessment of the economic success of an acquisition has been based on the return on investment several years after the acquisition; a consideration of the share prices of both the buyer and seller at the time of the bid and subsequently; the subjective opinions of managers involved in both the buyer and

seller companies; and whether the acquisition has been retained by the buyer.
EXHIBITS 17.7 TO 17.8

- There are three broad types of alliance: joint venture, strategic investment in a partner and consortium. The main advantage of alliances is the access to complementary resources at relatively low initial cost; the main disadvantage is the on-going costs. There are four main steps in alliance formulation: an internal strategic analysis; partner assessment; preparation of the joint business case; and preparation of the alliance contract. Of particular concern are the five elements in the test of whether a partner is suitable or not.   EXHIBITS 17.10 TO 17.12

- The sources of funds of particular concern to parents are long-term funds. These are of two main types: equity and long-term debt finance.

SELF-CHECK

1 Reconsider the learning outcomes for this chapter. Check that you feel confident that you can carry out the activities listed there.

2 Having read this chapter, you should be able to define the following terms:

acquisition	consortium	merger
alliance	debenture	strategic investment in a partner
alternative investment market	internal development	synergy
bank term loan	joint venture	takeover

MINI-CASE

Argos[e]

In February 1998 Great Universal Stores (GUS), the retail, mail-order and financial services group, launched a hostile £1.6 billion bid for Argos, the retail chain.

Argos pioneered catalogue selling on the high street, offering a no-frills approach to shopping. Customers select from a catalogue, fill in an order slip that is checked for availability and pay at a till; then wait for the purchase to be retrieved from the warehouse behind the store. Because most Argos shoppers choose from their own catalogues before arriving at the outlet there is less need for display space, glitzy window displays and lavish shop fittings. Location is also less important, enabling Argos to exploit many secondary shopping sites.

By the mid-1990s there were more than 400 catalogue shops. Argos claimed to be the country's leading discount retailer, the second biggest jeweller after the Signet group, one of the three largest toy retailers and a leader in the sales of small electrical appliances such as kettles and shavers. Argos became a leader in the use of computers for placing orders, controlling stock and analysing which lines should be added or dropped from each edition of its twice-yearly catalogue.

Recently, however, its value-for-money appeal has been challenged. The revival of Woolworth and Signet, previously weak high-street competitors, now offered Argos customers a more exciting customer-friendly shopping experience. Littlewoods, the mail-order and football pools group, has expanded its own Argos lookalike, Index, into a direct-mail operation offering its customers home shopping convenience. Complaints of long queues and poor customer service at Argos hit its vital Christmas sales for two con-

e   Prepared by C.J. Wood, Department of Strategic Management and Marketing, Nottingham Trent University.

secutive years. After three profit warnings from Argos in one year and a halving of its share price, GUS made its bid.

In the year ending March 1998, the GUS group generated pre-tax profits of £555 million, compared with £554 million the previous year. GUS's turnover and profit are principally derived from the business divisions listed in Exhibit 17.13.

EXHIBIT 17.13

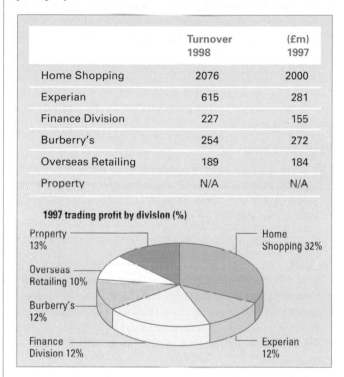

	Turnover 1998	(£m) 1997
Home Shopping	2076	2000
Experian	615	281
Finance Division	227	155
Burberry's	254	272
Overseas Retailing	189	184
Property	N/A	N/A

1997 trading profit by division (%)

Property 13%
Overseas Retailing 10%
Burberry's 12%
Finance Division 12%
Home Shopping 32%
Experian 12%

Despite long-term decline, 'agency' catalogues continue to account for the great majority of sales in the Home Shopping Division. Self-employed agents earning commission recruit customers using all-purpose catalogues and offering easy access to credit through instalment payments. However, today's 'agent' usually sells only to family and close friends using the commission as a personal discount. To maintain their market-leading position Lord Wolfson, the chairman of GUS, saw the bid as an opportunity to take Argos customers already familiar with catalogue buying from retailing into direct mail order. Fashion retailers like Next had already spotted the growing market for more specialised direct-mail selling. The *Next Directory* successfully transformed the catalogue market offering well-made clothes from stylish catalogues, with delivery within 48 hours. Wolfson argued that a takeover would enable Argos to introduce mail-order sales to its 14 million customers by using GUS's established delivery infrastructure.

Burberry's manufacturing and retailing division sells worldwide a range of luxury apparel, watches and jewellery. From its mail-order activities GUS developed the Finance Division and Experian, its information services business. Through acquisition Experian has become a global business providing large databases of public and proprietary information on customers, businesses, motor vehicles and property to support its clients in a wide range of commercial decisions.

Much of the current enthusiasm for home shopping stems from interest in the Internet and digital television. Sales on the Internet are doubling every year, driven not only by customers with time-pressed lifestyles seeking greater convenience but by prices that usually offer savings of at least 10% over high-street stores. With estimates suggesting that the worldwide on-line market will be worth £40 billion by 2001, most major retailers, including GUS, are investigating the potential of Internet shopping.

Argos's bid defence centred on revitalising the core high-street business, coupled with plans to open a further 200 stores. A stock enquiry and reservation telephone system for a 'call and collect' service as well as next-day local delivery for a £5 charge would offer customers greater convenience. A home shopping venture with Littlewoods was also proposed.

Despite a spirited defence by Argos, in April 1998 GUS ultimately emerged triumphant in the takeover battle after making an increased offer worth £1.9 billion. However, City analysts were concerned that even at the old bid price GUS would have to raise Argos's forecast net profit in 1998 by 50% merely to get a return equal to its own cost of capital.

Discussion point 17.7

What is the basis for Argos's competitive advantage?

- Critically appraise Argos's strategic position in the late 1990s.
- Is the acquisition of Argos an appropriate development of GUS's corporate strategy?
- Will GUS be able to turn round Argos's performance?

FURTHER
DISCUSSION
POINTS

1 For GSM:
    - What was the rationale for each of the five acquisitions that GSM made?
    - In particular, what did GSM get from the Primographic acquisition?
    - Use Exhibit 17.8 to analyse how GSM has gone about its acquisitions.
    - What forms of alliance is GSM engaged in?
    - Would any new formal alliance make sense to GSM? If so, what strategic goal would it support?
    - In Section 17.4 several sources of new ideas were described. Has GSM used any of them?
2 Exhibit 17.6 displays the culture of two organisations. How does this form of representation fit with the cultural web described in Chapter 2?
3 What sorts of cultural difficulties do you think might arise in an alliance between a Japanese and a northern European company?
4 Why are the anti-takeover ploys listed in Exhibit 17.9 considered unethical? Can any be justified on ethical grounds?

ASSIGNMENTS

1 Write an account of what is happening in one currently active acquisition. Information will be available in the financial sections of the broadsheet newspapers, especially the *Financial Times* and *The Economist*. The companies' Web pages are also likely to be a valuable source. In particular:
    a) plot the share price movements before and after the acquisition;
    b) determine the rationale that is stated for the acquisition by the companies involved and see the commentators' reactions.
2 Write an account of what is happening in one currently developing alliance. Information will be available in the financial sections of the broadsheet newspapers, especially the *Financial Times* and *The Economist*. The companies' Web pages are also likely to be a valuable source. In particular:

a) plot the share price movements before and after the alliance is announced;

b) determine the rationale that is stated for the alliance by the companies involved and see the commentators' reactions.

FURTHER READING

Two books are suggested to those wishing to consider sources of funding in more detail and to see worked examples. These are Richard Pike and Bill Neale, *Corporate Finance and Investment: Decisions and Strategies*, 2nd edn, Prentice Hall, 1996; and J.M. Samuels, F.M. Wilkes and R.E. Brayshaw, *Financial Management and Decision Making*, International Thomson Business Press, 1999.

CHAPTER NOTES AND REFERENCES

1 Marsh, P., 'Two blueprints for the engine of progress', *Financial Times*, 2 July 1998, p. 18.

2 Buzzell, R.D. and Gale, B.T., *The PIMS Principles: Linking Strategy to Performance*, Free Press, 1987.

3 Pinchot III, G., *Intrapreneuring: Why You Don't Have to Leave the Corporation to Become an Entrepreneur*, Harper & Row, 1985.

4 Extracts from the cases ARM Ltd, the chipless chip company, ITNET, and Pearson plc.

5 Peters, T.J. and Waterman, R.H., Jr, *In Search of Excellence: Lessons from America's Best-run companies*, Harper & Row, 1982.

6 Ohmae, K., in the BBC programme *Globalisation*, 1997.

7 Clarke, C.J., 'Acquisitions – techniques for measuring strategic fit', *Long Range Planning*, Vol. 20, No. 3, 1987, pp. 12–18.

8 Kay, J., 'Facing supermarket forces', *Financial Times*, 23 June 1999, p. 17.

9 Harnischfeger, U., 'Wal-mart shakes up Germany's food shopping sector', *Financial Times*, 23 June 1999, p. 32.

10 Hunt, J., 'Changing pattern of acquisition behaviour in takeovers and the consequences for acquisition processes', *Strategic Management Journal*, Vol. 11, 1990, pp. 69–77.

11 Porter, M.E., 'From competitive advantage to corporate strategy', *Harvard Business Review*, May–June 1987, pp. 43–59.

12 Ravenscraft, D.J. and Scherer, F.M., 'The profitability of mergers', *International Journal of Industrial Organization*, Vol. 7, No. 1, 1989, pp. 101–16.

13 *Ibid.*

14 Franks, J. and Harris, R., 'Shareholder wealth effects of corporate takeovers: the UK experience, 1955–1985', *Journal of Financial Economics*, 1986, pp. 225–49.

15 Mercer Management Consulting, *Making Mergers Work for Profitable Growth*, 1 Grosvenor Place, London SW1X 7HJ, 1997 (quoted by Holder, V. 'The secret of living happily ever after', *Financial Times*, 26 May 1997. This study was for acquisitions valued at $500 million or more.

16 See Section 10.5.2.

17 Gillies, M., 'Brands learn staying power', *The Guardian*, 'Management', 26 June 1999, p. 20, quoting research by Ernst & Young and ACNielsen-BASE.

18 Mercer Management Consulting, *op. cit.*

19 Datta, D.K., Rinches, G.E. and Narayanan, V.K., 'Factors influencing wealth creation from mergers and acquisitions: a meta analysis', *Strategic Management Journal*, Vol. 13, No. 1, 1992, pp. 67–84.

20 Cannella, A.A. Jr and Hambrick, D.C., 'Effects of executive departures on the performance of acquired firms', *Strategic Management Journal*, Vol. 11, special edition, pp. 137–52.

21 Caves, R.E., 'Mergers, takeovers and economic efficiency foresight v. hindsight', *International Journal of Industrial Organization*, Vol. 7, No. 1, 1989, pp. 151–74.

22 Kitching, J., *Acquisitions in Europe: Causes of Corporate Successes and Failures*, Business International, 1973; and 'Why do mergers miscarry?' *Harvard Business Review*, November–December 1967, pp. 84–101.

23 Hunt, J., *op. cit.*

24 Bleeke, J. and Ernst, D., 'The way to win cross-border alliances', *Harvard Business Review*, November–December 1991, pp. 127–35.

25 Hunt, J., *op. cit.*

26 Kitching, J., *op. cit.*

27 Hunt, J., *op. cit.*

28 *Ibid.*

29 Kitching, J., *op. cit.*

30 Hunt, J., *op. cit.*

31 *Ibid.*

32 Cowe, R., 'Making sense of mergers', *The Guardian*, 'Management', 6 February 1999, p. 24.

33 Mercer Management Consulting, *op. cit.*

34 Moran, J., 'Review of enterprise computing', *Financial Times*, 25 February 1999, p. 4.

35 Simonian, H., 'The integrator arrives', *Financial Times*, 3 February 1999, p. 19.

36 Cowe, R., *op. cit.*

37 Dess, G.G. and Miller, A., *Strategic Management*, McGraw-Hill, 1993, p. 177.

38 Hamilton, R., Morison, I.C. and Ul-Haq, R., 'Strategic alliances – an alternative schema', Loughborough University Business School, Research Paper Series, No.3, 1995.

39 Lei, D., 'Offensive and defensive use of alliances', *Long Range Planning*, Vol. 26, No. 4, 1993, pp. 32–41; Lorange, P., Roos, J. and Bronn, P.S., 'Building successful strategic alliances', *Long Range Planning*, Vol. 25, No. 6, 1992, pp. 10–17; Gugler, P., 'Building transnational alliances to create competitive advantage', *Long Range Planning*, Vol. 25, No. 1, 1992, pp. 90–9.

40 Hamel, G., 'Competition for competence and inter-partnership learning within international strategic alliances', *Strategic Management Journal*, Vol. 12, 1991, pp. 83–103.

41 Porter, M.E., *The Competitive Advantage of Nations*, Macmillan, 1990, p. 613.

42 Lorange, P., Roos, J. and Bronn, P.S., *op. cit.*

43 Pekar, P. and Allio, R., 'Making alliances work – guidelines for success', *Long Range Planning*, Vol. 27, No. 4, 1994, pp. 54–65.

44 Brouthers, K.D., Brouthers, L.E. and Wilkinson, T.J., 'Strategic alliances: choose your partners', *Long Range Planning*, Vol. 28, No. 3, 1995, pp. 18–25.

45 Bleeke, J. and Ernst, D., *op. cit.*

46 Doz, Y.L., 'The evolution of cooperation in strategic alliances. Initial conditions or learning process?' *Strategic Management Journal*, Vol. 17, No. SISI, 1996, pp. 55–83.

47 Lei, D., *op. cit.*

48 Pekar, P. and Allio, R., *op. cit.*

49 Bleeke, J. and Ernst, D., *op. cit.*

50 Lorange, P., Roos, J. and Bronn, P.S., *op. cit.*

51 Turpin, G., 'Strategic alliances with Japanese firms – myths and realities', *Long Range Planning*, Vol. 26, No. 4, 1993, pp. 11–17.

52 *Ibid.*

53 *BDO Stoy Hayward Guide to the Alternative Investment Market*, BDO Stoy Hayward.

54 *Ibid.*

55 Samuels, J.M., Wilkes, F.M. and Brayshaw, R.E., *Financial Management and Decision Making*, International Thomson Business Press, 1999, p. 215.

56 *Ibid.*

CHAPTER

18 On-going portfolio management

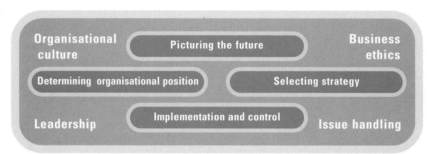

t his chapter is the last of the set of three that consider the distinct characteristics of parenting. The general direction of the corporation and the identification and establishment of the SBU and competence portfolios were considered in the two preceding chapters. This chapter deals with the on-going management of the chosen portfolios.

The chapter begins with a restatement of the scope of on-going portfolio management. The corporate organisational structure – the way in which the SBUs and the competences owned by the organisation might be structured – is then discussed in detail. The special features of maintaining alliances are considered. The next several sections explore how a parent can support the SBUs and the competences: providing corporation-wide services, including the important one of public relations; improving the performance of individual SBUs, including the forms of control that the parent can use to control its SBUs; improving the relationships between SBUs; and the nurturing of competences. Finally, there is a consideration of corporate governance.

Changes to the composition of a corporation's portfolios may be the most high-profile of activities in the world of business, but there are many 'bread-and-butter' activities that have as large if not a larger long-term impact on the success of a corporation. These on-going activities are also generally of considerably more concern to the corporation's subsidiary units. Thus it is important that leader-managers, both in the parent and in subsidiary units, understand what is involved.

LEARNING
OUTCOMES

When you have worked through this chapter, you should be able to:

- describe the different ways in which a corporation's businesses can be structured and explain the strengths and weaknesses of each structure;

- describe the ways in which competences can be structured;

- explain how a parent can best manage an alliance;

- list and critically examine the ways in which a parent can provide corporation-wide services;

- list and explain the ways in which a parent can improve individual SBU performance;

- list and explain the ways in which a parent can improve the relationships between SBUs;

- list and explain the ways in which a parent can nurture competences;

- explain the scope of corporate governance and what is entailed.

18.1 The scope of on-going portfolio management

The seven parenting roles in on-going portfolio management are listed in Exhibit 18.1. One significant consideration for SBU portfolio management is that the people who are parenting should have a good 'feel' for what makes the SBUs tick: they should have the tacit knowledge that allows them to see patterns in the situations in which the SBUs find themselves.

EXHIBIT 18.1

Parenting roles in on-going portfolio management

Determining the corporation's organisational structure

Supporting strategic alliances

Providing corporation-wide services

Improving individual SBU performance

Developing the relationships between SBUs

Nurturing competences

Maintaining appropriate corporate governance arrangements

18.2 The corporation's organisational structure

In a stand-alone business there is generally little contention as to where the functions should sit or who the heads of the functions should report to. However, since a corporation consists of (SBU) capabilities and (corporate) competences, the way in which units within the enterprise should be grouped and the associated lines of reporting and responsibilities become an issue. Broadly, the picture is as shown in Exhibit 18.2. The way in which the businesses in the corporation are structured depends on and reflects three features: the relationship between the parent and its constituent units; the relatedness of the SBUs to each other; and the degree of centralisation of the support services. The location of the competences, either within the businesses or held in dedicated, corporately controlled 'centres of excellence', is an important consideration, as are the linkages between the corporation and the (SBU) capabilities.

18.2.1 Parental relationships

The relationship between the parent and the rest of the corporation is obviously a significant feature of a corporation's organisational structure. This relationship is characterised by the number of the seven parenting roles that the parent wishes to

EXHIBIT 18.2

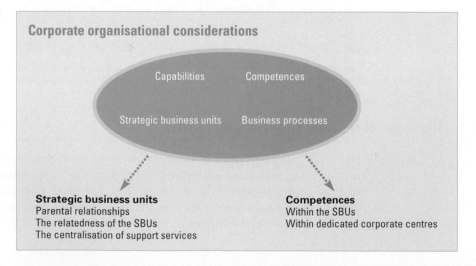

Corporate organisational considerations

Capabilities   Competences

Strategic business units   Business processes

Strategic business units
Parental relationships
The relatedness of the SBUs
The centralisation of support services

Competences
Within the SBUs
Within dedicated corporate centres

undertake. Two broad relationships can be identified, which lead to two types of structure: the holding company structure and the divisional structure. In the holding company structure the parent undertakes few of the parenting roles; in the divisional structure it tends to take on many of the roles.

The holding company structure

A holding company is a parent company that has shareholdings in one or more separate companies. These companies will almost always be operating companies, companies that themselves make offers and generate cash and profits. The holding company structure is shown in Exhibit 18.3.

In the holding company the linkages between the parent and its operating companies are kept to a minimum. The parent will restrict itself to providing very broad strategic direction, generally setting the boundaries on the scope of the businesses and setting financial targets for them. The parent will be concerned with maintaining appropriate governance arrangements. The parent will have some financial and legal expertise, but it is unlikely to be offered to the businesses. The holding company is the structure that suits a diversified organisation where the linkages between the businesses are effectively non-existent, or, rather, where the parent can't or doesn't want to add anything to what the businesses can do on their own.

The holding company structure has some advantages over a set of fully independent, stand-alone businesses. Its size may allow it to obtain finance at preferential rates. It can use its funds to subsidise the weaker or growing operating companies in its portfolio.[a]

EXHIBIT 18.3

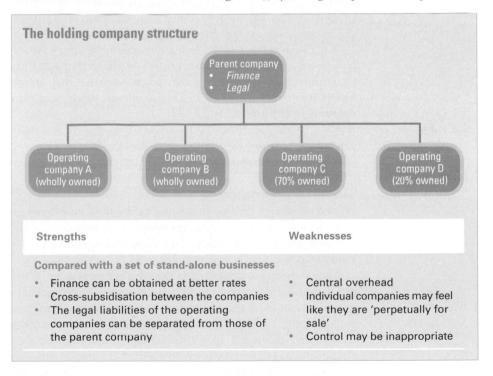

The holding company structure

Parent company
- *Finance*
- *Legal*

Operating company A (wholly owned) · Operating company B (wholly owned) · Operating company C (70% owned) · Operating company D (20% owned)

Strengths	Weaknesses

Compared with a set of stand-alone businesses

- Finance can be obtained at better rates
- Cross-subsidisation between the companies
- The legal liabilities of the operating companies can be separated from those of the parent company

- Central overhead
- Individual companies may feel like they are 'perpetually for sale'
- Control may be inappropriate

---

a   It could be argued that with the parent company keeping the operating companies at arm's length, it knows little more than the stock exchange and it should allow investors to make the investment decisions themselves.

EXHIBIT 18.4

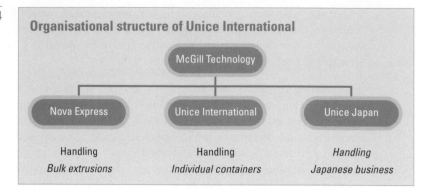

Organisational structure of Unice International

McGill Technology

Nova Express — Unice International — Unice Japan

Handling
Bulk extrusions

Handling
Individual containers

Handling
Japanese business

Rolls-Royce aero engines are in competition with those from General Electric and Pratt & Witney. GE generates only 8% of its turnover from aero engine-related business and Pratt & Witney just 27%, whereas Rolls-Royce generates a very large proportion of its revenues from aero engines. Rolls-Royce's competitors, especially GE, can fund development programmes much more easily than can Rolls-Royce.

Under UK law, the holding company is a separate legal entity to the operating companies and this allows the corporation to limit its liabilities: the liabilities residing with the companies rather than with the parent. This was the rationale for the holding company structure of Unice International,[b] a small company making frozen dessert-dispenser systems whose structure is shown in Exhibit 18.4. The intellectual property rights are held by the parent company and are protected from possible claims made against the three operating companies.

The disadvantages of the holding company structure *vis-à-vis* a set of stand-alone businesses are the, albeit small, central overhead that will be imposed on the operating companies and the feeling they might have that they are perpetually 'up for sale'. The parent company may also impose inappropriate controls on the activities of the operating companies.

DISCUSSION
POINT 18.1

In a holding company structure, what form of strategic objectives is the parent company likely to set for the operating companies?

The divisional structure

When considering divisional structures, 'division' means any grouping of capabilities. Usually, but not always, these groupings are equivalent to SBUs and thus a division contains one or more SBUs. The divisional organisational structure is shown in Exhibit 18.5.

The divisional structure offers the advantages associated with many of the roles of the parent listed in Exhibit 18.1. It can provide corporation-wide services, such as personnel and IT, that are more efficient and effective than those of independent SBUs could provide for themselves, and it can help improve individual SBU performance, for example through help with planning. It can improve the relationships between SBUs, releasing synergies between them. Very importantly, a divisionalised corporation can develop competences that may be used by several SBUs. The disadvantages are the central overhead and a potentially inappropriate parental influence.

b The company features in the case 'Shane McGill and One-shot'.

EXHIBIT 18.5

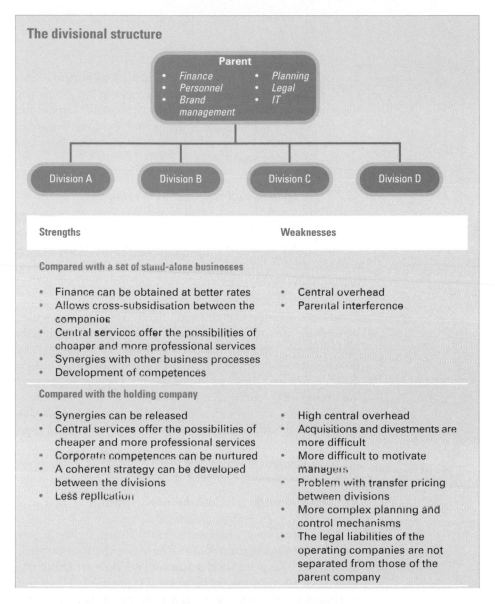

The divisional structure

Parent
- Finance
- Personnel
- Brand management
- Planning
- Legal
- IT

Division A   Division B   Division C   Division D

Strengths	Weaknesses

Compared with a set of stand-alone businesses

- Finance can be obtained at better rates
- Allows cross-subsidisation between the companies
- Central services offer the possibilities of cheaper and more professional services
- Synergies with other business processes
- Development of competences

- Central overhead
- Parental interference

Compared with the holding company

- Synergies can be released
- Central services offer the possibilities of cheaper and more professional services
- Corporate competences can be nurtured
- A coherent strategy can be developed between the divisions
- Less replication

- High central overhead
- Acquisitions and divestments are more difficult
- More difficult to motivate managers
- Problem with transfer pricing between divisions
- More complex planning and control mechanisms
- The legal liabilities of the operating companies are not separated from those of the parent company

Compared with the holding company, the divisionalised structure has a high central overhead because the parent carries out many more of the parenting functions. With such a slim head office, the holding company will put no effort into developing synergies, providing central services or nurturing corporate competences; indeed, corporate competences won't be recognised. Parents in a divisionalised structure can do all of these and produce a coherent strategy for the whole corporation. Replication of effort by the operating companies will be less than in a holding company. The planning and control mechanisms within the divisional structure will be more complex, and parents operating a divisional structure will need to consider their policy on the pricing of goods and services sold between their units. Parents in divisional organisations will find it harder than those within holding companies to set targets and the associated rewards and thus might find it harder to motivate the leader-managers in their units.

The holding company has companies within its portfolio, the divisional structure has divisions. The holding company carries out few of the parental roles, whereas the parent in a divisionalised company carries out many of them. A significant difference between the holding company and the divisional structure is the legal separation of liability between the parent and operating companies.

18.2.2 Companies and divisions – the relatedness between capabilities

The second consideration when selecting an appropriate SBU organisational structure is how to group the businesses in the divisions within the divisionalised structure and, less frequently, within the operating companies in a holding company. As a general rule, groupings will depend on the degree of relatedness of the activities of the constituent units.

The subdivisions between groups may be by product or by market. Exhibit 18.6a illustrates the product subdivision used by 3M. The assumption is that the relatedness between the activities of the automotive business is closer than that between those of any other business, and that the five businesses in the automotive and chemical industry group are more closely related to each other than to any other of the businesses within the industrial and consumer sector. Finally, the four industry groups that make up the industrial and consumer sector will be more closely related to each other than they are to any industry groups within the life sciences sector. Exhibit 18.6b illustrates a grouping that could form the basis for a division and subdivision grouping based on markets.

DISCUSSION POINT 18.2

In Exhibit 18.6, two structures, one based on products and one based on geographical areas, have been illustrated. What other possible structures are there?

A detailed example of a divisionalised structure is that of Lloyds TSB, shown in Exhibit 18.7.

If a corporation is composed of fairly distinct businesses, each selling one range of offers into one market, it would then be reasonable to arrange for the division to be made up of SBUs. This would be the case where the corporation consisted of national operations, such as retail banking. However, 3M provides an illustration of a corporation that is selling a great number of offers in a great number of markets. Here it wouldn't make sense to have completely separate production functions for each market, or separate salesforces for each product. Consequently, it makes sense to combine production and marketing in some way. The full-blooded way is to operate a matrix structure.

The matrix structure

In the matrix structure, each operating unit has responsibility for both the sales and marketing in an area and the products that are sold there. Above this level are one or more layers of marketing managers and product managers who have overall responsibility for marketing and for the product. The two sides to 3M's activities, juxtaposed in Exhibit 18.6, illustrate the problem: there will need to be someone or some unit responsible for marketing filtration products in Eastern Europe, for example.

EXHIBIT 18.6

Product and market corporate structures

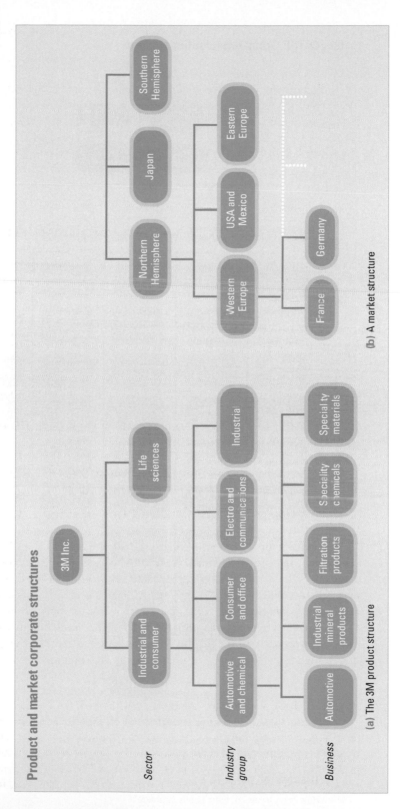

(a) The 3M product structure

(b) A market structure

EXHIBIT 18.7

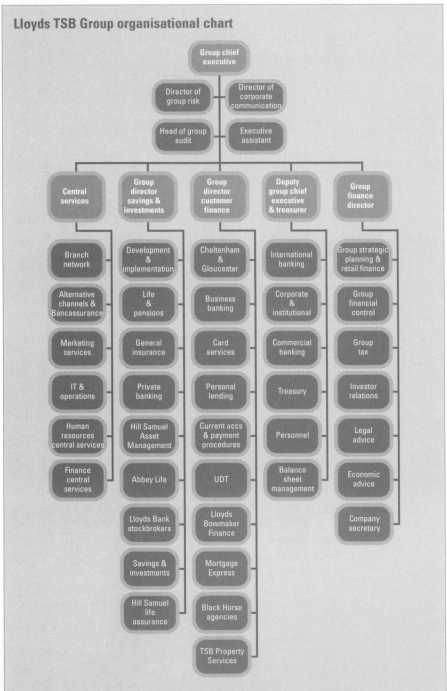

Lloyds TSB Group organisational chart

Source: Lloyds TSB Group plc internal planning documentation from summer 1997.

Note: Easter 1998 saw the introduction of two new executive positions, namely group director UK retail banking and group director wholesale markets & international banking.

Discussion point 18.2

How many levels are there in this structure?
- Which is the business level in this organisational structure?
- Which are the support functions?
- For Unice International and Lloyds TSB, are the subdivisions by market or by product?

A matrix structure is shown in Exhibit 18.8. Compared with an organisation based on almost autonomous SBUs the matrix structure has certain advantages. The salesforce is likely to be more efficient, being able to offer a wider portfolio of offers than would be possible if it were working for only one SBU. Brand/offer management will maintain the characteristics of the brand/offer over all markets. The downside of this is that the salesforce is likely to be less dedicated and less knowledgeable about the offers. Small decisions can be made locally and large decisions will be more informed, with the decision makers knowing both sides of the product–market situation. On the other hand, decisions are likely to take longer as two chains of command are involved. Having responsibility for both product and market should develop managers into more general managers, but at the cost of the dual chains of responsibility leading to greater management stress levels. Planning and control are likely to be more complex within a matrix structure. An example of a matrix organisation, that of a school, is also shown in Exhibit 18.8.

KEY CONCEPT   The relatedness between activities is the rationale for the grouping of units within a divisionalised organisation. For a simple divisionalised organisation there may be only one level of grouping; for a complex organisation there may be several. Groupings can be based mainly on the relatedness of products or on markets, giving rise to an SBU structure, or a combination of the two in a matrix structure. Within an SBU structure, each person has one line of command and responsibility and this leads to rapid decision making. Operating in a matrix organisation is more demanding, with two bosses to consider. However, the matrix organisation offers faster managerial development and more informed, albeit slower, decision making.

18.2.3   International configurations

Organisations that operate internationally have a special concern with organisation structure. Firms will begin in one country and almost invariably will initially have their production facilities and head office located there, in what Omhae[1] terms the *mother country*. Initially, they will almost always begin by supplying solely their home market. In wishing to move to supply foreign markets, there are two significant and perhaps conflicting pressures. First, there is the pressure to become and remain responsive to foreign markets – to satisfy the differing demands as they arise. Second, there is pressure to use the scope offered by operating abroad – both economies of scale and the ability to tap into the differing expertise that resides abroad. These two pressures suggest the four configurations that are shown in Exhibit 18.9.

Neither the exporting nor the multi-domestic firm exports much home-based production. The exporting firm is firmly based in its mother country, with any exporting likely to be on an opportunistic basis; certainly, the international operations are likely to be secondary to the domestic activities. The multi-domestic firm consists of several units operating almost independently, each in a home base that is similar to a mother country, having its own production capacity and a country head office. Each unit tends to export very little – almost all its production is destined for its own home market.

Both the colonial and the transnational are firms that export a considerable proportion of their home-based production. The colonial firm does this from its mother country, producing little abroad. A colonial (and an exporting) firm are characterised as selling a standard product in many countries. The Ford Motor Company has moved a considerable way towards this position.

EXHIBIT 18.8

The matrix structure

Parent
- Finance
- Personnel
- Brand management
- Planning
- Legal
- IT

	Area V	Area W	Area X	Area Y	Area Z
Offer group A					
Offer group B		*Operating units*			*Operating units*
Offer group C					
Offer group D					

Strengths	Weaknesses

Compared with SBU operations

Strengths	Weaknesses
• More efficient salesforce • Enables the characteristics of similar offers made in different markets to be controlled • Small decisions can be taken locally • Decision making is more informed and able to cope with increasing complexity • Management development will be enhanced	• Less effective salesforce • Large-scale decision making will tend to be slower and more diffuse • Dual responsibilities can cause confusion and tension • Acquisitions and divestments are more difficult • Change is more difficult to implement • More complex planning and control mechanisms

The matrix structure of a school

		Subject groups		
		Head of science	Head of languages	Head of history
Student groups	Year 7			
	Year 8			
	Sixth form			

EXHIBIT 18.9

International configurations

Pressure for international co-ordination	High	Colonial	Transnational
	Low	Exporting	Multi-domestic
		Low	High

Pressure for national market responsiveness

DISCUSSION
POINT 18.4

What are the organisational needs if a firm wishes to be a colonial firm?
- Is Ford an exporting or a colonial firm?

Bartlett and Ghoshal[2] consider that the transnational firm is the most effective configuration. It shares with the colonial firm the advantages of scope that a company with global reach can have (for example being able to use low-cost labour), yet it shares with the multi-domestic firm the advantages of being locally responsive – responsive to the tastes and standards of the local marketplace. Senior managers in such an organisation must think in terms of managing a network of associates rather than of operating within a hierarchy: a network of centres for each of research, development, component manufacture, assembly and distribution. In the ultimate, there would be no head office and no home country. Transnational organisations are currently fairly rare: ABB Asea Brown Boveri under Percy Barnevik is a company that would appear to be approaching the transnational form.

The Taiwan-based Giant Bicycle Company would appear to be acting as a transnational.[3] One of its biggest markets is the EU, and it manufactures in the Netherlands so as to be close to this major market, as well as in China and Taiwan. Three-quarters of the bikes it sells around the world are the same, but the other quarter has a regional flavour. Bikes are as much a fashion item as a mode of transport in some markets: in mid-1990 Giant introduced five to ten new models a year. As well as spreading its production it has designers in Taiwan, China, Japan, the USA and the Netherlands. Chinese and Japanese customers seek commuting bikes, the Dutch designers contribute ideas from the European racing scene and the US designers are working on mountain bike variants. The designers work together using computer-aided design facilities and get together twice a year in Taiwan.

18.2.4 Centralisation of support services

One of the abiding questions in organisations is where to locate the support services. Each operating unit will need to have some support services, but in a large company there is the question of how much of certain functions, such as accounting, IT and personnel, should be decentralised. Except to service its own very small requirements, the holding company offers no support services. The parent in a divisionalised company may control all the support services or it may delegate responsibility to the divisions and to the businesses. Sometimes all the functions will be present at all levels: for example, the parent formulating the overall personnel policy, but allowing the divisions and subsequently the businesses to interpret it as appropriate. Different interpretations would generally be called for if the company were a multinational, with several cultures and structures of employment law to contend with. IT is a function that has seen itself move from a very centralised function based on mainframes, through to decentralised computing as the cost of PCs fell to a level where their purchase was within middle managers' budgets, becoming partly recentralised once more in response to enterprise resource planning.

18.2.5 Production and markets

Exporting and colonial firms are characterised as selling standard products in all their markets. While this obviously suggests that its production facilities are standardised, it's important to realise that standardisation of production doesn't necessarily mean that there is standardisation of markets. Exhibit 18.10 illustrates this.[4]

The difference in prices reflects the different nature of the markets. Although Exhibit 18.10 applies to the EU, the same could be said about global markets. Commodity items such as metals and oil, and such items as aircraft and aircraft engines, are traded in global markets, but it's rarer for consumer goods or services to be global.

EXHIBIT 18.10

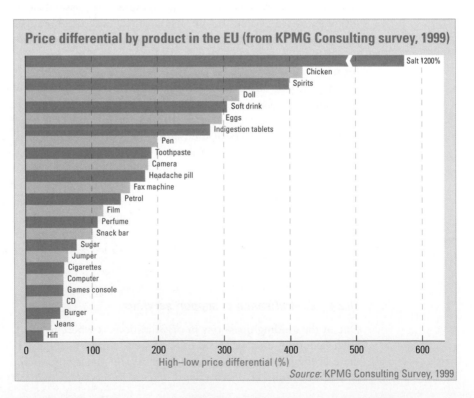

Price differential by product in the EU (from KPMG Consulting survey, 1999)

Salt 1200%
Chicken
Spirits
Doll
Soft drink
Eggs
Indigestion tablets
Pen
Toothpaste
Camera
Headache pill
Fax machine
Petrol
Film
Perfume
Snack bar
Sugar
Jumper
Cigarettes
Computer
Games console
CD
Burger
Jeans
Hifi

High–low price differential (%)

0   100   200   300   400   500   600

Source: KPMG Consulting Survey, 1999

KEY CONCEPT Four international configurations can be identified, characterised by the pressures to be responsive nationally and to co-ordinate international activities. A distinction must be made between international/global production and international/global markets: international/global production doesn't mean that there is a international/global market. In a truly global market customers can buy from anywhere in the world and prices are the same worldwide.

18.2.6 Competences

A key point about a competence is that it is available to many SBUs and not 'owned' by any one of them; it is a corporate resource. However, a corporation's competences may be located within particular SBUs, may be dispersed over several SBUs and local research and development (R&D) units, or may be located within divisional or corporate R&D units. These configurations are shown in Exhibit 18.11.

In (a), competences are shown residing totally within SBUs. SBU A is shown holding a competence involving two processes, and SBU C's competence involves three processes. In (b), the competence is considered to be more diffuse, with portions of it residing in several SBUs. For example, the skills and technology associated with adhesives resides in many SBUs within 3M; many competences reside in many centres and countries within ABB Asea Brown Boveri. In (c), the competence resides at the corporate level: for 3M, this was the case for many years with its competence in micro-replication, although now, with many consumer products available, the position is more akin to that shown in (b). Pattern (c) is typical of the big Japanese corporations.[5] Canon is a corporation operating pattern (c), where competences are held almost exclusively at the corporate level.[6] Matsushita has divisions of consumer electronics, industrial equipment, business machines, home appliances, lighting equipment systems products and electronic components. These divisions share R&D and use the output from the electronic components division and then compete in their own segments. Western companies also operate to pattern (c), for example IBM, Philips, ICI, DEC and Apple.[7]

The corporation may not own the competence it seeks to employ. One option is to use universities to carry out the basic research, with the application research and

EXHIBIT 18.11

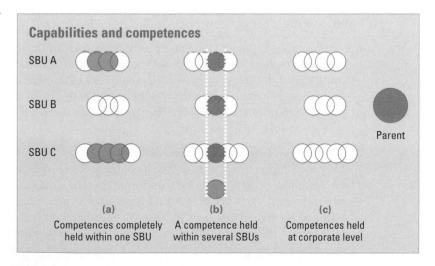

Capabilities and competences

SBU A

SBU B

SBU C

Parent

(a)
Competences completely held within one SBU

(b)
A competence held within several SBUs

(c)
Competences held at corporate level

development taking place within the corporation. For example, Rolls-Royce has for many years funded university departments through its University Techology Centre programme.

18.2.7 Linking (corporate) competences and (business) capabilities

It is becoming increasingly recognised that especially in areas of fast-moving technology, it is vital that technological competences are swiftly moved into existing SBUs or are used to develop new SBUs. The parent has an important role here, especially as competences are primarily the concern of the parent and particularly if they are held in a corporate centre or through a parental link with another institution, such as a university or a self-standing research institution. At microchip designer ARM a very significant role is played by the vice-president of business operations, who has the responsibility of ensuring that the technology developments of the R&D engineers flows to its worldwide markets.

18.3 Supporting strategic alliances

The discussion in the previous sections has been almost exclusively concerned with how to organise units that are owned by the corporation and controlled by it. In an alliance the parent needs to exercise influence rather than control, and the way forward has a different emphasis. In her search for lessons from productive alliances, Kanter[8] focused on the importance of intercompany relationships, noting that, in their preoccupation with the economies of a deal, companies frequently neglect the political, cultural and organisational aspects of a relationship.

Five main aspects of alliance management can be identified:

- Senior management involvement   The continual involvement of top management in an alliance is a way of developing a clear direction for the collaboration and creating a reservoir of goodwill to draw on if tensions develop in the venture at a later date.[9] Needless to say, the interest of senior management in any aspect of a business demonstrates its importance and sends a signal to the rest of the organisation that it is an activity that is valued and must receive appropriate effort and attention.

- The resources to share   Giving up autonomy over strategic resources and/or core competences can be one of the most difficult things for a company to contemplate.[10] Once they have been committed to an alliance, companies must share these resources with their new partner if resentment is not to develop, and recognise that they are no longer free to make decisions on how to use what was once exclusively their own.

- The quality of the alliance team   Alliances are typically difficult to work in. They are often in areas that stretch a company's expertise and knowledge, so there are few people to fall back on for advice and guidance. Alliances evolve and change quickly, bringing constant pressure to adapt, and there are often conflicts of interest that need to be resolved. Alliances need to attract and retain high-calibre staff, and to facilitate this the parent companies need to ensure that opportunities in the alliance are treated as high-quality, career-enhancing positions and not, for example, as pre-retirement jobs for ageing executives. They also need to consider the route back into the organisation for those individuals joining the alliance and appreciate the risks that these people are taking in joining a venture that doesn't necessarily have a long-term future.

In these circumstances compensation packages need to be entrepreneurial in structure and reflect the nature of the project.[11] This often leads to incentives different from those appropriate for the parent companies; in particular, careful consideration needs to be given to linking remuneration with performance against long-term strategic targets, as well as with the more traditional and shorter-term financial measures, since success in the early years is generally not as important as creating a positive environment for growing the alliance in the longer term.

- **The roles of team members**   Positions in new alliances, by their nature, are much more ambiguous than those in traditional organisations, which makes it more difficult to define precise responsibilities and duties. However, this ambiguity makes it more important to define roles carefully, not just as a way of telling individuals what their responsibilities are but also for communicating with the rest of the alliance. Role definition should be such that it fosters loyalty to the alliance, not to the parent, as this helps to develop the focus and motivation necessary to make the alliance work.

- **Interpersonal relationships**   This is key to the success of any alliance and is particularly important in 'relationship' cultures like those of East Asia. Although it's not easy to establish good relationships between firms from very different business cultures, it is even harder to sustain them. Operational and cultural differences will emerge after collaboration is underway, and these dissimilarities need to be worked out, and much more communication is required than anyone could have anticipated.[12] Theoretical synergies don't develop in practice until many people in both organisations know one another personally and become willing to make the effort to exchange technology, refer clients or participate in joint teams. Strong interpersonal relationships help resolve small conflicts before they escalate.

18.4   Providing corporation-wide services

It could well be that it would be inappropriate for each SBU independently to gain access to the same or similar resources. In some circumstances it makes sense for the parent to take responsibility for making resources available to all the SBUs. Considerations leading to the provision of services centrally are:

- **Scale effects**   There are many areas where either the parent has the capabilities that the businesses are too small to have, or alternatively it can strike a better deal when out-sourcing. One examples would be in IT, where the parent can get a better out-sourcing deal for the entire corporate requirements (as Rolls-Royce plc did when out-sourcing most of its IT to EDS). A particularly important area is where the parent is likely to obtain better rates when borrowing finance.

- **Specialist expertise**   There are several areas of expertise where it wouldn't make sense for a corporation to have several experts in its SBUs. The parent would be the natural home for expertise on employment law and on health and safety legislation, for example.

- **Day-to-day services**   There are many ways in which a parent can offer services of a bread-and-butter kind to the SBUs. They can provide such things as training, help with recruitment, running payroll applications and assistance in devising personnel practices.

- **Branding and reputation**   If a brand is to be an international one, then it's the responsibility of the parental brand managers to manage it. Similarly with reputation: many parents seek to use the reputation developed with one service/product to extend it to other services/products. A very good example of this is Virgin, which is using its brand name and the reputation of Richard Branson to spread its activities into financial services and train services. This is a prime example of 'corporate branding'.

- **Public relations**   Although individual businesses will be involved in public relations, it can become a parental concern with the large scale of lawsuits and the knock-on effects that bad public relations for a constituent unit can have on the whole corporation. Exhibit 18.12[13] illustrates this.

18.5   Improving individual SBU performance

There are three main ways in which the parent can improve individual SBU performance:

- **Senior SBU appointments and coaching**   One of the most significant roles for the parent is to determine who leads each of the constituent SBUs. A good choice can add great value. This is where the feel of the parent for the SBUs comes in. With this feel they have considerable knowledge of the sort of senior appointment to make. A further influence that the parent can have is in coaching SBU leaders to better performance.

- **Help to determine SBU strategy**   A parent can have a significant effect on the strategic direction of an SBU if it helps in strategy development and/or subjects the SBU's strategic management processes to rigorous appraisal. Such an appraisal can force SBU management to reflect more deeply on what it is doing and proposing, and also allows the expertise in the parent to be made available to the SBU. One of the parenting styles found by Goold and Campbell[14] was what they termed the strategic planning style, where the parent and each SBU worked together to formulate the SBU strategy. This joint approach allows the parent to expose potential synergies between SBUs and where competences could be used. It also allows the parent to input its own experience during the scenario-building processes. Exhibit 18.13 illustrates the process, while Exhibit 18.14 reproduces the planning *pro forma* used by Deutsche Bank to support its strategic planning style. Each year, each SBU completes this 'questionnaire' prior to discussions with the parent.

- **Imposing challenging strategic objectives**   The strategic planning style of relationship between the parent and its SBUs was only one of the three styles identified by Goold and Campbell.[15] The three styles are shown in Exhibit 18.15.

EXHIBIT 18.12

Law and the profits of PR (Monbiot, 1997)

Every month, the weapons mobilised in the public relations battle over the future of the planet become more sophisticated. A few weeks ago, a leak from PR company Burson-Marsteller revealed that it has been advising biotechnology companies to 'stay off the killing field' of the environment and human health, as 'the industry cannot be expected to prevail in public opposition to adversarial voices on these issues.' Other means had to be found of confronting opposition to genetic engineering.

This week, perhaps in response to similar advice, BP shifted the debate about its oil-prospecting work away from the Atlantic frontier and into the courts. On Monday, it began a suit against Greenpeace for the £1.4 million it claimed it had lost as a result of the group's occupation of a test-drilling rig near the Shetland Islands. If the organisation would not pay, BP said, it would hold three members of Greenpeace's staff personally liable. By Tuesday evening, the company was offering to abandon the suit if Greenpeace promised to keep out of its oilfields. BP has been deploying smart PR bombs throughout this ritual conflict. While Greenpeace sought to draw attention to climate change and the dumping of toxic residues on the ocean floor, BP concentrated on the safety of the activists chained to the oil rig, announcing that it would try to pull them off only if their lives were in danger. It succeeded both in drawing the press away from the critical issues and in presenting itself as a compassionate company, which puts human welfare ahead of filthy lucre. The sheriff evicting protesters at Manchester Airport deployed precisely the same tactic – the tunnellers, he said, were a danger to themselves, who had to be removed for their own good.

BP's lawsuit, which it delayed until police had removed the activists from the public eye, enabled it to drag the debate still further away from environmental arguments. Public discussion shifted to Greenpeace's assets and whether or not they should or could be seized. BP could distance itself from the dispute – arguing that the matter was now in the hands of the courts – while ensuring that the moral pressure remained on Greenpeace: if it did not pay up, it would expose its own staff to the suit. Now BP can pick up the mantle of magnanimity, while retaining a powerful new missile (the threat of reopening the case) with which to deter its opponents.

Had BP pursued its suit, seized Greenpeace's assets and, as some people predicted, wiped the organisation out, it would have found itself portrayed as an oceanic shark, snapping up defenceless tiddlers. But suits of this nature are seldom designed to succeed. In the United States they are so common that they have acquired a name of their own: 'strategic lawsuits against public participation', and the emphasis is firmly on the 'strategic'. About three-quarters of the charges of conspiracy, defamation or criminal liability that big companies pursue against American activists are dropped or thrown out of court, often after years of litigation. But both the charges themselves and the costs of fighting a case tend to stifle dissent, scaring protesters into mute acquiescence.

The first major case of this kind in Britain was pursued by the Department of Transport against people opposing its cutting through Twyford Down. The department's injunction named as many campaigners as it could identify, some of whom had only the most fleeting involvement in the protest. They were held 'jointly and severally liable' for the DoT's legal costs and damages – which amounted to around £2 million.

The department pursued them for three years, its demands for payment gradually falling from tens of thousands of pounds each, to £1000 to £500, before it quietly dropped the case altogether. But the lawsuit worked. Hundreds of people with assets kept away from Twyford Down, worried that they too might find themselves subject to the costs order. The campaign was left largely to the property-less and dispossessed, which helped the DoT to portray its opponents as a bunch of work-shy troublemakers, only protesting because they had nothing better to do.

The injunction's success, of course, was dependent on its failure. The last thing the department wanted to do was to seize the home of a respectable taxpayer. McDonald's twice flew senior managers over to England to try to stop the libel case it had initiated against two penniless protesters who had insisted on fighting to the end. Though they lost on several points of law, they won a resounding moral victory, as McDonald's was forced to carry out its threat to crush the butterfly on the wheel.

BP's lawsuit is one of many indications of an increasingly legalistic approach to public debate. Companies opposed by animal-rights protesters are now using the anti-stalking laws to stop them handing leaflets to their customers. Construction firms have used secondary-picketing legislation to deter roads protesters, while the 1994 Criminal Justice Act and the 1986 Public Order Act provide endless opportunities for criminalising dissent.

New legislation in the United States offers even more effective means of suppressing free speech: 14 states have now adopted bizarre 'food disparagement acts', banning insulting remarks about perishable food. Last year a group of ranchers filed a suit against the *Oprah Winfrey Show* after Oprah expressed her horror at the practice of feeding ruminant offal to cattle. She has kept her mouth sealed on this topic (if no other) ever since.

As both British and American laws tend to be more effective at protecting private property than public assets, the scope for retaliatory counter-suits is limited. Instead, environmentalists should continue to call the corporations' bluff, force them to pursue their suits and let them suffer the public humiliation of a brutal victory. Only then might the big companies be inclined to test their case not in the stuffy enclave of the courts but in the fresh air and open seas of public debate.

In **financial control** companies the parent plays little part in developing strategy and restricts itself to setting demanding financial targets. **Strategic control** parents combine well-developed strategic planning systems with demanding, short-term financial targets.

The characteristics of the two 'extreme' forms – strategic planning and financial control – are summarised in Exhibit 18.16.

DISCUSSION
POINT 18.5

Which style – strategic planning, financial control or strategic control – would most suit a holding company structure and which a divisionalised structure?

Inappropriate objectives set by a parent can be damaging. Illustrations of the consequences of inappropriate objectives are shown in Exhibit 18.17.

Interestingly, the corporation can also deliberately affect the performance of an SBU adversely in the interests of the corporation as a whole. Häagen-Dazs was a subsidiary of Pillsbury, a firm with a turnover in 1984 of $4 billion and which owned such well-known firms as Green Giant and Burger King. Häagen-Dazs management had threatened its distributors that it would cancel their contracts if they took to

EXHIBIT 18.13

Strategic planning in Lloyds TSB (McConchie, 1998)

There are three strands to Group Strategic Planning. Group consultancy working with businesses to develop value maximising strategies – helping them formulate strategy, helping them set milestones, helping them understand what the deliverables look like and the value of these deliverables, helping them understand the key value drivers and how they are going to change over time... it's very detailed, it's very interesting, it's extremely time consuming, it's very labour intensive. So that's one side. The second side is to do with monitoring, which will review and monitor the plan and report by exception to the main Board. They're also involved in group competitor analysis – they pool together a lot of competitor analysis that is taking place across the group and then provide a group perspective on it. Because sometimes you... might discover that one of our principal competitors in one area does not even appear on the radar in another area... What we do at Group is to have an understanding of capabilities. The chances are that if Hong Kong Bank is good in one area, if it puts its mind to it it can be good in another. So we would alert the business that didn't consider them as competitors that if push came to shove they could be and we would explain why and get them to take it into their thinking.

We ask a number of questions: what has this done to the competitive position within the market economics, have the value drivers changed? Is this now a different market to what it was originally? If so, how are we positioned in the new market compared with the old one? Do we have the tools to compete and be effective there? If so then carry on: if not, then is it helpful to the new direction or do we need something different?

I guess that you would say that the businesses knew an awful lot about how to run their business but very little about what the competition was doing and they were sort of reacting to it, whereas now the review has forced them to develop a sort of database and model of competitive behaviour, which is also a sort of reality check that does force them to consider not just how they will respond to changes in the market place, but also how the competition will respond.

(Interview with a senior strategist, Lloyds TSB)

distributing Ben & Jerry's ice cream. Ben & Jerry started a law suit and targeted the parent – through the Pillsbury Doughboy, the symbol of Pillsbury – with the slogan 'What's the Doughboy afraid of?' This was very embarrassing to Pillsbury, which forced the Häagen-Dazs management to sign an agreement not to put pressure on the distributors.[17]

18.6 Developing the relationships between SBUs

Porter[18] sees the main role of the parent as managing the relationships between the SBUs in the corporate portfolio. He sees releasing synergy as the *raison d'être* of the parent; for example through shared distribution or cross selling. More precisely, the parent needs to release the synergy that the businesses themselves are overlooking. The downside of synergy seeking may be a lack of focus; alternatively, the downside of focus is that the SBU optimises itself for a brief period of time and is unable to adjust to new market forces.

There are several ways in which SBUs can usefully collaborate:

EXHIBIT 18.14

The Deutsche Bank strategic planning framework 1997
GD Investment Banking (IB)

Contents

1   Market position and competitive environment
    1.1   Market position of the strategic business units
    1.2   External influences on the competitive position of the SBUs

2   Resource-based analysis of IB
    2.1   Resource endowment of the SBUs
    2.2   Valuation of SBU resources
    2.3   Confirmation of strategically critical resources

3   Resource-based strategic objectives and measures
    3.1   Qualitative objectives
        3.1.1.   GD objectives
        3.1.2.   SBU objectives
    3.2   Strategic measures
    3.3   Quantitative outcome

4   Divisional mission statement

1   Market position and competitive environment

1.1 Market position of the strategic business units
(Identify the current strategic business units of IB and evaluate their competitive position in the relevant regional markets. Consider market share, growth, products/services and profitability.)

1.2 External influences on the competitive position of the SBUs
(Describe the significant market trends which will influence the competitive position of the SBUs within the next few years. Particular reference is to be made to current and future trends in the economic environment, in technology, in the market/competitive structure, in regulation and in EMU.)

- Macro-economic trends
  (e.g. compare with brochure 'Mittelfrist-Ausblick 1997–2001' of db research)
- Technological trends
  (e.g. distribution channels, production processes, information systems)
- Market and competitive trends
  (e.g. consumer habits, mergers, market entrants/exiters, non-bank competitors)
- Regulatory trends
  (e.g. national/supranational regulation, taxation)
- EMU
  (e.g. chances, risks, costs, earnings)

2   Resource-based analysis of IB

2.1 Resource endowment of the SBUs
(Identify the important resources of the individual SBUs of IB on a disaggregated level of analysis. Distinction is to be made between tangible and intangible resources, and capabilities. Characterise the resources in terms of the categories indicated in the table.

Resources that do not qualify in regard to the five tests may be liabilities for the SBU. They are to be notified accordingly.)

- tangible resources
- intangible resources
- capabilities
- liabilities

Resources	Demand		Scarcity		Appropriability
	Does the resource create value to the customer? ('Utility')	Is the resource competitively superior? ('Comp. Superiority')	Is the resource hard to copy? ('Inimitability')	Is the resource hard to substitute? ('Non-substitutability')	Can DB capture the value created by the resource?
Resource 1	( )	( )	( )	( )	( )
Resource 2	( )	( )	( )	( )	( )
...	...	...	...	...	...

(+++) correct; (++) mainly correct; (+) partly correct

2.2 Valuation of SBU resources

(Evaluate the identified resources relative to those of the key competitors or other benchmark firms. Indicate to what extent the resources are and will be competitively critical for the SBUs. Include also those critical resources which the SBUs have yet to develop.)

	Which are the key resource competitors? (benchmark firms)	How does the resource rate vis-à-vis the peers?	Is the resource competitively critical for the SBU?	
	(Name)	(Score)	1997	2001
SBU A				
Resource 1				
Resource 2				
...				
SBU B				
Resource 1				
...				

1 = substantially weaker; 5 = substantially stronger   1 = not critical; 5 = absolutely critical

2.3 Confirmation of strategically critical resources
(Name the resources with criticality for prospective competitive advantages of the SBUs. Differentiate between SBU-specific resources and those with relevance at group division level. Substantiate your choice.)

3 Resource-based strategic objectives and measures

3.1 Qualitative objectives

3.1.1 GD objectives
(Identify and qualify maximum five strategic objectives for IB and the implications for the resource endowment associated with the objectives. Define and describe your future core SBU portfolio with reference to the regional scope. Reconsider your future core SBU portfolio on the premise of a cost-cutting target of 10% within 2 years (base year 1996) at group division level. Give reasons for your modifications.)

- Strategic GD objectives
- Implications for the resource endowment
- Strategic core SBU portfolio

Core SBU	Regional scope	Specification of core SBU
Core SBU 1	...	...
Core SBU 2	...	...
...	...	...

- Potential modifications of the strategic core BA portfolio to respect a 10% cost-cutting target

3.1.2 SBU objectives
(Identify and describe maximim three distinct strategic objectives for your core and non-core SBUs.)

- Objectives for core SBUs
- Objectives for non-core SBUs

3.2 Strategic measures
(Specify the measures you want to initiate (or have already initiated) in order to reconcile the resource endowment of IB with the strategic objectives. Potential acquisitions, co-operations, divestments, spin-offs, and structural and procedural measures are to be disclosed. Qualify these measures particularly with respect to the following categories: continuous investment in resources; upgrading of resources; leveraging of resources. Assess them regarding their relative contribution to the realisation of the strategic objectives, and give details about expected costs, inherent risks and the time-frame involved.)

3.3 Quantitative outcome
(Quantify the prospective outcomes of the strategic measures as per 2001 provided they will be implemented according to plan. Use the ratios as indicated in the table. The 1996 figures will have to be extrapolated from the latest available data.)

	1996	2001e
Gross performance		
Risk provisions		
Cost/income ratio		
Return on equity		
Return on assets		

4   Divisional mission statement

(Formulate a divisional mission statement – half a page maximum.)

Frankfurt am Main, June 2, 1997

EXHIBIT 18.15

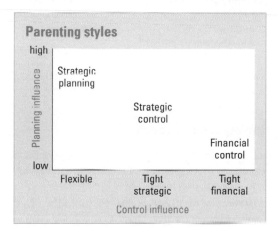

Parenting styles

- **Spreading best practice**   By which the parent encourages groups of SBUs to use each other as benchmarks and in this way spread best practice. This is spreading knowledge – of processes and of technology. In the past BAT Industries has grouped its worldwide tobacco operations into sets of triplets – for example, Brazil, Germany and the UK – with the members of the triplets looking at the other's activities to see what they could find of benefit to themselves.

- **Spreading skills**   Linked somewhat to spreading best practice. Skills are tacit knowledge that can't be codified, and the only real way of spreading these is to move the people who have these skills. The parent has the role through its personnel policies of moving its personnel around the corporation, inculcating others with the skills they have and learning new skills to pass on subsequently.

- **Sharing data**   It is useful, particularly in the financial services sector, to use customer data to cross-sell services. For example, someone with a mortgage will have their data available to the SBU that is selling insurance. The availablity of enterprise resource planning systems is an aid to this. The gains from data aggregation was the genesis of GUS's development of Experian.

EXHIBIT 18.16

Characteristics of the strategic planning and financial control styles

Strategic planning	Financial control
• The parent is deeply involved in SBU strategy development	• SBU managers are responsible for strategy development
• The SBUs are isolated from short-term financial pressures	• The parent exerts influence through short-term budgetary controls
• Synergies between SBUs can be exploited	• Few potential synergies are realised
• Fosters the creation of ambitious strategies	• There is a bias against investments with long lead times and paybacks
• A wide variety of views may be put forward	• Good at developing executives with a 'winner psychology'
• The SBUs will be less risk-averse	• SBUs will tend to be risk-averse, having to meet the monthy/quarterly financial targets
• SBU managers may have motivational problems as there may be little ownership of strategy	• Can be responsive to changing market conditions
• A diminished flexibility to respond quickly to changing markets	• Shakes managers loose from bad strategies
• The corporation may persist with losing strategies for too long	

EXHIBIT 18.17

Examples of counterproductive controls

One of the controls instituted by the National Health Service (NHS) on NHS hospitals covered the time patients in Accident and Emergency had to wait before receiving attention. In 1998 it was revealed that some hospitals were employing 'Hello nurses', who would greet patients when they first arrived: subsequently, the patients would be left for a considerable time before they were given medical attention. This subterfuge allowed hospitals to meet the letter of the targets set concerning delays in patient treatment if not the spirit.

Every police service in the UK has to report the incidence of serious crimes to the Home Office; less serious crimes are recorded locally but not reported to the Home Office. In 1999 it was reported that some police forces were massaging the crime rates and clear-up figures. The temptation, not resisted, was to downgrade crimes; for example muggings, which were a serious crime and had to be reported, were listed as theft. As theft was a crime which did not need to be reported, the reported crime rate was reduced. Reported clear-up rates were improved by encouraging people to admit to crimes they had not committed. On one occasion a criminal was allowed prison leave in exchange for admitting to stealing 70 cars that he had never even seen![16]

• **Co-operation when dealing with stakeholders** It can be beneficial for SBUs to share distribution channels or to combine when facing a powerful supplier. This allows start-up activities or activities with low activation rates to 'piggyback' on the activities of others.

18.7   Nurturing competences

The building and nurturing of competences are associated strongly with research and development (R&D).[19] The whole of an organisation's R&D should be seen as a continuous stream of competence-building projects, not as a series of isolated efforts. Hamel and Prahaled[20] describe how Canon overtook Xerox with a fraction of the spend on R&D through a focused R&D strategy. However, an R&D strategy can't sensibly be pursued in isolation from the rest of the corporation. The business strategy will concentrate on the broad range of products that the organisation wishes to have and the broad markets in which it wishes to compete. This strategy will be supported by the organisation's competence strategy, focused on the technologies the corporation needs if it is successfully to pursue its business strategy. The R&D strategy supports the firm's competence strategy and is focused on what is required to create and acquire the mastery of the identified technologies.

A corporation needs to manage its R&D centres actively. Since competence-building centres will be funded only if they are seen to be supporting the firm's technology and business strategies, the R&D centre needs to ensure that its outputs are made known to the businesses and to senior leader-managers. Research centres use a variety of means to publicise their activities throughout the corporation: through brochures describing the main activities, technical reports and conducting seminars.[21] Some research centres make a point of placing articles in corporate newspapers and house magazines. The most effective means of transferring technology, however, is to move people between the businesses and the R&D centres.[22] In this way tacit knowledge is also transferred.

The size of the research centre is significant: there appears to be a need to reach a critical mass. A study by the European Industrial Management Association[23] found in a survey of 57 companies that, without exception, the corporate R&D centre had either more than 100 people or fewer than ten people; there was no 'middle ground'. The centres with fewer than ten people were involved in co-ordination and planning and not in active research. Thus it would seem that 100 is the absolute minimum to provide a feasible R&D activity, although the size would depend on the number of technologies being supported. A minimum of ten people per technology has been suggested.[24]

R&D centres need to be controlled, and this is often difficult as many of the activities are unstructured and some of the activities will be long-term. A set of measures for research centres has been proposed:[25] along with the standard objectives for cost and productivity, other suggested measures are the number of new products per year, the timeliness of the centre's outputs, project durations and the level of 'creativity and innovation'. This latter category includes such things as the numbers of patents filed and publications achieved, and the number of presentations at conferences. These measures would appeal to the research staff themselves as it recognises the value of their work to the scientific community.

18.8   Corporate governance

18.8.1   What is corporate governance?

Corporate governance is about the way in which organisations are run and who should control them – the chairman, the chief executive, the board of directors, shareholders or other stakeholders such as the employees – and also about the process of governing – how decisions are to be taken and, if by vote, who has the right to vote. The controversy about the rights of stakeholders discussed in Chapter 1 is addressing one aspect of corporate governance.

18.8.2 The place of corporate governance within strategic management

Boards of directors in the UK have four principal roles,[26] which are:

- accountability   recognising responsibilities to those making a legitimate demand to know what the organisation is doing and intending to do;
- supervision   monitoring and oversight of management performance;
- direction   formulating the strategic direction of the organisation in the long term;
- executive action   involvement in implementing strategy.

Exhibit 18.18 indicates the distinction between governance and the rest of strategic management, with governance mainly concerned with accountability and supervision. In Germany, two-tier boards that recognise this split have existed for many years. Direction and executive action are the responsibility of a management board, while accountability and supervision are the responsibility of a supervisory board. Thus the supervisory board is responsible for governance. Other European countries, for example Austria, the Netherlands[27] and Switzerland, have a similar arrangement. In the UK and USA, there is no such clear separation and strategic management incorporates considerations of corporate governance in a fairly seamless way.

DISCUSSION
POINT 18.6

Who are the people or interest groups who might be able to make a legitimate demand for accountability of a profit-seeking organisation operating in the EU?

- Why do you think the term *corporate* governance is used rather than *business* governance?

EXHIBIT 18.18

Corporate governance and strategic management (after Tricker, 1984)

Accountability

Supervision

Corporate governance

Direction

Rest of strategic management

Executive action

18.8.3 The elements of corporate governance

Corporate governance has steadily moved up the list of concerns of business communities around the world over the last decade. The pressure in the USA was to address the 'unproductive biases' in the existing relationships between investors and directors, due in part to investors having much less information than directors. This concern found expression in the USA in the paper published by the Working Group on Corporate Governance.[29] As Exhibit 18.19 shows, the impetus in the UK came from the malpractices of the 1980s and the concerns that the financial sector had for the reputation of London as a financial centre. The concern in London stimulated the London Stock Exchange to set up a committee, chaired by Sir Adrian Cadbury, to consider the financial aspects of corporate governance. The committee's report is known as the Cadbury Report.[30] Since then there have been two further well-known UK reports that cover areas of corporate governance, the Greenbury[31] and Hampel[32] reports, named after their chairmen. The Greenbury Report covered the question of directors' remuneration and its disclosure, while the Hampel Report covered broadly the same area as Cadbury but with more emphasis on corporate performance in the balance between accountability and performance. Somewhat controversially, the Hampel Committee recommended that directors should be responsible for checking non-financial risks, such as those posed by environmentally unfriendly policies and changes in markets and technologies.

The main impetus for changes in corporate governance in the UK has stemmed from the Cadbury Report, mainly because, although the committee's recommendations aren't legally enforceable, they are backed by the London Stock Exchange. The exchange makes it obligatory for all listed companies to produce a compliance statement detailing where it does and doesn't comply with the Cadbury 'checklist'. The main Cadbury recommendations are shown as Exhibit 18.20.

Hampel and others have been critical of the checklist approach to governance shown by Cadbury, arguing that governance is more a matter of principles than hard-and-fast rules. Rather than 'box ticking', it is more important for companies to comply with the spirit of transparency and proper accountability, while not undermining corporate economic performance.

18.8.4 The future directions for corporate governance

The financial markets are truly global markets and thus there is a strong impetus for all the major centres to conform to the same standards on corporate governance, since those favouring the investor will naturally command the main share of investment. International institutional investors and the world markets for capital are the drivers for convergence. The likelihood of convergence of standards appears to be particularly strong within the EU.[33] Cadbury sees a convergence in governance standards and processes but, given the sharp differences between the UK and other European arrangements, not in structures. In 1998 and 1999 the OECD, the World Bank and the Commonwealth Association for Corporate Governance all produced statements on corporate governance, and Egon Zehnder International, a headhunting firm, organised the Global Corporate Governance Advisory Board involving the heads of large companies such as Société Générale, Daimler-Chrysler, Philips and the Industrial Bank of Japan.

EXHIBIT 18.19

A guide to corporate governance[28]

What is corporate governance? Sounds pretty boring to me

Not a bit of it. Corporate governance is one of the most exciting areas of debate in the business world today. It is tricky even to find two people who can agree on a definition of what it is. The bottom line is that it is about power – how it is used and controlled. The Report of the Committee on the Financial Aspects of Corporate Governance – otherwise known as the Cadbury Committee Report and widely recognised as the foundation stone of modern corporate governance in the UK – describes it as 'the system by which companies are directed and controlled'. The National Association of Pension Funds, the trade association for most of the UK's institutional shareholders, prefers a more watered-down version. It describes it as 'the nature of the relationship between companies and their shareholders'.

What sort of things does it involve?

Most people think that corporate governance is about shareholder activists making a lot of noise about what public companies get up to. The recent well-publicised effort by a minority of shareholders to get Shell to put in place new procedures for dealing with environmental and human rights issues won a lot of headlines. But these so-called shareholder revolts are rare, and corporate governance is mostly about institutional shareholders keeping a close eye, behind closed doors, on the companies in which they invest in order to safeguard the value of their investments.

The Cadbury Report was largely a reaction to the Robert Maxwell scandal and called on shareholders to ensure that companies follow best practice guidelines, or at the very least explain why they are not. Sometimes shareholders kick up a fuss if a company refuses to comply with a core Cadbury recommendation, such as separating the roles of chairman and chief executive, but normally only if the company's performance is poor. The Greenbury Report on executive pay, published in July 1995, came up with some new corporate governance recommendations covering how main board directors should be paid, and companies and shareholders are making some efforts to put these in place.

So why is there so much fuss about corporate governance?

Because an increasing number of people are keen for it to be about a lot more than cosy chats between City fund managers and company chairmen. They range from some in the Labour Party to PIRC, the corporate governance consultancy which specialises in leading shareholder actions, and the Centre for Tomorrow's Company, a think tank devoted to encouraging a more ethical approach to business.

Typically this group wants shareholders to become far more active in the companies in which they invest and, for example, to vote at annual general meetings. They also want companies to take more notice of their so-called stakeholders – that is, shareholders, customers, staff and so on. They believe that this will help improve companies' efficiency and profitability and therefore boost shareholder returns. Kleinwort Benson recently launched a fund which invests only in companies which comply with the Tomorrow's Company stakeholding criteria.

How is this affecting companies and institutional shareholders?

Quite a bit, leading some to talk of a corporate governance industry having developed in the UK. Pressure from pension fund trustees has led nearly every fund management group to publish its own corporate governance best practice codes for companies to follow, on top of the Cadbury and Greenbury guidelines. Institutional investors have also appointed full-time corporate governance managers to oversee how shares are voted at companies' annual and extraordinary general meetings. Company secretaries have taken on most of the responsibilities for corporate governance at large public companies.

But following the landmark British Gas annual general meeting in 1995, when 4500 shareholders turned up to lambast Cedric Brown, then chief executive, for accepting a large pay rise, chairmen and chief executives have become much more sensitive to possible action by shareholders.

Some senior business people, such as Sir Stanley Kalms, chairman of Dixons, the electrical retailer, are highly critical of these developments. He has said that corporate governance is 'running out of control' and lobbied to halt the formation of the Hampel Committee, the successor body to the Cadbury and Greenbury committees, because of fears that it would lead to yet more regulations.

Is Sir Stanley right to be worried about the Hampel Committee?

It is not due to report until later in the summer (1998) but the signs are that it is unlikely to recommend any dramatic changes to the current system. Sir Ronald Hampel, who chairs the committee and is also chairman of ICI, has talked of possibly scrapping some of the Cadbury and Greenbury rules that smaller public companies have to comply with, such as having a minimum number of non-executive directors. There is also talk of the committee sanctioning the payment of shares to non-executives instead of a cash fee. This is to overcome concerns that non-executive directors are being 'captured' by executive directors and are failing to represent the interests of shareholders firmly enough on boards. Some companies, such as Glaxo, are already starting to do this and in the USA it is now common practice. None of this should worry Sir Stanley.

Are there other things that might give him sleepless nights? Surely Labour cannot wait to introduce corporate governance reforms?

Not so. The corporate governance brief has been given by Tony Blair to Sir David Simon, former chairman of BP and recently appointed a minister in the Labour government. Sir David is also a member of the Hampel Committee and looks extremely unlikely to sanction the introduction of any radical changes. Before the general election, Tony Blair talked of stakeholding as his big idea, but there has been no mention of it since.

The biggest danger for the likes of Sir Stanley is coming from somewhere else – the USA. Shareholders in the USA have long taken a more aggressive stance on corporate governance and shown more willingness to oust poorly performing directors. Now those same shareholders are beginning to make their presence felt in the UK and other parts of Europe. For example, CalPERS, the US-based third largest public pension fund in the world, is planning to start publishing a target list of poor performers among UK companies in which it holds shares.

Another trend beginning to catch on here is the work of Al Dunlap, which specialises in turning around poorly performing companies in the USA. Al, whose catchphrase is 'if you want to have a friend, get a dog', is parachuted in by shareholders at companies where management has performed badly.

The debate on corporate governance seems to be particularly acute in the UK. Why is that?

A lot of it is to do with Margaret Thatcher and the range of labour, economic and market reforms she put in place in the 1980s. Short-term focus on shareholder value became all the rage and companies like Hanson prospered through executing a series of mega M&A deals. As a result customer and employee care played second fiddle to quarterly share price and dividend performance. Two recessions (and the break-up of Hanson) later, and shareholders and companies appear to have learned their lesson. Some spectacular crashes have led shareholders to use corporate governance to fill the gap between their desire for short-term performance and the need for all stakeholders to be brought along if companies are to achieve long-term improvements in shareholder value.

This process has put the UK light years ahead of continental Europe and Asia but it still lags behind the USA. While German company directors are still, for the most part, grappling with the concept of shareholder rights, Japan is an even bleaker land for holders of equity. In contrast, debate in the USA has moved on from stakeholding. In particular, executives and directors are being targeted, some activists suggesting that how they are paid and incentivised holds the key to improving company performance.

What about ideas – who is writing cutting-edge stuff on corporate governance?

There is no end of material to read on corporate governance, thanks to the seemingly endless number of conferences and seminar discussions on the subject. However, there are only three writers whose work, whether you agree or disagree with them, is required reading.

The first is John Plender, a journalist at the *Financial Times* and chairman of PIRC. He recently published *A Stake in the Future: The Stakeholding Solution*. Plender argues that the challenge for the new Labour government 'is to discover a distinctively British way of doing what comes more naturally to the Germans and Japanese', in other words, to find a more humane form of capitalism that gives ordinary people what former chancellor Lord Lawson has called 'a stake in the future'.

The second is Will Hutton, who recently followed up his best seller *The State We're In* with *The State to Come*. In his first book Hutton blamed a whole range of economic problems on the apparently short-term outlook of UK pension funds but now seems to have partially changed his view. 'We have to start . . . from where we are, with the institutions we have and in a highly open economy operating in a globalising market,' he states.

The third must is John Kay, who argues that the only way to create a market economy that commands wide support is to dispose of the notion that the functioning of markets depends on base and contemptible aspects of human behaviour. Happy reading.

Source: Mastering Management, Financial Times Pitman Publishing, 1997

EXHIBIT 18.20

The main recommendations of the Cadbury Committee (1992)
The Cadbury 'checklist'[25]

- The board must meet regularly and should have a formal schedule of matters that are for it to decide. Such matters would include the acquisition and disposal of significant assets, capital projects, authority levels and risk management policies.

- The board should include non-executive directors, who should be appointed through a formal process for specific terms, and reappointment should not be automatic.

- Non-executive directors should have a standing outside the company that ensures that their views carry weight. The majority of the non-executive directors should be fully independent and free from links with the company, apart from their fees and shareholdings. The fees for non-executive directors should reflect the time they spend on company business.

- There should be an accepted division at the head of the company, which will ensure a balance of power and authority such that no one individual has unfettered power of decision. Where the chairman is also chief executive, it is essential that there should be a strong independent element on the board, with a recognised senior member.

- Executive directors' terms of office should run for no more than three years without shareholder approval for reappointment.

- Executive directors' pay should be subject to the recommendations of a remuneration committee made up wholly or mainly of non-executive directors and chaired by a non-executive director. The full remuneration package of all directors – including performance-related elements, pensions contributions and stock options – should be disclosed in annual reports,

- Boards should have a separate audit committee with a minimum of three members and made up wholly of non-executive directors (of whom the majority should be independent). Non-committee board members should have the right to attend committee meetings, although the committee should meet with the external auditors at least once a year without executive directors being present.

A new development in the scope of corporate governance is expected from the Turnbull Committee, which will report towards the end of 1999. This has taken up the recommendation of the Hampel Committee and urges companies to monitor a wide range of non-financial risks. The report of this committee is considered the final element of a 'supercode of governance' that will bring together the recommendations of the Cadbury, Greenbury and Hampel committees.

During the 1990s the focus of attention has been on the roles and duties of boards. Boards have now become more accountable to investors, but investors aren't accountable to anyone. However, investors are now so powerful that the focus over the next decade may well be on them, and particularly on the institutional investor.

KEY CONCEPT   Corporate governance is concerned with how an organisation should be run. The main concerns are an organisation's accountability to legitimate outside parties and supervision of the activities of senior managers. One strand of governance is a consideration of the roles and rights of stakeholders.

SUMMARY

- There are seven roles that a corporate parent can undertake in on-going portfolio management: determining the corporation's organisational structure, supporting strategic alliances, providing corporation-wide services, improving the performance of individual SBUs, developing relationships between SBUs, nurturing competences, and maintaining appropriate corporate governance arangements. EXHIBIT 18.1

- The way in which the businesses in the corporation are structured depends on and reflects three features: the roles that the parent plays, the relatedness between the SBUs, and the degree of centralisation of the functions.   EXHIBIT 18.2

- There are two broad forms of relationship between the parent and the rest of the corporation: the holding company structure and the divisional structure. These differ as to the number of roles the parent undertakes. The relatedness between capabilities suggests two forms of structure within the companies of the holding company and the divisions within a divisionalised company: the SBU and the matrix structures. International operations call for international structures and four are identified. International production doesn't necessarily mean that international markets are the same. Competences can be located within one or more SBUs or in dedicated, corporately controlled 'centres of excellence'.   EXHIBITS 18.3 TO 18.9, EXHIBIT 18.11

- Supporting strategic alliances requires that the parent considers five factors: senior management involvement, the resources to share, the quality of the alliance team, the roles of team members, and interpersonal relationships.

- Providing corporation-wide services covers scale effects, specialist expertise, the provision of day-to-day services, branding and reputation, and wide-ranging public relations.

- Improving individual SBU performance involves the parent making senior SBU appointments and coaching them in leadership and management, helping to determine SBU strategy and imposing challenging strategic objectives. Three planning and control styles have been found to be used by parents with their subordinate units. These are strategic planning, strategic control and financial control styles. EXHIBIT 18.15, EXHIBIT 18.16

- Improving relationships between SBUs involves the parent in setting up the conditions that wouldn't arise naturally for the SBUs to improve relations and in so doing release any synergy that there might be. The parent should set up conditions to support the spreading of best practice and skills, sharing data, and encouraging the SBUs to combine when and where appropriate in dealing with stakeholders.

- In nurturing competences, the parent must ensure that controls on competence are such as to allow creative freedom. It is important that research and development centres are linked closely to the business units, both through personal ties and through strategy: the research and development strategy supporting the competence-building strategy and with this strategy supporting the business strategy.

- Corporate governance is about the relationship between companies and their shareholders, particularly the balance of power between directors and investors. The board of directors in the UK has four principal roles: accountability, supervision, direction and executive action. The main thinking concerning corporate governance in the UK is that contained in the report from the Cadbury Committee. EXHIBIT 18.18, EXHIBIT 18.20

SELF-CHECK

1 Reconsider the learning outcomes for this chapter. Check that you feel confident that you can carry out the activities listed there.

2 Having read this chapter, you should be able to define the following terms:

colonial firm	exporting firm	multi-domestic firm
corporate governance	financial control style	strategic control style
divisionalised company	holding company	transnational firm

FURTHER
DISCUSSION
POINTS

1 Identify how each of the parental roles is being carried out in GSM:
- determining the organisational structure;
- supporting strategic alliances;
- providing corporation-wide services;
- improving individual SBU performance;
- improving relationships between SBUs;
- nurturing competences;
- maintaining appropriate corporate governance arrangements.

2 In Chapter 1 the strategic management environment was characterised as chaotic, complex, dynamic and turbulent – all generally increasing the level of uncertainty facing leader-managers. However, not all business environments are the same. Reflect on how changes in the environmental characteristics might affect the approach taken to on-going portfolio management.

3 Which form of organisational structure would suit Siemens (Mini-case 16.2)?

ASSIGNMENTS

Obtain a set of annual reports and accounts for an FT 100 corporation covering three or more years. Analyse these to identify:
a) the portfolio of businesses;
b) its structure (holding company or divisional structure);
c) its alliances, the rationale for these and how it manages them;
d) its method of control;
e) how closely it conforms to the Cadbury code.

FURTHER
READING

The book by Michael Goold, Andrew Campbell and Marcus Alexander, *Corporate-level Strategy: Creating Value in the Multibusiness Company*, John Wiley, 1994, considers many aspects of corporate-level strategic management.

The past, current and future of corporate governance are well covered in Sir Adrian Cadbury's article 'What are the trends in corporate governance? How will they impact your company?, *Long Range Planning*, Vol. 32, No. 1 1999, pp. 12–19.

Sytse Douma provides a concise exploration of corporate governance in The Netherlands and Germany in 'The two-tier system of corporate governance', *Long Range Planning*, Vol. 30, No. 4, 1997, pp. 612–14.

CHAPTER NOTES
AND REFERENCES

1 Ohmae K., in the BBC programme *Globalisation*, 1992.

2 Bartlett, C.A. and Ghoshal, S., *Managing Across Borders: The Transnational Solution*, Century Business, 1992.

3 Marsh, P., Interview with Antony Lo, CEO of Giant, *Financial Times*, 1 October 1997, p. 16.

4 KPMG Consulting, *Pricing Policy White Paper*, EMU Unit – KPMG Consulting, Reference:/a7724, p. 3.

5 Goold, M., Campbell, A. and Alexander, M., *Corporate-level Strategy: Creating Value in the Multibusiness Company*, John Wiley, 1994, p. 169.

6 Ouchi, W.G., *The M-form Society: How American Teamwork Can Recapture the Competitive Edge*, Addison-Wesley, 1986.

7 Hampden-Turner, C. and Trompenaars, F., *The Seven Cultures of Capitalism: Value Systems for Ceating Wealth in the United States, Britain, Japan, Germany, France, Sweden, and the Netherlands*, Doubleday, 1993, p. 193.

8 Kanter, R.M., 'Collaborative advantage: the art of alliances', *Harvard Business Review*, July–August 1994, pp. 96–108.

9 *Ibid*.

10 Lorange, P., Roos, J. and Bronn, P.S., 'Building successful strategic alliances', *Long Range Planning*, Vol. 25, No. 6, 1992, pp. 10–17.

11 Pekar, P. and Allio, R., 'Making alliances work – gudelines for success', *Long Range Planning*, Vol. 27, No. 4, 1994, pp. 54–65.

12 Kanter, R.M., *op. cit*.

13 McConchie, D., 'Patterns of strategic control: an investigation of British, French and German retail banking practice', PhD thesis, Loughborough University, 1998. Discussions with a member of the corporate planning team of Lloyds TSB, p. 199.

13 Monbiot, G., 'Law and the profits of PR', *The Guardian*, 21 August 1997, p. 19.

14 Goold, M. and Campbell, A., *Strategies and Styles: The Role of the Centre in Managing Diversified Corporations*, Basil Blackwell, 1987; Goold, M., Campbell, A. and Luchs, K., 'Strategies and styles revisited: strategic planning and financial control', *Long Range Planning*, Vol. 26, No. 5, 1993, pp. 49–60; and 'Strategies and styles revisited: "strategic control" is it tenable?', *Long Range Planning*, Vol. 26, No. 6, 1993, pp. 54–61.

15 *Ibid*.

16 *Dispatches*, ITV, 15 March 1999.

17 BBC, 'The ice-cream wars', first in the *Blood on the Carpet* series, 1999.

18 Porter, M.E., *Competitive Advantage: Creating and Sustaining Superior Performance*, Free Press, 1985.

19 Iansiti, M., 'Real-world R&D: jumping the product generation gap', *Harvard Business Review*, May–June 1993, pp. 138–47.

20 Hamel, G. and Prahalad, C.K., 'Strategy as stretch and leverage', *Harvard Business Review*, March–April 1993, pp. 75–84.

21 Parker, R.J., 'The strategic role of the research centre', MBA thesis, the Business School, Loughborough University, 1994.

22 Nonaka, I., 'The knowledge-creating

company', *Harvard Business Review*, November–December 1991, pp. 97–104.

23 European Industrial Management Association, *Role and Organisation of Corporate R&D*, EIMA, 1987.

24 Parker, R.J., *op. cit.*

25 Thor, C.G., 'Performance measurement in a research organisation', *National Productivity Review*, Vol. 10, No. 4, 1991, pp. 499–507.

26 Tricker, R., *Corporate Governance*, Gower, 1984.

27 Douma, S., 'The two-tier system of corporate governance', *Long Range Planning*, Vol. 30, No. 4, 1997, pp. 612–14.

28 *Mastering Management*, Financial Times Pitman Publishing, 1997.

29 Working Group on Corporate Govern-ance, 'New compact for owners and directors', published in the *Harvard Business Review*, July–August 1991, pp. 141–3.

30 The Cadbury Committee, *The Financial Aspects of Corporate Governance*, Stock Exchange Council, Gee Publishing, 1992.

31 Study Group on Directors' Remuneration, *Directors' Remuneration: Report of a Study Group Chaired by Sir Richard Greenbury*, Gee Publishing, July 1995.

32 Committee on Corporate Governance (the Hampel Committee), *Final Report*, Gee Publishing, 1998.

33 Cadbury A., 'What are the trends in corporate governance? How will they impact your company?' *Long Range Planning*, Vol. 32, No. 1, 1999, pp. 12–19.

PART 7

Case studies

The GSM Group

Background

The GSM Group has around 200 employees spread fairly equally across three sites: Thirsk and Wetherby in Yorkshire and Brecon in South Wales. It produces a range of products as shown in Exhibit 1 and services customers mainly in the electronics and automotive industries located worldwide.

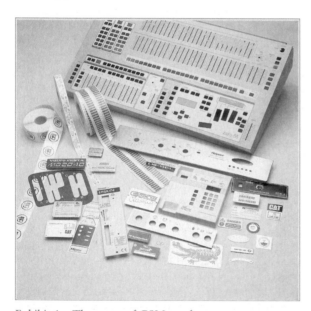

Exhibit 1   The range of GSM products

Thirsk produces labels and front panels for the electronics and many other industries in small and medium volumes and is equipped to react very quickly to customer demands. Brecon produces large-volume items – such as metal labels – mainly, but not exclusively, servicing automotive assemblers such as Ford and General Motors. Wetherby produces sheet metal kits for the electronics industry. Products from one plant are regularly used by another.

In reply to the question of what business(es) GSM is in, Barry Dodd, the owner-manager of the GSM Group, says:

We're engineers who print – we're not printers who dabble in engineering. Whilst we have several people with engineering degrees we don't have anyone with a degree in printing ... even though we are extremely competent in printing. The key to what we do is that we are dealing with the engineering industry – call it automotive, electronics, call it what you will. It's engineering of some description. We sell by knowing what the client is doing. Our technical skill is in precision engineering, precision metal punching, precision etching and precision printing.

The journey

Barry grew up in the USA, where his stepfather was a successful executive with AT&T. Because his stepfather was frequently promoted, Barry moved almost every year. His mother was also in full-time employment, so Barry was growing up in a culture where work and success were taken as the norm. He contrasts the US and UK view of success: 'In the States when you were in school and saw someone with a Cadillac the response was "I'm going to get a bigger one". In the UK the response is "How the hell did he get that?"'

Barry obtained an ICI scholarship to study for an honours degree in engineering and progressed to joining ICI as a graduate trainee. After two years he realised that working in a big company wasn't for him: he recalls sharing an office with a well-qualified 50-year-old engineer who was scared stiff of losing his job. So Barry left to become the technical director of a small engineering company. This was a disaster – although Barry confesses that he learned a great deal from his time there.

These experiences led Barry to decide to become his own boss, where he had control over his working life. In a chance meeting, Barry met Geoff Collier, a former senior manager he had known in ICI and who had left to become managing director of a printed circuit company. Both were interested in setting up an engineering company. They put together a list of criteria that they wanted in the product they would manufacture. The kinds of thing they came up with were:

- it had to be technically complicated enough that no one could set up in a garage and compete;
- there must be a UK-wide demand – and preferably an international one;
- it had to use printed circuit technology.

After extensive thought they decided to produce metal nameplates. They saw an increasing demand for these and thought that the ones then on the market were poorly made. However, they were setting up in an industry where they knew very little about the market and had no natural customers. They had to find all this out and that took time. As Barry ruefully recalls, 'Most people set up in an area they've already been working in, but we couldn't set up a polyethylene plant!'

This was in 1974. They decided not to borrow any money, because they didn't want to surrender any of the equity. In 1976 they purchased a site in Thirsk with 5000 square feet of factory space and set up GSM, a name derived from a wood carving hanging on the wall in Geoff Collier's house. The factory was inside a former Army compound, and they were able to build a new factory there on the parade ground when more space was needed. In 1987 Geoff retired, and Barry decided to purchase his partner's equity to avoid the company being sold out to a third party. In 1988, realising that he needed someone to support him with strategic thinking, Barry recruited Andrew Hall as general manager. Andrew had had considerable experience as a board director of plcs in several manufacturing industries, with companies of 2000 employees and above. As Andrew points out, 'Barry has been the main driver, but I think he realised that he needed a balance. I'm older than him and bring complementarity.'

In 1992, in the midst of the recession, GSM acquired a company from receivership called Edward H. Thew. This firm had been in business for 50 years and was a well-respected name on Tyneside producing very high-quality nameplates, labels and fascia panels. GSM had space in Thirsk at that time to take over production, with some people bussed in from Newcastle.[a] Barry recalls that he learned a lot from that acquisition, chiefly that GSM had concentrated on the Thew customers and neglected its suppliers. This may be a normal reaction, but it wasn't a good idea. He resolved to split GSM's time between customers and suppliers in any future acquisitions.

And the first subsequent acquisition came fairly quickly – at Christmas 1993, when GSM acquired Primographic, a firm producing labels for the automotive industry. The lead-up to this acquisition is both interesting and amusing. In 1983 five people from Nissan arrived to discuss using GSM as a supplier. Barry recalls:

They came with a fixed agenda for the day which went something like: 2 minutes past 9 arrive, 5 minutes past 9 presentation of business cards, 10 minutes past 9 introductions, at 11 o'clock GSM personnel will leave the room to allow Nissan ... and so it went on. GSM were the last people they looked at and at the end of the

[a] In 1999, some are still travelling from Newcastle.

day they said that we were nominated as a supplier. When we expressed surprise because we hadn't even quoted a price the reply was 'Oh, you'll be competitive'.

This meeting with Nissan was very consequential. The reason for the visit was that Nissan thought that its current supplier of vehicle identification number plates was perhaps not a good bet for the future. So it was looking for another supplier and was considering several companies. During the discussions with Nissan, it became obvious that its current supplier was Primographic. It was about to lose the Nissan contract and GSM to gain it. Barry had already looked at Primographic's accounts and so now knew it would be further in trouble and so he was ready to purchase. There was nothing wrong with Primographic in terms of quality; what was wrong was it didn't have the money to buy raw materials, so its delivery record was very patchy.

Primographic is located in Brecon and since it was a well-known name in South Wales for its high-quality products, it was decided to retain the name after takeover, as GSM Primographic. The Brecon factory is twice the size of that at Thirsk. The purchase brought with it big name customers, such as the Ford Motor Company, together with Ford's Q1 accreditation (Ford has its own quality system, a much tighter specification than ISO 9000).

There had been no investment in Primographic for six years, staff hadn't had a pay rise for four years and Primographic had had two receiverships in three years. So, although the people at Primographic could see the need for change, they were somewhat scared by their experiences. Brecon produced to a high quality but it wasn't innovative. Part of the struggle at Brecon was to alter expectations, and there had to be changes in the management to accomplish this. There's now a different general manager, a different quality manager and a different technical manager from the time of acquisition.

In early 1995, GSM acquired the firm of Alan Markovitz from receivership. This firm had been in business since 1957 and had aerospace quality approval and customers in the aerospace industry. There had been a management buy-in, which hadn't gone well. One of GSM's suppliers had alerted Barry to what had happened to Markovitz. The GSM team was very pleased with this acquisition; it had taken on a big firm of London accountants and won a very good deal – one that paid for itself within two weeks! Then in 1997 GSM acquired Thew Nameplates, a firm that had been set up by the former managers of Edward H. Thew and that had been competing directly with GSM. Thew ran into difficulties and GSM bought the good equipment it had and secured its client base.

Early in 1998 GSM made a further significant acqui-

GSM Graphic Arts Ltd	GSM Primographic	GSM Valtech Industries Ltd (Wetherby)
(Thirsk)	(Brecon)	

Exhibit 2   The GSM Group

sition, one that added the Wetherby site to the group as GSM Valtech and produced the group structure shown in Exhibit 2. Farnell plc, the largest distributor of electronic components in Europe, had packaged together all its manufacturing capability and sold it to the venture capitalist Cinven, which renamed it Advance International Group. In its turn, Advance International Group decided that it didn't want to be in sheet metalwork as this wasn't a core activity. It was a long-standing customer of GSM and approached GSM to offer its sheet metal factory at Wetherby. GSM thought that the metalworking skills at Wetherby were superior to those at Thirsk and, as the price was right, it acquired the factory. A team leader at Thirsk became the general manager, new equipment was bought, and 12 months later output had doubled and GSM had 28 external customers where it had none before. Although the factory at Wetherby is competitive on price as far as metal forming is concerned, the true strength is that it has moved to being an integrator, offering a range of skills that few other companies can match.

In 1999 the GSM Group had a turnover of £9 million. During the previous ten years revenues had grown tenfold. Throughout its life, GSM has never borrowed any money; now, with the good profits that it is generating, it doesn't need to. It is one of 120 companies which are regarded as exemplars by the UK's Department of Trade and Industry (DTI) and is visited by other organisations which wish to see how GSM has achieved its success. And these are large companies; ICI booked a dozen people to come and see GSM at £90 a head in January 1999, and American Airlines has taken all the available places for March.

Strategic thinking and strategic considerations

When pressed, Barry considers that GSM is in the nameplate industry. Although the competition is now global, the technology makes it very unlikely that firms in developing countries can compete. There is an enormous amount of knowledge in the product and systems; labels and nameplates need to be proof against petrol and urine, must pass the European rub test, must have low surface tension, need to operate down to −20°C and up to +60°C, must stick on to . . ., etc. etc. etc. There is a lot of technology and skills in the humble label! This range of technologies means that GSM has a well-contained if ill-defined set of competitors. Although it has no direct competitors that cover the range of products for either the automotive or electronic industries, there are around 100 firms in Europe which are doing some parts of its work.

The strategy at GSM has focused on the two growth industries that it wishes to be in – automotive and electronics. It has plotted where it wants to be in both industries and how it intends to get there.

• In electronics, GSM is intending to be a 'one-stop shop' in badging, labelling, fascias, chassis etc., offering a bespoke service to the electronics industry. Typical current customers are Zero88, the largest manufacturer of lighting equipment in the UK, Advance International Group, and Wayne-Kerr Electronics.

• In automotive, GSM decided to target one of the major car assemblers. It considered that Ford would be one of the winners in the global race that would result in only a few major car assemblers remaining.[b] It had the strongest contact with Ford among the big car assemblers after the Primographic acquisition. Although Ford was targeted for extra attention, GSM already had dealings with General Motors (GM) and Nissan and continues to work with these other assemblers.

Barry is clear that strategy is customer-driven, arguing that if you simply concentrate on what the customer wants now and what they are going to want in five years time, then you're heading in the right direction. It can be difficult to determine what customers want, but by being very close to major customers – designing jointly with their design teams, talking to them and listening – it is possible to get a very good feel for their requirements. Barry has said to his big customers that he is prepared to put a plant anywhere in the world if they will sign up to it; if Ford wants GSM to put a factory next door to its factory in Brazil then GSM will do it. GSM wants to make itself indispensable – and indeed indistinguishable from Ford's own in-house supply. This approach appears to be paying off. GSM's main car company clients have suggested that their suppliers talk to GSM, and so now it's being introduced into headlamp factories, brake factories and tyre manufacturers worldwide.

GM and Ford are in the process of demerging their suppliers and this presents a great opportunity for GSM, as do the recent acquisitions by Ford and GM of Volvo

[b] Ford's chairman, Jacques Nasser, predicted in 1998 that there would be six global players within the next decade – two in each of the USA, Europe and Japan.[1]

and Saab, respectively. The way ahead in the automotive business is to be in at the design stage of the car platform. That is what GSM is doing, not waiting for the design to arrive. GSM is able to plot through when a new platform will be required and when it will be designed.

GSM is one of only six firms in the UK that have been chosen by 3M to be 'supported converters'. 3M sees supported converters as vital in product testing and in delivering its products into markets, and has chosen GSM as a converter to the automotive industry, and so anything automotive is made available to GSM. Being a converter means that a firm has access to 3M technology at least six months ahead of competition and will be supported by 3M in its dealings with customers. A current example of conversion by GSM is the 3M laser-etchable roll label material, which is the core for the latest way of permanently marking plastic. GSM helped to launch this product for 3M and captured part of the market. GSM has some good IT people and a tie-up with a laser manufacturer, is able to put a package together and has sold three production-line systems to major automotive assemblers, linked to their CAM systems.

It is interesting how GSM became a 3M-supported converter, a process that took three years to achieve. Barry explains:

We always have a five-year rolling strategy for this company. And we had a strategy three years ago to become a significant supplier to Ford. We realised that if we didn't become that, we wouldn't supply them at all. I went to Detroit and I was able to talk to their senior people, because we were already a supplier. And I asked them what they saw as their needs for the next ten years from a supplier. I listened carefully, came away and got all our management team together and we set out our strategic objectives – one of which was that we needed an international liaison with a raw material supplier of repute. There were several that we could have chosen. 3M came out clearly as the best. We then had an exercise in raising the profile of GSM so that 3M and everyone else would know about us. We did this by myself becoming involved in outside organisations – things like YORTEK, the association of high-technology industries in Yorkshire, acting as an exemplar for the DTI, and assisting in the preparation of an Institute of Directors case on GSM. That's the sort of thing. And I've agreed to talk at various functions; for instance I'm giving a presentation for the DTI in Winchester on Partnerships with People.[c] When we finally approached 3M we found

that our two business plans were amazingly similar – in spite of the difference in size.

Barry raised the profile of GSM in other ways too. He is on the Regional Export Board and has been invited to No. 10 to share his views on industrial competitiveness with Tony Blair. He is a member of a business group of managing directors in Wales and is involved with the Welsh Development Agency. Until recently Barry was the only person involving himself in such networking, but now the general manager at Brecon is also getting involved, having been instrumental in setting up a Welsh automotive forum.

The development of the product range in electronics is interesting. The company began producing small labels for the electronics industry. Customers then wanted high-tech front panels and subsequently more complex metal shapes. Customers next began saying that what they really wanted was one supplier for all the non-electronic parts of their products. So now GSM is making everything that had originally been made by different suppliers and assembled by the electronics companies themselves – the metal box, back panel, inside metalwork, front panel – everything other than the electronic contents that go inside.

A number of companies have established full manufacturing capability in East Asia. So now all the electronics, not simply the box, are sourced there. So instead of GSM competing with UK manufacturers, it has to compete with East Asian manufacturers. It's not viable to ship simply a case from the East, but it is to ship the case plus the electronics because of the value added. Competition is really severe, particularly from China and South Korea, and it's not a case of differential labour costs. Raw material costs are much lower in South Korea, steel is cheaper and polycarbonate is about half the UK price. The computerised presses needed to make the boxes are half the price in East Asia, and injection moulding tools, which in the UK would cost £20,000, cost £3000. However, the East Asians are at a disadvantage in that they are ten weeks shipping time from their European customers, and this means slower response time and larger inventories.

Environmental legislation is tightening up with the requirement for much more recycling than formerly. For example, TV cases can no longer be dumped; they have to be recycled. Generally the TV cases have incompatible labels attached, but GSM is now making a polymer label that is totally compatible with all commonly used case materials. In Europe a number of companies that used to etch aluminium or stainless steel have stopped doing this because of environmental impact, the danger of contaminating water courses. This business came to the UK, but now the UK is catching up and the move is away from metals to plastics. There are now different ways of print-

[c] Short for the programme 'Competitiveness through partnerships with people', jointly sponsored by the DTI and the Department for Education and Employment.

ing on different substrates (such as laser etching), and adhesives have improved considerably and apply better in difficult situations. What were metal labels can now be made of plastic and put on a roll, which can be used in machinery for automatic labelling.

Acquisition strategy

From the earliest days Barry had kept a close watch on competitors. When in the late 1980s he was thinking of expanding, this interest focused on companies that had similar or complementary skills, that weren't doing very well and that had good customers. GSM realised that if companies have been happily supplied for several years, it is very hard to get them to change. For example, in the automotive industry if you haven't got a vendor number then you don't supply. One way of getting a vendor number is through acquiring a supplier that has. GSM is producing the profits to allow it to acquire, a position not shared by anyone else in the industry, although there may be venture capitalists around who might seek to enter the business.

GSM, like other firms, will always have trouble with customers changing suppliers when a company changes ownership, and this situation is exacerbated when the firm is bought from receivership. That is why GSM ensured that it looked after its new customers in the best possible way, better than they had ever been looked after, especially to secure the major customers. GSM obtained fixed assets with its acquisitions, but this wasn't a significant factor. As Barry remarks, 'Fixed assets are easy to acquire, it's what you do with them that matters. It's the systems and people that make the difference in any business.'[d]

One of Barry's criteria for acquisition involves location – that the site should be in a rural area. He argues that in rural areas you get a family atmosphere. In GSM's case employees want their relatives to work in their factories and GSM has a waiting list of people wanting to join it. Barry sees several reasons why rural areas are good:

People take ownership and there's little staff turnover. People in rural areas aren't a different sort of people, it's just the place affects people's attitudes. And we have no trouble attracting visitors.

Andrew concurs about Thirsk:

People like to come here, and they often stay for the weekend. The Yorkshire moors and dales are close by

and we're at the heart of Herriot country – a big difference from Birmingham, London and Stuttgart!

This is a deliberate part of GSM's sales technique.

In every acquisition Barry and Andrew worked together in every phase right from the first approach. Where an existing factory is to be retained, a cultural and organisational shift is required. The first thing they do is to get the incumbent management on board, getting them to come to Thirsk to see how GSM operates. In Wetherby there was a 90-day culture shift programme in which everyone was told of GSM's plans, teams were formed, team leaders were appointed, the morning briefing arrangements were set up and employment contracts were rewritten. Then the team leaders went to another of GSM's sites to talk with the team leaders who were operating there. This 90-day programme is only the start; it's recognised that it takes much longer to embed the culture.

Site operations

A general manager heads each of the three sites. The general managers aren't tightly controlled, but they do have profit targets to meet. There is a GSM philosophy about the way in which the factories should best be run, and so there is a fair degree of commonality about operations across sites. However, the work carried out at the sites – large production runs for the car assemblers in Brecon, smaller batches at Thirsk and metalworking at Wetherby – means that there are also distinct differences. The sites sell to each other, but there is no bar on them buying outside the group if this is more effective. Everyone in the company, including Barry and the general managers, has a contract that says that they are employed as a team member. Except for shift workers, everyone in the company starts at the same time in the morning, with no formal clocking in. Barry's base is at Thirsk, where he is the only person with an office. A dozen people have keys to the plant, allowing access at all times.

At each site manufacturing is split into about six teams ranging in size from six to 15 people, depending on the type of work being undertaken. The choice of team leaders is seen as a key issue for effective site operation. Team leaders are chosen by the site general and works managers, although there is often an obvious candidate. The mistake made in the past was to choose the most technically competent person to be the team leader. Now, although all the leaders are competent technically, or they wouldn't get the team's respect, they aren't always the most competent. The overriding consideration is that they must be communicators, and GSM provides team leaders with training in communication. Last year GSM wasn't happy with its team leaders' roles and they were redefined,

---

[d] Barry did buy a company that made aprons, strangely enough, because it had a very unusual drying system that he wanted. So this was one acquisition made to gain possession of a special piece of equipment.

Team leader's daily briefing sheet

WEEK NO. 9
DATE 4.3.99
DAY Thursday

ENGINEERING FINISHING TEAM
LEADER: D. HOGAN

INTAKE YESTERDAY	26.801
INTAKE WEEK	87.709
NO. QUOTES YESTERDAY	46
NO. QUOTES WEEK	171
INVOICED OUTPUT YESTERDAY	27.602
INVOICED OUTPUT WEEK	81.709
BUDGET FOR THIS WEEK	102.000
DAYS LEFT THIS WEEK	1
OUTPUT NEEDED	20.291
BUDGET FOR THIS MONTH	441.000
OUTPUT TO DATE	81.709
OUTPUT NEEDED	359.291
DAYS LEFT THIS MONTH	19

Checklist

COMPLEX ORDERS TAKEN YESTERDAY	See printout- DH
URGENT ORDERS CHASED – BB	Hughes Group/Advance Power
PROBLEM ORDERS ESP. CHASED	Volvo 29635
SIGNIFICANT PHONE CALLS	First order on its way from Czech R
TEAM GOOD NEWS	Jennys new baby (10lb boy)
VISITS, VISITORS	Customer 10.30 Lucas
BOTTLENECKS	CNC Punch
TEAM PROBLEMS	CNC Press Imping
CUSTOMER COPLAINTS	–
MACHINERY	Repair Guillotine, No 3 backstop
KAIZENS	2 current
TEAM MEMBERS' HOLS, ABSENCES, etc.	Tony on hols all next week

Exhibit 3   Team leader's daily briefing sheet

with all team leaders required to reapply for their jobs. One leader wasn't retained because he didn't want to go to visit customer sites, which was part of the new job specification.[e] A recent innovation is the appointment of deputy team leaders to stand in for the team leaders when they're away and be trained for subsequent team leader positions.

Each team operates as a mini-business and is in charge of its own day-to-day activities, such as the sequence in which jobs are tackled and the materials it wants the next day.[f] With this self-containment there is a need for a very good company communications system. Barry explains how it works:

At ten to eight each morning, the team leaders and the managers at each site will get together in the conference room and they go through a meeting with fixed agenda points and with the information specific to that day prepared by office staff prior to the meeting [see Exhibit 3 for an example of this briefing sheet].

The meeting lasts ten minutes and no more; people will leave in mid-sentence on the dot of 8 o'clock! Each person will know what the site produced the previous day, what it's hoping to do that day and details of any customers pulling jobs forward, any visitors we're having, what the significance of the visits is, the difficulties anyone is having with equipment – anything that may affect the work. People simply scan through the agenda information and pull out anything that they feel needs discussion to help them do their work.

At 8 o'clock each team leader goes to the team station. There the team leader briefs their team for five to six minutes, so that at five or six minutes past eight every person at every site knows what is happening.

GSM learned this system of daily briefings by hard experience. Years ago it had an 'end-of-month rush', with a great deal of output produced in the last few days of every

---

[e] Revealingly, he is still happy to work at GSM.
[f] It is intended to make the teams cost centres during the financial year 1999/2000.

month. Realising this was stupid, it moved to weekly targets – and then had an end-of-week rush. So now it's daily targets and no rush. One difference between GSM and other companies is a philosophy of dividing activities up and doing them in small packets, but doing it all the time. Instead of having a three-hour monthly meeting as other companies have, GSM has a ten-minute meeting every day – most importantly, with current information. Life is now much easier, as the quote in Exhibit 4 illustrates.

> The boss has mellowed. He used to be stressed out, carrying everything. Now the responsibility is shared out.
> Team leader, GSM Graphics[2]

Exhibit 4   Spreading responsibility

Salaries are important, since underpaid staff will perform grudgingly, but production bonuses aren't paid. At each team's briefing station there is a team board on which every skill that is needed by the team is listed and if a team member collects these skills they get more pay. The more jobs a team member can do the more valuable they are generally, and it makes them flexible. People don't get extra pay for doing a new job until they have proved they can do it. This is because it's far easier to ask someone to return to their previous job if they haven't got accustomed to the higher pay.

GSM is an ISO 9002 registered company and it audits all its activities. Every employee who has been with the company for six months gets their quality inspector's stamp when they've passed the GSM course. So everyone is their own inspector; they have their own numbered stamp to stamp an item off, having proved their competence in a particular area. As skills and experience build up, they can use their stamp in a wider range of activities.

GSM is happy to accept customers pulling jobs forward, and overtime is sometimes worked to accommodate this. GSM management is sure that there is some unnecessary overtime but is relaxed about this, arguing that the advantages associated with the freedom that GSM gives its team leaders far outweigh any extra costs. A 'fast delivery premium' is charged to the customer to cover overtime for any job needed in under seven days.

If a team thinks it wants another member, the leader asks the site general manager for permission to recruit. If recruitment is sanctioned, wage rates and duties are agreed. Advertising and interviewing of new team members are done by the present team members; management plays no part on the grounds that the teams are going to select people who they can work with. Team leaders don't have the authority to sack team members. Rudy Pearce, who was a team leader and is now the works manager at

Thirsk, points out: 'As a team leader, if someone wasn't working out in the team either personally or work-wise I could make recommendations to the works manager but couldn't sack anyone.' However, over the last few years no one has been sacked; what tends to happen is that anyone who doesn't fit in leaves of their own accord, or transfers to another team.

Every week a meeting is held to discuss what has happened over the intervening week in the factory. As Andrew explains:

> Every week I get together with the team leaders, the works manager, the quality manager and one or two other senior managers. We consider all day-to-day operational matters; we talk about the causes of any rejects from customers, other customer complaints, non-conformance within the factory, health and safety matters and we talk about training. We also talk about any projects that are going on. So there is a degree of control and it gives me a platform to voice any concerns I have. Otherwise it's got to be a fairly major issue for me to go to a team or a team leader and say, 'There's a problem. We must sit around a table and talk about it seriously.'

So rare is this that Andrew had difficulty thinking of a case where this had happened.

Kaizen – continuous improvement.

Kaizen is very, very active throughout GSM; 4000 suggestions for improvements have been made over the last four years from the Thirsk site alone. And these are suggestions that have actually been carried out.

When the scheme was launched there was a special prize for the person coming up with the most (accepted) *kaizens* in the first six months. The prize wasn't specified, because management wished to tailor the prize to the person getting it. One young chap came up with 14 suggestions. He was very keen on motor racing, so a day's racing was organised at the local motor-racing circuit. He loved it and came back with pictures that went into the local press.

Concentrating on time – not money – seems a very effective way of producing *kaizens* and (almost) everyone is involved. As Barry explains:

> If you get a team together and said 'Right guys, we want to save some money', it would be very difficult for them to come up with suggestions. However, if you say, 'Surely there's something in your job you feel's a waste of time. Tell me the most frustrating things in your job – things that really waste your time. Have you got any?' Nobody in the world will turn round and say, no, I haven't.

Ref. No: 7		Date: 20/6/99

Type of Report::	Non Conformance / Reject	
	Kaizen Proposal	✓

Section:	Artwork		Metal Preparation		Printing	
	Finishing		Engineering		Admin	
	Raw materials		Purchaser supplied		Miscellaneous	

Details:	Worksheet No		Customer	
	Purchase Order No		Supplier	
	Quantity rejected			
	Status	Tagged		Segregated

Reason for Non Conformity/Kaizen

Tinning Royal Mail badge pins is fiddly and time consuming using pliers to hold them and only a limited number can be done at one time.

Action required

Art Dept rework		Return to supplier		Re-print	
Replace/Repair/Credit		Obtain concession		Use alternative product	

Proposal

A piece of wood with two slots to put badge pins in to make the job easier and quicker.

Team Leader Assessment

This is a good idea that will enable us to save a considerable amount of time with a job of this size.

Corrective action

Comments:

Implement 21.6.99

Originator Janine Grange	Quality Inspector ....
Responsibility Paul Wright	Date 20/6/99...
Date Closed Out	

ISSUE: 2	DATE: April 99	SIGNATURE:

Exhibit 5   *Kaizen* form

Kaizens must be very easy to make. *Kaizen* forms – see Exhibit 5 – are dotted around on all the notice boards. The suggestees don't have to say how an issue should be tackled. The team leader is responsible for an initial filter and for taking the suggestions to a weekly meeting with the general manager and quality manager and others if needed. Inside of a week, a decision will be made whether to take the *kaizen* forward or not. Either way, the suggestee gets a response within a week. If it's decided not to proceed with the suggestion, the suggestee is told the reason why. If the suggestion is going to be progressed, then a timescale is put on its implementation together with a cost estimate. Money isn't the real motivator; for each *kaizen* the payment is only £5, a token way of saying thank you. But it's absolutely direct. Each person offering a *kaizen* can think, 'On Monday I came up with a suggestion, on Thursday it was accepted, on Friday I got my fiver. It's absolutely direct – and something to talk about in the pub!'

Exhibit 5 gives one example of a *kaizen*. A second is that undertaken by product development at Wetherby. They found that a customer spent a great deal of time unwrapping GSM products. So now products are delivered direct to the production line in returnable plastic crates with shaped foam inserts. The boxes fit into each other and come back on the lorry. So this *kaizen* got rid of a wrapping process at GSM, an unwrapping process at the customer and the cost of the wrapping.

With the *kaizen* approach in operation for so long it becomes more difficult to keep going. As Rudy says, 'We need to kick start the *kaizen* process from time to time to refresh it.'

As well as the *kaizen* forms, the set of order instructions that accompanies each job as it moves around the factory includes a piece of paper to allow people to write out in their own words a non-conformance statement, stating the problems they have had doing their job. For example: if only the plastic had been cut straight; if only the work sheet had said such and such; the next time this job comes up it's better if it's done this way, and so on. About 30% are improvement suggestions that are investigated further.

Training

GSM spends 1.4% of revenues on training, which is a much larger amount than most companies. This isn't a predetermined figure, just what has occurred, and is a level the firm is happy with. The profits are there to sustain this level – GSM's profits compare very favourably with similar businesses. All training is linked to the business plan, with every person having their own personal development plan that is reviewed every 90 days. As Andrew explains:

With Investors in People we decided that I would sit down with the team leader, the training manager and the team members individually, and discuss their training over the past three months and what was coming up in the next three months. And it would be a platform for me to tell them what the company was about to do, how the company had fared over the past, what was in the pipeline, the thinking and so on. This is done with every person individually, and it's a wonderful platform for me. I learn a lot – it's a relaxing atmosphere, but punchy. Getting up and addressing everyone *en masse* isn't the GSM style.

The proficiency of each team member, the training they are currently undertaking and their scheduled future training are all indicated on their team board. New technology is welcomed: 'people get into it straightaway and are keen to test out new equipment', notes Rudy. Training is generally provided by the skilled members in the team. Recently, some concern was expressed that the team leaders should have more external training. Eight people from the Thirsk site went off for one day a month for six months to an agency in Thirsk. They were the only people on the course, which was tailored to GSM's exact requirements, using GSM's own language: team leaders rather than supervisors and foremen, for example.

When interviewing, GSM looks for aptitude and attitude and in particular people skills. It's rarely looking for specific skills and so it isn't concerned with any so-called skills shortage because its training programme is so good that it can train people up itself. GSM looks within its own organisation, with all vacancies advertised internally first, and then gives fast-track training to people who are suitable. GSM has done this successfully many times. For example, three people are now on a website development course as it's in GSM's business objectives to establish a website in 1999; and one of the works managers came to GSM as a youth training scheme (YTS) trainee.

Operations and suppliers

For Ford, GSM operates a system whereby it interrogates Ford's parts requirements every day and decides what it will ship that evening, and thus what will be made each day. Its trucking system will arrive at the Brecon plant and the Ford requirements will be loaded. There is no human contact as it is all done through electronic data interchange (EDI). Ford demanded that all its suppliers establish EDI; it specified the system and the software but Primographic, as it then was, had to pay for it. EDI is now established at all three GSM sites.

GSM has made a great effort to keep the number of suppliers to a minimum, searching for single-source arrangements where possible. Currently it has around 50 suppliers that supply in any significant quantity. With the trust that tends to come from single sourcing, GSM expects prices to come down as raw material prices ease, and accepts the reverse situation. GSM discusses with each supplier exactly what it wants in terms of price, delivery, quality, and what the procedure should be if things go wrong; correspondingly, GSM guarantees to pay on the same day each month via BACS. GSM emphasises that it doesn't want to change suppliers and that suppliers would have to do something very wrong to be substituted. In the last ten years two metal suppliers have been changed, but the ink, paint and chemical suppliers have remained the same.

There are common suppliers to all sites for metals, adhesives, etc., with suppliers' prices checked on a continual basis. Suppliers supply within 48 hours or they cease to be suppliers. They supply into the site and put supplies where the team leaders want them. An interesting detail is that the racking for the supplies is made of such dimensions that supplies can't be overstocked: excess stocks simply can't get put into the racks!

Customer relations

Each site has its sales support team consisting of six people who are involved in all aspects of sales. However, the salesforce is common, in the sense that if one site has a client close to one of the other sites, someone from this second site will be charged with looking after that customer, unless there are specialist considerations. The team members spend a great deal of time on the phone, answering price, technical and order progress queries. Often a customer will know the application they want satisfying but it's up to the sales team to liaise internally to devise the means of achieving what is required. 3M provides technical specifications for its adhesives, for example, but for a particularly difficult requirement it would be consulted.

One recent development is to produce a superior form of nameplate. Anodising opens up the pores of aluminium, allowing the surface to be printed. The surface is then sealed by dipping it into boiling water for 25 minutes. The result is a nameplate impervious to bad weather, giving GSM a significant competitive advantage. A second development involved modifying cutting machinery. A customer had noted that their labels weren't adhering particularly well as the cutting of the labels out of the sheet left each with a very small raised rim, reducing significantly the area of contact of the adhesive surface. The solution that GSM came up with was to cut the sheet 'upside down', thus putting the rim on the front of the label. This could only be done by reconfiguring the cutting machine with closed circuit television cameras to allow the operator to see where to make the cuts.

The sales team issues and follows up quotations, which at the Thirsk site total about 40 per day. Thirsk has about 5000 customers, of whom around 2000 are very active. This is a tremendous strength, as Andrew points out:

This was one of the criteria that I used when I joined the company. I could see the range of applications of the labels. If the white goods industry went down, the brown goods industry would come up. It's like pressing a balloon; if you press at one point another part expands. So the safety factor is enormous.

Thirsk averages 800 live orders in the factory at any one time; Brecon has about 80. The turnover of the two factories is comparable.

The sales support team provides technical support for representatives and project managers, including the provision of samples and prototypes. It sends out mailshots to customers about new products and also sources special materials. Recently, one of the teams discovered that a cooker manufacturer was having problems with its control disc labels. GSM visited the manufacturer and suggested a new approach, using ultrasonic welding. GSM had no expertise in this area but was able to respond. This order is worth around £150,000 p.a.

At each point of customer contact GSM has timed responses, which, apart from the telephone rings, are strictly audited:

- no more than three rings on the telephone;
- a quotation within 24 hours (and usually within one hour);
- all customers who haven't accepted a quote within a further 48 hours will be chased;
- artwork proofs within 48 hours;
- customer told within one hour whether an order can be pulled forward.

GSM quotes a price within 24 hours in DM or euros to German customers in German, so that it can compare precisely GSM's prices and terms with those of German firms. To make life easy, the Germans pay into a DM account in Germany. Even in mid-1998 when the exchange rate was DM3 to the pound, GSM was still able to secure German orders. The power of the quick quotation was brought home to Barry when he was in GSM's front line on the sales desk. He saw at first hand that many times GSM was pricier than the opposition, but because it quoted within an hour, the customer had already placed the job when the opposition came in three days later with their price.

GSM has an open pricing policy. It is quite happy to give Ford its formulae for calculating prices – and it has –

and Ford has come back to discuss them. Ford knows that GSM will make a profit, it knows whether there is a possibility of reducing costs, and it knows what machines are used and how fast they run.

With some customers there is an on-going relationship. Some customers have come to GSM and copied its system, even making exact copies of the team boards. GSM operates a system whereby customer team leaders can talk to its people on the telephone. Team members occasionally work on the customers' production lines (for example with Nissan) to enable them to see what and how GSM products are used and to see other production processes.

If a mistake is made on a customer order, GSM finds that the best thing is for the team leader or manager to ring the customer and say outright, 'I've/we've made a mistake'. As long as this happens only occasionally, customers appreciate the frankness.

Planning, policy and the future

Barry, the general managers and two project managers form the strategy team. Barry has clear views on the importance of taking a strategic view:

It seems to me that there is a time in a company's development when one or two vital decisions have to be made – if you don't make these decisions then things start to drift away and thereafter it doesn't matter what decisions you make, you've lost. So there is a timeframe to make a decision. Digital printing technology is entering now and we've just got our foot in the door with our first digital printing system. There's a timeframe for that to happen – for us to be up front and leading. If we miss that boat, at some stage we'd be too late and lose part of our business.

Barry views clear goals and objectives as paramount:

Events happen around you that drive you off course. But you still need to hit the target. If you take the vague view of goals, you will be buffeted about and may not achieve your objective. So I don't like to do it that way. I much prefer to focus on what we're trying to achieve. If we sit down and say that the focus is no longer attainable and we intend to refocus, then that isn't buffeting; that's a strategic decision to move the goalposts. And there's nothing wrong with that.

GSM holds regular strategy reviews. Recently, Barry and the project managers spent the whole of one day discussing how they saw the automobile industry in two years time. Strategic initiatives are usually taken forward by setting up a project team to handle them. The teams contain about three to five people, almost always includ-

ing Barry. The team members are chosen because of their knowledge or their subsequent involvement in the initiative should it be carried forward. For example, a works or general manager from the factory most associated with the project would almost certainly be a member of the project team.

The project managers tend to be responsible for large customer-based changes. For example, when the Wetherby plant won the contract to take over all of a customer's metalwork manufacture, a project manager co-ordinated all the associated logistics and made sure that the customer's interests were taken care of. In the middle of 1999, a continuous improvement team leader (CITL) was appointed at Thirsk. As with most posts at GSM, this was an internal promotion, with training provided. While the *kaizen* committee deals with incremental process improvements, the CITL is concerned with site-wide issues. Their role is not necessarily to think of new ideas but to collate ideas from any source, get agreement on which initiatives to pursue and then to research their feasibility. For example, one potentially significant new area is the use of ultraviolet light to set adhesives, rather than using adhesives that contain polluting solvents. The CITL at Thirsk is researching this, talking to GSM's printers, 3M experts and so on to see whether the process will suit GSM. Another area is the use of pure water in the toilets, and recycling of the almost pure water used in the production processes.

So far, GSM has no Internet developments, although it has sent two people on an Internet training course. One reason for the slow progress is that Barry is the chairman of a regional IT group that has received £850,000 funding from the DTI to fund 100 companies in Yorkshire as exemplars of Internet practice. This group has the technical support of BT and ICL and, not unsurprisingly, GSM will be one of the chosen companies. By the end of 1999, GSM expects not only to have a website but to be engaged in e-commerce.[3]

Progress on strategic initiatives is fed into the general managers' meeting that is held every eight weeks to consider the more strategic issues of the company as they affect the sites. A written targeted business plan is produced annually for the subsequent 12 months. There is also a two-year, slightly more vague, set of targets, and then a 'wish list' of where GSM wants to be five years from the present. The business plan is continually audited; GSM looks at what it has achieved, why something hasn't been achieved and what changes are to be made. For example, at a recent meeting Barry began with an overview – a discussion of the products/markets the company wants to be in. Then the current customers and competitors were considered, especially if there have been any changes in the last two months. Next, the most appropriate way for GSM to benchmark itself was discussed. The agenda then focused more internally: on whether GSM's unique selling proposition was still current, its service levels, the equipment needs, the media presence required, and the marketing and sales status. It's at these meetings that customer/products with low profitability would be discussed; GSM is fairly ruthless in not continuing unprofitable activities.

Team leaders' conferences are held every six months, one for each site. All the team leaders, deputy team leaders, the general manager, the sales team and Barry meet in a hotel for the evening. They go through their objectives and ideas.

Decision making isn't democratic, although the process is such that everyone is listened to. The view is that committees can't make decisions, one individual has to do that. The view is also that if a decision is taken on reasonable grounds and it turns out to have been inappropriate, then that's no cause to get overly worried. What matters is the quality of the process: has it been logical and, very significantly, is it in the best interests of the customer.

GSM doesn't have a formal code of ethics. To quote Barry:

The one thing we are is that we're absolutely dead straight. As a company we'll tell it like it is. If we can't deliver something on Thursday afternoon and you seriously want it, we'll tell you now it's not going to happen. We've always done that and we've lost orders because of it in the past. But we don't end up with a web of deceit and silly happenings.

However, GSM does have a mission statement, reproduced as Exhibit 6. GSM is also run with few rules, although all staff are in post by 8am to hear the team briefing; only in exceptional circumstances will people be excused from this briefing, as it's considered vital in maintaining team cohesion.

During 1999, GSM is seeking to become an approved company to the environmental standard ISO 14001, which is concerned with everything to do with the environment – electricity use, water use, effluent, scrap, etc. Very few companies have attained this standard as yet. Seeking this standard is affecting GSM's products and processes.

GSM plans to have a yearly environmental audit that would interleave with its other audits, including its training audit, which is part of the Investors in People initiative and for which GSM won a regional training award in 1998. The firm is active in the local community. In Thirsk, it welcomes many students from the local school, and Barry attends its Prize Day. The social committee has donated a set of shirts to the local football team.

GSM has contingency plans in case of a fire at the factories, since customers can't wait. GSM knows it can

GSM GROUP
MISSION STATEMENT

GSM Group is committed to supplying metal & plastic components to all industries, realistically priced, with zero defects, delivered when required and produced profitably.

Our customers come first. GSM will always be helpful, friendly, responsive and pleasant to deal with.

Using the latest manufacturing techniques and quality systems GSM will maintain its leading position in UK industry.

Our team is dedicated to becomig the number one manufacturer in Europe by being more innovative, more cost-effective and consistently more reliable than any of our competitors.

By caring for all our team members, protecting the environment and being active in our community, GSM will be regarded as a good neighbour and a fine place to work.

Exhibit 6 GSM Group mission statement

double up on the shifts at Primographic and that people can be moved in coaches to Brecon and run the Thirsk production overnight. Similarly, Thirsk would run 24 hour a day and use two approved subcontractors to take a substantial part of the workload should there be a fire at Brecon. Some of Wetherby's key processes are duplicated at Thirsk and it would run 24 hours a day and be supported by an approved subcontractor. Computing cover is easy, as GSM operates the same systems at each of its three sites. GSM has a complete anodising plant off site; it was acquired in an acquisition and GSM kept it, as it is used as a selling point to customers: 'What other company can still be running the day after a fire?' And companies are well aware that such calamities can happen: Toyota had a single brake caliper plant for all its worldwide operations – in Kyoto – which was devastated by the earthquake of 1995. The whole of Toyota came to a stop.

One concern is a big lottery win. Almost all GSM employees are in one syndicate or another, and the risks to production of a big win are significant: all of the print team at Thirsk is in the same syndicate, for example. GSM tried to get insurance, but this would have cost almost as much as the winnings.

Intellectual property isn't safeguarded, with GSM believing that speed of innovation is what is vital, not patents or other forms of protection. There have been several times when it could have gone to court, but that would have wasted a lot of time and it wasn't sure of winning. GSM has low staff turnover, but it's relaxed about people leaving to join the competition.

References

1 Nasser quote from Brierley, D., 'Car makers run out of road', *The Independent on Sunday*, 'Business', 21 March 1999, p. 2.

2 Quoted in *Competitiveness through Partnerships with People*, jointly sponsored by the DTI and the Department for Education and Employment, 1997, p. 2.

3 GSM's website address is http://www.gsmgroup.co.uk

The life and times of an entrepreneur[a]

The formative years

Pete Parker had a very happy and comfortable childhood. His father was in middle management and his mother stayed at home looking after him and his brother. From the earliest age, he realised that he wanted things and that he had to work for them, but he had no particular ideas of starting his own business. Pete reflects on the first deal he ever made:

When I was at infants school there was a girl called Esmee Creswell who had the aluminium foil strips that I realised later were the 'chaff' used to foil radar. She came into school with a block of these strips for which I gave her the old 3p. And I started to sell these at 10 strips for a penny. There were lots of them and I made an enormous amount of money. All the kids were running around the school with these strips and they were all coming to me to get them. I distinctly remember that this was the first time I started dealing and making money. You know school crazes – yo-yos, matchbox guns. Well, I started this craze and I was king of the market there. I used to go home at night with my pockets bulging with money.

He recounts how he was always doing jobs. When he was at secondary school he marked up the papers and did three paper rounds each morning – and if he could, he would do another round in the evening. His father used to cut his and his brother's hair with a pair of clippers. Pete then used these to go round the local council estates and cut the children's hair in their own homes. He did a great many small jobs like that; to Pete it's a perfectly normal way of life.

Starting up

Pete was reasonably happy at school, but his abiding memory was that he wanted to leave, although he doesn't feel that the education system had in any way let him down. His first job on leaving school was as a dental mechanic, but after three months he realised that there wasn't a future in it. When he was 17 he started working for Gillette as a chemist in its laboratories. At that time he

was going to warehouses and buying all sorts of things – like shirts and Christmas crackers – and found that he could sell these around the factory very easily. There were thousands of people in the factory and trade was very good. He remembers his thoughts when the man in charge of the laboratory told him that he was taking his BSc and would then be getting a four-figure salary:

I thought, gee, four figures, and you're a really, really bright guy. And I'm pushing this trolley around the factory and I'm earning nearly four figures now. And you've had to work all this time to get yourself through. I thought this doesn't seem right. I'm never going to be as bright as you and so I might as well carry on as I am now.

Pete did carry on as before until he was told to leave. His studies on part time day release were going badly. They didn't interest him – especially as the end product only appeared to be £1000 a year! He had bigger goals than that. He also had a Saturday job selling clothing in a shop, which he felt he did well. The shop was one of a chain of menswear shops, the firm was reorganising, and it wanted Pete to oversee the whole chain. Pete thought about this as it was good money, but he wanted to be on his own. Although what he liked about being an entrepreneur was the style, the position and the money, the main driver was the freedom to make his own decisions. He started up a clothing business with a partner in Crayford in Kent. This venture failed miserably; it wasn't right and it wasn't in the right place. Pete found that he hated having to be in the shop at 9am, look after it and wait for people to come in; he was much happier with going out and finding the customers.

The go-go decade

It was the late 1960s, and with the failure of the Crayford venture Pete began work as a freelance sales agent selling ties. As he recalls:

The hardest thing in the world is selling ties – I'd far rather be selling jeans or shirts or something like that. However, ties were the only thing available – other people had been in the business far longer and had the good agencies. I had to start at the bottom.

Pete also took on other menswear agencies. Then he came across Ben, who was manufacturing shirts in the East End

[a] This case was prepared by Paul Finlay and Peter Jennings of The Business School, Loughborough University. © Paul Finlay and Peter Jennings, 1999.

of London. Pete had a reasonable eye for what would sell and he knew that, although the shirts weren't quite right, they could be made to be right. Pete and Ben started a small back-street business selling shirts with small motifs and Pete dropped the ties. They were selling into the big multiple outlets and so Pete made good contacts there which were to stand him in good stead later on. Things went very well, until the imports started coming in. Pete recalls ruefully that for the first time in his life he was affected by imports. Pete and Ben couldn't be competitive and the venture closed.

Pete was in his mid-twenties at this time and at home in the West End. As he puts it:

In the West End it's a bit incestuous – everyone knows everyone else. You walk around Great Portland Street and Mortimer Street and you see the people who go to the same shows, the same wine bars, the same coffee bars. They all know one another.

Pete got talking with the managing director of Smiths, a London-based firm that had a factory in Wakefield. He asked Pete to join them as a director. Pete had seen what this firm was doing and he liked it, so he agreed.

When he joined Smiths its turnover was around £750,000 and he built it up to £12 million. It was both importing and manufacturing. It was testing the water with its own manufacturing and then going overseas to get it made cheaper. Pete was well connected with the buyers of the large retailers, who would tell him what was selling, what they thought the next trend would be and what the competition was up to.

But Pete fell out with the managing director of Smiths and left. He started a partnership with Fernando, a Portuguese who was importing shirts in a very small way and whose father had an import–export business in Oporto. At that time you could start off a business in a small way as there was a reasonable number of small retailers, so you could build yourself up and then deal with the big retailers.[b] Pete went to Oporto to see what the set-up there was like and it seemed fine. Pete told Fernando that he could expand his operation if Fernando could deliver the goods. The business went quite well, but there was a clash of personalities. The success seemed to go to Fernando's head: he wanted to buy big cars, whereas Pete wanted to wait a little. his extravagance on the part of Fernando led to Pete severing the relationship. According to Pete, Fernando was following the classic route to failure:

You can earn a lot of money for three months and then you've got to wait nine months for some more work. You have the staff to pay and you buy big cars.

Lots of money was being earned in the West End in the early 1970s. Everything Pete earned was his own – there was no interest to pay, as Pete rarely borrowed money from the banks, believing that they throw money at you when you don't want it but won't give it to you when you do.

Then Smiths contacted Pete and enticed him back with an offer he couldn't refuse. But this only lasted a short time. Pete saw something that was so good that he had to put his whole effort into it. This was fleece miniskirts, which Pete introduced into the UK from an idea he got from the USA. Pete had always gone along to fashion shows and at that time was going to three or four shows a year. Sometimes he would go with the buyers of the big retailers, see what they liked and discuss with them how it would need to be modified. Pete thought he could do a range of the fleece miniskirts; it wasn't quite right for the Wakefield factory, but he knew it wouldn't take much to manufacture them. So he went to John, whom he'd known for several years while working in the West End and who could do this – John knew about the fabric, which Pete didn't. It was a full partnership – Pete didn't want this, but John did because he thought that Pete would learn about his connections as regards the fabric, since anyone can go into the suppliers and get the fabric if they have the money. As Pete recalls, 'It's dog eat dog in the West End – there're very nice people but you all know where you stand!'

Everything went very well. They moved out to South Kensington and subrented a factory to a Pole, who ran the factory with Polish workers. Pete recalls these people with a smile:

These guys were amazing. They were scientists and other educated people but they were hungry and they would work 24 hours a day seven days a week – except for the name days, when they got drunk and you couldn't do anything with them.

Pete and John branched out from miniskirts into tops. At that particular time there was a shortage of machinists, especially in central London. Pete had the confidence of the buyers – they could come down and see what was going on. They could sit opposite Pete and he could show them that he could produce what they wanted in an acceptable timescale. Imports were not such a threat as they had been with the shirts, because the miniskirts weren't as labour-intensive. They were very easy to cut and had few seams; so easy were they to make that people who had never seen a sewing machine could be employed.

---

[b] This isn't the case at the end of the 1990s, as the big retailers have a much greater percentage of the market.

The operation appeared to be going very well, as indeed it was, but things started to go wrong. Pete had been dealing with the customers, not concerning himself with the financial side. He was on holiday one Easter believing that the partnership had assets of £50,000. Pete says he can remember the feeling of foreboding as if it were yesterday:

It was a warm day and I was lying on the beach and thought, 'This just can't be right.' I phoned up John and said he must look at these figures again – instead of being 50 grand up I felt we were nearer 50 grand down!

When Pete got back from holiday he and John had a very acrimonious break-up – this was a partnership that went down screaming. John was both incompetent and wanting to start his own company doing something else. They had a joint overdraft secured on their houses. Although he retained his house Pete lost everything else; his beloved Jaguar had to be sold and he ended up with a small Fiat. He had to take his eldest daughter Alex out of private school in a leafy suburb of Weybridge in Surrey. It was a very poignant moment. As Pete recalls:

As I walked down the corridor there were lots of the children's pictures on the wall showing scenes of where they had been on holiday – Bermuda, Cyprus and so on. And Alex had done a painting of a house with the caption 'This year we didn't go on holiday because we're poor'.

The London entrepreneur

So Pete had to do something. There were two possibilities for him in the UK: work for the major multiple retailers and obtain very small margins, but get paid; or work for the smaller companies, which was risky, and possibly not get paid. Pete went for the secure route. His strengths were his contacts with the multiple stores; his weakness was that he had no money. He went to see a buyer for one of large multiples with whom he'd always had a very friendly relationship and told him of his situation. The buyer asked how he could help. Pete had for many years had a dormant company – for just such a situation – and he asked for an order for this company. So now he had an order, a beginning.

Pete then made an appointment with all the banks except for his own bank, which knew his financial predicament in detail! He went to a branch of Lloyds and discussed his situation with the manager. Pete told him what was going on and showed him the order. He remembers the interchange very clearly:

He asked what amount I needed to satisfy that order. I said ten grand. I wasn't sure that I could raise this. The bank manager asked me whether I had a credit card. I said yes. He then asked me what the credit limit was: I said ten grand. And how much have you outstanding he asked: three grand. So, if you put up £5000 from your credit card, I'll put up the other £5000.

So now Pete had his £10,000. Then the buyer for the high-street retailer told Pete what he wanted and Pete set about getting it made in a factory in Nottingham, after he bought the required fabric. Halfway through getting it made the mechanic at the factory rang him up one Friday night to tell him that Frank, the owner, had 'done a runner' to the States. The letter that the mechanic had received from Frank said that he had sent the keys of his house and the factory to the bank manager – he owed the bank about £30,000 – and said 'it's all yours'. And in the factory was Pete's fabric, which the bailiffs would impound! On the Saturday Pete went to Nottingham and to the factory with the mechanic and took all the firm's books back to the Savoy Hotel and went through them. He knew, having been in this situation himself, what to look for; he knew where the pressure was coming from. He knew he must not lose the fabric; it was in fluorescent colours which, once they're dead, are very, very dead.

Pete wondered if there was a chance of hanging on to the factory and getting his fabric made up so he could complete his order. No one except the mechanic knew that Frank had gone. The situation was that Frank owed the landlords rent and the tax authorities a little bit of PAYE and VAT. Because he'd had problems with landlords before, Pete phoned them and told them exactly what had happened. Pete said he would pay the rent from that day. The landlords were very understanding on the phone, but 20 minutes later the bailiffs were in – the landlords had instructed them to do so.

So the bailiffs came in and ticketed up everything, and Pete wasn't able to progress his order. The bailiffs pointed out that the machinery must be worth far more than the £5000 that would secure the factory for him. So Pete had to get £5000, which he succeeded in doing. He then had to do a bit of jiggery-pokery with the bailiffs and he managed to get everything in the factory and to pay the landlords. Now Pete had machinery worth £10,000 at auction. He then made the order but wondered whether he could run the factory long-term. Pete contacted his friendly high-street store buyer and said he'd like a meeting since, before running the factory on a longer-term basis, he wanted to know the strength of their relationship. The buyer said that he would support Pete if he went to live near the factory; at that time Pete was still living in Weybridge. Pete wasn't too keen on this, being a southerner, but he had to do it.

In Nottingham Pete went through the wage bill, which

was all on the computer – the firm was early into comput-ing – and it was clear that an enormous amount of dead wood was being carried. So he wrote new contracts for the staff he wished to retain and made the others redundant. This caused a lot of problems and he had a demonstration outside the factory. Pete made the front page of the local newspaper, the *Nottingham Evening Post*, with the head-line 'London entrepreneur colludes in factory closure', alleging that Pete was trying to get out of paying his creditors. This was untrue, as Frank had provided his house. As Pete ruefully remarks: 'All on the back of a Barclaycard!'

Pete couldn't afford solicitors – he'd always kept away from them as he believes that they cost you a fortune. Pete knew of the small business support services, including the local chamber of trade, but didn't turn to them; he believed that although they would try to be helpful, they weren't equipped to resolve non-standard issues. So he read up all he could on company law and got in touch with the DSS. Pete says that he has found with people like the DSS that it's best to be honest with them – tell it how it is. If they come along afterwards and you've been hiding something, you can be in a lot of trouble. He told them they could come in and have a look at the computer records, but that he must make some of the people redun-dant. After a lot of negotiation and discussion he was able to do so. The DSS weren't very helpful; apparently they're used to things falling into well-specified categories and Pete's situation wasn't one of these.

The mechanic had been retained as the factory man-ager, but in the end he departed in tears – he just couldn't handle the responsibility. Until then Pete had never run a factory, and that's when he and his wife seriously looked for property in Nottingham. Now he had to learn pretty quickly. The thing about a factory is that there's a big wage bill – the gap between the wages and output is very small. Pete knew that he had to look at the weakest link in his set-up. Getting orders was no problem and neither were the designs, but matching the response times required by the big retailers was vital. They would run trial designs in which they would want a pack of 12 garments – four blue, four pink and four orange, say – and they would put these trial packs in their outlets and then three days later they would phone you up and specify the order: perhaps 40,000 and in a particular ratio of colours. It's not poss-ible to hold big stocks because no one knows what the order will be, and the dyer has to turn round things very quickly.

Obtaining the fabric and getting it dyed were potential bottlenecks in responding to orders. To cope with the first issue Pete got in five knitting machines. He says he's never too worried by machines; when he buys he gets

good ones that he can always sell, and there are plenty of firms you can lease machines from. Dyeing is a big oper-ation and so Pete couldn't get involved in that. To pre-vent the dyers holding things up, Pete made a point of always paying them within seven days, and in this way got good service.

Simply manufacturing plain garments wasn't very prof-itable – what Pete had to do was make them look good, and the best way to make a garment look good was to put a print on it. Pete out-sourced his printing to three print-ers. The owner of the best printers was about to retire, so Pete decided to buy him out.

In the early 1990s the Department of Trade and Industry (DTI) ran a scheme under the slogan 'We're doing well, but we're not doing great' whereby it paid two-thirds of the cost of a firm's employing a consultant. Pete didn't know much about factories and thought he must be able to do better. The factory supervisor was a machinist whom he'd promoted. Pete recounts an interest-ing tale:

I decided to go for the scheme. First a consultant's consultant comes down to see whether I can be consulted by the consultant. He agreed that I could. Then a consultant comes down. He talks to me to decide which of his consultants should consult with me. When he comes, this guy says he knows what I need and where I'm going wrong. The problem is that you've no planning, he says. I didn't see how I could plan, with such short calls. You don't know what's running through your factory; I said I did, I've got it in my head. The guy said this was no good as no one else could get at the data. Fine, if you can show me how to do it. This guy got a board – which I had to pay for – and spent ages drawing lines on it and sticking stickers on it. I asked him what he had been doing previously. He had been working in a factory and he had to leave – the factory went bust! The consultant was explaining how I had to move the stickers across the board and, lo and behold, a retailer phones up and says, 'Pete, someone has let us down – can you do us a favour by pulling an order forward by a couple of weeks? Can you do it?

I had a large order going through for another high-street retailer. This retailer paid 40 days, the retailer on the phone seven days. The 40-day chap could wait. Plus they had done me favours. I said to my supervisor that we had to change the schedules – get the stuff off the machines and start the new job. The consultant said I couldn't do it. I said I can. And each time as he gesticulated and turned round, the stickers were sticking on him until he looked like a Christmas tree. You'll never run a factory like that, he says. I said I probably couldn't run a factory like that, but I could run my accounts like that. That's the most important thing. But you'll never ever be anything if you keep doing things like that. More stickers over him!

The planning board was never used. The consultant's consultant said he hoped Pete was satisfied. The consultant's report was massive and Pete was asked to sign that it was good value for money. Pete refused to sign as it was totally useless. A chap from the DTI asked Pete to sign, saying that Pete wouldn't need to pay his third. Toing and froing about payment went on for two years!

After this Pete was becoming computerised. A management information system was implemented, which Pete says is the best management tool he has ever had. In the factory the whole system ran on barcodes, providing Pete with a readout every day to tell him how many hours were needed on each machine to do something. So he was in a position to tell an enquirer if something could be made to a certain timescale. Pete showed all the staff what the computer could do: that he could tell how they were working and that there was full control of inputs.

However, he was being swamped by paperwork and bureaucracy as well; for example, the need to provide reasons for someone leaving; providing employee and output statistics, which take a long time to assemble; dealing with visits from the Health and Safety Executive; and keeping accident books. Employment legislation was becoming stricter; it was becoming very difficult to sack anyone – and, by extension, impossible to hire anyone. Even if someone was on drugs there's great difficulty in dismissing them. If women become pregnant you must give them maternity leave and re-employ them after three months. Pete had many letters from the DSS saying that he had no right to fire someone and that he must re-employ a previous employee. The no-win/no-fee situation had made matters much worse. Someone who had worked for Pete for three months two or three years previously put in a claim that she had lost a finger. She didn't win, but Pete had to defend it. It seemed to him that everyone had a down on him for employing people; in Pete's view he ought to be given a medal for employing them.

Even with a £4 million turnover, Pete was wondering whether he should continue. Margins were thin and being eroded all the time by imports. He found it difficult to gauge the effect of what he was doing on the bottom line. Pete realised that he didn't like handling the workforce, which numbered about 80 people. It didn't appear worth the hassle anymore and so he decided to pack it in. He spoke to his bank manager, who said he was mad. He told his accountant, who also thought he was mad. The general consensus was that it was a good business. But Pete didn't think so. As he put it to his bank manager:

The business is good for you and for the accountants. It's good for the multiples, it's good for the staff – some of whom are earning more than I am – but not good for me.

In 1996 he put the company into liquidation to avoid the £80,000–90,000 in redundancy pay that he would otherwise have been forced to meet. Every creditor was paid apart from the people claiming redundancy. To achieve this, Pete held back an order until the business was liquidated, and accepted payment for the order into his new firm.

Pete considered many facets of the clothing industry and looked at where he could earn a living without the factory. First of all he did some orders on a CMT (cutting, making, trimming) basis at another factory, but this wasn't very successful. He tried a second factory, but the margins were still very slim – and not worth the effort for the £500–600 he earned; he had to get the orders, find the factory and get the orders packed. Pete had kept the print operation from the liquidation, four or five staff and his secretary. The print operation was appealing because it could make money and it wasn't labour-intensive. And there was very good machinery there. It was a part of the business that ran OK, but Pete had never looked at it closely. It had been neglected. It was the profits from the printing operation that had allowed Pete to pay his creditors.

The lucrative niche

Pete needed to go out and get some good printing orders, but not with the big multiples as they couldn't now generate the margins that they had done before. He knew that if he found the right customer his output was good enough quality. He found a factory making children's nightwear that had five printers working for it. The print standard was poor and the designs were very average; this was Pete's chance, and he offered to do 5000 free prints. This initial approach developed into a good business relationship. Pete was on his way again, but not without hiccups: the chap who had been running the printing machine left at a week's notice!

Pete couldn't find a printer at such short notice and so he had to learn from scratch how to print. He had got several big orders, but he didn't even know where the switch was to turn on the machine! So he shadowed the machine operator, writing everything down on a clipboard. Pete called in all the reps that he was buying from – inks, meshes and screens – and asked what he did with this, and this, and so learned from them. He was learning by trial and error. A woman working the machine didn't know how to set it up and because of his eyesight Pete couldn't register the fine work. But together they triumphed.

Pete has optimised the business and it's now very tightly managed – because he could put the time and effort into it.

He wishes he had done this before. He explains how he has cut his weekly ink bill from £150 to less than £25:

When a company goes down, and they are always doing it, their assets are sold at auction. I go along, not to buy the machinery, but to buy the inks. Inks cost between £50 and £60 for a 5-litre drum and at auction you can buy a room full for £40–50. No one wants to buy the inks – often I'm the only bidder. People don't want to buy them because they've been opened. But there's no contamination and no drying out.

Pete retains very good relationships with the ink suppliers. Much of the time this is because he needs information about lines that are being discontinued, which they sell to Pete because he pays quickly – although they know Pete buys the cheap inks at auction. They will give technical information because allegedly printing is a very technical business, and Pete can pick up the phone and talk to someone for advice.

Printing is by far Pete's biggest turnover, but he is involved in other merchandise, such as buying and selling fabric, and recently he bought a parcel of 10,000 books. He could take on more orders but doesn't want to; as it stands he has no problems if work becomes slack. As Pete explains:

If I got bigger I would be more vulnerable if things go quiet. If I don't get any work for six months I don't care very much. I've got one person full time, two or three casuals and someone to come in over a weekend or if I have to work a 24-hour shift. I've just done 30,000 T-shirts all on a night shift that hasn't affected my business at all. I'm very, very flexible, with a good, solid little business. If I got bigger I'd have to buy a new machine – a good machine at auction is £20,000; a new one is £80,000. To move I'd need a crane and would incur all sorts of costs and it would take a year to get expenses back. It would take five years to pay for a new machine.

Pete doesn't meet the store buyers any more. The factories that he now deals with are suppliers to the second-line retailers. The buyers for these retailers will have ideas for designs for the clothes they are selling – a well-known cartoon character, for example – and will ask their suppliers (the factories) to come up with proposals. The design can't be exactly the same as the cartoon character, but they can be close. The factories then ask people like Pete to provide these designs.

Another route is for Pete to provide the factories with a portfolio of designs. Pete likes computers and was one of the first people to get actively involved commercially. In the evening he's happy sitting at the computer watching TV in one square and developing designs in the other. The factories sometimes give a theme but these are fairly obvious – the millennium and football for boys. Girls are much easier

to design for. Pete gets his design ideas from all over the place; for example shops, TV, the occasional trade show and foreign travel. After some discussion with the factories Pete finalises the designs. The factory cuts out the panels that will go on the garment, sends these to him and Pete prints the design on to the panels. The panels are then sent back to the factory to be incorporated into the garment.

Pete now does all his designs on a computer. This saves a lot on money on photographic materials but also has the advantage that if Pete finds that he has a lot of one colour of ink he can fit his designs around this. The thing that he finds a bit frustrating is that he could send JPEG files of the designs straight to the customer, but the buyers don't want to know. They aren't yet geared up to using IT at all – not even the Internet. He could alter designs straight under their eyes, but they want a more personal approach.

There are a host of printers, both in the UK and abroad, selling on price alone, because they have low-paid workers and work the machines for more hours per day. They also sell their designs to others, tend to economise on the ink they use and try to win on every order. Average margins are low; a child's pyjamas could be imported and sold to the store groups for £2. To compete with them Pete can't charge more than 25p per print. The advantage that Pete has is that he offers many more designs than the importers and can react much faster. Pete knows how the factories operate – he's run one – and so he does two things: he's always producing designs for them, and he doesn't push over-hard for fast payment. He also stresses that what he won't do is sell a design as an exclusive that he has already sold to another factory. And he won't sell the same design the second time without getting agreement from the first buyer. Because his factory is on a sound footing he can afford to give credit. The firms competing only on price won't give credit and will start withholding merchandise if payment isn't made promptly. Pete always gets the job done when he says it will be done.

There have been big changes in technology, especially in litho printing, and especially with simple stuff and very small runs. It's now easy to obtain a transfer from a computer linked to a laser colour printer, using one transfer per garment. Pete is involved with large-scale printing, doing 5,000–10,000 units a day, and hasn't been affected. The specialised stuff, where you just print four T-shirts, for example, is a lucrative area. Pete has to go through the same process with four garments as with 4000, so it's not viable to do small orders.

Pete uses Sage software for bookkeeping, a system handed down from the larger firm. He doesn't use a spreadsheet, as he makes all the decisions and he can retain all the information mentally. Strategy formulation is totally ongoing, with no goals set down in any formal way.

Shane McGill[a] and One Shot®

Frozen dessert[b] dispensing will never be the same again. The One-Shot® process is rapidly gaining ground as the most efficient and certainly the most hygienic way of dispensing frozen desserts. This has come about through the innovation and tenacity of one man – Shane McGill.

> One-Shot® to become the world leader in the frozen dessert dispensing field by offering perfect portion control of a complete range of frozen desserts having total product integrity using advanced equipment that is under continuous development, offering solutions to all customers' needs.

Exhibit 1   Mission statement

There is nothing remarkable in McGill's upbringing. He is from a working-class family, one of three children, with a father who had been badly injured at Dunkirk at the beginning of the Second World War. Shane passed the 11+ exam and went to Gravesend Grammar School. As he recalls, he was only interested in rugby and maths and he had gone to the wrong school: he should have gone to the technical school. At 16 he was told by Mr Stevens, the headmaster, 'I think it better you leave the school, my little cherub, as you will be much better off outside the school than inside the school – that is my decision.' So he left and became a grease monkey in an engineering workshop. He soon realised that this was a dead end and so he undertook a five-year engineering apprenticeship. It was during this period that he made his first invention, a potato-packing machine to fill potato sacks in the potato field without needing electricity. During the apprenticeship, McGill also worked in an engineering design and drawing office.

Soon, however, McGill was made an offer he couldn't refuse: he was offered a company car and twice his current salary to move into sales and marketing with a company that imported machine tools, printing machinery and Italian ice-cream-making equipment. McGill recognises today that this move into sales and marketing was vital for his later career. In his view, good engineers don't generally make good entrepreneurs – quite the opposite. As he says,

The UK has the greatest number of inventors that file patents per inhabitant than any other country – I mean real patents with real value – yet they probably have the greatest failure rate as innovators.

McGill isn't a corporate man, so when he was 28 he decided to leave this company and to set up selling industrial ice-cream-processing equipment with a colleague. When that partnership ended a few years later, he started his own business and extended the range of equipment that he sold by also importing printing and packaging machines. Within nine years he employed more than 30 people. One of the printing machines he sold was also capable of printing chocolate ice cream bar wrappers better and cheaper than the competition, and he seized the opportunity to diversify into printing these wrappers. Life was looking good – he had just invested over £1 million in this new printing venture for chocolate ice cream bars when a supermarket rang to tell him that the ink used in the printing was toxic. 'I became famous as the man who made chocolate bars taste of petrol,' he quips.

McGill can laugh at this now but as he himself puts it: 'Within 48 hours of feeling like a millionaire I could just about afford to pay for a taxi home. The bank took everything – the house, the cars, the lot.' Happily, the relationship that he had built up over a decade with the Italian ice cream equipment manufacturers was to stand him in good stead: within a month the firm had guaranteed a £100,000 overdraft with his bank, thus allowing him to carry on buying stock and financing the new business. So he started again, selling the same equipment from his base in Warwick.

Fairly soon afterwards, the Italian company sold out to the Alfa Laval food machinery group and this set McGill thinking about his next move. The opportunity came at a dairy show in Chicago when he saw a machine that sparked off an idea for eliminating the hygiene problems associated with soft ice cream dispensers. When in use these machines are left with traces of ice cream and, unless properly serviced, these are a health hazard. McGill rang up his wife from Chicago and asked her to find him a patent agent.

Once he got home he filled an empty Coca-Cola bottle with ice cream using a refuse bag with the corner cut off, like a cook's piping bag. He then screwed a tap on the end of the bottle and got his son to stand on the bottle. He opened the tap and out came ice cream. From that moment his wife also believed it would be a winner. The demonstration proved that frozen ice cream could be squeezed out with the pressure simultaneously helping to soften it during extrusion. It also helped show how the potential health hazards of soft ice cream dispensing could be eliminated.

But not all was plain sailing. The invention was to be turned into the Supanova® system, whereby the ice cream

---

[a] © Leen Valley Associates, 1999.

[b] Frozen desserts include ice cream, frozen yoghurt, sorbet, etc.

would be packed into concertina plastic containers at ice-cream dairies, frozen and delivered to the point of sale, where they would be dropped into a refrigerated cylinder inside a dispensing machine. Each sale would be made by simply using an air-operated plunger to dispense ice cream every time the tap was opened. This was simple, with little in the way of complicated machinery and with little cleaning to do.

In 1987 the first patent for the Supernova® was filed. However, the banks refused to help. Touting the idea around a dairy show in Frankfurt, McGill bumped into a colleague who ran a company in the USA. He offered to help McGill by developing and manufacturing the machines in return for a licence to sell them in North America with royalties to McGill. In 1988 McGill met an expert in plastics at a plastics exhibition, who assisted in the packaging design and manufacture of the concertina container. After a year of development, the first prototype of the Supanova® dispenser was achieved.

The contacts that McGill had made through many years in the ice cream business stood him in good stead yet again. However, when he first started it was very hard. Although the dairies didn't want to pack the concertina initially, they would do so if the customer wanted it. McGill had to be pragmatic in the early days by using smaller dairies that probably would not be his strategic partners today. It was very much a chicken-and-egg situation. The first major sale in the UK was to Pizza Hut, and by 1994 McGill had 265 machines installed in its outlets. However, the Supernova® achieved only moderate success: the problem was that the 10-litre container in the Supanova® meant that only one flavour of ice cream could be dispensed from each dispenser. Also the dispenser still required some cleaning and so the problem of hygiene still hadn't been solved in an industry employing many low-paid and transitory employees who were often poorly trained and badly supervised. However, sales of the Supanova® did provide sufficient income for McGill to try other things. Fortunately, a Californian company requested a patent licence for McGill's technology in 1993 and has paid substantial royalties to McGill ever since.

The birth of One-Shot®

Although the Supanova® system was reasonably successful, it wasn't the world-beater that McGill wanted. His customers were telling him of the limitations in the Supanova® and he realised that he hadn't cracked the problem of hygiene – of particular importance as hygiene regulations were being stiffened and standards raised worldwide. But he was convinced that he was on the right track. It was these pressures and McGill's drive that created the One-Shot® system.

The One-Shot® system grew out of the experience with the Supanova®. This time each portion of frozen dessert is packed in its own individual container (specially developed by McGill Technology and termed 'the intelligent container'). These containers are made from polyethylene and are recyclable. The containers are packed by a licensed One-shot® ice cream dairy producer under strict hygiene standards. After packing, the product is deep frozen to lock in the flavour and dispatched to the point of sale to be used in dedicated dispensers. The containers are kept in a cooled cabinet next to the dispenser and are inserted into the dispenser when required, thus allowing any type and flavour of frozen dessert to be sold in any sequence. The hygiene problem with frozen dessert dispensing was solved by including a hole in the base of the container through which the frozen dessert is extruded. In operation, the operator simply selects the chosen flavour from the cabinet, pulls off the tab that covers the extrusion hole and inserts the container into the dispenser. They then pull a handle, which operates a valve to actuate a plunger that pushes the ice cream out of the container. The container is then removed from the dispenser and disposed of. No frozen dessert touches the dispenser and thus there is no need to sanitise it. Exhibit 2 shows the dispensing mechanism and the intelligent container.

Product integrity is more than keeping the product hygienic. There is also the question of consistent high quality and avoidance of cross-contamination with other flavours. In a soft-serve machine the product is continuously 'churned', so the quality varies throughout the day and there may also be product flavour cross-contamination. Hand dipping relies totally on the operator to avoid cross-contamination and to control portion size. With One-Shot®, the intelligent container, the cooled cabinet and the dedicated dispenser allow full product integrity to be maintained.

In mid-1998 the significant breakthrough occurred. After numerous sales trips in two years, McGill clinched a

Exhibit 2

£7 million order to supply 4400 ice cream machines to the 7-Eleven retailer chain in Japan. By the end of 1998 the chain was already selling millions of containers a month. Recently, a deal has been finalised with a major US corporation, with McGill anticipating delivering 3,000–5000 machines per year into the USA.

Company structure and personnel

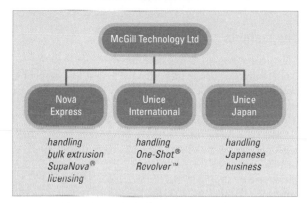

Exhibit 3   Holding and operating companies

McGill's company structure is shown in Exhibit 3. The holding company for McGill's activities is McGill Technology Limited. It legally owns the intellectual property rights to all patents, designs, knowhow and trade marks. McGill Technology now has around 100 patents – the first was on the Supanova® container and the latest ones are for the new Revolver™ milkshake concept using microwave technology. There are three operating companies controlled by McGill Technology: Nova Express, handling the bulk extrusion systems, Unice[c] International, responsible for One-Shot®, and Unice Japan, which has been set up specifically to handle the rapidly growing Japanese business.

McGill explains the rationale for the company structure:

Why run the greatest firm in the world for 20 years and make one mistake and lose it all? Why make a target for all the people prowling about? UK corporate law is presently flexible enough to allow companies to protect themselves in a group structure. The holding company owns everything and licenses to the trading/operating companies who then get on with selling and sublicensing. We also have separate independent segments, each one being an attractive opportunity for disposal at some future date.

---

[c] pronounced 'you nice'.

McGill Technology and its operating companies are 'lean manned'. Apart from McGill himself there are only four other UK employees, who all work in or out of the same office in Addington, Kent: his wife Shirley, who controls the finances; the company secretary, Freda Wells, who has been with the company for five years; Nick Delany, who supports Shane in sales and marketing; and Steve Garsden, who is in charge of order processing and the link to established customers. Surprisingly, perhaps, McGill denies that he is making all the decisions. He believes in training and empowerment and in 'management by suggestion'. Every day, they are asking how they can do something better, and often all five people take part in brainstorming sessions.

McGill has never sacked anyone: his secret is to employ the right people in the first place: 'Seek out high IQ people, keen on their job, give them human respect, treat them as equals, don't try to be a smart-arse, and don't forget to have a laugh with them.' He believes very strongly in training, with all his staff responsible for, yet supported in, their own training.

The office in Addington is solely concerned with innovation, sales and marketing. All the financial aspects such as invoicing are undertaken by an accounting firm in Coventry, run by Colin Beale, who is the company's finance director and a long-term personal friend of McGill. Beale comes down to Addington one or two days a week and travels with McGill overseas. The main control document is a four-weekly profit and loss account – although McGill doesn't think this is very important: he knows where he stands now on a daily basis, although this wasn't always the case!

A fairly strict demarcation is made between the on-going activities and innovation. McGill has a business plan for on-going activities that is strictly followed, with firm sales, promotional and marketing plans. Having said that, the plans are adaptable should anything untoward or exciting happen. McGill is convinced that there is no room to be number 2 and this view is known to all the staff: 'Already in Japan we're number 1, in France and Norway number 2 – in another three years we'll be number 1 worldwide in our niche.'

Unice International operations

Unice International is responsible for selling the One-Shot® system worldwide, excluding Japan. This system consists of filling machines and adaptation kits for the ice cream dairies, the containers for the frozen desserts and the dispensing machines with support for tempering cabinets in retail outlets. All sales are though stocking distributors worldwide.

At present the filling and dispensing machines are made under licence solely by a Kent engineering company, Kentinentel Engineering of Borough Green, but in the future Unice may have other licensees in other countries. The cabinets to hold the frozen dessert containers are made in the UK, Denmark and the USA. Although Unice sells the machines, it doesn't have anything to do with selling spares for them or their maintenance; this is handled by Kentinental and its stocking distributors. The users of the dispensers can't use a tempering/storage freezer cabinet that hasn't been tested and approved by Unice in the UK.

The intelligent containers are made in or close to the markets where they will be used; in the case of Europe they are made by another Kent firm, Blowspeed of Ramsgate, in the USA by Berry Plastics, and by three licensees in Japan. Three years ago McGill had to get Berry Plastics to buy into the tooling investment programme to produce the containers. It spent several hundred thousand dollars at a time when there wasn't a single container being used. As McGill says, 'That's sales and marketing! To put this system in place requires a lot of contacts.' The machines and containers are made under licence and neither McGill Technology nor Unice International has any equity stake in these manufacturers.

The frozen desserts need to be specially formulated to ensure that they come out at the right texture. Unice has two strategic partners to help the dairies get the consistency right, one in the USA and one in Denmark. The dairies generally have their own filling machines, but they need advice on how to handle the intelligent container. This isn't always easy – either the dairies put new parts on existing machines or they install new filling machines as specified by Unice. Either McGill himself or another consultant advises them on how to do this.

McGill believes in having strategic partnerships: a small number of contacts that he can trust, work with and, if necessary, develop. He is his own lawyer, writing the contracts with his strategic partners. He is able to do this as he has a database of 'template' contracts for many countries. For some esoteric contracts lawyers are asked to look over what is proposed, but the problem with using lawyers, as McGill sees it, is that lawyers make too many mistakes – not mistakes in law, but they don't know what the company is trying to achieve. McGill has confidence in what he's doing because he doesn't ever expect the contract to be used. In his view:

A contract is the last thing that gets signed, not the first. If you only want to get a contract signed to guarantee some money, don't run a business. It means that you have no relationship, no chemistry, there's nothing built up. We don't do that.

Although a heads of agreement is usually signed, McGill sits down with his potential partners and works with them on their operational plan; no contract is signed until everyone is satisfied that the arrangement will work. In McGill's view, there is nothing worse than locking a partner into a contract that they don't want. McGill sees contracts being for the partners' benefit; for him it's just a final backup because the partners want it. McGill has never had to go to law (yet!) over a distributor's contract.

The markets

The major potential markets are the USA and Japan. Apparently the UK is difficult to sell to – lots of people with independent ideas, who don't buy much, with the rest of Europe also somewhat slow compared with other areas. This will change as the products are accepted.

McGill believes that unless you have exclusivity, strategic partnering doesn't work. Thus he normally operates on the basis of one distributor per country or per niche/sector. In Japan the arrangement he has with his strategic partner, Magna International, is for it to do almost everything – it finds the customers for the One-Shot® system, takes delivery of the UK-manufactured dispensers and distributes them, organises the making of the intelligent containers, seeks out the dairies and installs the UK-manufactured filling machines or adapts those machines already installed. The Japanese are very hygiene-conscious, and this may be why One-Shot® found its first major sale in Japan.

The US operation is run very differently. McGill's son Gary, who is married to an American, runs the US office in Maryland. McGill himself has bought a house there, not for his retirement, but to live there for six months of the year – to be nearest his biggest market. Unice has approved the dairies and has linked up with ConAgra, a food group with a multibillion-dollar turnover that has the number 1 brand in the world for low-fat ice-cream, called Healthy Choice. Its brand name will now be on Unice's dispensers. McGill has forged strategic relationships with Unice, the machinery distributor, the dairy packers ConAgra, and Berry Plastics, which makes the intelligent containers.

Unice's marketing strategy has been also to promote to the national accounts directly, using fax, e-mail and direct mail, for which they have a mass mailing computer system. This is McGill's 'attack list'. McGill pays $5000 p.a. to an organisation in the USA to provide him with a list of national accounts with more than 100 outlets in the USA. Currently there are 900+ of them that need to be contacted annually, leaving the distributor to seek out the smaller operators. Everything is on the database and potential customers can be picked out by state, city, etc. There are around 3000 named senior executives in the list – 2.5 people per national outlet, with the names guaranteed never to be older than three months. McGill has the view that Unice must use the best-quality brochures: 'We don't send out junk – junk is wasting money.' Unice has produced a range of movie films loaded on to CD-ROMs to operate on both Mac and PC computers.

Unice mails the national accounts roughly twice a year – not always selling, sometimes just promoting the brand. It also mails to all the frozen-food distributors for Healthy Choice ConAgra. Unice's office in the USA will now arrange to have someone liaise personally with all the frozen-dessert distributors and the national account executives – someone has to contact these 3000 people personally over the next 12 months. McGill is not a believer in trade shows for major selling initiatives and leaves this job primarily to his stockists. Each distributor should know its own potential outlets, and their dealer network will know further outlets in their own localities.

In the USA and elsewhere there is a general tightening of hygiene laws, with outlets now having to take all the protective measures they can so as not to offend. McGill believes that quality levels in restaurant kitchens are often unbelievably poor. Many soft-serve machines require disciplined cleaning. The brand equity of a product often depends on a $5 per hour operator with little training or understanding of the laws!

McGill takes a direct line with his presentations to US managers. His general message is:

Many food service operators take hard drugs. The majority don't wash their hands after going to the men's room. Although people generally don't die from a lack of hygiene, such lack of hygiene is certainly not good for your health! At the moment legislation isn't tough enough so operators often don't take enough care. But legislation is getting tougher. Gentlemen, you know what's happening and you know how unhygienic your operations can be. Is it ethical not to use One-shot®?

It appears to be a message that's getting across!

Innovation and entrepreneurship

McGill sees his personal drive coming from a desire for his family and friends to remember him as an achiever and to be recognised more widely as a successful innovator. This looked unlikely to be fully achieved when he suffered the second of his two heart attacks in 1994 and had to have a quadruple bypass operation. He has total belief in his mission and only sleeps for four hours a night. He can work mentally 24 hours a day, but physically it's a differ-

ent matter: he hasn't been in a garden for 35 years and uses his car whenever possible. McGill has no interests other than watching football on TV, fishing and meeting people. He is hyperactive with some stress but doesn't believe this is worry stress.

McGill estimates that 75% of his time is spent on sales and marketing, with the remaining 25% on innovation/development. McGill's way of innovating follows a fairly standard pattern – after the initial idea, that is. He simply does a sketch of what he wants and gets someone to flesh out the detail. Some £200,000 has been set aside to invest with the developers of the milkshake machine to develop a working model. They will do this within four months.

More and more of McGill's meetings are with major customers who like the One-Shot® concept but want McGill to use his technology to develop a special machine for them. These projects can take two to three years to complete.

The years he has spent as an innovator have convinced McGill that there are really only two things that an entrepreneur needs to worry about, innovation and marketing. Nothing else in a company matters – everything else you can buy in. You need to have luck, be bloody-minded and never listen to your bank manager – but don't tell him so! And in McGill's case, a wife who understood what he wanted and was trying to do; willing to risk the house because, as he says, 'there's no money out there from anyone to assist inventors in the UK.'

McGill stresses the importance of marketing:

What is the use of having the greatest invention in the world if it can't be brought to market? The current market leader is not necessarily the largest market share holder – but the most innovative company! If you are not bloodying your nose in today's warp-speed economy, we have a name for you. Dead! If people did not do silly things, nothing intelligent would ever get done. In our company, you'll be fired for not making mistakes. We do not merely want to be considered just the best of the best. We want to be the only ones that do what we do. Our job is to give our customers what they never dreamed they wanted! The way you dress, how you say good morning in the office, the documents you send out: everything you do and speak is marketing.

No company can be unethical to get business, but McGill is frank enough to admit that he might have been ultra-pragmatic when he was starting up. What he wants now is for his company to have the reputation of being the best bunch of guys to deal with, supplying the best answer to meet all customers' needs.

Professional service firms

McGill has a scathing view of professional service firms, viewing them purely as salespeople. But he is philosophical about them, believing that there's no point kicking and screaming, as that's the way the world works. He believes the adage that banks will only lend you an umbrella when the sun is shining. As he recounts it:

The banks demand a business plan which you spend three months preparing at great cost and all they do is ignore the first 158 pages and look for the security on the back page. They want to lend money to property companies – in good times – successful companies and high-tech companies. One man from a bank wouldn't lend the money on the grounds that he'd just got divorced and remarried. 'If it goes wrong and they fire me I'll be in dead trouble,' was his rationale. The bank's senior management supported their manager. Everyone – in government, in the banks – says they will help you – but there's nobody there.

McGill recalls a discussion with another bank manager when seeking a £25,000 loan:

He remarked that my balance sheet was lousy and suggested that I capitalise the cost of my patents – to the tune of what they cost to obtain – and then a loan would be more likely. I pointed out that if I did that then I'd have to pay corporation tax. What's the point of doing that to get a loan from the bank – of almost nothing? The real problem is that the banks don't like extroverts – which is generally what innovators are – especially entrepreneurs. They want you to be an accountant!

McGill does, however, pay great compliments to Barclays in Coventry, which was the one exception that recognised the future and supported Unice some years ago.

He believes that special grants are of limited value: the lead time to obtain the relatively small grants available simply holds the entrepreneur back. Some years ago McGill got a professional company to devise a business plan and he sent it to 100+ investment companies. He was turned down by all of them on the grounds that the plan didn't meet their criteria. When he phoned some of them to find out which criteria the plan failed to satisfy, he found them rather evasive. After probing, the one criterion that the plan failed to satisfy was always the security. 'If you've got a house and a crappy business plan you can borrow money; if you've got a good business plan and no house then you can't. That's about it' is how he sums it up.

Although McGill believes that patent agents never tell you the truth about the costs, he is very complimentary about his patent agents and about his US lawyer. All are

McGill's friends – that's the way he works – and they do a great job because they are friends, not because they are professionals. McGill works very closely with the patent agent; he drafts out the specification and the agent puts it into patent language. The original patents for One-Shot® were taken out in 1992 and 1993; now McGill is going to go for about 120 patents over the next three to five years.

The nestable container that is used with One-Shot® represents Unice's income and must be protected. McGill first patented the nested container and then the system. In effect it's possible to keep dividing up a patent for 17 years; the more extensive your original filing, the more you can divide. But this costs a lot of money, so initially it is very tempting to economise on patents. Unice is often in litigation in the USA against patent infringement. McGill has had some good litigation wins in the USA and made money with the SupaNova® system and so is in the enviable position of being able to make a thorough job of subsequent patents.

The future

Ice cream isn't the only growing trend: frozen milkshakes, slush and frozen carbonated beverages are even bigger. People are eating out much more than they used to and in developing countries are becoming more quality- and health-conscious.

Although McGill has recently bought a house by the sea in Maryland, it's unlikely he will ever retire. He will be putting quite a lot of his effort into the milkshake venture with Revolver™. Every milkshake cup will have a whisk, like the blade of a blender, inside it. McGill has done his marketing and knows it will sell, so now he is having the machine made. He believes he must establish the market first, arguing that if he doesn't then there's no point in spending development money. He knows that the plastic container can be made for the right price and that the dairies want to pack the product. The cost of development is around $1 million from start to entry time into the marketplace. Setting up strategic partnerships takes a lot of time, and the tooling for the plastic containers will cost more than half a million dollars. Revolver™ has an operational plan to launch the milkshakes now.

McGill doesn't believe that there is any future for a national producer – except for the very small guy like himself, or the very large operators. He works with low fixed and higher flexible costs, which represent 60% of the total operating costs, and in an emergency could be cut overnight. The engineering company Kentinental now employs extra people because of Unice International's growth.

McGill's reasoning is as follows:

Our sort of company is the only way to survive in the future. How can you survive in the future when everything is just pressing a button? In the future, there's no space for a middle-sized company – the small companies will be like us with a tight system – just pressing a few buttons and involved in innovation and marketing. Global markets are killing the middle-sized business. Global markets strongly imply global supply. A global player must operate with good strategic alliances to survive.

The future for McGill looks secure. He predicts that he won't be involved in so much development, since he has revolutionised frozen-dessert dispensing and has products for the next three decades. Not all will be plain sailing, however. The old ways of dispensing desserts will hang on for some time yet because they are backed by powerful companies. But gradually McGill's better technology is likely to win. He sees himself as the president of his company, dealing with the 20 or 30 presidents of the major worldwide corporations. He intends to bring in half a dozen boy racers – good people to fulfil his dream.

McGill himself has recently taken to writing books under the pseudonym of Richard Head. His next book is called *Patently Obvious*, based on the past ten years of his company's development in a highly spoofed way. As he says, never let an impasse stop you!

There is more on One-Shot® at the company's website, http://www.one-shot@aol.com.

Dutton Engineering[a]

The journey

Ken Lewis was an apprentice toolmaker/engineer who wanted to branch out on his own, believing that he could do better than his current employer. He recalls: 'My vision was to have the best-operated sheet metal shop in Bedfordshire.' He was given a £1000 loan by his parents but couldn't augment it with a bank loan. However, one of the banks that had turned down his application considered Ken's track record to be good and suggested that he work with another of its clients, a precision stainless steel fabricator based in the north of England that wished to expand south. So Ken joined with one of the fabricator's accountants to set up and manage the new operation, initially based near Luton, Bedfordshire, and called Dutton Engineering (Woodside). Later, the firm moved to new premises in Sandy, Bedfordshire.

Ken started in a shed with one employee in 1972. In 1983 he bought the firm in a management buyout, and by 1989 it had 40 employees with a turnover of £1 million. In 1989 Ken sold a 51% share in Dutton to John Glasse, an accountant who had worked in industry for many years. Ken realised that he needed someone who was as involved in the business as he was whom he could confide in and discuss developments with. By 1996 there were 25 people employed with a turnover of £2 million and at the beginning of 1999, 40 people were turning over £2.2 million. The firm's main output is high-precision stainless steel boxes to protect electronic equipment (see Exhibit 1). In 1998 a survey found that Dutton's added value per employee was £80,000 p.a., compared with the average for the metal-forming businesses in the Eastern region of £37,000.

Exhibit 1

[a] © Leen Valley Associates, 1999.

In 1994, Dutton won the DTI (Department of Trade and Industry) Wedgwood Trophy for the best feedback from visitors, taking the award away from the previous year's winners, Nissan. In 1996, out of the 140 SMEs (small and medium-sized enterprises) that formed a nucleus of 'best practice' firms in the DTI-sponsored 'Inside UK Enterprise' programme, Dutton was voted the best by the visitors who came to see the firm.

This very profitable position and these awards had been achieved during a journey spanning 16 years since the management buyout in 1983.

The conversion

The journey began in earnest in 1984 when, after a full year of preparation, Dutton became one of the first metal formers to achieve the quality standard BS 5750 (now ISO 9000). However, Ken saw this achievement as merely a useful accolade to obtain some customers – he didn't feel it was really very useful. His views are summed up by Dr Albrecht, chairman of the TQS Group:

The ISO 9000 and BS 5750 approach is a ticket to mediocrity, not to competitive excellence. At its worst it is a slavish belief in the superiority of diagrams and manuals over human intelligence. At its best it does little more than force people to spend more time thinking about the processes than about getting the work done. There are better ways, and they all rely on mobilising the intelligence of all the workers in the company.

So obtaining ISO 9000 had little effect on internal operations. But during the early 1980s two things happened to change Ken's life for ever. The first involved his new TV set. He had owned a black-and-white Ferguson set that was forever being sent back for repair. In 1983 he bought a Japanese colour TV that worked faultlessly. This gave him the first inkling as to why the Japanese were steadily eroding the market shares of the UK car, motorbike and TV producers. He needed to know more, and in 1985 he went on a three-week visit to Japan. This was a great eye-opener. He and the rest of the group he was with were struck by the trust they saw between the people on the shop floor and management, and the trust between suppliers and customers. This confirmed Ken's view that 'There are very few basically corrupt people: if they are corrupt it's because management is corrupt.' Ken returned to Sandy full of enthusiasm and started to try out a few ideas. For example, the Japanese moved their employees between companies. At that time Ken had an interest in another sheet metal firm and, as Dutton was short of welders, he had two welders from the other company move to Dutton to help out. Dutton employees didn't make it easy for these 'guest workers'. They were afraid that Ken would send them to work in the other factory. This and other initiatives failed. It was very disappointing, to say the least.

The Dutton way

Domino is a maker of ink-jet printers located about 20 miles from Sandy that had been spun off from research at Cambridge University. In 1985, Domino started on a total quality management (TQM) programme and by 1988 was ready to enrol its suppliers, as it was seeking partnership arrangements with them. Domino invited all its 250 suppliers to an awareness programme and offered to help any of them to introduce TQM into their own organisation. Only Ken took them up on this offer – Dutton at that time did not have the money to undertake such a change on its own.

A year elapsed before TQM was launched at Dutton in 1989. This was because there were three main features of TQM that were hard for employees to understand and implement:

- what quality meant – conforming to standard or delighting the customer?
- the concept of internal customers;
- that quality had to do with everyone in the organisation.

A big-bang launch was decided on. Rather than call the changes TQM, it was decided to encapsulate them in 'The Dutton Way'. The Dutton way is to 'eliminate waste and fire fighting by working smart, not hard, and having fun at work'. The factory was shut down for a day and all the staff went to a conference centre, where Ken and some Domino experts explained and discussed the new TQM thinking. The staff were quite excited by this; some long-serving people, with over 30 years working in industry, had never experienced anything like this – off site and training! After a very enjoyable lunch, questions and answers and the issuing of baseball caps, everyone came away hyped up and ready to go.

The Dutton way contained five goals:

1 To simplify the manufacturing process   This initially meant restricting Dutton's activities to those things in which it could excel. Then it came to mean that Dutton would need to work much more closely with customers' design departments so that what was required took account of Dutton's manufacturing processes – and took advantage of Dutton's particular strengths. Customers know about electronics but not about boxes, but they used to design boxes that Dutton couldn't make or could only make at great cost.

2 To reduce working inventory   This meant building partnerships with companies in the supply chain.

3 To increase the skills flexibility of the workforce   Ken was very concerned with developing a learning organisation.

4 To maintain and improve product quality   In the first instance this meant installing systems to measure quality. Later, it meant establishing and cultivating a continuous improvement culture. These initiatives culminated in the Dutton mission statement (see Exhibit 2).

5 To be very customer-focused   This required Dutton to get closer to the customer, finding out exactly what they required to meet their goals.

Little actually happened after the launch, and Ken wondered why. He came to the following conclusion:

The problem lay with the managers – they had become managers because of their technical ability and few of

Exhibit 2

Dutton Engineering (Woodside) Ltd
Our
Quality
Policy

We must ensure that our present and future customers are always satisfied with the products and services which we provide.

EVERY DUTTON CUSTOMER MUST FIND THAT
❖ They can communicate with us.
❖ We listen and respond to their needs.
❖ We are reliable and do what we say we will do.
❖ We deliver the right products on time, every time.
❖ We are aiming for zero defects in all our products, services, information and advice.

The aim of Dutton's Zero Defect Policy is not restricted to products alone, but also applies to those tasks carried out by all employees.

Zero Defect Quality demands that each of us is right first time in every task we undertake.

Total customer satisfaction will only be achieved when we conduct our internal daily operations as if we were each other's customers.

Nº1

Our collective task is to increase customer satisfaction

them had verbal and people skills. Changing the attitudes of others is, in my experience, very difficult, particularly at management level. This brought about the rather hard-nosed expression at Dutton, 'If you can't change the person, change the person.'

Inspection

A particular problem lay with inspection. The three inspectors couldn't really inspect all the work of the factory. Skilled staff would ask them to check each hole marking in the sheet steel before drilling the hole, and such was the confusion and overwork that if the hole was slightly in the wrong place, the driller would simply leave the piece of work for an hour or so and then resubmit it – and it generally passed the second time. One factor that weighed heavily with Ken was that he had paid out £50,000 each on two apprentices for years of academic and practical training, yet their work had to be inspected by someone else.

The inspectors were there because of Dutton's defence contracts. Up to the early 1990s, a considerable proportion of Dutton's work was for the Ministry of Defence. This had a significant impact, because the firm fell into line with the requirement to have inspectors in the factory inspecting all aspects of the work. It also had a big impact because pricing was on a *cost plus* basis, meaning the Ministry of Defence didn't negotiate a fixed price for a product but paid the firm its costs plus an addition for profits. This environment was corrosive to standards and to cost control; if Dutton was about to lose money on a contract, then it simply asked for more money – and got it, with the taxpayer eventually paying. However, the defence contracts were becoming less significant to Dutton.

The quality manager, who was in charge of inspection, was against alteration of the inspection procedures. However, a good opportunity arose to change the whole inspection philosophy; the quality manager was a heavy smoker, and he left in the wake of the introduction of a no-smoking policy. So Ken called everyone to a series of meetings about the inspection. This was the start of empowering the workforce, although the final decision rested with Ken. While there was general agreement that inspection had become a bit of a joke, there was also a worry that people would have to take on more work. Also, some people didn't have the confidence to take responsibility for a whole job and welcomed inspection.

One Friday, Ken decided to stop inspection and moved the three inspectors to jobs on the factory floor starting the following Monday. Immediately, the quality of the work carried out in the factory improved. Previously, quality had been lost between the various operations. Following the closure of the inspectorate, the amount of data recorded about jobs was reduced to almost zero – and it was found that nobody had been looking at the data anyway! Staff taking control of quality was a watershed change and led to the move to team working.

The quest for understanding

Ken was very keen that everyone knew the impact their activities were having on everyone else. As Mike Nash, who has been with Dutton since 1990, recalls:

Ken got all the management team over a 12-month period to give two- to three-hour presentations where they told us what their job entailed and what value they added to Dutton. This was to stop the perception that I as a shop floor worker had that they didn't add any value. My view was that they came in a grey suit, sat in front of a computer screen all day drinking coffee and I was doing all the work. I was convinced after the first presentation that this manager did add value and I understood what he did, and the impact he was having on me doing a bad job. For example, if you wanted a job card – and we couldn't start a job without one because we were working to BS 5750 – you had to go to the office to get one. Getting one could take a week! This was making me do a bad job: by the time the card came out I'd missed the delivery date. I told the manager, 'You might come out and shout at me for not supporting the customer, but that was because of the system which you're making me work in.' So we started to talk with one another. Now we can get a job card within 30 seconds. However, increases in understanding weren't all one way. We didn't understand why we had to fill in the job cards. Once this was explained and the importance of filling the cards in correctly was emphasised, we then did fill in the cards properly.

Tina Mason, who was the business manager at the time, recalls the situation:

We had to make the workforce more knowledgeable about the marketplace; what we had been doing was shielding them from the realities. We needed to be pro-active with the biggest driver – the customer – and let the workers hear them say directly that they want it cheaper, faster, better. The perception was that management was saying that simply to get more profit out of them. The shop floor didn't know how much a product cost, because management was taking the view that if you tell the shop floor how much we're making they will want a pay rise. So people were given an understanding of how the budgets worked, how costings worked, where the money was made and lost. Then how they themselves can make a difference; in the early days they couldn't affect sales very much, but they could make a direct impact on the cost of sales. For example, *kaizen* eliminate waste, cell manufacture reduces cycle times and good supplier relations keeps stock levels down – they can see that. And we pressed the message, 'Do you wait for the drivers of change to impact you so hard that you are forced into a particular direction? Or should we be in control – make change go in more of the direction we want it to go?' Once you hit the buffers, it's difficult to change track.

As with most organisations, some people accepted change readily, others more slowly and some didn't think it was for them at all. One factor leading to the job cards being filled in correctly was that Ken decided to do away with 'clocking in', throwing the clock into a skip and telling the shop floor workers that they were to be trusted, just as management was, to start work at 7.30am and work until the job was done. This indicated that nominal times weren't as significant as real times. Later, in an effort to ease the filling of the cards, a computer system was installed on the shop floor. It was designed by the IT manager, who had worked on the shop floor before spending five years away getting qualifications in sheet metalwork. Unfortunately, the workers couldn't work the keyboard quickly enough and people were standing around waiting to input data. The solution was to buy a touch screen and to use barcodes. The manager learned that whatever system was introduced, it had to be simple.

The move to team working

Up to 1992, the factory was organised along functional lines with fitters, welders, etc. operating in separate sections. Ken decided that the firm had to operate as teams. Realising that the team leaders would be pivotal people, he asked anyone – anyone at all who thought that they could be a team leader – to give him a 10-minute presentation as to why they should be a team leader. Of the five foremen, only one was chosen to be a team leader, and over the subsequent few months those not selected left the company. Only one other person was chosen as a leader, a shop floor worker. Thus two teams were formed: one team looked after Domino and the other team looked after all the others. Dividing the people into the two teams raised some problems; dividing by skill, whereby half the welders were in each team, for example, made sense, and who made up the halves was decided by the management team taking into account what they knew of how well people got on with each other. The team leaders were sent on a Dale Carnegie team working training course. Before the

Christmas shutdown in 1992, the factory was operating in sections; after the New Year it resumed with the two teams. The teams were assigned work that needed similar treatment so that products no longer needed to pass through the whole factory.

The team leaders turned out to be excellent, but the teams didn't work well. Dutton attempted to build team spirit in a number of ways. It began by having each team attend a half-hour sit-down meeting every Monday morning. While these meetings highlighted several issues, including pay differentials, they showed that team building is far more than putting eight people in a room and telling them that they are a team. These meetings were quickly abandoned, being considered by the team members themselves as 'unproductive'. They moved to daily meetings with the adage 'Ten minutes on your feet, not half an hour on your seat!'

There was the question of giving the teams a name. While thoughts such as the speedy team and the champion team were considered at first, the teams rejected these in favour of the prosaic – the red and the blue team. Within a few weeks management was asked to buy coloured polo shirts. These are worn with pride, and on the odd day a team member isn't wearing this official shirt they can expect some serious leg-pulling. What Dutton has realised was that as well as having a balance of technical skills in a team it needs a balance of personalities.

The fact that the teams were given responsibility for customer relations was significant. Team leaders and team members went to visit customers' sites, and got to know the customers and their requirements. In this way the teams developed common ownership of the products they were making. Ken estimates that it took around two years for the teams to build up to this level of ownership. According to Mike, the cultural change was from an *I* to a *we* culture. Management didn't realise the damage that the ex-foremen were doing when placed in teams; the shop floor workers knew this and had tried to involve them fully. But the foremen had had been manipulating the system, for example working overtime themselves and making sure it was available to their favourites. Moving to a *we* culture broke this power. In the end the teams wanted the ex-foremen to leave, and they all did so within 18 months.

Dutton had a nominal 39-hour week for its production operatives. Generally, the staff did their work in four days and so had a three-day weekend. Stockpiling finished goods when they were otherwise underemployed and working overtime when demand was high was the basis of meeting fluctuations. Ken believes that overtime is pernicious:

Overtime isn't determined by customer demand, it's determined by the standard of living that the people think they should have. If overtime isn't forthcoming in the normal way, they are clever enough to manage things to get it.

In 1992, Tina read about a new way of working, termed annualised hours. This was a system that she knew had been employed in a very cyclical business, contract grass-cutting equipment. With annualised hours, the contract specifying that a number of hours should be worked each week was replaced by one where the contract was for a number of hours per year. Under annualised hours, when demand is high people work longer hours; when demand is low they work fewer hours. Over the whole year the time worked is the same as with weekly contracts.

Tina approached Ken and was given the go-ahead to investigate annualised hours further. She did nine months research, which included talking to a wide spectrum of people at Dutton and taking the most sceptical people from the shop floor to see the system in operation, reasoning that it was important to get the real barriers out in the open early on. Tina recalls the reaction:

I showed them the principle and asked if it could be refined to work at Dutton. The general view was that it should be feasible and it had its attractions, but they couldn't be sure. What the sceptics didn't realise until rather late was that annualised hours would transform the organisation in such a way that their manipulation of overtime would cease. There was more discussion, leading to a draft proposal including the new contract. People were asked to go and discuss with their families, and get all the what ifs? out of the way. After much preparation and discussion, the question of annualised hours was put to the vote of the whole workforce. Only two employees voted against the new scheme and it was implemented on 1 April 1994.

Mike and Tina identified two types of people opposed to change: the blockers, who were against change, and the terrorist blockers, who spoke the words that management wanted to hear but also spoke those that the shop floor people wanted to hear, playing one off against the other. All sorts of tactics were used to block change: changes were shrugged off as flavour of the month, proposals were rejected on the basis that something similar had failed at a previous workplace. If a *kaizen* was being put forward that threatened the status quo in a significant way, then the urgency of production work was cited and the proposal was put on one side with the promise, never kept, of doing it later. Other blockers agreed to implement a change and simply didn't do it. By the time their failure had been realised, many excuses could be put forward. And there was the genuine fear that you might continuously improve yourself out of a job.

Tina reflects on how she would have managed the changes in hindsight:

I would work harder on changing deeply held values, because you can move so much faster when this has been achieved. If you can get a few people to change on day 1 then you get others to join in. I now believe that people can change – team working is an example of a change of values. If you understand people you can change them. However, I believe in a twin-track approach, working on both values and behaviours.

The move to annualised hours was a catalyst for further change decided by management. One problem with jelling the team members into a team arose partly because there were 18 different rates of pay for the 20 people in the teams. So Ken ordered just one pay rate – the maximum rate of £14,500. Everyone was raised to this level, but with no overtime payment.

The distinction between hourly and monthly paid employees was abolished, with everyone moving to monthly pay and all having the same sickness benefits and pension rights. This was a big change for people who had little or no experience of this in their families. And the old job descriptions were done away with, leaving only two descriptions, production operative and administrative operative. There was some small resistance from one or two people who had 'skilled' in their job titles, but this soon evaporated. These changes weren't put to the vote.

Employees at the top of the scale didn't like the new salary scales, because they lost overtime and their differentials with other, apparently less skilled people. The flat pay scale didn't work as well as expected and it was realised that there had to be better pay for the real performers. So a three-tier salary scale was instituted: £14,500, £15,500 and £16,500. This was much better received.

Team working

At the beginning of 1999 there were five teams in the factory. The teams are mini-businesses 'owned' by the team members and responsible for all contact with established customers. One team is responsible for Dutton's major customer, another for two customers, a third for four customers, a fourth for six customers and the fifth for all the other customers. They know the customers and they agree delivery times. And the customers know the team – some know every member of the team! The teams are responsible for all the day-to-day operational needs: manufacturing techniques, job allocation, choice of consumables and work scheduling are all left to them. The teams are supported by three members of management: the chief executive, the IT manager and the bookkeeper, with management's role in day-to-day operations simply being to provide the 'infrastructure' within which the teams can flourish. The teams have boards on which they record how they are progressing. The boards contained monthly figures on sales, stock turn, on-delivery performance, rejects, profits and value added per employee. Flipcharts (for learning/explaining) are on the shop floor for each team

The experience has been that teams seem to work best if kept to around eight members. Teams now seem fully established. Two examples of the team spirit are the following. Ken recounts:

Staff can use their own cars to go 100 miles on business and we pay the petrol costs without quibble. A man whose main task was to polish the boxes prior to their being packed took it upon himself to visit a new customer in Thetford, Norfolk. When he got there he introduced himself as from Dutton (every member of staff can do this – there is no need for management to be involved) and asked to see the goods inward people. They wondered who he was and what his job was. When he told them he was a polisher they couldn't believe it: why should a polisher come to see them? 'Because I'm a member of the team that made the boxes,' was the reply. The polisher enquired about the quality of the boxes and about the quality of the packaging. So impressed was the client that he took the polisher to meet the purchasing function. Again impressed, they asked him if Dutton could make some other stainless steel fabrication. The polisher said they could, and this contact resulted in £300,000 worth of new business.

The second example of team spirit is shown by the saga of the forklift trucks. Ken bought one without consulting the workforce. When it wouldn't work, it was left for some time until it was fixed. Later, the teams wanted a replacement. Although £10,000 was set aside for one, they went round and bought one for £3000. When something went wrong with it they got it repaired immediately.[b]

Generally, the teams are responsible for recruiting extra members. As Ken says, 'A poor performer can hide from management, they can't hide from the team.' Selection is on attitude rather than qualifications or experience. As Tina remarks:

Once team working is embedded in a team they drive it – they have the set of expectations of what is the Dutton way. If you joined the team they would expect you to be a team member, to join in and to be multiskilled. The culture is now so deeply embedded that taking on the

new people is OK. We rewrote the book and now they own the book.

The teams are very supportive of the new team members for, say, a month, but after that they are fairly ruthless. However, even though the team working method is explained to prospective employees, a fair proportion don't like the responsibility of being a team member. The traditional way of working in a factory is to put your card in the clock and then stand around until someone tells you what to do. If they've done this for 20 years, it's difficult for them to change; for example, people want their work inspected, they don't like talking to customers, paperwork or discussing matters with management. These people leave voluntarily, they don't have to be dismissed. The teams are getting better at induction and recruitment as they get more experienced and many more people are retained than previously. Twice Ken has had to step in and suggest strongly that a team is working too many hours and that they ought to recruit another team member.

Every six months the teams sit down with Ken to discuss what their customer orders are and how they think the work is progressing. Ken requires a margin of 15% from each team. If things are going well, the team can ask for a salary rise to be split among the team members. All staff participate in an equal share of 20% of total Dutton profits. Recently, the teams have been able to decide how to split the sum total for salaries. Interestingly, two of the teams decided to revert to total equality of earnings.

By 1999, there are no longer team leaders but cell coordinators: the team leaders evolved themselves out of a job. The team leaders solved problems and talked to management where necessary. The teams are now self-managed, with co-ordinators who don't organise the team but simply bring issues to their notice. This move to self managed teams came about in a rather odd way. The management team decided that the leaders of two teams were getting stale and decided to swap them over. The leaders didn't want to move, and they were popular with their original teams. The teams realised that the new leaders didn't know their customers or the detail about the products they made, and reasoned that the new leaders couldn't help them and they were better off solving their own problems. The co-ordinator was now a team choice rather than a person whom managers had installed.

Kaizen – continuous improvement

Prior to Ken's trip to Japan, a suggestion scheme had been tried but was only of very limited success: either the suggestions were turned down or not considered for many weeks. An award scheme for innovation was tried, but again failed, because people didn't like having their sug-

---

[b] Ken isn't supposed to know that the truck needed repair.

Ref. No:		Date:	

Type of Report::	Non Conformance / Reject	
	Kaizen Proposal	

Work Centre   701 – Guillotine   702 – Sawing   703 – CNC Punching   704/705 – Folding
706 – Drill B / Sharp   707 – Drill Ped'st'l & Bench   708 – P / All & Hare Punch
709 – Inserting 7 Nutserting   710 – Grindmasters   711 – Assembly
799 – Shop Floor (Linish / Pt No / Fly)   Welding   Packing & Despatch
601 – Iridite & Etching   602 – Wet Paint   603 – Powder Paint
604 – Masking & Hooking-up   605 – Silk Screening Radan (E2I)

Part No.	
Purchase Order No.	
Quantity Rejected	
Customer	

Reason for Non Conformity/Kaizen

Action Required

Rework		Return to Supplier		Repair	
Replace		Obtain Concession		Credit	

Kaizen Proposal

Team Leader Assessment

Corrective action

Preventive action

Comments:

Implement

Originator	Quality Inspector
Responsibility	Date
Date Closed Out	

Exhibit 3

gestions turned down publicly by management. It was time to try the Japanese approach – *kaizen*, or continuous improvement.

The role for senior management in the *kaizens* is not hands-on; this is left to the team leaders and to the middle managers. The senior managers' role is to encourage and inspire the team leaders to implement the scheme. Dutton deliberately kept the *kaizen* form – see Exhibit 3 – extremely simple, realising that many people, especially in operations, aren't used to filling in forms.

At Dutton, the *kaizen* forms are kept by the team leaders. This means that when a team member thinks of an improvement, it's natural that they first discuss it with the team leader. It's also natural for team leaders sometimes to help team members fill in the forms. The form is filled in down to and including the effect that it's thought the *kaizen* will have. The team leader evaluates the suggestion and gives the go-ahead if they think it's appropriate. Once the go-ahead is given, the team leader will encourage the proposer to get the necessary resources to carry out the improvement. Once implemented, the team leader passes the *kaizen* form to the managing director. The involvement of the managing director is to show top management commitment and to show employees that their efforts are being recognised and appreciated at the highest level. After signing, the form is passed to accounts for immediate payment. The payments are for £5 or £15, the particular amount depending on the team leader. At the start, Ken put controls on the number of £15 awards that could be given, with the edict that only one in four awards should be worth £15. However, the team leaders were so concerned about overpayment that Ken had to intervene to ask them to make more awards for the higher amount.

The very first *kaizen* from the shop floor at Dutton involved scrap bins. For ten years the bin had been located in one of the car-parking slots and was one of the first things that the visitor saw on arriving at the site. The bin was moved on to some spare ground and in the process (which the suggestee hadn't foreseen) created another parking space worth perhaps £250 a year.

Ken himself produced a very visible *kaizen* early on. Every morning he would kick a wooden wedge under a door to keep it open. During the day it would work loose, often at very awkward times. Ken's *kaizen* was to go to the local hardware store and buy a hook and eye, get hold of an electric drill from the maintenance department and fit the fastenings. The great merit of this particular *kaizen* was that it was a highly visible improvement, done by the boss and the sort of thing that was within everyone's abilities.

Dutton calculated the costs and savings associated with the first 100 *kaizens,* and these are shown in Exhibit 4.

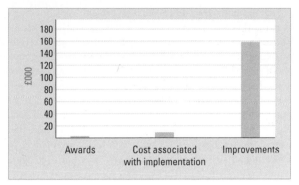

Exhibit 4   The first 100 *kaizens* costings (Lewis and Lytton, 1997)

Dutton spent £750 in awards and £1670 for the labour, materials and equipment to carry out the *kaizens* – a total of £2420. The first year's savings were £160,000. Fewer formal *kaizens* are now suggested: the culture has moved on to a view that as well as doing your job you also improve your job. If there is a need to spend money or a need for someone else's help, then the formal *kaizen* route is still needed – otherwise just get on with it. It took about two years to move to this point where people feel that improvement is just part of the job.

Mike recalls:

We used to look to the inspectors for inspection and managers for bright ideas. Now we were doing both. We were bringing our brains to work, not just our brawn. Previously we hadn't been allowed to use our brains.

Supplier and customer relationships

Dutton has very close relationships with all its suppliers, and over 90% of raw materials and consumables are delivered using a *kanban* system (the exception is the stainless steel). Each supplier has a pass that gives them access to the factory during normal working hours and allows them to deliver to the team positions inside the factory. The replenishment system is extremely simple, using two boxes, with each box holding just over a week's supply of components. When the first box is emptied the operator places the component ticket in a central position on the component rack and starts on the second week's box. In the meantime, the empty box is collected by the supplier and refilled with a further week's supply of components. The replenished box is replaced on the next supplier visit. There is no formal goods-inward inspection, as the suppliers are trusted. Thus most of the time the teams can simply get on with their jobs without thinking about supplies.

Along with the simplified component replenishment system, there is a very simple invoicing system. One of Dutton's trading conditions is that suppliers invoice only once per month. Invoices come on a computer disk coded according to Dutton cost centres. If suppliers are asked for something outside of the *kanban*, they ask for a job number against which the item is delivered. Between 1991 and mid-1994 the purchase invoice orders processed each month fell from almost 200 to 60. In 1991 Dutton had over 250 suppliers, of whom around 100 were core; in 1994 it had just under 60 suppliers, of whom ten were core.

A similar scheme is operated for finished goods and goods for painting. Only one delivery firm is used, and it comes into the end of each team's 'production line' and use the team's forklift to load. One invoice a month is received from the paint and delivery firms.

Because supplier relationships are so important to Dutton, and because it expects to put considerable effort into developing them, it is very careful whom it selects as a supplier. The procedure to find top-class suppliers is very thorough. First, some trial business is conducted with a supplier who has ISO 9000 or similar accreditation. If this trial is successful, Dutton gets a team together from the parts of the business that will be directly affected, and this team reviews all aspects of the potential supplier's performance. Very many features are considered and placed within the formula set out in Exhibit 5.

supplier rating = 0.3 × culture + 0.25 × product quality + 0.25 × delivery + 0.2 x price

Exhibit 5   Supplier assessment

The highest weighting is given to 'culture', with Dutton arguing that it would find it difficult to have a long-term relationship with another organisation that worked in a different way. The cultural assessment includes judging the quality of the paperwork it sends out, how the firm responds to problems and how pro-active it is. Equal weightings are given to product quality – the technical aspects of the supplier's products – and to delivery performance. Price is only weighted at 20%: Dutton has found that if the other three factors aren't good then any price advantages tend not to be translated into cost advantages: the consequences of deficiencies in cultural fit, quality and delivery performance are likely to outweigh any price advantages.

What isn't acceptable is for unexpected price rises to be imposed. One supplier put up its prices by 2% without informing Dutton. Dutton's systems were good enough to pick this up immediately and the supplier wasn't used again. Every year, Dutton holds a suppliers' day, when it discusses where Dutton is heading and what it feels it will want from its suppliers over the coming years. There is a 'Supplier of the Year' award, which is much sought after.

The move to self-managed teams released the very experienced former team leaders. They became the nucleus of a five-person support team that was responsible for product and customer development. The old way of obtaining orders was to respond to a request from a customer; typically, a drawing was sent in the post asking for a quote and Dutton responded. Now when Dutton receives a request to quote a member of the support team contacts the firm and asks to meet them. In a half-hour meeting they can be told how Dutton has re-engineered other clients' products to be more cost-competitive, how Dutton has the latest production equipment, the quality of Dutton's design facilities, and so on. Naturally, the prospective client gets very interested. It has been found that a very experienced person at the initial customer meeting can influence the way things go, and the former team leaders in the support team are ideal for this.

To be taken seriously, Dutton has to have a CAD/CAM system that is as good as those of its customers. The team uses the CAD/CAM system for product development, leading on to ordering all the stainless steel and working it to provide the components that the factory teams need. This involves punching out the panels required and bending them to the required shape. Thus the support team is an internal supplier to the factory teams.

The support team creates *kaizen* project teams when responding to a significant customer request for change, such as a cost down. This team would include the members of the new support team, someone from the factory team that services the customer, selected suppliers and the customer.

Training and development

A strong thread throughout all Dutton does is an emphasis on training. Anyone can go and do any sort of evening course and the firm will pay. It can be anything at all – needlework, if that's the thing. But few employees have taken up this offer. Tina has reflected on why this should be so:

I think it's partly a reflection of the busy lives we lead and this means that you have to be highly motivated to spend an evening a week on a course. There are also some barriers about what is seen as classroom learning – involved with words rather than with doing.

Those who have taken up the offer have mostly chosen to study information technology or language courses, especially as the firm is now doing work for German clients. Ken is fairly clear that you have to be very careful with managers:

Never talk to managers about training – they've had bad experiences about it. Always say 'let's talk about strategy' and they're quite happy.

Ken is very keen on Dutton being a learning organisation. Every team member is taught cost accounting and estimating by senior Dutton people. Ken says he teaches all the cost accounting the teams need in just 2½ hours, whereas it takes years to train a skilled metal craftsman! The skilled workers teach their colleagues the basics of their skill; for example, a skilled welder will teach basic welding to others so that when the workload demands it, the unskilled welder can do the unskilled portion of the welder's job. Initially, skilled workers didn't want to do this: knowledge is power, and it was another thing they had to do. Dutton wanted staff to have one core skill and around three other skills; in the event, many workers have ten or 12 skills. In general, people took to this form of working, as it made their day much more interesting. It also had the spin-off that when talking to customers, the shop floor workers knew much more about the range of production processes.

Over a considerable period Ken used to invite employees on a one-to-one basis to have lunch with him, where, among other things, he would learn of the employee's hobbies. He builds on these; for example, the IT manager was taken from the shop floor because he was interested in computers and given the extra training required.

Control

One source of Dutton's success is that it controls the time taken for all its activities, because the labour costs make up such a large proportion of costs. For example, in the early days making the tea was taking around five hours a week; as soon as this was recognised a vending machine was installed. This control has now been extended: teams are charged for the factory space they use, and this has led one team to come in during their weekends to build upwards!

This detailed concern with time and costs has led to three out-sourcing decisions. All salaries and PE11D tax forms are done outside for £40 per month. Dutton used to do its own gardening, but it is now subcontracted to a landscape gardener, and it immediately won for Dutton the best-kept factory premises award in Sandy. Dutton used to have a van to deliver finished goods, but now a single-sourced contractor is employed to deliver all goods in the UK and continental Europe.

Looking to the future

The support team now looks for new customers and new markets. New customers are found at exhibitions, where team members also collect intelligence on competitors. The trend is towards single sourcing, and the competition is becoming global. Competition is also becoming more severe; a box selling for £300 in 1990 is now selling for £200 and the competition is coming in at £150.

There is the 'green' trend to consider: there is so much congestion in the south-east of the UK that local supply is becoming important. Ken is thinking of getting the firm that paints the boxes to locate in the new premises he has recently purchased right next door to his Sandy factory, as it takes time to take items to the painter and back again.

The journey continues

In the early 1980s, Dutton had 40 employees and a turnover of £1 million. Quality was poor and only 60% of orders were delivered on time, even though there was on average six weeks from taking an order to delivery. There were four stock turns a year. At the beginning of 1999 40 people were employed, the turnover in 1998 was £2.2 million, and 99.9% of deliveries were within 24 hours of the agreed time. It takes ten days to get the materials, and Dutton can react in eight hours. There are now 100 stock turns per year. The 40 employees in 1999 were a very different mix to those employed in the 1980s. As Ken succinctly put it

In the early 1980s 12 of the 40 weren't bashing metal – they weren't directly adding value. The firm in 1999 had only three employees who weren't bashing metal.

Ken's goal as he moves towards retirement is to increase turnover from £2.2 million to £5.4 million in the next five years – when he will be 65 and thinking of selling up. So the journey continues.

Acknowledgement

I'm very much indebted to Ken Lewis for the time he made available to facilitate the writing of this case and for allowing me to quote extensively from the book he wrote with a colleague: Ken Lewis and Stephen Lytton, *How to Transform Your Company and Enjoy It!* 2nd edn, Management Books 2000, 1997.

BDHTBWA[a]

Introduction

BDHTBWA began life in Manchester in 1964 as the advertising agency BDH Communications, when Ken Boden, Mike Dyble, Geoff Hayes and Win Higgenbotham broke away from Osbourne-Peacock to form their own advertising agency. It remained privately owned until 1988, when it was sold to the moderately sized but ambitious London-based firm of Gold Greenlees Trott (GGT). This firm had a similar beginning to BDH Communications, being set up by three people covering the four areas necessary in an advertising agency – Mike Gold, a media specialist who also looked after the financial side, the client-oriented Mike Greenlees, and Dave Trott, the creative genius, the man behind such ads as 'lip-smackin', thirst-quenchin', ace tastin', motivatin', good buzzin', cool talkin', high walkin', fast livin', eva givin', cool fizzin' . . . Pepsi'.

GGT became a publicly quoted company but remained relatively small until 1997, when it embarked on an intensive acquisition strategy. This included the purchase of the French company BDDP, which gave GGT international coverage. One problem with this acquisition arose with the BDDP associate company in New York, Wells Rich Greene, which ran the Procter & Gamble account. After GGT's purchase, some senior managers left, taking the P&G account with them – an account representing around 15% of GGT's revenue. In 1998, GGT was taken over by the American multinational Omnicom, which became the world's largest marketing communications group as a result. It operates four strategic global networks: TBWA, DDB, BBDO and DAS. BDH Communications became part of TBWA. What was BDH Communications became branded BDHTBWA and is now the Manchester office of TBWA – part of a global network of around 100 offices in 62 countries.

BDHTBWA itself employs around 150 people. This office is quite imposing: in 1997 the firm bought a redundant church and had the inside gutted and replaced with a striking, purpose-built interior that supports the culture of openness that the firm wishes to foster. So conducive is it to working that some clients prefer to come to Manchester for meetings rather than have BDHTBWA staff visit them.

Marketing communications[b] covers a range of activities to support the marketing of products and services, both inside and outside organisations. The main activities include advertising – which may be defined as the generation of messages in the mass media outside the organisation – sales promotions such as point-of-sale material, direct mail and trade videos, public relations and personal selling. Although advertising is still the main activity within marketing communications, non-advertising activity now probably represents around 40% of marketing communications activity and is growing. This trend is highlighted by Saachi and Saachi Advertising recently dropping the 'Advertising' from its name. Several agencies now specialise in one form of communication, such as direct mail or public relations.

The organisation structure of BDHTBWA is shown in Exhibit 1. Central Services is purely financial, concerned with total financial performance and liaison with TBWA and Omnicom head offices.

Around 80% of BDHTBWA employees work in BDH Communications, which generates around 80% of the approximately £60 million billings (revenue) that BDHTBWA achieved in 1998. BDH Communications concentrates on developing branding strategies and brand positioning and is engaged in devising advertising and point-of-sale material. Compendium specialises in technological communications, particularly for information technology companies, focusing on the newer media channels such as the Internet, intranets and CD-ROMs. Almost all of its work is for its 'own' clients, with very little in support of BDH Communications. One major client is the telecommunications giant Ericsson, which is making great efforts to communicate a consistent brand identity across its international activities. Insight engages in strategic design, with roughly 50% of its effort servicing BDH Communications and 50% working with its own clients.

Exhibit 1   The BDHTBWA organisation

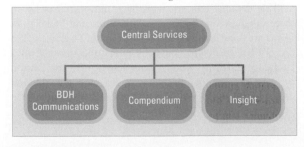

[a] This case was prepared by Mark Davies and Paul Finlay.
© Mark A.P. Davies and Paul N. Finlay, 1999.

[b] An alternative name is *marketing services*.

At one end of the scale, a client may feel that it needs its logo updating; at the other Insight might redesign the whole of a client's corporate identity, involving such things as the motif on company transport, logos, letterheads, package design and the redesign of the head office reception area.

The Manchester agency is headed by the chairman and the chief executive. Two joint managing directors, one with a client services background and the other a creative background, are responsible for the operations of the agency. There is a deputy managing director, two creative directors and several more directors responsible for key clients. Central Services is responsible for administration and contains the finance department, headed by the finance director. Since much of the liaison with Omnicom head office concerns financial matters, this is one of the key responsibilities that he shares with the chief executive and chairman.

The marketing services 'industry'

Ignoring the single-person consultancies, there are around 2000 marketing communications agencies operating in the UK. The top 20 agencies by turnover in 1998 are listed in Exhibit 2.[1] The top five regional agencies are listed in Exhibit 3.[2]

The move to global branding – and thus the need for global communication – is a powerful force for change in the marketing communications industry. Although the core product can be different – for example Coca-Cola is sweeter in the USA than in Europe – global brands require

Exhibit 2   Top UK marketing services agencies, by billings (Campaign Report, 1999)

Agency	Billings £m	Staff
Abbott Mead Vickers BBDO	356	320
Saachi & Saachi	267	480
J. Walter Thompson	259	321
Ogilvy & Mather	243	303
Publicis	231	241
BMP DDB	224	461
TBWA GGT Simons Palmer	205	250
McCann-Erickson (London)	203	310
DMB&B	194	219
M&C Saachi	187	208

Agency	Billings £m	Staff
BDHTBWA	52	120
McCann-Erickson (Manchester)	42	320
J. Walter Thompson (Manchester)	23	115
The Leith Agency	20	45
Yellow M	19	63

Exhibit 3   Top UK regional marketing services agencies, by billings (Campaign Report, 1999)

absolute consistency of theme, with campaigns tailored to particular regions. This is the position with Disney: Mickey Mouse is the same all over the world. Global branding begets global marketing communications agencies.

One appeal of global advertising is that it can present a global company/product/brand image. In the early 1990s, the Italian apparel firm Benetton created a very controversial worldwide advertising campaign. This campaign replaced 50 different ones that the company had in 50 different countries. The advertising was to create the message directly from the company without showing a product. This campaign included ads showing people of different races laughing, hugging and kissing; and photos of an oil-coated bird, a newborn child with the umbilical cord still attached, and a man dying of AIDS. According to Luciano Benetton, chairman of the company, these ads were a consequence of the company's seeing the world as a whole. They wanted to touch themes that were common to countries worldwide. This advertising has been both award-winning and banned.[3]

A second advantage of internationalisation is that it lowers the costs of preparing and implementing advertising campaigns. In the mid-1990s, the large, US-based Colgate Palmolive company saved a lot of money when it replaced 20 separate local advertising campaigns for laundry detergent with a series of successful commercials developed in France. This single campaign ran in 30 countries.[4]

Finally, an international stance on advertising can reduce message confusion in areas where media overlap is likely, for example Germany/Austria/Switzerland and Denmark/Germany, and where there is considerable country-to-country mobility (for business people, for example).

The globalisation of brands and agencies means that there has been a very strong polarisation, with the major multinational companies and the small breakaway agencies prospering. The middle-sized agencies are finding it very difficult to survive, as the takeover of GGT reflects. The bigger the multinational agencies get, the more dissatisfied people there are in them who can leave to set up their own agencies and take clients with them. As these breakaways prosper and get bigger, they need access to international-sized resources and they tend to sell out to the big players. And so the cycle continues. The picture in a few years time is likely to be of only six or seven global players, a declining number of privately owned, medium-sized players and an ever-regenerating number of new entrants.

The multinationals are termed *networks* or *agency groups*: they marry the reach of an international agency to the national standing of the indigenous agency. A few networks include alliances between independent agencies, but in general they consist of wholly owned subsidiaries or joint ventures. Typically, the international agency will buy roughly 50% of the equity in the national business in a joint venture; for example, the London office of BBDO is allied with Abbott Mead Vickers in a joint venture to form Abbott Mead BBDO, now the biggest agency in Britain. Although a few countries prevent foreign ownership – Indonesia is one such example – in general international branding is carried through, often with the addition of yet more initials, it would seem!

There is a difference between some of the London and other capital city agencies and the regional agencies. In the capital cities there is scope for the very specialised – niche – communications agencies specialising in only one or two forms of communication, perhaps only newspaper advertising or TV commercials. The regional agencies, on the other hand, have traditionally supplied an integrated service, bringing together all the channels of communication that best satisfy client needs. The regional agencies are what is termed *media-neutral*.

To illustrate the importance of integration and its facets, one of BDHTBWA's joint MDs drew the diagram shown as Exhibit 4.

Exhibit 4 The communications pyramid

The full-service ad agency – a one-stop shop – would have TV production facilities and a department looking after print production: anything that ends up being printed, such as press adverts, direct mail and in-store literature. It would also have creative, design and media planning and buying departments and a client service department to look after the finance, planning and administration to satisfy clients' needs.

The one-stop agency is under pressure from the more narrowly focused firms, which are becoming increasingly popular with clients as the clients become more confident of what they are wishing to do – they seek an *à la carte* operation. For example, there are the media independents who specialise in the planning and buying of media space, and indeed niche players who don't buy but who concentrate on devising media strategies. For example, will a TV campaign involve a consistent intensity of advertising throughout a two-month period or will initial hefty advertising be followed by a much lighter 'drip'? Media buying is concentrating into bigger and bigger operations. A media buyer for Unilever will be buying £600–700 million per year and will be able to demand rebates of up to 20%. There are only three sales houses in the UK selling TV advertising time for all the TV companies. There are TV production companies such as Howell Hendry Chaldicott Lury and Brasserie, which provides bespoke TV advertisements for companies. There are the production houses that engage in finished artwork and printing. There are planning consultancies that offer planning strategy research.

Boots is a company that operates *à la carte* – it uses the creative agency JWT to help determine its main messages and for TV advertising, an internal production facility to produce in-store literature and the media-buying company BMP. It uses JWT and other agencies for planning consultancy, 24 design agencies for packaging design, four design agencies for developing new store concepts, Mindshare for Internet/digital TV developments and four direct mail agencies.

This fragmentation isn't necessarily client-driven – it's also being driven by people in the industry wanting to make money. The problem for the one-stop agencies is that it's the very best people who have the confidence to leave a larger organisation and set up on their own, so the one-stop agencies aren't only competing with people who have lower overheads, they are also dealing with people who can offer high quality. To make the whole picture even more complex, these specialist firms also work for the full-service companies. Here are the elements of the virtual one-stop firm; indeed, totally virtual one-stop firms now exist.

It's all too easy to open the door with a lower-priced offer, not necessarily sustainable over a longer timescale.

Undercutting is rife; unfortunately, the focus isn't on adding value – if it were, margins would be greater. The standard commission rate is 15%, which can deliver reasonable net margins, but every further fragmentation of the industry tends to lower that rate, until now 10% is the start of negotiations. This leads to margins being achieved that are leading many firms into marginal profitability. As Rupert Howell of Howell Hendry Chaldicott Lury said, 'The one thing I fear most in this industry is a bad negotiator.' A bad negotiator strikes a deal delivering very low margins, which then provide the benchmark for future deals affecting the whole industry.

Time to market is an important feature of production house work, but less so for the creative aspects of marketing communications.

While there is sharp competition between agencies and from production houses, the most dangerous competition is from the management consultancies, such as McKinsey, Price Waterhouse/Coopers, and Deloitte and Touche. The problem has been highlighted by Martin Sorrell, the founder and chief executive of WPP Group, the world's second-largest communications company, as illustrated in Exhibit 5.

Management consultants are seen as having greater intellectual credibility than the marketing communications agencies. Their deficiency is in creative skills, but it is quite possible that they can develop these. They have unrivalled access to corporate clients – particularly at the highest levels – often through the network of contacts that consultants have with their former business school colleagues.

Most competitive pressures come on price rather than on value added. Agencies have great difficulty in demonstrating analytically the value added of their work. The problem they have is that the value of their work isn't measurable until after it has been employed. Marketing communication acts over a long period of time – it isn't just immediately after an advertisement has appeared on TV, for example; an advertisement generally needs to be seen more than once for communication of the message to be effected.

Clients can also have very fixed views. To quote Roger Ward, one of two joint MDs of BDHTBWA:

> It's the only industry that I know where you pay people hundreds of thousands of pounds to do something and these people have very strongly held views about what is required. Do you tell a brain surgeon how to operate? The clients are strongly tempted to back their own judgement rather than that of people who have specialised in the field for many years.

The marketing communications industry has a code of practice that is self-regulated through the Advertising Standards Authority (ASA). All ads in non broadcast media (direct mail, cinemas, cassettes and teletext) must adhere to the British Code of Advertising Practice, and all TV ads must fit the requirements of the Independent Television Commission Code of Programme Sponsorship. The aim is to ensure that ads are legal, decent, honest and truthful. There are additional restrictions applying to advertising to children and to special products such as alcohol. However, there is evidence that the ASA is something of a lame duck. *Which?* magazine[6] complained about 14 ads, four of which the ASA put through its formal complaints procedure. Three months later, when it published its report, no ruling on any of the four complaints had been given. During this time the ads had been free to run. Even with an adverse ruling, there is little the ASA can do to punish companies: it can't force companies to tell customers that they have been misled and it can't fine persistent offenders. (This is in sharp contrast to the practice in the USA, where the sanction of 'corrective advertising' – i.e. a public apology – is always a threat). A rarely used sanction is to refer an ad to the Office of Fair Trading, but the procedure is bureaucratic; by the time referral has been authorised, the damage has often already been done.

For the last 15 years, the Institute of Practitioners in Advertising has sponsored trade competitions. Agencies and their clients are asked to demonstrate how they planned and evaluated specific ad campaigns. There are several categories of award, for example for established and new consumer goods and services and campaigns with small budgets. These awards recognise the broader effects of advertising, taking into account such things as the

Exhibit 5   Sorrell and the threat from consultancy firms[5]

Sorrell sees a problem: management consultants. They get paid to give advice that Sorrell thinks WPP should itself be giving – and getting paid for. In recent years he has become vexed that WPP clients like Unilever ask the likes of McKinsey for advice on marketing strategy. 'They get paid millions for doing things we could do better.' Sorrell bristles at an incident that took place four years ago. Unilever, the maker of such well-known brands as Ragu pasta sauce and Dove soap, hired McKinsey to determine whether supermarket brands were cutting into the Anglo-Dutch consumer goods company's sales. '[WPP's agencies] have got billions of man hours invested in those brands and know more about them than anyone else,' he says. 'It seems incredible to me that we did not have a role in that.'

Sorrell, who has flouted conventional thinking before, now wants to build a separate consulting business at WPP, a plan that others say is risky – and unnecessary. WPP has bought three small consultancy firms this year, and more may be in the offing.

boosting of morale of the entire company's workforce or the morale of the sales team.

Agency operations

The creative agencies such as BDHTBWA have three main types of employee. There are the *creatives*, who are responsible for the overall message that is to be conveyed, for thinking up slogans, devising body copy and deciding on the details of the campaign. There are the *suits* – the account handlers – who deal directly with clients and who are responsible for relationships with clients, including financial relationships. And there are the *planners* (or the *intelligentsia*, as one agency director has called them), who are engaged in project planning and in planning and buying media space and in the printing of media. In the smaller agencies very junior people are interacting with many different people internally and with clients. They realise very early on to use personal relationships rather than authority to get things done.

The way in which agencies work is that small teams of people work on an account, with little linkage between the team and other people in the agency except for a general flow of ideas. Thus the agency is very vulnerable to people leaving; every defection will cause a wobble in the account, the size of the wobble depending on the contribution and seniority of the leaver. Some agencies have policies of rotating people through accounts, keeping continuity through a few very senior people retaining contact with the accounts. With this arrangement the client is continually meeting people who have to go through the learning curve.

The first point of contact for a new client would be with one of the account executives. The initial meeting would explore the nature of the issue, in particular whether marketing communications can solve the problem. The issue could be the underlying costs of the client's operations, reflected in the price of its offer or in the offer quality rather than in its promotion. Also discussed would be the aim the client has for the marketing communications – do they want to increase awareness of the brand or do they simply think that the agency that they have been using has become stale? Assuming that these initial discussions suggest that the agency might be suitable, the agency would show the client a portfolio of their activities in the same or similar sector. The client is likely to shortlist three or four agencies on this basis.

Contract terms would then be discussed. While marketing communications agencies can add millions to an organisation's profits, they aren't always remunerated in a way that is linked to the value they add. Remuneration is generally on the basis of media expenditure or on time spent. There is a trend to some sort of performance-related element being written into contracts, following the practice in some US agencies. Performance-related remuneration will tend to make the communications campaign 'media-neutral', in the sense that there's little tendency to use expensive media to boost earnings. If the costs looked satisfactory, the client would probably opt for an initial three- or six-month contract with the agency.

The first major briefing session would then take place. The client should provide a written brief of what it wants in terms of the broad aims from the communication, the target audience (dinkies, woopies, etc.[c]) and the objectives of particular advertising. In practice, some clients never provide a written brief. A typical briefing session would include the client brand and assistant brand managers and, from the agency side, the account executive, an assistant account executive and a media planner. A junior creative may also attend. It's likely that further follow-up meetings would be held to resolve any problems with the brief and finally an agreed brief would be written. The time from discussing terms to finalising the brief would typically be a month.

Surprisingly, this brief is generally only for the client and the account manager. The creative who will be working on the account is not given this brief; instead, the suit will interpret the brief to provide a second brief for the creatives to work from, detailing the form of media it is thought will be used, the target audience, the main themes, the positioning and any express requirements of the client (such as the size of the client's logo).

The creatives will then produce rough ideas of what they think the campaign material should be in terms of the messages, colours, etc. The media strategy will be devised in terms of which media to use, how much and when to use it. On an on-going basis the agency will engage in internal review – sometimes involving board members.

During the campaign, the clients will probably attempt to track the effectiveness of the campaign, perhaps using a market research agency. The agency is also likely to be doing the same.

Relationships are very, very significant. To quote Roger Ward:

We are the classic people industry. Relationship management is the key to the whole process. Everything is about personal contacts and about negotiation and brokerage. Of first importance are the relationships with clients, but the relationships internal to the BDH come a close second. No particular relationships are always of paramount importance: it depends on the nature of the

---

[c] Dual income, no kids; well-off older people.

business. Sometimes it's the relationship between the creatives and the suits, sometimes between the suits and the planners. But it's a truism that if you are an account manager you have to get along with the creatives or your life is a misery.

But every single client is being approached many times by your competitors. It's a dog-eat-dog situation. Competitors will pick over the bones of a (past) campaign and explain to the client what went wrong and how they would have done things differently. This is very unprofessional, in the sense that it's inconceivable that accountants and lawyers would openly attack the work of other accountants and lawyers.

There is a minimum size of planning department needed to provide all the resources. And in terms of intellectual resources the bigger the better – there is a lot of feed-across and synergy providing more knowledge and more creativity. The key thing for agency success is to have bright people – ten dull people aren't equal to one bright spark. How ever big the agency, an account will be serviced by between five and 25 people, and it is the calibre of those people that counts, not how good the other people in the agency are. Agency size is only important if the best people are being attracted to the large agencies, which can possibly afford to pay the best wages. There is a brain tendency to the larger agencies, but there isn't a brain drain, because in the small organisations the best people have more authority and tend to be offered equity in the company. The smart clients will go to an agency, see whether they like it and if they do, select the good people from within the agency. They will back the small breakaway agencies – of the best people – because they can get great deals from very good people.

Sheer scale doesn't necessarily mean quality. It probably means that you do well on media buying but not necessarily on value added. Media buying revolves around two things, volume and the relationships between the buyer and the seller. Small regional shops can outbuy the big London agencies – partly because of relationships and partly because they are big fish in a smaller pond and can utilise this.

BDHTBWA

Around half of new client business comes as a result of active marketing carried out by the business development department responsible for the marketing and selling of the agency. The leads are generated by public relations and via four direct mailings per year. Of particular importance is being cited in the trade press for excellent communications campaigns, through winning IPA awards. Recently BDHTBWA won four out of five pitches and eight out of 15 area effectiveness awards. The people associated with winning these awards are held in high esteem – they are heroes.

The other new business – where people approach BDHTBWA – comes from personal recommendation and from existing clients moving off to new organisations. This latter means of getting business is, of course, rather a two-edged sword.

BDHTBWA is typically associated with quality and highbrow communications. While it's one of the big three – nowhere as big as McCann-Erickson – it is somewhere that everyone wants to work.

Leadership and issue handling/decision making

In general, the marketing communications industry isn't very hierarchical, although some agencies are. It's an industry where very bright people in their early twenties are given huge responsibilities. BDHTBWA is a collective, like a classic legal or accountancy practice. There are lots of partners who see themselves as equals whatever their titles and whatever their status or how good they are. The firm can be described as fairly informal – lots of people in open-necked shirts, collaborative, open, friendly, considerate, sometimes acting as an extended family. In BDHTBWA it's difficult to see one person getting the power to be autocratic.

The chairman and chief executive are responsible for making all the senior management appointments. There are generations of senior managers. There were the founders, who sold out, and over the last four years the present chairman and chief executive have been in the process of handing over to the next generation to take the agency on for the next ten years. The important factor that is taken into account is who has had the most influential effect on the growth of the agency.

Every so often the directors meet for brainstorming, in what are called *hub meetings*. The firm Red Spider is used to facilitate the meetings, but as it charges £10,000–20,000 per meeting, it's only used on important issues – perhaps once every two months. Away days are used for issue handling. Power is less to do with title and more to do with the contribution that someone is making to the business. In an attempt to reduce hierarchy, meetings are held with round tables. Flipcharts are used extensively and wire runners have been installed in the main meeting room to facilitate their use. And this is even though the firm is very used to IT. Many issues aren't handled through board meetings, simply lots of conversations. A consensus is sought within the senior directors. The chairman and chief executive are used to making as many decisions outside board meetings as within it.

BDHTBWA has a written code of ethics, mainly about treating people as you would like to be treated yourself. It has a policy of never forcing someone to work on a piece of business that they have moral objections to; for example, some employees wouldn't work on a tobacco company account. When asked if BDHTBWA had a mission statement, Roger Ward resignedly said:

We have had loads of them – I could pull out loads – but whether we have one that I can go outside and ask 100 members of staff if they know what it is and get an affirmative answer is debatable. If you haven't got one that you can apply that test to then you haven't got a mission statement.

BDHTBWA has what the MD describes as a mantra, which is set out in reception and is on the agency's letterhead. It is ECPA, the key principles of the business:

Effective	BDHTBWA must provide marketing services that are effective for the client.
Creative	The effectiveness should come mainly through creativity.
Proven	BDHTBWA will prove the effectiveness of its creativity.
Accountable	BDHTBWA is committed to being held accountable for everything it does.

ECPA is the yardstick by which BDHTBWA judges all its work and what it sells its services on. These are the important features to be successful in marketing communications; BDHTBWA believes that it has the edge in most of these areas but particularly in the creative side (as the awards it has recently won testify) and in its ability to prove their effectiveness. One major plank in BDHTBWA's strategy is to *get price off the table*. It believes that clients should pay a premium for superior work.

Controls

Organisationally, BDHTBWA tries to be as unstructured as possible – but it is structured when it needs to be. It has very strong, albeit standard, financial controls, both to record how well it's doing and to forecast the likely future financial position. Reporting and invoicing are both done on a monthly cycle. There is a 'work-in-progress management system', which is administered by the account groups, who have weekly team meetings to check on progress and where individual responsibilities are assessed and perhaps reassigned. Formal sign-off and approvals procedures vary by account – they can be very structured or unstructured depending on individual preference and on the way the client wants to work. The balanced scorecard isn't used and indeed BDHTBWA tends to eschew

management theories. It has tried process re-engineering and other things but these weren't very effective and gave the management a reputation for meddling! The biggest control feature in BDHTBWA is common sense and being close to the client. BDHTBWA lets people operate in a way that suits them.

A major control is through recruitment – making sure that the right kind of people are recruited. BDHTBWA had run a very successful graduate recruitment scheme, with up to eight graduates per year. Every one of them stayed for at least 12 months, but very soon thereafter they left for another agency, usually in London. Now BDHTBWA recruits more widely, taking on some graduates, some people from other agencies and some people from other areas of the job market. The recruitment process is the same for all the types of people that BDHTBWA needs – creatives, suits and planners – but the criteria used in selection are different.

The recruitment process used by BDHTBWA may appear to be rather unscientific. Everything from psychometric testing, graphology, formal presentation, through to the pub test – taking potential employees to the pub and seeing how well you like them – has been tried. The belief in BDHTBWA is that none of these approaches is any more successful than any other. True headhunting has been tried, which involved all the managers being tested so that the consultants could match candidates with the culture of the firm. The best candidate they unearthed was someone who had been fired from BDHTBWA eight years before! To quote Roger Ward:

The one thing that seems to work is that the more people that see a candidate the better, and getting them to give some sort of presentation and then the pub test.

Intellectual property is safeguarded in several ways. First, BDHTBWA attempts to have terms of business that let it retain the intellectual property rights to its proposals and creative work. Almost without exception, clients don't want to agree such terms and try to insist that the rights pass to them. The argument that the agency gives is that no one knows the true value of the creativity that has gone into the work for the client, who may be paying a very small amount and drawing on years of creativity within the agency. An ad, or rather a series of ads, builds brand value and corporate reputation, which can easily be understated at the time the agency is remunerated.

For example, BDHTBWA created the Silentnight beds hippo and duck advertising campaign. This was a massively successful advertising and marketing strategy. It won a national marketing award and an IPA effectiveness award and it helped to take the agency from a loss to a £16 million profit in two years and the share price from

22p to 385p. The profits on spin-off sales of branded merchandise in such things as pyjamas and bed linen were equivalent to £4 million extra revenue on bed sales. Silentnight went on to use the duck and hippo advertising strategy in international markets. After a seven-year relationship, Silentnight decided to move its account away from BDHTBWA and had to pay BDHTBWA for the right to continue to use the duck and hippo characters. Interestingly, the rights were of little use to BDHTBWA except in association with Silentnight, since Silentnight had trademarked the characters and owned the registration and would have assumed the rights that come to it under the passing-off laws. All BDHTBWA would have been able to do would be to stop Silentnight using the characters.

The way to protect intellectual property rights is to sell them in a commercially sensible arrangement. One approach is to retain some sort of usage licence arrangements, perhaps based on getting some fraction of any money that the client gets on sales. A second approach is to take a percentage of expenditure if the client wishes to use BDHTBWA's creations in international markets.

References

1 *Campaign,* 'The Top 300 Agencies', Campaign Report, 26 February 1999.

2 *Ibid.*

3 Lynch, C., 'The new colors of advertising: an interview with Luciano Benetton', *Hemispheres*, 23 September 1996, p. 6.

4 *Business Week*, 'Make it simple', 9 September 1996, pp. 97–100, quoted in Albaum, G., Strandskov, J. and Duerr, E., *International Marketing and Export Management*, 3rd edn, Addison-Wesley, 1998, p. 456.

5 Harper, C., 'A battle cry from adland', *The Independent on Sunday*, 'Business', 20 September 1998, p. 29.

6 *Which Report*, 'Don't be had by financial ads', June 1997, pp. 12–15.

Eversheds[a]

History and present organisation

Eversheds is an amalgamation of 21 like-minded commercial law firms across England and Wales that were brought together during the late 1980s and the 1990s. The regional presence can in each case be traced back to what were major regional law firms; for example, in the East Midlands the Nottingham law firm Wells and Hind, which was set up in the 1830s, joined Eversheds in 1989. A big change occurred in 1995, when the major London law firm Jaques and Lewis joined Eversheds, giving it a much stronger presence in London. Prior to 1995, the individual firms had retained reference to their original names; for example, in the East Midlands the firm was known as Evershed, Wells and Hind. The association with Jaques and Lewis, however, was the catalyst needed for rebranding, and from that time all the firms were known simply as Eversheds. Eversheds is now the third largest law firm in the world in terms of people employed, with a total complement of 3200, of whom 1500 are lawyers[b] and 150 are non-legal consultants. There are 350 partners, of whom 200 are equity partners, i.e. who own the firm. In 1998–99 total fee income was £177 million and profits were £211,000 per equity partner.[1]

Eversheds operates in England and Wales[c] through seven regions: the north-east (with offices on Teesside and in Newcastle), the East Midlands (Derby and Nottingham), Wales and the west (Cardiff and Bristol), Birmingham, the north (Leeds and Manchester), the east of England (Cambridge, Ipswich and Norwich) and London. Overarching the seven regions is the national board, consisting of the chairman, the vice-chairman, the managing partner (client services), the director of international development and the managing partner from each of the regions. The board meets monthly, and the members talk once a week using a group conferencing facility.

Eversheds wants to be the first-choice legal advisers to major businesses in each of its regions. As part of meeting this aim, all offices are staffed to be the first point of contact with clients and all provide advice in the following five core areas:

1. **Corporate finance**   for example, the buying and selling of companies.
2. **Commercial law**   for example, an agreement between a supplier and a buyer.
3. **Commercial litigation/dispute management**   for example, handling disputes between businesses.
4. **Commercial property**   all types of property buying and selling.
5. **Employment law**   for example, unfair dismissal.

It's not feasible for each office to have an expert in every specialist area of commercial law; for example, while all offices have commercial lawyers, they don't all have dedicated environmental law experts. To be able to provide expertise in many areas requires a large number of solicitors, and this was the rationale for the creation of Eversheds – to provide each lawyer and therefore clients in each region access to a depth and scale of expertise unrivalled by any other regional law firm. Centres of excellence in particular areas of law have emerged in different offices. For example, Leeds has some of the best environmental lawyers in the country, and a large and growing team of tax lawyers in Nottingham supplies tax advice across the whole of Eversheds.

Unlike a limited company, partners are personally liable for the debts of the firm. John Sarginson, the managing partner of the East Midlands partnership, is certain that limited liability partnerships will come – partly because the law firms want to bring more cash into their businesses and partly because law firms are now compelled to run as businesses, and thus should be treated like every other business. Some lawyers find there's a tension between their work as lawyers and their working for a business. John Sarginson is firmly of the view that merely practising the law is now an outmoded concept, and that Eversheds is a business selling legal services to its commercial clients.

Regional strategic concerns

Strategy development is undertaken formally each year when each region reviews its business plan. The focus is on a few key issues: the match of the core services with the specialisms; getting the balance right between national and regional activities; and deciding which expertise should be recruited or augmented. An in-depth meeting every half year is held between the managing partner and the heads

---

[a] © Leen Valley Associates, 1999.

[b] This represents approximately 2% of the practising lawyers in England and Wales.

[c] Scotland has a different legal system to the rest of the UK and Eversheds doesn't deal with Scottish law matters.

of the departments to monitor progress against all the business plan objectives – financial, business development, and the career development of individual staff.

The East Midlands region provides an example of how Eversheds is organised and operates regionally. The heads of department and the heads of the support staff report directly to John Sarginson, who prides himself on knowing all the parts of the business – managing by walking around. He has set himself the goal of changing the culture, helping people to be less reactive and more proactive. In his words: 'I don't simply want complaints – I want people to identify their problems and to work with me and others to find solutions.'

Traditionally, financial controls in a legal business meant little more than checking the bank balance and seeing what was owed by clients: now the concern is much more with looking seriously at cash and work flows and seeing what will be filling the lawyers' desks in a year's time. Some client profitability analysis is undertaken. A local company that is a constant client and where there is only one person to deal with can be very profitable: one person to bill, one person to chase, one point of contact to discuss matters. There are some clients who have more sophisticated demands and need progress to be reported in detail and sent to many parts of the world. Eversheds carries this as part of its overhead and can't charge for doing it. It has, however, developed a sophisticated approach to client relationship management which makes this a key part of its business service for all clients.

Every member of Eversheds is assessed through the use of a personal balanced scorecard. Traditionally in law firms the career prospects for non-lawyers were limited. Now there are many finance, IT and HRM personnel and they have career prospects as good as in any other professional services firm. To devise a career progression for secretaries has been more difficult, but this is now being achieved. In John Sarginson's view secretaries have thought of themselves as audio typists: now they are being developed into departmental administrators and PAs.

It's always difficult to meld together the workings of teams and thus, not unexpectedly, Eversheds has had to put in place measures to speed up the process of integration among its seven regions. As Simon Slater, the director of business development (UK and international) explains: 'Ten per cent of our profits go into a pool for redistribution to be used to recognise what we call Evershedian behaviour: which is to look outside your own office, to share contacts and to refer clients to another office if it's more appropriate to do so. We are trying to get people to think less in terms of their own backyard.'

Legal entrants to Eversheds come from law school as trainee lawyers and train for two years to qualify as solicitors. Solicitors are promoted to associate and then to senior associate and from there to partner. Historically, as with many law firms, promotion has been on seniority, with people simply drifting up the ladder. Now the criteria for promotion are much more rigorous. Lawyers are very poachable, and the market for good lawyers is fiercely competitive, with many people getting offers from other firms, particularly local firms. Teams are poached as well as individuals. Most of the research suggests that people in legal jobs rarely move simply for money, although John Sarginson is of the view that money plays a bigger part than the research indicates.

Links with clients

Every client is allocated to a partner, who has overall responsibility for the client–Eversheds relationship. A client may make a formal approach and invite tenders for work. The client would then automatically have access to a partner, because it will be the partner who had led the team that has won the tender who then leads the client–Eversheds relationship. Contacts may come from social meetings and then the partner who is assigned to head the client–Eversheds relationship will be the partner who is best placed to supervise the initial work required. When the initial work has been completed, Eversheds makes a point of remaining in contact with the client – perhaps through invitations to the client's workplace, perhaps a telephone call three to four months later to enquire how things are going. Whatever the subsequent work from the client, the same partner would remain responsible for the client–Eversheds relationship. Historically, lawyers have considered clients to be 'their' clients, not the clients of Eversheds. Eversheds has moved a long way from that position, particularly in the last three to five years.

Historically, law firms weren't good at investigating the financial standing of new clients. Things are very different now, and the financial position of new clients is checked. Another difficulty is that sometimes people at a client's business ask for work to be done but when the bill is presented the lawyers find that the person didn't have a budget to pay for the legal advice. So now some clients have imposed a requirement on Eversheds that lawyers should only take instructions from named people, and some give an order number for billing purposes, which is logged into Eversheds' system. As John Sarginson remarks: 'If three years ago someone had said that this arrangement would apply, I would have said that they had got it wrong. Now the clients are accountable to budget holders in their own firms, and the management of legal expenditure is more tightly controlled.'

At present Eversheds is investing heavily in IT systems

and expects to see the way it does business transformed in the next ten years. In a typical office 95% of all employees have computer screens on their desks, and almost all the information brought in from the outside is by IT. For example, as part of Eversheds' property law information system, the *Estates Gazette* daily property law bulletin comes into the property lawyers' screens every morning. On a point of law, lawyers would simply access the journals database to see what the latest situation was. *The Times Law Reports* are brought in from outside and a major number of the most important legal textbooks are now available on line; for example, the White Book, the litigators' guide to the law courts, is available. Precedents as to how contracts should be written are available, and a lawyer will interrogate the Eversheds' precedent bank to find a contract and clauses that most nearly fit the particular situation being addressed. Eversheds is still paper-driven, however, in the sense that once an article has been found the lawyer would probably go along to the library and get that article.

In the very near future there will be a type of client who will want to access the relevant core legal information and will ask the solicitor to add expertise in the more esoteric areas. The large City firms are convinced that their larger clients will in future be buyers of legal information themselves.

Some lawyers subcontract, and Eversheds does some work for smaller solicitors. It also works for firms of accountants, especially high-grade tax work, where it does not have the required expertise.

Partnering

A recent development in the way clients and law firms work together is partnering. This method originated in the USA and has been developed by Du Pont, which wished to cut the cost of its legal function and to exert greater control over the way in which legal matters were handled. Most of the main features of the 'Du Pont legal model' and its links with Eversheds are described in Exhibit 1.

Du Pont publicises its legal partners with testimoninals run as adverts in the legal press and invites partners to its annual retreat and to attend its joint Du Pont–legal partner mini-college. A critical component of a Du Pont legal partnership is a change from the conventional billing practice of using hourly rates to one based on value. The key principle of value-based billing is that the law firm gets paid for value and results, not on how long it takes to provide them. Du Pont has invested in an intranet to link with all its legal partners and a computerised case management system to track progress on every legal matter.

A review by Arthur Andersen in 1995[2] showed that Du

Pont Legal had achieved significant cost savings, and in particular:

- expensive firms were replaced by more economical ones;
- firms still working with Du Pont had invested in creating long-term relationships through rate reductions and improved efficiency;
- by directing a significant volume of work to preferred law firms, Du Pont was able to maximise savings;
- the average length of a piece of work was reduced by one-third.

Simon Slater considers that the Du Pont way of operating is one that only relatively few companies will want in the medium term. He sketched Exhibit 2 to illustrate where he saw Eversheds positioning itself.

Eversheds has now produced a partnering model of its own to accommodate its own performance matrix, and has trained some partners, lawyers and non-legal consultants in the partnering concept.

Dispute management

Traditionally, lawyers believed that their litigation brief was simply to beat the opposition. About two years ago, Eversheds made a firm decision that this approach added little value for clients. There are many alternatives to litigation: negotiation, mediation, conciliation, determination of a result by an expert, use of a tribunal, or 'mini-trials'. These alternatives are often to be preferred to litigation on cost grounds and because the parties to a dispute very often have to maintain some sort of *modus vivendi* with each other after the dispute has been resolved because their commercial relationship will continue, e.g. landlord and tenant, major customers and major suppliers. John Sarginson stresses that there's nothing that clients find more commercially distracting than litigation, and so if you find a way out of this the client is very pleased. Eversheds now trains its lawyers to determine where clients wish to take a dispute. The lawyers put a monetary value on the benefits associated with the various ways a dispute might be approached.

Educating lawyers to assess quickly the information they're being given by a prospective client in order to make a proper assessment of the appropriate fee is hard work, as there's a very strong tendency to bid low. Eversheds regularly holds training sessions to remind its lawyers of the pitfalls in estimating and remind them of all the little bits and pieces that go into servicing a client. Fee estimates are generally approved by a partner, but there isn't an absolute embargo on a lawyer giving estimates, since clients want a quick response on fees, and with a business

The Du Pont legal model

In 1992 Du Pont, the US chemicals group, set about shedding some of the burden of more than $1 billion in operating costs.

As Howard Rudge, senior vice-president and general counsel, put it: 'Like a balloonist trying to gain altitude, it was eyeing its cargo, wondering what was essential and what was excess baggage.'

No area was to be immune from scrutiny in its search for ways to climb higher, faster, better – and cheaper, not even the internal legal operation.

To shave $100 million off the legal budget it turned to outside consultants for help in restructuring its corporate legal department – redesigning processes and refocusing incentives to reward quality and efficiency.

What emerged was the Du Pont legal model, a framework for improving the quality and efficiency of the legal function and for monitoring continuous improvement. Du Pont then set about restructuring its relationships with its outside legal advisers on the basis of 'partnering'.

The idea of abandoning the old arm's-length client/service provider relationships and replacing them with true partner relationships with each side sharing goals, visions and information and enjoying mutual benefits had been around in manufacturing for many years, but it was new to the legal arena.

The first task was to reduce the company's panel of 315 law firms some of which had been working for the company since the American Civil War – to a manageable size using the model's convergence process.

After a series of beauty parades, the company ended up with a panel of 34 outside law firms and suppliers. In 1994 the legal budget was $157 million but by 1997 it had dropped to $67 million.

Pleased with the success it had achieved in the USA, in 1996 Du Pont turned its attention to Europe and to the UK. Three law firms were shortlisted for the company's legal work in the UK and after another beauty parade a team led by Paul Smith from the national law firm Eversheds was selected.

Joining the Du Pont 'wheel' required a considerable investment of time and money by Eversheds. Information technology systems had to be set up for reporting, billing and sharing information and for handling monthly review meetings.

Eversheds was obliged to adopt Du Pont's early case assessment model, under which both sides are obliged to sit down within three months of a legal matter arising and, through a cost–benefit analysis produce a strategy document for handling it.

The document addresses such issues as the company's commercial objectives in handling the matter, what budget should be attached to it, whether it should be litigated at all costs and what resources each side is prepared to commit.

Eversheds soon found this to be a great discipline. 'It avoids all those problems three years down the line when you've spent a fortune and the client turns round and starts to question the whole thing,' Mr Smith says.

The early case assessment technique has proved so popular with other clients, resulting in considerable savings in litigation costs, that Eversheds has asked Nottingham Law School to train all its litigators in the technique.

The partnering arrangement with Du Pont has also been a commercial success for Eversheds, generating £3.5 million in fees, and by adapting the Du Pont model to the needs of other clients Eversheds has now entered into partnering relationships with Nissan, BTR and BBA.

The big difference is that partnering involves performance metrics

Mr Smith believes that Eversheds is the only firm offering partnership arrangements in the UK. Other firms have invested in client care programmes, but most of those involve a relationship partner visiting the client once a year and asking 'how is it for you?'

'Using a manufacturing analogy, it's equivalent to checking the quality of the product when it's in the consumer's stomach, whereas partnering involves monthly review meetings allowing you to fix the problems on the production line,' he says.

Partnering also requires a different mindset, he says. Firms are encouraged to criticise the client, and this takes some getting used to.

However, the big difference in approach is that partnering involves performance metrics and the concept of continuous improvement. In the USA, where the partnering relationship mainly revolves around litigation, Du Pont is able to benchmark its 34 law firms against each other.

It is able to produce tables which show by different categories of case, such as contract claims or personal injury actions, what the average legal costs of such cases were in, say, 1994 and 1996, and what the percentage change in costs was between the two years, what the average length of those cases was in 1994 and 1996, the percentage change over the two years and the numbers of cases in each category dealt with in those two years and the percentage change between the two.

Du Pont also produces charts for individual law firms showing their performance against the average length of time it took all 34 law firms to dispose of cases in different categories.

In the UK, however, Eversheds has nobody to benchmark itself against and so it has to measure against its previous year's performance. But with the end-goal being to get its legal budget down even further is there not a danger that by continuously improving year after year the return for doing the work will begin to dwindle?

Du Pont rewards the firms on its 'wheel' by recommending them to other companies. 'I go to the US and Howard Rudge introduces me to other corporates. He says: "In the UK our lawyers are Eversheds, we encourage you to use them." When that comes from the general counsel of the world's largest chemical company that's a pretty good recommendation and we have already acquired a large number of US clients as a result.'

In the short term, Mr Smith believes Eversheds will enjoy a considerable competitive advantage from partnering. If the world tips into recession and companies in the USA, the UK and elsewhere all begin to eye their cargo for excess baggage he may well turn out to be right.

Source: Robert Rice, 'Partnerships made to measure up', *Financial Times*, 20 October 1998, p. 17.

Exhibit 1

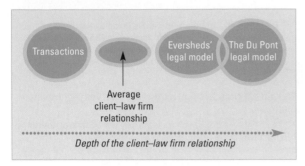

Exhibit 2   The spectrum of the client–law firm
relationship

the size of Eversheds to demand that a partner always approve the estimate is unworkable. Eversheds is breaking away from using hourly rates, since clients are very clear that they want fees to be event-driven rather than time-driven.

Business risk management

As well as dispute managment Eversheds has moved decisively into risk management, arguing that legal issues are either at the heart of many risk management areas or a powerful thread within them. Simon Slater explains the risk management service that Eversheds offers:

It's a service designed to encourage firms to take a more strategic approach to managing their risks. They wouldn't necessarily use lawyers to solve a specific problem but would turn to lawyers to advise them of the legal and commercial dimensions. This service isn't designed to appeal to the fear factor in a business, but to demonstrate how the Board can create/improve shareholder value by reducing risk and improving business relationships. It's quite a crowded market place, with about a dozen other types of company selling risk management services, and before getting involved in this I asked what were the special competences that a law firm has to help in this regard? In fact, we believe that our approach is more holistic than that offered by the accountancy firms.

Eversheds' risk audit service is effectively based around a set of 'What if?' questions in all the important risk areas: for example, insurance, product liability and employee liability. An example of such a set of 'What if?' questions is given in Exhibit 3.

Exhibit 3   Insurance risk

One way in which certain risks can be controlled as part of an overall risk management strategy is to transfer such risks to a third party – an insurer. The relationships an organisation creates with its broker and insurers are accordingly key risk management relationships and their proper operation and management are very important.

Your lawyers will frequently need to work alongside your broker and insurers to give advice on coverage, programme structure and policy compliance, through to dispute resolution and claims handling.

Which risks are covered and which are not?

We carry out comprehensive reviews of insurance programmes to appraise which risks are covered, the extent of such cover and when and how the policies will respond.

What can we do fo help you to avoid claims being rejected?

We advise on best practice to ensure that your insurance cover is not jeopardised by any innocent or negligent failure to disclose proper information at the proposal stage, or by any failure to comply with the conditions of the policy thereafter.

Is your insurance programme structured in its most cost-effective manner?

We have experienced commercial insurance lawyers who can review your needs and, in conjunction with your brokers, assist you in ensuring that you have the most cost-effective insurance programme in place for your business.

What if your insurer rejects a claim?

We can assist you in the resolution of any disputes you may have with your insurers, brokers or other insurance professionals. Our in-depth knowledge of insurance law coupled with our connections in the marketplace will minimise the likelihood of rejection by your insurers.

Are you happy with the way in which your claims are handled?

Many businesses do not realise their insurers will often be happy for them to determine the appointment of the adjusters and lawyers to handle their insurance claims, particularly where the business bears a significant proportion of the risk by retaining a high level of deductible. We provide claims handling and claims litigation services aimed at meeting your insurers' requirements whilst simultaneously protecting your interests.

Do you make full use of claims information to reduce future risks?

We have developed data retrieval systems which plot claims trends thereby enabling you to identify the most regular causes of your claims. This information is fed back to you for internal risk management purposes and is designed to prevent the recurrence of such claims. This has the combined benefit of reducing the actual cost to your business of claims at the same time as improving the safety and efficiency of your business operation.

The competitors

The large City law practices that make up what is known as the 'magic circle' – Slaughter and May, Freshfields, Linklaters, Allen and Overy and Clifford Chance – carry out a much larger volume of international work than Eversheds. This is based on a consistent flow of lucrative merger and acquisition work; for example, they handled the legal aspects of the Glaxo-Wellcome/SmithKline Beecham and ASDA/Wal-mart mergers. While not in the magic circle, legal practices like Eversheds are attractive to the big firms, as Exhibit 1 illustrates. Firms like Eversheds can do substantial, but not the mega, merger and acquisition work, and clients say that they enjoy dealing with lawyers who are near at hand on a personal level for day-to-day business law advice and from whom they think they get good value for money. In Loughborough, 3M used Eversheds in the litigation surrounding its faulty hip joints. 3M was happy to use Eversheds because it could get access to the quality of advice that an international firm demands. John Sarginson thinks that a firm like 3M wouldn't have been happy to have used the old, purely regional Wells and Hind to undertake its work.

There is growing national competition from the big five accountancy firms (Andersen Worldwide, Deloitte Touche Tohmatsu, Ernst & Young, KPMG and Price Waterhouse Coopers). They have very substantial market

Firm	Global revenues 1998 ($bn)
Price Waterhouse Coopers	15.3
Andersen Worldwide	13.9
Ernst & Young	10.9
KPMG	10.4
Deloitte Touche Tohamatsu	9.0

Source: Kelly, 1998.

Exhibit 4 The size of the big five accountancy firms

power[3] (see Exhibit 4), and they offer one-stop consultancy.

The big five accountancy firms are expanding their legal side, as Exhibit 5 exemplifies, and both John Sarginson and Simon Slater see them as a potential challenge to firms like Eversheds. To quote Simon Slater:

The reason that accountants are so keen to get into bed with lawyers is because they know that lawyers have a broader and deeper relationship with their clients because of the sheer number of specialist services in a law firm – from advocacy right through to venture capital, with employment, tax, intellectual property and numerous

Exhibit 5

PWC plans to build $1 billion global law firm network

PWC, the giant professional services firm, aims to build the fifth largest law firm in the world in the next five years with $1 billion in fees and 3000 lawyers.

It is about to open talks with potential partners in London and New York.

Gérard Nicoläy, global leader of PWC's legal network, announcing details of a deal to create Spain's second biggest law firm, said: 'We want to give a signal to the key law firms in the UK that we are ready to start merger discussions.'

It is understood PWC will be looking at the middle tier of City law firms and may also consider an additional merger with a strong provincial legal network.

Mr Nicoläy said he hoped PWC's legal practice in London would have 400–500 lawyers within two years. Regulatory constraints in the USA meant PWC would probably seek an associate law firm in New York.

'We want to become one of the top five legal firms in the world within the next five years,' he said.

PWC's move mirrors that of fellow Big Five accountant Arthur Andersen, which already has a legal network in 31 countries around the world. It acquired J & A Garrigues, Spain's largest law firm, in 1996. However, in recent months its efforts to rival the leading US and UK international law firms have suffered a setback following the collapse of merger talks with Wilde Sapte in London and the closure of its Hong Kong law firm.

The collapse of the Wilde Sapte merger raised doubts that any Big Five accountancy firm could build a comprehensive legal network to rival the big US and UK-based international law firms.

There are big disparities in earnings between partners in accountancy firms and lawyers. Business lawyers working in PWC's associated law firm in London are understood to earn an average of £170,000 – compared with £850,000 at Slaughter and May, the UK's most profitable law firm. Middle-tier earnings are lower and weaker in recession. Yesterday, lawyers said PWC would face similar problems to Andersen in trying to attract a City of London law firm. 'I don't think they will find any takers at the moment,' said one partner at a leading firm.

But Mr Nicoläy said the success of putting together the legal networks of Price Waterhouse and Coopers & Lybrand – the two firms which merged last year – showed that cultural differences would be overcome. PWC now has 1200 business lawyers in 38 countries.

PWC plans to create a global network of stand-alone legal firms. A global brand name would be chosen soon.

Mr Nicoläy said the PWC legal network would specialise increasingly in areas such as mergers and acquisitions, corporate restructuring, information technology issues, intellectual property issues, and employment law.

Source: Jim Kelly and Robert Rice, 'PWC plans to build $1bn global law firm network', *Financial Times*, 7 January 1999, p. 24.

others in between – a very broad range of specialist areas.

In mid-1999 the USA agreed to allow multidisciplinary partnerships, particularly those between accountants and lawyers, thus opening up the way for the Big Five to form global legal networks, where they can link up their legal and tax activities. The idea seems to be to form 'parallel' legal practices – stand-alone global legal networks tied to the main firm.[4] However, there are difficulties with the combined approach. Some £50 million of Eversheds fee income comes from litigation and dispute management. If it were to merge with a large accountancy firm, then there could be relationship difficulties caused by the litigation against the audit clients of the accounting firm.

Simon Slater sees considerable opportunity for legal firms that are the size of Eversheds.

The big five accounting firms are organised around eight major lines: audit, tax and legal, management consultancy, business assurance, insolvency and corporate rescue, forensic accounting, IT consultancy, and change management. Clearly within each there will be specialities. Eversheds itself has 30 specialist service lines. Having 30 businesses is perhaps too many in which to invest adequately, and we've identified 15 of these for priority investment. First there are the five core skills-based practice groups. Then there are six or seven other specialist areas, such as tax, pensions, intellectual property, and environmental law. Then there are around six or seven major sectors that we are concentrating on; for example, the biosciences, the media, telecommunications, and banking and financial services.

Another difference from the accountancy firms is that law firms probably have a better market knowledge of an industry than the big five accountants. The accountants tend to have a product-based approach – 'we have this so let's sell it' – whereas lawyers have a market-led approach.

There is commercial pressure for law firms to operate internationally. The very large London law firms have offices in many of the major commercial centres – Singapore, Hong Kong, New York, etc. Slaughter and May have set up what they term their 'legal best friends' in Europe – they have a strong association with the best or second best legal practices in each commercial centre in Europe and work exclusively with them. For other firms the way to internationalisation has tended to be through the development of a more formal relationship between a law practice in the UK and a chosen firm in each of several important countries, especially in Europe. Linklaters seems to be at the forefront of this, but as Exhibit 6 illustrates, it's unlikely to be plain sailing.

In John Sarginson's view:

The best friend relationships have not been a success. The best way forward is that at the end of the day the firm that you're using in Frankfurt, Paris or Milan will be your firm – that you will have a financial interest in it. But the scope of investment in the development of international people businesses is such that it's a slow process to develop.

Simon Slater echoes this view:

An association may be a stepping stone to the development of a single firm. But it's very difficult to have control over quality and reputation if you don't have any equity in the business and your name isn't associated with the business.

An even looser relationship model has been used by several law firms. They have joined such associations as ALFA and Commercial Law Affiliates – European groupings of lawyers, and the World Law Group. The firms in these associations refer work to associate firms in other legal jurisdictions. However, these arrangements often don't include any exclusivity in the referrals.

Eversheds has an office in Brussels with four partners/lawyers, which it set up and expanded following the pattern of the large City firms. Eversheds also has an office in Copenhagen with seven partner/lawyers. This was acquired following an approach by a very ambitious law firm – one whose focus is shipping law – which asked to join Eversheds. Both the Brussels and Copenhagen offices trade under the name Eversheds.

Through its incorporation of 25 partners from the splintering Frère Cholmeley Bischoff partnership in August 1998, Eversheds acquired four offices in continental Europe: in Paris (25 partner/lawyers), Monaco (eight), Moscow (15) and Sofia (35+). The Paris office is staffed by around 25 US, UK and French nationals practising international law. This is a centre of excellence that happens to be in Paris: it isn't yet staffed by French people practising French law for French companies. Moscow is a joint venture with a local Russian firm that has several large US firms as clients. The Bulgarian operation is in association with a local firm. In London there is a German desk of some 20 people advising German clients about both Germany and the UK. Currently, ten of Eversheds' partners are located outside the UK and 10% of its fee earners are overseas. Eversheds has no intention of setting up in the USA. This is partly because the investment would be too large and also because it might jeopardise the good relations that exist with US firms which provide Eversheds with a good flow of work.

Eversheds needs to be able to provide its clients with

Alliance in Euroland

To investment bankers it is a 'no-brainer'. Legal services, just like investment banking, consulting and accountancy services, require global reach and depth. But as other professions have rushed to consolidate, the natural caution of lawyers has left them playing catch-up.

Until last week, that is. Then came the move by Linklaters, the UK international law firm, and four other leading European commercial law firms, to form Europe's biggest international law practice and the second largest in the world. Linklaters brings the international dimension and London's financial savvy, while its European allies contribute in-depth knowledge of continental legal systems and lists of clients busy preparing for life in Euroland.

Charles Allen-Jones, Linklaters' senior partner, believes its move will wrongfoot competitors. 'There's no doubt there will be a lot of head-scratching over this everywhere' he says.

But Linklaters' competitors are not so sure. There are three reasons they believe the alliance will have its work cut out to succeed.

First, there is the question of whether the new international 'firm', as Linklaters refers to itself, is really an integrated single unit – or merely a loose alliance of five separate law firms.

If it's a merger then it's quite significant. If it's not, it's not,' says Harrold Voss, a senior partner of Bruckhaus Westrick Heller Löber, the leading German law firm.

Linklaters & Alliance, as it is to be known, is clearly not a fully fledged merger. The participants admit as much. 'We are not merging at this point. It is a co-operation,' says Michael Oppenhoff, senior partner of Oppenhoff & Rädler, the German member of the group. 'This is an interim period, but the (eventual) aim is clearly to integrate.'

If it is not yet a merger, Linklaters insists it is more than an informal alliance. From the start of operations in November, there will be some profit sharing. This will increase once the new practice has established a common system of accounting and brought the profitability levels of the Belgian, German, Swedish and Dutch members into line with that of Linklaters. Oppenhoff's profitability runs at about half Linklaters' levels.

The 'firm' hopes for full integration within two years. But rivals with similar experience believe that may be over-optimistic.

'It took us a long time to get the arrangement with Deringer to a basis where it was workable, and that's on a much smaller scale,' says Anthony Salz, senior partner of Freshfields, the UK international law firm, which earlier this year tied up with the German counterpart Deringer Tessin Hermann & Sedemund. 'It is a different task to take such a differential group of people and integrate them.'

Neither is time on the new alliance's side. Investment bankers say that while Linklaters & Alliance may enjoy a period of grace, it will not last for ever. 'They may be given a little bit of lead-in time but not a lot,' says one US banker based in Frankfurt. 'People want a high-quality integrated service now.'

The second potential pitfall is that the new alliance is not a truly pan-European practice. There are important gaps still to be filled in Italy, Spain and France.

True, Germany is the really big prize, but Linklaters realises that its inability to provide an integrated one-stop approach in Germany has, until now, left it at a disadvantage. A cursory glance at some of the most significant German transactions of recent years shows they have been dominated by the US law firms.

The Deutsche Telekom partial privatisation – at $13.3 billion the biggest of 1996 – was handled by two US law firms, Clearly Gottlieb Steen & Hamilton and Sullivan & Cromwell. More recently, the Daimler/Chrysler merger and the Deutsche Börse/London Stock Exchange link have been handled by another US law firm, Shearman & Sterling.

Linklaters & Alliance will clearly make headway in Germany. But there are other important markets where the new alliance will still not have adequate coverage.

While its UK rivals Freshfields, Clifford Chance and Allen & Overy have forged links with Italian law firms and are busy doing deals such as the Banca di Roma privatisation, Linklaters has missed out on big Italian privatisations. The pattern repeats itself, albeit to a lesser extent, in France and Spain. Linklaters' move will do little to address this shortfall.

Rivals believe these gaps in its network will hold the new alliance back. But investment bankers are not so concerned. 'If they can actually make work what they have put together, it's already quite a piece of the jigsaw,' says one London-based US investment banker.

Of more concern to investment bankers is Linklaters' third potential stumbling block: its relative lack of expertise in US law.

The increasingly important part played by the US capital markets in the restructuring of European industry calls for expertise in US securities law. Linklaters has some US law capability. But it is not clear whether this will be enough to satisfy the demands of global investment banks for a fully integrated global legal service. 'I'm not sure they have the US angle covered. That's key for us – strength and depth in US law capacity,' says one US investment banker.

To be fair, it is not just Linklaters that is likely to suffer from lack of US expertise. Freshfields, Allen & Overy, Clifford Chance and Linklaters have all hired US securities lawyers in recent years in an attempt to persuade banks they can handle the US end of multinational transactions.

Such a strategy takes time to succeed. There are signs that the investment banks, already critical of the failure of lawyers to match the pace of consolidation in their own industry, may not be prepared to wait.

The message to Europe's law firms is that if they want to become truly integrated global legal service providers, they may have to enter into a new set of mergers – this time with their transatlantic cousins.

Source: **Robert Rice, 'Alliance in Euroland',** ***Financial Times*, 29 July 1998, p. 24.**

Exhibit 6

some form of legal service throughout the world, and it does this by being able to recommend solicitors in places where it doesn't have a presence. It's able to do this through its membership of the World Law Group.

Simon Slater sees two paradoxical trends – globalisation favours a convergence of lifestyle yet a divergence of taste. 'The impact on legal practice is likely to be that both the very large and small business advisers will become more important,' he explains.

In five years time there will be 10 major players in Europe and Eversheds wants to be one of them. At least four of them will be accountancy firms. Globally there may be 10 law firms and it's very unlikely that Eversheds will be one of them without merging with another international legal or accounting firm. There are also likely to be smaller niche firms in such areas as shipping, telecommunications and pharmaceuticals operating globally. For example, there is a very small firm called Wiggin and Co. which has offices in Cheltenham, London and Los Angeles, focused on high net worth individuals in the media and entertainment. People in the media and entertainment tend to use the same lawyers for both their personal and business activities. The firms in the UK under most threat are those lying between the top 10 and the top 30 – neither big nor niche players although some niche firms have become medium-sized through pursuing successful strategies.

References

1 Philip Hoult, 'Composing a Song for Europe', *Legal Week*, 15 July 1999, pp. 10–11.
2 The Du Pont legal model.
3 Jim Kelly, 'Big five power ahead on back of consulting boom', *Financial Times*, 22 December 1998, p. 15, quoting Lafferty's *International Accounting Bulletin*.
4 Jim Kelly, 'All together now . . .', *Financial Times*, 17 June 1999, p. 35.

The Gallup Organization, London[a]

Introduction

The Gallup Organization, in recent years, has been the product of two traditions in social scientific research, namely survey technologies and the systematic assessment of human potential. The latter area of interest was originally cultivated by a mid-west American company, SRI Ltd, which actually acquired both the US Gallup in 1988 and the UK Gallup a few years later. These acquisitions helped establish the modern Gallup Organization and led to its development as an international social science-based consulting and research company with offices around the world, including China and India. The aspect of Gallup's work in the UK for which it is most widely known is, of course, political opinion polling. Indeed, the Gallup name predominantly features in people's minds as synonymous with the polling of public attitudes to the social and political issues of the day. The salience of this facet of the Gallup brand is such that it has reached the pages of the *Oxford English Dictionary*. But the full range of Gallup's practices spans more widely across such activities as:

- automated telephone employment screening;
- an Internet questionnaire (strengths finder) for individual self-development and assessment;
- structured interviews for staff selection and development (including leadership);
- market research, including brand evaluation;
- customer service quality measurement;
- employee surveys and organisation development.

Revenues in the first half of 1999 were, proportionately, about 30% in selection and development work, 15% from employee surveys, 30% from market opinion research and 20% from customer service quality evaluation. Despite their high profile, less than 5% of the revenue was actually generated by political opinion polling activities. The range of activities extends to the provision of strategic consulting on the linkages between talent, management styles, employee engagement and customer loyalty. The 'mission' of Gallup embraces these diverse activities. Its purpose is summed up simply in two brief phrases:

> **DISTILLATION OF THE MISSION OF GALLUP**
> 'To help people be heard'
> 'To identify and develop the talents of people'

[a] This case was prepared by Dr Jonathan Hill of the Gallup Organization.

Such ideals are put into practice through the core tasks of asking questions, studying the answers and reaching the results.

The company as a whole has expanded over the years, and a recent shareholders meeting (the organisation is employee-owned) heard that the following increases had taken place.

	1978	1998
Number of offices worldwide	13	32
Value of common stock	$0.22	$62.00

The shares are appraised semi annually by a third-party professional group, Mercer Capital Management Inc.

The Gallup office, London

While part of the internationally organised Gallup practices, the Gallup office in London has its own history and distinctive features. For many years the only talent selection and development practice outside the USA was managed from the UK office. Even earlier, in the 1930s, the first Gallup surveys of UK public opinion were published for the general reader to peruse in the columns of a widely read national newspaper of the time (*The News Chronicle*).

Currently, the Gallup office in the UK is in Kingston-on-Thames, and each of the major practices is represented there. A telephone survey centre is staffed by 100 survey interviewers, handling several different languages, and conducting social and market research across Europe. A smaller, but growing, call centre of interviewers provides a specialist service in recruitment campaign management and screening candidates for jobs. An expanding group of around 20 analysts and researchers is complemented by a team of technical and communication specialists totalling 100 people. Vacancies are advertised on the Gallup website.

The key element in developing a social scientific research organisation is the finding and keeping of high-quality professional and support staff. A recent Gallup job advertisement, for example, invited candidates to apply for the position of director of research for the survey practice, indicating that the salary with performance bonus should exceed £100,000 per annum. Questions embedded in the advertisement were placed to help candidates evaluate their own potential in response to the following bullet point posers:

- Are you recognised as an authority within the area of survey research?
- Could you inspire a team of talented individuals to deliver exceptional market research information to our clients?
- Do you pride yourself on being able to impart knowledge in a creative and enjoyable manner?
- Are you ambitious to achieve more?
- Can you build supportive relationships with associates and clients?

The text goes on to explain that Gallup's reputation rests on its ability to deliver research-based solutions to enhance business growth. The quality of the research has to be matched by the quality and depth of relationships between Gallup staff and their clients. The type of staff which Gallup employs includes client directors, research directors, sales specialists and technical and support specialists. The UK managing director, Jill Garrett, is a former secondary school headteacher with an in-depth background in talent research, mentoring and institutional turnaround. Her principal contribution is to provide visionary, value-based leadership to all the practices, although she also works closely with two key clients as a client director. For every position in Gallup the staff are hand-picked through a searching process of telephone interviews, carefully structured and tape-recorded with each candidate's consent. These interviews, which are sometimes fully transcribed, are scored by analysts who have themselves undergone rigorous selection and lengthy training. This process is essentially the same talent identification and development process sold as a service to Gallup's clients. The clients tend to be among the most prominent in their sectors, and some of the key client relationships have endured for 10 years or more.

The Daily Telegraph is the purchaser of political survey results, including election-related issues and politician popularity indices. Business clients include several leading companies, such as Standard Life, Glaxo-Wellcome, Citibank, Audi Merrill Lynch and IBM.

Many of the Gallup staff, all of whom receive per-formance-related monthly financial bonuses, are incentivised through measurement of the quantity and quality of their work for clients. At a monthly 'celebration of excellence' those Gallup associates with outstanding contributions for the month are given additional recognition and appreciation by their colleagues. A saying of the cur-

rent chairman of Gallop, Don Clifton, is that 'there is no talent without celebration'.

The external interface of Gallup

Competition takes many forms, but not always on a head-to-head basis, except in bidding for some of the largest research and consultancy contracts. Gallup's combination of talent research and survey is a very distinctive blend. But in specific fields the principal UK competitors include the survey providers (such as Market and Opinion Research International) and the psychometric publishing houses (such as Saville and Holdworth Ltd. in research, design, and print psychological tests). The large management consultancies are a further source of competition, where Gallup aims to outperform in several ways: on the product front, by the research and development of distinctive and comprehensively tested instrumentation (interviews and questionnaires), through the combined application of both qualitative and quantitative methods, and through sustained attention to implementing change. On the service front, competition is expressed through the employment and retention of outstanding salespeople, researchers and client service staff. The Gallup International Research and Education Centre in the USA provides the latest in ideas and applications from world-leading authorities in several social science disciplines. Gallup associates, for the most part, are engaged in continuous learning to maintain their cutting-edge awareness and skills in, for example, questionnaire design, structured interview validation and data capture, analysis, processing and communications. At international level there are fewer competitors since global reach is relatively rare. In the UK, the competition is fierce on practically all fronts. Overall policy and strategy is set in the United States, with some discretion on tactics and operations established in London.

A popular business book 'First … break all the rules', published in 1999 by Simon & Schuster, has been written by two Gallup consultants, one British, one American. Marcus Buckingham and Curt Coffman, the consultants concerned, also feature on Gallup's website at http://www.gallup.com, where they have their own management column. The book and website contribute to the Gallup marketing strategy, providing a resource for presentations to clients and prospects in order to facilitate cross-selling and integrated service provision across all the practices.

A key challenge for Gallup in the UK is to extend the business awareness of its full range of practices, building on its fame in political polling but bridging across several

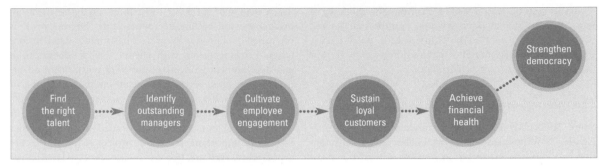

Exhibit 1   The Gallup path

spheres of activity. The explanatory model for achieving the bridging process is the Gallup path; a simplified format is shown in Exhibit 1.

The link to democracy is distinctive but reflects the traditions of Gallup in empowering the public viewpoint through the sharing of information, systematically collected.

The flow chart is presented to Gallup's clients and prospects to help conceptualise the integrated nature of the solutions proposed. At each stage in the model, Gallup research mainly focuses on the proven association between social science discoveries and business outcomes. For example, in the field of 'employee engagement', Gallup analysts have studied the most consistently observed correlations between employee attitudes and organisation performance. These results were obtained in the USA but are now in the process of replication in the UK. The findings shown in Exhibit 2 are drawn from a statistical 'meta-analysis' of questionnaire items from Gallup employee surveys with clients.

The statement with which people in the more productive business units agreed or strongly agreed was 'The mission of my company makes me feel my job is important'. Other similarly thought-provoking items are contained in Exhibit 2.

Exhibit 2   Questionnaire items with meta-analytic correlations (r) that are generalisable across organisations = x

Questionnaire Items		Organisation performance		
	Customer satisfaction	Profitability	Productivity	Employee retention
1 On a five-point scale, where 5 is completely satisfied, and 1 is extremely dissatisfied, how satisfied are you with your company as a place of work?		✗	✗	✗
4 At work, I have the opportunity to do what I do best every day.	✗	✗		✗
6 My supervisor, or someone at work, seems to care about me as a person.	✗	✗	✗	✗
10 The mission/purpose of my company makes me feel my job is important.			✗	
12 I have a best friend at work.	✗		✗	

These results, which would challenge the thinking of most British blue-chip companies, suggest that shared values ('mission') may make a difference to productivity, while caring supervisors may make a difference to all four indices of business unit performance.

The internal organisation of Gallup in the UK

Some of the key relationships, internally, are shown in Exhibit 3. With customer service quality and client retention in mind, the organisation revolves around the client service director roles. Their responsibility is for expanding business through exceptional client relationships of an enduring kind, fed by innovative social science discoveries which make business sense. These discoveries may well challenge conventional thinking: for example, the employee survey item 'I have a best friend at work', which repeatedly correlates with customer satisfaction and productivity. Surrounding the client service directors are 'leaky teams' of specialist researchers, analysts, client co-ordinators and technical/support staff. Survey work is organised on a project-by-project basis under detailed contractual arrangements with clients. Talent identification and development work may start with recruitment advertising campaigns, or executive team-building analyses, or seminars in leadership, or talent spotting through structured interview applications. In each practice, as the size of the project grows, systematic detailed pricing becomes ever more important to contain project scope and secure profitability. Staff are, in consequence, expected to observe the disciplines of time sheet management and project control.

Key meetings include an executive meeting of client directors, a cross-functional business development group (which embraces sales, marketing and research) and specific research project groups. Daily communication with Gallup's US research headquarters is maintained by e-mail and by telephone. Company conferences provide a

Exhibit 3   The Gallup Organization London office: key relationships (summer 1999)

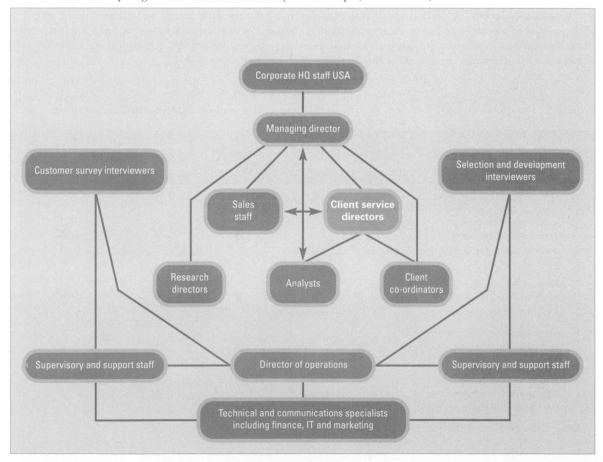

forum for the exchange of the latest scientific discoveries in social research, and the monthly 'celebrations of excellence' provide a chance for some informal chat as well as personal recognition over a buffet meal. An annual celebration of excellence is the largest gathering at which individual staff achievements from the preceding year are picked out and applauded. The meetings all provide opportunities for forward-looking presentations concerning company mission and strategy. The 'celebrations of excellence', in particular, also involve some drama, humour, kidding and teasing of a friendly and positive kind, but the principal strategy is a challenging one: to grow an integrated research and measurement-based consulting company, with strong international linkages, focused on high client service standards.

Gallup staff are developed according to the same research-tested principles shared with clients. One way to summarise the principles is through the Gallup talent equation:

> TALENT × (RELATIONSHIPS + EXPECTATIONS + RECOGNITION/REWARD) = INCREASED PERFORMANCE and GROWTH

Talent is the capacity for achieving high performance. But talent is socially constructed and depends crucially on the right developmental relationships (coaches, mentors or managers/supervisors), which channel the right expectations and appreciations towards their protégés. (All Linford Christies had a good coach; every Elton John had a good 'granny'.)

Gallup staff have the opportunity to build close developmental relationships with colleagues, and this is also important for staff retention. Unless staff are retained, clients cannot easily be retained. Performance-related pay helps focus staff minds on their individual contribution to business growth. Gallup staff tend to know their 'personal bests' in terms of measured performance for a month's work. They are all aware of their personal strengths through various feedback instruments and interviews. Colleagues tend to know each others' strengths. Clarity about personal strengths is a fundamental tenet of the organisation.

Future challenges

The Gallup company internationally achieved an average growth of 30% over the past 10 years. One of the challenges will be to staff for continued growth on an on-going basis, matching resources to client expectations and commitments. Another will be to introduce systems and structures to support but not dominate staff individuality in work performance. In the UK office new recruitment is always on the minds of the executives. But to find just one exceptional selection and development analyst, for example, may involve the assessment by interview of over 100 applicants. So the search is continuous. International experience and cross-cultural adaptability will be further sieves in future as the future strategic move into Europe takes place.

Technology-based solutions, such as IVR (interactive voice recording), help speed up and streamline data capture for both survey and selection purposes. Analysis, too, can be semi-automated with automated report protocols. But consulting relationships of a close, confidential, yet growing kind need the fuel of useful discoveries from the client's own data and actionable outcomes. The human qualities of integrity, courage and empathy on the part of consultants are not amenable to technological replacement.

For Gallup UK the challenges will include the customisation and anglicisation of US-built instruments, growth into Europe and the development of supervisory frameworks around which the staff can continue to improve their talents.

Internationally, the strategic issues will include the management of multi-country projects to involve local representation and central guidance in the most effective balance; and the design of payment schemes to further incentivise and stretch the performance of all staff for both short-term and long term engagement with clients.

Dr George Gallup

George Gallup founded the Gallup Poll at Princeton, New Jersey, which became the world's first system to objectively and scientifically measure public and customer opinion. He was also the inventor of market research.

The very existence of the Gallup Poll has changed the quality of political debate. The Gallup Poll makes it increasingly difficult for individuals to claim 'I am right', to claim they alone 'know what's best' for the public now that accurate scientific measurement of the public/customer viewpoint is possible.

As inventor of market research and the Gallup Poll, Professor George Gallup has so empowered the public viewpoint that his invention may be the greatest act of democracy ever performed by any scientist.

His research covered the fields of health, religion, politics, journalism, advertising, entertainment, business, education and human thinking. Few others have had the opportunity to notice and record the views of so many humans on so many aspects of their existence, and in so many parts of their world.

A lesser known side of Dr Gallup was his interest in humans and the factors which influence their opinions, attitudes, thinking and aspirations. He said: 'Teaching people to think for themselves was the most important thing in the world to do.'

Born in Jefferson, Iowa, in 1900, he attended the University of Iowa and spent ten years as a teacher at Drake, Northwestern, and Columbia universities. He had a strong interest in education and what could be done to improve it. He had more than ten honorary doctorate degrees from colleges and universities around the world. George died at his Switzerland home in 1984.

Rose Bearings[a]

Background

Rose Bearings is based in Lincolnshire, England, employing a total of 575 people producing high-tech bearings. It is a wholly owned subsidiary of the Minebea Group of Japan, a global company specialising in the mass production of miniature ball bearings and electronic components.

The company has two divisions, one at Skegness employing 350 people producing miniature ball bearings, and one at Lincoln employing 225 people designing and manufacturing high-tech rod end and spherical bearings.

Very broadly, the bearings made by Rose can be considered to be of two types: miniature and high-tech rod end and spherical bearings. The miniature bearings are typically used in domestic appliances, air-conditioning units, computers, printers, photocopiers, fax machines, power tools and extensively in car components (for example wiper motors, alternators and speedometers). The growth in the use of miniature bearings has been and continues to be enormous, directly attributable to the growth in sales of sophisticated consumer products. The high-tech rod end and spherical bearings are designed to cope with misalignment in linkages and structures. Typical applications include racing car suspensions and in aircraft. Typical aircraft applications include bearings for landing gear, engine thrust reverser actuators and flying control actuators.

For this case study the concern will be solely with the rod end and spherical bearings. Typical examples are shown in Exhibit 1.

The bearings are made from many different materials, and Rose has considerable expertise in their manufacture: carbon and alloy steels, aluminium alloys, bronzes, nickel alloys, and titanium. Rose also has considerable expertise in the tribology of metal-to-metal and self-lubricating bearing interfaces.

Each of the two types of bearing is made in two forms, depending on the way in which lubrication is provided. One form is the metal-to-metal bearings, where, as the term suggests, the two moving metal parts are in direct contact with each other except for lubrication supplied externally. The second form of bearing is the self-lubricating bearing, where a liner is fitted between the moving

[a] This case was written by David Shore, MBA student, studying at the Lincoln campus of the University of Lincolnshire and Humberside.

Exhibit 1   Typical examples of Rose bearings

parts and no additional lubrication is needed. The liners are made from such materials as PTFE. Rose has perfected unique processes for making the liners but has not patented them. Given that it has marketed the joint, patent protection cannot be obtained so Rose has to rely on its internal security for protection.

History to 1988

The origins of Rose Bearings lie with William Rose, a barber in Gainsborough, Lincolnshire, at the turn of the twentieth century. At that time, tobacco was sold loose by barbers and William saw the need for a simple packaging machine that would weigh out and wrap tobacco in one-ounce packs without having to touch the tobacco by hand. He founded Rose Brothers in Gainsborough and the company grew to become a very successful packaging machine manufacturer; indeed, it is believed that Cadbury's Rose's chocolates are named after the company, as Rose developed the first machine capable of wrapping multiple-shaped sweets.

During the Second World War, a German fighter aircraft was shot down over Lincolnshire. The Ministry of Defence found a revolutionary type of bearing used in its flying controls and wanted to develop a similar bearing for use in British aircraft. Rose Brothers was approached as a potential manufacturer, as it was already carrying out development work for the ministry. Rose Brothers became the first manufacturer of this revolutionary type of joint in the UK, and products of this type became nationally known as Rosejoints®.

Rose Bearings was formed in 1947 as a division of Rose Brothers of Gainsborough. The company began to thrive during the 1950s principally manufacturing bearings for the aircraft and packaging machine industries. The company merged in the early 1960s with Forgrove of Leeds, another packaging machine manufacturer. The Forgrove bearing factory in Skegness was merged into Rose Bearings and the Gainsborough operation was relocated to the village of Saxilby, close to Lincoln. Rose Bearings was essentially a country craft firm carrying out finishing work on the output from the bearing preparation plant in Skegness. Later, Rose Bearings was sold to Baker Perkins, later to become APV Baker.

Rose Bearings continued to thrive and grow during the 1960s and 1970s, principally manufacturing rod end and spherical bearings. However, by the mid-1980s East Asian competitors were able to sell into the marketplace at prices below Rose's manufacturing costs. Also, the aerospace industry in particular was beginning to demand purpose-designed products. It was apparent that a major change was needed. APV Baker wasn't willing to invest in the bearing side of the company as it didn't consider bearing manufacture as a core business. Towards the end of the 1980s, the management of Rose took the unusual step of asking APV Baker to sell the business to another company to which its activities would be better aligned and thus obtain the investment needed. As a consequence, the company was sold in 1988 to the Minebea Group.

The years of turbulence – 1988–92

Very quickly after the takeover in 1988, Minebea acquired a new factory on the outskirts of Lincoln. The Skegness factory became solely a ball-bearing plant making standard ball bearings and reporting directly to Minebea, with no formal links with the Lincoln operation. The preparation work that had been carried out in Skegness was relocated to the new factory. As only a few personnel transferred from Skegness, recruitment was needed at Lincoln.[b] Minebea had superior liners to Rose and the liner technology was introduced into Rose, where it was independently improved to fit Rose's requirements.

Minebea at that time had a highly entrepreneurial

focus. The Minebea philosophy was to diversify – in terms of both its products and its customers. The company was a sales-led organisation with the sales team charged with winning orders at the market price.[c] Minebea's established manufacturing plants had no input to the marketing and sales strategies but were sufficiently flexible and innovative to be able to cope with the demands placed on them; they were exceptionally good at innovating in manufacturing methods to provide good margins at the prices obtained. For example, the Japanese were continually improving their manufacturing methods through using faster machines, introducing robotics and employing dedicated production lines, which their high volumes would support.

After Minebea took over Rose, a similar spirit of entrepreneurship was injected, particularly into the sales team. The Minebea sales-led strategy was implemented within Rose, but with no consideration of the markets in which Rose was operating. The sales manager took over from the technical manager responsibility for applications engineering – designing bearings with and for specific customers. Responsibility for estimating the cost of these new products was transferred from production engineering to sales, and market pricing was used. Almost immediately the sales team was bringing in enquiries at a prodigious rate. These enquiries included products that were not within Rose's core capabilities.

The huge influx of orders caused absolute chaos in the production department. The sales department was taking orders using standard lead times. No consideration was given to the capacity within the factory, or to the lead time required to develop the engineering and manufacturing techniques required for the influx of new products. Rose didn't have the capability to innovate in manufacturing that the Japanese had.

In 1989 new production and operations managers were appointed from outside Rose and the Minebea Group. Although turnover had increased by around 30% within one year, by 1990 the company was in severe trouble; Rose had gone from a modest profit to a loss of almost £1 million. Overheads had increased due to the financial costs associated with the new factory and the investment in machine tools financed by Minebea. The reaction of the sales department was to inject even more orders, which crippled the factory and exacerbated the situation.

By this time Rose's customers were in despair. Within 12 months the company, which had previously held an enviable reputation for product quality and delivery

---

[b] Personnel were recruited so quickly and with such little concern that in 1998 Rose was still suffering from this rapid recruitment and the poor choice of personnel that resulted.

[c] A market price is the price needed to obtain the customer's order, with no consideration as to the actual manufacturing costs.

reliability, had experienced production line stoppages and lengthened lead times.

Minebea had a European sales operation, NMB Minebea, with offices in Frankfurt, Milan and Paris and in the UK (at Bracknell). In 1991 Minebea combined Rose's salesforce with that of NMB Minebea. By the end of 1992 it was obvious that the combination was a disaster. Minebea was upsetting the customers; it was acting as a buffer between the customer and the technical expertise at Rose. It was decided to put Rose's sales and marketing back under Rose's control, but working with the European Minebea sales arms. Rose regained the authority to set prices for its products.

This was the time of the Gulf War, and the bottom dropped out of the aerospace market, one of Rose's largest markets. Losses had increased to such a level that in April 1992 20% redundancies were announced.

But this wasn't the end of Rose's *annus horribilis*. The end of 1992 saw four major product problems, two of which eventually led to legal action against the company. The first two problems involved bearings that hadn't been properly heat-treated; since these bearings were used in critical aircraft applications, it nearly involved the grounding of large fleets of aircraft fitted with them. To Rose's credit, the factory opened over Christmas – even on Christmas Day – to provide replacements. These two problems had been caused by a lack of attention to detailed specifications.

The second two cases involved product failure. The first was caused by a subcontractor who had used incorrect materials in bearings for the Channel Tunnel shuttle trains. The second case was caused by Rose not knowing all of the parameters associated with the use that the bearings were being put to, i.e. a lack of contract review.

The years of tranquillity – or stagnation? 1993–98

In the middle of 1992, the managing director left and Ron Chapman, who was running the Skegness plant, was appointed the new managing director, heading both the Lincoln and Skegness factories. He got rid of the production and operations managers – the outside appointments – and appointed from within. He also replaced the quality manager through early retirement and so was beginning to build a new management team.

At about the same time, Minebea had run into trouble. The thirst for increased sales had resulted in diversification away from its core products into areas such as semiconductors, furniture and pig farming. The Japanese banks which were funding the organisation were very concerned with Minebea's very high gearing. They appointed one of their directors to the board of Minebea.

The appointment of the bank director to the board provoked an administrative approach within the group. The decision was taken to dispose of the group's non-core businesses, and this was accomplished very quickly. Minebea embarked on development of its core products and became even more innovative in its production methods. These moves proved to be highly successful.

At Rose, the new administrative focus had a dramatic effect. Major decisions were now very short-term and made on a purely financial basis. The financial manager was monitoring all expenditure – almost nothing could happen without his permission. For many years, Rose had spent around £10,000 each year to exhibit at the Farnborough Air Show. In 1990 the marketing department had spent in excess of £100,000 on its exhibit. As a result of this increase, the financial manager stopped all advertising in trade journals and prevented Rose having an exhibit at the 1992 show. This had an almost devastating effect on Rose's business within the aerospace industry, with customers losing confidence in Rose and beginning to doubt Rose's long-term future, with the result that some large orders were lost.

This strong administrative focus caused more problems. Although it was considered imperative that the company return to a profit-making position, most decisions were being taken with no consideration of the company's future needs. For instance, during the redundancy process Rose lost most of its expertise in the manufacturing and technical areas, particularly in production control, and much engineering experience was lost. Capital investment was halted, with the consequence that Rose was not able to invest in either machine tools or information systems. The lack of new machine tools caused Rose to start to become uncompetitive, because its competitors were achieving lower costs with their more modern, faster machines. The lack of up-to-date information technology stifled the innovation of new business processes, and Rose was carrying far more indirect employees in order to operate manual systems.

One of the main problems at this time was the lack of an effective marketing function. One major difficulty that marketing had lay with the research and development (R&D) department. Due to the administrative approach being adopted, product development was halted, and this meant that development in liner technology ceased. R&D expenditure was kept to a minimum; what R&D was undertaken by the three people in R&D was limited to troubleshooting in the factory and assisting with the manufacture of specialist parts. The litigation cases had made Rose's management very nervous and therefore there was a tendency to avoid the risks involved in employing new technologies in Rose's products and processes.

Historically, the product development carried out by the R&D department was projects that the department deemed were 'what the customer needed'. No market research was carried out and large amounts of engineering and production resources had been spent on projects that led to low sales. On the other hand, Sales had been pushing for the development of 'me too' products, under the belief that because other companies offered these products Rose should do so as well.

There was also a damaging conflict between marketing and purchasing concerning market forecasts. Market information was poor; for instance, Airbus was responsible for 30% of Rose's turnover, but Rose had very little information as to the quantity of which product went on to which Airbus variant. As a consequence, purchasing was reacting to customer orders and was in a poor position to develop relationships with its raw materials suppliers. As most of the raw materials are fairly exotic, it was almost impossible to procure them within acceptable lead times. Additionally, there was an added cost involved as purchasing was spot buying from a host of different suppliers, who were taking advantage of the urgency of Rose's situation. This use of many suppliers prevented Rose working with its suppliers on quality concerns. As a consequence, production was spending time rectifying faults and sending items back to suppliers for rework or replacement – incurring extra costs and causing production delays.

Customer relations were also being damaged by poor delivery times. Sales was responsible for providing customers with delivery times, but because of poor production control and poor communication between sales and production control, there was considerable delay before the customer could be given a date – and often this date wasn't adhered to. The control system was so poor that management only knew of delivery problems when the customer alerted them to it! It would have been surprising if customers hadn't lost confidence in Rose's delivery performance.

Marketing was responsible for setting prices for Rose's products, and the official policy was to use cost-plus pricing. However, the costing system was unreliable and therefore marketing set prices to beat the competition. The competitive advantage that Rose had with products that had a longer working life was ignored. Customers would get a lower-priced quotation from competitors who were offering lower-quality products in order to induce Rose to lower its prices. (It was subsequently found that Rose was losing money on 75% of sales at this time.)

Finished goods inventory presented another problem. The sales department created buffer stock to mitigate delivery problems and had been over-ordering to get round batch size constraints imposed by production. As a consequence, Rose was holding £500,000 in redundant inventory. The sales department had also allowed customers to cancel orders without penalty.

Arguably, the most damaging aspect of the administration phase was that decision making was effectively taken away from management. The resultant low management morale inevitably communicated itself to the rest of the workforce. Low motivation and absenteeism became a severe problem. Product quality began to suffer, and there was a general slowing down of the workforce, which caused an increase in production costs. Once again, Rose was heading towards a loss-making situation.

A new sales and marketing manager was appointed from within the company in 1994. One of the first things he did was to undertake market research with Rose's 20 most important customers, who accounted for approximately 75% of its sales. The results of a series of face-to-face meetings with these firms were surprising. Despite the problems Rose had been facing, particularly with late deliveries, the customers still linked the Rose name with quality and reliability. Of great significance was that Rose's products were giving long service life, due to its superior technology. The aerospace industry customers indicated that there was an increasing requirement for larger-size, high-technology, value-added bearings, with which Rose wasn't currently involved. The exciting aspect was that Rose had the technology and machine capacity to deal with these. Less exciting – but no less valuable – was the realisation that came out of the customer discussions that considerable rationalisation of the Rose product range was possible. Rose had the registered trade mark Rosejoint®, which had not been used for many years, and this was used to brand the resulting new rationalised range of bearings. Discussions with distributors of bearings showed that Rose's brand name was very valuable to them; by using the brand name, Rose's products could be sold at a premium price.

In 1996, the finance manager died and this position was filled by Mark Stansfield, the management accountant. In November 1997 Ron Chapman retired and in March 1998 Mark Stansfield was appointed general manager of the Lincoln plant, reporting directly to Minebea in Japan.

In 1996, it was realised that the liner system that Rose used was becoming outdated. Competitors were able to offer bearings with a longer life than Rose's and obtain a very healthy margin from them: they could offer a bearing for £120 that Rose had to sell at £20. In 1997, after a search, Rose found a new form of PTFE material that could be used as a liner and developed it.

Although there had been investment in the Lincoln site

Year end March	1994*	1995	1996	1997	1998
Turnover (£m)	3.1	7.1	8.8	10.6	11.8
Profit/(loss) (£m)	(0.8)	(0.5)	0.1	0.3	0.8
WIP (months)	1.7	1.7	1.9	2.1	2.1
Inventory (months, sales)	1.2	1.1	1.0	0.8	0.7

*for six months

Exhibit 2   Rose Bearings Ltd, Lincoln division

in the years since 1992, it had tended to be in such things as perimeter security rather than in Rose's core activities. In 1997 there was the start of reinvestment in the CNC machine tools that are particularly suited to the small batchwork that Rose specialised in. Their acquisition had a very significant impact on Rose's manufacturing costs.

Turnover and profit figures for Rose are set out in Exhibit 2.

Current situation

Relationships within the Minebea Group

Minebea Co. Ltd of Japan has a total of 35,000 employees with manufacturing sites in China, Germany, Japan, Singapore, Thailand, the UK and the USA and sales offices in many countries. Expansion of manufacturing facilities in Thailand and China has been undertaken to increase capacity and to keep costs low. It has given Minebea the added advantage that the plants are close to the customers in these developing economies.

Minebea principally manufactures high-precision miniature ball bearings, computer power supplies, disk-drive assemblies, spindle motors, stepper motors, fan motors, loudspeakers and keyboards. Sales of standard yet high-precision ball bearings represent 30% of the group's turnover. Minebea is the world's largest producer of high-precision miniature ball bearings having an outside diameter of under 22 mm. Minebea's current worldwide production capacity is 125 million bearings per month.

There are three sister organisations within Minebea involved with rod end and spherical bearings: a factory in Japan about twice the size of the Lincoln plant and a company in the USA about three times the size. Each company operates fairly autonomously, with very little interaction between them. In terms of 'spheres of influence', the Japanese company sells into East and South-east Asia, the US company sells into the USA and South America, and Rose sells into Europe. However, there has

been some encroachment of the Japanese company into Europe of late.

Minebea has a low profile within Rose – there are no obvious signs that Rose is owned by it. The name 'Minebea' doesn't feature on Rose's letterhead or on the company sign or anywhere in reception; in Rose's sales literature the only mention is one reference to the head office tucked away in the corner of a page. Minebea provides financial targets for Rose and investment support – and early on provided some technological help – but otherwise Rose's management is left to devise its own strategy to meet Minebea-specified objectives.

Customers and markets

Until about ten years ago, the vast majority of Rose's customers would buy directly from the Rose catalogue. However, the current situation is markedly different in that around half of Rose's customers now use its specialist design and manufacturing skills to obtain bearings to suit their special requirements. Now 80% of Rose's sales come from the UK, with the remaining 20% coming from mainland Europe. The East and South east Asian and American markets are basically closed to Rose, as these are serviced by its sister plants in Japan and the USA. Rose has two sales engineers in the UK, and its European interests are looked after by Minebea's sales offices, where Rose has one sales engineer allocated to it in each office.

Currently Rose's sales are increasing, mainly due to the buoyant nature of the aerospace industry. Around 50% of Rose's sales are to Airbus Industrie partners and subcontractors. It is a first-tier supplier to British Aerospace with bearings for main landing gear, the Anglo French company Messier-Dowty with bearings for both the main and nose landing gear, the UK firm Rolls-Royce with engine bearings, the UK firm Lucas Aerospace with flight control actuator bearings and thrust reverser bearings, and the two Belgian firms Asco and Sonaca with slat-knuckle bearings.

The current boom in the civil aircraft market is predicted to end in the early 2000s, when aircraft production rates will possibly halve. In addition, the economic turmoil in the mid- and late 1990s in Asia has brought into question the business that Airbus Industrie is predicting.

Rose is currently using its advanced capabilities in bearing design in the car industry; for example, it supplies bearings to a British company that makes steering columns for Audi and VW cars. The car industry now makes up 20% of Rose's turnover. Expansion in the car industry is one possibility for Rose, linking with the second-tier suppliers to supply the subassemblies that the car assemblers require, and continually seeking longer-lasting components. However, the trend throughout Europe is for governments to press the case for fewer cars and more public transport – for high-speed trains and urban trams. Currently around 5% of Rose's turnover comes from this area, and this area is being targeted for future business.

There has been a change in customer characteristics over the past 15 years. Customers, particularly within the aerospace industry, have increasingly demanded higher-specification bearings in terms of loading and life, and also in terms of intricacy and shape. And there is a continuing emphasis on testing of outputs. There has been an increase in out-sourcing and a consequent expansion in the activities of their buying offices. They now rely heavily on MRP systems, with the consequence for Rose and its competitors that there has been a shift to vendor-driven scheduling, demanding very precise delivery patterns – almost to JIT standards. In both the aerospace and car industries the shift has been towards more quality and more focus on whole-life costs. In general, the time to market forced on Rose's customers has been reduced significantly. In both the aerospace and railway markets, total cost of acquisition has become a major issue. In particular, reduced maintenance and increased life are important: the move is towards *fit and forget*.

The annual world aerospace market for high-tech bearings is estimated to be around £60 million, with the European market around £25 million. Rose has approximately 30% of the market and so is a big player – and in the UK it has around 70% of the market. Potentially the market in rail transport is greater because as trains run faster and customers are demanding greater comfort, pressure grows to use aerospace technology and the higher-tech components that are used there. There are only four major railway systems competitors in the European arena: Adtranz, a subsidiary of Daimler-Benz; Siemens; Bombardier, a Canadian company with interests in Germany; and GEC-Alsthom. These are easy to identify and so are their suppliers – who are Rose's potential customers. The key to entering this market is to sell to the suppliers to GEC-Alsthom, which supplied the Trains de Grand Vitesse to the French Railways and has over ten years of experience of their running.

The knowledge that customers have of their application varies widely. At one end of the spectrum there are customers who provide Rose with a complete specification of the bearing they require – the loading that the bearing will be subjected to and the materials they want it to be made from. At the other end there are customers who will simply describe their application in general terms and ask Rose to design an appropriate bearing.

Until recently, the procedure that Rose adopted was for a sales engineer to visit the customer to discuss requirements and then to write a report for others within the company. This has become too sluggish, and the recently established practice is for a small project team to be set up, often consisting of a sales, a production and an application engineer, and for this team to visit the customer's site. Customers are encouraged to visit the Rose factory to discuss their requirements – and especially for them to understand the constraints that Rose is operating under and the effect of these constraints on lead times.

Ultimately, Rose designs and produces drawings of the bearing and moves on to produce what is termed a *first article*. This prototype and a report on its characteristics are then provided to the customer for acceptance. This acceptance and the subsequent firm customer order initiate production.

A recent departure for Rose is its collaboration with two aerospace companies to develop titanium bearings.

Competition

Rose's competition comes principally from Ampep in the UK, Frankenjura of Germany, Sarma in France, Aurora, Barden and Transport Dynamics in the USA – and from Minebea itself! In general, the US companies have been kept very busy due to the buoyancy of the aerospace market, and they are full of orders for Boeing. However, Rose is now coming under pressure to reduce prices in the face of increased competition from US suppliers, who have begun to take Airbus Industrie seriously.

Ampep and Sarma are both subsidiaries of the SKF group of Sweden, the largest bearing manufacturer in the world. Both have the considerable resources of this group to draw on, particularly in research and development and manufacturing technology. Ampep in particular is very strong in bearing interface technology, and indeed has given Rose serious competition in the helicopter bearings market, which demands this technology. However, both companies are unable to machine the intricate larger bearings that Rose – uniquely – can do. At times Ampep and Sarma seem to be in competition with each other, which has confused and frustrated many customers. Both are experiencing delivery problems and have increased their lead times.

There are many producers of standard bearings, principally in East Asia. Their quality is good, their prices are low and they have set up good distribution networks within Europe, with distributors who are generally able to service customer requirements from stock. The products are relatively simple to produce. Apart from the Japanese manufacturers, they do not yet have the knowhow in bearing interface technology or the capability to manufacture complex bearings. Thus they are currently unable to attack the specialised aerospace market. Additionally, to enter the aerospace market they will have to obtain the necessary approvals on safety grounds from the national civil aviation authorities (and the Joint Airworthiness Authority) and this requires a long-term effort.

Manufacturing

PRODUCTS AND MATERIALS

Bearings are important components in most equipment with moving parts, as they act as supports for moving elements. They must therefore be capable of withstanding high and varying loads, while providing low values of friction to prevent overheating and failure. Bearings are therefore produced from a range of materials according to the strength and speeds required, and manufactured to high standards of precision in order to reduce friction and guarantee accurate movement of the machine components. From a design perspective, bearings are usually defined as being 'plain bearings', where the moving components are separated by a film of lubricant and/or a low-friction lining material; or 'rolling bearings', where the moving elements are separated by a series of rollers (either cylindrical or spherical in shape) that have a small contact area. From a marketing perspective, bearings are usually classified into 'standard' bearings, which are produced in high volumes to meet a wide range of applications, or 'special-purpose' bearings, which are specially designed to meet particular demands of load, speed, configuration or size that are beyond the capabilities of standardised products.

Special-purpose bearings therefore require innovative designs to ensure that the product's configuration and materials meet the specific requirements of customers' products' working environments, and this design work is required anew for each application if no previous design can be used. In addition, it is important to carry out research and development on new materials for increased strength and reduced friction, and possible new configurations for future applications in order that the company's products can remain competitive.

PROCESSES AND MATERIALS

Precision bearings require precise manufacturing processes for individual components and also for assembly. It is usual for the raw materials to be purchased either as bar or tube, as some of the main components are annular in shape. In some cases, however, it may be necessary to buy 'forgings' in view of the higher strength obtained from forged components, or to compensate for higher forging costs through reduced production costs during the early stages of manufacture ('machining'). It may frequently be necessary to wait some time to receive supplies of certain exotic materials that are only produced intermittently, and it may also be necessary to wait for supplies of forgings

compared with bar or tube, as special forging tools may have to be made. The longest supply times are therefore usually for forgings produced from exotic materials.

The first stage in the manufacture of roller bearings is the machining of components from bar, tube or forgings. In low- and medium-volume production conditions this machining is usually carried out on 'computer numerically controlled' (CNC) machines, which can cut components to a high precision and geometric integrity. This precision and geometric integrity are important, as the removal of large amounts of material in subsequent operations may be uneconomic, and imperfections in geometric integrity cannot usually be removed during finishing operations. CNC machines are viewed as being flexible in operation as they can be quickly changed over for the production of different components compared with the specially tooled machines used in high-volume conditions; although these latter machines do have the advantage of being able to carry out several operations simultaneously. Furthermore, as a result of improvements in machine design, CNC machines are frequently more productive than manually operated machines for low- and medium-volume work, although manually operated machines may still be preferred for very low-volume work and unique components.

The components are hardened using either a heat treatment or electrical process, and subsequently toughened in order to withstand high levels of load and shock. The components are then finished using very precise grinding processes that can achieve higher levels of finish and precision than machining, particularly with hardened components, although the rates of metal removal are slower for grinding than for machining. Specialised lining materials may be fitted to these components if required, which may also need to be an additional finishing process with the lining *in situ*. The precision-produced components are then prepared for final assembly, which is also carried out in accurate, clean and temperature-controlled conditions.

MANUFACTURING STRATEGY

To be successful in the manufacture of special-purpose bearings, it is important to source from suppliers who can guarantee consistent quality and timely supplies; and to be equipped with CNC metal-cutting machines and precision grinding equipment, together with the manpower with the skills to operate, service and maintain this equipment. In addition, extremely clean and temperature-controlled conditions are required for finish grinding, inspection and assembly. Furthermore, an adequate system of traceability is required in case of subsequent problems in service.

In a manufacturing strategy, therefore, it is important to have CNC and grinding machines of the requisite accuracy and productivity housed in facilities with high levels of cleanliness and temperature control, and capable of providing the required support services. In particular, flexibility in operation will be required in special-purpose bearing production because of variations in size and product mix. This demands automation and equipment design that will support rapid changeover rather than rapid production rates, particularly as each new product may present particular problems during machining because of differences in materials and configuration. In addition, these day-to-day activities of process selection and modification require to be supported by longer-term process development work for improved precision and productivity, and the introduction of new lining materials. New manufacturing investment may be focused on critical components that are subject to load bearing, friction and relative motion, rather than other peripheral components such as housings. Other components may be purchased more cheaply from outside suppliers provided that reliable deliveries can be guaranteed.

In addition to these technological requirements, it is also important that a company has sufficient capacity to cope with demand, and that this capacity should be able to be rapidly increased or decreased (usually by changes in working patterns in view of the scarcity of the required working skills). Furthermore, it is imperative to have the requisite production planning and control systems (such as MRP) to schedule a complex series of manufacturing processes under conditions of varying demand.

Rod end and spherical bearings are made in small batches, typically anywhere between two off and 500 off, and this causes a very large number of batches in manufacture – it has become normal to have over 1000 batches on the shop floor at any one time. This has proved to be very difficult to control: part-due and late deliveries have increased and overtime has become a financial drain. This method of operation has also been physically and mentally stressful for some employees.

Capacity planning is based on sales forecasts, but Rose only manufactures once a customer order has been received. The factory runs a full 37-hour day shift and a skeleton 37-hour night shift. Rose has some extremely modern CNC machine tools that are being used to reduce operations, and therefore cost, on the higher-quality, intricate bearings. Towards the end of 1998 Rose took delivery of three state-of-the-art grinding machines and three, six-axis twin-spindle/twin-turret lathes, which together will reduce machining times and cost significantly. It now has excellent manufacturing facilities. Rose is following the Minebea strategy of vertical integration within manufacturing.

Responsibility for the provision of samples and prototypes lies with manufacturing with little input from research and development. Rose is unable to produce samples and prototypes within reasonable periods. It is continually having to interrupt manufacturing in order to produce them and this exacerbates its delivery problems. Rose is also taking too long in the design and engineering of these new products, therefore reducing the available manufacturing time still further.

The main material inputs are fairly specialised alloy steels. There are several mills that produce these but they have traditionally given poor service, partly because bearing manufacturers constitute such a small proportion of their customers (their major customers being the car assemblers). Rose gets its metals from around six specialist stockists who specialise in each of the metals needed. It has built good relationships with stockists concerning consignment stocks (pulling off material as it is needed) and who now prepare the metals more for Rose's machining operations than previously. As a simple example of this, Rose used to buy in bars of metal and cut these in its factory; the suppliers have the scale and equipment to do this more cheaply than Rose can.

Quality is of particular concern to Rose. Bearings for the aerospace industry are 100% inspected, with every important dimension measured for conformance with specification. Rose is considering putting in statistical quality control procedures, but this is difficult with small batch sizes. A quality manager was recruited towards the end of 1998 to release the engineering manager to concentrate on more central engineering matters. To maintain accreditation with the Civil Aviation Authority, Rose has to be prepared for visits from its officers.

One feature of manufacturing is Rose's realisation of the very important role that the section heads play and can increasingly play: they are no longer seen as the mouthpieces of management but encouraged to suggest changes in operations. Towards the end of 1998, a common, Japanese-style uniform was accepted for all non-management grades in the factory.

Research and development (R&D)

Historically, the company has responded to changing customer needs by investing in R&D to develop the bearing interfaces needed to meet the higher specifications, and by investing in the machine tools necessary to process the larger, more intricate bearings. In addition, production support staff have been employed to enhance the engineering and quality functions. However, R&D since 1992 has suffered somewhat in the administrative focus. Spending has been kept to a minimum, with the result that R&D has been reduced to that of basically supporting manufacturing and the necessary testing of bearings requested by Rose's customers. Research into PTFE liner systems, which are important to Rose's superior bearing interface technology, has almost ceased.

Goals for Rose

Rose has been set the following goals and policies by Minebea:

1 To increase turnover at the rate of at least 10% per annum and to achieve initially 10% gross profit margin before tax rising to 30% by fiscal year 2000.

2 To reduce work in progress to one month, and to reduce inventory to the value of one month's sales.

Pearson Education and higher education publishing[a]

Background

Addison-Wesley is a long-established US publisher and one of the largest global educational publishers. It sells books, multimedia and learning programmes in all major academic disciplines to the primary, secondary, higher education, professional and English-language teaching (ELT) markets throughout the world.

In 1988 Addison-Wesley was acquired by Pearson plc and in 1995 it was merged with Longman, the world's leading publisher of ELT materials and a Pearson-owned company, to become Addison Wesley Longman. In 1996 Addison Wesley Longman acquired HarperCollins Educational Publishers, consisting of HarperCollins College and Scott Foresman, and Pearson merged these operations with Addison Wesley Longman.

In the summer of 1997 Peter Jovanovich was hired from McGraw-Hill with the directive from Pearson's new CEO, Marjorie Scardino, to 'Make us the biggest educational publisher in the world'. This he succeeded in doing when, early in 1998, he led the negotiations that culminated in Pearson acquiring the US publisher Simon & Schuster.

When presenting an analysis of the Pearson group to UK investors in mid-1999, the US presenter summed up Pearson Education with the charts in Exhibit 1.[b] In these diagrams, 'International' means non-US.

The imprints are mostly English-language, but Markt und Technik is German, Alhambra Longman is Spanish and Cuisenaire is French. There is a small amount of publishing in Italian for the higher education market. As Claire Tavernier, business development manager at Pearson Education, explains:

> We're the leader in English language teaching. In Europe, Pearson is present in some niches – for example in IT publishing – and where we are present we tend to dominate. But they are small niches. Campus Press is the Number 2 IT publisher in the French market, Markt und Technik has a 35% share and is by far the biggest IT publisher in Germany. We also have 30% of the Polish ELT market.

Within what is termed the international market, Pearson's major schools markets are the UK, South Africa and Australia, with a small presence in Spain and Hong Kong. The higher education market is predominantly the UK, with some English-language higher education books sold in continental Europe – particularly in Scandinavia and the Benelux countries. The professional market is more

Exhibit 1   Pearson Education profile, 1998

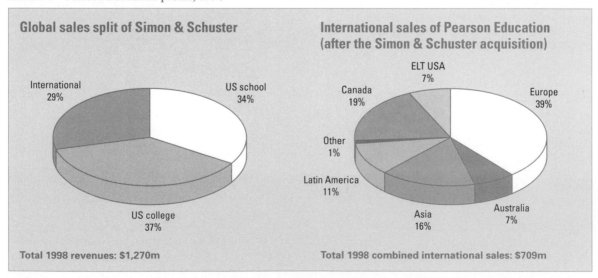

Global sales split of Simon & Schuster

- International 29%
- US school 34%
- US college 37%

Total 1998 revenues: $1,270m

International sales of Pearson Education (after the Simon & Schuster acquisition)

- ELT USA 7%
- Canada 19%
- Europe 39%
- Other 1%
- Latin America 11%
- Asia 16%
- Australia 7%

Total 1998 combined international sales: $709m

---

[a] This case was written by Paul Finlay.

[b] ELT in the USA is English as a second language.

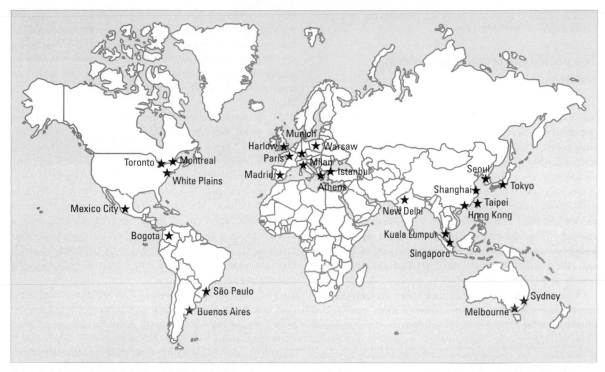

Exhibit 2   Pearson Education publishing offices

international. ELT sales in the UK are mainly to the language schools.

Pearson's international publishing locations are shown in Exhibit 2. It has marketing offices in practically every country.

Pearson's main competitors in order of market share in its international markets are shown in Exhibit 3.

According to Andy Ware, a former head of publishing at Addison-Wesley:

The university presses such as Oxford University Press and Cambridge University Press match Pearson's range of publishing but don't have the same textbook orientation. The strongest UK competition is within Reed (Butterworth-Heinemann), Macmillan, Thomson, Blackwell and Routledge. None of these is able to match Pearson's global sales network. Reed and Thomson do have greater 'verticality' than we do, benefiting from extensive schools and professional publishing. However, the benefits of vertical publishing should not be overstated in connection with most higher education subjects.

The market leaders in all fields are operating in a very similar manner with similar quality. In the ELT market, however, an Israeli company has come into the market and aggressively gone for the cheap and poorer-quality

Higher Education	Pearson McGraw-Hill ITP
ELT	Pearson Oxford University Press Macmillan/Heinemann
School	Pearson Reed Elsevier ITP Macmillan Oxford University Press
Professional	Pearson IDG Sybex Microsoft Press John Wiley & Sons McGraw-Hill

Exhibit 3   Pearson Education's main international competitors

end. Innovations are very easy to copy and little is sustainable.

The number of major global players has fallen from ten to six over the last two years. US publishers have downsized their local publishing operations and have focused on selling rights to their US books. Wiley is the only publisher expanding its UK output.

The publishing process for academic textbooks[c]

The commissioning editor is the first point of contact between the publisher and potential author. Their responsibility is to manage a list of books within defined subject areas and within a generally agreed publishing strategy, identify specific titles they want to publish, and decide who they would like to write them. Although the commissioning editor generally works to a 'hit list' of desired titles, this is constantly under review as the needs of the market and availability of authorial expertise changes. They will then approach the author with the idea and between them will agree on an outline of the book that the market needs, defined in a proposal which is drawn up by the author.

This is a somewhat idealised scenario, however, as commissioning editors also receive a large number of unsolicited approaches and proposals by potential authors. They must evaluate these as well and consider which ones they want to take further and which to reject.

Proposals are detailed descriptions of the book, giving information on the target audience, a comparison with competitors – including unique or distinctive aspects of the project that will convey competitive advantage – a detailed table of contents, and estimates of the length and numbers of figures, table and diagrams. It will often but not always also include a sample chapter, to give an idea of the writing style of the author.

The aim of the proposal is to produce an overall vision for the book that will serve as a guide to both author and publisher during the writing process. It's vital at this early stage that both parties share their vision for the finished project, otherwise there is great potential for conflict later. It's therefore very important that author and commissioning editor communicate openly with each other. In many ways the commissioning editor's primary responsibility is the successful management of this relationship. The authors are a significant resource to a publisher and authors generally want to go to large publishing houses.

The commissioning editor understands the market in terms of the competition, size, needs of lecturers and students, but usually does not have detailed knowledge of the subject areas they are responsible for. They can't therefore evaluate a proposal on their own in terms of its academic content. They pay a number of reviewers, who will be

experts in the subject, and for the most part will also be teaching the subject to the target group of students. The precise number of reviewers varies considerably depending on the project. For a book with a small market it may be as few as three or four; for core textbooks aimed at courses with large student numbers it can be as many as 20.

Reviewers will comment anonymously on the details of the proposal, with criticism and suggestions for improving the book. The commissioning editor and author will together decide which comments and suggestions are most useful to the development of the text, and agree on any changes to the proposal that may be necessary in the light of this feedback. The commissioning editor then has to project sales and costs of the project, based upon what's known about it at that time. This will be done in consultation with the sales and production departments with their knowledge of the market and costs of preparing and manufacturing a book.

The commissioning editor will then make a brief presentation, outlining the details of the project to a committee of senior managers drawn from the editorial, sales, marketing and production functions. Once approved, a contract is drawn up which marks a firm commitment to the project from both publisher and author. Contracts are fairly standard, the most important aspect of them being the author's rate of royalty and any advances, and the specified delivery dates for the manuscript. Important aspects of the manuscript, especially those which can have an impact on the cost of the book, such as number of words, tables and diagrams, may also be specified.

The contract having been signed, it is then down to the author to write the book, which can take any time between a few weeks or months and several years. The commissioning editor will maintain regular contact with the author, providing advice and help whenever necessary.

During this period a lot of work goes into further refining the project. Textual and pedagogical features, often very specific to the subject of the book, may be developed by both author and commissioning editor. Often a specialised development editor will work alongside the commissioning editor and author in this task, especially for more complex books. A text and page design will also often be developed at this point.

When the book is complete in manuscript form it is sent out for a further review. This is designed to make sure that it has delivered what was decided on in the proposal, and that there is nothing missing that should be there, that it is correct and written to an acceptable standard according to the market needs. Reviewers may suggest a number of changes and these are taken into consideration by the commissioning editor and author, with a period of time

---

[c] I'm indebted to Richard Beaumont, a former Addison-Wesley commissioning editor, for writing this section.

given over to making any revisions. When both author and commissioning editor are happy with the manuscript it is accepted as a final draft and work begins on the production of the book.

First the manuscript is copy-edited, which involves a very careful checking process, making sure the text is consistent, the bibliographical details are accurate and that there are no typographical or grammatical errors. Once this has been done it is sent to a typesetter, who transforms the basic text into the design that has been agreed upon for the final book, carefully laying out each page, including all the diagrams and tables, adjusting the text to fit the page size of the book itself. This process generates a set of page proofs, which begin to show for the first time what the final book will look like and how many pages it will run to. Page proofs are then sent back to the author to make sure that no errors have crept into the text. A professional proofreader is also used as an added measure. At this point a cover design is produced.

Once the author and the publisher are happy that the page proofs are correct, a film of the book is produced, which is similar to an overhead transparency acetate, for each individual page. Film is then used to make up a set of lithographic plates. Each plate can contain up to 32 individual text pages. Finally, the plates are used to transfer the text on to paper, which is then folded, bound together with the cover and trimmed to produce the final product.

The time between having a final manuscript and the finished book available to the customer can vary enormously but on average is six or seven months.

The markets

Overall, the market for books and particularly educational books is very buoyant. There is a focus on education by the political parties in many countries, with spending consistently outstripping GDP growth, the rise of the English language making English language publishing a global market and the drive to improve educational standards being a worldwide phenomenon. There is also a move towards a continuous learning model, whereby people take charge of their own adult education and training, and continue to learn throughout their lives, with a growth in distance learning.

The 'harder' the subject the less it is influenced by cultural factors and the more uniformly it can be treated around the world: for example, computing is very similar the world over, as is much of engineering. However, the humanities and social sciences have different traditions and cultural features, and here there can be wide country differences. The Benelux and Nordic countries use English-language texts quite widely and have curricula similar to the USA, and only at the very basic levels would they use their own languages. France and Germany are very different: own- and original-language books are used at undergraduate level, although English-language books are quite widely used at postgraduate and professional level. In terms of curricula France and Germany tend to go their own way. The countries of southern Europe tend to use their local language – with many original-language books rather than translations.

The not-invented-here syndrome is well represented in the USA: Andy Ware can count on the fingers of two hands books with UK authors and not US co-authors that have become Number 1 or 2 in the USA. Canada, Australia and New Zealand are very similar markets to the USA, with the same academic model and with the same textbooks used, albeit with adaptions, for the local market (local economic examples, use of local currency, etc.). The Asian markets are very open to English-language texts from the UK and the USA.

The UK market

Pearson Education publishes in 15 higher education (HE) subject areas, as shown in Exhibit 4.

Exhibit 4   UK higher education enrolments, 1998

Subject area	UK enrolment (000)	Change on previous year
History	28 (+ 20 combined studies)	3%
Literature	28 (+ 20 combined studies)	2%
Linguistics	5	15%
Law	54	5%
Economics	22 (+ 80 services)	0
Politics	17	1%
Sociology	56	1%
Psychology	31	2%
Business	212	2%
Geography	18	0
Chemistry	22	(2%)
Biological sciences	83	10%
Maths	10 (+ 42 service)	4%
Engineering	122	(13%)
CS (acad)	76	10%
CS (prof + trade)	n/a	n/a
Total	1,700	3%

Source: **Higher Education Statistics Agency April 1998.**

The total number of UK HE enrolments is 1.7 million, up 3% on 1996. This splits into 37% science and technical, 63% social sciences and humanities – an increase of 5% towards science and technical.

The UK market trends can be summarised as follows:

- The government has reaffirmed its intention to lift the cap on student numbers, with a target of 45% of young people enrolled in post-16 education by 2002 (up from 32%). This should create an extra 500,000 students, although expansion plans are likely to favour further education (FE) over HE.
- Credit accumulation and transfer schemes are being considered and will blur the lines between FE and HE, swelling HE numbers by increasing throughput to HE courses from FE.
- Fees and the withdrawal of the maintenance grant are currently discouraging applications and pushing those students who are applying towards vocational courses (e.g. design) or to courses leading to a profession (e.g. law, business, finance, computing/IT).
- University for industry, individual learning accounts and greater funding for FE will increase the proportion of mature/adult students, which could work either to *inhibit* textbook sales (greater sophistication of purchase decision, other commitments for funds), or to *stimulate* them (greater purchasing power, greater perception of value).
- IT developments will create more pressure for electronic licensing of materials by higher education institutes (HEIs), e.g. the HERON initiative. This is likely to have a negative impact on sales of supplementary reading texts but not adoptable texts.
- Increases in class sizes are pushing lecturers towards adopted textbooks placed at the heart of the teaching process and away from the more traditional recommended reading list.
- Lower entrance qualifications for HE students drive a need for lower-level introductory textbooks with greater pedagogy, as well as foundation-level textbooks in many subject areas, notably maths.

The US market can be characterised by the following:

- Growing enrolments.
- Moderate price increases for texts, which are acceptable.
- Publishers using technology to increase revenues through companion websites.
- Professional education experiencing double-digit growth.
- Increase in distance learning, adult education and corporate training, which is not only creating new niche markets for textbooks but also for new on-line or computer-based offers.
- Industry consolidation amongst publishers in recent years, which has helped profitability and will keep margins high over the next few years.

While educational systems and funding vary considerably across Europe, the trends in Western Europe may be summarised as follows:

- While school enrolment is flat or declining, university enrolment has been growing as a larger proportion of an age group goes to university.
- Efforts are being made to harmonise higher education by creating diplomas recognised across Europe – master, doctorate, etc.
- Increasing numbers of students studying in other European countries through exchanges, etc., which increases the market for English-language texts.
- At the same time, regionalisation of education – the *Lander* in Germany have a lot of independence; regions in Spain have increased independence in their curriculum development and can teach in the local language (Catalan, Basque, Galician).
- Pressure on the price that can be charged for new books, because of the large second-hand and photocopy markets.
- Consolidated or consolidating markets with very strong national players – Havas and Hachette in France, Santillana and Anaya in Spain, Zanichelli in Italy, Klett and Cornelsen in Germany, Wolters Kluwer in the Netherlands and Scandinavia.
- Emergence of a few cross-national players: the most obvious is Havas, which acquired Anaya in Spain, but also Wolters Kluwer (Netherlands, Scandinavia, UK)
- The emergence of internationally recognised universities with often at least one curriculum in English, e.g. Bocconi in Italy, St Gallen in Switzerland, Insead in France, Rotterdam University in the Netherlands, is leading to a greater use of English-language texts, especially in business and management subjects.

Sales and marketing

In the higher education market, students are having more and more say in what they do or don't buy: they are looking for value for money to help them pass their degree. In 1998 Addison-Wesley talked to a lot of students and found that price wasn't as critical as content and whether the book was appropriate to their course. However, getting a book on to lecturers' reading lists is vital, and to get students to buy the listed books is of course paramount.

In the USA, the modules follow a very set pattern, whereas in the UK, although the first year is rather standard, courses fragment as years go by. Thus publishers are more interested in the first year, where sales can be large. However, fragmentation gives a lever into the market for niche titles and new entrants.

Although students aren't generally conscious of the imprint they are buying, lecturers do have some brand recognition, and this is useful to publishers as lecturers are more willing to talk with their salespersons. It's considered that a brand name puts the publisher into the top five rather than the top 20 books the lecturer might look at. And a lecturer may wish to publish with a well-known imprint.

Imprints are seen as extremely important, since they allow a publisher to cover more of the market. In the Pearson stable, Prentice Hall, Allyn & Bacon and Addison-Wesley have different images and people expect different things from them. Claire Tavernier reinforces this view:

Prentice Hall and Addison-Wesley are very strong brands, and immediately after the Simon & Schuster acquisition the thought was to lose the Allyn & Bacon imprint. But this didn't happen as it was realised that this would lose Pearson market share.

However, in science for example, Pearson would use the Addison-Wesley or Prentice Hall brands rather than any other; for computing, the Addison-Wesley brand. Where there are two or three brands of roughly equal size and clout then Pearson intends to keep the brands and have internal competition, but with books in the same area positioned so that they aren't competing directly – only obliquely.

Salespersons are trained to do 'corridor sales' – selling in a minute or so to a lecturer who is on their way to a lecture or to the car park. The publisher emphasises the currency of their product and strives to keep their books current, especially if they have the market leader. There is strong inertia for a lecturer to keep recommending the same book – the book that they know. Awareness of the marketplace has become more important as the input has broadened – so now many students are of different ability and background to those of ten years ago.

Distribution

Book adoption in the UK is serviced mainly by campus or high-street bookstores and there are no signs that this will change. However, there is pressure on shelf space for supplementary reading texts, titles that have a general interest readership and professional/trade computing titles. Increased public relations activities (for example, press reviews and newspaper articles) and special/corporate sales activity will be needed to drive through sales of this type of product. This requires more resources in sales and marketing.

In the UK a few chains control the retail book trade – HMV (Dillons), WH Smith and Waterstones. Andy Ware says that when he joined the publishing trade as a rep he was told that the publisher–retailer relationship was 'like a knife-fight – each has a knife and each is holding the other's wrist.' However, the bigger you are the smaller discount you need to give to the bookshop and Pearson will be the biggest academic bookseller in the UK, Europe and the USA.

Publishers need good relations with the campus bookshop. As Andy points out:

If these relationships aren't good there may be some problems: they won't collaborate with you on a certain promotion; they won't carry an extra range of books that you are trying to convince them is the next big thing in a certain area, they don't want to add to the core recommendations – to carry the more 'marginal' books that might be extra reading. Some publishers in the US tried to contact the student directly, saying that if you buy from us we will give you a certain amount of discount, but this didn't work very well. It's very difficult to track the student market by individual.

In the first two or three weeks of the semester, campus bookshops must have books available: if a student can't get the book in this time then it's unlikely they will get it subsequently. Publishers have to have the stock to supply a bulk order, and this is especially difficult when a book is first published as it's difficult to know how the book will sell.

Electronic developments

Peter Brimacombe, Pearson's strategy and development executive, considers the possibilities of linking traditional book publishing with the Internet. 'The opportunities are enormous – for companion websites, interactive testing and a million and one exciting things. There could be password controls to give access for the period of the course to help control second-hand book sales and photocopying. The investment needed will be large and there will definitely be economies of scale.'

In the USA, Jim Behnke, the head of the higher education division of Addison-Wesley, left the company in the mid-1990s feeling he was getting no further and set up a small on-line publishing company specialising in the life sciences. He developed a presence there, delivering educational material to both lecturers and students via his

Exhibit 5   Significant new media activities

website. The company is called Peregrine. Addison-Wesley bought it in 1997 and Jim became a president of Addison-Wesley heading up the Internet business.

In the USA all universities have Internet access. In Europe bandwidth problems are still there and take-up is slower.

Pearson Education's Internet offerings in the USA are shown in Exhibit 5.

There is more on Financial Times and Pearson at the companies' websites, htpp://www.ft.com and htpp://www.pearson.com respectively.

Wynnstay & Clwyd Farmers plc[a]

Introduction

Wynnstay & Clwyd Farmers plc is a public limited company registered under the Companies Acts 1985 and 1986. It is a broadly based agriculture supply business operating throughout the principality of Wales and the border counties of Shropshire and Cheshire. Since its establishment over 80 years ago, the organisation's reputation for quality products and efficient service has allowed it to grow into one of the most successful regionally based farm supply businesses in the country.

The organisation was originally established in 1917 as a Farmers' Requisite Co-operative. The business gradually grew through expanding its product range and geographical area of operation. This growth included a series of joint ventures and acquisitions, particularly during a period of severe rationalisation that took place in the agricultural supply industry during the late 1980s and 1990s.

In 1992 members took the significant step of converting the organisation from a co-operative society to a public company, for the sound economic reasons of securing the business capital base and releasing the true worth of the company for the shareholders. Although the business is controlled as a public company, its shares remain 'unquoted', which means they will not be traded on any official stock exchange but will be actively available within the company's internal market.

Wynnstay as a co-operative

Wynnstay and Montgomeryshire Farmers' Association was formed in 1917 by a group of tenant farmers under the leadership of Lord Wilkins as a co-operative supplier of agricultural inputs to the farmer members. The membership fee was £1.

The basic objectives of all concerned were to:

- improve the production of farmers through the supply of quality inputs at fair prices and on reasonable terms;
- develop an efficient marketing system for the produce of the farmer members.

The co-operative grew in the 1920s and 1930s with the

merger of a large number of small village co-operatives in the region.

By the mid-1980s, the co-operative had a membership of 1200 farmers and was trading under the name of Wynnstay and Clwyd Farmers' Co-operative Society Ltd.

Co-operative management

Co-operative management has some distinct cultural differences to that of a public limited company. The British co-operative movement dates back to 1845, when the first retail co-operative was formed in Rochdale, Manchester, by a group of factory workers. The philosophy and the principles laid out by those pioneers are still in practice in co-operatives all over the world. Co-operatives are based on values of self-help, self-responsibility, democracy, equality and solidarity. In the tradition of their founders, co-operative members believe in the ethical values of honesty, openness, social responsibility and caring for others.

The original co-operative principles of the founding members were:

1. Open and voluntary membership.
2. Democratic control – one member one vote.
3. Limited interest on capital.
4. Dividend on purchase.
5. Neutrality in politics and religion.
6. Cash payments in buying and selling.
7. Promotion of education.

Definition

A Co-operative is an autonomous association of persons united voluntarily to meet their common economic and social needs through a jointly owned and democratically controlled enterprise.

Co-operatives collaborate locally, regionally, nationally, and internationally in federations, alliances and other joint activities so that they can meet needs most effectively. (ICA Congress, 1995)

Co-operative principles

The co-operative principles are guidelines by which co-operatives put their values into practice. During the last 150 years, the co-operative principles set out by the

[a] This case was prepared by Nimal Wijayaratna. © Nimal Wijayaratna, 1999.

pioneers have been subject to periodic discussions and debate among the international co-operative organisations. Since its creation in 1895, the International Co-operative Alliance (ICA) has been the final authority for defining co-operatives and for elaborating the principles on which co-operatives should be based. The alliance has made three formal declarations on co-operative principles, the first in the 1930s, the second in the 1960s and the third in 1995. The first two declarations were to adopt the original principles. But a major change came in September 1995.

Seven co-operative principles were declared by the ICA on 23 September 1995 in Manchester. These are given below:

1 Voluntary and open membership Membership is open to all persons able to use their services and willing to accept the responsibilities of membership.
2 Democratic member control Members have equal voting rights (one member one vote irrespective of the number of shareholdings).
3 Member economic participation Members contribute equitably to, and democratically control, the capital of their co-operative. Members usually receive limited compensation, benefiting in proportion to their transactions with the co-operative.
4 Autonomy and independence Co-operatives are autonomous, self-help organisations controlled by their members.
5 Education, training and information Co-operatives provide education and training for their members, elected representatives, managers and employees so they can contribute effectively to the development of business. They inform the general public about the nature and benefits of co-operation.
6 Co-operation among co-operatives Co-operatives serve their members most effectively by working together through local, national, regional and international structures.
7 Concern for community Co-operatives work for the sustainable development of their communities through policies approved by their members.

The adoption of these principles by the ICA does not, however, automatically enforce acceptance and adherence to them in any or every co-operative society. It remains for the members and the board directors of each co-operative formally to adopt the principles as a policy by which the co-operative will be guided.

Member involvement

The basis of co-operatives is the member, whose interests and needs must at all times be reflected in the objectives and work of co-operative organisations. The members of most co-operatives relate to their organisation in three ways:

1 They are owners. They should attend meetings, vote in elections, make decisions on matters referred to them by the board and assist in the promotion of their organisation.
2 They are users who patronise their co-operative, constructively suggest how it might be improved and appreciate what their patronage brings.
3 They are investors, minimally if that is all that is required.

Each of these relationships has its own responsibilities and rewards. The business is conducted for the mutual benefit of members, and members' benefits stem from participation in the business.

Legal requirements of a co-operative society

1 Business conducted for mutual benefits of members and members' benefits to stem from participation in the business.
2 Control to be vested in members and not in accordance with their financial interest. (In general, one member one vote).
3 Interest on share and loan capital not to exceed a rate necessary to obtain and retain capital required to carry out objects.
4 Profits, if distributable, to be distributed among members in relation to the extent they have traded or taken part in the business.
5 No artificial restriction of membership with the object of increasing value of property rights and interests.

Essentials of co-operative management

The professional managers of co-operative organisations have to acclimatise to the co-operative management environment that prevails in it. The first and foremost principle of co-operative management is its democratic character:

● One member one vote.
● Joint and several responsibility.
● Answerable to the general body.
● The general body has the supreme power to undo or to carry out decisions already taken or proposed to be taken.
● Aim to afford best services to members, employees and society.
● Democratic way of management includes absolute faith, tolerance, justice for all, freedom of expression and opinion, work under a board of elected directors, and promotion of the overall interest of the whole membership.

Conversion process

From its humble beginning in 1917, Wynnstay and Clwyd Farmers managed its business as a farmers' co-operative and developed into a major agriculture supply and marketing organisation in the region.

By 1990, the society had 2000 farmer members. Over the years, farmer shareholders of the Wynnstay and Clwyd Farmers' Co-operative Society Ltd built up considerable shareholdings, most of which were accumulated from initial direct investments of only a few pounds. The strong financial base put Wynnstay and Clwyd Farmers Ltd in the forefront of farmer-owned businesses in the UK. In 1990, the board believed that the strong financial position would enable it to take advantage of the rapidly changing conditions of the agriculture sector.

The value of a share in the society has been £1. It never changed during the period of its existence. Only a limited interest was paid and the share value remained constant. In a co-operative society, members can withdraw their shares and accumulated interest at any time. At this time (1990/91), the board was considering converting the society to a public limited company.

The chairman of the society, Mr J.E. Davies, put the initial proposal for conversion to the members through the 1990/91 annual report of the society. He said:

The Society has now been in existence for seventy four years and the pace of change in the agricultural industry has never been greater. For several years, the Board of Directors has been reviewing the finances of the Society and this has been referred to by my predecessors in earlier reports. They now believe, largely due to the financial strength of the business, that the time is right to convert the Society to a Public Limited Company.

This decision has not been taken lightly and is a culmination of a great deal of research, examining many possibilities and looking closely at the pattern of other businesses not only in Great Britain, but also in Southern Ireland and France. The conclusion that has been reached is that the business needs a much more stable financial base, to enable it to take advantage of the changing conditions in the Agriculture Industry.

Recessionary conditions of the 1980s have meant that the farmers are both unable and unwilling to invest in their agricultural co-operatives. During this period members have withdrawn in excess of one million pounds in cash, in terms of bonus and interest on share capital, at a time when they have only re-invested approximately £10,000 in new membership fees.

The management of the Society as custodians of the members' worth, have during that period enhanced the Balance Sheet so that every one pound of member's equity invested in the Society has an underlying net asset value of about three pounds.

Market conditions have tightened considerably at the same time, and we have seen examples where profitability in the larger co-operatives has become marginal or at worst non-existent forcing them into drastic action.

Your Board of Directors are determined that the financial base of your Society is further strengthened at a time when the Balance Sheet is already strong.

A booklet containing the details of the proposal was sent to the members for consultation purposes, culminating in a special general meeting held in the spring of 1992.

Members were understandably concerned about the potential loss of farmer control once the conversion had taken place. The conversion was a major change for the farmer members, who had enjoyed the privilege of participating in the decision-making process since its inception. They were also worried about the loss of ownership of the society. The society would be deprived of its co-operative culture, principles, values and image. They would inherit a corporate culture based on share value and profitability. Some of the members resisted the change. One director resigned on the grounds that the 'one member one vote' principle would be lost to the members as a result of the conversion.

In explaining the strategy for the conversion process, the chairman said:

I would make several points regarding this. Most importantly, a golden share will be issued which will be managed by a Board of Trustees and will be used in certain pre-determined situations to ensure farmer control. The Board will also have the right of veto on the transfer of shares to any individual or organisations they decide are not suitable shareholders. In addition there will be written into the constitution a maximum of a 5% shareholding. As no new shares will be issued at conversion, all shares will be held by the original farmer members. This will mean that there will be no dilution of farmers' holdings and they will therefore have firm control over the business, that control only being forfeited if they, the shareholders, choose to sell out.

This argument was further substantiated by the fact that in a co-operative society, the members cannot sell their shares, only withdraw them if they so want. Any number of shares withdrawn by members means that the society would lose an equal amount of value from the share capital. In a public limited company, the shares are not withdrawn but sold whenever the shareholders want to do so. This process retains the capital in the company as against the co-operative system, where the capital is lost to the business when shareholders withdraw their shares.

Change of status

The board of directors informed the members through a booklet of the proposal to change the status of the co-operative society to a public limited company and the reasons for the change. They set out the following timetable for the conversion process.

February 1992	Farmers' briefings
February 1992	Annual report and conversion proposal published
12 March 1992	First special general meeting
27 March 1992	Second special general meeting and AGM
1 April 1992	Conversion date
30 June 1992	Inaugural share-dealing day

Reasons for change

As a co-operative, the society's share capital is very fluid, with new shares issued to new members and old shares constantly being redeemed by withdrawals. This fluctuation obviously has been a concern, as the society was never sure of exactly how much capital it will have access to in the future. This makes long-term investments and decision making very difficult. Under the proposed company structure, the share capital is fixed, which enables the company to know reasonably well what it will have available for the future.

A further reason to change relates to the requirement to secure capital in the future from the retained profits of the organisation. The society's taxation position was changing as the effects of capital allowance changes were beginning to bite. Higher tax bills would invariably result in fewer transfers to reserves if no action were taken to secure greater retention.

The new company shares would acknowledge the inherent value of the organisation by allowing the shareholders to benefit from the net worth of the company that they own, which in financial terms would be considerably above the existing par value of the shares. Under the co-operative structure, the £1 par value of each share cannot change, and under normal circumstances a member could obtain only that amount for each share they hold.

The only way shareholders in the co-operative could obtain the 'true value' of their shares would be to wind up and asset strip the organisation. Tradable shares under the new company structure would be able to reflect their true value, which it anticipated to be higher than the existing par value, giving all existing shareholders an immediate capital gain. Shareholders would also benefit from the receipt of traditional corporate dividend based on earnings per share, while the company would also organise other commercial benefits for farmer trading shareholders.

The board's proposals

The proposal of the board for the conversion to a public limited company put before the members read as follows:

The Board wish to convert the Society to an unquoted Public Limited Company registered under the Companies Act 1898.

This structure has been selected as it not only provides the required financial base, but also, because of the strict legislation governing P.L.C.s, it provides the enhanced protection that an organisation as large and with as many members as Wynnstay requires. The proposal needs the passing of a Special Resolution at a general Meeting, which will require subsequent ratification at another meeting a fortnight later. If the membership approve this proposal then all existing share capital in the Society will be converted into shares in the new company, which will be able to float in value. The new company will arrange four pre-set dealing days each year on which shares may be bought or sold at a price that will have been previously set by a firm of independent accountants.

This price will obviously be dependent on a number of factors including asset value, company profitability and dividend policy. The price will be notified on a regular basis in all company publications such as the new style customer newspaper. The Board is very confident that the share dealing mechanisms that will be put into place will result in an active market at a fair price, with members being able to realise their investment if they wish to do so, as easily as under the current structure, but at a better price.

Independence Safeguards

A number of farmer members have expressed concern about the possibility of the company being taken over after conversion, possibly by a competitor or other organisation who would not be interested in supporting local agricultural needs. In practical terms there will be no greater risk of this occurring under the new structure than there would under the existing co-operative legislation, as has been demonstrated in Ireland where several Agricultural Co-operatives have been taken over in recent years. But the Board has acknowledged these concerns and does not wish to be complacent about the possible problem and have therefore constructed a number of safeguards to be written into the Articles [rules] of the company to prevent this occurring. These include:

- A rule that any individual, company or group of people or organisations will not be able to hold and obtain voting rights of more than 5% of the issued shares.
- The issue of a 'Golden Share' to an independent Board of Trustees consisting of prominent members of the Agricultural community including Alex Carlisle, QC, MP, and hopefully representatives of farming unions, which would have majority voting power under a number of special circumstances such as an attempt to overturn the rules preventing take-over.
- The ability of the Board to reject the request to purchase shares from people it did not think fit to admit to membership.

The Board and Management are confident that these and other safeguards will ensure the long-term financial and commercial independence of Wynnstay & Clwyd Farmers Plc.[1]

The special general meeting and the subsequent annual general meeting were held at Oswestry in the spring of 1992. Out of a possible 2000 farmer members, 450 turned up for the meeting; 76% voted in favour of the resolution giving the board powers to convert the society to a public limited company.

The strategy of the board to achieve this aim has been to contain costs, exercise strong control over debtors and stock, and expansion through acquisitions and joint ventures.

As a member of the co-operative society, the farmer members received a 'share pass book', which contained the details of limited shareholdings and financial transactions each member had with the society. On the establishment of the public limited company, new share certificates were issued to all members registered on 1 April 1992. The price of one share in the co-operative was £1 and now it is worth £4.

One year after the conversion, Mr J.E. Davies, chairman of the Wynnstay & Clwyd Farmers plc, assessed the situation and said in his report in 1993:

In the Co-operative, farmer shareholders built up considerable holdings over the years, most of this accumulated from initial direct investments of only a few pounds. These shares together with last year's distributed profits of approximately £200,000 were converted on the first trading day into shares in the new company valued at £1.53 each, representing a 53% gain in value over the Co-operative shares valued at £1.00. In addition, the Board is recommending a dividend for this year, subject to shareholders' approval, of 6p per share, and the auditor has indicated at the next trading day, on the 31 March, shares will rise by 7p to £1.60.

These transactions have resulted in the average shareholder, who before conversion held 675 shares with net worth of £675, now having shares together with proposed income totalling £1,291, representing an overall return of 90%. The directors believe that this return adequately rewards shareholders for their loyalty during last year. The Board is delighted to welcome the staff as shareholders in the new company, as a result of conversion.

The financial report of Wynnstay & Clwyd Farmers Co-operative Society Ltd for the year 1990/91 (the year before conversion) and the financial report 1998 of Wynnstay & Clwyd Farmers plc are shown in Exhibits 1 and 2.

Shareholder information

Shareholders in the company are mainly its farmer customers and members of staff. This makes it relatively easy for the company to keep in contact with its shareholders, as they are usually in day-to-day trading or employment contact. It makes the company responsive not only to the needs of its customers but also to the aspirations of the shareholders. As well as this informal contact, the company produces a bi-monthly customer/shareholder newsletter, which not only contains company and product information but also the latest situation regarding shares and their price. The company also produces an informative annual report, which attempts to give shareholders and other interested parties information about the company's business and performance over and above what is required by law. This is an attempt to educate the farmer shareholders on the developments within the company, particularly as regard to their shareholdings, because the majority of the farmer shareholders were members of the original farmer supply co-operative society.

Through these publications and other informal methods, the shareholders are able to obtain the information they require to make their investment decisions with regard to their shareholdings in the company.

Share dealing

The internally created market for shares in the company is operated under a strict set of guidelines, and the company auditors will independently set the share price.

The market in shares operates on four dealing days per year, 31 December, 31 March, 30 June and 30 September, with the company registrar matching previously identified buyers with sellers who have indicated their willingness to sell.

Wynnstay & Clwyd Farmers Ltd.

Group Profit & Loss Account

year ended 31st October 1991

	Note	1991 £	1991 £	1990 £	1990 £
TURNOVER	1		23,338,707		21,671,404
TRADING PROFIT			686,342		626,106
Trading profit is stated after charging:					
Hire of plant		65,938		81,160	
Bank and loan interest		180,696		219,983	
Auditors' remuneration		16,000		11,000	
Depreciation of owned fixed assets	4	303,240		303,280	
Depreciation of assets held under finance					
Leases and hire purchase contracts	4	77,238		62,664	
Pension costs	11	82,257		79,283	
Share of associated undertakings' results	5	34,928		(7,182)	
and after crediting:					
Other income		27,358		48,839	
Taxation	2		(199,000)		(36,000)
Profit after taxation and					
Balance carried forward			487,342		590,106
Profit and loss account brought forward			590,106		–
			1,077,448		590,106
Distribution of profit					
Interest on share capital 1989/90		(108,573)		–	
Dividend to memebers 1989/90		(67,191)		–	
Staff bonus 1989/90		(72,800)		–	
			(248,564)		–
Profit and loss account carried forward			828,884		590,106

Exhibit 1

A minimum of two weeks prior to the next dealing day, the company will publish the independent auditors' latest valuation of the shares, which will act as the basis price for the matched bargain in trading to take place on that forthcoming dealing day. Potential buyers or sellers of shares will then have a minimum of one week to consider whether they wish to deal or not.

When a member has decided that they wish to deal at the given valuation, the appropriate form must be lodged with the company secretary at least one full week before the relevant dealing day (lodgement day).

To buy shares, the applicant must submit a 'buy request form' and submit it along with a cheque made payable to Wynnstay & Clwyd Farmers plc for the amount calculated on the application form. To sell shares, the member must complete and submit a 'sell request form' and submit it along with their share certificate to the company secretary.

When these buy and sell request forms have been successfully matched on the dealing day, a share transfer form will be sent to the selling member and on the receipt of that signed form the company secretary will register the share transfer and forward the sale proceeds to the seller.

It is company policy that no buyer applicant's cheque will be cashed until their application has been successfully matched with a sale, resulting in no cash flow disadvantage if a request to buy is unsuccessful.

Where a buy application needs to be scaled down because of insufficient shares being offered for sale, the applicant's cheque will be cashed and a refund cheque from the company sent along with the share certificate on allocation.

Where, for the same reason, a seller's request needs to be scaled down, a replacement share certificate will be issued along with a cheque for the proceeds of the shares that were successfully matched and sold.

Wynnstay & Clwyd Farmers Ltd.

Balance Sheet

as at 31st October 1991

	Note	1991 £	1991 £	1990 £	1990 £
Fixed assets					
Tangible assets	4		2,127,468		2,020,424
Investments	5		329,253		95,699
			2,456,721		2,116,123
Current assets					
Stocks	6	2,234,776		2,640,571	
Debtors	7	2,950,244		2,713,434	
Cash		1,423		1,897	
		5,186,443		5,355,902	
Creditors: amounts falling due within one year	8	(3,778,713)		(3,821,233)	
Net current assets			1,407,730		1,534,669
Total assets less current liabilities			3,864,451		3,650,792
Creditors: amount falling due after more than one year	9		(48,253)		(132,016)
Provision for liabilities and charges	10		(15,000)		(15,000)
Net assets			3,801,198		3,503,776
Financed by:					
Share capital			1,252,130		1,212,200
Loan capital			103,017		119,231
General reserve			1,582,239		1,582,239
Profit and loss account			863,812		590,106
Members' equity			3,801,198		3,503,776

Approved by the board on 16th January 1992 and signed on their behalf:

Director	Director	Secretary
J. E. Davies	R. G. Jones	B. B. Harris

Exhibit 1 (continued)

The business

The business is highly diverse and centres on feed manufacture, fertiliser distribution and retail; the latter is focused on both farmers and the country dweller. The company has a substantial stake in a number of joint ventures involved in fuel distribution, pig production, livestock marketing, feed blending and grain trading.

Business sector performance

The company's business performance breakdown for financial year 1997 is given in Exhibit 3.

Mission statement

Wynnstay & Clwyd Farmers Plc is committed to becoming the leading supplier of products and services in the rural economy of which it is part of the essential fabric.

Consolidated Profit and Loss Account
for the year ended 31st October 1998

	Notes	Total 1998 £'000	Total 1997 £'000
TURNOVER	1(c)		
Continuing operations		52,035	46,760
Acquisitions		286	6,683
		52,321	53,443
Cost of sales	2	(41,474)	(43,218)
GROSS PROFIT		10,847	10,225
Selling, distribution and administrative costs	2	(9,313)	(8,165)
Associated undertakings results	10	(12)	(110)
OPERATING PROFIT			
Continuing operations		1,546	1,963
Acquisitions		–	(13)
		1,546	1,950
Profit on sale of fixed assets in continuing operations		42	16
Acquisition reorganisation costs		–	(199)
Permanent diminution in carrying value of livestock	4(a)	(248)	–
PROFIT ON ORDINARY ACTIVITIES BEFORE INTEREST		1,340	1,767
Interest payable	3	(165)	(195)
PROFIT ON ORDINARY ACTIVITIES BEFORE TAXATION	4	1,175	1,572
Tax on profit on ordinary activities	6	(250)	(550)
Profit on ordinary activities after taxation		925	1,022
Dividends	7	(240)	(232)
RETAINED PROFIT FOR THE YEAR	18	685	790
Earnings per share	7	51.02p	59.18p
Fully diluted earnings per share	7	45.29p	47.00p

There were no recognised gains or losses other than those shown in the above profit and loss account.

The notes on pages 13 to 26 form part of these accounts.

A statement of movement in reserves may be found in note 18.

Exhibit 2

To do this, Wynnstay & Clwyd Farmers Plc recognises that it must excel in terms of Value, Quality, and Development of its products, services and people.

In so doing Wynnstay & Clwyd Farmers Plc will optimise the returns to all stakeholders and so retain wealth within the rural based communities it serves.

The main divisions of the company

The company has five main operational divisions.

Animal compound feed manufacture

The company operates one of the country's most technically advanced feed mills situated in the village of Llansantffraid, on the mid-Wales/Shropshire border. It produces a full range of compound and liquid feeds for all classes of stock: dairy and beef cattle, pigs, sheep, chickens, turkeys and ostriches. The production has been consistently upgraded to improve efficiency and quality, and is supported by full nutritional and technical advice teams.

Consolidated Balance Sheet
for the year ended 31st October 1998

	Notes	Group 1998	Group 1997	Company 1998	Company 1997
		£'000	£'000	£'000	£'000
Fixed assets					
Tangible assets	8	4,603	4,923	4,071	4,296
Investments in subsidiary undertakings	9	–	–	2,770	2,682
Investments	10	730	397	706	426
		5,333	5,320	7,547	7,404
Current assets					
Stocks	11	5,073	4,846	4,348	4,615
Debtors	12	7,713	7,992	5,891	6,187
Cash and bank balances		2	2	426	–
		12,788	12,840	10,665	10,802
Creditors: amounts falling due within one year	13	(8,985)	(8,704)	(7,893)	(8,237)
Net current assets		3,803	4,136	2,772	2,565
Total assets less current liabilities		9,136	9,456	10,319	9,969
Creditors: amounts falling due after more than one year	14	(602)	(739)	(602)	(739)
Provisions for liabilities and charges	15	(99)	(41)	(88)	(30)
Net assets		8,435	8,676	9,629	9,200
Capital and reserves					
Called up share capital	16	1,830	1,787	1,830	1,787
Share premium account	17	1,141	1,036	1,141	1,036
Reserves	18	5,464	5,853	6,658	6,377
Shareholders' funds	19	8,435	8,676	9,629	9,200

Reistered number: 2704051

The financial statements were approved by
the Board of Directors on 19th January 1999

J.E. Davies   Directors
B.P. Roberts

The notes on pages 13 to 26 form part of these accounts.

Exhibit 2 (continued)

All feeds are heat treated by means of expanders – and unique products have been developed for poultry production, where heat treatment plays an important role in disease control. The plant has a capacity of approximately 4000 tonnes per week. The company has gained an ISO 9002 quality award for the mill. Feed blends have become popular in the country over the last few years, and in 1995 the company opened a blending facility at Tern Hill in Shropshire in conjunction with KW Agriculture. The company works on an agreed capital expenditure programme to upgrade the technology of production and acquisition of new machinery. This strategy has proved to be highly successful, as the company is now in a position to produce a wide range of custom mixes based on quality raw materials. Before conversion, the co-operative did not have sufficient capital strength to invest in new technology or expansion of product lines.

Wynnstay feed	36.7%
Other feed	17.1%
Retail	8.0%
Arable	22.3%
Animal health	5.8%
Livestock	4.4%
Grain	5.7%

Exhibit 3   Business performance[2]

According to the managing director, Bernard Harris, the company operates a 'quality policy' for animal feed manufacturing and supply. The quality policy states:

Wynnstay & Clwyd Farmers plc is committed to becoming the leading supplier of agri-products and services in the rural economy of which we are part of the essential fabric.

To do this, we recognise that we must excel in terms of value, quality and development of our products, services, and people.

Our mill in Llansantffraid is one of the most modern in Europe and can produce in excess of 110,000 tonnes of animal feed per year. It is our policy that the feed produced should be of the highest standard of quality in order to satisfy the requirements and expectations of our customers.

The quality of our product is assured by utilising appropriate manufacturing methods and quality systems. These methods and systems are based on satisfying or exceeding the requirements of the Ministry of Agriculture, Fisheries and Food, trading standards and ISO 9002.

The aims of this policy are achieved by following quality procedures, which are regularly reviewed and improved upon to ensure customer specifications are satisfied.

The implementation of our policy is the responsibility of the Company's Personnel and Compliance Manager who has the necessary authority from the Managing Director and Board.

This Quality Policy and all documented manuals and procedures are issued with the authority of the Managing Director and Board and the system the company's documentation describes is a mandatory obligation for all employees.

Our ethos is to achieve and maintain a reputation for quality which makes Wynnstay 'First for Feed'.

We have now established ourselves as a major regional producer of pig feeds, both to our contract production units (Partnership in Pigs) as well as to third party producers. Sheep feed sales are also buoyant. Our policy of working closely with producers helped us to improve our market share. The sheep feed market is particularly receptive to the concept of single ingredient declaration and producers appreciate having full knowledge of the feeds that they are purchasing.

An open policy of declaration is critical in restoring both the farmers' and food chain's confidence in the animal feed industry.

The 'mad cow disease' (BSE) problem demonstrated the importance of food safety and the catastrophic consequences that can result from the loss of consumer confidence. Other problems such as the outbreak of E. coli and the on-going salmonella situation in poultry will continue to make headlines, and the livestock industry and its suppliers have to take all the necessary steps to ensure that the UK produces some of the safest food in the world. This is a major challenge faced by animal feed manufacturers and suppliers. The company operates a policy of not using meat and bonemeal in its mill and at the time of the BSE crisis, unlike some of its competitors, was not affected by the cost of disposal of materials held in stock, or the recall of contaminated feed.

The company instigated a campaign to urge all animal feed manufacturers to declare their feeds singly (the ingredients used for each feed), rather than adopting a category system that enabled manufacturers to state ingredients as a whole. While this did not have a direct bearing on the BSE situation, it is a major factor in restoring the image of compound feeds to the farmers and to the food chain. At the height of the crisis, farmers were appearing almost daily in the media, repeatedly stating that they had little or no knowledge of the ingredients contained in the compound feeds they had been buying. The effect of this on the public at a time of maximum media exposure was very damaging, both for the image of farmers and, more importantly, for the feed industry that was supplying them.

British agriculture was severely affected by the worldwide ban on the export of British beef, which resulted in a chain of suppliers having to cut down their activities. Furthermore, it has been affected by the strength of sterling, which has reduced the prices of milk, meat and grain. In addition, it also encouraged importation of all classes of meat from around the world, which particularly depressed pig meat prices. However, this situation has brought about some respite in raw material costs and cheaper grains for the animal feed manufacturers and suppliers, and helped the feed business, although a fall in the market for ruminant feeds intensified the competition considerably.

Fertiliser and arable

Operating in a mixed farming environment, the company makes the most of the opportunity to supply the grassland and arable farms with a range of quality products. In fertiliser, the Wynnstay Group is one of the country's largest distributors and benefits from its close geographical proximity to one of the largest manufacturing plants in Europe, situated at Ince, in Chester.

The company's arable business is supplemented by supplying quality, locally processed cereal seeds together with its own range of grass mixtures. It also distributes a full range of agrochemicals. It employs specialist staff for this purpose.

The company has a policy of using quality raw materials in its feeds, making it one of the largest consumers in the area of locally produced cereals. It works closely with its joint trading partner, Shropshire Grains Ltd, for the procurement of significant quantities of wheat, barley, field beans and peas.

A specialist herbage seed department stocks a wide range of both grass and clover seeds and can produce mixtures to meet individual customer requirements. A comprehensive range of Staylush grass seed mixtures is available for distribution. This department markets cereal and maize seeds together with peas, beans and all root crops.

Wynnstay is a major distributor for Kemira, the largest manufacturer of compound fertiliser in the UK. The company also markets a range of blended fertilisers as required by the farming community.

The lack of low-priced imports of ammonium nitrate from Eastern Europe, coupled with greater demand throughout the EU, has rapidly changed market conditions, and the main suppliers are being forced to control supplies. Although the market is likely to be more competitive in the future, in the medium term it is forecast that fertiliser supplies in Europe will remain tight, with the former Soviet Union countries consuming much more of their own production. However, the company believes that its strategy of building up the market in fertilisers will keep it in good stead, while the logistics of supply will become more difficult. This will enable the company to build on its considerable fertiliser business and seek opportunities to expand it wherever possible.

Retail depots

An area of significant growth in recent years and high hopes for the future is the group's chain of retail outlets. Currently, there are 14 retail depots located in significant market towns throughout mid- and North Wales and Shropshire. The chain is currently undergoing a rebranding process to ensure that the success achieved over recent years is built on for the future.

These retail depots supply approximately 9000 different product lines ranging from household goods to country clothing and specialised animal health products. The goods from these depots can be purchased by farmer members and non-members alike.

Wynnstay has a well-trained retail management team which focuses on expanding the business to country dwellers and the farming community. Countrywise stores are targeted at both the country dweller and the urban population within their catchment area. Pet food, clothing and footwear, household items and gardening are focused on the general public. In money terms, sales in the retail business have grown by 56% since the conversion.

Supply of fuel and vehicle maintenance

The group completes its product range to farms and other customers with the supply of all types of fuel and lubricating oils, with a Fina authorised distributor service provided from operating locations at Chester, Llansantffraid, Market Drayton and Craven Arms.

A fully equipped Shell service station, a transport maintenance company in Welshpool and a specialised facility at Llansantffraid provide vehicle maintenance services.

Transport

The company has its own fleet of vehicles, which enables it to achieve its distribution targets effectively and efficiently. It provides dedicated vehicles for specific poultry customers to transport veterinary medicines used in disease control. In fact, this service is extended to its trading partners in the blending plant, to further improve their vehicle utilisation.

Changing government legislation requires haulage companies to exercise greater control over the delivery of raw materials into feed plants. In order to meet this requirement, the company acquired the Jack Jones transport company, with which it had a long association, and now plans to build up a substantial integrated haulage fleet. The company intends to expand its transport facilities from in-house requirements to competitive services to third parties.

Corporate governance

The board of Wynnstay & Clwyd Farmers plc has recognised the need for corporate governance, although the company is not listed. In order to develop corporate governance, it adapted the aims contained in the Cadbury Committee report. Corporate governance for the company was set up in 1995. Where applicable, the board complies with the code of best practice and has taken additional measures to ensure sound corporate governance, including the adoption of a set of guidelines for the conduct of directors and senior staff in regard to their responsibilities for the management and conduct of the company.

The board has established an audit and remuneration committee, whose tasks include detailed consideration of capital projects, internal controls and company-wide remuneration matters prior to making recommendations to the board.

The board recognises its overall responsibility for the group's system of internal financial control and has established a control structure to provide reasonable, but not absolute, assurance against material misstatement or loss. The key procedures within the control structure are as follows:

- Managers at all levels in the group have clear lines of reporting responsibility.
- Comprehensive financial reporting procedures exist with budgets, covering profits, cash flows and capital expenditure being prepared and adopted by the board annually. Actual results are reported monthly to the board and results compared with budgets and last year's actual. Revised forecasts are prepared as appropriate.
- There is a structured process for appraising and authorising capital projects with clearly defined authorisation levels.

The directors adopt the 'going concern' concept in preparing financial statements, with the expectation that the company has sufficient resources to continue its operations for the foreseeable future.

As a result, the auditors were not required to perform any additional work necessary to express a separate opinion on the effectiveness of the company's corporate governance procedures, or on the ability of the company to continue in operational existence.

Expansion strategies

Wynnstay & Clwyd Farmers plc continues to look for opportunities to further its growth through acquisitions and joint ventures. It has been a successful strategy since its conversion to a public limited company. The company is quite happy to work with like-minded people who bring specialist expertise to a number of joint ventures, involved in agricultural merchanting, fuel distribution, poultry production and, increasingly important, livestock marketing.

The following joint ventures and acquisitions are on record since the conversion, and the strategy seems to have worked well for the expansion and growth of the business.

Joint ventures

1992 Wynnstay Fuels Ltd, a business selling and distributing all farm, commercial and domestic fuels and lubricant requirements.

1992 Wynnstay Country Lamb, the marketing agent for finished lambs exported to Spain under the Volac marketing initiative. This partnership was an important step in forming a farmer-controlled marketing organisation for livestock in the area.

1993 Wynnstay Country Farmstock, a business extensively involved in the marketing of sheep, cattle and pigs from third parties and also managing the company's contract pig units.

1994 E.W. Webster Ltd, one of the foremost independent turkey-breeding companies in the UK with a significant export trade to Europe, both for leading commercial strains and its own niche speciality breeds.

1995 The Wrexham Grain Company, a successful grain procurement and marketing company in North Wales.

Acquisitions

1993 L.N. Jones animal feed manufacturers, an acquisition aimed at expanding the business further into Cheshire and adjoining areas.

1995 Jack Jones & Company, a haulage business serving both agricultural and construction industries.

1995 Retail division of G.S.L. Farm Suppliers, North Wales.

1997 Griffith & Simpson Ltd, one of the largest independent agricultural merchants in the Midlands. This acquisition gave the company the opportunity to expand further into Shropshire and surrounding counties.

1997 Shropshire Grains Ltd, an opportunity to enter into quality grain marketing and integrate company activities in the area, including Griffith & Simpson together with its other businesses in Cheshire, and L.N. Jones.

All acquisitions and joint ventures are within the company's region of operation.

The future

The agricultural supply industry in the UK, in particular the feed sector, is grappling with the problems of huge overcapacity. The problems in the beef sector, which threatened to spill over to sheep meat, compounded by the strength of sterling, have made conditions difficult for companies like Wynnstay & Clwyd Farmers plc. However, the company remains optimistic and continues to follow a policy of expanding the business geographically, while at the same time broadening the base of its activities within the agricultural field.

References

1   *Progress through Evolution*, Wynnstay & Clwyd Farmers Ltd, 1991.
2   Wynnstay & Clwyd Farmers plc, annual report, 1997.

ARM Ltd: The chipless chip company[a]

Background

As more than four billion microchips are produced annually in the world and relatively few are used in the central processor of PCs,[1] the main concern for chip makers and ancillary businesses is with digital appliances other than the high-profile computer. These appliances include computer peripherals such as modems and printers; portable devices such as mobile phones and personal organisers; automotive applications such as engine management systems and airbag controllers; and the consumer multimedia market such as games and set-top boxes.

Microchips can be single-purpose (application-specific) or multipurpose. Single-purpose chips have a single 'dedicated' design and tend to be cheap to make, while multipurpose chips have the advantage of flexibility because they can be programmed for many specific purposes. Electronic engineers refer to high-level microchip design and construction as 'architecture'. There are two broad categories of chip architecture, one built around complex instruction set computing (CISC) and one around reduced instruction set computing (RISC). CISC typically has 300 instructions and is the choice for the Wintel (Windows/Intel) *de facto* standard that dominates desktop PC applications. In such applications high speed is important and power consumption is of little concern. However, in many applications, particularly in the portable market, performance is a lesser consideration and cost and power consumption are much more significant factors. In these cases modern RISC architecture is more appropriate because the chips use less power and are cheaper to make. ARM Ltd is in the forefront of low-cost, high-performance, power-efficient RISC technology.

Company history

In the 1980s, the standard UK schools' computer was the BBC Micro designed by Acorn Computers. Acorn wanted to produce a more powerful computer and needed an improved microprocessor. The Acorn engineers had heard of the RISC architecture and decided to develop their own chip based on it to increase performance, but also focusing on low cost to meet their tight budget constraints. They had to design their chip to a very tight cost

ARM's vision

ARM's vision is to establish its architecture as the standard for embedded RISC processors for use in a wide range of high volume applications, in the embedded, portable and consumer multimedia markets.

Exhibit 1

budget, whereas the competing American RISC technology designs at that time were focused on performance only.

Acorn got the first RISC chip operating successfully in 1984, and it became the basis for the Acorn RISC machine, called the Archimedes. Acorn designed the chip and got the firm VLSI Technology to produce it. However, Acorn realised that it faced an ever-increasing R&D budget for further chip development and, although VLSI had interested Apple in supporting the R&D, Apple didn't want to be dependent on a competitor for its chips. It was happy to enter an alliance and in November 1990 Apple, Acorn and VLSI established a joint-venture agreement with a capitalisation of £3.25 million. The joint venture company was named ARM, with ARM now standing for Advanced RISC Machines. The joint venture was set up under the holding company ARM Holdings Ltd, with a board consisting of two Acorn directors, two Apple directors and the CEO of the operating company ARM Ltd.[b] At its birth, ARM Ltd consisted of 12 engineers and was headed by Robin Saxby, who had been headhunted for the job of CEO.

Robin Saxby

Robin Saxby graduated with a B.Eng. in electronics from Liverpool University at 21 and went to work designing colour TV receivers for the TV group Rank Bush Murphy. The receivers were based on microchips, which in those days contained 50 transistors; today's chips contain 10 million. He spent four years there and then in 1973 moved to Pye, a subsidiary of Philips. He had the view that professional electronics must be more professional than consumer electronics and he thought that he would learn much more there. This turned out to be rather dull; most

[b] VLSI didn't have a seat on the board as it held only a small share.

of the work was with the Post Office (what is now BT) and mainly about standards.

At roughly the same time as he joined Pye he gave a talk at the Royal Television Society entitled 'TV and chips', with the thrust that money could be saved and time to market could be reduced using chip technology. The audience contained a manager from Motorola, which was setting up a new operation and wanted commercially oriented engineers. Motorola tried to get Robin to join them for over a year. They got their man when they asked him, 'What colour would you like for your Cortina 2000GXL?'[c] Married and with a car that was falling apart, Robin decided to stop being a design engineer and become a sales engineer. He quickly became a divisional manager. The last job he had with Motorola was in charge of the European microsystems business.

While he worked with Motorola Robin didn't live in the USA but was a very frequent visitor. He feels that he imbibed the US culture when he joined Motorola – everyone used Christian names, management was very approachable, there was little hierarchy, there was a 'get on with it' culture. He appreciates this way of commercial life but he also likes aspects of other cultures, in particular the Japanese team-working and consensus culture. He has tried to build the best of all worlds into the ARM culture, which he characterises as 'work hard and have fun', reasoning that it's difficult for engineers to be creative unless their workplace is a good place to be in.

In 1984 he got a headhunting phone call for a chief executive's job, to head the security division of Henderson Garage Doors. As Robin recalls:

Quite an interesting experience. In a big corporation like Motorola you are very protected, very cosseted from the issues, and here I was in charge of the lot – global operations, legal, sales, marketing, the factories ... I joked that it was like a Harvard Business practical with a vengeance.

Robin was running the high-tech end of Henderson, but for him it was low-tech. He recalls that during the time he was at Henderson, he was being asked by European Silicon Structures to join it. At that time it was one of Europe's best-funded start-ups with $100 million behind it. After two years with Henderson, Robin joined European Silicon Structures in phase two of the management build-up. He became president of the US sister company, called United Silicon Structures, which was losing money, and his job was to cut the operation down to size and turn the company around. He stayed with European Silicon Structures for five years. Again, he commuted to the USA, as his wife didn't want their children

educated in American schools. He spent two or three weeks a month in Silicon Valley, where he was the president of United Silicon Structures as well as retaining his European job as chief executive of European Silicon Structures.

Robin has had some formal management training. When he first started at Rank, he thought he would go into management and started a diploma in management studies at what was then the London Polytechnic. But there was a conflict: he was going to these courses for which he was paying and also giving lectures at Essex Polytechnic on TV and circuit design, for which he was getting paid. He had almost completed the first year of the DMS when he had to make a choice and he chose to concentrate on the paid work. However, he believes that the year on the diploma course was a good grounding in basic management. With Motorola he got on average one week's useful training per year. When he first became a director he took several of the Institute of Directors' courses and also solicited advice from those who had done it before.

Robin is a member of various government and industry advisory panels and a frequent speaker at international events.

The early ARM years

After five years with European Silicon Structures, Robin received a headhunting call about ARM. He talked over the proposal with a friend who was a partner in a venture capital company. His friend warned him off taking the job, saying that joint ventures never work. Robin soon found out why his friend was so sceptical.

The problem was that there were representatives of both Acorn and Apple on the board and not only would they each have their own agendas (one was a specialist in finance and another a specialist in marketing), they were also both customers of ARM Ltd. Their priority wasn't to make ARM Ltd successful in its own right – that was a secondary consideration – what mattered to them was to protect the Acorn and Apple interests. As Robin wryly remembers, 'It was a bit like "if we get the technology we want you can turn ARM into a business". And I very much wanted to turn ARM into a business.' The ARM management realised that if they ran ARM very lean and mean and made a profit very early on, they would be less dependent on the joint venture shareholders. ARM broke even in 1992 and was making money in 1993. Since then all the growth has been self-funded.

Early in 1993 Nippon Investment and Finance, a Japanese venture capital company, asked ARM if it could invest in it. As ARM wanted to penetrate the Japanese market, it thought it useful to have some local help and

---

[c] The answer was white with black upholstery.

accepted the investment. The stake also provided security in case the business didn't take off as was hoped; it provided an extra £650,000.[d] The original business plan was for ARM to float or be sold, but getting the corporate investors to agree what to do was challenging. There couldn't be an initial public offering (IPO) unless the founders sold some shares, because if a firm wants to go public in London it has to have 25% of its shares on the market. The upshot was that all the stakeholders except the staff sold 20% of their shares at the IPO.

ARM Holdings plc was listed on the London Stock Exchange and on NASDAQ[e] on 17 April 1998. ARM Limited, its wholly owned subsidiary, is the principal operating company. All employees are granted stock options, and ARM employees own around 3% of the company, with a further 3.6 million shares under option. Robin explains the reason for the flotation:

The reason we needed to float the company was because our major assets are people. All employees are shareholders, but unless you're publicly quoted who knows what the price is. Our competitors were primarily Silicon Valley start-ups and the challenge realistically was we would have lost staff. It was a strategic decision. But the other factor was that creating a public company was a way of dissolving the joint venture. At the time of flotation neither Apple nor Acorn were significant customers and so we were in another phase of life. Flotation wasn't to get money to expand.

Jonathan Brooks, the chief financial officer, explained one of the advantages of the double flotation:

In the last market turndown we didn't get dumped in the way we might have been if we'd been a pure Nasdaq stock. European investors are more stable and we like that stability, but if we were just listed on London I doubt our share price would have gone up as much as it did. It was the movement on Nasdaq that pulled it up and that was because a lot of technology stocks were going up.[2]

Currently, ARM Holdings has three executive officers from ARM Ltd on the board: Robin Saxby, chairman and CEO, Jonathan Brooks, the chief financial officer, and Jamie Urquhart, the chief operating officer. The ARM Holdings board meets quarterly. Apple's holding is now less than 10% and Acorn's is now zero. More than 90% of the shares are in public hands, including those of employees.

---

[d] In the event this wasn't needed.

[e] North American Securities Dealers Automated Quotation. Equivalent to London's Alternative Investment Market (AIM).

ARM Ltd

ARM designs high-performance, low-cost, power-efficient RISC microchips and the related software, and licenses them to chip manufacturers and applications software developers. A sample of the end products that are 'ARM-powered' is shown in Exhibit 2. Embedded within these products are chip designs of the sort shown in Exhibit 3. In 1998 about 50 million products with ARM chips inside them were manufactured (compared with 10 million in 1997). ARM undertakes no manufacturing.

ARM also receives income from the sale of software and hardware development tools, design consulting services, and from offering support, maintenance and training. In 1998, the breakdown of revenues was as shown in Exhibit 4.

In 1998, new licence fees accounted for the majority of sales. However, royalty payments, based on a set percentage of a licensee's net sales price per chip, are likely to become more significant. In the early days licences generated cash quickly, but this is no longer so important an issue. ARM receives a royalty of between 1 and 5% of the chip price depending on how complex the design is. A chip is roughly 10% of the factory price of a mobile phone.

The structure of the microchip design business is shown in Exhibit 5.

Many end products, such as a mobile phone, an airbag for a car or a computer games console will include microchips. These will be made by chip manufacturers such as Alcatel and Texas Instruments. To be effective the microchips need to be allied to software, from such sources as ARM, Symbian (the joint venture of Psion with Nokia, Ericsson and Motorola) and the chip manufacturers themselves. This software and the combined hardware–software product are supported by development tools. ARM's areas of expertise are shown within the ellipse in Exhibit 5.

A corresponding example for PCs is that Dell makes the end product by buying in chips from suppliers such as Intel. It also buys in software such as MS-DOS and the Windows operating systems from Microsoft. Supporting the Intel chips are the designers of the chips, and supporting MS-DOS and Windows are software designers. Both sets of designers use design tools. ARM is bringing computer-type design techniques to the embedded market.

ARM is a globally oriented organisation with European offices in Cambridge, Maidenhead, Munich and Paris, East Asian offices in Seoul and Tokyo, and US offices in Austin in Texas, Los Gatos in California, Seattle in Washington and Boston, Massachusetts. These locations and the numbers of staff are indicated in Exhibit 6.

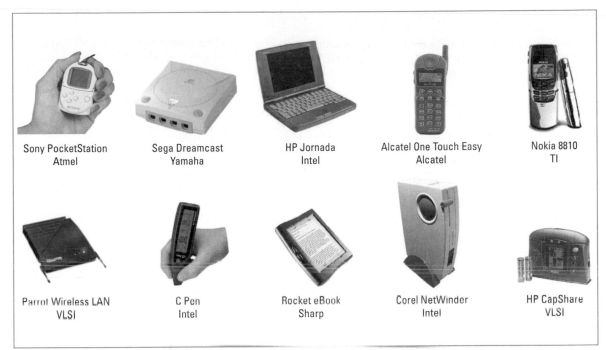

Sony PocketStation
Atmel

Sega Dreamcast
Yamaha

HP Jornada
Intel

Alcatel One Touch Easy
Alcatel

Nokia 8810
TI

Parrot Wireless LAN
VLSI

C Pen
Intel

Rocket eBook
Sharp

Corel NetWinder
Intel

HP CapShare
VLSI

Exhibit 2   New announced ARM-powered end product examples

Mobile phones

In 1998 an estimated 70% of ARM-enabled products were in mobile phones (which means that over 20% of all mobile phone processors in the world were based on the ARM architecture). Thus the mobile phone market is very important to ARM. The growth of the mobile phone sector is shown in Exhibit 7.

This sector is particularly important as Nokia, the largest maker of mobile phones, has estimated that by 2004 it expects more users to be connected to the Internet via mobile smart devices than via PCs. Symbian aims to promote the EPOC-32 software as the *de facto* operating system for mobile communications and ARM is supporting it. However, ARM is hedging its bets; it also has designs available for Windows CE, the main rival to Symbian.

Competition and collaborations

Two vertically integrated semiconductor producers, Hitachi and Motorola, are well established in designing and manufacturing embedded RISC-based chips. Hitachi's SH products are widely used in video games. The nearest technical equivalents to ARM's designs are PowerPC made by IBM and Motorola, the i960 and x86 from Intel, MIPs by MIPS Technologies and the 68000 from Motorola. MIPS Technologies is a US-based company that is closest to ARM in terms of the way it operates, but there is little overlap at present between ARM and MIPS applications areas.

With the older mobile phones, around 150 different microcontroller architectures were available from around 200 vendors. In general, one manufacturer wouldn't license its designs to another. But the end product manufacturers such as Nokia want multiple sourcing, and some of the vertically integrated companies have only grudgingly allowed access to their designs. In general most licensees aren't as good as the licensor. What ARM has done is to say that all chip suppliers will be treated equally. ARM offers an open rather than a closed model – and this is an approach that finds favour with the end product manufacturers as they aren't tied to any one chip manufacturer. Now firms like Nokia are saying to the chip makers that they must use ARM. The vertically integrated competitors are fighting back against the open standard that ARM is offering, saying that they will license their technology to their competitors.

The world of chips isn't straightforward. Intel appears as likely to be an ARM customer as a competitor. In May 1998, Intel acquired Digital Equipment Corporation and with it Digital's licence to ARM technology. Intel has subsequently increased the designs it licenses from ARM to include the StrongARM range, although it has retained its own RISC chip design team. Motorola is a 31% shareholder in ARM licensee Symbian.

ARM offers a range of microchip designs, from the central processing units that are at the heart of a microprocessor to complete microprocessors, which will typically include memory and interfaces with input and output units. Primary examples are:

Central processing units	
ARM7	Small, fast, low-power, integratable 32-bit RISC processor core. Used in portable telecommunications.
ARM7TDMI	This is the company's most widely licensed product. It combines an ARM7 instruction set with additions to reduce memory size and system cost. Typical applications are digital cellular phones and hard disk drives.
ARM9TDMI	Provides more than twice the performance of the ARM7TDMI core. Typical applications are networking and TV set-top boxes.

Microprocessors	
The ARM710 family*	Low-cost, low-power, packaged general-purpose system microprocessors with cache, memory management and write buffer. Applications include handheld computing, data communications and consumer multimedia.
ARM940T, 920T families	Low-cost, low-power, high-performance general-purpose system microprocessors with cache, memory management and write buffer. Target applications are advanced engine management, instrumentation, safety systems, TV set-top boxes, portable computers and high-end printers.
StrongARM	Very high-performance yet affordable general-purpose microprocessor jointly developed with Digital Equipment Corporation and subsequently licensed to Intel.
ARM7500, ARM7500FE	Highly integrated single-chip RISC computers. They are based around a cached ARM7 32-bit core, they have memory and I/O controllers, on-chip video controller and colour palette, and stereo sound ports. The ARM7500FE adds floating point and DRAM support. Applications include TV set-top boxes and network computers.
ARM7100	High-integration microcontroller designed for smart mobile phones, handheld games, portable instruments. Built around the ARM710 microprocessor, the ARM7100 integrates LCD control and the other peripherals required for handheld computing applications. Manufactured under license by Cirrus Logic.

The most significant architectural advantage of ARM's products is the proven industry-leading performance in low power consumption or MIPS per watt. At a low cost per MIPS of processing power, ARM's partners offer among the most competitively priced products in their class, enabling rapid growth of new consumer products.

For example, the ARM7TDMI central processing unit provides 690 million instructions per second per watt (MIPS/watt) and the StrongARM microprocessor yields performance over 250 MIPS at less than 1W of power consumption.

*Includes ARM710, ARM710T, ARM720T, ARM740T

Exhibit 3   Examples of ARM's microchip designs

As a result, the industry is now more willing to out-source and to collaborate. According to Robin:

In the past people like Texas Instruments, Intel, Alcatel, Sharp and Sony would each design their own proprietary standards and the architectures for their own embedded products. What we are saying is don't design your own thing, come to ARM as a standard and we will license the technology to you. You can add your own differentiated technology on top of what we do to make

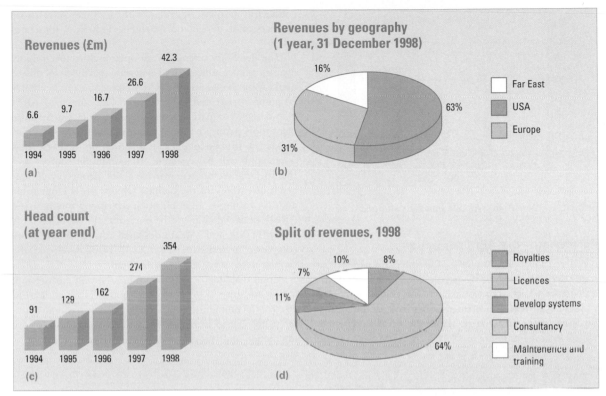

Exhibit 4   ARM statistics

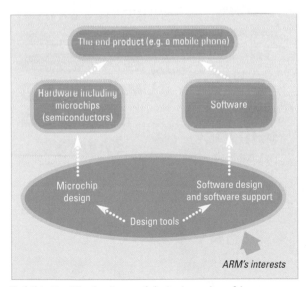

Exhibit 5   The business of designing microchips

Exhibit 6   ARM's global operations

more successful products for you. In joining the ARM community you get software, design tools and so on. Our key customers are our semiconductor partners, our key competitors are semiconductor companies and ARM is saying why do you want to compete? Why not collaborate?

This is the rationale underlying the partnering arrangements that ARM is fostering.

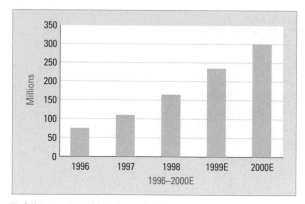

Exhibit 7   Worldwide mobile handsets shipped[3]

Partnering – the ARM community

ARM's vision is to establish its architecture as the standard for embedded RISC processors. To accelerate the acceptance of its architecture and the products that use its designs, ARM has created a network of three main types of partner in what it terms the ARM community: 30 microchip manufacturers, which ARM terms semi-

conductor partners, together with a range of software partners, and design tool partners. Exhibit 8 illustrates this.

The flexibility offered by an open architecture rapidly enables semiconductor and software partners to design applications based on the ARM architecture and facilitates on-going design and maintenance. The combined ARM chip design, compatible software and associated development tools ensure the end product manufacturers, such as Nokia in mobile phones and Bosch in airbags, that microchips will be available from multiple sources and that the architecture will provide a well-defined evolutionary route. Many of the designs are upwardly compatible and, for example, an application developed for the basic ARM7-designed chip can be ported to the more versatile ARM7TDMI and ARM8-designed chips. While more complex chip designs are continually being developed, the simpler designs are still being licensed.

Good dialogue is vital to sustain a strong partnership, and one feature of the ARM community is a high level of electronic communication, through e-mail and videoconferencing. But in Robin's view, you also need face-to-face interaction and you do need critical mass:

Exhibit 8   Leveraged partnership model

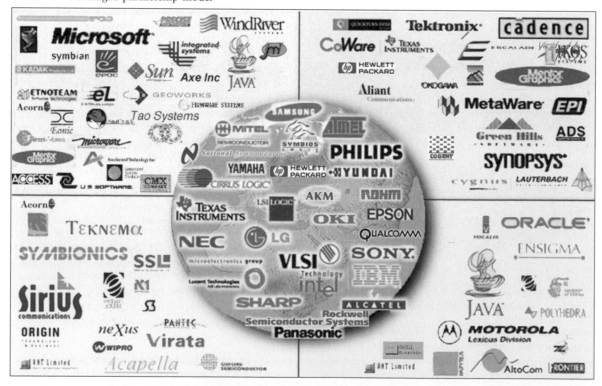

Clusters are important, especially intellectual clusters. A large part of our world is still Silicon Valley – Intel, LSI Logica have head offices there and many other industry opinion leaders are there. That's why Reynette is there. Our design team in Austin focuses on high-performance design. In Silicon Valley it's software porting work. In Seattle we're near to Microsoft and Texas Instruments is in Houston. We are where our partners are. So you have critical mass but this doesn't mean that everyone needs to be in the same room. If you stay in the same room you become inward looking. I'm a member of the electronics community in Silicon Valley just as I am in Cambridge.

Potential partners are now knocking at ARM's door. ARM has limited resources and it has to prioritise who it will work with because partnerships involving technology transfer take time and effort to achieve. ARM agrees a strategy statement with each new partner in which the partner commits itself to contribute to the ARM community. So ARM is asking for more than just money from a partnership. Partners are part of the project in all design development: they influence the technology, bring engineering resources, provide test sites and engage in joint project development. However, licensees aren't exclusively ARM licensees: they still have their own design teams and also often license technology that competes with ARM's.

Although potential partners are knocking on ARM's door, ARM is still very pro-active. Its efforts in the automotive industry are an example of this.

The automotive industry is destined to be a very large one for chip manufacturers and designers, with chips used in engine management, suspension control, airbag control, anti-skid braking and in all the information systems that are touted to aid driving and ease traffic flows. Automotive electronics has a design cycle of ten years, because all the enabling technologies have to be in place before the moves finally get underway. As Robin puts it:

There isn't an automobile that's been fitted with an ARM chip as yet, although one should be announced towards the end of 1999. We're working with the top 20 customers and the top 20 application areas and the top 20 chip suppliers. The electronics are supplied by people like Bosch, ACDelco (General Motors' (GM) division that includes electronics), Ford's electronics division and Lucas. Some of the car companies are very vertically integrated although this is diminishing with the demergers of GM's and Ford's components businesses into Delphi Automotive Systems and Visteon respectively. This is what Tim's gang are trying to crack. Some of Tim's people are wholly focused on the car industry. TI[f]

is a major supplier to the car industry and Oki is the equivalent in Japan. We pick the best in each area and so get to market faster. It would only be by 2005 that we might become the global standard in automotive chips.

Once a year, ARM holds a partner meeting in the vacation period at a Cambridge college. Typically about 300 people will attend. ARM has close links with universities, especially Cambridge with its research expertise and its supply of students. ARM also works with Manchester, Harvard and Stanford universities, wherever the best work is going on.

ARM is very concerned with branding, its image, trade marks and patents. It does virtually no advertising; instead, its staff are active at events where there are awards for the best technical papers, and where new developments are announced. ARM staff also go to all the appropriate trade shows, where they promote its development tools. ARM has good brand awareness within the business-to-business community, but a much lower one among consumers. Consumer branding is considered important over time, and all end product partners have to put the 'ARM powered' slogan in their adverts (equivalent to the 'Intel inside' advertising).[g]

Management structure

The management structure in 1988 is shown as Exhibit 9. It's a global arrangement, with Robin in Maidenhead, Jamie in Cambridge, Jonathan in London and Tim in Los Gatos.

The chief finance officer's concern is with the financial and legal side of company affairs, particularly with patents. Patents are vital: if ARM didn't have patent protection its licensees wouldn't pay the royalties. So patents are a must, but they aren't infallibly strong. ARM currently has 55 basic patents. The chief operating officer is responsible for research and development and for the products and services that ARM provides. The head of ARM Inc. is responsible for global sales and marketing. Robin sees his job as concentrating on strategy and pulling everything together.

The total number of company employees in mid-1999 was about 390. Operations account for about 170, with 70 in sales and marketing. The R&D engineers work on either product development or design consulting, according to demand. A very significant role is that played by Warren East, who has the responsibility of ensuring that the technology developments of the R&D engineers flow to the markets.

---

[f] Texas Instruments

[g] For example, Nokia phones have a little label saying 'ARM powered' on them.

Exhibit 9   Structure of ARM Limited

Operational structure

The design and tool development side of the company is structured into six distinct yet integrated units providing comprehensive support to system designers. In chronological order of when they were established these are:

1   The product licensing business unit licenses the ARM architecture, chip designs and software tools. ARM's major revenue stream is from licensing and royalties from its semiconductor partners.

2   The support services business unit provides support, maintenance and training to ARM partners and systems companies, assisting with software applications and porting. This group also runs ARM training courses for ARM partners and their customers.

3   The design consulting business unit works with partners to deliver ARM expertise to end product manufacturers who are designing using the ARM architecture. Specific consulting services include feasibility studies and software design.

4   The development systems business unit provides designers with a fully integrated development environment combining software tools and hardware/software co-design support.

5   The software systems business unit covers two areas:

•   the porting of operating systems to the ARM architecture. Examples are JavaOS from Sun Microsystems and Windows CE from Microsoft;

•   work with specialist applications software vendors to deliver applications software, for example audio/speech coders, Chinese character input and modem software.

6   The electronic design automation business unit works with third-party partners to provide ARM licensees with automated design tools.

ARM splits itself into the most appropriate units, based on the view that small units are easier to handle and 30–40 people is the maximum size of a unit. The software business unit is becoming large and is likely to be split in the near future.

Sales and marketing

Most of the field sales staff are organised into three market segments:

1   Embedded control applications, which span a wide spectrum, from mass storage, security, automotive and instrumentation to printers, smart cards, modems and communications systems. Critical needs for this segment are low cost, and design and software support.

2   Consumer multimedia applications, which demand low cost, high performance and software support, include several high-volume markets as well as emerging ones like network computers. Among designs well suited for ARM implementation are digital cameras, game machines, digital TVs, TV set-top boxes, intelligent terminals and satellite global positioning devices.

3   Portable products include handheld PCs, pagers and cellular phones, including emerging smart phones. The crucial needs of chips used in these mobile devices are low power consumption, low cost and software.

A fourth group focuses on partner management.

Strategic considerations

Robin explains the reasons why the chip industry is changing:

It's because of 3 main factors:

•   Everything is getting so complicated – with 10 million transistors on a chip – that no one or small group of engineers can get their heads round all of them. With the earlier chips you didn't need the software tools and other bits to make them work. Now things are much more complex and we're now designing at a higher level.

The culture and value norms which evolve within an organisation and which ultimately pervade all individual and organisational activities are fundamental components of the motivational climate of that organisation and ultimately relate directly to individual job satisfaction and job performance.

Recognising this as fundamental, ARM has sought consistently, since its formation in 1990 and throughout its years of growth into a public company, to build and sustain a culture which reflects and supports a set of core values which all members of the company can endorse and which they feel are appropriate for ARM – a culture which attracts people to ARM.

Whilst any concept as intangible as culture is difficult to explain, the following phrases have frequently been used to demonstrate an attitude or value which represents a desirable component of 'the ARM culture'.

- portraying a *'can do'* approach to any request or challenge
- treating time as a valuable and scarce resource – *every deadline is urgent*
- seeking *understanding of customer and partner* perceptions and perspectives
- respecting and appreciating *colleagues' contributions*
- developing *team working* and peer relationships
- *contributing to change* in the interests of organisational growth
- *sharing knowledge* openly whilst respecting confidences

- *developing mutual trust* with colleagues, partners and customers
- striving for *continuous improvement* in performance standards and deliverables
- promoting *creativity and innovation*
- investing personal time and effort in *self-development and betterment*
- *fulfilling* leadership roles *in relation to tasks, teams and individuals*
- being pro-active and taking *initiatives*
- building *re-usable* working methodologies and processes
- promoting and exploiting ARM's *progressive and leading edge* market position
- nurturing and propagating *ARM's greatest asset – its people* and their ideas
- respecting, valuing and exploiting ARM's *geographical and cultural diversity*
- balancing *hard work and fun*

Through these, ARM seeks to be a *'premier global company'* widely respected throughout the world for the calibre and status of its people, the efficacy of its business model, the uniqueness of its partner and customer relationships, the innovativeness and usefulness of its progressive, leading edge technologies and for having *ARM technology everywhere*

Exhibit 10   The ARM culture

- The cost of manufacturing in the semiconductor industry is now horrendous: a manufacturing plant will now cost at least $3 billion. So depreciation is horrendous. So if you don't keep factories full, then you lose a lot of money: keep them full and you make a lot of money. To keep the factories full, you need to be able to make chips for many customers. The time to market of the design activity is a limiting factor.
- Software is becoming a bigger and bigger proportion of the cost of the product. In the past, integrated chip companies could do everything themselves; now time to market and the greater complexity strongly suggest that collaboration with specialists is appropriate.

The learning curve in chip design appears to be very strong. Every design can be continuously improved, with developments being incremental rather than transformational. Patents have been successful in protecting from reverse engineering, but ARM has had to send cease and desist letters to some companies – which worked. Because ARM's products are a complex linkage of hardware design and software, they're very difficult to copy successfully.

For technology to take off, global standards are needed. The mobile phone is an example of getting it (almost) right; GSM (general system mobile) is the standard used across Europe, Hong Kong and some other places and CDMA is a competing standard used in the

USA. Smart card technology is an example of getting it wrong (so far). ARM is involved in the most advanced smart card technology; however, until there is agreement on a standard, smart cards won't be brought to market, except in areas where there is strong local support such as France.

Although the quality of ARM's relationships with its partners is vital to its success, so too are its internal relationships. One of the challenges with a fast-growing company is that people forget the strategy and forget to check the direction they're going in. ARM is running six global operations conferences in 1999. These are two-day off-site meetings involving a series of workshops to discuss strategy and such matters as how to exploit ARM's success, its intellectual property and its new software. It's at these workshops that new staff are told the ARM culture and older members are reacquainted with it. The culture of ARM is illustrated by the briefing notes used by Robin at the workshops and reproduced as Exhibit 10.

Most of the staff have electronic engineering backgrounds, but the field staff also need negotiating and legal skills because all ARM's designs are patented and licensed. Although ARM is very actively pursuing the burgeoning automotive market, it doesn't recruit from the car industry:[h] it recruits engineers because it's selling to the

---

[h] Unless from the electronics division of the car companies.

engineers in the car industry. These staff are developing new areas and need considerable technical competence. ARM also has key account managers who build up relationships once the technical aspects have been finalised, and they may not be engineers. Pay is related to performance, and design engineers get bonuses if a patent on which they've worked is filed.

Everyone in ARM is responsible for their own education. There's a performance appraisal review process, but the culture is that if anyone wants training, and it makes sense in the light of ARM's vision and strategy, then ARM will pay for it. For example, one of ARM's lawyers in the UK wants to take the American Bar exams and ARM will pay for their airfare. Several people are studying part-time for MBAs at Cranfield and elsewhere, and some people are studying part-time for MScs at Manchester University. All staff attend at least one major company learning event each year. There is the two-day globalisation conference for all staff, the ARM partners' meeting is attended by many staff, and there is an annual global sales conference, which in 1999 was in Mexico. Very often outside consultants are used to give a wider view.

An intranet using Lotus Notes is the main form of electronic communication within ARM. In 1998 a very close look was taken at how information was communicated and knowledge developed, with the aim of improving information and knowledge management. ARM saw the challenge as how to make knowledge usable and useful without being bureaucratic; how to have simple systems that give a snapshot of everything that is going on. ARM has recently hired a senior IT person to improve knowledge and information management.

ARM uses the expression 'less is more': the executive summary is more useful than reams of paper. No executive information systems software is used, but spreadsheets are. Industry standard packages are invariably used, as befits a global company. However, it is stressed that what matters are face-to-face meetings; the danger that ARM sees is that people work in their small groups and tend to become inward-looking.

Strategy development

ARM has a vision and within this vision plans two to three years ahead. It has a strategic plan and an operational plan with an annual budget. Strategic thinking is part of the general way of life for the executive team and every operational decision is part of the strategy. The weekly executive team meetings are used to fine-tune the strategy. ARM doesn't really believe in formal techniques; for example, it doesn't use the balanced scorecard at present, but it is open to new ideas. The simple executive summary is vital – that is ARM's tool.

In the executive team everyone owns something – someone will be mainly responsible for monitoring environmental issues, for example. Mike Muller is the person mainly responsible for highlighting strategic trends and he participates in industry standard working groups, talks to banks, etc. Leadership is a team effort, with every decision being unanimous. The leadership style is described as 'Come on, we can do it'. All developments are apparently coming from below the top team. As Robin puts it:

All we say is, 'The industry is going this way, have you thought of this.' We set direction, we hire people and we set up the mechanism for them to get approval for resources. Anyone in the company can put a proposal to the board. Someone puts up a proposal, saying the competition is doing this or that, I think this is very important etc., here's my project proposal and they will argue for it. Then I ask Jonathan what the financial risk is and David about the legal aspects. This is what we do at the operational meetings. Every project needs approval.

The quest continues

ARM believes that it will take to 2010 before it can get to the point of being the global standard for embedded RISC processors. So the quest continues. In mid-1999 the company was worth £1.4 billion, so some investors must believe that this is possible.

References

1 Murphy, D., 'Surfing with the oven', *Financial Times*, 18 September 1998, p. 12.
2 Franklin, C. 'Soaring chip sales put more strength in Arm', *Sunday Times*, 7 February 1999.
3 Report on ARM Holdings plc (ARMH.O/ARM.L), 'License to kill', Goldman Sachs International, 14 April 1999.
ARM Internet address http://www.arm.com

ARM, StrongARM and ARM Powered are registered trade marks of ARM Ltd.

'ARM' is used to represent ARM Holdings plc, its operating company ARM Limited, and the regional subsidiaries ARM, INC., ARM KK, ARM Korea Ltd.

Thorntons[a]

Foundation and development

Thorntons, the UK's largest manufacturer and retailer of specialist chocolates, was founded in 1911 by Joseph Thornton, a commercial traveller engaged in selling confectionery. Tired of travelling, he opened his own shop in the city of Sheffield. His two sons, Norman and Stanley, joined him to combine their abilities in retailing, devising recipes and manufacturing, to provide freshly made confectionery, manufactured in the shop in which it was sold.

The benefits of self-manufacture and product innovation were soon to become apparent. During the 1920s several product lines were established that have continued to the present day. In 1925 a recipe for special toffee, based on cream, butter and eggs, gave the business an outstanding product. The self-manufacture of Easter eggs, decorated in the shop to include names and messages, added to the range of freshly made and fresh-tasting confectionery.

By the Second World War Thorntons had established 35 shops in the Midlands and the north of England, half of which were later destroyed by bombing. The 1950s provided a period in which the company re-established itself. With the ending of the post-war rationing of sweets in 1952, a period of rapid expansion began.

In 1953 Stanley and Norman Thornton visited Switzerland to find out how Thorntons could make what was regarded as the very best of chocolates. The visit included the Basle School for Swiss Chocolatiers and the recruitment of an outstanding student, young Swiss confiseur Walter Willen, who was to stay with Thorntons until his recent retirement. Walter Willen created the original recipes for Thorntons' Continental chocolates, a range that was to become the largest-selling specialist assortment of chocolates in the UK.

Thorntons began to develop sales outside the UK and by 1982 the value of its exports to Europe and Australia had reached £300,000. Attracted by the prospect of further sales outside the UK, the company decided that the massive potential of the US market offered the best vehicle for expansion. Thorntons opened two shops in Chicago, with the longer-term intention of operating a 100-shop chain throughout the USA.

[a] This case was written by Dr David Jennings of Nottingham Business School, Nottingham Trent University. © D. Jennings 1999.

Going public

By the late 1980s, Thorntons was operating the largest chain of quality confectionery shops in the UK and was well known for its freshly made style of chocolate and toffee confectionery. The product was delivered weekly to the shops from the company's own factories at Belper, Sheffield and Alfreton, where its purpose-built factory was one of the most modern plants of its type in Europe. The number of retail outlets had increased to around 270, 170 company-owned shops and 100 franchised outlets operating in towns too small to merit a Thorntons-owned shop. Further sales were achieved through the company acting as a supplier to Marks & Spencer. In addition, the company owned the Mary Morrison chain of 25 greeting card shops in Scotland. This chain was not considered to be central to Thornton's core business and in 1990 Mary Morrison was sold to Hall of Cards for £2 million.

The company had developed its product range to focus on the rapidly growing higher-value and gift market through a range of chocolate assortments, Easter eggs, special designs (such as a white chocolate 'snowman') and liqueur chocolates. With sales of £46 million and a pre-tax profit of £6 million, Thornton's believed that there was scope in the UK for a further 130 retail outlets. Although Thorntons was achieving success in the UK, the venture into the USA, showing little prospect of profit, had recently been closed.

The directors believed that the time had arrived for the stock market flotation of Thorntons through the public offer of 27% of its equity. Flotation was intended to achieve a number of benefits, raising new money to enable the company to expand the chain of UK shops, with the expansion concentrated in the south-east, away from the company's heartland in the Midlands and the north; growth was to be achieved either organically or by acquisition. Growth was also anticipated through acquisitions in Europe, where markets were believed to be more similar to the UK than had proved to be the case with the venture in the USA. In addition, the flotation would help some of the family members – six Thorntons were directors of the company – to leave the company to develop other interests. With the offer of shares eight times oversubscribed, share trading began at a good premium.

European and UK developments, 1988–96

Within three months of flotation Thorntons had made its first European acquisition, Gartner, based in Antwerp, a specialist in high-quality chocolate and fresh cream products with sales mainly through patisseries. With net assets of £196,000, Gartner had a turnover of £1.7 million. Thorntons established an integrated manufacturing and retail operation, distributing Gartner's products through Thorntons retail network as well as selling its own confectionery to the Belgian company's customers.

In the following year Thorntons acquired two French confectionery retailers, Candice-Martial SA and Société Nouvelle de Confiserie (SNC) for a total of £8.65 million. Candice, previously owned by Nestlé SA, had 55 retail outlets based mainly in the Paris area selling confectionery and ice cream. After reorganisation by Nestlé, which had resulted in a pre-tax loss of £760,000 for the previous year, the company's trading was showing significant improvement. SNC had 11 confectionery outlets in the Normandy and Brittany region. The French and UK factories were to contribute to the supply of each other's markets.

In the UK a variety of factors affected the level and pattern of Thorntons' sales. Sales of the company's confectionery were highly dependent on a number of seasonal events. The six weeks before Christmas provided 30% of turnover. Easter, Valentine's Day and Mothering Sunday accounted for a further 25% of sales. The concentration of sales into short periods made the company particularly vulnerable to conditions at those times. While snow might be part of the image of Christmas, poor weather conditions were only one of many factors, along with the development of superstores and Sunday trading, that could result in reduced high-street shopping activity. Similarly, the recessionary conditions of the early 1990s reduced high-street trade and the occurrence of impulse buying by passers-by. At other times of the year unseasonally hot weather could reduce the demand for chocolate by as much as 20% of a month's sales. Even the occurrence of events such as a general election could disrupt demand; in Easter 1992 a post-election rush of spending, with subsequent queues at Thorntons shops, prompted some consumers to go elsewhere. The problems of seasonality were exacerbated by the company's products having a comparatively short shelf life due to the high quality of their ingredients.

Thorntons developed a number of strategies to counter the effects of seasonality. The company introduced a range of ice creams as a counter-seasonal product. Although the value of the UK premium ice cream market had doubled in five years, Thorntons' own sales of ice cream, at 5% of total company sales, were too small to offset the periodic fall in confectionery sales.

Thorntons had a 1% share of the daily confectionery market and a 6% share of the confectionery gift market. Determined to reduce further the effect of seasonal variations in sales by expanding day-to-day sales of confectionery, the company changed its promotional message. However, finding the right marketing approach proved elusive. In 1994 the Christmas sale of speciality boxed chocolates fell compared with the previous year, a decline attributed to the day-to-day focus of the television advertising campaign. While the number of customers had been sustained there was an increase in the purchase of cheaper, loose chocolates rather than boxed. The group responded by appointing its first marketing director and changing the advertising campaign.

While the majority of Thorntons' sales were made through the company's own shops, use was also made of other forms of distribution, including franchising. In certain respects franchising provided a cost-effective way to achieve distribution coverage; however, it did not provide the customer with the same experience as shopping in a Thorntons-owned shop and occasionally it could be difficult to maintain standards. Franchising could also provide surprises. In 1995 the company lost 15 franchised outlets following their takeover by Clinton Cards, a company that did not normally sell confectionery. The retailing of greetings cards represented the principal business of a high proportion of Thorntons franchisees.

Progress was made in developing the company's commercial customers. Thorntons had a long-standing supply arrangement with Marks & Spencer and in 1991 Sainsbury's was added to Asda as a supermarket outlet for the company's products, with the range of chocolate products broadened to suit supermarket shelves. The supply of chocolates and ice cream to commercial customers continued to increase, to £14.8 million in 1992. Commercial customers' products differed by style and recipe from those provided through Thorntons' own outlets, and regular customers would not be sure that they were made by Thorntons.

The attempt by the group to enter the European market began to show disappointing results. Although several of the acquisitions had well-established brand names, including the well-known Martial brand, there were marked differences between the UK and French markets. While Thorntons' UK sales divided 80% to chocolate and 17% to toffee, the French market divided equally between chocolate, ice cream and sugared confectionery. The French preferred bitter chocolate. Sales relied less on Christmas and Easter, with a greater emphasis on gifts for weddings, births and christenings. In addition to different sweet-eating cultures, the French operations demonstrated differences in working culture.

In 1991 Thorntons (France) made a loss of £850,000. The losses continued and were worsened by high French interest rates, the severity of the downturn in the French economy and the devaluation of sterling. In 1993 the loss reached £1.8 million. Thorntons' chairman and chief executive, John Thornton, concluded: 'We had a strategy that we believe would have worked in the end, but we are not a large enough company to sustain large losses over a long period.' Thorntons provided £7.75 million to cover the cost of restructuring the French operations, including the sale of 25 Martial stores to provide a smaller, high-quality, profitable core. The cumulative cost of the French initiative had reached £20 million.

The European operations continued to make a loss, £395,000 in 1995. Thorntons began to plan for the conversion of many of the remaining shops to the Thorntons brand, with the aim of increasing the synergy with the core Thorntons business. In the UK market Thorntons continued to develop the products and packaging within the core chocolate gift ranges. The Continental range was developed to include a 'French' dark chocolate selection and a 'Belgian' milk and white chocolate selection. A new Classics traditional assortment and a Premier Selection of hand-finished chocolates were established to top the company's range. Product development was complemented by a programme of shop refurbishment to enhance both image and selling environment. Around 15 shops a year were to be relocated to reflect changes in retail shopping patterns. In addition, the management of franchise operations and the company's own shops was unified to increase the consistency of quality, standards and service.

A change of direction

Thorntons' chairman and chief executive, John Thornton, had joined the company in 1966. After holding senior positions on the production side of the business, he was appointed production director in 1977, managing director of the UK business in 1982 and chairman and chief executive in 1987. During the latter part of 1995 the company announced that it was seeking a new person for the position of chief executive. In January 1996 Roger Paffard became chief executive of Thorntons, with John Thornton as chairman. Roger Paffard's previous position was that of managing director of Staples UK, the office superstore joint venture between Kingfisher and Staples of the USA. Joining Staples in 1993, he had presided over the expansion of the out-of-town superstore business. Announcing the appointment, John Thornton described Mr Paffard as 'energetic with a strong retail background'. Roger Paffard demon-

strated his faith in the company by purchasing 73,000 shares at 135p, just 10p above the price at flotation in 1988.

Further changes to the board of directors included the departure of the UK managing director, the appointment in 1995 of the company's first marketing director and in June 1996 the appointment of the company's first retail director and a director for operations.

In March 1996 the company announced a fall in interim profits, from £9.62 million to £7.63 million for the 28 weeks to 6 January. Although the trading period had encountered difficulties, a warm summer and the loss of franchised outlets to Clinton Cards, sales had increased from £58.4 million to £59.1 million. As part of a three-year redesign plan the company had spent £1.1 million on store refurbishment during the year. The new-look stores achieved a sales increase of 8%. Costs, however, were increasing faster than sales. At the same time, losses for the French operation amounted to £494,000 on sales of £2.2 million.

The new management team undertook a comprehensive review, which resulted in a number of changes to the group. To improve efficiency and cut costs, packaging was to be concentrated at the Belper packing and manufacturing site, providing annual savings of £250,000 at a cost of £750,000. The Belgium business, Gartner Pralines, was to be sold for a nominal sum. The disposal would cost £900,000 but would save £650,000 a year. The third of Gartner's output that had been produced for the UK would be replaced by production at the group's main plant at Alfreton.

Within the year a buyer was also found for the 21 shops remaining in operation in France. Losses for the year had reached £655,000 on net assets of £3.9 million. The sale, again for a nominal sum, was to Jeff de Bruges, a company specialising in retailing chocolate, with 160 outlets in France and ten abroad.

With regard to UK operations, the new chief executive concluded that the company's existing shops were 'tired and increasingly off-pitch'. Many of the shops were too small and in poor locations. The group, it appeared, had become a manufacturing rather than a retail led business, the product range had not been fully updated and, he concluded, Thorntons needed to return to its retail roots. With the aid of retail consultants, Thorntons undertook a review of its UK market and operations. The review concluded that there was still significant potential to increase the UK retail chain.

By October 1996 a further three-year plan had been developed that included the closure of 126 shops and the opening of 216, taking the total from 269 to 359 shops. There was to be an emphasis on developing larger and better prime location sites in such locations as malls, shopping centres and small market towns. Expansion was particularly targeted towards London and the south. The aim was to provide a 60% increase in total floor space by the year 2000, with annual sales per shop of £350,000 (as against £232,000 in 1996). Achieving these targets would require an ambitious programme of investment, averaging £17 million a year for three years. In addition, the product range would be developed to provide a wider range of products.

1998

One of a number of ways in which Thorntons' confectionery was distinctive concerned the freshness of the product; at the extreme a chocolate egg might reach the retail outlet within less than a week of manufacture. For other manufacturers, addressing the wider chocolate market, the inclusion of vegetable fat (other than cocoa butter) resulted in products with a shelf life of up to two years. Although Thorntons' own research indicated that freshness was not the first concern for consumers when purchasing a gift of chocolates, the company believed that it was essential to maintain the customer's experience of a fresh product. As a consequence many retail outlets, corner shops, garages and most of the supermarkets were not suitable for the product, even if the company wished to achieve sales through those outlets. For similar reasons, care had to be taken in selecting and controlling franchised outlets.

The quality of the product was ensured by Thorntons' use of quality ingredients (the champagne truffles contained Moët and Chandon champagne, for example) and through the manufacturing expertise the company had developed. All but a few products – such as solid chocolate bars, chocolate buttons, jelly beans and much of the ice cream – were made in house, a practice that also ensured the exclusivity of Thorntons' recipes. The retail outlets provided a good quality of service and offered the inclusion of personalised messages, written in icing, on such gifts as Valentine's Day chocolate hearts and the two million Easter eggs sold by the company each year. At extra cost, products could also be purchased gift wrapped.

The combination of providing a fresh product together with the need to meet a seasonal pattern of demand placed particular pressures on the company's manufacturing facilities. A proportion of the Christmas product could be produced up to six months in advance, maintaining freshness through chilled storage. Thorntons' chocolates were enrobed in chocolate, rather than moulded. Their handmade appearance made the labour-intensive process of packing boxed chocolates less open to automation than was the case for moulded chocolates (with their more uni-

form shape and size) produced by companies such as Cadbury. The seasonal demand for the labour-intensive task of packing required 700–800 casual workers, with consequent falls in efficiency. Seasonal demand also required the use of temporary staff in the retail outlets to meet a sales pattern that could move within a few days from weekly sales of £6000 to £60,000.

By 1998 Thorntons, the UK's only dedicated high-street retailer of confectionery, had come to see itself as a market-led, retail-driven business, selling into a market that could be defined in a number of ways. As a gift the boxed chocolates competed with a wide range of products in the £5–10 price range, provided by high-street specialist retailers such as Body Shop, Sock Shop and Wax Lyrical. The same market was also addressed by postal gifts such as flowers and wine. The company's Continental range of chocolate, the best-selling specialist chocolates in the UK, had no large direct competitors in the UK. However, to an extent, supermarkets, the Boots, Marks & Spencer and BhS retail chains and Woolworth, with its large range of confectionery, offered some competing products, including imported chocolates.

The company's advertising slogan ('Chocolate heaven since 1911') and shops had become a widely accepted part of UK retailing. In an independent market research survey consumers, asked to rank their typical high street, included Thorntons in fifth place. However, establishing and maintaining shops required a considerable commitment of resources. For a new shop the average cost of fitting out was £80,000–100,000. To account for wear and tear, the shop investment was written off over a four-year period.

Thorntons had markedly increased the rate and scope of product innovation, repackaging and relaunching the Classics range, adding Swiss and Austrian selections to the core Continental range and introducing an Awesome American range. In 1997, 27 new countlines had been introduced, providing a fivefold increase in the range available. The ice-cream range was expanded and a children's range introduced, with product themes including dinosaur eggs, fossils and dalmatian spots. In 1998 a further 132 new and updated products were introduced. Widening the product range to include a greater emphasis on countlines, acting as a snack or impulse buy, attracted a wider range of customers, but it also brought Thorntons into competition with the products of such companies as Nestlé and Cadbury. Overall, Thorntons' prices ranged from a £50 Easter egg or £30 boxed assortment (previously £20 represented the top of the range), through self-selected assortments, to 19p for a single, individually boxed chocolate.

Sales from the new ranges were over £5.5 million in

1998, but not all of the new products were to prove successful. Within the year 15 of the new products were discontinued due to their failing to reach an acceptable level of sales. In 1998 the company had begun a £3 million programme to install EPOS in the shops but, because of a lack of timely performance information, the loss from discontinued products was disproportionate.

In addition to developing products and packaging (packaging provided a large part of the products' perceived value), Thorntons had begun the introduction and evaluation of a series of distribution innovations with the aim of achieving a less seasonal sales pattern. Eleven Café Thorntons had been opened. Each café explored a different type of location and format providing for the sale of light refreshments, including chocolates, and confectionery sales. A mail order service had been introduced with a range of confectionery gifts, some combined with other items such as a bottle of champagne or a luxury Christmas pudding. Outlets were also being developed and evaluated at selected railway and airport locations. Some airlines were being supplied, mainly to gain prestige sales to first- and club-class passengers. Gaining access to overseas airports was seen as an important stepping stone into overseas markets, where sales had increased to £757,000.

Thorntons' existing channels of distribution were targeted for further expansion to increase the total of wholly owned shops to 507 by 2001, together with 200 franchised outlets. Some of the existing franchisees had come to be seen as inappropriate because they occupied a major or non-viable location. In addition, while some franchisees had been very committed, others operated units that had become rather run down. Thorntons' efforts were aimed at replicating the customer's experience of the company's own shops; to that end a new look and layout were trialled for the franchise outlets. Overall sales growth was aimed to increase by 15% a year.

During 1998 Thorntons' sales increased to £133 million, with sales in the company's own shops, including 100 new shops, growing to £105.9 million, on like-for-like growth of 9.6%. Sales to commercial customers had reached £17.4 million, the main customer remaining Marks & Spencer. However, profit growth, at 9%, fell short of the company's own target. Partly this was due to margin erosion as a result of renting costly external warehousing space ahead of the availability in 1999 of the company's new £14 million warehouse and the higher than expected discounting costs on the 15 underperforming new product lines.

The introduction of new products had achieved a number of beneficial effects, increasing the number of male customers, children and teenagers and lowering the overall age profile of the customers. Although 50% of turnover was still derived from 12–16 weeks of sales (for Christmas, Easter, Valentine's Day, Mother's Day and Father's Day) the new products had helped to reduce the extent of the variations in production. However, seasonal demand remained difficult to meet. During the Christmas 1998 period consumers had tended to delay their seasonal purchases; when demand finally occurred it ran ahead of the capacity of the shops. Tired of queuing, customers went elsewhere. Sales for the Christmas season were down

Exhibit 1   Thorntons Group financial information (£m)

	1986	1988	1990	1992	1994	1995	1996	1997	1998	
Sales	42.5	52.5	76.2	84.3	96.6	95.6	97.6	111.3	132.8	
Operating profit	5.3	6.9	10.0	10.4	12.6	10.1	5.8	11.3	12.9	
Profit after tax	2.8	4.8	7.9	6.3	7.8	6.7	(15.1)	8.6	9.0	
Fixed assets	18.5	27.3	49.0	52.3	51.0	50.4	45.1	52.1	86.2	
Net assets	17.4	32.6	39.1	48.0	47.3	50.1	33.3	38.4	44.8	
Number of UK outlets										(2001 target)
Own shops				243	263	269	300	344	507	
Franchised				189	150	129	202	151	200	
Number of employees										
Management & administration							209	188	206	
Management, admin. & distribution				474	489					
Selling & distribution							1526	1705	2123	
Sales					1401	1432				
Manufacturing					957	909	1187	1482	1755	
Total employees					2832	2830	2922	3375	4084	

UK per capita consumption of confectionery is one of the highest in the world. Within the UK market chocolate confectionery is viewed as an affordable treat, as part of snacking or a gift. In recent years increased consumer spending confidence has boosted demand for luxury chocolates, a trend shared with other products such as wine. The main UK confectionery manufacturers have responded rapidly to this trend by launching their own premium ranges. Premium chocolates generally have a continental image and are frequently imported from Belgium. The UK confectionery market is highly competitive with a great deal of product and packaging innovation. Manufacturers have tended to focus effort on the chocolate sector, with its higher margins. The sector has demonstrated strong value growth. New chocolate products include larger-size countlines and premium boxed chocolates.

UK confectionery sales (£m)

	Total	Chocolate	Sugar
1993	4415	3038	1377
1995	4643	3208	1435
1997	5109	3571	1538

Chocolate market: subsectors

	Value share 1997	Value growth 1993–97
Countlines	43.9%	22.2%
Moulded bars	16.9%	36.2%
Boxed chocolates	16.3%	(9.2%)
Seasonal products	12.2%	26.3%
Bagged self-lines	10.6%	16.9%

- **Countlines** Wrapped chocolate bars designed for one person to consume. Products include KitKat (Nestlé Rowntree), 16% of countline sales value, Mars Bar 12%. Advertising expenditure, 1996, KitKat £4 million, Mars Bar £1–2 million.

- **Moulded bars** Chocolate as slabs or segmented; the product can be separated to be shared.

- **Boxed chocolates** Sales declined by 2% in 1997 to £583 million; this decline is partly due to the increasing number of luxury products and gift goods within other subsectors of the chocolate market; for example some moulded bars have been turned into suitable gift goods as 1kg bars, combining novelty and value for money. Cadbury's Roses was the leading brand of boxed chocolates in 1997 with a 15% share of subsector sales. Thorntons

Continental had a 6% share, Ferrero Rocher 5%, Dairy Box (Nestlé Rowntree), 5%. Advertising expenditure, 1996, Cadbury's Roses £2–3 million, Ferrero Rocher £2–3 million.

- **Seasonal products** Grew by 7.9% in 1997 to £436 million, Easter chocolate accounted for 66% of the sales of seasonal chocolate, with Cadbury's having a 50% of the Easter market. In 1998 Woolworth stocked 153 different varieties of Easter egg, 79 of which were exclusive to its stores. Selection packs account for over half of Christmas chocolate sales. Increasingly manufacturers are linking with companies, such as Disney, to use film and cartoon characters to add appeal for younger consumers.

- **Bagged self-lines** Smaller chocolates sold in bags; examples include Smarties, M&M's, Mars Miniatures.

Chocolate confectionery: manufacturers

	Market share	
	1993	1997
Cadbury Schweppes	29%	28%
Nestlé Rowntree	25%	25%
Mars	22%	22%
Suchard/Philip Morris	4%	4%
Other manufacturers	20%	21%

Consumers: percentage of adults, 1997, regularly purchasing

	Chocolate bars	Chocolate slabs	Boxed chocolate
Male	51%	11%	5%
Female	53%	14%	7%
Age			
15–24	75%	10%	8%
25–34	60%	13%	7%
35–54	53%	15%	5%
55+	35%	12%	5%

Distribution

In 1997, 45% of chocolate confectionery sales were through multiple grocers (1993, 40%), CTNs 19% (1993, 22%), department stores 10% (1993, 12%), garage forecourts 8% (1993, 7%).

Despite the predominance of sales through multiple grocers brand sales accounted for 94.8% of chocolate confectionery sales in 1997. Price cutting is most apparent in the major multiples. The average retailer margin for chocolate confectionery is 25%, excluding VAT, with seasonal lines having higher margins.

Exhibit 2   The UK confectionery market

by 3.8% on a like-for-like basis, franchised sales fell 13.1% and commercial revenue 6.1%. The chief executive, Roger Paffard, said that he anticipated continuing rough trading conditions in 1999.

By the end of 1998 the group's manufacturing had been consolidated to two factories, Belper and Alfreton, with Belper producing toffee, fudge and nougat, all of the sugar confectionery, boiled sweets and the group's production of ice cream. Overall, Thorntons self-manufactured 70% of the product range. During 1997–99 the company planned to invest a further £35 million at Alfreton in manufacturing capacity and automation, consolidating packaging operations to the Alfreton site.

ITNET: Our mission – to be the best out-sourcing services company

The origins of ITNET

Through to the mid-1980s, Cadbury Schweppes plc had a Management Services Division to ensure cost-effective information technology (IT) services. In 1987 the division was transformed into a free-standing unit within Cadbury Schweppes, with the objective of developing external sales as well as continuing to meet the IT needs of the Cadbury Schweppes group. The unit showed its strength when, in 1989, it won a major contract with Birmingham City Council. This contract led to a doubling of ITNET's staff and reduced the proportion of its £20 million turnover derived from Cadbury Schweppes sources to under one-third.

However, the board of Cadbury Schweppes realised that the incumbent ITNET management team wasn't sufficiently commercially focused. In 1991 a new management team was put in place and this set a new strategy – to focus on IT out-sourcing. IT out-sourcing was a new and rapidly growing market in which (external) firms ran the IT operations that weren't core to an organisation's business. As Dr Claire Forrest, director of corporate marketing and planning, puts it:

It's running the basic applications, ensuring that the handle got turned every day. Organisations could get on with their real business knowing that their people would get paid, the factory lines would run and invoices would be taken care of.

Consistent with this focus on out-sourcing, ITNET disposed of its peripheral activities, including hardware maintenance, acting as an agent for AS400 computers, and software development. ITNET started with what it knew – a well-established mainframe business, but as during the 1990s there was also the need to manage PCs and client servers, it developed an expertise in this new area. Development tended to be on a trial-and-error basis – through supporting existing customers as they moved some of their activities away from the mainframe.

By 1992 turnover was £34 million, with substantial contracts with Hertfordshire County Council and CBM Packaging. ITNET had also developed software to assist Birmingham City Council exchange data with over 400 of its schools.

In 1992 ITNET was awarded BS5750 accreditation for customer delivery. In 1993 it was voted best out-sourcing supplier in *Computing* magazine's awards for excellence. New customers included Premier Brands, Express Foods, Lawnet, the City of Westminster Council and Brent Council.

By the end of 1994 the number of ITNET staff had grown to 830 and it was working from seven sites, providing out-sourcing services to around 30 companies across the UK. ITNET was again voted best out-sourcing supplier in the *Computing* awards for excellence, and it achieved ISO 9002 accreditation for one of its divisions. The Distributed Services Division was set up in 1994 as a direct result of the growth in distributed computing. The division supported over 6000 PCs and 170 local area networks (LANs). New customers included Camelot, Esso Petroleum, The Cheese Company and the London boroughs of Croydon and Bexley.

Most of ITNET's business involves three- to five-year contracts, so it knows when cash is coming in. The public sector tends to pay in advance, so ITNET has a very secure cash flow but pays for this somewhat through narrow margins of around 7–8% return on sales, about the average for this industry sector. ITNET doesn't sell technology; it's a service organisation focusing on costs.

The management and employee buyout

In 1995 Cadbury Schweppes no longer saw ITNET as a core business and decided it wanted to sell. It had received offers for ITNET and thus had a good estimate of its value. The management team immediately wanted to bid via a management and employee buyout. ITNET's management team negotiated a three-month protected period, during which Cadbury Schweppes wouldn't accept any outside bids and the team could put together a bid. The team brought in the venture capital company 3i to provide cash and give strategic support as it had considerable experience in buyouts. The Bank of Scotland provided traditional bank support with additional funding. The price/earnings ratios in the IT sector at the time were around 17 and the price paid to Cadbury Schweppes was £32.5 million; 50.1% of the shares were owned by management and staff, 37.4% by 3i and 12.5% by Cadbury Schweppes. The board comprised the executive directors and three non-executive directors, one each from Cadbury Schweppes, 3i and the Bank of Scotland.

This case was prepared by Grahame Boocock and Paul N. Finlay. © Grahame Boocock and Paul N. Finlay 1999.

3i played an important part in the post-buyout phase. It understood planning, and it acted as a sounding board and guide, although it wasn't involved in the operational side. 3i and the bank had to approve the financing arrangements for new big contracts. The bank was taking a banking risk and required ITNET to satisfy three covenants every quarter, involving its cash position, the value of the business and the relation between debtors and borrowers. The new finance director who came in at the time of the buyout arranged for these to be measured on a daily basis, with a focus on the debtor position. At the buyout, debtor time was around 77 days and this has been reduced to 32–33 days – a considerable boost to cash flow.

Of the 50.1% of shares owned by directors and other staff, 25.1% was owned by the directors, who had to put in cash of their own. The other 25% was put in an employee trust, and shares were made available to employees through their distribution in lieu of bonus over a three-year period for those employees who opted to join the share scheme – and 75% did. The reason for this was that the directors didn't want people to own shares by dint of having more money than anyone else. To give equal access to share ownership, the award of shares was related to the performance appraisal process.

Consolidation

The shares, which weren't traded externally, were valued by Price Waterhouse once a year based on ITNET's assets and contracts. Every year there was an internal trading period when employees who wanted to sell their shares and those who had left ITNET, who had to sell their shares, could do so, and new people could buy shares. The demand for shares exceeded their supply. Originally it was planned that in three years time the ownership would be reviewed – a trade sale or a flotation was mooted – so everyone knew there was an end date to this particular distribution of shares. Staff who joined in the first year saw their shares growing (internally). Shares were issued at 19p, the subsequent year they were at 228p, and the following year they were at 409p and, not unnaturally, this created a very positive attitude to share ownership and owning the company.

ITNET had to be very careful around the time of the buyout to ensure that customers were confident that the company would be stable and the staff would stay. ITNET reaffirmed its commitment to continuous improvement with a substantial investment in a new customer service centre and in Enterprise Management – software to manage its services across multiple users. ITNET attained the Investors in People accreditation. Local sponsorship of Industry Links with Education saw ITNET and a local school working together on a variety of projects; for example, designing Internet home pages, providing advisers to a young enterprise company and distributing software via an electronic bulletin board. New customers included BAA, BASF, Signet Group, English Heritage, Colchester Borough Council and the London Borough of Wandsworth.

By 1996 ITNET was employing 1200 people on 12 sites throughout the UK. The fastest-growing area was desktop management, with ITNET supporting and managing over 20,000 PCs. ITNET managing director Bridget Blow won the NatWest Midlands Businesswoman of the Year award. In 1997 ITNET won the first UK Arthur Andersen Award for Best Practice in Motivating and Retaining Employees. New clients included Merck, Argos and Savacentre, the RAC, Forte Hotels, BA Pensions, Glaxo Wellcome and the London Borough of Sutton. ITNET set up a customer service centre, which was the consolidation of 19 help desks around the company – involving lots of training and new technology.

Strategically, ITNET knew it wasn't growing as quickly as its competitors. IBM, CSC and EDS had taken the high ground and were servicing the multinationals. ITNET competed with the mid-sized players, who focused on national markets: Cap Gemini, Sema and a subsidiary of ICL. Claire explains:

We were finding that we were constrained in the size of the contracts we could get. We were a £60 million turnover company and if we went for a £10 million contract the client would see this as a very large proportion of our turnover, and would prefer to give the contract to a £150 million turnover company. So size was a constraint on growth. We won a BAA contract to look after their mainframe systems for £2 million and this was OK, as it was well within ITNET capability. In 1997 we bid to take over the IT for Ernst & Young – a £12 million contract – and we got down to the last two in the bidding. When the proposal went to the Ernst & Young partners they gave the contract to Sema, because they believed that it was too big for us. At that time the contracts were getting more complex; in the £12 million contract you would have a complete range of technologies, you wouldn't just have a set of things that logically sat together, we would be supporting all their offices throughout the UK, their help desks, their mobile phone users, the whole of a complex environment to take over. Turnover is a surrogate for complexity – but it's also a surrogate for financial stability. A lot of customers ask to see your top ten list of clients and to see where they stand in relation to the others, arguing that if you lost a big customer you would have a problem.

Conversely, we've picked up customers on renewal, from clients who think that their supplier has got too big and isn't now giving them the attention they should. It's a matching thing. For example, Iron Trades, a medium-sized insurance company, used IBM and IBM grew massively in this time. On renewal, the company turned to ITNET. They asked what number customer they would be in our list: we wrote back and said number 12 and that reassured them.

The worry for ITNET was that if it stayed the same size it would get squeezed between the big players and the specialist firms that only work in one area. For example, FI is a specialist in managing applications and it does not become involved with data centres, help desks, etc.: if an applications-only contract came up it would tend to win it. ITNET considers itself to be a specialist out-sourcing company and feels that it must be able to support all the technologies it is asked to by its clients.

The flotation

After the buyout the company had approaches on a regular basis for a trade sale. Rumours in the market that other companies were interested in ITNET was very unsettling for customers who had signed long-term contracts. ITNET had said that in the three-year post-buyout period it would review the ownership of the company, and conditions were then right for a stock market flotation. The company had reached the point where it needed to clear debt off the balance sheet in order to fund growth. ITNET was growing at 18–20%, which was good but wasn't at the same rate as its competitors, which were growing at 40% and 50% a year, largely through acquisitions. ITNET's organic growth was comparable, but the competitors were growing through acquisition as well. Debt was holding ITNET back, and a policy of funding acquisitions through issuing further debt didn't look sensible. The buyout financing structure prevented ITNET moving quickly enough. It had had a look at acquisition targets but, before it could react, competitors had moved in and made an offer.

In 1998 ITNET became a listed company. The flotation price on the London Stock Exchange was £3.50 per share, valuing the company at £245 million. The float was timed perfectly and was very successful. The p/e ratio for similar stocks was around 50. The City liked the £240 million long-term order book.[a] Also, IT stocks had become mainstream and pension funds were putting IT stocks in their portfolio, which they hadn't been doing before. There was a shortage of stocks, and the majority of IT companies aren't large. Part of the reason for the flotation was to

enable ITNET to finance the continuing expansion of its businesses and fund any suitable acquisitions. Another motivation was be able to continue to incentivise employees. ITNET wanted to continue with its share ownership culture, and it had issued all its shares. With the number of staff growing rapidly there was a danger of a two-tier culture developing – those with a shareholding and those without.

ITNET believes that going public has improved its profile substantially and allowed it to bid successfully for larger contracts. Recently it won a £60 million contract with a London borough and won its largest ever commercial contract with London Transport, worth £25 million over five years.

Post-flotation

The turnover and pre-tax profit figures in the years since its foundation are shown in Exhibit 1.

Since the flotation the staff have learned that share price isn't always determined by performance. ITNET's share price has moved up and down, irrespective of what it has been doing. ITNET floated at 350p, and its shares have been up as high as 519p. From February to June 1999 its shares came down steadily to 336p, and within a week they shot up to 390p for no obvious reason.

One of the reasons for the flotation was to permit ITNET to move quickly to acquire. In 1999 it acquired a small, highly technical and innovative company in Coventry called Technosys. Technosys is a Microsoft/ e-commerce consultancy with 80 staff and a £6 million turnover with Internet and e-commerce skills that ITNET doesn't possess, but no out-sourcing capability. ITNET wanted to buy and Technosys wanted to sell as it was having difficulty getting large contracts. Customers weren't happy giving contracts of mission-critical systems to a small company. ITNET intends to keep this company and ITNET separate, with ITNET selling Technosys into its customer base to increase its sales from existing accounts but also to help retain control of the account and prevent competitors gaining a foothold.

ITNET wants to work in Europe but doesn't bid for continental work at the moment. The way it intends to enter continental Europe is through its present client base – following its customers there. ITNET is helping Cadbury Schweppes to implement Enterprise Resources Planning[b] across Europe and has already implemented it in Russia and Poland, supported from the UK.

---

[a] In mid-1999 it was £320 million.

[b] Enterprise Resources Planning is an umbrella term for integrated business software that provides an organisation-wide information structure integrating management functions across geographical sites.

	1989	1990	1991	1992	1993	1994	1995	1996	1997	1998
Turnover	20	27	30	24	44	50	59	69	82	106
Pre-tax profit	–	–	–	2.6	3.1	3.8	4.4	5.5	6.3	7.6
Turnover from Cadbury Schweppes (%)	100	95	90	50	40	25	16	12	10	6

Exhibit 1   Turnover and pre-tax profit (all figures £m)

LawNet is a consortium of over 80 independent solicitors' practices working from nearly 200 offices spread throughout England, Wales , Scotland, Northern Ireland and the Channel Islands. LawNet provides services and advice to member solicitors and gives them the opportunity to share their experiences. To facilitate essential communications between members, LawNet needed a nationwide information network.

LawNet Chose ITNET, a leading IT services provider, to plan, design and implement a UK wide Lotus Notes network and associated applications. ITNET's solution allowed existing documents to be scanned in and word-processed documents from other systems to be integrated into a database. ITNET performed a number of roles, including hardware specification and supply, testing and integration and writing bespoke systems for LawNet. It has also provided training for staff using the system.

This network now enables member solicitors to access information databases of legal precedents, reports and case studies from anywhere in the country through their own desktop or portable PC. Business information of all types can be shared, including text, financial data, graphics, images and even sound and video. LawNet's member solicitors, working in different practices, can exchange information with each other, their clients, major institutions, information providers and other contacts such as barristers. Members can also share and exchange information with one another on specialist fields of interest, or exchange briefs with regularly used chambers.

Roger Herbert, managing director of LawNet, commented: 'Lotus Notes provides the ideal environment for our members to share information and using ITNET's technical expertise and business knowledge has provided us with the most efficient and cost-effective solution.'

Source: **Extract from ITNET case study in Groupware Technology.**

Exhibit 2   Groupware technology and LawNet

The markets

The IT software and services market in the UK is worth around £16 billion annually.[c] ITNET operates in the out-sourcing subsector, which is worth about £4 billion. The Computing Software and Services Association lists around 90 out-sourcing companies operating in the UK. The top ten companies take 80% of the market. ITNET is ninth in the list, and only ITNET and one other company are British.

Initially ITNET restricted itself almost completely to IT out-sourcing, which involves the running of all or part of the IT functions of another organisation. Very significantly with IT out-sourcing, the organisation's employees cease being on the organisation's payroll and become staff of the firm offering the out-sourcing service. The Birmingham City Council contract that ITNET won in 1989 meant that 200 staff were transferred from the city payroll and became ITNET employees. Thus IT out-sourcing poses the challenge of changing the culture of the out-sourced employees to that of ITNET.

In the early 1990s IT out-sourcing was often a reaction by finance directors to the poor service and high costs they saw as associated with their IT department. However, during the last three or four years things have changed, with IT directors now owning the out-sourcing agenda. They realise that their departments can't do everything for their companies and tend to concentrate on the strategically interesting bits, allowing another firm to run the day-to-day operations and the transition into the new technologies: for example, from mainframes to PCs and client servers.

ITNET followed this transition from mainframes and then moved to undertake other types of work: for example, networking, as Exhibit 2 illustrates, and latterly into Internet developments and enterprise resource planning. These can result in large change contracts as companies change processes to take advantage of the new technologies. This sort of work is being undertaken by the big systems integrations companies like Logica and Admiral, which specialise in implementation but don't normally undertake on-going operation and management. This means ITNET is now meeting new competitors that have not traditionally undertaken out-sourcing work.

A new development area is business process out-sourcing, whereby not only the IT is out-sourced but also the administration it's supporting, and thus IT is a smaller part of the whole. An example is given in Exhibit 3.

---

[c] The figure in 1998 from Holway Ltd.

When an organisation spends £10 million each month on wages and salaries, entailing production of 200,000 payslips annually for more than 11,000 full- and part-time staff, administering the payroll has to be taken seriously. The London Borough of Bexley, for which payroll management meant employing 19 dedicated staff, understood the situation better than most: 'Being paid the right amount on time is something most people take for granted – unless something goes wrong,' said Bexley's paymaster, Peter Nash.

Whilst the importance of payroll management was always clear to the council, it was equally clear that payroll was a 'non-core' activity, which did not contribute directly to the provision of local services. Bexley's payroll had been streamlined during recent years, with staff numbers reduced through natural wastage and many procedures simplified. Much time had been invested in an internal refocusing with a reinforced emphasis on service quality. 'We had excellent people, working efficiently to provide a good service,' says Nash.

Because of the government's timetable for compulsory competitive tendering (CCT), the council knew that it would eventually need to re-examine the way in which a number of financial functions, including payroll, were managed. 'The Council decided to take the voluntary route, rather than wait for CCT to happen,' says Peter Nash. 'It gave greater flexibility, with more time to examine the alternatives in depth.' The council also decided not to submit an internal bid for the payroll business.

Having made the decision to out-source, the council received a number of replies to its advertised invitation to tender. It then drew up a shortlist of six potential out-sourcing suppliers for closer analysis. At this point, the project team, headed by the council's assistant financial controller David Bunker, tested the options against the strict criteria that had already been established. A major council consideration was its staff; it was particularly concerned that an out-sourcing company could demonstrate a good history with regard to staff relations. The selection process avoided the traditional 'beauty parade' of brief presentations by out-sourcing companies followed by a direct staff vote. Instead, Peter Nash and his senior staff met each of the short-listed companies for detailed discussions. Meanwhile, regular briefings solicited the opinions and questions of Bexley's other payroll personnel and kept them informed of progress. Equally high on the task force agenda was the question of service quality. Having worked hard to achieve high standards internally, the council was not prepared to compromise them in an out-sourcing agreement. It was, therefore, particularly important that a prospective partner could show a successful track record, not just in out-sourcing generally but also in payroll administration specifically. ITNET, for example, had been succesfully administering payroll for local government organisations for many years.

And, of course, there was the question of cost. However attractive a proposition might be in all other areas, the council still had to maximise value for money. As quotes arrived, it was soon clear that this would not be a problem. 'Out-sourcing the payroll services to another organisation makes excellent financial sense: over the next five-year term we'll make savings of £250,000,' commented Christopher Duffield, executive and director of finance at the London Borough of Bexley. 'Naturally, this wasn't our only consideration. We sought a company that would provide a high-quality service and place a lot of importance in other areas, such as staff relations.'

By September 1994, ITNET had been chosen as the preferred supplier. The company's excellent reputation for the service quality and personnel relations had preceded it and had been borne out by the council's thorough examination of the facts. Just as important, from Bexley's viewpoint, was that ITNET offered the most economically advantageous solution. Of the council's 19 payroll administration personnel, 17 had transferred to ITNET under TUPE* regulations and relocated to newly refurbished premises by the time the contract began in January 1995. The remaining two stayed with Bexley, with new responsibilities primarily involved in monitoring service quality. The council was pleased to have its payroll managed at a lower cost with no loss of service quality, but how have the transferred staff reacted to the change?

Peter Nash, now ITNET's site manager with responsibility for Bexley's payroll, has no doubts about what the transfer has meant:

Following the initial, brief feelings of strangeness that come with a move into the private sector, the new methodologies make obvious sense. There is more internal monitoring, adding a little to the administration load, but it is appreciated for the undoubted improvements it has already brought to our cost efficiency. We are already delivering the same quality of service at a lower cost and are working on the longer-term aim of raising value still further.

The new ethos of empowerment is also very welcome; the whole environment is now team-driven, with many former management responsibilities devolved to team leaders. As for the service itself, there was only limited room for growth while we remained an internal department. As part of the ITNET, the business grew, through further out-sourcing contracts, within the first six months, creating new opportunities for individual career progression.

Payroll consultant Mandy Vennard, previously a senior pay officer, agrees:

We expected growth, but not quite so soon. What's also impressive is ITNET's human resources expertise and focus. As one example, training is on the basis of individual need, not set rules and regulations. If one of us needs particular training, ITNET ensures that it is provided, whether internally or via training specialists. This applies at every level – and ITNET's flatter structure means that there are fewer levels than in local government. There is also much more variety and scope.

Moving from pay clerk to ITNET payroll administrator, Andrew Lemon confirms the greater variety for individuals. His responsibilities have broadened to include being the site's health and safety representative. 'Overall the work is much the same, of course, because we are still managing Bexley's payroll,' he adds. 'But, moving to ITNET has definitely brought positive changes. We are working for customers now, rather than colleagues, and there seems to be more pride in doing a good job.'

In out-sourcing payroll management to ITNET, Bexley has achieved its aims, with lower costs, maintained levels of service quality and undoubted benefits for its former employees. Perhaps the last word should be given to the transferred staff. Andrew Lemon sums it up in this way: 'Looking back, we were all a bit apprehensive about how out-sourcing might work. Working for ITNET, it is clear that this was the only way to go.'

Source: **Extract from ITNET case study in Payroll Management.**
* TUPE stands for transfer of undertakings and protection of employment. This is an EU regulation designed to protect staff at transfer.

Exhibit 3 Payroll management and Bexley Borough Council

Claire explains ITNET's repositioning in response to this out-sourcing movement:

We had to develop expertise in business process management. At the moment this is focused purely on local government authorities because they're the ones coming forward with contracts. For example, ITNET goes in and takes over not just the IT payroll but also payroll administration, which for local government is complex with many intricate pay scales and terms and conditions – teachers, groundsmen, cleaners etc. We do all the liaison with BACS,[d] if there's a problem we talk to the employee, we change the tax codes and so on. All the payroll staff come on to the ITNET payroll and these contracts are more 'people' based than IT contracts.

Claire muses on political developments:

I thought that there would be a political shift after 1997 with less work going out to tender. But in fact more of the London boroughs have come out to tender after Labour told them it was now politically correct. Now it's not compulsory to out-source they're all out-sourcing. Sheffield has let the biggest out-sourcing contract in the whole market. Recently we took on a contract with the London Borough of Hackney to collect their council tax community charge and administer their housing benefit payment and 240 people transferred to ITNET.

With these developments ITNET isn't ignoring its main *raison d'être* – to run IT operations effectively. It has five revenue and benefits contracts with different London boroughs. Each borough will have the same technology, the same software platform and the same call centre arrangements. ITNET's strategic aim is to build large processing centres. It won't then need all the people that are currently employed and should be able to reduce transaction costs significantly by reducing headcount.

Competition in business process management is coming from several quarters. There is some element of globalisation, where a global company wants a global IT out-sourcing supplier, but this isn't a strong trend. There are the Big Five consulting firms which are particularly strong in finance administration; for example, Andersen's do all the financial administration for BP, Conoco and other oil companies, and Ernst & Young and Shell have established a joint venture. Capita, a competitor of ITNET, has followed a different strategy to ITNET, with less emphasis on IT and a focus on a few business processes, whereas ITNET looks to service business processes that have a high IT content.

Another set of competitors is developing among firms that traditionally haven't possessed any superior IT skills but have offered other specialist services. For example, Hays is a large company involved in distribution and logistics that is now offering to undertake the IT that supports these services. It has bought a small IT out-sourcing company to augment its skills.

The ITNET organisation

ITNET has split its sales and marketing into two sectors – public sector and commercial, with about 30 people in each. Behind them there are three operating divisions that are the 'factories for deliverables':

- applications management involving enhancement, managing, installing and changing applications and project managing. An example of an application management contract is that with the RAC, running their membership systems.
- infrastructure management operating and managing the mainframe, midrange and desktop computers and other infrastructure needed for IT operations.
- business processes management undertaking to run the whole of a business process including the IT component. For example, payroll administration, and revenues and benefits administration.

The main interface to customers is via a highly developed customer service centre, employing 90 staff who handle around 2000 calls a day.

Getting work

ITNET does not advertise, instead relying completely on direct marketing, and so it has to identify its markets and the targets within them. In local government ITNET will have 30 clients that it focuses on at any one time. ITNET directs its attentions to many people in a target authority at the appropriate time (when a contract is about to be renewed, for instance). The sort of people targeted would be the senior managers in the central IT department, the human resources department, the functional departmental heads who might be looking for lower costs and better service, the chief finance officer, and the chief executive. ITNET is now well known and asked to bid for contracts.

In the commercial sector, there are around 3000 organisations that are being pursued at any point in time. Direct mail, telephone sales and seminars are used in the marketing approach. On the new business side, what ITNET tries to do is to create a relationship with a customer before it prepares a tender. ITNET has found that once it goes to the formal process and a relationship hasn't been built beforehand, then the chance of getting the contract is small. Out-sourcing is an enormous decision – with the

---

[d] Bank Automatic Clearing System.

organisation's people, IT infrastructure and software being transferred to the out-sourcer and the new arrangements can't be trialled beforehand.

ITNET undertakes little market research. Since ITNET takes on long-term service contracts, the accounts teams have the aim to sell more services to present clients: ITNET works through its present customers. For example, a number of its commercial customers are moving to the enterprise resources planning software SAP.[e] SAP tends to be implemented by the Big Six consultancies, and it's difficult for ITNET to enter this market. But in order not to lose these customers ITNET has recognised that it should concentrate on managing the on-going support and development. So it has set up an SAP business unit, is recruiting staff experienced with SAP and is now bidding that service to other clients. SAP activity will provide £4 million of turnover in 1999. ITNET is supporting SAP in its existing customers Trebor Bassett Ltd and Cadbury Ltd and has recently taken on Forte as a new customer. Claire puts the response of ITNET this way:

ITNET must be good at recognising when to shift gear. When both the market people and the techies are saying it's a good thing to support SAP then response is very rapid – we set up the unit in one month, pulling together a fragmented team of SAP technicians, sales and product managers.

The process of bidding

Public sector work is advertised in the *European Journal*. An authority placing an advert could get 50–60 'requests for information', some of which could be from continental Europe. The requests for information ask for a short document from bidders saying why they are fit to bid. From this number the authority would select six or seven to make a bid, and following the bid would probably select two to negotiate with. The final decision isn't always made on price, although in the public sector the winning bid must be close to the lowest-priced bid. Largely the decision is a culture-based decision, with questions such as: can we work with these people for the next five years? Is the culture match good? Are these people flexible enough? Flexibility is significant; in the London Transport contract public–private partnerships will be set up in the near future and the contract will demand that eventually ITNET will be working with five partners. So ITNET will be moving the contract forward without renegotiating it.

One of the criteria for success is how clearly the bidder has articulated what exactly the organisation is going to get. The bidder also has to demonstrate its methodology – how the outputs will be achieved. Competitors who come into the market have to make several bids before they are successful, because they have to learn how to bid. When ITNET started to bid for revenues and benefits administration work it lost the first four bids; it wasn't worried because it knew that it had to learn. ITNET would expect to earn double the revenue from the contracted amount in a contract with commercial clients because of the extra functionality that will subsequently be asked for.

ITNET only bids for around 20 contracts each year and is winning six to eight of these. This high win rate indicates that ITNET's process is very effective, reflecting the time and effort that it puts into building up relationships. ITNET has a policy of never taking on a loss leader – if a contact won't make the right margins then the company will walk away.

After every bid, win or lose, a full debrief is undertaken. An independent person from one of the marketing departments will meet the client and discuss where ITNET was in terms of price and where it stood on the other criteria compared with its competitors. For example, did the winner perhaps show a greater strength in depth in an important area than ITNET could demonstrate? ITNET also finds out what the factors were that gave it competitive advantage when it has won.

ITNET's 'Take On and Bid Guide' is a living document in that it's updated as more learning comes about and it's very well protected. It's on a server, but people wanting to see it have to go to the person who owns the take on and bid process and ask for a copy. Also ITNET has a competitive database with all the contracts that have been let since 1991, which again is very well protected, and if anyone wants information from it they must go to the process owner.

Every bidder must exercise due diligence in the bidding process. In due diligence the bidder checks that what has been said by the organisation is true: for example, has the organisation got the number of workstations that it says it has? Are the skills of its people as stated? Is the stated software on the computers? How many help desk queries are there per week?[f] Sometimes bidders can carry out due diligence examinations before putting in their bid, sometimes the facility is only available after winning the contract subject to due diligence. Sometimes due diligence has to be completed within two weeks and so if it's a big contract half a dozen people work on the job.

ITNET estimates that a bid costs £50,000 on average.

---

[e] SAP is the Enterprise Resources Planning (ERP) software sold by SAP, the world leader in ERP with a 17% market share.

[f] When ITNET takes over a help desk the number of calls rockets initially, largely because people can now get through. ITNET anticipates a 30% increase is calls.

Implementation

Claire emphasises the role of innovation:

Innovation isn't a key skill in our day-to-day operations but pro-actively seeking continuous improvement is: Could we cut this out? Can we do this in two days or less? Clients now take better and cheaper services with outsourcing as a given. They now want you to tell them how you will help them to develop their IT to suit the way their business is changing. For example, they say we're going to develop an Internet service in this way and we want you to support it. They don't ask us what they should be doing, just how to do what they want.

When ITNET first takes over a contract, the operation goes from being an in-house department dependent on people to becoming a service that delivers an agreed set of outputs, irrespective of who does it. So ITNET first consolidates by putting in procedures to support the processes, and then gets the people to change to a service orientation. Claire sums up the position as follows:

Customers start by asking 'Will Joe Bloggs be doing this' and we need to change that to 'Is my report going to be here on Friday?' We need to change people from being concerned with the process to being concerned with the outputs of the process. A major challenge with IT and business process management is to spread the ITNET way of doing things and the ITNET culture to the new sites, which can be a long way from ITNET head office and still located within the customer organisation.

When ITNET takes over a contract it spends a lot of time supporting the new staff. At first they are very much site-oriented but over time they become integrated into ITNET. One of the advantages for staff is that they aren't restricted to one little IT department – they can go on to work as an IT specialist in other parts of the country. The ex-City of Birmingham Council employees are now working all over the country with ITNET.

ITNET has never lost a major contract so far and has gained contracts from its competitors. If a contract is lost, staff that have worked on that contract for some time would get transferred. For example, IT staff who worked for English Heritage were transferred to ICL when it won the initial contract, and then transferred to ITNET when it won the contract at renewal. Some of the people ITNET inherited might be ICL people and some originally English Heritage employees. When an out-sourcing contract is about to be put out or renewed, the star performers tend to be taken off the dedicated areas and absorbed into the main part of the organisation. Thus ITNET sometimes inherits people that the organisation might have had diffi-culty transferring elsewhere. Some people find life with ITNET very liberating and succeed, whilst other don't like the culture and leave. Some don't come up to ITNET standards, so ITNET needs to be very good at easing them out of the company. Many government organisations find this difficult and carry weak performers, but ITNET can't afford to. All ITNET's performance and pay systems are linked to performance: if someone isn't performing they don't get a pay rise of any sort. ITNET does make some redundancies, for example, if it consolidates hardware into the central data centres.

All contracts will have some support provided. The first point of call is the ITNET call centre, which is manned by 80 people, who are split into customer groups, and the call-handling service will channel the query to the appropriate best person available. If it's a very large contract, there will be a local support team on site. For smaller contracts then someone from the ITNET pool will go to the site to sort things out.

Strategic planning and thinking

The executive members of the board have worked together since 1992. They are a very cohesive unit operating a very open environment – there are very lively debates. The two sector directors and three operational directors are very involved. The CEO seeks consensus but only up to a point. The finance director does the sanity check on the market sector proposals. He has a spreadsheet financial model that works out the consequences of decisions down to earnings per share, although the model isn't used interactively in meetings. One day planning sessions are booked at the beginning of the year. One particular meeting agreed the top-down goals for the coming year's planning cycle with the finance director checking that they would give the earnings/share profile that ITNET requires. ITNET has a meeting set up with the marketing managers for later in the year when, for the first time, a set of computer-based modelling tools will be used; these include Ansoff's Matrix the Boston Consulting Group matrix and the Directional Policy matrix. This is from a company that uses the models – not a vendor of the package.

In its strategic planning ITNET undertakes a formal analysis of competitors and highlights the important market trends, analysing how the product managers are developing their products. The analysis is down to the level of revenue by major product area (for example, desktop management and SAP). Claire has identified strategic issues and options over the next three years, e.g. that ITNET must reduce its dependence on mainframe activity, it must be in a position to support SAP, and how to replace revenue streams that are declining such as supporting bespoke legacy applications. ITNET only considers scenarios in the sense that it looks at the sensitivities in the plan. ITNET does 'what if?' analysis rather than rigorously developing scenarios. No formal forecasting tools are used.

New product areas are popping up in the company. ITNET has a monthly development executive meeting where the management team look at projects (ITNET also has a monthly operational meeting), new organisational structures, problems, etc. Anyone can present their ideas at this meeting. Generally, they would have discussed their proposal with Claire and/or the business development manager and would have worked with the individual to build a case for the initiative and positioned it within ITNET's strategy. One recent presentation was from someone who had an idea about a product for the Internet, which the board agreed to give space and time to nurture.

The ITNET culture is strong, with one important plank being the single status of all employees.[g] Reward packages (salary and the quality of company car) are related to market worth. There are no special car parking spaces for senior staff. Directors have offices but are often in the open plan area. The culture pushes responsibility down the organisation, with the aim of allowing the people who are close to the customers to make the decisions that relate to them. The culture may be described as a 'blame-free culture' where it's acceptable to get things wrong as long as you learn from your mistakes, reflecting on what happened and realising why it happened. The management style is based on enpowerment supported by coaching (e.g. individuals are encouraged to take ownership of projects with their manager's help). ITNET was chosen by the Industry Society as a case study for its new liberating leadership video and course. The CEO goes to every site every year, talks to small groups and gets very direct questions posed to her.

ITNET doesn't have a code of ethics but it does have a mission statement, which is produced as Exhibit 4, and a set of labels and behaviours to describe the way thing should be done.

Claire describes how the mission statement is used.

We have a set of labels setting out how we'd like customers to describe us. And a set of behaviours. They are posted on the walls. 'Service with integrity' is one of the labels. The mission is widely known mainly because people are appraised not only against objectives but also against how they have been achieved – against the behaviours. If you've upset a customer, not followed important company procedures, or not worked as a team member you won't get a bonus.

Making decisions quickly is important and is encouraged. For example, if someone in reception thinks that something needs doing for customers, then they will do it. Management training emphasises that managers should act as they want others to act: for example, if they don't pick up the phone within three rings they can't expect their staff to do so.

Employees have become more demanding about their careers. On the technical side they expect to be moving and developing skills, and ITNET encourages them to build their CVs – for internal purposes! ITNET will support any skill that is useful to the company; for example, it supports marketing people getting their Institute of Marketing qualifications. All the large sites have a learning centre with computer-based training, and people who buy books put them in the library and then get the cost reimbursed. The continuous improvement mentality leads to continuous learning and always trying to learn from mistakes. ITNET constantly looks at the performance figures: for example, how many failures in the network occurred last month and what are those responsible going to do about it. Customer surveys are carried out every month as standard. From time to time ITNET does a higher-level customer survey, asking what it is like to be an ITNET customer overall.

E-mail is Lotus Notes-based, and many projects have Lotus Notes databases. ITNET is currently piloting its own intranet. The Internet is used as a marketing and recruitment tool. Initially ITNET was finding it difficult to recruit the 30 people a month it needed in addition to the people who joined through the contracts. It assessed its recruitment procedures from end to end and set up a dedicated recruitment centre. Having a very slick process made sure that candidates got an offer really quickly, and organisational recruitment is now successful with a 10:9 offer to acceptance ratio.

ITNET has well-defined objectives for customer satisfaction and retention goals, although it doesn't use a balanced scorecard.

There is more on ITNET at the company's website, http://www.itnet.co.uk.

---

[g] Except for the legal requirement to have directors.

Our mission statement

Too many organisations are guilty of setting 'empty' or 'unrealistic' mission statements. ITNET's mission is customer-focused, quality-driven, challenging but above all realistic, measurable and achievable. Within the organisation, staff have demonstrated their commitment to the company mission by identifing service standards against which they wish their customer performance to be measured.

The mission:
'To be the best out-sourcing services company'

What our definition of 'best' is based upon:

QUALITY CUSTOMER SERVICE
Delivering what was agreed with the customer
Getting it right first time
Setting industry-leading customer satisfaction standards
Always looking for opportunities to impress the customer

FINANCIAL PERFORMANCE
Exceeding shareholders' expectations
Ranked as a successful performer in our industry

EMPLOYEES
Having employees who are customer-focused, demanding, pro-active, flexible and team-oriented
Earning the means to reward top-performing staff in the top 25% of our industry

REPUTATION
Enjoying a distinctive reputation for service with integrity
Being rated as one of the best employers in the industry

Total customer satisfaction

ITNET is committed to total customer satisfaction. This is fundamental in helping to deliver the mission.

Satisfied customers almost always come back. They will motivate others through word of mouth. On the other hand, dissatisfied customers will tell someone else about their unhappy experience. This will cause us not only to lose them, but also to lose other potential customers.

Research statistics show that for every individual who complains, 24 others do not. Moreover, research has found that every dissatisfied customer will tell 20 to 30 other people over a period of time.

At ITNET, we must constantly strive to improve our customer service. We believe there is no measure of the quality of work other than the customer perception.

People values/behaviours

'Best' means being an industry leader in customer satisfaction, financial performance, employee satisfaction and market reputation. In achieving this mission, ITNET places a very high value on consistent quality, customer service and high performance and expects every member of staff to have a personal vision of what these values mean.

As a result, we expect to see certain key behaviours adopted throughout the company. It is our vision that:

Customer focus		Rating
Understands customer needs	Clearly understands who his/her customers are, both internal and external. Vividly understands customer expectations and the required deliverables. Understands the impact of ITNET's service on the customer. Understands the key issues in the customer's business. Treats the customer with respect.	
Strives to inprove performance	Pro-actively improves the quality of the service to assist the customer's business and add commercial value to ITNET's business. Identifies suggestions to reduce customer's costs, increase the customer's revenue and improve the customer's service.	
Adds value	Takes opportunities to surprise the customer pleasantly.	
	TOTAL CUSTOMER FOCUS RATING	

Culture		Rating
Works to high quality standards	Has pace and a sense of urgency. Takes pride in own and company services. Intolerant of poor quality. Is keen to succeed and will persevere to see things through. Imposes standards of excellence on self rather than having standards imposed by others.	
Accepts responsibility	Delivers what was promised. Does not promise what cannot be delivered. Owns own career.	

Exhibit 4   Section 2 – our culture

	Identifies and addresses own training and development needs. Accepts own accountabilities.
Good communication skills	Demonstrates excellent communication skills
Works effectively as a team member	Keeps other team members informed of progress/issues. Understands the effect of his/her behaviour on others. Has respect for the other members of the team. Understands the needs of others. Jumps into the same ship as colleagues when appropriate.
Adopts a pro-active approach	Takes action to achieve goals beyond what is called for. Is flexible, demonstrates a 'can do' attitude and wants to learn. Will question traditional assumptions. Helps to turn mistakes into development opportunities. Does not wait for 'others' to do something.
Is change-oriented	Takes an optimistic approach and will bounce back from setbacks. Difficult to upset, takes things in stride and maintains a sense of perspective. Can adapt to a variety of situations. Maintains stable performance under pressure. Reacts to change in a positive and supportive manner.
	TOTAL CULTURE RATING

Process	Rating
Knows/understands process	Understands the relevant organisational and management processes within both own and other divisions. Recognises own accountabilities within the processes, in particular with the deliverables and customer dependencies.
Measures effectiveness of the process	Constantly reviews work standards and process and continually strives for improvement. Pro-actively recommends improvements where applicable. Documents processes and is aware of how changes in own processes or poor quality impacts on other related processes and deliverables.
Models on best practice eleswhere	Shows desire to learn from best practice elsewhere.
Delivers	Adopts agreed processes readily. Delivers high quality work to agreed process.
	TOTAL PROCESS RATING
	OVERALL APPRAISAL RATING

Management	Rating
Demonstrates an appropriate management style	Creates a positive climate. Provides coaching, training and development to achieve business objectives. Involves others and is able to build co-operative teams in which group members feel valued and empowered and have shared goals. Listens. Does not assign blame when mistakes are made. Gives honest and timely feedback on individual performance. Gives recognition for work well done. Encourages people to give their best. Sets goals for the team. Implements plans and ideas. Takes responsibility for all aspects of the situation.

Exhibit 4   Section 2 – our culture (continued)

Makes decisions effectively	Has confidence in own judgement.
	Expresses confidence in the future success of the actions to be taken.
	Will anticipate problems and revise plans in accordance with change.
	Understands the organisation and perceives the impact and the implications of decisions on other parts of the organisation.
Inspires others	Presents ideas clearly with ease and interest so that the other person (or audience) understands what is being communicated.
	Uses open and probing questions, summaries, paraphrasing etc. to understand the ideas, concepts and feelings of another.
	Status-free.
	Positive attitude.
	Leads as a role model to make team act out the ITNET behaviours.
	Has vision, can see beyond the obvious and immediate.
	Paints a vivid pricture of what is required.
	Has influence with customers and colleagues.
	Confident of own persuasive skills and can gain support for ideas, strategies and values.
	Actively participates in and facilitates team effectiveness.
Results-oriented	Wants to do things better, to improve, to be more effective and efficient.
	Sets high standards for the team and individuals.
	Measures progress against targets.
	Can plan for long-term objectives.
	Is capable of formulating detailed short-term plans.
	Will take control and organise resources to make sure things happen.
	Has regular meetings with customers to gain feedback and measure performance.
	Has the ability to solve problems.
	Shows concern for all aspects of the job.
	Checks process and tasks accurately.
Business awareness	Demonstrates sound financial acumen.
	Understands the external marketplace.
	Forecasts accurately.
Demonstrates intellectual flexibility	Holds different options in focus simultaneously and evaluates their pros and cons.
	Can appreciate events, issues, problems and opportunities from the viewpoint of others.
	Able to 'see the wood from the trees' and think logically.
	Can evaluate both verbal and numerical alternatives effectively.
	Can reason with complex information.
TOTAL MANAGEMENT RATING	
OVERALL APPRAISAL RATING	

Vocabulary

As the company has developed its culture, a corporate vocabulary has become established. Phrases in common usage which describe some of the right and wrong attitudes found around the business are as follows.

- 'Flat world thinking' – Traditional views lacking imagination, reflecting old values and beliefs.
- 'Outside your comfort zone' – An uncomfortable experience or opportunity not relished by the individual as it is outside the domain he/she is used to.
- 'Rock the road' – An obstacle which an individual is concentrating so hard on that he/she cannot see ways around.

- 'Broken windows' – An undesirable state of something that people have come to live with and regard as acceptable due to the passage of time.
- 'What good looks like' – The way in which our culture suggests something should be done or someone should act.
- 'Thinking outside the nine dots' – Looking for creative solutions and questioning barriers that others have taken for granted.
- 'Remember the boxing ring' – A reminder that you don't always have to have the solution identified before you commit to deliver one.
- 'Playing blue' – Acting in the best interests of the organisation as a whole rather than looking after personal self-interests.

Exhibit 4   Section 2 – our culture (continued)

Superdrug[a]

Introduction

In 1966 Ronald and Peter Goldstein opened a shop on Putney High Street to initiate what was to become a key force in personal care retailing – Superdrug. By 1983 it had become a public limited company, and in 1987 its 339 stores were integrated into the Kingfisher group.

Throughout its history new formats have been developed as a response to trends in consumer markets; for example, 1991 saw the introduction of fragrance counters, with pharmacy counters soon to follow in 1992. In 1995, a new concept store was trialled that incorporated a clearly defined vision for the future. This concept is now being developed across the company with an anticipated deliverable benefit of £8.75 million per annum. Superdrug is firmly established in the toiletries and cosmetics retail sector; by 1998 it was the number 2 UK toiletries and cosmetics retailer. Its 705 stores are mainly in high-street locations with an average turnover per store of just under £1 milliom and average size of around 3000 square feet.

The consumer offer is perceived to consist of a combination of quality with good value for money, with both branded and own-brand products. The own-brand component within Superdrug has been increasing, with over 1400 own-brand products introduced in 1997.

The Kingfisher Group

The Kingfisher Group consists of several well-known UK retail businesses that span a wide range of shopping experiences and offers, as Exhibit 1 shows. These include B&Q in the DIY/gardening sector, Comet in the home appliance/electrical goods sector, Woolworth with its variety sector presence, Superdrug in the health and beauty sector, and the less recognised names of Chartwell (property development) and Darty (French electrical retailer).

Kingfisher's goal is to be one of Europe's most profitable volume retailers. It intends to achieve this by concentrating on markets centred on the home and family – markets that it feels that it knows and understands – and

by developing strong retail brands with leading positions in these markets. Its focus is to build on existing businesses using opportunities for internationalisation of its operations where appropriate.

The toiletries and cosmetics market

The UK toiletries and cosmetics sector consists of a number of varying retailers, reflecting the fragmented nature of the market; these include the retail pharmacy/drugstores, grocery multiples, and specialist health and beauty retailers.

The retail pharmacy/drugstore sector is dominated by Boots the Chemist and Superdrug, which accounted for 38.5% of the toiletries and cosmetics market (Exhibit 2).

The grocery multiple sector is more fragmented, with four key players accounting for 36.3% of the toiletries and cosmetics market (Exhibit 3).

Three key players among the specialist health and beauty retailers account for 10.7% of the toiletries and cosmetics market (Exhibit 4).

Within the toiletries and cosmetics retail marketplace a number of key issues are evident:

- After the recession of the early 1990s, spending on cosmetics and toiletries was quick to recover. There has been growth in real terms since 1993.
- Retail concentration continues as multiple retailers pursue their expansion and take over independent pharmacies.
- The distribution base is widening as other retail outlets carry basic ranges of toiletries.
- The grocery multiple sector has overtaken retail pharmacy/drugstores in toiletries and cosmetics sales. Retail pharmacy operators have responded by refocusing on healthcare.
- Own-label merchandise is in favour, with 38% of Mintel's respondents saying that they buy own-label toiletries more frequently than branded products. Consumers still prefer the image and assurance of major brands when purchasing cosmetics.
- Further growth in natural-based products is predicted alongside manufacturers seeking to incorporate scientific developments into their products in order to provide added consumer benefits. Own-label markets will also become more discriminating, with retailers further exploiting their brand names.

---

[a] This case was written by Helene Hill of the Department of Retailing and Marketing, Manchester Metropolitan University. The information presented in this case is based on interviews with staff from a number of perspectives: strategic management, regional management, and store at both shop floor and management level.

	Superdrug	B&Q	Woolworth	Comet	Darty	Chartwell
% of group operating profit	8	33	20	6	22	12
Market share ranking	#2	#1	#1	#2	#1	na
Market % share (1997)	10.7	19	*	11.7	13.4	na
Number of stores	705	282	781	232	156	na

* Category	%	Estimated position
Entertainment	14.6	1
Confectionery	4.1	1
Stationery	5.0	2
Children's wear	6.6	3
Toys	14.2	2

na: not applicable

Source: Kingfisher website

Exhibit 1   The Kingfisher Group

	Market share		% change	Operating profit (£m)	Net profit margin %
	1992	1997			
Boots the Chemist	27.9	27.8	−0.1	132.1	12.9
Superdrug	8.2	10.7	+2.6	134.6	6.2
Others	9.7	4.1	−5.6		

Exhibit 2   The retail pharmacy/drugstore sector

	Market share		% change	Operating profit (£m)	Net profit margin %
	1992	1997			
Tesco	8.5	12.9	+4.4	148.1	5.8
Sainsbury	8.8	10.5	+1.7	95.2	6.2
Safeway	6.0	6.5	+0.5	130.7	7.0
Asda	5.0	6.9	+1.0	176.0	5.3
Others	10.2	6.6	−3.6		

Source: *Mintel Toiletries and Cosmetics, 1998*

Exhibit 3   The grocery multiple sector

- It is forecast that there will be fewer, larger suppliers, and the move towards stronger own-brand labels will cause both diversification and merging of the suppliers to the sector.
- Grocery multiples are expected to add to their existing growth patterns, partly facilitated by further introductions of in-store pharmacies, better display techniques and further consolidation of their strengthening own-label brands.

The model for change: living the mission

There are a number of elements within the Superdrug strategy: understanding consumer needs, the integral role

	Market share			Operating profit (£m)	Net profit margin %
	1992	1997	% change		
The Body Shop	1.8	3.0	+1.2	119.3	12.8
Avon	6.5	3.4	−3.1	na	na
Department/variety stores	6.2	4.3	−1.9	*	†

* Operator	Operating profit (1997)		† Operator	Profit margin (1997)
House of Fraser	53.8		House of Fraser	3.1
Debenhams	180.3		Debenhams	9.9

na: not applicable

Source: *Mintel Toiletries and Cosmetics, 1998*

Exhibit 4   The specialist health and beauty sector

of brand development, the importance of distribution networks, the increasing significance of store format and presentation, the pivotal role of innovation and new product development and, finally, the company culture and strategic planning process, which must tie all of these facets together with systems, procedures and personnel to achieve the Superdrug aims and missions. The mission is 'to be the customer's favourite, up-to-the-minute health and beauty shop, "loved" for its value, choice, friendliness and fun'. Some of Superdrug's strategic terminology is set out in Exhibit 5.

An extensive strategic change programme has been devised to advance Superdrug towards its future vision. It has been named Living The Mission (LTM). The programme was initiated by holding a competition in which staff at all levels were invited to take part, asking for ideas for a mission statement based on Superdrug's key principles. This approach sought to ensure that staff 'bought into' the mission and could associate with the mission statement. The programme was underpinned by the principles of total quality management (TQM). All areas of the company have been affected and involved. Three factors deemed to be pivotal in gaining a competitive advantage were the focus for action: improving core processes that would deliver a competitive edge, focusing on customers, and providing staff support.

The LTM programme facilitates the achievement of the company vision in three ways.

First, the company mission is translated into seven 'stands'[b] that staff can associate with. These stands are:

● Superdrug's primary market focus will be on health and beauty.

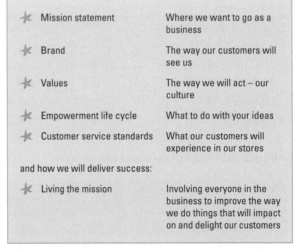

Mission statement	Where we want to go as a business
Brand	The way our customers will see us
Values	The way we will act – our culture
Empowerment life cycle	What to do with your ideas
Customer service standards	What our customers will experience in our stores
and how we will deliver success:	
Living the mission	Involving everyone in the business to improve the way we do things that will impact on and delight our customers

Exhibit 5   Some of Superdrug's strategic management definitions

● Superdrug offers superior value.
● Superdrug offers superior choice.
● Superdrug has its finger on the pulse.
● Superdrug goes the last mile for the customer.
● Superdrug is friendly and fun.
● Superdrug creates winning teams.

The second facilitating feature was the Superdrug brand. The essence of the Superdrug brand is 'accessible value and choice in a shopping experience that makes me feel good about myself'. This brand essence is a central feature in the new concept stores under development, and it is this new store concept that epitomises the future for Superdrug. This is reflected in the current training programme for store staff. The training that all staff undergo

[b] 'Stand' appears to be a term specific to Superdrug and means 'what they stand for'.

before commencing work in these new concept stores is similar in outcome to that of the LTM programme for existing stores. Both training programmes reflect a united approach to retailing, including both old-style community stores (secondary pitch sites) and transit stores (stores located on expressways), and the newer concept stores (stores on a primary pitch/location that have undergone significant refurbishment and redevelopment in a new store format). The additional burden that existing stores must overcome is how to move from the old style to the new way of 'living the mission'.

The third component of the LTM programme consists of the values that the people in the company must believe in and share. These result in the way in which all personnel conduct themselves as representatives of the organisation. The most important values are delighting the customer, winning, generosity of spirit, constructive rigour, straightforwardness, diversity and, finally, Involvement, Ownership, Pride and Excellence of execution (IOPE).

In summary, the stated overall aims of the LTM programme are to:

- continuously improve the way we meet our paying customers' requirements consistent with our mission and brand;
- harness everyone's commitment and potential through Involvement, Ownership, Pride and Excellence of execution (IOPE);
- get things right, on time, first time, every time at the lowest cost.

The programme's broad aims and strategies must be operated at the regional and store levels, particularly in the area of store standards, and the mission statement was seen as a mechanism to facilitate this. The broad outlines were translated into the following issues for store management:

- Understand and focus on our paying customers.
- Live IOPE, train everyone in TQM values and TQM management/improvement tools and techniques.
- Develop team working.
- Plan up-front with clear, measurable, owned, time-dated objectives.
- Continuously improve – plan, do, measure, improve, share.
- Recognise and celebrate successful involvement.
- Management lead by example.

Implementing the LTM programme

With 705 stores and 12,355 employees in the whole organisation, a key issue for Superdrug was how this pro-

gramme was going to translate into a plan of action across the various functions and levels of the company that would ensure a consistency of experience, in terms of training, process and measurement of outcomes.

The roll-out of LTM was segmented into the three core areas of the company: distribution, head office and stores.

Distribution

The roll-out programme below was followed within the distribution function:

Management	2 days	20 senior managers
Supervisors	2 days	40 supervisors
Improvement groups	2 days	30 staff

Head office

Within the head office functions the following structure was used to roll out the LTM programme training.

Champions	2 days	20 senior managers
Functional	1 day	380 head office staff
Internal customer	$3 \times \frac{1}{2}$ day	380 head office staff

Stores

Across the 705 stores, personnel needed to be given a consistent presentation of the LTM programme. Serious consideration had to be given, therefore, to how this would be rolled out at store level. The structure at the operational store level is more complicated than either distribution or head office, and this resulted in the segmentation of personnel for training according to varying management levels, down to store staff, and also for the presenters who would, unequivocally, be responsible for the training sessions given to all stores. This led to five separate phases in the roll-out: presentation to regional staff, area staff, presenters, store staff, and the follow-up team time sessions.

All personnel associated with the stores would need to understand and behave in a manner that reflected the principles underlying LTM. This was especially important in relation to personnel who operated outside individual stores. For example, visiting area and regional managers would be expected to 'live the mission' on store visits, otherwise this strategy would be perceived by staff in store as not being important. Therefore, potentially, there are many breaking points in this chain: any person failing to 'live the mission' is signalling its lack of importance to their junior staff, who may, as a consequence, be less likely themselves to 'live the mission' and value its significance.

All 60 regional and area staff received two days training, and the 800 area and store management staff were given a one-day session.

The presenters, 120 store managers, were given a three-day training session before they rolled out this programme to the stores. The selected store managers presented the sessions in the region from which they originated, and thus a store manager wouldn't necessarily be presenting LTM to their own staff. The time required to present to other stores was included alongside their normal working hours within their own stores. The training session consisted of all personnel being given their prepared training programme material: a large number of overhead slides, set exercises and video material. The presenters' training session included the external consultant who had designed the material for the programme. The sessions gave the trainers the opportunity to look through the material, discuss its contents and test small sections of the total package. The second component of the training session, facilitated by an internal person, consisted of presentation skills training. The total programme took six months to complete.

The initial LTM session within stores

Each store had an initial four-hour training session for all staff who could attended, whether full-time or part-time. This initial training session introduced LTM, its aims and objectives, why it was important, and the role that each individual and team played in the achievement of the objectives. Every member of staff was given an LTM booklet to be used both as a tool for conducting the reflective and practical exercises and as a tool to facilitate every individual having a personal record of the training session, its contents and key learning points. The half-day workshop session was followed up approximately four weeks later with another four-hour session. All remaining issues would be covered in regular monthly team time sessions held in the stores.

The starfish

The key issues at store level, which were introduced and explored within the workshop session, have been exemplified visually by the starfish framework for customer service standards, as shown in Exhibit 6. This represents the brand identity and, importantly, is used as an outline for plotting and measuring the attainment of key customer service goals within all stores.

The five legs of the starfish reflect the five aspects of service standards within each store, seen from the customer's perspective. All of these standards can be seen to relate directly to issues of managing service-based operations. Here the emphasis requires additional consideration beyond that of product, price, promotion and place, into that of physical surroundings, process (what the shopping experience consists of) and personnel. The aim of the

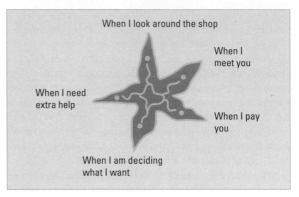

Exhibit 6   Service standards

company was to position itself in this market with the fun, friendly and helpful image, and to move away from the 'white coat' style which is associated with Boots. The five aspects considered from the customers' perspective are illustrated in Exhibit 7 and were:

- **When I look around the shop**   This issue covers cleanliness, signage and layout of the store.
- **When I meet you**   This aspect tackles personal appearance and the manner of all store personnel when interacting with customers.
- **When I'm deciding what I want**   When consumers are in the store this area gives consideration to product knowledge, clarity of pricing and special offer displays, and availability of products when requested.
- **When I pay you**   This aspect of service focuses on both cleanliness and speed of till areas, but also the manner in which staff involve themselves when customers pay for their purchases, e.g. offering to gift wrap perfume, and packing of goods.
- **When I need extra help**   The focus of this aspect is on the manner in which staff make consumers feel at ease with their shopping experience, and that they are aided where possible to make it as positive an experience as possible.

The measurement of service standards

The starfish is used as a tool for measuring service standards. All stores are provided with a large starfish that allows the achieved standards to be plotted along the five axes. This is used both to highlight areas for improvement and to make progress within the store on all of these aspects. The starfish focuses on customer service standards. The other main measures concern productivity and people, e.g. shrinkage levels, takings and what individual staff have highlighted as areas for improvement in the store.

Service standards

I'm a customer here
1) When I look around the shop:

- I don't see any litter on the floor.
- There is no dust or dirt on the shelves.
- I don't find leaking, dusty, out-of-date damaged products.
- I can find things I want to buy within 2 minutes.
- I can get my double buggy around.
- I can get what I want without moving anything.
- I don't see tatty signs or posters.
- I can pick up a basket.

Service standards

I'm a customer here
2) When I meet you:

- I can tell you work here and what your name is.
- You are clean, smart and look the part.
- You look me in the eye and smile.
- You stop what you are doing to help me.
- You also say hello, goodbye and thank you.
- When I need help, you're there.

Service standards

I'm a customer here
3) When I'm deciding what I want:

- You can tell me about the products and help me to make the right choice.
- You take me to a product if I can't find it.
- You check in the warehouse when the product is not on the shelf.
- If you haven't got what I want and you can't get it quickly enough you tell me where I can get it.
- You never walk in front of me while I'm looking.
- Your testers are available for me to try.
- I can always tell what the special offers mean.
- I can see the price of every product.

Service standards

I'm a customer here
4) When I pay you:

- I'm given a receipt and the right change.
- My bags are packed with care and are easy to carry.
- You offer to gift wrap my perfume.
- Tills are never dirty or cluttered.
- There are never more than three people in front of me at the till.
- If I've missed a good deal, you tell me.

Service standards

I'm a customer here
5) When I need extra help:

- I'm never embarrassed if I have asked for something personal.
- When I need more help than most, you give it to me.
- When I have an accident in your shop it's never a problem.
- When I bring things back I'm treated the same way as when I bought them.
- You answer the phone with hello, the shop name and your name.
- If you promise to call me back you always do.

Exhibit 7   Service standards

Central to this measurement of standards is the process by which they are decided and agreed. The second follow-up session on the LTM training programme involves store team members discussing and deciding on a rating for their store on all axes at that particular point in time. It also requires the store team to devise action plans, which will allow them to improve on all aspects of their service standards, productivity and people issues. This process includes part-time, full-time, shop floor and management levels. The decisions form the basis of their LTM contract:[c] how these targets will be achieved, and who will be responsible for ensuring that they are. There is no fixed formula as to how the store should implement this

---

[c] This LTM contract isn't a formal document, simply a tacit agreement.

measurement; precisely how to proceed becomes part of the store team's decision.

These service standards provide for an overall view of how the store is performing and integrate into the programme of store visits made by area and regional management.

The role of innovation in LTM

In 1997, Superdrug introduced over 1400 own-brand products. The importance of new product development and innovation is apparent in a number of ways. 'Innovation and learning' is one of the five elements within the Superdrug balanced scorecard, integrated alongside the other four key areas headed under values, processes, customers service standards and financial. The importance of innovation and new product development is also implicitly reflected within the LTM stands. For example, the 'need for continuous improvement' requires innovation, 'offering superior choice' involves developing new products and services, and 'has its finger on the pulse' is reflected in appropriate product ranges and service levels.

LTM embraces many levels and types of change and innovation, from 'new product development' as a more radical change at the strategic level, to steady in-store improvements at the operational level.

Facilitating and organising different levels of innovation

At the strategic level, major changes are initiated by appointed strategic project teams that focus on approximately seven or eight key initiatives. While these teams operate at a strategic level, the original ideas behind these projects may have been suggested and developed at any level in the organisation, although the tendency is for them to have been initiated at a senior level. This is partly a consequence of store staff's lack of confidence and motivation to suggest potential projects. The lack of confidence arises for several reasons: the belief that their ideas won't be taken seriously; the view that a development role in the store isn't part of their remit; and a lack of sufficient time to undertake additional roles. All of these concerns reflect the company culture that LTM is attempting to address.

The existing procedures in Superdrug do state that all ideas will be given consideration. It is only to be expected that not every idea suggested will automatically be accepted: similar ideas may already be in the system, or ideas may not be in line with the overall corporate mission and aims. Existing procedures specify that any individual whose idea has been rejected will be told of this and the reasons for rejection justified. The existing systems are also being developed in an attempt to ensure that staff, when proposing ideas, do think of all the implications of the idea and assess whether it complements the brand essence and is a cost-effective use of resources. Project proposals are assessed by considering:

- their fit within the balanced scorecard/key growth areas of the company;
- the resources required (staff levels and numbers);
- the success criteria for the proposed project;
- any assumptions/risks implicit within the project;
- the main obstacles to the success of the proposal.

Such measurement ensures that the value of each project and the associated risks are consistently considered and extensively evaluated.

At the operational store level, the focus of innovation is placed more on steady improvement. This is facilitated by a number of mechanisms.

First, improvement groups have been formed to look at a particular issue that has arisen. Such groups may consist of regional managers, area managers, store managers and occasionally store staff. The choice of group members is based around the necessary skills for the task to be performed, and also the types of team member that will ensure more effective teamwork.

The second way in which steady improvement is advanced is by the use of the customer service standards starfish framework and the LTM contracts, which are an integral part of the innovation programme. All issues that arise are discussed in the monthly team meetings held in each store. As part of a drive to reward and recognise successful innovation at store level regarding the main areas of measurement, the current Premier Crew store competition has been undertaken to select and reward the most successful stores throughout the UK. This also feeds into best practice.

The final aspect of steady improvement is focused on the individual store employee. One of the key elements in LTM revolves around what is termed the 'empowerment cycle'. This cycle is a model of operating that encourages all staff to suggest ideas for improvement, ensures that the ideas be taken through a series of stages to focus the idea further, and ensures that all implications are considered. The operation of the empowerment cycle would be done with the help of the store manager.

All of these action plans need to be incorporated into the broader strategic business framework. For example, an outcome of the empowerment cycle may be an improved way of operating that can then be fed into the area's model of best practice. A central belief is that success should be widely publicised, since this both gives positive reinforcement to such behaviour and enhances the likelihood that these improvements will be spread through the organisation. Communication of best practice is pivotal for overall corporate improvement throughout the stores. As indicated previously, while in theory staff are willing to suggest ideas, the extent to which they have been thought through, or their ability to complement the brand, is sometimes limited. It was also highlighted that time was a major factor that would inhibit the ability to consider these issues in any depth. Measures of innovation are also taken at store level, e.g. the number of ideas per store, and the number of ideas implemented per store. Overall, measurement is a major tool used by Superdrug at all levels to assess the progress of the LTM programme.

Acknowledgements

The author would like to thank Superdrug and Kingfisher for their active support in developing this case study. Particular thanks go to Peter Raine (head of total quality, Superdrug), Tony Mann (category general manager, Superdrug), Peter Geddes (head of marketing, Superdrug), John Phipps (regional manager, Superdrug) and all staff in the Sheffield Meadowhall and Manchester Piccadilly stores.

PowerGen: Strategy and corporate planning[a]

The privatisation of the electricity industry

Prior to the reorganisation of the electricity industry in England and Wales in 1989 and its subsequent privatisation in 1991, the Central Electricity Generating Board (CEGB) was responsible for the generation and transmission of electricity.

By the mid-1980s the number of power stations was declining, from 262 in 1958 to 79 in 1986. At the same time the technical complexity of power stations was increasing. In 1987 the CEGB reorganised to reflect these changes, adopting a structure based on functional specialisation, replacing regional management by providing resources on a national scale to address the generic problems of the power stations.

In 1990 the CEGB's generating activities were split between three companies, non-nuclear generating capacity was divided to form two organisations, National Power and PowerGen; nuclear generation formed the basis for a third company, Nuclear Electric. The CEGB's transmission function (the national grid) was placed within the joint ownership of the 12 electricity supply companies, the regional electricity companies (RECs). The RECs were to continue their function of supplying electricity to the final customer, metering and billing. Until 1998 customers with a demand below 100kW were to be exclusively supplied by the local RECs, after which time the market was to be opened to competition. Supply to customers above 100kW was progressively opened to all competitors in 1990 and 1994.

The reorganised industry was to be regulated by a director general of electricity supply, whose duties included the promotion of competition in the generation and supply of electricity.

PowerGen's functions were conferred in March 1990. In March 1991 PowerGen was privatised through the sale of 60% of its shares in a public offer (the remaining 40% in 1995). At vesting, PowerGen was allocated 21 power stations, generating approximately 30% of the electricity supplied to the transmission and distribution networks in England and Wales (National Power 48%, Nuclear Power 17%). Over 94% of PowerGen's output was generated

from coal and dual-fired (coal/oil) power stations, all of which were first commissioned in the mid- to late 1960s and early 1970s.

The generators were to sell electricity into an electricity pool, from which the suppliers (RECs) would buy. The pool operated on the basis of competitive bidding by generators. The national grid determined which sets of generating plant needed to run to meet demand. The bid price of the last set required (i.e. the most expensive) became the price for that (half-hour) period.

As pool prices could vary significantly over short periods, they were often hedged by agreements between a generator and a supplier to specify a price and quantity for a particular time. The contracts resulted in payments by generator to supplier when the pool price exceeded the agreed price, or supplier to generator when the pool price was lower than the strike price.

PowerGen

Organisation and planning, 1989–92

In 1988 the McKinsey consulting company was employed to help develop a strategy and organisational structure for PowerGen. A structure was proposed that was based on well-defined functional responsibilities and few layers of management (Exhibit 1, asterisks indicate those involved in managing the planning process). Each function formed a division, within which units were termed business units.

The McKinsey review also considered the planning process, recommending a five-stage process (Exhibit 2) that was introduced in 1990, along with the new organisation structure.

The planning process was led and managed by the commercial division, within which a large group of planners assisted the development of corporate strategy and the company's diversification through the new business development unit. The planning process retained a high degree of centralisation. Staff in the business planning and development department constructed a number of scenarios concerning market share, pool prices and competitor analysis for the core business (the generation division). The decisions that could be made by each unit (power station) were essentially those that had been available to them within the CEGB, with planning focused on developing the resource implications of a centrally determined strategy. The plans from the business units were aggregated to pro-

[a] This case was written by Dr David Jennings of Nottingham Business School, Nottingham Trent University. © D. Jennings 1999.

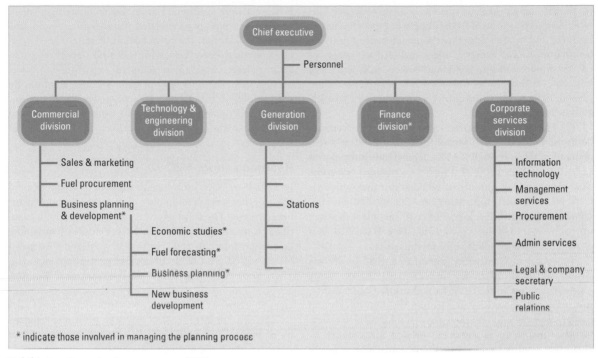

Exhibit 1 Organisation structure: 1990

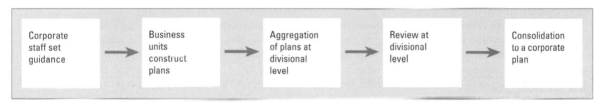

Exhibit 2 Corporate planning cycle, 1990

vide divisional plans. Financial projections from these exercises were consolidated by the finance division.

Strategic development

The centralised approach to planning associated with the CEGB began to lose relevance with the opening of the market for electricity, the wholesale electricity pool (April 1990). The operation of the pool became the focus of PowerGen's strategy, requiring the development of both a strong commercial orientation and increased operational flexibility.

At an early stage PowerGen's chief executive (and from 1996 also chairman), Ed Wallis stated that the company was 'first and foremost, a power generation business'. 'We concentrated our early energies on totally reshaping the core electricity business' to become 'a low-cost producer on a world class basis.' In addition, the company would 'seek

the opportunity to reintegrate generation with supply', implying merger with a regional electricity company.

PowerGen began to develop its generating capacity to better fit commercial and environmental requirements, through improving the flexibility of the coal units and developing gas-fired stations. By October 1990, plans had been announced for three CCGT power stations at a cost of £500 million. By 1996 the three gas-fired stations would provide over a third of PowerGen's output. Similar investments were being made by National Power.

Gas has numerous benefits for a generator. Compared with coal-fired stations the plant has relatively low capital costs, a shorter construction time, operates at high efficiency and productivity levels and has a lower emission of pollutants than coal generation. At the same time the availability of gas-fired technology lowered the barriers facing would-be entrants to electricity generation.

In gas supply the privatised company British Gas retained effective control of the supply of North Sea gas to business and households. PowerGen formed a joint venture with Conoco, Kinetica. Plans included the supply of gas to power stations, including PowerGen's, and large businesses with factories near the route of its £200 million pipeline. The pipeline was projected to supply 20% of UK gas consumption.

The national grid forecast a growth in electricity demand of only 0.6% a year for the period 1990–97, with demand peaking at 50,000 MW, against industry capacity of 61,000 MW in 1990/91. PowerGen engaged in a series of power station closures that would adjust the company's capacity to the new operating and commercial environment; this included the closure of coal-fired plant that was up to 34 years old. By April 1993, PowerGen had shut down 3275 MW of plant since privatisation.

The company's strategy anticipated that PowerGen would suffer an inevitable reduction in market share together with pressures for price reduction. Consequently, the company recognised that growth in the medium and longer term would require the establishment of new income streams in other energy-related areas where its core competences could create value. Early attention was given to developing a portfolio of new businesses based in the UK; international developments were believed to take longer to contribute to profits.

Upstream gas activities were seen as a logical extension of PowerGen's downstream activities, and assets were acquired in the North Sea and Liverpool Bay. Downstream, there was the partnership in the gas supply and transportation company, Kinetica. Also in the UK, Combined Heat and Power (CHP) was established to design, install, own and operate plant providing combined heat and power under agreements with specific industrial companies.

Overseas, the increasing international demand for power and the opening up of electricity markets to foreign investment presented opportunities for PowerGen's diversification. In the USA, the world's biggest energy consumer, energy demand was predicted to grow by 30% over the next two decades. Within the developing countries the rate of growth in electricity consumption was considerably greater than that in the UK, China and India averaging increases of 9 and 10% respectively between 1985 and 1991. The tendency throughout the developing countries for utilities to charge too little for the power they generated would require in some cases considerably higher prices (as much as a 50% increase) to attract outside capital investment. Projected investments also faced the possible effect of depreciating exchange rates over the 20-year life of most investments and future changes in government regulation of the industry. Nevertheless, the growth

prospects were sufficiently attractive to invite investment proposals from power-related businesses around the world. In addition, the privatisation of state-owned utilities presented PowerGen with potential opportunities to enter markets and apply acquired expertise in project management, the operation of plant and deregulation. By the middle of the 1990s, PowerGen had made power station and mining acquisitions in eastern Germany and Hungary, with construction projects in Portugal and Indonesia.

Reorganisation, 1992

In 1992 PowerGen introduced a number of organisational changes that were profoundly to affect the corporate planning process. The company was reorganised from a functional form to three divisions: New Ventures (containing PowerGen International, North Sea (gas) and Combined Heat and Power), UK Electricity (UK generation, including sales and marketing) and Engineering and Business Services (Exhibit 3). Each division was given its own managing director.

The existing large, central planning team was replaced by planning staff within the divisions. A smaller central strategic planning function was introduced, responsible for both corporate strategy and corporate planning. The separate task of financial planning was located within the finance department.

All business units became either profit or cost centres. The business units were given a wider role in decision making, with their managers provided, often for the first time, with a profit-and-loss format and support from finance staff newly located in their division.

In the New Ventures division the business units were to have considerable influence over their own revenue. North Sea Gas actively bought and sold gas, Combined Heat and Power had its own client contracts. The increased freedom also extended to UK Electricity. The power station managers were empowered to take a wide range of decisions that would reduce costs, including through questioning the purchase of a range of central services. The process of devolution and the internal market extensively reduced PowerGen's central staff and helped to empower business-level management.

Within the new structure the planning process operated at a number of levels. The central strategic planning staff developed the corporate strategy. Each unit in the organisation produced a business plan, which was consolidated by the divisional board and again at corporate level to form the corporate plan. Guidance for the planning exercise was provided by corporate-level planning staff. The guidelines included overall business and economic assumptions, scenarios and profit targets (in place of

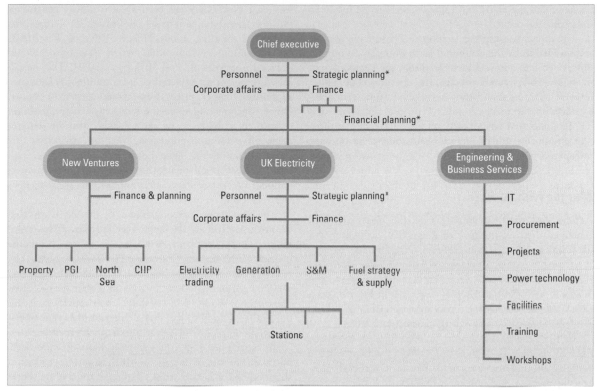

Exhibit 3   Organisation structure: 1992

expenditure limits for various categories of spend), anticipated output required from each power station and, for a non-generating unit, the corporate challenges and targets that the business unit was expected to contribute to achieving. The challenges and targets encouraged units to explore their potential rather than meet a set target.

The scope of options available to the business units had been considerably widened and provided with a commercial focus. The level of detail required in business unit plans was reduced to provide a plan that could be expressed in a few sheets of paper. The time required to carry out the corporate planning process had also changed, from a year, or more, to a nine-month process.

Planning problems: 1993–94

During 1993–94 several developments occurred that would affect the future profitability of the core business, UK Electricity. These included an agreement with the industry regulator to cap wholesale prices in the electricity pool and also for the company to sell 2 GW of power plant. The effect on profit forecasts was compounded by an unexpected increase in electricity supplied by Nuclear Electric.

For any organisation, planning is inherently an iterative process, but during the 1993–94 planning cycle

presentation of the corporate plan to the board was delayed by the need for substantial reworking of the plan to reflect PowerGen's financial priorities more fully. The 1993 planning cycle revealed a rift between strategic decisions and the group's financial requirements. In part the problem was seen as a result of the way in which planning responsibilities had been assigned within the company. The company's strategic planner, reporting to the chief executive, was responsible for both the development of corporate strategy and production of the corporate plan, an arrangement that limited the influence of the finance department in shaping the corporate plan early in the planning cycle. Responsibility for the plan and for managing the corporate planning process was passed to the director of finance, effectively increasing the influence of financial considerations in the planning process.

The planning difficulties also reflected a failure by the centre to communicate scenario information fully. The centre had considered that such an event as 'capping' could occur, but had not communicated that early enough for it to be a part of the context for developing the business plans. PowerGen adopted the practice that, as part of the strategic review, the core businesses should themselves develop a number of scenarios as to how the market might develop, and the plans that followed were to be robust to those possibilities.

The difficulties experienced in the 1993 planning cycle were added to by the divisional form of organisation that PowerGen had adopted in 1992. From the perspective of managing the planning process, the divisions could add a level of bureaucracy to the process and affect communication with the business units. Priorities and issues that were identified at corporate level were filtered, and often new arguments added, before their address by business unit planners.

Merger with an REC

At the end of 1995/96, sales to the electricity pool remained the core business of PowerGen, accounting for 70% of group turnover. PowerGen continued to face increasing pressures on market share and lower electricity prices. Although overall electricity demand in England and Wales in 1995/96 had risen by over 3% in the year, as a result of the continuing economic upturn and a cold winter, PowerGen's share of the market had fallen.

In 1995 the government's 'golden share' in the RECs expired, leading to a flurry of takeover activity with a range of UK and overseas companies, from within the generating industry and outside it, bidding to acquire RECs. Motives varied but included the belief that the five-yearly review of prices left the RECs comparatively weakly regulated: domestic electricity prices had fallen by only 4% since privatisation. PowerGen made an agreed offer of £1.9 billion for Midlands Electricity plc, a regional electricity company. Although this was the sixth bid that had occurred for an REC, and the government had recently allowed Scottish Power's £1.1 billion offer for Manweb, the industry regulator voiced concern. The merger, together with a similar proposed merger by National Power with Manweb, was referred to the Monopolies and Mergers Commission (MMC).

As an REC, Midlands had a local monopoly of supply in its geographical area for customers of less than 100 kW, customers whose annual electricity bills ranged from £12,000 (small business) to £300 (domestic customer). In total RECs had 23 million such customers, accounting for half of all electricity demand by volume and two-thirds by value. In the over 100 kW (competitive) market – large customers throughout England and Wales – MEB had a 6% share. PowerGen was the largest supplier to that market, with a share of 16%. Under its operating licence MEB was allowed to generate up to 88 MW, 15% of its requirements at vesting, and had interests in five power stations with a total capacity of 2688 MW.

Analysis presented to the MMC pointed to the conclusion that PowerGen had been able to use its generating facilities (non-baseload) to set pool prices for a large proportion of the time, about 35%, in 1995/96. The MMC considered that without the merger that figure would reduce to between 27 and 30% by 2000/01. The merger raised the prospect of acquired information and influence supporting higher prices than would otherwise occur. Other concerns addressed the industry regulator's ability to enforce prohibitions on cross-subsidy and the requirement for economic purchasing. At the same time the increased size of the merged company and its wider skill base was seen as enhancing the ability to compete in international markets, where international energy companies were emerging.

The overall conclusion arrived at by the MMC was that the adverse effects of the merger need not justify its prohibition. The government, however, decided to block the merger. However, chief executive Ed Wallis responded by restating his intention to buy an REC, although accepting that PowerGen might have to wait until after the next general election. Wallis predicted that merger activity was leading to the creation of five or six super-utilities that would emerge to dominate the privatised electricity market.

In November 1996 the company had sufficient cash, partly due to sale of its stake in MEB, to carry out its third share buy-back in two years, totalling a third of its shares since the completion of its privatisation in 1995.

Reorganisation, 1996

By the mid-1990s several of the businesses within the New Venture division had developed to a stage where they justified their own management, on a level with that of UK Electricity. In addition, within the core, the signalled liberalisation of the electricity market (1998) argued for sales and marketing to be given greater autonomy and separation from generation.

In September 1996 PowerGen underwent a reorganisation that reflected these developments, replacing the divisional form of organisation with new clusters of business units (Exhibit 4). Each cluster, such as UK Production, was headed by a managing director. Typically the MD was assisted by a finance manager whose role included, as part of their financial responsibilities, managing the planning process. Similarly, it was common practice for a specific member of staff to be given the role of developing business unit strategy.

The reorganisation improved the focus of unit managers on the particular circumstances associated with their businesses; it also enabled corporate staff to develop targets that more exactly addressed the individual business.

Within the new structure a group MD had been estab-

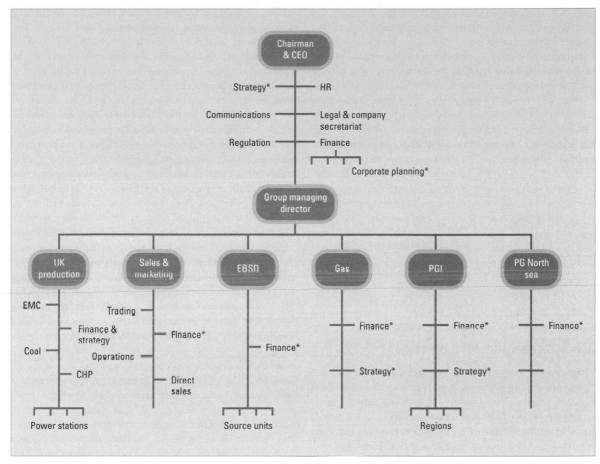

Exhibit 4   Organisation structure: 1996

lished to act as MD responsible for all the business units. The role of the chief executive focused on the development of corporate strategy, the finance director was mainly concerned with the financial aspects of plans, and the group MD was concerned with business unit strategy. As a team they engaged in a continuing dialogue concerning the overall strategic and financial direction of PowerGen. The corporate strategist (with a team of three staff) and corporate planner (four staff) assisted this debate and the development of business strategies and plans.

Environment and scenarios

A number of developments acted to increase the environmental complexity and uncertainty facing PowerGen. These included industry and geographical diversification, increasing competition in the UK generation industry (the core business for revenue) and the actions and reactions occurring at the company/regulator/government interface. As a consequence, the company placed a great deal of

effort into managing the interface with regulatory, political and environmental developments, continually absorbing the external perspective and assessing its implications for strategic options.

Prior to the planning cycle, in July and August, a number of scenarios were developed. The past practice of centralised scenario development had been replaced by a devolved process based on one or more business units and the corporate strategist.

The principal scenario exercises in the planning round primarily concerned the inputs and outputs of PowerGen's businesses, the markets and prices for gas, coal and electricity. Price information was developed in the context of the larger, world pictures, with the prices based on views concerning possible futures that may, for example, include the composition of the industry, how those in the industry might behave, the role of wider sources of supply, such as Russian gas, and conditions in the UK energy markets.

Other scenarios were also developed; for example, as

part of strategy development for UK production a scenario would be developed for the evolution of the UK electricity market. Given that PowerGen was a major supplier, the company would have some influence in how that situation might develop. In such a case the scenario exercise became part of strategy development.

Scenarios came to be developed by a team drawn from a number of functions and businesses to represent the various groups with a significant interest in the output from the scenario. The team would be led by a representative of the unit that either has the most expertise or involvement in the area on which the scenario was focused. In general, outside experts were not involved as team members; however, the advice of external people was sought and they made presentations to the team. The scenarios were developed by trying to identify the key drivers for the industry. This involved the use of quantitative trends and qualitative analysis concerning industry structure, government intervention and the behaviour of the various players in the market. Brainstorming then focused on how different futures might evolve. Information from the scenario exercises formed part of the planning guidance.

The corporate planning process, 1996–98

The planning system encouraged initiatives by the business units within a corporate context; it also addressed the need for co-ordination between a number of the business units. In the UK, PowerGen was seeking to build an integrated gas and electricity business. The businesses that made up the UK electricity and gas value chain had to have consistent strategies and objectives for achieving that end. There was also a need for co-ordination between UK generation and the developing overseas operations, a skills transfer that required integration of human resource planning. The planning cycle is detailed in Exhibit 5.

FINANCIAL AND STRATEGIC OVERVIEW

The on-going examination of business unit strategy at business and corporate level made it unnecessary to have a comprehensive review prior to the planning cycle. However, as preparation for the planning cycle, there were strategy debates for particular business units during July/August. In developing and appraising options, the business units used whatever strategic techniques they thought appropriate. Throughout the organisation technique was seen as secondary to the quality of debate that was achieved.

During September each business unit provided an update of the plan for the previous year, taking account of developments in strategy and the market context, together with the options that the business believed were open to it. A base case for the business unit's plan was agreed, forming the option that it was expected would be developed in the subsequent business planning. Business unit strategy was established before developing detailed planning guidance. Partly this reflected the need for co-ordination. However, there was scope for flexibility: issues affecting business unit strategies often emerged and had to be addressed within the subsequent stages of the corporate planning process, prior to board approval.

Following its consolidation this information was examined by the corporate staff for its strategic and financial fit against the overall priorities of the company. Conclusions from this comparison supported the development of guidelines, the corporate context of strategic and financial priorities and targets agreed with each business unit within which business planning was conducted.

PLANNING GUIDELINES

Typically this stage in the planning process involved a great deal of discussion and lobbying between the corporate strategy and planning staff and business unit managers. The guidelines were formally agreed with the chief executive or the group managing director.

Guidelines differed between business groups and were further developed within each business group before becoming a basis for business unit plans. In UK production, particular attention was given to short-term profit. For PowerGen International (PGI) the objectives included the size of developments and when they were to occur, the plant capacity to be achieved in each country, the profit level in five to ten years time, the number of projects to be delivered each year to achieve those objectives, and the required level of resources to achieve those outcomes. More immediate targets would also typically refer to the human resource developments that were required to underpin the longer-term achievements.

Exhibit 5: 1998 Corporate planning cycle

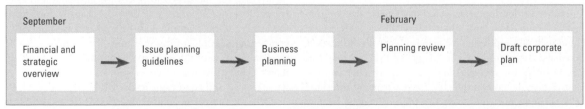

September .... February

| Financial and strategic overview | → | Issue planning guidelines | → | Business planning | → | Planning review | → | Draft corporate plan |

BUSINESS PLANNING

All units, including corporate staff units, produced a plan with a five-year horizon. Typically a plan was a brief document clearly stating the business unit objectives and how they expected to meet them, the key issues facing the business, how the business was going to develop and the expected financial performance.

PLANNING REVIEW

The planning review stage involved the corporate planning staff, business planners and business directors. Once business units had submitted their individual plans, the team examined the overall financial picture that the plans presented and whether in total they met the group requirements. This led to feedback into the business reviews, where the group MD and financial director reviewed the plans of individual business units with the unit's MD.

The final stage in the planning process involved amalgamating the business plans and drafting the corporate plan.

PERFORMANCE REVIEW

Following the presentation of the plan to the board, the performance of the managing directors of the various businesses was reviewed. A bonus scheme operated with three components: individual performance, the performance of the director's business and corporate performance. While corporate performance typically involved earnings per share, business performance included the year's contribution to achieving the longer-term key achievements that the business was trying to deliver over the next five years, such as market share, developing the business's capabilities and other forms of business development. All of the financial and strategic targets were specified in the business plan for the previous year.

Industry and company developments, 1998

During 1997/98 competition from over 30 other generators contributed to a further fall in PowerGen's share of UK generation, by 2.1% to 19.5%. In the supply of electricity to industrial and commercial customers, the company retained its leading position with a market share of 16%.

In the same period the upstream gas business, PowerGen North Sea, delivered a strong performance. This was originally established to secure low-cost gas to support PowerGen's CCGT programme and to enable the group to gain expertise and knowledge of the business. Further growth would require the injection of considerable capital and the decision was taken to find a buyer for the business.

PowerGen was involved in the production, transportation, marketing and trading of gas, meeting its own long-term needs through long-term contracts with gas producers. In gas supply PowerGen had achieved agreements to supply gas for household use, as well as electricity, to two of the regional electricity companies. PowerGen already supplied 10% of the industrial and commercial gas market.

PowerGen's combined heat and power business successfully commissioned a further two new CHP plants, for Conoco and Iggesund Paperboard, bringing the total of PowerGen's CHP capacity to 180 MW of electricity on five sites.

In international activities, by 1998 PowerGen had achieved a total committed investment of £700 million in plant and projects overseas. The operations in Australia, Hungary and Germany had produced improved results, although continuing difficult market conditions in Australia (accounting for 55% of the company's operational overseas generating capacity) depressed the company's international profits. During the next two years the completion of major projects in India, Indonesia and Portugal, to a total of 5455 MW, would more than double PowerGen's international operating capacity. A further three projects in Hungary, India and Thailand, totalling 2367 MW, were due to come into operation by 2002/03. By 2001 PowerGen expected to earn £100 million a year from outside the UK.

Within the UK the increased use of gas and the consequent loss of jobs in the coal-mining industry became a politically sensitive issue for the power industry. In 1997 the newly elected Labour government announced its intention to limit further construction of gas-powered generating plant. The industry regulator observed that this would not be a barrier to industry entry, arguing, if necessary, for the break-up of National Power and PowerGen. The government announced its intention to review the operation of the electricity pool and prices in distribution. Government proposals included replacing the pool with bilateral trading arrangements between large users (big industrial consumers and supply companies) and the generators, in an attempt to lower the wholesale price of electricity.

The government continued to hold a 'golden share' in both PowerGen and National Power, protecting them from takeover. Nevertheless, a consortium of overseas financial and industrial companies had planned a hostile bid for National Power with the intention of demerging the company, whose share price was depressed by a profit warning and potential power plant disposals. It was not clear that the government would oppose an offer that promoted competition and assisted realisation of its energy policy.

By 1997 only one REC remained independent, Southern Electric, with more than half the original 12 companies held by US companies. In September 1998 PowerGen was given government permission to proceed with a second bid to acquire East Midlands Electricity from Dominion Resources, an American utility, for £1.9 billion, £300 million more than Dominion had paid 18 months earlier. A further referral to the MMC would have delayed the signing of long-term coal contracts, which the government believed would safeguard thousands of jobs in the mining industry. The government's condition for the merger was that PowerGen would carry out the disposal of two large coal-fired power stations, amounting to 4002 MW of its 13,600 MW coal- and gas-fired capacity. The disposals were expected to raise about £900 million.

The acquisition of EME provided PowerGen with its long-sought integration with the supply industry, in addition enabling the company to sell both electricity and gas to household customers. The merger also provided a wider base of expertise for PowerGen to use in bidding for overseas contracts, many of which involved running distribution networks as well as generation.

In September 1998 the liberalisation of the under 100 kW (household) market began, to be completed during 1999. Liberalisation replaced the monopoly supply of the RECs with a competitive market in which consumers were encouraged to find best value from over 15 potential suppliers, whose offers included lower prices and the dual supply of gas and electricity. At an early stage British Gas had succeeded in attracting 400,000 electricity customers. Its 150 door-to-door salespeople, together with sales through the Sainsbury supermarket chain, were intended to raise the total to 3.5 million customers.

PowerGen's vision was to build one of the world's leading integrated electricity and gas businesses, using the experience gained in the UK liberalisation process as a basis for developing opportunities in other liberalising markets. PowerGen had entered into negotiations with Houston Industries, America's ninth largest utility, to form a £10 billion group. Previous merger talks with

another US company, Cinergy, had broken down in 1997, partly due to strains between the two chairmen. Houston was also to be deterred, this time by the prospect of a changing UK regulatory climate that might include the forced divestment of a substantial part of PowerGen's generating capacity. Other US companies had started to lose interest in the UK for similar reasons, including the government's imposition in 1997 of a windfall tax on industry profits (£202 million for PowerGen) and the increasing level of competition in the domestic market.

PowerGen continued to assess opportunities to enter the US market, creating a new holding company, PowerGen 1998, to more easily meet US regulatory demands in the event of a merger and to increase the financial flexibility of the group.

Between April 1990 and March 1994 prices paid to generators were set by the pool without an upper limit. For the period April 1994 to April 1996, the DGES obtained voluntary undertakings from PowerGen and National Power to bid into the pool in such a way that average pool prices would be below a specified level, 'the cap'.

In 1996 the Monopolies Commission concluded that within the electricity pool market share by output (nonbaseload sector) was a broad indicator of a generator's ability to set pool prices. CCGT (gas-powered plant) can be technically operated as 'baseload' (continuous demand) as well as 'mid-merit', which involves turning the plant on and off at least once in 24 hours. The report of the MMC concluded that market shares of around 17% for PowerGen and 21% for National Power would provide a 'broadly satisfactory competitive environment' in generation.

In 1996 PowerGen and National Power completed an undertaking to the DGES by disposing of a total of 6000 MW of plant through a leasing arrangement to Eastern Electricity. By 1998 Eastern had become a vertically integrated company (generator and REC) with a 9% share of

Exhibit 6   Market share

	Generator's share of total output of electricity in England and Wales (%)							
	1991	1992	1993	1994	1995	1996	1997	1998
National Power	45.5	43.5	40.9	35.0	34.0	32.6	24.1	20.9
PowerGen	28.4	28.2	27.0	26.0	26.0	24.2	21.5	19.7
Nuclear Electric	17.4	18.6	21.4	23.2	22.2	22.3	24.2	24.7
Scottish and French interconnectors	7.1	8.0	8.2	8.0	8.7	8.5	9.3	9.1
Others	1.6	1.7	2.5	7.8	9.1	12.4	20.9	25.6

the generation market. In that year evidence emerged that the Eastern group had been able to use its capacity to achieve higher pool prices. The development of market share over the years is given in Exhibit 6.

The industry regulator estimated that, as a result of 'gaming', in December 1998 wholesale (pool) prices for electricity had been £90 million higher than they should have been, a figure equal to 10% of that month's pool sales. PowerGen's performance and group interests are set out in Exhibits 7 and 8, respectively.

| | Years ended (£ million) | | | | | | | |
	1991	1992	1993	1994	1995	1996	1997	1998
Turnover:								
Generation (pool)	2412	2667	2537	2225	2252	2184	2071	1897
Direct sales to end customer	239	430	651	707	615	674	656	622
Other energy and hydrocarbon sales	–	–	–		18	75	128	156
Gas trading and retail	–	–	–	–	–	–	43	257
Total turnover	2651	3097	3188	2932	2885	2933	2898	2932
Sources of profit								
Operating profit/loss:								
Generation	237	323	422	509	547			
Direct sales	7	(1)	28	(18)	–			
Other	(3)	3	(1)	(14)	(16)			
International operations	12	12	9					
Combined heat and power	(1)	1	5					
Operating profit	241	325	449	477	531	693	511	*591
Profit before tax	272	359	425	476	545	687	577	**211

* 1998, before exceptional items of £369m for plant rationalisation and restructuring costs, £339m of which follows a review of the company's UK plant portfolio in the light of increased competition and market changes.

** Pre-tax profit is before windfall tax.

Operating profit margin (%)	9.1	10.5	14.1	16.3	18.4			
Average number of employees	8840	7771	5715	4782				
Employees: UK business					4122	3558	2833	2865
International business					49	590	534	591

PowerGen does not analyse its results by business segment in its statutory accounts, figures for 1991–1995 are from the company's submission to the MMC.

Source: 1991–1995, MMC
1996–98 PowerGen Co. Report

Exhibit 7   PowerGen performance

By 1998 PowerGen held a 100% interest in the following group undertakings:

PowerGen CHP Ltd
Sale of energy services involving the construction of combined heat and power plant

PowerGen North Sea Ltd
Oil- and gas-related activities

Kinetica Ltd
Transportation and marketing of natural gas in the UK

Wavedriver Ltd
Development of electric-vehicle-related technology

Csepel Power Company
Generation and sale of electricity (Hungary)

It also held the following investments in associated undertakings:

	% of capital held by the group
Yallourn Energy Australia, mining of brown coal and production and sale of electricity from coal-fired power station	49.95
Saale Energie Germany, holding and management company for the group's interest in Schkopau power station	50
MIBRAG mbh Germany, mining, refinement and sale of brown coal and generation and sale of electricity	33.33
Turbogas Produtora Energetica Portugal, construction of gas-fired power-station plant	49.99
PT Jawa Power Indonesia, construction of coal-fired power-station plant	35
Gujarat Torrent Energy Corporation India, construction of gas-fired power-station plant	27.8
Cottam Development Centre UK, construction and operation of gas-fired power-station plant to develop, test and commercially operate the next generation of gas-powered plant technology, a joint venture with Siemens	50

Exhibit 8   PowerGen: group and associated undertakings

Pearson plc[a]

In the four years leading up to 1997 Pearson had spent £2 billion buying bits and pieces with little to show for it. The idea seemed to have been to model Pearson on the big media companies pursuing ownership of diverse media assets, as indicated by the start-up of Pearson New Entertainment, which involved electronic publishing, video and magazines. At the end of 1996 Pearson plc saw itself 'as an international media group with a diverse range of skills in newspaper, magazine and book publishing, on-line and software services, television, and visitor attractions. The Group focused these core skills through separate business divisions on three key markets worldwide: information, education and entertainment. Pearson also has significant interests in investment banking.'[1]

The three market areas were as follows.

Information: The information division encompassed a wide portfolio of information services worldwide. Its printed products included national and international business newspapers, professional books, magazines and periodicals. It also provided information services. The major holdings at the end of 1996 were:

- Financial Times Newspapers – printed in ten centres covering Europe, North America and Asia;
- Financial Times Information – providing electronic business and specialist financial information worldwide;
- Les Echos – France's leading business daily newspaper and the flagship of a group that includes many other business and professional titles, including a twice-weekly medical newspaper;
- Recoletos – one of Spain's leading newspaper and magazine publishers. Its titles include the country's premier business daily, its premier sports daily and a daily newspaper for doctors;
- Pearson Professional – publishing books, periodicals and screen-based services for professional communities worldwide under the brand names of the Financial Times, Pitman Publishing and Churchill Livingstone.

Education: The education division was one of the world's top educational publishers, selling books, multimedia and learning programmes in the school, higher education, professional and English language teaching markets through-

out the world. The major imprints at the end of 1996 were Addison Wesley, Longman, and Benjamin Cummins.

Entertainment: The entertainment division produced, distributed and broadcast television programmes, was a leading international trade book publisher, ran visitor attractions and produced consumer magazines, videos and software. The major holdings at the end of 1996 were:

- Penguin – publishing English-language consumer books, fiction and non-fiction, in hardcover and paperbacks. Joined by Putnam Berkley, the US trade publisher, in 1996;
- The Tussauds group – was the largest European operator of leading visitor attractions specialising in exhibitions and theme parks, including Madame Tussauds, Alton Towers, Warwick Castle, Chessington World of Adventures and a 40% holding in Port Aventura, a major theme park near Barcelona;
- Pearson New Entertainment – publishing special interest consumer magazines, videos and related new media especially for 'boys of all ages';
- Mindscape – developing and publishing consumer software for personal computer and video game systems;
- Pearson Television – was the UK's largest international television producer. It sold its formats worldwide and also had interests in distribution and broadcasting. It produced and sold programmes under the Thames, Grundy, Alomo, Witzend and ACI brands. It had a 24% stake in the UK's Channel 5.

Investment banking: Pearson had a shareholding in Lazard Partners, a 50% interest in Lazard Brothers and a 9% stake in the partnership profits of Lazard Frères, Paris, and Lazard Frères, New York.

In January 1997 Marjorie Scardino became CEO of the Pearson Group after four years running The Economist, where she was credited with the 78% growth in sales and 130% increase in profits between 1992 and 1996.[2] From the beginning of 1997 to the middle of 1999 she embarked on a very significant corporate change programme. A list of her disposals and acquisitions is given in Exhibit 1.

By mid-1999 the Pearson Group had four sets of businesses built around strong brands – The Financial Times group, Pearson Television, Penguin and Pearson Education, as Exhibit 2 illustrates. However, as Mrs Scardino is reported as saying, 'What we've been trying to

---

[a] This case was prepared by Paul Finlay.

Date		Unit	Area of expertise	Cost/price (millions)
M	sold	Mindscape	Educational software	
	sold	TVB	Hong Kong broadcaster	
	sold	6.3% stake in Société Européenne des Satellites		
Oct 97	bought	All-American Communications	World's largest owner and distributor of game shows (including *Blind Date* and *The Price is Right*) and owns US drama series, including *Baywatch*	$373
	announced	Expansion of Financial Times in USA		£100
		Specialist law and tax publishing	'Must have' technical and proprietary information for lawyers	£70
Apr 98	sold	Future Publishing, Edicrop Publications SA and Futurenet	Consumer magazines, including computing and the Futurenet website	£142
May 98	bought	Pasha Publications Inc.	Leading provider of energy market and pricing information	$18
Jun 98	sold	Port Aventura	Spanish theme park	£58
Aug 98	sold	4.8 million shares in Flextech	Broadcast media company	£28
Aug 98	alliance	Pearson companies Rough Guides and Headland Digital Media link with the industry leader in web-based travel reservations systems Internet Travel Network (to put the guides on the Internet)		
Sep 98	sold	20% stake in *Canadian Financial Post*	Financial newspaper	C$34
Oct 98	sold	The Tussauds group	Leisure, including Alton Towers	£352
Nov 98	bought	Mastrofilm	Italian drama production company	
Nov 98	bought	30% of Unidad Editorial SA	Publishers of *El Muño*, one of Spain's leading newspapers	£44
Nov 98	bought	50% stake in Economica SGPS publisher	Publisher of Portugal's leading financial daily *Diário Económico* and weekly newspaper *Semanário Económico*	£6
Nov 98	bought	Simon & Schuster's education, reference, business and professional divisions	Academic and professional publishers	$4600
Jan 99		Appleton & Lange	Medical texts and education products for the academic, clinical and consumer marketplaces	
		Jossey-Bass	Key topics in management of businesses	
Jan 99	bought	10.9% stake in E-Pub Holdings	A leading US-based on-line entertainment company with the website Uproar	
Feb 99	sold	Extel research products	Data on over 15,000 companies principally in the UK	$19
Jun 99	link	Telefonica takes a 5% stake in Pearson	Telefonica bought the stake from Financiere et Industrielle Gaz et Eaux. It has interests in Spain and Latin America	
Jun 99	sold	Macmillan Library Reference	Library reference books sold to Thomson Inc.	$96
Jun 99	sold	Lazard stake	Sold to Financiere et Industrielle Gaz et Eaux.	£410

Exhibit 1   Major changes in the Pearson Group, 1997–99

Date	Unit		Area of expertise	Cost/price (millions)
Jun 99	sold	Macmillan General Reference	Sale of business reference books and magazines to IDG Books Worldwide	$83
Jul 99	bought	Thomson Financial Securities Management	Provides securities pricing service (especially in the municipal bond market) and other specialist information to the global financial information community	$150
Sept 99	sold	4% indirect stake in BSkyB	Sold to Vivendi	£408

Exhibit 1   Major changes in the Pearson Group, 1997–99 (continued)

Exhibit 2

do is figure out whether there is any connection between them. Some synergies are showing up: Pearson Education and the Financial Times are making a joint push in management education.'[3]

Pearson's financial position at the end of 1998 is set out in Exhibit 3.

At the end of 1998 Pearson had offices in 53 countries with a total staff of 20,000. In 1999 it spent £14 million on giving each of its 13,000 eligible employees a 3% bonus and 15 free shares to celebrate its 20% growth in earnings per share. Pearson is considering a secondary listing on the New York Stock Exchange, mainly to give the company greater flexibility to reward its US-based staff, who now comprise half of Pearson's total staff, with equity.

The Financial Times group

The *Financial Times* is the world's leading international business newspaper, with a worldwide circulation of 385,000 in early 1999, of which 210,000 were non-UK sales. In 1998 Pearson announced that it was investing £100 million over the five years to 2002 to strengthen the *Financial Times* in the USA and Europe and to make it into a global brand. The *Financial Times* was relaunched

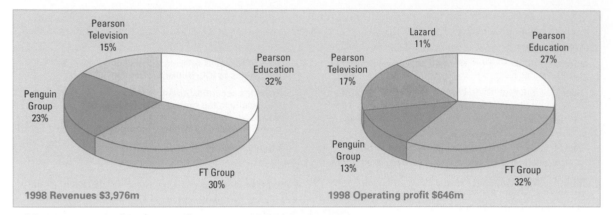

Exhibit 3   Pearson plc – 1998 performance

in the USA with a separate editorial team, and the US circulation grew from 32,000 at the beginning of 1997 to 70,000 at the end of 1998.

There are now articles in the US edition that don't appear in the UK or European editions. Previously, what had occurred was that the same articles would appear, but the US-oriented articles would be positioned more prominently than the UK-originated articles: the same content but a different format. In the USA, the big story would almost certainly centre around Wall Street and/or the White House, and now this comes first, with other news following.

All editions and editorial staff have full access to a database of articles held by the *Financial Times*, and the original idea was that each local editorial staff could simply translate these to the local language; similarly for material in *Les Echos,* which would be translated for use in the *Financial Times.* However, it's now realised that news must be combined with the appropriate local background – news of a channel ferry blockade by French lorry drivers is news, but this would be added to quite differently in France than in the UK. The reporters getting the news are a shared resource – while the customers get what they want by relating the news to their own viewpoint.

A joint venture with Gruner & Jahr in Germany was initiated to launch a German-language business newspaper, drawing on the editorial content of the *Financial Times.* Gruner & Jahr is the magazine and newspaper division of Bertlesmann, Europe's biggest and the world's third largest media group. Until recently, the *Financial Times* was heavily UK-focused: now there are Asian, UK, European and US editions: the one brand the *Financial Times* now offers a focused product in each of its major marketplaces.

In September 1998 Pearson sold its 20% stake in the *Canadian Financial Post* following a policy of disposing of its passive investments.

The Financial Times group doesn't just consist of the *Financial Times* itself: there are several businesses associated with the newspaper:

- FT Electronic Publishing – provides corporate clients with general news and analysis and with specialist company and market information, and financial data. It generates more advertising revenue than any other UK site and had over 1.5 million registered users worldwide, with the majority outside the UK.[4]
- FT Business – produces specialist information on particular industries – energy, media, telecommunications and finance. In finance, for example, it publishes the UK's premier personal finance magazine, *Investors Chronicle,* along with the *Banker, Money Management* and *Finance Advisor* for professional advisers.
- FT Asset Management – the leading global provider of end-of-day pricing and valuation of securities to fund managers, reporting on 3.5 million securities through its EXSHARE. In 1999 FT Asset Management sold Extel, a business providing data on over 15,000 companies, principally in the UK, to Primark, a US-based company that wished to add UK companies to its large US database.

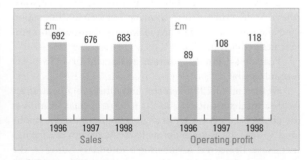

Exhibit 4   FT group

- FTSE International – a joint venture with the London Stock Exchange to provide the professional investment community with the leading UK indices. Together with the Amsterdam Stock Exchange, it publishes the Eurotop family of indices.
- AFX News – a news agency jointly owned by the Financial Times group and Agence France-Presse. It's a global provider of real-time financial and business news.
- Group Les Echos – France's leading business daily newspaper and the flagship of a group that includes many other business and professional titles, and Recoletos, which publishes *Expansión*, the leading Spanish business and financial newspaper.
- Pearson also owns 50% stakes in *Business Day* and *Financial Mail*, South Africa's leading business publisher.

The sales and operating profits over the three years 1996–98 are shown in Exhibit 4.

Pearson Television

Pearson moved into television through its acquisition of Thames Television when it lost its broadcasting licence in 1993. Acquisition has been an important element of Pearson Television's growth strategy.

Some TV production companies are tied to a broadcaster, whilst others are independent. Although Pearson owns 24% of the UK's Channel 5, it considers itself as an independent because it doesn't have management control over the channel. Pearson Television is the world's biggest independent production company, with over 150 programmes and with over 200 million viewers a month in 30 countries. Seventy per cent of its revenues are from outside the UK. Pearson Television has interests in game shows (*Family Fortunes*, *The Price is Right*), whereby Pearson owns the format and takes those formats internationally (*Family Fortunes* is *Family Feud* in the USA and *Une famille enor* in France). Pearson Televison has an extensive library of game show formats, owning 70% of all formats worldwide. It also makes what are called 'industrial dramas', soap operas with a heavy production schedule – several shows per week off the same set and production assets: for example, *The Bill*, *Neighbours* and *Baywatch*. Pearson Television has a strong presence in the USA through All-American, in Australia with Grundy, Italy with Mastrofilm, and in the UK with Alomo, Witzend and ACI. It's developing a presence in Latin America and Asia, but the downturn in these regions' economies has slowed this development. Pearson Television distributes programmes worldwide through Pearson Television International.

In November 1998 it launched its own website at

Exhibit 5   Pearson Television

www.pearsontv.com, containing everything you might wish to know about Pearson TV shows.

In January 1999 Pearson Television took a 10.9% stake in E-Pub Holdings, a leading US-based on-line entertainment company. This was so that Pearson Television could exploit its world's largest catalogue of game show formats on the Internet. E-Pub distributes through its website, *Uproar*, a website visited by nearly 4 million contestants per month.

The sales and operating profits for Pearson Television in 1996–98 are shown in Exhibit 5.

Pearson Television has made an investment in television broadcasting with its holding in MRTL, a new channel in Hungary, with a joint venture with a local investor and a broadcaster. Eighteen months after launch the Hungarian channel is now the most watched channel in Hungary. Pearson was approached by CLT-Ufa, the broadcasting arm of Bertlesmann, with which Pearson had a joint venture in Germany producing drama. Pearson didn't look to enter the Hungarian market but reasoned that this was a good opportunity to get a toehold in the huge Eastern European market for a relatively small investment, entering with a known partner and into one of the more stable Eastern European countries.

Penguin

Penguin has a catalogue of 40,000 English-language titles and is the world's leading children's publisher by revenue, and includes Ladybird books and Beatrix Potter. Recently the Ladybird production facility in Loughborough was closed down and integrated into Penguin's, and this led to the drop in operating profit in 1998. Penguin sells in 120 countries, with 50 million books sold in 1998. The sales and operating profits over the three years 1996–98 are shown in Exhibit 6.

Pearson Education

In the summer of 1997, Peter Jovanovich was hired from McGraw-Hill with the directive from Mrs Scardino to 'Make us the biggest educational publisher in the world'. This he succeeded in doing when, early in 1998, he led the negotiations that culminated in Pearson acquiring publishers Simon & Schuster for $4.6 billion (£2.8 billion). It was rumoured that the first offers were at $3.8 billion.[5] The merger of Pearson and Simon & Schuster is expected to produce savings of $130 million per year by 2000.[6] The one-off cost of the full integration of the two businesses is expected to be around $270 million. Initial financing for the acquisition was met by $6 billion of new bank facilities, which were used to refinance existing facilities. The $6 billion comprises a £2.5 billion five-year reducing loan, a £2 billion five-year reducing revolving credit facility and a $1.5 billion 364-day facility.

The educational imprints now owned by the Pearson group include Addison Wesley, Allyn & Bacon, Globe Fearson, Longman, Modern Curriculum Press, Pitman, Prentice Hall and Silver Burdett Ginn. In 1999 these imprints were consolidated into Pearson Education.

The Economist

Pearson own 50% of the shares in *The Economist*, the weekly global magazine of business, politics and finance. The other 50% is held by a conglomerate of private investors and parties with a personal interest in the paper and who strongly defend its editorial independence. *The Economist* has its own management structure: Pearson personnel are on the board, but they have no say in day-to-day management. The *Financial Times* and *The Economist* do collaborate – because both managements think this is a profitable thing to do. Not surprisingly, *The Economist* and the Financial Times group have collaborated more closely since Mrs Scardino became the CEO of Pearson.

The Economist is highly profitable. In 1998 it produced close to $40 million (£26 million) in profits and circulation has risen from 300,000 in the mid-1980s to 700,000 in mid-1999. Although a British paper, the UK readership is just one-sixth of the total. One in three of its American readers is a millionaire, and this accounts for the high volume of upmarket advertising it carries.

Pearson Technology Centre

Pearson plc provides central IT services to the whole of the group through the Pearson technology centre. For example, the centre manages all of Pearson Education's databases and co-ordinates IT investment across the group. It's a spin-off from the Simon & Schuster merger and is totally an internal operation located in the USA. It's planned to have branches in other places – probably the first of these will be in the UK.

Headland

Headland was the on-line division of Mindscape that was retained when Mindscape was sold. It's Pearson's on-line

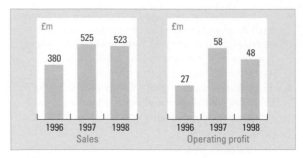

Exhibit 6   Penguin

publishing company which develops the authoring tools and digital publishing support for websites for all Pearson companies. It provides support to all the businesses in Pearson: for example, it supports the Rough Guides travel site, the Higher Education companion website, and The KnowZone with Scott Foresman–Addison Wesley. It does have a few projects with outsiders, but almost all of its activities are for Pearson companies.

Group strategy matters

Pearson plc effectively has a two-tier board system. The board of directors is made up of the chairman, the chief executive officer, the director of people, the finance director, the head of Pearson Television, and five non-executive directors. Beneath this is the Pearson management committee, composed of the CEO, the finance director, the director of people and the four people who are both chairpersons and chief executives of the four sets of businesses.

When Mrs Scardino took office she promised double-digit growth in earnings. Pearson used to be cash-rich and, deliberately through the Simon & Schuster acquisition, has increased the pressure on senior management to deliver. Strategy is developed both through regular strategy meetings and in a more *ad hoc* manner. Often Mrs Scardino will ask a senior manager to prepare a strategy paper for the next board meeting. This strategy paper will outline how a set of businesses is to develop and any investment needed. Each senior manager has to explain the strategic direction for their units and state how they will look in three to five years time. The CEO is keen on her senior managers having a vision – a clear direction and a reasoned pathway. Senior managers will also come along with projects outside of the planning process.

Peter Brimacombe, Pearson's strategy and development executive, sketches the strategy of the group:

Group strategy is to have a portfolio of assets that maximise the value of the Pearson Group. Competencies undersit our strategic thinking but you won't hear corporate executives talking about them. They don't talk about a collection of assets either. They talk about a great business that's good at doing something; for example, the *Financial Times* has the ability to deliver high-quality news information and analysis. But there is a search for synergy.

Claire Tavernier, the business development manager at Pearson Education, expands on this:

Pearson Television may be thinking of developing an educational channel or educational programmes, and would look to Pearson Education for content. Pearson Television has put together a new animation business and turned to Penguin with their children's characters. And Penguin's consumer appeal adds to the allure of the English-language teaching business – and we have a joint venture between Pearson Education and Penguin.

It appears that the media industry in which Pearson is operating values size. According to Claire Tavernier:

We need to attract creative talent and to do so it's very appealing to be a world-ranking media business. When the *Financial Times* went into Germany to form a joint venture with Bertlesmann it was much more powerful to say that it's Pearson talking to Bertelsmann rather than saying it's the Financial Times Group. In the media world aura or size matters, and in Europe there are only four or five media conglomerates – Bertelsmann, United News Media, Havas, Holtzbinde and Pearson, and thus only four who could have struck a deal with Bertlesmann. It helps us to be Pearson.

In January 1999 it was decided to establish Financial Times Management. This was a business that brought together the distance learning management education operations of the Financial Times group with the extensive intellectual properties of Pearson Education. It's aimed at providing both individual and company training. The newly appointed head reports directly to Mrs Scardino. This is a Pearson approach to fledgling businesses of great potential. New businesses are left alone to get on with things – and can thus react very speedily – but at the same time they have direct access to resources should they be needed. This approach can only be used in a few key strategic areas, but it can be, and has been done, at levels other than the very top of Pearson; for example, the head of the new animation business reports directly to the head of Pearson Television.

Budgets are developed each year. Detailed budgets are created for one year ahead, less detailed ones for the subsequent two years. The top line budgets are then monitored by the centre. There are three objectives by which the operating companies are measured – revenue growth, rate of profit growth and cash conversion – how much of the profit growth comes through to the centre. Bonuses are paid to senior managers on their achievement of these performance measures. Investments are more closely monitored than previously: the monitoring now includes the less obvious investments associated with on-going internal development, not simply with high-profile activities such as acquisitions.

The Pearson Group has no mission statement. It has set out its values as a company that 'always strives to be imaginative, brave and decent' and allows the individual businesses to develop mission statements if they so wish within this value framework. Peter explains what this means:

'Brave' means being prepared to take difficult decisions and to pursue significant and ambitious business opportunities; 'imaginative' means doing things differently where possible, and trying to change our structure; and 'decent' means how we treat people, particularly our three main stakeholders – shareholders, customers, and the people who work for and with Pearson – staff, authors, freelancers and actors.

The Pearson culture is to get the best talent and provide editorial independence. All the Pearson businesses are about creative people developing offers that can then be taken out into the marketplace: a creativity coupled with a sound commercial approach. The management team in Pearson believes it can transfer this culture across to all businesses.

The management team meets twice a month. Financial reports from the four groups go to the finance and strategy group at the centre, are bound in a pack with commentaries from the operating units and the finance and strategy group. The CEO reviews progress and talks to each operating unit about its performance. The board meets nine times a year and reviews quarterly performance and takes major strategic decisions.

Pearson follows a fairly open management style. After the annual presentation of the results to the staff, Mrs Scardino, who encourages staff to e-mail her, had 4,000 e-mails from throughout the organisation.

References

1 Pearson Annual Report, 1996.
2 Dawn Hayes, 'Scardino plays it by the book', *The Independent of Sunday*, Business Bloomberg, 24 May 1998, p. 2.
3 'Educating Pearson', *The Economist*, 23 May 1998, p. 86.
4 Pearson press release, 24 November 1998.
5 Jim Milliot, 'Top of the class in America', *The Independent of Sunday*, Business Bloomberg, 24 May 1998, p. 2.
6 Pearson press release, 24 November 1998.

There is more on Financial Times and Pearson at the companies' websites, http://www.FT.com and http://www.pearson.com, respectively

Adtranz (UK & Ireland)[a]

Background/history

Adtranz (UK & Ireland) has a history which goes back over 150 years. Originally, the company was the workshop arm of the nationalised railway company, British Rail, known as British Rail Engineering Limited (BREL). Privatisation of the industry has meant that the company has undergone many changes, but it has emerged a much leaner and stronger organisation.

1989 – BREL became the first British Rail-owned company to be privatised. It was bought by ABB 40%, Trafalgar House 40% (now Kvaerner) and a management–employee buyout (MEBO) 20%.

1991 – ABB took majority control of the company and launched an 'Operation Recovery' programme to make the culture of the business more customer-focused. (Trafalgar House believed that the rail market was not profitable, and MEBO could not get parent company guarantees.)

1992 – The company became ABB Transportation Ltd.

1992 – The privatisation of the UK's entire railway network was announced, leading to a three-year hiatus in investment. In this period, the company was forced to close its main plant in York and reduce its workforce significantly. However, the company further strengthened its maintenance and signalling operations through the acquisition of three new maintenance depots and Interlogic (part of the signalling arm of British Rail).

1996 – On 1 January 1996, ABB and Daimler-Benz merged their transportation interests on a 50:50 basis. The company's formal name became ABB Daimler-Benz Transportation, but for marketing purposes it chose the name Adtranz, incorporating both parent companies and implying 'A to Z' solutions. Overcapacity in the industry had led to pressure for a merger. (ABB and Daimler-Benz were fourth and fifth in the world.) This, coupled with the increasing trend towards globalisation, was the reason behind the merger. However, to justify a 50% stake, Daimler-Benz paid a substantial amount of cash.

Adtranz was headed by Kaare Vagner (CEO) and employed approximately 25,000 employees in over 60 group companies. It had marketing, engineering and manufacturing bases in some 40 countries, ensuring a global presence, with international group corporate centres located in Berlin, Brussels, Zurich and Singapore.

Adtranz could now draw on an immense pool of knowhow, from aerospace innovations in satellite technology put to use in signalling systems, to car designers creating new low-drag locomotive cabs, to a long-standing commitment to rail systems. The result of the merger was the world's most complete railway systems provider, offering customised solutions with a product ranging from diesel and electric locomotives, high-speed trains, light rail vehicles, metros, transits and people movers, through to signalling, fixed installations and customer support.[1]

1997 – The privatisation of the UK's railway network was complete. Further orders for new trains continue to be placed.

1998 – Adtranz (UK & Ireland) appoints a new chief executive officer, Per Staehr, who strongly believes in the future of the UK's railways:

Rail in the UK is in a new era of growth. Congested roads and railways are reaching bursting point. Environmental pressure grows. Rail must – and I believe will – play an increasing role in establishing the 'seamless integrated transport system' for the new millennium. In our newly privatised railway industry there is constant exposure to the public. The key to success is product reliability, the commitment of employees and suppliers, and competitive costs. Our first and foremost aim is to deliver what we promise to our customers, and in doing so, we will assist in growing their business. Together, we will strive towards making rail the first choice in transportation. I firmly believe in the future of

---

[a] This case study was prepared by Kevin Waring. © Kevin Waring, 1999.

the rail industry and in 'speaking railways'. In the UK, there is no real – and immediate – alternative to rail.

Rail privatisation has been spreading all over the world at a fast pace. What started in the UK some years ago is now underway throughout Europe, as well as in Asia and Latin America.

In the 'good old days', Adtranz worked mainly with one customer per country, the national railways. It is now, however, facing an increasing multitude of customers locally. This is being addressed by the strategy and organisational structure, in terms of a decentralised and increased marketing responsibility. Adtranz faces ever-increasing competition per country as more and more newcomers are entering the national markets. In line with these global developments and challenges, Adtranz has strategically based its organisation's efforts on a 'centre of expertise' concept. This is a concept already successfully implemented in the automotive and airline industries – designed to cope with changing market conditions. Today, modular product platforms offer basic standards and allow a multitude of pre-designed options. This allows customers to select from a comprehensive range of features fitting their specific market requirements.[2]

ABB

ABB was formed in 1988 when the Swedish company Asea merged with Brown Boveri of Switzerland to create a global engineering giant with a turnover in excess of $30 billion and with 210,000 employees worldwide. The merger decision was preceded by only six weeks of negotiations, conducted without investment bankers by both companies' top management and their major shareholders, namely Peter Wallenberg for Asea and Stephan Schmidheiny for Brown Boveri. Asea's CEO, the then 46-year-old Percy Barnevik, became CEO of ABB.

ABB's roots are in electrical engineering, having a strong local presence in over 100 countries and with global expertise in production, supply and finance – giving access to many new customers for Adtranz. ABB's research and development is focused on customer needs, having its unique expertise in cultural and business diversity, establishing cross-border teams.

ABB has been divided into 1300 identifiable companies and 5000 profit centres. These are aggregated into 59 business areas and eight business segments. The business segments are power plants; power transmission; power distribution; electrical equipment; transportation; environmental controls; financial services; and other activities.[3]

All segments are responsible for organising manufacturing around the world and for product development. All are headed by a 12-member executive board in Zurich, Switzerland.

The organisation chart for ABB can be seen in Exhibit 1.

Daimler-Benz

Daimler-Benz has a history that dates back more than 100 years. Daimler-Benz's roots are in mechanical engineering and particularly transportation. The expertise in areas such as rail vehicle assembly and diesel drives is Daimler-Benz's key input to Adtranz. Today, Daimler-Benz is Europe's largest industrial corporation, with a turnover in excess of DM100 billion and with a portfolio of 23 business units focusing on transportation services. The business units are organised into four divisions – passenger cars, commercial vehicles, aerospace and services, as well as in the directly managed industrial holdings.[4]

AEG Daimler-Benz Industrie is a business unit within the technologically integrated Daimler-Benz group. AEG has been a supplier for more than a century in all fields of rail passenger and freight transport found throughout the world. AEG Daimler-Benz Industrie consists of six business segments: rail systems – rail wayside systems (i.e. point machines, barriers, etc.), rail vehicles, AEG transportation systems (AEG); microelectronics; diesel drives; power engineering; automation; and other activities.

The organisation chart for Daimler-Benz can be seen in Exhibit 2.

Current situation in the public transport industry

Transportation has reached global dimensions, with the various flows of traffic inexorably growing together to form one complex system. Increasing internationalisation calls for mutually compatible transport technologies that overcome any borders between systems. However, individualised solutions are needed that are adapted to the respective local, economic and ecological conditions.

Rail systems will be of crucial importance for the future development of passenger and freight transport. At the same time, rail, with its high potential, will play an ever-increasing role in intermodal transport when it comes to the best combination of all modes. Rail in this serves as the interface between ships, automobiles and aeroplanes, forming the link between urban, regional and international traffic.

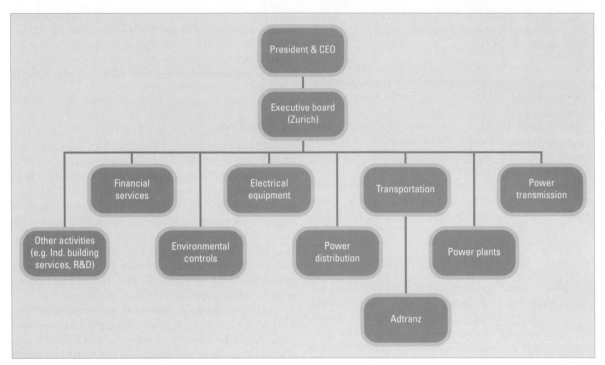

Exhibit 1   ABB organisation chart

Exhibit 2   Daimler-Benz organisation chart

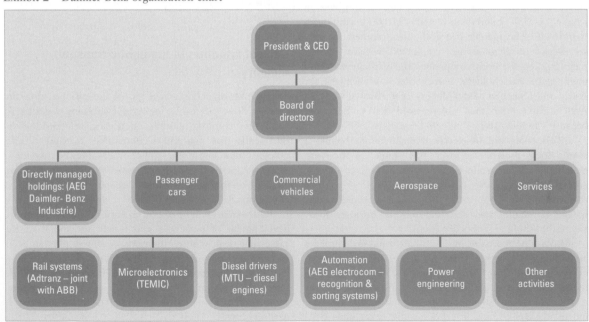

The last ten years have seen a major change in the 'public transport industry' within the UK. Privatisation in most sectors in the early 1990s has meant that operators need to pull out of the 'dark ages' and make their business reliable and profitable. During the final years of British Rail, no new rolling stock orders were placed and the infrastructure was slowly falling apart – and yet people were wanting to use the trains. The government allowed the UK's railways to fall into decline while talk of privatisation was going on.

There are many reasons why, at the end of this century, we are witnessing a rail renaissance. The uncontrolled growth of road transport points towards severe problems; however, there are now restrictions upon new motorway building within the UK. Twenty per cent of the total global carbon dioxide emissions now come from traffic – feeding the greenhouse effect. Coupled with the impact on the landscape and the problem of congestion, the railways are an increasingly environmentally friendly transport option.[5] Toxic emission levels caused by railways are almost negligible in comparison with cars, and in terms of primary energy consumption rail systems are substantially better than cars, not to mention the enormous environment bonus of rail against air travel (rail vehicle engines typically run at very low revolutions, around 2000rpm compared with jet engines at around 10,000rpm and hence use much less fuel, particularly at take-off, when jet engines have to be at full throttle).[6]

The future in the UK

There are currently 25 train operating companies (TOCs) in the UK which run passenger trains. The 25 TOCs came into the passenger rail business knowing they had to increase rail usage while agreeing to reduce public subsidy. As a group of private businesses, they took on an immense set of challenges, including that of maintaining the benefits of the network as a whole for passengers. While each TOC has separate and clearly understood obligations and objectives, there is also a collective recognition of their role as participants in a national drive to rejuvenate Britain's railways.

This is why the companies, through their association (the Association of Train Operating Companies – ATOC), have from the start argued in favour of a directing force, near to the centre of government, to co-ordinate and drive the many policy decisions attached to this boldest of political–commercial ventures. From its inception in 1996, ATOC has called for strong government to provide a clear and coherent programme for the railways.

Strategy is a keyword in the government's vocabulary, something apparent in the 1998 Integrated Transport White Paper (the first transport policy white paper for 20 years), which said: 'It is clear from our discussions with train operators ... that the industry wants leadership and focus that only the government can provide; and that the level of long-term investment is directly related to the clarity of that strategic vision.'

ATOC has therefore welcomed the creation of the Strategic Rail Authority (SRA) to complement and reinforce its members' private enterprise skills and commitment to running world-class railways. It believes the SRA should occupy this strategic vacuum in the following interlocking ways, with the emphasis firmly on strategy – and not operations:

- by acting as an engine for growth;
- by giving strategic focus, especially with regards to investment;
- by being an industry champion.

Deputy Prime Minister John Prescott, in a speech to the House of Commons in July 1998, said: 'The rail industry needs a stable framework to deliver long-term investment and better services for passengers. In the next six years, 17 of the franchises come up for renewal. Some train operators want early renegotiation of their franchises.'[7]

Competition – major players in the industry

Globally, there are four significant organisations that design and manufacture rolling stock and signalling systems:

- Adtranz (global) – 14% global market share;
- Alstom (UK/France) – 12% global market share;
- Siemens (Germany) – 12% global market share;
- Bombardier (Canada/Europe) – 8% global market share.

The remaining 54% global market share is divided between numerous organisations, some of the larger being Fiat (Italy) and CAF (Spain); 10–15% is the combined Japanese contribution, while the North American locomotive market accounts for around 5–6%.

There are other smaller manufacturers of rolling stock. One such organisation is the Central Japan Railway Company, which is developing magnetically levitated vehicles specifically for the home market. Within the UK there is also RFS(E) Ltd – Rail Freight Services Engineering – based in Doncaster, which is a shunting locomotive manufacturer with aftersales support, and Thrall Europa, part of America's second largest freight company (Thrall Car), which builds freight wagons for EWS (English, Welsh & Scottish). In Germany smaller manufacturers include Vossloh AG and Schaltbau Group. Vossloh AG own the former Siemens diesel locomotive factory, and the Schaltbau Group is involved in vehicle re-manufacturing/rail traffic systems.

Whether global or local, the major players compete for similar business. The mass transportation global market is aggressive and profits have been depressed in recent years to remain competitive – particularly in privatised markets. One result of privatisation has been to force rolling stock prices down. However, due to Adtranz's global presence, every market becomes local, and economies of scale from its global reach can be drawn upon – unlike any other competitor.

Bombardier in the UK currently has the Virgin Cross Country contract to supply diesel multiple units, some of which will be tilting trains. Including the maintenance contract the total value is around £1 billion. Bombardier has about 13,000 employees worldwide in transportation and has strengths in the following areas:

- extensive product line covering all transportation modes from electric/diesel urban-type vehicles to light rail and intercity trains;
- turnkey capability, i.e. can carry out infrastructure work;
- a strong strategic position in the USA and European facilities in Germany, Austria, Belgium, France and the UK.

Alstom currently has numerous contracts globally; some of the UK-based ones include Virgin West Coast Mainline (54 × eight-car tilting trains), electric multiple units for Gatwick/South West Trains/ScotRail, diesel multiple units for First North Western/First Great Western and London Underground Jubilee/Northern Lines, all adding to around £900 million. Alstom has about 21,000 employees worldwide in transportation and has strengths in the following areas:

- standard product platforms for vehicle systems;
- a profitable order book;
- high-speed intercity dominance;
- very strong procurement management.

Customers

To explain how the rolling stock industry works and who its customers are, it is best to focus on the UK market as this is particularly interesting. In the UK there are three financiers which emerged out of privatisation – the rolling stock leasing companies or ROSCOs as they are known – Porterbrook, Angel Trains Contracts and Forward Trust (along with one recent addition called GATX), and 25 customers called train operating companies (TOCs) – such as

Midland Mainline, ScotRail, Central, Connex, Anglia Virgin.

In the newly privatised railway industry in the UK the process of actually purchasing new rolling stock is a complicated process. First, there has to be a perceived need that more trains are required. This may start with the results of market research carried out by the TOCs. The situation is that the TOCs buy the trains, which are financed by the ROSCOs for a defined period of time. Therefore, the TOC would most likely be unable to satisfy the market needs unless more vehicles were leased from the ROSCO. Currently, TOCs are buying new vehicles with a commitment to lease until the end of their franchise period. On this basis the ROSCOs can investigate the feasibility of financing new rolling stock.

Tender requirements vary from specific TOC infrastructure to vehicle interior requirements. A ROSCO would have less contact with Adtranz than the TOC since the TOC defines the performance specification along with its own colour scheme for, say, seats on the inside to logos on the outside. Other options a TOC may wish to specify include catering facilities, disabled areas, layout of seats, luggage racks, seat reservations, etc., although satisfying the build requirements isn't where a contract ends. Many of the recent UK-based contracts also contain work packages covering maintenance – planned and unplanned. These too have a set of performance criteria defined by the TOC but indirectly by OPRAF (Office of Passenger Rail Franchising). The ROSCO, however, has a constant presence at all contract negotiations and reviews to ensure that the residual value of their vehicles is maximised, as the trains will be still running after the current TOC franchise commitments go under review.

Current contracts contain the usual penalty clauses for late delivery, but also penalties on the train manufacturer for trains not running or being delayed due to faults.

Adtranz and its organisational structure

Adtranz's global reach is supported by the company's organisational structure, ensuring that each local Adtranz transportation company can draw upon the resources and expertise of the whole group to deliver customised system solutions. The structure combines both ABB and Daimler-Benz organisations, ensuring there is no duplication or overlapping of resources and activities.

To eliminate duplication and overlapping, Adtranz's organisational structure consists of five distinct business segments (A, B, C, D and E), with profit and loss responsibilities for defined worldwide regions and countries, as well as specified products under the leadership of a group executive board member for each segment. In order to speak with one voice in the marketplace, and to ensure the setting up and defining of the product portfolio, eight centres of product expertise have been created. These centres of expertise (CoE) have responsibilities for marketing, design and manufacture, and the CoEs relating to each specific business segment can be seen in Exhibit 3. Exhibit 4 shows the organisational structure of Adtranz.

CoEs report directly to the head of each relevant business segment. Each CoE keeps all rail transportation companies (RTCs) informed of any developments and in turn feedback is given to the CoE. This is done through regular meetings.

The CoE concept refers to Adtranz products, i.e. multiple units, locomotives, light rail, etc. The CoEs are designated to the appropriate business segments as follows:

- have full technical product responsibility;
- manage the product portfolio for a specific vehicle category;
- develop vehicle concepts based on worldwide markets.

Customer support is the odd one out. It is responsible for fleet maintenance of rolling stock for numerous operators, from collision damage to spares supply and heavy main-

Business segment	CoE	Location
A	Multiple units (i.e. regional trains)	Vasteras (Sweden)
A	Intercity trains	Vasteras (Sweden)
A	Automatic guided train systems	Pittsburgh (USA)
B	Electric locomotives/ power heads	Zurich (Switzerland)
C	Diesel locomotives	Kassel (Germany)
C	Light rail vehicles	Nremberg (Germany)
D	Customer support	Derby (UK)
E	Metros	Derby (UK)

Exhibit 3   Adtranz centres of expertise

tenance. Globally, the customer support CoE originated through there only being Africa and Derby as customer support centres; during reorganisation Derby became the CoE due to its greater experience.

Each of the products that are the responsibilities of the

Exhibit 4   Organisational structure of Adtranz (global)

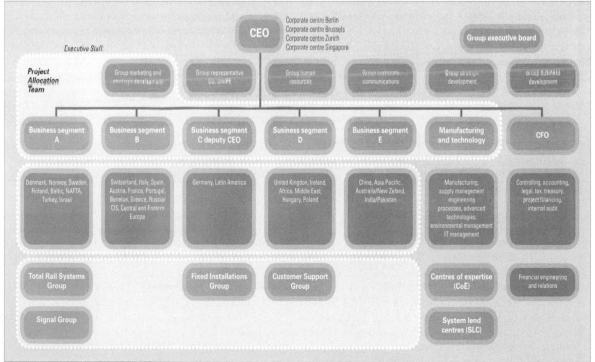

CoE can be broken down into a number of parts or sub-systems, i.e. body shells, bogies, etc. System lead centres (SLCs) are set up to provide a support role to the CoEs of the subsystems, whilst execution of allocated production orders are carried out within a manufacturing facility, known as a regional transportation company (RTC).

Adtranz (UK & Ireland) is manufacturing 'Eurotrams' for Strasbourg in France. Under normal conditions, France falls within the group's business segment B, not business segment D, which Adtranz (UK & Ireland) is in. This example highlights the standardised cross-border approach to design and manufacture. Countries fall within certain product groupings purely through the past work that has been carried out there and through superior knowledge.

Adtranz encourages continuous learning and knowledge generation at all levels. Knowledge can be tapped into easily where it is needed through the clear product responsibilities defined earlier. For example, the Derby site has recently become the CoE for metros due to the design and development done of the body shell (by Derby Bodyshell SLC). In addition, sales and marketing has carried out heavy marketing and bidding in the Far East for metro vehicles. Other crucial areas for design such as bogies can be sourced from Germany – the bogie SLC. When it comes to manufacture, the inherent modular concept means that Derby or any other RTC could potentially assemble metro vehicles – usually the RTC local to the customer.

The railway industry stands on the threshold of deep structural change. Politicians, operators and manufacturers have a lot of homework to do, according to Andrew F. Saxe, an internationally respected railway consultant. Adtranz is rising to this challenge with its innovative modular product platforms. The increased use of prefabricated modules is a must to optimise ease of maintenance and life-cycle costs. Adtranz's organisational structure and culture supports innovation. For example, Germany is the SLC for bogies, while they can be manufactured in Derby. An RTC like Derby, while able to manufacture bogies, cannot develop bogie designs independent of the German SLC – or even modify system designs without prior approval. Therefore the SLC has responsibility for the engineering and application design of its systems but can draw from the expertise elsewhere within the group if necessary.

Adtranz (UK & Ireland) organisation

Exhibit 5 shows the organisational structure of Adtranz (UK & Ireland). It is broken down into a number of areas, including rolling stock (GB ROS), customer support (GB CUS), total rail systems (GB TRS) and signalling. Within GB ROS are rail products, such as bogie manufacture, and rail projects, where complete vehicles (such as 'Turbostar') are assembled. Within GB CUS there is train part services (TPS), satisfying all spares and logistics needs for maintenance, and train maintenance services (TMS), carrying out all kinds of planned and unplanned maintenance.

Exhibit 5 Organisational structure of Adtranz (UK & Ireland)

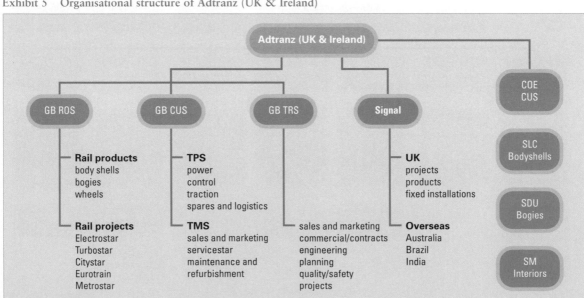

Manufacturing

Rail projects are managed per project by a decentralised 'one roof' concept. This concept allows all functions of project management, procurement, finance, engineering and manufacturing to be housed together in one office per project.

Exhibit 6 shows an exploded view of a rail vehicle,

Exhibit 6 Exploded view of vehicle assembly philosophy

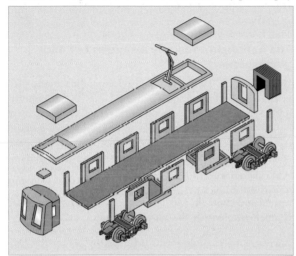

and this is essentially how a rail vehicle is built at Adtranz. Roof, underframe and body sides will be fitted out first. Simultaneously, the cab and intermediate end will be fitted out. The sides, roof and underframe are then brought together and joined to form a tube. The ends are capped, with the cab and intermediate end forming the shell of a rail vehicle. From here the interior and heavy underframe rafts are fitted. On the underframe items such as the engine are supplied on a raft and fitted.

This modular approach allows Adtranz a simple way in which solutions can be tailored to meet the customers' needs, both in operation and interior layout.

References

1 'Daimler-Benz', Daimler-Benz UK plc, 1996.
2 'Modular Product Platforms', Adtranz, March 1998.
3 'We Speak Railways', Adtranz, Germany, 1997.
4 ABB Deutschland, Prof. Hugo Uyterhoeven, Harvard Business School, 12 May 1993.
5 'A New Dimension of Sustainable Transport Development', Adtranz, Ake Nilsson and Kaare Vagner, 1998.
6 'Daimler-Benz', Daimler-Benz UK plc, 1996.
7 *Rail Magazine*, ABC Consumer Press, Nigel Harris (managing ed.), March 24–April 6 1999.

European telecommunications champions: preparing for global competition[a]

Introduction

Between the 1910s and 1970s, most telephone systems in Europe were controlled by state-owned national monopolies called postal, telegraph and telephone (PTT) agencies. International telephony was administered by a cartel comprised of the largest European PTTs and American Telephone and Telegraph (AT&T). The major European PTTs and their favoured equipment suppliers were protected from domestic and international competition until the 1980s and 1990s. The traditional arrangement of closed national systems is now being transformed into a new, more open and competitive domestic and international structure. Following the lead taken by the USA, UK and Japan, countries throughout the world have privatised state-owned PTTs to form public telecommunications operators (PTOs) and liberalised telecommunications markets. A new international political economy is emerging in telecommunications services as PTOs face strong competition at home and the rise of global telecommunications companies operating in international markets.

This case study addresses the internationalisation strategies of the largest and most internationally active PTOs in the European Union (EU): British Telecommunications (BT), Deutsche Telekom, France Telecom, KPN Telecom of the Netherlands, Telia of Sweden, Telefónica of Spain and Telecom Italia. It deals with the period prior to full liberalisation of the EU telecommunications market on 1 January 1998. In order to prepare for domestic and international competition, the major European PTOs have expanded in foreign markets and formed global strategic alliances. It is widely expected that only a few large operators with a strong international presence will survive intensifying competition and a growing concentration of market power in the late 1990s. Many of these operators, such as BT and KPN Telecom, maintain that competitive success in global markets can only be secured from a strong home base.

[a] This case was prepared by Dr Willem Hulsink (assistant professor with the Department of Strategic Management and Business Administration, Rotterdam School of Management, Erasmus University, Rotterdam) and Dr Andrew Davies (research fellow, SPRU – Science and Technology Policy Research, University of Sussex). © Willem Hulsink and Andrew Davies, 1999.

The national environment and globalisation

This section examines the shift from a universal model based on the PTT structure of national monopolies towards a new globalised telecommunications environment.

The national monopoly arrangement and globalisation

Until the early 1980s, national telecommunications provision consisted of standardised and basic voice telephony, telegraph, telex and leased-line services supplied by a national monopoly or regional and long-distance monopolies working in close co-operation. In most European countries, telecommunications provision was a legal monopoly placed under the control of state-owned PTTs. PTTs were considered to be natural monopolies that had to be owned and controlled by governments rather than private companies to ensure the supply of an efficient and universal service. Under this national monopoly arrangement, the strategy of the PTT coincided with national telecommunications policy. Under the accounting rate system, an international cartel of PTTs agreed prices and conditions for international telecommunications, which were charged in excess of the cost of delivering calls. Common standards and rules to ensure joint service provision were regulated by the International Telecommunications Union (ITU).

While most PTTs were not involved in equipment supply, they were surrounded by a few preferred equipment suppliers that were dependent on PTT contracts and prevented from serving foreign competitors. In the UK, for example, the telecommunications service monopoly controlled by the Post Office was closely linked to an oligopolistic club of domestic equipment manufacturers, including General Electric Company (GEC), Plessey and Standard Telephone Company (STC).

It should be recognised, however, that national PTT monopolies were not universally adopted throughout Europe. Sweden, for example, never held a statutory monopoly. Televerket, the Swedish national telecommunications operator, had a monopoly that extended from services into equipment provision. Televerket encompassed an equipment manufacturing arm, called Teli, which was its parent's prime supplier and prevented Televerket being captive to Ericsson, the largest Swedish telecommunications equipment supplier. In Denmark and Finland, national telecommunications provision was divided among a number of regional monopolies controlled by local authorities or private interests connected to a state-owned, long-distance monopoly PTT operator. In Finland, the numerous regional telephone operators maintained competition between suppliers by ordering equipment from domestic (Nokia) and foreign suppliers (Ericsson, Siemens and Alcatel). Despite these exceptions, however, telecommunications systems throughout Europe were characterised by some form of monopoly and were contained within the boundaries of the nation-state.

In the 1980s and 1990s, a number of forces have exerted pressure on the closed and stable structure of national telecommunications systems and brought about a shift from monopoly to greater domestic and foreign competition:

- **Technical change** New technologies (e.g. fibre-optic transmission, computer-controlled switching, cellular radio and the Internet) provide opportunities for contestibility and market entry, as new companies challenge traditional PTTs by offering access to cheaper and more innovative telecommunications services. A small number of global operators now use network-management technologies to provide services, such as virtual private networks, at low cost across national borders. National markets are often no longer sufficient in size to recover the high costs of R&D and investment in new network technologies.

- **Markets** PTOs and new operators are offering a range of new services (data, multimedia, mobile communications, Internet access, etc.) and moving into new geographical markets to meet unsatisfied user requirements and proliferating market demands. PTOs are extending their geographical presence throughout the world and developing innovative new services by entering into joint ventures, alliances, mergers and acquisitions to meet the global telecommunications needs of multinational corporate customers. More recently, international operators have been attracted into foreign markets to supply cable TV, multimedia and Internet services through mergers and alliances with partners from previously separate broadcasting, computing and information industries.

- **Neo-liberal policies** Deregulation and liberalisation, which first took place in the USA and later in the UK and Japan, has since spread throughout the world as national governments and the EU implement policies to liberalise telecommunications markets, privatise PTTs and establish regulatory authorities that are separated from PTO operations and in some cases

independent of government (e.g. Oftel[b] in the UK). The monopoly held by European PTOs was abolished on 1 January 1998, when the European Commission (EC) liberalised all telecommunications markets, including infrastructure and voice telephony.

Since the UK's decision to privatise, liberalise and re-regulate domestic telecommunications markets in the early 1980s, other European countries have opened up telecommunications markets to greater competition. In theory, the EU's decision to sanction full competition in infrastructural and voice telephony markets on 1 January 1998 appears to symbolise the end of the national monopoly in European telecommunications. In practice, however, European governments have used a mixture of policy and regulatory instruments to create distinctive governance regimes and patterns of domestic competition:

- **Privatisation** Corporatisation is a stepping stone in the transition from a publicly controlled PTT to a private corporation, called a public telecommunications operator (PTO). Privatisation involves a change from public to private ownership through the sale of PTO shares. While privatisation does nothing to liberalise the market, it provides some of the conditions to prepare PTOs for competition: (1) changes from civil servant status to more flexible personnel policies; (2) changes from a functionally integrated hierarchy to profit-driven and decentralised multidivisional organisation; and (3) an opportunity to form strategic alliances and take out equity stakes in foreign PTOs.

- **Liberalisation** The shift from monopoly to competition is brought about by three forms of liberalisation: (1) licensing new companies; (2) structural separation of the integrated structure of the PTT, e.g. divestiture, horizontal separation of posts and telecommunications, or vertical separation of networks and services (into wholesale and retail companies); and (3) asymmetrical regulation to promote competition by protecting new entrants and curtailing the incumbent operator.

- **Regulatory reform** Competitive markets have to be regulated by the separation of the former PTT's operational and administrative tasks. (1) Operational tasks remain in the hands of PTTs, which have been granted an (exclusive) concession for the provision of basic services. (2) Regulatory authorities are responsible for controlling prices, enforcing licence conditions and ensuring quality of service and fair competition. Regulatory authority can be located in

---

[b] The UK regulatory body the Office of Telecommunications.

Ranking 1997	Company	International revenue 1996 $m	Total revenue 1996 $m (rank)		Employees 1996	% State ownership
1	Deutsche Telekom	6,961	40,945	(1)	201,060	74
2	Cable & Wireless	4,597	9,918	(6)	37,448	0
3	BT	2,949	24,344	(3)	127,500	0
4	France Telecom	2,845	29,095	(2)	164,720	100
5	Telecom Italia	1,835	19,320	(4)	86,030	65
6	Swiss Telecom	1,568	7,794	(8)	21,204	100
7	KPN Telecom (NL)	1,265	8,253	(7)	32,277	44
8	Telefonica (Spain)	1,047	11,325	(5)	67,217	21
9	OPT (Austria)	859	5,313	(10)	53,555	100
10	Telia (Sweden)	775	6,459	(9)	34,192	100

Source: adapted from *Communications Week International*, 24 November 1997

Exhibit 1   Top ten European PTOs, ranked by international telecommunications revenue

single-industry regulators (e.g. Oftel) that are independent of government, or assigned to departments of government, as in continental European countries.

In response to the globalisation of telecommunications markets, several EU member states have embarked on programmes of privatisation, liberalisation and re-regulation to prepare national PTOs for strong competition at home and opportunities to expand abroad in liberalised markets. The largest PTOs in Europe ranked by international revenue and total revenue are shown in Exhibit 1. Although these figures indicate the contribution of domestic telecommunications markets to the size of a PTO, they do not capture the degree to which PTOs have become internationalised.

Often the rhetoric about globalisation misses the point that the nation is becoming more, not less, important in a competitive global telecommunications market. The idea that one near-universal model of a PTT monopoly is being replaced by another based on competition obscures significant differences in national governance regimes.

In practice, two quite different types of governance regime have emerged out of the restructuring in national telecommunications environments during the 1980s and 1990s. The different ways in which policy and regulatory instruments are used by governments to promote and shape the outcomes of competition in national telecommunications markets reflect a more fundamental difference between two models of capitalism (see Exhibit 2).

	Strategies towards structuring the home market and international environment
Anglo-American liberalism	Strong domestic rivalry to promote international competitiveness (e.g. USA, UK)
Continental mercantilism	Promotion of national champions in sheltered home markets as springboard for foreign expansion (continental Europe)

Exhibit 2   Diverging national approaches

Anglo-American liberalism

The Anglo-American liberal market model of regulatory reform followed by the UK and USA draws inspiration from Adam Smith's sources of entrepreneurial initiative and free trade. In this model, individual or private interests take precedence over collective and public interests. It assumes an atomised market with little social cohesion and government interference, which is seen to promote efficiency, risk taking, innovation and entrepreneurial investment.

Radical policies of competition at home and free trade abroad championed by the USA and UK emphasise how 'domestic rivalry' is in the nation's interest, since it promotes internationally competitive players that will generate early-mover advantages in global competition. Companies that have capable, home-based competitors are forced into becoming pioneering global businesses seeking access to foreign markets. With a century-long tradition of antitrust action under the Sherman Act, the US government has shown its commitment to breaking up monopolies – such as Standard Oil, American Tobacco and AT&T – in the interest of competition. The Monopolies and Mergers Commission (MMC) in the UK performs a similar function. The EU is now following the USA and UK in adopting stronger pro-competition policies since the Commission's decision to fully liberalise the telecommunications industry in 1998.

The Anglo-American model emphasises the early introduction of domestic rivalry and the end of the public utility concept in telecommunications. In this view, only the free play of market forces can determine which part of telecommunications remains a natural monopoly. Deregulation and divestiture of AT&T in the USA in 1984, and liberalisation and privatisation of BT in the same year, injected competition into the traditional monopoly framework. While the US and UK governments have encouraged foreign competition in their home markets, this is balanced by a requirement for the investors' home countries to reciprocate by opening up their markets (see Exhibit 3). In order to prevent hostile takeovers of domestic operators by foreign companies, the US government has restricted foreign ownership of domestic operators to 20 per cent. Rapid implementation of open and competitive telecommunications markets is well suited to the USA's and UK's interest in gaining early access to other European countries before their PTOs are in a position to offer strong competition.

Continental European mercantilism

The continental approach to industrial policy owes more to the ideas of Colbert, the seventeenth century founder of selective government regulation to support strategic French enterprises. In the tradition of French mercantilism, the essential characteristics of Colbertism are protectionism and enlightened state intervention. Colbertism is a carefully organised system of selective state intervention, regulatory protection and subsidies run by a technocratic elite to assist backward national industries in catching up with enterprises in the leading industrial nations.

In contrast to Anglo-American antitrust policies, countries on mainland Europe – such as France, Germany, the Netherlands and Switzerland – have traditionally tolerated market dominance – such as monopoly, oligopolies and cartels – in strategic national industries. In the post-war years, continental European countries have developed a social partnership ideology, involving co-operation between management, employees, banks, government and other stakeholders (e.g. consumers) and long-term considerations, such as investment, training, employment and R&D.

Continental European governments support national industries in international markets by taking protectionist, or mercantilist, measures: public procurement programmes, R&D subsidies, trade-related investment measures, export financing, local content requirements for foreign investors, exclusive rights to home-based companies, etc. Their aim is to retain domestic autonomy in strategic industries by restricting real competition at home and thereby creating a favourable environment to prepare 'national champions' for international competition. In the 1960s, European governments encouraged the formation of one or two chosen national champions from a number of existing firms in computing and aerospace industries, because they believed that too much domestic competition prevented companies achieving the scale and strength to challenge foreign competitors. In return for being responsive to the nation's needs, national champions were entitled to be subsidised and protected by their national government.

Despite the widespread acceptance of liberal policies, national control of telecommunications service provision in varying forms continues to be the favoured route to success in global markets in several continental European countries, including France, Germany, the Netherlands, Sweden and Switzerland (see Exhibit 3). As in the airline industry, European governments are seeking to turn their

Exhibit 3   Strategies of nation-states

		Home market preferences	
		Domestic protection	Domestic rivalry
International market preferences	Mercantilism/strategic trade	France Germany Italy	Finland
	Liberalism/free trade	The Netherlands	UK USA

former PTTs into national champions by carefully reorganising and changing the legal status and names of their PTTs. Less emphasis is placed on free markets and more on the preparation of PTOs for commercial success, while minimising the risks and harmful shocks of competition.

Whereas the UK adopted a 'big bang' approach by simultaneously privatising BT, sanctioning domestic competition and establishing an independent regulator as early as 1984, continental European countries have delayed the move towards fully competitive telecommunications markets. For example, despite early signs that the Netherlands might be one of the first continental European countries to follow the UK's liberal approach, PTT Telecom was corporatised in 1989 under the control of KPN, a postal and telecommunications holding company, and policies to privatise KPN and liberalise the market have been delayed. Competition in the Dutch telecommunications infrastructure was introduced in 1996 and voice telephony in mid-1997, just prior to EU liberalisation. While Germany sanctioned limited domestic competition prior to the EU's 1998 deadline, other countries such as Spain and Switzerland preferred to wait for EU liberalisation.

However, there are differences between continental countries, indicated by the timing, speed and selectivity of privatisation, liberalisation and independent regulation. For example, France, Germany and Switzerland have been slow to move on all three fronts. Sweden has moved ahead with liberalisation but delayed privatisation. The Netherlands has adopted a more balanced and incremental approach to reform along the three dimensions by establishing a fully competitive market in 1997. Spain has privatised Telefonica, but liberalisation of domestic telecommunications is delayed until October 1998.

In continental countries that were quicker to liberalise telecommunications markets, new entrants have experienced difficulties in getting established. For example, Esprit Telecom, the foreign-owned reseller of international sellers, accused PTT Telecom of charging inflated prices for leased lines and filed a complaint with DG XIII, the EC's telecommunications directorate, charging the Dutch regulator with not implementing open network provision (ONP) directives, which require that leased lines should be provided at cost price. The complaint was only withdrawn after the Dutch government forced PTT Telecom to reduce its leased-line charges. Similarly in Germany, a recent attempt by Deutsche Telekom to offer substantial bulk discounts to large business users to pre-empt competition was strongly opposed by new entrants. After the EC intervened in favour of the new entrants, Deutsche Telekom was forced to modify its plans.

Programmes of reform were delayed while governments satisfied the requirements of various interests that were opposed to corporatisation and privatisation, particularly trade unions, PTT employees and opposition parties. Although they differ in timing and emphasis, these PTOs have capitalised on their remaining monopoly periods to build up profits and reserves, pay off debts and mobilise support from management, employees and other stakeholders for potentially unpopular policies to privatise and restructure national monopolies. Priority was given to internal corporate restructuring, privatisation and tariff rebalancing – a precondition for competition so that prices are more closely aligned to costs – while liberalising peripheral markets such as value-added services and terminal equipment.

Continental PTOs receive government assistance through the shelter of supportive legal and regulatory regimes, rather than direct subsidies, to protect PTOs from destructive competition and tolerate their attempts to control new markets. Unlike the UK, where Oftel is independent of government, responsibility for regulation in continental European countries has been assigned to departments of government that are ill equipped to prevent the abuse of monopoly power or disinclined to favour new entrants. With the exception of the Netherlands, these countries delayed the establishment of an independent regulator until the EU's deadline for full competition on 1 January 1998.

Innovation and internationalisation strategies of Europe's major PTOs

The two contrasting models of governance create the domestic environment within which PTOs must innovate and achieve competitiveness in global markets. Before describing the different approaches to globalisation, it is important to explain how the different national environments shape the innovation strategies pursued by European PTOs and their orientation towards globalisation. Exhibit 4 summarises the paths of globalisation pursued by the leading (European) telecommunications operators, dealing with strategies via collaboration or internal growth.

Many of the leading offensive innovators in world telecommunications originate from the highly competitive US market. It was MCI and Sprint, the new long-distance operators allowed into the market after divestiture in 1984, that encouraged AT&T to accelerate its investment in digital switching and fibre-optic transmission during the late 1980s.

More recently, WorldCom, a new type of entrepreneurial telecommunications operator, has entered the scene, which is not tied to the sunk costs in older technologies and bureaucratic management structures of the

Towards internationalism		Towards innovation	
		Defensive	Offensive
	Collaborative	Deutsche Telekom NL PPT TeleDenmark	AT & T BT
	Internal	Cable & Wireless	WorldCom

Exhibit 4   Telecommunications companies' strategic pathways

traditional PTOs. Whereas traditional PTOs are deeply involved in many domestic telecommunications activities, WorldCom is entirely focused on the global end of the spectrum. WorldCom operates a high-volume and low-unit-cost fibre-optic local and long-distance network with access to the Internet to provide global services to business users. WorldCom also provides a radically different approach to international expansion compared with the more defensive route favoured by traditional operators of entering into strategic alliances with other PTOs.

Compared with Continental European PTOs, BT was quicker to follow an aggressive strategy of growth through a merger with MCI. However, its global ambitions were thrown into disarray in October 1997 when WorldCom's offer to take over MCI was accepted. In contrast to most of the traditional PTOs, WorldCom has grown internationally largely through acquisitions, such as MFS (operating fibre-optic metropolitan area networks in financial centres throughout the world) and UUNet (Internet access service provider).

The emphasis placed on domestic rivalry or protection, and the orientation towards internationalisaton, are reflected in the emergence of the three different innovation and internationalisation strategies pursued by European PTOs. Exhibit 5 illustrates the international orientation of different European PTOs and strength in their home markets.

Domestic protection without internationalisation

The traditional policy of protecting national PTOs from foreign competition inside their home market with little or no attempt to venture abroad continues to serve as a model for restructuring in several continental European countries, such as Austria, Belgium, Greece, Ireland, Italy and Portugal. These are inward-focusing PTOs, which have maintained traditional commitments to domestic equipment suppliers, often benefit from government-subsidised R&D, and have built up a dominant position in services in a bid to defend against foreign competition.

While Italy's national PTO has made little attempt to internationalise, it has attempted to remain dominant in its home market. The Italian telecommunications sector is controlled by Stet, the state-controlled telecommunications holding company, and its various subsidiaries, including Telecom Italy (the national PTO), Telecom Italia Mobile, Italtel (the equipment manufacturer) and Finsiel (a software house).

There are various reasons for this defensive national approach. Europe's peripheral regions, such as Greece, Ireland and Portugal, have prolonged the domestic voice and infrastructural monopoly beyond the EU's 1998 deadline in order to prevent wasteful competition during the roll-out of their national networks. In countries such as Belgium and Austria, with strong trade unions, there is

Exhibit 5   Strategies of PTOs

International stance		Domestic interest	
		Strong presence	Weak presence
	Inward-looking	Austrian PTT France Telecom	Alternative carriers: Enertel NL
	Outward-looking	BT	Infonet SITA Cable & Wireless

concern about job losses, the end of civil servant status, and issues concerning social cohesion, such as universal service and regional development.

Domestic rivalry and first-mover internationalisation strategies

In following the USA, the UK became the first European country to establish domestic competition in national telecommunications markets. Competition occurred in two phases. In a duopoly period from 1984 to 1991, a newly privatised BT faced duopoly competition from Mercury (a company established by C&W, the UK's second international operator, which was privatised in 1981). In this period, Mercury played the role of an offensive innovator. Mercury's investment in new fibre-optic transmission and digital switching technologies in the mid-1980s stimulated BT into responding by modernising its network, reducing prices, and increasing productivity by adopting a new form of corporate organisation. The need to recoup the large costs of R&D and fixed capital investments provided BT with a strong incentive to extend market share by supplying new services and expanding into new geographical markets.

Mercury gradually increased its share of the long-distance market to capture around 24% by 1994. During the duopoly period, however, BT benefited from a regulatory safety net that prevented Mercury from challenging the incumbent's market dominance. Indeed, the USA has gone further than the UK in promoting domestic rivalry. In 1984 AT&T's national monopoly was broken up into seven regional monopolies to promote home-based long-distance competition with new entrants such as MCI and Sprint. Divestiture preserved AT&T's strength by allowing it to retain its long-distance operations, equipment supply and its world-renowned research base – Bell Laboratories – but prevented AT&T using a monopoly to cross-subsidise competitive services. The UK preferred a regulatory remedy that allowed BT to preserve a dominant position through its control of local monopoly and competitive long-distance services. As a result, Oftel was preoccupied in the duopoly period trying to prevent BT abusing its dominant position to compete with Mercury.

A second period opened in 1991 when the duopoly between BT and Mercury was abolished to promote open competition in most market segments. BT now faces competition from around 150 new entrants but is banned from providing entertainment TV over its local network until 2001 to protect foreign-owned cable TV companies and other new entrants while they establish a viable market share.

Since 1996, however, a process of concentration has signalled the return to duopoly or oligopoly in UK telecommunications markets. In October 1996, C&W

announced the formation of Cable and Wireless Communications (C&WC), a major new national telecommunications company intending to obtain economies of scale and scope by operating across local, long-distance and international markets. C&WC was formed out of a merger of Mercury, its UK long-distance subsidiary, and three cable TV companies (Nynex CableComms, Bell CableMedia and Videotron).

In consequence, BT is being put to the test in its home market by stronger competition and an increasingly adversarial regulatory environment, with a regulator seeking stronger powers to protect new entrants. BT claims that unfair competition from mainly foreign-owned cable TV companies and prohibitive price controls in the UK have encouraged its expansion abroad.

The experience of early domestic rivalry has encouraged BT not only to innovate more offensively at home but also to follow AT&T's lead in seeking to be among the first PTOs to develop a presence in global markets. Therefore, by comparison with PTOs on the continent, BT has become an offensive innovator at home and has captured some first-mover advantages in new geographical markets.

Initially, however, there was a lack of strategic focus due to unsuccessful attempts to enter equipment supply. In 1990, for example, BT sold its stake in Mitel, the loss-making Canadian equipment manufacturer for a quarter of the original price. AT&T made similar losses through its forays into equipment supply (e.g. NCR and Olivetti). By the mid-1990s BT had abandoned its attempts to move into equipment supply and focused on service provision. BT and C&W have continued to grow in foreign markets by making acquisitions or taking equity stakes in telecommunication operators, equipment, value-added services, broadcasting, computing and cable TV companies, and by winning licences for mobile communications. C&W already had major international operations and major investments in other national networks, such as Hong Kong Telecom.

BT spent $4.3 billion on a 20% stake in MCI to form Concert, a joint-venture global telecommunications company offering voice and data telecommunications services to large international business customers. At the beginning of 1997, BT was involved in a merger with MCI as well as over 80 alliances, joint ventures and foreign investments in 23 countries. After a long period of negotiation, in August 1997 BT announced an expenditure of $19 billion to gain full control of MCI, the second largest long-distance operator in the USA. However, the merger between BT and MCI was prevented in October 1997, when WorldCom announced its intention to purchase MCI.

National champion and catch-up internationalisation strategies

On the continent of Europe, the main PTOs following internationalisation strategies are Deustche Telekom, France Telecom, PTT Telecom, Telia and Swiss Telecom. From inside a largely sheltered home market, these PTOs have engaged in a variety of defensive innovation strategies. In contrast to the UK, where the coercion of competition forced BT to become a more aggressive innovator, continental PTOs have used the home market as a test bed for experimenting with new technologies and services, and to prepare for international expansion and the influx of foreign competition. While these European PTOs are currently behind AT&T, BT and newcomers such as WorldCom in the race to become global operators, they have enjoyed the time and space to learn from the successes and failures of the first movers, such as AT&T's and BT's misplaced emphasis on manufacturing in the late 1980s.

The main European PTOs have used their protected domestic markets to experiment and gain experience with new network technologies and services, before moving into unfamiliar foreign markets. France Telecom is an example of a relatively efficient national PTO with the technological capabilities to face up to foreign competition without relying on a strategy of domestic rivalry. Under the umbrella of state support and guidance, France Telecom has become a leader in the provision of a range of high-quality services, such as Minitel, ISDN and the Transpac data network, and it operates one of the world's most efficient national digital networks. During the 1980s, however, France Telecom failed to anticipate the demand for cellular telephony, mainly because of the absence of competition in this market segment. The widely used but outdated Minitel system has hindered the rapid diffusion of the Internet. France is lagging well behind the USA, UK and Scandinavian countries in the provision of Internet access.

International expansion has been achieved by entering into 'non-aggression pacts' with like-minded partners on the continent that are of a similar size, in strategically placed or adjacent markets, and following a similar protectionist strategy. France Telecom and Deutsche Telekom have linked up with Sprint to form Global One, which awaits the approval of the EU and US antitrust authorities. In 1992 PTT Telecom BV and Telia of Sweden established Unisource NV, a joint-venture company, to provide the largest of multinational corporate customers with pan-European services in competition with the largest global operators. Swiss PTT joined Unisource as an equal partner in 1993, and Telefónica of Spain temporarily joined under the same conditions between 1995 and 1997, before linking up with Concert. In December 1994 Unisource, together with AT&T, set up a joint company called Uniworld to provide pan-European services, and WorldPartners (a partnership between Unisource, AT&T, KDD of Japan and Singapore Telecom) will provide worldwide coverage.

Exhibit 6 offers an overview of the main strategic alliances in the industry.

Conclusion

National telecommunications policies and regulatory frameworks influence the innovation strategies of PTOs and their approaches to internationalisation. Whereas

Exhibit 6   Internationalisation strategies and strategic partnerships of PTOs

Company or strategic alliance	Concert	Cable & Wireless	Global One	Worldpartners	WorldCom
Constituting partners	BT (UK)	C&W (UK) Hong Kong Telecom/ China Telecom	Deutsche Telekom France Telecom Sprint	AT&T (US) Unisource (EU) KDD (J) Singapore Telecom	WorldCom (US) MCI (US) MFS (US) UUNet (US)

Privileged or associate partners	Telenor (N)
	TeleDanemark
	Telecom Finland
	NTT-IBM (J)
	Banco Santander (ES)
	Nazionale del Lavoro (I)
	VIAG (FRG)
		Telecom Italia
		Comvik (S)
		Vebacom (FRG)
		Bouygues Telecom (F)
			Telmex
			Enel Telecom (I)
			Telecom Argentina
				PTT Telecom
				SwissCom
				Telia (S)
				Korea Telecom
				Telecom
				   New Zealand
				Telstra United of
				   Canada
					Telefonia (ES)
					Telecom Portugal

WorldCom's rapid growth and profitability are linked to its strategy to become a truly global operator, the traditional PTOs continue to rely on their home markets and a growing number of multi-domestic activities. However, the main European PTOs are attempting to gain stronger positions in global telecommunications markets by pursuing two different strategies of internationalisation.

First, the UK's big-bang approach to telecommunications reform forced BT, C&W, Vodafone and other UK operators into following offensive innovation strategies, by encouraging the introduction of radical technical and organisational innovations, and entering foreign markets. As in the USA, the early introduction of capable home-based competitors was the key factor behind BT's transformation into a more innovative and international company. For example, BT is operating in other domestic markets in collaboration with second national infrastructure operators, such as Telfort in the Netherlands. Expansion abroad provided opportunities to extend its global reach, establish an international reputation with large corporate customers, enter new geographical markets, and diversify into new products and services. But costs were incurred in being a first mover, such as the misplaced emphasis on equipment supply, as well as the high restructuring costs of shedding labour in home countries.

Second, the leading continental European PTOs and their governments have followed a catching-up strategy of encouraging foreign expansion while restricting competition and new entry at home. Their national governments have sought to exploit the advantages of protected domestic markets. Privatisation, liberalisation and independent regulation have been delayed to provide valuable time to restructure the PTO and mobilise widespread support from domestic stakeholders in preparation for global competition. Some of the high social and economic cost risks incurred by the first movers have been minimised under domestic protection. These PTOs have been able to capitalise on their remaining monopoly periods, using a largely protected home market as a test bed for experimenting with some of the new technologies and services already commercialised by AT&T and BT. But the pursuit of defensive strategies has prevented continental PTOs gaining a lead in promising new markets, such as global business networks, or recognising new possibilities when they first emerge, as in mobile communications or Internet access.

Protection in their home markets provided the basis to launch these national champions in 'non-aggression pacts' with like-minded continental partners in global markets. However, despite the huge financial resources of the largest continental PTOs, even companies as powerful as Deutsche Telekom and France Telecom have merely focused on imitating the successes of the offensive innovators. Such strategic alliances among continental PTOs may serve to block potentially ruinous international competition threatened by the large price reductions and new services offered by competitors such as WorldCom using low-cost alternative networks.

Notwithstanding the fact that the corporate strategies of PTOs will continue to reflect the historical and institutional specificity of their home bases, their entry in each other's sheltered markets and the formation of transnational carriers and alliances of operators to provide worldwide services suggest that telecommunications is definitely advancing towards a more dynamic and internationally integrated industry. This may raise, however, the possibility of pan-European and international regulatory problems between PTOs and their home and host national regulators and among the multinationalising companies themselves regarding market access, trade reciprocity and fair competition. These problems will need to be addressed by the relevant international regulatory, trade and competition authorities, including a future European Federal Communications Commission, possibly a revitalised International Telecommunications Union, and/or – most likely – the World Trade Organisation. So, despite the deregulation of the old telecommunications regime, a new form of global governance will eventually still be needed to shape and supervise the next crucial stage in the transition from a national monopoly to a fully global and competitive sector.

Glossary

Absolving (an issue) Ignoring an issue and hoping that it will go away.

Acceptability (of a strategy) How welcome a strategy is to all the organisational stakeholders.

Acquisition The action by which one company purchases a controlling interest in another company.

Adaptive control The form of control in which the system adjusts itself to new environmental conditions.

Added value The benefit from carrying out some process. In accountancy terms it is the difference between the revenue obtained from the sale of a product or service and the costs directly associated with it.

Agent An element in the distribution chain. Agents don't normally own the goods they sell and they generally carry stock and take responsibility for credit risks.

Agent for change A person who seeks to initiate and manage a planned change process.

Alliance (strategic) A durable relationship established between two or more independent firms, involving the sharing or pooling of resources for undertaking activities of strategic importance to one or more of the partners.

Alternative investment market The organisation set up by the London Stock Exchange to provide a market for the shares of small and/or youthful companies.

Appropriability The ability of a firm to retain the rewards that 'should' come to it as the generator of a competitive advantage.

Architecture The linkages between resources within a business. These linkages are not restricted to the relationships between people but include all the linkages within and between the organisation's processes and capabilities.

Assets The resources, processes and capabilities that the organisation owns.

Associate company A company in which another company holds a significant equity interest, where this interest is less than or equal to 50%.

Assumption control Focused environmental monitoring of the assumptions under which strategy has been selected.

Augmented product/service The core product/service with additional features that constitute the product or service that is bought.

Balanced scorecard A set of strategic goals that balance several perspectives: the past and the future; the internal and the external; the financial and the non-financial; and those of different stakeholders.

Bank term loan A loan offered by a bank for a period longer than one year.

Basic asset A building block of an organisation that can be recognised and evaluated by outsiders.

Behaviour The way a person or group does something. Thus behaviour is readily observable.

Belief The feeling that something is true or definitely exists. Beliefs are not observable; they must be inferred from individual and/or group behaviour, and/or stated views.

Benchmarking The process of comparing a firm's offers and processes with those of comparable firms in order to identify where improvements can be made.

Best-owner test Whether the corporation is the best possible parent for a business.

Better-off test Whether the corporation will be adding more value with a business in its portfolio than without it.

Bill of exchange A commitment to pay a specified sum at a later date. A bill can be referred to as a bill, draft or acceptance, and often comes with a label; for example, bank draft, bank bill, time draft and banker's acceptance.

Brand   A name, symbol or design used to identify offers from one seller and to differentiate them from competitive offers.

Brand stretching   The use of a well-respected brand name with a new offer.

Breach of confidence   A form of intellectual property right that offers protection for information such as customer lists, knowhow and trade secrets. It is often the only form of protection when something is still in its infancy.

Bribe   An amount of money or something valuable given covertly to someone to persuade them to do something that they wouldn't do otherwise.

Business   An organisation undertaking a set of processes to provide a well-defined offer in a well-defined market.

Business process   A process carried out to further the aims of a business. It is performed by using a procedure to combine basic assets with explicit and tacit knowledge.

Business intelligence system   A system for systematically gathering, analysing and disseminating information about the business environment.

Buy (access to resources)   The process whereby a business gains access to the results of another firm's capabilities through market transactions.

Capability   A set of business processes that affect the offer a customer receives.

Causal forecasting   A forecasting method whereby future data values are obtained from extending past, explicitly formulated cause-and-effect relationships.

Change agent   A person who implements change.

Chaos   The situation in which broad patterns are predictable but detailed features within these broad patterns are completely unknowable.

Charismatic transformation   The style of change management appropriate for transformational change where key interests accept the need for such change. The appropriate style is collaborative or consultative.

Climate   The quality of the feelings that people have about an organisation's culture and about what they are asked to do.

Climate control   The process aimed at establishing and maintaining a favourable business environment.

Closed-loop control   Control in which there is direct feedback from outputs to inputs.

Cluster   A grouping of businesses in the same geographical location that includes competitors, suppliers and other elements of the value chain.

Coalition   An informal group of people pursuing shared objectives.

Coercive power   The power that results from the ability to punish people who won't behave as required.

Cognitive coathanger   A broad generic mental model on to which detail particular to a specific situation can be added to form a mental model applicable to that situation.

Collaborate (access to resources)   The process whereby a business augments its capabilities with the resources of another, independent, organisation.

Collage   A picture that has been made by sticking together pieces of paper, cloth, photos, etc. More generally, something made by combining a number of different things.

Colonial firm   A firm that sells a standard product in many countries, with a considerable proportion of its production coming from its mother country, with little produced abroad.

Committee   A formal group of people selected by a larger group to consider, investigate or take action in regard to specified matters.

Common interest organisation   A type of stakeholder that exists to distort markets in their favour. Such organisations include the professions, trade associations and trade unions.

Competence   A collective learning in the organisation, especially how to co-ordinate diverse production skills and integrate multiple streams of technologies.

Competence-based approach   The approach by which the competences of the corporation are a fundamental basis on which strategy is developed.

Comparator group   A group of businesses that operate in a similar way and thus whose levels of performance are appropriate for purposes of comparison.

Competitive advantage   An advantage in the competitive arena that is reflected in the ability of the firm to earn returns on investment persistently above the average for the arena.

Competitive arena   At the minimum, the competitive arena is defined by all competing businesses whereby an increase in total market share by one business automatically leads to a decrease in the market share of at least one other business. More widely, it may include potential competitors.

Competitive group   A subset of all the businesses in the competitive arena that are competing to serve a defined market segment.

Complexity   The need to mesh together many different forms of information to achieve understanding and to allow reasoned action to be taken.

Conglomerate   A corporation in which there is little or no significant offer or market relatedness between the businesses in its portfolio.

Connection power   The power that results from personal and professional access to key people and information.

Consolidation   The market share option whereby a firm seeks to maintain its market share.

Consortium   An alliance between a number of partners for a very specific purpose. This purpose is usually a project, where the collaboration runs for the duration of the project.

Consumer surplus   The difference between the value of an offer and its price.

Copyright   A form of intellectual property right that offers protection for tangible expressions of an idea in the form of the following kinds of original materials: literary works, artistic, dramatic and musical works, sound recordings, films, and broadcasts and cable programmes.

Core product/service   That part of a product or service that provides the core benefit.

Corporate branding   A brand strategy whereby a firm makes its name the dominant brand identifier across all its offers.

Corporate governance   The way in which organisations are run and controlled.

Corporate venturing   A form of capital injection that a large company can make into a small company. The large company might take an equity stake, usually a minority equity stake, to gain access to the small company's innovative R&D or to an innovative product.

Corporation   An organisation consisting of more than one business.

Creativity   An experience or flash of insight whereby two bodies of thought, considered remote from each other, are suddenly brought together.

Crisis control   The process of managing potentially damaging, rapidly arising issues.

Critical offer feature   A characteristic of an offer that must be present for an offer to appear credible and have the potential to win sales.

Culture   The shared norms of behaviour, values and assumptions that knit a community together.

Cultural web   The manifestations and fundamentals of culture – the intermeshing of the webs of behaviours and beliefs.

Cultural onion   The view of culture as consisting of three layers. The outer layer consists of the norms of behaviour, the middle layer consists of organisational values, while the inner layer consists of the group's paradigm.

Cybernetic control   A form of control in which the controls are set from outside the system being controlled.

Cycle time   The time it takes to convert a customer need into an offer that satisfies that need, or the time taken to convert an idea into a product or service that is ready for the market.

Debenture   A loan arrangement in which a company agrees to meet a series of interest payments and pay back the sum borrowed at the end of a fixed period – usually more than ten years.

Decision making   The process of considering optional courses of action.

Decision taking   The act of irrevocably committing resources.

Deferred tax   The postponed payment of tax due.

Delphi technique   A means of obtaining judgemental forecasts from a group without many of the biases inherent in face-to-face group discussions.

Demerger   The process whereby a corporation splits its activities into two or more self-standing groups of businesses.

DEEPLIST   An acronym that can be used as a checklist to help identify the important factors in the remote environment The DEEPLIST acronym stands for Demographic, Economic, Environmental, Political, Legal, Informational, Social and Technological.

Design right A form of intellectual property right that offers protection to facets of an offer that are functional. (This is in contrast to registered designs, which apply to visually appealing characteristics of an offer.)

Designed physical system A system not including humans that has been constructed for a purpose.

Dictatorial transformation The style of change management appropriate for transformational change where key interests oppose it. The appropriate style is directive or coercive.

Differentiation The distinguishing of one offer from another in order to achieve superior value.

Discount house A company that buys bills of exchange at a lower (discounted) price than the face value of the bills.

Discovery The finding out of something that already exists yet was unseen or unknown.

Disintermediation The process by which a process in the value chain is made redundant.

Distributor An element in the distribution chain. Distributors have exclusive or preferential rights to purchase the goods and services they sell. They provide all or some of aftersales service, market feedback, forecasting and sales reports, and sales and distribution management.

Dissolve (an issue) Changing the context in which the issue has arisen so that the issue no longer exists.

Diversified Refers to a corporation engaged in a range of business activities.

Divestment The process whereby a parent sells off a business or a competence.

Divisionalised company A company organised into divisions, which are groupings of businesses. The parent carries out many of the possible parenting roles.

DIY (internal development) The process whereby new capabilities and competences are developed in-house. This can be achieved either by redeploying resources that are already available in the firm or by buying in individual resources or processes, which are then melded into the required sets of new processes.

Dominant coalition The group of people in an organisation that are in a position to decide policy and how issues are handled.

Double-loop learning The transformational learning resulting from changes in the deeper mental models that constitute a person's mindset.

Dynamism The rate of change of features in the environment.

Economy of scale The situation whereby the unit costs associated with an offer decrease with the number of offers made per period.

Economy of scope The situation whereby the cost of providing two distinct offers from the same organisation is less than the cost of providing both separately.

Emergent strategy A strategy that is developed in response to environmental influences. The strategy will become evident in retrospect from the strategic pathway chosen.

Entrepreneur A person who continually seeks opportunities where they can innovate and drive change, and who seeks the power and independence necessary for success.

Entrepreneurship What an entrepreneur does.

Equity The value of a company's shares after debts have been paid.

Ethical Conforming to the rules or principles of behaviour for deciding what is right.

Ethics Rules or principles of behaviour for deciding what is right and wrong.

Expert power The power that comes from the superior expertise that the leader has, or is believed to have.

Explicit knowledge Knowledge that can be coded so that it can be passed on in a formalised manner. It tends to be public, defined, documented and objective.

Exporting firm A firm based in its mother country, with any exporting likely to be on an opportunistic basis. International operations are likely to be secondary to the domestic activities.

Externality Costs not absorbed in a product or service and not paid for directly by the customer; the costs are borne by the wider community.

External relationship The linkage between a firm and an external stakeholder. External relationships are most often relationships between people but can be wider than that – for example, the e-commerce between suppliers and buyers.

Extranet Communications between organisations conducted through a private network that operates under the transmission control protocol/international protocol (TCP/IP).

Factoring The arrangement whereby a third party, a factor, takes responsibility for invoicing and debt collection. For this they receive a percentage of the invoice value of the debts owing to the company.

Familiar issue One of the three types of strategic issue. Familiar issues are characterised by being relatively simple to deal with as they are met on a regular basis and have limited consequences, and being only mildly controversial since they are mainly influenced by internal interest groups.

Feasibility (of a strategy) Whether an intended strategy can be implemented. Feasibility is concerned with whether the resources can be obtained and processes devised to support the proposed new pathway within suitable timescales.

Feedback The process whereby the outputs from a system are reintroduced as inputs to it.

Feedforward The process whereby knowledge about the future inputs to a system is used to alter the system prior to the inputs being received.

Financial control style One form of parenting style in which the parent plays little part in developing strategy and restricts itself to setting financial targets.

Forced evolution The style of change management appropriate for incremental change where key interests oppose the change. The appropriate style is directive or coercive.

Forecast A statement about the future.

Formalism A moral code based on universal moral principles that apply to everyone equally.

Franchising The arrangement whereby the franchise holder undertakes specific activities such as the manufacture, distribution and selling of an offer. The franchiser is responsible for the brand name, marketing and offer development.

Globalisation The process whereby an organisation's operations span the world and the strategic position of competitors in national markets is affected by their overall global positions.

Harvesting The option whereby a firm allows its market share to fall.

Heuristic Rules of thumb developed from experience (rather than from theory).

Hire purchase An arrangement whereby a company, typically a finance company, buys equipment which the firm can then use for a series of rental payments. After all the payments have been made the firm will become the owner of the equipment.

Holding company A company in which there is a legal separation of liability between the parent and operating companies. The parent carries out few if any of the parental roles.

Horizontal diversification The enlargement of a firm's capabilities into a competitive arena not within its current value chain.

Horizontal integration The merging of a firm's operations with those of another in the same competitive arena.

Human activity system A system that takes account of human volition, beliefs and behaviours.

Human rights The concept that natural laws exist through which a person or group has an entitlement to be treated in a certain way. These laws take priority over the laws devised by humans.

Immediate operating environment The part of the operating environment that encompasses the markets in which the business is operating, and takes heed of the barriers to entry and to the threat of substitutes.

Implementation control The form of control focused on the achievement of strategic change.

Incremental change An alteration to the outer ring of the cultural onion – the behaviours – that does not disturb the more deeply held beliefs in an organisation. Incremental change is associated with doing things better or doing more of them.

Industry A grouping of business activities made by government agencies for purposes of data recording as one of the bases for governmental policy decisions. The definitions used take into account a number of different factors, including the nature of the process or of the work done, the principal raw material used, the type or intended uses of the goods produced or handled and the types of service rendered.

Influence   The application of power.

Information   Data that are perceived by an employee to be of use or potential use in their job.

Information appliance   Any device that can be connected via a network to a source of information.

Innovation   The commercial exploitation of an invention.

In-sourcing   The process whereby activities are brought into the business's value link.

Intellectual capital   The intellectual material that has been codified, captured and used to produce a higher-valued asset. It includes such items as patents and computer systems. It is calculated by subtracting the financial capital of the firm (book value or some variant of it) from its market value.

Intellectual property   Assets that can be traded (bought, sold, hired or rented) and that are intangible, as opposed to the physical assets such as buildings, machinery or stock.

Intelligence   The outcome of the meshing and reconciliation of a set of information.

Intended strategy   A strategy consisting of a set of actions planned to achieve well-defined organisational goals.

Internal development   The process whereby new capabilities and competences are developed in house. This can be achieved either by redeploying resources that are already available in the firm or by buying in individual resources or processes, which are then melded into the required sets of new processes.

Internationalisation   The extension of operations to more than one country.

Internet   An international network of computers offering e-mail, Web, UseNet and mailing list groups operating under the transmission control protocol/international protocol (TCP/IP).

Intranet   Communications within an organisation that operates under the transmission control protocol/international protocol (TCP/IP).

Intrapreneur   An entrepreneur acting within an organisation of which they are a part.

Intrapreneurship   What an intrapreneur does.

Invention   The act of creating or producing by use of the imagination.

Issue   A development, trend or event that potentially could have a high impact on an organisation's overall performance but is controversial in that it is likely that reasonable people may have different views about its probability of occurrence and on the most appropriate way to handle it.

Issue handling   The process of dealing with an issue.

Joint venture   An arrangement where two or more independent firms enter into a durable relationship to pursue jointly a common goal by establishing a distinct organisational structure with a number of dedicated resources and a number of the characteristics of an independent firm.

Judgemental forecasting   A method of forecasting that relies on expert judgement. It is used where future data values are required in situations where little directly relevant experience exists and where it is hard to articulate this experience.

Knowledge   The result of meshing together and reconciling pieces of information and their subsequent internalising.

Knowledge age   The period of history that many commentators believe we are now entering, where the major source of wealth becomes the possession of knowledge.

Knowledge management   The systematic capture and structuring of knowledge within an organisation in order to improve business performance.

Law of requisite variety   For a system to be able to maintain itself it must have at least as much variety as the environment in which it is operating.

Leader   A person who operates on the emotional and spiritual resources of the organisation – they deal with values, commitment and aspirations.

Leader-manager   A person who combines the qualities of a leader and a manager.

Leadership   The process of moving a group in some direction through mostly non-coercive means. Effective leadership is that which produces movement in the long-term best interests of the group.

Leading indicator   A variable where a change in its value precedes a change in the variable whose value is to be forecast.

Learning organisation   An organisation skilled in continually seeking out knowledge deficiencies, acquiring, creating, spreading and managing knowledge, and expert at modifying its behaviour to reflect its new knowledge.

Legitimate power   The power that comes from the socially accepted duty for people to do as the leader says.

Leasing   An arrangement similar to hire purchase, but with the difference that at the end of the lease period the firm using the equipment doesn't become the owner of it.

Licensing   An arrangement whereby the right is given to manufacture a product or offer a service for a fee or a royalty.

Liquidation   The process whereby the assets of a business or competence are broken up and either sold or used elsewhere in the organisation.

Machiavellian   Using clever but somewhat unethical methods to achieve an objective.

Management buyin   A form of divestment whereby a management team from one organisation buys an equity stake in an existing company and takes over managerial control.

Management buyout   A form of divestment whereby the current management of a business purchases the business assets from the corporation of which it is a part.

Manager   A person who directs and controls the physical resources of an organisation, concerned with efficiency and with mastering routines.

Market   A group of individuals or organisations that have the willingness, need and authority to buy and sell similar offers, and where buyers can readily substitute one offer for another.

Market-based approach   An approach to strategy in which the market is the major focus for decision.

Market segment   A group of buyers who have similar offer needs.

Market segmentation   The act of dividing the market into distinct groups of buyers who might require separate offers.

Market niche   A narrow segment, often a part of the market only profitably served by one firm and not being pursued by larger firms.

Market share   The sales of a firm relative to the total sales made in its market or market segment.

Market penetration   The market share option whereby a firm seeks to increase its market share with its present offers in its present markets.

Market substitute   The replacement of one offer by another from a competitor already in the competitive arena.

Maximin   An ethical procedure for reconciling the utilitarian, efficiency-focused approach with the procedural, fairness-focused approach. In the maximin approach inequalities are permitted as long as they result in the greater good for the poorest in the group.

Megatrend   A very long-term trend that may take decades to work itself through. The trends influence, and are part of, the remote environment.

Metaphor   A way of describing something by comparing it to something else that has similar qualities. Something that is intended to represent a more general idea or quality.

Merger   The coming together of two organisations, often of a broadly similar size. Negotiations are generally friendly as the coming together is mutually desired and instigated.

Mindset   A constellation of concepts, values, perceptions and practices that form a particular individual vision of reality.

Mission   A statement of the organisation's function in the eyes of the outside world: in terms of what the organisation is, why it exists and the unique contribution it can make. A mission statement provides a 'road map' for stakeholders, particularly for employees.

Model   A simplified representation of reality created for a purpose.

Mortgage   An arrangement whereby an individual or a company can convert some of its assets into funds and continue to be able to have use of the assets, with the individual or company retaining the benefits of ownership.

Multi-domestic firm   A firm consisting of several units operating almost independently in different national markets, each having its own production capacity and a country head office. Each unit tends to export very little – almost all its product is destined for its own home market.

NAFTA   North American Free Trade Agreement – a wide-ranging trade agreement between Canada, Mexico and the USA.

Negative feedback   Feedback that negates the variance that has been detected.

Norm   Acceptable behaviour by members of a group.

Objective   A statement of what is to be achieved and when results are to be accomplished.

Occupation-based labour market   A market in people that focuses on well-defined disciplines and skill sets, where the requirements are set externally. An example is accountancy, where the accounting bodies set the qualification standards.

Offer   A product or service made available for purchase.

Offer enhancement   A small-scale change to a product or service. Enhancements are often the changes that are required to keep the product/service viable in the current marketplace and require little in the way of changes to current processes.

Offer enlargement   A large-scale change to a product or service requiring access to new capabilities. An offer enlargement generally leads to the creation of a new business.

Offer extension   A change to a product or service larger than an offer enhancement and achieved through extensions to the processes that the business already possesses.

Open-loop control   Control in which there is no direct feedback.

Operating costs   The costs incurred in the day-to-day running of an organisation.

Operating environment   The elements of an organisation's environment that the organisation can influence.

Operational control   A form of control that is internally focused to make the present processes more efficient.

Order-qualifying feature   A characteristic of an offer that must be present at a threshold level for a sale to be possible.

Order-winning feature   A characteristic of an offer where the likelihood of making a sale depends on the magnitude of the characteristic.

Organisational development   A top management supported long-term effort to improve an organisation's issue-handling and renewal processes.

Organisational structure   The sum total of ways in which the organisation divides its labour into distinct tasks and then achieves co-ordination between them.

Organisation-based labour market   A market in people that focuses on membership of a particular organisation. Skills are developed that the organisation needs and promotion is from within the organisation.

Out-sourcing   The practice of handing over the management and operation of certain functions to a third party. Thus activities are removed from the business's value link.

Paradigm   A constellation of concepts, values, perceptions and practices shared by a community that forms a particular vision of reality, which is the basis of the way a community organises itself.

Passing off   The situation where the offers of one business are confused with those of another. Passing off can only be challenged when a reputation has been established.

Parent   The people in a corporation who aren't affiliated to any of the constituent businesses and who have the ultimate responsibility for the performance of the corporation's businesses.

Parenting   The distinct characteristics of corporate strategic management: i.e. those aspects that aren't present at the business level.

Participative evolution   The style of change management appropriate for incremental change. The appropriate style is collaborative or consultative.

Patent   A form of intellectual property right that gives the inventor the right for a period of time to stop other people making, using or selling the invention without the permission of the patent holder. A patent is concerned with the technical and functional aspects of a product.

Perfect competition   The situation in a market that ensures that the customer can buy an offer at the lowest price – and correspondingly the producers obtain just those profits that allow them to continue to exist but to do no better than that.

Personal power   The power that results from being supported and trusted by colleagues and subordinates.

Plan   A set of proposed actions.

Policy   A rule or guideline which expresses the limits within which action should occur.

Portfolio   A collection of items. A business has a portfolio of offers; a corporation has a portfolio of businesses.

Post-capitalist   The period of history that many commentators believe we are now entering in which capital ceases to be the most important source of wealth generation.

Positive feedback   Feedback whereby the variance between the objective and the actual is used to increase the size of the variance, and thus tends to lead to instability.

Power   The capacity to make someone else act according to one's preferences, even if that isn't in accordance with the other's own preferences.

Predetermined factor (in a scenario)   A factor that has a known and ordained value. In the scenario-building process the value of a predetermined factor is the same in all the scenario end-states.

Predetermined forecast   A forecast based on variables whose future values are effectively already known.

Preresolving (an issue)   An apparently appropriate response is available prior to the issue arising.

Price   The sum of money that a customer pays for an offer.

Primary stakeholder   A stakeholder who operates in a market, for either capital, labour, information or goods and services.

Principle of benefaction   The ethical principle of making an exception to a rule when greater overall good or satisfaction will occur by doing so.

Principle of membership   The ethical principle of according people in a group the same treatment because this leads to group cohesion.

Pro-active control   The form of control that is exercised to prevent a variance between the desired and actual outcomes occurring.

Problem solving   The process of moving from a less to a more satisfactory state.

Proceduralism   The ethical code resulting from the combination of formalism and human rights.

Procedure   The way a set of actions needs to be performed.

Process   A series of actions involving resources taken in order to achieve a particular result. A business process is performed by using a procedure to combine basic assets with explicit and tacit knowledge.

Product   Generally a tangible thing whose ownership changes when it's bought.

Programme   A step-by-step sequence of events necessary to achieve objectives within the limits set by policy.

Programmed response   An immediate reaction to an issue. It is a 'cognitive shortcut' or heuristic whereby a set of decision rules have been internalised and are used when the individual or organisation thinks appropriate.

Project   A set of processes aimed at achieving a well-defined objective within a specified timescale.

Public relations   The process of looking after a firm's reputation with the aim of earning understanding and support, and influencing opinion and behaviour.

Publicity   An act or public device designed to attract public attention or support. It isn't controlled by the organisation; rather it originates from other sources.

Purpose (in a mission)   The organisation's 'reason for being' – its overarching strategic aim.

Quality   The standard of an offer. One offer is of a better quality than another if more people would buy it if the price of the two offers were the same.

Rational   Open to evidence, with logical analysis used in coming to a conclusion.

Reactive control   A form of control that is exercised after a variance between the desired and actual outcomes has occurred.

Referent power   The power that comes to someone who is a role model for others: someone that others seek to emulate.

Refreezing   The process by which new ways of thought and behaviour are locked in place in the minds of individuals and in the organisation's procedures.

Registered design   A form of intellectual property right that gives a monopoly for the outward visual appearance of a product or set of products.

Related diversification   A diversification where the activities of the different businesses have some significant commonalities.

Relationship   The linkage between parts of the organisation and between the organisation and its external stakeholders.

Remote environment   The elements of the organisational environment over which the individual business has no significant influence but which may have a major effect on it and on its operating environment.

Reputation   The way in which the market deals with offer features that customers cannot easily determine for themselves.

Requisite variety (law of)   The law of requisite variety states that for a system to be able to maintain itself it must have at least as much variety as the environment in which it is operating.

Resolving (an issue)   The process of seeking a way of handling an issue that is 'good enough' rather than an optimum one.

Resource   Something that can be used to create value. Four types of resources can be identified: basic assets, explicit knowledge, tacit knowledge and procedures.

Resource-based view   The view of a firm as composed of a unique set of resources and that competitive advantage originates from their utilisation.

Reverse engineering   The process by which an offer is analysed to determine how it has been made in the case of a product, or provided in the case of an offer.

Retained profit   Profit held back within the firm and not dispersed.

Reward power   The power that results from the ability to reward required behaviour.

Risk   A management definition of risk is the same as that for uncertainty, where a particular action will lead to one of several possible outcomes. However, a specialist risk analyst's definition of risk is the state where there are several possible outcomes and the probability of their occurrence is unknown. In 'extremely risky' situations, it may not even be possible to identify all the possible outcomes.

Rumour   A proposition that is unverified and in general circulation.

Sale and leaseback   An arrangement whereby a business can convert some of its assets into funds and continue to be able to have use of the assets. The business gives up ownership of the assets.

Satisficing   Finding a satisfactory or 'good enough' course of action.

Secondary stakeholder   A stakeholder who isn't active in a market but who requires the organisation to perform to acceptable standards.

Sector   A group of industries that are related through the processes and/or products or services they provide.

Scenario   A narrative providing an internally consistent view of how the future might plausibly turn out. It consists of the scenario end-states and the logic by which they are thought to arise.

Scenario end-state   One situation at the end of the timeframe being considered in the scenario-building process.

Scenario logic   The logic underpinning the move from the present to a scenario end-state.

Scenario variable   A variable whose values differentiate one scenario end-state from another.

Self-defeating forecast   A forecast whereby people believe that something will happen; they change their behaviour, and this then 'defeats' the forecast.

Self-fulfilling forecast   A forecast whereby people believe that something will happen; they act upon this view, and their actions bring about what was forecast.

Significant operating factor   An element of a business's operating environment that is strategically significant.

Service   An offer that generally doesn't result in the customer owning anything that has a resale value.

Single-loop learning   The incremental learning that comes from the cycle of implementation, monitoring to obtain feedback information on the consequences, understanding this information and the subsequent implementation of incremental change. The learning that takes place is rather superficial learning in the sense that it leaves untouched a person's deeper mental model.

Skill   The ability to do something well, especially because it has been learned and practised.

Small and medium-sized enterprises   An SME should not have a workforce exceeding 500, net fixed assets exceeding €75 million or more than one-third of its capital held by a larger firm.

Soft information Information that lacks objectivity and is generally qualitative.

Solving (an issue) The process of seeking the best outcome when handling an issue.

Stakeholder Individuals and groups who are affected by the activities of the organisation.

Strategic business unit A strategic business unit has a distinctive business mission, sensibly independent of that of any other business in the corporation, and contains all the important components essential to the conduct of its business mission; for example, technology, operations and marketing. It is able to manage its strategy in a manner that is independent of other businesses within the corporation (although not of the strategy of the corporation itself), and it offers a well-defined product or service in a well-defined market (and is not predominantly a supplier to other units in the corporation).

Strategic control style One form of parenting style that combines well-developed strategic planning systems with demanding, short-term financial targets.

Strategic fit The match between what is proposed and the organisation's aspirations and capabilities, and whether the proposed strategy is a suitable response to environmental events and trends.

Strategic goal A general statement of organisational direction: where it wishes to go and when it wishes to get there.

Strategic group A group of businesses which are likely to respond similarly to environmental changes and be similarly advantaged/disadvantaged by such changes.

Strategic investment in a partner An arrangement whereby a firm takes a minority equity stake in another firm, which remains independent.

Strategic issue An emerging development, trend or future event that potentially could have a high impact on the organisation's overall performance, is controversial, in that it is likely that reasonable people may have different views about its impact, and is likely to have strategic consequences. There is the implication that the various ways in which the issue may develop might mean that different strategic directions should be taken.

Strategic management The process of managing the mix of goals and the strategic pathway that serve to define what the organisation is (or wishes to be),

where it is going, when it wants to get there and how in general it is to get there. It also includes the processes of monitoring and controlling the strategy of the organisation.

Strategic management substitute The replacement of the offers made by all the businesses currently operating in a competitive arena by an offer from a business not yet in the arena and which satisfies the customer need in a different manner to the incumbents. The organisations in the competitive arena cannot respond except through changes that are very costly in time, money and/or emotional effort.

Strategic pathway The pattern of actions used to attain a strategic goal.

Strategic planning The systematic process by which the results of strategic thinking are formalised and plans devised to support strategy implementation and control.

Strategic resource An asset that is important to strategic positioning and that allows an organisation to offer appropriate critical offer features, currently or in the future.

Strategic thinking The creative thinking and learning process that allows an organisation to be positioned for maximum effect.

Strategy The long-term direction and scope of an organisation. It is the combination of strategic goals and strategic pathways. Strategy can be summed up in the phrase *not in the face of the enemy*.

Structure The sum total of the ways in which an organisation divides its labour into distinct tasks and then achieves co-ordination between them.

Structured process Stable, repetitive activities or procedures that can be systematised.

Structural asset The advantage a business enjoys because of the structure of the competitive arena. The advantage is not associated with current superior performance; it's the legacy of largely fortuitous positioning.

Subsidiary company A company with a parent that either controls the composition of its board of directors or holds more than half the equity share capital.

Substitute (in strategic management) The replacement of the offers made by all the businesses currently operating in a competitive arena by an offer from a business not yet in the arena and which satisfies the customer need in a different manner to the incumbents. The organisations in the competitive arena cannot respond except through changes that are very costly in time, money and/or emotional effort.

Supply chain management   The physical management of materials from suppliers to the customers' warehouses.

Surveillance control   A form of control whereby unfocused environmental monitoring is undertaken to provide early warning of changes in the business environment.

Sustainable competitive advantage   A sustainable competitive advantage will have been achieved when a firm receives a return on investment that is greater than the norm for its competitors, and when this enhanced return persists for a period long enough to alter the relative standing of the firm amongst its rivals.

SWOT analysis   The process of determining organisational position *vis-à-vis* its competitors and within its environment.

SWOT table   A concise statement setting out a firm's strengths and weaknesses *vis-à-vis* its competitors, and the opportunities and threats that the environment poses.

Symbol   Someone or something that represents a particular quality or idea.

Synergy   Where the whole is more than the sum of the parts. This is popularly stated as either $1 + 1 = 3$ or $2 + 2 = 5$.

Tacit knowledge   Knowledge that is personal, ill- or undefined and subjective, and hasn't been codified.

Tactics   Activities conducted within current resources. It is summed up in the phrase *in the face of the enemy*.

Takeover   A hostile acquisition.

Technology   Knowledge about scientific, business or industrial methods, or knowledge about the use/application of these methods.

Term loan   A loan offered by a bank for a period longer than one year.

Theology   A set of beliefs and ideas that spring from a divine rather than a human source.

Time series analysis   A method of forecasting whereby future data values are obtained by directly extending past data.

Tractable issue   One of the three types of strategic issue. They are characterised by being mildly complex, are met with only rarely, contain little that is contentious and, although many internal interest groups will be affected, the consequences of the issue aren't serious.

Trade credit   The credit obtained from suppliers or given to customers.

Trade mark   Any sign that distinguishes the offers of one particular organisation or sole trader from other organisations and sole traders.

Transformational change   Alteration in one or more assumptions in the organisational paradigm, and with it the values of the organisation. Transformational change is associated with doing things very differently or doing different things.

Transnational firm   A firm that combines the advantages of scope associated with global reach with the advantages of being responsive to the tastes and standards of the local marketplace.

Turbulence   The situation in which the environment is changing in an irregular, unpredictable way.

Utilitarianism   A moral code based on the view that actions aren't good or bad in themselves but are to be judged on their consequences. The consequences are to be viewed in terms of the 'happiness' that results.

Uncertainty   The imprecision associated with the values of a factor. It reflects the number of feasible futures facing an organisation.

Unfreezing   The process of loosening the hold of the established behaviours, values or the organisational paradigm.

Unrelated diversification   A diversification where the activities of the different businesses have no significant commonality.

Unstructured process   Novel activities requiring judgement.

Value (in culture)   The beliefs of an individual or group. They are of two sorts: the ethical stance on what is good and just; and the organisation's general goals and ideals.

Value (in an offer)   The price that a customer is prepared to pay for an offer.

Value (in a mission statement)   What the organisation considers important in its dealings with its stakeholders. A value is often associated with a constraint on behaviour.

Value added   Turnover minus bought-in materials and services.

Value chain   The linked set of processes involved in the transformation of raw materials into the products and services finally consumed.

Value link   A model of a business that emphasises its internal architecture and its external relationships, and describes the way in which a business combines its processes.

Venture capitalist   There are two forms of venture capitalist. There are individuals who obtain funds from a variety of sources and pool these to support projects for a specified period of time and then liquidate them. There are the subsidiaries of major financial institutions, banks and insurance companies that channel money into risky enterprises.

Vertical diversification   An enlargement of a firm's capabilities in order to undertake operations in a different competitive arena but within the same value chain.

Vertical integration   A vertical diversification in which a company's operations in one competitive arena are used mainly by the same company's operations in another arena.

Virtual private network   A secure network connection with messages travelling over the public Internet. It is a cheaper alternative to a company leasing its own direct network connection.

Vision   An overarching goal, often articulated in a phrase of only a few words, summarising an attractive and challenging future.

Vortex issue   One of the three types of strategic issue. They are characterised by being the most complex types of issue, involving many internal interest groups and external stakeholders. They are the most controversial of all strategic issues, being contentious, having serious consequences and being heavily influenced by external stakeholders.

Web of behaviours   The manifestations of culture – the behaviours in an organisation.

Web of beliefs   The set of organisational values and the organisational paradigm.

Whistleblowing   The act of informing on the behaviour of someone or some group that is acting unethically or illegally, to agencies outside the organisation in which the behaviour is taking place.

Wisdom   Knowledge coupled with judgement.

World Wide Web   A global multimedia information system accessible by any user anywhere on the Internet. Documents are hypertext, which means that they provide links to other documents.

Zone of comfortable debate   Issues that involve a consideration of possible changes to norms of behaviour.

Zone of disturbing debate   Issues that involve a consideration of values.

Zone of uncomfortable debate   Issues that involve a consideration of possible changes to elements of the organisational paradigm.

Index